PSYCHOLOGY

THIRD EDITION

Stephen F. Davis
EMPORIA STATE UNIVERSITY

Joseph J. Palladino
UNIVERSITY OF SOUTHERN INDIANA

Prentice Hall, Upper Saddle River, New Jersey 07458

Library of Congress Cataloging-in-Publication Data

Davis, Stephen F.
    Psychology / Stephen F. Davis, Joseph J. Palladino. — 3rd ed.
      p.   cm.
    Rev. ed. of: Psychology 2. c1997.
    Includes bibliographical references and index.
    ISBN 0-13-932583-2
    1. Psychology.   I. Palladino, Joseph J.   II. Davis, Stephen F.
Psychology 2. III. Title.
BF121.D35 1999
150—dc210   99-21562
                             CIP

To Kathleen and Jennifer Marie, Karin Marie, and Sharin Marie

Editorial Director: **Charlyce Jones-Owen**
Editor-in-Chief: **Nancy Roberts**
Executive Editor: **Bill Webber**
Editorial Assistant: **Tamsen Adams**
Editor-in-Chief of Development: **Susanna Lesan**
Development Editor: **Susan Moss**
AVP/Director of Production and
    Manufacturing: **Barbara Kittle**
Managing Editor: **Mary Rottino**
Project Manager: **Maureen Richardson**
Manufacturing Manager: **Nick Sklitsis**
Prepress and Manufacturing Buyer: **Tricia Kenny**

Assistant Creative Design Director: **Carole Anson**
Cover & Interior Design: **Tom Nery**
Photo Research: **Diana Gongora**
Image Specialist: **Beth Boyd**
Manager, Rights & Permissions: **Kay Dellosa**
Director, Image Resource Center: **Melinda Reo**
Line Art Coordinator: **Guy Ruggiero**
Electronic Art Creation: **Maria Piper, Dartmouth**
    Publishing, Inc.
Copyeditor: **Barbara Sutton**
Proofreader: **Judy Coyle**

Photo and text credits appear on pp. 780–785, which constitute a continuation of the copyright page.

This book was set in 10.5/12 Fairfield Light by TSI Graphics and was printed and bound by Courier, Kendallville. The cover was printed by The Lehigh Press, Inc.

Printed in the United States of America
10 9 8 7 6 5 4 3

ISBN 0-13-932583-2

Prentice-Hall International (UK) Limited, London
Prentice-Hall of Australia Pty. Limited, Sydney
Prentice-Hall Canada Inc., Toronto
Prentice-Hall Hispanoamericana, S.A., Mexico
Prentice-Hall of India Private Limited, New Delhi
Prentice-Hall of Japan, Inc., Tokyo
Pearson Education Asia Pte. Ltd., Singapore
Editora Prentice-Hall do Brasil, Ltda., Rio de Janeiro

Brief Contents

Contents

Chapter 5

States of Consciousness   189

Chapter 6

Basic Principles of Learning   233

Chapter 7

Memory   275

Chapter 13

Psychological Disorders 531

Chapter 14

Therapy 579

Chapter 15

Health Psychology 625

Chapter 16

Social Psychology: The Individual in Society 669

About the Authors

STEPHEN F. DAVIS is Professor of Psychology at Emporia State University in Emporia, Kansas. He received his bachelor's and master's degrees in psychology from Southern Methodist University and his Ph.D. in experimental psychology from Texas Christian University. His research, which always includes student assistants, has investigated such diverse topics as academic dishonesty, learning versus grade orientation of students, Type A personality, and the behavioral effects of ingesting toxic metals. He is the author of more than 225 journal articles and more than 750 convention presentations.

Steve's teaching abilities have drawn acclaim on the national level. In 1988 he received the National Distinguished Teaching of Psychology Award from the American Psychological Foundation. He was awarded the Teaching Excellence Award from Division Two (Society for the Teaching of Psychology) of the American Psychological Association in 1989. His professional accomplishments also include serving as president of the Southwestern Psychological Association, the Southern Society for Philosophy and Psychology, and Division Two of the American Psychological Association. He also served as the National President of Psi Chi (the national honor society in psychology). He has been elected as a Fellow of the American Psychological Association, the American Psychological Society, and the American Association of Applied and Preventive Psychology.

JOSEPH J. PALLADINO is Professor of Psychology at the University of Southern Indiana in Evansville, Indiana. He received all his academic degrees from Fordham University, including the Ph.D. in general-theoretical psychology. His numerous articles and presentations have covered topics such as sleep and dreams, the death penalty, extra-credit opportunities, teaching methods, and techniques to encourage research by undergraduate students.

Joe founded the Mid-America Undergraduate Psychology Research Conference in 1982. The Mid-America Conference for Teachers of Psychology, which he founded in 1984, has become the model for regional teaching conferences. His contribution to the continuing education of teachers was recognized by the Faculty Service Award presented by the National University Continuing Education Association in 1991. In 1990 he received the Teaching Excellence Award from Division Two (Society for the Teaching of Psychology) of the American Psychological Association. He was elected to Fellow status in the American Psychological Association in 1989 and served as the president of Division Two in 1991–1992. He has also served Division Two as a consulting editor and the methods and techniques editor of *Teaching of Psychology*, and as chair of the program committee. In his spare time, he enjoys writing the column *On the Light Side* with Mitch Handelsman of the University of Colorado and speaking to faculty on "The Humor of Teaching; the Teaching of Humor." *On the Light Side* appears in the Psi Chi newsletter, *Eye on Psi Chi*. In addition, he creates cartoons to accompany the column, and several of these now appear in this textbook.

Preface

To the Instructor

We began the first edition of this text with the premise that introductory psychology may be the only psychology course your students ever take. With that in mind, we set out to write a text that would make the beginning psychology course an engaging, relevant, and interactive experience. This philosophy was maintained in the second edition and continues in this, the third edition.

Between the two of us, we have taught introductory psychology for over 50 years. Our experience has taught us that students would rather be "talked with" than "talked to." We hope that as students read the third edition of this book they will have the feeling they are engaging in a conversation with us. We have also attempted to convey the excitement and love of psychology that we hope characterize our own classes.

Objectives of the Third Edition

The objectives of the first two editions continue in the third edition. First, we believe that psychology has much to offer individuals, groups, and society as a whole. Psychology is a dynamic and ever-changing discipline that is constantly seeking new ways to apply the knowledge gained from research. Hence, we stress the wide range of **practical applications** of psychological research.

Second, we believe that it is extremely important for students to learn about the various methods used by psychologists to answer the questions they pose. We believe that a thorough understanding of **research methods** will make students better consumers of psychological information. Therefore, we have taken special care to delve into the whys and hows of research methods.

Third, we have tried to put the material we discuss into **historical perspective.** We believe that the history of psychology is best understood when it is integrated into the discussion of key topics throughout the text. As you use this text, you will find that we discuss topics such as the discovery and function of neurons, the development of phobias, and the concept of stress in historical context.

Finally, throughout the book we have paid careful attention to the issue of **human diversity.** We are convinced that a multicultural perspective is an integral part of the day-to-day work of psychologists and that the findings of cross-cultural research have wide-ranging significance.

To integrate these themes into the text, we have incorporated numerous special features—which are described in some detail later in the Preface—and have worked diligently with the staff at Prentice Hall to create a text design that is consistent with our goals. We have tried to make each paragraph and section flow into the next without interruptions. Because students usually see boxed material as peripheral and often do not read it, there are no "boxes" to disrupt the flow of the text or distract the reader.

Organization of the Third Edition

As we examined the numerous introductory psychology textbooks available to instructors, we decided that the most effective approach is to provide an interactive framework, numerous illustrations, and pedagogical aids designed to help students study and review material as they progress through each chapter. The 17 chapters of this text follow the sequence that has become standard in introductory psychology textbooks, beginning with the nature of psychology and its biological foundations and ending with maladaptive behaviors, therapy, health psychology, social psychology, and industrial/organizational psychology. One chapter not always found in other texts is Chapter 11, Sex and Gender. We believe that this topic is important enough in today's world to warrant an entire chapter.

The major organizational changes in the third edition include the inclusion of the new chapter on industrial/organizational psychology (Chapter 17) and the expansion of Chapter 4 to include material on both emotion and motivation. Other changes are detailed, on a chapter-by-chapter basis, below.

Changes in the Third Edition

In preparing the third edition we enhanced our coverage of several key topics and also introduced relevant and exciting new material.

Chapter 1 - Psychology, Research, and You
- Chapter reorganized to facilitate flow of material.
- Added material on use of statistics by psychologists.
- Introduction of the Cultural and Diversity Perspective.

Chapter 2 - Biological Foundations of Psychology
- Added material on cranial nerves, MRI, and spatial and temporal summation.
- Section on the endocrine system expanded.
- Material on the biology of motivation moved to Chapter 4.

Chapter 3 - Sensation and Perception
- Added material on converting light waves into neural signals, the volley principle, feature detectors, sensorineural deafness, and location and operation of the taste buds.
- New section on "Contemporary Issues and Findings in Perception Research."

Chapter 4 - Motivation and Emotion
- Based on reviewer comments we reconstituted this chapter as motivation and emotion.
- Expanded coverage of sexual behavior.
- Material on the biological bases of hunger made more accessible and tied to the material in the Health Psychology chapter.

Chapter 5 - States of Consciousness
- Expanded material on melatonin.
- Added material on siestas, culture and dreams, the drug Rohypnol, and marijuana.

Chapter 6 - Basic Principles of Learning
- New material on experimental neurosis added to the section on generalization and discrimination.
- Added material on overshadowing, shaping, decision-making strategies, social communication of taste preferences, and reinforcing alternative behaviors.

Chapter 7 - Memory
- Chapter format reorganized to facilitate presentation of material.
- New Myth or Science feature on eidtic imagery.
- Added material on transfer-appropriate processing, parallel distributed processing, memory illusions, and acronyms and acrostics.

Chapter 8 - Thinking and Intelligence
- Added material on cultural views of intelligence.
- Added material on Gardner's multiple intelligences and a comparison with Sternberg's theory of intelligence.
- New figure and discussion of heritability and age.

- New table illustrates application of Sternberg's theory of intelligence to the teaching and evaluation of students.

Chapter 9 - Developmental Psychology I
- Material on language development repositioned in this chapter.
- Added material on Bowlby's Ethological Theory of Attachment, transductive reasoning, Vygotsky's theory of scaffolding.

Chapter 10 - Developmental Psychology II
- Added material on adolescence, young-old and old-old, identity achievement, and teenage pregnancy.

Chapter 11 - Sex and Gender
- Material on sexual harassment in elementary school to graduate school has been added.
- Material on women's career opportunities and male/female salary differences has been added.
- Cross-cultural material on views of masculinity and feminity has been added.
- Added material on Steele's vulnerability hypothesis to explain, in part, differences between males and females on mathematics and spatial reasoning.

Chapter 12 - Personality
- Added information to help students interpret scores on the Sensation Seeking Scale.
- Added a questionnaire on the Big Five Factors.
- New material on the methods used to translate the MMPI for use in other languages and cultures.
- New material on culture and the conception of the self.

Chapter 13 - Psychological Disorders
- Added material on the following topics: double depression, suffocation theory of panic disorder, generalized anxiety disorder, effects of comorbidity, culture-bound syndromes, viral theories of schizophrenia, and types of antisocial personality disorder.

Chapter 14 - Therapy
- Revised and updated table on drug treatments.
- Added coverage of typical and atypical antipsychotics as well as anticonvulsants used to treat bipolar disorder.
- Expanded list of self-help groups with Web site addresses.
- Revised material on deinstitutionalization, drug treatments, psychosurgery for OCD, and token economy.

Chapter 15 - Health Psychology
- New questionnaire on hostility.
- New questionnaire on nicotine dependence.
- Material on body mass index with instructions for calculating and interpreting BMI added.
- Added material on a global perspective of HIV.

▨ Updated material on optimism, PTSD, and research on the effects of hostility.

Chapter 16 - Social Psychology: The Individual in Society

▨ Added material on distinctiveness to the section on attributions.

▨ Added material on the sleeper effect to the section on persuasion.

Chapter 17 - Industrial/Organizational Psychology

▨ Available as a supplement with the second edition, this chapter has been added to the text.

▨ The material focuses on personnel selection, performance appraisal, training, and human factors psychology.

Pedagogical Aids

In developing this book we have created a variety of pedagogical aids that will make the study of psychology more interesting and effective for your students. These are described briefly here.

Chapter in Perspective Each chapter begins with a brief discussion of how the material covered in the chapter fits with the "big picture." We show students how chapters build on one another and fit together to create a more complete understanding of behavior as we progress from the chapters that emphasize the more basic processes to those that deal with more complex behaviors.

The Cultural and Diversity Perspective In the first two editions of this book we have woven cultural and diversity material throughout the text—a tradition we continue in this edition. However, to highlight this important emphasis in psychology more clearly, we have included a specific section on *the Cultural and Diversity Perspective* in each chapter.

Myth or Science In each chapter we have highlighted paragraphs in which we compare the findings of psychological research with widely held popular notions. These discussions should help your students evaluate the claims made in "pop psych" writings.

Psychological Detective Several times within each chapter the reader is asked to consider a question or questions about the topic under discussion. The question may deal with issues such as research ethics, how to conduct research, or the importance of a particular research finding. The reader is asked to supply an answer to the question before reading further.

Review Summaries and Study Breaks Each chapter contains several Review Summaries, each of which is followed by a Study Break. Because a basic pedagogical principle tells us that students learn best when they learn small chunks of information, these summaries should help students master the material. They can then use the Study Breaks to test their mastery of the material they have just reviewed and to prepare for quizzes and exams.

Hands On In keeping with the interactive, hands-on emphasis that distinguishes this text, each chapter also features a questionnaire or a similar interactive exercise, identified by a small "hand" symbol. These questionnaires and exercises bring your students into direct contact with the material presented in the chapter.

Marginal Definitions The definition of each key term is presented in the margin on the page where the term is introduced. Because so much of the terminology will be new to your students, we believe it is important to provide instant access to these definitions.

Multimedia, Internet, and the World Wide Web

The New Psychology Interactive Center Prentice Hall and Peregrine Publishers are proud to present a melding of two acclaimed interactive learning resources: Prentice Hall's *Companion Website* ™ with Peregrine's *The Psychology Place*.

Available at *http://www.prenhall.com/davis*, this new **Interactive Psychology Center** provides materials to help students review chapter content and then test their knowledge of what they've read. It provides exciting World Wide Web destinations where students can find related information that expands on material found in their text. Chat rooms and Message Boards allow students to share their ideas about psychology with students from their own classroom or from colleges across the country.

In addition, over 600 articles, demonstrations and interactive exercises from *The Psychology Place* have been keyed to each chapter to provide extra information for motivated students.

The Interactive Psychology Center contains materials for instructors as well.

Both the Instructor's Resource Manual and our new Media Users Guide provide helpful information for instructors and students on how to get the most out of this unique resource.

WebCT

For instructors interested in distance learning, Prentice Hall and WebCT Educational Technologies offer a fully customizable, online course with www links, online testing, and many other course management features using the popular WebCT online course architecture. See your local Prentice Hall representative or visit our special Demonstration Central Website at *http://www.prenhall.com/demo* for more information.

Ancillary Program for Instructors

Instructor's Resource Manual. We believe that you will find a wealth of helpful information and other resources in the Instructor's Manual written by Alan Swinkles (St. Edwards University) and Traci Giuliano (Southwestern University). These experienced teachers bring a number of innovative ideas to the IRM for our third edition, including expanded "Lecture Enhancers" as well as demonstrations, activities and student assignments. Each chapter contains detailed information regarding how resources in the Interactive Psychology Center (particularly from The Psychology Place) can be used as homework assignments or in-class activities. The manual also offers a number of cross-cultural and multicultural resources and teaching ideas for each chapter.

Test Bank. The authors' involvement in all aspects of the ancillary program for the Third Edition is clearly illustrated in the Test Item File, which was written by Joe Palladino. Drawing on his experience as a graduate student in Dr. Anne Anastasi's Test Construction class at Fordham University, Joe carefully reviewed and rewrote the items to improve clarity and coverage of the material and to ensure that the vocabulary level is accessible to students. Joe continues to teach and do research in the area of Psychometrics.

The total number of items has been expanded for the Third Edition, and an increased number of items are now written in the question format rather than the incomplete stem format. The items continue to be coded as either definitional/factual or applied/conceptual.

Interactions. One of the innovations our text has long been known for is our newsletter, *Interactions*. This newsletter provides research updates, lecture enhancers, demonstrations, and a column called Teaching Issues," which has covered topics such as cheating, extra credit, and legal issues in grading. Each feature is tied to chapters and pages in the text and is written so the material can be incorporated into your class presentations. The issues can be added to the *Instructor's Resource Manual*.

Prentice Hall Test Manager. *Psychology, Third Edition* is now accompanied by the best-selling test-generating software on the market. The software runs on IBM (DOS and Windows), Macintosh and Apple IIE. It contains the following modules:

- GRADE: Gradebook
- GUIDE: Tutoring system
- PAINT: Creates graphical artwork and illustrations;
- Online Network Testing. Tests are created through the custom-test software, administered through the On-line Testing, and then transferred to the gradebook for evaluation.

Prentice Hall Transparencies for Introductory Psychology Series V. Add visual impact to the study of psychology with our collection of four-color transparencies. Designed in a large-type format for lecture settings, many of these quality illustrations are not found in the text and offer a wealth of additional resources to enhance lectures and reinforce student learning.

Powerpoint Slides and Electronic Text Art. A set of Powerpoint Slides and nearly all of the line art found in the text is available on a CD-ROM and can also be downloaded from the Faculty Section of the Psychology Interactive Center.

Teaching Psychology, 2/E
Fred W. Whitford, Montana State University
Teaching Psychology serves as a guide for new instructors or teaching assistants to manage the myriad tasks required to teach effectively from the start.

ABCNEWS **ABC News/Prentice Hall Video Library** Prentice Hall has assembled a collection of feature segments from award-winning news programs. The following libraries are currently available to qualified adopters: ABC News Videos for Introductory Psychology Series III consists of segments from such programs as *Nightline, 20/20, Prime Time Live*, and *The Health Show*. A summary and questions, designed to stimulate critical thinking for each segment, are included in the *Instructor's Resource Manual*.

The Alliance Series: The Annenberg/CPB Collection. The Alliance Series is the most extensive collection of professionally produced videos available with any introductory psychology textbook. Selections include videos in the following Annenberg series: *The Brain, The Brain Teaching Modules, Discovering psychology, The Mind, and The Mind Teaching Modules*. Available to qualified adopters. Please contact your local Prentice Hall representative for more information.

Ancillary Program for Students

Practice Test and Review Manual. Prepared by Professor Scott Bailey of Texas Lutheran University, this 256 page manual is provided at no charge with the purchase of each new text. It encourages students to reinforce their learning by providing chapter reviews and self-tests. Each chapter opens with a "Do You Know" section that piques student interest by expanding upon the information presented in the text and presenting it in different ways. After the review and testing sections, each chapter concludes with a useful tip for developing useful study habits that students can take well beyond their introductory psychology course.

Media User's Guide. Beginning in January, 2000, the *Media User's Guide* will be provided to students at no charge with the purchase of a new text and will include:

- written explanations and navigational instructions for using the *Interactive Psychology Center* (see above description under *Multimedia, Internet, and the World Wide Web*).
- summaries of the content of every article, demonstration and exercise found in *The Psychology Place*
- a hands-on *Internet Tutorial* that features web sites related to psychology.

Students who use this guide should have no trouble taking advantage of everything the web has to offer for their introductory psychology experience.

 The New York Times Supplement. The core subject matter provided in the text is supplemented by a collection of time-sensitive articles from one of the world's most distinguished newspapers, *The New York Times*. Also included are discussion and critical thinking questions that relate psychological perspectives and topics in the text to issues in the articles.

Supplementary Textbooks Available for Course Packaging

A variety of Prentice Hall textbooks are available for packaging at reduced prices to enhance the introductory experience:

The Psychology Major: Careers and Strategies for Success by Eric Landrum (Idaho State University), Stephen Davis (Emporia State University), and Terri Landrum (Idaho State University). This 160-page paperback provides valuable information on career options available to psychology majors, tips for improving academic performance, and a guide to the APA style of research reporting.

Forty Studies That Changed Psychology, Third Edition by Roger Hock (Mendocino College). Presenting the seminal research studies that have shaped modern psychological study, this brief supplement provides an overview of the environment that gave rise to each study, its experimental design, its findings, and its impact on current thinking in the discipline.

How to Think Like a Psychologist by Donald McBurney (University of Pittsburgh). This unique supplementary text uses a question-answer format to explore some of the most common questions students ask about psychology.

A Guide to the Brain: A Graphic Workbook, Second Edition by Mark B. Kristal, SUNY at Buffalo. This study aid helps students learn the names and locations of the most important structures and functions of the brain and nervous system. The Second Edition offers more review exercises, expanded figures, and brief concept summaries.

Acknowledgments

No textbook is the product of the authors' efforts alone. In preparing **Psychology, Third Edition** we have benefited from the insights of many colleagues in the discipline. We would like to express our thanks to the following individuals, who reviewed the first, second, and third editions of this text.

Ruth L. Ault, Davidson College, NC
William A. Barnard, University of Northern Colorado, CO
Joe Bean, Shorter College
Angela Becker, Indiana University Kokomo
Barney Beins, Ithaca College, NY
Daniel Berch, University of Cincinnati
Joy L. Berrenberg, University of Colorado at Denver, CO
Amy D. Bertelson, Washington University, MO
Deborah L. Best, Wake Forest University, NC
Michael Best, Southern Methodist University, TX
Jeanine R. Bloyd, Spoon River College, IL
Ross Buck, University of Connecticut
Peter Carswell, Asheville-Buncombe Technical Community College
Avi Chaudhuri, McGill University
Ronald Comer, Princeton University, NJ
Gary Coover, Northern Illinois University, IL
Catharine L. Cowan, Southwest State University, MN
Michael Crabtree, Washington and Jefferson College, PA
W.A. Cronin-Hillix, San Diego State University, CA
Denys deCatanzaro, McMaster University
Patricia Decker, DeVry Institute of Technology
William Domhoff, UC Santa Cruz
Betty Dorr, Fort Lewis College
Robert Emery, University of Virginia
Robert Emmons, University of California—Davis, CA
Roberta A. Eveslage, Johnson County Community College, KS
Sandra R. Fiske, Onondaga Community College, NY

Karen E. Ford, Mesa State College
Charles Brewer, Furman University, SC
Grace Galliano, Kennesaw State College, GA
Tracey Geer, University of Arizona
Judith Gibbons, St. Louis University
Peter J. Giordano, Belmont University, TN
Nuria Giralt, University of Arizona
John Governale, Clark College, WA
Richard A. Griggs, University of Florida, FL
Sid Hall, University of Southern Indiana
Wayne Hall, San Jacinto College Central
Bernice B. Harshberger, Carteret Community College
Diane Herbert, SUNY Farmingdale
David K. Hogberg, Albion College, MI
Phyllis A. Hornbuckle, Virginia Commonwealth University, VA
James Huntermark, Missouri Western State College
Ted Jaeger, Westminster College
John Jahnke, Miami University
George G. Janzen, Ferris State University, MI
Laurie L. Jensen, Northern State University
James M. Jones, University of Delaware, DE
William Kelemen, University of Missouri St. Louis
Mark Kelland, Lansing Community College
Allen Keniston, University of Wisconsin—Eau Claire, WI
Stephen Klein, Mississippi State University, MS
Randy Larsen, University of Michigan, MI
Leslie Joy Larson, SUNY Farmingdale
Neil Lutsky, Carleton College, MN
Salvador Macias III, USC—Sumter
Harold L. Mansfield, Fort Lewis College, CO
Janet R. Matthews, Loyola University, LA
Ron Mosher, Rock Valley College
David Murphy, Waubonsee College
David E. Neufeldt, Hutchinson Community College, KS
Michele Paludi, Union College
Jeffrey Pedroza, Lansing Community College
Marites Pinon, Southwest Texas State
Tom Marsh, Pitt Community College

Retta E. Poe, Western Kentucky University
Janet Proctor, Purdue University, IN
Neil Salkind, University of Kansas
Connie Schick, Bloomsburg University
George Schreer, Plymouth State College
Alan Schultz, Prince Georges Community College, MD
Matthew J. Sharps, California State University—Fresno, CA
Craig A. Smith, Vanderbilt University
Randolph A. Smith, Ouachita Baptist University, AR
Steven M. Smith, Texas A&M University, TX
Susan Nash Spooner, McLennan Community College
Michael J. Strube, Washington University, MO
Christopher Taylor, University of Arizona
Larry R. Vandervert, Spokane Falls Community College, WA
Eva D. Vaughan, University of Pittsburgh, PA
Wilse Webb, University of Florida—Gainesville, FL
Robert A. Wexler, Nassau Community College
Gordon Lee Whitman, Sandhills Community College
Patrick S. Williams, University of Houston—Downtown, TX
Janice Yoder, University of Wisconsin
Otto Zinser, East Tennessee State University, TN

The editorial team at Prentice Hall deserves special praise. We would like to thank Editor-in-Chief Nancy Roberts, Executive Editor Bill Webber, Editor-in-Chief of Development Susanna Lesan, Development Editor Susan Moss, Production Editor Maureen Richardson, and Editorial Assistant Tamsen Adams. We would also like to thank Guy Ruggiero, Assistant Manager of Art and Electronic Artist Maria Piper. Thanks to all!

Finally, we express our deepest appreciation to our own teachers. Among them we count Anne Anastasi, Virginia Chancey, David Landrigan, Wayne Ludvigson, Alvin North, and Jack R. Strange. Special thanks to "The Teacher of Teachers," Bob Daniel.

S.F.D.
J.J.P.

CHAPTER 1

Psychology, Research, and You

Chapter in Perspective

This chapter introduces you to psychology, a field that has grown tremendously over the years. Here we describe the methods psychologists use to gather information about the numerous problems and areas they research, examine the historical development and growth of psychology, and look at the different types of jobs that psychologists currently hold. In addition to introducing you to the broad and exciting field of psychology, we also indicate how you can become a knowledgeable consumer of psychological research. The results and claims of psychological research fill our daily lives; we need to know how to evaluate them. Once we have put contemporary psychology in perspective in this chapter, we will be ready to examine its special topics in greater detail in subsequent chapters. ▪

Almost every day we encounter events in our lives or in the mass media that involve what we call "psychology." These events cover a wide variety of topics. Consider the following examples.

1. Patty's friends have convinced her to take one of the many tests they have located on the Internet. Patty has always wanted to know her IQ, so she selects an IQ test with a picture of Albert Einstein at the top.

She answers multiple-choice questions such as "What is the color of the sky at night?" and "The color of the sky is caused by." After she completes the test, she is told her score is 48 and is able to view a list of people who had received high scores on this test. Because her score of 48 is toward the top of the list and more than 162,000

Social psychologist Stanley Milgram investigated the factors that produced unquestioning obedience. Such factors may have contributed to the deaths of millions of people in Nazi concentration camps during World War II.

individuals had visited this Internet site, Patty is convinced she has a high IQ. We will have more to say about Patty's IQ test in Chapter 8.

2. At a university on the other side of town, Keith is enrolled in a history class that covers the events leading to World War II. Today's lecture deals with the atrocities committed in the Nazi concentration camps. Keith hears how millions of Jews, gypsies, and members of other devalued groups were forced onto trains and taken to concentration camps as part of Adolf Hitler's "Final Solution." The instructor graphically depicts the conditions endured by prisoners at camps like Dachau and Auschwitz. The examples include unprovoked beatings, separating children from their parents, and using gas chambers to kill hundreds of people at a time. Keith tries to comfort himself with the thought that such unspeakable cruelty could never happen anywhere else. Nevertheless, as he walks to his next class, a psychology course, he cannot stop thinking about the lecture. Will his psychology class help him understand what he heard in his history class?

After Keith takes his seat, the psychology instructor begins the class by asking, "How much electric shock, from 0 to 450 volts, would you administer to someone as part of a psychology experiment?" Keith learns that a social psychologist, Stanley Milgram (1974), conducted a study in which people were asked to administer shocks to others as part of what they believed was an investigation of how people learn. Although no shocks were actually delivered, the participants were unaware of this fact. They continued to administer "shocks" even when they believed the shocks could be harmful. Keith is both surprised and saddened by the results of Milgram's study, which we discuss in more detail in Chapter 16.

3. Later that week a mentalist known as Kreskin comes to town for a performance. Mentalists claim to be able to read minds and communicate with an audience by transmitting thoughts rather than by using the "normal" senses—speech, vision, hearing, and so forth. Kreskin tells the audience he is thinking of two simple geometric figures, one inside the other, and is projecting them onto his "mental screen" so that the audience can receive them: "OK, I am thinking of a triangle inside a circle—did anyone get that?" Hundreds of hands go up. Kreskin quickly adds, "Or a circle inside a triangle." The receptive audience applauds enthusiastically and is eager to see more.

Next Kreskin tries to "send" the audience a number between 1 and 50. "I'll make both digits odd, but not the same odd digit. For example, 15 would be OK, but 11 wouldn't do because the two odd digits are the same. I'm projecting it on my mental screen." He pauses and then asks, "How many got 37?" Hands go up across the auditorium. He adds, "I started to think 35, but . . . " More hands go up, and the audience applauds again (based on Marks & Kammann, 1980).

Some students who attended the performance are fascinated by what they witnessed, but they are not convinced that any unusual mental powers were responsible for what they observed. How could they test Kreskin's ability to read minds? Did the show provide sufficient evidence to prove the existence of such mental powers? Or is mentalism the practice of "sleight of mind," as critics (Gordon, 1987) have said? We have more to say about Kreskin later in this chapter.

Becoming a Psychological Detective

You could probably put yourself in one or more of these real-life situations. Each one poses questions that psychologists might ask and try to answer. A psychologist has earned a doctoral degree and is interested in the behavior of human beings and animals. We define **psychology** as the science of behavior and mental processes. Although this definition emphasizes behavior, it does not exclude the rich inner life that we all experience; it includes dreams, daydreams, and other inner experiences. As a science of behavior and mental processes, psychology provides the tools we need to answer questions about IQ testing, ethics in research, the validity of mentalism as a psychological fact or event, and countless other issues.

To understand each of these situations, you need to be clear about what happened before you can determine why and how each one happened. For example, was Patty's IQ score an accurate indication of her intellectual ability? Will most people administer a 450-volt shock to another person as part of a study of learning? How did Kreskin transmit geometric figures and numbers to members of the audience? Answering such questions helps you understand similar situations and provides the tools you need to answer questions about other situations.

How can you learn to be a psychological detective when every day you are bombarded by information designed to influence your opinion, persuade you to buy products, entertain you, or inform you about the world (Pratkanis & Aronson, 1991)? The information flows from newspapers, radio, television, family and friends, and advertisements. Often it takes the form of headlines like the following:

> Miracle Happy Pill Banishes the Blues
> You'll Read 200% Faster with Better Comprehension
> Recovered Memories Point to a History of Abuse
> Hidden Messages in Rock Songs Linked to Suicides
> Three-Year-Old Psychic Predicts the Future

To evaluate such information, psychologists have found certain techniques to be helpful in thinking critically. We introduce these techniques in the next section, but first let's consider a common alternative: folk wisdom.

When we try to understand events in the world around us, we sometimes turn to what is known as *folk wisdom*. Table 1-1 contains examples of folk wisdom in the form of proverbs. Read each proverb and decide whether you agree with it.

Such efforts to explain events are usually presented in ways that can never be proved wrong (Stanovich, 1992). Look at the list of proverbs again and notice that the proverbs in List B contradict those in List A. Folk wisdom can provide an explanation for every conceivable event—as well as for its exact opposite (Teigen, 1986). Hence folk wisdom answers all situations but explains none. If folk wisdom does not provide helpful guidance in understanding our world, where can we turn?

The answer is to look for insights and explanations through psychological methods. Psychologists are trained to ask good questions, to gather useful information, to arrive at appropriate conclusions, and to develop and ask further questions based on the information collected. But there are right and wrong ways to ask questions and arrive at conclusions. Becoming a good psychological detective requires practice. To understand the need to practice the skills of a psychological detective, let's journey back to England in 1920.

Arthur Conan Doyle's Belief in Fairies

After World War I, spiritualism sparked interest on both sides of the Atlantic. Almost every city had several *mediums*—people who claim that they can contact the spirit world and communicate with the dead during a séance (Hines,

psychology
Science of behavior and mental processes

TABLE 1-1 Folk Wisdom

This test of folk wisdom includes general principles of behavior. Read each proverb, and decide whether you agree with it. Notice how proverbs of the same number from List A and List B contradict each other.

LIST A

1. Look before you leap.
2. You can't teach an old dog new tricks.
3. Out of sight, out of mind.
4. Two heads are better than one.
5. A penny saved is a penny earned.
6. Opposites attract.

LIST B

1. People who hesitate are lost.
2. It's never too late to learn.
3. Absence makes the heart grow fonder.
4. If you want something done right, do it yourself.
5. Nothing ventured, nothing gained.
6. Birds of a feather flock together.

1988). The participants in a séance hold hands as they sit around a table in a darkened room. Strange things often seem to happen during a séance: Spirits are heard to speak through floating trumpets, cool breezes and touches are felt, and tables tip over even when no one has touched them.

Sir Arthur Conan Doyle, the creator of the master detective Sherlock Holmes, was deeply interested in spiritualism. His interest started as a hobby but later became the focus of his life because he wished to communicate with his son, who had been killed in World War I. In fact, Doyle believed he had spoken with his son on several occasions (Hanson & Hanson, 1989).

In May 1920, Doyle heard reports that fairies had been photographed; he greeted the reports with enthusiasm because they seemed to confirm his belief in the existence of the spirit world. The photographs had been taken by two young girls who said they had observed the fairies in a nearby field. Doyle dismissed the possibility of fraud because the girls were young and did not know how to use photographic equipment (although one of the girls had worked in a photography shop). In 1921, he presented the results of his investigation in a book, *The Coming of the Fairies.* Doyle's authoritative statements led many people to believe the photographs were genuine, and hundreds of people wrote to him describing fairies they had seen in their gardens (Randi, 1987).

Modern technology has shown the fairies to be a hoax. Computer enhancement of the photographs reveals the supposed fairies were actually cardboard cutouts from a children's book suspended by almost invisible threads.

What lessons can we learn from the story of the fairies? First, although prominent public figures may have great credibility, their statements should not

Frances Griffiths is shown with some of the cardboard cutouts she used to convince Sir Arthur Conan Doyle that she had contacted the fairies.

keep us from asking our own questions. Second, we should be aware of the potential for **bias,** or preconceptions that can cloud our observations, influence the questions we ask, determine the methods we use, and influence our interpretation of the data we gather. Before Conan Doyle had seen the photographs of the fairies, he was already convinced of the existence of a spiritual realm. Unlike Sherlock Holmes, the fictional detective he had created, Doyle did not require stringent proof of "what I hear with my own ears or see with my eyes" (Hanson & Hanson, 1989, p. 96). In short, he allowed his beliefs to cloud his thinking, something all of us probably do from time to time. Had Doyle been a good detective, he would have recognized the potential for bias, asked good questions, and arrived at appropriate conclusions.

Mentalism Revealed

Let's turn our attention to one of the situations described at the beginning of the chapter. Are you convinced that Kreskin can transmit his thoughts without using the "normal" senses? Does he have some special mental power?

Kreskin claims that he can communicate numbers and geometric figures by transmitting his thoughts to the audience without speaking or writing. Up to now, most people have believed thoughts can be communicated only if they are spoken or written. What a dramatic discovery it would be if Kreskin actually transmitted his thoughts. Imagine the implications. Could mental powers be used to influence the behavior of others? Would we all be subject to interference from the nearest mentalist? Would politicians hire mentalists to influence the way people think and vote?

To begin our examination of Kreskin's feats, we now introduce one of the important features of our book: the Psychological Detective sections, which pose questions about the material you are reading. A Psychological Detective section may ask you to collect data to answer a question, to suggest an explanation for a finding presented in the text, or to try your hand at solving a problem. Here is your first opportunity to sharpen your thinking skills by becoming actively involved with the material you are reading.

Psychological Detective

Let's do some detective work. Returning to page 4, carefully reread the description of Kreskin's transmission of numbers. Within the range that Kreskin stated, how many numbers actually were possibilities? Write down all the numbers Kreskin could possibly transmit, according to his statement to the audience.

If you decided there were 50 numbers, you would be mistaken. Remember, Kreskin said that single-digit numbers were out, as were two-digit numbers that included an even digit. When you complete your list, you should have only eight numbers. So Kreskin told the audience he would transmit one of eight possible numbers, making his task easier than it appeared at first, but still not a simple feat to accomplish.

Give Kreskin's instructions to several friends, and ask them which number comes to mind. You will find that many people select 35 or 37. Why? A key to understanding this feat is Kreskin's use of 15 as an example of an acceptable number and 11 as an unacceptable number. Researchers have determined that this simple statement leads many people to think about numbers in the thirties (Marks & Kammann, 1980).

bias
Beliefs that interfere with objectivity

Notice that we have mentioned only two numbers. Kreskin takes credit for transmitting not one number but two. We doubt that anyone in the audience would stand up and say "Wait a minute, you said you were sending one number, but now you're talking about two." By selecting two numbers, Kreskin increases the odds that members of the audience will choose the "right" number. You can accomplish the same feat (although it doesn't seem to be much of a feat now) without resorting to explanations that involve mentalism.

Kreskin also said he would transmit two geometric figures, one inside the other. Try asking some friends to think of two geometric figures, one inside the other. We doubt that your friends will think of a hexagon, a parallelogram, a pentagon, or another less common figure. Most likely, they will think of common figures such as a circle, square, or triangle. You begin to see that Kreskin's accomplishments are not feats of mentalism; rather, they show how much he knows about the way people think. In fact, if Kreskin "projected" a parabola inside a parallelogram onto his "mental screen," most of the audience would still think of a triangle inside a circle or a circle inside a triangle.

Remember, it is important to be clear about exactly what is claimed. Notice, for example, that Kreskin changed the rules as the performance proceeded. First, he said he would send one number; later, he took credit for sending two numbers. No one protested. Then he said he would send two geometric figures, one inside the other. Later he was given credit for sending the two figures regardless of which was inside the other.

Next, focus on the evidence used to support Kreskin's claim. We should ask good questions about the evidence and collect useful data if necessary so that we can arrive at defensible conclusions. You have already learned a bit about asking good questions, and you have collected some data from friends to help you understand a claim of mentalism.

The Law of Parsimony.   In studying the claim of mentalism, you have learned to apply the **law of parsimony.** Suppose we have two or more explanations for an event or claim. Which one should we accept? Assume for a moment that all the proposed explanations explain the event or claim. The law of parsimony tells us to adopt the explanation that requires the fewest assumptions.

In the case of Kreskin's performance, there are two competing explanations: (a) Kreskin can transmit information without using the normal senses, or (b) the information Kreskin chooses for transmittal does not even need to be transmitted because people would supply it themselves without reading anyone else's "mental screen." Research conducted by psychologists supports the second explanation (Marks & Kammann, 1980). Most members of the audience never stopped to consider the alternative explanation: They would have thought of the number 35 or 37 and a circle in a triangle or a triangle in a circle no matter who was standing on the stage. The supposed transmission of numbers has been described as "a remarkable psychological force" (Gardner, 1956, p. 173); however, the method of transmitting numbers and geometric figures has been available in the literature on magic for several decades. The magician's explanation does not require us to propose special mental forces or powers and the ability to use these powers to transmit thoughts. To understand these "magic powers" we need to understand that magicians and mentalists base their acts on their understanding of the way people think.

One of our goals in writing this book is to help you become a better psychological detective—capable of asking good questions, collecting useful information, arriving at defensible conclusions, and being aware of your own biases and those of others. The process we discuss can be applied to the story of Doyle's fairies, to Kreskin's claim of mentalism, to the newspaper headlines we

law of parsimony
Principle that simple explanations of phenomena are preferred to complex explanations

listed earlier, to the other scenes we used to introduce this chapter, and to countless events you experience each day.

Guidelines for the Psychological Detective

"Critical thinking is the reasoning we do in order to determine whether a claim is true" (Gray, 1991, p. 1). One objective of this text is to show you how to evaluate critically the information you read and hear in the media and elsewhere. How do you know what to believe? How do you separate sense from nonsense?

The following are some guidelines you can use in evaluating a statement or claim.

What is the statement or claim, and who is making it?   Before accepting a statement or claim, consider the possibility of personal bias. When we realized Kreskin's stake (a good show and a handsome income) in claiming powers of mentalism, we examined his actions more closely. Was he transmitting one number or two? one geometric figure inside the other or vice versa?

Whenever a person makes what seems like an extraordinary claim, always ask yourself if he or she has anything to gain by making that claim. Salespeople have a personal stake in convincing you to purchase the products they sell. For example, car dealers want new customers to know that past buyers have been satisfied, and to prove their point they often offer the results of surveys. Car manufacturers mail surveys to recent buyers to determine their level of satisfaction. According to *Consumer Reports* ("Selling It," 1991), some car dealers have offered their customers incentives to complete these surveys—but only if they take the survey to a dealer, who is more than happy to help them complete it!

Besides considering the influence of personal bias, we should also evaluate the authority of the person making the claim. Authority figures often provide helpful insights, but we should not be blinded by those insights. Remember, credibility does not automatically transfer from one field to another.

For example, in the fall of 1990, Iben Browning, a climatologist with questionable credentials as an "expert" on earthquakes, predicted that a quake would occur in the central United States. Many seismologists believe that an earthquake will indeed occur along the New Madrid fault (centered in Missouri) during the next 100 years. Browning, however, predicted the day the earthquake would occur—December 3, 1990. Widespread media coverage of the prediction led many schools and businesses to close for the day, but no earthquake occurred. Why did so many people believe Browning? One important reason is that they were impressed with his credentials as a climatologist and mistakenly considered him an expert on earthquakes as well.

We have focused on the potential for bias among those who make some claim. We must recognize, however, that the very assumptions we hold can themselves create biases that in turn influence our views of claims, questions, or proposed solutions to a problem. The influence of bias is not limited to the experts; we are all subject to its influence and must strive to recognize its sometimes subtle effects. Table 1-2 contains a series of seemingly simple questions. Try answering them, and then check to see if your answers are correct.

Is the statement or claim based on scientific observations?   Many people support conclusions about behavior by citing personal experiences or anecdotes. For example, you may think that you succeeded on an exam because you sat in your "lucky seat." Personal experiences are also frequently offered as proof of the quality of particular products, ranging from detergents to cars.

TABLE 1-2 Simple Questions That May Reveal Some Evidence of Bias

Answer each of the following questions as well as you can. Then compare your answer with those on page 43.

1. Is the sun closer to the Earth or farther from the Earth during the winter months, or is the distance the same in summer and winter?

2. Whose face appears on a penny?

3. Who stole the greatest number of bases in a single season of professional baseball?

4. Can you transform the following figure into a perfect square using just one straight line?

Source: Adapted from Beins, 1993.

Whenever you come across such a claim, ask whether it is justified. For example, does the fact that one customer is satisfied with a product prove that the product is consistently satisfactory? Critical thinking also requires us to question where the facts came from. Was the information based on scientific research, or was it based on casual observation? Later in this chapter we discuss several research methods that psychologists use to collect data for answering questions. Only one of these methods, the experimental method, can provide the basis for cause-and-effect statements.

Popular sources ranging from such tabloids as the *National Enquirer,* the *Star,* and the *National Examiner* to more respected newspapers such as *The New York Times* and the *Philadelphia Inquirer* often print news related to psychology. Only about 40 percent of these articles, however, specify the research methods on which the claims in these news stories are based (Evans et al., 1990). Thus many sources of the claims we read in the print media pay little attention to the process of scientific inquiry, which makes it difficult for us to evaluate these claims.

What do statistics reveal? Many students are fearful of statistics in any form, yet we use statistics all the time, although not always wisely. Never hesitate to ask for numbers to support a claim, but be sure you understand them.

Claims are often presented as some type of average. An average conveys information about the middle of a distribution or collection of numbers. There are actually three types of averages, however, and you need to know which type is being presented and whether it is appropriate.

When evaluating claims, we need to know whether the findings could have occurred by chance. Researchers usually report the likelihood that their findings might have resulted from the operation of chance alone. Findings that exceed chance occurrence are said to be *statistically significant.* It is important to remember that you cannot tell if a finding is statistically significant just by looking at the results; a statistical test needs to be performed.

TABLE 1-3　**Cause and Effect**

Consider each of the following statements. Does one of the factors in each statement cause the other? If not, what other factors might be involved?

1. The phone always rings when I'm in the shower.
2. I lose my keys only when I'm in a hurry.
3. People always call at the wrong time.
4. It always rains just after I wash the car.
5. An item goes on sale the day after I buy it.
6. The doorbell always rings just as the baby is going to sleep.

Such tests, and other statistical topics, are covered in Appendix A. We encourage you to read this material at this time; it will improve your ability as a psychological detective.

Are there plausible alternative explanations for the statement or claim?　Researchers frequently report that two variables (behaviors or events) are related. When we deal with an association between two variables, called a *correlation,* we must consider the possibility that the relationship is actually due to a third variable. The fact that two events are correlated does not prove that one of the events caused the other; however, knowing the relationship between two events helps us to make predictions about when events will occur in the future. For example, whenever the moon is full, the police report more crimes and emergency rooms treat more accident victims. Is there a relation between the full moon and these occurrences?

One study actually indicated a relation between the full moon and increases in accident rates and incidents of violence. Closer inspection revealed, however, that the researchers had inadvertently selected periods when the full moon occurred on weekends. Because accident rates are higher on weekends than on weekdays, it is not surprising that these studies found a relation between the full moon and higher accident rates. Researchers who have examined broader periods have consistently failed to find such a relation (Rotton & Kelly, 1985).

Although all the world's events demand an explanation, some are mere coincidences. Consider the statements in Table 1-3. Did one of the factors cause the other, or are there other factors involved?

Among the many claims we encounter every day are ones about drugs and other remedies. Patients may respond to drug treatment even if the treatment contains no active ingredient. Why? How you respond to a drug depends on many factors, including your beliefs about the drug's effectiveness. If you expect that a drug will give you relief from some ailment, that belief itself may bring about a reduction in the symptoms. This response is termed the **placebo effect.** The claims made for drugs often sound quite impressive; when judging a drug's effectiveness, however, we need to know how many patients may have improved because of the placebo effect alone. Only when we have undertaken a study to obtain this comparative information can we judge the true effectiveness of a drug.

We have presented four guidelines that can be helpful in evaluating a claim:

1. What is the claim, and who is making it?
2. Is the statement or claim based on scientific observations?

placebo effect
In drug research, positive effects associated with a person's beliefs and attitudes about the drug, even when it contains no active ingredients

3. What do statistics reveal?

4. Are there plausible alternative explanations for the statement or claim?

Using these guidelines does not guarantee that you will always arrive at a complete and accurate understanding of any claim or proposed explanation. Not even a well-conducted, scientific experiment can guarantee that you have found truth. Depending on the specific type of experiment conducted, the culture in which the experiment is conducted, and the personal interpretation of the results, different views of "the truth" may exist. The guidelines do, however, help you avoid certain pitfalls that can easily lead to inaccurate conclusions.

In the next section we examine the methods psychologists use to answer research questions. These techniques truly are the tools of the psychological detective.

Review Summary

1. The events of our daily lives pose questions that psychologists can answer. In answering these questions, **psychology** can help us develop the skills needed to evaluate claims critically.

2. The case of Sir Arthur Conan Doyle and the photographs of alleged fairies teaches us the importance of asking good questions and demonstrates the importance of being aware of how **bias** can influence the questions we ask and the conclusions we draw.

3. When there are two (or more) competing explanations for an event or claim, the **law of parsimony** indicates we should select the one requiring the fewest assumptions. Applying this law to Kreskin's claims of mentalism leads us to conclude that he does not have special mental powers; rather, he understands how people think and bases his act on that knowledge.

4. By asking good questions, collecting useful data, and arriving at defensible conclusions, we can become good consumers of psychological research.

5. In evaluating causal or research claims, we need to know exactly what the claim is and who is making it. Authority figures often have great credibility, but their expertise does not transfer from one field to another, and their pronouncements should not be accepted uncritically.

6. Determining whether claims are based on scientific observations is also important. Even though science does not guarantee the researcher will find truth, conclusions based on systematic and empirical (objectively quantifiable) observations of large samples are stronger than those based on a few personal testimonials.

7. Understanding and using statistics is a great aid in evaluating claims. Useful measures include three types of averages. Psychologists usually report the likelihood that their findings might have resulted from chance alone.

8. We need to realize that a relationship between two events does not prove that one of the events caused the other. We should consider alternative explanations that might account for a particular event or claim.

Study Break

1. Psychology is the science of
   a. behavior and mental processes.
   b. behavior.
   c. mental processes.
   d. human behavior and mental processes.
2. What is the major problem in relying on folk wisdom or proverbs to explain behavior?
   a. Folk wisdom and proverbs cannot be refuted because they can account for any event.
   b. Folk wisdom and proverbs are never correct.
   c. Folk wisdom and proverbs are too vague.

   d. Folk wisdom and proverbs provide no insight into behavior.
3. Randy is a tremendous fan of the Minnesota Vikings football team. In fact, he will, with little provocation, engage you in a debate about whether they are professional football's greatest team ever. Randy <u>may</u> be showing
   a. critical thinking.
   b. personal bias.
   c. an ignorance of statistics.
   d. the law of parsimony.

4. Read each of the following claims and assess its validity by using the guidelines for the psychological detective presented on pages 9–11.

  a. Students in an introductory psychology course were intrigued by the topic of dreams; they posed questions about dream recall, the meaning of dreams, and the presence of color in dreams. They decided to conduct a survey to answer their question about color in dreams. The students reported whether color appeared in any dream they had the previous night. Only 2 of the 50 students reported color in their dreams. The class concluded that we rarely dream in color.

  b. A testing firm reported the results of a taste test of two colas under the heading "Fizzy Beats Foamy." The company concluded that "an amazing 60 percent said Fizzy tastes as good as or better than Foamy."

  c. In the disorder known as *autism,* the affected person tends to avoid human contact and displays little or no ability to speak; many people with this disorder are also mentally retarded. To help autistic persons to communicate, researchers developed a technique in which an assistant guided an autistic person's arm to point to letters on a keyboard and thus spell words. With this assistance, people who were previously unable to communicate reportedly learned how to spell correctly, to construct grammatically correct sentences, to write poetry, and to solve math problems. Critics were skeptical, however. They noticed that the autistic persons rarely looked at the keyboard while the assistant guided their arms.

Research Methods in Psychology

Brandy and Michael spent Saturday afternoon surfing the Internet. They were amazed at the variety of sites they visited. One site described the growing phenomenon known as "road rage" (Davis, Evans, & Farris, 1997). They wondered what causes such aggressive behaviors in motorists. Another site (Davis, 1997) described a new disorder that involves people becoming hooked on or addicted to the Internet. Again, they wondered about the causes. Later they came across a site where they could order a product being advertised by a well-known celebrity. They wondered if the product was as good as the celebrity claimed. ***How would psychologists answer the kinds of questions asked by Brandy and Michael?*** ▪

The science of psychology is concerned with events like these and the ones described at the beginning of this chapter. The goals of psychology are to describe such events, to make predictions about the conditions that gave rise to them, and then to use that knowledge to predict and, possibly, to control events in the future.

As we noted, psychology is the scientific study of behavior and mental processes. What makes psychology a science? Psychologists share a basic assumption with all other sciences: Physical and psychological events have causes that can be uncovered through scientific investigation. Scientists do not rely on guesswork, hunches, or unsystematic collections of personal experiences. Rather, they use a system of investigation known as the **scientific method.** Like all scientists, psychologists begin their work by making very careful and precise observations of different phenomena or events. They then use the information they have obtained to develop explanations for the phenomena they have observed, which we call **theories.** From these theories

scientific method
System of investigation in which a person makes careful observations of a phenomenon, proposes theories to explain the phenomenon, makes hypotheses about future behaviors, and then tests these hypotheses through more research and observation

theory
Explanation for a phenomenon based on careful and precise observations

psychologists develop **hypotheses,** which are predictions about future behaviors. They then test these hypotheses through more research and observation.

How do psychologists collect the data they need to develop theories and test hypotheses? Psychologists use a number of research methods, including case studies, naturalistic observations, and experiments. Each of these methods has strengths and weaknesses, and all of them contribute to our knowledge of claims and events. The choice of the specific method used usually is determined by the type of problem being investigated. Let's look more closely at each of the methods that psychologists use.

The Case Study

The **case study** (sometimes called a *clinical study*) is an in-depth analysis of one person. This method was used in the 1800s by the physician Paul Broca, who discovered the brain area responsible for the language difficulties experienced by one of his patients (see Chapter 2). It was subsequently popularized by Sigmund Freud (see Chapter 12) and a Swiss scientist, Jean Piaget (see Chapter 9). A major advantage of the case study is that concentrating on one person (or sometimes a few people) allows researchers to gather a great deal of detailed information. The goal of a case study is to use the information obtained from one person to understand the behaviors of others. The case study is often an excellent source for suggesting research ideas that can be explored with other methods.

One potential disadvantage of the method is that what we learn by studying one person may not necessarily apply to other people. For example, an intensive study of the interpersonal behaviors and personality attributes of the president of the United States may not tell us much about such behaviors and attributes in other American men or women. The president lives in unique circumstances and leads a life that few people can relate to. Findings that have limited applicability are said not to *generalize*.

Naturalistic Observation

In contrast to the casual, informal observations of behavior that each of us makes every day, scientists make formal, recorded observations of events. The goal of such **naturalistic observation** is to describe the settings, frequency, and characteristics of certain behaviors. For example, psychologists interested in the use of seat belts have stationed themselves at the exits of shopping malls to see how many drivers used them. They have also observed whether children riding in the cars used seat belts. When psychologists make naturalistic observations, they observe behaviors as they occur, without intervening or altering the behaviors in any way.

The observers must be careful not to affect the behaviors they observe and record. Observations that interfere with the behavior being studied are termed *reactive*. Have you ever noticed someone in a restaurant watching you while you are eating? If so, you are familiar with a reactive observation. Try to remember if the observer's scrutiny may have changed your behavior in any way. For example, did you check to see if you had food on your clothing or face, or did you make an effort to use your best table manners? Psychologists who make naturalistic observations try to make sure that they themselves are not observed—they try to "blend in with the surroundings" so that they are not noticed by the persons being observed. Another method is to find some way to gather data without being physically present. For example, if you wished to study the aggressive behavior of young children, you might arrange to have their classroom and playground behavior at a day-care center or school recorded by a concealed videocamera (Pepler & Craig, 1995).

hypothesis
Prediction about future behaviors that is derived from observation and theories

case study
In-depth study of a single person that can often provide suggestions for further research

naturalistic observation
Study of behavior in its typical setting, with no attempt to alter it

By using a one-way mirror, the researcher can make naturalistic observations of the children at this day care center.

Correlational Research

Imagine that it is your senior year in high school and you are faced with all the choices and decisions involved in getting ready to go to college. Before applying to the college of your choice, you likely took an entrance examination, such as the Scholastic Aptitude Test (SAT) or the American College Test (ACT). What purpose do tests such as the SAT and ACT serve? Psychologists believe that the scores on these tests are related to (*correlated with*) your performance as a college student. For example, certain researchers (Hopkins, Stanley, & Hopkins, 1990) say that "the College Board's Validity Study Service has conducted more than 2,000 studies in almost 700 colleges; the mean validity coefficient for freshman GPAs [grade-point averages] for the SAT was .42" (p. 347). This means that scores on the SAT enabled educators to predict how a student would do during his or her first year in college. Keep in mind, though, that just because two variables are correlated, even highly correlated, one variable does not *cause* the other. In this case, SAT scores are related to—but do not actually cause—grade point averages.

Figure 1-1 presents two possible **scatterplots**—graphs that illustrate the relationship between two variables (in this case, SAT scores and first-year [freshman] grade-point average). In these examples, each dot in the scatterplot represents one student. The location of the dot is determined by both the student's SAT score (along the vertical axis) and his or her freshman grade-point average (along the horizontal axis). If the relationship between SAT scores and grades was perfect—that is, if the student with the highest SAT score had the highest grade-point average and so on down the line—the dots would fall on a straight line from the lower left to the upper right, as in Figure 1-1A. The collection of dots in Figure 1-1B looks more like a large oval running from the lower left to the upper right of the diagram; the higher the SAT score, the greater the *tendency* to have higher grade point averages. Hence there is some predictability here, but it is not perfect.

Scatterplots tell us whether the values of two variables are correlated—whether they tend to occur together. We can summarize the information presented in a scatterplot with a single number, a bit of shorthand that is very helpful when you do not have a scatterplot handy. This number, known as a

scatterplot
Figure that illustrates a relationship between two variables

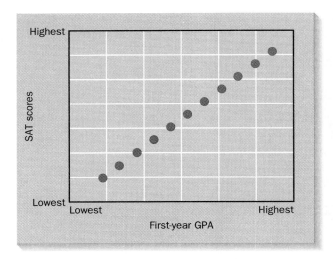

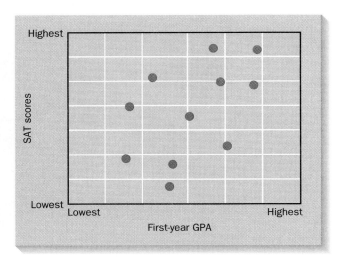

A   B

FIGURE 1-1 Scatterplots indicating (A) a perfect positive relationship and (B) a moderate positive relationship between SAT scores and first-year grade-point average (GPA).

correlation coefficient, is symbolized by the letter *r* (see Appendix A). A correlation coefficient can have a value ranging from +1.00 to −1.00—no higher and no lower. The number tells you the strength of the correlation, and the sign tells you the direction of the relation. What do those numbers mean? First, disregard the sign (+ or −) in front of the numbers for a moment. The higher the *r*, the stronger the relationship. Thus if *r* is .70, the two variables are more strongly associated than they would be if *r* were .30. If *r* is 0, the two variables are not related at all.

The sign (+ or −) tells us the *direction* of the relationship. A plus sign tells us that as the values of one variable (such as SAT scores) increase, so do the values of the other (e.g., grades). Thus values of both variables are headed in the same direction; they are *positively correlated*. Consequently, if SAT scores are high, grade-point averages also tend to be high. Similarly, the number of hours students study for an exam and the grades they earn are positively correlated. By contrast, a minus sign tells us that the values of the two variables travel in opposite directions; they are *negatively correlated*. As the values of one variable increase, the values of the other tend to decrease. For example, students who study a great deal should make fewer errors on an exam. Those who do not study much would probably make more errors. The variables of study time and errors on an exam are negatively correlated.

Psychological Detective

The two variables in our preceding example were SAT scores and grade-point averages. Before reading further, make a list of some factors that could be responsible for the association between these two variables.

correlation coefficient

Number ranging between +1.00 and −1.00 that represents the degree and direction of relationship between two variables

One factor that could explain the association between SAT scores and grades is the possibility that certain students (especially those with higher SAT scores) were raised by families that stressed enrichment and learning activities. This family influence provided information and experiences that contributed to higher SAT scores and better study habits (i.e., higher grades). We highlight this possibility because a correlation between two variables does not mean that one variable causes the other. The two variables may be related because of the influence of a third variable. Correlations do allow us to make predictions, however; the larger the correlation, the better the prediction.

survey method
Research method that involves collecting information from a selected group of people who are representative of a larger group

Survey Research

Psychologists and other social scientists devised the **survey method** of research to gather data from a sample that represents a larger population. Surveys are often used because they can be efficient ways to collect large amounts of information. They can be conducted in face-to-face interviews, by telephone through written questions, and even by computer.

An interest in understanding violence might lead researchers to ask, "How much violence exists in our society?" We could answer this question by asking every person in the country whether he or she had been the victim of a violent crime (such as robbery or assault) during the past year, but this kind of approach would be extremely expensive and impractical.

Psychological Detective

Suppose that we decided to answer our question by examining the number of violent crimes reported to the police. Can you think of why this approach might not provide an accurate estimate of the amount of violent crime in our society? What are some ways the type of survey used might influence the type of information that is produced? Write down some reasons before reading further.

The number of violent crimes reported to the police would not reflect the actual amount of violent crime in society because many crimes are never reported to the police. In 1988, the U.S. Department of Justice found that only 37 percent of all crimes were actually reported to the police; that is, for every

Surveys are a means of collecting large amounts of information. Face-to-face interviews allow interviewers to ask for clarification of answers.

FIGURE 1-2 Results of the Department of Justice's National Crime Victimization Survey.

Source: U.S. Department of Justice, 1997.

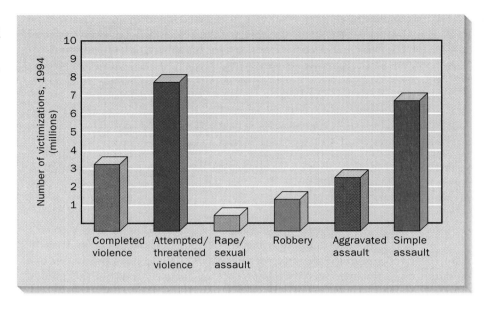

37 crimes reported, 63 were not reported (Jamieson & Flanagan, 1988). To counteract the problem of underreported crimes, the Justice Department collects data on crime victimization in its annual National Crime Victimization Survey. The survey depends on victims' reports; therefore it cannot assess the frequency of murder, a crime that is typically reported to police or discovered by them. How "violent" crimes are defined also will influence the number of crimes that are reported. Is death or hospitilization included in the definition? Is property damage a requirement? These features of the survey will have a direct influence on the number of violent crimes that are reported.

Researchers asked residents age 12 or older in 48,000 housing units a series of questions about their experiences with crimes in the previous year. This sample is extremely large, and researchers usually can conduct such large studies only with the resources available to the federal government. There were 43 million victimizations (some people are victims of more than one crime) during 1993. Of these crimes, 11 million were crimes against persons, and 32 million were crimes against property. This survey was repeated in 1994. Figure 1-2 shows some of the results of the survey of crime victimizations in 1994 as they pertain to crimes of violence (U.S. Department of Justice, 1997).

When conducting a survey, researchers must obtain a **representative sample**—one that is selected to reflect the characteristics of a larger group (the *population*). The researcher tries to make sure that the sample is a miniature version of the population. You see the survey method applied every November, when news anchors announce election winners based on information from polling researchers, with only 2 percent of the vote tabulated. How can anyone make a prediction based on 2 percent (or even less) of the vote? News organizations can make these predictions because their polling experts have identified key areas within the state that represent the entire population from the standpoint of gender, ethnicity, and political preference; thus a small but representative segment of the population can be used to predict the way the entire population voted.

Obtaining a representative sample is not the only important consideration when conducting surveys. Questions must be carefully worded to elicit meaningful and useful responses. Consider a survey of the number of headaches reported

representative sample
Sample selected so that it reflects the characteristics of a population of interest to the researcher

by respondents. When the question was phrased "Do you get headaches frequently, and, if so, how often?" the average number of reported headaches was 2.2 per week. When the word *occasionally* was substituted for the word *frequently* the average number of headaches reported was only 0.7 per week (Loftus, 1975). The respondents' answers may also depend on whether researchers include a "Don't know" option (Schuman & Presser, 1981). The absence of a "Don't know" response seems to create subtle pressure to offer opinions, even on fictitious, or imagined, issues (Bishop, Tuchfarber, & Oldendick, 1986). Survey questions are sometimes slanted in ways that invite biased results. For example, in 1993, H. Ross Perot and his United We Stand organization conducted a nationwide survey. Skeptical of the results, *Time* and CNN asked Yankelovich Partners, a professional survey company, to conduct two surveys of random samples of the U.S. population. One sample was given Perot's version of the questions; the second sample was asked similar questions that had been rewritten to reduce the potential for bias. Perot phrased one question this way: "Should laws be passed to eliminate all possibilities of special interests giving huge sums of money to candidates?" The Yankelovich version was "Should laws be passed to prohibit interest groups from contributing to campaigns they support?" The results were eye-opening. To the Perot version, 80 percent of respondents said yes and 17 percent no. In the Yankelovich survey, 40 percent favored the passing of such laws, whereas 55 percent supported the right to contribute (Moore & Parker, 1995). As we noted earlier, the nature of a survey and the way a project is conducted can result in different views of the true state of affairs.

The Experimental Method

The research methods covered so far can provide useful leads, strong data, and excellent descriptions. Yet, as we saw with correlational research, those methods cannot provide us with cause-and-effect statements. By contrast, the **experimental method** can provide such statements. Therefore it is considered the most powerful research method.

The logic of the experimental method starts with a *hypothesis,* or testable prediction, about which variable or variables cause the behavior under consideration. For example, what variables could conceivably affect violent behavior? Some possibilities are crowding, frustration, and hot weather. Each of these variables could affect the probability that an act of violence might occur.

In the logic of an experiment, such variables are called **independent variables.** The psychologist's goal is to manipulate one or more independent variables to determine the effect on a **dependent variable**—a behavior that shows the outcome of an experiment by revealing the effects of an independent variable (see Smith & Davis, 1997). In the study of violence, hitting a person could be a dependent variable; the number of hits might change if we manipulated an independent variable that actually affects the probability of violence, such as observing an aggressive model. Researchers are careful to offer clear and precise definitions for both the independent and dependent variables. Such definitions, known as **operational definitions,** allow other researchers to replicate (repeat) an experiment exactly as it was originally done in order to verify the findings. In a simple case, some participants in the experiment are exposed to the independent variable; they constitute the **experimental group.** Other participants are not exposed to the independent variable; they constitute the **control group** that will be compared with the experimental group on the dependent variable. If our independent variable had an effect on violence, the value of the dependent variable (number of hits) exhibited by the control group and the experimental group would be quite different.

experimental method
Research method that involves manipulating independent variables to determine how they affect dependent variables

independent variable
Variable manipulated by a researcher to determine its effects on a dependent variable

dependent variable
Variable that shows the outcome of an experiment by revealing the effects of an independent variable

operational definition
A careful and precise definition that allows other researchers to repeat an experiment

experimental group
The group in an experiment that receives the effect of the independent variable being manipulated

control group
A comparison group in an experiment that does not receive the effect of the independent variable being manipulated

Let's consider a classic experiment. In the 1960s, Albert Bandura and colleagues (Bandura, Ross, & Ross, 1963) conducted a study to determine whether children learn aggressive behaviors by observing the actions of others. They hypothesized that children who observed an adult behaving aggressively would be more likely than children who observed an adult *not* behaving aggressively to exhibit aggressive actions. Nursery school children were assigned to two groups; one group observed an aggressive adult model, and the other group observed a nonaggressive model. The *independent variable* in this experiment was observing an aggressive or a nonaggressive model. Later, all the children were given an opportunity to hit a Bobo doll (see Figure 1-3A); therefore, the *dependent variable* was the number of blows directed at the Bobo doll. Bandura and colleagues found that children who observed an aggressive model engaged in more aggressive behavior than those who observed a nonaggressive model. The independent variable (observing an aggressive model) led to a higher rate of aggression (hitting a Bobo doll)—the dependent variable. Although the research demonstrated that modeling can play a part in causing children to act aggressively, you need to keep some other factors about the experiment in mind. The specific details of the experiment, such as the type of participants, age of the models, sex of the models, measure of aggression, and so forth, may have influenced the results. Possibly other procedures, participants, and measures of aggression would have produced different results. Such considerations clearly point to the need to replicate or repeat research; they also highlight the care that experimenters must take in conducting and interpreting their research.

Psychological Detective

Suppose that Bandura and colleagues had assigned all of the boys to the group that observed the aggressive model and all the girls to the group that observed the nonaggressive model. Could they conclude that boys were more aggressive because they observed an aggressive model? Give this question some thought, and write down your response before reading further.

If all the boys had been assigned to the group that observed an aggressive model, we could not conclude that the aggressive model was responsible for their aggression in the second part of the experiment. Boys might be more aggressive than girls no matter what kind of model they observed. The logic of the experimental method requires that the *only* difference between groups be the independent variable (or variables) manipulated by the experimenter—in this case, the type of model observed. If you hold all other variables that could also influence the results of the experiment—known as **extraneous variables**—constant, you may identify the cause of the behavior under consideration. If all of the boys had been assigned to the aggressive-model group, there would be two possible explanations for any increased aggression: being a boy and observing an aggressive model.

In general—and this was also true for the study by Bandura and colleagues—we need to select two groups that are as much alike as possible before an experiment begins. One way to accomplish this objective is to use the procedure called **random assignment,** or assignment of participants to two or more groups on the basis of chance. Random assignment usually results in two groups that are quite similar in many characteristics. In this case, we would probably have about the same numbers of boys and girls in each group (see Figure 1-3B).

extraneous variables
Variables, other than the independent variable, that can influence the outcome of an experiment

random assignment
Assignment of experimental participants to two or more groups on the basis of chance

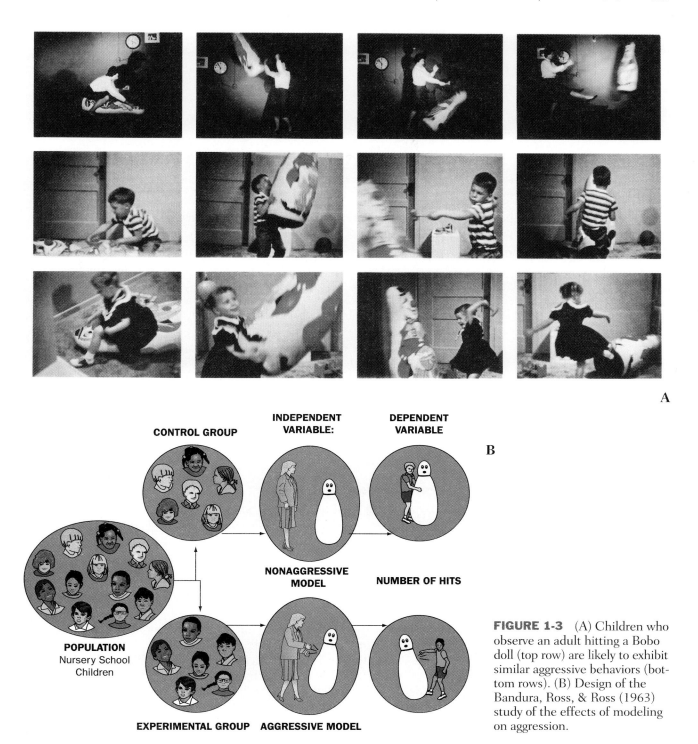

FIGURE 1-3 (A) Children who observe an adult hitting a Bobo doll (top row) are likely to exhibit similar aggressive behaviors (bottom rows). (B) Design of the Bandura, Ross, & Ross (1963) study of the effects of modeling on aggression.

In the coming chapters, you will see these research methods applied to answer questions about a wide range of behaviors. Examining the Study Chart should help you understand the differences among these methods. Remember that each method can make a contribution to our understanding and that the methods are often used in combination.

In this section, we have seen how, through careful design and execution, experimental research can show cause and effect. Once a research project is

Research Methods in Psychology

Method	Description
Case study	Use of information obtained from one person or a few people to illuminate the behaviors of others and to suggest further research.
Naturalistic observation	Observation of behaviors as they occur, without any intervention or alteration.
Correlational research	Research in which data on the incidence of two variables are analyzed to determine the extent to which those variables tend to occur together.
Survey research	Research in which information is gathered from a representative sample of a larger population, using face-to-face or telephone interviews or written questions.
Experimental method	Research technique in which an independent variable (or variables) is manipulated to determine whether it affects a dependent variable—a behavior that is the outcome of an experiment.

completed, however, the results must be analyzed before they can be understood and shared with other professionals.

Statistics and Psychologists

The practice of doing experiments created the need for methods to summarize experimental results before researchers presented them to the scientific community.

Psychological Detective

Why is it necessary to summarize research data before disseminating them? Jot down some answers to this question before reading further.

If you are conducting an experiment and a coworker simply hands you a sheet of paper with several hundred scientific observations on it, you are no closer to having an answer to your research question than before you started. You need to make sense out of the data that have been collected. Psychologists have turned to a branch of mathematics called *statistics* for assistance. **Statistics** involves the summarization, analysis, and interpretation of data. The two main branches of statistics assist your decisions in different ways. **Descriptive statistics** are procedures used to summarize a set of numbers so that you can understand and talk about them more intelligibly. **Inferential statistics** are procedures used to analyze data after an experiment is conducted to determine if an independent variable had a significant effect. Let's see how these two branches of statistics operate.

Descriptive Statistics. The test you took Tuesday was just returned. The score on your paper is 67. What is your reaction? Because you do not have enough information to know whether your score of 67 is good or bad, a reaction of uncertainty and confusion is understandable and predictable.

statistics
Branch of mathematics that involves the collection, analysis, and interpretation of data

descriptive statistics
Procedures used to summarize any set of data

inferential statistics
Procedures used to analyze data after an experiment is completed; used to determine if the independent variable has a significant effect

Psychological Detective

What additional information do you require to judge the quality of your work? Give this question some thought and write down your answers before continuing.

Your first response may have been, "How did the rest of the class do?" You're on the right track, but let's see if we can be a bit more precise. First, we need to know what the typical score was. When we report the typical score in a set of numbers, we are presenting a **measure of central tendency.** Undoubtedly you are already familiar with one measure of central tendency, the *arithmetic mean,* which is calculated by dividing the total of the scores by the number of scores. By itself, however, a measure of central tendency does not provide enough information for you to fully understand your test score of 67; you also need to know about the variability or spread of the other scores in the class. **Measures of variability** provide information about the variability or spread of the scores in a set of data. If all of the scores are clustered closely around the *mean* or other measure of central tendency, then you will view the score of 67 differently than if the scores are spread out widely. Measures of central tendency and variability are the primary descriptive statistics used by psychologists; they are described in more detail in Appendix A.

Inferential Statistics. When an experiment is conducted we hope that the manipulation of our independent variable (IV) will have a pronounced effect on the dependent variable. Typically the effect of the IV is evaluated by the difference between the groups in the experiment; the larger the difference, the greater the effect of the IV. Not all differences between groups, however, are attributable to the influence of the IV. Sometimes the differences are due to chance variation among the participants who are in the groups. Even though we may select our groups randomly, they will never be perfectly identical. So how does the experimenter distinguish between differences among the experimental participants and differences caused by the IV? *Inferential statistics* offer a solution to this dilemma. Conducting an inferential statistical test allows the researcher to mathematically evaluate the difference between the groups in an experiment and decide whether the observed difference occurred frequently or rarely by chance. If the difference occurs *rarely* by chance, then the experimenter concludes that the result is "significant" and that the difference was caused by the IV. Further discussion of inferential statistics and a sample inferential statistical test are found in Appendix A.

Research, however, is not conducted or reported in a vacuum; psychologists are obligated to adhere to a code of ethical behavior.

Research Ethics

Let's return to the 1963 Milgram study described at the beginning of this chapter (see p. 4). Imagine being a participant and being asked to administer 450 volts of electric shock to another person. How would you react if you agreed to administer the shock? Later you are told that no shocks were actually delivered, but you realize that if they had been delivered, you might have killed someone. Clearly, there is the potential for long-term, traumatic effects on the research

measures of central tendency
Descriptive measures of a set of data that tell us about a typical score

measures of variability
Descriptive measures that tell us about the amount of variability or spread in a set of data

participants in this experiment. This example highlights a major concern for researchers: how to conduct research in an ethical manner.

The American Psychological Association (1992) has adopted ethical guidelines that prescribe standards of conduct for the professional work of psychologists in their roles as researchers, clinicians, and teachers. These guidelines include several general principles. For example, psychologists must maintain high standards of competence in their work, including recognizing the limitations of their expertise. They also must show respect for the rights and dignity of people, such as rights to privacy and confidentiality.

The ethical guidelines for conducting research require that all research proposals be reviewed to ensure compliance with the guidelines. Each proposal must be approved by an institutional review board (IRB) established by a college, university, or other organization where research is conducted (Smith & Davis, 1997).

Protection from Harm. What's more, the ethical guidelines state that psychologists who conduct research using human participants must ensure they are protected from physical and psychological harm. For this reason, the study conducted by Milgram several decades ago would not be permitted today. Although no shocks were actually given, the study required the participants to obey the experimenter despite the moral imperative that they not hurt another person. This type of conflict is certainly unpleasant and could cause psychological harm to some people.

Psychologists today are very careful to follow the ethical guidelines for research. Consider the work of two psychologists who studied the relationship of handedness (preferred hand) and life expectancy. Diane Halpern and Stanley Coren "did not want to appear to be ghouls or to be insensitive to people's feelings when they were grieving over the death of a loved one" (Coren, 1992, p. 216). First, they consulted a bereavement counselor who suggested that they not contact anyone unless at least nine months had passed since the loved one's death. The counselor also suggested that they make the contact as gentle as possible and not follow up or press people for responses. The researchers decided that they would not contact next of kin if the death had been a result of murder or suicide or if the deceased was a child age 6 or younger. Their research proposal was evaluated and cleared by a university research ethics committee. Despite their precautions, a few people they contacted did become upset by questions about deceased loved ones (Coren, 1992). Figure 1-4 shows the postcard the researchers used.

The results of this study show that being left-handed was associated with reduced longevity (Coren, 1992; Coren & Halpern, 1991). Left-handed people died at an earlier age (mean of 66 years) than right-handed people (mean of 75 years). Other researchers have not found handedness to be associated with earlier death (Harris, 1993; Salive, Guralnik, & Glynn, 1993), although these findings have been disputed (Halpern & Coren, 1993). Study of the possible relationship, if any, between handedness and death continues; the research is conducted in accordance with established ethical principles designed to protect participants (in this case, the relatives of deceased persons) from any harm.

Confidentiality. The ethical guidelines also require that any research records associated with a person's name or identity be kept confidential. For example, Halpern and Coren "kept no records as to whom we contacted, and there was no identifying information on any of the materials that we sent" (D. F. Halpern, personal communication, August 3, 1992). In other cases, psychologists may use code names or numbers for their participants so that information cannot be associated with the actual names of people who have taken part in research.

Please answer the following questions about the deceased person:

Circle one

1) Hand used for writing	Right	Left	Don't know
2) Hand used for drawing	Right	Left	Don't know
3) Hand used for throwing a ball	Right	Left	Don't know

4) Did this person suffer from any allergies? If so, explain: _____

_____

5) Cause of death (circle one and explain at the bottom
   a) medical
   b) accidental
   c) don't know

_____

_____

Thank you. Please deposit this card in a mailbox at your earliest convenience.

FIGURE 1-4 Postcard used in Coren and Halpern (1991) study of the effects of handedness on life expectancy.

Source: Halpern, 1991.

Voluntary Participation. Participants, including college students in introductory courses, must be told that their participation in research is voluntary. They cannot be coerced into participating. College students may be part of a pool from which researchers draw participants for their studies. If a student objects to participating, he or she must be given an opportunity to select other ways to earn the same amount of credit or to complete the course requirement. In other words, no one may be punished for not participating in research. To enable potential participants to make proper judgments about their participation, the researcher must describe the procedures of the experiment and obtain a written agreement to participate, which is called an **informed consent.** This document indicates that the participant knows the nature of the research and what he or she has agreed to do before participating.

Deception and Intimidation. Some experiments require the use of deception. For example, researchers would be unable to study the true effectiveness of drug treatments without the use of placebos. Participants who are given placebos are led to believe they are taking the actual drug so that researchers can assess the influence of expectations on the drug's effectiveness. When psychologists use deception in their research, they must **debrief** the participants immediately after the study or provide a complete explanation of the deception.

informed consent
Written document in which a person who might be involved in a research study agrees to participate after receiving information about the researcher's specific procedures

debriefing
Procedure during which a complete explanation of research that has involved deception is provided to a participant

Psi Chi Newsletter 22, no. 1 (Winter 1996). Reprinted with the permission of Psi Chi.

During the debriefing participants are allowed to ask questions and the researcher checks for possible negative aftereffects of the deception. In addition, participants in psychological research have the right to end their participation at any time. Researchers cannot use any form of threat or intimidation to force them to complete tasks in a study.

The Ethics of Research with Animals.   As you will see throughout this book, many of psychology's most enduring findings have resulted from research with animals (Domjan & Purdy, 1995; King & Viney, 1992). For example, much of our knowledge about the structure and functioning of the brain (Chapter 2), sensation and perception (Chapter 3), motivation and emotion (Chapter 4), basic processes of learning and conditioning (Chapter 6), developmental processes (Chapters 9 and 10), and maladaptive behavior (Chapter 13) is the result of animal research. Yet the use of animals in psychological research has not gone unchallenged (Mukerjee, 1997).

The ongoing debate between advocates of using animals in research and those who deplore such efforts has been heated and emotional at times (Galvin & Herzog, 1992). Animal rights activists view the use of animals in psychological and medical research as cruel and unnecessary. What's more, they note that such research often involves stress, pain, punishment, or social and environmental deprivation (Bowd & Shapiro, 1993; Rollin, 1985). On the other hand, the value of animal research has been defended by arguments that such research has led to improvements in human welfare (Baldwin, 1993; Miller, 1985). Psychological and medical researchers point out that some types of research could not be conducted without using animals. The American Psychological Association (1992) has adopted a set of seven principles for the ethical treatment of animals, including consideration of the following:

1. Justification for the research to be conducted: Is this an important piece of research? Have procedures not involving the use of animals been considered?
2. Qualifications of the personnel involved: Has the head of the research team received proper training in animal experimentation?
3. Care and housing of the animals: Will the animals be cared for appropriately, and will their quarters allow appropriate exercise?
4. Acquisition of the animals: Will the animals be acquired from a licensed, approved supplier?
5. The experimental procedures to be used.
6. The conduct of field research: Will the study of animals in the natural setting disturb their habitat?
7. The educational use of animals.

Researchers who use animals in their research are subject to a long list of regulations, including local, state, and federal laws. These regulations seek to define under what circumstances it is acceptable to sacrifice animals for research. Moreover, the regulations often mandate certain requirements concerning food, cage space, and veterinary care.

A number of factors influence individuals' judgments about the ethics of using animals in research. These factors are complex and include the similarity of the animals to humans, their "cuteness," and the perceived importance of the research to alleviating human suffering (Herzog, 1990).

The influence of the animal rights movement is evident. A decline in the number of studies using certain animal species such as cats, dogs, and rabbits may be due, in part, to the attention that the animal rights movement has focused on this issue (Viney, King, & Berndt, 1990). Moreover, researchers are now looking for ways to reduce the number of animals used in research. For example, they are investigating alternatives to the use of animals for testing potentially toxic chemicals. The new methods do not involve testing intact higher animals, such as dogs and cats; instead, they rely on bacteria, cultured animal cells, or fertilized chicken eggs (Goldberg & Frazier, 1989). Such methods, however, do not eliminate the need for animals in certain types of research. Opinions on the use of animals in research will no doubt continue to be highly personal, emotional, and strong.

Now that we have discussed the need to be a good psychological detective and the methods used by psychologists to conduct and analyze their research, it is time to stand back and get a general overview of the field of psychology before we begin our chapter-by-chapter coverage of specific psychological topics. A brief review of the history of modern psychology and a consideration of the activities of contemporary psychologists should prepare you for this more in-depth coverage.

Review Summary

1. The goals of psychology are to describe, predict, and control behavior. These goals are accomplished by using the **scientific method,** which is systematic and empirical (based on observable events).

2. A **case study** is an in-depth analysis of a single person or event. Although the findings of a case study may apply only to the person who was studied, they may provide direction for further study using other methods.

3. To study behavior in real-life settings, psychologists often use **naturalistic observation.** This technique also may suggest research projects using more controlled approaches. In using naturalistic observation, the onlooker must be unobtrusive and avoid influencing the behavior being studied.

4. Correlational research tells whether the values of two variables are related. Although correlational methods do not inform us about causality, they can provide useful insights and help us to make predictions.

5. By asking questions of a **representative sample,** researchers using the **survey method** can provide useful information about a much larger population. The wording of the questions can influence participants' responses.

6. Because it can generate cause-and-effect statements, many psychologists believe that the **experimental method** is the most powerful research approach. By manipulating an **independent variable** (the cause), the researcher determines whether it influences the **dependent variable** (the effect). Despite these strengths, the results and interpretation of a scientific experiment can be influenced by the specific way the research is conducted, the culture in which the research is conducted, and the experimenter's personal biases.

7. Statistics is a procedure that involves the collection, analysis, and interpretation of data. **Descriptive statistics** are used to summarize data, whereas **inferential statistics** are used to determine if the results of an experiment are significant.

8. Measures of central tendency provide information about the typical score in a set of numbers. **Measures of variability** provide information about the variability in a set of data.

9. The American Psychological Association has established ethical guidelines for making decisions about research with both human and animal participants.

Study Break

1. When people attend sporting events and see a television camera focused on them, they often act silly. This effect is most nearly <u>opposite</u> of what research technique?

    a. case study
    b. experiment
    c. naturalistic observation
    d. correlational study

2. Which aspect of a correlation coefficient tells you the <u>direction</u> of the relationship between the variables? Why?

3. The experimenter assesses the outcome of the experiment by measuring the _____ variable.
   a. dependent
   b. independent
   c. controlled
   d. extraneous

4. What kind of statistical procedure is used to analyze data after an experiment is conducted to determine whether the independent variable had a significant effect?
   a. descriptive
   b. inferential
   c. summary
   d. biased

5. Discuss one of the strengths and one of the weaknesses of naturalistic observation as a research technique. What is a reactive measure? How can it be avoided?

6. In each of the following sets of correlation coefficients, which one represents the strongest relationship? Why?
   a. +.25   −.30   +.10
   b. +.65   −.88   −1.00
   c. −.20   −.05   +.33

7. "Correlation does not imply causality." What does this statement mean?

8. What do we mean when we say that a sample must be representative?

9. Identify the independent variable and the dependent variable in each of the following situations:
   a. A researcher is interested in how fast college students can turn off a buzzer when it sounds. The participants are tested under two conditions: dim light and bright light.
   b. The Board of Directors of the National Football League has decided that half of its teams will sell beer until the end of the game; the other half will stop sales at the end of the third quarter. The board is conducting a study to determine whether the timing of beer sales influences the number of fights and arrests that occur at games.
   c. An industrial psychologist has developed two possible packages for a new shampoo that will be on the market soon. She is interested in seeing which package has the greater sales appeal.

The Origins of Modern Psychology

Some friends came over the other day and were talking about the courses they are taking at the university. Several of them are enrolled in a psychology course. They are fascinated by the topics covered and wonder whether psychology has always been part of the university curriculum. *What are the origins of scientific psychology?* ■

Although people have observed and studied human behavior for millennia, scientific psychology is a relatively new discipline. The origins of modern psychology can be traced to the University of Leipzig in Germany, where the first laboratory devoted to the scientific study of psychology was established in 1879.

Wundt and Structuralism

Wilhelm Wundt (1832–1920) is credited with establishing the first psychology laboratory (Bringmann, Bringmann, & Ungerer, 1980). Because the profession of psychology was not a career choice at that time, Wundt was originally trained as a physician. His mission in establishing the laboratory was to describe the contents of the conscious mind. Wundt and his student Edward B. Titchener (1867–1927), who brought Wundt's type of psychology to the United States, wanted to study psychology in the same way that a person would study physics or chemistry. If

Wilhelm Wundt is credited with establishing the first psychology laboratory in 1879.

researchers could break down the contents of the mind into basic units like the basic elements of matter in chemistry, they could identify the structure of conscious experience and describe its major components (e.g., feelings, sensations, images). This approach to psychology became known as **structuralism.**

Titchener's research depended on a method called **introspection,** in which participants gave verbal reports of their conscious experiences. For example, participants given an orange would not describe it as a fruit but would instead describe its color, shape, and texture and other aspects of their own experience of the orange. Across a variety of tasks, however, the participants had difficulty producing similar reports; this fact raised questions about the existence of any common elements of conscious experience. Structuralism was replaced by other approaches, and at times conscious experience was not even considered a legitimate subject of psychological research.

During the past decade or two, psychologists have rediscovered conscious experience and investigated it using more sophisticated techniques than those available to the structuralists at the end of the nineteenth century (Coon, 1993; Gardner, 1985). Today a rapidly growing area of psychology has broadened the early interests of structuralists; it is called **cognitive psychology.** Cognitive psychologists are not interested in the structure of conscious experience; instead, they study higher mental processes. Their research is designed to determine how we store and recall information, solve problems, and make decisions (Bourne et al., 1986). We discuss the cognitive perspective in greater detail later in this chapter.

Functionalism

A new approach to psychology developed in the United States in the late 1800s. **Functionalism** was concerned not with the structure of the mind but with the purposes of consciousness—what the mind does and why. One early proponent of functionalism, William James (1842–1910), was especially interested in what he termed the "stream of consciousness" (Simon, 1996). Because consciousness was like a continually flowing stream, it could not be easily broken down into its elements as Wundt had hoped. According to James, if it were broken down into elements, it would lose its reality.

Functionalists wanted to see how people use information to adapt to their environment (Fancher, 1996). James and his functionalist colleagues were among the first applied psychologists; they were interested in the practical aspects of psychology, such as creating optimal conditions for learning or selecting the right workers for various jobs. Functionalism reached its peak in 1906 with James Rowland Angell's presidential address to the American Psychological Association. During its influential period, functionalism was associated most strongly with James Rowland Angell at the University of Chicago and Robert S. Woodworth at Columbia University.

Gestalt Psychology

A group of psychologists who termed their approach **Gestalt psychology,** which was noted for emphasizing that perception of a whole differs from that of individual stimuli, spearheaded the challenge to the structuralists' notion that conscious experience could be broken down into elements (Ash, 1995). The key members of this group were Max Wertheimer (1880–1943), Wolfgang Köhler (1887–1967), and Kurt Koffka (1886–1941). The Gestalt

structuralism
Earliest approach in modern psychology, founded by Wilhelm Wundt; its goal was to analyze the basic elements of conscious experience

introspection
Structural psychologists' major method, in which participants reported the contents of their conscious experience

cognitive psychology
Study of higher mental processes, such as thinking, knowing, and deciding

functionalism
Approach to psychology that focused on the functions of consciousness

Gestalt psychology
Approach to psychology most noted for emphasizing that our perception of a whole is different from our perception of the individual stimuli

FIGURE 1-5 Although a strip of film contains a series of separate images, we perceive those images as continuous when they are projected on a screen. This phenomenon, known as *apparent motion,* gave rise to the Gestalt school of psychology.

Ivan Pavlov. His studies of digestion in dogs led to important observations about how animals associate events in their environment.

John B. Watson. The founder of behaviorism declared that psychologists should limit their research to observable behaviors.

behavioral perspective
Perspective that focuses on observable behavior and emphasizes the learned nature of behavior

approach started in Germany in 1912, when Wertheimer (King et al., 1994) described the visual illusion called *apparent motion,* in which a rapid sequence of stationary images creates the illusion of movement, as in a movie (Rock & Palmer, 1990; see Figure 1-5). Soon Gestalt psychologists were describing other phenomena that supported their contention that what we perceive is different from the sum of its parts. We perceive unified forms, rather than bits and pieces. Because the German word *Gestalt* can be translated as "pattern," "shape," or "configuration," Gestalt psychologists have made their greatest contributions in the area of perception, as we see in Chapter 3.

The Behavioral Perspective

The **behavioral perspective,** unlike the approaches we have discussed thus far, focuses on observable behaviors; thus it does not speculate about mental processes such as thinking. Moreover, this perspective emphasizes the importance of learning in understanding how various behaviors occur.

In the early 1900s the Russian physiologist Ivan Pavlov (1849–1936) was studying digestion in dogs when he noticed a curious phenomenon. When the dogs were about to be fed, they began salivating at the sight of the food or the jangling of keys used to unlock the rooms where they were kept. The dogs seemed to have learned an association between certain sounds or sights and being fed. As we see in Chapter 6, this simple observation led to the development of our understanding of how organisms learn to associate events in their environments.

The American psychologist John B. Watson (1878–1958) read about Pavlov's work and saw great promise in it. Watson believed psychology should be concerned not with the mind or consciousness but solely with observable behaviors. He asserted that the application of rigorous scientific principles, as used in Pavlov's laboratory, could lead to major advances (Buckley, 1989). Watson developed and applied his principles in the laboratory under strictly controlled conditions. Laboratory animals made excellent subjects for his research, which he later expanded to human participants.

The behavioral tradition started by Pavlov and continued by Watson found many strong proponents. The most notable was B. F. Skinner (1904–1990), who has been called the "greatest contemporary psychologist" (Fowler, 1990). In some ways, Skinner's approach to psychology was simple: Behavior changes as a result of its consequences (Bjork, 1997). Thus environmental consequences, rather than free will, shape human behavior. The behavioral psychologist's goal is to identify and change the environmental conditions that control behavior (O'Neill, 1995).

Skinner's followers used many of his basic principles to alter human behavior in a variety of settings (Martin & Pear, 1996). Some of Skinner's methods have been used to teach schizophrenic patients to speak after years of being mute, to improve safety in manufacturing plants, and to teach basic skills to mentally retarded persons. If you have ever visited an amusement park that features trained dolphins, seals, whales, or other animals, you have seen an application of Skinner's principles (see Chapter 6).

Sigmund Freud and the Psychodynamic Perspective

Historically, Skinner's approach followed the development of Watson's behaviorism. At about the same time Watson was defining psychology as the study of observable behavior, however, Sigmund Freud (1856–1939), across the Atlantic, was delving deeply beneath observable behaviors (Gelfand & Kerr, 1992). Few people have had such a profound impact on the way we think about ourselves as Freud, and few have been—or continue to be—so controversial (Crews, 1996).

Freud was trained as a neurologist, rather than a psychologist. The patients who came to him suffered from a variety of anxieties and other disturbances. Freud and his followers developed the **psychodynamic perspective,** which suggests that both normal and abnormal behaviors are determined primarily by unconscious forces. The term *psychodynamic* is used because these forces are believed to interact with one another. Freud's experiences in treating his patients convinced him that the unconscious mind exerted great control over behavior. Among the observations that led him to this conclusion were "slips of the tongue," in which the patients' true feelings were apparently revealed, and analysis of his patients' dreams. Freud came to believe that the mind often disguises dreams so that the dreamer is not aware of their true meaning (see Chapter 5).

Freud also focused on early childhood experiences as a major influence on personality development. According to Freud, if you want to understand a person's personality, you must examine his or her early experiences, which could have long-lasting effects. Freud gained great fame and notoriety by suggesting that people (even children) are driven by motives that are sexual in nature.

In treating his patients, Freud first turned to hypnosis (see Chapter 5), but he abandoned it when he determined that not everyone could be hypnotized. The treatment approach for maladaptive behavior that he eventually developed, known as **psychoanalytic therapy,** attempts to bring unconscious causes of distress to the conscious level. According to Freud, once the sources of distress are brought to awareness, they can be changed.

The Humanistic Perspective

Over time, the psychodynamic and behavioral approaches were questioned. Many psychologists viewed the behavioral approach as cold and unappealing. To these psychologists, the notion that all behavior is controlled by environmental circumstances left no room for personal freedom, and the suggestion that we are doomed to behave in environmentally determined ways was unattractive. These critics believed that behaviorists seemed to avoid the unique and positive qualities of human behavior, such as creativity and love. What's more, the argument went, their views of human nature were either neutral or negative.

B. F. Skinner. His principles provided the basis for many applications of psychology.

Sigmund Frued. His influence can be seen not only in psychology but in many other fields.

psychodynamic perspective
View taken by Sigmund Freud and his followers suggesting that normal and abnormal behaviors are determined primarily by unconscious forces

psychoanalytic therapy
Treatment for maladaptive behavior developed by Sigmund Freud; its goal is to bring unconscious causes of behavior to the conscious level

To some, the psychodynamic approach was no more appealing because its proponents viewed behavior as resulting from irrational forces that are not even under conscious control. Psychoanalysts studied people suffering from a variety of pathological problems, whereas behaviorists attempted to identify conditions that influence behavior by studying lower animals under controlled laboratory conditions. Critics argued that neither of these perspectives led to a true understanding of human behavior because neither focused on the creative potential and psychological health of human beings. As a result, a new approach to psychology developed. Emphasizing free will and individuals' control of their own behavior, the **humanistic perspective** was characterized by a distinctly positive view of human nature. Humanistic psychologists viewed themselves as a "third force" because they were an alternative to the behavioral and psychodynamic perspectives in psychology (DeCarvalho, 1990, 1991, 1992).

The proponents of this approach, notably Carl Rogers (1902–1987) and Abraham Maslow (1908–1970), focused on the freedom they believed characterizes human behavior. According to the humanists, people have choices in their lives, and we cannot understand their choices by studying animals in laboratories or people experiencing adjustment problems.

Rather than attempting to develop general principles, Rogers and Maslow sought to understand each person as a unique individual. Humanists believe each person experiences the world differently. One of the most important humanistic principles is that all human beings have a basic need to grow to their fullest potential. The humanists' major contributions to psychology have been their dramatically different view of human nature and the development of a variety of psychotherapeutic techniques (Barton, 1992).

The Physiological Perspective

As we discuss in Chapter 2, every behavior of human beings and animals is related to some physiological change within the body. These physiological changes are the focus of psychologists interested in the **physiological perspective.** Physiological psychologists have a special interest in the functioning of the brain and the rest of the nervous system (Kalat, 1998). To assess neurological function they now use sophisticated equipment that can create images of the brain. These imaging techniques reveal differences in the functioning of various areas of the brain depending on the task given to a person.

Physiological psychologists also study how our nerve cells, called *neurons,* communicate with one another through special chemical substances called *neurotransmitters.* Scientists have identified a number of different neurotransmitters; each seems to play a special role in a variety of normal and abnormal behaviors. Most drugs influence our emotions and behaviors by altering levels of these neurotransmitters in the body.

During recent years physiological psychologists have shown a special interest in the influence of heredity on personality characteristics, abilities, and the potential for developing certain abnormal behavior patterns. A number of psychologists are examining the wide range of physiological changes that occur when we are under stress. Their research has determined that illness is not simply a function of the presence of disease-causing viruses or bacteria. More and more, psychologists are investigating how personal factors such as how we deal with stress can influence our health status.

humanistic perspective
Approach to psychology associated with Abraham Maslow and Carl Rogers; emphasizes free will and individuals' control of their behavior

physiological perspective
View that behaviors and mental processes can be understood and explained by studying the underlying physiology

The Cognitive Perspective

Because they focused only on observable behaviors, the behaviorists did not study cognitive processes—processes such as thinking, remembering, and determining how material is organized and stored in the mind—as part of the mainstream of psychological research. Consequently, from the 1920s to the 1960s psychologists gave little research attention to these processes. Certain psychologists, however, disagreed that observable behavior should be the sole subject matter of psychology. For example, the Gestalt psychologists advocated the study of cognitive processes. Psychologists George Miller and Jerome Bruner established the Center for Cognitive Studies at Harvard University in 1960, and Ulrich Neisser published the book *Cognitive Psychology* in 1967. The appearance of a widely read article supporting the study of cognitive processes (Lieberman, 1979), combined with the ability of the computer to simulate human thought processes, generated considerable interest and research. Many psychologists have accepted the **cognitive perspective**—where the focus is on how thought occurs, memory processes, and information storage and utilization—and currently conduct research in the area of cognitive processes.

These different perspectives are summarized in the Study Chart on page 34. You should review this material at this time.

Mary Whiton Calkins, the fourteenth president of the American Psychological Association, was the first woman to be elected to that position.

The Cultural and Diversity Perspective

Attend a major meeting of psychologists and you are likely to be surrounded by dozens of different types of psychologists. Many are employed by colleges and universities, where they may teach, conduct research, or work in a psychological clinic sponsored by the university. The presence of women and minority psychologists provides a vivid contrast to the Caucasian, male-dominated field of only a few years ago. Psychologists are beginning to realize that the culture in which research is conducted; the gender, ethnicity, and personal biases of the researcher; and the gender and ethnicity of the research participants all influence our research results and contribute to our conception of "truth." Psychology is becoming more diverse, but this has not always been the case (Bohan, 1992a, 1992b).

In the past, numerous barriers limited access to the field, especially for women and ethnic minorities. For example, Mary Whiton Calkins (1863–1930) completed her work at Harvard University, where she was a student of William James, but the university refused to award the doctoral degree she had earned because it did not grant degrees to women (Furumoto, 1979). Despite this setback, Calkins had a distinguished career in teaching, founded one of the first psychology laboratories in the United States, and was the first woman to be elected president of the American Psychological Association (Madigan & O'Hara, 1992).

In some cases, marital status and family ties hindered the careers of the first female psychologists. For example, the noted researcher Christine Ladd-Franklin "was not considered a suitable candidate for any regular academic position" because she was married (Furumoto, 1992, p. 180). Similarly, the tradition of the eldest daughter taking care of her aging parents cut short the budding career of Milicent Shinn, the first woman to receive a Ph.D. from the University of California at Berkeley in 1898. Shinn established herself as a leading expert on the mental and physical growth of infants and seemed poised for an eminent career in psychology until her parents' illness forced her to return to her family farm (Scarborough & Furumoto, 1987). Her career stopped completely at that point and was never resumed.

Christine Ladd-Franklin was a noted researcher who was denied a regular academic position because she was married.

cognitive perspective
View that focuses on the study of how thought occurs, how our memories work, and how information is organized and stored

STUDY CHART

Major Perspectives in Psychology

Perspective	Description	Key Figures
Structuralism	Attempted to identify the basic elements and structure of conscious experience	Wilhelm Wundt (1832–1920) and Edward B. Titchener (1867–1927)
Functionalism	Concerned with the purposes of consciousness—what the mind does and why—and how that information could be put to practical use	William James (1842–1910) and James Rowland Angell (1869–1949)
Gestalt psychology	Made major contributions to understanding how we perceive the world as different from the sum of its individual elements	Max Wertheimer (1880–1943), Wolfgang Köhler (1887–1967), and Kurt Koffka (1886–1941)
Behavioral	Focuses on observable behaviors without speculating about mental processes such as thinking; a major emphasis is that learning plays a key role in controlling and influencing all behaviors	John B Watson (1878–1958) and B. F. Skinner (1904–1990)
Psychodynamic	Based on the belief that the unconscious mind exerts great control over behavior and that early childhood experiences are a major influence on personality development	Sigmund Freud (1856–1939)
Humanistic	Focuses on the creative potential and psychological health of human beings while emphasizing the individual's interpretation of events	Carl Rogers (1902–1987) and Abraham Maslow (1908–1970)
Physiological	Focuses on the underlying physiology involved in all forms of behavior and mental processes; uses increasingly sophisticated research tools to investigate brain functioning and conduction of nerve impulses; also investigates the role of heredity in normal and abnormal behavior patterns	Karl S. Lashley (1890–1958)
Cognitive	Focuses on the processes of thinking, memory, and organizing and storing information	George Miller (b. 1920), Jerome Bruner (b. 1915) and Ulrich Neisser (b. 1928)
Cultural and diversity	Focuses on the influence that different cultures and diverse individuals have on the research process and the results of that process	Janet Hyde and David Matsumoto

A century after Harvard refused to award Calkins a doctoral degree, women are entering the field of psychology in great numbers (see Figure 1-6). Women outnumber men two-to-one as undergraduate psychology majors and now earn more doctoral degrees in psychology than men.

The struggle of racial minorities to become recognized professionals parallels that of the early women psychologists. Robert Guthrie (1998) summarized the struggles of African-American psychologists in his influential book *Even the Rat Was White*. For example, he indicates that professional training was not an option for black Americans during the late 1800s and early 1900s. It wasn't until 1920 that Francis C. Sumner (1895–1954) became the first African American to receive a Ph.D. in psychology. Subsequently, Sumner established the psychology program at Howard University and turned it into the major source for doctoral degrees for

FIGURE 1-6 Percentages of doctoral degrees in psychology awarded to men and women.

Source: Henderson, Clarke, & Woods, 1998.

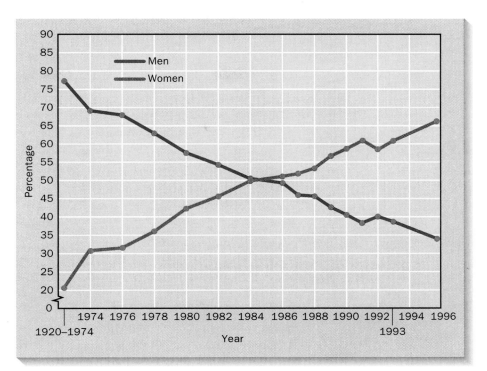

Milicent Shinn was the first woman to receive a Ph.D. from the University of California at Berkeley. She later abandoned her career to care for her aging parents.

Kenneth B. Clark was the first African American to serve as president of the American Psychological Association

African-American students during the first half of the twentieth century. Sumner has been followed by a succession of eminent African-American psychologists such as James Arthur Bayton (1912–1990), who achieved national recognition for his marketing research.

Doctoral degrees in psychology were not granted to African-American women until the 1930s. Two women in this group are noteworthy. Inez Beverly Prosser (1897–1934) was the first African-American woman to receive a doctoral degree in educational psychology; she received this degree from the University of Cincinnati in 1933. Unfortunately, her career was cut short by a tragic automobile accident one year later. Ruth Winifred Howard (b. 1900) received her Ph.D. in psychology in 1934 from the University of Minnesota. She was the first person to publish research on triplets.

Until recently, few members of racial minority groups obtained jobs in psychology. Today the number of minority candidates receiving doctoral degrees and finding employment in psychology is increasing (Howard et al., 1986). In fact, in 1970 the American Psychological Association elected an African American, Kenneth B. Clark (b. 1914), as its president. Clark is noted for his research on the harmful effects of segregation, which was cited by the Supreme Court in the landmark 1954 case, *Brown* v. *Board of Education.* His wife, Mamie Phipps Clark (1917–1983), received her doctoral degree in psychology from Columbia University in 1944 and achieved considerable recognition through her research and publication on such topics as "The Development of Consciousness of Self and Emergence of Racial Identification in Negro Preschool Children," which appeared in a 1939 issue of the *Journal of Social Psychology.*

An Asian American, Richard Suinn, was elected president of the American Psychological Association in 1997. However, attaining prestigious offices in professional associations is not the only visible sign of the influence of culture and diversity.

Cultural & Diversity Perspective

Dr. Mamie Phipps Clark conducted important research on consciousness of self and social identification in African American preschoolers.

Appreciating Differences

THE IMPACT OF DIFFERENT CULTURES AND DIVERSITY ON PSYCHOLOGY IS SEEN IN contemporary psychological literature. Studies on diverse groups and topics—such as gender issues, ethnic groups, national cultures, sexual orientation, and persons with disabilities—abound in the psychological journals. It is arguable (Matsumoto, 1998) that there is a revolution afoot in the field of psychology; there is a move toward a cultural psychology where such topics are the rule rather than the exception. Psychologist David Matsumoto believes that

> the psychological principles we derive about people may be consistent or discrepant across cultures. To the extent that differences do exist, it is important for all of us to appreciate how cultural factors moderate our psychological processes. In gaining such appreciation, we can learn how our own viewpoint, developed within our own cultural framework, can distort our interpretation of others' behaviors. At the same time, we need to know what kinds of cross-cultural similarities exist in psychological principles and basic processes. Knowledge about these similarities as well should help us in our endeavors to apply these principles to improve our lives. (Matsumoto, 1997, p. 2)

In previous editions of this book we have woven cultural and diversity material throughout the text—a tradition we continue in this edition. However, to highlight this important emphasis in psychology more clearly, we have included a specific section on the *Cultural and Diversity Perspective* in each chapter. Without question, the good psychological detective will take cultural and diversity factors into account when evaluating the research results reported in the coming chapters. Keep these issues in mind as you read this text and become involved with the Psychological Detective activities.

Present-Day Psychology

Psychologists today are interested in a diversity of topics. In fact, there are few endeavors that would not interest at least one of the more than half-million psychologists in the world (Rosenzweig, 1992).

Present-day psychologists do not align themselves strictly with any of the approaches we outlined in our earlier discussion of the origins of psychology. Instead they tend to choose the approach they consider appropriate to each issue under consideration. Because they use several approaches, many psychologists have adopted an **eclectic approach** to psychology.

Most psychologists earn an advanced degree, usually a doctorate. In a number of states a person cannot assume the title of *psychologist* unless he or she meets certain standards of education and training set by a state board. Psychologists all over the world are working to establish legal status for their profession. Their purpose is to protect the public by ensuring that people who represent themselves as psychologists have appropriate training and professional experience.

Although all psychologists share a keen interest in advancing our knowledge of human and animal behavior through research, some psychologists, by choice, engage in little or no research. A rapidly growing number of psychologists have entered what are termed *health service provider* or *direct service specialties* (A. Howard et al., 1986). These psychologists are interested primarily in the applications of psychology. As you can see from Figure 1-7, the largest specialty in psychology is a direct service one, clinical psychology.

eclectic approach
View of psychology that combines several different approaches

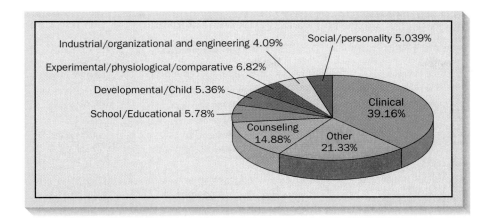

Industrial/organizational and engineering 4.09%
Social/personality 5.039%
Experimental/physiological/comparative 6.82%
Developmental/Child 5.36%
School/Educational 5.78%
Counseling 14.88%
Clinical 39.16%
Other 21.33%

FIGURE 1-7 Specialties in psychology. Note: Figures are based on a survey of doctoral recipients, 1986–96.

Source: Henderson, Clarke, & Woods, 1998.

Psychological Specialties

Clinical and Counseling Psychology. Most students who major in psychology are interested in the work done by clinical psychologists. More and more students want to "work with people." Although most psychologists work with people in one way or another, those involved in **clinical psychology** specialize in helping people with behavioral or emotional problems adjust to the demands of life.

Clinical psychologists are frequently confused with psychiatrists (Murstein & Fontaine, 1993). Members of these two professions share an interest in diagnosing and treating people who are experiencing various behavioral and emotional problems. Clinical psychologists and psychiatrists differ, however, in the advanced degrees they obtain and in other aspects of their training. After completing an undergraduate degree, clinical psychologists earn a doctoral degree (Ph.D. or Psy.D.), which usually takes four or more years. They then complete an internship of at least one year to develop their diagnostic and therapeutic skills; during this time they are supervised by experienced clinical psychologists.

By contrast, **psychiatrists** are medical doctors; they have earned an M.D. After graduating from medical school, they complete a three-year residency, often at a major psychiatric hospital. Although some aspects of the training of clinical psychologists and psychiatrists are similar, there are major differences. For example, psychiatrists are trained in the medical assessment of disorders and hence are more likely to view the disorders as caused by medical conditions. Their treatments reflect this medical orientation—they are likely to prescribe drugs to alleviate their patients' symptoms.

A specialty that has much in common with clinical psychology is **counseling psychology;** counseling psychologists also administer psychological tests and provide therapy. One difference between clinical and counseling psychologists involves the types of clients they see. Counseling psychologists often work with clients who have less serious problems than those of patients seen by clinical psychologists. For example, the counseling psychologist is more likely to deal with people who are having difficulty dealing with everyday problems, such as a physical handicap or a vocational decision.

Other Specialties. Many people believe that psychologists are engaged exclusively in providing diagnostic and therapeutic services to sufferers of mental disorders; however, there is a wide range of specialties beyond clinical and counseling psychology. For example, you may hear the term *experimental psychologist* used to describe psychologists who conduct experiments on learning, motivation, and

clinical psychology
Specialty of psychology that involves the diagnosis and treatment of psychological disorders

psychiatrist
Medical doctor with specialized training in the medical treatment of mental and emotional disorders

counseling psychology
Specialty of psychology that deals with less serious problems than those treated by clinical psychologists

TABLE 1-4 Research Psychologists and Their Interests

AREA OR SPECIALTY	DESCRIPTION OF RESEARCH INTERESTS
Animal behavior	Behavior and basic learning processes; comparative studies using different species
Biopsychology/ neuropsychology	Physiological mechanisms of learning, memory, and behavior
Cognitive processes	Mental processes used to take in, store, and utilize information in thinking, remembering, and making decisions
Cross-cultural	Research conducted to determine whether results are universal or culture-specific
Developmental	Processes of growth, development, and change throughout the entire life span
Educational	Application of psychological findings and principles to the classroom
Motivation	Causes and consequences of motivation in animals and humans
Personality	Factors that make individuals unique, as well as factors that are shared
Psychometrics	Theoretical and practical aspects of psychological testing and measurement
Sensation and perception	Process of sensory input and the use and interpretation of sensory information
Social	Influence of other people on behavior

physiological processes. Because many different types of psychologists conduct experiments, the term **research psychologist** is more appropriate. Table 1-4 summarizes these research specialties. Often you will find research psychologists dividing their duties between conducting research and teaching at a college or university.

Because modern psychology is identified so highly with the United States, we may have a tendency to view our psychological research as applying to all other cultures. The view that other cultures are an extension of your own is called **ethnocentrism** (Smith & Davis, 1997). **Cross-cultural psychology** is a branch of psychology that seeks to determine if research results are universal (that is, if they can be generalized or applied to other cultures [Matsumoto, 1994]). As psychologists recognize the increasingly diverse nature of their field, the importance of cross-cultural research is clearly highlighted. The understanding of "human" behavior requires that we know which of our findings are universal and which are limited to specific cultrues.

research psychologist
Psychologist whose primary activity is to conduct and report the results of experiments

ethnocentrism
The view that other cultures are an extension of one's own

cross-cultural psychology
Branch of psychology whose goal is to determine if research results can be applied to other cultures

Psychological Detective

How might cultural differences affect the development and conduct of psychological research? Write down some possibilities before reading further.

The different attitudes, values, and behaviors held by different cultures can influence the choice of research problems, the research hypothesis that is developed, the variables that are studied, and even the type of survey or questionnaire that is used. In short, culture has the potential to influence all aspects of psychological research. Hence we must be very cautious in generalizing results from one culture to another. Finally, keep in mind that there are numerous different cultural groups within the United States; their differences must also be considered. Just because a piece of research was conducted in the United States does not guarantee that its results are applicable to all Americans. Clearly, these cross-cultural issues must be the concern of all research psychologists.

School psychologists are employed by school systems as consultants to other educational personnel. They may administer psychological tests to evaluate problems in academic skills or conduct evaluations of behavioral and emotional problems experienced by school-age children (Shapiro & Ager, 1992).

Industrial and organizational psychologists (also known as **I/O psychologists;** see Chapter 17) are concerned with all aspects of work and the structure and function of organizations. Their responsibilities vary with the employer, but they may be asked to design a system for selecting employees or to implement an employee assistance program to deal with alcoholism, drug abuse, and stress both on and off the job. Once new employees are hired, I/O psychologists may assist in designing and evaluating programs to train them for their new jobs. In addition, they may be asked to design methods to measure worker productivity, increase worker motivation, evaluate work schedule efficiency, or design systems for resolving disputes within organizations (Jewell, 1998).

Some I/O psychologists are involved in the design of equipment and manufacturing plants. When they design equipment, they take into consideration the relationship between the worker and the equipment and, also, the capabilities of the worker. These psychologists are also called *human factors psychologists* and they work in a specialty that is called *ergonomics.*

Consumer psychology is the scientific study of the behavior of consumers. Although your last purchase of a portable cassette player or a hair dryer may have seemed an unremarkable event, such apparently casual events provide the basis for consumer psychologists' questions. They may want to know how you became aware of the product, how you went about evaluating various brands, or what made you select a particular brand.

A recent addition to the list of psychology's specialties is **health psychology.** This diverse and rapidly growing specialty is concerned with the relations between psychological factors and health. Health psychologists work to promote

school psychologist
Psychologist whose specialty encompasses diagnosing and treating learning disabilities and providing consultation on other problems of school-age children

industrial and organizational (I/O) psychologist
Psychologist who applies psychology to problems of businesses and other organizations

consumer psychology
Specialty of psychology that studies consumers and the choices they make

health psychology
Subfield of psychology that is concerned with how psychological and social variables affect health and illness

The work of industrial/organizational psychologists is quite varied. For example, they are involved in such projects as the developments of an ergonomic keyboard which better matches the equipment and the operator.

forensic psychologist
Psychologist who applies psychology to law and legal proceedings

sport psychologist
Psychologist who provides services to athletes and coaches based on psychological principles

neuropsychologist
Psychologist trained in the diagnosis and rehabilitation of brain disorders

health and prevent illness; they study the causes and treatments of illness and the ways people cope with their illnesses (see Chapter 15). They also investigate ways to reduce risk for disease by changing unhealthy or harmful behaviors (Rice, 1992; Taylor, 1990). For example, they may investigate the effects of exercise on cholesterol levels and subsequent heart attacks, or they may evaluate techniques to encourage the practice of safe sex. Because stress is an ever-present part of our lives, health psychologists also try to increase our understanding of the factors related to stress and to discover ways to alleviate its negative consequences. For example, health psychologist Tom Boll is using psychological tests and other measures to select potential heart transplant patients who are best able to handle the stress of the operation (De Angelis, 1992).

Emerging Specialties.   Psychology is not a static science; its proponents continually strive to discover new arenas for research and application. Among the recent additions to the field are forensic (legal) psychology, sport psychology, and neuropsychology.

   Forensic psychologists work within the legal system; they may work in a prison to evaluate incoming prisoners or assist in selecting a jury for a trial (Weiner & Hess, in press; Wrightsman, Nietzel, & Fortune, 1994). Carefully wording the questions asked of prospective jurors can help identify potentially biased jurors, who can then be excused from service (Cutler, Moran, & Narby, 1992; Goodman, Loftus, & Greene, 1990). Forensic psychologists also provide testimony as expert witnesses (see Chapter 7). For example, psychologist Elizabeth Loftus has testified many times about how stress affects the accuracy of recalled events, how observing violent crimes affects eyewitness identifications, or how police lineups can sometimes lead witnesses to an incorrect identification of a suspect (Loftus, 1991).

   Sport psychologists apply the theories and knowledge of psychology to enhance athletes' performance (Wann, 1997). They may consult with coaches about the use of specific coaching techniques or provide supportive therapy and encouragement to players recovering from injuries. They also help athletes improve their performance by using techniques such as relaxation and imagery (Green, 1992; Murphy, 1994). Since 1978, sport psychologists have been part of the team of experts who help U.S. athletes prepare for the Olympics.

   Given that Congress designated the 1990s as "the decade of the brain," it is not surprising that one of the emerging specialties in psychology is concerned with brain functioning (see Chapter 2). **Neuropsychologists** are trained to diagnose disorders of the brain. Using various tests, they try to identify specific brain areas that may be malfunctioning. They often conduct research to identify early symptoms that predict the development of disorders such as Huntington's disease (Diamond et al., 1992). They also devise rehabilitation programs to help patients regain as much of their abilities as possible after suffering brain damage, strokes, or traumatic brain injury (Diller, 1992).

Review Summary

1. The history of modern psychology began in 1879, when Wilhelm Wundt established the first psychology laboratory at the University of Leipzig in Germany. The goal of Wundt's school of psychology, known as **structuralism,** was to identify the elements of conscious experience by using the method of **introspection.**

2. Another perspective, which came to be known as **functionalism,** focused on the purposes of consciousness and was especially concerned with the applications of psychology. **Gestalt psychology** is concerned primarily with our perception of our environment. **Cognitive psychology** studies higher mental processes such as thinking, knowing, and deciding.

3. Influenced by the Russian physiologist Ivan Pavlov, John B. Watson was interested in how the environment affects behavior. Because consciousness cannot be observed directly, Watson defined psychology as the study of observable behavior. The **behavioral perspective** was continued by B. F. Skinner, probably the best known and most influential psychologist of our time.

4. Sigmund Freud's **psychodynamic perspective** focused on unconscious determinants of behavior. Freud also developed a treatment approach known as **psychoanalytic therapy.**

5. Dissatisfaction with both the behavioral and the psychodynamic perspectives led psychologists Abraham Maslow and Carl Rogers to develop the **humanistic perspective.** Humanists believe that other perspectives pay too little attention to uniquely human characteristics such as free will and individual control.

6. The **physiological perspective** focuses on the underlying biological bases of all forms of behavior.

7. The field of psychology has begun to recognize the contributions made by women and ethnic minorities, and additional contributions from these groups can be expected in the future. The *Cultural and Diversity Perspective* focuses on such research contributions.

8. Most psychologists have earned a doctoral degree (Ph.D. or Psy.D.). Although many psychologists teach and engage in research, a growing number provide direct services to clients.

Study Break

1. The origins of modern, scientific psychology can be traced to
   a. Wilhelm Wundt.
   b. William James.
   c. Max Wertheimer.
   d. Ivan Pavlov.
2. John B. Watson believed that psychology should involve the study of
   a. the mind.
   b. the brain.
   c. consciousness.
   d. behavior.
3. What barrier toward becoming a psychologist did Mary Whiton Calkins face in the late 1880s?
   a. As a woman, she could not complete graduate courses at Harvard.
   b. As a woman, Harvard would not award her the doctoral degree she earned.
   c. Women could not establish psychological laboratories in the United States at that time.
   d. She was not allowed to join the American Psychological Association.
4. What is the current sex representation in psychology?
   a. Men earn more doctoral degrees than women.
   b. Women and men earn approximately equal numbers of doctoral degrees.
   c. Women earn more doctoral degrees than men.
   d. Psychology does not categorize doctoral degrees by gender.
5. Each of the following descriptions could apply to one of the historical perspectives on psychology discussed in this chapter. Which perspective best fits the description?

   a. believes unconscious forces are the most significant determinants of behavior
   b. is concerned with the biological processes involved in a behavior
   c. is interested in the elements of consciousness
   d. believes the whole is different from the sum of its parts
   e. is interested in studying decision making and problem solving
6. Identify the person who is most likely to have made each of the following statements.
   a. "I never received my Ph.D., although I earned it."
   b. "The study of my patients convinces me that unconscious forces lie beneath many of their disturbances."
   c. "What impresses me about human behavior is the freedom each of us has to make choices."
   d. "I was kept from joining several 'men-only' research societies."
7. Name the type of psychologist (or specialty) described in each of the following:
   a. was asked to diagnose and treat a 35-year-old man who hears frightening voices every day
   b. helped an out-of-work auto mechanic decide on a new career
   c. designed a survey to determine whether purchasers of a liquid detergent were satisfied with the product
   d. testified as an expert witness on factors that influence the accuracy of eyewitnesses

ANSWERS TO STUDY BREAKS

Pages 12–13

1. a
2. a
3. b
4. a. The claim of not dreaming in color is not based on scientific observation. Moreover, this finding also could be explained by other factors, such as poor recall for one's dreams.
  b. There are several problems with the finding that "an amazing 60 percent said Fizzy tastes as good or better than Foamy." We really do not know who participated in the taste test; perhaps, they were paid employees of the Fizzy Company. The 60 percent figure that seems to support the company's claims is misleading at best. What if 90 percent of this number feel that both brands taste equally good? That leaves only 10 percent who like Fizzy better than Foamy, and 40 percent who like Foamy best. Much more information is needed.
  c. There is no indication that the autistic individuals had anything to do with the movement of their arms. It is likely that the facilitator is responsible for the results we are considering.

Pages 27–28

1. c
2. The plus or minus sign in front of the correlation coefficient tells you whether the relationship is positive (plus sign) or negative (minus sign).
3. a
4. b
5. The main advantage of naturalistic observation is that behaviors are observed as they occur in the real-life setting; there is no interference with them. A disadvantage is that the researcher has no control over the research and cannot reach any firm conclusions concerning the cause(s) of the behavior in question. A reactive effect occurs when the participants know they are being observed and change their behaviors. Being inconspicuous will help deal with the reactivity problem.
6. a. −.30 **b.** −1.00 **c.** +.33
7. Just because the two variables are correlated, we cannot say that one caused the other. The relationship may have been caused by a third factor that we are not aware of.
8. A representative sample reflects the characteristics of the population, so our conclusions are more likely to generalize to that population.
9. a. The independent variable (IV) is the lighting conditions (dim and bright); the dependent variable (DV) is reaction time.
  b. The independent variable is length of beer sales (stop at end of third quarter or sell for entire game); the dependent variable is the number of fights and arrests.
  c. The independent variable is the two shampoo packages; the dependent variable is sales appeal.

Page 41

1. a
2. d
3. b
4. c
5. a. Psychodynamic
  b. Physiological
  c. Structuralism
  d. Gestalt
  e. Cognitive
6. a. Mary Whiton Calkins
  b. Sigmund Freud
  c. Abraham Maslow
  d. Christine Ladd-Franklin
7. a. Clinical psychologist
  b. Counseling psychologist
  c. Consumer psychologist
  d. Forensic psychologist

ANSWERS TO QUESTIONS IN TABLE 1-2

Page 10

1. The answer depends on the hemisphere you are in when you answer the question. For people in the Northern Hemisphere, the Earth is closer to the sun from September to May; for people in the Southern Hemisphere, the Earth is closer to the sun from May to September. The degree of warmth is not associated with distance from the sun; the tilt of the earth as it receives the sun's rays determines warmth.

2. It depends. If the country minting the coin is the United States, the answer is Abraham Lincoln (you may be aware of the much older and very valuable "Indianhead" pennies). In Canada, the Queen of England appears on a penny.

3. The answer is Sophie Kurys, who played for the Racine Belles in the Women's Professional Baseball League in 1946; she stole 202 bases.

4. The answer is simple, provided that assumptions do not get in your way. Extend the line on the right side downward and you will produce the number 4 (a perfect square).

CHAPTER 2
Biological Foundations of Psychology

Clockwise from the bottom Sunday, August 16, 1998, are, Griffin, Anne Rain, Christopher and Emily Tanner, fifteen-year-old quadruplets who are about to start tenth grade. They are two girls, two boys, two blondes, two brunettes, two left-handers and two right-handers.

Chapter in Perspective

This chapter begins our in-depth exploration of the various areas of psychology. As you progress through this book, you will notice that our general plan is to move from basic and elemental topics to general and broad ones. Notice we did not say that we would progress from the simple to the complex. As you read about the nervous system, the endocrine system, and our basic biological processes in this chapter, we are sure you will agree that these topics are far from simple. The activities of sensing, processing, and responding are vital to our psychological makeup and to our ability to adapt to our constantly changing environment. In subsequent chapters we expand our discussion of biological psychology to include such topics as how we receive and process information from the environment (Chapter 3) and the various states of consciousness that we may experience (Chapter 5). From time to time throughout the book we will return to a consideration of the physiological basis of behaviors to help explain more general topics such as human development (Chapters 9 and 10) and various types of abnormal behavior (Chapter 13). ■

The study of the relationship between biological functions and psychological functions is one of the most rapidly expanding, complex, and fascinating areas of psychological research. Knowing how the human body and brain work helps us to understand many areas of psychology: the nature of personality, the causes of certain abnormal behaviors, our reaction to stressful situations, the effectiveness of some types of therapy with certain patients but not with others, and much more. Recognition of the potential importance of physiological processes in understanding behavior has caused Congress to designate the 1990s as "the decade of the brain."

Biopsychology, Neuroscience, and the Evolutionary Perspective

As you walk past the offices in the psychology department, you notice some of the faculty have listed their research specialties. One faculty member is a biopsychologist, another specializes in neuropsychology, and a third is a comparative psychologist. Psychology is truly a diverse field. ***Do these research specialties have any similarities? What are their differences?*** ■

As you can see from Table 2-1, several types of psychologists are interested in studying the relationship between behavior and physiological processes. The main differences among these researchers concern the focus of their research and the tools they use to relate physiology to behavior.

Many of these researchers have adopted an **evolutionary perspective** (Gray, 1995), which focuses on the role played by a particular physical structure or behavior in helping an organism adapt to its environment over time. Charles Darwin (1859), who popularized the theory of evolution, maintained that evolution unfolds according to the principle of **natural selection,** which states that the strongest or most fit organisms are those that have adapted best to their environment. These organisms are more likely to survive and to pass on their characteristics to future generations. Therefore researchers who work from an evolutionary perspective consistently ask what role a physiological structure or behavior plays in helping the organism survive and adapt to its environment.

evolutionary perspective
Interest in the role a physiological structure or behavior plays in helping an organism adapt to its environment

natural selection
The principle that the strongest or most fit organisms are the ones that adapt best to their environment

TABLE 2-1   Psychologists Who Study the Relationship between Physiological Processes and Behavior

TYPE OF PSYCHOLOGIST	RESEARCH EMPHASIS
Physiological psychologist, biopsychologist, behavioral neuroscientist	Relating brain and nervous system physiology to behavior
Comparative psychologist	Relating and comparing the behavior of different species
Neuropsychologist	Testing of brain-injured individuals to determine the location, extent, and nature of the damage and its effects on adaptive behavior

In addition to studying the process of natural selection, researchers are also intent on discovering the actual genetic material responsible for the structure or behavior under investigation. We say more about genetics in Chapter 9. We encourage you, however, to keep the evolutionary perspective in mind as you read this book. See if it can help you understand why a particular behavior or physical structure developed.

Sensing, Processing, and Responding

The topic of your most recent psychology class was the biological or physiological basis of behavior. By the end of the class, you were beginning to see how important it is to understand these aspects of behavior; the new concepts were starting to fall into place. Then your instructor provided some real food for thought. You were told that the study of the brain may be the brain's greatest challenge. *How can the study of the brain provide the greatest challenge for the brain?* ▨

The nervous system, which includes the brain, is the most complex machine ever constructed; it is infinitely more complex than the most sophisticated computer (Fishbach, 1992). Hence understanding the brain is the greatest challenge for the brain. Our examination of the brain begins with an overview of how humans relate to their environment.

To survive, human beings must be able to perform three interrelated activities: sensing events, or stimuli; processing stimuli; and responding to stimuli. A **stimulus** is a feature in the environment, such as a traffic light, raindrops, the smell of smoke, or a sunset, that may provoke a response. The specialized cells that sense such stimuli are called **receptors.** We discuss several receptors, such as those located in the eyes and ears, in Chapter 3. For now, remember that we are concerned with a chain of events that typically begins when a stimulus activates a receptor.

The second activity in the chain is making sense of, or *processing*, the information that reaches the receptors. This processing typically takes place in the brain. Once we've made sense of the sensory input, we may need to respond to it. Therefore the third activity occurs when the brain sends messages to the muscles to produce a response. As you can see in Figure 2-1, these three activities are involved in an event as common as slamming your hand in a car door. First, you sense pressure and pain. Then you realize (very quickly) that something is wrong (processing). Finally, you take action to correct the situation (responding).

The Nervous System

One of your classmates, Bryant, has a major test next week, and he is worried about it. At night he sleeps fitfully; during most of the day he feels tense. He has been keeping to himself more than usual and has even refused to answer the phone on occasion. You agree with Bryant's friends that he is more irritable than usual. Obviously, the impending test is the cause of his irritability. **What can be done to make Bryant feel better?** ▨

stimulus
Environmental feature that provokes a response

receptors
Specialized cells that are sensitive to specific types of stimulus energy

| Sensing | Processing | Responding |

FIGURE 2-1 An example of the activities involved in sensing, processing, and responding to stimuli. It's raining and you are in a hurry to get inside. In your haste you slam the car door on your hand. As you feel the pressure and pain (Step 1: sensing), you realize something is terribly wrong (Step 2: processing) and you need to do something to free your hand (Step 3: responding).

The activities of sensing, processing, and responding, in which Bryant is engaged, are coordinated and controlled by the nervous system. The nervous system has two main divisions (Figure 2-2): the **central nervous system (CNS)** and the **peripheral nervous system (PNS).** The CNS consists of the brain and spinal cord; the PNS connects the outer portions, or periphery, of the body with the CNS.

 The nervous system has two halves, one for the right side of the body and one for the left. These two halves of the brain are called *hemispheres.* The right hemisphere receives input from the left side of the body, and the left hemisphere receives input from the right side of the body. This process, in which each hemisphere receives input from the opposite side of the body, is called *contralateral conduction.* Conduction of information from the hemisphere to the same side of the body is called *ipsilateral conduction.* The basic cells of the nervous system are **neurons,** and we say more about them shortly. First we take a closer look at the peripheral and central nervous systems.

The Peripheral Nervous System

The PNS consists of all the parts of the nervous system that lie outside the CNS. If we think of the nervous system as a computer, the PNS would consist of the "peripherals"—such as the monitor, keyboard, or printer—that transport information in and out of the central portion of the computer. The two major divisions of the PNS are the somatic division and the autonomic division (see Figure 2-2).

The Somatic Division. The **somatic division** of the PNS makes contact with the environment. It consists of nerves that connect receptors to the spinal cord and brain, as well as nerves that go from the brain and spinal cord to the muscles. The nerves that carry information from the receptors to the brain and spinal cord are known as **afferent (sensory) nerves;** those that carry information from the brain and spinal cord to the muscles are known as **efferent (motor) nerves.** The somatic division is involved in sensing and responding, Steps 1 and 3 of the chain of events described in Figure 2-1. When you slam a car door on your hand, you feel pressure and pain (Step 1) because afferent nerves have conveyed information to the CNS to be processed. Efferent nerves then convey information from the CNS so you can make a response (Step 3) to correct the situation. Because the responses we make are often planned and organized, the somatic division is said to be a *voluntary* system—that is, one that is under our control.

The Autonomic Division. The **autonomic division** of the PNS affects our organs and glands in ways that regulate bodily functioning. Because the autonomic division operates without our conscious awareness, it is said to be an *automatic* or *involuntary* system. The autonomic division has two main components: the sympathetic division and the parasympathetic division.

---

central nervous system (CNS)
Division of the nervous system that consists of the brain and spinal cord

peripheral nervous system (PNS)
Division of the nervous system that consists of neural fibers lying outside the brain and spinal cord

neurons
Basic cells of the nervous system

somatic division
Division of the peripheral nervous system that consists of nerves coming from the receptors to the brain and spinal cord, as well as nerves that go from the brain and spinal cord to the muscles

afferent (sensory) nerves
Nerves that carry information from the receptors to the spinal cord and brain

efferent (motor) nerves
Nerves that carry information from the brain and spinal cord to the muscles

autonomic division
Division of the peripheral nervous system involved in the control of bodily functioning through organs and glands

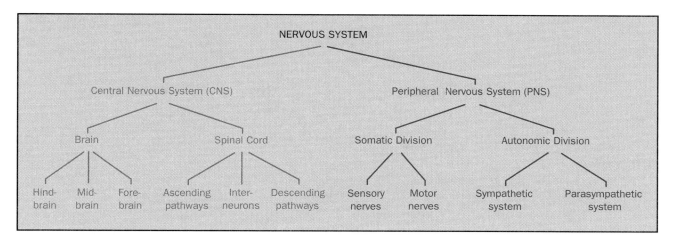

NERVOUS SYSTEM

Central Nervous System (CNS) — Peripheral Nervous System (PNS)

Brain — Spinal Cord — Somatic Division — Autonomic Division

Hind-brain | Mid-brain | Fore-brain | Ascending pathways | Inter-neurons | Descending pathways | Sensory nerves | Motor nerves | Sympathetic system | Parasympathetic system

FIGURE 2-2 Major divisions of the nervous system—the peripheral nervous system (PNS) and the central nervous system (CNS). The CNS consists of the brain and spinal cord. The PNS connects the outer portions of the body with the CNS.

The Sympathetic Division. The **sympathetic division** mobilizes the body in times of stress or danger. In other words, your body is prepared for "fight or flight" when the sympathetic division is active (see Chapters 4 and 15). Have you ever been scared by a loud clap of thunder? Did your heart start to race? Did your skin tingle? Did your muscles feel tense? These reactions were produced by the sympathetic nervous system.

Psychological Detective

Let's say that you have shut your hand in a car door. After this happens, the sympathetic nervous system is hard at work. You become prepared for fight or flight, mostly flight in this case. Imagine yourself in this situation. Which sympathetic processes are in operation? Write down the processes that you would experience and then read further.

The reactions that you experience when you shut your hand in the car door or that Bryant has been exhibiting as his test approaches (see page 47) are evidence that the sympathetic division is at work. During these times the body is prepared for action by a series of coordinated changes, including enlargement (dilation) of the pupils of the eyes, acceleration of the heart, inhibition of digestive activities, and release of sugar (glucose) to produce energy. The almost constant activity of the sympathetic nervous system keeps Bryant on edge. Wouldn't you feel irritable if you were constantly prepared for fight or flight?

Look at the left side of Figure 2-3 to see the major sympathetic responses. Are there any that you are not experiencing when you are scared out of your wits at a horror movie? Most likely you experience all of them in this rather stressful situation. Notice that some of these processes involve an increase in a particular bodily function, whereas others involve a decrease in function.

The Parasympathetic Division. The **parasympathetic division** is responsible for returning the body to a restful or balanced state when fight-or-flight responses are no longer needed. We can now answer the question we asked earlier: "What can be done to make Bryant feel better?"

Bryant will feel better when his parasympathetic system is allowed to operate. The parasympathetic system slows the processes that have been accelerated by arousal of the sympathetic system. For example, when the

sympathetic division
Subdivision of the autonomic nervous system that is responsible for mobilizing the body in times of stress, preparing for fight or flight

parasympathetic division
Subdivision of the autonomic nervous system that is responsible for returning the body to a resting or balanced state

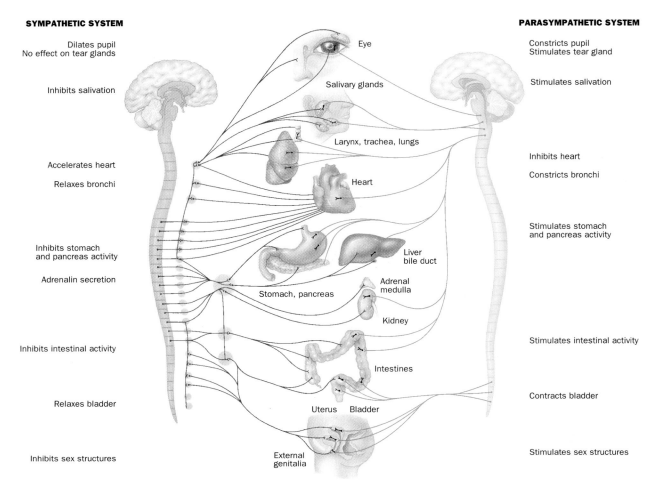

SYMPATHETIC SYSTEM

Dilates pupil
No effect on tear glands

Inhibits salivation

Accelerates heart

Relaxes bronchi

Inhibits stomach
and pancreas activity

Adrenalin secretion

Inhibits intestinal activity

Relaxes bladder

Inhibits sex structures

PARASYMPATHETIC SYSTEM

Constricts pupil
Stimulates tear gland

Stimulates salivation

Inhibits heart

Constricts bronchi

Stimulates stomach
and pancreas activity

Stimulates intestinal activity

Contracts bladder

Stimulates sex structures

Eye

Salivary glands

Larynx, trachea, lungs

Heart

Liver
bile duct

Adrenal
medulla

Stomach, pancreas

Kidney

Intestines

Uterus   Bladder

External
genitalia

FIGURE 2-3 The sympathetic and parasympathetic divisions of the autonomic nervous system and their functions.

Source: Shaver & Tarpy, 1993.

parasympathetic division is operating, the pupils of the eye constrict, or close, and heart rate slows. These effects, and others that are shown on the right side of Figure 2-3, return the body to a more normal or balanced state of functioning, characterized by an optimal range of physiological processes, called **homeostasis.** Before the test, Bryant can assist his parasympathetic system by listening to his favorite CD or not thinking about his test for a while. (See Chapter 15 for techniques to help cope with stress.) Once Bryant takes the test, the stress will be relieved and his body will return to a homeostatic state.

The Central Nervous System

The other major division of the nervous system, the CNS, consists of the brain and spinal cord (see Figure 2-2). You can think of the CNS as analogous to the engine of a car or to central processing unit (CPU) of a computer. The following sections discuss the main components of the CNS.

The Spinal Cord. The spinal cord is tucked safely into a protective jacket known as the vertebral column, which in humans is made up of 24 bones called

homeostasis

Tendency of the body to maintain a balanced state; characterized by the functioning of an optimal range of physiological processes

CROSS SECTION OF SPINAL CORD

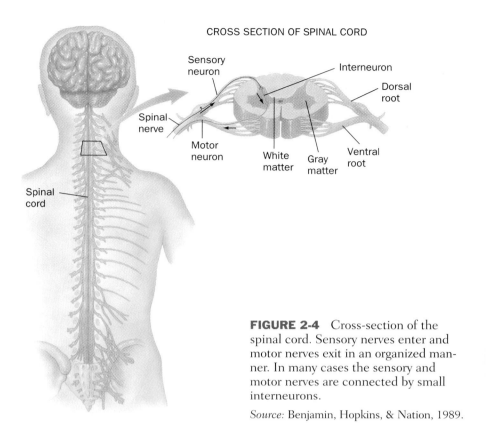

FIGURE 2-4   Cross-section of the spinal cord. Sensory nerves enter and motor nerves exit in an organized manner. In many cases the sensory and motor nerves are connected by small interneurons.

Source: Benjamin, Hopkins, & Nation, 1989.

vertebrae. The sensory nerves of the PNS enter the spinal cord and the motor nerves exit the spinal cord between the vertebrae in an orderly manner (see Figure 2-4). The sensory nerves enter the back or *dorsal* portion of the spinal cord; the motor nerves exit from the front or *ventral* portion. The H-shaped center portion of the spinal cord shown in Figure 2-4 is called the *gray matter* because it is largely composed of gray-colored cell bodies. The surrounding portion, called the *white matter,* consists of afferent neurons that ascend to the brain and efferent neurons that descend to lower portions of the peripheral nervous system. Figure 2-4 also shows the small neurons, called *interneurons,* in the spinal cord. The interneurons send information either directly to a motor nerve so a response can be made or sent up the spinal cord for processing by the brain.

When information provided by the sensory nerves does not have to travel all the way to the brain to produce a response, automatic behaviors known as **reflexes** are produced. The message that brings about a reflex typically takes a shorter journey than it would if it had gone to the brain for further processing. For example, if I were to hit your knee lightly with a hammer, your leg would jerk reflexively—that is, automatically and involuntarily. As you can see in Figure 2-5, when the knee-jerk reflex occurs, the sensory information produced by hitting your knee enters the spinal cord and contacts the efferent nerve, which returns a signal almost immediately to your leg to produce movement. Similarly, an object placed in an infant's mouth stimulates a sucking reflex. Because reflexes are automatic, we may not even realize that they have occurred. When you slammed the car door on your hand, and perhaps before you even felt pain, your first response—probably a reflex—might have been to jerk your arm back. Reflexes occur very rapidly. For example, the reaction to a painful stimulus occurs in approximately 0.8 millisecond (a millisecond is one one-thousandth of a second).

reflex
Automatic behavior in response to a specific stimulus

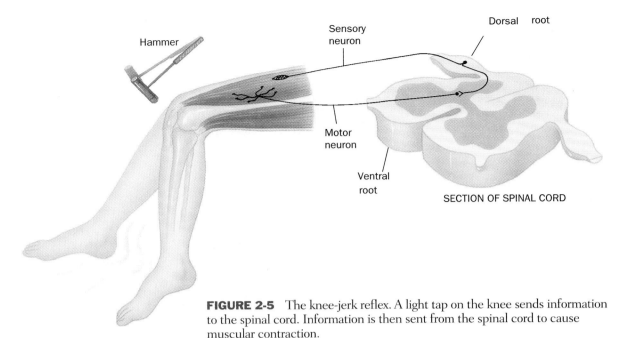

FIGURE 2-5 The knee-jerk reflex. A light tap on the knee sends information to the spinal cord. Information is then sent from the spinal cord to cause muscular contraction.

hindbrain
Oldest of the three main divisions of the brain; its major structures are the medulla, pons, and cerebellum

medulla
Structure located in the hindbrain that regulates automatic responses such as breathing, swallowing, and blood circulation

pons
Structure of the hindbrain that connects the two halves of the brain; has nuclei that are important for sleep and arousal

cerebellum
Structure of the hindbrain that coordinates muscular movements

cranial nerves
The twelve pairs of nerves that control the sensory and motor information from the skin and muscles of the head and internal organs

The Brain. Although some of your behavior consists of reflexes such as knee jerks and the attempt to yank your hand out of a car door, many of your more complex actions are a result of processing that occurs in the brain. What would you do if your hand were stuck in a car door and you couldn't pull it free? Let's follow that information as it is sent up the spinal cord to the brain. (Bear in mind that although it takes us some time to describe these travels, the entire process happens in milliseconds.)

Initially the information travels upward in a group of nerves called a *tract;* its ultimate destination is the brain, which sits on top of the spinal cord. The three main divisions of the brain are the hindbrain, the midbrain, and the forebrain. A detailed cross-sectional view of the various divisions of the brain and their respective structures is shown in Figure 2-6.

The Hindbrain. As the information about what has happened to your hand leaves the spinal cord, it passes through structures located in the **hindbrain.** The major components of the hindbrain are the medulla, the pons, and the cerebellum. From an evolutionary perspective, these are the oldest parts of the brain, and they have important survival functions. For example, the **medulla** controls automatic responses such as breathing, swallowing, and circulation of the blood. When the hand-in-the door information reaches and activates the medulla, that structure may cause your breathing to increase. The **pons** (from the Latin for "bridge") connects the two halves of the brain at the hindbrain level; this part of the hindbrain is important for sleep and arousal. The **cerebellum** coordinates skilled movement sequences that deal with objects in motion. Without the control exerted by the cerebellum, we would have great difficulty performing such behaviors as pointing to a moving object. Cerebral palsy, whose major symptom is a lack of coordinated movements, is a condition caused by damage to the cerebellum.

Eight of the twelve pairs of nerves from the skin and muscles of the head and internal organs connect to the brain at the pons and medulla in the hindbrain. These twelve pairs of nerves are known as **cranial nerves;** most of them have both afferent and efferent fibers. The remaining four cranial nerves connect to the brain at the midbrain and forebrain levels.

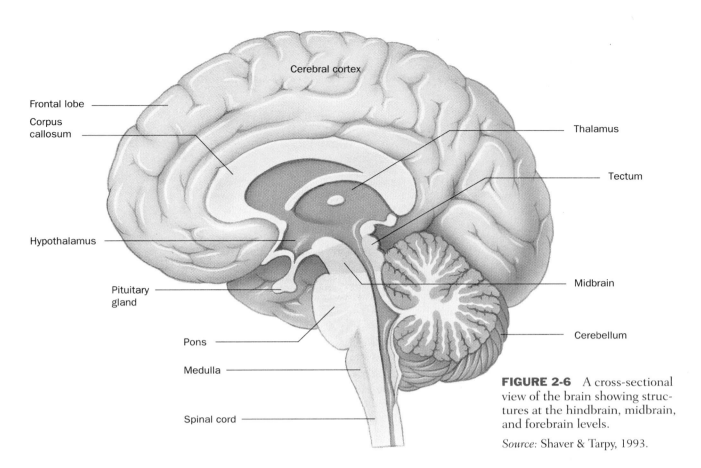

FIGURE 2-6 A cross-sectional view of the brain showing structures at the hindbrain, midbrain, and forebrain levels.

Source: Shaver & Tarpy, 1993.

The Midbrain.   Continuing its trip to the higher brain centers, the information about your injured hand passes through the **midbrain.** Together the hindbrain and midbrain are known as the *brain stem* because they form the stem or stalk on which the remainder of the brain rests. The roof of the midbrain, called the *tectum,* is important in the processing of sensory information.

The midbrain also is composed of nerve pathways that go *to and from* higher brain centers. Psychologists have found that this complex network of fibers, known as the **reticular formation,** is very important in controlling our level of arousal or alertness. Actually, the reticular formation reaches all the way from the hindbrain through the midbrain and into the forebrain.

When you first moved into your new dormitory room or apartment, you probably did not sleep very well for several nights. Every little noise probably sounded like a cannon going off in your bedroom. Now that you are accustomed to your new environment, you can (and do) sleep through everything (except classes). Your reticular formation was involved in this change because it acts like a gatekeeper. When we need to be aware of new and unfamiliar information, such as the sound of an ambulance or a fire engine, the reticular formation allows it to pass on to higher brain centers for processing. Familiar information that is of no immediate consequence, such as the sound of a refrigerator motor or air conditioner, is blocked by the reticular formation, and we do not become aware of it.

The Forebrain.   As the injured-hand information leaves the brain stem and moves upward, it enters the **forebrain.** Examination of the forebrain reveals that this part of the brain is divided into two distinct halves with duplicate

midbrain
Major division of the brain that contains fibers known as the reticular formation

reticular formation
Nerve fibers passing through the midbrain that control arousal

forebrain
Major division of the brain that consists of subcortical structures and the cerebral cortex

FIGURE 2-7 Viewed from below (left), the corpus callosum is seen as a broad band of fibers that connects the two hemispheres of the brain and allows information to be passed between them. In the human brain the corpus callosum is approximately the size of a small banana.

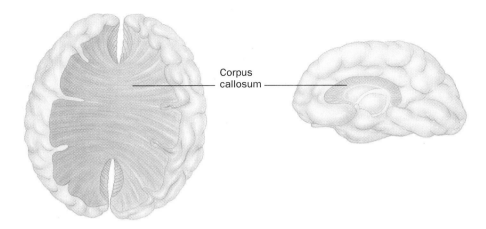

Corpus callosum

corpus callosum
Wide band of neural fibers that connects the two hemispheres of the brain

subcortical structures
Structures of the forebrain, such as the amygdala, hypothalamus, and thalamus, that are located beneath the cerebral cortex

cerebral cortex (cerebrum)
The convoluted (wrinkled) outer layer of the brain

limbic system
System of interconnected subcortical structures that regulates a variety of emotions and motivated behaviors, such as hunger, thirst, aggression, and sexual behavior

thalamus
Subcortical structure that relays incoming sensory information to the cerebral cortex and other parts of the brain

structures in each half. These two halves or hemispheres are connected by a wide band of fibers known as the **corpus callosum** (see Figure 2-7). The two hemispheres of the forebrain communicate with each other through the corpus callosum (Allen et al., 1991).

Within the forebrain, the areas that the information about your injured hand encounters first are collectively known as **subcortical structures** because they are located beneath the other main division of the forebrain, the **cerebral cortex** (also known as the **cerebrum**) or outer covering of the brain. Several of the major subcortical structures are summarized in Table 2-2 and appear in Figure 2-6. Spend a few minutes familiarizing yourself with these structures and their functions, and refer to Figure 2-6 from time to time so that you know the location of each one.

The **limbic system** is a group of interrelated subcortical structures that are involved in the regulation of emotions and motivated behaviors such as hunger, thirst, aggression, and sexual behavior. Table 2-2 describes several components of the limbic system.

The **thalamus** is of special importance because it sends sensory information to the cerebral cortex and other parts of the brain. Because so much information comes into and goes out of the thalamus, it is called the great relay

---

TABLE 2-2   Selected Subcortical Structures and Their Functions

Limbic system
A group of structures involved in the control and direction of emotional behavior; includes the amygdala, involved in emotional reactivity, aggression, and the processing of odors; the hippocampus, involved in emotional reactivity and the storage of memories; and the septum, involved in emotional reactivity.

Hypothalamus
Some neurons in the hypothalamus are involved in the control of arousal, emotionality, food and water intake, sexual behavior, and body temperature; considered by some researchers to be part of the limbic system. Other hypothalamic neurons control pituitary hormone production and release.

Thalamus
A structure that integrates incoming, sensory information and relays it to appropriate areas of the cerebral cortex.

Basal ganglia
A group of structures located near the thalamus that are involved in the control of slow, voluntary movement, such as standing, sitting, and walking.

station of the brain. A large number of nerve fibers radiate from the thalamus and route information to specific areas of the cerebral cortex (Barth & MacDonald, 1996). For example, some fibers go to your sensory cortex, whereas others go to your motor cortex (see Figure 2-10 on page 57).

The major structures of the brain are summarized in the following Study Chart.

You may be wondering how sensory information gets to the correct location for processing. It is easier than it might seem. Remember that nerve tracts bring sensory information up the spinal cord and then through the brain stem. When these tracts reach the thalamus, each goes to an area that is appropriate for the information it is carrying. There is an area for vision, one for audition (hearing), one for taste, one for touch, and so on for all the other senses, except the sense of smell, which is processed in the olfactory bulb. Information is then relayed from these areas to appropriate areas of the cortex.

Ultimately, the information about your hand being caught in the car door reaches the appropriate areas in the cerebral cortex. As we saw in Figure 2-6, the cerebral cortex covers the subcortical structures we have been discussing. As Figure 2-8A shows, the cortex in lower animals such as rats or frogs is quite smooth and not very thick. The more complex the brain, the rougher the cortex (Figure 2-8B). The human cortex has a very wrinkled and crumpled appearance that resembles a cauliflower (Figure 2-8C); in prehistoric times, when the human brain began to develop, a great deal of growth and expansion took place in the cerebral cortex. Because the brain was confined within the bony case of the skull, this growth caused the expanding cortex to wrap around subcortical parts of the brain and take on its characteristic pattern of ridges and valleys (called *fissures*). This great expansion and development of the cerebral cortex sets the human brain apart from the brains of lower animals.

Because the ridges and valleys are similar from one person to the next, they are used as landmarks to locate specific areas of the cortex, called *lobes*. Figure 2-9 shows the locations and functions of each of the four lobes—the frontal,

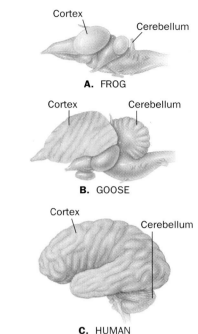

FIGURE 2-8 (A) The cortex of a frog is quite smooth. (B) The cortex of a more complex brain, such as that of a goose, is more wrinkled. (C) The cortex of the human brain is very wrinkled and crumpled.

STUDY CHART

Major Structures of the Brain

Structure	Location	Function
Medulla	Hindbrain	Controls autonomic responses such as breathing, swallowing, and blood circulation
Pons	Hindbrain	Serves as a bridge to connect the brain's two halves
Cerebellum	Hindbrain	Coordinates muscular movements
Reticular formation	Midbrain	Controls levels of arousal or alertness
Corpus callosum	Forebrain	Allows the forebrain's two hemispheres to communicate
Cerebral cortex (cerebrum)	Forebrain	Handles sensory processing, motor control, and memory formation and storage
Limbic system	Forebrain	Regulates emotions and motivated behaviors such as hunger, thirst, aggression, and sexual behavior
Thalamus	Forebrain	Integrates incoming information and relays it to the cerebral cortex

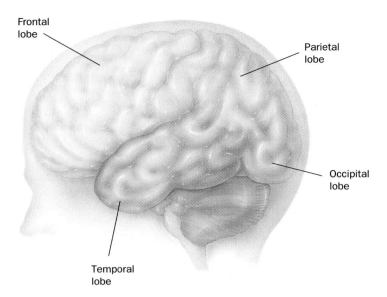

Frontal lobe

Parietal lobe

Occipital lobe

Temporal lobe

FIGURE 2-9   Locations and functions of the four lobes of the cerebral cortex. *Frontal lobe:* Involved in the control of (1) major body movements (motor cortex; see Figure 2-10), (2) precision movements (premotor cortex), (3) decision making (prefrontal cortex), and (4) speech production. *Temporal lobe:* Serves a variety of functions, including memory, development of some aspects of personality, processing of auditory information, and limited control of sexual behavior. *Parietal lobe:* Contains major sensory areas of the cortex. The sensory information, however, is received from the opposite side of the body. Thus the left parietal lobe receives information from the right side of the body, and vice versa. *Occipital lobe:* Contains the primary visual-processing areas of the cortex.

Source: Shaver & Tarpy, 1993.

temporal, parietal, and occipital lobes—in each hemisphere. (Remember, there are two halves, or hemispheres, of the brain. The cortex of each hemisphere has four lobes.) Notice that several of these lobes are separated by various fissures.

Psychological Detective

The earliest studies of brain activity were concerned with the functions of the cortex in animals. There was no way, however, to examine the subcortical structures without also damaging the overlying cortex. What problems would this arrangement create for researchers trying to learn the functions of subcortical structures? Analyze the situation, and write down some possible answers before reading further.

Studying the Functions of the Brain.   Identifying the parts of the brain does not necessarily tell us the functions of those parts. How have psychologists learned about these functions? How do we know, for example, that the hippocampus, a part of the limbic system, is involved in memory or that a portion of the frontal lobe of each hemisphere controls motor responses?

Early Surgical Approaches.   Early experimental research on the cortex yielded vital information. By surgically removing or destroying a brain area or electrically stimulating brain activity, researchers discovered the

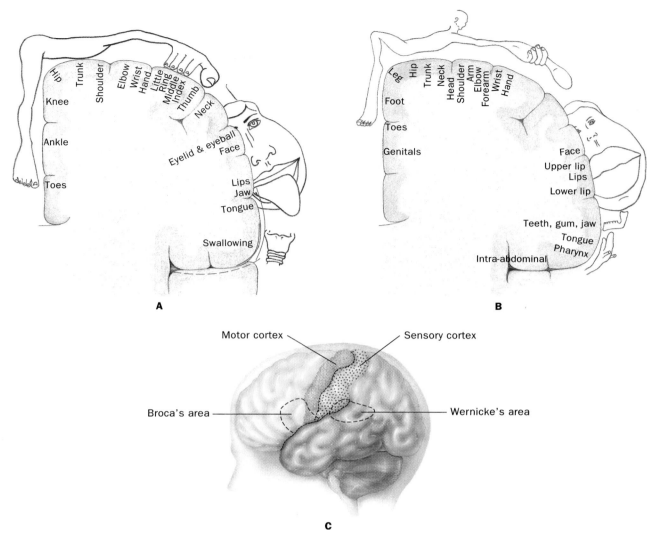

FIGURE 2-10 (A) Map of the sensory cortex. More important senses occupy larger areas. (B) Map of the motor cortex. More important motor functions occupy larger areas. (C) Location of motor and sensory cortex, as well as Broca's and Wernicke's areas.

Sources: Benjamin, Hopkins, & Nation, 1989; Shaver & Tarpy, 1993.

sources of many cortical functions. They identified areas of the cortex that control various sensory and motor functions and created "maps" of cortical functions.

Figure 2-10A presents a map of the sensory cortex. Notice how the parts of the body that are most important in dealing effectively with the environment have the largest brain areas. For example, information received from your fingers is more important to your survival than information received from the middle of your back. Therefore, more brain area is devoted to the fingers than to the back. A similar map of the motor cortex is shown in Figure 2-10B. As with sensory abilities, more cortical area is devoted to the motor functions that are most important to survival. Because the use of our hands is so important to survival, large motor areas are devoted to manual dexterity.

The French physician Paul Broca (1824–1880) introduced the case study method for studying brain functioning.

The Case Study Method.   In 1861, the French physician Paul Broca popularized another technique for understanding the brain—the clinical or case study method. As we saw in Chapter 1, in this method a single patient is studied intensely. Broca had been treating a terminally ill patient who was nicknamed "Tan" because this was one of the few sounds he could make. Tan's vocal system was not paralyzed, and he could understand what was said to him. After Tan's death, Broca autopsied his brain and found a damaged area in the frontal lobe of the left hemisphere. Broca correctly concluded this area was responsible for the ability to produce speech. In recognition of his discovery, this speech area is called *Broca's area.* A second area, *Wernicke's area,* is responsible for speech comprehension. These areas are shown in Figure 2-10C.

The story of Phineas Gage (Harlow, 1868) is an even more fascinating case study of brain function. Gage, a railroad employee, was working with dynamite when an explosion blasted an iron tamping rod completely through his skull. Figure 2-11 shows the relative size of the rod that went through Gage's head and the path it took. Surprisingly, Gage was not killed in the accident; however, a variety of problems became evident after the accident. Before the accident, Gage had been an excellent worker who got along well with others and carried through with his plans. After the accident, he continually made plans he never carried out. He also used gross profanity, refused to listen to others if what they said interfered with what he wanted, and was moody. This case study continues to provide researchers with a glimpse of the functions of the frontal lobes of the human brain (Damasio et al., 1994).

Brain Damage.   The study of people who have suffered from some type of brain damage also provides an abundance of information about brain functioning. A **stroke,** or temporary loss of blood flow to the brain that is also referred to as a *cerebrovascular accident,* is the most common form of brain damage experienced by adults (Ginsberg, 1995). Direct injury produced by a blow to the head or gunshot wound is equally common.

By comparing a person's behavior, thought processes, and intelligence before and after brain damage, *neuropsychologists* can learn a great deal about specific functions of the brain. Such comparisons are typically made with a large battery of tests that evaluate basic sensory abilities, such as vision and hearing, intelligence, memory, and language (Lezak, 1995). As we discuss later in this chapter, the neuropsychological approach to studying brain functioning has grown rapidly in recent years.

Stereotaxic Surgery.   In 1904, two brain researchers, Victor Horsley and R. H. Clarke, produced a device that made studying subcortical structures possible (Valenstein, 1973). Before the invention of this device, subcortical structures could be examined only by removing or damaging the cortex that covered them. The **stereotaxic instrument** holds the organism's head in a fixed position and allows an electrode (a fine piece of specially treated wire) to be inserted into a specified subcortical area of an anesthetized patient. The electrode is thin enough that it does not damage the cortex as it passes through it. The electrode can be used to record electrical brain activity, to stimulate brain activity with a mild electric current, or to destroy a brain area by *lesioning,* or destroying the area bypassing a strong electric current through it. All three procedures (recording, stimulating, lesioning) provide information about the functions of various subcortical structures and are commonly used to study brain functioning in animals. The stereotaxic instrument also is used to inject chemicals into selected brain areas. These chemicals can be used to stimulate or destroy brain areas or create a genetic mutation (Joyner & Guillemot, 1994).

stroke
Temporary loss of blood flow to the brain; also known as a *cerebrovascular accident*

stereotaxic instrument
Instrument that holds the head in a fixed position to allow precise surgery on subcortical structures

The stereotaxic instrument depicted in Figure 2-12 is used for the study of human brains. Stereotaxic instruments are individually created for each species and have been used on a variety of animals and humans. The use of this technique raises ethical questions, such as the risk that the operation will change the patient's personality. On humans, stereotaxic surgery is a last resort. The purpose is to destroy a brain area that is believed to be malfunctioning and creating serious behavior problems. For example, parts of the amygdala (a subcortical structure in the limbic system involved in the control of emotional behavior) may be destroyed in an attempt to control excessive, unprovoked violence (Mark & Ervin, 1970).

The Electroencephalograph. More recently developed techniques enabled researchers to examine brain functions and anatomy without having to resort to autopsy or stereotaxic surgery. In 1929 Hans Berger developed the **electroencephalograph (EEG),** a device that monitors and records the brain's electrical activity. To make an EEG recording, a technician places several round metal discs, called electrodes, on a patient's scalp (see Figure 2-13). These electrodes sense the brain activity occurring in the region beneath them and transmit this information to the EEG system, which amplifies the signals. These amplified signals activate a pen that records the type of electrical activity (known as *brain waves*) occurring in the region monitored.

Brain waves (identified by Greek letters) are distinguished by their frequency, which is measured in cycles per second (called *hertz,* abbreviated *Hz*), and their amplitude, which reflects strength. *Alpha waves* are fast waves (8 to 12 Hz) that are not high in amplitude. *Beta waves* are very fast (13 to 30 Hz) but

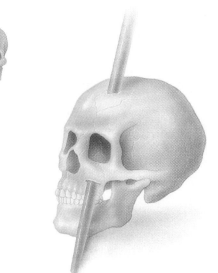

FIGURE 2-11 Phineas Gage had an iron bar blasted through his head and lived to tell about it! The relative size of the iron bar that passed through his head is shown on the left. The path the bar took is shown on the right.

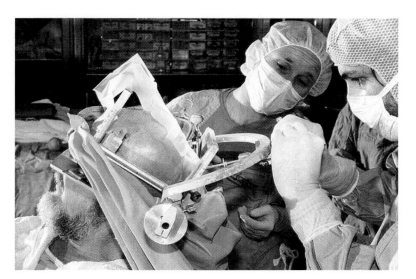

FIGURE 2-12 A person in a stereotaxic instrument. This instrument allows the researcher to insert a fine piece of wire called an electrode into subcortical brain areas. The electrode can be used to record brain activity, stimulate a brain area, or completely destroy or lesion a specified area.

electroencephalograph (EEG)
Device that monitors and records electrical activity of the brain

positron emission tomography (PET)

Imaging technique that involves monitoring the metabolic activity of the brain

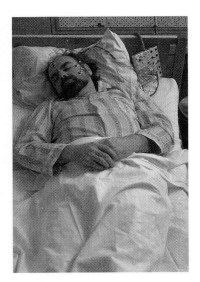

FIGURE 2-13 EEG participant with scalp electrodes in place.

not high in amplitude. *Theta waves* (3.5 to 7 Hz) are irregular in frequency and low in amplitude, whereas *delta waves* are quite slow (below 3.5 Hz) and quite high in amplitude. These different types of brain waves are associated with different states of consciousness. (See Chapter 5 for more about the states these brain waves represent.) Because of the more general nature of the EEG, more detailed technology has been developed to determine exactly which brain areas are involved with the behavior in question.

Magnetoencephalography is a relatively new technique that is similar to the traditional EEG procedure (Hari, 1994). When using magnetoencephalography, researchers measure the brain's magnetic fields to determine electrical activity; it is easier to conduct and more precise than the traditional EEG procedure.

Computerized Brain Imaging. The advent of computers has led to major advances in the study of brain processes. With the newest techniques, brain activity is measured, and then a computer uses the measurements to produce a brain image. The three most widely used brain-imaging techniques are the PET scan, the CT scan, and the MRI process (Gilman, 1992).

Positron emission tomography (PET) provides information about the brain's metabolic activity. In this procedure the patient is injected with a radioactive form of glucose (blood sugar). Because active neurons require larger amounts of fuel, the radioactive glucose accumulates in the most active areas of the brain (Phelps & Mazziotta, 1985). The PET procedure scans the brain and monitors the radioactivity of various brain areas. Figure 2-14 shows patterns of brain activity during auditory stimulation (Figure 2-14A) and in an Alzheimer's patient (Figure 2-14B). The areas of highest glucose utilization (highest activity) are shown in yellow and red. Clearly, the activity of these two brains differs drastically. Although the PET scan provides very useful information, it is time-consuming and requires the patient to be conscious and able to process the stimuli that are presented.

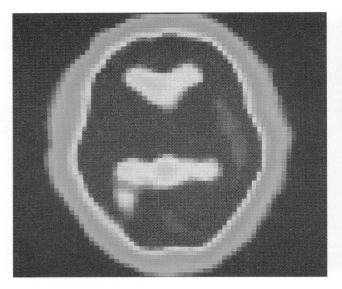

A

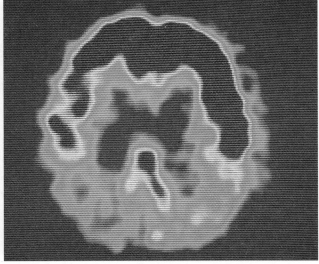

B

FIGURE 2-14 Color photographs of PET scans conducted (A) during auditory stimulation and (B) on an Alzheimer's patient suffering from memory loss. Red and yellow indicate the greatest amount of brain activity; blue indicates the least amount.

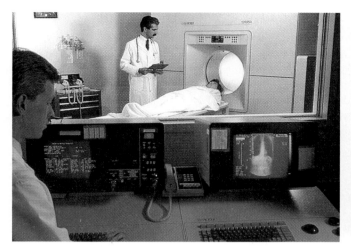

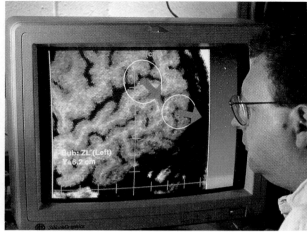

A

B

FIGURE 2-15 (A) A patient preparing for a CT scan is about to be positioned in the gantry. (B) The result of a CT scan showing the structure of an isolated portion of the brain.

If you were to undergo a **CT** or **CAT (computerized axial tomography)** scan, an imaging technique involving computer interpretation of a large number of X-ray films, you would find yourself lying on a table with your head positioned inside a large collarlike structure called a *gantry*. Figure 2-15A shows a patient about to be put into a gantry. An X-ray machine located inside the gantry can be completely rotated around the patient's head while the X-rays are taken. The patient remains in the CT scanner for 15 to 30 minutes. With this procedure a computer combines the X-rays to produce an image. Because many different X-rays are taken from a variety of angles, multiple brain images can be produced. Figure 2-15B shows the result of a CT scan.

The third brain-scanning technique, the **MRI (magnetic resonance imaging)** process, uses a strong magnetic field and radio waves, rather than X-rays (Warach, 1995). With this process, a patient's head is positioned within a strong magnetic field, which causes the hydrogen atoms in the brain cells to become aligned—that is, to spin in the same direction. Radio waves directed at the brain cause the spinning hydrogen atoms to emit a signal. The denser or thicker the tissue, the greater the number of hydrogen atoms and, therefore, the stronger the signal. A computer amplifies and analyzes signals from the hydrogen atoms to construct a picture of the brain tissues. The MRI procedure takes about twice as long as a CT scan, but the results are often worth the extra time. If you compare Figures 2-15B and 2-16, you will see that the details produced by the MRI process (Figure 2-16) are superior to those of the CT scan (Figure 2-15B).

If you have a heart pacemaker or any other type of metal implant, the MRI process, with its strong magnetic field, will not work well. (According to several reports, technicians who forgot to take off watches and jewelry have been dragged across a room by the MRI magnet!)

Although the standard MRI technique produces excellent structural images, it is not capable of depicting *ongoing* (temporal) brain activity. **Functional magnetic resonance imaging (fMRI)** is a modified version of the standard MRI procedure that provides both excellent structural views *and* temporal changes in brain activity (Cohen, Noll, & Schneider, 1993). The fMRI procedure has been used effectively at Massachussetts General Hospital to chart the course of activity in different parts of an addict's brain during cocaine ingestion.

computerized axial tomography (CT or CAT)

Imaging technique that involves the production of a large number of X-rays interpreted by a computer

magnetic resonance imaging (MRI)

Imaging technique that involves the use of radio waves and a strong magnetic field to produce a signal that can be interpreted by a computer

functional magnetic resonance imaging (fMRI)

A modification of the standard MRI procedure that allows both structural and temporal images to be gathered

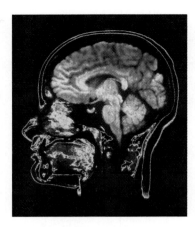

FIGURE 2-16 The magnetic resonance imaging (MRI) procedure provides the neuroscientist with a detailed image of the living human brain.

Psychological Detective

A construction worker suffered a head injury that may have resulted in brain damage. If you were on duty in the emergency room when the patient arrived, what technique would you use to diagnose the extent of any possible brain damage? Your choices include the EEG, a CT scan, a PET scan, and the MRI process. Think about the situation, and write down the procedure you would recommend. Why did you make this choice?

Because of the time involved, MRI is not used when quick evaluations are needed. For example, victims of automobile accidents typically require the quicker CT scan. The PET scan and EEG procedure would not be used because they are not designed to detect damaged tissue.

In this section you have learned about the nervous system, its major components, and the ways psychologists study these structures. We next turn our attention to the individual cells that make up the nervous system.

Review Summary

1. The **evolutionary perspective** stresses the role that physiological structures and behaviors play in an organism's survival and adaptation to its environment. The principle of **natural selection** states that the strongest or most fit organisms survive because they best adapt to the environment.

2. We use the processes of sensing, processing, and responding to interact with the environment. The nervous system, which is divided into the **central nervous system** (**CNS**—brain and spinal cord) and the **peripheral nervous system** (**PNS**—all parts of the nervous system outside the CNS), coordinates these three activities.

3. The PNS is composed of the **somatic division** and the **autonomic division.** The somatic division consists of **afferent (sensory) nerves** that run from the receptors to the brain and **efferent (motor) nerves** that run to the muscles. The autonomic division consists of the **sympathetic division,** which mobilizes the body's resources, and the **parasympathetic division,** which returns the body to a normal state of **homeostasis.**

4. The spinal cord is composed of sensory (afferent or ascending) and motor (efferent or descending) nerves and small interneurons that may connect the sensory and motor neurons.

5. The brain is divided into the **hindbrain** (which handles survival functions and motor control), the **midbrain** (where the **reticular formation** is located), and the **forebrain** (which consists of two hemispheres joined by the **corpus callosum**).

6. The cerebral cortex covers the forebrain and is divided into four areas or lobes: frontal, parietal, temporal, and occipital. A group of **subcortical structures** involved in such activities as emotion, memory, eating, drinking, and sexual behavior are located beneath the cortex. These structures include the **limbic system, thalamus,** *hypothalamus,* and *basal ganglia.*

7. Early studies of brain functioning involved stimulating or removing portions of the cortex. The **stereotaxic instrument** allowed examination of the subcortical structures without damaging the cortex.

8. The **electroencephalograph (EEG)** provides an investigator with a chart of a person's brain waves. Images of the structures of the brain can be produced by computerized techniques such as the **PET (positron emission tomography)** scan, the **CT** or **CAT (computerized axial tomography)** scan, the **MRI (magnetic resonance imaging)** process, and the **fMRI (functional magnetic resonance imaging)** process.

Study Break

1. What is the evolutionary perspective?
2. On your way to class you see a $5 bill in the street.

Because you want something more than a soda for lunch, you claim the bill as yours. For this situation, describe each of the steps involved in interacting with the environment—sensing, processing, and responding.

3. For each of the following activities, indicate whether the sympathetic or parasympathetic division of the autonomic nervous system is involved.
   a. A sinking feeling in the pit of your stomach tells you that you are lost in a run-down section of a large city at night and have no money to make a phone call or catch a bus.
   b. Getting psyched up before a football game; you are ready to devastate the opponents.
   c. You are shivering in a cold wind.
   d. Soothing music helps calm you after a very frustrating test.

4. Which of the following are reflexes? Explain why.
   a. deciding to go to a show on Friday night
   b. blinking when a puff of air hits your eye
   c. a baby's sucking when a pacifier is placed in his or her mouth
   d. jerking your hand out of very hot water
   e. remembering how good a slice of pizza tasted
   f. the downward curling of your toes when someone tickles the bottom of your foot
   g. calling home to ask for a loan

5. Name the three main divisions of the brain.
6. The limbic system is a group of structures that are involved in which activities?
7. Cells that detect stimuli are called
   a. receptors.
   b. effectors.
   c. neurons.
   d. sensory tracts.
8. Which division of the nervous system makes contact with the environment?
   a. Sympathetic
   b. Parasympathetic
   c. Autonomic
   d. Somatic
9. The fibers that connect the two hemispheres of the brain are known as the
   a. reticular formation.
   b. cerebral cortex.
   c. corpus callosum.
   d. thalamus.

Neurons: The Cells of the Nervous System

In 1906, an English physiologist named Charles Scott Sherrington (1857–1952) was conducting research on reflexes in dogs. Shortly after he pinched a dog's foot, the foot would rise reflexively. Because he had disconnected the dog's brain from its spinal cord, Sherrington was confident that he was observing reflexive behavior. But he did not understand the delay that occurred between the time he pinched the dog's foot and the time the foot was raised. The length of the neurons that ran from the foot to the spinal cord and from the spinal cord to the muscles that controlled the foot had been carefully measured. Sherrington also knew the speed at which the neural impulse traveled. The reflex simply took too long to occur. ***What makes Sherrington's observation one of the most important in the history of psychology?*** ■

As we mentioned earlier, the nervous system is composed of cells called *neurons*. Like other cells in the body, neurons have a nucleus, are enclosed in a membrane, and contain an assortment of smaller structures. Unlike other cells, however, neurons are able to communicate or interact with one another. Neurons come in a variety of sizes and shapes. Motor neurons usually have longer distances to travel, so they tend to be large. Interneurons are small, so a large number of them can occupy a given area. The greater the number of neurons in an area, the more complex the interconnections among them.

Charles Scott Sherrington (1857–1952) deduced the existence of the synapse from the speed of reflexive foot raising in dogs.

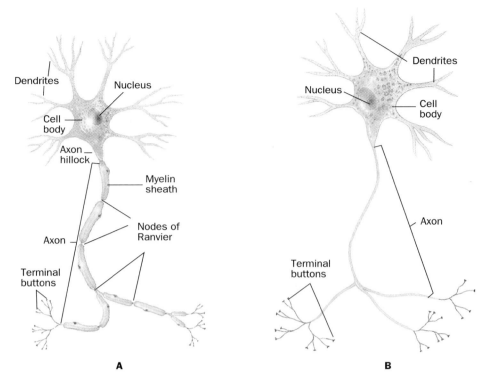

FIGURE 2-17 The basic structures of all neurons are the dendrites, cell body (soma), axon, and terminal buttons. In some neurons the axon may be covered by a fatty myelin sheath (A), whereas in others the axon is not covered (B).

Source: Shaver & Tarpy, 1993.

Components of the Neuron

The two neurons in Figure 2-17 are similar in that they each have a cell membrane, dendrites, a cell body (soma), an axon, and terminal buttons. First we look at these common components and what they do; then we consider the part that makes these neurons different—the myelin sheath.

The Cell Membrane.   The cell membrane surrounds the entire neuron to give it shape and keep the cell's internal fluids, known as the cytoplasm, inside. The cell membrane, however, is *semipermeable*: It allows some—but not all—substances to pass through it.

Dendrites.   The short, branchlike structures of neurons, called **dendrites,** receive signals or information from the receptors (such as the eye) or from other neurons. Most neurons typically have many dendrites. Hence it is possible for a single neuron to receive signals from many other neurons.

The Soma (Cell Body).   Once a signal has been received by the dendrites, it passes through the **soma** (cell body). Like other cells, the soma of the neuron contains a nucleus and is involved in the metabolic, or energy regulation, processes of the cell. The soma relays the neural signal from the dendrites to the axon.

The Axon.   The **axon** is the part of the neuron that transmits signals to other neurons and to muscles and glands. Only one axon leaves the cell body of each neuron. Whereas most dendrites tend to be rather short, axons vary

dendrite
Short, branchlike structures of a neuron that receive information from receptors and other neurons

soma
Cell body of a neuron

axon
Part of a neuron that transmits information to other neurons and to muscles and glands

greatly in length, depending on the location of the neuron. The axons of some neurons located in the cerebral cortex are microscopic; others are quite long. For example, the axon of a motor neuron can stretch from your spinal cord all the way to your hand.

Terminal Buttons. Although only one axon leaves the cell body, it may branch one or more times before reaching its target. Because the axon branches, the same signal can be sent to several different neurons. Most axons have several small knobs, known as **terminal buttons,** at their ends. The terminal buttons store neurotransmitters prior to their release and are directly involved in transmitting a signal from one neuron to the next.

The Myelin Sheath. Now that we know the structures common to all neurons, we examine the differences between the two neurons shown in Figure 2-17. Unlike the axon of neuron B, the axon of neuron A is covered by a **myelin sheath,** a fatty protein substance that increases speed of transmission.

The myelin sheath is composed of **glia cells,** another special type of cell found in the nervous system. Glia cells are considerably smaller and more numerous than neurons; there are about ten glia cells for every neuron. In addition to comprising the myelin sheath *(myelination),* glia cells remove waste material (Sontheimer, 1995), occupy vacant space when neurons die, and help guide the migration of neurons to their correct destination during the development of the brain (Kimelberg & Norenberg, 1989).

The myelin sheath is critical to rapid neural transmission. Consider what happens when you accidentally put your hand on a hot stove. It is important that you remove it—immediately! Even though a signal is transmitted rapidly down the axon, motor axons are very long; therefore anything that speeds up the transmission will help. Accelerating the transmission of the neural signal is the function of the myelin sheath. The sheath covers the axon entirely except at small, regularly spaced gaps, called **nodes of Ranvier** (see Figure 2-17A). We say more about the myelin sheath and the nodes of Ranvier on page 73.

About 50 percent of the axons in the nervous system have myelin sheaths. Most of the long motor neurons in the peripheral nervous system are myelinated; many of the very short axons found in the brain are not. When you stop to think about the frequent need for quick motor responses, myelination of the motor neurons makes sense.

Psychological Detective

What happens when the myelin sheath degenerates? Review what you have learned about the myelin sheath and give this question some thought. Write down your answer before reading further.

The most common disease caused by degeneration of the myelin sheath in the CNS, **multiple sclerosis,** begins with degeneration of small patches of myelin. As the disease progresses, the entire myelin sheath is destroyed. The physical symptoms associated with multiple sclerosis include weakness, tremors, and visual disturbances, but the most prominent symptom is **ataxia,** loss of motor coordination (Vickrey et al., 1995).

terminal buttons
Structures located at the ends of the axon in which neurotransmitters are stored before release

myelin sheath
Fatty protein substance that covers some axons, increasing speed of transmission

glia cell
Special type of cell found in the nervous system that forms the myelin sheath

nodes of Ranvier
Regularly spaced gaps in the myelin sheath

multiple sclerosis
Disease caused by degeneration of myelin in the central nervous system

ataxia
Loss of motor coordination

The Synapse and Neurotransmitters

You now know the components of neurons, but how do these special cells work? In this section we explore how neurons are organized and how information is transmitted from one neuron to another.

The Synapse.   To send messages, neurons must be aligned and organized in a particular manner. Because a signal is sent from one neuron to the next through the terminal buttons of the axons, the most common arrangement is for a neuron's terminal buttons to be near, but not touching, the receptive dendrites of neighboring neurons. This arrangement, which is diagramed in Figure 2-18, is called a **synapse.** The membrane on the side that sends the message is called the *presynaptic membrane.* The membrane on the receiving side of the synapse is called the *postsynaptic membrane.*

The most common synapse consists of three parts: a terminal button to send the signal, a dendrite to receive the signal, and the gap between the two, which is called the *synaptic cleft.* The synaptic cleft is microscopic—two one-hundredths of a micrometer (a micrometer is one one-thousandth of a millimeter)—yet the neurons never touch each other. To give you a better idea of the size of the synaptic cleft, it would take more than 12.5 million of them to fill an inch.

How many synapses are in the brain? This is a difficult question to answer. Estimates of the number of neurons range from 10 billion to 100 billion. Each neuron may make between 5,000 and 50,000 contacts with other neurons. Thus using the most conservative estimate of 10^{10} (10 billion neurons) with 10^4 (10,000) connections each gives us 10^{14} (100 trillion) synaptic connections (Hooper & Teresi, 1987).

Neurotransmitters.   If there is a gap between the neurons, why doesn't the signal stop when it arrives at the terminal buttons? The answer to that question involves special chemicals called **neurotransmitters.**

The discovery of neurotransmitters is a fascinating story. Recall the description of Charles Scott Sherrington at the beginning of this section. As we mentioned, Sherrington was studying reflexive foot raising in dogs when he observed that reflexes occurred more slowly than the speed of the neural impulse

synapse

Site where two or more neurons interact but do not touch

neurotransmitters

Chemical substances, stored in the terminal buttons, that facilitate the transmission of information from one neuron to another

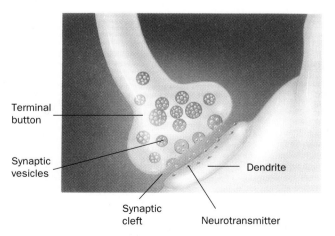

FIGURE 2-18   The synapse typically consists of terminal buttons containing synaptic vesicles and dendrites. The terminal buttons and dendrites are separated by the synaptic cleft.

Source: Shaver & Tarpy, 1993.

in the axon would predict. Sherrington reasoned that another process must be involved. Because Santiago Ramón y Cajal (1852–1934) had previously demonstrated that neurons are separate units of the nervous system, Sherrington concluded that the process he inferred must occur in the space separating the neurons—that is, in the synapse.

Sherrington proposed that the transmission of impulses across the synapse must involve special chemicals that are now termed neurotransmitters. Neurotransmitters are stored in tiny packets, called **synaptic vesicles,** located in the terminal buttons. When the neural signal reaches the terminal buttons, it causes calcium ions to rush into the terminal buttons. (Ions are electrically charged particles. We say more about them on page 73.) This influx of calcium ions results in the synaptic vesicles releasing the neurotransmitter into the synaptic cleft. As the neurotransmitter enters the cleft, it contacts the post-synaptic membrane (usually the dendrite) of the next neuron. When the molecules of the neurotransmitter contact specially shaped receptor sites located on the postsynaptic membrane, they attach or bind to them, thereby allowing the neural signal to be transmitted from one neuron to the next. This "lock and key" arrangement is diagramed in Figure 2-19.

When the neurotransmitter occupies the appropriate receptor site, depending on the type of neurotransmitter and the location of the synapse in the nervous system, one of two things occurs. The neuron that is receiving the neurotransmitter may become more likely to transmit the message to subsequent neurons; this process is called *excitation.* In other instances the neuron that receives the neurotransmitter becomes less likely to transmit the message to subsequent neurons; this process is called *inhibition.* Because a receptor site accepts only a neurotransmitter molecule of a particular shape, the synapse must be made up of terminal buttons containing the appropriate neurotransmitter and a postsynaptic membrane with matching receptor sites. Otherwise the message will not be transmitted from one neuron to the next.

Several neurotransmitters are described in Table 2-3. It is likely that additional neurotransmitters will be discovered in the future.

The importance of neurotransmitters in even basic behaviors like moving is evident in the case of John, a 50-year-old carpenter. Several years ago John noticed that his fingers felt stiff and that he sometimes had slight hand tremors. This condition became progressively worse until he was unable to work. What caused John's motor control problems, and what can be done to help him?

synaptic vesicles

Small pockets or sacs located in the terminal buttons that contain a neurotransmitter

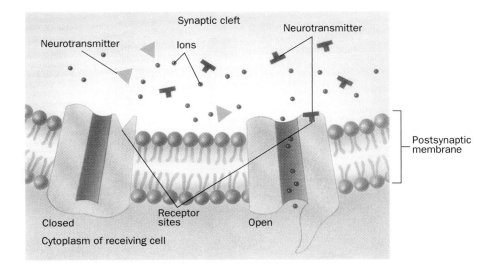

FIGURE 2-19 The lock-and-key arrangement of neurotransmitter and receptor site.

TABLE 2-3   Selected Neurotransmitters: Their Effects, Locations, and Functions

NEUROTRANSMITTERS	EFFECTS	LOCATION	FUNCTIONS
Acetylcholine	Excitatory or inhibitory	Brain spinal cord, synapses of the skeletal muscles, and parasympathetic nervous system	Involved in muscle movement and also memory; Alzheimer's disease is associated with its low levels
Norepinephrine	Generally excitatory	Brain stem (nerve tracts extend to many areas of the brain and spinal cord) and sympathetic nervous system	Involved in sympathetic nervous system activity; influences arousal, mood, and and reward centers; cocaine and amphetamines block reuptake
Serotonin	Inhibitory or excitatory	Brain stem (nerve tracts extend to many areas of the brain and spinal cord)	Involved with mood, appetite, and sleep induction
Dopamine	Inhibitory or excitatory	Brain (three major circuits: hypothalamus, pituitary, midbrain)	Involved in movement and reward centers; destruction of dopamine-secreting neurons can lead to Parkinson's disease; implicated in the development of schizophrenia
Gamma-aminobutyric acid (GABA)	Inhibitory	Local transmission in CNS	Involved in levels of excitablity; drugs used to treat anxiety increase the ability of GABA to bind to postsynaptic sites, which leads to reduction of arousal
Endorphins and enkephalins	Inhibitory	Throughout CNS and PNS	Drugs such as morphine bind to endorphin and enkephalin receptors and reduce pain
Substance P	Excitatory	Spinal cord, brain, and sensory neurons associated with pain	Involved in pain transmission pathways

Sources: Leavitt, 1995; Seeley, Stephens, & Tate, 1995.

John is suffering from Parkinson's disease, which can result from brain infections, injury, strokes, or tumors. Regardless of which of these events happened to John, we know that the motor effects, such as stiffness, tremors, and slow movements, are caused by reduced levels of the neurotransmitter dopamine in the brain. Administration of L-dopa, the chemical from which dopamine is produced, increases the amount of dopamine and improves the motor behaviors of patients suffering from Parkinson's disease.

Unfortunately, this treatment is not a cure. The positive effects of L-dopa wear off after about four years; patients gradually lose sensitivity to the treatment, which begins to work for shorter and shorter periods of time (Youdim & Riederer, 1997). Also, L-dopa treatments produce harmful side effects such as nausea, sleep disorders, and disturbances of thought processes (Obeso et al., 1989). Although a solution to these problematic side effects has not been found, researchers are on the trail of several promising leads. For example, it may be possible to transplant normal dopamine-producing tissue into the damaged brain areas (Björklund, 1992).

Clearing the Synapse.   How does the neurotransmitter get out of the synaptic cleft? If you think about that question for a moment, the importance of clearing the synaptic cleft becomes apparent. It's like your telephone. If you talk to only one person and never hang up, only one message can be sent and received. You must hang up to receive additional calls. Likewise, the synapse must be cleared, and cleared rapidly, before additional signals can be transmitted.

The synapse is cleared in one of two ways, depending on the neurotransmitter involved. With the first method, the neurotransmitter (e.g., acetylcholine) is broken down and removed from the synaptic cleft. For example, almost as soon as the acetylcholine affects the next neuron, an enzyme, acetyl-cholinesterase, begins to break it down. Once the acetylcholine is broken down and the receptor sites are unoccupied, the postsynaptic membrane is ready to receive another signal. This rapid breakdown is important for the production of rapid motor responses as in playing the violin or the piano.

The second method for clearing the synapse, **reuptake,** involves taking the neurotransmitter back into the terminal button from which it came. Once the neurotransmitter has had its effect on the postsynaptic membrane, it reenters the terminal buttons in the presynaptic membrane, is repackaged into synaptic vesicles, and is ready to be used again. All neurotransmitters, except acetylcholine, are removed from the synapse by the process of reuptake.

Neurotransmitters and Drug Action. Understanding the way neurotransmitters operate has led to increases in our knowledge of how drugs affect the functioning of the brain and, consequently, our behavior. Many drugs exert their effects by influencing the operation of a neurotransmitter.

Agonists. Drugs that promote or enhance the operation of a neurotransmitter are called **agonists.** One of the most common agonists, caffeine, is a CNS stimulant (Hughes et al., 1992; Scheibel et al., 1992). Caffeine does not stimulate the CNS directly. Rather, it acts indirectly by interfering with the effects of *adenosine*. Adenosine inhibits the release of the neurotransmitter glutamate (Silinsky, 1989), which is a CNS stimulant. Therefore, as you consume caffeine, the inhibitory effects of adenosine decrease, allowing the stimulating effects of glutamate to increase (Landoldt et al., 1995; Rainnie et al., 1994).

Have you wondered how much caffeine you consume during a day? When are your peak consumption periods? If you complete the questionnaire in Table 2-4, you will have your answers. Typical caffeine consumption rates for college students are given on page 85.

Some agonists eliminate the enzyme that breaks down the neurotransmitter in the synapse. Without the enzyme, the neurotransmitter remains active in the synaptic cleft for a longer period, resulting in a more intense response. For example, the drug physostigmine inactivates acetylcholinesterase, the enzyme that breaks down acetylcholine. Thus the acetylcholine remains active longer. Drugs like physostigmine produce a wide range of behavioral effects that may include nightmares and vivid dreaming (see Chapter 5), as well as parasympathetic effects such as decreased heart rate and constriction of the pupils of the eyes.

The benzodiazepines are a class of drugs that occupy receptor sites and increase the ability of the receptors to bind to or accept a neurotransmitter. Although the name *benzodiazepines* may not be familiar, you have probably heard the trade names Valium, Librium, and Xanax. These drugs are most often prescribed to reduce anxiety, but they also promote sleep, relax the muscles, and decrease the likelihood of convulsions. Benzodiazepines work by enhancing the ease or tightness of binding of the neurotransmitter gamma-aminobutyric acid (GABA) (Breier & Paul, 1990).

Another class of drugs, known as *tricyclic antidepressants,* is often used to relieve depression (Julien, 1995). These drugs block the reuptake of the neurotransmitters norepinephrine and serotonin into the terminal buttons (see Chapter 14). When reuptake is blocked, these neurotransmitters remain active in the synapse for a longer time period than usual. Because depression is alleviated when the effective levels of norepinephrine and serotonin in the synapse are raised, researchers have proposed that depression may occur when abnormally low levels of these neurotransmitters are present (Schildkraut & Kety, 1967; Jaskiw & Weinberger, 1992).

reuptake
Method of clearing a neurotransmitter from the synaptic cleft, in which the neurotransmitter is taken back into the terminal buttons

agonist
Drug that enhances the operation of a neurotransmitter

TABLE 2-4 Caffeine Consumption Questionnaire (CCQ)

Answer the following questions about your caffeine usage. Respond to items that you consume at least once a week.

Coffee (5-ounce servings per week)	Morning 6 A.M.–12 noon	Afternoon 12 noon–6 P.M.	Evening 6 P.M.–2 A.M.	Night 2 A.M.–6 A.M.
Regular (brewed)				
Percolated	_____	_____	_____	_____
Drip	_____	_____	_____	_____
Regular instant				
Decaffeinated				
Brewed	_____	_____	_____	_____
Instant	_____	_____	_____	_____

Tea (5-ounce servings per week)

Cocoa (5-ounce servings per week)

Chocolate (8-ounce servings per week)

Soft Drinks (12-ounce servings per week)	Morning 6 A.M.–12 noon	Afternoon 12 noon–6 P.M.	Evening 6 P.M.–2 A.M.	Night 2 A.M.–6 A.M.
Coca-Cola Classic	_____	_____	_____	_____
Diet Coke	_____	_____	_____	_____
Dr. Pepper	_____	_____	_____	_____
Mountain Dew	_____	_____	_____	_____
Mr. Pibb	_____	_____	_____	_____
Tab	_____	_____	_____	_____
Pepsi Cola	_____	_____	_____	_____
Diet Pepsi	_____	_____	_____	_____
RC Cola	_____	_____	_____	_____
Mello Yello	_____	_____	_____	_____

Over-the-Counter Drugs (tablets per week)				
Vivarin	_____	_____	_____	_____
NoDoz	_____	_____	_____	_____
Excedrin	_____	_____	_____	_____
Vanquish	_____	_____	_____	_____
Anacin	_____	_____	_____	_____
Dristan	_____	_____	_____	_____
Dexatrim	_____	_____	_____	_____

This is the CCQ as administered to students. To score the questionnaire, yielding a milligrams-per-week measure, use the following caffeine amounts: percolated, 110.0 mg; drip, 150.0 mg; regular instant, 66.0 mg; decaffeinated brewed (drip or percolated), 4.5 mg; decaffeinated instant, 2.0 mg; tea, 45.0 mg; cocoa, 13.0 mg; chocolate, 6.0 mg; Coca-Cola Classic, 42.0 mg; Diet Coke, 46.0 mg; Dr. Pepper, 61.0 mg; Mountain Dew, 49.0 mg; Mr. Pibb, 40.0 mg; Tab, 46.0 mg; Mello Yello, 52.0 mg; Pepsi Cola, 37.0 mg; Diet Pepsi, 36.0 mg; RC Cola, 24.0 mg; NoDoz, 100.0 mg; Excedrin, 65.0 mg; Vanquish, 33.0 mg; Anacin, 32.0 mg; Dristan, 16.2 mg; Dexatrim, 200.0 mg; Vivarin, 200 mg.

Source: Adapted from Landrum, 1992; © 1988 R. Eric Landrum.

Antagonists. Drugs that block the operation of a neurotransmitter are called **antagonists.** They attach to postsynaptic receptor sites and block the neurotransmitter from attaching there. By stopping the action of the neurotransmitter, they prevent transmission of signals. For example, the drug haloperidol (Haldol) attaches to dopamine receptors and blocks them; as a result, less dopamine binds to the receptors on the postsynaptic membrane. As we shall see in Chapter 13, researchers believe that some psychological disorders result from high levels of dopamine. Haloperidol is effective in the treatment of these disorders because it reduces the level of dopamine.

Other drugs block the storage of the neurotransmitter in vesicles. When the synaptic vesicles empty their contents into the synaptic cleft, a reduced amount of the neurotransmitter is released, and the effect on the postsynaptic membrane is less than normal. The blood pressure drug reserpine, which affects dopamine synapses, operates in this manner. Reserpine destroys the membrane of the synaptic vesicles that contain the dopamine. With no membrane to protect it, the dopamine is destroyed by an enzyme contained inside the terminal button. As a result, there is less dopamine to be released into the synaptic cleft.

Neuromodulators. The search for neurotransmitters has led to the discovery of other chemicals, **neuromodulators,** that are capable of influencing the transmission of signals between neurons. Whereas the release and action of a neurotransmitter are confined to synapses located in a specific area, the distribution of a neuromodulator is more widespread, and its activity may be somewhat indirect and longer-lasting. Some neuromodulators appear to produce their effects by facilitating the release of neurotransmitters; others seem to inhibit the release of neurotransmitters.

One of the best-known neuromodulators, morphine, is used to relieve pain. Consider the case of Kevin, who broke his leg while playing football in high school. The injury was so severe that Kevin had to be hospitalized and given morphine injections to reduce the pain. How does morphine work? Such drugs affect synapses that transmit pain signals. Somehow they block or inhibit transmission of the neural signal at these synapses. Perhaps the body produces a substance that is similar to morphine—otherwise, would it have developed receptors for such substances?

This question led researchers Candace Pert and Solomon Snyder to seek and locate the receptors that are sensitive to chemicals like morphine (Pert & Snyder, 1973). Clearly, these receptors are not there just to receive external substances like morphine, so the next piece of the puzzle involved identifying the endogenous (internal) chemicals that naturally occupy these receptors. In 1975, researchers found two of these painkilling chemicals produced by the body, which are called **opioid peptides** (Hughes et al., 1975); other substances of this kind have been found since then. Although each of these chemicals has a technical name, they are generally referred to as *endorphins* and *enkephalins.*

How do morphine and the opioid peptides function as neuromodulators? **Substance P,** a neurotransmitter located primarily in the spinal cord (Levine, Fields, & Basbaum, 1993), is believed to play a major role. When you are experiencing pain, it is a good bet that substance P has been released. Painkillers, such as the opioid peptides and morphine, appear to block the release of substance P. When opioid peptide receptor sites, which are located on the terminal buttons (but not in the region of the synaptic cleft), are occupied, the release of substance P is blocked. When opioid peptide receptor sites are not occupied, substance P is released, and pain signals are readily transmitted. The proposed interaction between the opioid peptides and substance P is diagramed in Figure 2-20. We say more about pain in Chapter 3.

antagonist
Drug that blocks the operation of a neurotransmitter

neuromodulators
Chemicals that may have a widespread or general effect on the release of neurotransmitters

opioid peptides
Painkillers that are produced by the body

substance P
Neurotransmitter involved in sensing pain

FIGURE 2-20 Diagram of the relationship between opioid peptides and substance P.

Source: Shaver & Tarpy, 1993.

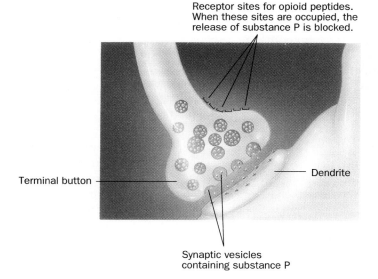

Psychological Detective

 What causes the release of opioid peptides? The body must store and release them as needed, because if they were present all the time, we would never feel any pain. Give this matter some thought, and write down some possible answers before reading further.

Pain itself appears to be one stimulus that releases the body's natural painkillers. The first perception of pain causes the release of the opioid peptides, which in turn block the release of substance P and thereby reduce the pain. This sequence explains how athletes are able to continue playing despite injuries and conditions that should be painful.

Humans have an elaborate and complex system to sense pain and then block it (Fernandez & Turk, 1992). Would it be better if we did not sense pain at all? Consider the case of Miss C., who had been insensitive to pain from birth (Melzack & Wall, 1982):

> The young lady . . . seemed normal in every way except that she had never felt pain. As a child, she had bitten off the tip of her tongue while chewing food and had suffered third-degree burns after kneeling on a radiator to look out of the window. . . . She felt no pain when parts of her body were subjected to strong electric shock, to hot water . . . , or to a prolonged ice-bath. Furthermore, she could not remember ever sneezing or coughing, the gag reflex could be elicited only with great difficulty, and corneal reflexes (to protect the eyes) were absent. (pp. 16–17)

Miss C. was unusual because she lived into her teens. Most people who cannot sense pain die at an early age. To adapt to and survive in our environment, we must be able to sense occurrences that could lead to injury or illness.

The Nature of the Neural Signal

At the beginning of the chapter we mentioned that the basic function of the nervous system is to receive information or signals from specialized cells called receptors. As demonstrated in the example of closing your hand in a car door, much of this information is processed further by the brain and then translated into some form of action. Now we turn our attention to the neural signals themselves. To understand the signal, we must consider the inside and outside of the neuron at the same time.

If you were to examine the chemicals on the outside of the semipermeable cell membrane of the neuron and compare them with those found on the inside of the cell membrane, you would notice a difference in very small electrically charged particles called **ions.** There are two types of ions, positive (+) and negative (−), resembling the two poles or ends of a battery. The most important negative ion is chloride (Cl−); potassium (K+) and sodium (Na+) are the most important positive ions.

When the neuron is not sending or receiving a signal, it is in a **resting state,** with more negative ions on the inside than on the outside. Relative to the outside, the inside of the neuron is about −70 millivolts (a millivolt, mV, is one one-thousandth of a volt) when the neuron is in the resting state. Because of this unequal distribution of electrically charged ions, we say that the neuron is *polarized,* like a battery that has stored an electrical charge. This −70 mV difference in electric charge between the inside and outside of a neuron at rest is called the *resting potential.*

What happens when the neurotransmitter enters the synaptic cleft? One of two reactions may occur. The presence of the neurotransmitter may result either in **depolarization** (a process in which the neuron becomes *less* negatively charged) or **hyperpolarization** (a process in which the neuron becomes *more* negatively charged). As you will see in a moment, the reaction that occurs is determined by the type of neurotransmitter and the location of the synapse. Acetylcholine is an excellent example of the location effect because its presence at synapses located in some parts of the body, such as the skeletal muscles, results in depolarization, whereas its presence at synapses located in other parts of the body, such as the heart, results in hyperpolarization.

Depolarization and Excitatory Synapses.

When excitatory neurotransmitters occupy the appropriate receptor sites, they cause the cell membrane to allow some positive ions from the outside to pass inside. The increase of positive ions on the inside of the neuron causes the resting potential to change; it may drop from −70 to −68 mV. As you just learned, this change, which brings the potential closer to zero, is called depolarization. If enough of the neurotransmitter is present to cause the dendrite and soma to depolarize to between −65 and −60 mV, the neuron generates its own signal. At this threshold (the minimum amount of change required for the neural response to occur) the axon membrane suddenly allows large quantities of positive (Na+) ions to rush inside. In less than a millisecond (one millisecond is one one-thousandth of a second) the neuron changes from −60 to +40 mV, completely reversing its electrical nature or polarity. This reversal from −60 to +40 mV on the axon is the neural signal we have been talking about. We call it an **action potential,** or *all-or-none response:* When the axon fires, it does not fire more or less than it did last time. If an action potential occurs, it has the same magnitude each time.

Once the dendrite and soma reach the threshold level, the action potential rapidly spreads down the axon until it reaches the terminal buttons, where it causes the release of a neurotransmitter. The action potential, or signal, is nothing more than an exchange of ions. For axons that do not have a myelin sheath, this process of ion exchange takes place along the entire axon. If a myelin sheath is present, the ion exchange occurs only at the nodes of Ranvier. Hence there is less work to be done, and the action potential arrives at the terminal buttons more rapidly. The large myelinated axons in your legs may transmit action

ions
Electrically charged particles

resting state
Electrical charge (−70 mV) of a neuron when it is not firing

depolarization
Process in which the electrical charge of the neuron becomes less negative

hyperpolarization
Process in which the electrical charge of the neuron becomes more negative

action potential
Reversal in electrical charge of a neuron that occurs when the neuron fires

refractory period
Brief period following an action potential when the neuron is returning to the resting state and cannot be fired

potentials at speeds as fast as 100 meters per second (224 miles per hour), whereas small, unmyelinated axons (such as the ones in your brain) may conduct action potentials at speeds as slow as 1 meter per second (2.24 miles per hour).

At the same time that the action potential is being transmitted, the initiating neurotransmitter is being cleared out of the synaptic cleft. Removal of the neurotransmitter causes the receiving neuron to return to the resting state and allows it to generate another action potential—that is, to fire again. The period during which the neuron is being reset—when positive ions are pumped to the outside of the cell—is called the **refractory period.** Actually, the refractory period consists of two stages. During the *absolute* refractory period, the neuron cannot fire again. During the *relative* refractory period, the neuron can be fired, but it is more difficult to do so because the electrical charge has dipped below the resting potential. When the neuron returns to the resting state, it can be fired normally. This entire process is diagrammed in Figure 2-21.

Remarkably, the action potential and the refractory period occur within 2 milliseconds. Many messages can be transmitted when neurons fire 500 or more times per second! The rate at which neurons fire is important because stimulus magnitude or intensity is indicated in this manner. Strong stimuli produce a high rate of firing, whereas weaker stimuli produce a lower rate of firing. For example, the pressure from a handshake results in a low rate of firing compared with the pressure of shutting your hand in the car door.

Hyperpolarization and Inhibitory Synapses.   Not all neurons respond to the presence of a neurotransmitter by depolarizing or showing an action potential; the result may be just the opposite. In these cases the neurotransmitter is inhibitory and causes additional negative ions to cross the cell membrane and enter the neuron. When inhibition occurs, the neuron becomes more negative than it was during the resting state—that is, it becomes hyperpolarized. For example, the resting potential may change from -70 to -72, -73, or -74 mV. Because the threshold for firing is between -65 and -60 mV, an action potential is harder, if not impossible, to generate when a neuron is hyperpolarized. The electrical state of the neuron is moving away from the threshold level.

Some acetylcholine synapses in the parasympathetic system reflect this inhibitory nature. When acetylcholine is released, the neurons hyperpolarize, and the result is a decrease in a parasympathetic activity such as heart rate.

FIGURE 2-21 The sequence of events involved in firing a neuron (generating an action potential) and resetting it consists of Time (1) Resting (-70mV), Time (2) Threshold (-68mV), Time (3) Action Potential ($+40$ mV), Time (4) Absolute Refractory Period, Time (5) Relative Refractory Period (e.g., -73mV), Time (6) Resting (-70 mV). The entire process is completed within 2 milliseconds.

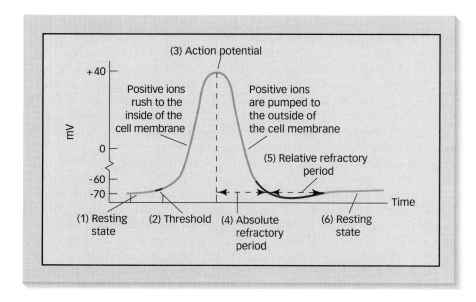

Review Summary

1. The cells that make up the nervous system, **neurons,** are composed of dendrites, a **soma** (cell body), an **axon,** and **terminal buttons.**

2. Dendrites receive signals from adjacent neurons; **axons** transmit signals. The tips of the axon, or **terminal buttons,** contain chemicals, known as **neurotransmitters,** that enable the signal from one neuron to be relayed to other neurons across the synaptic cleft, a small gap that separates neurons. The **myelin sheath** consists of glia cells and covers the axons of some neurons (except at the **nodes of Ranvier**) to increase the speed of transmission of the neural signal. The **synapse** is the site where two or more neurons interact but do not touch.

3. Neuromodulators, which have more widespread and indirect effects than neurotransmitters, also influence transmission between cells.

4. Agonists are drugs that promote the action of a neurotransmitter, and **antagonists** are drugs that block or oppose the action of a neurotransmitter.

5. The neurotransmitter must be removed from the synaptic cleft before another signal can be transmitted.

Removal is accomplished either by destroying the neurotransmitter or by taking it back into the terminal buttons **(reuptake)** and repackaging it into **synaptic vesicles** to be used again.

6. Ions (electrically charged particles) are found on the inside and outside of the semipermeable cell membrane of the neuron. When a neuron is in a **resting state,** more negative ions are on the inside of the cell (measured at −70 mV) than on the outside.

7. Neurotransmitters stimulate the cell membrane to allow ions to enter the neuron. Depending on the location and type of neurotransmitter, its effect is either to **depolarize** (the neuron-positive ions move inside the neuron; the result is excitation) or to **hyperpolarize** it (additional negative ions move inside; the result is inhibition).

8. If depolarization of the dendrite and soma reaches the threshold level (−65 to −60 mV), the axon quickly reverses its electrical charge (to about +40 mV), and the signal is transmitted to the next neuron. This reversal in electrical charge is known as the **action potential.**

Study Break

1. What are the basic building blocks of the nervous system?

2. Match each of the following structures with the appropriate description:

a. Dendrites	**1.** Receives information from other neurons
b. Axon	**2.** Bare spots on the axon
c. Soma	**3.** Speeds the neural impulse on its way
d. Terminal buttons	**4.** Transmits information to other neurons, muscles, and glands
e. Myelin sheath	**5.** Stores neurotransmitters
f. Nodes of Ranvier	**6.** The cell body

3. What is the approximate electrical charge of a neuron in the resting state? What might it become if the neuron depolarizes? After it hyperpolarizes?

4. What is the relationship between depolarization and the threshold? Explain what happens if the threshold is reached. Where do neurotransmitters come from, and how do they enter this process?

5. Once a neurotransmitter has been released, it must be removed from the synapse before the neuron can fire again. Explain how this is accomplished.

6. In which ways may a drug influence the operation of a neurotransmitter?

7. What is a neuromodulator? How does it differ from a neurotransmitter?

8. Glia cells make up the _____ of a neuron.
   a. terminal buttons
   b. myelin sheath
   c. cell membrane
   d. soma

9. Parkinson's disease is caused by reduced levels of the neurotransmitter
   a. dopamine.
   b. acetylcholine.
   c. serotonin.
   d. GABA.

The Split-Brain Operation and Neuropsychology

The following case history was reported by Oliver Sacks (1985), a former professor of clinical neurology at Albert Einstein College of Medicine:

Dr. P. was a music teacher who had some very peculiar visual problems. Frequently, he was seen patting parking meters, which he mistook for children. ***What caused Dr. P.'s visual problems?*** ◼

Being able to diagnose and treat a case like this reflects the progress that has been made in applying our knowledge of the brain and its functions to real problems. Much has been achieved to date, and the 1990s, "the decade of the brain," promises to produce even greater discoveries.

The Split-Brain Operation

Earlier in the chapter we described the two hemispheres of the cerebral cortex, which are connected by the corpus callosum. Figure 2-7 shows the corpus callosum (about the size of a small banana) and the fibers that connect it to each hemisphere. For years psychologists wondered what would happen if the corpus callosum was cut, eliminating communication between the two hemispheres. Would there be two independent minds inside one head? In the early 1960s, two neurosurgeons, Philip Vogel and Joseph Bogen, discovered that cutting the corpus callosum reduced seizures in untreatable epileptics (Bogen, Fisher, & Vogel, 1965). Even though we do not know exactly why this operation controls seizures, it is still performed as a last resort in severe cases of epilepsy.

Initially no other changes were noticed in patients who had this operation; however, research by Nobel Prize winner Roger Sperry (1964) and his colleague Michael Gazzaniga (1967) produced some startling findings. They showed that in people with a severed corpus callosum the two hemispheres appeared to be doing different things. Indeed, it was as if there were two minds in one head! For example, the right hand might unbutton the patient's shirt, while the left hand buttoned it. Such conflicts typically occur shortly after surgery and tend to subside as the two independent hemispheres learn to work together (Myers & Sperry, 1985).

Let's look at the logic behind the Sperry and Gazzaniga testing procedure. Figure 2-22 shows the transmission of visual information from the left and right visual fields to the brain. If you carefully trace the pathways, you see that when the corpus callosum is cut and the person focuses on the center of the visual field, information presented to the left visual field of each eye goes only to the right hemisphere, whereas information presented to the right visual field goes only to the left hemisphere. In people with an intact corpus callosum, information presented to only one hemisphere is quickly transmitted to the other. In short, in a person with a severed corpus callosum, the two hemispheres of the brain cannot communicate with each other.

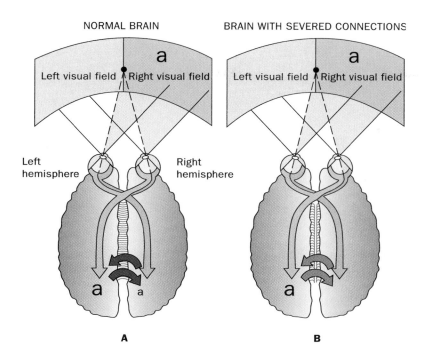

NORMAL BRAIN   BRAIN WITH SEVERED CONNECTIONS

A   **B**

FIGURE 2-22 Transmission of visual information to the brain. All information from the right visual fields goes to the left hemisphere, whereas information from the left visual fields goes to the right hemisphere. In Part A, the image in the right visual field will travel over the corpus callosum to the right hemisphere. In Part B, the corpus callosum is severed, so the image cannot be transferred to the right hemisphere.

Psychological Detective

Assume that you have undergone this operation. You are seated in the testing apparatus, wearing a special set of glasses that allows a technician to present a visual stimulus separately to either your right or your left visual field. What kind of responses might you be required to make when an object is presented to you? Will the response you are able to make differ depending on which hemisphere receives the information? Write down and explain your answers to these questions before reading further.

Suppose that we flash a picture of a baseball in your right visual field and ask you to name the object. If we trace the visual input, we find it ends in the left hemisphere. Responsibility for naming the object falls on the left hemisphere. If we switched visual fields, the right hemisphere would be involved. Such tasks pose major problems for patients with a severed corpus callosum; they can name an object only when it is presented to the right visual field. If, however, the task is reversed, so that when the patient is shown the word *baseball* in the left visual field and told to select what was seen from a group of objects on a table with the left hand, the left visual field–right hemisphere combination can perform the task whereas the right visual field–left hemisphere combination cannot (see Figure 2-23). Why?

Studies like those just described support the conclusion that the left hemisphere is involved in speech and language production. Thus you can easily identify a baseball or a cup of coffee when it is presented to your right visual field because this information is processed in the left hemisphere. In addition, the left hemisphere operates in a very logical, sequential, and analytical manner (Bradshaw & Nettleton, 1981). If your left hemisphere is dominant, people might describe your mind as operating "like a computer."

Although the right hemisphere has only limited language functions (Levy, 1983), it is essential for adding emotional content to our speech (Shapiro & Danly, 1985). It is also important for spatial abilities such as recognizing complex geometric patterns

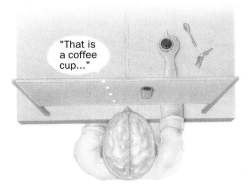
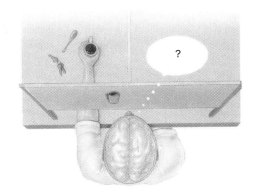

FIGURE 2-23   Testing the split-brain patient. In the left panel, the image of a coffee cup is projected on the right side of the screen and transmitted to the patient's left hemisphere. The patient is able to select the object by touch from a group and identify it verbally. When the image of the cup is projected on the left side of the screen and transmitted to the right hemisphere (right panel), the patient is able to locate the object by touch but cannot identify it verbally.

Source: Shaver & Tarpy, 1993.

(Clarke, Assal, & deTribolet, 1993) and people's faces and selecting objects. The right hemisphere operates in a more holistic or all-encompassing manner. A person whose right hemisphere is dominant might be described as more creative and insightful.

We do not want to leave you with the impression that the split-brain operation leaves the patient in an unusual or abnormal state. Other than having some trouble maintaining attention, split-brain patients do not suffer deficits in intelligence or motivation (Hoptman & Davidson, 1994).

Myth or Science

This proposed difference between the hemispheres has generated a great deal of interest and research. For example, it has become commonplace to talk about "left-brain" and "right-brain" people. It has even been suggested that public schools should gear their curricula more toward either right- or left-brain abilities. Thus the impression that one type of ability is better or more desired than the other has been created. Thankfully, educators finally seem to have realized the value of having and using the abilities provided by both hemispheres. For example, the standards for teacher training established by the National Council for the Accreditation of Teacher Education (1990) stress both the acquisition of a knowledge base (a left-brain function) and an understanding of the overall flow of the educational process (a right-brain function). Likewise, Kalat (1998) indicates that "for any individual, the balance of activity shifts from one hemisphere to the other, in accord with the task, and every task activates both hemispheres to some extent" (p. 380).

Brain Asymmetries

brain asymmetries

Differences between the two hemispheres of the brain

Much of the research on the structure and functioning of the brain has focused on differences, known as **brain asymmetries** or imbalances, between the two hemispheres. (If the hemispheres were really identical, they would be symmetrical.) One approach used in these studies is to look for physical differences such as size and weight (Crichton-Browne, 1980), structure (Eidelberg & Galaburda, 1982), and distribution of neurotransmitters (Perrone & Vignolo, 1982).

A second approach is to look for functional asymmetries, or what the hemispheres do differently. This approach has produced a great deal of valuable and informative data. As we have seen, the left hemisphere is involved in language production and speech, while the right hemisphere is important for spatial abilities. Research on aphasia and apraxia has filled in some of the specifics.

Aphasias. The term **aphasia** refers to a loss of the ability to speak or understand written or spoken language. Did you say to yourself, "Aphasias must involve the left hemisphere?" The point at which the damage occurs will likely determine the type of aphasia that occurs. For example, Paul Broca's case study of Tan (see page 58) involved *nonfluent aphasia,* an inability to produce speech that is caused by damage to the left frontal lobe.

In 1874, Carl Wernicke found that damage to a portion of the left temporal lobe (see Figure 2-10) produces a deficit in speech comprehension. Such damage may result from an infection, a tumor, or a birth defect. Patients suffering from Wernicke's aphasia do not have trouble producing words and sounds; their speech just doesn't have any meaning. These patients simply do not understand written and spoken language; they suffer from *afluent aphasia.*

Although the aphasias revealed by Broca's and Wernicke's patients are the two most common, other types have been identified. For example, *optic aphasia* refers to the ability to read only one letter at a time (Buxbaum & Coslett, 1996), whereas a person suffering from *word deafness* cannot understand spoken language despite the presence of normal hearing and reading abilities (Davis, 1993).

Apraxias. **Apraxias** are deficits in nonverbal skills. As you might suspect, apraxias involve damage to the right hemisphere. Depending on the site of the damage, one might observe a *dressing apraxia,* in which a person has trouble putting clothing on one side of the body, or a *constructional apraxia,* in which a person cannot copy a simple drawing.

Sacks (1985) reported an interesting apraxia that involved the inability to smell odors. After a head injury, a gifted young man suffered complete loss of his sense of smell. This loss was a terrible blow to him: "It was like being struck blind. My whole world was suddenly radically poorer" (Sacks, 1985, p. 159). Some time passed, and he felt he was regaining his ability to smell. Once again he could savor the fine aroma of his favorite pipe. Examination showed that he had not regained any ability to smell, however: His memories of favorite aromas were taking over and making his world more complete. In addition to the scent of his pipe, he could smell a cup of coffee and the aromas of spring.

In addition to apraxias, the right hemisphere controls *prosody,* the ability to express emotion. People suffering from *motor aprosodia* speak in a flat monotone regardless of their real feelings. Such people simply cannot display emotions.

Neuropsychology

Our interest in the functioning of the human brain has grown to the point that a new specialty has developed within psychology. Known as *clinical neuropsychology* (see Chapter 1), this specialty is the study of the relationship between the brain and behavior (Beaumont, 1988). Neuropsychologists study people who have suffered some type of CNS damage. Such people often display a bewildering array of symptoms. Brian Kolb and Jan Whishaw (1990) describe such a case: "A 22-year-old woman was referred to us by a clinical psychologist to assess the possibility of . . . [brain] dysfunction. She had on several occasions

aphasia
Loss of the ablity to speak or understand written or spoken language

apraxia
Deficits in nonverbal skills

engaged in bizarre behaviors such as undressing in public and urinating on other people and on one occasion had attacked her roommate" (p. 770).

Neuropsychologists try to understand how the normal nervous system functions by observing the changes that occur after the brain has been damaged. Because they are dealing with human patients, ethical considerations prohibit neuropsychologists from manipulating independent variables directly. Therefore the case study approach is used to evauate patients who have suffered accidents or diseases that produce brain damage. Not surprisingly, major advances in neuropsychology have been recorded after each major war in which a large number of injuries occurred.

Neuropsychologists seek to determine which area of the brain is responsible for a certain ability or function. To accomplish this goal, they must show that damage to a particular brain area leads to the loss of a particular function but not of others. They must also show that the function under study is not affected by damage to other brain areas.

Recall the case of Dr. P., the music teacher who mistook parking meters for children. His problem, known as *visual agnosia,* the inability to identify objects visually, was caused by a tumor in the visual area of his brain. Despite these problems, Dr. P. was able to continue teaching music until the last days of his life. Were Dr. P.'s problems limited to parking meters and children? To determine the extent of his problem, he underwent extensive visual recognition tests. When looking at a rose, for example, he described it as "a convoluted red form with a linear green attachment." The researchers concluded that he was suffering from visual agnosia—he simply did not recognize or remember anything he saw. Once he even mistook his wife's head for his hat—he tried to lift it from her body and put it on his head.

Psychological Detective

How would you prove that Dr. P.'s problem was limited to visual ability? He could also have lost other abilities such as hearing and smelling. Give this potential problem some thought. Think of and write down some possible experiments that could be conducted to obtain this information.

When Dr. P.'s other senses were tested, he did quite well. He identified a rose immediately after he smelled it, and he recognized his music students instantly when he heard their voices. Dr. P.'s problems were strictly visual.

In addition to conducting tests to determine which brain areas regulate which processes, neuropsychologists frequently coordinate and direct treatment programs that use the skills of other professionals, such as speech therapists and occupational therapists. Thus the neuropsychologist may assume the role of a rehabilitation or guidance specialist.

The Endocrine System

Reuben has been experiencing an unusual problem recently. The amount of food he eats has increased significantly, yet he is hungry all the time. He has even lost weight. An examination of Reuben's work schedule and home life indicates that he has few worries and experiences little stress. *What is the cause of Reuben's problem, and what can be done about it?* ▪

Besides the nervous system, which is crucial to the activities of sensing, processing, and responding, another system plays a major role in shaping and controlling behavior and mental processes. The **endocrine system** consists of a number of glands that produce chemicals known as **hormones.** When stimulated, the endocrine glands secrete (release) hormones into the bloodstream. The blood flow carries the hormones throughout the body and, ultimately, to their target, which may be another gland located some distance away. Numerous monitoring stations or structures in the body detect levels of hormones in the bloodstream. As we discuss the endocrine system, keep in mind that it can, and does, interact with the nervous system.

Major Endocrine Glands

The locations of some of the major endocrine glands are shown in Figure 2-24. A brief description of the function of each gland follows.

The Pituitary Gland.   The **pituitary gland,** located below the hypothalamus, is often called the master gland because its secretions control many other glands. Two distinct areas make up the pituitary gland. The *posterior pituitary* is responsible for the release of *vasopressin,* a hormone that helps regulate fluid balance in the body, and *oxytocin,* a hormone that stimulates uterine contractions during labor and the release of breast milk. Among the hormones secreted by the *anterior pituitary*

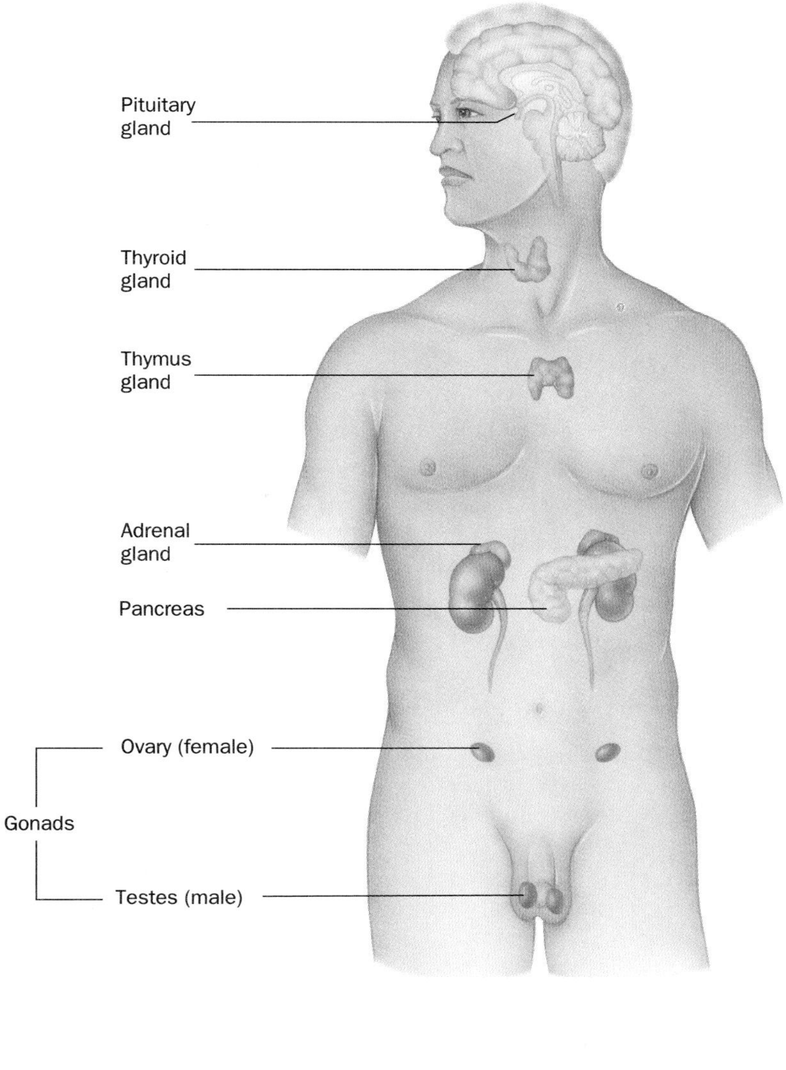

endocrine system
System of glands that produce and secrete chemicals

hormones
Chemicals produced by the glands of the endocrine system that are carried by the bloodstream to other organs

pituitary gland
Gland located below the thalamus and hypothalamus; called the master gland because its secretions control many other glands

Pituitary gland

Thyroid gland

Thymus gland

Adrenal gland

Pancreas

Ovary (female)

Gonads

Testes (male)

FIGURE 2-24 Locations and functions of the major endocrine glands.

are prolactin, a hormone that stimulates the secretion of breast milk; *somatotropin,* a growth hormone that acts directly on bones and muscles to produce the growth spurt that accompanies puberty; and *thyroid-stimulating hormone,* which stimulates the thyroid gland to regulate the release of its hormone, thyroxine. The anterior pituitary also releases *adrenocorticotropic hormone* (ACTH), which has been linked to learning and memory. ACTH causes the adrenal gland to secrete *cortisol,* which accelerates the production of energy-producing glucose during stress.

The release of these pituitary hormones clearly reflects the interplay that occurs between the nervous system and the endocrine system. The hormones released by the posterior pituitary are actually produced by the hypothalamus and transported to the pituitary gland for subsequent release. What's more, the hypothalamus secretes *releasing hormones* that are responsible for the secretion of the hormones produced by the anterior pituitary.

The Thyroid Gland. This gland, which is shaped like a butterfly, is located below the *larnyx* (voice box). When activated by thyroid-stimulating hormone released by the anterior pituitary, the *thyroid* secretes thyroxine, which is important in regulating growth and metabolic rate. Secretion of thyroxine in appropriate amounts is especially important to the development of infants. Undersecretion of thyroxine, known as *hypothyroidism,* results in a small, dwarflike person. Oversecretion of thyroxine, known as *hyperthyroidism,* results in Grave's disease, which is characterized by insomnia, protruding eyes, and a wild stare.

The Pancreas. Located near the stomach and the small intestine, the *pancreas* secretes one of the best-known hormones, *insulin.* For the cells of the body to use blood sugar—called glucose—a proper level of insulin must be maintained in the bloodstream. (Insulin allows blood sugar to enter the cell and be processed.) People suffering from diabetes mellitus are deficient in insulin; therefore, their cells do not receive an adequate supply of nourishment.

Recall Reuben from the opening vignette. Reuben is a diabetic; no matter how much food he eats, there is not a sufficient amount of insulin to allow his cells to use the glucose he is ingesting. He continues to overeat because his cells are starving (Lindberg, Coburn, & Stricker, 1984), and he is losing weight because most of his glucose is excreted unused.

The pancreas provides a good example of the feedback system of the endocrine glands. When you eat a meal and the food is broken down into glucose, the rise in glucose level in your blood signals the pancreas to secrete insulin. As the blood glucose level drops, the amount of insulin secreted by the pancreas decreases.

The Gonads. The *gonads*—*ovaries* in women and *testes* in men—produce sex hormones (androgens in men; estrogens in women) that activate the reproductive organs and structures at puberty. These hormones also affect the appearance of secondary sex characteristics (such as facial and body hair, change of voice, and development of breasts). Testosterone level is also related to aggressiveness (Dabbs & Morris, 1990); higher levels of testosterone can result in greater aggressiveness.

The Adrenal Glands. The *adrenal glands* are divided into two distinct areas— the *adrenal medulla* (the inner core) and the *adrenal cortex* (the outer layers that surround the core). When you experience stress, the adrenal medulla secretes *epinephrine* and *norepinephrine* (originally called adrenaline and noradrenaline, respectively), which, in addition to being neurotransmitters, are important in sympathetic nervous system activity. As we have seen, when the adrenal cortex is stimulated by the pituitary hormone ACTH, it secretes *glucocorticoids,* steroid hormones that are involved in the production of glucose. The glucocorticoids also increase the strength of muscle tissue under conditions of stress. This increase in strength is the reason that some athletes take steroids before a major game or competition. Despite their appeal to athletes, steroids can have severe side effects, such as nausea, muscle pains, atrophy of the testicles in men, cessation of menstruation in women, and severe depression (Pope & Katz, 1987).

Although it is easy and convenient to talk about the endocrine system and the nervous system as if they were completely independent, they are not. You can clearly see this interaction in the case of the adrenal medulla and the sympathetic nervous system. When you are under stress, the adrenal medulla secretes epinephrine and norepinephrine, preparing you to make a fight-or-flight response.

The Liver. The liver produces hormones (*somatomedins*) that stimulate growth. As we discuss in the next section, this endocrine gland may play a prominent role in some cultural differences.

Physiology and Alcoholism SOMETIMES PHYSIOLOGICAL DIFFER- ences, even those involving the endocrine glands, can be the cause of cultural differences. Such is the case with the low levels of alcohol abuse shown by Southeast Asians.

When researchers were unable to isolate psychological and cultural beliefs and practices that would explain the very low levels of alcohol abuse, they sought a physiological explanation. They systematically traced the path that alcohol takes once it enters the body and looked for deviations from normal.

The physiological processes of the liver offered promise in helping unravel this mystery. Normally, our liver *metabolizes* (converts) the alcohol we drink into acetaldehyde (a poison). The acetaldehyde is then metabolized into acetic acid, a harmless substance. As researchers found, however, many Southeast Asians are physiologically unable to convert acetaldehyde into acetic acid; the acetaldehyde simply accumulates and makes them sick (Tu & Israel, 1995). To avoid becoming sick is a simple matter—just decrease the intake of alcohol. The result is low levels of alcohol abuse.

We are not saying that all cultural differences are due to physiology; clearly many differences are *not* due to such factors. On the other hand, researchers must be sensitive to the possibility of such physiological effects if we expect to fully understand human behavior.

Cultural & Diversity Perspective

In this chapter we have examined the biological foundations of psychology: the nervous system, especially the brain, and the endocrine system. We have seen how these systems are involved in sensing, processing, and responding to stimuli in our environment. In the next chapter we look more closely at these processes. We explore the ways in which specialized receptors in the nervous system sense stimuli and how the resulting sensations are processed to produce the perceptions that are the raw materials of psychological functioning.

Review Summary

1. The split-brain operation involves severing the corpus callosum to help reduce epileptic seizures. The study of split-brain patients provides information about the functions of the two hemispheres of the brain. The left hemisphere is responsible primarily for language abilities and the production of speech, as well as rational and logical thought, whereas the right hemisphere is better suited to dealing with spatial relationships and the perception of more holistic concepts.

2. Studying the human brain yields information about **aphasias** (language deficits) and **apraxias** (nonverbal deficits).

3. Neuropsychologists study the relationships between the brain and behavior and frequently coordinate and direct treatment programs for brain-injured patients.

4. A major system that affects behavior is the **endocrine system,** which produces and secretes chemicals (**hormones**) that regulate body functions. Among the major endocrine glands are the **pituitary gland,** the thyroid gland, the pancreas, the gonads, and the adrenal glands.

Study Break

1. Explain how the two hemispheres of the brain can be separated. Why has this operation been performed? What are its consequences?
2. What is a brain asymmetry? In what two main ways have such asymmetries been studied?
3. What term describes the condition of a person suffering verbal deficits? What term applies to a person with deficits in nonverbal skills such as getting dressed or copying a drawing?
4. Some people cannot express emotion openly. In some cases—for example, when a child has been severely punished for displaying emotion—this may be a learned reaction. However, this behavior can also be caused by damage to a hemisphere of the brain. Which hemisphere? What term is used to describe an inability to express emotion?
5. Both the nervous system and another system play a role in determining behavior. What is that other system?
6. What is a hormone, and what does it do?

7. A language deficit or difficulty is an
   a. apraxia.
   b. aprosodia.
   c. aphasia.
   d. alexia.
8. How do neuropsychologists try to understand how the nervous system functions?
   a. inflicting damage to the brains of animals
   b. studying electroencephalograph recordings
   c. manipulating independent variables in neural experiments
   d. observing what changes occur when the brain has been damaged
9. Which endocrine gland controls several other glands?
   a. thyroid
   b. pituitary
   c. pancreas
   d. adrenal

ANSWERS TO STUDY BREAKS

Pages 62–63

1. Based on the theory of Charles Darwin, the evolutionary perspective focuses on how and why a particular physiological structure developed over time.
2. Sensing—seeing the $5 bill; Processing—deciding you need the money for lunch; Responding—picking up the $5 bill
3. a. Sympathetic
   b. Sympathetic
   c. Parasympathetic
   d. Parasympathetic
4. a. Not a reflex—voluntary behavior is involved
   b. Reflex—involuntary response
   c. Reflex—involuntary response
   d. Reflex—involuntary response
   e. Not a reflex—voluntary behavior is involved
   f. Reflex—involuntary response
   g. Not a reflex—voluntary behavior is involved
5. Hindbrain, Midbrain, Forebrain
6. Motivation and emotion
7. a

8. d
9. c

Page 75
1. Neurons
2. a. −1
   b. −4
   c. −6
   d. −5
   e. −3
   f. −2
3. −70mV; −69mV or −68mV; More negative
4. As the neuron gradually depolarizes, it approaches threshold. If threshold is reached, the neuron reverses polarity and "fires." Neurotransmitters, which are stored in the terminal buttons, are released when the neuron fires. Neurotransmitters allow the electrical change to be conducted from one neuron to another.
5. Neurotransmitters are either destroyed by enzymes or taken back into the terminal button to be reused (reuptake).

6. A drug may act as an agonist and increase the effectiveness of a neurotransmitter. Drugs may also act as antagonists and decrease the effect of a neurotransmitter.
7. Like neurotransmitters, neuromodulators affect the transmission of information between neurons. They are, however, more widespread or generalized than neurotransmitters.
8. b
9. a

Page 84

1. The two hemispheres can be separated by cutting the corpus callosum. This operation is performed in cases of untreated epilepsy. The epileptic condition is alleviated, and researchers have found that the abilities of the two hemispheres appear to differ. The left hemisphere appears to be analytical, logical, and involved with language. The right hemisphere is important for spatial abilities.
2. A difference between the two hemispheres. Physical and functional asymmetries have been studied.
3. Aphasia; Apraxia
4. Right hemisphere; Prosody
5. Endocrine system
6. Hormones are chemicals produced by the endocrine system. They are carried by the blood to influence target organs and other glands.
7. c
8. d
9. b

ANSWERS TO THE CAFFEINE CONSUMPTION QUESTIONNAIRE (IN MILLIGRAMS PER WEEK)

Page 70

	OVERALL RANGE	MALES	FEMALES
Highest 10 percent	1,276–11,595	1,301–11,595	1,201–6,198
	1,006–1,275	1,071–1,300	700–1,200
	661–1,005	913–1,070	630–699
	534–660	601–912	501–629
	451–533	461–600	441–500
	350–450	346–460	350–440
	226–349	226–345	251–349
	151–225	151–225	151–250
	71–150	71–150	71–150
Lowest 10 percent	0–70	0–70	0–70

Source: Landrum, 1992.

CHAPTER 3

Sensation and Perception

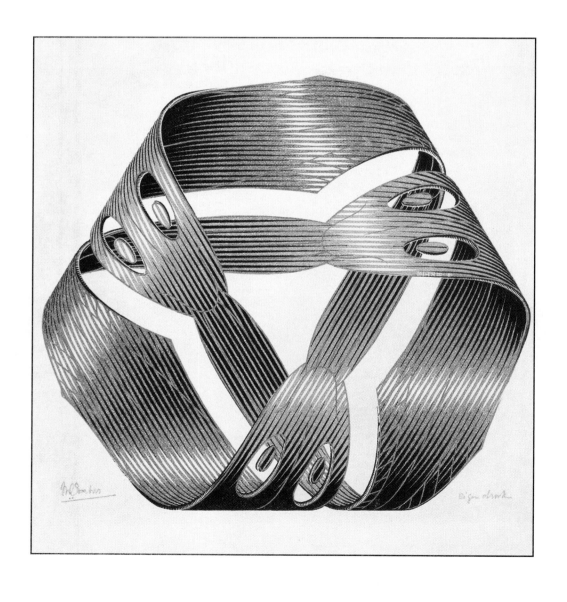

Chapter in Perspective

In Chapter 2 we discussed the importance of our physiological makeup in adapting to the demands of our constantly changing environment. In Chapter 3 we take our discussion of the biological foundations of behavior one step further. First, we examine the systems that receive sensory information about vision, hearing, taste, smell, body position, and movement. Once we determine the nature of this sensory information, we then see how we process or perceive this information to bring meaning to it. Keep in mind that this meaning varies according to experience and culture. For example, many people in the United States report seeing the "man in the moon" when they look at the moon on a clear night. Native American participants, however, report seeing a rabbit, whereas Chinese participants see a woman trying to escape from her husband (Samovar & Porter, 1991).

As you read the remainder of this book, keep in mind that the basic building blocks of sensation and perception are crucial to various states of consciousness (Chapter 5), emotional behaviors and reactions to stress (Chapters 4 and 15), learned responses (Chapters 6 and 7), maladaptive responses (Chapter 13), and our interactions with other people (Chapter 16). Without adequate sensory input and perceptual processing, these and other more elaborate systems simply would not perform appropriately. ▪

Sensation, Perception, and Psychophysics

For some time you have been planning to have several friends over for dinner—not carry-out pizza, but something you prepare yourself. The big day is here; you've spent the whole afternoon in the kitchen. The aromas filling your apartment suggest that a superb meal is in the making. To be sure that everything tastes as good as it smells, you sample the offerings frequently. The more you sample, however, the less satisfied you are. The spicy sauce tastes bland, and the potato dish does not seem to have any flavor. Some additional spices will cure this problem, you hope. *Are more spices the solution to your problem?* ▪

The problem just described has to do with how we experience and understand our world—that is, it is concerned with the processes of sensation and perception.

Sensation and Perception

In Chapter 2 we discussed the sensitivity of specialized cells, called *receptor cells,* to specific types of environmental stimuli. **Sensation** refers to the activation of these receptors, and sensations can be viewed as the basic building blocks of perception. **Perception** is the process of organizing and attempting to understand the sensory stimulation we receive. When the receptors are stimulated, information can be transmitted to the brain. Transmission of neural impulses to the brain is not, however, enough to give us an understanding and awareness of our surroundings.

If the receptors do not receive stimulation from the environment or are unable to process the information they receive, no information is transmitted to the brain, and perception does not occur (Dennett & Kinsbourne, 1992). For example, people who are colorblind cannot tell from their perception of color when a traffic light is red or when it is green; because they cannot sense color information, they depend on brightness and position cues to determine the color of the signal.

It sounds simple—activate the receptors (sensation) and then transmit the information to the brain to make sense of it (perception). As you will see, however, the process is more complicated than that.

To activate a particular receptor, a specific type of energy must be present—light waves for vision, movement of air molecules for hearing, molecules in a liquid solution for taste, and so forth. If you shine a flashlight in your ear, do not expect to have a visual response; there are no light-sensitive receptors there.

As we saw in Chapter 2, neurons operate on the basis of changes in electrical charge and the release of chemical substances called neurotransmitters. Somehow, the physical energies of light and sound waves and those of odor and taste molecules must be changed into electrochemical forms the nervous sys-

sensation
Activation of receptors by stimuli in the environment

perception
The process of organizing and making sense of sensory information

The sights, sounds, and odors of a large city provide ample stimuli to activate the sensory receptors (sensation). The brain will interpret these stimuli (perception).

tem can process. This process of converting the stimulation received by the receptors into electrochemical energy that can be used by the nervous system is called **transduction.** When you hear a sound, for example, sound waves cause a number of very fine hairs located in your inner ear to bend. These hairs are your auditory receptors. If they are bent sufficiently, the first neuron in the auditory pathway will fire (display an all-or-none response). Now auditory information can be transmitted to your brain.

Continued presentation of the same stimulus, however, causes the receptors to become less sensitive to that particular stimulus. This process, known as **adaptation,** occurs very rapidly when odors and tastes are involved. In some cases—for example, when a sewer is clogged—adaptation is highly desirable. In other situations, such as when preparing dinner for your friends, adaptation may be disadvantageous. Think back to the cooking scenerio at the beginning of this chapter. Are more spices the solution to your tasting problem? Because your repeated tastings have caused your receptors to adapt, a stronger stimulus (in this case, more spices) is now required to activate them. Therefore adding spices may create a bigger problem than the one you think you have. Your guests, whose receptors have not adapted the way yours have, will find the meal very spicy!

Psychophysics

Before we explore how our sensory systems operate, let's take a look at the methods used by early researchers, known as *psychophysicists,* who studied the relations between the mind and the body. At the same time Wilhelm Wundt was founding psychology (1879), a group of German psychophysicists were studying the relationship between stimuli and the participant's experience. The basic procedure they used is clear and straightforward. A stimulus was presented, and the individual was asked to indicate whether the stimulus was perceived (when only one stimulus was presented) or if the stimulus that was presented differed noticeably from a comparison stimulus that was also presented. In short, they studied the relationship between the mind and the body.

transduction
Conversion of stimuli received by the receptors into a form (patterns of neural impulses) that can be used by the nervous system

adaptation
Loss of sensitivity to a stimulus by the receptors as a result of continued presentation of that stimulus

Ernst Weber (1795–1878) studied the smallest detectable difference between two stimuli.

Ernst Weber (1795–1878) was interested in determining the smallest detectable difference between two stimuli. For example, can you tell that a 105-watt light bulb is brighter than a 100-watt bulb? Would you notice that a 95-watt light bulb is dimmer than a 100-watt bulb? Weber's research indicated that the amount of change required to perceive such a difference could be described by the formula $K = \Delta I/I$. This formula, known as **Weber's law,** indicates the change in stimulus intensity (ΔI) divided by the comparison intensity (I) is equal to a constant (K). The constant would be the same for all tests of the same sense, but it differs from one sense to another. For example, the constant for identifying noticeable changes in auditory intensity is 5 percent, whereas the constant for vision is 8 percent.

Weber's study of the **just noticeable difference (jnd),** or the smallest difference between two stimuli that is noticeable 50 percent of the time, gave psychology one of its first laws. By showing that the amount of stimulus increase or decrease required to notice a change, divided by the original stimulation, was a constant, Weber showed how the mind (our perceptions) could be related to the body (the physical stimulation we receive).

Thresholds

How intense does a stimulus need to be in order for it to be noticed by a receptor? Through his study of sensory thresholds, Gustav Fechner (1801–1887) refined and expanded the work Weber had begun. Fechner studied both the absolute threshold and the differential threshold. To determine the **absolute threshold,** one asks, "What is the smallest amount of stimulus energy that must be present for perception to occur 50 percent of the time?" As you can see from Table 3-1, the absolute threshold for each of our senses is astonishingly low. To determine the **differential threshold** or **jnd,** we investigate the amount of stimulus energy that must be added to or subtracted from an existing stimulus for a participant to notice a difference (i.e., to produce a *just noticeable difference*) 50 percent of the time. For example, a psychophysicist studying the differential threshold might be interested in how much the intensity of a light or a tone must be increased (or decreased) for a test participant to notice the change. Think back to the cooking vignette that opened this chapter: When you were trying to decide how much spice should be added, you were dealing with a differential threshold problem.

Although Fechner's research on the absolute and differential thresholds was important, it failed to take into account two factors: (a) the condition under which the stimulus was perceived and (b) the nature of the perceiver. Both factors are important in determining thresholds. For exam-

Weber's law

The observation that the amount of stimulus increase or decrease required to notice a change, divided by the original stimulation, is a constant

just noticeable difference (jnd)

Smallest difference between two stimuli that is noticeable 50 percent of the time by participants

absolute threshold

Minimum amount of energy required for conscious detection of a stimulus 50 percent of the time by participants

differential threshold

Smallest amount of stimulation that must be added to or subtracted from an existing stimulus for a person to be able to detect a change 50 percent of the time (see jnd)

TABLE 3-1 Examples of Absolute Thresholds

SENSE	THRESHOLD
Vision	A candle flame at 30 miles on a clear, dark night
Audition	The tick of a watch 20 feet away in a quiet room
Olfaction	One drop of perfume diffused throughout a small house
Gustation	One gram of the bitter substance denatonium saccharide diffused in one million grams of water
Touch	An insect wing falling on your cheek from a distance of 1 centimeter

ple, the task of determining either the differential or the absolute threshold for a light is much more difficult in a brightly lit room than in a darkened room. In a brightly lit room, distinguishing changes in the target stimulus (signal) from the background illumination (noise) is more difficult than in a darkened environment. **Signal detection theory,** or the contention that the threshold varies with the nature of the signal and noise, was developed to explain the difficulties one might encounter in distinguishing a certain stimulus from the background or noise (Swets, Tanner, & Birdsall, 1961). Signal detection problems occur frequently in everyday life. How often have you thought you heard (or later learned that you failed to hear) the ringing of your doorbell or telephone while you were watching television or listening to music?

The importance (or lack of importance) of detecting the signal also influences our detection of it. If your car is in the repair shop and you are waiting for a call telling you that it is ready, detecting the signal (hearing the phone ring) is very important. You can afford to make a few mistakes (for example, picking up the phone only to hear the dial tone), as long as you answer it when the repair shop calls. Such mistakes are called *false positives* because we mistakenly believe that the awaited signal is present. A radar operator who is monitoring for incoming enemy aircraft cannot afford to make any false positive mistakes; such errors would result in a full-scale alert and the mobilization of many personnel. By the same token, the radar operator cannot afford to overlook any incoming enemy aircraft. Such mistakes are called *false negatives*. Such errors might prove to be costly in terms of loss of life and property. These decisional factors are called *receiver operating characteristics*; they are important to a complete understanding of whether a stimulus is detected.

The study of thresholds is more than a collection of laboratory results; direct applications exist in everyday life. For example, how much sugar should a restaurant manager add to the iced tea to satisfy customers' requests for sweetened tea? With too little sugar, the tea does not taste sweet; too much sugar results in needless waste and an unacceptable taste. Likewise, the owner of an ethnic restaurant must take into account the fact that many customers may not be familiar with the type of food being served. If it is very spicy, like Indian curry, the "hot" threshold may be quite low. Here's another example. To conserve energy, light bulb manufacturers want to reduce the power consumption of their product. Can the typical light bulb be reduced from 100 watts to 95 watts without customers noticing that the light is dimmer?

With this general information about sensation, perception, and the methods of psychophysics in mind, we can now look at several of our sensory systems to see how they operate.

Sensory Systems

If you spend time watching other people, you will notice they blink frequently. Although the rate of blinking varies from one person to another, the average rate is about one blink every four seconds (Records, 1979). When the air is dry, the blink rate goes up. Why? Because blinking moistens the delicate surface on the front of the eye and keeps it from drying out. *How else is blinking related to our sensory processes?* ▨

Many people would argue that vision is the most important and most highly valued sense. Ask several people which of their senses they would least be willing

signal detection theory
The contention that the threshold varies with the nature of the stimulus (signal) and background stimulation (noise)

FIGURE 3-1 The visible spectrum and the three characteristics—wavelength (hue or color), amplitude (intensity or brightness), and saturation (purity)—of the visual stimulus.

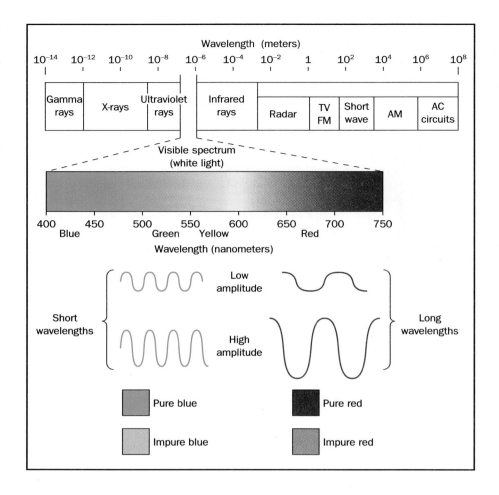

to lose, and almost all of them would say vision. We fear blindness because we are primarily visual creatures. Why? Our brain has more neurons devoted to vision than to hearing, taste, or smell (Restak, 1994).

What adjustments would you have to make in your lifestyle if you lost your sight? Compare these changes to the adjustments that would be required if you lost your sense of smell. Given the importance of vision and the ease with which the eyes can be studied, it is not surprising that vision is the sense that has been studied most thoroughly.

Vision

To appreciate our visual abilities, we need to know two things: what we see and the components of our visual system.

What We See: The Visual Stimulus. Vision is a process that involves the reception of electromagnetic waves by visual receptor cells. This kind of energy travels in waves that vary greatly in length. For example, gamma waves are very short, whereas some of the waves involved in broadcasting are miles long (Block & Yuker, 1989). We measure **wavelengths,** or the length of light waves, in nanometers (nm), which are billionths of a meter. The only light waves that humans can detect have wavelengths between approximately 380 nm and 760 nm (see Figure 3-1). This range of stimuli is called the *visible spectrum.* Different wavelengths are associated with different colors. For example, we see a wavelength of 425 nm as violet and a

wavelength
Physical length of a light wave measured in nanometers

The red car is a source of *reflected light,* whereas the light bulb is a source of *radiant light.*

wavelength of 650 nm as red. Thus the psychological counterpart of wave-length is *hue* or color.

Light waves can differ in two additional ways: amplitude and saturation. **Amplitude** refers to the strength or intensity (brightness) of the light. **Saturation** refers to the "trueness" or purity of the colors we perceive. The more saturated a color seems, the more likely you are to be seeing only one wavelength.

To understand the concept of saturation we need to distinguish between radiant light and reflected light. With **radiant light,** visible energy is emitted (released) directly by an object. There are only a few sources of radiant energy: the sun, light bulbs, and other hot, energy-releasing objects. If you place a piece of red cellophane in front of a light bulb, you will see a red light because red wavelengths are shown through the red cellophane. Similarly, you would see blue light with blue cellophane and green light with green cellophane.

What happens when you simultaneously look at red and green lights? As you can see in Figure 3-2A, you will perceive yellow. If you add a blue light to the red and green mixture, you will see white. Why? Because the three primary wavelengths are added together and are being sensed at the same time. *Adding the three primary wavelengths results in the perception of white (in other words, no specific wavelength is dominant)*

With **reflected light,** by contrast, energy is reflected by objects. Most of the light waves we receive are not radiant; they are reflected from objects in our environment. In other words, the light waves strike an object and bounce off it; we receive the waves that have bounced off the object. You perceive the colors of grass, a rose, and your sweater owing to the reflection of light from those objects.

Psychological Detective

What is it about reflected light waves that enables us to see different colors (wavelengths)? Spend a few moments thinking about the process that might make the reflection of different wavelengths possible. Here's a hint: When light strikes an object, are all the different wavelengths reflected to your eye? Write down your suggestions before reading further.

amplitude
Strength or intensity of a stimulus (brightness for visual stimuli; loudness for auditory stimuli)

saturation
Trueness or purity of a color

radiant light
Visible energy emitted by an object

reflected light
Energy that is reflected by objects

FIGURE 3-2 The additive and subtractive processes of color mixing. (A) When lights are mixed, wavelengths are added. For example, red and green lights combine to form yellow. (B) When paints are mixed, wavelengths are subtracted. For example, red, yellow, and blue paints combine to form a dark or blackish color.

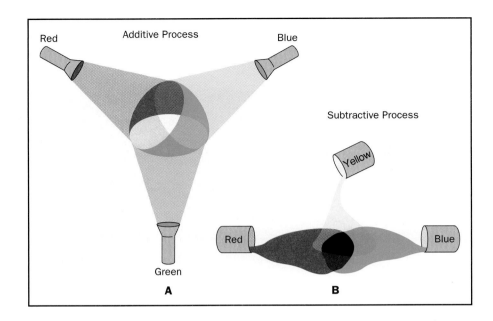

Knowing that objects absorb light waves in addition to reflecting them should help you understand the reflection of different colors. If all of the light waves are absorbed, the object or surface appears black; by contrast, if all of the light waves are reflected, the object or surface appears white. We see colors when certain wavelengths are reflected and others are absorbed. As you can see in Figure 3-2B, when red, yellow, and blue paints are mixed, all wavelengths are absorbed or subtracted, and the result is black because no hue is reflected.

If a surface reflects only one wavelength, the color you perceive is pure. The degree of purity decreases as the number of different reflected wavelengths increases.

How We See: The Visual System. Vision entails a complex chain of events. The structures of the eye are depicted in Figure 3-3. Take some time to familiarize yourself with them as we trace how light waves travel through the eye.

Initially, light waves pass through the protective *cornea.* The cornea is transparent but becomes an opaque, whitish covering, known as the *sclera,* over the rest of the eyeball. In addition to its protective function, the cornea helps focus the light waves.

After striking the cornea, light waves enter an open area called the *anterior chamber.* Here they pass through the *aqueous humor,* a clear fluid with the consistency of jelly that helps supply nourishment to the structures of the eye. Then the light waves are funneled through the small opening known as the *pupil.* The pupil is surrounded by a colored membrane, the *iris,* which changes shape to regulate the size of the pupil and therefore the amount of light taken in.

Next the light passes through the *lens.* The lens, which is supported by two powerful *ciliary muscles,* is elastic; it can change shape to focus the visual image. Changing the shape of the lens to assist in the process of focusing is known as **accommodation.** The *rectus muscles* move the entire eyeball to provide the best view or image. Movements of the eyes in the same direction (up, down, left, or right) are called **conjunctive eye movements.** Movements of the eyes in opposite directions (either inward or outward) are called **vergence eye movements.**

After passing through the lens, the light waves enter a second, larger open space called the *posterior chamber.* Another clear, jellylike fluid, the *vitreous humor,* fills the posterior chamber. The vitreous humor also provides nourish-

accommodation
In focusing, action of the ciliary muscles to change the shape of the lens

conjunctive eye movements
Movements of the eyes in the same direction

vergence eye movements
Movements of the eyes in opposite directions

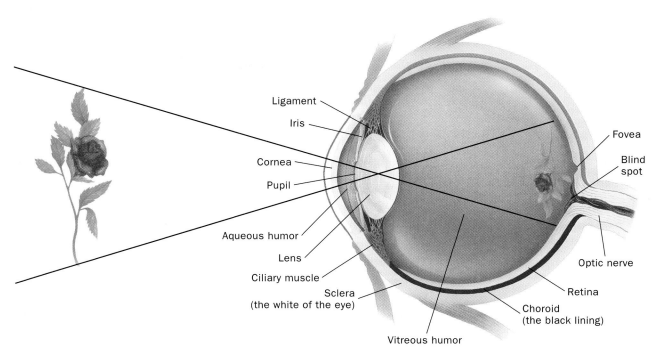

FIGURE 3-3 Structures of the eye.

Source: Pinel, 1993.

ment and helps give shape to the eye. Finally, the light waves strike the **retina,** the light-sensitive tissue at the back of the eye that contains the visual receptors (rods and cones). Figure 3-4 shows that the retina is made up of several layers: the ganglion cell layer, the bipolar cell layer, and the photoreceptor layer.

This explanation would be much simpler if we could tell you that when the light waves strike the retina, they first stimulate the receptors and then progressively activate layers of cells located toward the back of the retina, with the optic nerve exiting at the very back of the retina and going to the brain (see Figures

retina

Tissue that contains the visual receptors, located at the back of the eye

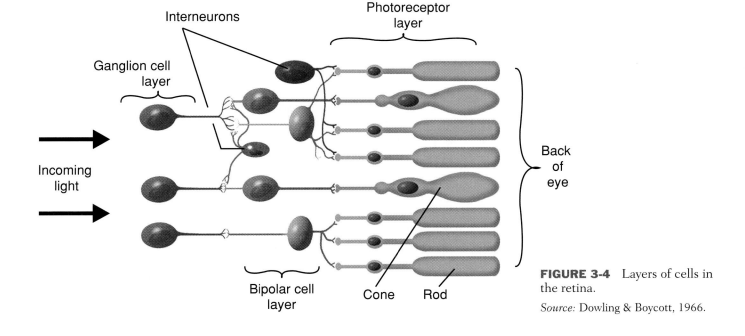

FIGURE 3-4 Layers of cells in the retina.

Source: Dowling & Boycott, 1966.

bipolar cells

Cells in the retina that connect the receptors to ganglion cells

ganglion cells

Cells in the retina whose axons form the optic nerve

blind spot

Location at which the optic nerve leaves the eyeball; contains no receptors

optic chiasm

Point at which the optic nerve fibers from each eye join; fibers from the nasal half of the retina cross to the opposite hemisphere of the brain

3-3 and 3-6). In reality, however, the reverse is true: After light strikes the surface of the retina, it must travel through several layers of cells before it activates the visual receptors, which make up the back layer of the retina (see Figure 3-4). Light waves cause the receptors to change their electrical charge. If that change is great enough, the **bipolar cells** fire. If enough bipolar cells fire, the next layer of cells, the **ganglion cells,** fire. The axons of the ganglion cells come together to form the optic nerve, which carries visual information to higher brain centers.

Why are our visual receptors "wired" backwards? The arrangement may seem impractical, but it is the only way the receptors can be positioned close to the blood supply that lies behind the retina to receive the proper nutrients and maintain their correct biochemical status.

At the point where the axons of the ganglion cells come together and leave the eyeball, there are no receptors. This area is known as the **blind spot.** If you follow the directions in Figure 3-5, you will experience your own blind spot.

Psychological Detective

As we suggested at the beginning of this section, blinking may have more to do with sensation than just keeping the eyes moist. When you blink, light does not enter your visual system. Because no light is being processed during a blink, you should experience fifteen or more brief visual blackouts each minute. Can you explain why we do not experience such blackouts? Write down some possible reasons before reading further.

Frances Volkmann, Curnin Riggs, and Robert Moore (1980) proposed that when the brain signals the eyelids to close in a blink, it also stops or inhibits activity in the visual system. When the blink is completed, the visual system returns to its normal functioning. Thus information about visual blackouts simply is not transmitted or processed.

The Visual Pathway. The pathway taken by the optic nerve is diagrammed in Figure 3-6. The optic nerves from each eye join at the **optic chiasm,** which is located on the underside of the brain just in front of the

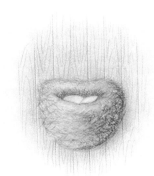

FIGURE 3-5 Hold the book about 20 inches in front of you. Close your left eye and stare at the X with your right eye. Gradually move the book toward you. The bird that is approaching its nest will disappear when its image is focused on the blind spot. As the book continues to move toward your eyes, the image will reappear as it moves off the blind spot. Do you now understand how you may miss things because they were in the blind spot of your eye?

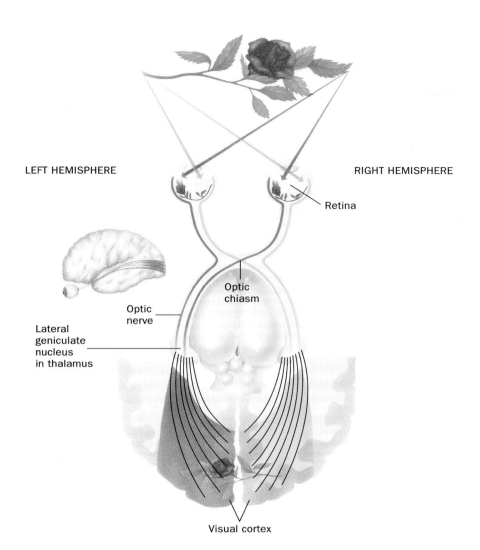

FIGURE 3-6 Pathway taken by a visual stimulus from the eye to the brain.

LEFT HEMISPHERE

RIGHT HEMISPHERE

Retina

Optic chiasm

Optic nerve

Lateral geniculate nucleus in thalamus

Visual cortex

pituitary gland. The fibers from the nasal half (closest to the nose) of the retina cross to the opposite hemisphere; those from the peripheral (outlying) half of each retina continue to the hemisphere on the same side of the body. The next stop is an area in the thalamus, the relay station in the forebrain (see Chapter 2). Ultimately, the visual information is received by the occipital lobe of the cortex, where higher-level visual processing begins (Knierim & Van Essen, 1992; Zeki, 1992).

The Visual Receptors.   Because they are so important to what we see, the visual receptors, the rods and cones, deserve special attention. The **rods** are the most prevalent visual receptors. They have a lower threshold and lower acuity (sharpness of perception) than cones and do not detect color. By contrast, the **cones** are less prevalent, have a higher threshold and higher acuity, and are able to detect color. The rods are slender and cylindrical, whereas the cones are much broader (see Figure 3-4). An examination of the retina shows that there are many more rods (120 to 125 million) than cones (6 to 7 million). What's more, most of the cones are found in one area, the **fovea,** an indented spot in the center of the retina (see Figure 3-3). Both the rods and cones contain light-sensitive chemicals called *photopigments.* When light strikes the rods and cones it causes a chemical reaction in these photopigments (Wang et al., 1994). This change hyperpolarizes

rods

Most prevalent visual receptors; have lower threshold and lower acuity than cones and do not detect color

cones

Visual receptors that are less prevalent than rods; have a higher threshold and higher acuity and are able to detect color

fovea

Indented spot in the center of the retina that contains only cones

(see Chapter 2) the rods and cones and releases their inhibitory influence on the bipolar cells (Lamb & Pugh, 1990). With this inhibition removed, the bipolar cells exhibit excitation, and a message is sent to the brain.

Look again at Figure 3-4. Do you see that the cones have a more direct, or one-to-one, hookup with the bipolar cells? Compare this arrangement with that of the rods: Many rods synapse on one bipolar cell. Which receptor do you think provides more detailed and precise information? Perhaps an analogy will help you understand the cones better. Suppose that you are having a one-on-one discussion with a classmate about the next psychology test. Each of you knows exactly what the other is saying. This conversation is like the information sent by the cones to the bipolar cells—it is clear and direct. In comparison, information transmission from the rods to the bipolar cells would be like members of a large class heatedly discussing politics. Because of the size of the class, you often cannot tell exactly who is talking at any given moment.

To experience the difference in the precision, or acuity, of the rods and cones, hold this book about 12 inches from your face and look straight at it. Position the book so that the line of type you are reading is focused on the center of the retina, that is, directly on the cone-rich fovea. Now move the book down or from side to side. Do not move your eyes. Keep looking straight ahead and try to read the line on which you are focused.

Psychological Detective

As you vary the book's position, the type should appear blurred and more difficult to read. Why? Figure 3-7 provides a clue. Give the situation some thought, and write down some possibilities before reading further.

As you move the book, the specific line you are trying to read moves away from the fovea and falls on areas containing more rods. The lowered acuity of the rods causes the image to become blurred. That is why you hold documents with fine print, like your apartment lease, right in front of your eyes: to focus the print on the cones in the fovea (see Figure 3-7).

We have said that rods and cones differ in two important respects: Rods have a lower threshold than cones, so less light is required to activate them, and cones are used for color vision (Table 3-2). Rod vision is like black-and-white television—you can adjust brightness levels, but you see only black, white, and gray. Therefore if illumination is decreased gradually you should be able to watch objects lose their color. Use Figure 3-8 to demonstrate this phenomenon.

Theories of Color Vision.   Researchers have long known that the sensation of color is transmitted to the brain by cones in the retina; until recently, however, they have not known exactly how this happens. Two theories, originally proposed in the 1800s, have guided our progress toward understanding this process. The **trichromatic theory** was originally proposed by Thomas Young in 1802 and modified by Hermann von Helmholtz in 1852. Young and Helmholtz believed there are three types of cones, each responding to one of the three primary colors: red, green, and blue. What about all the different shades of color that we see? According to the trichromatic theory, different shades are created when we receive sensory input in different amounts or proportions from the three types of cones.

trichromatic theory
Color vision theory stating that there are three types of color receptors

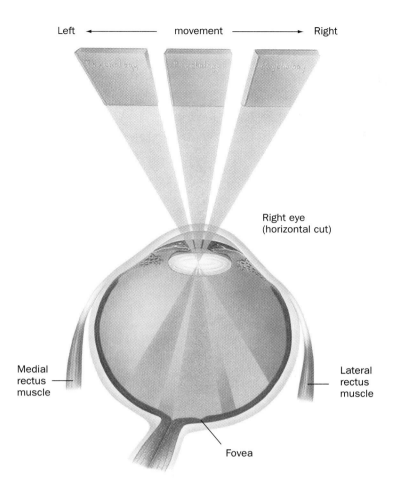

Left ← movement → Right

Right eye
(horizontal cut)

Medial
rectus
muscle

Lateral
rectus
muscle

Fovea

FIGURE 3-7 When the book is moved up or down or from side to side, the image on which you have focused moves away from the fovea, which contains most of the cones, to the peripheral retina, where the rods are found in great numbers.

FIGURE 3-8 Watch the rose turn black! Under high levels of illumination we are using our cones and can see color. As we experience lower levels of illumination, however, we shift to rod vision and cannot see color. To experience this shift, find a room in which the lighting can be decreased gradually with a dimmer switch. Slowly turn the intensity of the lights down, and you will see the rose change from red to black—the point at which you have shifted from cone to rod vision.

There is some support for this theory. In the 1960s, researchers (such as Brown & Wald, 1964) identified three types of cones in the retina, each of which is sensitive to one of the primary colors. These three types of cones are sensitive to wavelengths of either 445, 535, or 570 nm. As you can see by comparing these values with those in Figure 3-1, Young and Helmholtz were a bit off in proposing red, green, and blue wavelengths; blue-violet, green, and yellow-green wavelengths are the maximally sensitive wavelengths (Pick & Reid, 1995).

If the trichromatic theory goes so far toward accounting for color vision, do we even need to discuss the second theory of color vision? For several years after the existence of three types of cones was verified, researchers did not think so.

TABLE 3-2 Differences between Rods and Cones

RODS	**CONES**
1. Are numerous and found primarily in the peripheral retina	**1.** Are concentrated primarily in the fovea
2. Have a lower threshold for activation	**2.** Have a higher threshold for activation
3. Have lower acuity	**3.** Have higher acuity
4. Do not process color	**4.** Process color

Continued research, however, has provided support for another theory of color vision. When it was originally proposed in 1870 by Ewald Hering, the **opponent-process theory** stated that the cones are arranged in pairs; red is paired with green, whereas blue is paired with yellow. The operation of one member of a pair directly inhibits or opposes the operation of the other member. For example, if a red cone fires, the green cone paired with it is inhibited, and vice versa.

As knowledge of the retina grew, the opponent-process theory was abandoned when the trichromatic theory was verified. By the late 1960s, however, brain researchers (such as De Valois & Jacobs, 1968) who recorded the signals from single neurons discovered that some pairs of cells respond as Hering had said. These cells are not cones, however, and they are not located exclusively in the retina. These *opponent-process cells* are found in the lateral geniculate nucleus (LGN), an area of the thalamus (see Figure 3-6). Opponent-process cells also exist in the bipolar-cell layer of the retina. Therefore the trichromatic theory accounts for color processing by the cones in the retina, whereas the opponent-process theory accounts for color processing by the bipolar cells and the thalamus.

Opponent-process cells may also be responsible for the production of color afterimages. A **color afterimage** is the perception of a color that is not really present; it occurs after viewing the opposite or complementary color. For example, after staring at a red object, you will see a green afterimage when the object is taken away (see Figure 3-9); green is the opposite or complementary color to red. According to the opponent-process theory, continual viewing of red weakens the ability to inhibit green; adaptation has occurred.

Psychological Detective

Having learned some of the basics of color vision, now consider a challenging question. Do other animals, such as dogs, cats, and birds, have color vision? If we were testing a primate (gorilla) for color vision, we could present a colored piece of plastic and require the animal to select the same color from a large group of equally bright plastic pieces to receive a reward. How would you test other animals? Write down some possible testing procedures before reading further.

Psychologists have shown that many primates can match colors successfully, but demonstrating color vision in other animals is more difficult. Consider the case of an Asian elephant named Ruby (Gilbert, 1990). Keepers at the Phoenix, Arizona, zoo noticed that Ruby continually made marks in the sand with a stick. In 1987, one of Ruby's trainers had seen

> an elephant in southern California who had learned to paint. She thought of Ruby and decided to offer her some lessons. Ruby immediately showed interest and within a week had mastered the basic techniques. She has become increasingly adept with brushes, and her present paintings are generally much more intricate than the first, rather crude ones. (Gilbert, 1990, p. 50)

A session with Ruby occurs in the following manner. An elephant trainer

> brings out an easel, a stretched canvas, a box of brushes (like those used by human water colorists), and jars of acrylic paints fixed onto a palette. With the marvelously manipulable tip of her trunk, Ruby taps one of the pigment jars and then picks a brush. The [trainer] dips the brush into this jar and passes it to Ruby, who begins to paint. Sometimes she asks, in her own way, to have the same brush refilled repeatedly with the same color. Or she may

opponent-process theory
Color vision theory stressing the pairing of color experiences; activation of one process can inhibit its partner

color afterimage
Perception of a color that is not really present; occurs after viewing the opposite or complementary color

FIGURE 3-9 Color afterimages. Stare at the dot in the center of the four color patches for 1 minute. Now stare at the dot in the center of the right panel. The color afterimages you see will be the opposites of the first ones you looked at.

change brushes and colors every few strokes. After a time, usually about ten minutes, Ruby puts her brushes aside, backs away from the easel and indicates that she is finished. (Gilbert, 1990, p. 40)

Ruby and an example of her artwork are shown in Figure 3-10. How did the trainers discover that Ruby had color vision? They noticed she was matching the colors she painted with those she saw in her environment. If people wore red on a particular day, she painted with red. If yellow vehicles were outside her enclosure, she painted with yellow.

Ruby's artwork has become very popular; her paintings sell for several hundred dollars apiece. The proceeds go to the Phoenix Zoo Conservation Fund to pay for further research on behalf of Ruby and other endangered species. No one is sure how many other animals have color vision (Fischler & Firschein, 1987); it is an exciting challenge to complete the list.

Color Deficiencies. People who suffer deficits in color vision are said to be color deficient. In rare instances they can see no color; these people are called **monochromats.** Monochromats possess only one type of cone; as a result, in affected people the brain treats all received light waves as the same, and only shades of gray are perceived.

monochromat
Person who sees only shades of gray owing to a rare form of color deficiency

FIGURE 3-10 Ruby the elephant admires a painting she has just completed. Ruby painted *Fire Truck* after seeing a fire engine and its blue-clad rescue squad in action.

dichromat

Person who has trouble seeing one of the primary colors (red, blue, or green) owing to a form of color deficiency

anomalous trichromat

Person with a form of colorblindness in which one of the three primary colors (red, blue, or green) is processed incorrectly

You can experience what it is like to be a monochromat. Because rods are monochromatic receptors, they process only shades of gray. The next time you are in dim light and cannot see color, you will know how true monochromats perceive the world.

Two other types of color-deficient people are dichromats and anomalous trichromats. A **dichromat** has trouble seeing one of the primary colors (red, blue, or green). A person with this deficiency lacks one type of cone and therefore has trouble with the opponent-process function. If the deficiency involves a red or green cone, the person sees only blues and yellows. If the deficiency concerns the blue cones, the person sees only reds and greens. Special tests have been developed to evaluate color deficiencies. One of these test patterns is shown in Figure 3-11. If you do not see a number there, you may have trouble with red-green color vision.

Anomalous trichromats are able to see three distinct colors. One of the three colors, however, is not processed the way it is in a normal-sighted person (Dartnall, Bowmaker, & Mollen, 1983). As a result, the colors an anomalous trichromat perceives differ from those seen by people with normal vision. For example, a person who does not process red or green may confuse these colors with browns and tans.

Because more males than females suffer from these difficulties, color deficiencies may have a genetic or hereditary basis (Sekuler & Blake, 1990). Factors such as diabetes, a diet lacking in vitamin B12, or a change in the lens of the eye, which filters color, can lead to an acquired color deficiency. For example, as we grow older, the lens becomes yellow and loses some of its ability to filter short wavelengths. This change can lead to color confusion, especially between blues and greens. Color confusion may become a life-threatening problem for elderly people dealing with colored medicine capsules. Peter Hurd and Julia Blevins (1984) investigated this problem in a

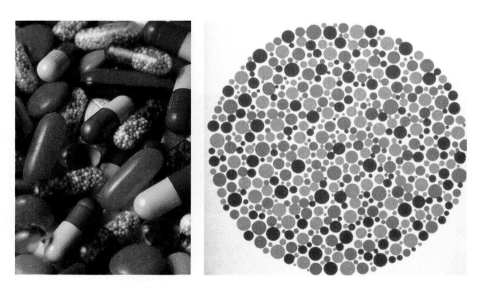

FIGURE 3-11 A test for color deficiency. All of the dots in this pattern are of the same brightness. Only the difference in wavelength allows one to see a number. Individuals who do not see the number may have trouble with red—green color vision. Elderly people may have trouble distinguishing between blues and greens. This visual difficulty may become life-threatening if medicine capsules are confused.

group of elderly people (average age, 70.9 years) who had difficulty discriminating between blue and green capsules, as well as among different shades of blue, yellow, and green.

Review Summary

1. Sensation refers to stimulation or activation of the receptors. Sensations are the basic building blocks of **perception,** the process of interpreting or making sense of our sensory input.

2. Receptors for each sensory system respond to only one type of environmental stimulus. **Transduction** is the process by which the receptors change the energy they receive into a form that can be used by the nervous system. **Adaptation** occurs when continued presentation of the same stimulus results in a loss of sensitivity.

3. Psychophysicists, such as Ernst Weber and Gustav Fechner, studied the relationship between the mind and the body. **Weber's law** relates the amount of change in a stimulus and the conscious experience of change in the stimulus. Fechner studied the smallest amount of energy that could be detected 50 percent of the time (the **absolute threshold**) and the smallest change that could be detected 50 percent of the time (the **differential threshold** or **just noticeable difference [jnd]**).

4. The visual receptors, the **rods** and **cones,** respond to a limited range of light waves, the visible spectrum.

Light waves differ in terms of **wavelength** (hue), **amplitude** (intensity), and **saturation** (purity).

5. The **cones** have greater acuity, respond to color, and have a higher threshold for activation; the **rods** have lower acuity, respond to black and white and shades of gray, and have a lower threshold.

6. The visual receptors are located in the **retina** at the back of the eye. To reach the receptors, light waves pass through several other structures in the eye, as well as several layers of retinal cells.

7. Two theories of color vision have been formulated. The **trichromatic theory** proposes that there are three different types of cones; the **opponent-process theory** argues that color-sensitive cells are arranged in pairs. Both theories are supported by research findings.

8. Dichromats lack the ability to see one of the three primary colors. **Anomalous trichromats** can see three colors, but one color is not processed normally. **Monochromats** are unable to see color.

Study Break

1. Sensation refers to
   a. activation of the receptors.
   b. attempting to understand the stimulation we receive.
   c. reduction in sensitivity of receptors to a particular stimulus.
   d. converting stimulation received by receptors into electrochemical energy.
2. Match each term with its characteristic.
   a. Differential threshold   1. Sensitive to color
   b. Absolute threshold   2. Activation of receptors
   c. Sensation   3. Minimum amount of energy
   d. Rods   4. Less visual acuity
   e. Cones   5. Minimum change in energy
   f. Wavelength   6. Hue
3. What process transforms energy that stimulates sensory receptors into a form that the nervous system can transmit?
   a. Sensation   b. Perception
   c. Transduction   d. Thresholding
4. The process by which receptors become less sensitive to repetitions of the same stimulus is called
   a. adaptation.   b. transduction.
   c. sensation.   d. perception.
5. You are watching TV while expecting an important phone call. Periodically you think you hear the phone and pick up the receiver only to hear a dial tone. According to signal detection theory, you have just made a
   a. false negative move.   b. false positive move.
   c. true negative move.   d. true positive move.
6. Your red sports car has been a source of great pride for several years. Lately, however, your car doesn't

seem as red as it used to be: The paint seems dull. Which characteristic of the visual stimulus is involved here? Why?

7. "We can see only a small portion of the visible spectrum." Explain this statement.

8. It is early in the morning, and you are trying to get dressed in the dark to avoid waking your roommate. You get to school and notice that you have put on one red sock and one green sock. Why did this mismatch occur?

9. Which sensory receptors receive information related to color?

a. rods   **b.** cones
c. sclera   **d.** transducers

10. Alex's hospital chart has the following notation: "Patient is a monochromat." Assuming this notation is accurate, what would you conclude about Alex?
    a. He sees only bright colors.
    b. He cannot distinguish colors.
    c. He prefers one color over others.
    d. He can pay attention to only one input at a time.

Audition (Hearing)

Next to vision, the sense of hearing, or **audition,** is our most important link to the environment. Just as we see light waves, we hear sound waves. In this section we explore what we hear (the auditory stimulus) and how we hear (the auditory system).

What We Hear: The Auditory Stimulus. Have you ever stopped to ask, "What is a sound wave?" To understand audition, we need to answer that question. A *sound wave* is essentially moving air. Objects that vibrate cause air molecules to move, and the movements of these molecules make up sound waves. Examples of sound waves are shown in Figure 3-12.

Like light waves, sound waves have three distinct characteristics: wavelength (frequency), amplitude (intensity), and purity (also known as *timbre*). Shorter wavelengths occur more frequently; longer wavelengths occur less frequently. Frequency is measured in cycles per second and expressed in **hertz (Hz).** People with longer vocal cords have lower voices (lower frequencies) than people with shorter vocal cords because the longer vocal cords of lower-voiced people do not vibrate as rapidly.

As with light waves, the amplitude, or height, of the sound wave affects its intensity. Greater amplitude results in a more intense sound. The volume control on your CD player adjusts the amplitude or intensity of the sound you hear. The amplitude of sound waves is measured in **decibels (db).** Decibel levels represent the amount of energy producing the pressure of the vibrations we perceive as sound; the greater the pressure, the stronger or more intense the vibration (see Table 3-3, p. 109).

Just as we seldom see pure colors, we do not hear only one pure tone at a time. Consider the variety of sounds you hear when you listen to the radio. Then add your roommate talking, traffic noise from the street, and a ringing phone. The purity or *timbre* of a sound wave can be measured, but we do not experience many pure tones in our lifetimes.

Like the visual receptors, the auditory receptors are sensitive to a limited range of sound waves. Basically, we hear sounds with wavelengths between 20 and 20,000 Hz. Even within this "normal" range of hearing, we do not hear all sounds equally well. As you can see in Figure 3-13, there is a relationship between the frequency of a sound and the threshold at which we hear it. Our hearing is more acute at 1,000 Hz; greater intensity (amplitude) is required if we are to hear tones at lower and higher frequencies. Thus to hear all of the low and high frequencies on a CD, we would need to turn the volume up very high.

audition
Sense of hearing

hertz (Hz)
Unit of measure (in cycles per second) of the frequency of a sound wave

decibel (db)
Unit of measure of the amount of energy producing the vibrations we perceive as sound

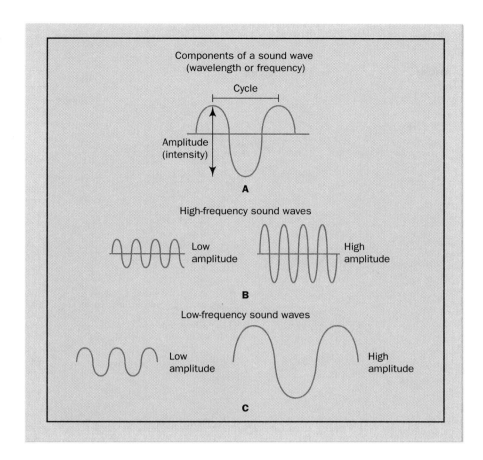

FIGURE 3-12 Sound waves are measured in terms of the number of times the wave repeats itself each second. Each repetition is called a cycle. Cycles per second are also called hertz (Hz). The greater the hertz, the higher the pitch of the sound. Some objects vibrate more strongly than others. This difference in vibration results in varied amplitudes or intensities of the sound waves. The stronger the vibration, the more intense the sound.

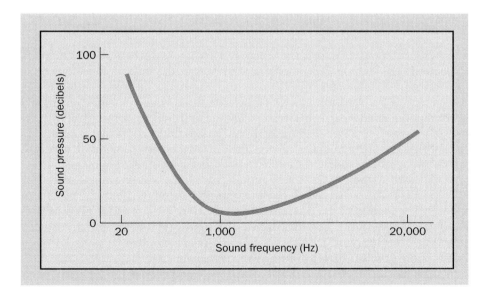

FIGURE 3-13 Threshold at which we hear different frequencies (pitches). Greater intensity is needed to reach threshold for very high and very low tones, whereas tones of around 1,000 Hz require much less intensity.

How We Hear: The Auditory System. The remarkable range of our auditory ability suggests the presence of an intricate system. A diagram of the auditory system is shown in Figure 3-14. The auditory system is divided into three components: the outer ear, the middle ear, and the inner ear.

FIGURE 3-14 (A) The auditory system. (B) The inner ear and auditory receptors.

Source: Shaver & Tarpy, 1993.

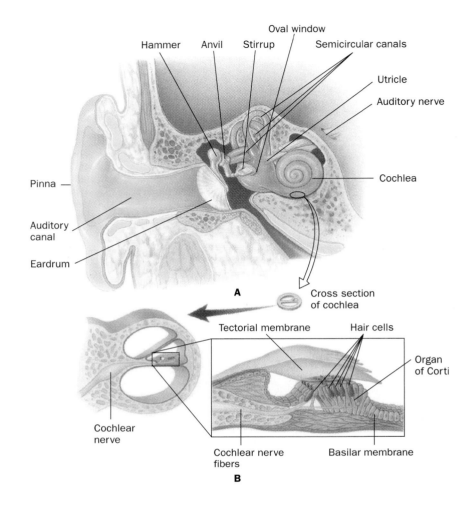

ossicles

Three bones (hammer, anvil, and stirrup) located in the middle ear that conduct sound from the outer to the inner ear

oval window

Structure that connects the middle ear with the cochlea of the inner ear; its movement causes fluid in the cochlea to move

basilar membrane

Membrane located in the cochlea of the inner ear; movement of cochlear fluid causes it to vibrate

organ of Corti

Structure located on the basilar membrane of the inner ear that contains the auditory receptors

tectorial membrane

Membrane located above the organ of Corti in the inner ear

The outer ear, especially the *pinna,* gathers sound waves and starts them on their way to the auditory receptors. The sound waves are then funneled down the *auditory canal.* Ultimately they strike the *eardrum* and cause it to move. Movement of the eardrum in turn causes the three bones (hammer, anvil, and stirrup) of the middle ear, collectively called the **ossicles,** to vibrate. The *hammer* (malleus), which is attached to the eardrum, strikes the *anvil* (incus). The anvil in turn strikes the *stirrup* (stapes). The stirrup is connected to the **oval window,** which connects the middle ear to the snail-shaped *cochlea* of the inner ear.

Look at Figure 3-14B as we continue with the chain of events. When the stirrup causes the oval window to vibrate, fluid located in the cochlea is set in motion. The motion of the fluid produces vibration in the **basilar membrane.** This vibration in turn causes the **organ of Corti,** which rests on it, to rise and fall. When the organ of Corti moves upward, the hair cells that project from it brush against the **tectorial membrane** located above it.

The hair cells are the auditory receptors. Contact with the tectorial membrane causes them to bend; when they bend, they depolarize (Fettiplace, 1990). Sufficient depolarization of the auditory receptors causes the neurons that synapse with them to fire. The axons of these neurons come together before they leave the cochlea to form the *auditory nerve* which transmits auditory information to higher brain centers. From the cochlea, the auditory nerve travels to the medulla, where some fibers cross to the opposite hemisphere. The remaining fibers do not cross. The next stop is the thalamus. Ultimately the information reaches the temporal lobe of the cortex for processing.

Psychological Detective

If the hair cells are the auditory receptors and they are activated by being bent, how is information about different tones conveyed to the brain? Give this question some thought, and write down some possible answers before reading further.

Specific hair cells differ from one another. Some convey information about low frequencies, whereas others convey information about high frequencies. The procedure by which we hear different frequencies, however, involves more than the specific hair cells that have been activated.

At present there are two theories to explain how we hear different tones or pitches. The older **place theory,** proposed by Hermann von Helmholtz in 1863, says that hair cells located at different places on the organ of Corti transmit information about different pitches. For example, bending hair cells located near the oval window results in the perception of higher frequencies, whereas bending those located farther away results in the perception of lower frequencies. The place theory says that what you hear depends on which hair cells are activated. For this theory to be correct, the basilar membrane has to vibrate in an uneven manner, which is exactly what happens with frequencies above 1,000 Hz. This uneven vibration, known as a *traveling wave,* is caused by the differential thickness of the basilar membrane. The basilar membrane is thinnest near the oval window and becomes progressively thicker (von Bekesy, 1956).

"What about frequencies below 1,000 Hz?" you might ask. Here the **frequency theory** of Ernest Rutherford applies. In 1886, Rutherford suggested that we perceive pitch according to how rapidly the basilar membrane vibrates. The faster the vibration, the higher the pitch, and vice versa. The frequency theory works fine with frequencies up to 100 Hz; typically, however, neurons do not fire more than 100 times per second. How do we get from 100

place theory
Theory stating that the basilar membrane vibrates at different places to create the perception of different pitches

frequency theory
Theory stating that the basilar membrane vibrates at different rates to create the perception of different pitches

STUDY CHART

Characteristics of Light and Sound Waves

Characteristic	Description	Unit of Measurement	Visible/Audible Range
Wavelength (frequency)	Length of the wave, represented by the distance between the crests of successive waves	Light: nanometers (1 nm—one billionth of a meter) Sound: 20—20,000 Hz	Light: 380—760 nm Sound: hertz (Hz; cycles per second)
Amplitude	Strength or intensity of the wave, represented by its height	Sound: decibels (db; amount of energy producing the wave) Light: foot-candles (ft-c; usually measured with a light meter)	Sound: 0—180 db Light: varies according to receptor rods more sensitive than cones
Saturation	"Trueness" of the color/sound percentage	Presence of wavelengths other than the target wavelength	Depends on percentages of other wavelengths

to 1,000 Hz, where the place theory begins? The *volley principle* (Rose et al., 1967) suggests a likely possibility. According to this view, at frequencies above 100 Hz auditory neurons do not all fire at once; instead they fire in rotation or in volleys. For example, for a 300 Hz tone, one group would fire at 100 Hz, to be followed by a second group that also fired at the next 100 Hz interval, and then by a third group that fired at the next 100 Hz interval. The activation of these three groups of neurons would tell the nervous system that you had heard a tone of 300 Hz.

Certainly the ability to discriminate among various pitches is an important attribute. Equally important is our ability to locate sound in space. Think of how confusing your world would be if you could not tell where sounds were coming from. Driving would be a nightmare, you could not tell when people were talking to you unless you saw their lips moving, and it would be impossible to find a lost child by hearing a call for help.

Two mechanisms help us locate the source of a sound. The first is blockage of certain sounds by the head. Because the head partially blocks sound waves coming from the opposite side of the body, those sounds are a bit weaker and are perceived as farther away. For example, if someone on your right side is talking to you, the sounds of his or her speech enter your right ear unblocked. Your head, however, partially blocks these sounds before they enter your left ear. In this way the sounds entering your right ear are a bit stronger than those entering your left ear, and you are aware that the person is on your right. Similarly, your ears help block sounds coming from directly behind you.

The second mechanism is time delay in neural processing. The brain also processes the difference in time when a sound enters one ear and when it enters the other ear to enable you to locate sounds in space. If a sound is presented on your right, it enters your right ear first, then enters the left ear. Even though the time difference may be only a few milliseconds, it is enough time for your brain to process and help you locate objects in space.

Hearing Disorders.   For a number of years, reports in the media have warned that loud noises such as those from rock concerts, jet planes, sirens, and air hammers can cause hearing damage. If you are like most people, you probably want to know if these claims are true. Some damage-risk comparisons are presented in Table 3-3. It turns out that extended exposure to sounds with intensities of 70 db or more can result in hearing loss. As the decibel level increases, the exposure time needed to produce damage decreases. In other words, the louder the sound, the shorter the exposure time before your hearing is damaged. Are you doomed to suffer from hearing loss? Contemporary living involves potentially dangerous sounds; however, the extent of exposure to them is often within your control.

Many people have hearing problems. Three such problems have been studied extensively: conduction deafness, sensorineural deafness, and central deafness. The first two may be caused by exposure to very loud noises. **Conduction deafness** refers to problems associated with conducting or transmitting sounds through the outer and middle ear. In addition to excessive exposure to loud noises, common causes of conduction deafness are excessive ear wax or damage to the hammer, anvil, or stirrup. **Sensorineural deafness** is caused by damage to the inner ear, especially the hair cells. Noise that is sufficiently loud to cause the hair cells to break can be a cause of this type of deafness. **Central deafness** is caused by disease and tumors in the auditory pathways and auditory cortex of the brain. Although sensorineural and central deafness can be inherited, they can also develop from exposure to measles and other contagious diseases before birth, inadequate oxygen supply during birth, and childhood diseases such as meningitis (Cremers & van Rijn, 1991).

conduction deafness
Deafness owing to problems associated with transmitting sounds through the outer and middle ear

sensorineural deafness
Deafness caused by damage to the inner ear, especially the hair cells

central deafness
Deafness resulting from disease and tumors in the auditory pathways or auditory cortex of the brain

TABLE 3-3 **Various Sounds, Their Decibel Level, and the Risk of Damage to the Auditory System**

DECIBEL LEVEL	SITUATION	HARMFUL EXPOSURE TIME
180	Rocket launch	Immediate permanent hearing loss
150	Jet plane, shotgun blast	Any exposure dangerous
120	Rock concert (near speakers)	Immediate danger
100	Chain saw	Damage in 2 hours
90	Truck traffic, lawnmower, motorcycle	Damage possible in less than 8 hours
80	Heavy city traffic	Damage possible after 8 hours
70	Constant exposure to a noisy restaurant	Critical level—prolonged exposure can result in damage
60	Normal conversation	No danger

Conduction deafness can be treated; hearing aids are often used to offset hearing loss resulting from damage to the bones of the middle ear. Sensorineural and central deafness are treatable only with cochlear implants, which stimulate the auditory nerve, or surgery of the auditory portion of the central nervous system.

American Sign Language

WHEN WE THINK OF A LANGUAGE, WE TEND TO THINK OF AN ORAL-AUDITORY one—that is, one that is heavily dependent on *audition*. Not all languages fit into this category, however. A prominent example is **American Sign Language (ASL),** a *manual-visual* language developed within the American deaf community that is distinct from oral-auditory languages. People who use ASL communicate rapidly via thousands of manual signs and gestures. Words are assembled from hand shapes, hand motions, and the positions of the hands in front of the body (see Figure 3-15).

Facial expressions and pantomimes of emotions such as lifted eyebrows punctuate and place emphasis in sentences. Facial expressions may also serve as adverbs: For example, a slight display of the tongue as if in distaste during the sentence "I slept" turns the meaning to "I slept badly." Although they do not involve spoken words, sign languages are legitimate languages with their own rules and syntax (Pinker, 1994). In fact, they are produced and processed by the same parts of the brain involved in spoken language (Meier, 1991; Sacks, 1989). What's more, deaf children reared in an environment in which they have no access to spoken language and were not taught sign language sometimes invent their own sign language (Meier, 1991; Sacks, 1989).

Until recently, the education of the deaf population emphasized lip reading and speech training to the exclusion of sign language. Approximately 90 percent of deaf children are born to hearing parents who were discouraged from signing to their deaf children because the use of sign language might impede progress in learning English. Consider the case of Joseph: "At the age of 11 and with no language at all, Joseph just entered a school for the deaf. Apparently he was born deaf, but this was not realized

Cultural & Diversity Perspective

American Sign language (ASL)

A manual-visual language developed within the American deaf community

FIGURE 3-15 Examples of hand symbols that indicate words in American Sign Language. In the past sign language was thought to be a form of pantomine that relied on the similarity of its symbols to the ideas they represent. Some signs, called *iconic,* seem to reflect the objects they represent; however, most of the signs are complex, abstract symbols.

Source: Meier, 1991.

until he was four years old. Up to that time his failure to understand speech at the normal age was attributed to retardation and then to autism. Although he had never been exposed to sign language, he was deriving great joy from what he was picking up. In fact, he wanted to stay at school all the time because going home meant returning to a communicational vacuum" (Sacks, 1989, pp. 38–39). In recent years, however, such policies have begun to change as a result of pressure from the deaf community. Today ASL is recognized as a legitimate language, and many deaf people emphasize learning sign language over speech therapy.

The Chemical Senses: Taste and Smell

Unlike humans, many animal species rely heavily on the chemical senses (taste and smell); hence these are sometimes called *primitive senses.* Taste involves the mixing of molecules in a liquid, and smell involves the mixing of molecules in the air.

Taste (Gustation). Few people would disagree that **gustation** (the technical term for taste) is a meaningful and often enjoyable link with our environment. As one researcher has described it, "The tongue is like a kingdom divided into principalities according to sensory talent. It would be as if all those who could see lived to the east, those who could hear lived to the west, those who could taste lived to the south, and those who could touch lived to the north. A flavor traveling through this kingdom is not recognized in the same way in any two places" (Ackerman, 1990, p. 139). Because taste receptors adapt so quickly and because tasting typically does not occur without smelling, our knowledge of the sense of taste is not, however, as complete or as accurate as it could be.

gustation
Sense of taste

What We Taste: The Gustatory Stimulus. The stimuli for taste are molecules dissolved in a liquid. But how do we account for the distinctive

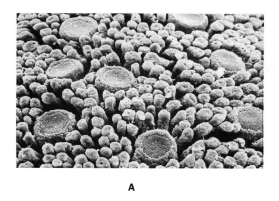

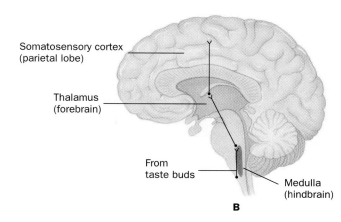

A

B

FIGURE 3-16 (A) The large, round tastebuds are clearly visible in this photograph. (B) Pathway of the gustatory nerve.

tastes of dry foods? If you think of the saliva that is produced when you eat dry foods, you know the source of the liquid. Have you ever eaten dry cereal as a snack? The first few bites are likely to be bland and dry, but when your saliva starts flowing the full flavor of the food comes through.

How We Taste: The Gustatory System. Once molecules are in solution, they can come into contact with the taste receptor cells, which are located in structures known as **taste buds** (see Figure 3-16A). Each taste bud contains approximately 20 taste receptors. The taste buds line the walls of small bumps on the tongue and throat called **papillae** (Latin for "bumps"). Although the primary locations of the taste buds are the tip, back, and sides of the tongue, some taste buds are located in the back of your throat, on the roof of your mouth, and inside your cheeks.

Individual taste receptor cells do not last forever; with a life expectancy of only ten days to two weeks, the cells within a taste bud are continually being replaced (McLaughlin & Margolskee, 1994). The number of taste buds increases during childhood to a maximum of about 10,000. At approximately age 40 the trend reverses, and our sense of taste declines (Schiffman, 1983).

How do the taste receptors work? Although researchers are not absolutely sure, the most credible theory advanced to date suggests that molecules in the solution attach to or fit into receptor sites. The actual taste receptor sites appear to be located on microscopic hairs, known as **microvilli,** that project from the tips of the taste receptor cells. Researchers believe that the receptor sites have different geometric shapes, so the shape of the molecule determines whether it fits into a specific receptor site (Tetter & Gold, 1988).

For nearly a century, researchers have agreed with the proposal that we are sensitive to at least four primary tastes: sweet, sour, bitter, and salty (Henning, 1916; Scott & Plata-Salaman, 1991). Hence it is reasonable to suppose that there are at least four different types (shapes) of receptor sites. The arrangement is like a key fitting into a lock. In this case, the key is the molecule and the lock is the receptor site. Once the sites are occupied, depolarization occurs and information is transmitted through the gustatory nerve to the brain (see Figure 3-16B). A number of molecules can occupy a receptor site: The better the fit, the greater the depolarization (McLaughlin & Margolskee, 1994). Keep in mind, however, that the lock-and-key theory is not absolute. Even though a receptor signals a certain taste more than others,

taste buds
Structures that contain the taste receptors

papillae
Bumps or protrusions distributed on the tongue and throat that are lined with taste buds

microvilli
Hairs that project from taste receptors

it can also contribute to the perception of other tastes (Erickson, DiLorenzo, & Woodbury, 1994).

Psychological Detective

This four-taste, lock-and-key theory sounds reasonable, but has it occurred to you that we experience more than four tastes? With only four proposed types of receptor sites, how do you explain the wide variety of tastes that we are able to experience? Write down some possible answers before reading further.

The explanation of our ability to experience a variety of tastes despite the existence of only four types of receptor sites appears to lie in the *pattern or combination* of neural activity the gustatory nerve sends to the brain (Pfaffmann, 1955; Hettinger & Frank, 1992). For example, one taste could be represented by considerable activity from all receptors except the salty ones, whereas a second taste could be represented by high activity levels of only two types of receptors.

As Figure 3-16B shows, the gustatory nerve goes from the taste buds to the medulla in the hindbrain (see Chapter 2), where they synapse. From there the information travels to the thalamus and is then relayed to the somatosensory cortex, located just behind the central fissure (see Figure 2-9 on page 56). At this point you are able to determine the nature of the taste you have experienced.

Throughout the world, humans have learned to like many tastes. Because various food sources are more plentiful in different locations and countries, cultural and ethnic differences in tastes have developed. As Diane Ackerman (1990) points out, "Many people eat rodents, grasshoppers, snakes, flightless birds, kangaroos, lobsters, snails, and bats. Unlike most other animals, which fill a small yet ample niche in the large web of life on earth, humans are omnivorous. Diversity is our delight" (p. 133).

Smell (Olfaction).   Unlike animals that rely on their sense of smell for survival (Menco, 1992), humans typically do not pay much attention to odors unless they are unusually bad (like 3-week-old perishable garbage) or unusually pleasant (like a freshly baked pizza). **Olfaction,** the ability to sense odors, is not crucial to our survival, but certain odors—such as those of leaking gas, spoiled food, or smoke—are important. Even if olfaction is not essential for survival, consider how bland our world would seem if we could smell nothing. Humans can recognize approximately 10,000 scents; many animals, such as bloodhounds, can detect and discriminate among many more (Axel, 1995).

What We Smell: The Olfactory Stimulus.   Odors are produced by molecules in the air. The more easily a substance's molecules mix with the air, the easier it is for us to smell it. Gasoline molecules mix with air quite easily and are readily detected; glass molecules do not mix well. Can you describe the smell of glass? Although no one can describe the smell of glass, some people cannot even describe the smell of common odors. More than 2 million Americans have a significant loss in the ability to smell. This condition, called *anosmia,* can result from genetic defects, aging, viruses, allergies, or certain prescription drugs. The most common cause, however, is head trauma, which can shear off axons that run from the olfactory nerves to the brain (Freedman, 1993).

olfaction
Sense of smell

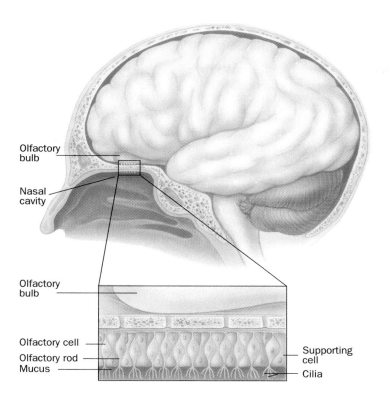

FIGURE 3-17 The location of the olfactory receptors makes them very difficult to study.

Source: Shaver & Tarpy, 1993

How We Smell: The Olfactory System.   Olfaction is not considered a major sensory system in humans and therefore has not received as much research attention as vision and hearing (Geldard, 1972). What's more, the location of the olfactory receptors makes it difficult to examine them directly. You may be surprised by that statement until you realize that the nose does not contain the olfactory receptors; its function is to collect and filter the air we breathe (Negus, 1956). As you can see in Figure 3-17, the olfactory receptors are located in an area of tissue of about 2.5 centimeters (1 inch) square in each nasal cavity (Breer & Boekhoff, 1992).

We have about 10 million olfactory receptors, each of which has six to twelve hairlike projections called *cilia.* Like taste receptors, olfactory receptors are continually dying and being replaced (Moulton, 1974; Wang, Wysocki, & Gold, 1993). The life span of an olfactory receptor is about 5 to 8 weeks.

In 1991, Linda Buck and Richard Axel identified several specific olfactory receptor sites. Other researchers (Raming et al., 1993) have since identified additional ones. In fact, there may be as many as 100 different types of olfactory receptor sites. Although researchers do not know a great deal about how they work, the olfactory receptors appear to operate under the same type of lock-and-key principle as the taste receptors (Amoore, 1970). When air molecules of a certain shape fit into a receptor site (Gesteland, 1986), the receptor depolarizes and a message is sent to the brain (Mori, Mataga, & Imamura, 1992). The olfactory nerve takes a somewhat different route to the brain from the other senses we have discussed. The first step is a synapse in the *olfactory bulb,* which is located near the optic chiasm on the underside of the brain. From there some of the olfactory nerve fibers go to the amygdala, which, as noted in Chapter 2, is part of the limbic system. From the amygdala the olfactory nerve travels to the thalamus and hypothalamus and then on to the cerebral cortex for higher-level processing.

The link between odors and memories is familiar to everyone. Charles Dickens claimed that a mere whiff of the type of paste used to fasten labels to bottles would bring back with unbearable force all the anguish of his earliest years, when bankruptcy had driven his father to abandon him in a hellish warehouse where such bottles were made. Do you ever find that the smell of gasoline, pizza, fresh-baked bread, after-shave lotion, sweat, perfume, or pine trees evokes memories? Likewise, many travelers also comment that different countries and cultures have their own unique smells. How old are these memories? How vividly do you recall them? Are there emotions attached to them?

A number of odors are associated with very emotional memories (Engen, 1987). This is a natural consequence of the fact that the limbic system, the emotional center of the brain, is involved in the processing of odors. Diane Ackerman (1990) described the memories that are triggered by odors in the following manner: "Smells detonate softly in our memory like poignant land mines, hidden under the weedy mass of many years and experiences. Hit a tripwire of smell and memories explode all at once. A complex vision leaps out of the undergrowth" (p. 5). Manufacturers of cologne and perfume have long taken advantage of their knowledge of the involvement of the limbic system in processing odors.

Myth or Science

 Sometimes the outlandish claims that characterize much popular psychology actually lead to scientifically sound experiments and meaningful discoveries. For example, in the early 1980s, most people scoffed at the proposal that spraying a fragrance in the air would improve productivity, dismissing it as just another advertising gimmick. Research, however, has actually supported this claim. For example, certain psychologists (Warm, Dember, & Parasuraman, 1991) found that men and women who smelled a pleasant peppermint odor performed significantly better on a boring computer task than comparable participants who breathed only unscented air. Another researcher (Griffin, 1992) reported similar results in a large commercial firm in Tokyo and in New York subway cars.

Do men and women differ in their sense of smell? The olfactory systems in men and women appear to be structurally the same, but there may be sex-based differences in sensitivity and odor memory. William Cain (1982) investigated this question by presenting 80 different odors to men and women. The participants sniffed each odor several times and then were told what the odor was. A series of odor recognition tests followed; women outperformed men on the majority of these tests. Among the 63 odors women learned to identify better than men were those of cigarette butts, leather, pipe tobacco, ginger, honey, and machine oil. Men learned the smells of such things as after-shave, ammonia, bourbon, and bubble gum more readily than women did. We do not know the reason for these results, but it seems that in general women have better odor memory than men. Perhaps these results also mean that women have a better sense of smell in general. It will be interesting to see what answers further research brings and to determine if there are cultural differences as well.

The Interaction of Smell and Taste.   So far we have treated smell and taste as if they were independent; however, these two sensations interact quite dramatically to determine flavor—remember how your food tasted the last time you had a head cold? One set of researchers (Mozel et al., 1969) reported the results of an experiment that proved the interdependence of smell and taste in experiencing a flavor. In this study they placed a drop of a certain flavor on a participant's tongue and asked the person to identify the taste. When participants could smell normally, they were correct on most tries; when the experimenter prevented them from smelling the flavor, however, they were often unable to identify it. For example, when participants could taste and smell coffee, its flavor was identified correctly nearly 90 percent of the time. When they were permitted only to taste, its flavor was identified correctly less than 5 percent of the time.

You can demonstrate this phenomenon yourself. Cut an apple and a potato into small pieces. Close your eyes, hold your nose, and have a friend put a piece of apple (or potato) into your mouth. Can you tell whether you were given an apple or a potato? When we must rely on taste alone, we often confuse various flavors (Mozel et al., 1969; McBurney, 1986). Thus odor is an important cue to what food we are eating and how it should taste.

The interaction of taste and smell does not end with the demonstration that odors and odor memories influence our perception of taste. Researchers have also found that when an odor component is added to a taste, the sensation of taste—not that of odor—is amplified (Murphy, Cain, & Bartoshuk, 1977). Prove it for yourself: Start eating with your nose closed, then add the odor component by opening your nostrils. The flavor will seem to come alive in your mouth; chewing releases chemicals into the nasal passages.

Other Sensory Systems

Vision, hearing, taste, and smell are important senses; however, they are not our only ones. If you have ever ridden a roller coaster at an amusement park, ridden in a fast-moving subway train that stopped suddenly, worn a piece of clothing that was too small, or put your hand into a pan of scalding water, you are well aware of your other senses. In this section we discuss three of them: the vestibular sense, the kinesthetic sense, and somatosensory processing.

Vestibular Sense.   The **vestibular sense,** which originates in the inner ear (see Figure 3-14), provides information about the body's orientation and movement. The vestibular system consists of the three semicircular canals in the inner ear and the utricle. The **semicircular canals** are located at right angles to each other to provide information about movement in all directions. Each semicircular canal is filled with a jellylike fluid that moves as the head moves. Movement of the fluid in the canal causes hair cells located in the canal to bend. Bending the hair cells sends information about movement to the brain (Gresty et al., 1992).

The **utricle,** a fluid-filled chamber located in the inner ear, operates on the same principle as the semicircular canals and serves as a gravity detector. To experience the vestibular system, move your head and continue reading. You should have no problem. Now try moving the book while you are reading. The act of reading should be noticeably harder. Why? Because our head movement activates our vestibular system. When we sense movements of our eyes, head, and body, we can make adjustments to keep our world in some perspective. This perspective helps us to orient ourselves to our environment.

Kinesthetic Sense.   Have you ever sat on one leg or kept an arm in an awkward position until it tingled or "went to sleep"? Remember how difficult

vestibular sense
System located in the inner ear that allows us to make adjustments to bodily movements and postures

semicircular canals
Fluid-filled passages in the inner ear that detect movement of the head

utricle
Fluid-filled chamber in the inner ear that detects changes in gravity

The vestibular system is active during Olympic skater Michelle Kwan's performance.

it was to walk or move your arm under those circumstances? The reason for the difficulty is that when this tingling sensation occurs, you no longer have adequate information to determine the location of your leg or arm. Such information about our muscles and joints constitutes our **kinesthetic sense.** Sense receptors located in the joints and muscles send information to the brain concerning muscle tension and joint position. The brain combines this information with other sensory input, such as vision and audition, to help you determine the location of your limbs. The importance of kinesthetic information is most apparent in the performance of skilled activities, such as gymnastics, swimming, dancing, playing basketball, and driving a car. Such activities require input from a variety of sensory systems, including the kinesthetic sense. As you will see in the next section, sensations from the skin also provide valuable information.

Somatosensory Processing.   Somatosensory processing involves several kinds of information that are sensed by receptors in the skin (Iggo & Andres, 1982). A microscopic view of the skin yields an amazing picture (see Figure 3-18).

Some sections of our skin are packed with a variety of receptors that respond to some form of somatosensory information—touch or pressure, pain, and temperature. The wide variety of skin receptors for touch or pressure are called *mechanoreceptors*; the receptors for temperature are called *thermoreceptors*. Moving from the outer to deeper layers of the skin, we find the following somatosensory receptors:

> *Meissner corpuscles*—receptors for light touch, as when something rubs against you or you move your fingers over an object
>
> *Merkel disks*—receptors that are activated by the steady pressure of small objects
>
> *Ruffini endings*—receptors that are activated by the pressure of larger objects and stretching of the skin
>
> *Pacinian corpuscles*—receptors that are very sensitive to touch
>
> *Free nerve endings*—receptors that are sensitive to temperature and pain

Pain.   The sensation of pain is caused by a harmful stimulus such as extreme heat or cold, toxic chemicals, or breaking or invasion of the skin. The general term for receptors that respond to painful stimuli is *nocioreceptors*. Think of the different types of pain you have experienced. A bright, sharp pain can be caused by pinprick, whereas a dull, chronic pain can result from physical overexertion. Because pain warns us of impending injury, it helps us adapt to the environment.

One theory of pain, the **gate control theory** (Melzack & Wall, 1965), has greatly influenced our understanding of pain. According to this theory, pain impulses are transmitted from the receptors (free nerve endings) to the spinal cord. The axons of the pain neurons release substance P (see Chapter 2) in the spinal cord (Piercey et al., 1981; Levine, Fields, & Basbaum, 1993). In turn, substance P causes neurons in the spinal cord to send information about pain to the brain for processing and perception.

Thus the painful stimulus, in conjunction with substance P, opens the pain gate. How is the gate closed? Neurons that descend from the brain to the spinal cord release opioid peptides (see Chapter 2) called **endorphins.** In turn, the endorphins block the release of substance P (Reichling, Kwait, &

kinesthetic sense

System of receptors located in the muscles and joints that provides information about the location of the extremities

gate control theory

Theory of pain stating that the release of substance P in the spinal cord produces the sensation of pain

endorphins

Opiatelike substances produced by the body that block pain by inhibiting the release of substance P

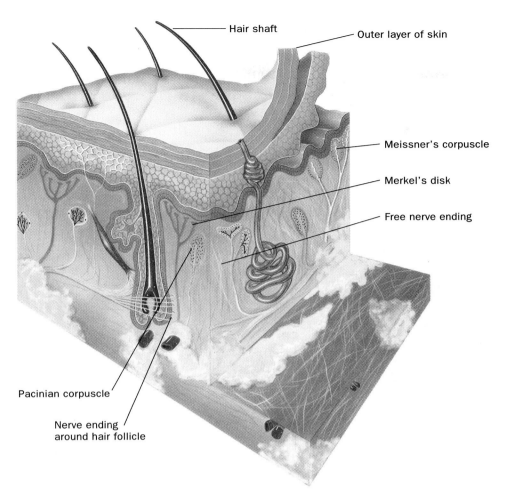

Hair shaft

Outer layer of skin

Meissner's corpuscle

Merkel's disk

Free nerve ending

Pacinian corpuscle

Nerve ending
around hair follicle

FIGURE 3-18   Cross-section of the skin showing several of the receptors located there.

Source: Shaver & Tarpy, 1993.

Basbaum, 1988), and the pain gate is closed. Pain and stressful or thrilling situations are among the conditions that elicit the release of endorphins.

Is pain perceived similarly by all people? Evidently not. For example, Hall and Davies (1991) found that varsity female athletes had higher pain thresholds than female nonathletes. Likewise, cultural differences in the response to pain have been reported. For example, Nepalese participants have higher pain thresholds than Western participants (Clark & Clark, 1980).

The **somatosensory receptors** work together to provide comprehensive information concerning the types of objects we encounter. Once the somatosensory information has been sensed, the sensory nerves travel up the spinal cord and synapse in the thalamus. The sensory information is then relayed to the somatosensory cortex, which is located in the parietal lobe (see Chapter 2), for higher-level processing. As you saw in the map of the sensory cortex (Figure 2-10A), the areas of the skin with the most receptors send information to larger areas of the cortex.

The following study chart summarizes the properties and operation of the five major senses.

somatosensory receptors
Receptors in the skin that provide sensory information

STUDY CHART

The Five Senses

Sense	Receptors	Objective Stimulus	Subjective Experience
The ability to detect stimuli	Specialized cells that allow us to experience this sense	Energy or chemicals that cause these receptors to fire	What we experience when these receptors fire
Vision	*Rods and cones* in the retina	Electromagnetic waves between 380 to 760 NM	LIGHT
Hearing (Audition)	*Hair cells* in the basilar membrane	Molecules that vibrate between 20-20,000 Hz	SOUNDS
Taste (Gustation)	*Microvilli* on the tongue	Molecules of substances dissolved in a liquid	TASTES
Smell (Olfaction)	*Olfactory cells* in the walls of the passageway between the nose and the throat	Molecules of substances in the air	ODORS
Touch (Somatosensory)	*Mechanoreceptors* in the skin which respond to skin deformation *Thermoreceptors* in the skin which respond to changes in temperature *Nocioreceptors* in the skin which respond to painful stimuli	Skin indentation, vibrations, and hair movements; changes in temperature; and mechanical or thermal stimuli that begin near levels which can produce tissue damage	PRESSURE TEMPERATURE PAIN

Review Summary

1. Audition, the sense of hearing, is initiated by the movement of molecules in the air. Vibration of the eardrum starts a chain reaction that results in movement of fluid in the inner ear and the bending of specialized hair cells, which are the receptors for hearing.

2. The pitch or frequency of a sound wave is determined by the location of the hairs that are activated (**place theory**) and the rapidity with which the basilar membrane vibrates (**frequency theory**).

3. Hearing disorders can result from damage to the bones of the middle ear (**conduction deafness**), the inner ear, especially the hair cells (**sensorineural deafness**), or the auditory nerve and auditory cortex (**central deafness**).

4. The chemical senses include the sense of taste (**gustation**) and the sense of smell (**olfaction**).

5. Molecules in solution stimulate taste. Hairs, located on structures known as **taste buds,** serve as the receptors. Although receptors may respond to several tastes, each one is maximally sensitive to one of four tastes: sweet, sour, bitter, or salty.

6. Molecules in the air stimulate the sense of smell. Hairs located in the nasal cavity serve as the receptors. Olfaction has a direct connection to the limbic system; as a result, many of our memories involving odors are highly emotional.

7. The **vestibular sense** enables us to adjust to different bodily movements. The **kinesthetic sense** allows us to determine the position of our extremities. **Somatosensory receptors** for pressure, pain, and temperature are located in the skin.

Study Break

1. Describe what causes a sound wave. How are sound waves measured?
2. Match each term with a term closely associated with it.

   a. Hertz (Hz)
   b. Pacinian corpuscle
   c. Decibels (Db)
   d. Microvilli
   e. Semicircular canals
   f. Substance P
   g. Kinesthesis

   1. Taste receptors
   2. Vestibular sense
   3. Somatosensory processing
   4. Position of arms and legs
   5. Pain
   6. Frequency
   7. Intensity

3. While attending a rock concert, you notice that it seems easier to hear the vocals than the electric bass. Assuming that both have the same intensity, how would you explain this difference?
4. Distinguish between the place theory and the frequency theory. Which is correct?
5. We can locate sounds around us through
   a. volume of sound and timbre of sound.
   b. the volley principle and volume of sound.
   c. timbre of sound and differences in time for sound to reach each ear.
   d. volume of sound and differences in time for sound to reach each ear.
6. What are the four primary tastes? Explain how we are able to experience such a wide range of flavors.
7. What term describes the loss of the sense of smell?
   a. kinethesis
   b. olfaction
   c. anosmia
   d. paranomia
8. Distinguish between the stimuli for taste and smell.
9. Why has research on the olfactory system not progressed at a rapid rate?
10. Distinguish among vestibular, somatosensory, and kinesthetic processes.

Perception

Spring break is over, and you are driving back to school. Having savored every minute of your leisure time, you get a late start and skip lunch and dinner. Now it's 9 P.M., and you have become painfully aware of every sign on the highway that mentions food. The other signs are a blur; in fact, you aren't even sure that there have been any other signs. At last you reach the exit for the fast-food place you've been reading about for the past 25 miles. You pull off; after a burger, fries, and a shake, you're back on the road. *Why did you fail to perceive the other billboards?* ▪

As we discussed at the beginning of this chapter, perception is the process of organizing and making sense of the stimuli in our environment. Because we rely so heavily on the visual sense, much of our knowledge about perception has been learned through research on vision. Thus to understand perceptual processes, we focus on visual perception. Many of the processes that we discuss also apply to other senses, however, as you read this section, try to use these principles to describe the perception of sounds, tastes, and odors as well as pressure, pain, and temperature.

Like so many areas in psychology, perception is not a simple and straightforward matter. Because our motives (needs, drives, and even prejudices) may distort or determine what we perceive, our discussion of perception begins with a description of how attention is influenced by motivation.

Motivation and Attention

We do not perceive everything in our environment; our motives greatly influence our perceptions. Similarly, certain stimuli are more likely than others to attract our attention.

Motivational Influences. Think back to our opening vignette—to the part about noticing only those billboards advertising food. In this scenerio, why did you fail to perceive the other billboards? Those other billboards certainly activated your receptors (sensation), but you did not perceive them because they were not related to hunger, your dominant motive at the time. Now that your need for food has been satisfied, you begin to notice other things. You glance at your instrument panel and panic—the gas gauge reads "empty"! Now you become aware of an entirely different set of billboards—those advertising gas stations.

Attention. We cannot possibly attend to and process all of the stimuli received by our sensory systems at any one moment; some of them must be filtered out. Have you ever tried to listen to two friends talk to you at the same time? This is an example of the need to filter information. You can re-create such a situation by conducting a dichotic listening exercise (Goodwin, 1988).

In *dichotic listening* experiments, a different message is presented to each of a participant's ears, and the participant is asked to recall both messages. These experiments usually involve the use of a tape recorder and special headphones. However, three people, minus this equipment, can accomplish the same goal. The procedure is as follows: Place three chairs side by side. You, the participant, sit in the middle chair. Have a person seated on your right and a person seated on your left read different passages at the same time. After a fixed amount of time, such as 20 or 30 seconds, try either to repeat verbally or write down whatever you can recall. You can create interesting variations of this basic procedure, such as a male voice in one ear and a female voice in the other ear, or fast reading in one ear and slow reading in the other. When you try to listen to both messages, you will probably find yourself switching back and forth between them and becoming quite confused.

Dichotic listening tasks are designed to study **divided attention,** the ability to attend to more than one message or type of information at the same time. Research in this area has uncovered some intriguing information about human perception. For example, we hear (and understand) much more than the information of which we are consciously aware. This fact is demonstrated by the famous "cocktail-party phenomenon" (Cherry & Bowles, 1960). With this phenomenon, the scene is a typical weekend party—lots of people doing lots of talking. You are having a conversation with five or six friends when suddenly you hear your name mentioned in a conversation on the other side of the room. Your name was not shouted, and you are not aware of anything else that was said—only your name. Clearly, you have been listening to and processing other conversations during your conversation with your friends. Only when the content included something important, like your name, did the conversation enter your consciousness and sharpen your awareness or perception.

The cocktail-party phenomenon demonstrates that attention can be divided. The ability to listen to two messages at once might be very beneficial. Can you do anything to make this task easier or more effective? The answer is to practice. The more you practice at processing two separate messages, the more skilled you will become at it. Also, you will find that it is easier to divide your attention when you are processing different *types* of information. For example, most of us have little difficulty listening to a CD while driving. We divide our attention between the visual stimuli involved in driving and the auditory stimuli produced by the CD. This type of divided attention is easy to accomplish on a monotonous interstate highway or in a familiar neighborhood, but what happens when you

divided attention

The ability to process more than one source of stimulation at the same time

find yourself in rush-hour traffic in a strange metropolitan area? Many people turn the volume of the music down or turn it off completely. The shift in attention from the music to the demands of the signs and traffic around them shows selective attention at work.

In addition to needs, motives, and prejudices, certain aspects of stimuli determine which ones get our attention. For example, people generally pay more attention to stimuli that are larger, louder, or more colorful than others. You can watch television commercials any night of the week to see how advertisers exploit this phenomenon. What's more, your attention is attracted to stimuli that stand out from or contrast with the objects around them.

When something happens unexpectedly our attention is attracted very quickly. When contrast and surprise combine, our attention is commanded even more quickly. If your instructor wore pajamas to class, for example, this unusual occurrence would catch your attention immediately.

Although motivation and attention are important aspects of perception, they do not provide the complete picture. Once a stimulus has attracted our attention, there are basic perceptual abilities that we use to respond to it.

The cocktail-party phenomenon. You can hear something that is very important to you, such as your name, even though it is said in a normal manner across a noisy room.

Basic Perceptual Abilities: Patterns and Constancies

We perceive objects in our environment as having features such as pattern, constancy, depth, and movement. Our perception of these objects and their features is so automatic that we often take them for granted. However, they are crucial components of perception. In this section we describe them in detail.

Pattern Perception.   Among the most basic perceptual abilities is the ability to perceive patterns. To survive in modern society, we must be able to perceive a staggering number of shapes and figures. A few of the patterns we deal with every day are the letters of the alphabet, traffic signs, friends' facial features, food items in the grocery store, the buildings in an apartment complex, and the automobiles in a parking lot. Psychologists refer to the ability to discriminate among different shapes and figures as **pattern perception.** Although some cortical cells appear to function as *feature detectors* that are sensitive to specific shapes, such as lines, bars, or edges, we still need to translate these features into a perception of our environment (Hughes, Nozawa, & Kitterle, 1996). There are several theories concerning the process of pattern perception.

One popular theory of pattern perception (Hubel & Wiesel, 1979) suggests that specialized cells in the occipital lobe (see Chapter 2) are responsible for the perception of patterns. For example, simple cells respond to bars or edges in a particular orientation. In turn, the responses of the simple cells appear to be received by complex cells that are also located in the occipital lobe. Complex cells respond when *moving* bars or edges of a particular orientation are presented. Once these separate elements have been sensed, the brain assembles them, and we can identify the object in question as one that we have, or have not, seen before.

The **feature analysis theory** of pattern perception (Lindsay & Norman, 1977) states that we perceive basic elements of an object and mentally assemble them to create a complete object. As when a house is built, various pieces

pattern perception
The ability to discriminate among different figures and shapes

feature analysis theory
Theory of pattern perception stating that we perceive basic elements of an object and assemble them mentally to create the complete object

perceptual constancy
The tendency to perceive the size and shape of an object as constant even though its retinal image changes

shape constancy
The tendency to perceive the shape of an object as constant despite changes in its retinal image

size constancy
The tendency to perceive the size of an object as constant despite changes in its retinal image

are put together until the structure is completed. In short, we start from the bottom and work up to a completed and recognizable building. Once the object has been assembled, it is matched against items stored in memory. If there is a match, we are able to identify the item. If there is no match, we probably search for the memory that resembles it most closely.

In terms of perceptual processes, your perceptual experience starts with receptor activity and works toward progressively higher brain centers. This process of starting with basic elements and working toward a more complex perception is known as a *bottom-up model*. If, however, we look at the task of recognizing words, this *bottom-up model* of feature analysis runs into problems. Several studies (such as those by Johnston & McClelland, 1973, 1974) have shown that we can recognize an entire word better than we recognize individual letters. These results suggest that, at least in some instances, we use a *top-down approach* in which the whole object is recognized before its component parts are identified. But top-down processing results in mistakes when the word is not perceived correctly, such as reading the word *house* for the word *horse*.

Perceptual Constancies. You do not have to treat every perceptual change as if your environment had changed completely. Once you have identified an object, you continue to recognize it even if its location and distance from you change, thereby casting a different image on your retina. A change in the retinal image does not signal a change in the object. This tendency to perceive the size and shape of objects as relatively stable despite retinal changes is called **perceptual constancy.** The importance of perceptual constancies should be obvious; they allow us to deal with our environment as relatively stable and unchanging.

Shape Constancy. **Shape constancy** means that your perception of the shape of an object as viewed from different angles does not change even though the image projected on your retina does so. In other words, the shape of an object is perceived independently of the image it casts on the retina. This phenomenon is easy to demonstrate. Look at this book from a number of angles. You see nothing but a book being held in different positions. The same could be said for the opening and closing of a door or the image of a car making a left turn in front of you. The image on your retina changes dramatically, yet the object you perceive does not. Almost any moving object displays the principle of shape constancy. For the perception of shape constancy to occur, however, the object must be familiar and must be seen in an identifiable context. If there is no context or background to which the object can be related, it appears to float in space, and you cannot judge its correct orientation; shape constancy disappears.

Size Constancy. **Size constancy** also helps us to maintain consistency in our perceptual environment. As objects move toward us, their retinal images enlarge; as they move farther away, their retinal images diminish. We do not perceive the size of those objects as changing, however, instead we perceive the objects as moving toward or away from us. Size constancy depends on our familiarity with the object and on our ability to judge distance. When we are dealing with familiar objects and can easily judge distances, we are more likely to perceive the size of the objects as being constant. When we are dealing with unfamiliar objects and our ability to estimate distance is poor, the objects may appear to change size.

To understand this point, consider a classic example. C. M. Turnbull (1961), an anthropologist, was studying the BaMbuti Pygmies in the dense for-

Can you tell the size of this object? When we can't rely on cues for distance or the size of other objects, size constancy is not good. See the end of the chapter for another photo that gives you a better idea as to the size of this object.

est of the Belgian Congo. During his studies, Turnbull traveled from one group of Pygmies to another. On one trip, which took him across the plains, he was accompanied by a youngster, Kenge, who had spent his entire life in the dense forest. Having never been on the plains, Kenge was unable to judge distances and determine the size of unfamiliar objects. A distant herd of buffalo presented a major problem; Kenge "tried to liken the distant buffalo to the various beetles and ants with which he was familiar" (Turnbull, 1961, p. 305). Imagine Kenge's surprise when, as they drove closer to the buffalo, he thought he saw the animals grow steadily larger. Clearly, our culture and experiences influence our perceptions of real life and of pictures (Deregowski, 1980).

Because they are automatic processes, size and shape constancy may seem rather simple; however, these constancies involve much processing. We are using familiar background objects for purposes of comparison (size constancy) and to anchor our perceptions (shape constancy). If the background objects are eliminated and we are confronted with an unfamiliar object, however, we have difficulty perceiving its correct size and distance. For example, without distance cues and other objects with which to make comparisons, we cannot judge size well. Similarly, without a background to anchor our perceptions, moving objects may appear to change shape rather than simply to move in space (see Figure 3-19).

A classic experiment in which participants judged the size of familiar circles (Holway & Boring, 1941) demonstrates the importance of these cues. When background and depth cues were present, the participants were very accurate in their size estimates. As these cues were eliminated, the participants depended increasingly on the images cast on the retina and on their memories of the size of familiar objects (Schiffman, 1967).

Auditory constancies are another important aspect of perception. We perceive words as the same when they are spoken by many people with very different voices. Likewise, a melody is recognizable even when it is played on different instruments and in different keys.

Depth Perception. In addition to a world of constancies, we experience a third dimension, **depth perception.** For decades psychologists have been puzzled by the question of how we are able to perceive depth or distance. The surface of the retina is two-dimensional (top to bottom, side to side), yet we are

depth perception
The ability to perceive our world three-dimensionally

FIGURE 3-19 Examples of size and shape constancy with an indication of the influence of supporting cues. Notice the hand drums that these women are holding. Even though the drums cast very different images on the retina, shape constancy dictates that they will all be seen as drums, and not as three different shapes.

able to judge distances and locate objects in space (three-dimensionally) quite well. Two main types of cues, binocular and monocular, are used to create our perception of depth. **Binocular cues** involve the use of both eyes, whereas **monocular cues** are processed by only one eye.

Binocular Cues.   Among the most important binocular cues are adjustments of the eye muscles and binocular disparity. Let's consider eye muscle adjustments first. Our eyes are supported by muscles that move the eyeball to allow us the best possible view. They also provide feedback for judging distance. When objects are near, the eyes rotate toward a center point. You can feel the muscle tension when you look at objects that are very close. To experience this sensation, focus on this sentence and gradually move the book closer to your eyes. The closer the book gets, the more eye muscle strain you feel; the farther away the book is, the less eye muscle strain you experience.

If you open and close one eye and then the other, you do not see exactly the same thing with each eye. The closer the object, the greater the difference between what the two eyes see. This difference occurs because each eye sees from a different angle, a phenomenon known as **binocular disparity.** When the images from both eyes merge in the brain, a sense of depth is created. Researchers have identified cortical cells that respond to binocular disparity (Ohzawa, De Angelis, & Freeman, 1990), assuming that the activity of these cells is a primary cue for depth. You can easily demonstrate binocular disparity by closing one eye and aligning your two index fingers. Now switch eyes. Are the fingers still aligned? This misalignment is even greater when the fingers are closer to the face, as compared with when they are at arm's length.

Monocular Cues.   Monocular cues, which can be perceived by either eye alone, also help determine depth (Stoner & Albright, 1993). For example, when the ciliary muscles change the shape of the lens in accommodation, the muscle adjustments are sensed and are used to help determine distance.

Artists use numerous monocular cues—including *superposition* (near objects partially obscure more distant objects), *texture gradient* (the texture of a surface becomes smoother with increasing distance), *linear perspective* (parallel lines appear to converge as they recede into the distance), and *relative brightness* (brighter objects appear closer than duller-appearing ones)—to create the illusion of depth. These cues also operate in our day-to-day environment, as you can see in Figure 3-20. After you have studied the figure, look around the room you are in and identify other examples of these cues.

In addition to demonstrating the importance of binocular and monocular cues for depth perception, psychologists have investigated whether this perceptual ability is innate or learned. For example, Eleanor Gibson (Gibson & Walk, 1960) has successfully used the visual cliff (see Figure 3-21) to test depth-perception ability in human infants and children as well as in a variety of animals. The visual cliff consists of a two-sided chamber; the bottom of one side of the chamber is shallow and within easy reach, whereas the bottom of the other side is deep. Both sides of the chamber are covered by glass. A test participant is placed on a small platform in the center of the visual cliff and must choose between crawling to the shallow and deep sides. Human infants avoid the deep side from the time they are mobile. Thus humans perceive depth from about 6 months of age. Gibson's research on perception is so significant that she was awarded the National Medal of Science by President

binocular cues
Cues for depth perception that involve the use of both eyes

monocular cues
Cues for depth perception that involve the use of only one eye

binocular disparity
The difference between the images seen by the two eyes

FIGURE 3-20 Monocular cues for depth perception: superposition and brightness (left); texture gradient and linear perspective (center); and texture, linear perspective, and superposition (right).

George Bush in 1992, the highest honor that can be bestowed on a scientist by the president of the United States.

Gestalt Principles of Perceptual Organization

The founders of Gestalt psychology (see Chapter 1)—Max Wertheimer, Wolfgang Köhler, and Kurt Koffka—proposed we are born with the ability to organize the elements of our perceptual world in very predictable ways. The goal of these automatic organizing processes is to produce the best or most complete perception of our environment. Among the most familiar of these processes are figure-ground distinctions and the grouping of elements.

Figure and Ground. The Gestalt psychologists emphasized that one of the ways in which we organize our perceptual world is by sorting stimuli into figure and background (or ground). The figure is the focus of our attention; the ground constitutes the remainder of our perception. An example of **figure-ground relationships** is shown in Figure 3-22. Notice what we focus on—the figure—tends to be smaller, more colorful, or brighter than the background.

Sometimes these automatic processes can trick us. Look at Figure 3-23 and decide what is figure and what is ground in each example. In each instance the figure-ground relationship is unclear or ambiguous, and the task is much more difficult than that in Figure 3-22. When we are confronted with ambiguous figures like those in Figure 3-23, we are able to organize the material in at least two ways. Which do you see

figure-ground relationship
Organization of perceptual elements into a figure (the focus of attention) and a background

FIGURE 3-21 The visual cliff. Will the child perceive depth or move onto the glass that covers the deep side of the visual cliff?

FIGURE 3-22 Example of figure—ground relationships. Notice that what we perceive as figures tend to be smaller, more colorful, or brighter than the background.

first? That may depend on the caption (Did it say "young woman" or "old woman" first?) or on the features that first attracted your attention. Once you have seen both figures in an ambiguous drawing, you can easily reverse the figure-ground relationship.

How often do you encounter figure-ground problems in your day-to-day activities? For example, while driving have you ever stopped next to a large truck at a traffic light? Suddenly you feel yourself moving backward! Have your brakes failed? Your foot is on the brake, and you push it harder. Nothing happens, however—the backward motion continues. Only then do you realize that the truck—not your car—is moving.

Unconsciously you perceived your car as the figure and the larger truck as the ground. Because figures normally move across a background, you perceived yourself, rather than the truck, as the moving object. Can you think of other examples of how your perceptions have been fooled by unusual figure-ground relationships?

Principles of Grouping. In addition to showing that we perceive figure-ground relationships, the Gestalt psychologists demonstrated that we organize our perceptions by grouping elements. The way we group perceptual elements is extremely important. Think of how much trouble you would have if you had to deal with every perceptual element independently. The letters you are reading fall into groups we call words. What would reading be like if you had to think about every single letter? What would it be like to listen to someone speak if you couldn't group the sounds into words? We function more effectively and efficiently when we organize perceptual elements into groups.

Several conditions promote the grouping of perceptual elements. Although we discuss these conditions separately, keep in mind that more than

A Letters or objects?

B Vase or faces?

C Young woman or old woman?

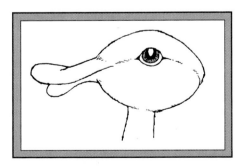

D Rabbit or duck?

FIGURE 3-23 Examples of ambiguous or unclear figure-ground relationships. Which object do you see first in each picture? Does it make seeing the other figure more difficult?

one of them can operate at a time. See how many of these conditions you notice in your day-to-day life.

With **proximity,** one of the most elementary Gestalt grouping principles, items that are close to each other are perceived as a group. The words strung together on this page are an example of proximity. According to the Gestalt principle of **similarity,** items that are alike are grouped together: XXXOOO, perceived as three Xs and three Os. These two principles are illustrated in Figure 3-24 (items A, B, and C). Do they operate effectively with senses other than vision? Think about musical melodies or spoken words. What would they be like if you had to pay attention to each separate note or sound?

The Gestalt principle of **good continuation and direction** says that we perceive continuous, flowing lines more easily than choppy or broken lines. What do you see in item D of Figure 3-24? A diamond between two parallel lines is an organization of elements that emphasizes the continuous lines at the sides. You could also, however, see a W sitting on top of an M. Try it. Although this perception is possible, it is more difficult to achieve because it involves breaking the continuity of the lines on the sides.

When you look at item E in the figure, you probably see two overlapping circles. This drawing illustrates the Gestalt principle of **inclusiveness,** which says that a smaller figure's identity may be lost within a larger, more complex figure. It is easier to see two overlapping circles than three separate elements. If we label and identify the separate figures, all of them are more easily seen.

Now examine F in Figure 3-24. What do you see? It's a bicycle, of course, but is the drawing complete? To complete the picture and identify the object, you had to create the missing pieces perceptually. This process illustrates the Gestalt principle of **closure,** which says that organizing our perceptions into complete objects is easier than perceiving each part separately.

proximity
Gestalt principle stating that perceptual elements that are close together are seen as a group

similarity
Gestalt principle stating that perceptual elements that are similar are seen as a group

good continuation and direction
Gestalt principle stating that smooth, flowing lines are more readily perceived than choppy, broken lines

inclusiveness
Gestalt principle stating that the identity of a smaller figure may be lost within a larger, more complex figure

closure
Gestalt principle stating that organizing perceptions into whole objects is easier than perceiving separate parts independently

Perception of Movement

Suppose you are on your way to your next class when you notice a message on an electronic sign. It is one of those signs, like a theater marquee, that has letters and words that appear to move across it. Our perception of separate

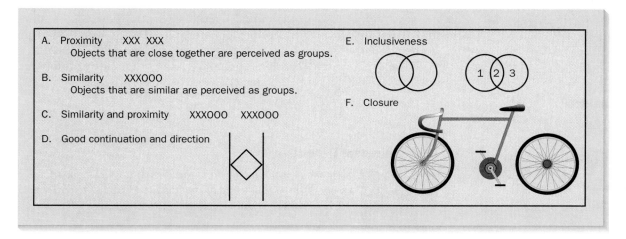

FIGURE 3-24 Examples of the Gestalt principles of grouping. The grouping of perceptual elements allows us to deal more effectively with our environment.

When you see "moving" words, such as the ones on this building on Broadway in New York City, you are experiencing *apparent* motion. The words do not actually move.

words is created because of the proximity of the letters that make up each group (word) and the spaces between successive groups of letters. Unlike the letters you are reading in this text, the letters on the electronic sign are made up of separate, unconnected points—and we connect them using the principle of closure.

This sign, however, adds another dimension to our consideration of perception. Although the words do not really move across the sign, they appear to do so. **Apparent motion** is the illusion of movement in a stationary object. In the electronic sign, it is created by turning the lights on and off in a particular sequence. How prevalent is apparent motion? Consider movies, television, and videocassettes. All of these forms of entertainment rely on the brain's ability to create the perception of motion from a series of still pictures.

Motion is so important that your brain creates the illusion of movement even when there is none. This phenomenon, known as the *autokinetic effect,* keeps the visual receptors from adapting. If your receptors adapted, vision would cease. To demonstrate the autokinetic effect, you will need a small flashlight, some string, and a very dark room. Hang the flashlight, pointed down, from a light fixture or ceiling fan. Turn the flashlight on and all the other lights in the room off. Sit on the floor, and stare at the flashlight. Within a minute or less the light should appear to move, usually in an elliptical (egg-shaped) pattern. Your brain has created the perception of motion.

Perceptual Hypotheses and Illusions

We have said that perception involves the brain's attempt to interpret and make sense of the stimuli we receive from our environment. Constancy, figure-ground relationships, and grouping processes help us develop educated guesses, or inference, about the nature of those stimuli. Such inferences are called **perceptual hypotheses,** and they routinely shape our perceptual experience. Much of the time our perceptual hypotheses are accurate, but sometimes they are wrong. For example, how often could you have sworn that your professor said a paper was due next Thursday, rather than next Tuesday? Have you ever been absolutely sure that a traffic light was green, not red?

It is easy to trick our senses into developing an incorrect perceptual hypothesis. Such incorrect perceptual hypotheses form the basis for **perceptual illusions,** or misperceptions or interpretations of stimuli that do not correspond to the sensations received by the eye (Block & Yuker, 1989). The case in which grass looks greener on the other side of the fence is an example.

apparent motion
Illusion of movement in a stationary object

perceptual hypothesis
Inference about the nature of stimuli received from the environment

perceptual illusions
Misperceptions or interpretations of stimuli that do not correspond to the sensations received

Psychological Detective

How many times have you heard people say, "The grass looks greener on the other side of the fence"? Usually this statement refers to the fact that most of us fail to appreciate what we have and long for what we do not have. Does real grass on the other side of a real fence actually appear greener? Give this question some thought. Write down your answer, and the reasons for it, before reading further.

The answer to the greener-grass question is yes, and there is an explanation. When you look directly *down* at the grass in your yard, you see both green grass and the dark brown soil in which it is growing. These colors blend together. When you look at the grass *across* the fence, however, you are not looking straight down, and therefore you do not see the brown soil. Hence you perceive the grass on the other side of the fence as being a purer shade of green. Your senses are tricked into believing that the grass really is greener on the other side of the fence.

The development of incorrect perceptual hypotheses is at the heart of perceptual illusions. Some of our favorites are shown in Figure 3-25. Look at each and decide what perceptual hypothesis you have developed for it. Figure 3-25D, which depicts the Ebbinghaus Illusion, suggests that our perceptual hypotheses are influenced by contrast or the tendency to accentuate differences. In this illusion, big circles make a central circle appear small, whereas small circles make a central circle look larger. What aspects of the other drawings trick the visual system causing us to develop incorrect perceptual hypotheses?

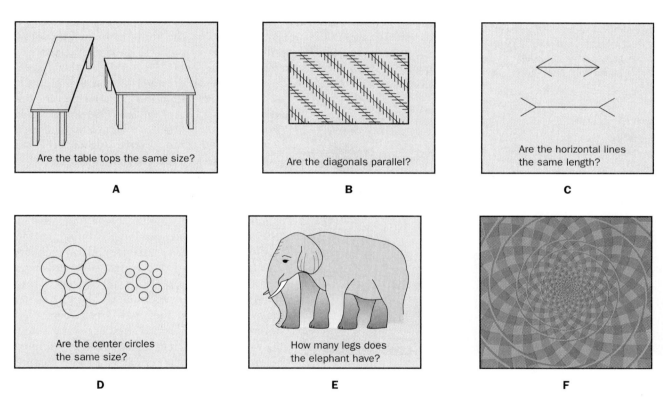

FIGURE 3-25 Perceptual hypotheses may be the cause of many illusions. (A) Because it is narrow, the table on the left is perceived as being longer than the table on the right is wide; it is not. (B) The short crossing lines (some people call them feathers) help create the perception that the longer lines are not parallel; they are. (C) The < > symbols or "wings" at the ends of the top lines and the > < symbols at the ends of the bottom line create the illusion that the top line is shorter than the bottom line. The amount of error in judging the Muller-Lyer illusion depends on a number of factors such as the angle of the wings and their length. (D) Because it is surrounded by several larger circles, the center circle on the left is perceived as smaller than the center circle on the right (Ebbinghaus Illusion). The two circles are exactly the same size. (E) Even though we know that an elephant has only four legs, the additional leg shapes are compelling cues. Are the elephant's real legs dark or light in color? (F) Fraser's spiral creates the illusion of a spiral. If you check carefully, there is no spiral, just a series of concentric circles.

visual search

Identifying the presence of a target stimulus among a group of other, distractor items

One of the most fascinating perceptual illusions is the Ames room. Figure 3-26A shows the view that you would have if you were looking into the Ames room. Notice how much bigger the woman on the right appears. How can this be? People are not supposed to vary this much in height. The explanation is in Figure 3-26B. Although you assume the room is perfectly square, it is not square. The floors you thought were level are not level. The woman is actually closer to you and casts a larger image on your retina. Without information to tell you that one person is closer and on a floor that slants upward, you conclude that this person is abnormally large.

Contemporary Issues and Findings in Perception Research

FIGURE 3-26 If you assume that the Ames room is a regularly shaped room with a normal ceiling height, then the person in the right corner appears much larger that she should be.

Source: Seaman & Kenrick, 1994.

Parallel Processing, Visual Search, and The Application of Basic Perceptual Research. During "the decade of the brain" (see Chapter 2) research on perceptual processes has progressed rapidly. According to Woods and Krantz (2000), recent advances in the study of brain functioning promise to change our conception of sensory processes and perception. For example, studies of the human visual cortex (Zeki, 1993) indicate that sensory processing does not occur in a strictly sequential manner, such as that proposed by Hubel and Wiesel (1979). The picture that emerges is of a *parallel processing system* (Friedman-Hill & Wolfe, 1995) in which information flows both from lower to higher levels *and* from higher to lower levels in the brain.

For example, research on the basic process of vision (Neitz, Neitz, & Jacobs, 1995) indicates the existence of *five* different cones that are genetically coded (Neitz, Neitz, & Grishok, 1995): one for short wavelengths (blue), two for medium wavelengths (green), and two for long wavelengths (red). Even though we possess more than three cones, the *trichromatic theory of color vision* (see p. 98) is not in danger. It appears that the signals from the two green cones are summed together before they leave the retina; likewise, the two red signals also are summed before they leave the retina. This more complex arrangement allows us to understand why people can strongly disagree on certain colors; different proportions of wavelengths supplied by the two red cones and the two green cones result in the perception of different colors (Neitz, Neitz, & Jacobs, 1993). The challenge to researchers in this basic area of sensation and perception is to work out the details of this more complex processing system and its physiological basis.

Exciting breakthroughs also are occuring in the study of higher-level, more cognitive processes, such as visual search (Geisler & Chou, 1995). **Visual search** is the process of identifying the presence or absence of a target stimulus among a group of other, distractor

A

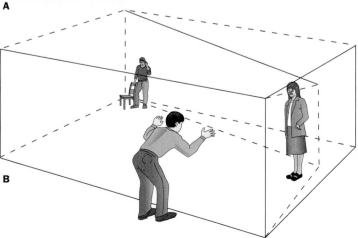

B

items. Research on this topic shows that when stimuli have high salience (that is, when they are relevant, meaningful, or distinctive), visual search is done efficiently, rapidly, and in a parallel manner. Indeed, such high-salience stimuli seem to "pop out" from the distractors. Such features as color (D'Zmura, 1991), motion (Nothdurft, 1993), brightness (Gilchrist et al., 1997), and prior experience with the target (Lubow & Kaplan, 1997; Wang, Cavanagh, & Green, 1994) help create the pop-out effect. The combination of these features (e.g., color and form [D'Zmura, Lennie, & Tiana, 1997]), however, can result in a more lengthy and difficult visual search. There are several notable applications of visual search research to real-life situations in which target stimuli must be detected from distractors. These include controlling air-traffic (Vortac et al., 1993), driving an automobile (Lajunen, Hakkarainen, & Summala, 1996), and monitoring visual displays (Liu, 1996).

Basic perception research also is playing an important role in our understanding of the family of learning problems known as *dyslexia*. For example, a recent psychophysical study has provided data showing that dyslexia is linked to abnormal neural develoment (Stein & Walsh, 1997). Moreover, children with the most common form of dyslexia, *specific reading disability*, have been shown to have a variety of perceptual difficulties. These difficulties include an impaired ability to distinguish among phonemes, or the smallest units of speech (Merzenich et al., 1996); problems with motion perception (Cornelissen et al., 1998; Eden et al., 1996); and difficulty with nonverbal auditory perception (Tallal, 1980). The more we know about dyslexia, the better we are able to confront problems associated with this learning disability.

Without question, basic perception research has provided important information and promises to yield additional real-life applications in the future. It also has the potential to tell us about social processes.

Perception Is Affected By Social Context.   Because most stimuli have physical properties that can be described precisely, it is easy to get the impression that perception is a rather automatic and mechanical process. In fact, some psychologists have held this view for years. The view is beginning to change rather dramatically, however, specifically, researchers are showing that even basic perceptual phenomena can be influenced by *social* context. Consider an intriguing research project from the University of Amsterdam, Holland (Stapel & Koomen, 1997).

Do you remember the Ebbinghaus illusion (see Figure 3-25D)? In this illusion the perceived size of the center circle is influenced by the size of the circles that surround it: When the surrounding circles are large, the center circle is seen as smaller, and vice versa. Stapel and Koomen wondered if this effect could be obtained when stimuli other than geometric figures were used. If the effect could be obtained with non-geometric figures, they then wondered if other factors influenced it. To answer these questions, they conducted two experiments. In both experiments, college students estimated the size of a human face that was surrounded by faces or other objects.

In the first experiment the target stimulus (a face) was surrounded by (a) identical faces, (b) same-gender faces, (c) different-gender faces, or (d) nonperson objects (trucks or handbags). The results showed that the magnitude of the illusion was greatest when the target stimulus was surrounded by identical stimuli. Thus the target face was seen as being largest when it was surrounded by small, identical faces. As you can see in Figure 3-27, same-gender faces produced the next largest contrast, followed by different-gender faces, and nonperson stimuli. Clearly, the type of stimulus that surrounds the target has a significant effect on your perception of the target: not all stimuli are perceptually equal.

FIGURE 3-27 Results from Stapel and Koomen's Experiment 1, showing the magnitude of the size contrast illusion as a function of physical appearance of context stimuli. Illusion magnitude is defined as the difference between the targets in two types of stimulus configurations: the target stimulus surrounded by small context stimuli versus the same target stimulus surrounded by large context stimuli.

Source: Stapel and Koomen (1997).

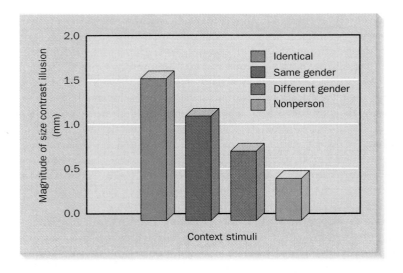

Psychological Detective

The results of this experiment suggest the operation of a general underlying principle. Spend a few minutes reviewing the results of this study, making sure to consult Figure 3-27. Collect your thoughts and then write down your impression of the general principle.

The results of Experiment 1 indicate that the greater the *similarity* between the target in the center and the surrounding stimuli, the more pronounced the illusion (the greater the perceived contrast). Stapel and Koomen refer to this effect as "similarity breeds comparability"—that is, the more similar the target and the surrounding objects, the more likely you are to compare them and experience the illusion. This general principle was given an interesting and important twist in Experiment 2.

The same stimuli from Experiment 1 were also used in Experiment 2. Some participants, however, were given a social description of the target and surrounding faces before they judged the size of the target. For example, one group was told the faces were *all* students. These social descriptions had the effect of increasing perceived similarity of the target and surrounding stimuli. Thus comparability of the stimuli was greater and the magnitude of the illusion also was increased. For example, even though the target face was female and the surrounding faces were male, when participants were told they were all students (or lawyers), the size of the illusion increased and did not differ from the illusion that occurred when the faces were identical. Thus nonphysical (social) factors can—and do—influence our basic perception of human and nonhuman objects. We encounter the influence of social context again when we discuss social psychology (Chapter 16).

Now that we have examined both standard and contemporary perceptual phenomena, we turn our attention to an area that always receives considerable media attention—paranormal phenomena.

Paranormal Phenomena

Thousands of handbills were distributed, posters were displayed, and newspaper advertisements were placed to announce the first

public appearance of a famous psychic who had spent years being tested in laboratories around the world. Extra chairs were brought in to accommodate the huge crowd that wanted to see and hear the lecture and demonstration. The psychic began by showing plants perceiving animosity or affection from people. Next he drew some geometric figures that matched those drawn by a member of the audience. Finally, from about 20 feet away and using only the power of his mind, he caused a large heavy rocking chair to move back and forth (Gordon, 1987). ***What do people believe to be the cause of such phenomena?*** ▪

According to a 1990 survey (Gallup & Newport, 1991) of more than 1,000 adult Americans, 93 percent believe in at least one *paranormal* (literally, "beyond normal") or *psychic* phenomenon, and almost half believe in five or more. Belief in such phenomena is widespread among college students. One-third of them express belief in reincarnation; a similar number believe that communication with the dead is possible. Over half believe that their dreams predict events such as the death of a family member or a natural disaster (Messer & Griggs, 1989).

Undoubtedly you have heard about **extrasensory perception (ESP)**, which refers to experiences or behaviors that occur without sensory contact—in other words, without the use of our sensory receptors. The term *ESP* is reserved for paranormal phenomena that do not involve the senses. The most frequently mentioned examples of ESP are clairvoyance, telepathy, and precognition. *Clairvoyance* (from the French for "clear seeing") is the claimed ability to "see" information from objects or events without direct contact with the senses. If you could tell us what was in a closed box that you had never seen, you might be demonstrating clairvoyance. *Telepathy* is the claimed ability to perceive the thoughts or emotions of others without the use of recognized senses. An example is Kreskin's supposed transfer of thoughts from his mind to the audience (see Chapter 1). *Precognition* is knowledge of a future event or circumstance obtained by paranormal means. *Psychokinesis* (once known as *telekinesis*) is the claimed power of the mind to influence matter directly. Because psychokinesis does not involve perception, some researchers do not consider it an example of ESP.

The term *parapsychology* is often used to refer to "the study of paranormal phenomena, which are considered to be well outside the bounds of established science" (Hines, 1988, p. 7). Some psychologists (Zusne & Jones, 1982) prefer the term *anomalistic psychology*, which describes the phenomena as apart from normal experiences but avoids any suggestion that they are unexplainable. The events and behaviors are indeed unusual, but Zusne and Jones believe they can be explained, as we will see in the following sections.

Skeptical Scientists

The study of paranormal phenomena dates from the late 1800s, when there were numerous investigations of *spirit mediums*—people who claimed that they could receive messages from the dead. Modern laboratory research on paranormal phenomena began with the work of Joseph Banks Rhine (1895–1980), who coined the term *extrasensory perception* in 1934. Rhine established a laboratory at Duke University and devoted his career to the study of parapsychology.

Many of Rhine's experiments used a deck of Zener cards, which consists of five each of the following designs: circle, cross, rectangle, star, and wavy lines. In a typical study, the participant's task was to guess the design on each

extrasensory perception (ESP)

Behaviors or experiences that cannot be explained by information received by the senses

card as an experimenter selected it from the deck. Using statistical procedures, Rhine compared each person's success with the success rate that could be expected on the basis of chance—which is 20 percent, or one in five correct. A number of participants did better than chance and seemed to defy those odds. Unfortunately, some of the best performers apparently may have had an opportunity to cheat. What's more, success rates exceeding chance may also have been due to irregularities in the cards that participants could use as clues. For example, with the right light it was sometimes possible to read the symbol through the back of a worn card.

Beginning in the 1960s, parapsychologists devised new ways to test ESP because they believed methods relying on Zener cards were not like the circumstances in which paranormal phenomena might occur in daily life. For example, these researchers believed that paranormal phenomena were associated with hypnotic, dreaming, and meditative states. The new testing method involves the study of telepathy between a sender and a receiver.

The receiver is put in a soundproof room, with halves of table tennis balls taped over the eyes and headphones placed over the ears. A red floodlight is directed toward the eyes, and white noise (a combination of many frequencies) is played through the headphones. Researchers believe that all of these efforts produce what is called the *Ganzfeld* ("total field") that might allow weak signals of paranormal phenomena to come through.

Meanwhile, a sender is put in a separate soundproof room with a randomly selected visual stimulus (such as a picture) that serves as the target for the session. The sender then concentrates on the target for 30 minutes. At the completion of a 30-minute *Ganzfeld* period, the receiver is presented with a series of stimuli (usually four) and is asked to rate the degree to which the stimuli were the target.

One report on *Ganzfeld* research led some researchers to conclude there was evidence to support ESP (Bem & Honorton, 1994); others were much more skeptical. Because people often show a bias in favor of selecting early items in a series, the researchers noted the possibility of problems in randomization that may have caused the target to be the first or second item during the judging series. We often show a bias in favor of selecting early items in a series. There is also the possibility that the experimenter inadvertently cued the receiver during the judging stage (Blackmore, 1994; Hyman, 1994).

Psychologist and magician Ray Hyman (1989) reviewed a number of studies of ESP phenomena and concluded that most contained flaws. For example, the participants may have found inconspicuous ways to divert the researcher's attention or to look for relevant information, or the researcher may not have been able to see the participants at all times. Hyman notes that he has "always been struck by the fact that the optimal conditions for the occurrence of psychic phenomena within a given setting seem to coincide with just those conditions I would require in order to pull off my deceptions" as a magician (p. 212).

The claims offered by supporters of ESP are sometimes presented in ways that make designing a definitive test difficult, if not impossible. (Recall the guidelines for evaluating claims presented in Chapter 1.) For example, when participants have done worse than expected on the basis of chance, parapsychologists have taken it as evidence of what has been termed *psi-missing*, or purposely giving the wrong answer. Such claims put critics in the position of playing a game of "heads I win, tails you lose." On the basis of such findings, James Alcock (1989) concluded that parapsychology has failed to produce scientific evidence of its validity. It is not surprising that parapsychology has been termed a "controversial science" (Broughton, 1991).

Most scientists agree that allegedly paranormal phenomena can be explained without resort to nonnormal evidence. Paranormal explanations would require that we rewrite well-established scientific principles to account for them. The law of parsimony (see Chapter 1) suggests that we look for explanations that require fewer assumptions, provided they can explain the phenomenon in question.

A Believing Public

"Evidence for paranormal claims comes in many guises," one researcher observes. "The overwhelming bulk of the evidence comes from personal experience, anecdotes, and folklore. Although psychologists and other scientists realize that such evidence is unreliable, almost every believer has become convinced because of such evidence" (Hyman, 1989, p. 15). According to Wayne Messer and Richard Griggs (1989), over 40 percent of college students reported having experienced dreams that predict the future (precognitive dreams). The accuracy of these dreams can be checked by keeping a written dream diary (Alcock, 1981). Even people who claim that their dreams "always come true" find that this is not the case when they use a dream diary to check their accuracy.

The surveys cited earlier indicate that many people believe in psychic phenomena. Why? The answer is simple: Many people have psychic experiences, or at least experiences they interpret as such. Psychologists suggest that paranormal experiences are an inevitable consequence of the way we perceive and remember information (Blackmore, 1992; Hines, 1988). Explanations that rely on some proposed "will to believe" do not enhance our understanding.

We can be fooled by our experiences in much the same way we are fooled by the visual illusions described earlier in the chapter. One illusion that encourages belief in paranormal phenomena like ESP occurs when we consider coincidences, such as dreams that come true, as evidence of a connection. We have all had an experience similar to this: "He called me today after we hadn't heard from each other in 15 years. I had been thinking about him just a few hours earlier. I know it's not a coincidence—it must be ESP." No doubt the experience is real, but its origins lie in our internal processing, not in the external world. Coincidences do happen!

Imagine sitting in front of a computer designed to generate heads or tails in a coin-tossing game. Your task is to guess whether a head or a tail will appear on the screen. How many correct guesses (called "hits") do you think you will manage in 20 trials? ESP believers guessed that they would average 7.0 hits; nonbelievers guessed an average of 9.6 hits (Blackmore & Troscianko, 1985). Moreover, the believers were more likely to decide they had influenced the computer, even when the computer was generating a random series of heads and tails. Why? As mentioned earlier, believers underestimate the number of correct guesses achieved by chance alone. People who consistently underestimate chance occurrences may look elsewhere for explanations, and paranormal explanations may look attractive. Underestimating chance underlies the tendency to interpret ordinary coincidence as psychic events and thus strengthens belief in such phenomena.

The media also affect belief in the paranormal, although they may reflect rather than cause the beliefs. Simply stated, paranormal phenomena sell—whether they be ghosts, reincarnation, or spoon bending (Feder, 1988). Newspaper stories of alleged paranormal phenomena are often reported as facts, with extensive coverage of the proponents' views and less attention to the skeptics' views (Klare, 1990).

The role of the media is especially prominent in the popularity of predictions, or precognition. One famous psychic, Jeanne Dixon, makes a living by

"The Amazing Randi." Magician James Randi has offered $10,000.00 to anyone who could demonstrate paranormal power under satisfying observing conditions.

producing a steady flow of predictions. But she is by no means alone. Mathematician John Paulos (1991) uses the label "the Jeanne Dixon effect" to describe situations in which a few correct predictions are widely heralded while thousands of false ones are ignored: "The phenomenon is quite widespread and contributes to the tendency we all have to read more significance into coincidences than is usually justified" (p. 384). Some examples of failed predictions hold great lessons for the study of supposed paranormal phenomena. For example, in early 1998 the Psychic Friends Network (a cable television station that provided psychic readings to callers) filed for bankruptcy. Apparently, none of the psychics employed by the network foresaw its impending demise.

A Final Word.   There is a wide variety of paranormal phenomena, and many people report personal experience with some of them. Scientists and believers disagree about what constitutes proof of such phenomena. Believers present anecdotes and point to laboratory research. Skeptics point to flaws in the laboratory research, and psychologists offer explanations for many of these personal experiences. Because psychologists can point to reasons that such phenonena may not occur, they cannot disprove them; the burden of proof for such extraordinary claims rests with the people making the claim.

Although the methods of studying paranormal phenomena have improved, "the goal of a conclusively convincing demonstration or a repeatable experiment has not been achieved" (Blackmore, 1994). At the beginning of this century, the magician Harry Houdini challenged mediums to produce phenomena he could not duplicate. No one succeeded. Since 1964, the magician James Randi has offered $10,000 to anyone who could demonstrate paranormal power under satisfactory observing conditions (Randi, 1987). Again, no one has succeeded. Should we therefore dismiss even the possibility of paranormal phenomena? Before we do, let's consider an important history lesson: Some phenomena that in the past were considered to be paranormal, impossible, or even fraudulent have since been verified to be real.

As late as the 1700s, most people believed that the notion of rocks falling from the sky was ridiculous. Anyone suggesting the possibility was met with jeers that might be similar to the reception often given to present-day reports of unidentified flying objects. Despite these reactions, what was once believed to be impossible is indeed possible: Meteorites do fall from the sky. Perhaps the lesson of history is twofold: First, a certain amount of humility in what we believe becomes us; second, we can be open-minded without neglecting the need for empirical evidence.

Review Summary

1. Perception is the process of organizing and making sense of the stimuli in our environment. Our motives help determine which stimuli we perceive.

2. We engage in *selective attention* because we cannot process all of the stimuli we encounter. Dichotic listening experiments study **divided attention.** With practice we can learn how to divide our attention effectively.

3. To attract our attention, stimuli should be more colorful, larger, and louder than other stimuli in our environment.

4. The ability to discriminate among shapes and figures is known as **pattern perception.** The **feature**

analysis theory states that we perceive the elements of an object and then combine them to produce our perception of the object (bottom-up processing). Other research has shown that we perceive the object before we perceive its elements (top-down processing).

5. We experience **perceptual constancies** when our perception of an object does not change, even though the retinal image changes. **Size constancy** and **shape constancy** depend on the presence of a background and our ability to judge distance.

6. The Gestalt psychologists demonstrated that we actively organize our perceptual world into meaningful groups or wholes. The **figure-ground relationship** is one of the most basic perceptual organizations. Additional principles for the grouping of stimulus elements are **proximity, similarity, good continuation and direction, inclusiveness,** and **closure.**

7. Perceptual hypotheses are inferences about the nature of the stimuli we sense. **Perceptual illusions** and ambiguous figures may cause us to develop incorrect perceptual hypotheses.

8. Parallel, as opposed to sequential, processing appears to characterize much of our perceptual activity. Parallel processing is seen in **visual search** where a target stimulus must be distinguished among a group of distractors.

9. Basic perception research has been applied to the learning disability *dyslexia.* Children suffering from *specific reading disability* have trouble distinguishing between phonemes, have problems with motion perception, and have difficulty with auditory perception.

10. Perception may be influenced by the social context. For example, the Ebbinghaus illusion is influenced by the type of social stimuli used.

11. Extrasensory perception (ESP) refers to the occurrence of experiences or behaviors in the absence of an adequate stimulus. Such occurrences are considered to be paranormal, or beyond our normal sensory abilities. Clairvoyance, telepathy, precognition, and psychokinesis are examples of paranormal phenomena. Parapsychology, or anomalistic psychology, is the study of such phenomena.

Study Break

1. What is selective attention? Why is it an important feature of the perceptual process?
2. Why is trying to listen to your roommate and the radio at the same time an example of dichotic listening, whereas watching the evening news on TV is not?
3. According to feature analysis theory, how do we identify objects that we perceive?
4. You are often accused of "jumping to a conclusion" and frequently find that you did not hear exactly what you thought you had. Which theory of perception do you seem to be following?
   a. top-down   **b.** bottom-up
   c. parallel processing   **d.** modular perspective
5. What is meant by perceptual constancy? Give examples of shape and size constancy.
6. Depth perception is difficult to explain because our perceptions are three-dimensional despite the fact that the image cast on the retina is
   a. positive.   **b.** negative.
   c. distorted.   **d.** two-dimensional.
7. What is a figure-ground relationship? What features characterize figures?
8. A student club at school invited a psychic to perform several feats during the lunch hour. One of the feats involves "physically" moving a pencil across a table without touching it. What psychic ability does this represent?
   a. clairvoyance   **b.** precognition
   c. psychokenesis   **d.** telepathy
9. Two poker players tell you that the key to their success is ESP. Bob claims that he can read minds; Ray says he knows in advance what cards he will receive. What abilities do they claim to possess?
   a. Ray claims to have precognition; Bob claims to have telepathy.
   b. Bob claims to have clairvoyance; Ray claims to have telepathy.
   c. Ray claims to have telepathy; Bob claims to have telepathy.
   d. Bob claims to have clairvoyance; Ray claims to have precognition.
10. A computer is programmed to generate a random series of symbols, either heads or tails. One at a time, ESP believers and nonbelievers take turns sitting at the computer and guessing which symbol will be flashed on the screen across fifty trials each. At what number would someone who believes in ESP be more likely to estimate the number of "hits" correctly guessed by chance?
    a. 30   **b.** 25   **c.** 18   **d.** 0

ANSWERS TO STUDY BREAKS

Pages 103–104

1. a
2. a-5, b-3, c-2, d-4, e-1, f-6
3. c
4. a
5. b
6. Purity. Your aging paint is reflecting more than just the wavelength for red; the result is a color that seems less red than it did when your car was new.
7. Our visual receptors are sensitive only to wavelengths between 380 and 760 nm.
8. The intensity of your socks, the visual stimulus, in the dark was not sufficiently strong to activate your cones; hence you were unable to perceive colors and mistook the red and green socks as being the same color.
9. b
10. b

Page 119

1. Movement of air molecules causes a sound wave. Sound waves are measured in decibels.
2. a-6, b-3, c-7, d-1, e-2, f-5, g-4
3. Sounds with lower frequencies are more difficult to hear than sounds with higher frequencies.
4. Place theory states the vibration of *certain* hair cells results in perception of a certain pitch. The frequency theory states that the frequency of neuronal firing determines the pitch that is perceived. Both theories are valid. The frequency theory works well for pitches of 1,000 Hz and below, whereas the place theory works well for pitches above 1,000 Hz.
5. d
6. The four primary tastes are sweet, sour, bitter, and salty. Our ability to sense more than four tastes appears to be based on the fact that different *patterns* of information can be sent by the four nerves for the primary tastes.
7. c
8. Gustatory (taste) stimuli are molecules in a liquid solution, whereas olfactory stimuli are molecules in the air.

9. Research in olfaction has not progressed at a rapid rate because olfaction is not considered one of the major senses *and* because the olfactory receptors are rather inaccessible and difficult to study.
10. The vestibular sense provides information about the body's orientation and movement. The somatosensory processes provide information from the skin (temperature, touch, pressure, and pain). The kinesthetic sense provides information about the location of your extremities.

Page 137

1. Selective attention involves attending to some stimuli and not others. It is important in helping organisms concentrate on the stimuli that are most relevant at the time.
2. Trying to listen to your roommate and the radio at the same time is an example of dichotic listening because there are two auditory stimuli. Watching the evening news on television involves an auditory stimulus and a visual stimulus.
3. We identify the elements or features of the object in question; then we assemble these features to create the complete, identifiable object (i.e., bottom-up processing).
4. a
5. A perceptual constancy involves the perception of a stable object, despite a changing retinal image. An example of shape constancy would be the perception that an airplane does not change shape as it rises into the sky and the retinal image of the plane changes. The fact that the same plane is seen as moving farther away, and not physically changing shape, is an example of size constancy.
6. d
7. The figure-ground relationship is the organization of the perceptual stimuli we receive into a figure and a background. Figures typically are smaller, brighter or colorful, and display motion.
8. c
9. a
10. c

ANSWER TO QUESTION

Page 122

With the appropriate cues to distance and size, the object you saw on p. 122 may be much larger than you thought it was.

CHAPTER 4

Motivation and Emotion

Chapter in Perspective

In the opening chapters we are laying the groundwork for considering the complex processes observed in animals and humans. So far we have described the methods psychologists use to answer the questions they pose; we have also showed how you can become educated consumers of information. We now consider two related topics, motivation and emotion, which together will help us further understand complex human behaviors.

The term *motivation* is derived from the Latin word *movere*, which means "to move." Motivation is concerned with the causes of behavior—that is, what "moves" organisms to behave. We begin the chapter with a discussion of theories of motivation and then talk about some specific motives. Our journey toward developing an understanding of behavior has included a discussion of our nervous system and our sensory apparatus. We now know more about how the nervous system communicates and how the brain makes sense of the environment. Evolution was the backdrop for our discussion of the nervous system in Chapter 2. We next turn to an element of our behavior that has some significant evolutionary advantages—emotions. Think of the times you have experienced positive or negative emotions. How do such experiences impart any advantages? As we explore this topic, you will see that the brain plays a crucial role in regulating emotions. Because culture can affect all forms of behavior, we explore similarities and differences in emotional expression around the world. In the last part of this chapter we see how the cognitive evaluation (appraisal) of situations affects our emotional responses. ▪

What Is Motivation

After two hours of hiking, Dan and Dana stop for a drink to quench their thirst. Later in the day they stop to eat some of the food they brought along. While sitting and relaxing, they talk about what they will do the next day, and decide to climb a mountain because "it is there." They also decide to add to their rock collection by picking up some specimens as they hike. *Why were these behaviors performed? What caused them?* ▪

Such questions are the core of the study of motivation, which has three aspects: (1) the factor or motivational state prompting the behavior, (2) the goal(s) toward which the behavior was directed, and (3) the reasons for differences in the intensity of the behavior.

Some examples are easier to explain than others. We understand why Dan and Dana drank water and why they ate. When it comes to climbing the mountain and collecting rocks, however, the explanations are not as clear.

Combining the three aspects, we define **motivation** as physiological and psychological factors that account for the arousal, direction, and persistence of behavior. Note that motivation is considered a hypothetical state. We cannot directly see or touch it; we infer it from observable behaviors. Consider two rats that have learned to engage in a behavior (pressing a lever) to receive food in their specially constructed cage. Once this behavior has been learned, what causes it to be performed again? Perhaps the sight of the cage or the lever elicits the lever-press response. Although these stimuli may influence the rats' behavior, there is another equally important factor—hunger. If the rats are hungry (a motivational state), they press the lever to obtain food (the goal).

Why does one rat make twice as many responses (and receive twice as many food pellets) as another rat? If the first rat has not been fed for 24 hours, whereas the second rat was fed 12 hours earlier, we conclude that differences in *motivational state* influenced the behavior. In other words, the first rat is hungrier. These three aspects fit together this way: The hungry rat presses the lever (behavior) to obtain food (goal); the hungrier the rat (level of motivation), the more frequent the lever presses.

Theories Of Motivation

motivation
Physiological and psychological factors that account for the arousal, direction, and persistence of behavior

Our opening vignette tells us something else about motivation: It can be complex. Why do people collect rocks? To understand this complexity, researchers have proposed several theories (Franken, 1998). One group of theories focuses on the biological factors such as hunger; a second group focuses on cognitive processes. Abraham Maslow's theory considers *both* physical and cognitive factors. The following sections examine these three approaches to motivation.

Biological Theories

Biological theories stress the importance of biological or physiological processes in determining behavior. Among these processes are unlearned behaviors that are part of an organism's repertoire from birth. When such unlearned behaviors are more complex than simple reflexes, such as the eye blink, they are called **instincts.**

Instinctive behaviors are triggered or released by specific environmental events called *releasing stimuli.* Instinctive behaviors shown by members of one species are not displayed by members of a different species. Thus instinctive behavior is unlearned, species-specific, and triggered by a releasing stimulus. For example, bats feed on moths. Bats locate objects through the use of sonar waves, which are similar to radar. The sound of the sonar waves serves as a releasing stimulus for the moths, triggering erratic flights to safety in the nearest patch of grass.

Ethology.   The *ethologist* Niko Tinbergen (1951) was interested in studying reproductive and aggressive behavior in a species of fish known as the three-spined stickleback. During the spring, physiological changes cause male sticklebacks to develop a red spot on their belly. Tinbergen determined that this red spot is a releasing stimulus.

What behavior does the red spot release? Tinbergen showed that male sticklebacks establish territories and build tunnel-like nests. When another male swims into one of these territories, the presence of the intruding male releases a characteristic threat display by the territory's "owner" (see Figure 4-1).

Do instincts also direct human behavior? The ethologists' research prompted speculation on human instincts. Robert Ardrey (1966) suggests a case for humans having an instinct to establish and defend territories. He notes a "parallel between human marriage and animal pairing" and "between human desire for a place that is one's own and the animal instinct to stake out such a private domain" (Ardrey, 1966, p. 101). We hear people discuss a "maternal instinct" and an instinct to be aggressive. Although such behaviors may be instincts in some lower animals, there is no convincing proof of it in humans. Moreover, it is difficult to rule out the influence of learning in such situations. Although attempts to explain human behavior by using the concept of instincts failed, psychologists continued and expanded their interest in the influence of biological factors on behavior (Franken, 1998).

FIGURE 4-1 The male stickleback on the right has assumed the head-down, threat posture because of the intruding male on the left.

Source: Tinbergen, 1951.

Frank and Ernest

Reprinted by permission of Tom Thaves.

instinct
Unlearned behavior that is more complex than a reflex

sociobiology
The study of the genetic and evolutionary basis of social behavior

drive
Internal motivational state created by a physiological need

homeostasis
Tendency of the body to maintain an optimum, balanced range of physiological processes

drive-reduction model
Theory that views motivated behavior as directed toward the reduction of a physiological need

Sociobiology. According to its leading proponent, Edward O. Wilson, **sociobiology** is the "systematic study of the biological basis of all (animal and human) social behavior" (1975). Sociobiologists view the primary goal of motivated behavior as ensuring that the individual's genes survive (Wilson, 1975). This view of behavior as largely instinctual results in some interesting predictions. For example, sociobiologists stress the survival of the individual rather than that of the group. When individuals survive, their genes survive and are more likely to be passed on to the next generation. Likewise, sociobiology can explain and even predict the occurrence of altruism. Both humans and animals make what appear to be unselfish sacrifices—and may even die—for others because this behavior helps perpetuate their genes. How can death perpetuate one's genes? If you die while saving a close relative, your genes survive because your relative's genetic makeup includes many of the same genes. The closer the relative, the more genes you share and the more likely the occurrence of altruistic behavior. Thus sociobiology predicts that you would be more altruistic toward your brother than toward your second cousin.

This controversial view of behavior has both supporters and opponents. One of the primary arguments against sociobiology is that it discourages social reforms (Geertz, 1980). Opponents note that if social behavior is genetically determined, there is no reason to try to improve society. Therefore, for example, the conditions of the homeless are beyond our control.

Internal States, Drives, and Drive Reduction. When John B. Watson founded behaviorism, his goal was to understand the relationships between environmental stimuli and responses. He reasoned that if we understood those relationships, we could make accurate predictions about which behavior would occur when a certain stimulus was present. According to behaviorists, an unchanging situation or stimulus should evoke the same response every time it occurs. This proposal ran into difficulty, however.

Although environmental stimuli may remain constant, behavior does not always follow suit. For example, Curt Richter (1922) found that the activity level of female rats peaked every fifth day, even though they were tested in the same apparatus. Why? Richter noticed that this increase in activity coincided with the *estrus* or sexual receptivity cycle. He concluded that the estrus cycle created an internal motivational state that influenced the rat's behavior. An internal motivational state that is created by a physiological need is known as a **drive.**

Drives can activate more than one response. If food is not freely available, a hungry rat may try other responses that have allowed it to secure food in the past. What would you do if you had no money to buy lunch? You might search your car for change. You might ask a friend for a loan, or you might check vending machines for change that people have forgotten. Motivated behavior is goal directed; the internal motivational state of hunger is prompting or driving your behaviors toward the goal of obtaining food. A variety of behaviors can be used to achieve most goals.

Clark Hull (1943, 1952) used the concept of drives to link physiological processes and behavior. Figure 4-2 illustrates how drives operate. The drive is created by a physiological need, such as lack of water. Once created, the drive can activate several responses, including learned ones such as lever pressing. The goal of these responses is to do or secure something that reduces the drive, thereby returning the body to a more normal state. This state, which may be viewed as the optimum, balanced range of physiological functions, is called **homeostasis.** Because Dan and Dana were thirsty, they drank some water; later they were hungry, so they ate. In both cases they were returning their bodies to the more balanced state of physiological functioning that existed before they were in a thirsty or hungry state. We can say that the **drive-reduction model** views motivated behavior as occurring to reduce a physiological imbalance and return the organism to homeostasis.

According to the drive-reduction theory, the strength of a particular drive determines our behavior. During a storm, people are more concerned with reaching shelter than with what they are going to eat at their next meal.

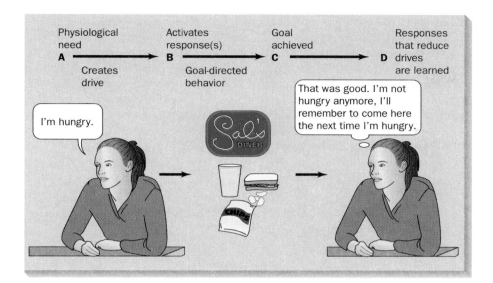

FIGURE 4-2 A drive is created by a physiological need (A). This drive activates responses (B). These responses are directed toward achieving a goal that reduces the drive by satisfying the need (C). Responses that reduce drives are learned (D).

Source: Scherer & Wallbott, 1994.

Drive reduction signals the organism that a particular need has been reduced and that behaviors designed to reduce other current drives can be engaged. Theorists like Hull view drive reduction as a necessary condition for learning; behaviors that result in drive reduction are learned. Each time a behavior results in drive reduction, the strength of the habit (or tendency) to perform that behavior increases slightly. When a behavior has been followed by drive reduction many times, the habit strength, or tendency to perform under similar situations, is very high. When you are hungry at noon, what behavior are you most likely to engage in?

The strength of each drive determines our behaviors; we seek to reduce the strongest drive first, then the next strongest. When you are caught in a blizzard at noon, it is more important to find shelter than to have lunch. Once you have reached shelter, you can deal with your hunger. After your hunger has been satisfied, you can repair your ripped parka. Because new drive states are continually created, we never completely reduce all of our drives and reach a condition of complete homeostasis.

Optimum-Level Theories. Why would monkeys press a lever for nothing more than the opportunity to watch a toy electric train (Butler & Harlow 1954)? Why would monkeys work for hours on a complicated lock that provided no reward other than opening it (Harlow, Harlow, & Meyer, 1950)? Why do humans spend hours trying to solve crossword puzzles? Drive theory might explain these behaviors in terms of the reduction of some type of *stimulus drive,* including curiosity, exploration, and manipulation. Ask yourself what you would do under the following conditions: (a) a helicopter hovers nearby, and (b) while in an art museum you see a sign that says Do Not Touch. When a stimulus drive is sufficiently strong, it elicits behaviors such as looking up at the helicopter or touching the work of art. Successful completion of these behaviors reduces the drive. Consequently, the frequency of these behaviors should increase.

Although this analysis seems to make sense, the definition, creation, and measurement of a *stimulus drive* such as curiosity is not as straightforward as the definition, creation, and measurement of the hunger drive. We

These monkeys spent hours just opening and closing the latches. Some researchers suggest that their curiosity drive is high.

can restrict food intake to create hunger, but what do we restrict to activate the curiosity drive?

Is there another way to view the behaviors just described? Consider an experiment (Haber, 1958) in which human volunteers were first adapted (became accustomed) to 68 degree water. Later they rated water that was slightly above or slightly below 68 degrees as pleasant, whereas they rated much cooler and much warmer water as unpleasant or aversive.

Psychological Detective

 Stop for a moment and think about the results of the Haber study. What information do they provide about motivated behavior? How would a drive-reduction account of motivation explain these results? Write down some possible answers before reading further.

These results suggest that we do not always seek to reduce stimulation as drive-reduction theory predicts; rather, experiencing change in stimulation is important. The 68 degree water to which volunteers were adapted was boring; a change in stimulation was pleasant. If however, the change in temperature was too great, it was perceived as unpleasant. Other instances in which stimulation may be sought include riding a roller coaster, singing in the shower, and changing radio stations to hear something different.

Organisms seem to seek an optimum level of arousal or change in stimulation. This optimum level differs from one person to another and depends on the level of stimulation to which the person has become accustomed. In general, stimulation that is too far above or below an optimum level is perceived as unpleasant. This **optimum-level theory** allows us to make interesting predictions. Because people in urban and rural areas have adapted to different levels of stimulation, they should react differently to reduced sensory experiences. (People who live in urban areas have adapted to high levels of noise and stimulation, such as incessant honking in traffic; people in rural areas have adapted to lower levels of stimulation, such as birds singing.) Sensory deprivation represents a greater change for urban individuals than for rural residents, so they should rate this change as more unpleasant. This prediction was tested by comparing the reactions of two groups of men living in Norway (Haggard, As, & Borgen, 1970). Men who lived more solitary lives on the frozen tundra were less distressed by sensory deprivation than men who lived in the urban surroundings of Oslo.

Optimum-level theory is an important addition to our list of motivational theories because it helps us understand our need for change. Some people move to the country to get away from the hectic pace of life in the big city; others move to the excitement of the big city to escape the boredom of the country. Clearly not all of our motives are innate (instinct theory) or designed to reduce needs (drive-reduction theory).

Cognitive Theories

Cognitive theories of motivation stress the processing and understanding of information. When you are hungry, you do not always eat just to reduce a drive. You make decisions about what and where you will eat. Cognitive theories view individuals as thinking about, planning, and exercising control over their behavior. The most prominent cognitive theories are cognitive-consistency theories and Maslow's hierarchy of needs.

optimum-level theory
Theory that the body functions best at a specific level of arousal, which varies from one individual to another

cognitive theories of motivation
Theories that stress the active processing of information

FIGURE 4-3 Examples of low and high levels of cognitive dissonance. Participants were instructed to select which of two gifts they would like to receive. The desirability of all gifts was rated before these selections. (A) Low level of cognitive dissonance: When one gift was low in desirability and the other was high, the choice was easy, and cognitive dissonance was low. Little change in evaluation of these two gifts occurred. (B) High level of cognitive dissonance: When *both* gifts were high in desirability, the choice was much more difficult. After the choice was made, the chosen gift was rated more positively, whereas the rejected gift was rated more negatively.

Source: Adapted from Brehm, 1956.

Cognitive-Consistency Theories. The basic premise of cognitive-consistency theories is that we are motivated to achieve a psychological state in which our beliefs and behaviors are consistent; we perceive inconsistency between beliefs and behaviors to be unpleasant (Elliot & Devine, 1994). Students who think about studying but never get around to it need to achieve consistency between their thoughts and actions. They may achieve consistency by deciding they are too tired to study. You might think of this motive as the need to achieve psychological homeostasis.

Cognitive Dissonance. Leon Festinger (1957) proposed that a psychological state known as **cognitive dissonance** (see Chapter 16) occurs when a person has two inconsistent or incompatible thoughts or cognitions. Because cognitive dissonance is an unpleasant or aversive state, we seek to reduce it and instead create *cognitive consonance*—the state in which our cognitions are compatible with one another.

An example of cognitive dissonance and its resolution is shown in Figure 4-3. The experiment involved participants who were instructed to select one of two gifts (Brehm, 1956). Before picking a gift, participants rated the desirability of the items. When they chose between a highly desirable gift and a less desirable gift, the decision was easy. The decision was more difficult when the choice was between two very desirable gifts.

Psychological Detective

Why was cognitive dissonance aroused in participants who chose between two desirable gifts? How did the participants reduce this dissonance? Write down some possible answers to these questions before reading further.

cognitive dissonance
Aversive state produced when an individual holds two incompatible thoughts or cognitions

Choosing one gift means rejecting the second. When the second gift was less desirable, the decision was quick and easy. But choosing between two equally desirable gifts created a conflict. Once such a difficult decision has been made, most of us wonder whether we made the best decision. The gift we chose may not be perfect; the rejected gift might have been better. This conflict, called *postdecisional dissonance* (Aronson & Mills, 1959), is reduced by raising one's evaluation of the chosen item and decreasing the evaluation of the rejected item. These changes in evaluation occur after the decision has been made; the two items are no longer rated as equally desirable. In this way cognitive dissonance is reduced.

Dissonance occurs in situations other than choosing between two desirable items. Here are three examples of other situations in which cognitive dissonance might occur: forced compliance, exposure to information that contradicts one's beliefs, and challenges to one's opinions (Festinger, 1957). In a forced-compliance situation, people are required to convince others that a boring task (such as adding columns of numbers) is actually exciting. The participants' appraisal of the boring task improves, and dissonance is reduced. When we are exposed to information that contradicts our beliefs, dissonance is aroused, and we are likely to seek additional information that supports our belief. For example, smokers have been bombarded by reports of the dangers of smoking. They may search for reports that support their smoking behavior and may even focus on examples of people who have smoked for decades with no apparent ill effects. Dissonance is also created when our opinions are challenged. Consider your reaction when your political beliefs are challenged. The agreement of others who hold opinions similar to yours reduces the dissonance you experience.

Incentive Theories.   Not all motives can be explained as instinctual behavior, a reduction in drive, or the resolution of cognitive dissonance. How many times have you dreamed of owning a new car? Perhaps you want a new red convertible; you save your money and one day you are driving it. What motives are involved? How would a drive-reduction theory of motivation explain your desire for the convertible? It is difficult to imagine a physiological drive that has been reduced by your car-buying behavior. Nor is it likely that the car is a releasing stimulus for instinctive behavior. Because drive-reduction and instinct theories do not explain behaviors like car buying, some theorists stress the importance of incentives or goals in motivating our behaviors.

Drive-reduction theories say that our biological drives push us toward goals. By contrast, **incentive theories** see motivated behavior as being *pulled* by the incentive or goal; the larger or more powerful the incentive, the stronger the pull. It is more compelling to argue that we are pulled by the lure of our dream car than to depend on the idea that we have a car-buying drive.

Maslow's Hierarchy of Needs

incentive theory
Theory that views behavior as motivated by the goal the organism seeks to attain

hierarchy of needs
Maslow's view that basic needs must be satisfied before higher-level needs can be satisfied

Abraham Maslow's (1970) **hierarchy of needs** combines biological and psychological aspects of motivation (see Chapter 12). According to Maslow, five categories of motivated behavior can be ordered in a hierarchial fashion along two dimensions: (1) the *type* of motivation (from innate, physiological motives to more psychological, learned motives), and (2) the *strength* of the motivation (from strongest to weakest). This arrangement of motives is shown in Figure 4-4. The strongest and most physiologically based motives involve satisfying basic or survival needs such as hunger and thirst.

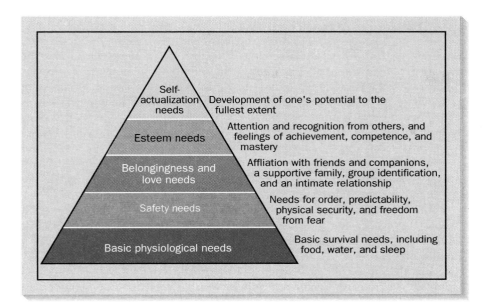

FIGURE 4-4 Maslow's hierarchy of needs. Lower needs must be satisfied before an individual can focus on needs at the next level.

According to Maslow, we attempt to satisfy stronger basic motives before trying to satisfy motives that are higher in the hierarchy. Thus basic *physiological* needs (such as hunger) must be met before safety needs (security) can be satisfied. *Safety* needs are satisfied by a stable job, insurance, and a financial reserve for emergencies. Once safety needs have been met, we can proceed to meet belongingness and love needs (such as having close relationships and friendships). Once these needs have been met, we may turn our attention to *esteem* needs.

There are two basic sources of esteem: self-esteem (competence) and the esteem we receive from others (status). If esteem needs are not met, feelings of helplessness and inferiority are likely to occur. For the few people who successfully satisfy their physiological, safety, belongingness, and esteem needs, yet another need, *self-actualization,* emerges.

Self-actualization comes from developing one's unique potential to its fullest extent. Each of us strives to become the very best (mathematician, editor, and so on) that our potential allows us to become. Because our struggle to satisfy needs that are lower in the hierarchy is a continuing one, only a small number of people achieve self-actualization. For example, Maslow believed that Thomas Jefferson and Abraham Lincoln were self-actualized.

Because people strive to satisfy successively higher needs, Maslow's theory is often characterized as a growth theory of motivation. We grow as individuals as we satisfy needs at progressively higher levels of the hierarchy, and this growth influences how we behave when we are later forced to confront lower-level needs again. For example, we might expect prisoners of war to be concerned only with their survival. Individuals who have experienced higher motives, however, may perform remarkable acts of unselfish behavior under the most terrible circumstances (Frankl, 1959). Many prisoners in Nazi concentration camps gave their food, clothing, and even their lives for others.

Critics point out that not everyone proceeds through the hierarchy as Maslow outlined. What's more, in some societies people experience difficulty in meeting their basic needs, yet they may be able to satisfy higher needs, as when a couple struggles to establish a family and to make ends meet while growing closer to each other as a result of their struggle.

self-actualization
Need to develop one's full potential

The Role of Learning

Imagine you did not have cats as pets when you were younger; however, some friends persuaded you to adopt a stray kitten. Now you are convinced this was a bad idea. Each evening, when you settle into your favorite chair to watch the evening news, the kitten launches a sneak attack. After a week of this behavior, you become tense as soon as you sit in your favorite chair. It does not matter whether the kitten is in the room. The sound of the evening news increases your anxiety. When you leave the room, you immediately feel better.

We do not have to learn to be hungry or thirsty, nor do we have to learn that food or liquid will satisfy these needs. During our lives, however, we acquire or learn many motives and goals.

Your favorite chair and the evening news have become stimuli that elicit tension and anxiety. You find these feelings of tension and anxiety unpleasant and are motivated to reduce them when they occur. This is an example of a **learned motive.**

A similar procedure and logic can be applied to the learning of goals and incentives. Many of the goals and incentives that motivate our behavior are learned and hence are termed **learned goals** or **incentives.** Consider money, diamonds, gold, and concert tickets. An infant's response to these objects will quickly convince you that they do not possess intrinsic value; we must learn their value before their acquisition is reinforcing.

Dealing With Multiple Motives

How many times did the following scene occur when you were a child? Dinnertime is an hour away; you feel as if you will die of hunger before then! You see the refrigerator and think a little ice cream before dinner would taste great. No one is around; you could get the ice cream in a heartbeat. What if you got caught? The penalty would be severe, and you have been warned on more than one occasion not to eat just before dinner. *How can this dilemma be resolved?* ▪

Both drive-reduction theory and Maslow's hierarchy of needs may make you think that people deal with only one motive at a time. A moment's reflection will convince you this is not the way the real world operates. We are frequently confronted by several motives. Psychologists (Lewin, 1938; Miller, 1944) have identified four situations involving multiple motives: *approach-approach, avoidance-avoidance, approach-avoidance,* and *multiple approach-avoidance.* In each situation, satisfying one motive leaves one or more others unsatisfied. These four situations are diagrammed in Figure 4-5.

Basic Conflicts. In *approach-approach* conflict you are confronted with two desirable goals you would like to satisfy. Satisfying one motive, however, prevents you from satisfying the second. Suppose you are trying to decide whether to spend your savings on a new car *or* a vacation. The desire for each goal is high, but your savings will pay for only one; a choice must be made. If either goal can be made a bit more attractive than the other, you will be able to make a choice and resolve the conflict (Figure 4-5A).

In an *avoidance-avoidance* conflict you must choose between two unpleasant alternatives. For example, many college students find themselves

learned motives
Motives that are learned or acquired

learned goals (or learned incentives)
Goals or incentives that are learned

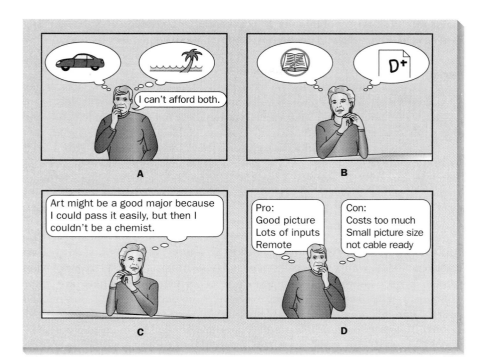

FIGURE 4-5 Dealing with several motives at the same time. (A) An approach-approach conflict. (B) An avoidance-avoidance conflict. (C) An approach-avoidance conflict. (D) A multiple approach-avoidance conflict.

faced with a choice of studying *or* not studying and failing. Because both alternatives are unpleasant, the avoidance-avoidance conflict is difficult to resolve and frequently involves procrastination. How many of your classmates put off their studying until the last minute?

Rather than dealing with two unpleasant alternatives, people caught in avoidance-avoidance situations may exhibit a third type of behavior: They may leave the situation. Rather than studying or accepting failing grades, a student may choose to withdraw from school. Thus two unpleasant alternatives are avoided (Figure 4-5B).

In an *approach-avoidance* conflict only one goal is involved. This goal, however, has both good and bad aspects. Are you willing to accept the negative

Approach-avoidance conflicts result in vacillation; one moment you feel that the decision should be yes, and the next moment that it should be no.

aspects of the goal to obtain its benefits? College students who frequently change their majors may be dealing with approach-avoidance conflict. Choosing one major involves sacrificing other choices and possibilities (Figure 4-5C).

It might seem that the approach-avoidance conflict would be easy to resolve—just make a choice and the agony will be over. Although this solution sounds simple, it is often difficult to accomplish. For example, the hungry child stands in front of the refrigerator, knowing dinner is an hour away. Some ice cream would satisfy the hunger, but what about the punishment? How could this dilemma be resolved?

In an approach-avoidance situation the positive values of the goal attract you, and the negative features of the same goal repulse you. The result is vacillation; one moment the answer is yes; the next moment it is no. Only when one motive (attraction or repulsion) becomes stronger than the other will this conflict be resolved. Often the immediate temptation of the ice cream outweighs the threat of punishment at a later time.

Multiple Approach-Avoidance: Several Goals With Good And Bad Features.   Suppose you need a new television and have decided to shop around. As you weigh the pros and cons of various brands, you are overwhelmed by indecision. Which one will you buy? Each set has good and bad features. You are caught in a multiple approach-avoidance situation.

Multiple approach-avoidance conflicts are similar to many daily experiences in which we are attracted to and repulsed by a variety of goals. By continuing to evaluate the features of the various brands, costs, and dealer reputation, you can resolve the TV set problem without much difficulty. When, however, such conflicts occur over interpersonal relationships that may have several positive and several negative factors, such as marriage or divorce, they can have serious long-lasting effects (Figure 4-5D).

Review Summary

1. Motivation   refers to physiological or psychological factors that account for the arousal, direction, and persistence of behavior. The aspects of motivation are (a) a motivational state that prompted the behavior, (b) the goal toward which the behavior is directed, and (c) reasons for variability in the intensity of the behavior.

2. Biological theories of motivation stress the importance of biological processes in the determination of motivated behavior.

3. Instincts are unlearned, species-specific behaviors that are more complex than reflexes. Instinctive behaviors are triggered by environmental events known as releasing stimuli.

4. Internal motivational states or **drives** are created by physiological needs, such as the need for food. Drives produce motivated behavior. Because drives are aversive, the goal of motivated behavior is drive reduction.

5. Behaviors that successfully reduce drives are learned. Unlike drive-reduction theories, **optimum-level theories** propose that there is a level of arousal at which organisms function best. To reach this level, the organism may actively seek added stimulation or arousal.

6. Cognitive theories of motivation stress the active processing of information. Cognitive-consistency theories stress the need to achieve a psychological state in which one's thoughts are consistent. **Cognitive dissonance** occurs when the presence of two incompatible thoughts creates an aversive state that the organism is motivated to reduce.

7. Incentive theories of motivation stress the goals toward which the organism is pulled.

8. Maslow's theory of motivation combines biological and psychological factors. Motivational needs are arranged hierarchically from basic physiological needs to **self-actualization.**

9. Learned motives and **learned goals** or **incentives** play a major role in our everyday lives. Learned incentives can reinforce the learning of new responses.

10. Several situations involving multiple motives have been identified: *approach-approach conflicts, avoidance-avoidance conflicts, approach-avoidance conflicts,* and *multiple approach-avoidance conflicts.*

Study Break

1. Describe the three general aspects of motivation?
2. Indicate which type of motivational theory (instinct, drive reduction, cognitive dissonance, incentive) is exemplified by each of the following behaviors:
   a. Birds build nests in the spring.
   b. You stay up late to finish reading an exciting novel.
   c. Although you don't like chicken, you eat your roommate's chicken leftovers because there is nothing else in the house and you haven't eaten anything the entire day.
3. You have only $100.00 remaining from your paycheck. This amount is just enough to do only two of the following:
   a. Pay your electric bill.
   b. Go to a new play that you want to see.
   c. Buy next week's groceries.
   According to Maslow, which two will you choose? Why?
4. Identify each of the following as an approach-approach, avoidance-avoidance, approach-avoidance, or multiple approach-avoidance conflict:
   a. You want to buy a new car, but the monthly payments are too high.
   b. You go to the video store with enough money to rent one movie. You cannot decide between two great new releases.
   c. "It's a dirty job, but somebody has to do it." That statement describes the condition of your apartment and the need to clean it.

Specific Motives

As part of a project for a class on advertising, Scott and Jane are collecting information on the motives they believe advertisers use to attract people to purchase products. They conclude that many advertisers gear their advertisements toward arousing the sexual motive, even in cases when the product has little to do with sexual behavior. *Why do advertisers use sexual motives to try to sell their products?* ▪

Up to this point we have concentrated on a theoretical overview of motivated behavior. These theories try to provide insight into *all* motivated behavior, without focusing on any given motive. Psychologists are interested in specific motives, as well as the big picture offered by theoretical overviews. Here we will focus on four specific motives: hunger, sex, achievement, and affiliation.

Hunger

Drive theories of motivation view hunger as a physiological need that pushes us to behave in particular ways: We eat because we must do so to survive. Incentive theories stress the attractive properties of the food we plan to consume and where we plan to eat. We could say that according to drive theories we eat to live, whereas according to incentive theories we live to eat. Regardless of which motivational theory you espouse, questions about hunger need to be answered. What are the physical signals for hunger. Where are these signals processed and translated into action?

At early explanation for hunger proposed that blood glucose (blood sugar) is an important hunger signal (Mayer, 1953). When our supply of glucose is high and the cells of the body are able to use it, hunger is low. As the blood sugar supply decreases, hunger increases. This *glucostatic theory* is helpful in explaining short-term variations in hunger.

The amount of fat the body has stored also seems to serve as a hunger signal (Teitelbaum, 1961). This *lipostatic theory* proposes that a person's

Sex is a powerful motive that advertisers frequently use to entice us to buy their products.

long-term weight fluctuates around a **set point** or normal level of body weight. When a person's weight falls below the set point, fat is withdrawn from the fat cells and a hunger signal is sent to the brain. When fat cells are full, no signal is sent. That fat stores can be monitored and kept within a rather narrow range over time supports the lipostatic theory (Friedman & Stricker, 1976).

Researchers focused on the hypothalamus as the brain structure that received hunger signals (Grossman, 1990). With rats serving as the experimental animals, researchers found that surgically removing (lesioning) two areas of the hypothalamus yielded different results. Lesions in the lateral (side) hypothalamus reduced food intake; lesions to the ventromedial (front center) hypothalamus increased food intake. Lateral hypothalamic lesions may result in starvation and death, yet removing the ventromedial hypothalamus does not create an animal that overeats until it dies. These animals become quite obese, but their weight eventually stabilizes at a new, higher level. This finding has been interpreted as evidence that the body's set point is reset for different levels of fat (Nisbett, 1972).

These areas of the hypothalamus are important in determining eating behavior, but they are part of a complex system. For example, a bundle of nerve fibers that passes close to the lateral hypothalamus is also important in regulating hunger. What's more, cholecystokinin, an intestinal hormone, appears to be another stop-eating signal (Kalat, 1995). More recently, researchers have found that the hormone, leptin, is involved in regulating body fat. What has become clear is that the regulation of hunger and body fat is a much more complex phenomenon that was originally believed (Stephen et al. 1998). We will have more to say concerning factors that influence hunger and how obesity affects our health in Chapter 15. We will also describe two eating disorders, *anorexia nervosa* and *bulimia nervosa*.

Sex

A glance at television, magazine, and newspaper advertising will convince you that sex is a powerful motive. Although sex is usually categorized as a biological motive, it differs from other biological motives such as hunger and thirst. Sexual behavior is required for survival of the species, but lengthy sexual deprivation does not lead to a person's death, as does deprivation of food and water. What's more, hunger and thirst are aversive states that we seek to reduce; by contrast, sexual arousal is a pleasurable state. Also, sexual behavior, unlike hunger and thirst, is influenced by several factors (Jones & Barlow, 1990). In this section we examine the influence of external factors, hormones, and brain mechanisms on sexual behavior.

External Factors.   In many species, sexual responsiveness in the male is linked to external cues. For example, the odor emitted by a female dog when she ovulates is an external cue for sexual advances by male dogs. Such odors, called **pheromones,** are created by chemicals that elicit a particular response in a species. Sexual pheromones do not, however, always elicit sexual behavior. For example, the odor of a strange male mouse causes pregnant female mice to abort (Parks & Bruce, 1961).

Although the existence of human pheromones has not been convincingly demonstrated, there is interesting speculation on the subject. According to researchers, the menstrual cycles of college women living in the same dormitory became synchronized during the first four months of dorm life. What's more, similar *menstrual synchrony* has been found among lesbian couples (Weller & Weller, 1992). The convergence of the menstrual cycles of women who live in close proximity to one another might be due to

set point
A range of weight that the body seems to maintain under most circumstances

pheromones
Chemical odors emitted by some animals that appear to influence the behavior of members of the same species

an as yet unidentified pheromone transmitted from one woman to another (McClintock, 1971).

Although the importance of external sexual stimuli cannot be disputed, internal factors such as hormones and brain mechanisms are also important determinants of sexual behavior.

Hormones. As we described in Chapter 2, there are two major groups of sex hormones: *androgens* (notably testosterone) and *estrogens* (notably estradiol). Although many people believe men and women have entirely different sex hormones, men and women have measurable quantities of estrogen, progesterone, and testosterone (Franken, 1998). The amounts of these hormones differ in men and women: testosterone dominates in men, estradiol in women.

Sex hormones are highly significant in directing sexual behavior in lower animals; in directing sexual behavior of humans, however, the role of hormones is less clear (Wallen, 1990). Castration may result in a decline in sexual desire in men (Money, 1980), but this operation does not end sexual activity. On the other hand, studies relating estrogen level and sexual interest have failed to detect a strong relationship between hormone level and sexual interest or activity (Abplanalp et al., 1979).

Brain Mechanisms. In addition to its involvement in determining hunger and thirst, the hypothalamus regulates sexual behavior. External signals, (such as odors, visual signals, and sounds) and internal stimuli (such as the rise and fall of estrogen levels in females) stimulate the hypothalamus to release chemicals known as *releasing factors* that cause other glands to release their hormones. In turn, these releasing factors stimulate the pituitary gland to secrete follicle-stimulating hormone (FSH) and luteinizing hormone into the bloodstream. FSH in turn stimulates ovulation in the female and sperm production in the male, whereas luteinizing hormone stimulates the ovaries to secrete estrogen and the testes to secrete testosterone. As the female's estrogen level declines at ovulation, stimulation of the hypothalamus to secrete the releasing factor is reduced. A reduction in sexually arousing external stimuli results in a decrease in the production of hypothalamic releasing factors in men and women.

Human sexual behavior—in contrast to that of many other organisms—is a function of the interplay of genetic, prenatal, and environmental factors; thus human beings are not slaves to hormone levels. We can become sexually aroused by a various stimuli, from smells to sights to fantasies. This observation accounts for some unusual sexual behaviors and arousal patterns that occur in humans but not in lower animals (see Chapter 13).

Although the factors controlling sexual behavior are complex, male sex drive is related, in part, to levels of circulating testosterone. Therefore attempts to alter aggressive, inappropriate sexual behavior such as urges to engage in sex with children (*pedophilia*) have focused on the use of medications. Antiandrogen drugs lower testosterone levels profoundly but reversibly; the drug *medroxyprogesterone acetate* (MPA or Provera) has been prescribed for aggressive sexual deviations. It is given via injection into muscle tissue from which it is slowly released into the bloodstream, where it acts to lower testosterone levels (Kufka, 1997).

The Sexual Response. Alfred Kinsey and colleagues (Kinsey, Pomeroy, & Martin, 1948; Kinsey, et al, 1953) conducted pioneering research on sexual behavior. Among other things, they found that the incidence of premarital intercourse, masturbation, and homosexuality was higher than had previously been believed.

One criticism of the Kinsey surveys was the participants were not a randomly selected group. A more recent survey updated and expanded the Kinsey surveys of several decades ago. The University of Chicago's National Opinion Research Center conducted a survey of more than 3,000 randomly selected American men and women (Laumann et al., 1994). The participation rate in this survey was quite high—80 percent of individuals contacted agreed to answer questions concerning their sexual behavior (see Table 4-1).

William Masters and Virginia Johnson (1966) conducted the first laboratory research on sexual responses. Their study of the physical changes during intercourse led to identification of four phases of the sexual response: *excitement, plateau, orgasm,* and *resolution.* Each phase is characterized by specific physiological and behavioral changes (see Figure 4-6); this pattern varies, however, from person to person and in any individual at different times and under different circumstances (Masters et al., 1994). For example, physiological responses can be sluggish as a result of high levels of alcohol, fatigue, or recuperation from previous illness.

Masters and Johnson (Masters et al., 1994) found that the sexual response is not just a genital event; in fact, many body systems are involved. For example, during sexual arousal our sensory awareness changes dramatically. The sense of touch can become magnified in intensity as sexual involvement heightens. What's more, the senses of vision and hearing are often diminished when sexual arousal is very high. These changes in sensory awareness at high levels of sexual arousal may explain why some people may be surprised to discover they have been scratched or bitten during sexual activity (Masters et al., 1994).

During the excitement phase, sexual arousal increases rapidly; heart rate, blood pressure, and respiration increase. Arousal continues to build, but at a slower rate, during the plateau phase. Orgasm occurs when sexual arousal reaches maximum intensity, with respiration, heart rate, and blood pressure increasing even further at this stage. Whereas women are capable of multiple orgasms, men rarely experience than one orgasm during an episode of sexual intercourse. During the resolution phase, physiological changes associated

---

TABLE 4-1   Results of Survey of Sexual Behavior

	DEGREE OF APPEAL TO MEN AGED 18–44 (IN %)				DEGREE OF APPEAL TO WOMEN AGED 18–44 (IN %)			
	Very	Somewhat	Not Really	Not at All	Very	Somewhat	Not Really	Not at All
Vaginal intercourse	83	12	1	4	78	18	1	3
Watching partner undress	50	43	3	4	30	51	11	9
Receiving oral sex	50	33	5	12	33	35	11	21
Giving oral sex	37	39	9	15	19	38	15	28
Active anal intercourse	5	9	13	73	—	—	—	—
Passive anal intercourse	3	8	15	75	1	4	9	87
Group sex	14	32	20	33	1	8	14	78
Same-sex partner	4	2	5	89	3	3	9	85
Sex with a stranger	5	29	25	42	1	9	11	80
Forcing someone to do something sexual	0	2	14	84	0	2	7	91
Being forced to do something sexual	0	3	13	84	0	2	6	92

Source: Laumann et al., 1994.

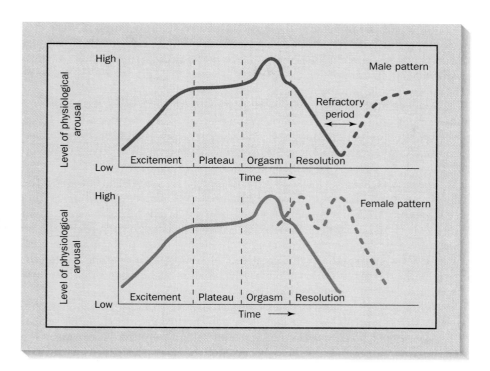

FIGURE 4-6 The four stages of the human sexual response cycle. Although men and women share the basic response cycles (excitement, plateau, orgasm, resolution) there are some differences. Following resolution, men enter a refractory period during which they are not sexually excitable. On the other hand, women may experience several orgasms before entering resolution.

Source: Masters & Johnson, 1966.

with sexual arousal gradually decline. If orgasm has not been experienced, however, the resolution phase is extended. Men become much less responsive to stimulation after orgasm; this unresponsiveness is known as the *refractory period.*

In addition to describing the stages of the human sexual response, Masters and Johnson investigated conditions that impair sexual activity. People with *sexual dysfunctions* are unable to function normally in their sexual response. Among the common sexual dysfunctions are *premature ejaculation*—the tendency to reach orgasm and ejaculate with minimal sexual stimulation before, or shortly after, penetration and before the man wants it to occur (American Psychiatric Association, 1994). In *female orgasmic disorder* a woman repeatedly experiences delayed orgasm or rarely has one at all (American Psychiatric Association, 1994).

Even though their original research project focused on the physical aspects of sexual behavior, Masters and Johnson found that many sexual dysfunctions require psychological treatment. They believe couples, not individuals, have sexual problems, therefore they emphasize treating both partners in cases of sexual dysfunction. One of their techniques, *sensate focus,* is based on the belief that sexually dysfunctional couples have lost the ability to think and feel in a sensual way as a result of stress and pressure they associate with intercourse. They need to be reacquainted with the pleasures of tactile contact. Each partner learns that being touched is pleasurable, and that exploring and caressing the partner's body can be stimulating. During the early stages of treatment, intercourse is prohibited because requiring it might increase tension.

Achievement

Most people are sure they understand what achievement is and can provide examples of achievement-related behavior, but it is difficult to define achievement precisely: "Achievement behaviors are those behaviors concerned with manipulating the environment according to rules and standards" (Hoyenga & Hoyenga, 1984, p. 374). **Achievement** consists of three components:

achievement

Manipulation of the environment according to established rules to attain a desired goal

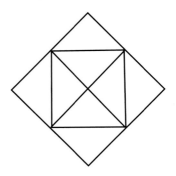

FIGURE 4-7

(1) behaviors that manipulate the environment in some manner, (2) rules for performing those behaviors, and (3) accepted performance standards against which people compete and compare their performance. Studying hard to earn good grades is an example of achievement behavior; the grades are the achievement toward which the behavior is aimed.

Achievement and competition permeate society. The prevalence of achievement-oriented behaviors has prompted theorists to propose the existence of an achievement motive. Because achievement behaviors are directed toward attaining a pleasurable award/goal or avoiding an aversive event, incentive theories are often used to explain achievement behaviors.

David McClelland (1958, 1985) and John Atkinson (1974) have used the Thematic Apperception Test (TAT) to measure levels of achievement motivation (see Chapter 12). When you take the TAT, you are asked to create a story about a series of pictures that depict people in ambiguous situations. Participants are believed to attribute their own motives to the figures in the ambiguous pictures. Participants whose stories have a great deal of achievement content are considered high in the achievement motive; participants whose stories contain little achievement content are considered low in this motive.

Whereas McClelland stresses the need to succeed, Atkinson stresses the need to avoid failure. The difference between the two needs can be illustrated by two students who earn As in the same course, but for different reasons. One student is motivated to earn the A because of the pride that comes from mastering the material. The other student earns the A to avoid the shame associated with failing or making a lower grade.

Consider an example. Chris volunteered to take part in a psychological experiment. The first task she was asked to complete was to make up a story about each of a series of pictures (TAT). After relating her stories, she was given a stack of cards with a figure (see Figure 4-7) printed on each.

Her task was to trace around the figure without retracing a line or lifting her pencil. She was told that "The probability of success on this task is 70 percent." Thus the chances of succeeding were more than two times greater than the chances of failing. After trying to trace the same diagram on several cards, however, Chris decided she did not want to experience any more failures, so she quit. She wondered how many cards were traced by the experiment's other participants.

There are numerous examples of achievement-oriented behavior every day; they include academic achievements and sports achievements. Some achievements result in recognition in the form of praise, plaques, or ribbons; for many forms of achievement the personal satisfaction is all that matters to the participants.

What does this experiment tell us about the need to achieve? Before we go any further, we should point out that the pattern used in this research, the Euler diagram, is not solvable. You cannot trace around the entire figure without retracing a line or lifting your pencil.

How was Chris's need to achieve evaluated? The content of the stories provides a measure of achievement motivation. Is achievement the only motive TAT stories measure? No, as Atkinson demonstrated; the motive to avoid failure also can be measured. Recall that Chris wondered how other participants were doing. What if there were two groups—one composed of participants high in the need to achieve and the other of participants high in the need to avoid failure? Would you predict that the response of these two groups to this unsolvable task would differ? What about after several failures? Achievement-motivated participants would be energized to continue responding in order to achieve. The participants who were motivated to avoid failure should stop tracing sooner in order to avoid further failure. When such an experiment was conducted, these were exactly the results that were obtained (Feather, 1961). Participants with a high need for achievement attempted more tracings than participants with a strong desire to avoid failure. The need to achieve is a powerful motive that influences the behavior of both children and adults, but it is more complex than many of us believe.

According to a well-known song, "People who need people are the luckiest people in the world." Stressful circumstances probably increase the need for affiliation. The opportunity to be with others would be welcome at such times.

Affiliation

Imagine that you have volunteered to participate in an experiment in which you may receive electric shocks. You find yourself sitting in the waiting room. Would you rather wait alone or with other people who are also going to participate? Research using situations like this one indicates that many of us have a need to be with others (Latané & Bidwell, 1977). The need to be with others and avoid being alone is termed **affiliation.** Like achievement motivation, the need for affiliation is measured through responses to TAT cards.

The presence of a need to affiliate was also demonstrated in an ingenious study in which sensitivity to various types of visual stimuli was evaluated (Atkinson & Walker, 1956). After an assessment of the strength of affiliation, male college students were shown a series of blurry slides for a very brief period and were then asked to identify each picture. Men who scored high in need for affiliation identified significantly more slides of faces than men who were low in need for affiliation. In other words, faces were relevant stimuli for men who had a high need for affiliation. It appears, therefore, that affiliation with others is a powerful motive in many people.

affiliation
The need to be with others and avoid being alone

Review Summary

1. According to the *glucostatic theory,* low blood sugar (glucose) levels signal hunger and high blood sugar levels signal that the organism is full. This theory accounts for short-term fluctuations in hunger. The *lipostatic the-* ory, which stresses stored fat levels, accounts for long-term fluctuations in hunger that are thought to vary around a **set point** weight or normal level.

2. Although sex is classified as a biological motive, it is different from other biological motives in important ways. Sexual behavior is influenced by external factors, brain mechanisms, and hormones.

3. Pheromones are chemicals that elicit a response in members of the same species.

4. The display of sexual behavior in lower organisms is closely tied to hormone levels in the blood. Human sexual behavior results from a complex interplay of genetic, hormonal, and psychological factors.

5. Achievement consists of behaviors that manipulate the environment, rules for those behaviors, and standards for judging performance. The need to achieve can be measured by responses to the Thematic Apperception Test (TAT).

6. Affiliation refers to the need to be with other people.

Study Break

1. In the middle of the afternoon you are hungry. You munch a candy bar and your hunger is gone. Which theory of hunger does this example illustrate. Why?

2. Damage to which of the following areas of the brain is most likely to affect an animal's hunger?
   a. frontal lobes
   b. hypothalamus
   c. hippocampus
   d. parietal lobes

3. Which of the following is an example of an androgen?
   a. estrogen
   b. testosterone
   c. provera
   d. pheromone

4. What are the stages of the Masters and Johnson sexual response cycle?

5. After years of blaming each other for their sexual problems, a couple seeks therapy. The therapist recommends sensate focus. How will the therapist explain this treatment?
   a. "Let's analyze the primary cause of your problems."
   b. "Here are changes in your diets that can increase hormone levels."
   c. "I want the two of you to spend time caressing and exploring each other's bodies and experiencing the pleasure of touch."
   d. "I want you to daydream about each other and then engage in sexual intercourse each night for at least one week."

6. Describe the three components of achievement behavior. Why is each a necessary ingredient of achievement?

The What and the Why of Emotion

Tim stands in front of the microphone to deliver a presentation. The room is not really hot; it only seems that way to Tim. As he begins to speak, a strange sensation grips his throat. He tries to clear his throat, hoping the words will pass his cotton-dry lips. He is holding the podium so tightly his hands ache. The growing restlessness in the audience is not a real threat, yet Tim acts as if it were. His heart begins to race. Tim hopes no one sees the perspiration soaking his body. The rational part of his being tells him his imagination has gotten the better of him, yet he cannot shake the dread that has taken hold of his body. ***What does Tim's experience tell us about the study of emotion?*** ■

Imagine life without emotion: There would be no joy associated with great art; vicious crimes elicit no anger or disgust. As we watch our favorite team, we would never experience the thrill of victory or the agony of defeat. Without emotion, life would be listless and colorless, like a meal in need of seasoning. But emotions do more than provide color and spice; they can actually help us survive.

Not long ago, many scientists considered emotion trivial, not worthy of study. Let poets and philosophers analyze emotions, they argued. Scientists focused on the rational part of human nature. Emotions, they argued, represent the animal, irrational side of human nature capable of disrupting rational thought. This disregard of the emotional part of human nature has changed; an expanding body of research has focused on the what, why, and how of emotions.

The common term for what Tim experienced is *stage fright,* an extreme example of emotion. Significant increases in heart rate, feelings of distress, and elevated levels of hormones related to stress occur during stage fright (Fredrikson & Gunnarsson, 1992). Tim's experience echoes what happens when we face real threats such as losing control of a car on an ice-covered road. This phenomenon can tell us how the study of emotions connects our present with the past.

Your heart pounds, your mouth is dry, and the pupils of your eyes are dilated. These physiological changes are the result of the activity of the sympathetic branch of the autonomic nervous system (see Chapter 2), which prepares us for fight or flight. We burn energy at a higher rate than normal in this state of heightened arousal, so we perspire to cool down.

Eventually the parasympathetic branch of the autonomic nervous system takes command to calm the body and return all systems to normal resting levels. We now know that spending extended periods of time in the aroused state that accompanies some emotions can have devastating effects on the body and on our health (see Chapter 15).

But what is emotion? Like many terms we use each day, *emotion* is not easy to define. Try describing what you know about the term. You decide emotion is different from rational thought; it is not the same as information acquired through our senses or the same as information stored in memory. Emotions do not last long (Ekman, 1992a). When the subjective feelings associated with emotions stretch on for a period of time, we call them *moods.*

The word *emotion* is derived from the Latin word meaning "to move"; the prefix *e-* means "away." As the preceding vignette reveals, **emotion** can be described as a state that has several components. Thus our definition of emotion encompasses physiological indices such as changes in heart rate, overt behaviors such as facial expressions and tightly grabbing the podium, and elicitors of emotion such as concern about giving a talk. But a key question remains: What is the purpose of our emotions?

Relating Emotions and Behavior

In his book *The Expression of Emotion in Man and Animals,* Charles Darwin (1872/1965) suggested that emotional expressions have a biological basis. According to Darwin, animals and humans share similar facial and postural expressions that have common origins and functions. For example, both humans and higher primates seem to frown; most animals bare their teeth during anger or rage. Later we will see that the facial expressions humans display during emotional reactions are quite similar across cultures.

But why would such expressions be passed down from species to species and across generations? Darwin argued that these expressions communicate information about events that help organisms adapt. For example, the ability to

emotion
Physiological changes and conscious feelings of pleasantness or unpleasantness, aroused by external and internal stimuli, that lead to behavioral reactions

communicate fear of a predator is important to prey animals; emotions can also communicate a willingness to fight an enemy.

Emotions can increase the chances of survival by providing a readiness for actions such as fighting predators that have helped us survive throughout our evolutionary history (Plutchik, 1993). For example, fear quickly drives blood to the large muscles, making it easier to run; surprise raises our eyebrows so the eyes widen to collect more information. Some gestures associated with emotional reactions may have descended from our human ancestors who did not have a well-developed spoken language; they may have relied on nonverbal communication to promote survival. In summary, emotions warn us of danger, guide us to what is desirable and satisfying, and convey our intentions to others.

The Physiological Components of Emotions

Fourteen-year-old Matilda Crabtree planned to go to her friend's house to spend the night; her parents would go to visit friends. When her parents returned at about 1 A.M., they heard noises and suspected a burglar. They did not know Matilda and her friend had returned home and were making noises as they hid in a closet ready to spring a practical joke. Bobby Crabtree picked up his pistol and walked toward Matilda's bedroom. As he entered the room, Matilda jumped out of the closet and yelled, "Boo!" A shot rang out; a bullet lodged in Matilda's neck. She died 12 hours later. In an instant, fear mobilized Bobby for actions meant to protect himself and his family. Evolution had prepared him for a rapid response. In the split second he will remember the rest of his life, he did not have time to recognize his daughter's voice (Nossiter, 1994). ***What brain circuits are involved when we react instantly to events such as our suspicions that a burglar might be in the house?*** ■

If asked to provide a definition of emotion, many people offer examples of physiological activity. Why? Our body's generalized arousal is often the most perceptible sign of emotion to the person as well as to observers. You can imagine what was going on in Bobby Crabtree's body as he made his way to confront a suspected burglar. That arousal motivates or moves us toward a course of action that may help us survive. At times, however, emotions can be disruptive, as any student who has suffered test anxiety knows.

The First Theories

Given the prominence of the physiological components of emotion, it is not surprising that the first theoretical explanations of emotion focused on this component. We will turn to these explanations next.

The James-Lange Theory.   In 1884, William James (1842–1910) proposed a theory that was independently proposed in 1885 by a Danish physi-

Matilda Crabtree was shot by her father, who mistook her for a burglar. Her father's action was an instantaneous reaction to a perceived threat that left him no time to determine that the person he was shooting was his own daughter.

ologist, Carl Lange (1834-1900); it is referred to as the **James-Lange theory** of emotion.

Before the James-Lange theory, it was assumed that an internal or external stimulus triggers an emotion and the emotion in turn produces physiological changes. The sequence stimulus → emotion → physiological changes is called the **commonsense view of emotions.** The James-Lange theory reversed the commonsense notion that perception of an emotional event caused a physiological state that we label as emotion.

James believed the order of the last two events should be reversed: stimulus → physiological changes → emotion. Thus the James-Lange theory states that physiological changes occur *before* the emotion and actually create the feelings we label as an emotion. For example, the feelings you experience while listening to "The Star-Spangled Banner" are a result of physiological changes. The sounds of the music are received by the sensory cortex, which activates the sympathetic branch of the autonomic nervous system. Then impulses from the sympathetic division are sent to the cortex to create the appropriate emotional feeling. In other words, the physiological changes precede and produce the emotion: We feel sorry because we cry, afraid because we tremble, and not the other way around.

Today scientists know a lot more than James and Lange did about the physiological changes associated with emotion. As a result, they have several criticisms of the James-Lange theory. For example, sometimes we experience emotion before the body's systems have had time to react, as the case of Bobby Crabtree reveals. What's more, if emotion is equivalent to general physiological arousal, how do we sort out differences between fear and love, excitement and joy, and so on? There is no doubt that physiological arousal plays a part in emotion, but it does not necessarily *cause* emotion.

TABLE 4-2 **Percentage of Participants Reporting Physiological Changes with Specific Emotions**

EMOTION	CHANGE REPORTED	PERCENTAGE OF PARTICIPANTS
Anger		
	Faster heartbeat	50
	Tensed muscles	43
	Faster breathing	37
Fear		
	Faster heartbeat	65
	Tensed muscles	52
	Faster breathing	47
Joy		
	Increased temperature	63
	Faster heartbeat	40
	Decreased muscle tension	10
Sadness		
	Crying/sobbing	55
	Faster heartbeat	27
	Tensed muscles	27
Shame		
	Increased temperature	40
	Faster heartbeat	35
	Lump in throat	24

Source: Scherer & Wallbott, 1994.

James-Lange theory
Theory that physiological changes precede and cause emotions

commonsense view of emotions
View that emotions precede and cause bodily changes

Cannon-Bard theory
Theory that the thalamus relays information simultaneously to the cortex and to the sympathetic nervous system, causing emotional feelings and physiological changes to occur at the same time

The Cannon-Bard Theory.   The James-Lange theory was criticized by Walter Cannon and his colleague Philip Bard, who argued that the physiological changes that occur during emotional episodes are not diverse or complex enough to account for the range of emotions we experience. What's more, Cannon (1927) believed that many physiological changes, especially those involving hormones, are too slow to serve as the basis of emotions. The fear you feel when an airplane pilot announces "a problem with our engines" is instantaneous and precedes physiological changes such as the release and influence of epinephrine (adrenaline). This sequence of reactions contradicts the James-Lange theory.

Cannon and Bard created a theory of emotions that focuses on the thalamus, a relay point for sensory information traveling to the cerebral cortex (see Chapter 2). According to the **Cannon-Bard theory,** information from incoming emotional stimuli is relayed simultaneously to the cortex and to the internal organs of the sympathetic system. Thus our emotional feelings do not depend on the occurrence of bodily changes (James-Lange theory), nor do the bodily changes result from a prior emotional feeling (commonsense view). The feeling and physiological components of an emotion occur simultaneously.

The Cannon-Bard theory may reconcile differences between the commonsense view and the James-Lange theory, but it is not perfect. Karl Lashley (1938) noted that the Cannon-Bard theory places heavy responsibility on the thalamus. For this theory to be correct, the thalamus must be capable of interpreting and relaying the full range of both physiological and emotional reactions. It is doubtful the thalamus is this versatile. Although the thalamus does relay information, it appears that other areas of the brain are required to interpret this information fully.

Physiological Differences among Emotions

Although it may be difficult to distinguish one emotion from another solely on the basis of physiological changes, some differences offer important cues. People cry when they are sad, sometimes when they are happy, but almost never when they are angry (Scherer & Wallbott, 1994). Klaus Scherer and

FIGURE 4-8 Physiological (autonomic nervous system) differences in emotions. Heart rate increases in anger, fear, sadness, and happiness; finger temperature increases in anger and decreases with fear.

Source: Levenson, Ekman, & Friesen, 1990.

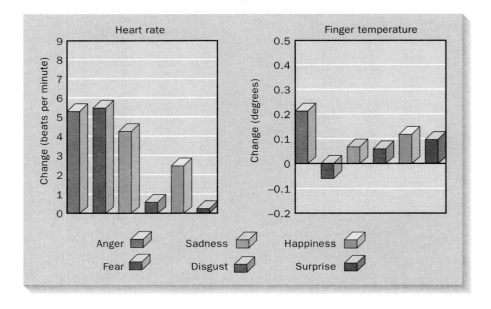

Harald Wallbott (1994) asked almost 3,000 students from 37 countries to describe various emotional experiences. They found widespread agreement about the primary physiological sensations that occurred (see Table 4-2).

Establishing the physiological specificity of emotions does not require that every emotion have a unique physiological signature, only that some emotions differ from others in consistent ways. Finding such evidence has not been easy because emotions generally last a few seconds (Edwards, 1998). What's more, researchers must find a way to elicit an emotion before it can be studied. In one method (Ekman, Levenson, & Friesen, 1983; Levenson, Ekman, & Friesen, 1990), students and actors followed instructions to create facial expressions. Look in the mirror and follow these instructions: "Pull your eyebrows down and together. Raise your upper eyelid. Push your lower lip up and press your lips together" (Levenson, Ekman, & Friesen, 1990, p. 365). You have just portrayed anger. The researchers coached participants to help them comply with the instructions; then they recorded autonomic nervous system indices while participants held the expressions.

Evidence based on this type of research suggests that there are several differences among emotions. One consistent finding is the tendency for anger to be associated with cardiovascular changes (Cacioppo et al., 1993). Heart rate increases with anger, fear, and sadness; it decreases with disgust (see Figure 4-8). Compared with anger, fear is associated with lower blood pressure, cooler surface temperature, and less blood flow to the body's periphery (Levenson, 1992, 1994). Our language reflects some physiological differences: We use phrases such as "blood boiling" when discussing anger, the description "white with fear" reflects the cooler skin temperature associated with this emotion.

Robert Levenson and his colleagues (1992) traveled to western Sumatra, in Indonesia, to study the Minangkabau, an agrarian society that has a female-oriented socioeconomic organization. This society emphasizes external aspects of emotion and has a strong prohibition against public displays of anger. Levenson and his colleagues found evidence of similarities and differences between the Minangkabau and Americans. Young male participants who posed the facial expressions of emotions had the same physiological distinctions found among Americans. This finding suggests that the posed faces cause autonomic changes that are prewired and largely culture-free. The sensory signals from facial muscles did not, however, produce the same subjective feelings that they did in Americans.

We can observe physiological patterns in certain emotions such as embarrassment, which can lead to *blushing*. Imagine this scenario: You are in a room with other people waiting to listen to a tape of *your* singing. As the tones come over the sound system, capillaries in your cheeks, ears, and neck, (the "blush region") fill with blood, raising the temperature and making your skin hot (Shearn et al., 1990). Blushing in darker-skinned people can appear as a further darkening of the skin, or it may not be observable by others at all (Leary et al., 1992).

Although Darwin (1872/1965) thought this peculiar human expression served no function, blushing seems to communicate the message that the person values the positive regard of others. Almost all people have blushed, although those who are especially concerned with how others evaluate them are more prone to blush (Leary & Meadows, 1991; Leary et al., 1992). Threats to one's public image, such as being made to look incompetent, are strong elicitors of blushing; simply being the center of attention, however, may be sufficient to cause some people to blush. Blushing can also occur when we are praised or told we appear to be blushing (Leary et al., 1992).

We know that particular physiological changes occur with certain emotions in people everywhere, from Baltimore to Borneo (Mesquita & Fridja, 1992). But some differences in physiological reactions may result from cultural influences. For example, in the United States and other countries that encourage individuality, emotional expressions tend to last longer and are more intense (see the discussion of individualism and collectivism in Chapter 16).

The importance of physiological aspects of emotion leads to questions about which parts of the nervous system are significant. Clearly the brain has a key role to play in emotions, as it does in most of our behaviors.

The Role of the Brain

The size and development of the cortex separates more developed animals such as primates from lower animals. The cortex (called the rational part of the brain) grew from what could be called the emotional part of the brain. Our sophisticated cortex provides a range of emotions and more options following emotional arousal. A rabbit being chased by a predator has few responses to its deathly fear—either it runs faster than ever, or it loses the race and its life. By contrast, the highly evolved human cortex offers several options: run, fight, dial 911, and so on (Goleman, 1995).

The *limbic system* (see Chapter 2) may be the most important part of the brain in emotions. This network of structures located beneath the cortex includes the *amygdala,* the *hippocampus,* and the *hypothalamus.* Although the hippocampus had been viewed as involved in emotion, its primary role appears to be in processing memories. The amygdala—a small, almond-shaped structure—receives sensory inputs and is essential in evaluating the emotional meaning of stimuli. Research has substantiated the importance of the amygdala to emotions; for example, animals whose amygdala is removed lack fear and rage responses.

Joseph LeDoux (1996) has found that the amygdala reacts instantly to sensory inputs and can trigger the fight-or-flight response while the cortex is evaluating inputs and making a decision. This sequence of brain activity helps us understand Bobby Crabtree's rapid response in firing his gun.

LeDoux focused on fear because it occurs across cultures and in many species and plays a key role in some psychological disorders (see Chapter 13). Using rats as his experimental animals, LeDoux played a tone and applied a brief electric shock to the rat's feet (see Chapter 6).

Psychological Detective

Think of yourself as one of LeDoux's rats. Each time you hear a tone, you also receive a mild electric shock to your foot. How would this experience change your behavior? Write down your answer before reading further.

Later when the tone was sounded again (without the accompanying electrical shock), the animals froze, and their blood pressure and heart rates increased. The rats seemed to have learned to fear the tone.

LeDoux used electrodes to trace nerve impulses that carried information about the sound from the ear to the thalamus. From the thalamus, the information sped to the cortex, where it was evaluated; then the impulse went to the amygdala. The pathway from the thalamus to the sensory cortex to the amygdala involves several neural links that add time to the process.

There was a second route followed by the signal carrying information about the tone—straight from ear to thalamus to amygdala (see Figure 4-9). But why would two routes, one cortical and one subcortical, carry the same information? The shorter (subcortical) route conserves time, which permits emotional responses to begin in the amygdala before we completely recognize

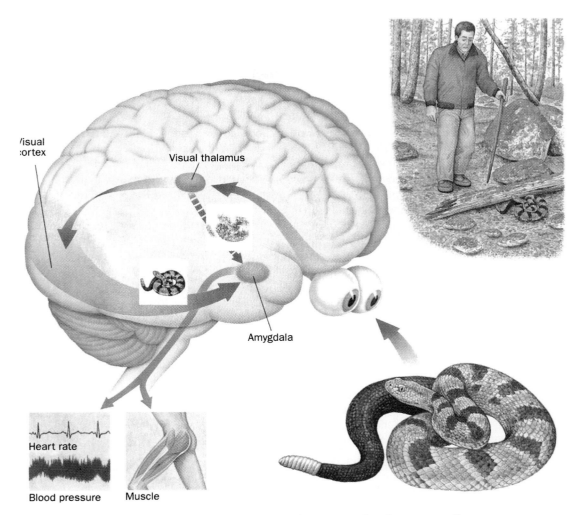

FIGURE 4-9 Cortical and subcortical paths of information related to potentially fear-inducing stimuli. Information about a visual stimulus first travels to the thalamus, which passes the information directly to the amygdala (red). This rapid transmission provides a quick response to potential danger (green). The thalamus also sends the information to the visual cortex, where greater perceptual sophistication and added time lead to a determination that there is a snake on the path (blue). Relaying this determination to the amygdala leads to increases in heart rate and blood pressure and muscle contraction. If, however, the cortex had determined that the object is not a snake, the message to the amygdala would reduce the fear response.

Source: LeDoux, 1994, p. 56.

what we are reacting to or what we are feeling (LeDoux, 1994). As LeDoux explains, "Failing to respond to danger is more costly than responding inappropriately to a benign stimulus" (p. 56).

Researchers continue to discover information on the amygdala's role in emotions. For example, human participants who were taught to associate a visual cue with shock exhibited increased blood flow to the amygdala when they saw the cue later. In other research, patients with a damaged amygdala rated faces with negative expressions to be as trustworthy as faces with positive expressions (Mlot, 1998).

The Brain's Hemispheres and Emotions.   Clearly subcortical areas are involved in fear, but the entire brain plays a role in emotion. Physicians, clinical neuropsychologists, and family members of people who have suffered brain damage have noted that right hemisphere damage often leaves victims emotionally indifferent. These observations are consistent with research on brain activity during emotional expressions. Stroke patients with right-hemisphere damage have trouble expressing emotion and perceiving emotional signals from others. These people may understand the statement "I am angry" but fail to detect the speaker's tone of voice or angry facial expression. Patients with right-hemisphere disease or damage have more difficulty than patients with left-hemisphere damage in processing facial expressions or emotionally charged speech. Recall that the right hemisphere is specialized for perceiving emotion from facial expressions (see Chapter 2).

When normal people report negative emotions such as fear or disgust, there is increased activity in their right hemisphere; the left hemisphere is more activated during positive emotions such as happiness (Davidson, 1993; Ekman, Davidson, & Friesen, 1990). Richard Davidson (1993) has proposed that the frontal regions of the left and right hemispheres are specialized for approach and withdrawal processes, respectively.

Lack of Emotion.   Although we think all humans share and express emotions, some people have difficulty in expressing their emotions and understanding the emotions of others (McDonald & Prkachin, 1990). As a result, these people find it difficult to maintain relationships; their lack of emotional responsiveness often infuriates their partners. This emotional difficulty, called *alexithymia,* is derived from Latin: *a* (without words), *lex* (word), and *thymia* (feeling). Thus, the word refers to a deficiency characterized by having no words to describe feelings (Linden, Wen, & Paulhus, 1995). Consider the following case:

> Gary, a successful 35-year-old surgeon, is articulate and reflective when discussing art and science. By contrast, he has difficulty speaking about his emotions and is unresponsive to the emotions exhibited by others. After he married Ellen, she was often angry with him, although he rarely understood why. She urged him to begin psychotherapy. During a group therapy session, he said, "I don't naturally express my emotions" and was relieved to hear that others had similar problems. When someone described him as too intellectual, he smiled in agreement. Gary described his difficulty with emotion: "I have no strong feelings, either positive or negative." (Swiller, 1988)

People with alexithymia lack self-awareness; they rarely cry, are described as colorless and bland, and are not able to discriminate among different emotions. They are often at a complete loss to know what others around them feel. These people tend to be men who come from families that did not permit the free and open expression of feelings. What's more, their families provided little positive communication and few models for expressing emotions (Berenbaum & James, 1994).

Although alexithymia is not an officially recognized psychiatric or psychological diagnosis, interest in this condition has grown because it is associated with physical symptoms, drug problems, and stress-related disorders (Bach et al., 1994; Taylor, 1994).

The Opponent-Process Theory.   Did you ever wonder why depression may follow a joyous event or why guilt follows on the heels of careless abandon or why satisfaction occurs after completing a nagging job? Richard Solomon's (1980, 1982) **opponent-process theory** of emotion (not to be confused with the opponent-process theory of color vision discussed in Chapter 3) states that once a particular emotional reaction has been activated, the brain tries to achieve homeostasis by initiating the opposite reaction. For example, if the initial emotional state is pleasant,

opponent-process theory
Theory that following an emotional response, the brain initiates the opposite reaction in an attempt to achieve homeostasis

the second emotional state is unpleasant. To simplify the discussion, Solomon calls the first emotion the "A process" and the second, or opposing, emotion the "B process." The following example illustrates these processes.

"There is no way that someone could convince me to sky-dive!" Those were your thoughts before your friend persuaded you to try it. The fear you felt just before and during that first jump was almost unbearable (A process). Once you were safely on the ground, the feelings of fear were replaced by a feeling of elation (B process). Perhaps the experience was not so bad. A dozen jumps later, the intense fear has been replaced by mild anxiety, and the elation you experience after the jump has increased dramatically. What can we learn about emotion from this sequence?

Solomon's opponent-process theory makes two interesting predictions concerning the effects of repeated emotional experiences. The A process should decrease in strength, and the B process should increase in strength. The more sky dives you make, the less terrified you should be, and the more you should enjoy the experience (see Figure 4-10). These effects, once again, show the importance of the brain and the entire nervous system in understanding emotional responses.

Evaluating the Lie Detector

What a boost it would be to police if we could attach electrodes to a suspect, ask questions, monitor physiological indices, and determine if the person tried to be deceptive. The premise of lie detection is this: A specific physiological change tells us that a person has been deceptive.

You may be surprised to learn that the device we call a *lie detector* does not actually detect lies. What we call a lie detector is really a **polygraph** (literally, "many writings"), an electronic device that simultaneously senses and makes records of several physiological indices, including blood pressure, heart rate, respiration, and *galvanic skin response* (GSR)—changes in the skin's ability to conduct electrical current that are associated with levels of perspiration.

Although most state and federal courts prohibit testimony based on lie detectors (Saxe, 1994), police often use them to clear suspects, to verify witness statements, or to find new leads. Polygraphs were used frequently in the past in preemployment screenings and to uncover employee theft; now

polygraph
An electronic device (often called a lie detector) that senses and records changes in several physiological indices including blood pressure, heart rate, respiration, and galvanic skin response

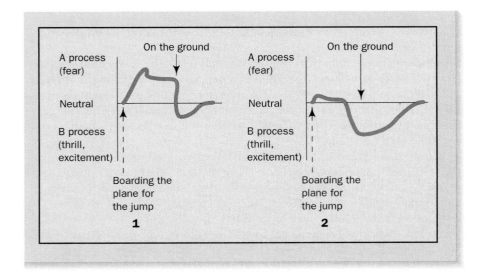

FIGURE 4-10 (1) Your initial sky dive is a terrifying experience (A process). Only after you are safely on the ground do you feel the thrill and excitement (B process) of having made a successful jump. (2) After several successful sky dives, the fear (A process) is much less, and the anticipation of the thrill and excitement (B process) is stronger and occurs earlier.

Administration of a polygraph test typically involves the use of electrodes to measure several physiological indicators thought to be related to deception.

FIGURE 4-11 A record of a polygraph test. Most polygraph methods involve comparing an individual's physiological arousal to different questions. For example, a participant would not be expected to exhibit much physiological arousal when asked, "Is your name John Donald?" If the person had stolen an expensive camera, polygraph examiners expect to see physiological arousal to the question, "Did you steal a camera?"

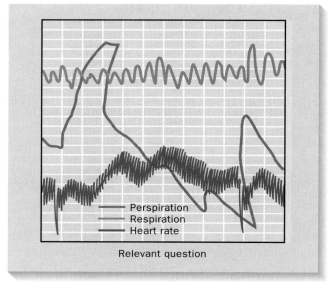

the *Employee Polygraph Protection Act of 1988* prohibits most employment-related uses.

One method of administering a polygraph test—the *guilty knowledge test* (GKT)— was designed to reveal whether a person has specific information relevant to a crime (see Figure 4-11). The questions focus on pertinent details of the crime that only the guilty party and the police know. Thus only the guilty person is expected to react strongly to the relevant details of the crime (Rosenfeld, 1995).

Because polygraph tests measure physiological responses, efforts to modify these responses can affect test accuracy. The methods used to alter physiological responses—called *countermeasures*—include drugs, *physical methods* (such as biting the tongue), and *mental methods* (such as counting backward by sevens). In one study, half the guilty people defeated the polygraph test (were judged innocent) by using physical or mental countermeasures when questions were asked (Honts, Raskin, & Kircher, 1994). The use of countermeasures is a serious—perhaps insurmountable—problem for examiners because it is difficult to detect.

Psychological Detective

 Imagine you have been "hooked up" to a polygraph. An examiner walks into the room and requests that you answer all questions truthfully. What physiological changes might occur as you answer the questions? Why do you think these changes would occur?

Polygraph tests have been viewed as an invasion of privacy and criticized on ethical, legal, and scientific grounds. Perhaps the most compelling criticism is that the basic premise is faulty: "If there were a specific lie response, then modern psychophysiological techniques would probably allow us to detect it and the dream of a genuine lie detector would be a reality" (Lykken, 1981, p. 51). The physiological changes thought to reveal deception could, however, result from anxiety about being interrogated, anger at being asked to take the test, or fear from pondering the consequences of "failing" the test. You might react in any of these ways if you were "hooked up" to a polygraph. In short, we cannot measure deception directly (Ford, 1996; Iacono, & Lykken, 1997).

The most common error in using a polygraph is identifying an innocent person as not telling the truth, called a *false positive* (Lykken, 1981). Such errors can occur at a rate as high as 50 percent (Kleinmuntz & Szucko, 1984). Thus efforts to identify guilty persons inevitably identify some honest people as deceptive (Saxe, 1991).

We have seen that physiological components of emotion are important in describing our own emotions and the emotional reactions we perceive in others. Unfortunately, focus on physiological components has led to the controversial lie detector. As we will see, we must consider other components of emotions to develop a more complete picture.

Review Summary

1. Emotion is the awareness of a feeling elicited in response to an environmental stimulus, accompanied by physiological changes and certain behaviors.

2. Darwin proposed that emotions may be innate behaviors, passed on genetically, that help organisms adapt to their environments.

3. The **commonsense view of emotions** states the sequence of events in emotional responding is emotional stimulus → emotion → physiological changes.

4. The **James-Lange theory** states physiological changes precede and actually create emotions. The sequence of events in emotional responding is emotional stimulus → physiological changes → emotion.

5. The **Cannon-Bard theory** stresses the role of the thalamus in simultaneously relaying emotional input to the cortex and sympathetic system.

6. There are some physiological differences among the emotions such as increased heart rate in anger.

Blushing is elicited by a number of circumstances that usually involve concern about how others evaluate the person.

7. *Alexithymia* is a marked inability to experience and express emotions.

8. The **opponent-process theory** states that an initial emotional reaction is followed by the opposite reaction in an attempt to produce homeostasis. With repeated experiences, the initial reaction gradually diminishes while the second reaction gains strength.

9. The **polygraph** records physiological indices that proponents view as indicating deception. Physiological changes can, however, result from anxiety, anger, or fear. Failure to recognize possible causes of arousal can lead to *false positive* errors—incorrectly identifying people as being deceptive.

Study Break

1. What is Darwin's view on the functions of emotions in animals and human beings?
2. Give an example of the type of evidence Darwin used to support his view of the functions of emotion.
3. You are walking in the forest and see a bear. What happens as this point according to the James-Lange theory?
   a. Physiological changes followed by fear
   b. Fear followed by physiological changes
   c. Physiological changes and fear simultaneously
   d. Physiological changes and context appraisal followed by fear
4. According to LeDoux's research, which part of the brain plays an especially important role in learning a fear reaction?
   a. amygdala
   b. cerebellum
   c. hypothalamus
   d. corpus callosum
5. How do researchers elicit emotional reactions in research designed to study physiological changes associated with different emotions?
6. What pattern of brain activity is most likely to occur while a person is experiencing happiness?
   a. Elevated activation in the cerebellum
   b. Elevated activation in the hippocampus
   c. Elevated activation in the left hemisphere
   d. Elevated activation in the right hemisphere
7. Which of the following is most characteristic of a person who is described as exhibiting alexithymia?
   a. is in a constant state of fear
   b. has difficulty finding words to discuss emotions
   c. reacts very strongly with anger to any provocation
   d. is adept at decoding emotion from voice only
8. What is the literal meaning of the word *polygraph*?
   a. lie detector
   b. many writings
   c. deception recorder
   d. physiological detector

The Expressive Components of Emotions

For a research project, you are asked to look at photographs of facial expressions and select the emotion exhibited from a list. The task is easy, and you finish quickly. As you leave, you ask the researcher about the purpose of the research. She says you participated in a study of the universality of emotional expressions. *Are the same emotional expressions recognized around the world?* ■

The face is a like a bulletin board. How would you know a friend is afraid, angry, or happy? Consistent with evolutionary theory, the face plays an important role in communicating emotion to others, so it is not surprising that a great deal of research has focused on two related questions: Are the same emotions recognized around the world, and how many emotions exist?

Universal Elements in the Facial Expression of Emotion

Evidence for the universal occurrence of facial expressions of emotion comes from several sources. Observations of the emotional expressions of infants during the first months of life show that even infants born blind and deaf display the same facial expressions in similar situations (Galati, Scherer, & Ricci-Bihi, 1997). For example, one emotion observed in babies is disgust. This expression may have evolved from sensory experiences that kept animals from eating spoiled food (identified from an offensive smell).

TABLE 4-3 **Percent Agreement across Cultures in Recognizing Basic Emotions**

	HAPPINESS	SURPRISE	SADNESS	FEAR	DISGUST	ANGER
Germany	93	87	83	86	61	71
Italy	97	92	81	82	89	72
Japan	90	94	87	65	60	67
Sumatra	69	78	91	70	70	70
Turkey	87	90	76	76	74	79
United States	95	92	92	84	86	81

Source: Ekman et al., 1987.

Eventually disgust came under some voluntary control; facial expressions of disgust now occur as responses to circumstances that have less to do with the taste of foods and a lot to do with reactions to moral offenses, foul language, or poor hygiene (Rozin, Lowery, & Ebert, 1994).

Paul Ekman and his associates (1987) asked thousands of people around the world to play a game of "name that emotion" (see Table 4-3). They concluded that people from Western and Eastern literate cultures, including Germany, Japan, and the United States, associate similar emotions with certain facial expressions. In fact, even people from an isolated preliterate culture in New Guinea readily identified photographs of various emotions, although they exhibited some difficulty distinguishing fear from surprise (Ekman, 1994b; Izard, 1994). These people could not have learned the meanings of facial expressions through media exposure. The researchers reversed the design and found that the people of New Guinea posed facial expressions that were understandable to Western observers.

No one has found people who smile when they are disgusted or frown when overjoyed. These findings support the notion that we are genetically wired to express different emotions. "It makes sense that there should be similarities across cultures. Human beings belong to the same species: our brains, our bodies, our autonomic nervous systems, our hormones, and our sense organs are similarly constructed" (Ellsworth, 1994, p. 25).

How Many Emotions Are There? The negative emotions—including anger, disgust, and fear—seem to have distinctive facial signals. By contrast, the facial expressions of positive emotions are more blurred. Why? From an evolutionary perspective, it is probably sufficient to know that an emotion is positive without knowing the specific emotion.

There are at least six emotions recognized everywhere: anger, disgust, fear, happiness, sadness, and surprise. Agreement is highest for facial expressions of happiness. There is some disagreement about the universality of other emotions such as contempt, guilt, interest, and shame (Ekman, 1992a; Matsumoto, 1992), and as we will see later, some models of emotion suggest that there are more than six primary emotions.

The labels we use to describe emotions are a shorthand for a number of processes and responses: physiological changes, facial expressions, appraisal of the preceding event, memories, and expectations. What's more, distinctions blur easily, making it difficult to agree on the specific label for an emotion. When does impatience become anger? Within each of the basic emotions, related facial expressions share core properties; thus they can be viewed as

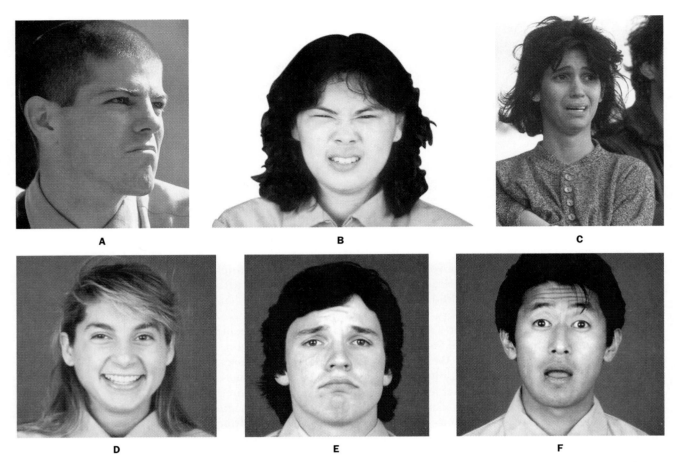

Facial expressions of six basic emotions. Each emotion involves a blueprint of movements of several sets of muscles: the brow and forehead; eyes, eyelids, and root of the nose; and the lower face.

A. Anger: Eyes have a penetrating stare; vertical crease in the brow; lids are tensed; lips are pressed together or opened and pushed forward.

B. Disgust: Raised cheeks, wrinkled nose; lower lip either pulled up or lowered and slightly protruding; upper lip is raised; lower eyelid is pushed up, and brows are lowered.

C. Fear: Eyebrows are raised and drawn together; wrinkles in the middle of the forehead; eyes are open and tense; mouth is open; lips may be drawn back tightly.

D. Happiness: Raised cheeks; raised corners of the mouth and crow's feet (wrinkles from the outer corner of the eyes); teeth sometimes are exposed.

E. Sadness: Uplifted inner corner of the eyebrows; lowered upper eyelids; raised corners of the upper eyelid; downturned lips.

F. Surprise: Raised brow; the eyes are open wide; dropped jaw; wrinkled forehead; open mouth.

variations within a family reflecting the level of intensity (arousal) of an emotion, whether the emotion is controlled, whether it is simulated or spontaneous, and the specifics of events that provoked the emotion (Ekman, 1993). For example, there is a questioning surprise and a dumbfounded surprise. The intensity of anger is conveyed in 60 facial expressions, which range from minor annoyance to uncontrollable rage.

Robert Plutchik (1980) has developed a visual vocabulary that allows him to talk about and compare emotions. He proposes eight basic emotions: acceptance, anger, anticipation, disgust, fear, joy, sadness, and surprise.

"HERE ARE THE SIX PRIMARY EMOTIONS RECOGNIZED AROUND THE WORLD."

"RESEARCHERS HAVE RECENTLY DISCOVERED A NEW EMOTION...."

These primary emotions can be viewed as polar opposites, and each emotion exists in varying degrees of intensity. Plutchik uses the primary emotions as building blocks that can be combined to create more complex emotions just as primary colors are combined to form different hues. The result is Plutchik's *Emotion Solid*—a three-dimensional structure consisting of eight groupings of primary emotions arranged in tiers representing degrees of intensity and purity.

Each color in Figure 4-12 (p. 176) represents a different emotion; anger is presented as red, terror as green. Notice that each color is brightest at the top of the figure; the brighter the color, the more intense the emotion. If you are so angry that you are throwing things against the wall and screaming, you are in a rage, which would be at the top of the anger section. If someone just cut in front of you in line at the supermarket and you are not in a hurry, you might be merely annoyed. The emotions at the top level exist in pure form only; those at lower levels can be combined to create other feelings. For example, combining fear and surprise yields awe; hostility is a blend of anger and disgust. Opposites such as fear and anger may not blend at all; a person experiencing both may feel pulled in two directions at once.

The Facial Feedback Hypothesis. Recall the emphasis Darwin placed on facial expressions of emotions. The **facial feedback hypothesis** is a direct extension of Darwin's (1872/1965) view that the intensity of an emotion is strengthened when it is accompanied by muscular activity and weakened when it is not accompanied by such activity (Cacioppo, Bush, & Tassinary, 1992; Izard, 1990). The facial feedback hypothesis states that feedback from facial expression affects emotional expression and behavior.

Darwin based his views on speculation and conjecture. How could a researcher demonstrate that facial features can influence our emotions?

Psychological Detective

 Suppose you have volunteered to be a participant in an experiment on motor activity. You are sitting with a pencil clenched in between your teeth. A few minutes ago, your task was to cross out some letters. Now you are judging how funny each of a series of cartoons is. This task does not seem to have much to do with motor ability; humor is more of an emotional response. How does holding a pencil in your teeth relate to the facial feedback hypothesis? Think about this question, analyze the situation, and write down some answers before reading further.

facial feedback hypothesis
Hypothesis that making a certain facial expression will produce the corresponding emotion

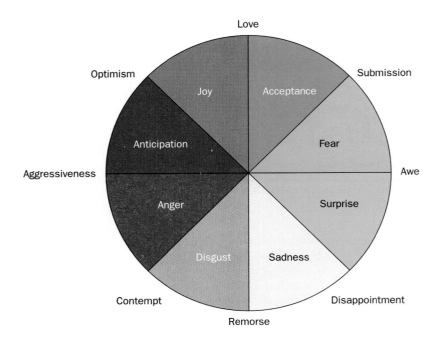

FIGURE 4-12 (A) The eight basic human emotions and some combinations, according to Robert Plutchik.
(B) Changes in intensity can modify each of Plutchik's eight basic emotions.

Source: Plutchik, 1980.

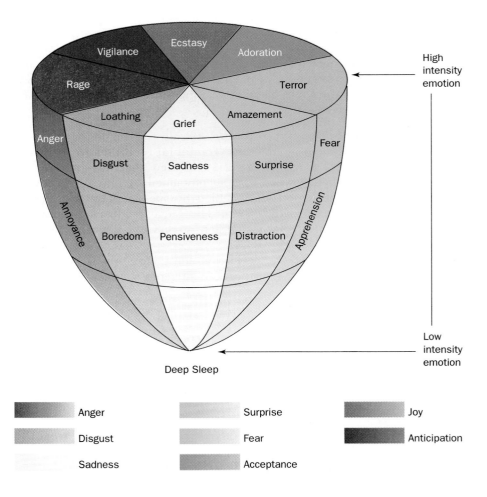

College students were told they were going to participate in a study of psychomotor ability "using parts of their body that they would normally not use for such tasks" (Strack, Martin, & Stepper, 1988, p. 770). The students held a pencil in their mouth and then engaged in tasks that required writing. One group held their pencils with their lips, which prevented use of the muscles involved in smiling. A second group of students held the pencils in their teeth, which allowed them to use those muscles.

The dependent variable (see Chapter 1) was students' ratings of the funniness of a series of *Far Side* cartoons. If the facial feedback hypothesis is correct, students who held pencils in their teeth and could smile should have rated the cartoons as funnier than those who held pencils in their lips and could not smile. The results confirmed this prediction: The same group of cartoons was rated as funnier by the participants who held the pencils with their teeth than by those who held the pencils with their lips.

A second study confirmed and extended this finding (Martin, Harlow, & Strack, 1992). Participants who held their faces in an expression of happiness while they read a story rated the story more positively than those who had angry faces while reading the story. The level of arousal also influenced the intensity of the emotion: Participants who had exercised for 90 seconds before reading the story had stronger emotions than participants who had not exercised. There are two versions of this theory. One says that manipulating facial muscles brings forth emotional experiences in all of its aspects. The other says that the feedback from the facial muscles affects the emotion's intensity.

Display Rules: The Effects of Culture

EVEN IF CERTAIN EMOTIONS ARE UNIVERSAL, WE MUST RECOGNIZE THAT CULTURE can influence their expression. Some differences in emotional expression can be accounted for by **display rules**—cultural norms that tell us which emotions to display, to whom, and when (Ekman, 1993). Which emotions we display depends on the situation and who is present. For example, only the really brave or independently wealthy fail to smile in reaction to a joke told by the boss. These requirements or expectations can lead us to exhibit emotions we may not actually feel or to fail to exhibit emotions we do feel.

Paul Ekman showed a stress-inducing film of surgery to male college students in Tokyo, Japan, and Berkeley, California (Ekman & Friesen, 1971). At first the participants watched the film while alone; later a scientist (dressed in a lab coat) entered the room and sat down while the participants watched the film. Videotapes recorded by a hidden camera revealed that students of both countries exhibited similar distressed expressions when they were alone. In addition, they reported similar feelings and had similar physiological responses. When talking to the researcher, however, the Japanese students remained composed, whereas the American students openly displayed their feelings. Why did the two groups behave differently? Compared with Americans, the Japanese are more sensitive to status differences (Barnlund, 1989); their display rules discourage them from displaying negative emotions in the presence of individuals of higher status. Thus they expressed the same emotions as the Americans when they were alone, but they did not exhibit those emotions when the scientist was present (Matsumoto, 1994b).

Cultural & Diversity Perspective

display rules
Culturally specific rules for which emotions to display, to whom, and when they can be displayed

Other examples of display rules abound. For example, the Utku Eskimos strongly condemn feelings of anger, and certain Arab groups view a man's failure to respond with anger as dishonorable (Ellsworth, 1994). Display rules also influence the perceptions of emotions in others. For example, compared with Americans, Japanese people perceive less intense emotions whether viewing faces of Americans or Japanese (Matsumoto & Ekman, 1989).

Smiling.   Smiling is a social act; we rarely smile when we are alone (Provine, 1997). It is such a prominent social signal that we can recognize a smile at 300 feet away (Blum, 1998). Smiles can reflect enjoyment resulting from amusement, pleasure, praise, or relief. We also smile, however, when we are not experiencing true enjoyment: A "false smile" is made deliberately to convince another that enjoyment is occurring; a "masking smile" conceals negative emotion; a "miserable smile" acknowledges a willingness to tolerate unpleasant circumstances (Ekman, Davidson, & Friesen, 1990). Thus at times the universal facial expression of happiness can be deceiving.

Psychological Detective

Think of a time you have smiled when you were not experiencing enjoyment. How might that smile differ from smiles of true enjoyment? Give this question some thought, and write down your answer before you read further.

FIGURE 4-13 Two major muscle groups are involved in a smile. The genuine or Duchenne smile of enjoyment involves the orbicularis oculi muscles, which wrap around the eyes and crinkle the outer corner of the eyes. The zygomatic muscles run from the cheekbone to the corner of the mouth, and pull the lips upward.

Source: Martini, 1992.

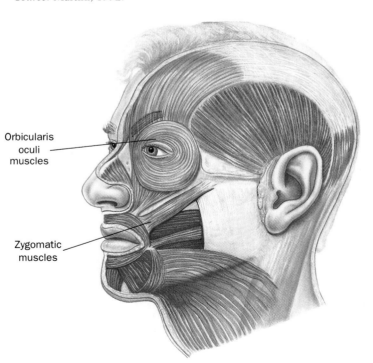

Orbicularis oculi muscles

Zygomatic muscles

A French physician, Guillaume Duchenne de Boulogne (1806–1875), suggested that genuine smiles of enjoyment result from contraction of two facial muscle groups (see Figure 4-13): the *zygomatic muscles* and the *orbicularis oculi muscles*. Although at least 18 different smiles can be identified (e.g., cruel, false, and polite smiles), only the *Duchenne smile* reveals true enjoyment. Duchenne noticed when people put on a phony smile, they smile with their cheeks, not their eyes. Why? The *orbicularis oculi* (which wraps around the eye) is not under voluntary control, so smiles of faked enjoyment do not activate this muscle. Now you understand why you have difficulty smiling naturally when photographers ask you to "Say cheese" (Damasio, 1994). The zygomatic muscles pull up the lip corners toward the cheekbone. The orbicularis oculi muscles pull skin above and below the eye toward the eyeball, resulting in these changes in appearance (see Figure 4-14): The cheeks are pulled up, the skin below the eye may bag or bulge, the lower eyelid moves up, and wrinkles known as crows' feet may appear at the outer corner of the eye socket (Frank & Ekman, 1993). Duchenne smiles last longer than faked smiles; their occurrence is related to ratings of enjoyment, whereas the occurrence of other smiles is not (Ekman, Friesen, & O'Sullivan, 1988).

FIGURE 4-14 Paul Ekman demonstrates the difference between a faked smile and a genuine (*Duchenne*) smile of enjoyment. Can you tell the difference? One key to differentiating a genuine smile from a faked smile is to observe the area near the eyes. Crow's feet appear with a genuine smile (*right*).

Source: Michael Klauseman/NYT Pictures.

Nonverbal Communication

Imagine spending an hour among people who speak another language. You might be surprised that you can learn a lot about people even if you do not speak their language. What's more, you would find it almost impossible *not* to communicate. For example, your quizzical facial expression right now sends a message that you are experiencing doubt. When we communicate by using body movements, gestures, and facial expressions rather than words, we are using **nonverbal communication.**

Tone of voice and posture convey information that is different from what we verbalize. Someone who claims to be fine but is sobbing is viewed differently from when he or she is smiling. Consider the word *no*. It can be a simple, unemotional response to a question. If it is uttered while you are stomping your foot and pounding the table, however, the meaning becomes "Absolutely not!" Add a rising inflection, and it is converted into a question. A crooked smile and a slight hand wave alters the meaning to disbelief (Ruchlis, 1990). Thus nonverbal cues can overshadow the literal meaning of the words we use (Archer & Akert, 1984).

Body Language. In addition to facial expressions, we communicate messages about our feelings through gaze, gestures, posture, and walk. The following examples can convey emotion: the "high five," handshakes, and putting a hand on a person's shoulder. We will look briefly at several types of body language: emblems, illustrators, regulators, and adaptors.

Emblems are nonverbal gestures and movements that have one- or two-word translations (see Figure 4-15); they are also called *symbolic gestures* (Rime & Schiaratura, 1991). We use emblems intentionally to communicate a specific meaning (Richmond & McCroskey, 1995). Nod your head and most people know you mean "yes." There is general agreement on emblems for "I warn you" and "It's cold" (Kleinke, 1986), although emblems may not have the same meaning across cultures (Ekman, Friesen, & Bear, 1984).

Ask a restaurant server in southern Italy for something not on the menu and the likely response is not a side-to-side head shake but a quick upward head toss often accompanied by a "tsskk" sound. Winston Churchill, prime minister of Great Britain during World War II, used the "V for victory" (palm forward). Change the gesture to the palm-back position, however, and it becomes a gross insult (Morris, 1994).

Nonverbal cues like the stance and expression of this police officer can arouse specific emotions.

nonverbal communication
Communication that involves movements, gestures, and facial expressions

Former British Prime Minister Winston Churchill's famous "V for victory" sign can take on very different meanings if the position of the hand is reversed.

paralanguage
Communication that involves aspects of speech such as rate of talking and tone of voice, but not the words used

Illustrators are nonverbal gestures or movements made while speaking that accent or emphasize words. Unlike emblems, however, they do not communicate specific meanings. Illustrators such as waving your arms or pounding a table may enhance your words, but they do not stand alone (Ekman, Friesen, & Bear, 1984). We use illustrators to clarify verbal statements or a point by drawing a picture or pointing. Illustrators also communicate intensity of emotion: Active gestures indicate strong intensity, whereas gestures such as shrugging indicate weak emotional involvement.

Regulators are actions such as eye contact and head nods that coordinate the flow of communication among two or more people. They are used to begin conversations and to signal when a listener is ready to speak and a speaker is ready to listen. The most common regulator for initiating an interaction is the handshake.

Adaptors (or *manipulators*) are movements or objects manipulated for a purpose; we use these when we find ourselves in a particular mood or situation. They include what we do with our bodies (scratching, grooming) or with objects (doodling, fiddling with a pencil or pen). Adaptors have no specific meaning, although they generally increase when people become uncomfortable (Ekman, Friesen, & Bear, 1984).

Paralanguage. A great deal of nonverbal communication occurs by way of vocal expression such as tone of voice, rate of speech, pauses, sighs, loudness, emphasis, and even silence. Silence, for example, frequently accompanies sadness, shame, guilt, fear, and disgust (Scherer & Wallbott, 1994). **Paralanguage** involves communication above and beyond the specific spoken words. As Richard Weaver (1993) explains, "It is not what you say, it is *how* you say it. And the *how* is conveyed by paralanguage" (p. 269).

Emotions are often associated with marked shifts in tone of voice. The frequency (pitch; see Chapter 3) of vocalizations increases in many emotions. Although emotions presented at similar levels of arousal (intensity) cannot be

FIGURE 4-15 Gestures that have specific meanings are called emblems; the meaning of these gestures may vary from culture to culture.

Sources: Ekman, Friesen, & Bear, 1984; Morris, 1994.

"I am impatient." Frequently occurs when we have been kept waiting or when we are impatient because something is not happening. Considered a symbolic form of "running away," this emblem might be associated with the urge to get up and go. In evolutionary terms, our hands were once our front feet. Rhythmical tapping of the foot has the same meaning. The use of these gestures is widespread.

"Shame on you!" One forefinger is rubbed up and down the other, which symbolizes friction. Used in North America.

"Everything is fine", or "good." The ring gesture displayed with the thumb and forefinger tips has been known for about 2,000 years. It is used throughout North America and Europe. In Germany, Greece, Turkey, the Middle East, and parts of South America, it symbolizes an orifice and can be a sneering insult. In Belgium and France, the ring symbolizes a zero, indicating that an individual or an object is worthless. In parts of southern Italy, it is a vulgar expression for rectum. In Japan, the ring is a symbol for a coin, and the gesture is usually asking for money or commenting on the cost of something.

"No good." The thumb is jerked downward several times or may be held in an inverted position. Originated in ancient Rome to represent the stabbing of a defeated gladiator. When the audience wanted the man to be killed, they thrust their thumbs downward as if plunging a sword into his body. Its use is widespread.

distinguished from one another, utterances associated with various emotions are usually presented at different intensity levels. These differences allow us to recognize different emotions from the voice alone at better than chance levels. Sadness and anger are the easiest emotions to recognize, followed by fear (Pittam & Scherer, 1993).

Gender Effects

A frequently asked questions about emotion is, Do men and women differ in their emotional reactions or their ability to detect (decode) emotions in others? Robert Rosenthal and his colleagues (1979) developed the *Profile of Nonverbal Sensitivity (PONS)* to measure the ability to read emotional cues. The *Interpersonal Perception Test (IPT)* consists of 30 brief videotaped scenes used to evaluate and teach about forms of communication. For example, one scene shows a man telling two versions of his life: a true version and a fabricated one. Viewers are asked to determine which version is the lie and which the truth (Costanzo & Archer, 1989, 1991). Across ages, cultures, and stimulus persons, studies using tests such as these show that women are more accurate than men in decoding emotion from nonverbal cues offered by the face, body, and voice (Hall, 1984). Objective observations support the common stereotype that, compared with men, women exhibit a greater degree of facial expressivity of positive and negative emotions except anger (Brody & Hall, 1993; Kring & Gordon, 1998; Grossman & Wood, 1993).

One possible explanation for these differences is that women are expected to be nurturing and are often the primary caregivers in the family and workplace (e.g., nurse, teacher). These roles and occupations require sensitivity to others' needs and emotional expressions; men's typical roles are less likely to emphasize emotional responsiveness (Brody & Hall, 1993; Grossman & Wood, 1993). There are also differences in infancy and preschool years: A greater variety of emotions are displayed to, and discussed with, infant and preschool girls than boys (Brody & Hall, 1993).

Researchers have also examined facial muscle differences in men and women exposed to slides of positive and negative stimuli. Women exhibit a higher level of facial muscle movement than men, which suggests that the self-reports on emotional responsiveness are accurate. These differences occurred when the participants were given no clear instructions concerning the appropriate emotional response; thus participants probably relied on their knowledge of the typical roles that men and women engage in. When participants were given instructions that associated either an increase or a decrease in emotional responsiveness with psychological adjustment, there were no differences between men and women.

Neuroscientists have also addressed questions about differences between men and women in judging emotions from facial expressions (Gur et al., 1995). Volunteers judged whether the face of a man or a woman showed happiness or sadness. When judging facial expressions of happiness, men and women were almost infallible. The results were different, however, when they judged sad faces. Women correctly identified a sad face 90 percent of the time whether presented by a man or a woman; in contrast, men recognized sadness on the faces of men 90 percent of the time (same as the women) but were only 70 percent correct when judging sadness on women's faces. The findings make sense in evolutionary terms; men would need to be especially vigilant about men's faces, lest they miss early hints that they were about to be attacked (Begley, 1995).

Review Summary

1. There is strong evidence for universal recognition of at least six basic emotions: anger, disgust, fear, happiness, sadness, and surprise.

2. Robert Plutchik has offered a model of how emotions can be combined to yield blends that differ in intensity.

3. The **facial feedback hypothesis** contends that feedback from facial muscles affects our experience of emotion.

4. **Display rules** are culturally specific prescriptions that tell us which emotions to display, to whom, and when. Such rules account for some cross-cultural differences in the expression of emotion.

5. A real smile of enjoyment, the *Duchenne smile,* involves activation of muscles that are not activated during faked smiles.

6. **Nonverbal communication** involves communication through body language, movements, and gestures. There are four major categories of body language: *emblems, illustrators, regulators,* and *adaptors.* The meaning of certain gestures varies with the culture.

7. **Paralanguage** involves communication through tone of voice, rate of speech, pauses, sighs, and loudness.

8. Compared with men, women report more emotional experiences and greater comfort with emotions. One possible explanation is that women's roles and occupations require greater sensitivity to the emotional expressions in others.

Study Break

1. Which emotion is recognized most easily across cultures?
   a. fear
   b. anger
   c. disgust
   d. happiness
2. Describe the key elements of Plutchik's model of emotions.
3. Which of the following is the best indication that a person who is smiling is experiencing true enjoyment?
   a. crow's feet   **b.** raised eyebrows
   c. right-hemisphere   **d.** increased blood flow
       activation   to the amygdala

4. You are taking part in a fun experiment—you get to watch comedy movies. In which condition will you find the movies funniest?
   a. You hold a pencil in your lips.
   b. You hold a pencil in your teeth.
   c. You wrinkle your nose while watching the movies.
   d. You wrinkle your forehead while watching the movies.
5. Give an example of each category of body language: emblems, regulators, adaptors, and illustrators.

The Cognitive Components of Emotions

Being a parent is a tough job. Make no mistake: Marie and Joe's teenager is well behaved, respectful, and earns good grades. In their state a person can obtain a driver's license at age 16, which Marie and Joe insist is too young. On a typical summer night, their daughter is out with friends. Marie and Joe hold a vigil for her safe return. As the family curfew approaches, they pace as several thoughts run through their minds. They are not sure what they are feeling. Is it anger, or is it fear? When their teenager arrives home safely, they feel relief. Does that mean that they were anxious, fearful, or what? ***How do we determine which emotions we are experiencing?*** ■

Among the situations that can elicit emotional responses are interpersonal actions and natural events such as thunder. But does the event itself lead to emotional responses? Does our language play a role in emotion? And how does our interpretation of an event influence our emotions? These are some of the topics we explore as we continue our study of emotions.

The Language of Emotion

The words we use to describe our experiences are important. Cultures and languages vary in the number of terms they use to describe emotion. English has a larger word pool than other languages. More than 2,000 English words describe emotions, compared with 1,500 words in Dutch, 750 in Taiwanese, 230 in Malay, and 7 among the Chewong, a society of hunter-gatherers living in the rain forest of Malaysia (Russell, 1991).

Some differences in the words used to describe emotions are worthy of note. For example, the Japanese translation for the English word *depression, yuutsu,* does not capture the English meaning. How do researchers know this? They asked people in different cultures to provide free associations to the words under investigation (Russell & Sato, 1995).

Some English words describe categories of emotion that have no equivalents in other languages; other languages have emotion words with no equivalents in English. For example, in English we distinguish *apprehension, horror,* and *terror* as degrees of fear. In contrast, the Australian aboriginal language uses one word, *gurakadj* (Russell, 1991). The English language distinction between *shame* and *embarrassment* is not made in Japanese. Although the Tahitians have 46 words for types of anger (English has *annoyance, rage, fury,* and so forth), they have no concept of sadness. Of course, the fact that a language has no word for an emotion does not mean that the emotion does not occur in that culture, only that the emotion is not represented by a single term (Ekman, 1993).

There is no English word for certain emotions found elsewhere; the German word *schadenfreude* (literally, "harm joy") refers to the pleasurable feelings one person derives from another person's misfortune. The Japanese word *ijirashii* refers to feelings associated with seeing someone praiseworthy overcoming an obstacle (Russell, 1991). The Japanese word *amae* literally means sweet dependency, and specifies an interdependent relationship involving the expectation of acceptance and care by others (Matsumoto, 1996). The importance of *amae* to the people of Japan exemplifies how emotional life is shaped by culture. In community-oriented cultures like Japan, emotions focus not on the individual's needs and abilities but on feelings that emphasize the links among people.

The Schachter and Singer Appraisal Model.   These language differences suggest that how we think about events may affect emotional experiences. Along similar lines, Stanley Schachter and Jerome Singer (1962) proposed a theory that stresses physiological processes and the evaluation of context as determinants of emotion. According to Schachter and Singer, physiological arousal is an *undifferentiated* state that can be given a number of labels. The labels we use to describe our emotions depend on our immediate environment and what is on our mind at the particular moment.

How could you test this theory's predictions? Creating a context in which a specific emotion is experienced seems easy enough. People could interact with a confederate of the experimenter who pretends to be experiencing a particular emotion such as euphoria (happiness). The confederate's behavior creates a context that suggests an interpretation of the events. We need to find some way to create the physiological changes in each test participant.

The emotion this person is feeling is clear; however, we are not sure what led to this particular emotional reaction. If the same situation occurred to another person, the response may have been quite different depending on how the situation was appraised.

Injections of epinephrine (adrenaline), a substance that increases heart rate and creates generalized arousal (sympathetic activation), were used to create physiological changes similar to those experienced during a genuine emotional reaction. To disguise the drug effects, participants in the experimental groups were told they were receiving a vitamin supplement called Suproxin, which would produce no noticeable effects. Then each of the participants was put in a room with a confederate who acted either euphoric or very angry. The control participants who were told what physiological effects would occur did not experience these emotions.

Because the participants in the experimental group could not attribute their physiological arousal to any external causes, they attributed it to the presence of an emotional reaction. When asked what type of emotion they were experiencing, the individuals who had interacted with the happy confederate said they were happy; those who interacted with an angry confederate reported being angry. Thus the context in which an emotion is experienced plays a role in deciding which emotion is felt.

Other Appraisal Theories of Emotion. In the 1960s, several psychologists developed similar theories to suggest that emotions result from the way we interpret or appraise our environment (Ellsworth, 1994; Roseman et al., 1995). These *appraisal* theories elaborate Schachter and Singer's claim that differences in emotion result from differences in how perceivers interpret their environment. If people interpret their environment differently, they will experience different emotions. For example, a specific situation does not produce shame; a person's interpretation of an event produces shame (Lewis, 1993a). Sorrow is different from anger because people see the situation differently. What separates appraisal theories from Schachter and Singer's efforts is these theories' attempt to define the kinds of interpretation that contribute to different emotions (Ellsworth, 1994; Lazarus, 1994).

Similar emotions appear in most cultures because events that occur are similar, as are appraisals of those events (Lazarus, 1994). Moreover, observers distinguish which emotion someone is experiencing not so much from the expression as from knowledge of which emotions are likely to occur in a given situation. Different cultures emphasize or deemphasize certain emotions, however. Suppose two people from different cultures have experienced a failure in school. In one culture, it is not desirable to blame failure on lack of effort. In the other culture, it is not desirable to blame failure on a lack of ability. In the first case, to suggest that failure is due to lack of effort can lead to shame or anger. In the second case, such an explanation has little or no emotional spinoff; lack of effort might even provide a socially acceptable excuse for failure. Thus cultural values that define what is offensive or threatening shape the appraisal of events and the emotions experienced (Lazarus, 1994).

Psychologist Robert Zajonc (1980) has argued, in contrast, that emotion does not even require prior cognition; the two are basically separate. This approach does make some sense from an evolutionary perspective because emotions preceded a cognitive response in evolution; therefore we do not need cognitive appraisal in order to experience some emotional reactions. One of the best examples of emotion without cognition is the rapid fear response that we discussed earlier in this chapter.

The Development of Emotion

Emotions in infancy range from general distress to pleasure. Joyful expression emerges as infants smile and appear to show excitement and happiness when confronted with familiar events such as the faces of people they know. Sadness emerges at about 3 months in connection with the withdrawal of positive stimulus events (Lewis, 1993a).

Early on, children learn that emotional expression is more than making faces and sounds; it requires timing, an understanding of context, and knowledge of the audience receiving the communication. By the age of 2, most toddlers have begun to work this out. For example, a child who is hurt while playing and begins to cry may stop and look around to find someone to hear the cries. Determined to find an audience for the emotional expression, the child walks closer to the house, spots Mom or Dad within earshot, and begins to cry in earnest.

Young children are better at identifying the feelings appropriate to a particular situation when they feel close or have ties to it. For example, they are more likely to remember and recognize basic emotional reactions on television programs when humans are involved than when puppets or cartoon characters are used. Among the possible reasons for this finding is that human faces and gestures may be more understandable than the expressions of cartoon or puppet characters (Hayes & Casey, 1992).

At approximately 3 years of age, the emotions a child experiences become highly differentiated (Lewis, 1993a). What accounts for this major change? The answer is that the child develops some fairly sophisticated cognitive abilities that set the stage for a new set of emotions. The child has acquired a sense of self-awareness, a set of standards, an understanding of what constitutes success or failure, and the ability to evaluate his or her behavior as compared with the standards. These abilities are the basis for the self-conscious emotions— the negative emotions of shame and guilt and the positive emotion of pride (Lewis, 1993b, 1995). These emotions are also intimately connected and can lead to other emotions such as anger and sadness (Lewis, 1992). Shame results when an individual senses having failed to live up to his or her standards (Lewis, 1992). The shamed person wishes to hide, disappear, or die. This intensely negative and painful emotion can disrupt behavior, confuse thinking, and render the person speechless (Lewis, 1993b).

Guilt (or regret) is produced when a person evaluates his or her behavior as a failure and focuses on the specific features of the self or actions that led to the failure. These people are pained by the evaluation of the failure, but they direct the pain to the cause of the failure or the object of the harm. Guilt is

Emotional expressions that resemble those seen in adults are observed in children under 1 year of age. Which emotions do you believe these children are expressing?

associated with some corrective action taken to repair the failure and prevent it from happening again. Therefore guilt is not as intensely negative as shame and does not lead to confusion and loss of action.

Pride and shame are quite different from happiness and sadness. If you win a lottery, you will probably feel quite happy about the money, but you would not feel pride, because winning is not viewed as having anything to do with your behavior. You might feel sad if you were not able to do something, but if it was not your fault, you would not feel shame or guilt.

Emotional Intelligence. The term *emotional intelligence* describes such qualities as the abilities to motivate oneself, to persist in the face of frustrations, to control impulses, to delay gratification, to regulate one's mood, and to keep distress from swamping the ability to think, empathize, and hope (Goleman, 1995). This concept recognizes the fact that brain power as measured by tests of intelligence and standardized achievement tests is not necessarily as important for success as the qualities just outlined, which have gone unrecognized.

Many people do not even recognize which emotion they are experiencing. For example, they may not realize that they are actually angry at a person for dying. Or consider a parent who yells at a child who has just run into the street. Is the parent expressing anger at the act of disobedience or fear at what could have happened? Recognizing which emotions we are feeling is a key element of emotional intelligence because it helps individuals understand how their thinking can be affected by the emotions they are experiencing.

Some impulses appear easier to control than others; anger is one of the hardest to control, perhaps because of its evolutionary value in priming people to action. Dwelling on anger actually increases its power. To control anger, the body needs a chance to use up the adrenaline through exercise, relaxation techniques, or the well-known admonition to count to ten. Understanding how anger can affect our behavior is an excellent example of emotional intelligence in action (Goleman, 1995). In fact, education may someday include training in self-awareness, self-control and empathy, and the arts of listening, resolving conflicts and cooperation" (Sleek, 1997). To those who argue that schools have too much to teach students already without adding instruction in emotional intelligence, proponents of such instruction suggest that it would be easier to teach students who can maintain their emotional equilibrium in the face of a wide variety of stressors at home and in the community (Sleek, 1997).

Review Summary

1. Languages and cultures differ in the number of words that describe categories of emotion. Some words refer to emotions that are not described in all cultures or languages.

2. Schachter and Singer proposed a theory that described emotion as beginning with undifferentiated arousal. The specific emotion label we use to describe the arousal depends on our interpretation of the context.

3. Appraisal theories of emotion propose that how we make judgments about events leads to emotional reactions. Cultural values can influence people's emotions.

4. A key cognitive ability is evaluating one's behavior in relation to internal or external standards. This ability is the basis of the self-conscious emotions such as shame, guilt, and pride.

5. The concept of *emotional intelligence* includes such abilities as motivating oneself, persisting in the face of frustrations, and controlling impulses, as well as being aware of the emotions one is experiencing.

Study Break

1. Give examples of words from other cultures that describe categories of emotion that do not have counterparts in English.
2. You are walking in the forest and see a bear. According to Schachter and Singer, what happens at that point?
   a. Physiological changes, followed by fear
   b. Fear, followed by physiological changes
   c. Physiological changes and fear simultaneously
   d. Physiological changes and context appraisal, followed by fear
3. How did Schachter and Singer create physiological arousal similar to that experienced during emotional reactions in their experimental participants?

   a. Participants were given epinephrine injections.
   b. They had them exercise before entering the laboratory.
   c. Participants watched a frightening movie before the experiment began.
   d. They told the participants that a dangerous chemical was leaking from an adjacent laboratory.
4. Which of these is considered a self-conscious emotion?
   a. fear
   b. shame
   c. disgust
   d. happiness
5. Define the term *emotional intelligence*.

ANSWERS TO STUDY BREAKS

Page 153

1. The factor or motivational state that prompts the behavior; the goal toward which the behavior is directed; reasons for differences in intensity of behavior.
2. a. instinct
   b. incentive
   c. drive reduction
3. Buy next week's groceries and pay your electric bill. These two needs are more basic and lower in the hierarchy of needs than going to a play.
4. a. approach-avoidance
   b. approach-approach
   c. avoidance-avoidance

Page 160

1. Glucostatic theory. The candy bar provides sugar, which can be used quickly.
2. b
3. b
4. Excitement, plateau, orgasm, resolution
5. c
6. Behaviors that manipulate the environment, rules for performing these behaviors, and accepted performance standards against which performance is evaluated/compared. These three components are needed to explain the full range of achievement motivated behaviors.

Page 172

1. According to Darwin, emotions involve expressions that communicate information about present or future events that help organisms adapt to their environments.
2. Darwin pointed to animals' baring their teeth during anger to support his view on emotion.
3. a
4. a

5. One method of eliciting emotions in order to study physiological differences is to ask research participants to follow muscle-by-muscle instructions to create facial expressions associated with different emotions.
6. c
7. b
8. b

Page 182

1. d
2. Plutchik proposed that eight basic emotions can be viewed as polar opposites; each emotion exists in varying degrees of intensity. These primary emotions are building blocks that can be combined into the more complex emotions.
3. a
4. b
5. Emblems—nodding your head to indicate "yes" regulators—eye contact and head nods that coordinate the flow of communication in a conversation
   adapters—doodling, fiddling with a pen or pencil
   illustrators—waving your arms or pounding a table to enhance your words

Page 187

1. The German word *schadenfreude* means "harm joy" and the Japanese word *ijirashii* refers to feelings associated with seeing someone praiseworthy overcoming an obstacle.
2. d
3. a
4. b
5. Emotional intelligence is the ability to motivate oneself, to persist in the face of frustration, to control impulses, to delay gratification, to regulate one's moods, and to keep distress from affecting the ability to think, empathize, and hope.

CHAPTER 5

States of Consciousness

Chapter in Perspective

Our journey toward understanding behavior has led us to the study of several fundamental processes—the functioning of the brain and the nervous system, the ability to sense and perceive our environment, biological and social motivations, and emotional reactions. Our focus on these fundamental processes continues as we investigate changes in our awareness. The term *consciousness* is puzzling and difficult to define. As you read these words, you are conscious, but how does brain tissue make one conscious?

In this chapter we learn that our ability to sense or perceive stimuli can be influenced naturally by ongoing bodily changes called *biological rhythms.* Changes in our awareness can also be brought on artificially—through the use of drugs or perhaps through induction of a hypnotic state. Our discussion will include evidence that social factors can also affect our awareness.

Like the ocean tides, most of our internal biological processes follow a rhythm of alternating high and low levels. Some biological processes are accompanied by changes in our awareness or level of consciousness. For example, the rhythm of sleep and wakefulness is accompanied by the change in consciousness we call dreaming. For centuries people have found ways to alter their consciousness through such means as drug use or hypnosis. These are just some of the topics we encounter in this chapter. ■

What Is Consciousness?

To fulfill a requirement in a psychology course, Amy agrees to participate in several research projects. For the first one, she must carry a beeper with her throughout the day. The device sounds at irregular intervals to alert her to write down whatever she is thinking at the time. When her participation in the project is completed, the researcher tells her the topic of the research was consciousness. *How do psychologists define consciousness?* ■

To be conscious is to be aware, but aware of what? Psychologists define **consciousness** as personal awareness of feelings, sensations, and thoughts. Driving through an unfamiliar city would provide ample opportunities to understand changes in your level of consciousness. You are aware of increased feelings of tension; you grip the steering wheel tightly. Your mouth has gone dry; beads of sweat cascade down your face. You see cars weaving in and out of traffic as if they were performing a high-speed ballet. You see a big truck behind you in your rear-view mirror—or is it in your trunk? You start thinking that you shouldn't be driving in this city during rush hour. Finally you reach the outskirts of the city and enter the suburbs. You see a snazzy sports car speed past you, and you picture yourself behind the wheel. Wait a minute! You just passed your exit!

As we noted in Chapter 1, William James described consciousness as a stream. Like a stream, consciousness is continuous, can change, and has depth. But the stream of consciousness is personal; it is very much your own. Let's return to your drive through an unfamiliar city. Throughout the drive, your awareness of external stimuli—such as other cars—and internal stimuli—such as the seat belt against your body—probably changed. What's more, as you left the city, you daydreamed about a sports car. During this fantasy, your attention was directed inward and away from external sources of stimulation. To drive through the city, you had to focus your attention on the events around you; it was no time for consciousness to wander. But once you left the city, your attention could stray, and you missed your exit. We often engage in everyday behaviors without being completely aware of them—that is, they can occur outside of consciousness.

This form of consciousness involving fantasy, occurring while you are awake, is called **daydreaming.** Almost all people daydream, although the frequency drops as we get older (Giambra, 1989). Most daydreams are spontaneous images or thoughts that pop into our mind for a brief time and are then forgotten. We can, however, become adept at using daydreams to solve problems, to rehearse a sequence of events, or to find new ideas. Some daydreams are deliberate attempts to deal with situations like a boring job by providing some internal stimulation. Nevertheless, the content of most daydreams is related to such everyday events as paying bills or selecting clothes to wear. About two-thirds of daydreams are related to the daydreamer's immediate situation. Contrary to popular belief, a small proportion of all daydreams involves sexual content (Klinger, 1990). Nevertheless, approximately 95 percent of men and women report having had sexual daydreams at some time (Leitenberg & Henning, 1995).

consciousness
A person's awareness of feelings, sensations, and thoughts at a given moment

daydreaming
A form of consciousness involving fantasies, usually spontaneous, that occurs while a person is awake

Psychologists have devised ingenious ways to investigate changes in our consciousness, particularly daydreaming. For example, they have equipped people with beepers that sound at random intervals to signal them to report their thoughts in writing (Klinger, 1990). These beepers are one of the methods used to study daydreaming. The advantage of this method is that it does not rely on memory.

The experience of daydreaming is different from normal waking consciousness, and for that reason it can be called an **altered state of consciousness.** During the course of a day, however, our consciousness can change even more dramatically. For example, the use of alcohol or other drugs often leads to major changes in consciousness and observable behavior. As we later discuss, some researchers consider hypnosis to be an altered state of consciousness. Likewise, the rhythmic changes of sleeping and dreaming dramatically alter personal awareness. We discuss the study of sleep and dreams as we investigate both consciousness and the biological rhythms of life.

The Rhythms of Life

A jet flying from Taiwan to Los Angeles lost power in one engine and fell about six miles, resulting in injuries to two passengers and structural damage to the aircraft. Although the power loss was an accident, the pilot may have failed to monitor the instruments carefully. Investigators determined that the accident occurred five hours beyond the time when the pilot was accustomed to going to sleep (Lauber & Kayten, 1988). Tim, a worker in a nuclear power plant, read a newspaper account of the accident and wondered whether working the night shift might affect his ability to monitor instruments and make critical decisions. *What are the effects of shift work on alertness and decision making?*

All living organisms exhibit built-in rhythms or cycles of internal biological activity called *biological rhythms.* Biological rhythms such as the heartbeat that are shorter than 24 hours are called *ultradian rhythms.* Ones that are longer, such as the menstrual cycle, are known as *infradian rhythms.* Some of the most important biological rhythms, however, occur on a daily schedule.

Circadian Rhythms

Internal biological changes that occur on a daily schedule are called **circadian rhythms** (*circa,* "about"; *dies,* "day"). Most of us have a single sleep period every 24 hours. The sleep-wake cycle is just one of our circadian rhythms; scientists can detect peaks and valleys in body temperature, heart rate, and hormone levels during a 24-hour period. For example, levels of the stress hormone *cortisol* are negligible an hour or two before sleep, begin increasing before we awaken, and reach a peak at or near awakening (Moore-Ede, Sulzman, & Fuller, 1982). Circadian rhythms are also important in detecting diseases and in planning drug treatments (Lamberg, 1994; Office of Technology Assessment, 1991). The results of medical tests can depend on when the test is given; drugs that help at one time of day may harm at another. The peak times for a number of indicators of health and disease are shown in Figure 5-1.

altered state of consciousness
State of consciousness that is different from normal waking consciousness

circadian rhythm
Internal biological changes that occur on a daily schedule

FIGURE 5-1 Biological processes that follow a circadian rhythm peak at the same time every day. Researchers and physicians are becoming more aware of the effects of circadian rhythms on biological and psychological measurements.

Source: Morris, 1989.

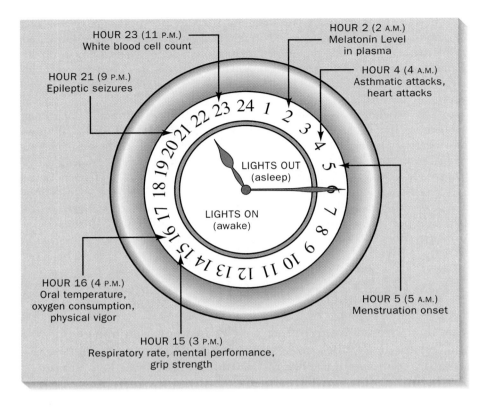

HOUR 23 (11 P.M.)
White blood cell count

HOUR 21 (9 P.M.)
Epileptic seizures

HOUR 2 (2 A.M.)
Melatonin Level
in plasma

HOUR 4 (4 A.M.)
Asthmatic attacks,
heart attacks

LIGHTS OUT
(asleep)

LIGHTS ON
(awake)

HOUR 16 (4 P.M.)
Oral temperature,
oxygen consumption,
physical vigor

HOUR 15 (3 P.M.)
Respiratory rate, mental performance,
grip strength

HOUR 5 (5 A.M.)
Menstruation onset

The Sleep-Wake Cycle. *Chronobiology* is the branch of science that investigates and applies information about biological rhythms. To determine what controls our biological rhythms, researchers have observed volunteers who were isolated from all time cues—no watches, television, radio, or newspapers—in caves or special apartments. What happened in a world without time cues? If before the experiment the volunteers typically went to sleep at midnight and awoke at 8 A.M. during the experiment, they began sleeping at 1 A.M. and awoke at 9 A.M. on the first day. On the next day they might begin their sleep another hour later (2 A.M.) and rise at about 10 A.M. Day by day their sleep cycle shifted later in the day, yet they maintained a systematic sleep-wake rhythm.

Why does our sleep-wake cycle shift? The answer lies in the *suprachiasmatic nucleus (SCN)*, a pinhead-sized collection of neurons located in the hypothalamus (see Chapter 2), just above the optic chiasm (Meijer & Rietveld, 1989). These neurons receive information about light and dark from the eyes and its own nerve pathways (Moore-Ede, 1993). The neurons serve as an internal clock that exerts indirect control over neurons throughout the body. Although this internal clock is accurate within a minute or two each day, it must be reset every day because it tends to run on a 25-hour cycle, not a 24-hour day (Moore-Ede, 1993).

Exactly how the biological clock operates is still under investigation. Researchers suspect, however, that the hormone *melatonin*, produced by the pineal gland (a pea-size structure at the center of the brain), is involved (Delagrange & Guardiola-Lemaitre, 1997). Bright light suppresses production of melatonin; darkness triggers secretion of the hormone. Because of its effects on our circadian rhythms, melatonin is sometimes referred to as "nature's sleeping pill." Synthetic forms of it have been used to treat insomnia (Garfinkel et al., 1995), although definitive evidence for its effectiveness as a significant sleep-inducing agent is still a topic of debate (Mendelson, 1997; Sack et al., 1997). What's more, further research needs to be done on possible long-term effects of this treatment.

Although the public has embraced melatonin, most researchers are cautious in their assessments of this hormone that has been touted as a cure for everything from insomnia to cancer (Cupp, 1997; Zhdanova, Lynch, & Wurtman, 1997).

The 25-hour sleep-wake cycle in a laboratory is described as a *free-running cycle* because there are no external signals to reset the internal clock. Outside the laboratory, sunlight is the most important cue that resets the internal clock to a 24-hour day. However, meals, social interactions, and even alarm clocks also influence circadian rhythms (Moore-Ede, Sulzman, & Fuller, 1982).

Psychological Detective

 We experience the effects of our 25-hour internal clock almost every week. Many people wake up Monday morning feeling exhausted and wanting more sleep. What happens over the weekend to create such feelings? How does the 25-hour internal clock explain how we feel on Monday morning? Think about these questions, and write down your answers before reading further.

On weekends, when we are freed from the demands of external schedules, we tend to sleep and awaken later than we normally do during the school week or workweek. Like volunteers isolated from time cues, our sleep-wake cycle stretches to 25 hours, thus moving our sleep later in the 24-hour day. We often go to sleep later on Sunday than we do on weekdays, but on Monday we must awaken in time for work or school. Because our sleep-wake cycle has shifted, the clock on the nightstand may say it's 7 A.M., but our internal clock tells us that it is much earlier and we should still be asleep.

Body Temperature.   You might be surprised to find your body temperature is not a constant 98.6 degrees; rather, it fluctuates 2 to 3 degrees over the course of a day (see Figure 5-2). The 24-hour (circadian) rhythm of body

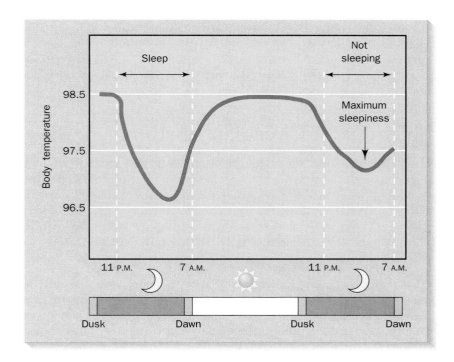

FIGURE 5-2 The circadian rhythm of body core temperature. If you have ever "pulled an all-nighter," you probably felt chilly in the middle of the night. Even if the temperature in the room remained the same, your internal body temperature would fall, and you would also find it increasingly difficult to concentrate.

Source: Moore-Ede, 1993.

temperature is controlled by the SCN (Coleman, 1995). Body temperature is related to our level of alertness and our sleep-wake cycle. In fact, observations of circadian cycles in free-running situations show that sleep is associated more with our body temperature at bedtime than with the number of hours we have been awake (Czeisler et al., 1980).

High temperature typically corresponds to higher levels of alertness; low temperature generally corresponds to reduced alertness and motivation. Body temperature reaches its lowest point of the day during sleep; it then rises after we wake up and peaks in the afternoon. The body is primed for high levels of efficiency in the afternoon.

The sleep-wake and body temperature cycles are typically synchronized. When we are deprived of time cues or when we travel through time zones or change work shifts, however, these cycles can become uncoupled and cause problems such as fatigue and sleepiness.

Have you heard the terms *owls* and *larks* applied to people with different sleep habits. Larks (*morning type*) get up easily and are more alert in the morning than in the evening; they find it difficult to sleep late and fall asleep quickly in the evening. The lark's peak temperature occurs early in the day; around 8 A.M. By contrast, owls (*evening type*) are more alert at night, able to sleep late in the morning, and take a long time to fall asleep at night. The owl's temperature peaks later in the day, around 8 P.M. or later. These individual differences in the sleep-wake and temperature cycles seem to be influenced by genetic factors (Hur, Bouchard, & Lykken, 1998).

Problems with Circadian Rhythms

Our 25-hour internal clock provides the flexibility needed to adjust to the seasons, with their accompanying changes in the number of hours of daylight. However, the modern era has stretched our body's ability to adapt. For example, the ability to travel great distances through many time zones in very little time has given rise to the phenomenon known as **jet lag,** the temporary maladjustment that occurs when a change of time zone causes biological rhythms to be out of step with local time.

Jet Lag. Hop on a jet in New York, and two hours later you can be in Chicago; the change of one time zone requires only a minor adjustment of your internal clock. A trip from New York to London takes about seven hours on a jet traveling through five time zones. You might be in London at 8 A.M., but your body thinks it's the middle of the night (3 A.M. in New York). Your circadian

jet lag

Temporary maladjustment that occurs when a change of time zones causes biological rhythms to be out of step with local time

rhythms are not synchronized with your surroundings; as a result you are likely to experience the symptoms of *jet lag*: fatigue, irritability, difficulty concentrating, insomnia, and disturbed appetite (Waterhouse, Reilly, & Atkinson, 1997).

Psychological Detective

Your travel plans call for several long-distance trips by jet that take you across the country and around the world. Which direction of travel would be easier to adjust to: east to west or west to east? Why? What could you do to adjust to the time changes brought about by your travel?

Jet lag has little to do with the length of your flight; the key is the number of time zones you cross. Increase the number of time zones you cross, and you increase the need for adjustment (see Figure 5-3). If you travel from New York to Lima, Peru—directly south through the same time zone—you do not need to reset your internal clock. But a trip from Los Angeles to Hong Kong takes you through several time zones, requiring a major adjustment. The direction of travel influences the speed with which the body adapts. A westward trip—say, from New York to San Francisco—is equivalent to delaying your sleep by three hours and is called a *phase delay*. If you travel eastward from San Francisco to New York, you shorten the day to 21 hours, which is known as a *phase advance*. Phase delays (east-west travel) coincide with the body's tendency to extend the sleep-wake cycle to 25 hours. Therefore, it is easier to adapt to phase delays than to phase advances (west-east travel).

If you travel great distances and expect to experience jet lag, here is some advice. During short stays, eat and sleep on your home time so you don't need to reset your internal clock. For longer stays, start adjusting before you leave by eating meals according to the time of your destination. When you arrive at your destination, use the most powerful time cue—sunlight—to reset your internal clock to local time (Czeisler et al., 1986). However, the timing of your exposure to strong light is a key factor (Waterhouse, Reilly, & Atkinson, 1997). The biological clock interprets exposure to bright light near the end of the usual sleep period (e.g., 4 A.M.) as a dawn signal (a new day is starting) that can advance the clock and initiate a period of activity. By contrast, exposure to bright light near the end of the normal active period (awake hours) delays the clock and makes people want to go to sleep later than their normal time (Coleman, 1995).

Shift Work.
Consumers need and want products, protection, and entertainment around the clock. Rotating work shifts fulfill the demand for 24-hour-a-day staffing of manufacturing plants, hospitals, and recreational facilities. However, there are some problems associated with shift work.

At the beginning of this section you met Tim, who was concerned that rotating shift work might affect his alertness and decision-making capacity in his job at a

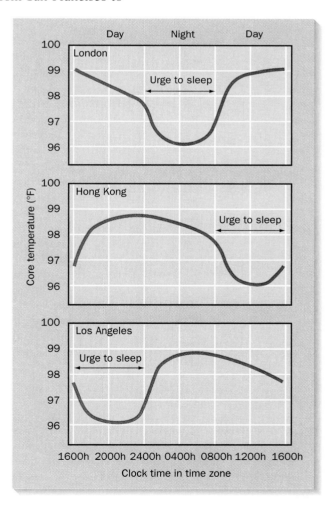

FIGURE 5-3 The effects of traveling eight hours through several times zones is evident in the desynchronization between time of day and an individual's core body temperature. This figure illustrates what would happen to a person who begins travel from London and journeys to Hong Kong or Los Angeles (eastward, phase advance; westward, phase delay).

Sources: Waterhouse, Reilly, & Atkinson, 1997.

nuclear power plant. Tim is not alone: More than 22 million Americans work a shift other than the day shift (American Sleep Disorders Association, 1994). Many of them report symptoms like those of jet lag as well as a number of social and family problems (Monk & Folkard, 1992).

Let's take a closer look at Tim's rotating schedule. At the end of a day shift, he heads home and retires for the night at 11 P.M. After one week on the day shift, he rotates to the night shift, working from 11 P.M. until 7 A.M. Trying to sleep at 2 in the afternoon is almost impossible because his body is not ready for sleep. It is, however, ready for sleep when he arrives at work!

Shift work often leads to a cumulative sleep loss. As many as 75 percent of night shift workers experience sleepiness on every night shift, and 20 percent report having fallen asleep on the job (Akerstedt, 1991). Charles Pollak, head of New York Hospital's sleep clinic, says the sleepiness resulting from shift rotation "doesn't make it difficult to walk, see, or hear. But people who don't get enough sleep can't think, they can't make appropriate judgments, [and] they can't maintain long attention spans" (Toufexis, 1990, p. 78). The number of on-the-job errors peaks during the night shift, which can adversely affect work performance and even compromise public safety (Scott, 1994). The sleepiness resulting from rotating shift work can interfere with a person's ability to administer drugs to patients, to navigate a plane, or to operate a nuclear power plant. Sleepiness was a factor in serious accidents at two nuclear power plants (Chernobyl in the Ukraine and Three Mile Island in Pennsylvania) and the *Exxon Valdez* oil spill in Alaska. Moreover, an investigation of the 1986 explosion of the space shuttle *Challenger* cited errors in judgment that were related to sleep loss and rotating shift work during the early morning hours (Report of the Presidential Commission on the Space Shuttle *Challenger* Accident, 1986). Sleep deprivation and sleep disorders contribute to accidents, reduced productivity, and higher medical costs (Fritz, 1993; National Commission on Sleep Disorders Research, 1992).

Improving Shift Work.   A typical rotation schedule calls for a week each on the day, night, and evening shifts, in that order. Although a week on a shift is not enough time for workers to adjust to their new schedule, they are often required to shift again at the end of the week. This rotating schedule is the equivalent of working successive weeks in Denver, Paris, and Tokyo (Coleman, 1986).

Researchers have some advice for people who schedule or work rotating shifts (Akerstedt, 1991; Czeisler, Moore-Ede, & Coleman, 1982). Workers should rotate in a "clockwise" direction (from days to evenings to nights) so that the changes are phase delays, not phase advances. If you work from 7 A.M. to 4 P.M. and go to sleep at 10 P.M., it would not be difficult for you to delay your sleep until after the evening shift ends at 11 P.M. When shifts rotate in a "counterclockwise" direction (from days to nights to evenings), workers must try to sleep during the time they had been working. The advantages of rotating in a clockwise direction can be enhanced by allowing workers to spend more than one week on a shift so that they have more time to reset their internal clocks. Rotating shifts in a clockwise direction has been shown to improve the satisfaction of both workers and their families, increase productivity, and lead to fewer accidents (American Sleep Disorders Association, 1994).

Review Summary

1. Consciousness is personal awareness of feelings, sensations, and thoughts. Changes from normal consciousness are known as **altered states of consciousness.** One common change in consciousness is **daydreaming.**

2. A number of biological processes follow regular rhythms or cycles that vary in length. The study of biological rhythms, *chronobiology,* includes research on the effects of such cycles on the diagnosis and treatment of diseases.

3. Circadian rhythms are biological changes that occur on a daily schedule, including the sleep-wake cycle and the body temperature cycle.

4. Circadian rhythms are controlled by the *suprachiasmatic nucleus (SCN)* which is located in the hypothalamus and acts as an internal clock. Levels of a hormone secreted by the pineal gland, *melatonin,* are affected by light and darkness; thus melatonin may play a role in controlling biological rhythms. By isolating volunteers in an environment without time cues, researchers have found the *free-running* sleep-wake cycle extends to about 25 hours. To correspond to the 24-hour day, the cycle must be reset every day by external cues, especially sunlight.

5. Jet travel and shift work can disrupt the sleep-wake cycle. The symptoms of **jet lag** result from the difference between our internal clock and the time in our environment. It is easier to adapt to *phase delays,* resulting from east-west travel, than to *phase advances,* resulting from west-east travel.

Study Break

1. What do psychologists mean when they use the word *consciousness*?
2. According to researchers, which of the following is a common daydream?
   a. Winning a Nobel Prize
   b. Writing the world's greatest novel
   c. Dealing with an everyday situation
   d. Punishing oneself for thinking about sex
3. Tim is a volunteer in a laboratory study of free-running circadian rhythms. Without any time cues, Tim's sleep-wake cycle is likely to average about _____ hours.
4. Where in the brain is the internal clock located? Which hormone secreted by the pineal gland plays a role in controlling our biological rhythms?
5. Which *one* of the following journeys would be classified as a phase advance of your sleep-wake cycle?
   a. Paris to Detroit
   b. Rome to Denver
   c. New York to Miami
   d. Chicago to London
6. The new Mega-Store opening in town will be open 24 hours. The store manager hired a consultant to design the best possible rotating shifts for full-time employees. Which of the following is likely to be the schedule the consultant recommends?
   a. 2 shifts of days, then 2 on evenings, and 2 on nights
   b. 1 week on days, 1 week on nights, and 1 week on evenings
   c. 2 weeks on night shift, 1 week on days, and 2 weeks on evening
   d. 2 weeks on days, 2 weeks on evenings, and 2 weeks on nights

The Study of Sleep

Sara and Jim are fascinated by their infant daughter. They frequently tiptoe into her room at night to check on her. At times they notice that her body is completely still, yet her eyes dart quickly back and forth. They had not realized it is possible to see someone's eyes move beneath closed eyelids. They wonder what those eye movements mean. ***What is the significance of the eye movements that occur while we sleep?*** ▪

 Much of what we know about sleep is derived from research conducted in sleep laboratories since World War II. Researchers representing several disciplines—including neurology, psychiatry, and psychology—have probed thousands of people in search of solutions to the mysteries of sleep and dreams.
 Hans Berger's invention of the *electroencephalograph (EEG)* in 1929 made it possible to study the living brain without entering it (see Chapter 2). Although the EEG was a significant advance, the major breakthrough in studying sleep was the observation of the eyes of sleeping people. One research team

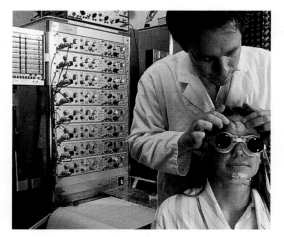

Polysomnograph amplifies and records signals associated with physiological changes that occur during a night in a sleep laboratory.

attached electrodes next to the eyes of the sleeping people to provide a continuous record of periods during which the eyes moved back and forth (Aserinsky & Kleitman, 1953). Researchers coined the term *rapid eye movement (REM)* to describe this phenomenon.

At the beginning of this section you met Sara and Jim, who were curious about their daughter's eye movements during sleep. We now know they were observing REM sleep. What is the significance of the eye movements? When awakened from REM sleep, people report dreams about 80 percent of the time, compared with about 14 percent in people awakened from non-REM sleep (Dement, 1978).

A Night in a Sleep Lab

A posted request for sleep study volunteers catches your attention. Imagine being paid for sleeping! You call the researcher, who tells you she is interested in the sleep patterns of college students with part-time jobs. You arrive two hours before your usual bedtime. A technician attaches several dime-sized electrodes to different parts of your body. The electrodes detect physiological changes that occur during the night. The information is fed to a **polysomnograph** (*poly,* "many"; *somni,* "sleep"; *graph,* "written or drawn"), an instrument that amplifies signals and produces a record on paper, disk, or tape of these physiological changes.

The technician attaches several electrodes to your scalp to measure brain waves. Two more electrodes, one near each eye, provide data for the *electro-oculograph (EOG),* which detects eye movements. An electrode under your chin measures muscle activity; your heart rate is monitored by an *electrocardiograph (EKG).* When other devices that measure breathing, oxygen in the blood, and temperature are added, you look and feel like a robot.

You are ushered into a soundproof room, where every movement and sound you make will be recorded. Apprehensive about possible equipment malfunction, you find fearful thoughts running through your mind. The first night's sleep may be atypical compared with a night at home; as a consequence, researchers usually discard the first night's data (Toussaint et al., 1997). The next night, having adapted to your new surroundings, you sleep comfortably.

The Stages of Sleep

During a typical night you pass through five stages of sleep: REM sleep and four other stages of sleep known as Stages 1, 2, 3, and 4. During each stage of sleep, a distinctive "signature" of brain waves appears on the EEG record (see Figure 5-4). Let's take a closer look at these stages.

NREM Sleep.   You begin sleep with Stage 1 and then progress to Stages 2, 3, and 4. At each step the task of being roused from sleep becomes more difficult. These four stages are known collectively as **non-REM (NREM) sleep.** You typically spend a few minutes in Stage 1, a transitional phase between wakefulness and sleep; Stage 2 sleep occupies about 50 percent of an adult's sleep. The EEG heralds the arrival of Stage 2 with the appearance of sleep spindles, bursts of activity on the EEG record, and K complexes, large deflections in the waveform (see Figure 5-4). Finally, we descend to Stage 3 and 4, which together are known as **slow-wave sleep** or delta sleep. Waking someone from slow-wave sleep is quite difficult; people awakened from this deep sleep are likely to be disoriented and groggy. Delta waves first appear in Stage 3, in which they account for 20 to 50 percent of the brain waves. By Stage 4 sleep, delta waves make up more than 50 percent of the brain waves. Sleep

polysomnograph
Instrument that amplifies and records signals associated with biological changes taken during a night in the sleep laboratory

non-REM (NREM) sleep
Sleep stages 1, 2, 3, and 4; NREM sleep consists primarily of Stages 3 and 4 early in the night and Stage 2 later on

slow-wave sleep
Deep sleep of NREM stages 3 and 4, characterized by delta waves

patterns may vary from one person to another but generally progress as outlined in Figure 5-5. As you can see, from the deep sleep of Stages 3 and 4 a person ascends through the lighter NREM stages and then enters a dramatically different stage of sleep called REM.

REM Sleep. What makes REM sleep so different from the other sleep stages? At one time sleep was viewed as a "time out," like turning off your car's motor; however, this view is now considered wrong (Dement, 1986). During **rapid eye movement (REM) sleep**—a sleep stage characterized by rapid eye movements, dreams, high brain activity, and muscle paralysis—the brain is more like a parked car with its motor racing. The signs of activity are all obvious: Heart rate and respiration are more variable than they are during NREM stages. Men have penile erections; women experience an increased blood flow in the genital area. This indication of sexual arousal is not related to erotic dreams, however, the EEG record of a person in REM sleep resembles that of an awake person (review Figure 5-4). Intense activity of neurons throughout the brain make a PET scan (see Chapter 2) look like a lit Christmas tree; brain temperature increases as more blood flows to the brain (see Figure 5-6). As we saw in Figure 5-5, adults spend 20 to 25 percent of the night in this supercharged stage of sleep.

Let's return to our description of a night in a sleep lab. The lab technician attached an electrode to your chin to detect muscle activity. Why? During REM

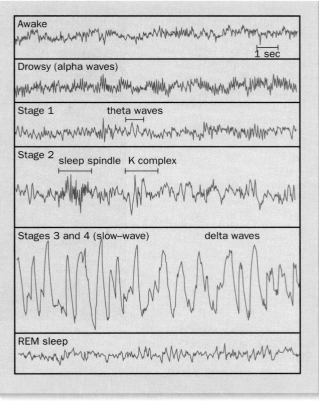

FIGURE 5-4 EEG markings from a recording made in a sleep laboratory. Each stage of sleep has its own identifying marks on the EEG record.

Source: Hauri, 1992.

rapid eye movement (REM) sleep

Sleep stage characterized by rapid eye movements, dreams, high brain activity, and muscle paralysis

FIGURE 5-5 The stages of sleep throughout the night. The cycle of sleep follows a rather consistent pattern throughout the night and from person to person. Each sleep cycle lasts about 90 minutes and consists of a series of NREM stages followed by REM sleep. Most slow-wave sleep occurs during the early part of the night; most REM sleep occurs during the later part of the night. REM periods generally become longer during the night.

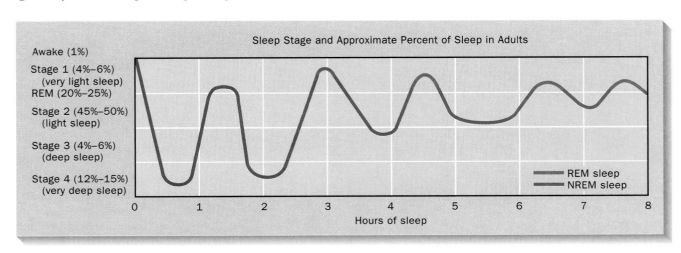

FIGURE 5-6 Positron emission tomography (PET) scans of the brain during REM sleep (left), NREM sleep (right), and waking hours (bottom). The colors red and yellow indicate higher levels of metabolic activity. Note the similarity in the level of activity during REM sleep and waking hours.

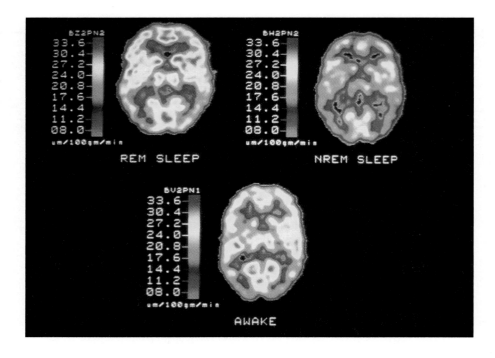

FIGURE 5-7 Sleep length over the life span. Sleep length drops rapidly from infancy to adolescence and then changes at a much slower rate.

Source: American Medical Association, 1984.

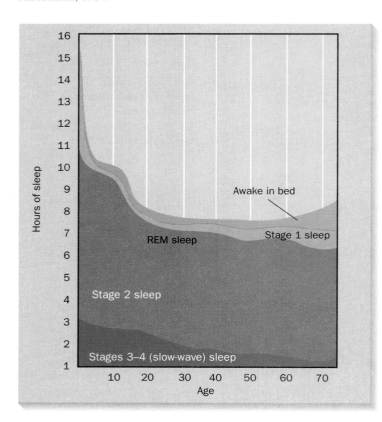

sleep, activity in your skeletal (voluntary) muscles is suppressed, leaving you essentially paralyzed; this paralysis shows up first in your chin and neck. This curious combination of an active brain with inactive muscles led researchers to describe REM as "paradoxical sleep."

The end of the first REM period marks the end of a sleep cycle—the period from the beginning of sleep to the end of REM sleep—which takes about 90 minutes (Allen, 1997). The sleep cycle repeats itself, with some changes, four to six times a night in most adults (review Figure 5-5).

Changes in the sleep cycle during the night involve slow-wave and REM sleep. The amount of slow-wave sleep decreases during the night; most of your slow-wave sleep occurs early. The length of REM episodes increases during the night: The first REM period may be five to ten minutes long; the final one can last 30 minutes or more.

Differences in Individual Sleep Patterns

As you can see in Figure 5-7, the amount of time people sleep varies with age. During the first week of life, most infants sleep about 16 hours a day; some newborns, however, sleep as little as 11 hours and others more than 20. These large differences are likely due to genetic factors; sleep length is more similar in identical twins than in fraternal twins (Heath et al., 1990; Webb & Campbell, 1983).

Sleep length decreases with age through adolescence, but it does not change much from early adulthood to the seventies. Should you worry if you don't sleep seven or eight hours, as the average adult does? When it comes to sleep, one size does not fit all. Two of every ten adults sleep less than six hours a night, and one in ten sleeps nine hours or more (Hauri & Linde, 1990). How do you assess your own need for sleep? The key question to ask is, "Are you refreshed after you awaken?" For an increasing number of people, the answer is no.

The *multiple sleep latency test* is a sensitive indicator of a person's level of sleepiness. With this technique, researchers ask you to try to fall asleep every two hours during normal waking hours. If you fall asleep, they wake you and repeat the request later. Falling asleep easily is a sign that your daily amount of sleep does not satisfy your need. Numerous such observations have convinced some sleep experts that "most people no longer know what it feels like to be fully alert" (Coleman, 1995, p. 67). Consider the following: Prior to Thomas Edison's invention of the light bulb, most adults slept ten hours each night. During the course of the next century, average hours of sleep per night decreased to approximately eight hours a night (National Commission on Sleep Disorders Research, 1993). This spiraling decrease continues: A survey of adults reveals that the average amount of sleep is now approximately seven hours per night (Gallup Organization, 1995). The National Sleep Foundation (1998) called 1,000 randomly selected women and determined that they slept on average 6 hours and 41 minutes during the workweek, and seven hours and 16 minutes on weekends. Sleep researcher James Maas (1998) sees serious problems in this declining sleep length: "The third of your life that you should spend sleeping has profound effects on the other two thirds of your life, in terms of alertness, energy, mood, body weight, perception, memory, thinking, reaction time, productivity, performance, communication skills, creativity, safety, and good health" (p. 6).

Contrary to common belief, older people do not need less sleep than younger adults. They do, however, awaken more often during the night; consequently, their sleep is more fragmented (see Figure 5-8). The *sleep efficiency index*—the proportion of bed time actually spent sleeping—reveals what happens to sleep as we grow older. Sleep efficiency is above 95 percent for men and women through their thirties; however, it drops to about 80 percent among people in their seventies. Sleep efficiency drops in older people for two reasons. First, the deep sleep of Stage 4 is either markedly reduced or completely absent. Second, elderly people spend more time in the lighter stages of sleep, which makes them more susceptible to awakening.

Most adults have just one period of sleep every 24 hours; babies have six to eight sleep periods a day. The next time you hear someone say that he or she "slept like a baby," point out that a baby's sleep consists of several short episodes of sleep. Over time those short episodes consolidate (see Figure 5-9); by 6 months of age, about 80 percent of babies sleep through the night (Webb, 1992).

Toddlers are likely to have two episodes of sleep a day (night sleep and an afternoon nap). Most children stop napping when they attend elementary school, yet as many as 50 percent of college students take naps either every day or occasionally to compensate for lost nighttime sleep. In addition to college students, many other normal healthy adults nap. Some famous nappers include Wolfgang Mozart, Napoleon Bonaparte, and Winston Churchill. Many adults nap once or more a week, most often when their night sleep is inadequate. Although some nappers experience *sleep inertia*, a temporary feeling of impairment that follows awakening, naps typically improve both mood and performance (Dinges, 1989).

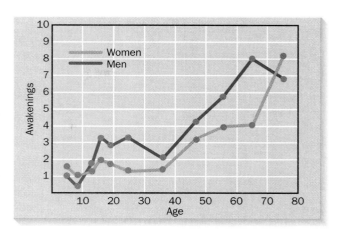

FIGURE 5-8 Number of awakenings during the night. The number of awakenings increases dramatically among elderly individuals. The numerous awakenings are one primary reason why some elderly individuals report that their sleep is less restful than it had been in the past.

Source: Hartmann, 1987.

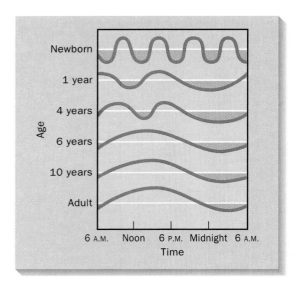

FIGURE 5-9 Sleep periods (shaded time periods) at different ages. As most parents know, newborns have several periods of sleep that are spread across the 24-hour day, with no differentiation as to night and day. These sleep periods quickly consolidate into one long period, primarily at night, plus a nap. Most adults have a single, long period of sleep, usually during the night; however, some adults nap (not shown in this figure), thus exhibiting a pattern that is common at a younger age.

Source: Moorcroft, 1993.

One type of nap, the *siesta*—a one- to two-hour nap, usually taken in the afternoon following a noon meal—is considered, in part, a culturally determined sleep practice. The practice developed as a way to avoid the hottest part of the day in tropical climates such as the Mediterranean countries of Spain and Italy and parts of Central and South America. After a siesta, people return to work during the cooler hours of the day. Most people who take a siesta reduce their amount of nighttime sleep; thus the combination of nighttime sleep and a siesta is within the average range. An added advantage of siestas is that they counteract the body's normal postlunch dip in alertness. The increasing rate of industrialization, however, has reduced the frequency of the practice (Kribbs, 1993).

Sleep Deprivation

If you live to be 75 years old, you will spend one third of your life (about 220,000 hours) sleeping. Why? One way to answer this question is to deprive people of sleep and watch what happens.

In January 1959, a 32-year-old disc jockey named Peter Tripp decided to go without sleep for 200 hours as a publicity stunt to raise money for charity. Undaunted by experts who warned of the risk of death, Tripp persevered. When he found it extremely difficult to stay awake after 135 hours, he turned to stimulants. The stimulants (amphetamines) altered his perceptions: Specks of dust became insects; a bureau drawer burst into flames. Yet he hosted his show, "Your Hits of the Week," between 5 and 8 P.M. each day, without giving any hint of what he was enduring. After 201 hours without sleep, he slept for 13 hours; the only symptom he experienced as a result of his ordeal was a slight depression that lasted a few months.

In 1964, Randy Gardner, a 17-year-old California high school student, resolved to set a new world record for sleep deprivation. Gardner used no stimulants—not even coffee—during his 264 hours without sleep (Gulevich, Dement, & Johnson, 1966). On the first night after setting the record, he slept less than 15 hours.

These people extended the limits of sleep deprivation without suffering any apparent serious long-term consequences. In fact, "systematic studies of total sleep deprivation in humans revealed no permanent effects and few profound deficits" (Anch et al., 1988, p. 9).

Both Peter Tripp and Randy Gardner appeared to go without sleep for several days. We now know that total sleep deprivation is almost impossible except in rare neurological disorders. People who undergo long periods of sleep deprivation experience lapses of attention, forgetfulness, and impaired performance. Why? The answer seems to be *microsleeps,* which are episodes of sleep (up to 30 seconds) that intrude on wakefulness. As the period of sleep deprivation gets longer, the microsleeps become longer and more frequent; total sleep deprivation does not occur for very long in humans. Most cases of total sleep deprivation are not really total. Although microsleeps do not compensate for all of the lost sleep, they reveal how powerful the urge to sleep can be when we try to deny it for extended periods.

The Functions of Sleep

What purpose does sleep serve? The answer to this seemingly easy question has proved elusive. Attempts to answer the question have focused on REM sleep and slow-wave sleep as well as on the overriding question of why we sleep at all.

Researchers have deprived people of REM sleep by waking them whenever they entered this stage. When REM-deprived people were allowed to sleep without interruption on subsequent nights, they exhibited an increased percentage of REM sleep, a phenomenon known as the **REM rebound.** The body apparently needs REM sleep because it attempts to recapture some if it is lost. But demonstrating a need does not tell us what purpose it serves.

There is a clue in the fact that half of a newborn's 16 hours of sleep per day is spent in REM; premature babies spend even more than half of their sleep in REM (Roffwarg, Muzio, & Dement, 1966). Why do babies spend so much time in REM sleep? REM sleep—a period of high activity in the brain—may provide babies with the stimulation they cannot provide for themselves. This stimulation may be necessary for brain development. The function of REM sleep in adults is still not certain; however, some evidence suggests that it may play a role in consolidating or strengthening memories (Barinaga, 1994).

Randy Gardner, who went without sleep for 264 hours, is shown here after his first recovery sleep. Sleep researcher William Dement, who monitored Gardner's sleep deprivation, looks on.

Myth or Science

Evidence suggesting that memories may be consolidated during REM sleep leads us to ask this question: "Can we learn new material while asleep?" The popular press has heralded sleep learning as an easy way to learn. Imagine playing a tape of course material while you sleep and waking the next morning with the material in your memory. Unfortunately, laboratory evidence reveals that although we may process some sensory information during sleep, as when we awaken to the sound of a fire alarm or a crying baby, we do not retain information for later recall. Some people who appeared to retain information from their sleep were actually awake, based on EEG records, during the playing of the tape. Thus sleep learning appears to be a myth born of wishful thinking (Badia, 1993).

The commonsense notion that sleep restores fatigued bodies is difficult to reconcile with certain facts. If you spend most of the day in bed, for example, you will still sleep that night even though your energy expenditure and the wear and tear on your body have been minimal. This observation reflects the built-in nature of the circadian sleep-wake cycle, which causes sleepiness at about the same time every day. Starvation, surgery, and other physical demands, however, sometimes lead to increases in slow-wave sleep. This deep sleep is the stage during which rest and repair are likely to occur.

But why do we sleep at all? Wilse Webb (1988) suggests that sleep developed in each species in ways that increased survival. Whether a species adapts best by sleeping a lot or a little depends on two factors: the animal's vulnerability to predators and its need for food. Animals that are at great risk from predators must be alert because periods of inactivity put them in grave danger. Deer and sheep do not sleep much. By contrast, lions may sleep for two or three days after consuming a meal of gazelle or antelope because they have so few enemies (Hobson, 1989).

Sleep Problems

The growing number of clinics that diagnose and treat sleep disorders attests to the fact that sleep is not always peaceful and restful. Sleep disorders range from annoying to life-threatening and can be divided into three

REM rebound

An increase in the typical amount of REM sleep following reduction of REM sleep owing to sleep deprivation or the use of certain drugs that reduce REM sleep

WHEN HE WAS A CHILD, BOB'S PARENTS REPEATEDLY TOLD HIM TO "TRY HARDER" TO FALL ASLEEP.
AT AGE 50, HE FINALLY REALIZES THAT WAS **NOT** VERY GOOD ADVICE.

Source: From *Eye on Psi Chi Newsletter* 2, no. 3 (Spring 1998). Reprinted with permission.

categories: insomnia, hypersomnias, and parasomnias (see Study Chart on p. 205).

Insomnia. "I couldn't sleep at all last night; I was tossing and turning." If this condition sounds familiar, you are not alone. Each year, approximately 35 percent of adults experience this condition, termed **insomnia,** which is characterized by various forms: difficulty falling asleep, staying asleep, frequent awakenings, or poor-quality sleep. Of these affected persons, about half view the condition as serious (Mellinger, Balter, & Uhlenhuth, 1985). Insomnia is a very common complaint, but fortunately it usually lasts less than three weeks (Reite, Nagel, & Ruddy, 1990).

Not only does insomnia come in several forms, but it has a variety of possible causes. Most cases of insomnia are related to life stress or the disruption of circadian rhythms owing to jet lag or nighttime work. Too much caffeine and illnesses that result in physical or psychological discomfort are also significant causes of brief bouts of insomnia (Pagel, 1994). Chronic cases are often associated with emotional problems, especially anxiety and depression (Buysse et al., 1994; Pagel, 1994).

The most common form of insomnia is difficulty falling asleep, known as *sleep-onset insomnia* (Pillitteri et al., 1994). Most people fall asleep within 15 minutes after their head hits the pillow; others toss and turn. This type of insomnia is usually associated with stressful events and disappears when those events end. For example, you may toss and turn the night before an important test or interview, but the next night you probably will have no trouble sleeping. If the insomnia continues and becomes chronic, however, you most likely will search for a cure. You take pills for all kinds of other ailments, so why not for sleep problems?

Over-the-counter (nonprescription) sleep aids are frequently used to treat insomnia (Pillitteri et al., 1994). These drugs contain an antihistamine that causes drowsiness that can extend into waking hours and can affect our ability to drive.

A number of prescription drugs are available to treat insomnia. Although sleeping pills do not cure insomnia, they do provide relief from the symptoms (Gillin & Byerley, 1990). The use of sedative or hypnotic drugs to treat insomnia has declined, however, as a result of growing recognition of their side effects and other problems (Pagel, 1994). For example, if you use them every night, they may lose their effectiveness in a few weeks as your body adjusts to them. Sleeping pills that reduce REM sleep can cause a REM rebound when you stop taking them. During succeeding nights, insomnia may return along with nightmares produced by the additional REM sleep.

Such psychological treatments as relaxation and stimulus control are quite effective in reducing sleep latency (the amount of time required to fall asleep) and increasing sleep time (Murtagh & Greenwood, 1995). The *stimulus control* method—used for sleep-onset insomnia—is a set of rules designed to establish better sleeping habits. People with sleep-onset insomnia are instructed to lie down to sleep only when sleepy, not to use the bed for anything except sleep and sex, and to get out of bed if unable to sleep (Bootzin, Epstein, & Wood, 1991). These suggestions are also elements of good sleep hygiene; in fact, the best way to deal with insomnia is to practice good sleep hygiene. For example, maintain a regular sleep schedule and avoid caffeine. Table 5-1 lists several suggestions to help you sleep better.

insomnia
Complaints of difficulty falling asleep, staying asleep, frequent awakenings, or poor-quality sleep

STUDY CHART

Common Sleep Disorders

Disorder	Description
Insomnia	Difficulty falling asleep (sleep-onset insomnia), staying asleep, frequent awakenings, or poor-quality sleep. Treated with over-the-counter sleep aids that contain an antihistamine, sedative or hypnotic drugs, or a number of psychological treatments such as relaxation and stimulus control.
Narcolepsy	A potentially serious disorder consisting of daytime sleepiness and symptoms related to the intrusion of REM sleep into the waking hours, including cataplexy (sudden muscle weakness related to strong emotions). Treatment consists of stimulant drugs and antidepressant drugs; afternoon naps may be helpful.
Sleep apnea	Frequent pauses in breathing, especially in overweight males, causing hundreds of brief awakenings during sleep. Treatments include CPAP, changes in sleep position, weight loss, and tongue-retaining devices.
Sudden infant death syndrome (SIDS)	The leading cause of death in infants between 1 month and 1 year of age. Placing the infant on the side or back to sleep may reduce the incidence of SIDS.
Sleepwalking	A parasomnia that occurs out of Stage 4 sleep, especially in children, and may reflect the immaturity of the nervous system. Preventive measures such as locking windows and doors can reduce the chance of injury.
Enuresis	Bedwetting that can be treated with the urine alarm (pad and buzzer).
Sleep terror	Partial awakening from Stage 4 sleep accompanied by a high level of physiological arousal; may occur simultaneously with sleepwalking. Children typically do not recall any of the terror.
Nightmare	A frightening dream that occurs during REM and therefore is likely to occur near the end of sleep when REM periods are longer.

Hypersomnias.   Although our culture does not recognize excessive daytime sleepiness as a serious complaint, it can be a symptom of a serious medical disorder. **Hypersomnias** are sleep disorders that are characterized by excessive daytime sleepiness. They include narcolepsy and sleep apnea.

Narcolepsy.   Imagine that you feel sleepy every day. Your eyes droop as you struggle to remain awake, but sleep wins, and your head plunges to your chest. Excessive daytime sleepiness, regardless of the amount of nighttime sleep, is one of the symptoms of **narcolepsy** (*narce,* "numbing"; *lepsis,* "attack"), a life-long sleep disorder that afflicts about 300,000 Americans (American Narcolepsy Association, n.d.). Daytime sleepiness, however, can be caused by many factors, so careful diagnosis in sleep disorders clinics is needed to determine its cause.

   Now imagine a friend who suddenly collapses to the floor while telling you a joke. Your friend has just experienced one of the symptoms of narcolepsy—*cataplexy* (*cata,* "down"; *plexis,* "strike"), a sudden loss of muscle tone often triggered by strong emotion. Attacks of cataplexy range from partial muscle weakness to an almost complete loss of muscle tone that lasts between a few seconds and a minute. Two other symptoms of narcolepsy are *hypnagogic hallucinations*—intense, vivid dreams that occur at the beginning of sleep— and paralysis at the beginning of sleep or upon awakening.

   One victim of narcolepsy continually fell asleep while in high school and college. Repeated bouts of sleep led to 15 automobile accidents by age 25; fortunately, no one was seriously injured (Fritz, 1993). Narcolepsy usually begins

hypersomnias
Sleep disorders characterized by excessive daytime sleepiness

narcolepsy
Sleep disorder characterized by excessive daytime sleepiness and attacks of muscle weakness induced by emotion (cataplexy); the symptoms are due to the intrusion of REM sleep into waking time

in adolescence or early adulthood; however, 10 to 15 years may elapse before a correct diagnosis is made.

Psychological Detective

Narcolepsy consists of several symptoms that share a common connection. Use what you have learned about sleep to suggest what is wrong with the sleep of people who have narcolepsy that could cause these symptoms. You need to analyze each of the symptoms to find the connection. Write down your answer before reading further.

Sleep researchers have found that narcolepsy occurs when REM sleep intrudes into wakefulness. A review of the symptoms reveals how they are related to REM sleep. For example, the loss of muscle tone in cataplexy is consistent with the paralysis of skeletal muscles that occurs during REM sleep. The exact mechanism that causes REM to spill into waking time is not yet understood, although narcolepsy seems to be genetically transmitted. There is no cure for narcolepsy, but stimulant drugs can reduce the sleepiness, and antidepressant drugs can control the cataplexy. A long afternoon nap helps some victims ward off the attacks of sleep (Garma & Marchand, 1994).

Sleep Apnea.   Another major hypersomnia is seen in the case of a 59-year-old lawyer who fell asleep during a conference with a client. His spouse provided the clue to the diagnosis: Her husband's snoring was so loud that she had found it necessary to sleep in another room (Hartmann, 1987). Between 10 and 30 percent of adults snore with no serious consequences. For about 2 percent of middle-aged women and 4 percent of middle-aged men, however, loud snoring can be a sign of a serious sleep disorder, characterized by pauses in

---

TABLE 5-1   Suggestions for Good Sleep

1. Maintain regular sleep and waking times to establish a consistent circadian rhythm.

2. Avoid extreme temperature and noise. Reduce the amount of light entering the room.

3. Take time to "wind down" before you head off to sleep; establish relaxing presleep rituals such as soft music or a warm bath.

4. If you are unable to fall asleep within 15 to 20 minutes, get up and go to another room. Stay up as long as 30 minutes, then return to the bedroom to sleep. If you still cannot fall asleep, get up again. The goal is to associate the bed with falling asleep quickly.

5. Don't take your worries to bed. If you must worry, set aside some time earlier in the day. Don't make the bed the place to agonize over your problems.

6. Avoid alcohol, caffeine, and nicotine. Large doses of alcohol disrupt sleep. Caffeine and nicotine are stimulants, which cause arousal rather than sleep. Moreover, chronic use of sleeping pills can be ineffective and even detrimental to good sleep.

7. Eat light snacks which may help you sleep, especially if they contain L-tryptophan, which is found in milk, cheese, and other foods.

8. Exercise during the day promotes slow-wave sleep, but do not exercise within three hours of bedtime because its arousing effect can delay sleep.

Source: American Sleep Disorders Association, 1994; Hartmann, 1987; Hauri, 1991, 1992.

breathing during sleep. **Sleep apnea** (from the Greek word for "absence of breathing") is a serious, potentially life-threatening condition in which the flow of air to the lungs stops for at least 10 to 15 seconds (Brock & Shucard, 1994). There are two forms of sleep apnea: central and obstructive. *Central sleep apnea* (the less common form) occurs when the brain fails to send the appropriate signals to the muscles for breathing. *Obstructive sleep apnea* is far more common and occurs when air cannot flow into or out of the person's nose or mouth despite continued efforts to breathe (National Institutes of Health, 1995). After going without oxygen for as long as 90 seconds, the brain signals an emergency wake-up to fill the lungs with air.

Apnea victims may awaken hundreds of times a night, yet they become accustomed to the multiple awakenings. The risk of developing sleep apnea is higher among men and obese people (Brock & Shucard, 1994); sleep apnea also substantially increases their risk of death (Schmidt-Nowara & Jessop, 1995). Despite the serious health consequences associated with sleep apnea, at least 80 percent of all cases are likely to be unrecognized (Young et al., 1997).

Some cases of sleep apnea respond to changes in sleep position or weight loss; in other cases tongue-retaining devices or jaw retainers may be used to keep the airway free of obstruction (Pascualy & Soest, 1994). A very effective treatment for apnea is *continuous positive airway pressure* (CPAP, pronounced "see-pap"). At night a mask placed over the patient's nose is connected by a tube to a machine that maintains a flow of pressured air to the lungs to prevent airway collapse. Although CPAP therapy is effective, many patients stop using it because it is uncomfortable (National Commission on Sleep Disorders Research, 1992). In other cases, surgical procedures, including laser procedures, are used; for example, some excess, soft tissue at the back of the throat is shrunk or removed to enlarge the breathing passage.

Parasomnias.　The **parasomnias** are undesirable and/or distressing sleep behaviors other than insomnia and hypersomnia that occur exclusively during sleep or that are exacerbated by sleep. This diverse group of disorders ranges from bedwetting to nightmares. The disorders occur more frequently in children than in adults, perhaps reflecting the immaturity of a child's nervous system. Although many parasomnias disappear over time without treatment, some are potentially dangerous and even deadly.

sleep apnea
Sleep disorder characterized by pauses in breathing during sleep; most prevalent in older, overweight males

parasomnias
Sleep disorders, other than insomnia and hypersomnia, which occur more frequently in children and often disappear without treatment

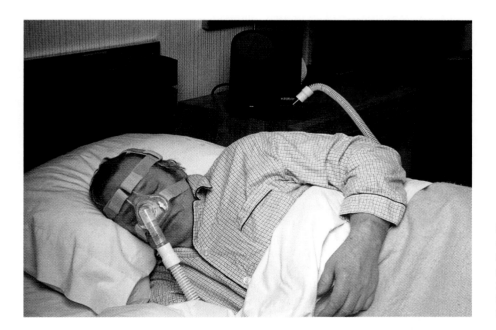

Sleep apnea can be treated with continuous positive airway pressure (CPAP). The mask over the sufferer's face is connected to a mechanical device that maintains a steady flow of air to keep the airway from collapsing.

Sleepwalking. As many as 20 percent of the population have experienced one or more episodes of **sleepwalking;** most of these episodes occur in children between the ages of 4 and 12 (Anch et al., 1988). In the movies, sleepwalkers walk about with their arms stretched out in front of them. In real life, however, a typical episode involves merely sitting up in bed. When a sleepwalker does get out of bed, he or she is likely to stumble about in a disoriented state and may turn on the lights, eat cat food sandwiches, or walk through open doors or windows. Although a sleepwalker's eyes are likely to be open, the person's EEG shows an unusual mixture of the brain waves associated with deep sleep and relaxed wakefulness.

Here is some helpful advice for parents of sleepwalkers: Remove any electrical cords that might cause tripping; locate the sleepwalker's bedroom on the first floor; and lock windows and doors. In most cases sleepwalking occurs for a few years and then disappears without treatment.

Psychological Detective

 Sleepwalkers can engage in some odd behaviors if they ramble about the house. Does this mean they are acting out a dream? Give this question some thought, and write down an answer before reading further.

Because the skeletal muscles are paralyzed during REM sleep, sleepwalkers do not act out their dreams. Instead, sleepwalking occurs during Stage 3 and 4 sleep and hence is more likely to occur during the first third of the night (Keefauver & Guilleminault, 1994; review Figure 5-5).

Although sleepwalking is closely associated with slow-wave sleep, another sleep disorder that occurs out of REM sleep resembles sleepwalking. *REM sleep behavior disorder (RBD)* is a syndrome of injurious or disruptive behavior that emerges during REM sleep (Schenck & Mahowald, 1990). RBD occurs primarily in older men; the average age of onset is in the fifties (Schenck, Hurwitz, & Mahowald, 1993). The behavior may consist of sitting up, jumping out of bed, running, and punching. As a result, both victim and spouse are frequently injured. One suspected cause is subtle age-related changes in the brain that affect the mechanism that usually suppresses voluntary muscle activity during REM sleep. RBD can be treated effectively with a mild tranquilizer.

Enuresis. **Enuresis** (bedwetting) is a childhood sleep problem that affects about 5 million children in the United States. Sleep specialists do not consider it a disorder unless the child is at least 5 years old (Friman & Warzak, 1990). Like other childhood sleep disorders, enuresis may reflect an immature nervous system. The tendency to develop enuresis runs in families; children with enuresis may inherit a delay in the development of the bladder muscles needed to control urination while sleeping.

Drug treatment of enuresis can pose health risks, and the drugs are often ineffective in the long run (Friman & Warzak, 1990). Other approaches to dealing with enuresis include waking the child periodically throughout the night and rewarding the child for sleeping through the night without wetting the bed. A common treatment is the "pad and buzzer," or urine alarm (Friman & Warzak, 1990; Houts, 1991). A urine sensor, either placed under the bedsheets or sewn into the child's underpants, is connected to a buzzer that sounds when the first drops of urine fall on it. The resultant awakenings make the child aware of bladder pressure. Once children have gained this awareness, they awaken spontaneously before beginning to urinate. Most children outgrow enuresis, as they do sleep terrors and sleepwalking, which suggests all three are related to delayed maturation.

sleepwalking
A parasomnia that occurs during Stage 4 sleep, most often consists of sitting up in bed

enuresis
Bedwetting, a sleep disorder that occurs primarily in children

Sleep Terrors.　**Sleep terrors** (also called *night terrors*) are intensely frightening experiences that begin during Stage 4 sleep. About 5 percent of children between ages 2 and 5 experience sleep terrors; the disorder usually disappears as the child matures. The first sign of a sleep terror is often a blood-curdling scream, usually followed by sitting up in bed. The accompanying physiological arousal is remarkable: Heart rate can triple in a minute, breathing is labored, and the sleeper becomes soaked with perspiration. Children are unable to recall the experience, which often terrifies their parents. By contrast, adult victims of night terrors (who have the experience very rarely) tend to recall the event in detail.

　　Nightmares are frightening dreams that occur during REM sleep; however, they are mild compared with sleep terrors. The dreamer experiences moderate anxiety and can often recall the disturbing dream. Young adults seem to experience about one nightmare per month; nightmare frequency in the general population is not related to anxiety levels (Wood & Bootzin, 1990).

Psychological Detective

Suppose you are the only technician working in a sleep laboratory. Two people are scheduled to spend a night in the laboratory in separate rooms; one suffers from sleep terrors and the other suffers from nightmares. You want to be present to observe each of the disorders, but you can't be in two places at once. If both people begin sleeping at the same time, can you accomplish your objective? Give this question some thought, and write down an answer, with reasons, before reading further.

　　Sleep terrors are a Stage 4 sleep disorder; they occur early in the night, usually within two hours after the person has fallen asleep. Nightmares take place during REM sleep, so they are likely to occur closer to the time of awakening, when REM episodes are longer. Even though you are the only technician on duty, you should be able to observe both the sleep terror and the nightmare.

SIDS.　Each year, more than 6,000 apparently healthy infants are found dead in their cribs after a night's sleep or a midday nap. **Sudden infant death syndrome (SIDS)** is the sudden death of an apparently healthy infant under one year of age that is not explained by an autopsy and investigation of the child's history and death scene. SIDS is the leading cause of death between the ages of 1 month and 1 year; most cases occur between two and four months of age (Sears, 1995). We do not know what causes SIDS, but we do know that certain factors increase the likelihood that it will occur. Sleeping in the prone position (on the belly) increases the risk of SIDS, as do a recent illness, sleeping on a soft mattress, and elevated room temperature. The specific means by which these factors contribute to SIDS is not yet known. One possibility is that the soft bedding material obstructs the air passage. Another possibility is that soft mattresses reduce air movement, which can increase the likelihood that the baby will rebreathe the carbon dioxide that was just exhaled (Ponsonby et al., 1993). Infants who have died of SIDS have a deficiency in the binding of the neurotransmitter acetylcholine (see Chapter 2) in the medulla—the part of the brain that controls breathing. This deficiency seems to render these infants less able to respond with protective reflexes that ensure proper breathing when their oxygen level drops (Kinney et al., 1995).

　　A national public health campaign, using the slogan "Back to Sleep," has encouraged caregivers to place infants to sleep on their side or back. In several countries these campaigns have led to decreases of approximately 50 percent in the SIDS death rate (Dwyer et al., 1995; Willinger, 1995). In addition, some

sleep terror
Partial awakening from Stage 4 sleep characterized by loud screams and extreme physiological arousal

nightmare
Frightening dream that occurs during REM sleep

sudden infant death syndrome (SIDS)
Unexpected death of an apparently healthy infant up to age 1 that is not explained by autopsy, medical case information, or an investigation of death scene

caregivers now use electronic monitors that track an infant's breathing and sound an alarm if it should stop.

Dreams: Nighttime Theater

Psychologist Calvin Hall (1966) describes a **dream** as "a succession of images, predominantly visual in quality, which are experienced during sleep" (p. 3). Opinions vary about the importance we should attach to this succession of images, but Hall believes that interpreting our dreams can enhance our self-knowledge.

As typically defined, dreams occur during REM sleep; however, do not let the association between REM and dream reports lead you to conclude NREM is a mental wasteland. When awakened from NREM sleep, people are likely to report some mental content. There are, however, qualitative differences between REM and NREM reports. REM dream reports are more vivid, more visual, more dramatic, more emotional, and more active. NREM reports tend to be just the opposite; they often resemble thoughts and are more concerned with current problems than REM dreams.

Why We Forget Our Dreams. Dream recall varies from one person to another. To study why we forget our dreams, psychologist David Cohen randomly divided college students into two groups and asked both groups to write down their dreams upon awakening (Cohen & Wolfe, 1973). Students in the experimental group called the weather information number and recorded the weather prediction before writing down their dreams. Those in the control group spent about 90 seconds (the time required to call the weather report) lying in bed before writing. Obtaining the weather report had a dramatic effect on dream recall: 33 percent of the students who called for the weather report recalled a dream, compared to 63 percent of those who did not call. Cohen concluded that engaging in various activities after we awaken interferes with our ability to remember our dreams.

Culture and Dreams

IT DOESN'T MATTER WHERE YOU LIVE OR WHO YOU ARE; FALL ASLEEP AND AT SOME point you will dream. Although some people claim they never dream, when awakened during the night in a sleep laboratory they inevitably report dreams. Whether a person remembers a dream upon awakening in the morning depends, in part, on factors such as interference but also on how one's culture views dreams.

Different cultures place varying emphases on dreams and support different beliefs concerning dreams. For example, many people in the United States view dreams as irrelevant fantasy with no connection to everyday life. By contrast, people in other cultures view dreams as key sources of information about the future, the spiritual world, and the dreamer. Such cultural views can influence the probability of dream recall. In many modern Western cultures, people rarely remember their dreams upon awakening. The Parintintin of South America, however, typically remember several dreams every night (Kracke, 1993), and the Senoi of Malaysia discuss their dreams with family members in the morning (Hennager, 1993).

Some cultures view dreams as real acts or channels of communication. A story of a missionary in one such culture illustrates the point: The missionary was amazed by the frequency of reports of adultery confessed by his converts. Later he discovered they were confessing sins they had carried out during their dreams. Among the Parintintin people, having an erotic dream may mean the

dream
A succession of visual images experienced during sleep

other person is thinking about the dreamer with desire. The Arapesh of New Guinea believe dreaming of someone else in an erotic manner is equivalent to actual intimate contact (Kracke, 1993). Similarly, the Senoi view dreams as a "co-reality" with waking life; to them, the dream world exists along with the waking world. If something occurs in one, it also occurs in the other. The Senoi believe that dreams reflect ongoing life events, and thus view them as an important guiding force in their lives. Moreover, Senoi children are encouraged to report dreams and to use them to manipulate reality (Hennager, 1993).

A method of analyzing dreams proposed by Calvin Hall (called *content analysis* of dreams) has been used to study dreams in a number of cultures. The results reveal both consistencies and differences that may reflect cultural emphasis on dreaming as well as differing cultural experiences. For example, the dreams of college students in the Netherlands contain fewer examples of physical aggression than the dreams of Americans. Perhaps this difference in dream content reflects the fact that the United States is the most violent industrialized nation, whereas the Netherlands is one of the least violent (Domhoff, 1996). The dreams of Japanese college students have fewer animals than the dreams of Americans. One possibility for this finding is the dreams reflect the primarily urban settings and the relative absence of pets in Japan. The dreams of Japanese students also contain more familiar than unfamiliar people compared with the dreams of Americans. Perhaps people in a society that emphasizes collectivism do not readily view others as strangers (Domhoff, 1996).

"Dreams are just taped replays of your day."

Reprinted with special permission of King Features Syndicate.

Interpreting Dreams.   According to Sigmund Freud (1900/1965), the dream you remember in the morning is the manifest content. If you told someone the dream you had last night, you would be reporting its **manifest content.** Freud believed, however, that we must probe beneath the obvious content for the deeper underlying meaning—that is, we must seek the **latent content.** The latent content is transformed into the manifest content by a process called *dream work.* Analysis of the manifest content would reveal attempts to fulfill wishes, especially of a sexual or aggressive nature, of which the dreamer was not consciously aware. These wishes are thus expressed in a symbolic form, which is the manifest content of our dreams.

Calvin Hall (1966) saw symbols in dreams that he believed explained rather than disguised or distorted meaning. For example, although a number of dream symbols can represent sex organs (sticks or knives may represent the male sex organ; ovens or chests may represent the female sex organ), most people understand the symbols; thus they do not hide meaning. Hall also found a number of common elements in his analysis of thousands of dreams. For example, most dreams include about two characters besides the dreamer, men dream about men more than about women, women dream about men and women equally, unpleasant emotions outnumber pleasant emotions, and hostile acts outnumber friendly acts.

Dreams can also be interpreted literally and symbolically. What does this mean? A literal interpretation of a dream about losing a possession may mean exactly that—that the object was lost. Because some dreams cannot be interpreted literally, however, they must be interpreted symbolically. Consider the dream of flying. Because we cannot fly under our own power, dreams of flying should be interpreted symbolically. One talk show host frequently dreamed of flying. What is a possible interpretation? His dreams of flying occurred when his show had gone particularly well; hence the dream expressed a feeling of "being on top of the world" (Faraday, 1972).

manifest content
According to Freud, the dream as reported by the dreamer

latent content
According to Freud, the deeper underlying meaning of a dream, connected by symbols to the manifest content

activation-synthesis hypothesis

Explanation of dreams that suggests that they result when the cortex seeks to explain the high level of neuronal activity occurring during REM sleep

Brain researchers J. Allan Hobson and Robert McCarley (1977) offer a different approach to explaining dreams. Their **activation-synthesis hypothesis** begins with the different ways brain cells turn on and off during waking as well as during both REM and NREM sleep. As we have seen, the brain is very active during REM sleep. Hobson and McCarley believe that dreams arise during REM sleep from random bursts of activity from nerve cells in the brain stem. The cortex of the brain then tries to make sense of these haphazard signals. Nevertheless, dreams can be disjointed and jumbled because they begin as random signals. Hobson and McCarley also draw parallels between brain activity and the characteristics of our dreams. For example, the brain centers responsible for motor activity fire furiously during REM sleep, but motor movement is blocked in the spinal cord and brain stem. Rapid firing of neurons also occurs in the brain centers responsible for the sense of balance, which may account for dream reports of flying. Remember, the eyes are moving rapidly, so it is not surprising that dreams are characterized by vivid visual imagery. Although this theory offers a physiological basis for dreams, it does not explain why certain themes may consistently appear in a person's dreams. This consistency is hard to explain if dreams are the result of random signals (Cartwright & Lamberg, 1992).

In sum, there are a number of approaches to the study and interpretation of dreams. For theorists who emphasize the personal meaning of dreams, dream interpretation involves symbols that may not be difficult to understand. By contrast, the activation-synthesis hypothesis states that the cortex creates dreams to explain elevated levels of brain activity during REM sleep. No one explanation of dreams is likely to satisfy everyone.

Review Summary

1. The major breakthrough in the study of sleep was the observation of *rapid eye movements (REM)*. Measures of physiological processes such as the *electroencephalograph (EEG)* also aid sleep research.

2. A sleep cycle lasts about 90 minutes and starts with **non-REM (NREM) sleep.** We descend through NREM Stages 1 to 4 and then ascend through them to **rapid eye movement (REM) sleep.** In the average adult, this cycle repeats itself about four to six times each night.

3. Average sleep decreases from about 16 hours at birth to about 7 to 8 hours in young adulthood, with little change thereafter. Observations of sleeping people suggest that many people are not getting enough sleep. Sleep efficiency (time in bed actually asleep) is lower among elderly people, who experience less slow-wave sleep and spend increased time in the lighter stages of sleep. Naps are more common than many people believe.

4. Sleep-deprived persons experience *microsleeps*, which can cause poor performance on tasks requiring attention.

5. REM sleep deprivation leads to the **REM rebound,** an increase in the amount of REM sleep. Infants spend about 50 percent of their sleep in REM,

perhaps to provide stimulation needed for brain development. Sleep may have evolved to fill time, but the amount of sleep in each species depends on vulnerability to predators and the need to find food.

6. Most cases of **insomnia** are of short duration. Sleeping pills have limited usefulness and should be used with care. The *stimulus control* method is an effective treatment for many cases of sleep-onset insomnia.

7. Hypersomnias are sleep disorders that are marked by excessive daytime sleepiness. **Narcolepsy** is characterized by daytime sleepiness, *cataplexy,* and other symptoms consistent with the intrusion of REM sleep into waking hours. Overweight, middle-aged men are susceptible to **sleep apnea,** which consists of frequent pauses in breathing during the night.

8. Parasomnias are sleep disturbances other than insomnia and hypersomnias. **Enuresis** (bedwetting) is a common disorder in childhood and can be treated with the urine alarm. **Sleepwalking** and **sleep terrors** are associated with Stage 4 sleep, tend to occur in children, and usually disappear without treatment. *REM sleep behavior disorder* occurs in older men and consists of aggressive actions during REM sleep. **Nightmares** are bad dreams that occur during REM sleep. **Sudden infant death syndrome (SIDS)** is the leading cause of death for infants between 1 month and 1 year of age. Placing infants to sleep on the side or back may reduce the incidence of SIDS.

9. As typically defined, dreams are associated with REM sleep, although NREM sleep is not a mental void. Freud suggested that dreams serve to fulfill wishes, especially of a sexual or aggressive nature.

Analysis of the **manifest content** of a dream yields the dream's **latent content,** or supposed true meaning. Waking activities can interfere with the ability to recall dreams.

10. The **activation-synthesis hypothesis** suggests that dreams result from attempts by the brain to make sense of high levels of neuronal activity.

Study Break

1. People observed in a sleep laboratory have several measuring devices attached to them. Name the device used to measure each of the following physiological indicators:
   a. Heart rate
   b. Brain waves
   c. Eye movements
2. If awakened at random, who is most likely to be in REM sleep?
   a. a 1-year-old child
   b. a 15-year-old adolescent
   c. a 35-year-old adult
   d. a 65-year-old adult
3. If you awaken a 27-year-old person from sleep at a randomly selected point of sleep, which of the following stages is most likely to be the one the person was in at the time of the awakening?
   a. Stage 1
   b. Stage 2
   c. Stage 3
   d. REM sleep
4. Give two reasons why the sleep of older people is less efficient than that of younger people.
5. Researchers have not found a complete answer to the

question "Why do we sleep?" One intriguing possibility is that the sleep time of various species is designed to provide a period of immobilization. Their length of sleep, in turn, depends on several factors; name two.

6. Identify the sleep disorder that is most likely afflicting each of the following people:
   a. Al experiences extreme daytime sleepiness and collapses to the floor after he tells a joke.
   b. Sixty-year-old Mel loves his wife very much, so he is puzzled to learn that he has attacked her during the night.
   c. A newspaper article described the death of 4-month-old Jessica from what was described as "the leading cause of death in children between the ages of 1 month and 1 year."
   d. Several times during the past two months, 3-year-old Tom has screamed loudly while asleep. When his parents rush to him, they find that his heart appears to be racing and he is soaked in perspiration.
   e. Because John feels sleepy every day and has felt this way for several years, his physician recommends that he be examined at a sleep disorders clinic, where they find that he awakens hundreds of times each night.

Hypnosis

Last week Beth and George attended a stage hypnotist's performance. The audience eagerly anticipated the show, and they were not disappointed. During the course of the show, an audience member was hypnotized and instructed to stretch his body across two chairs—head and shoulders on one chair and feet on the other. Then the hypnotist stood atop this "human plank" to show that a hypnotized person can support the hypnotist's entire weight. *Does hypnotism explain the human plank demonstration?* ▨

You may have seen performances by stage hypnotists or read advertisements claiming that hypnosis can help us lose weight, stop smoking, or study more effectively. The power attributed to hypnosis has intrigued and challenged practitioners, researchers, and theorists for more than a century.

The History of Hypnosis

In the eighteenth century, hypnosis was called *mesmerism,* after the Austrian physician Franz Anton Mesmer (1734–1815). Mesmer captured the imagination of many residents of Paris by claiming he could cure everything from toothaches to paralysis. He believed that the atmosphere was filled with an invisible magnetic force that he could accumulate in his body and transfer to the bodies of sick people. Patients who hoped to be healed sat around a tub filled with water, iron filings, and ground glass. Then Mesmer made a grand entrance and passed iron rods over the patients or touched them with a wand. The patients started shaking; their arms and legs moved involuntarily; some fainted. Mesmer assured them that several treatments would reestablish their bodies' magnetic equilibrium and cure their ailments. Countless testimonials attested to the healing power of the magnetic fluid.

The medical and scientific communities viewed Mesmer's treatments with skepticism and petitioned for an investigation. In 1784, a commission chaired by Benjamin Franklin concluded that the patients' reactions were due to imagination, not magnetism. Mesmer was discredited, but his technique survived to be used by others. In 1843, James Braid, a Scottish surgeon, changed its name to *hypnosis.*

Hypnotic Induction

John Kihlstrom (1985) defines **hypnosis** as "a social interaction in which one person, designated the subject, responds to suggestions offered by another person, designated the hypnotist, for experiences involving alterations in perception, memory, and voluntary action" (p. 385). Some theorists view hypnosis as an altered state of consciousness, called the *hypnotic trance;* others claim that hypnotized people behave in accordance with their expectations about hypnosis. To understand why these different views persist, we need to take a closer look at the phenomenon of hypnosis and how it is produced.

Human response to hypnotists' communications led researchers to the concept of *suggestibility,* or "hypnotizability." People clearly differ in suggestibility—that is, in how readily they follow a hypnotist's suggestions. About 5 to 10 percent of adults are so unresponsive to suggestion they cannot be hypnotized.

A hypnotist needs to create a situation in which people are especially likely to follow suggestions, instructions, or requests. This process is known as *hypnotic induction.* Traditional hypnotic induction involves having the subject gaze at an object, inducing relaxation, fostering imagination, and encouraging drowsiness.

Suppose you have agreed to be hypnotized. The hypnotist may tell you to "relax and concentrate" on an object such as a watch. "You are becoming more relaxed. Your eyelids are becoming heavier. You are becoming sleepy." Although the word *hypnosis* is derived from the Greek word for sleep, hypnosis is not sleep. The EEG of a hypnotized person indicates relaxation, not sleep.

After a brief induction such as the one just described, the hypnotist uses a number of tests to judge your degree of suggestibility. You may be asked to "lock the fingers of both hands together so tightly they cannot be separated." Can you separate your fingers? Such tests allow hypnotists to determine whether you are susceptible to hypnosis. If you are, you are likely to be highly hypnotizable 25 years from now because susceptibility to hypnosis appears to be quite stable over time (Piccione, Hilgard, & Zimbardo, 1989).

hypnosis
State of heightened susceptibility to suggestions

Hypnotic Phenomena

A hypnotist *cannot* make you do anything you would not do otherwise. Hypnosis does not endow you with superhuman strength; you will not be able to lift a car while hypnotized unless you can lift it while not hypnotized. Hypnosis depends on establishing a positive relationship between the hypnotist and the hypnotized person (Levitt, Baker, & Fish, 1990).

In this section we examine some of the claims made for hypnosis. We begin with some of the more dramatic claims—those dealing with pain reduction and medical treatment.

Pain Reduction and Medical Treatment. Since the 1800s, numerous researchers have described the use of hypnosis to reduce the pain of surgery, childbirth, burns, cancer, and dental procedures. The lack of proper controls in the reported cases should make us skeptical, but it does not preclude the possibility that some people benefit from such treatment.

Psychological Detective

 An advertisement for pain-free dentistry attracts your attention, but you have some questions about the treatment. A friend tells you he has had several dental procedures done under hypnosis and has felt no pain. What components of hypnosis might be helpful in reducing pain or alleviating certain medical problems?

Several elements of hypnotic induction could help reduce pain. First, relaxation, which is typically included in the induction, can help reduce pain. Second, the hypnotist's encouragement may help patients who are experiencing pain. Third, in helping people withstand pain, repeated presentations of the hypnotic induction are more effective than a single presentation (Price & Barber, 1987). The multiple presentations may serve as relaxation reminders or may distract the person from the experience of pain.

In addition to alleviating pain, hypnosis has been used to combat common medical problems. Nicholas Spanos (1991) reviewed the effectiveness of hypnosis in treating medical conditions such as asthma and behavior problems such as smoking. There were few differences between treatments with or without hypnosis. Spanos concluded that the benefits that did occur were due to the patients' attitudes and expectations rather than to any intrinsic effect of hypnosis.

Memory Effects. After a hypnotic session, some hypnotized people may report that they cannot remember events that occurred during the session. Perhaps these lost memories can be recovered when the hypnotist gives a particular signal. Hypnosis has been proposed as an aid to memory, which would be a major benefit to the police. Witnesses or victims of crimes do not have photographic memories, and the stress associated with traumatic events like observing a murder or suffering an assault makes it difficult to remember the event clearly.

The use of testimony that has been hypnotically refreshed but not confirmed by physical evidence has, however, aroused serious concern (Giannelli, 1995). When people undergo hypnosis to refresh their memories, their recall often contains distortions and false memories. Yet they tend to be more confident of the accuracy of those memories than people who have not undergone hypnosis (Spiegel & Scheflin, 1994; Steblay, Mehrkens, & Bothwell, 1994). As one expert observed, "Researchers in the field of hypnosis have known for well over a century that false memories can be implanted in individuals through the use of formal hypnotic procedures or even through simple suggestion" (Yapko, 1994, p. 96).

Perception.   Among the various perceptual effects reported by people who have been hypnotized are positive and negative hallucinations. *Positive hallucinations* are reports of seeing an object that is not really present. For example, a hypnotized person may report petting an imaginary cat. With *negative hallucinations,* a hypnotized person fails to perceive an object that is present. For example, he or she may walk into a chair in the middle of a room.

A clever approach to testing the validity of hypnotically induced perceptual changes is to give a hypnotic suggestion of deafness and ask a hypnotized person to read aloud. His (or her) words are played back to him a half second after they are spoken; this delay is confusing for the average hearing person. If hypnotic deafness had been induced, the delayed feedback would have no effect; however, studies have found that it has as great an effect on hypnotized people as it does on those who have not been hypnotized (Baker, 1990).

Age Regression.   In the phenomenon of *age regression,* hypnotized people are given suggestions that allegedly lead them to relive events that occurred when they were younger—often during childhood—and to feel and act like a child of that age. The changes observed in adults who have responded to such suggestions can be dramatic and seem to offer convincing evidence that age regression has occurred.

Are the changes attributed to hypnotic age regression different from those that could occur in someone who has not been hypnotized? In one study, 92 percent of hypnotized people who had regressed to their tenth birthday correctly identified the day of the week on which the event took place, and 84 percent of those who had regressed to their fourth birthday did the same (True, 1949).

Psychological Detective

These findings are impressive, but are you convinced that the study participants recalled the day of the week of their fourth or tenth birthday? Can you recall the day of the week of your last birthday? Subsequent researchers found a major flaw in this study that explained the high rates of recall. Can you think of a research flaw that might account for these results? Write it down before reading further.

The hypnotist-experimenter who conducted this study had a perpetual calendar on his desk. As he questioned the participants, he could have subtly cued the correct answer when asking such questions as "Was it Wednesday?" When other investigators corrected this methodological flaw, they could not replicate the finding.

Hypnotic regression has been used to take people on even more impressive journeys—journeys to previous lives. In hypnotic *past-life regression,* people are said to report prior lives as well as events from earlier times. Such reports, however, depend in part on suggestions by the hypnotist. If the hypnotist expresses little belief in past-life regression, participants report few such experiences (Spanos et al., 1991). Past-life reports are also sprinkled with errors of historical fact that people from the relevant historical period would be unlikely to make. For example, one person claimed to be Julius Caesar, emperor of Rome, in 50 B.C. Do you see the problem? The designations B.C. and A.D. were not used until centuries later (Spanos, 1987–88).

Explanations of Hypnosis

As noted earlier, researchers are divided in their explanations for hypnosis. According to the *cognitive-social view,* the phenomena we label *hypnotic* occur when someone enacts the role of a hypnotized person. This view suggests that hypnosis is not an altered state of consciousness.

One of the problems in viewing hypnosis as an altered state of consciousness is that it is difficult to know when a person is hypnotized. Veteran hypnosis researcher Ernest Hilgard (1991) admits "it would be more comfortable for the investigator if there were some precise indicator of the establishment of a hypnotic condition, but so far that has eluded investigators" (p. 39). Moreover, some of the feats attributed to hypnosis can also be accomplished by people who have not undergone hypnotic induction.

At the beginning of this section we met Beth and George, who attended a stage hypnotist's performance. They were amazed when a hypnotized person who was stretched across two chairs was able to hold the weight of the hypnotist on his chest. Do we need the concept of hypnosis to explain this human plank demonstration? The photograph on this page shows two people, neither of whom is hypnotized, performing the human plank. The demonstration works if the hypnotist is not very heavy and does not remain in position for long. If Beth and George had known what you now know, they would not have been so amazed.

If the shoulders and feet are properly supported, the weight of a person standing on the chest of the human plank can be supported. The weight is carried by the strong muscles of the shoulders, back, buttocks, and legs. If, however, these muscles are weak or if the chairs slide, serious injury can result.

Psychological Detective

 The cognitive-social perspective views hypnotized people as behaving the way they believe hypnotized people behave. If you were participating in an experiment on hypnosis, how would you behave as a hypnotized person? Give this question some thought, examining your expectations about hypnosis, and write down an answer before reading further.

Robert Baker (1990) asked several students to undergo hypnotic induction before making an instructional videotape. When he found that he needed more volunteers, he asked studio personnel to fill in, although they were not hypnotized. They all behaved so similarly that the audience could not distinguish the fill-ins from those who had undergone hypnotic induction. All participants sat with their eyes closed, looked sleepy, and complied with requests to lower and raise their hands. When told that their chairs were burning hot, everyone got up. This demonstration reveals that people easily conform to their perceptions of what hypnotized people do, which is to respond automatically to suggestions (Lynn, Rhue, & Weekes, 1989).

Earlier in this chapter we mentioned pain reduction as a claim made for hypnosis. Among the most striking demonstrations of pain reduction through hypnosis are those occurring during dental procedures or childbirth. Ernest Hilgard (1991) has proposed an explanation of hypnotic phenomena that originated in studies of people experiencing painful stimuli. Hilgard suggests that hypnosis involves a **dissociation,** or splitting of conscious awareness. Examples of dissociation can occur in ordinary activities. Have you ever been reading a book only to find that you had no idea what you had read for the past several minutes? Your eyes were following the text, but your mind was daydreaming; the act of reading and the memory of what you read were dissociated from the experience of daydreaming.

Hilgard proposes that some people, when facing painful stimuli, can dissociate the experience so successfully that one part of the mind is aware of the

dissociation
Splitting of conscious awareness that is believed to play a role in hypnotic pain reduction

pain while another is unaware of it. These parts of the mind are separated and have no knowledge of each other. But what type of person is capable of dissociating consciousness in this way? Researchers have found that an excellent predictor of hypnotizability is a tendency to become heavily involved in imaginative activities and to have exceptionally vivid images that occur without much deliberate effort (Wilson & Barber, 1983). These fantasy-prone people spend about half their time absorbed in fantasy. In fact, their sexual fantasies are so powerful they claim to be capable of achieving orgasm without physical stimulation. Their very vivid imaginations can serve a useful function by enabling them to alter consciousness in ways that are adaptive—for example, by using dissociation to deal with pain.

There are competing explanations for hypnosis; in fact, experts disagree as to whether hypnosis is a phenomenon that even needs explanation. Obviously, more research must be done in this area.

Review Summary

1. Hypnosis can be traced to the eighteenth century, when Franz Anton Mesmer claimed he had the power to induce magnetic equilibrium in the bodies of his patients.

2. Hypnosis can be defined as a heightened state of suggestibility. Contrary to the popular view that it is an altered state of consciousness, evidence shows it does not differ from a state of relaxation.

3. Hypnosis has been used to reduce pain in various kinds of medical treatments. It is not clear, however, what aspect of hypnosis may be responsible for pain reduction; relaxation, distraction, and expectations seem to play significant roles.

4. Hypnosis has been used to improve recall; however, hypnotically refreshed memories tend to contain distortions and false reports.

5. In hypnotic *age regression,* a hypnotized person appears to return to childhood or perhaps even to past lives. Research indicates age regression results in the reporting of fantasies or memories suggested by the hypnotist.

6. There are competing explanations of hypnosis. The *cognitive-social* explanation suggests that the observed phenomena can be explained by the relationship between the hypnotist and the hypnotized person, as well as by widely shared expectations about the procedure. Another explanation, offered by Ernest Hilgard, suggests that **dissociation,** or a separation of parts of the mind, may be at work in cases of hypnosis.

Study Break

1. What force did Mesmer claim to harness in his efforts to cure various ailments?
   a. the soul
   b. magnetism
   c. a "virtual essence"
   d. sleep juice
2. A person is hypnotized and is given the posthypnotic suggestion she is deaf. How would a researcher test the validity of the suggestion for deafness?
   a. Play the hypnotized person's favorite music
   b. Check the level of delta waves in the brain
   c. Feed back her reading with a delay of about a half-second
   d. Watch her body movements to detect any hint that she can hear

3. What are the key elements of hypnotic induction?
4. There is controversy concerning whether hypnosis can reduce pain or cure medical problems. What elements of hypnosis may be responsible for reports of pain reduction in hypnotized patients?
5. Early research on the effects of age regression through hypnosis seemed to suggest that hypnosis could bring back memories of an earlier time. What serious flaw was identified in this research?
6. Describe the effect that hypnosis seems to have when it is used to refresh a person's memory; for example, that of a witness to a crime.
7. What does Hilgard mean by dissociation, and how does he use this concept to explain hypnotic phenomena, especially pain reduction?

Altering Consciousness with Drugs

psychoactive substances
Chemicals that affect consciousness, perception, mood, and behavior

Two middle-aged couples having dinner at a fancy restaurant were talking about taxes, politics, and drugs. They agreed that they would never use any drugs that could affect their minds. Halfway through the meal, they asked the waitress to bring them another bottle of wine. Later they had several cups of coffee with their chocolate pie. After dinner, they went for a walk and smoked a few cigarettes. *Are illicit drugs the only substances that can affect consciousness, perception, mood, and behavior?* ■

As we write this chapter, we hear and read reports concerning drug use from around the country. Almost every day police find another crop of marijuana; the tragic results of drinking and driving frequently appear in the media.

Many people use the term *drug* to refer to illegal, possibly addicting substances, as opposed to the medicines taken to cure illnesses. Actually, the term refers to both legal and illegal substances; a drug is any chemical that modifies physiological functioning. **Psychoactive substances,** which include many illegal or illicit drugs, are chemicals that can alter consciousness, perception, mood, and behavior.

The two couples just described claimed they would never use any drugs that could affect their minds. Yet within just a few hours, they used three legal psychoactive substances: alcohol (in wine), caffeine (in coffee and chocolate pie), and nicotine (in cigarettes). When they said they would never use drugs, they meant illegal or mind-altering drugs; they were assuming that the legal substances they were using would not affect their minds. But as we will see shortly, they were mistaken. The most common psychoactive substances can be divided into four categories on the basis of their effects: depressants, stimulants, opioids, and hallucinogens (see Table 5-2).

The National Household Survey on Drug Abuse estimates that 13 million people (age 12 and older) in the United States used an illicit drug in the month prior to the survey. Marijuana, the most commonly used illicit drug, was used by 77 percent of current illicit drug users. The 1.7 million cocaine users represented a significant drop from the peak of 5.7 million in 1985 (U. S. Department of Health and Human Services, 1997). Every year, surveys of high school seniors provide statistics on the percentage who use various drugs. Figure 5-10 shows the percentage of high school seniors who are

FIGURE 5-10 Percent of twelfth graders who have used any illicit drug, several specific illicit drugs, or alcohol in the 30 days prior to being surveyed for the University of Michigan's Monitoring the Future study.

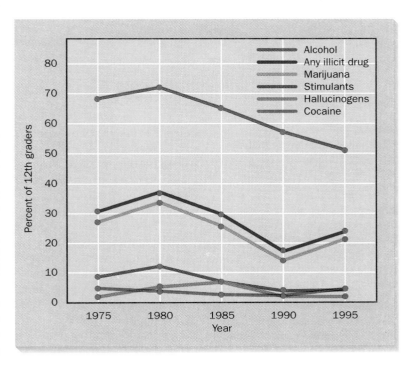

TABLE 5-2 The Effects of Major Drugs

DRUG	SOURCE	COMMON OR SLANG NAMES	MEANS OF ADMINISTRATION	TYPICAL REACTIONS
Depressants				
Alcohol	Fermenting sugar and yeast	Booze, juice, sauce	Taken orally	Tension reduction, reduced inhibitions, relief from anxiety, drowsiness
Barbiturates	Synthetically derived	Barbs, blues, yellow jackets	Taken orally, injected	Tension reduction, reduced inhibitions, relief from anxiety, drowsiness
Stimulants				
Amphetamines	Synthetically derived	Uppers, speed, crank	Taken orally, injected	Increased alertness, elevated mood, reduced fatigue, increased motor activity
Cocaine	Coca plant	Coke, rock, blow	Taken orally, (chewed), injected (snorted), smoked	Increased alertness, elevated mood, reduced fatigue, increased motor activity
Opioids				
Morphine	Opium poppy	White stuff, M, morf	Taken orally, injected, inserted rectally	Relaxed euphoria, sedation, reduced apprehension
Heroin	Morphine	Junk, china white, smack	Injected, smoked, inserted rectally	Relaxed euphoria, sedation, reduced apprehension
Hallucinogens				
Lysergic acid diethylamide (LSD)	Ergot fungus on rye	Acid, LSD-25, blotter acid	Taken orally	Illusions, hallucinations, distortions in time, anxiety, enhanced sensory experience
Marijuana	*Cannabis sativa* (hemp) plant	Pot, grass, weed	Taken orally, smoked	Euphoria, relaxed inhibitions, increased sense of well-being

substance abuse
Pattern of substance use that has detrimental effects on a person's health and safety and on social and occupational roles

substance dependence
More serious pattern of substance use than found in substance abuse; popularly called *addiction* and often characterized by drug tolerance

tolerance
Need for increasing dosages of a drug to achieve the same effect as earlier doses

current users of several drugs (used the drug in the 30 days prior to the survey) across a number of years.

The effects of most psychoactive substances can be explained by the changes they cause in the action of neurotransmitters (see Chapter 2), especially in the brain. Thus most psychoactive substances can have wide-ranging effects.

The regular and excessive use of drugs can lead to a pattern of maladaptive behavior known as a *substance use disorder* that includes substance abuse and substance dependence (American Psychiatric Association, 1994). **Substance abuse** occurs when use of a substance disrupts family and social relationships, interferes with work, and/or creates health and safety hazards for the abuser.

People who display **substance dependence,** a more serious disorder that is popularly called *addiction,* develop a physical dependence on the substance in addition to a pattern of abuse. Physical dependence is evident in the phenomenon of **tolerance,** which occurs when a person needs increasing

CONSEQUENCES OF AN OVERDOSE	MEDICAL USES	EFFECTS ON NEUROTRANSMITTERS
Disorientation, loss of consciousness, lack of coordination; at very high levels, death owing to cessation of respiration	Antiseptic	Enhances the activity of GABA, inhibits acetylcholine, augments the action of dopamine; alters the processes of neuronal membranes such as ions and neurotransmitters
Impaired motor and intellectual performance, coma and death at high doses when mixed with alcohol	Sedative, sleeping pill, anesthetic, anticonvulsant	Enhances the activity of the inhibitory neurotransmitter, GABA
Anxiety, suspiciousness, paranoia, hallucinations	Treatment of attention-deficit hyperactivity disorder, narcolepsy; diet aid in weight-loss programs	Blocks the reuptake of dopamine and norepinephrine
Anxiety, suspiciousness, paranoia, hallucinations	Local anesthetic	Blocks the reuptake of dopamine and norepinephrine
Possible death owing to depression of the respiratory system	Painkiller, cough suppressant	Inhibits the release of substance P and increases the release of dopamine
Possible death owing to depression the respiratory system	—	Inhibits the release of substance P and increases the release of dopamine
"Bad trip," characterized by anxiety, panic attacks, or serious psychotic reactions	—	Interferes with the normal action of serotonin, which in turn triggers response that involve several other neurotransmitters
Impaired learning and coordination, dizziness, paranoia, hallucinations	Reduction of nausea and vomiting associated with chemotherapy for cancer, reduction of intraocular pressure in glaucoma	Affects specific brain receptors, which are structurally similar to opioid receptors

doses of a substance to achieve the effect formerly obtained from a smaller dose. **Withdrawal,** characterized by changes in behavior, cognition, and physiology, may then occur if the person stops taking the substance or reduces the amount taken. The symptoms of withdrawal range from irritability to a craving for the substance that can begin within hours of taking the last dose.

In the remainder of this section, we take a closer look at each of the major categories of psychoactive substances.

Depressants

Depressants are drugs that slow functioning of the central nervous system. Among the depressants are alcohol and barbiturates. **Alcohol** is one of the most widely used psychoactive substances in the United States and throughout the world. Barbiturates are less common but are still readily available.

withdrawal
Changes in behavior, cognition, and physiology that occur when stopping or reducing the heavy and prolonged use of a psychoactive substance

depressants
Drugs that slow the activity of the central nervous system, including alcohol and barbiturates

alcohol
Depressant psychoactive substance, also known as ethyl alcohol or ethanol

Among the factors responsible for drinking are social pressures and the expectation of positive effects of alcohol.

Alcohol.   Along with nicotine and caffeine, alcohol might be called an unrecognized drug. We are so accustomed to consuming alcohol that "to drink" often means to drink alcoholic beverages unless otherwise specified. The following are some significant facts about alcohol use in the United States:

- Alcohol contributes to 100,000 deaths and an annual economic cost of $100 billion; approximately 40 percent of traffic fatalities are alcohol-related.
- A survey of college students found that 50 percent of men and 39 percent of women engaged in binge drinking (drinking five or more drinks in a row for men or four or more for women during the two weeks prior to the survey). Binge drinking was associated with health and other problems such as personal injuries and property damage.
- In 1995, high school seniors had a 3.5 percent rate of daily use of alcohol; 81 percent had used alcohol at some time during their lives (Johnston, O'Malley, & Bachman, 1996; Secretary of Health and Human Services, 1997; Wechsler et al., 1994).

The use of alcohol is associated with a range of medical and mental health problems. Heavy alcohol use is linked to several forms of cancer, antisocial personality disorder (see Chapter 13), and heart damage (O'Connor & Schottenfeld, 1998; Secretary of Health and Human Services, 1997). *Moderate* consumption of alcohol, however, is associated with a lower risk of heart disease; the exact mechanism by which this occurs is not known, although alcohol seems to reduce cholesterol levels (Zakhari, 1997). Public health officials hesitate to call for consumption of alcohol to reduce heart disease risk for fear that such a call would be misinterpreted. Alcohol is the primary contributor to cirrhosis, a disease of the liver that is the eleventh leading cause of death in the United States (Dufour, 1995). Thus it is important to identify and treat alcohol abuse or dependence as early as possible. The questionnaire in Table 5-3 is designed to help people determine whether they have a problem with alcohol.

TABLE 5-3   Alcohol Use Disorders Identification Test (AUDIT) Core Questionnaire

The World Health Organization developed this self-report questionnaire as a measure of alcohol consumption, symptoms of dependence, and personal and social harm owing to drinking, especially in the past year. The AUDIT is effective in detecting hazardous or harmful drinking as well as confirming cases of alcohol dependence.

1. How often do you have a drink containing alcohol?
   (0) Never
   (1) Monthly or less
   (2) 2 to 4 times a month
   (3) 2 to 3 times a week
   (4) 4 or more times a week

2. How many drinks containing alcohol do you have on a typical day when you are drinking?
   (0) 1 or 2
   (1) 3 or 4
   (2) 5 or 6
   (3) 7 to 9
   (4) 10 or more standard drinks

3. How often do you have six or more drinks on one occasion?
   (0) Never
   (1) Less than monthly
   (2) Monthly
   (3) Weekly
   (4) Daily or almost daily

4. How often during the last year have you found that you were not able to stop drinking once you had started?
   (0) Never
   (1) Less than monthly
   (2) Monthly
   (3) Weekly
   (4) Daily or almost daily

5. How often during the last year have you failed to do what was normally expected from you because of drinking?
   (0) Never
   (1) Less than monthly
   (2) Monthly
   (3) Weekly
   (4) Daily or almost daily

6. How often during the last year have you needed a first drink in the morning to get yourself going after a heavy drinking session?
   (0) Never
   (1) Less than monthly
   (2) Monthly
   (3) Weekly
   (4) Daily or almost daily

7. How often during the last year have you had a feeling of guilt or remorse after drinking?
   (0) Never
   (1) Less than monthly
   (2) Monthly
   (3) Weekly
   (4) Daily or almost daily

8. How often during the last year have you been unable to remember what happened the night before because you had been drinking?
   (0) Never
   (1) Less than monthly
   (2) Monthly
   (3) Weekly
   (4) Daily or almost daily

9. Have you or someone else been injured as a result of your drinking?
   (0) No
   (2) Yes, but not in the last year
   (4) Yes, during the last year

10. Has a relative, friend, doctor, or other health worker been concerned about your drinking or suggested you cut down?
   (0) No
   (2) Yes, but not in the last year
   (4) Yes, during the last year

Scores of 8 or above are associated with hazardous or harmful alcohol use.

Source: Bohn, Babor, & Kranzler, 1995; Saunders et al., 1993.

Effects of Alcohol.   The alcohol in beer, distilled liquor, and wine is ethyl alcohol, or ethanol. This colorless liquid contains a relatively high number of calories but virtually no vitamins or other nutrients. Drinking alcoholic beverages adds calories to your diet at the same time it slows your rate of fat metabolism. The fat that is not broken down is deposited on your hips, thighs, and stomach (Suter, Schutz, & Jequier, 1992).

Alcohol content varies with the beverage: Beer is 3 to 6 percent alcohol, wine 8 to 20 percent, distilled beverages 40 to 50 percent. Typical servings of these beverages (e.g., beer, 8 to 12 ounces; wine, 5 to 6 ounces; distilled beverages, 2 ounces) contain similar amounts of alcohol, so the effects of alcohol do not depend so much on what you drink as on how much you drink.

BLOOD ALCOHOL CONCENTRATION (B.A.C.) CHART
(PERCENT OF ALCOHOL IN BLOODSTREAM)

YOUR WEIGHT ▼	NUMBER OF DRINKS CONSUMED *								
	1	2	3	4	5	6	7	8	9
100	.029	.058	.088	.117	.146	.175	.204	.233	.262
120	.024	.048	.073	.097	.121	.145	.170	.194	.219
140	.021	.042	.063	.083	.104	.125	.146	.166	.187
160	.019	.037	.055	.073	.091	.109	.128	.146	.164
180	.017	.033	.049	.065	.081	.097	.113	.130	.146
200	.015	.029	.044	.058	.073	.087	.102	.117	.131
220	.014	.027	.040	.053	.067	.080	.093	.106	.119
240	.012	.024	.037	.048	.061	.073	.085	.097	.109

USE CAUTION	DRIVING IMPAIRED	LEGALLY DRUNK
Response time affected	Crash risk quadrupled at .080%	

NOTE: .100 OR ABOVE IS LEGALLY INTOXICATED [756]

DO NOT DRIVE

* ONE DRINK = 1 oz. of 80 proof alcohol; 12 oz. bottle of beer; or 3 oz. glass of wine.

FIGURE 5-11   Blood alcohol concentration (BAC) levels. The concentration of alcohol in the blood is related to body weight and the number of drinks consumed. The BAC levels in this chart assume that the drinks have been consumed in one hour. At the same weight and after consuming identical amounts of alcohol, women will typically have a slightly higher BAC than men.

Source: Washington State Liquor Control Board.

Your body can break down alcohol before it affects you if you consume it slowly, but few people consume it slowly enough (the liver can break down the alcohol in one drink per hour). The amount of alcohol in the blood depends in part on how long it takes the stomach to empty its contents into the small intestine, where most of the alcohol enters the bloodstream. If you slow the stomach's emptying time, you slow (but do not stop) the release of alcohol into the blood. One reason to eat food while drinking alcoholic beverages is that the presence of food in your stomach slows the emptying process.

Blood alcohol concentration (BAC) is the percentage of alcohol in the blood; a BAC of 0.05 percent is 5 parts of alcohol per 1,000 parts of blood. Many states use a BAC of 0.10 as the legal definition of intoxication, although some states have lowered it to 0.08. As you can see in Figure 5-11, your BAC depends primarily on your weight and the number of drinks you have consumed. A person who weighs 120 pounds will have a much higher BAC than one who weighs 240 pounds if they both consume the same number of drinks. A woman who weighs the same as a man and consumes the same amount of alcohol, however, will nevertheless have a slightly higher BAC level. This sex difference in BAC levels may be due to differences in the efficiency of one of the enzymes that breaks down alcohol. For reasons that are not yet understood, the enzyme is not as efficient in women as it is in men (Braun, 1996). With a BAC of about 0.32, you could endure surgery without awareness; BAC levels of 0.40 and higher can paralyze the part of the brain (the medulla) that controls breathing and thus cause death.

Alcohol affects virtually all organs of the body, especially the brain. Did you ever wonder why some of your friends behave in outrageous ways at parties after having consumed alcohol? Alcohol depresses brain areas that inhibit behavior, thereby allowing the person to engage in behaviors that might not otherwise occur. Even at low levels, alcohol quickly affects vision, reaction time, muscle coordination, and judgment.

One reason people drink alcohol is the expectation of positive effects: They believe alcohol helps them feel better, overcome a gloomy mood, or fall asleep more easily (Stacy, Widaman, & Marlatt, 1990). In low doses, alcohol reduces anxiety in nervous or shy persons, but in higher doses, it interferes with sexual performance (Crowe & George, 1989). Shakespeare summarized the effects of alcohol on sexual arousal in these words from *Macbeth* (act 2, scene 1): "It provokes the desire but takes away the performance."

People who have been drinking alcoholic beverages may end up in a sexual or driving situation that seems to contradict their usual attitudes and intentions. Why? Alcohol leads to an altered state of consciousness characterized by decreased capacity to attend to the information presented. In one study, sober and intoxicated college students expressed equally negative attitudes when they were asked general questions about drinking and driving. When asked more specific questions, however, such as "Would you drink and drive only a short distance?" intoxicated students were less likely than sober ones to say no (MacDonald, Zanna, & Fong, 1995). Thus intoxicated persons may attend only to the most salient cues at the moment, such as the desire to get home as quickly as possible. This *alcohol myopia* (Steele & Josephs, 1990) may account for a number of instances in which intoxicated drinkers engage in behaviors that contradict attitudes they express while sober.

A number of studies suggest that alcohol and aggression are related. For example, 42 percent of violent crimes reported to police involved alcohol, and estimates for specific crimes are even higher (National Institute on Alcohol Abuse and Alcoholism, 1997). Recent laboratory research has clarified our understanding of the association between alcohol and aggression. At low BAC levels, our expectations seem to play a significant role in the effects of alcohol; however, at higher levels, the biological effect of alcohol on the central nervous system, especially the brain, is the prime determinant of its effect. Violence is more likely to occur at higher BAC levels (Chermack & Taylor, 1995). The specific mechanism that accounts for increased aggression after ingestion of high doses of alcohol is not known. Alcohol has a wide range of effects that may play a role. For example, high doses of alcohol reduce fear, which may diminish the concern about potential harm resulting from aggressive actions.

One serious consequence of long-term heavy consumption of alcohol is a form of withdrawal called *delirium tremens (DTs)*. The symptoms include severe anxiety, a fast pulse, and even death. Vivid hallucinations, especially of small, quickly moving insects or animals, also occur and can heighten the person's anxiety. The hallucinations may result from REM rebound, because alcohol suppresses REM; when alcohol is withdrawn, a great deal of REM returns.

Another long-term consequence of alcohol use is *Korsakoff's syndrome,* a severe brain impairment characterized by forgetting incidents of one's daily life as soon as they occur. Consequently, people with this syndrome virtually live in the past. For example, a person who developed Korsakoff's in the 1960s might believe the president of the United States today is John Kennedy (Oscar-Berman et al., 1997). An alcoholic's diet is often lacking certain vitamins; a deficiency in thiamine (a B vitamin) plays a crucial role in the development of Korsakoff's syndrome. Moreover, extensive use of alcohol can damage brain areas that are important to memory, such as the hippocampus (Berman, 1990).

Factors that Influence Alcohol Use.

Drinking patterns vary among different populations within our society. For example, men drink more than women and experience more adverse consequences of drinking (U.S. Department of Health and Human Services, 1993). According to an annual survey of drug use by high school seniors, 3.6 percent of boys but only 1.4 percent of girls use alcohol on a daily basis. Thirty-five percent of high school senior boys drank five or more drinks in a row in the two weeks prior to the survey versus 21 percent of the girls (Johnston, O'Malley, & Bachman, 1996).

In the United States the one-year prevalence of alcohol abuse and dependence (commonly called *alcoholism*) is approximately 7 percent of people over age 18, a total of about 13 million people. The rates of alcohol abuse and dependence vary according to a number of factors, especially the person's sex (Grant et al., 1994). The rates of alcohol abuse and dependence are higher for men than for women (see Figure 5-12). Age is also a factor: The 1-year prevalence of problem drinking is much higher among persons aged 18 to 29 than at other ages (Grant et al., 1994).

Both physiological and social factors play important roles in alcohol consumption. About 50 percent of East Asians have a deficiency in the enzyme that breaks

Magnetic resonance images (MRIs) of the brains of two men, one with and one without a history of heavy alcohol consumption. The dark areas reveal enlarged ventricles (fluid-filled spaces) resulting from a loss of brain tissue. Changes such as this one are common in persons who have consumed large amounts of alcohol for many years.

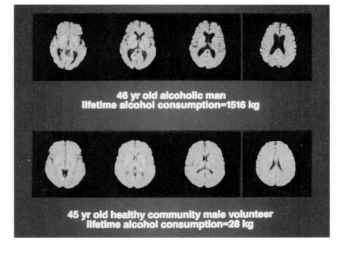

Approximately 40 percent of highway deaths are related to alcohol use.

barbiturates
Depressant drugs that are used to induce sleep but can be deadly when combined with alcohol

FIGURE 5-12 One-year prevalence rates of alcohol abuse or dependence in the United States. Note that for each ethnic group, the rates for men are significantly higher than those for women.

Source: Grant, Harford, Dawson et al., 1992.

down alcohol in the body (see page 83). As a result, they may experience flushing when they consume as little as one drink. This reaction involves a reddening of the face and neck that may be accompanied by headaches, nausea, and other symptoms. Therefore Asians are often thought to be unlikely to become problem drinkers. Asian Americans in the United States report lower levels of alcohol drinking than Caucasians, which may be due to this reaction (Akutsu et al., 1989). Surveys of drinking among men in Korea and Japan, however, have found alcohol abuse and dependence at least as high as it is in the United States (Helzer et al., 1990; Yamamoto & Lin, 1995). By contrast, Chinese people in Taiwan drink significantly less than Koreans and Japanese do, and they are less likely to develop alcohol abuse and dependence. Korean and Japanese men often feel social pressures to drink, even though their capacity to handle alcohol is limited. By contrast, Chinese culture advocates moderation in the use of alcohol (Yamamoto & Lin, 1995).

Barbiturates. **Barbiturates** are commonly called "downers" because they depress the functioning of the central nervous system. Depending on the dosage, their effects range from mild sedation to coma (Julien, 1998). At very high doses, barbiturates can lead to serious withdrawal symptoms, including life-threatening convulsions.

Because most barbiturates cause drowsiness, in the past they have been used to treat insomnia. This use has declined dramatically, however, as physicians have recognized that barbiturates do not induce a natural sleep; rather, they suppress REM and Stage 4 sleep. Moreover, it is easy to take a lethal overdose of barbiturates. A person with a sleep problem might seek a prescription for a barbiturate and then either knowingly or unknowingly also consume some alcohol. The two drugs can combine to reduce the activity of the central nervous system, sometimes leading to death. In fact, many of the effects of barbiturates are indistinguishable from those of alcohol.

Because barbiturates have been used to induce sleep, they have been called *sedative-hypnotics*. Their use as sleep-inducing drugs has generally been taken over by *benzodiazepines* (see Chapters 2 and 14), which are generally considered safer than barbiturates. In addition to their use in treating sleep-related difficulties, benzodiazepines are also used in the treatment of anxiety, agitation, and to relax muscles (McKim, 1997). One of the benzodiazepines, *Rohypnol,* is known on the street as rophies, Mexican Valium, and Roach. Its detrimental effects on memory and its quick action as a sedative that can last for eight hours have led to its nickname, the "Forget pill" or "Forget me pill." The pill has been slipped into drinks of unsuspecting women who have been raped.

Stimulants

Stimulants are drugs that speed up the activity of the central nervous system. Among the most common stimulants are a group of synthetic drugs called **amphetamines** such as *Benzedrine* and *Dexedrine*. A similar drug called *Methedrine* (methamphetamine) is known on the street as *meth* or *ice* when it is sold in a crystallized form (McKim, 1997). Also known as "uppers" or "speed," these drugs stimulate the release of the neurotransmitters dopamine and norepinephrine (see Chapter 2). In low to moderate doses, amphetamines increase alertness, elevate mood, reduce appetite and the need for sleep, and induce euphoria. Larger doses of amphetamines cause irritability and anxiety or bring on a serious reaction that is indistinguishable from paranoid schizophrenia (see Chapter 13).

Amphetamines were formerly used in weight-loss programs because they increase metabolism, but they are rarely used for that purpose today because their rapid tolerance can lead to serious physical and psychological effects. Among the few appropriate medical uses of amphetamines are the treatment of narcolepsy and *attention-deficit hyperactivity disorder (ADHD)* in children (Julien, 1998). Children with this disorder display high levels of activity and are inattentive and impulsive. Although amphetamines would appear to be the last drug to give to a child with ADHD, they have a paradoxical effect on such children: The drug allows them to focus their attention, which, in turn, calms them down. When amphetamines are administered continually over time, however, the drug's calming effect tends to diminish. *Ritalin,* an amphetaminelike drug, is the most frequently prescribed drug for the treatment of ADHD in children.

Another stimulant, *cocaine,* is extracted from the leaves of the South American coca plant. For centuries, inhabitants of the Andes Mountains have chewed coca leaves to counteract fatigue. Popular views of cocaine have changed dramatically over the years. In the 1800s, cocaine was hailed as a wonder drug and used in cold remedies. Sigmund Freud heralded it as a cure for depression, fatigue, and alcohol problems (Julien, 1998; Karch, 1998). Until 1903 it was an ingredient in Coca-Cola. During the 1960s and 1970s, cocaine use increased and was often associated with glamorous industries and lifestyles, such as show business and professional sports. The high cost of cocaine made it more accessible to economically prosperous people.

Cocaine can be eaten, injected into the veins, smoked, or inhaled through the nose. When it is injected, its potency is increased greatly, making this practice very dangerous and potentially lethal. *Crack* is a purified form of cocaine that is very potent when smoked. The term *crack* derives from the crackling sound heard when the drug is mixed with chemicals and heated (Langton, 1991).

Cocaine gets to the brain very quickly, where it acts to increase the release and block the reuptake of dopamine and norepinephrine. A rapid and powerful high is followed by a dramatic low that creates a craving for more of the drug. Laboratory animals have been observed to self-administer cocaine until they died (Siegel, 1989). Cocaine also increases heart rate and blood pressure, raises mental awareness, and reduces fatigue. These effects are similar to those of amphetamines, although they do not last as long.

About 10 percent of Americans aged 12 and older have used cocaine at least once (U.S. Department of Health and Human Services, 1997), although the number of users has declined since the 1980s. The availability of cocaine has not changed significantly, but perceptions of cocaine's risk and disapproval of its use have increased (Bachman, Johnston, & O'Malley, 1990).

stimulants
Drugs that increase the activity of the central nervous system

amphetamines
Stimulants that are used to treat attention-deficit hyperactivity disorder and narcolepsy

opioids

Drugs that reduce pain

hallucinogens

Drugs that can cause changes in thinking, emotion, self-awareness, and perceptions; these changes are often expressed in hallucinations

lysergic acid diethylamide (LSD)

Powerful hallucinogen derived from the ergot fungus found on rye

Although it is not generally considered a drug and certainly does not require a prescription, *caffeine* is a widely available and frequently used stimulant. Caffeine is found in a variety of foods and drinks, including coffee, tea, chocolate, soft drinks, and some nonprescription drugs. Heavy and continuous use of food products that contain caffeine is responsible for many cases of insomnia. The effects of caffeine are not as severe as those of other stimulants because large amounts of caffeine would be necessary to cause similar symptoms.

Also included in the category of stimulants is *nicotine*, a potent substance that activates the brain, heart, and nervous system. Next to caffeine, nicotine is the most widely used stimulant in our society. Found in tobacco products, it increases blood pressure and heart rate, and it stimulates the body's fight-or-flight response. There are at least 1,200 toxic chemicals in tobacco smoke, many of which cause cancer. Cigarette smoke contains tar; a number of gases, including carbon monoxide; and, of course, nicotine. The surgeon general of the United States (U.S. Department of Health and Human Services, 1988a) cited cigarette smoking as the largest single preventable cause of premature death in the United States. Nevertheless, millions of Americans continue to smoke. We discuss the health problems associated with smoking in more detail in Chapter 15.

Opioids

The **opioids** are a group of naturally occurring and synthetic drugs (see the discussion of opioid peptides in Chapter 2). This family of drugs is also called *narcotic analgesics* because they produce analgesia (loss of sensitivity to pain) and make a person sleepy (McKim, 1997). *Opium* is derived from the unripe seedpod of the poppy plant; it may have been used as early as the Stone Age. Two of the drugs derived from opium are *morphine* and *codeine* (Julien, 1998); of the two, morphine is the more powerful painkiller. Also included in the opioid category is *heroin,* a synthetic compound that is produced from morphine. In recent years there has been an increase in heroin use and a shift from injecting it to smoking or sniffing heroin with improved purity levels. People who use opioids at first experience a sleepy, pleasant euphoria and relief from anxiety and stress. Continued use, however, leads to tolerance that makes it impossible to feel any pleasurable effects. Today the primary medical uses of opioids are pain relief (analgesia), relief of coughing, and treatment of diarrhea.

The opioids are highly addictive and potentially dangerous. Depending on the dosage, the method of administration, and the user's tolerance level, their effects can range from mild sedation and relaxation to paralysis and death. Opioids are also associated with very powerful withdrawal effects. Withdrawal from opioids produces *agitated dysphoria,* a condition whose symptoms include pain throughout the body, as well as sweating and stomach upset that may be mistaken for flu symptoms.

Hallucinogens

Hallucinogens are drugs that can change a person's perception, thinking, emotions, and self-awareness. They have been used for thousands of years in magical, mystical, and religious ceremonies. This class of drugs, sometimes called *psychedelic drugs,* includes compounds that are natural in origin as well as a growing number of drugs produced in laboratories. Hallucinogens can produce hallucinations, time and space distortions, and symptoms similar to those found in severe psychological disorders.

Lysergic acid diethylamide (LSD) is a colorless, odorless, and tasteless drug derived from the ergot fungus that grows on rye. Usually taken by

The seedpod (top) of the poppy plant is the source of opium, which can be processed into morphine and codeine.

mouth, LSD is rapidly absorbed by the body, and a small amount finds its way to the cortex. The effects of LSD depend on the amount taken; the user's personality, mood, and expectations; and the surroundings in which the drug is used. Physical effects include dilated pupils, elevated temperature, and increases in heart rate and blood pressure. Sensations and feelings, however, are much more dramatic than the physical signs. A user may feel several emotions at once or swing rapidly from one emotion to another. Larger doses can produce delusions and hallucinations such as changing colors and shapes. Another reaction to the use of LSD, the *flashback,* is most likely to occur in people who are chronic users of hallucinogens. Without having taken the drug again, the person suddenly experiences a recurrence of aspects of an earlier drug experience, complete with feelings of paranoia and perceptual distortions.

Phencyclidine piperidine (PCP) can have depressant, stimulant, hallucinogenic, or analgesic effects, depending on the dosage. PCP can be taken orally, smoked, or inhaled through the nose ("snorted"). It is frequently mixed with other illicit drugs, and for this reason it is difficult to obtain accurate reports of the extent of PCP use.

The varied effects of PCP include euphoria, very unpleasant feelings, distorted sensations, hallucinations, and even a tendency to commit violent acts. A particularly dangerous effect of PCP is a type of dissociation in which sensory inputs are so distorted that the user experiences no pain. In this condition a user might incur serious physical injury without realizing it.

Almost 70 million Americans (32 percent) aged 12 and older have used **marijuana** at least once in their lives, and 18 million (9 percent) had used marijuana within the past year (National Institute on Drug Abuse, 1997). Marijuana is the most commonly used illicit drug in the United States. Marijuana consists of the dried leaves and flowers of the *Cannabis sativa* (hemp) plant; it can be smoked, eaten, or drunk. *Hashish,* or "hash," is a more potent form of marijuana made by pressing resin from the leaves or flowers of the cannabis plant.

Of the more than 400 compounds found in marijuana (Grinspoon & Bakalar, 1993), one is an important psychoactive ingredient—*delta-9-tetrahydrocannabinol* (THC). This compound is rapidly absorbed into blood and tissue throughout the body, including the brain. It stimulates nerve receptors in the cortex and hippocampus, which suggests that the body produces its own version of the substance (Matsuda et al., 1990). These receptors are located in areas responsible for motor activity, concentration, and short-term memory; marijuana is known to be able to disrupt all three areas (Cowley, 1997). The by-products of THC can be detected for days or weeks following even brief use of marijuana.

The subjective experience of the marijuana high is influenced by the person's expectations about how he or she will feel, the amount of the drug taken, and its potency. Small to moderate doses of THC usually lead to feelings of well-being and euphoria; large doses can cause paranoia, hallucinations, and dizziness (Fackelmann, 1993). The most common effects of THC are an increase in heart rate and bloodshot eyes; however, attention, short-term memory, and coordination can be impaired (Grinspoon & Bakalar, 1993; Leavitt, 1995).

At one time marijuana was portrayed as a "killer weed" that drove people to insanity and violence. Nevertheless it became widely used during the 1960s and 1970s. Since 1979, however, its use has declined, largely because of growing disapproval and concern about perceived risks (Bachman et al., 1988), but use of the substance may be on the rise, especially among persons aged 12 to 17 (Chalsma & Boyum, 1994; Bachman, Johnston, & O'Malley, 1998).

Marijuana appears to have few serious medical effects (Grinspoon & Bakalar, 1993). For example, reports that marijuana suppresses the immune system are contradictory (Hollister, 1988). Some of these studies are flawed by use of very high concentrations of marijuana to produce suppression of the

phencyclidine piperidine (PCP)
Powerful hallucinogen that can have unpredictable depressant, stimulant, hallucinogenic, or analgesic effects

marijuana
Substance derived from the *Cannabis sativa* plant

immune system. There is one well-confirmed physical effect of marijuana: harm to the pulmonary system. Marijuana contains more tar and carbon monoxide than tobacco smoke, and marijuana smokers inhale more deeply than tobacco smokers. Most marijuana smokers, however, do not smoke as much marijuana as tobacco smokers smoke tobacco (Grinspoon & Bakalar, 1993).

Recent reports about the effects of marijuana have been more balanced than those of earlier years. In fact, some researchers have noted that THC may have medical benefits such as reducing side effects of chemotherapy and treating glaucoma (Grinspoon & Bakalar, 1993). These claims are controversial; for example, although marijuana may reduce the pressure in the eye that occurs with glaucoma, it may also reduce the blood supply to the optic nerve (Cowley, 1997). The controversy over the use of marijuana will continue. In 1996, voters in Arizona and California passed a proposition allowing the use of marijuana for medical treatment (Julien, 1998). Although the intention was to make marijuana available to AIDS sufferers, people in chronic pain, and cancer patients undergoing chemotherapy, cannabis clubs have sprung up to provide marijuana for potential users.

Interest in the potential medical uses of marijuana led voters in two states to approve its use. As a result, cannabis clubs were started as some people interpreted the law more broadly than was originally intended.

Review Summary

1. Psychoactive substances are chemicals that affect consciousness, perception, mood, and behavior. Regular and excessive use of drugs can lead to **substance abuse** or **substance dependence.**

2. Alcohol use is associated with a range of medical and psychological consequences, including cirrhosis of the liver. Its major effect is on parts of the brain responsible for inhibiting behavior.

3. The effects of alcohol are related to *blood alcohol concentration (BAC),* an indication of the amount of alcohol in the blood. Your BAC is determined by how much you drink, the time you take to drink it, your weight, and whether you have consumed food before or while drinking.

4. Expectations about the effects of alcohol can influence drinking patterns. The relationship of alcohol to violence, however, seems to be due to its biological effects, not to expectations.

5. The rate of alcohol abuse and dependence is higher in men than in women.

6. Like alcohol, **barbiturates** are depressants; they slow the activity of the central nervous system.

7. Stimulants such as **amphetamines** speed up the activity of the nervous system. One of the most widely used stimulants is *caffeine,* which is found in foods such as chocolate and beverages such as coffee. *Nicotine,* a major component of tobacco smoke, is associated with several preventable diseases such as heart disease. *Cocaine* can get to the brain quickly and cause a powerful high followed by a dramatic low.

8. Opioids, such as *morphine* and *codeine,* are drugs derived from the seedpod of the poppy plant; their primary medical use is to reduce pain. *Heroin* is a synthetic compound derived from morphine.

9. A variety of drugs known as **hallucinogens** can cause changes in perception, including hallucinations. Among the best-known hallucinogens are **lysergic acid diethylamide (LSD)** and **phencyclidine piperidine (PCP). Marijuana** consists of dried leaves and flowers from the *Cannabis sativa* plant. The active psychoactive ingredient in marijuana is delta-9-tetrahydrocannabinol (THC).

Study Break

1. Indicate whether each of the following is a depressant, a stimulant, an opioid, or a hallucinogen: ethyl alcohol, cocaine, caffeine, morphine, PCP, nicotine.
2. What processes or disorders are being described in the following examples?
   a. Despite regulations prohibiting alcohol use by pilots for eight hours before flight, Ted consumed ten beers before piloting a plane. He said that ten beers in him is not the same as ten beers in someone who has not been drinking as long as he has. On what concept is his argument based?
   b. After taking barbiturates for three years, Jack wants to stop. When he tries to do so, however, he experiences disturbing physical and psychological symptoms. What is the name of the syndrome Jack is experiencing?
3. Your friend frequently consumes seven or eight alcoholic beverages within an hour at parties. What is the term for this pattern of consumption?
4. In most states, intoxication, is legally defined as a blood alcohol concentration of how much?
5. Match the following items:
   1. Cocaine   a. Marijuana
   2. THC   b. Crack
   3. Analgesia   c. ADHD
   4. Ritalin   d. Hallucinogen
   5. PCP   e. Opioids
6. What are some of the factors that influence patterns of drinking alcoholic beverages? What is flushing, and how might it affect drinking patterns?

ANSWERS TO STUDY BREAKS

Page 197

1. *Consciousness* refers to our personal awareness of feelings, sensations, and thoughts at a given moment.
2. c
3. 25
4. Our internal clock (suprachiasmatic nucleus) is located in the hypothalamus. The hormone secreted by the pineal gland that plays a role in controlling our biological rhythms is melatonin.
5. d
6. d

Page 213

1. **a.** EKG   **b.** EEG   **c.** EOG
2. a
3. b
4. Compared to younger people, older individuals spend less time in the deep sleep of stage 4 and more time in the light sleep of stage 1. Consequently, they are more easily awakened.
5. vulnerability to predators and need for food
6. **a.** narcolepsy
   b. REM sleep behavior disorder
   c. sudden infant death syndrome (SIDS)
   d. sleep terror
   e. sleep apnea

Page 218

1. b
2. c
3. The key elements of hypnotic induction include relaxation, concentration, and listening to the hypnotist's commands.

4. Among the elements of hypnosis that might reduce pain are relaxation and distraction from the pain.
5. The researcher had a calendar on his desk that enabled him to know if the hypnotized person was correct. He apparently asked questions in a way that cued the correct answer.
6. When used to refresh memory, hypnosis can lead to distortions and false memories. People who have been hypnotized to refresh their memories often have increased confidence in their refreshed and often inaccurate memories.
7. Dissociation is a splitting of the mind. Hilgard proposes that some people can dissociate the experience of painful stimuli so that one part of the mind is aware of the pain and another is unaware of it. These parts are separated and have no awareness of each other.

Page 231

1. Ethyl alcohol is a depressant; cocaine is a stimulant; caffeine is a stimulant; morphine is an opioid, PCP is a hallucinogen; nicotine is a stimulant.
2. **a.** tolerance   **b.** withdrawal
3. binge drinking
4. .10
5. 1-b   2-a   3-e   4-c   5-d
6. Alcohol use is greater among men than women. Rates of alcohol abuse/dependence are highest for men between the ages of 18 and 29. Flushing is a physiological reaction to the use of alcohol that consists of reddening of the face and neck, headaches, and nausea. This reaction is the result of a deficiency in an enzyme that breaks down alcohol; it is found in about half of East Asians. Flushing may account for lower rates of problem drinking by some East Asians.

CHAPTER 6

Basic Principles of Learning

Chapter in Perspective

Nearly every organism must learn to survive in its environment. Indeed, the ability to adapt to the environment is often the key to determining which organisms survive long enough to pass on their genes to future generations. Hence, according to the evolutionary perspective we studied in Chapter 2, learning is an adaptive behavior that supports *natural selection*—the principle that the strongest or most fit organisms will adapt best to their environments—and promotes the survival of the fittest. We have already examined the physical structures (Chapter 2) and sensory and perceptual processes (Chapter 3) that we use to interact with our environment. In some cases our responses to environmental stimuli, such as reflexively blinking in response to a puff of air, are routine, very brief in duration, and never enter our consciousness. In other instances our awareness is critical when it comes to responding to and interacting with our environment. For example, we need to remember the painful consequences of touching a hot stove. Similarly, once a field rat has found a way into a farmer's corn crib, it is important for the rat to remember how to return to this food source on later occasions. These longer-lasting effects of interaction with the environment are the subject of this chapter

233

and the next. In short, they are what we mean when we speak of *learning*. In this chapter we discuss basic forms of learning. Keep in mind as you read that the *principles* we are describing are universal. Indeed, they are applicable across species, let alone cultures. On the other hand, the specific *contents* (what we learn) differ across individuals and cultures. More complex forms of human learning and memory are discussed in Chapter 7. ▪

What Is Learning

For a person who has grown up in a small town, driving in big-city traffic can be an anxiety-provoking experience. The fast pace and the large number of vehicles on the road can be overwhelming at first; with cars to the left and to the right, not much sanity appears to be in sight! After several months of driving to and from work during rush hour in Chicago, however, Belinda, who grew up in a small town, has become a real pro at driving in city traffic. *Why should Belinda's improved driving ability be considered an example of learning?* ▪

Most psychologists define **learning** as a relatively permanent change in behavior or the potential to make a response that occurs as a result of experience. This definition distinguishes learned behaviors from those occurring automatically in response to external events, such as shivering in a cold wind. By including the concept of experience in our definition, we can distinguish between learned behaviors and behaviors that become possible through development of our physical capabilities—that is, *maturation*. For example, when you were 2 years old, you did not have the strength to lift a 5-pound weight. By the time you were 10, however, lifting 5 pounds was an easy task because your muscles had developed sufficiently. You did not have to learn anything to be able to pick up the weight; maturation was responsible for your new ability.

To return to our question, why should Belinda's improved driving ability be considered an example of learning? Unless Belinda was very young at the time she began big-city driving, we can rule out maturation as a cause for the change in her behavior. Likewise, the change in Belinda's driving behavior is not an automatic response, like shivering in a cold wind. Rather, the repeated experience of rush-hour city driving has brought about a change in her behavior; she has *learned*.

In Chapter 3 we discussed how psychologists study color vision in animals like Ruby the elephant. Ruby's painting also provides us with a good example of learning. Initially, the sound of the word *paint* had no meaning, and Ruby made no response to it. After the word was associated (paired) with one of her favorite activities, Ruby began to squeal when her trainer said "paint." Ruby learned that this word signaled the opportunity to engage in an enjoyable activity. The elephant's response is an example of a relatively permanent change in behavior that occurs as a result of experience; she has *learned*.

learning
A relatively permanent change in behavior or the potential to make a response that occurs as a result of experience

In this chapter we first discuss two of the three basic types of learning, *classical, or respondent, conditioning* and *operant, or instrumental, conditioning.* Later in the chapter we explore the third basic type of learning, *observational learning.* The word *conditioning* refers to the fact that the learner forms an association, usually between a stimulus and a response or between two stimuli. You will see that although classical and operant conditioning are basic, recent research has shown that these forms of learning are far from simple.

Classical Conditioning

A psychology class is participating in an unusual demonstration of learning. First, the instructor passes a can of powdered lemonade mix around the room; each student puts a spoonful on a sheet of paper. Once all students have their own lemonade powder, they are instructed to wet one of their fingers. When the instructor says "now," each student puts a small amount of lemonade powder on his or her tongue with the moistened finger. The effect of putting lemonade powder on the tongue is predictable: The mouth puckers, and saliva begins to flow. The instructor has the students repeat this procedure several times during the class period until all the lemonade powder is gone. Before the class period ends, the instructor says "now" without warning. The students' mouths pucker, and saliva flows. **What is the purpose of this demonstration?** ▪

This demonstration exemplifies classical conditioning, which has become so closely associated with the Russian scientist Ivan Pavlov (1849–1936) that it is often called *Pavlovian conditioning.* Although Pavlov conducted much of his research with dogs, examples of classical conditioning can be found in many human behaviors. **Classical conditioning** is a form of learning that occurs when two stimuli—a neutral stimulus and an unconditioned stimulus—that are "paired" (presented together) become associated with each other. Think back to Ruby the elephant in Chapter 3. After the word *paint* was paired with a pleasurable activity, Ruby associated it with that activity. Similarly, the sight of the golden arches at McDonald's and the smell and taste of a juicy burger have occurred together, and as a result many people associate the golden arches with tasty fast food.

Pavlov and the Elements of Classical Conditioning

We have said that the procedure for establishing classical conditioning is to present two events—called *stimuli*—to a participant so that the pairing of these two events causes a participant or animal subject to make an association between them. At the start of conditioning, the first event, which in a laboratory setting may be the presentation of a light or a tone, is neutral—that is, not currently associated with the response to be established. What was the neutral stimulus in the lemonade example at the start of this section? Keep reading and you will find out. When this **neutral stimulus (NS)** is presented, the participant may notice that it is there, but it does not cause any particular reaction. By presenting the second event, called an **unconditioned stimulus (US)**, after

classical conditioning
Learning that occurs when two stimuli—a conditioned stimulus and an unconditioned stimulus—are paired and become associated with each other

neutral stimulus (NS)
Stimulus that, before conditioning, does not elicit a particular response

unconditioned stimulus (US)
Event that automatically produces a response without any previous training

Ivan Pavlov (1849–1936), a Russian physiologist, was awarded the Nobel Prize in 1904 for his research on the digestive system. Here Pavlov (seated, back to the camera) is shown in his laboratory studying classical conditioning in a dog.

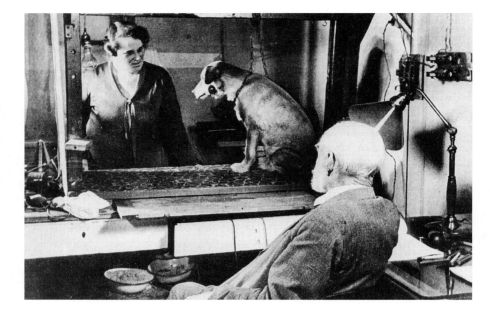

the NS, however, we transform the NS into a **conditioned stimulus (CS).** The NS becomes a CS because it is repeatedly paired with a US. This pairing eventually causes the participant to establish an association between the two events; the CS comes to *predict* the occurrence of the US. In the lemonade powder example the word *now* was the NS; it became a CS after it was paired with the lemonade powder.

As the term suggests, the US automatically produces a reaction; the participant does not have to be trained to react to it. The US never fails to produce the same reaction. Food in your mouth causes you to salivate; touching a hot stove causes you to jerk your hand away. In psychological terms, the US *elicits,* or calls forth, a *response.* The reaction that is elicited by the US is called the **unconditioned response (UR).** If you have a feeling that we have already discussed this type of response, you are correct. These URs are reflexes, just like those we described in Chapter 2. You do not have to learn a UR. For example, you do not learn to jerk your hand away when you touch a hot stove; you pull it away automatically. It is a built-in (unconditioned) response. What is the UR in the lemonade powder example?

When a participant associates the NS (e.g., a light or a tone) with the US, the NS is transformed into a CS that can elicit a response similar to the UR (e.g., a little less saliva). The response caused by the CS is known as the **conditioned response (CR).** When the CS elicits the CR, we say that classical conditioning has occurred. Pavlov (1927) used food as the US in his pioneering studies. While a metronome was ticking (CS) he placed a small amount of meat powder (US) into a hungry dog's mouth. The meat powder caused the dog to begin salivating (UR). Later, when just the sound of the metronome ticking was presented, the dog salivated (CR).

Let's return to the earlier demonstration in which lemonade powder was associated with the word *now* (Cogan & Cogan, 1984) so that you can experience classical conditioning firsthand. Think what occurred naturally (US-UR) and what was learned (CS-CR) and complete the blanks in this sentence to see if you can apply the terminology just described to the demonstration. "The CS, _____, paired with the US, _____, results in the UR, _____." The CS is the word *now.* The lemonade powder is the US; it automatically elicits the unconditioned response (UR) of puckering and salivating. Initially the word *now* is a

conditioned stimulus (CS)
Neutral stimulus that acquires the ability to elicit a conditioned response after being paired with an unconditioned stimulus

unconditioned response (UR)
Reaction that is automatically produced when an unconditioned stimulus is presented

conditioned response (CR)
Response elicited by a conditioned stimulus that has been paired with an unconditioned stimulus; is similar to the unconditioned response

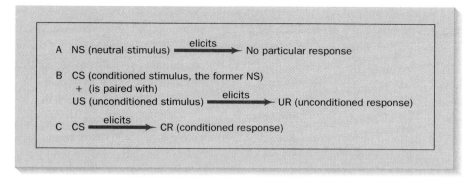

A NS (neutral stimulus) —elicits→ No particular response

B CS (conditioned stimulus, the former NS)
   + (is paired with)
   US (unconditioned stimulus) —elicits→ UR (unconditioned response)

C CS —elicits→ CR (conditioned response)

FIGURE 6-1 Using our symbols, we can describe classical conditioning in the following manner: (A) The NS originally does not elicit a specific response. (B) The NS (now called the CS) is presented just before the US. The US automatically elicits a UR. (C) Later, when the CS is presented by itself, a CR, which is similar to the UR, occurs. In short, a new response, the CR, has been conditioned to the CS because the CS has been paired with the US.

neutral stimulus. After it is paired with the lemonade powder several times, however, it becomes a CS and now elicits the conditioned response (CR) of puckering and salivating.

Let's put these elements together in another example. Suppose that your younger brother is just tall enough to reach a hot skillet on top of the stove. He grabs it and immediately drops it. His pain is obvious, and you try to comfort him. Finally his tears stop, and you put the incident out of your mind. Three days later, however, the same skillet is again on the stove. Your brother enters the kitchen, sees the skillet, and begins to cry. Clearly, the skillet has taken on a new meaning for him, showing that some stimuli are so memorable that they produce learning without the need for repeated pairing.

In classical conditioning terms, initially the skillet was a NS; after conditioning, it became the CS. The intense heat was the US, which always elicits pain and an avoidance response. Those responses—the pain and jerking the hand away or dropping the skillet—constituted the UR. Remember that the classical conditioning sequence involves first presenting the NS and then following it with the US. If these two events are associated, the NS becomes a CS that signals that the US is on its way.

After a conditioning experience of this type, when the CS is encountered alone, it produces a response, the CR, that is very similar to the UR. In our example the sight of the skillet reminds your brother of the pain he experienced. The classical conditioning sequence is presented in diagrammatic form in Figure 6-1.

Condition Your Friends

Hands On

THE EASE BY WHICH CLASSICAL CONDITIONING IS DEMONSTRATED IN CLASS CAN be duplicated in real life. This exercise, which was developed by Mark Vernoy, rests on the premise that most of us have been conditioned to flinch when we see someone stick a balloon with a pin. (The pin is the CS, the bang is the US, and the startle response is the UR.) "In this way we have learned that needles always pop balloons" (Vernoy, 1987, p. 177). By using the following procedure, you may be able to surprise your friends and observe classical conditioning at the same time.

According to Vernoy, "The equipment needed for this demonstration includes about 20 to 30 good-quality, round balloons and a needle. Any sharp sewing needle will do, but for dramatic effect I use a foot-long needle that I borrow from a colleague who is an amateur magician. You can acquire these needles at any good magic shop" (p. 177). The procedure is simple. Start by blowing up several balloons; 15 or 20 should be sufficient. Then have your friends pop 5 or 6 of them with the needle you provide. Next have your friends watch you use the needle to pop 5 or 6 more balloons. Once you have popped several of them, stick the needle into an area of the balloon where there is less tension (such as the nipple or around the knot). Because there is less tension at these points, the rubber is relatively thick, and the balloon does not pop when it is stuck. Your friends still flinch, however. Why? This reaction occurs because your friends have been conditioned to expect a loud bang. If you are using a foot-long needle, you can make the effect even more dramatic by passing the needle completely through the balloon (enter at the nipple and exit at the knot).

Psychological Detective

Think of your own examples of classical conditioning. You will probably find it easiest to start with the US, then decide what the UR is, and finally determine what CSs might readily occur in the presence of the US. Think of a food smell that makes you remember a pleasant childhood memory—perhaps cookies baking or the cinnamon smell of hot apple pie. Do you think of a particular event, and does your mouth water? The food you enjoy is the US. What is the UR? the CS? the CR? List those items, and then read the following section, in which you meet Scott, who is intensely afraid of closed spaces. After you finish reading about Scott, list the elements of classical conditioning that were involved in the development of his fear. (The answers to these two examples appear at the end of this chapter.)

As you read this and the other Psychological Detective sections in this chapter, keep in mind that researchers assume that these processes are universal. Do not tacitly accept this assumption; challenge it. See if you can think of any cross-cultural examples that do not conform to our expectations.

Phobias

When Scott was 3 years old, he was locked in an abandoned refrigerator by his playmates and nearly suffocated to death. Ever since then, he has avoided closed spaces. Now, 30 years later, he is still deathly afraid of closed spaces and anything that reminds him of them. He cannot stand to ride in an elevator and always takes the stairs, even in tall buildings. Even seeing a picture of a refrigerator makes him break out in a cold sweat. If you were unaware of Scott's background, his intense fear of closed spaces, such as elevators, compact cars, and small rooms might seem rather strange. Although you may not fear closed spaces to the same degree as Scott, chances are good that you are afraid of certain other objects or situations that most people do not fear. How do we acquire many of these apparently unrealistic, irrational fears?

Many of our fears and anxieties may have been classically conditioned, as in the case of Scott's fear of closed spaces. Because he was locked in an abandoned refrigerator when he was a child and nearly died of suffocation, Scott now fears anything that remotely resembles a closed space. Scott has a condition known as a *phobia;* more specifically, he is suffering from *claustrophobia* (*claustrop,* "enclosed place"; *phobos,* "fear"). A **phobia** is an irrational fear of an object, situation, or activity that is out of proportion to the actual danger it poses. Because phobias create so much anxiety that they interfere with normal functioning, they are classified as *anxiety disorders* (see Chapter 13).

Other people with phobias may not be able to recall a specific event that is the cause of the phobia. Thus many phobias exert their influence in a seemingly mysterious and potentially detrimental manner.

As you might expect, phobias can interfere with a person's daily activities. For example, a business executive suffering from *logophobia* (fear of words) would not do very well in the contemporary business world where meetings and reports (all filled with words) are the order of the day. Psychologists have developed a procedure, known as *systematic desensitization,* to help eliminate phobias. Basically, systematic desensitization involves classically conditioning a desired response, relaxation, to the phobic stimuli. Thus a person, like Scott, with claustrophobia is conditioned to relax in enclosed spaces. We discuss systematic desensitization in greater detail in Chapter 14.

John B. Watson (1878–1958), the father of behaviorism, used basic learning processes to understand the behavior of organisms.

John Watson, Little Albert, and the Ethics of Research

In 1913, John B. Watson proclaimed that psychologists should study only directly observable behaviors. As we saw in Chapter 1, Watson's approach to psychology was called *behaviorism.* The main business of psychology, according to the behaviorists, is the study of behaviors such as jogging in the park, leaving the scene of an accident, running through an airport so as not to miss a plane, and even expressing emotion. Anything having to do with thinking, feeling, or consciousness was not considered an appropriate subject of psychological study because those processes could not be observed directly.

The behaviorists' goal was to discover which observable stimuli elicit which responses (observable behaviors). In an experiment that applied this approach to human emotions, Watson and his assistant, Rosalie Rayner, classically conditioned a 9-month-old, "Little Albert," to fear a white rat (Watson & Rayner, 1920). At first Albert showed no fear of the rat and even allowed it to crawl on him. While Albert was playing with the rat, Watson hit a large steel rod with a heavy hammer, making a sudden, deafening noise. Not surprisingly, Albert was startled and scared. Each time the loud noise was paired with the presence of the rat, Albert cried in fear. After several pairings of the two stimuli, Albert started crying at the sight of the rat, even when there was no noise, and he eventually came to fear any object that resembled a rat, such as a white rabbit and even the white whiskers on a Santa Claus mask. Just as Scott developed a fear of closed spaces and things that reminded him of closed spaces, Albert developed a phobia for rats and ratlike objects. Unfortunately, no one followed Albert throughout his life; hence we do not know how long these phobias plagued him.

Let's analyze the elements of Little Albert's fear. What US was used? What was the UR? What were the CS and the CR? While you think about these questions, remember that the rat was also exposed to a frightening situation. For both

phobia
Irrational fear of an activity, object, or situation that is out of proportion to the actual danger

FIGURE 6-2 Conditioning "Little Albert" to fear a white rat. (A) Originally Little Albert had no fear of the white rat (the NS for Little Albert); the rat had no fear of Little Albert (the NS for the rat). (B) While Little Albert is playing with the rat, John Watson strikes a steel bar. The loud noise (US) elicits a startle and fear response (UR). The white rat (now the CS) is associated with the loud noise for Little Albert. Little Albert (now the CS) is associated with the loud noise for the rat. (C) Later, the white rat elicits fearfulness in Little Albert. Other objects, such as a rabbit, that are similar to the white rat now elicit fear in Little Albert, and the boy in turn elicits fear in the rat.

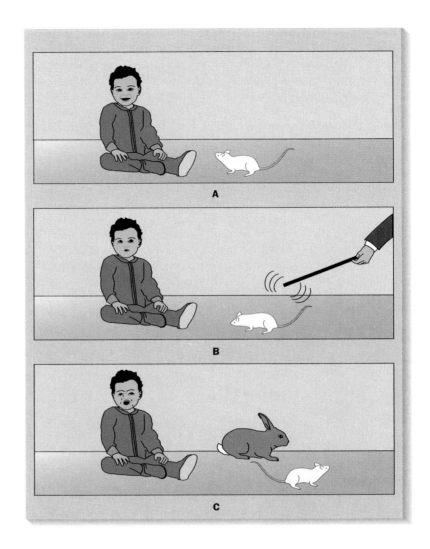

Little Albert and the rat, the US was the loud noise. The UR was the state of being startled and scared. For Albert, the CS was the rat; for the rat, the CS was Albert. The CR for both of them was fear of an object that signaled that a loud noise might follow. These relationships are diagrammed in Figure 6-2.

Psychological Detective

Although Watson's study is important because it was one of the first experiments to show that an emotional reaction, such as fear, could be classically conditioned, it raises some questions about the ethics of psychological research (see Chapter 1). Was it acceptable for Watson purposely to frighten Little Albert so intensely? Would you allow such an experiment to be conducted with your child? Would such a procedure be acceptable if the child's parents authorized it? Write down your responses and the reasons for them before reading further.

Ethical Principles of Psychologists and Code of Conduct, a manual published by the American Psychological Association, would probably say "no" to all of our questions (American Psychological Association, 1992). If Watson conducted his research with Little Albert in the 21st Century he would have difficulty meeting the ethical standards you read about in Chapter 1.

Pleasant Unconditioned Stimuli

Up to this point we have focused on unconditioned stimuli that produce disagreeable or unpleasant effects. Thankfully, the US does not have to be a painful event like heat, electric shock, or hitting your finger with a hammer (Capaldi & Sheffer, 1992; Owens, Capaldi, & Sheffer, 1993). A bite of your favorite food when you are hungry automatically causes you to salivate. Food in your mouth is the US; salivation is the UR.

Obviously, psychologists do not hide in restaurants to present a tone while you are eating, nor do most instructors bring lemonade powder to class with them. Yet people become classically conditioned in much the same way that Pavlov's dogs did. For example, the sights and sounds that accompany our meals can become conditioned stimuli. For many people, the unique decor of a restaurant or even an advertisement or menu may act as a CS. Have you ever found yourself salivating as you looked at the tempting pictures in an advertisement or browsed up and down the aisles of a grocery store?

Examples of classical conditioning of pleasant CRs abound in everyday life. Is there a particular song (CS) that prompts you to recall a happy moment (CR)? Do you know someone who purchases cars only of a certain color because that color was associated in the past with a favorite car?

Other Aspects of Classical Conditioning

Pavlov's research revealed several additional characteristics of classical conditioning besides those discussed so far. These findings fall into two categories: *acquisition,* or how we develop CRs, and *extinction,* or how we eliminate those responses.

Acquisition. Acquisition is the training stage during which a particular response is learned. Several factors influence the acquisition of CRs. Among them are the order in which the CS and US are presented, the intensity of the US, and the number of times the CS and US are paired. We now take a closer look at each of these factors.

Sequence of CS-US Presentation. The sequence in which the CS and US are presented influences the strength of conditioning (Keith-Lucas & Guttman, 1975; Sherman, 1978). The optimum sequence is for the CS to precede the US and remain until the US is presented. Other sequences, such as the CS coming on and going off before the US or the US preceding the CS, produce weaker conditioning.

Strength of the US. The stronger the US, the stronger the conditioning (Prokasy, Grant, & Myers, 1958; Holloway & Domjan, 1993). When Pavlov gave his dogs a small amount of food powder, they did not salivate as much as they did when he gave them a large amount of food powder. The hot skillet your younger brother grabbed on the stove was a painful and salient stimulus. Stronger USs elicit stronger URs; weaker USs elicit weaker URs.

Number of CS-US Pairings. The more times the CS and US are presented together, the stronger the CR becomes. It is easy to conduct research on

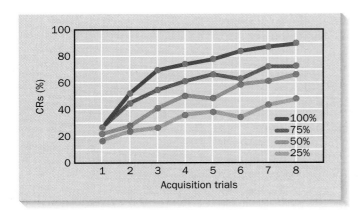

FIGURE 6-3 Patterns of acquisition in classical conditioning when the US is presented on different percentages of trials. The percentage of CRs decreases as the percentage of trials on which the US follows the CS decreases.

Source: Hartman & Grant, 1960.

extinction

The process of removing reinforcers, which leads to a decrease in the strength of a CR

the relationship between the CS and the US when we can use a laboratory setup such as Pavlov's. Under such conditions, the number of times the CS and US are presented can be determined precisely. The effects of varying numbers of CS-US pairings, however, can also be demonstrated in real life. If your little brother grabs the hot skillet more than once, the chances are good that his CR to the skillet will be stronger. If you have eaten at an exceptionally fine restaurant several times, your conditioned responses to the sight of the restaurant and its menu will be stronger than they would be if you had eaten there only once before. Figure 6-3 displays several patterns of classical conditioning acquisition; as you can see, as the percentage of pairings increases, acquisition of the CR becomes stronger.

Extinction.   Once a CR has been acquired, what can be done to extinguish or eliminate that response? The easiest procedure is to present the CS without the US and record how strong the CR is and how many times or how long we can present the CS alone before the CR disappears. The number of times the CS is presented without the US is a very important factor in eliminating the CR (Monti & Smith, 1976; Shipley, 1974). When Pavlov repeatedly sounded the tone (CS) without giving the dog any meat powder (US), the number of drops of saliva produced gradually decreased each time the tone was sounded. Similarly, if your brother grabs the skillet several times when it is cold, his fear decreases a little each time.

The process through which the strength of the CR is decreased is called **extinction** (Schreurs, 1993). The stronger the CR, the longer extinction takes. What takes place during acquisition influences the process of extinction. For example, the stronger the US and the more frequently it is presented during acquisition, the longer it will take to extinguish the CR (Hull, 1943).

Spontaneous Recovery.   At times a classical conditioning participant seems to "forget" that extinction has occurred. Consider Pavlov's dog once again. Only the CS (a bell in this case) has been presented to the dog several times during its daily extinction session. The CR (salivation) has

A bad fall on a ski slope can result in a classically conditioned fear that spontaneously recovers as you prepare to go skiing on subsequent occasions.

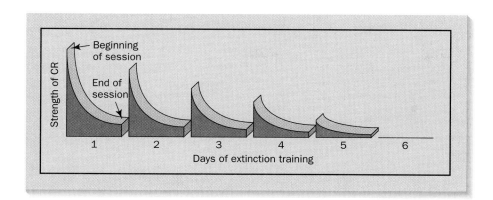

FIGURE 6-4 Extinction occurs when the tone (CS) is presented without food powder (US). By the end of each daily extinction session, the CR is quite weak. It regains some strength, however, by the start of the next session, a phenomenon known as spontaneous recovery. By the end of extinction, the CR is quite low, and the amount of spontaneous recovery may be undetectable.

decreased until it appears that the dog is not salivating. When the dog is returned to its cage, we might conclude that the extinction process is complete. When the CS is presented on the following day, however, the dog begins to salivate once more. Pavlov (1927) called this phenomenon **spontaneous recovery** because the CR recovers some of the strength it lost during the previous extinction session. This process is diagrammed in Figure 6-4. Notice that the amount of spontaneous recovery decreases from day to day until the CR finally does not occur at the start of a session. At this point extinction is probably complete.

Spontaneous recovery is not limited to laboratory experiments; it occurs in real-life situations as well. For example, assume you went skiing last winter and on the second day you had a bad fall. After summoning much courage and determination, you put your skis on and went back out on the slopes for the next two days. Thankfully, nothing adverse happened on those days; your fear seemed to be extinguished. Now, a year later, you have returned to the ski resort. You experience some apprehension as you pull on your ski boots. You thought the fear had disappeared—that it was extinguished—by the time you were finished skiing last year, but a bit seems to have returned (spontaneous recovery) this year.

Generalization and Discrimination.   Suppose that several days after your little brother made the mistake of grabbing the hot skillet, you and he are walking through the housewares section of a local department store when he starts crying and refuses to walk any farther. You look where he is looking and see a display of skillets. Is he afraid of them also? Yes, he is, and the more those skillets resemble the one at home, the greater is his fear.

Psychologists (such as Hovland, 1937; Razran, 1949) call this phenomenon, in which a response occurs to stimuli that are similar to a CS, **generalization.** By this they mean that the effects of classical conditioning may be applied (generalized) to other stimuli that are similar to the original CS; they "spread" from the original stimulus to others. For example, although Pavlov's dogs were conditioned to salivate in response to a specific tone (CS), they also salivated when other tones were presented. Likewise, we saw Little Albert's fear of the white rat generalized to other objects that were white and furry. An early study using humans as participants involved pairing a tone (CS) with a mild electric shock (Hovland, 1937). As you can see in Figure 6-5, when different tones were tested, the CR still occurred but was weaker than the response to the original tone.

It is easy to see how generalization occurs. If you have ever been stung by a wasp, you probably have a healthy respect for all flying insects, especially those that resemble wasps. Your response has generalized from one stimulus to many others. But if you are not stung every time you encounter a flying insect, many of these

spontaneous recovery
Reappearance of an extinguished CR after the passage of time

generalization
Occurrence of responses to stimuli that are similar to a CS

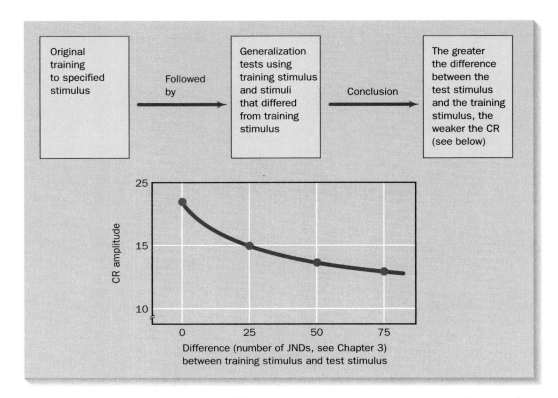

FIGURE 6-5 Diagram of the Hovland (1937) experiment on generalization of classical conditioning.

generalized responses will be extinguished. Thus as children we quickly discover that butterflies and moths do not sting, whereas hornets and bees do. We therefore come to fear the stinging insects but not the others. In other words, we learn to distinguish or discriminate between conditioned stimuli that accurately predict the occurrence of the US and those that do not (Bouton & Brooks, 1993; Nakajima, 1993). Through this process of **discrimination,** we have extinguished our fear of insects that do not sting but have retained our fear of insects that do.

Generalization and discrimination work in opposite ways. Whereas generalization makes you more likely to respond to a number of similar stimuli, discrimination narrows your response to the appropriate stimulus and no other. Discrimination thus requires stimuli that are clearly distinguishable (Brown, 1942; Gantt, 1971). For example, if you could not easily distinguish between insects that sting and those that do not, imagine how apprehensive you would be whenever you went outdoors.

Pavlov (1928) understood this principle and investigated it. First, he trained a group of dogs to discriminate between a circle and an ellipse; the circle was always associated with food. Once this association was made, Pavlov changed the ellipse over a series of presentations until it was indistinguishable from the circle.

Psychological Detective

What behavior(s) did Pavlov's dogs show when confronted by these two indistinguishable stimuli? Write down your answer before reading further.

discrimination
Occurrence of responses only to a specific CS

Because the dogs were unable to discriminate between the two stimuli, they salivated to both of them. They displayed other behaviors, however, that were not shown when they were able to discriminate between the two stimuli. They whined and yelped, became agitated, and tried to escape from their harnesses. To Pavlov's surprise, these behaviors continued outside the experimental room. Pavlov called these inappropriate behaviors *experimental neuroses* and believed that they occurred when an animal or human attempted to solve an insoluble discrimination. This analysis provides a clue concerning a possible origin of abnormal behavior in humans (see Chapter 13; Baumrind, 1983; Kazdin, 1978). As the next section shows, such agitation and apprehension can influence our motivated behavior.

Classical Conditioning and Our Motives

Even though Jim did not have cats as pets when he was a child, his friends persuaded him to adopt the cute stray kitten he found last week. Jim is now convinced this was a very bad idea. Each evening, when Jim has settled into his favorite chair to watch the evening news, the kitten launches a sneak attack. After a week of this behavior, Jim becomes tense and anxious as soon as he sits in his favorite chair, whether the kitten is in the room or not. The sound of the evening news increases his anxiety. When Jim leaves the room, he immediately feels better.

What is the relationship among the kitten's attacks, Jim's tension and anxiety, and motivation? Parts of the story about Jim and his cat may sound familiar. Can we describe the cat's sneak attack in psychological terms that you have already learned? Would certain responses automatically follow such an attack? If you said that pain, fear, or anxiety would follow, we would agree. What kind of stimuli automatically elicit a response? If you are thinking that unconditioned stimuli (USs) elicit unconditioned responses (URs), you are right again. What about Jim's favorite chair and the evening news program? What role do they serve? After these stimuli have been associated with cat attacks several times, they cause Jim to become tense and anxious. These are conditioned stimuli (CSs), and the tension and anxiety they produce are conditioned responses (CRs).

How is Jim's conditioned anxiety related to motivation? Through the process of classical conditioning, Jim's favorite chair and the evening news have become CSs that elicit tension and anxiety. Jim finds these feelings of tension and anxiety unpleasant and is motivated to reduce them when they occur by leaving the room. Motives that are acquired through the process of classical conditioning are called **learned motives.** Many other motives are acquired in this manner. Phobias are excellent examples of learned motives. Classical conditioning appears to be at the core of many of these unusual fears.

The same procedure and logic can be applied to the learning of goals and incentives. The importance of many of the goals and incentives that motivate our behavior is also learned through classical conditioning; hence they are termed **learned goals** (or **learned incentives**). Consider money, diamonds, gold, and concert tickets. An infant's response to these objects will quickly convince you that they do not possess intrinsic value; we must learn their value before their acquisition is reinforcing.

learned motives
Motives that are learned or acquired through the process of classical conditioning

learned goals (learned incentives)
Goals or incentives that are learned through the process of classical conditioning

Current Trends in Classical Conditioning

Our conception of classical conditioning has changed dramatically since Pavlov's time. We now know that conditioning is not an automatic process that simply links conditioned stimuli and unconditioned stimuli. Psychologists now place more emphasis on what information the CS seems to tell or convey to the participant.

Contingency Theory.   One principle that has emerged from this continued research is that the better the CS is able to *predict* the occurrence of the US, the stronger the conditioning will be (Bolles, 1979; Rescorla, 1968). (Recall that we encountered the importance of predictivity when we considered the sequence of CS-US presentation on page 241). A study of classical conditioning in two groups of rats clearly illustrates this point (Rescorla, 1968). For the first group the CS (tone) was always *followed by* the US (a shock). The animals in this group were called the *contingent* group because the occurrence of shock always followed (was contingent on) the tone. The animals in the second group heard the tone *before or after* the shock was presented. These animals were called the *noncontingent* subjects because the occurrence of shock did not always follow (was not contingent on) the tone. Because the tone perfectly predicted the US for the *contingent* animals, classical conditioning was strong. Classical conditioning was weaker for the *noncontingent* animals because the CS did not always precede the US.

This relationship should not be surprising. As we have seen, a strong and predictable CS is the goal of the acquisition or training process during which an association between the CS and US is formed. A particular CS predicts that a particular US is about to occur. For Pavlov's dogs, for example, the sound of the ticking metronome reliably predicted the delivery of food. Conversely, when we undertake extinction, we try to convince the participant that the CS will no longer be followed by—will no longer predict—the US (Delemater, 1995). The more reliable the CS is in predicting the US, the harder it will be to extinguish. As the next section shows, however, conditioned stimuli do not automatically become associated with unconditioned stimuli, even if they are predictable.

Blocking.   If classical conditioning simply involves the pairing of a CS and US, the time at which the pairing occurs should not make any difference. But it does. Animal researcher Leon Kamin (1969) demonstrated the importance of the timing of the pairing. In Kamin's study, one group of rats was classically conditioned by presenting a tone (CS) and following it with an electric shock (US). Once response to the tone was conditioned, a second CS (a light) also was presented before the shock. A second group of animals received only pairings of the light and the shock. Kamin then tested the strength of conditioning to the light. This experimental arrangement is shown in Figure 6-6.

Conditioning was weaker for the animals that received tone-shock pairings before tone and light were paired with shock. Stronger conditioning was shown by the animals that received only the light-shock pairing. Kamin reasoned that conditioning of the tone before presenting the light had blocked or reduced the conditioning of the light.

	Phase 1	Phase 2	Test Phase
Group 1	Tone (CS) ⟶ Shock (US)	Light (2nd CS) + Tone (former CS) ⟶ Shock (US)	Test for conditioning to the light
Group 2	No conditioning	Light (CS) ⟶ Shock (US)	Test for conditioning to the light

FIGURE 6-6   Diagram of the Kamin (1969) blocking experiment.

If you consider predictability, this interpretation makes perfect sense. If the tone had already been established as a predictable CS, another predictable CS was not needed (see Barnett, Grahame, & Miller, 1993; Williams, 1994). The prior condition **blocked** the light-and-shock association for the animals that had already received tone-and-shock pairings. Because light was the only CS presented to the other group of animals, it was conditioned strongly.

Overshadowing. With the blocking experiments we saw that previous experience with a CS *blocked* the conditioning of a second CS when it was presented in compound (together) with the first CS. What happens when two CSs are presented in compound and neither CS was experienced previously?

Research on **overshadowing** provides an answer to this question (Blaisdell, Denniston, & Miller, 1998). Most often, a stronger CR is shown to the more intense or salient CS (Klein, et al., 1984). Typically, the greater the difference in intensity or salience, the larger the difference in the conditioned responses. In overshadowing the more intense CS interferes with the association of the less intense CS and the US. For example, if a loud tone overshadows a weaker tone that is of a different pitch, then a stronger CR will be shown to the louder tone when it is presented by itself.

Taste-Aversion Learning and Preparedness

Suppose that you have just moved to a large metropolitan area, which is vastly different from the small town you left behind. For example, the variety of restaurants is amazing. Last night some friends took you to a seafood restaurant. The décor and atmosphere of the restaurant were intriguing, and the taste of the food was unlike that of any you had ever had. Unfortunately, however, during the night you came down with the stomach flu that had been going around. For the rest of the night you were nauseated or worse—not a pleasant experience. These events may not seem to involve learning, but as you will see, classical conditioning took place: You were conditioned to avoid seafood.

Taste Aversion. Does becoming nauseated after eating a food that is unusual to you have anything to do with learning? The notion of predictability is useful here. Whenever a person or animal becomes ill after consuming a food with a novel taste (taste-aversion conditioning), that taste (CS) may become an excellent predictor of illness.

Taste-aversion learning involves the development of an aversion to (dislike of) a flavor that has been associated with illness (Batsell & Best, 1992, 1993). In the mid-1960s, John Garcia and his colleagues demonstrated that when a novel flavor was used as the CS and illness or nausea was the UR, rats developed an intense aversion to the flavor (Garcia & Koelling, 1966). Classical conditioning of a tone and food occurs best when the tone is sounded one-half second before the food is presented, but strong taste aversions can be conditioned when illness occurs more than an hour after the taste is experienced (Garcia, Ervin, & Koelling, 1966).

There are two points of interest in these taste-aversion results. First, the flavor had to be novel for it to become associated with the illness. A flavor that has been consumed many times does not predict illness. Second, the time between the onset of the CS (taste) and the onset of the US (illness) can be quite lengthy, yet strong conditioning still occurs.

Preparedness. Certain stimuli, such as flavors, can be associated with certain unconditioned responses, such as illness, more easily than they can be

blocking
Situation in which the condition-ability of a CS is weakened when it is paired with a US that has previously been paired with another CS

overshadowing
Situation that occurs when a compound CS is paired with a US and the more intense (salient) CS elicits a stronger CR

taste-aversion learning
Development of a dislike or aversion to a flavor or food that has been paired with illness

preparedness

Theory that organisms are biologically ready or prepared to associate certain conditioned stimuli (CSs) with certain unconditioned stimuli (USs)

associated with other URs, such as electric shock. According to Martin Seligman (1970), animals seem to be biologically ready or *prepared* to associate certain CSs with certain USs. Some events seem to go together naturally, whereas others do not. For humans and many animal species, taste and illness form one such natural pairing; presenting a tone or light CS with an electric shock forms another natural pair. If instead we try to pair the tone or light CS with illness or the taste CS with an electric shock, we usually get very weak conditioning (Garcia & Koelling, 1966). Other pairings also are learned quite easily. For example, humans, as well as many household pets, seem prepared to associate the sight of lightning (CS) with the sound of thunder. **Preparedness** occurs when some species are more biologically ready to form certain associations; it may explain why some phobias are learned so easily (also see Chapter 13). We do not seem prepared, however, to associate loud noises with nausea or illness.

Psychological Detective

Preparedness may differ according to the species that is being tested. For example, birds use color, not taste, as an important cue in food selection. In birds, how would you determine whether color can be conditioned to an illness US more easily than a taste? Give this question some thought, and diagram an experiment to test it before proceeding.

Wilcoxin, Dragoin, and Kral (1971) answered this question in a convincing manner. As shown in Figure 6-7, they first presented blue, sour-tasting water (CS) to quail and then made the birds ill temporarily by giving them a nausea-producing drug. Later (after the birds became ill) they found that the birds had a strong aversion to the blue color but not to the sour taste. The findings suggest that the quail were unprepared—or, in Seligman's words, "contraprepared"—to make the taste-illness association. Preparedness theory suggests one important means by which animals adapt to the demands of their environments: They learn to avoid potentially dangerous stimuli that have made them ill on a previous occasion. Avoiding such substances increases their chances of survival. Birds, with their keen eyesight, are more likely to discriminate on the basis of color, whereas rats and mice, whose eyesight is poor,

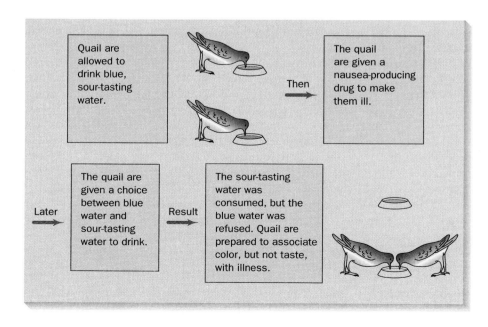

FIGURE 6-7 Diagram of Wilcoxin, Dragoin, and Kral's (1971) preparedness experiment.

are likely to discriminate on the basis of taste. Preparedness theory is a good example of the evolutionary perspective at work: Animals are prepared to make associations that help them adapt to the environment they inhabit.

Humans also form taste aversions quite readily. Think of the times you have been nauseated after eating. In most of these cases, had you just consumed a novel food or beverage? Will you ever consume that food or drink again? Chances are pretty good that you are saying "never," and you may be right. Such aversions do not extinguish very easily; they can last for 50 years or more (Garb & Stunkard, 1974).

Sometimes taste aversions have detrimental effects. For example, in children undergoing chemotherapy for cancer, very strong food aversions often develop that prevent proper eating. Ilene Bernstein and her colleagues (Bernstein, 1978; Bernstein & Webster, 1980, 1982) have applied their knowledge of taste-aversion learning to this problem. In one study, children were allowed to eat an unusually flavored ice cream (Bernstein called it "Mapletof") shortly before receiving nausea-producing chemotherapy. Later these patients ate less Mapletof ice cream than did a second group of patients whose treatment consisted of surgery rather than drug therapy. Children in the second group had also eaten some Mapletof ice cream before treatment. Because their treatment did not produce nausea, however, these patients did not associate the ice cream flavor with illness. Clearly the taste-illness pairing is crucial for the development of taste aversion.

Subsequent research demonstrated that consumption of the Mapletof ice cream before chemotherapy greatly reduced the patients' reluctance to consume their normal diet. After chemotherapy, patients who had previously eaten the Mapletof ice cream and had formed a taste aversion to this flavor were more willing to consume their normal diet than were patients who had not eaten any Mapletof ice cream. The formation of a taste aversion to the Mapletof ice cream tended to block the formation of taste aversions to other foods and thus helped the patients maintain their normal diet without becoming nauseated.

Review Summary

1. Learning occurs when experience produces a relatively permanent change in behavior.

2. Classical conditioning involves pairing an **unconditioned stimulus (US),** which automatically elicits an **unconditioned response (UR),** with a **conditioned stimulus (CS),** which is neutral at the start of conditioning. After several pairings, when the CS is presented by itself, it elicits a **conditioned response (CR).**

3. Intense, unrealistic fears, or **phobias,** for certain activities, objects, or situations may be caused by classical conditioning.

4. Watson and Rayner demonstrated that emotions can be learned by classically conditioning a child to fear a white rat. Watson's experiment, however, would not be considered ethical by present-day standards.

5. Not all unconditioned stimuli result in painful or unpleasant responses. Some stimuli, such as food, when paired with neutral stimuli, result in the conditioning of a pleasant reaction such as salivation.

6. When the US is intense and presented more frequently, stronger classical conditioning is produced.

7. The classically conditioned response is eliminated or **extinguished** when the US is removed or not presented. **Spontaneous recovery** of the CR occurs when time is allowed to pass between extinction sessions.

8. Generalization occurs when CRs are elicited by stimuli that are similar to the CS. **Discrimination** is the opposing process; it involves responding only to the appropriate CS.

9. Learned motives and **learned goals** are acquired through the process of classical conditioning.

10. For many species, the pairing of a novel taste with the experience of illness results in learning an aversion to that taste. **Taste-aversion learning** occurs readily in humans; birds, however, more readily associate a color with illness. **Preparedness** is evident when some species are more prepared to form certain associations than others.

Study Break

1. Have you ever found yourself salivating while walking through the bakery section of a supermarket? What was the US? the CS? the CR?

2. Complete the following:
   a. Before conditioning, the _____ is automatically elicited by the _____.
   b. The CR is strengthened if the _____ and _____ are paired frequently.
   c. Extinction of a classically conditioned response involves presentation of only the _____. In other words, the _____ is removed.
   d. Extinction causes the _____ to grow gradually _____.

3. State which aspect of classical conditioning is illustrated by each of the following situations:
   a. A tone sounds; half a second later, a puff of air is delivered to your eye and you blink. Once the conditioned eye blink has been established, the puff of air is discontinued and the tone is presented by itself a number of times.
   b. As a child you had the misfortune of sticking an object into an electrical outlet. The ensuing shock resulted in a strong conditioned fear of electrical outlets. Later it became apparent that you also had developed a fear of electrical cords and plugs.
   c. Your roommate went to a new pizza restaurant for dinner and developed a severe case of intestinal flu later that night. The pizza restaurant lost a customer.
   d. Children who play with large plastic bags sometimes become trapped inside the bag and nearly suffocate. If they are fortunate enough to be rescued, they will probably have a conditioned fear of closed spaces.

4. All of the following are changes in behavior that could be due to experience *except*
   a. learning.
   b. maturation.
   c. perception.
   d. conditioning.

5. In classical conditioning, what automatically produces a reaction?
   a. UR
   b. CR
   c. US
   d. CS

6. Explain how learned motives and learned goals are acquired.

Operant Conditioning

Bob's roommate, Greg, is a complete slob. In Bob's view, the condition of Greg's room is Greg's business, but the condition of the bathroom they share is another matter. Almost every week they have major arguments about cleaning the bathroom, and Bob ends up doing the cleaning. When the unfairness of the situation is more than Bob can stand, he tries a new approach. Whenever Greg does anything to help clean the apartment, Bob praises him: "Good job, Greg; the apartment really looks great." Gradually Greg begins helping on a more regular basis, and one week he even offers to clean the bathroom. ***What technique did Bob use to get Greg to help clean the apartment?*** ▓

We will now discuss the second basic type of learning, operant conditioning. In **operant conditioning,** also known as *instrumental conditioning,* an organism operates on its environment to produce a change. In other words, the organism's behavior is *instrumental*—it directly results in a change in the environment. As you will see, the type of change that is produced is a critical element of this type of learning.

operant conditioning
Learning that occurs when the participant must make a response to produce a change in the environment

Reinforcers

To return to our question, what technique did Bob use to get Greg to help clean the apartment? The answer is that he reinforced this behavior by praising it.

In some cases, operant behavior may result in the delivery of a stimulus or an event. When you insert money into a soda machine, for example, you receive a cold drink. When Greg cleaned the apartment, he received praise. In other instances, the operant behavior may result in the elimination of a stimulus or an event. For example, you have probably learned the quickest way to eliminate the sound your alarm clock makes early in the morning. These events are known as *reinforcers,* and they are at the heart of operant conditioning. We can define a **reinforcer** as an event or stimulus that makes the behavior it follows more likely to occur again (Skinner, 1938). For example, obtaining a cold drink from the soda machine and eliminating the annoying sound of your alarm clock are reinforcers. The behavior that a reinforcer follows can be thought of as the *target response*—it is the behavior that we want to strengthen or increase.

When rates of detection and punishment are very low, cheating rates may be very high.

Primary and Secondary Reinforcers. A **primary reinforcer** is a stimulus or an event that has innate reinforcing properties; you do not have to learn that such stimuli are reinforcers. For a hungry person, food is a primary reinforcer. A **secondary reinforcer** is a stimulus that acquires reinforcing properties by being associated with a primary reinforcer; you must learn that such stimuli are reinforcers. Money is a good example of a secondary reinforcer. By itself, money has no intrinsic value; children must learn that money can be exchanged for primary reinforcers such as ice cream and toys.

Positive and Negative Reinforcers. Primary and secondary reinforcers may be either positive or negative (Skinner, 1938). As we discuss positive and negative reinforcers, remember that regardless of whether a reinforcer is positive or negative, it always makes the target response more likely to occur again.

Positive reinforcers are events or stimuli such as food, water, money, and praise that are *presented* after the target response occurs. For example, a real estate agent earns a commission for each house she sells; the commissions reinforce her efforts to sell as many houses as possible. Your little brother is allowed to watch cartoons on Saturday mornings after he has cleaned his room; as a result, he cleans his room every Saturday. You have been praised for receiving good grades on psychology tests; the praise should encourage you to study even harder.

Psychological Detective

Can a positive reinforcer encourage unethical behavior? Consider the problem of cheating. Children are taught that cheating is wrong, but this behavior persists in most segments of our society. Why? Take a few moments to analyze the behavior of cheating in operant conditioning terms. Be sure to write down the target response and the reinforcers.

Suppose a student consults a concealed cheat sheet during a test. The target response is the act of cheating. The reinforcer is receiving a high (or passing) grade. Because the grade is given (presented), it is a positive reinforcer. Do threats of punishment serve to counteract this behavior? The answer appears to be no; the number of students who admit to having cheated on examinations is quite high: Between 40 and 60 percent of college students surveyed in three studies reported having cheated (Davis et al., 1992; Davis & Ludvigson, 1995; Jendreck, 1989). What's more, detection

reinforcer
Event that increases the frequency of the response that it follows

primary reinforcer
Stimulus that has innate reinforcing properties

secondary reinforcer
Stimulus that acquires reinforcing properties by being associated with a primary reinforcer

positive reinforcer
Event *presented* after the target response that increases the likelihood that this response will occur again

rates are low—frequently less than 2 percent (Haines et al., 1986). Thus a very small number of cheaters are caught, and even fewer are punished. The prospect of achieving an easy grade, coupled with a relatively low chance of getting caught, can be a powerful reinforcer of cheating on tests. The same analysis also applies to other familiar events. For example, the number of people who receive tickets for speeding on the highway is very low, relative to the number of people who speed.

Negative reinforcers are events or stimuli that are *removed* because a response has occurred. Examples of negative reinforcement include playing music to reduce boredom and cleaning your room so that your roommate will stop complaining that you're a slob. In these situations something stopped (boredom) or was removed (criticism) because you performed a target response. What response will occur the next time these unpleasant situations arise? If the negative reinforcer has been effective, the target response that terminated it is likely to occur again. The operation of positive and negative reinforcers is diagrammed in Figure 6-8.

B. F. Skinner and the "Skinner Box"

Probably no one has been associated more closely with operant conditioning than the late Harvard psychologist B. F. Skinner (1904–1990). Skinner was strongly influenced by John B. Watson's behavioral view of psychology (see page 239). As we have seen, Watson believed that if we could understand how to predict and control behavior, we would know all there was to know about psychology. Skinner therefore began to look for the stimuli that control behavior. The effects of reinforcement quickly impressed him as critical, and he devoted himself to studying

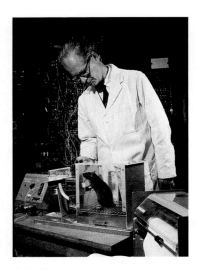

B.F. Skinner training a rat in a Skinner box.

negative reinforcer

Event *removed* after the target response, thereby increasing the likelihood that this response will occur again

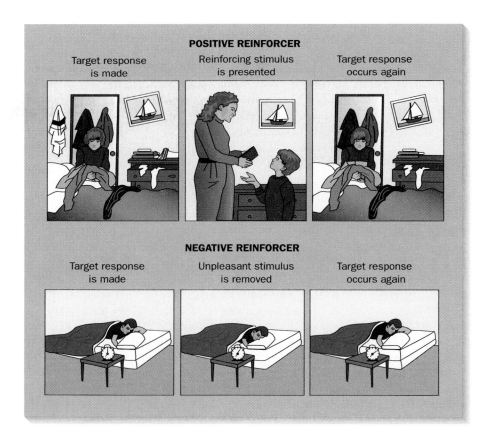

FIGURE 6-8 Diagram of the operation of positive and negative reinforcers. In the top panel the target response of picking up is reinforced with money (a positive reinforcer). In the bottom panel the target response (turning off the alarm clock) removes the loud noise (a negative reinforcer).

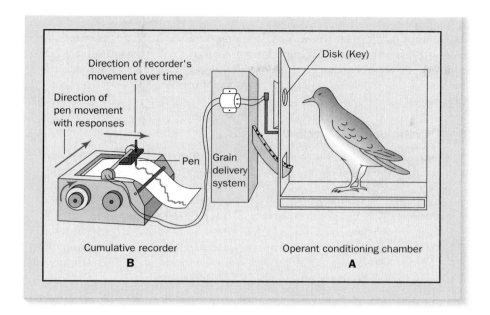

reinforcement and its influence on behavior. To isolate those effects, he developed a special testing environment; he called it an operant conditioning chamber, but it is usually referred to as a *Skinner box.* (See Figure 6-9A.)

In an operant conditioning chamber, the experimenter can present reinforcers, such as a piece of food for a hungry rat or pigeon, according to a preset pattern. Figure 6-9B shows the instrument, known as a *cumulative recorder,* that logs the participant's responses. The results sheet, known as a **cumulative record,** shows the rate of responding in a series of operant conditioning trials; the steeper the line, the higher the rate of responding. The preset pattern or plan for delivering reinforcement is known as a **schedule of reinforcement** (Skinner, 1938). Schedules of reinforcement are important determinants of behavior, and we say more about them shortly. But before we can impose a schedule of reinforcement, our participant or animal must be able to perform the target response, which is achieved through the process known as *shaping.*

Shaping

When you start training a rat in a Skinner box (see photo on page 252), you should not expect too much. The rat will not begin pressing the lever or bar as soon as it enters this new environment. You may have to help it to learn to press the lever or bar to receive food. The technique you will use is a form of operant conditioning called **shaping.** Shaping involves reinforcing successive responses that more closely resemble the desired target response; in other words, you are using the method of *successive approximations.* Although the concepts of shaping and successive approximations are reasonably clear, actually doing the job may be fairly difficult. The timing of reinforcement presentation is crucial; if reinforcers are not presented at exactly the right moment, an inappropriate response may be shaped.

For a rat learning to press a lever for food, the sequence of events might go as follows: When the rat is near the food dish, you drop a piece of food into it. Eating the food reinforces the behavior of approaching the dish. Once the rat has learned where the food is, you begin offering reinforcers only when the rat goes near the response lever. Gradually you make your response requirements

cumulative record
Results of a series of operant conditioning trials, shown as rate of responding

schedule of reinforcement
Preset pattern for delivering reinforcement

shaping
A form of operant conditioning in which a desired response is taught by reinforcement of successive responses that more closely resemble the target response

more demanding until the rat must actually touch the lever to receive the reinforcement. Once the rat has started touching the lever, you can require that the lever be pressed before the reinforcement is given. In this way you have gradually made the response that produces reinforcement that more closely resembles (*successively approximates*) the target response of pressing the lever. In short, you have *shaped* the rat's response.

Psychological Detective

Whether or not we realize it, shaping techniques have been used to help us acquire many new behaviors. Think about behaviors such as talking, writing, driving a car, and even thinking. These behaviors were gradually shaped and perfected through the appropriate delivery of reinforcers. Remember when you learned to drive? How were your driving skills when you first started driving? How are they now? In which ways were those skills shaped? Recall these behaviors and events and relate them to our discussion of operant conditioning before you read further.

The first time you sat behind the wheel, you were probably unable to drive around the block or parallel park like an experienced driver. To drive around the block, you had to become used to the rear-view mirrors, use the turn signals, apply the brakes, and perhaps shift gears. Then there was parallel parking, which required much practice. Your instructor reinforced good driving techniques with phrases like "Good job," "Excellent," and "Way to go." Gradually your skills improved until you could maneuver your car into a small space without any difficulty.

Now recall the case of the roommates Bob and Greg, who had trouble keeping their apartment clean. Bob was shaping Greg's behavior. At first he praised anything Greg did to help keep the apartment clean. Gradually he reserved his praise for greater efforts, until finally Greg was cleaning the apartment on a regular basis.

Schedules of Reinforcement

Once a target response has been shaped, the experimenter can arrange to have the reinforcer delivered according to a specific schedule (Ferster & Skinner, 1957).

Continuous Reinforcement. As noted earlier, a schedule of reinforcement is a preset pattern or plan for delivering reinforcement. The most basic schedule of reinforcement is one of **continuous reinforcement,** in which the participant is given a reinforcement after each target response. For example, a rat in a Skinner box receives a piece of food for each bar press; a salesperson receives a commission for each car sold; a soda machine delivers a cold drink each time you put money in it. A continuous schedule of reinforcement produces a reasonably high rate of responding. Once the reinforcer loses its effectiveness, however, the response rate drops quickly. Thus food pellets reinforce responding in a hungry rat, but they are not effective after the rat has eaten a large number of them.

Intermittent (Partial) Reinforcement. In schedules of reinforcement that do not involve the use of continuous reinforcement, some responses are not reinforced. The term **intermittent** or **partial reinforcement** is used to describe these noncontinuous patterns of delivering reinforcement. There are two main types of intermittent schedules, *ratio* and *interval*.

Ratio Schedules. When a **ratio schedule** is in effect, the number of responses determines whether the participant receives reinforcement. In some

---

continuous reinforcement
Reinforcement that follows every target response

intermittent, (or partial), reinforcement
Reinforcement that does not follow every target response

ratio schedule
Reinforcement schedule in which reinforcement is based on the number of responses; number may be set (fixed-ratio [FR] schedule) or may vary from one reinforcement to the next (variable-ratio [VR] schedule)

cases the exact number of responses that must be made to receive reinforcement is specified. For example, a pigeon may be required to peck a key five times before grain (a positive reinforcer) is presented. When the number of responses required to produce reinforcement is specified, the arrangement is known as a *fixed-ratio (FR) schedule*. Requiring a pigeon to peck five times to receive reinforcement is designated as a "fixed-ratio 5" (FR5) schedule. A continuous reinforcement schedule can be thought of as a "fixed-ratio 1" (FR1) schedule.

On other occasions we may not want to specify the exact number of responses. Sometimes the reinforcer will be delivered after 15 responses, sometimes after 35 responses, and sometimes after 10 responses, and so forth. Because the exact number of responses required for reinforcement is not specified, this arrangement is called a *variable-ratio (VR) schedule*. Typically the average number of responses is used to indicate the type of variable-ratio schedule. In our example, in which the values 15, 35, and 10 were used, the average number of responses would be 20 [(15 + 35 + 10)/3 = 20)]. This particular schedule would be designated as a "variable-ratio 20" (VR20) schedule.

Whether we are dealing with a VR or FR schedule, our participants usually make many responses. Frequent responding makes good sense in these situations: The more responses made, the more frequently the participant receives a reinforcer. Although both FR and VR schedules produce many responses, VR schedules produce somewhat higher rates of responding. These differences are shown in Figure 6-10.

When an FR schedule is in effect, the participant may pause for a brief period after the reinforcement has been delivered. This *postreinforcement pause* typically does not occur when a VR schedule is used. When an FR schedule is used, the reinforcer seems to serve as a signal to take a short break. If you were responding on an FR schedule, you might be thinking, "Five more responses until I get the reinforcer, then I'll rest for a bit before I start responding again."

Suppose that you have a job stuffing envelopes. For every 200 envelopes you stuff, you receive $10 (a positive reinforcer). To earn as much money as possible, you work very hard and stuff as many envelopes as possible. Every time the 200th envelope is completed, however, you stop for a minute to straighten the stack and count how many piles of 200 envelopes you have completed.

The duration of the postreinforcement pause is not the same for all FR schedules; the higher the schedule (the greater the number of responses required to produce a reinforcer), the longer the pause (Todd & Cogan, 1978). In addition, the more time expended in responding, the longer the postreinforcement pause will be (Collier, Hirsch, & Hamlin, 1972).

Now consider a case in which there is no postreinforcement pause. Last year Kim and some of her friends spent their spring break in Las Vegas. The slot machines proved to be Kim's downfall. Sometimes the jackpot bell rang and she collected a potful of quarters, which encouraged her to continue playing. Before she knew it, she had been putting quarters into the "one-armed bandit" for six hours straight. When she counted up her winnings and losses, she had spent over $250 just to win $33.50. Why did Kim put so much money into the slot machine?

The answer is that slot machines "pay off" on a VR schedule. As Kim put quarter after quarter into the machine, she was probably thinking, "Next time the bell will ring, and I'll get the jackpot." She knew that she would receive a reward (hitting the jackpot) at some point, but because slot machines operate on a

"Actually, he's easy to train, everytime I press the buzzer, he brings me food."

Reprinted by permission of Jerry Marcus

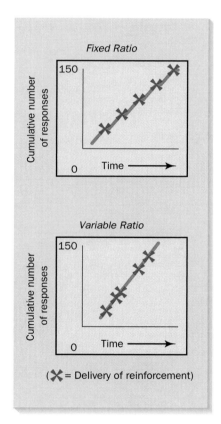

FIGURE 6-10 Examples of fixed-ratio (FR) and variable ratio (VR) response patterns. The steeper the slope of the line, the higher the rate of responding. Note that the responding ceases (flat line) for a brief period after reinforcement has been delivered under the demanding FR schedule. This pause does not occur when the VR schedule is in effect.

variable schedule, she could not predict *when* she would be rewarded. If you have ever become "hooked" on playing the lottery, you can understand this process.

Interval Schedules. The second type of intermittent schedule of reinforcement, the **interval schedule,** involves the passage of time. When an interval schedule is in effect, responses are reinforced only after a certain interval of time has passed. As with ratio schedules, there are two types of interval schedules, fixed-interval and variable-interval.

Under a *fixed-interval (FI) schedule,* a constant period of time must pass before a response is reinforced. Responses made before the end of that period are not reinforced. No matter how many times you check your mailbox, you will not receive mail until it is time for the daily mail delivery. Under an FI schedule, participants try to estimate the passage of time and make most of their responses toward the end of the interval, when they will be reinforced. If your mail always is delivered between 3:00 and 3:30 P.M., you won't start to check for it until that time. The longer participants stay on an FI schedule, the better they become at timing their responses (Cruser & Klein, 1984).

When reinforcement occurs on a *variable-interval (VI) schedule,* the participant never knows the exact length of time that must pass before a response is reinforced; the time interval changes after every reinforcement. Because a response can be reinforced at any time, it makes sense for the participant to maintain a steady—but not especially high—rate of responding. Think of the times you have called a friend on the phone only to get a busy signal. You probably did not start redialing at a frantic pace. Most likely you initially called back a few minutes later, and then a few minutes after that if you were not successful, and so on. You could not determine whether your friend was having several short conversations or a lengthy one—that is, you did not know when your dialing would be reinforced by the sound of a ringing telephone. Only time would tell. At some point your friend hung up, and you were able to get through. As time passed, your chances of getting through got better and better.

The average amount of time that must elapse before a response produces reinforcement under a VI schedule influences the rate of responding; the longer the interval, the lower the rate of responding. For example, pigeons reinforced on a VI 2-minute schedule responded between 60 and 100 times per minute, whereas pigeons reinforced on a VI 7.1-minute schedule responded 20 to 70 times per minute (Catania & Reynolds, 1968). The characteristic response patterns for FI and VI schedules are shown in Figure 6-11.

The following Study Chart compares classical and operant conditioning. Check your understanding of these basic forms of learning before reading further.

interval schedule
Reinforcement schedule based on the passage of time and in which a single response at the end of the designated interval is reinforced; intervals may be set (fixed interval [FI] schedule) or may vary from one reinforcement to the next (variable-interval [VI] schedule)

Myth or Science

When George Orwell's famous novel Nineteen Eighty-four was published in 1949, it presented a world in which Big Brother was constantly watching, and everyone's behaviors were conditioned. Books such as this were written at a time when B. F. Skinner and the principle of operant conditioning were first becoming known to the public. Because such principles were often misunderstood and misinterpreted, there was genuine fear that they might be used to turn people into conditioned robots capable of committing hideous crimes. The year 1984 has come and gone; even though an increasingly large body of scientific data about operant conditioning has been accumulated, we seem to be far from the conditioned robots portrayed by George Orwell.

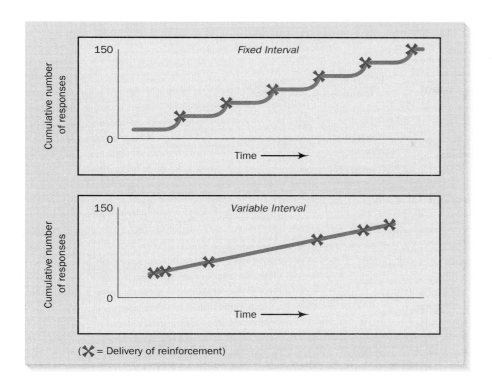

FIGURE 6-11 On a fixed-interval (FI) schedule, most responses are made toward the end of the interval when a response will be reinforced. Once the reinforcer has been delivered and the interval begins again, the rate of responding decreases drastically. Under the variable-interval (VI) schedule, the participant cannot predict the end of the interval and therefore cannot judge when to respond. A low, steady rate of responding is maintained.

STUDY CHART

Comparison of Classical and Operant Conditioning

Basic Process	Classical Conditioning	Operant Conditioning
	An unconditioned stimulus (US) causes an unconditioned response (UR); after pairing a conditioned stimulus (CS) with the US several times, the CS comes to elicit a conditioned response (CR).	Reinforcement (positive and negative) is used to shape a desired response; once the response is established, a schedule of reinforcement (fixed or variable; interval or ratio) may be implemented to maintain it
Training—acquisition of a new response	The CS and US are paired; after several pairings the CS comes to elicit a CR	Because the target response is followed by a reinforcer, its probability or rate increases
Extinction—Probability or frequency of a conditioned response is decreased	The CS is presented alone, and a decrease in the CR is observed	Reinforcement is discontinued and the rate of responding gradually decreases
Generalization—Responses are made to stimuli other than those used in training	Stimuli similar to the CS elicit the CR	Responding occurs when stimuli similar to the discriminative stimulus are presented
Discrimination—Responses are made only to the stimuli used in training	Stimuli that are similar to the CS do not elicit a CR	Only the discriminative stimulus results in responding

The Role of Cognition

In our study of classical conditioning, we encountered contingency theory and blocking (see pages 246–247). These processes indicate that classical conditioning is not simply mechanical; rather, mental activity or thought processes (cognition) are involved to some degree. The relation of cognition to basic learning processes, such as *insight learning* and *latent learning*, has been studied for many decades. Other behaviors with cognitive requirements—such as *serial enumeration, decision-making strategies, encoding of visual information,* and *social communication of taste preferences*—have emerged from the research laboratory only recently.

Insight Learning. The importance of cognition to operant conditioning can be seen in the process known as insight learning. **Insight learning** is a form of operant conditioning in which we restructure our perceptual stimuli (we see things in a different way), make an instrumental (operant) response, and generalize this behavior to other situations. In short, it is not blind, trial-and-error learning that develops gradually but a type of learning that occurs suddenly and relies on cognitive processes. It is the "aha!" experience we have when we suddenly solve a problem.

Classic research by the Gestalt psychologist Wolfgang Köhler (1927) exemplifies insight learning. Using chimpanzees as his test animals, Köhler gave them the following problem. A bunch of bananas was suspended out of reach of the apes. To reach the bananas, the apes had to stack three boxes on top of one another and then put together the pieces of a jointed pole to form a single, longer pole. After several attempts at jumping and trying to reach the bananas, Köhler's star pupil, Sultan, appeared to survey the situation (mentally rearrange the stimulus elements that were present) and solve the problem in the prescribed manner. Köhler believed that Sultan had achieved insight into the correct solution of the problem.

Consider the solution of a particularly difficult mathematics problem. You struggle and struggle to solve the problem, but nothing happens. In frustration you set the problem aside and turn to another assignment. All of a sudden you understand what is required to work the math problem successfully; you've had an "aha!" experience. How you perceive the situation has changed; insight has occurred. Once this problem has been solved, you are able to solve others like it.

Thus cognitive processes are important in helping us to adapt to our environment. As we shall see, other organisms—even rats—may use cognitive processes as they go about their daily activities.

Latent Learning. In his study of maze learning by rats, psychologist Edward C. Tolman presented very persuasive evidence for the use of cognitive processes in basic learning (Tolman & Honzik, 1930). Tolman is associated most often with his study of **latent learning.** Latent (hidden) learning occurs when learning has taken place but is not demonstrated. In one of his most famous studies, three groups of rats learned a complex maze that had many choices and dead ends. One group of rats was always reinforced with food for successfully completing the maze. These animals gradually made fewer and fewer errors until, after 11 days of training, their performance was nearly perfect. A second group was never reinforced; the rats continued to make numerous errors. The third (latent-learning) group of animals did not receive reinforcement for the first 10 days of training. On the eleventh day, reinforcement was provided. The behavior of these animals on the twelfth day is of crucial importance. If learning occurs in a gradual, trial-and-error manner, the rats' performance on the twelfth day should not have differed drastically from their performance on the eleventh day. If, however, the rats used cognitive processes to learn to navigate the maze, they would exhibit more dramatic behavior changes.

insight learning
Sudden grasp of a concept or the solution to a problem that results from perceptual restructuring; typically characterized by an immediate change in behavior

latent learning
Learning that has occurred but is not demonstrated

In fact, on the twelfth day these rats solved the maze as quickly as the rats who had been continually reinforced. How did these rats learn so quickly? Tolman argued that by wandering through the maze for 10 days before the introduction of reinforcement, these animals had formed a *cognitive map* of the maze. In other words, they had learned to solve the maze, but this knowledge had remained latent (unused) until reinforcement was introduced on the eleventh day. Then, on the twelfth day, these rats demonstrated that they knew how to get to the location of the reinforcement. Their latent learning had manifested itself.

Serial Enumeration.   **Serial enumeration** refers to the ability to remember a series of events and to respond appropriately the next time that series of events is encountered. Serial enumeration involves the use of cognitive processes.

Richard Burns and Walter Gordon (1988) have shown that rats are capable of serial enumeration. They trained rats to run a straight runway from a start area to a goal area, and they recorded the rats' speed. They reasoned that if the rats were given a different reinforcer each time they ran down the runway, the animals would be able to keep track of which trial they were running by the type of reinforcement they received. They trained the rats over a period of several days, always following a fixed pattern in which the rats received different types of reinforcers (such as rat pellets or breakfast cereal) after some trials and no reinforcement after others. After experiencing this pattern of reward and nonreward for several days, the animals should have been able to predict when a nonreward trial was going to occur by the type of reinforcer they received on the preceding trial. The results showed that this was indeed the case. Just as if a sign saying No Food had been posted on the runway, the rats used cognitive processes to learn to run more slowly on the trials that would not be rewarded. A study by Breukelaar and Dalrymple-Alford (1998) also demonstrated that rats have good timing (see also Crystal, Church, & Broadbent, 1997) and counting abilities, but these attributes are only used as a last-resort measure when other, less complex strategies have failed.

Decision-Making Strategies.   Several researchers have investigated the decision-making strategies used by animals as they forage for food. A wide variety of animals, ranging from black-capped chickadees (Roche, 1996) to rats (Roche & Timberlake, 1998), use very elaborate decision-making strategies as they forage for their daily food.

Encoding Visual Stimuli.   Contemporary researchers are not willing to simply state the physical nature of experimental stimuli they use in their research; they want to know how these stimuli are processed and represented by their animal subjects (Cook et al., 1997; Fetterman, 1996). For example, Spetch, Kelly, and Lechelt (1998) investigated how pigeons *encode* (process; see Chapter 7) visual information in a natural, outdoor setting. Likewise, Kirkpatrick-Steger, Wasserman, and Biederman (1998) investigated which features of a picture (line drawings of objects such as a water can and a desk lamp) were the most important cues for pigeons; they showed that although no single feature is crucial for object recognition, the overall organization of features is very important (see also Kirkpatrick-Steger & Wasserman, 1996).

Social Communication of Taste Preferences.   Bennett Galef Jr. and his colleagues at McMaster University have demonstrated that social interactions can influence the amount and kind of food an animal consumes. For example, naive (observer) rats that interact with demonstrator rats that have consumed a uniquely flavored food increased their subsequent intake of the unique flavor significantly more than did observer rats that interacted with demonstrators that consumed their normal diet (Galef, 1989, 1996; Galef & Stein, 1985). In some

serial enumeration
Ability to remember a series of events

manner the demonstrator rats communicated information about the food they had eaten. In a related experiment, Galef, Whiskin, and Bielavska (1997) found that rats that had learned a taste aversion (see page 247) to a specific flavor increased their consumption of that flavor after interacting with non–taste-aversion rats that had just consumed that flavor. Social interaction clearly influences how animals perceive, react to, and learn in their environments.

Thus cognitive processes appear to play a major role, even in the acquisition of basic learning phenomena (see Macuda & Roberts, 1995; Wilkie & Wilson, 1995).

Review Summary

1. Operant conditioning occurs when an organism performs a target response that is followed by a reinforcer.

2. All reinforcers increase the frequency of the response they follow. **Positive reinforcers** are presented after the target response has been made; **negative reinforcers** are taken away after the target response has been made.

3. Complex responses may be acquired gradually through the process of **shaping** and the use of **successive approximations.** Once a behavior has been acquired, it may be reinforced according to a particular **schedule of reinforcement.**

4. When a **ratio schedule** is in effect, the number of responses is important. **Fixed-ratio (FR) schedules** require that a set number of responses be made before a reinforcer is delivered; **variable-ratio (VR) schedules** require that the participant perform differing numbers of responses to obtain a reinforcer.

5. With an **interval schedule,** a certain amount of time must pass before a response is reinforced. With a **fixed-interval (FI) schedule,** the time interval is constant; the time interval changes after each reinforcer is delivered when a **variable-interval (VI) schedule** is used.

6. Ratio schedules generally produce higher rates of responding than interval schedules.

7. Insight learning involves restructuring our perceptual stimuli to achieve the solution to a problem. Such perceptual restructuring and solutions typically occur rapidly.

8. Latent learning occurs when learning has taken place but is not demonstrated until a later time.

9. Serial enumeration refers to the ability to remember a series of events correctly.

10. Current research on the role of cognition in basic learning processes includes an investigation of *decision-making strategies, encoding of visual stimuli,* and the *social communication of taste preferences.*

Study Break

1. For each of the following situations, find the response that is being reinforced, identify the reinforcer, and determine which schedule of reinforcement is being used.
   a. Playing the lottery has become popular in many states. People continue to line up to buy lottery tickets. Sometimes they win, and sometimes they lose.
   b. A friend has a part-time job making telephone calls to convince people to sign up for a credit card. For every 100 new customers who sign up, your friend receives a weekend vacation.
   c. Each morning, rain or shine, your dog, McDuff, comes to the back door to wait for his breakfast.

2. What is the effect of reinforcers on the target response?
3. For each of the following situations, indicate whether a positive or negative reinforcer is being used.
   a. A rat presses a bar to turn off an electric foot shock.
   b. A child digs through a new box of cereal to get a prize.
   c. A child pretends to be sick in order to receive extra attention.
   d. A student pretends to be sick in order to avoid having to make a presentation in class.

4. Explain why learning to play the piano would be an example of shaping. What would the reinforcer or reinforcers be in this situation?

5. Match each item in the left-hand column with the corresponding item in the right-hand column.

a. A set number of responses is required to produce a reinforcer	**1.** Insight learning
b. Ability to remember a series of events correctly	**2.** Latent learning
c. Learning has taken place but is not demonstrated until later	**3.** Fixed-ratio schedule
d. The time interval changes after every reinforcement	**4.** Serial enumeration
e. Result of the restructuring of our perceptual environment	**5.** Variable-interval schedule

6. In which type of conditioning is the learner's behavior important in bringing about the learning?
- **a.** backward conditioning
- **b.** classical conditioning
- **c.** operant conditioning
- **d.** Pavlovian conditioning

7. An event or stimulus that makes the behavior it follows more likely is a/an
- **a.** reinforcer.
- **b.** punishment.
- **c.** conditioned stimulus.
- **d.** unconditioned stimulus.

8. A graph that shows the pattern of a rat's responding in a Skinner box is a
- **a.** response pattern.
- **b.** cumulative record.
- **c.** shaping record.
- **d.** reinforcement pattern.

Punishment: The Opposite of Reinforcement

We have seen that the effect of a reinforcer (either positive or negative) is to increase the likelihood of a target response. A **punisher** has the *opposite* effect: to decrease the likelihood or rate of responding of a target response.

Everyone seems to have an opinion about the usefulness of punishment. The typical view is that punishment does not work very well. This philosophy seems to have originated with the educator E. L. Thorndike. In the early 1900s, Thorndike developed a very influential theory of learning. One of the main components of that theory was the **law of effect** (Thorndike, 1911), which stated that presenting a "satisfier" (a reinforcer) leads to the strengthening or learning of new responses, whereas presenting an "annoyer" (a punisher) leads to the weakening or unlearning of responses.

Thorndike later concluded that punishment might not be effective, but he may have been premature in dismissing the influence of punishment. We now explore different types of punishers as well as some guidelines for using punishment effectively.

Just as there are positive and negative reinforcers, there are positive and negative punishers. As you can see in Figure 6-12, positive punishers are aversive stimuli or events that are presented; negative punishers are pleasant stimuli or events that are removed. This might sound just like the description of reinforcement. Remember, reinforcement (positive or negative) increases the rate of responding, whereas **punishment** (positive or negative) decreases the rate of responding. For example, if a rat in an operant conditioning chamber receives a mild electric shock for pressing a lever, its rate of responding decreases. Similarly, if a child is scolded for playing in the street, that behavior is likely to occur less often. These are examples of positive punishers. Examples of negative punishers include taking away a child's allowance, grounding a teenager, or suspending a basketball player for violating training rules.

punisher
Stimulus that produces a decrease in responding; may take the form of presentation of a stimulus (positive punisher) or termination of a stimulus (negative punisher)

law of effect
Thorndike's view that reinforcers promote learning, whereas punishers lead to the unlearning of responses

punishment
The process of using a punisher to decrease response rate

FIGURE 6-12 Diagram of the operation of positive punishers and negative punishers.

POSITIVE PUNISHER

An undesired behavior is | Followed by the *presentation* of an aversive stimulus | Result: A decrease in the undesired behavior

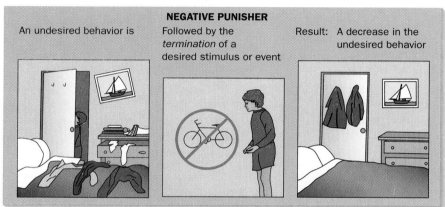

NEGATIVE PUNISHER

An undesired behavior is | Followed by the *termination* of a desired stimulus or event | Result: A decrease in the undesired behavior

Psychological Detective

We have examined how to present reinforcers to obtain a high rate of responding. How can punishment be administered so as to maximize its effects? Select an undesired behavior that you would like to see decreased or eliminated and then formulate specific answers to this question and write them down before reading further.

How and when should punishment be used? Azrin and Holz (1966) and Axelrod and Apsche (1983) have suggested several procedures that should be followed if punishment is to be used effectively:

1. The punisher should be delivered (positive) or taken away (negative) *immediately after the response that is to be eliminated.* Slapping your cat for digging up your African violets while you were out will have no effect except perhaps to make you feel better. Why not? The cat will not see any connection between the earlier, undesirable behavior and the current punishment.

2. The punisher should be *strong enough to make a real difference.* Being grounded for two days may not matter very much, but being grounded for two months is a different story. Most people consider the use of extremely strong punishers, particularly those involving physical or violent punishment, unacceptable, if not ethically wrong. We do not want to inflict so much punishment that real damage results.

3. The punishment should be administered *after each and every undesired target response*. Punishment is not as effective when you do not punish all of the undesired responses; it must be administered consistently. Thus if you want to stop a child from using "bad" or offensive language, you should punish the child every time he or she uses it. Permitting even one episode of the undesired behavior to occur after previous punishment greatly decreases the effectiveness of the punishment.

4. There should be *no unauthorized escape from the punisher*. If the punishment is not applied uniformly, its effects will be weakened. Rats are very clever; frequently they learn how to hang upside down from the top of a cage to avoid an electric shock to their feet.

5. If you use punishment, be prepared for the possibility of *aggressive responding*. Rats do not like to be shocked, children do not like to have their television privileges taken away, and spankings can elicit behaviors other than crying. Children who are spanked may retaliate by kicking and biting. Note that aggressive responding may be directed toward a person, an animal, or an object that cannot retaliate, such as a pet dog or cat; such behavior is called *displaced aggression*. Nor does aggressive behavior always end when the punishment ends. As a child, did you ever try to "get even" with your parents after being punished? In short, punishment can teach a child to use force or other violence against people.

6. Provide the person with an *alternative desired behavior* that can gain a reinforcer for the person. Simply giving a child a spanking for playing in the street may not be especially effective if there is nowhere else to play. Clearly, it is very difficult to use punishment effectively. Perhaps the best solution is to reinforce an alternate desired behavior. The use of "redirecting" as a disciplinary technique in child-care settings provides an example. When a child engages in an inappropriate behavior, the child is removed from the "scene" and given another, appropriate activity to engage in. Praising the child for success in this appropriate activity is reinforcement of an alternate, desired behavior.

The following Study Chart summarizes the difference between reinforcement and punishment.

STUDY CHART

Positive and Negative Reinforcement Compared with Positive and Negative Punishment

Reinforcement	Results in an increase in responding
Positive	A stimulus is presented after a target response; an increase in responding occurs, (e.g., receiving good grades increases the amount of time one studies)
Negative	A stimulus is removed after a target response; an increase in responding occurs, (e.g., if playing music reduces boredom, the frequency of playing music increases)
Punishment	Results in a decrease in responding
Positive	A stimulus is presented after a target response; a decrease in responding occurs (e.g.,washing a child's mouth out with soap for cursing reduces the number of curse words the child says)
Negative	A stimulus is removed after a target response; a decrease in responding occurs (e.g., Saturday morning cartoon privileges are taken away because the child's chores have not been completed)

Extinction

Remember Kim, who put all those quarters into the slot machine? Is the machine really going to pay off with a big jackpot this time, or is the jackpot switch broken? Because she does not know, Kim continues to put coins into the machine, always hoping for a big payoff. She spends her entire bankroll of $250 just to win $33.50. Other people have been known to spend much more money playing slot machines. ***Why is it so difficult to stop playing a slot machine once you have started?*** ▮

In this section we examine the process by which learned responses are weakened and become less likely to occur. As with classically conditioned responses, this process is known as *extinction*. We also discuss how operant behavior can come under the control of certain stimuli. Let's begin with what is known as the *partial reinforcement effect*.

The Partial Reinforcement Effect

Every day you look in your mailbox for a letter from a friend. After ten months of looking, you are finally convinced your friend is not going to write; no letters have come, and there is no reason to expect any. Completely removing the reinforcer—in this case, your friend's letters—from the operant conditioning situation eventually results in extinction or elimination of the operantly conditioned response. There are some basic similarities between the way extinction is produced in classical conditioning (by omitting the US) and the way it is produced in operant conditioning (by removing the reinforcer).

So why is it so difficult to stop playing a slot machine once you have started? As you saw earlier in this chapter, intermittent or partial reinforcement schedules can produce very high rates of responding. This outcome is especially true of ratio schedules, in which the harder the participants work, the more reinforcement they receive. Because partial reinforcement schedules involve making a number of responses that are not reinforced, it may be difficult to tell when reinforcement has been discontinued completely and when it has merely been delayed. Because Kim cannot tell whether the slot machine is broken or whether it will pay off the next time she puts in a quarter, she continues to play. Many players stop only when all their money is gone.

Are you beginning to see a general pattern concerning extinction and operant conditioning? If reinforcement is delivered in a predictable manner, it should be easier to tell when it has been discontinued and when extinction has begun. Hence extinction should occur more rapidly following FR training than following VR training. Likewise, extinction should occur more rapidly following FI training than following VI training. What's more, it should be even easier to extinguish responding that has been conditioned through the use of continuous reinforcement than responding that has been conditioned through any partial or intermittent schedule.

All of these facts have been verified experimentally. This general pattern, termed the **partial reinforcement effect,** is well established (Amsel, 1962). Briefly, the partial reinforcement effect states that extinction of operant behavior is more difficult after partial or intermittent reinforcement than after continuous reinforcement. Have you ever taken pity on a hungry, stray cat and put out some food for it? Sometimes when it comes to your door you feed it, and other

partial reinforcement effect
Phenomenon in which extinction of an operant response following partial or intermittent reinforcement takes longer than extinction following continuous reinforcement

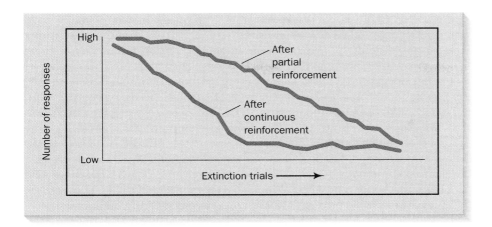

FIGURE 6-13 Extinction of a bar-press response after continuous and partial reinforcement.

times you don't. When you finally decide you are never going to feed the cat again, you find it *will not* go away.

Figure 6-13 shows differences in extinction after continuous and partial reinforcement training in a Skinner box. The same pattern of results has been shown for extinction after classical conditioning (Humphreys, 1939). Continuous reinforcement participants who received a puff of air (the US) on each of 96 training trials extinguished their conditioned eye-blink response more rapidly than partial reinforcement participants who received the US on only 48 of the 96 trials.

Operant Conditioning and Stimulus Control

Bringing a behavior under stimulus control means that a particular stimulus or signal tells the participant that its responses will be reinforced (Fetterman, 1993). In an operant conditioning chamber, for example, a green light or a tone can be a signal to a rat that pressing the lever will be reinforced. Such a signal is called a **discriminative stimulus.** When the light or tone is present, lever presses are reinforced under the schedule of reinforcement that the rat has experienced during training. When the discriminative stimulus is absent, the responses are not reinforced, and extinction occurs.

A vast number of discriminative stimuli are found in the real world. The Open sign in a store window is a discriminative stimulus signaling that the response of reaching for the door handle will be reinforced by your being able to enter the store and shop. The color of the traffic light at an intersection signals that the response of stopping your car (red) or proceeding through the intersection (green) will be reinforced by safe arrival at your destination. Your friend's mood serves as a signal that a response such as telling a joke or making a sympathetic remark will be appreciated.

In discussing classical conditioning, we saw that conditioning may become generalized—that is, a CR may occur in response to stimuli that are similar to the one used in training. Generalization also occurs in operant conditioning. In certain instances this generalization may be helpful. For example, in some towns the traffic light hangs over the center of the street, whereas in others it is at the curb. Moreover, the colors of the lights are not identical; some greens are bright, whereas others are dull. Yet in all cases we respond appropriately; we have generalized the appropriate responses that we made to similar stimuli in the past. We stop when we see a red light, whether it is bright or dull, overhead or at the curb—and we go when we see a green light.

The "open" sign is a discriminative stimulus signaling that the response of pulling the door handle will be reinforced by your being able to enter Mother Myrick's for an afternoon snack.

discriminative stimulus
Stimulus or signal telling the participant that responding will be reinforced

Generalization is not always desirable, however. Imagine a young child who runs to meet relatives whenever they come to visit. Would you want that child to run to adult strangers as well? In general, children must learn which behaviors are appropriate in different situations. They must learn, for example, that behaviors appropriate for a sports event are not appropriate for a wedding, even though both situations involve crowds of people. This discriminative training is accomplished by reinforcing responses only when the precise discriminative stimulus is present. Other responses, especially those made in the presence of similar but incorrect stimuli, are not reinforced; in other words, they are extinguished. Gradually we learn to respond only when the precise discriminative stimulus is present. If you stop and analyze what we have said about discrimination and generalization in operant conditioning, you will see that they are opposing processes, just as they are in classical conditioning.

Cultural & Diversity Perspective

The Snark Was a Boojum

IN 1950, THE EMINENT PSYCHOLOGIST FRANK BEACH PUBLISHED AN ARTICLE TITLED *The Snark was a Boojum.* Beach's message was simple and straightforward: Comparative psychology should, by definition, be based on studies of numerous species. According to Smith and Davis (1997), "Beach examined 613 research articles and found that 50% of them dealt with the rat, despite the fact that the Norway rat represented only .001% of all living creatures that could be studied" (p. 359). Beach felt that failure to heed this caution would result in comparative psychology silently fading away, just like the hunters in Lewis Carroll's *Alice in Wonderland* who encountered a snark that was a boojum.

Beach's cautions are just as relevent today as they were in 1950. In many respects psychology has become the science of the white rat and the American, male, college sophomore. These two types of participants appear far more often in the published research literature than other types of participants (Jones, 1994; Lee & Hall, 1994; Marin, 1994).

The intent of this feature is not to present specific cross-cultural and diversity findings but to alert you to the fact that psychologists probably should be concerned about looking for such influences in the area of basic learning processes such as classical and operant conditioning. Why is it difficult to point to such influences when basic learning processes are considered?

Part of the answer concerns the nature of the material: basic learning processes. Most researchers and students probably asume that basic processes apply to all animal species and people in all cultures; hence cross-species and cross-cultural studies are not needed. This assumption may be true, but we will never know for sure until such studies are conducted.

A second reason for the lack of comparative and cross-cultural data concerns the orientation of the researchers. This area of psychology traditionally has been *very* concerned with the methodology that is used in the experiments and in the creation of theories to account for the behaviors and phenomena that are observed. These interests shift attention away to the specifics involved in the conduct of the experiments and away from determining cross-species and cross-cultural effects.

Keep these concerns in mind as you read about basic learning processes. The future, we hope, will see a change in this state of affairs.

Observational Learning

Let's say you have given permission for your young son and daughter to participate in a psychological experiment at the local university. During the experiment each child watches an adult play with a large inflatable doll that can double as a punching bag. Because the doll's base contains sand, the doll bounces back when it is punched: It bounces back and then is ready for more punches. The adult gives the doll a merciless beating; then each child is given an opportunity to play with the doll. *What can this experiment tell us about learning?* ▪

observational learning (social learning theory)
Learning that occurs through watching and imitating the behaviors of others

vicarious reinforcement
Ability to imagine the effects of a reinforcer

vicarious punishment
Ability to imagine the effects of a punisher

For many years psychologists believed a participant must actually perform an operant response for learning to occur. In the early 1960s, Albert Bandura and his colleagues changed this view (Bandura, Ross, & Ross, 1963). As you will recall from Chapter 1, they found that children who observed an adult hitting and punching an inflatable Bobo doll were likely to repeat those behaviors when they were given a chance to play with the doll. Control participants, who had not observed the adult model, behaved less aggressively. Because the children made no responses while they were watching, the researchers concluded that simply observing the behavior and reinforcement (or punishment) of another participant could result in learning (Bandura, 1977). Such learning is termed **observational learning.** Because the observation of other people is a central factor in this form of learning, this approach is often called **social learning theory.**

If you stop to think about it, observational learning is the main way we learn about our culture and its customs and traditions. The key to observational learning appears to be that the participant identifies with the person being observed. If we put ourselves in the other person's place for a moment, we are better able to imagine the effects of the reinforcer or punisher. This phenomenon is called **vicarious reinforcement** (or **vicarious punishment**).

Observational learning, or *modeling,* as it is sometimes called, is a widespread phenomenon. It is even found among a number of animals. In one study rats that observed the extinction behavior of other rats subsequently stopped responding more rapidly than rats that did not observe extinction performance (Heyes, Jaldow, & Dawson, 1993). In another experiment, monkeys reared in a laboratory didn't fear snakes. After watching another group of monkeys react fearfully to snakes, however, the nonfearful monkeys also developed a pronounced fear of snakes (Cook et al., 1985).

SKINNER
TO ENTER, PRESS LEVER

PAVLOV
KNOCK, DO NOT RING BELL, DOGS INSIDE

BANDURA
PLEASE WATCH VIDEOTAPE ON HOW TO KNOCK

Palladino, Handelsman, & Butler

From *Eye on Psi Chi.* Reprinted by the permission of Psi Chi The National Honor Society in Psychology.

This 10-year-old Shoshone Indian boy learns traditional dances by viewing VCR tapes in his home.

Attempts to influence behavior through observational learning occur every day. Turn on the television and you are bombarded with commercials, which are nothing more than a form of observational learning. If you drive *this* kind of car, wear *these* clothes, use *this* brand of perfume, shower with *this* soap, use *this* shampoo, and eat *this* kind of breakfast, you will be rich, famous, powerful, sexy, and so forth, just like the models in the commercials.

According to the social learning theory proposed by Bandura (1986), for observational learning to be effective, the following conditions must be present:

1. You must *pay attention* to what the other person is doing and what happens to him or her.
2. You probably will not make the modeled response immediately, so you need to *store a memory* of the situation you have observed. For example, catchy advertising jingles that run through our heads continuously help us remember a particular commercial (see Chapter 7).
3. You must be able to *repeat or reproduce* the behavior you observed. It might be wonderful to dream of owning a Porsche, but most of us will never be able to reproduce the behaviors needed to obtain one, no matter how often we watch the commercial.
4. *Your motivational state must be appropriate* to the behavior you have learned through observation. Watching numerous commercials of people drinking a particular soft drink will not normally cause you to purchase one if you are not thirsty.
5. You must *pay attention to discriminative stimuli.* Sometimes we do not choose the best time and place to imitate someone else's behavior. For example, it would not be wise for teenagers to model some of their peers' behaviors at the dinner table.

The knowledge that children model the behaviors of adults has led to concern about the possible effects of filmed and televised violence on children. Many people fear that youngsters who witness violent acts on television and in films may repeat those acts in real life. Edward Donnerstein (1995), a psychologist at the University of California, Santa Barbara, indicates that "there is absolutely no doubt that higher levels of viewing violence in the mass media are correlated with increased acceptance of aggressive attitudes and aggressive behavior. This exposure in young children can have lifelong consequences." We have more to say about the possible effects of televised violence in Chapter 16.

To end our discussion of observational learning on a more positive note, we should point out that this technique has been used successfully to teach desired behaviors. For example, young children who have been taught to chew their food carefully find that swallowing a large medicine capsule whole can be a major obstacle. The observational learning technique, in which another person modeled the correct procedure for swallowing a capsule, was used to teach children how to swallow such pills (Blount et al., 1984).

The following excerpt is from a therapy session in which the therapist is trying to help a client, a male college student, overcome his fear of asking for a date over the telephone (Masters et al., 1987, pp. 100–101). Notice how the therapist models appropriate behavior in an attempt to extinguish the client's inappropriate responses.

CLIENT: By the way (pause), I don't suppose you want to go out Saturday night?

THERAPIST: Up to actually asking for the date you were very good. If I were the woman, however, I think I might have been a bit offended when you said, "By the way." It's like your asking her out is pretty casual. Also, the way you phrased the question, you are kind of suggesting to her that she doesn't want to go out with you. Pretend for the moment I'm you. Now, how does this sound: "There's a movie at the Varsity Theater this Saturday that I want to see. If you don't have other plans, I'd very much like to take you."

CLIENT: That sounded good. Like you were sure of yourself and liked the woman, too.

THERAPIST: Why don't you try it?

CLIENT: You know that movie at the Varsity? Well, I'd like to go, and I'd like to take you Saturday, if you don't have anything better to do.

THERAPIST: Well, that certainly was better. Your tone of voice was especially good. But the last line, "If you don't have anything better to do," sounded like you don't think you have much to offer. Why not run through it one more time?

CLIENT: I'd like to see the show at the Varsity Saturday, and if you haven't made other plans, I'd like to take you.

THERAPIST: Much better. Excellent, in fact. You were confident, forceful, and sincere.

Observational learning has also been used to reduce or eliminate phobias. In one case (Bandura, Blanchard, & Ritter, 1969) adults with an intense fear of snakes were shown live models handling live snakes. The patients were then encouraged to handle the snakes themselves. A final test indicated that these patients had less fear of snakes than those patients who had watched a film of people handling snakes and a control group who had received no treatment.

Behavior Modification

Your friend John is a junk-food addict. He just cannot pass up those extra cookies, a handful of potato chips, or what's in the candy dish. His bad habits are catching up with him. For the third time in the past five years his clothes are embarrassingly tight, his cholesterol

behavior modification
Using the fundamental principles of learning to change inappropriate behaviors

levels are dangerously high, and his health is generally poor. John is well aware of the negative effects of the junk food, but he just cannot stop his poor eating habits. *Can anything be done to change John's behavior?* ▪

Significant changes in behavior can be made through reinforcement and shaping. In 1962, Robert Watson started a new area of psychological research and treatment when he introduced the term *behavior modification*. **Behavior modification** has been defined as "the application of the results of learning theory and experimental psychology to the problem of altering maladaptive behavior" (Ullman & Krasner, 1965, p. 2). In other words, behavior modification, or "B-mod," as many people call it, uses the learning principles we have studied in this chapter to decrease undesired behaviors and increase desired ones.

For example, one researcher reported on the way consumption of junk foods was controlled by pairing the foods with cigarette smoking (Morganstern, 1974). The patient, who was nauseated by cigarette smoking, first ate some junk food and then smoked a cigarette and became nauseated. As we learned earlier in this chapter, such conditions produce a taste aversion. The patient developed a strong aversion to the junk food and avoided it. After the procedure was repeated for certain types of junk food, such as cookies and doughnuts, the aversion generalized to other types, such as ice cream. Possibly such a procedure would work with your friend John who cannot refrain from eating junk food. If John uses this procedure, however, he should keep in mind that taste aversions are developed most strongly with novel foods and flavors (see page 247). Under these conditions John will have to keep remembering the unpleasantness of conditioning and the aversion to junk food.

Reinforcers do not always have to be concrete items like food, candy, or money. Much behavior is shaped and reinforced by praise and attention; as in the driving example cited earlier in this chapter, words like "Good job" or "Way to go" are often used to make you feel proud and want to work even harder. Even exclamations like "Uh-huh" can serve as verbal reinforcers. To understand just how strong verbal reinforcers are, imagine what a phone conversation would be like if the person you were talking to never said "Uh-huh." Without the verbal reinforcers that indicate the person is paying attention and understands what you are saying, you might become flustered and unsure of yourself.

Behavior modification has been used in many different situations with a wide range of participants and problems. When applied correctly, it is very effective. We encounter this technique again in Chapter 14 when we discuss the wide variety of therapies that have been developed to help patients suffering from mental disorders of all kinds.

We have presented this chapter's various concepts and principles separately to make your learning and understanding easier. In reality classical conditioning, operant conditioning, observational learning, and punishment are not mutually exclusive. They can, and do, occur simultaneously.

Review Summary

1. The opposite of reinforcement, **punishment** decreases the rate or frequency of responding. Punishment involves either removing a **positive reinforcer** (negative punishment) or presenting a **negative reinforcer** (positive punishment).

2. Operant responses that are not reinforced each time during training take much longer to extinguish than ones that have received continuous reinforcement. This phenomenon is known as the **partial reinforcement effect.**

3. A **discriminative stimulus** signals that responses will be reinforced. Behavior is said to be under stimulus control when responding occurs only when the discriminative stimulus is present.

4. Observational learning takes place when we observe and identify with the behaviors of others. Advertisements and television commercials appeal to this process. Televised violence may result in observational learning and lead to an increase in violent behaviors.

5. Behavior modification is the application of the basic principles of learning to change or modify an undesired behavior or increase specific desired behaviors.

Study Break

1. For each of the following, indicate whether partial reinforcement is involved. If it is, indicate the likely schedule of reinforcement.
   a. Receiving praise for each good grade you make
   b. Sometimes getting caught for speeding
   c. Having never been caught for cheating in high school
   d. Occasionally finding money on the ground as you walk to class
   e. Playing basketball on a team that won 3 out of 15 games last year
   f. Driving around and around a full parking lot until someone leaves and you can park your car
2. Which of the following involve(s) observational learning?
   a. Learning to drive by taking a driver education course that emphasizes behind-the-wheel experience
   b. Pushing the remote control to change channels on the television
   c. Using a video to learn how to play golf
   d. Seeing friends go by on their motorcycles and saying to yourself, "I bet I can do that"
   e. Salivating every time you pass your favorite restaurant
3. What is the purpose of punishment?
4. As with reinforcement, there are two types of punishers; name them. Then indicate for each of the following situations which type of punishment is being used:
   a. Your Mexican dinner tasted terrible because the chef put too much spice in it.
   b. A student is given an F for cheating on an exam.
   c. Your roommates do not invite you to join them for dinner because you did not help clean the apartment.
   d. A police officer gives you a ticket for running a red light.
5. The effect of _____ is to decrease the likelihood or rate of a target response.
   a. positive reinforcement
   b. negative reinforcement
   c. punishment
   d. partial reinforcement
6. What is the partial reinforcement effect?
   a. Extinction after continuous reinforcement is more difficult.
   b. Extinction after partial reinforcement is more difficult.
   c. Learning under continuous reinforcement is more difficult.
   d. Learning under partial reinforcement is more difficult.
7. What two opposing processes are involved in creating discriminative stimuli?
   a. shaping and cognition
   b. discrimination and generalization
   c. positive and negative reinforcement
   d. observational learning and modeling
8. Concern has been raised about violence in television and films because of research evidence about
   a. modeling.
   b. classical conditioning.
   c. operant conditioning.
   d. negative reinforcement.

ANSWERS TO STUDY BREAKS

Page 250

1. US—the taste of the bakery goods you've eaten before; CS—the sight and smell of the bakery goods; CR—salivation

2. a. UR, US
   b. CS, US
   c. CS, US
   d. CR, weaker

3. **a.** Extinction
   b. Generalization
   c. Taste-aversion conditioning
   d. Conditioned phobia
4. b
5. c
6. Learned motives and learned goals are acquired through the process of classical conditioning.

Pages 260–261

1. *Lottery example:* a. Buying lottery tickets is the response that is being reinforced; b. Money is the reinforcer; c. A variable ratio schedule is being used. *Telephone call:* Making telephone calls is the response that is being reinforced; b. The vacation is the reinforcer; c. A fixed ratio schedule is being used. *McDuff waiting for breakfast:* a. McDuff coming to the door is the response that is being reinforced; b. Food is the reinforcer; c. A fixed interval schedule is being used.
2. Reinforcers increase the frequency of the target response.
3. **a.** Negative reinforcer
   b. Positive reinforcer
   c. Positive reinforcer
   d. Negative reinforcer
4. Beginning piano students do not possess the required skills to begin playing immediately. Musical skills—such as left- and right-hand dexterity and coordination, phrasing, and tempo—are acquired gradually. Praise from the music teacher and significant others would be one source of reinforcement; the student's own feeling of accomplishment would be another source of reinforcement.
5. **a**-3, **b**-4, **c**-2, **d**-5, **e**-1

6. c
7. a
8. b

Page 271

1. **a.** Partial reinforcement is not used; this is a continuous reinforcement schedule.
   b. Punishment, not reinforcement, is involved.
   c. Partial reinforcement is not used; this is a continuous reinforcement schedule.
   d. Partial reinforcement is involved. A variable ratio schedule is involved.
   e. Partial reinforcement is involved. A variable ratio schedule is involved.
   f. Partial reinforcement is involved. A variable interval schedule is involved.
2. **a.** Not observational learning
   b. Not observational learning
   c. Observational learning
   d. Observational learning
   e. Not observational learning
3. Punishment is used to decrease the frequency of the response it follows.
4. The two types of punishment are positive and negative.
   a. Positive
   b. Positive
   c. Negative
   d. Positive
5. c
6. b
7. b
8. a

ANSWERS TO PSYCHOLOGICAL DETECTIVE ON CLASSICAL CONDITIONING

Page 238

For the food example, the US is the food in your mouth, and the UR is salivation that occurs when the food is in your mouth. The CS is the name of the food that is spoken to you, and the CR is the salivation that occurs when you hear the name of your favorite food. In the example of Scott's fear of closed spaces, the US is being locked in the abandoned refrigerator and the UR is nearly suffocating. Anything that resembles a closed space is the CS, and the fear he has to closed spaces is the CR.

Memory

Chapter in Perspective

In Chapter 6 we examined the basic learning processes, especially classical conditioning and operant (instrumental) conditioning, that are characteristic of a wide variety of organisms. In this chapter we highlight some uniquely human aspects of learning and memory. We begin with early studies of memory, giving special attention to the pioneering work of Hermann Ebbinghaus. We then examine the phenomenon of memory in detail and discuss several recent developments in the study of memory. After a look at some techniques for improving your memory, we explore the physiological basis of learning and memory.

In addition to helping us adapt more effectively to our environment, the processes covered in this chapter clear the way for improved communication and the storage of knowledge. As you might have sensed, we are beginning to focus on the processes that define what makes us human and the way we function as individuals and as members of groups. In the succeeding chapters we will explore such topics as thinking and intelligence (Chapter 8); health psychology (Chapter 15); and development throughout the life span (Chapters 9 and 10). You will see how these processes also contribute to our ability to adapt effectively to our environment.

Before we begin an in-depth examination of memory, let's define our topic. This task may be more difficult than you think; memory is one of those abilities we take for granted. Certainly memory is related to learning. If we did not learn or acquire new knowledge, we would have nothing to store in our memories. In many instances memories last an incredibly long time. Putting these ideas together, we can tentatively define **memory** as a system or process by which the products or results of learning are stored for future use. ▪

Initial Studies

When Sue graduated from high school, she enrolled in a college several hundred miles from her home. After completing college, she accepted a job as a YMCA program director in a large metropolitan area. Because her trips back home were infrequent, she lost contact with her high school classmates. She has not seen most of them in years. Her twenty-fifth high school reunion is now approaching, and Sue wonders how good her memory is. How many of her former classmates will she recognize? *How good is our memory for faces after a long interval of time?* ▪

The scientific study of human memory is almost as old as scientific psychology itself. The pioneer in this area was Hermann Ebbinghaus, a patient and thorough German psychologist who conducted his studies of memory in the late 1800s and early 1900s (Ebbinghaus, 1885). Ebbinghaus asked questions such as "What conditions are favorable (or unfavorable) for linking or associating the words, sounds, and visual stimuli that make up our store of learned knowledge?"

Because everyday words already have meanings and associations attached to them (i.e., some learning already has taken place), Ebbinghaus decided not to use them as stimuli in his experiments. Instead, he invented special stimuli that he called *nonsense syllables*. **Nonsense syllables** are usually composed of three letters arranged in a consonant-vowel-consonant sequence. For example, *gok, taf, ceb,* and *tup* are nonsense syllables. Because nonsense syllables were supposed to have no meaning, Ebbinghaus believed that he would be able to study how associations between these stimuli are formed without any other factors, such as previous learning, complicating the results.

Armed with these new stimuli, Ebbinghaus began his studies with only one research participant: himself. In most instances the task consisted of memorizing lists of nonsense syllables. Before you start questioning the importance of studying how one learns a sequence of nonsense syllables, think about all the lists or sequences that we learn (Curran & Keele, 1993). Grade school children learn the alphabet, the names of the presidents, and the multiplication tables. As they grow up, they learn telephone numbers, ZIP codes, addresses, and lock combinations. Ebbinghaus's studies of lists were actually quite relevant.

Hermann Ebbinghaus (1850–1909) was a pioneer in the study of human memory

memory
System or process by which the products or results of learning are stored for future use

nonsense syllables
Stimuli used to study memory; typically composed of a consonant-vowel-consonant sequence

Psychological Detective

Ebbinghaus's next step was to devise a way to measure memory. Now, if someone says that all you have to do to measure memory is to ask a participant what he or she has learned, you might be skeptical. Measuring memory is more complicated than that. Before you read further, write down some ideas about how you might measure memory when a participant is learning a list of nonsense syllables. Be sure to identify the specific response you are measuring.

Ebbinghaus's method for measuring learning was called **serial learning** (also known as *ordered recall*). As a participant, you would be asked to repeat the material in the order in which it had been presented. This technique shows whether you have mastered the correct sequence (Baddeley, Papagno, & Andrade, 1993; Watkins & Le Compte, 1991). For example, if you dial 343-7355 on the telephone instead of 343-3755 (the number that was supposed to be learned), serial learning is not perfect.

A second method, **paired-associate learning,** was developed by another early German memory researcher, George Elias Müller, a few years after Ebbinghaus began his work. In this task you associate an unfamiliar word or nonsense syllable with a familiar word. This technique is often used to learn the vocabulary for a foreign language—remember the flash cards you used to learn Spanish or French? The test consists of presenting the familiar word and then producing the foreign word associated with it.

A third, more recent method of measuring learning is **free recall.** Here the task is to remember as many items as possible, regardless of their sequence. Naming the major parts of a neuron (see Chapter 2) or the components of classical conditioning (see Chapter 6) would be examples of free recall. Free recall is now the preferred method of measuring learning.

The Curve of Forgetting

An important finding of Ebbinghaus's research is the *curve of forgetting.* Ebbinghaus found that our memory for learned material is best right after the learning session. As time passes, we forget more and more. This basic finding has been replicated (reproduced) numerous times since Ebbinghaus discovered it. As you can see from Figure 7-1, Jenkins and Dallenbach (1924) found that participants recalled the most when they were tested immediately after learning. The participants learned a list of ten nonsense syllables and then were asked to recall the list one-half hour, and two, four, and eight hours later. Half an hour after the initial training session, the participants were able to recall only half of the list; their performance continued to deteriorate with the passage of time. The importance of these results is clear: You can expect your best recall shortly after a learning session. This is why students cram for a test as close to the time of the test as possible.

Recognition and Relearning

Two additional procedures for measuring memory, the recognition test and the relearning test, have been developed to supplement the three methods described in the last section. In the **recognition test,** participants are asked to pick out the items to which they were previously exposed from a longer list that also contains unfamiliar items (Haist, Shimamura, & Squire, 1992; Yonelinas,

serial learning
Learning procedure in which material that has been learned must be repeated in the order in which it was presented

paired-associate learning
Learning procedure in which items to be recalled are learned in pairs. During recall, one member of the pair is presented and the other is to be recalled

free recall
Learning procedure in which material that has been learned may be repeated in any order

recognition test
Test in which retention is measured by the ability to pick out previously learned items from a list that also contains unfamiliar items

FIGURE 7-1   Number of non-sense syllables recalled at various intervals following learning. In agreement with Ebbinghaus's research, the greatest decrease in recall occurred very shortly after learning had taken place.

Source: Jenkins & Dallenbach, 1924.

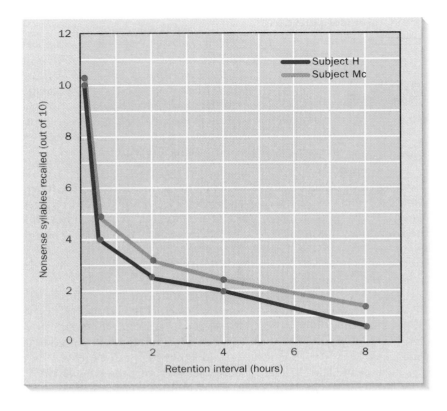

Hockley, & Murdock, 1992). This type of memory task is involved in taking a multiple-choice test. Recall Sue from this chapter's opening vignette. When she attends her high school reunion, Sue will be performing a similar task in attempting to recognize her former classmates.

How good is our memory for faces after a long interval of time? The results of a research project indicate that our ability to remember faces for a long time is quite good (Bruck, Cavanagh, & Ceci, 1991). The researchers asked participants to match current photographs of former high school classmates with photos taken approximately 25 years earlier. Those individuals did much better at matching photos than a group of participants who had not gone to high school with the people in the photos.

A **relearning test** is exactly what the name implies. After the passage of a certain amount of time (called a *retention interval*), the original material is learned again. For example, you might study a list of 15 nonsense syllables on Monday afternoon. You study the list until you can repeat it three times without an error; this level of performance, your *performance criterion,* is established by the researcher. One week later you study the same list. The researcher calculates the amount of time, or number of trials, it takes to relearn the material so that you can match your performance criterion, and the two scores are compared. If learning occurred more rapidly the second time you studied the list, this difference is reported as a **savings score** (or *relearning score*). A good example of relearning is studying for a comprehensive final exam. Chances are good that, with the right concentration, it will take you less time and effort to relearn the material.

Although the work of Ebbinghaus and other early psychologists provided a basic understanding of human learning and memory, much more has been discovered since then. Today few psychologists study how people learn lists of nonsense syllables; they are more interested in examining the processes by which

relearning test
Test of retention that compares the time or trials required to learn material a second time with the time or trials required to learn the material the first time

savings score
Difference between the time or trials originally required to learn material and the time or trials required to relearn the material

memories are formed and used. This shift in interest occurred because most psychologists abandoned the mechanical, association-based model of memory in which items were simply linked to other items. A new view of the mind began to emerge—one suggesting that the mind is an active agent with many other organizational properties. This developing view prompted different questions. How do we store items in memory? Once memories are stored, how do we retrieve them?

Traditional Models of Memory

Anne is phenomenal! She knows every client by name and can recall the details of particular accounts with ease. She always makes the right decision, often under extreme pressure, and never seems ruffled or disturbed. Business appointments with her are a pleasure. Her friends have frequently commented that her memory is "like a computer." *In what ways might a computer and human memory be alike?* ■

Human Memory as an Information Processing System

Much of what we have learned about human memory has been inspired by the development of computers. In what ways are a computer and the human memory alike?

Like the computer, human memory has been characterized as an information-processing system that has three separate stages: an input or encoding stage, a storage stage, and a retrieval stage during which an already stored memory is called into consciousness (see Figure 7-2). Let's take a closer look at each of these stages.

Encoding. In the **encoding** stage, sensory information is received and coded, or transformed into neural impulses that can be processed further or stored for later use. Just as the computer changes keyboard entries into usable

encoding
First stage of the memory process; in it information is transformed or coded (a transduction process) into a form that can be processed further and stored

FIGURE 7-2 Because it has separate encoding, storage, and retrieval stages, human memory is similar to an information processing system.

electronic symbols that may be stored on a computer disk, sensory information is transduced (see Chapter 3) so that it can be used and stored by the brain. In addition to transduction, a great deal of the encoding process appears to be devoted to rehearsing (practicing or repeating) the input, organizing it into groups, and relating the groups to already stored information. Encoding may even involve giving this information a special name or label.

Suppose that as you drive to school, you listen to a new song on the radio. The sounds are transduced into neural impulses, which are then recognized as making up a song. You remember hearing similar songs and label the one you are listening to as belonging to that group—for example, "love ballad." This procedure is very much like a computer program; information is encoded in the central processing unit, and the program is given a name that helps relate it to similar programs.

Storage.   The second stage of memory processing is **storage.** Like the computer program, the encoded information must be stored in the memory system if we plan to retain it for any length of time or use it more than once. Although some bits of information are stored briefly, used only once, and then discarded, others, like certain telephone numbers, are used frequently and are therefore stored on a more permanent basis.

Retrieval.   Once a computer program has been named and stored, we can "call it up" by its name and use it again. Human memory works in much the same way. When we recall or bring a memory into consciousness, we have retrieved it. This recall process is known as memory **retrieval.**

We do not store information in memory randomly. The information is organized and related to already stored information in such a way as to allow us to use certain cues to retrieve it.

storage
Second stage of the memory process; in it information is placed in the memory system. This stage may involve either brief or long-term storage of memories

retrieval
Third stage of the memory process; in it stored memories are brought into consciousness

Psychological Detective

To see how the retrieval process works, write down the name of your fourth-grade teacher. After you have done so, describe the process that led you to that particular name.

What memories does this grade school science class help you retrieve?

The words *fourth-grade teacher* are the stimuli that activated your memories of the fourth grade. As you retrieve these memories while searching for the name of your teacher, you may recall your school building, your fourth-grade classroom, the ride to school on the bus, and the names of your classmates. In turn, each of these memories could serve as a stimulus to retrieve related memories. There are probably many stimuli that could help you retrieve the name of your fourth-grade teacher.

In some instances the network of related memories is small and only a few specific cues will successfully retrieve a certain memory. For example, suppose you are in the supermarket trying to choose a brand of detergent when an apparent stranger begins a conversation with you. The "stranger" is talking as if you have known each other for some time, but you have no idea who this person is. Why do we find it so difficult to recall some people's names? Knowing about retrieval cues helps answer this question. When the stranger reminds you that you met last Saturday at a party, it is as though a light goes on. Suddenly you remember who this person is and where you met. Because you met under special circumstances, the party, only cues related to that situation will retrieve the memory of the meeting. When those specific cues are presented, the memory returns.

Myth or Science

How often have you heard it said that someone has a "photographic memory"? Although it is likely that nothing more than someone with a very good memory is being described, there are people who appear to have this ability. People with eidetic imagery *(the technical term for photographic memory) say that they can look at a written page, person, or drawing and then later mentally see that image (Guenther, 1998). It is truly as if these people take photographs and store them in their minds for future use. For example, when you need the information from a page in a book, you simply retrieve that page from memory and read it. Would this ability be great at test time!*

Leonardo da Vinci and Napoleon Bonaparte are two of the most famous people with photographic memory. Apparently Leonardo could draw detailed portraits of people after meeting them only once. Likewise, it is reported that Napoleon could glance at a map briefly and later recall the location of every stream, town, and hill. Clearly, there are some interesting processes of storage and retrieval occurring here.

The Atkinson-Shiffrin Model

Our encoding-storage-retrieval model of memory would serve our purpose quite well if we had only one type of memory to store. We have, however, at least three well-defined types of memory: sensory memory, short-term memory, and long-term memory. So the information processing model must be modified to read as follows:

Encoding --> "type" of storage --> retrieval

The rest of this section describes the three types of memory and the ways they are used in our daily lives. The memory model that we discuss is shown in

FIGURE 7-3 The Atkinson-Shiffrin (1971) model of memory.

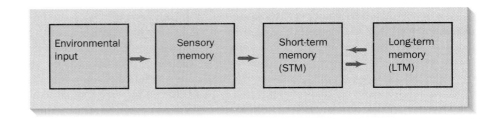

Figure 7-3. This influential model was developed by Richard Atkinson and Richard Shiffrin in 1971.

Sensory Memory.   **Sensory memory** is just what its name implies—a memory or storage of sensory events such as sights, sounds, and tastes, with no further processing or interpretation. Because sensory memory provides us with a fleeting image of the stimuli present at a particular moment, it has the potential to be huge. Because many stimuli are received all the time, sensory memory appears to last only briefly, about one-half of a second to one second, depending on which sensory system is involved.

Sensory information that is not selected for further processing by higher brain centers decays and is replaced by incoming stimuli. As you saw in Chapter 3, we cannot attend to and process all the stimuli we receive; some of them must be filtered out. Stimuli that we attend to will be those that are selected from sensory memory for further processing; other stimuli are lost.

After a moment's reflection, you ask, "If sensory memories last such a short time, how can you demonstrate that they really exist?" In a compelling set of experiments on this topic, a display of 12 letters was presented to participants (Sperling, 1960). The pattern might look like this:

D   C   R   M

Y   N   S   V

I   E   G   Z

In the original experiments, the entire pattern was flashed for one-twentieth of a second. The participants were then asked to recall and write down as many letters as possible. Typically they were able to identify only 4 or 5 of the 12 letters. That does not seem like good evidence for any kind of memory! Some changes made in later experiments, however, produced dramatic improvement. One modification involved assigning a different audible tone to each row of the stimulus pattern: a high tone to the top row, a medium tone to the middle row, and a low tone to the bottom row. As before, the entire pattern was flashed for one-twentieth of a second. Immediately afterward, one of the three tones was sounded, and the participants were asked to write down the letters in the row designated by the tone.

Imagine you are a participant in such an experiment. The pattern of letters has just been presented. Now you hear the medium tone, so you write down as many of the letters from the middle row as you can remember. How many letters do you think you will remember?

Sperling found that when tones accompanied the presentation of the letters, participants correctly identified three or four letters in a row, regardless of which row was signaled. Clearly, much more information was potentially available in memory than the original experiments had indi-

sensory memory
Very brief (0.5 to 1.0 second) but extensive memory for sensory events

cated. Because they did not know in advance which row would be signaled, the participants had to have a memory of all the letters when one of the tones was sounded. Time is important, however, when the tone was sounded a full second after the letters were presented, the participants could remember only one or two letters in the designated row. Thus a significant amount of information is lost from sensory memory very quickly after the stimuli are presented.

The amount of information lost from sensory memory is not a fixed quantity. Rather, it depends on the amount of processing effort that is expended in the next stage of memory. We can either process a few items very thoroughly and lose a great deal from sensory memory, or we can process a larger number of items less thoroughly and retain more from sensory memory (Kahneman, 1973).

Because it is important and easier to study, we have been talking exclusively about visual sensory memory. Do we have brief sensory memories for our other senses? Although not much research has been done on this topic, the answer appears to be yes.

Psychologist Ulrich Neisser (1967) proposed the existence of an auditory sensory memory. His proposal was supported by a study in which participants heard simultaneous lists of letters from three loudspeakers in different locations (Darwin, Turvey, & Crowder, 1972). If the students tried to report the letters from all three loudspeakers, they did poorly; if they were asked to repeat the letters from a specific speaker immediately after the list was read, they did much better. If a delay was imposed, their performance decreased noticeably. These results are very similar to those Sperling reported for visual stimuli. You can also experience auditory sensory memory. Hit your hands against the top of your desk. Do you still hear the sound for a brief instant after you have stopped? This sound is an *auditory sensory memory*.

Consider the following situation. Jim is sitting in class but is not really paying attention to the lecture. His mind is on the movie he is planning to see that evening. Without realizing it, he is rubbing one hand along the edge of the desk. After rubbing his hand on the desk several times, Jim becomes aware of his behavior. Each time his hand leaves the desk, he is sure he is still feeling the sensation. What causes the sensation that Jim experiences after he rubs his hand along the edge of the desk?

Sensory memory appears to be involved in the sensation Jim is experiencing. Try it yourself. Rub your hand quickly along the edge of your desk or a table—heel first, fingertips last. For a brief instant after your hand leaves the desk, you will have the sensation that you are still touching it. You have just experienced an example of *tactile (touch) sensory memory*.

What happens to the information that is selected from sensory memory and not lost? To answer this question we need to continue our exploration of the various types of memory.

Short-Term Memory. Once information has been attended to or selected from sensory memory, it is transferred to our conscious awareness (Engle, Cantor, & Carullo, 1993; Laming, 1992). According to Atkinson and Shiffrin (1971), information must be processed in **short-term memory (STM)** before it can be transferred to more permanent storage in long-term memory. What is this STM? As the name implies, STM lasts for only a short period—perhaps a few seconds. Although researchers have not determined exactly how long such memories endure, it appears that items are lost from STM in 10 to 20 seconds. For example, research in which participants recalled a three-letter stimulus found that recall fell from 90 percent

short-term memory (STM)
Memory stage in which information is held in consciousness for 10 to 20 seconds

correct immediately after presentation of the stimulus to 10 percent correct after 18 seconds (Brown, 1958; Peterson & Peterson, 1959). Why? Atkinson and Shiffrin suggest that two processes are at work: (1) Unless memories are practiced or rehearsed, they become weaker and fade away, and (2) to make room for new, incoming information, some of the memories in STM are pushed out or displaced. In the Brown and Peterson and Peterson studies, the participants counted backward by threes to prevent practice after learning the three-letter stimulus. Their results indicated that much of this displaced information is simply lost, but some is transferred to long-term memory.

Psychological Detective

Study the following phone numbers for 15 seconds:

316-343-5800
401-246-4531
912-692-3423

Now write them on a piece of paper without looking at this page. You probably found this task difficult. You would be able to handle two phone numbers better. Why? Write down some possible answers before reading further.

Exercises like this one, coupled with extensive research, prompted psychologist George Miller (1956) to propose that we can hold approximately seven items (plus or minus two) in STM at any one time. After a moment's reflection you are sure that this 7+/−2 proposal is incorrect. When we remember two telephone numbers, we are dealing with more than nine items (7+/−2). That would be true if you counted each digit separately. Phone numbers, however, are broken up by dashes. The result is that we are actually dealing with two groups of numbers (343, 5800) rather than with a series of individual numbers (3, 4, 3, 5, 8, 0, 0). When the area code is added (316-343-5800), there still are only three groups of numbers. Say your own phone number aloud. Did you hear the pauses? Those pauses separate the *chunks,* or clusters of information. With two phone numbers, each having an area code, you have only six chunks to remember.

Consider another example. Your friend Brian loves zoos. He works as a volunteer at the local zoo and spends many hours there. Whenever he travels, he makes it a point to visit every zoo he comes across. When he takes visitors to his local zoo, Brian amazes them by correctly identifying each animal. What memory technique is Brian using to remember the names of the animals?

The answer should come to you easily. When Brian originally learned the names of the animals, he set up several STM categories or groups. Each animal in the zoo was assigned to one of these categories. To recall the names, Brian first recalls the categories and then the animals in each category. For example, one category might be ducks. Within that category we could find mallards, mergansers, pintails, ruddy ducks, and black ducks.

These are examples of the principle of grouping or chunking. What Miller demonstrated is that although STM may be limited to five to nine items (7+/−2), each of those items may consist of a chunk or group of items. In this way the capacity of STM can be increased significantly.

George Miller, former president of the American Psychological Association, proposed that we can hold 7±2 items in short-term memory at any one time.

Psychological Detective

What would you do if you wanted to remember the following list? Study it for 15 seconds; then close your book and write down as many of the items as possible.

telephone	Ford	pine
poplar	fax machine	Chevrolet
oak	telegraph	walnut
Buick	Mazda	television
cedar	mail	audiocassette
Pontiac	maple	elm

working memory
Second stage of short-term memory; in it attention and conscious effort are brought to bear on material

There are 18 items in this list, considerably more than the magic number 7+/−2. Hence it will be difficult for you to remember each word by itself. If, however, you set up three categories (trees, automobiles, and communication devices) and put each item into the appropriate category, you should have no trouble remembering all 18 items (see Figure 7-4).

The original conception of STM posed a major problem: It was too short. Although 10 or 20 seconds was sufficient to input and store new information, it did not allow time for the processing of this information (Ashcraft, 1994). It appears that the initial 10- to 20-second STM period often leads to a second phase, **working memory,** where attention and conscious effort are brought to bear on the material at hand (Baddeley, 1992a, 1992b). For example, let's say you are listening to a lecture in which an interesting but complicated point is made. While you hold the sentence in STM, you retrieve word meanings from *long-term memory.* Then, in light of what you already know (retrieval from long-term memory), you use working memory to make sense of this new sentence you've just heard. Working memory seems to be an intermediate, processing stage between STM and long-term memory.

Long-Term Memory. What would your interactions with your environment be like if STM was the only type of memory you had? Because you lacked any

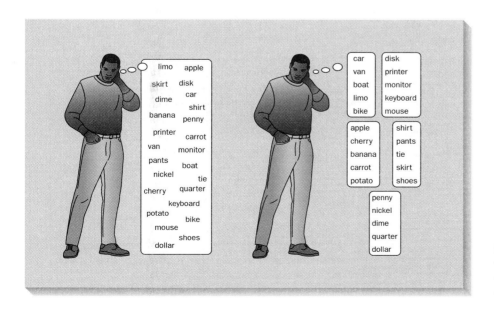

FIGURE 7-4 Chunking helps us create categories that increase the amount of information we can hold in STM.

long-term memory
Memory stage that has a very large capacity and the capability to store information relatively permanently

maintenance rehearsal
Rehearsal used when we want to save or maintain a memory for a specified period of time

elaborative rehearsal
Rehearsal in which meaning is added to the material to be remembered

capacity for permanent memory storage, you would have to learn the same things over and over again. (We describe a person who has only STM later in this chapter.) It is critical to be able to transfer information from STM to more permanent storage in **long-term memory (LTM)**. Atkinson and Shiffrin (1971) stress the importance of rehearsal or practice in this transfer. Items that are rehearsed seem more likely to be transferred than unrehearsed items. For example, you will remember your friend's new telephone number better if you repeat (rehearse) it several times than if you repeat it just once.

There are different types of rehearsal; some types aid in transferring information to LTM, and others do not. One researcher conducted a series of studies of a phenomenon known as *directed forgetting* (Björk,1975). In these experiments two groups of participants were asked to learn several lists of items, such as nonsense syllables or telephone numbers. Both groups were given the same amount of time to rehearse each list after it was presented. A retention test was given before presentation of the next list. Before beginning the experiment, one group was told to forget all the items from a given list immediately after the retention test. The second group was told to remember all the lists. A typical directed-forgetting experiment is diagrammed in Figure 7-5.

Although no differences were found between the groups in retention of individual lists of nonsense syllables, large differences were apparent on a retention test given after *all* the lists had been presented. The participants who had been directed to forget did much worse than those who had been directed to remember. These differences appear to be caused by different types of rehearsal.

Two types of rehearsal—maintenance and elaborative—have been studied. We use **maintenance rehearsal** when we want to save or maintain a memory (such as the telephone number for the pizza delivery you have just looked up or the material you tried to cram for a test) for a short period. Maintenance rehearsal ensures that the memory remains until it has been used and is then discarded; participants who are directed to forget use this type of rehearsal. Participants who are instructed to remember a list use **elaborative rehearsal,** which adds meaning to material that we want to remember. For example, you increase your chances of remembering someone's name if meaningful elements are present when you are introduced. Where does the person work or live? What are his or her hobbies? An introduction such as "I would like you to meet my friend Jason Downey. Jason works as the chief parole officer for the state. He is an avid sky diver" provides several elements that

> *Group 1:* Instructed to learn each list of nonsense syllables for a test and then forget the list before learning the next list
>
> *Group 2:* Instructed to learn and store all lists of nonsense syllables

Learn List 1	Test List 1	Learn List 2	Test List 2	Learn List 3	Test List 3	Test All Lists
	Both groups equal		Both groups equal		Both groups equal	Group 2 superior to Group 1 (evidence of directed forgetting)

FIGURE 7-5 Design of a directed-forgetting experiment.

are useful to memory. Earlier we saw that the more meaningful material is, the better it is learned. Elaborative rehearsal is an example of this process at work; it results in a more permanent memory and promotes the transfer of information to LTM (Bartlett, 1932). Unlike STM, LTM has a very large, if not unlimited, capacity.

Once a memory has been transferred from STM to LTM, it seems to be there on a somewhat permanent basis. If that is true, why do we forget? Some memory loss may be due to the fading or *decay* of memories, but much loss appears to be caused by interference. Old memories that are already stored may be recalled instead of the specific memory we are seeking. This effect is called **proactive interference.** Proactive interference occurs when old information hinders our memory of the new information. When you move to a new house or apartment, you have a new address and telephone number. How often do you find yourself using the old address or phone number? Sometimes this problem lasts for years. Another example of proactive interference can be seen every January, when millions of people continue to write the previous year on their bank checks.

Similarly, information that was learned *after* the material we want to remember may hinder the recall of the earlier learned material. This process is called **retroactive interference.** Sometimes it is important to remember old addresses and phone numbers, but try as we might, new addresses and phone numbers are the only ones that come to mind. The other information may be stored in LTM, but we simply cannot retrieve it. Proactive and retroactive interference are diagrammed in Figure 7-6.

What happens when we retrieve a memory from LTM? As we saw in Figure 7-3, the Atkinson and Shiffrin (1971) model suggests that when a memory is recalled from LTM and enters consciousness, it is placed directly into STM. There it may be combined with new information that has been received, creating a new memory. If this new memory is properly rehearsed, it may be transferred to LTM for more permanent storage.

proactive interference
Situation in which previously learned information hinders the recall of information learned more recently

retroactive interference
Situation in which information learned more recently hinders the recall of information learned previously

Proactive interference: Old memories are recalled in place of new memories.

Sorry, that's my old number.

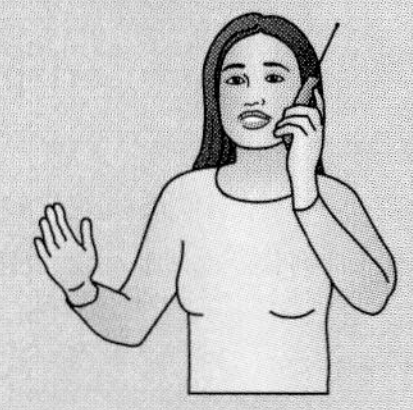

	Task 1	Task 2	Test
		Experimental group	
	Learn A	Learn B	Recall B
		Control group	
	Rest	Learn B	Recall B

Proactive interference occurs if B is recalled better by the control group. This result indicates that A interfered with the recall of B.

Retroactive interference: New memories are recalled in place of old memories.

Sorry, that's my new number.

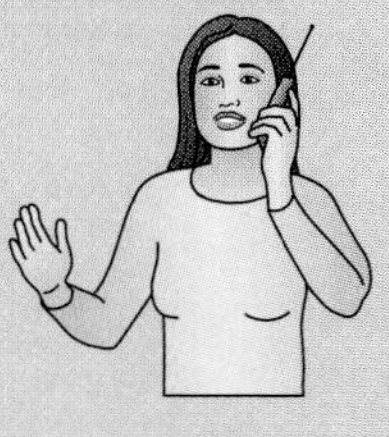

	Task 1	Task 2	Test
		Experimental group	
	Learn A	Learn B	Recall A
		Control group	
	Learn A	Rest	Recall A

Retroactive interference occurs if A is recalled better by the control group. This result indicates that B interfered with the recall of A.

FIGURE 7-6 Proactive and retroactive interference.

The Atkinson and Shiffrin approach is not the only model of memory that has been developed. We explore a second influential model, the Craik and Lockhart levels of processing model, in the next section.

Types of Memory according to the Atkinson-Shiffrin (1971) Model

Type	Description	Example
Sensory	Storage of a large number of sensory events for one-half to one second.	Rubbing your hand across a table top and feeling the sensation for a brief instant after you stop.
Short-term (STM)	Also called working memory. Lasts for a few seconds unless rehearsal takes place. Conscious awareness is involved.	Remembering the name of a person you just met.
Long-term (LTM)	More permanent form of memory storage. Rehearsal or practice is important for transferring memories from STM to LTM.	Your telephone number or home address.

Review Summary

1. Hermann Ebbinghaus conducted the pioneering research on memory in the late 1800s. Ebbinghaus devised **nonsense syllables,** which he believed had no meaning attached to them, in order to study how associations between stimuli are formed.

2. Through the use of **serial learning** Ebbinghaus determined that much of what we learn is forgotten very shortly after a learning session. Other methods include **paired-associate learning** and **free recall.**

3. These basic methods were developed and expanded by incorporating additional tasks, such as the **recognition test** and the **relearning test.**

4. The **savings score** is produced by the relearning method.

5. Some investigators have drawn a parallel between the computer and human memory. Computers and human memory have (a) an input or **encoding** stage, (b) a **storage** process, and (c) a **retrieval** process.

6. The Atkinson-Shiffrin model of memory proposes that memories can be processed in different ways.

There are three types of memory: sensory, short-term, and long-term.

7. Sensory memory is a very brief (lasting one-half to 1 second) memory for a large array of stimuli.

8. Short-term memory (**STM**) is more limited in capacity than sensory memory but lasts longer (10 to 20 seconds). **Working memory** is the second stage of short-term memory, where attention and conscious effort are brought to bear on material.

9. With practice or rehearsal, memories may persist even longer and ultimately be transferred to more permanent storage in **long-term memory** (**LTM**).

10. Memories may not be retrievable from LTM because they have faded or because of interference by other memories.

11. Proactive interference occurs when old material interferes with the retrieval of material learned more recently. **Retroactive interference** occurs when recently learned material interferes with the retrieval of material learned earlier.

Study Break

1. Kevin and Sharon are participants in a memory experiment. Their task is to learn a list of items such as *bok* and *gex*. What are these items called? Why are they used in the study of memory?

2. Once he has learned the list of items, Kevin's task is to reproduce them in the order in which they were presented. What is the procedure for measuring memory called?

3. Explain the statement "human memory is like an information processing system."

4. Indicate whether each of the following statements describes sensory memory, short-term memory, or long-term memory.
   a. Very large capacity
   b. Capacity of 7 +/− 2 items
   c. Permanent storage
   d. Lasts only .50 to 1.00 second
   e. Lasts 10 to 20 seconds
   f. Associated with chunks

5. Describe working memory. How does it differ from short-term memory?

6. Distinguish between maintenance rehearsal and elaborative rehearsal.

7. You cannot remember your friend's new address; only the old one comes to mind. This type of memory failure is an example of what process?

8. Your final exam was a nightmare. All you could remember was the material you had just learned; the older material seemed to have vanished from your memory. This type of memory failure is an example of what kind of interference?

9. A child learning to say the alphabet is an example of
   a. serial learning.
   b. free recall.
   c. paired-associate learning.
   d. recognition.

10. Ebbinghaus found that our memory is best immediately after we learn information, and we gradually forget more as time passes. This finding is known as the
   a. serial position effect.
   b. curve of forgetting.
   c. memory curve.
   d. free recall curve.

11. In a multiple-choice test, your memory is measured by
   a. recall.
   b. recognition.
   c. relearning.
   d. paired-associate learning.

Other Approaches to Learning and Memory

Myra volunteered to participate in an experiment involving memory. Her initial task was to read an article in a psychological journal. After reading the article, she was instructed to prepare a brief presentation about the article from the perspective of its author. Finally, Myra took a test that dealt with the content of the article. *What did these procedures have to do with memory?* ■

Although the STM-LTM model developed by Atkinson and Shiffrin makes good sense and has generated a large amount of research activity, it is not the only theoretical account of how memory works. In this section we examine several other models of the memory process.

The Levels-of-Processing Model

The **levels-of-processing theory** proposed by Fergus Craik and Robert Lockhart (1972) represents a radical departure from the Atkinson-Shiffrin model (Challis, 1993; Challis & Brodbeck, 1992). Craik and Lockhart proposed

levels-of-processing theory
Theory stating that deeper processing of information increases the likelihood that the information will be recalled

FIGURE 7-7 The Craik-Lockhart (1972) levels-of-processing model of memory.

that there is only one type of memory store and that its capacity is enormous, if not unlimited. Once memories have entered this store, they may be retained there for extremely long periods.

You may be thinking, "One large memory store in which memories last for long periods—that seems simple enough. If that's the way our memory is set up, however, why do we forget some things faster than others?" That question gets to the heart of Craik and Lockhart's view of memory: What really matters is the way we process information. Rehearsal is important, but *how* we rehearse is even more important. As you can see in Figure 7-7, Craik and Lockhart believe that we can engage in several levels of rehearsal or processing. The maintenance and elaborative rehearsal techniques discussed earlier are only two examples.

A very shallow or simple level might involve processing only the physical characteristics of an object. Thus we might characterize the object in Figure 7-7 as red and rectangular. At a deeper or more complex level of processing, we consider additional characteristics such as the fact that the object has pages. This addition is a form of elaborative rehearsal. Now we are dealing with a red, rectangular book. Adding or attending to *meaning* even more— that is, moving to an even deeper level of processing—we now consider what type of book this is and whether it will help us in any of our courses this semester. This last type of processing requires that we examine the book and compare it with other books and with information already stored in memory. Which courses are we taking? Which books are being used in those courses? Will this book help?

Geech © 1993 Universal Press Syndicate. Reprinted with permission. All rights reserved.

Craik and Lockhart suggest, however, that you do not automatically progress from one level to another simply because you spend more time processing. If all your processing time is spent at a very shallow level, your memory will be stored only in terms of shallow cues such as color, shape, or sound. When you want to retrieve this memory, only those shallow cues will be able to access and retrieve it. For example, if you listened only to the sound of a person's name, you might not be able to retrieve it later. The person's physical features, occupation, personality, address, and so forth would be of no help because those cues were not rehearsed when the memory was stored. The sound of the person's name is the only cue that will access the memory of the name. These physical cues are less meaningful; therefore, they do not remain in our memory store as long as more meaningful cues that are rehearsed at deeper levels of processing. In other words, the deeper the level of processing, the greater the likelihood the information will be stored. Time of processing is not as important as depth of processing.

The instructions given to research participants can have a dramatic effect on what is learned. In one study researchers demonstrated the effects that different types of processing can produce (Hyde & Jenkins, 1969). They instructed four groups of participants to study the same list of words. The specific instructions differed for each group, as shown in Table 7-1. A recall test was then given to all four groups. The test was a surprise for Groups 1, 2, and 3, but not for Group 4.

The results (see Figure 7-8) indicated that participants in Groups 1 and 2 remembered significantly fewer words than did participants in Groups 3 and 4. Because Groups 3 and 4 did not differ, we can conclude that the surprise value of the test did not produce these results. The groups differed in terms of the level of processing in which they engaged. Groups 1 and 2 never dealt with the words themselves—they just counted letters (Group 1) or marked e's (Group 2). Hence Groups 1 and 2 processed the information at a very shallow level. Because they had to take the words into account, the participants in Group 3 (who rated the pleasantness of the words) and Group 4 (who memorized the words for a test) processed the information at deeper levels and therefore remembered it better.

Consider the memory experiment described at the beginning of this section. What did these procedures have to do with memory? The experiment in which Myra participated was concerned with levels of processing. Unknown to Myra, other participants were required only to read the journal article; they were not required to prepare the brief presentation. When researchers designed the study, they hypothesized that preparing the presentation would require a deeper level of processing and result in better comprehension (Kixmiller et al., 1987). This prediction was borne out by the experiment's results.

Although many other studies have produced results indicating that depth or level of processing influences our memories, this theory has not gone unchallenged. Critics assert that the exact meaning of the term "level of processing" has not been specified. Without a clear definition of what a level is or

TABLE 7-1 **Instructions Given to Participants in the Hyde and Jenkins (1969) Experiment**

Group 1	Count the letters in each word.
Group 2	Mark all the e's in each word.
Group 3	Rate the pleasantness of each word.
Group 4	Memorize the words for a later recall test.

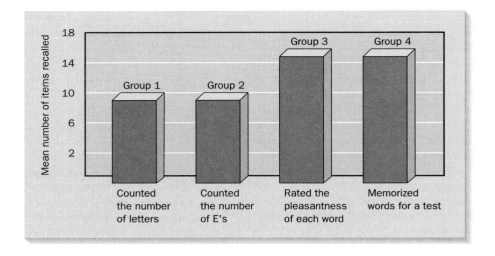

how to objectively measure it (Baddeley, 1998), it is difficult to know how many levels there are. Such criticism has encouraged some researchers (among them, Ellis, Thomas, & Rodriguez, 1984) to view different levels of processing in terms of the amount of cognitive or mental effort expended. In their view, the greater the effort, the deeper the level of processing.

In support of this proposition, several studies (e.g., Graf, 1982) have been interpreted as showing that better retention is linked to greater effort. For example, imagine you are part of an experiment in which the task is to learn words that rhyme. You are presented with a word such as *cat* and asked to generate a word, such as *bat*, that rhymes with it. Your task is to memorize the rhyming words that you have generated. Will you remember your rhyming words better than people who were asked only to memorize rhyming words that were presented to them? Because your effort in generating and memorizing the words was greater than their effort in merely memorizing them, the answer is yes.

Finally the levels-of-processing model assumes that processing occurs through a succession of independent stages; this assumption has yet to be verified. Because of such issues, other approaches have been developed.

Alternate Approaches

Transfer-Appropriate Processing. The transfer-appropriate processing (TAP) model proposed by Bransford, Franks, Morris, and Stein (1979) states that whether shallow or deep processing results in better learning and memory depends on the measure of learning or memory that is used. The best learning and memory occur when the encoding and retrieval processes are the same. For example, if shallow processing is applied at the encoding stage, then it should also be applied at the retrieval stage.

Although the considerations prompted by the TAP model have drawn critical attention to the way research in this area is conducted and have facilitated the study of *implicit* or *priming memory* (Roediger, 1990), it has not fostered the development of a new and elaborate system. The *parallel distributed processing* (PDP) model has assumed this role.

Parallel Distributed Processing. In Chapter 3 we saw that current research on perception stresses the notion of parallel processing: the brain may process information in several subsystems simultaneously. Such findings in the area of perception stimulated the development of the parallel distributed processing (PDP) model of human cognition and memory by James McClelland and David Rumelhart (1986; McClelland, Rumelhart, & Hinton, 1986). The basic view of this model is that mental processes and activities consist of a system of highly interconnected basic units (possibly composed of single neurons) that communicate with each other. According to Solso (1998), these "units are organized into modules, such as atoms are organized into modules" (p. 206). When information relevant to learning and memory is received, it is distributed to appropriate units and modules. The processing of information results in a change in the strength of connections between individual units. Thus information is stored in terms of the numerous connections among units. The stronger the connection, the easier it will be to retrieve the memory.

Remembering how to rollerblade is an example of procedural memory.

Different Types of Long-Term Memory

Recent research on human memory has demonstrated there is more than one type of long-term memory. We do not just place a memory into LTM (Atkinson-Shiffrin model) or simply process at a deeper level (Craik-Lockhart model). The type of information being processed influences the nature of the stored memory. Four major categories or types of LTM have been proposed: procedural, semantic, episodic, and priming or implicit. In addition, current research has improved our understanding of encoding, processing, and retrieval strategies. We examine some of these current approaches in the following sections.

Procedural Memory.   **Procedural memories** are the memories we use in making responses and skilled actions (Anderson & Fincham, 1994). Remembering how to ride a skateboard, water-ski, or play frisbee are examples of procedural memory. Procedural memories are often used at the same time as other types of memory. For example, remembering how to drive a car involves procedural memory. Remembering the traffic laws, however, does not involve the use of motor skills; it involves the memory of general principles. Memory for general principles is known as *semantic memory.*

Semantic Memory.   Our fund of general knowledge is stored in **semantic memory.** Because we are dealing with general knowledge, specific dates and times that pertain to people are not included in our semantic memories. Semantic memory includes concepts, the meanings of words, and facts (Lesch & Pollatsek, 1993; Rohrer et al., 1995). The following are some examples of items that might be stored in semantic memory:

1. Texas shares a border with Mexico.
2. $7 - 2 = 5$
3. Big cities tend to be rather impersonal.

Have you ever been asked a question you could not answer immediately, yet you felt the correct response was "on the tip of your tongue"? Such a question produces what is known as the **tip-of-the-tongue (TOT) phenomenon.** You know the answer is there, but you cannot retrieve it.

procedural memory
Memory for making responses and performing skilled actions

semantic memory
Memory for general knowledge

tip-of-the-tongue (TOT) phenomenon
Condition of being almost, but not quite, able to remember something; used to investigate the nature of semantic memory

Psychological Detective

Let's test your semantic memory. Write down the answer to each of the following questions before reading further.

1. *Which ocean is adjacent to California?*
2. *Which tree produces acorns?*
3. *What type of engine is used to power an automobile?*
4. *What does a bear do in the winter?*
5. *Which river separates Kansas from Missouri?*

How many of these questions produced a TOT response? Were you able to search your stored memories and find the correct answer? Because most TOT experiences seem to involve semantic memory, they have been studied thoroughly by psychologists who want to learn more about this type of memory and how it is retrieved. Apparently, we are very systematic and organized when we search our semantic memories (Reason & Mycielska, 1982). By observing how people search their stored knowledge, we can learn more about the vast network of semantic memories.

Hands On

TOT Phenomena and Memory

To get a better idea of how the TOT phenomenon is relevant to the study of memory, take the following test. Using strips of cardboard, cover both of the columns of the letters that follow and write down as many state capitals as you can. Then uncover the columns and see if these alphabetical cues aid your recall for those that were on the tip of your tongue. The answers can be found at the end of the chapter.

State	First Letter of Capital	State	First Letter of Capital
Alabama	M	Maryland	A
Connecticut	H	Massachusetts	B
Florida	T	Mississippi	J
Georgia	A	Nebraska	L
Idaho	B	New Jersey	T
Iowa	D	Oregon	S
Kentucky	F	Texas	A
Louisiana	B	Wyoming	C

Episodic Memory.   Our personal experiences are stored in **episodic memory.** These memories involve events that occurred at certain times with specific people, places, and things (Goldinger, 1996; Kliegl & Lindenberger, 1993; Levy et al., 1995). The following are some examples of episodic memories from your authors. What episodic memories do you have?

episodic memory
Memory of one's personal experiences

1. Being in Dallas, Texas, the day President John F. Kennedy was assassinated

2. Watching baseball pitcher Nolan Ryan strike out his 5,000th batter in 1989 and win his 300th major league game in 1990
3. Seeing tornadoes devastate Nashville, Tennessee, in the spring of 1998
4. Graduating from high school
5. Arriving on campus for the first day of college

Just as the TOT phenomenon has been studied to help us learn more about semantic memory, *flashbulb memories* have been examined to provide information about episodic memory. **Flashbulb memories** are memories of situations that are very arousing, surprising, or emotional. Our memories of such events are much more detailed than our memories of more usual, everyday episodes. You might think of flashbulb memories as similar to photos taken with a Polaroid camera. Push the button, and 60 seconds later you have a perfect re-creation of the scene that you can look at whenever you want. In your mind, the situation is illuminated just as it occurred. Because more effort is expended in the formation of flashbulb memories, such highlighting of details might lead to deeper levels of processing as well as provide more cues for retrieval.

Because flashbulb memories are tied to specific dates, places, and times, it is difficult to give examples that everyone can immediately identify. Some people vividly remember where they were when President Kennedy was assassinated in 1963, but others do not. Whereas the explosion of the space shuttle *Challenger* in 1986 and the tearing down of the Berlin Wall in 1989 may be no more than historical facts to some people, to others they are flashbulb memories.

Priming or Implicit Memory.   The recent addition of **priming** or **implicit memory** to the list of memory types may be one of the most important

"Where were you during the summer of 1998 when Mark McGwire and Sammy Sosa battled for the home run championship? These two baseball players provide flashbulb memories for many people."

flashbulb memory
Very detailed memory of an arousing, surprising, or emotional situation

priming or implicit memory
Unconscious memory processing in which prior exposure to stimulus items may aid in subsequent learning

advances in the study of memory (Goshen-Gottstein & Moscovitch, 1995a, 1995b; Poldrack & Cohen, 1998). According to Endel Tulving and Daniel Schachter (1990), "Priming is a nonconscious form of human memory, which is concerned with perceptual identification of words and objects and which has only recently been recognized as separate from other forms of memory or memory systems" (p. 301).

Because priming or implicit memory does not operate on a conscious level, it is difficult to detect and study. The first evidence for priming came from studies of *amnesia,* or memory loss (Warrington & Weiskrantz, 1968). Even though the amnesia patients had extremely poor memory for recent events, allowing them to study a group of words helped them later when they had to learn those same words. The earlier study period primed or sensitized them to the words they were to learn in the later session. Even though they had no *memory* of the first study session, the *primed* amnesiac patients performed better than other amnesiac patients and normal individuals who had not studied the items earlier. Somehow the earlier study session prepared (primed) the amnesiac patients to recognize the objects they were to learn. Subsequent studies (Schweinberger, 1996) of nonamnesic individuals have examined the timing and production of brain waves to study priming. Priming effects are revealed when appropriate brain waves are shown earlier in primed participants.

What is the purpose of priming? Although we still have a great deal to learn, priming apparently facilitates procedural and semantic memory processes by improving our ability to identify perceptual stimuli or objects we encounter (Rajaram & Roediger, 1993). At an unconscious level, priming memory alerts us that we have encountered a particular object previously (Musen & Squire, 1993). It is interesting that this priming effect is better when deeper levels of processing are involved (Hamann & Squire, 1996). Given the complexity of contemporary society, any assistance we can receive in such tasks will help us perform more effectively (Nelson et al., 1993).

STUDY CHART

Types of Long-Term Memory

Type	Description	Examples
Procedural	Memories used in making responses and skilled actions.	Remembering how to ride a bicycle, play tennis, or drive a car.
Semantic	Our store of general knowledge.	Water freezes at 32°F, Texas is the largest of the continental states, metabolism decreases when animals hibernate.
Episodic	Memories of personal events.	Your high school graduation, your first day at college, getting your driver's license.
Implicit (priming)	Nonconscious form of LTM that is related to identification of words and objects.	Allowing amnesia patients to study an object and later finding that learning is enhanced even though they do not remember seeing the object.

Retrieval

Last year during spring break, Jennifer paid a surprise visit to her former first-grade teacher. Even though the teacher had not seen Jennifer in ten years, she immediately said, "Well, Jennifer, how are you? Do you still have Buffy, your pet boa constrictor?" At times we are able to retain and retrieve some of the most remarkable memories. Conversely, sometimes things we should remember seem to be gone forever. For example, are you among the large number of people who seem unable to remember their license plate and telephone numbers?

Retrieval from Short-Term Memory.   As mentioned earlier, retrieval is the process by which we locate a memory that has been stored and then bring it into consciousness. Because most people have both extremely good and extremely poor memories, psychologists are interested in studying retrieval.

Psychological Detective

When you read the heading "Retrieval from Short-Term Memory," the following question may have occurred to you: "If the information in STM is already in our consciousness, why would we talk about retrieving it?" Give this question some thought, and write down some possible reasons before reading further.

A lengthy series of studies by S. Sternberg (1966, 1975) suggested that retrieval from STM is not instantaneous; we *do* have to scan our STM, locate an item, and process it. Sternberg arrived at this conclusion in the following manner. Participants were asked to hold a series of letters (such as B, Q, R, D, T, and P) in STM for later recall. But instead of being given the recall test they expected, they were presented with a letter, such as B, and were asked whether it was one of those in the list they were holding in STM. If retrieval was not involved, the participants should have responded almost instantaneously. As it turned out, they did not. What's more, as additional letters were added to the list held in STM, the participants took longer to answer. They were scanning the entire list in STM to match the test letter with those they had stored. The longer the list in STM, the longer the search process required to make a match.

Retrieval from Long-Term Memory.   The process of scanning items in STM to retrieve a specific memory is rather straightforward, but retrieval of long-term memories is a different story. Depending on the situation, various processes may be involved. For example, we have to distinguish between retrieval of memories in recognition tasks and retrieval of memories in recall tasks.

Which type of test would you rather take—an essay test in which you have to produce all of the answers or a multiple-choice test in which you have to recognize the correct answer? Most people prefer the multiple-choice test because it is easier; all you have to do is choose the right answer. Consider the following questions on material from Chapter 2. Which question do you think is easier?

1. Which of the following mobilizes the body for fight or flight?
   a. basal ganglia pathway
   b. sympathetic system
   c. hypothalamic system
   d. limbic system

semantic network
Network of related concepts that are linked together

schema
Grouping or cluster of knowledge about an object or sequence of events

2. Name the division of the nervous system that mobilizes the body for fight or flight.

If recognition tasks are easier, perhaps they do not require the same amount or type of retrieval processing. It may be simpler to retrieve memories through recognition. Many researchers supported this view until Tulving and his colleagues demonstrated that in some situations recall memory is actually superior to recognition memory.

Although one type of memory task is not always easier than the other, perhaps the process of retrieval is the same for both. John Anderson and Gordon Bower (1974) have proposed that recognition and recall use the same retrieval process. Both recall and recognition retrieval have an initial stage during which we search stored memories. Anderson and Bower believe that our search leads us to a large number of related words and phrases. In short, we do not store information as separate bits and pieces; much of it is stored as a semantic network of related items.

Semantic networks are formed by related concepts (called *nodes*) that are linked together (Collins & Loftus, 1975; Collins & Quillian, 1972). For example, mentioning the concept "newspaper" might activate the semantic network shown in Figure 7-9. The process of activating a network constitutes the retrieval process. The length of the lines, called *links,* that connect the various concepts in the newspaper network reflect the strength of the association; shorter links imply stronger associations. For example, the association between "newspaper" and "reporter" is stronger (shorter link) than the association between "newspaper" and "rain" (longer link). Note that in the semantic network every concept is related to the core concept—in this case, "newspaper." In some instances the relation is direct; in others, it is indirect.

Not all of our stored memories are arranged in semantic networks in which one concept triggers a network of related items. There are numerous occasions when we are required to use a grouping or cluster of knowledge about a sequence of events or an object. Such clusters of knowledge or typical ways of thinking about things are called **schemas** (Ahn, Brewer, & Mooney, 1992; Dopkins, Pollatsek, & Nordlie, 1994). For example, suppose that a friend asked you to tell her about the concert you went to last weekend. Because you

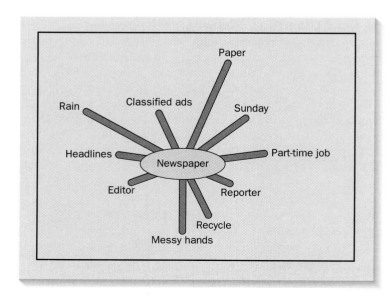

FIGURE 7-9 A semantic network for the concept "newspaper." Longer lines depict weaker associations (links); shorter lines depict stronger links.

have been to several concerts during the past year, you have an organized cluster of knowledge (a schema) about going to concerts. Thus your recall of last weekend's concert will be influenced by your schema for concerts and the specific events that occurred at the concert in question. Similarly, you have schemas for grade school, marriage, rude behavior, trendy clothing, and so on.

To get a better idea of the nature of semantic networks and schemas, let's say you have learned a list of words that included the word *horse*. Later in the day you take a recognition test in which you are given a longer list of words and are asked to pick out the ones you have learned. You come to the word *horse,* which serves as a retrieval cue for the semantic network that contains your horse-related memories. Now your job is to determine whether the word *horse* was on the list you learned earlier. Sorting through all of your horse memories could be a rather imposing and confusing task, especially if there are many strong links. On the other hand, the word *aardvark* should be easier to recognize as one of the words you learned because it should activate fewer links than *horse*.

The same process is involved when we retrieve memories under recall conditions. For example, an essay question on your psychology test might ask you to name the four lobes of the cortex. You start scanning your semantic network for items related to the concept "lobe of the cortex." You find a network of related information that includes subcortical structures, stereotaxic surgery, and a group of items that includes the terms *frontal, temporal, parietal,* and *occipital*—the four cortical lobes you've been looking for.

What about the next question on the test: "Explain the contributions of Ivan Pavlov"? In this case, you need to recall more than just names to answer the question; you need to activate an organized cluster of knowledge, a schema. Your schema for Pavlov contains the information the instructor wants. In fact, it contains even more than you need to recall. Could there be some way to retrieve only the desired memory?

Encoding Specificity. This question has been addressed in research by Endel Tulving (Tulving & Thomson, 1973; Tulving, 1983). Tulving's **encoding specificity** hypothesis states that the effectiveness of memory retrieval is directly related to the similarity of the cues present when the memory was originally encoded to the cues present when the memory is retrieved. In short, specific cues are encoded, and these cues, or very similar ones, should be present when retrieval is attempted. For example, if you study for a test in your bedroom, items in your room become stimuli that can help you retrieve the memories you stored while studying.

Have you ever had difficulty recalling material you have studied? Part of the problem may be that the studying took place in one location and the testing occurred in a very different place. Most of the effective retrieval cues (those in the room where you studied) were missing in the classroom where you took the test. Hence it was difficult for them to retrieve the needed information.

How can you solve this recall problem? Try to do some studying in the room where the test will be given. The cues in the room will be among those that can help you retrieve the memory. This principle has been verified by a large number of experiments (Greenspoon & Raynard, 1957; Smith, Glenberg, & Björk, 1978). If you cannot study in the room where the test will be given, try varying the locations where you study. This would prevent a single set of cues from becoming associated with the memory of the material you are learning. As a result, retrieval of your memories will be tied less directly to a specific set of environmental cues.

Eyewitness Testimony. One of the most intriguing applications of Tulving's encoding specificity hypothesis has been in the area of eyewitness

encoding specificity
Theory stating that the effectiveness of memory retrieval is directly related to the similarity of the cues present when the memory was encoded and when the memory is retrieved

testimony. Such testimony often plays an important part in jury trials. Consider the following incident that was related to us by a friend:

> Walking home from the bus stop, I stopped to wait for a light to change. There was a screech of brakes and a crash. In the intersection in front of me a fast-moving car had struck the side of another car and pushed it onto the sidewalk. Both cars came to a stop, and there was silence. The traffic light was leaning at about a 60-degree angle; the light was still red. I was about to leave when I realized that I was the only witness to the accident. I went up to the officers to give a statement. We sat in one of the police cars, and I described the accident. I spoke of standing on the corner, hearing the crash, and watching the cars slide across the intersection. Then I showed the direction from which each car had approached the intersection and stated that one of the cars had run the light as I waited for it to change. Just then the driver of one of the cars came up and overheard what I was saying. Angrily, he denied that his car had been where I said it was—as a matter of fact, he said, it had been going in the opposite direction! Nor, according to him, had the other car approached from the street beside me; it had been speeding, not running the light. Somewhat red in the face, I withdrew my statement and went home. To this day I have been unable to figure out what really happened.

Psychological Detective

Before reading further, analyze this situation, and write down some possible reasons for the inaccuracy of this person's eye-witness testimony.

What cues were present when the accident was observed? Are they the same cues that were present when the statement was made? No, the two sets of cues are quite different. Is it possible for the drivers of the two cars to modify the memories of the witness as they "discuss" what happened during the crash?

The possibility that eyewitness reports may be inaccurate has stimulated a large amount of research. One of the most startling findings concerns what can happen to a memory once it has been retrieved. Earlier we saw that when a memory is retrieved from LTM, it appears to be placed in STM for conscious processing. While this memory is in STM, however, it is possible to add new information to it and then reencode the modified memory. The next time you retrieve the new memory, your report may not correspond exactly to what actually happened because the new memory now contains the additional information.

This effect was tested in several ingenious experiments conducted by Elizabeth Loftus and her colleagues (Loftus, Miller, & Burns, 1978; Loftus, 1979). One of those experiments is diagrammed in Figure 7-10. In this experiment two groups of people watched a series of slides that showed an impending collision between a red sports car and another automobile. One group saw the red sports car approach a stop sign at an intersection. The second group saw the sports car approach a yield sign at the intersection. After the slide presentation was completed, the participants were asked a series of questions about what they had seen. For half of the participants in each group, the questions were consistent with what they had seen. In other words, if they had seen a stop sign, the questions referred to a stop sign, and if they had seen a yield sign, the questions referred to a yield sign. For the remaining participants in each group, the questions were inconsistent—if they had seen a stop sign, the questions referred to a yield sign, and vice versa. Finally, all participants were shown pairs of slides and asked to pick the one they had actually seen (a recognition test).

The results of Loftus's experiment were startling. As you would expect, a large number (75 percent) of the participants who were asked consistent questions after seeing the slides picked the slide they had seen. When they were asked inconsistent questions, however, only 40 percent were able to select the slide they had actually seen. The inconsistent questions altered their memory of the incident. Later, when they retrieved this memory, many participants reported an incorrect memory because they had encoded inaccurate information in their memory after being asked questions that were inconsistent (Ayers & Reder, 1998).

In addition to demonstrating the memory-altering effects of inconsistent questions, Loftus (1984) has shown that (1) participants have trouble distinguishing between individuals of other races, (2) violence interferes with memory retrieval, and (3) the degree of confidence of an eyewitness is not related to the accuracy of the memory. The problems and concerns that such results create for the credibility of eyewitness testimony are obvious.

State-Dependent Learning.   For a number of years psychologists have known that if you learn material under certain special conditions,

What you say you saw may not be what actually happened; our memories can be changed.

One group saw the red sports car approaching a *stop* sign.

Experimental Design

Step 1	Step 2	Step 3	Results
See slides of red sports car approaching a *stop* sign.	Answer questions about what they had seen. *Consistent* participants had questions about stop signs. *Inconsistent* participants had questions about yield signs.	View slides and pick those that actually were seen in Step 1.	Participants asked consistent questions in Step 2 were significantly more accurate in picking the slides they had seen than were the inconsistent participants.

The other group saw the red sports car approach a *yield* sign.

Experimental Design

Step 1	Step 2	Step 3	Results
See slides of red sports car approaching a *yield* sign.	Answer questions about what they had seen. *Consistent participants* had questions about yield signs. *Inconsistent participants* had questions about stop signs.	View slides and pick those that actually were seen in Step 1.	Participants asked consistent questions in Step 2 were significantly more accurate in picking the slides they had seen than were the inconsistent participants.

FIGURE 7-10   Diagram of the Loftus (1979) experiment on eyewitness accuracy.

Source: Loftus, 1979.

If you drink a stimulant, such as coffee, while studying, the state-dependent learning phenomenon predicts that you will be better able to retrieve your memories of the material you studied if you drink a stimulant beforehand

your retrieval of that material will be successful under the same conditions. For example, Randi drank a lot of coffee while she was studying for her last psychology test. As we saw in Chapter 2, coffee contains a generous amount of caffeine, a central nervous system stimulant, so Randi was quite alert during her study session. Her physiological state became one of the stimuli that were present when the memories of the material she was studying were encoded. The implication from Tulving's encoding specificity hypothesis should be clear: Randi's retrieval will be best when she is tested after drinking a considerable amount of coffee. In other words, material learned in a particular physiological state is recalled best in the same physiological state, a phenomenon known as **state-dependent learning.** State-dependent learning has been demonstrated in animals (Overton, 1964) as well as humans (Eich et al., 1975).

Gordon Bower (1981) extended this finding to include mood states, such as being happy or sad. His logic was simple. If you learn material while you are happy (or sad), you should retrieve that material more easily when you are happy (or sad). If the mood state that was present during learning differs from the one present during testing, retrieval should be more difficult (Weaver & McNeill, 1992).

As we saw in Chapter 3, odors can be linked to both emotions and memories. The link between odor and memory was tested experimentally by psychologist Frank Schab (1990). In this research Schab tested students who smelled an odor both while they were generating antonyms (opposites) to a set of stimulus words such as *large* and *beautiful* and while they were recalling those antonyms later. These students recalled more antonyms than other students who had smelled an odor only during the learning session or only during the test session. Three very different odors—a chocolate scent, an apple-cinnamon scent, and a mothball scent—were used separately to prove that this memory effect was not limited to one specific odor. The results clearly indicated that regardless of the odor type, participants who smelled the same odor during both training and testing remembered antonyms better than participants who smelled an odor only during training or only during testing.

The phenomenon of state-dependent learning indicates that memories acquired under a specific set of circumstances may be difficult to retrieve at another time or under different circumstances. Perhaps we have memories of events that occurred years ago waiting to be triggered.

The Repressed-Memory Controversy

One of the most dramatic and significant controversies in recent years involves reports of the sudden recall of repressed memories of childhood sexual abuse. Retrieval of such memories has been reported to occur decades after the abuse. The significance of this issue is evident in the fact that the American Psychological Association and the British Psychological Association have asked groups of experts to study the issue and write policy statements (Lindsay & Read, 1993). This issue continues to attract so much professional attention that in 1997 an entire issue of *Current Directions in Psychological Science* was devoted to this topic. The following cases illustrate the basis for the controversy.

Case 1. While Melody was in the hospital for treatment of depression, her therapist repeatedly suggested that her depression resulted from incest during childhood. After a few sessions, Melody reported that her father had raped her when she was 4 years old. When pressed for details, she wrote pages of her emerging repressed memories, including being molested by her father when she was 1 year old. She confronted her parents and consulted a lawyer about filing charges against her father. After leaving the hos-

state-dependent learning
Theory stating that when we learn something while in a specific physiological state, our recall of that information will be better when we are in the same physiological state

pital and consulting new therapists, Melody concluded that the abuse never occurred. She now says the memories were "a figment of my imagination encouraged by my therapists and the pop psychology books I was reading" (Wartik, 1993, p. 64). Melody is trying to make amends with her family. (Bower, 1993; Jaroff, 1993; Wartik, 1993)

Case 2: Claudia lost more than 100 pounds in a hospital program for treatment of obesity. While in the hospital, she had flashbacks of sexual abuse committed by her brother. After joining a therapy group for incest survivors, the memories of abuse flooded back. Her brother had died in combat in the Vietnam War more than 15 years before her memories surfaced. Claudia's parents had left his room untouched since his death. She searched his room and found pornographic materials, handcuffs, and a diary in which he had described sexual "experiments" with his sister. (Bower, 1993)

About half the states in the United States have extended the statute of limitations, allowing people who retrieve memories of abuse to sue alleged perpetrators within three to six years of the time the memories emerge. A growing number of victims have used these revised laws to file civil and criminal actions.

How are these memories retrieved? Psychotherapy (see Chapter 14) is the most common vehicle for the retrieval of memories of childhood abuse (generally incest). Typically a person (usually a 20- to 30-year-old woman) seeks therapy for any of a number of problems. Many therapists believe that childhood sexual abuse is associated with a range of problems. Consistent with this belief, some of them ask about the existence of childhood abuse in the first therapy session, and some even insist such abuse occurred, despite the client's denials.

Many therapists rely on memory recovery techniques they believe help their patients remember repressed memories of abuse. For example, 83 percent of a sample of therapists agreed with the statement "Hypnosis seems to counteract the defense mechanism of repression, lifting repressed material into conscious awareness" (Yapko, 1994, p. 57). Unfortunately, these memory-recovery techniques (such as imagery, dream interpretation, and journal writing) can also help people create compelling illusory memories (Ceci & Loftus, 1994; Lindsay & Read, 1993; Yapko, 1994). For example, it has been "known for well over a century that false memories can be implanted in individuals through the

George Franklin Sr., left, appears in a Redwood City, California, courtroom, Wednesday, Jan. 31, 1996. Franklin, 56, who was convicted for a 20-year-old murder based on the repressed memory testimony from his daughter, was ordered retried and the conviction overturned.

use of formal hypnotic procedures or even through simple suggestions, without formal hypnosis" (Yapko, 1994, p. 96).

What is the evidence for repression? The theory that memories can be repressed is a cornerstone of the debate (Arrigo & Pezdek, 1997). Yet after 70 years of looking, researchers have not found evidence that the process actually exists (Holmes, 1994).

In a typical evaluation of repression, participants learn groups of words. Then half of the participants are stressed by being told either that they failed a test or that they have some personality defect. The other participants are either told that they passed the test or they are given neutral personality comments. When asked to recall the words, participants exposed to stress recall fewer words. This result seems consistent with the notion that they had been repressing memories associated with stress. Later, when the stressed individuals are told that they had passed a difficult test or that the earlier test results had been false, they remember the words as well as the control participants did.

Researchers have found that the participants were *concentrating* on the experience of the stressful event instead of shutting it out, as repression suggests. Thus the participants recalled the words poorly because of the distraction created by concentrating on the stressful event, rather than because of repression. Critics argue, however, that laboratory studies of repression are not relevant to the kinds of real-life traumas that have been associated with repressed memories.

It seems possible that we can lose contact with memories for long periods of time; however, repression is an overused explanation of such memory failures. The more likely explanations are normal forgetting, deliberate avoidance, and *infantile amnesia,* or the inability to form memories before approximately age 3 (Ceci & Loftus, 1994).

There is no evidence that people who report memories of abuse are involved in any form of deliberate deception (Yapko, 1994). On the contrary, Loftus (Loftus & Ketcham, 1994) has shown that it is possible to create false memories of a childhood event (e.g., being lost in a shopping mall) that never happened. Not only do participants believe these created memories, but they also expand on them and provide details that were not even hinted at in the initial suggestions.

Perhaps the major problem in evaluating memories of childhood sexual abuse is that there is no way to distinguish true repressed memories from false ones (Lindsay & Read, 1993; Loftus, 1993). Ceci and Loftus (1994) write, "The point is not that suggestive memory work techniques unalterably lead to false memory, but merely that they may do so" (p. 359). There is a tragic risk of uncritical acceptance of allegations made by patients: "These activities are bound to lead to an increased likelihood that society in general will disbelieve the genuine cases of childhood sexual abuse that truly deserve our sustained attention" (Loftus, 1993, p. 534).

Memory Illusions

Clearly the false-memory research and the repressed-memory controversy have stimulated considerable research. Indeed, a new view of memory may be emerging from this research: "memory is fallible, quirky, and essentially reconstructive in nature" (Lynn & Payne, 1997, p. 55).

Because false memories "occur in many different contexts and can be quite compelling" (Payne et al., 1997, p. 56), several investigators view such occurrences as *memory illusions.* (Do you remember some of the visual illusions on p. 129? With visual illusions, we see things that don't exist.) In the case of memory illusions, we remember things that never happened.

The strength and believability of memory illusions are shown in studies in which lists of words were learned (Payne et al., 1996). In these studies participants claimed they remembered exactly who said the critical but *nonexistent* words. What's more, some participants refused to believe that the nonexistent words were not part of the original list, even when they heard a playback of the original tape. Other research clearly indicates that memory illusions are created for very complex situations, such as being hospitalized at a young age (e.g., Loftus, 1997). Memory illusions are *very* strong and believable. Moreover, they seem to operate much in the same manner as other, normal memory processes.

Even though memory illusions appear to operate similarly to other normal memory processes, there are some differences between them and true memories. Perhaps the most apparent difference concerns the amount of detail that is recalled: Greater detail is recalled with true memories (Mather, Henkle, & Johnson, in press; Norman & Schachter, in press).

What part of the brain is involved in creating memory illusions? Daniel Schachter and his colleagues were not content to speculate; they reported data suggesting that the right frontal lobe plays an important role (Schachter, 1997; Schachter et al., 1996). For example, a patient with damage to the right frontal lobe displayed significantly more memory illusions than did people without frontal lobe damage.

As we have seen, memory illusions are clearly relevant to eyewitness testimony. However, research has progressed far beyond demonstrating the fallibility of eyewitness testimony to examining specific factors, other than adding misleading questions and planting pieces of misinformation, that can create such memory illusions. For example, Maggie Bruck and Stephen Ceci (1997) demonstrated that interviewer bias is one of the factors leading to memory illusions. Likewise, research on the accuracy of memory recall under hypnosis indicates that such memories are no more accurate than those recalled under nonhypnotized conditions (Erdelyi, 1994). In fact, highly hypnotizable individuals report more memory illusions than do nonhypnotized persons (Lynn et al., 1997; Lynn, Myers, & Malinoski, in press). Although warning people of the possibility of suggestibility before hypnosis reduces the number of memory illusions, it does not eliminate them (Green, Lynn, & Malinoski, in press).

Clearly, memory illusions are very real and very prevalent. It will be interesting to see what future research will uncover.

Techniques for Improving Memory

Bradford is an art major who is having difficulty in his U.S. history course. He cannot remember such facts as the major battles of the Civil War. They have no meaning for him. His friends' advice has not helped. Bradford is very frustrated and is thinking of dropping the course. Yet he must pass this required course to complete his degree. *What can Bradford do to improve his memory?* ▪

Influential Factors

Psychologists have been trying to answer this question for a long time (Higbee, 1993). As you can see from Table 7-2, they have found several factors that influence learning and memory. Among those factors are number of study

TABLE 7-2   Factors That Influence Human Learning and Memory

FACTOR	EFFECT
Number of study sessions	The greater the number of study (learning) sessions, the better the learning and memory.
Distribution of study sessions	Study sessions should be spread out. Spaced practice is more effective than massed practice.
Meaningfulness of material	Material that is meaningful will be learned better and remembered longer.
Similarity of items	A group of items of the same general type will be learned better than a group of dissimilar items.
Serial position	Items at the beginning and end of a study session or list will be learned better than items in the middle.

sessions, distribution of study sessions, meaningfulness of material, similarity of items, and serial position.

Assuming that Bradford really has tried to study, the key to remembering the history assignment is finding some meaning in the material. As long as U.S. history has little meaning or relevance to him, he will have difficulty learning it.

Understanding the factors presented in Table 7-2 also helps us to answer the question "What is the best way to study for a test?" Bradford now knows he will do better on his tests if he studies as often as possible (increases the number of sessions) but takes several breaks between study sessions (improves the distribution of sessions). For the best learning to occur, the material he is studying should be meaningful (Moravcsik & Healey, 1995), and he should not try to study several different topics during the same session (maintain similarity of items). Finally, the **serial position effect** (Gershberg & Shimamura, 1994) indicates that he should give a little extra attention to the material he studies during the middle portion of a study session. You might want to try these procedures yourself; they could help raise your grades.

Processing Strategies

Now that you understand how to arrange your study sessions and the type of material that should be studied, you want to know more. Why do some people remember better than others? Do they have special secrets or tricks? This section describes some memory techniques that have been shown to work. These techniques, known as **mnemonic devices,** are procedures for associating new information with previously stored memories. Thus they are forms of elaborative rehearsal and result in deeper processing. To remember new material, you first recall previously learned (familiar) information and then recall the new information that has been associated with it. You can decide whether mnemonic devices really work. Like anything else, some practice is required to learn to use them effectively. Among the most common techniques are imagery, grouping, and coding.

Imagery.   Researchers have shown that if you create and use mental pictures or images of the items you are studying, you will remember better (Dewhurst & Conway, 1994; Paivio, 1971). Repeating items over and over again does little to help you remember them; however, visualizing them as you are learning can

serial position effect
Tendency for items at the beginning and end of a list to be learned better than items in the middle

mnemonic devices
Procedures for associating new information with previously stored memories

help you recall them. For example, if you are learning the components of classical conditioning (see Chapter 6), you should not simply think "CS," "US," and "CR"; rather, visualize a concrete example of each. The CS might be a noisy buzzer, the US a delicious apple pie, and so forth. This process of visualizing items as they are being learned is known as **imagery.**

Beyond this general finding, two more specific techniques for mental imagery have been developed. They are known as the method of loci and the pegword technique.

Method of Loci.   *Loci* is the Latin word for "places"; the already stored cues for the **method of loci** are specific places. When using this mnemonic device, you start with a set of familiar locations. For example, if you live on campus, you could list (in order) the major landmarks you see every time you go from your dormitory room to the student union. Such landmarks could include the door to your room, the staircase to the first floor, the outside door, a tree, a statue, the science hall, and so forth, until you enter the front door of the student union. Then you would assign to each location an item that you want to learn. So if you were trying to learn the parts of the brain, you could pair the medulla with your door, the cerebellum with the staircase to the first floor, and so on. Some people believe that the more bizarre the image, the better your recall. You could imagine an animated medulla hanging on your door. The cerebellum could become the staircase. To recall the parts of the brain in order, you would call up the mental image of the things you encounter on the way to the student union and remember the part of the brain associated with each location. This procedure may sound a bit complex, but it has been found to be highly effective.

Psychological Detective

 Don, the rock-and-roll expert, can name in order all of the songs on each of the most popular "oldies" rock CDs. Tonight Don is studying for a psychology test. During this study session, he listens to some of his favorite songs. Don hopes that rather than interfering with his studying, listening to music will help him to score higher on the test. He plays one type of music for each section of material he is studying. He studies the first section while Beatles music is playing; during the next section he listens to some Billy Joel, and so it goes for the rest of the evening. How will Don's unusual study session assist him when he takes the test? Write down an answer to this question before reading further.

Pegword Technique.   In the **pegword technique,** which is similar to the method of loci, you start with a list of items that you already know quite well. For Don to learn a set of items, all he has to do is assign one item to each song on a particular CD. When he is ready to recall the new information, he simply remembers the song titles and the item associated with each. Don is using the pegword technique to help him remember material for his psychology test. For example, basic learning terms (see Chapter 6) such as *CS, US, UR, CR, reinforcement,* and *extinction* may be associated with the titles on the Beatles CD. Items having to do with states of consciousness (Chapter 5) might be associated with titles on the Billy Joel CD. The main difference between the pegword technique and the method of loci is that in the method of loci you visualize specific *locations,* whereas in the pegword technique you think of an already established list of items.

imagery
Process of visualizing items as they are being learned

method of loci
Use of familiar locations as cues to recall items that have been associated with them

pegword technique
Use of familiar words or names as cues to recall items that have been associated with them

Grouping (Chunking). What is your telephone number? You will answer with a group of numbers, such as 316-555-5800. Since the first experiment on grouping (Bousfield, 1953), psychologists have consistently found that we tend to group or *chunk* items when we recall them. Several clustering strategies can be used. If you must learn material in a certain order, you can group together the first three or four items, the next three or four, and so forth. We use this method of grouping when we learn telephone numbers.

If the material does not have to be remembered in a particular order, the possibilities for grouping increase greatly. You can group items according to their type, their ending, their length, or any other way in which they are similar.

How would you remember the following words?

dolphin, green bean, Mickey Mouse, beet, Goofy, carrot,

minnow, squash, bass, Minnie Mouse, spinach, trout,

Pluto, salmon, celery, perch, Donald Duck

Study this list for one minute; then close the book and write down as many of the words as you can. Did you group the items into three familiar categories: fish, vegetables, and Walt Disney characters? If you did not use those three categories, did you use others? If so, how did they differ from the categories we proposed? Chunking seems to be used most frequently and effectively with short-term memory tasks, such as remembering a phone number or a list of words.

Coding. Items that are not very meaningful or relevant to the learner are not learned as well or as easily as more meaningful or relevant items. Some people create special codes to help them learn material that lacks relevance. They code the less relevant material in a meaningful form and then remember the coded items. It is important, however, to be able to decode the items once they have been learned. For example, the nonsense syllables *cib, xos,* and *gip* would be difficult to remember because they do not have high levels of meaning. What if we were to code each by printing it backward? In that case *cib* becomes *bic, xos* becomes *sox,* and *gip* becomes *pig.* These coded syllables are high in meaning and therefore are much easier to remember. When we want to recall the coded stimuli, all we have to do is reverse the order of the letters after the familiar words have been recalled.

Acronyms and Acrostics. The use of acronyms and acrostics are two popular coding techniques. An **acronym** is a word formed by the initial letter(s) of the items to be remembered. To remember the desired information you recall the acronym and then decode it. For example, to help remember the names of the Great Lakes all you need to do is recall the acronym HOMES and then decode it: H (Lake Huron), O (Lake Ontario), M (Lake Michigan), E (Lake Erie), and S (Lake Superior).

An **acrostic** is a verse or saying (often unusual or humorous) where the first letter(s) of each word stands for a bit of information. For example, let's say you are assigned the task of remembering the names of the first seven presidents of the United States in order. One approach would be to use rote memorization. On the other hand, you might do better, spend less time, and have more fun if you made up a little phrase such as this: "**W**ashington **a**nd **J**efferson **m**ade **m**any **a** joke." The first letter of each word in this saying stands for the last name of a president: George **W**ashington, John **A**dams, Thomas **J**efferson, James **M**adison, James **M**onroe, John Quincy **A**dams, and **A**ndrew **J**ackson. Students frequently create acronyms and acrostics when they study for tests.

acronym
A word formed by the initial letter(s) of the items to be remembered

acrostic
A verse or saying in which the first letter(s) of each word stands for a bit of information

Educating Children with Special Needs

BEGINNING WITH THE PASSAGE OF PUBLIC LAW 94-142 (THE EDUCATION FOR ALL Handicapped Children Act) in 1975, several pieces of legislation designed to increase appropriate educational experiences for the great diversity of children in the United States have been passed. The most recent legislation, the Individuals with Disabilities Education Act (IDEA), was originally passed in 1990 (PL 101-476). This law has been reauthorized (1997) and amended since that time. Basically, this legislation calls for (1) nondiscriminatory and multidisciplinary assessment of educational needs; (2) parental involvement in developing each child's educational program; (3) education in the least restrictive environment; and (4.) an individualized education plan.

These mandates make it clear that all students may not learn in the same manner. For example, even though some of the memory aids we've just discussed might work well for you, they may be inappropriate for children with special needs. In this section we examine the implementation of special learning techniques for several of two groups of children with special needs: (1) autistic and (2) gifted, creative, and talented persons.*

According to the U.S. Department of Education (1991), *autism* a developmental disability significantly affecting verbal and nonverbal communication and social interaction, generally evident before age 3, that adversely affects educational performance. Characteristics of autism include—irregularities and impairments in communication, engagement in repetitive activities and stereotyped movements, resistance to environmental change or change in daily routines, and unusual responses to sensory experiences. (p. 41271)

The Javits Gifted and Talented Education Act defines *giftedness* in this way:

> Children and youth with outstanding talent perform or show the potential for performing at remarkably high levels of accomplishment when compared with others of their age, experience, and environment.
>
> These children and youth exhibit high performance capability in intellectual, creative, and/or artistic areas, possess an unusual leadership capacity, or excel in specific academic fields. They require services not ordinarily provided by the schools.
>
> Outstanding talents are present in children and youth from all cultural groups, across all economic strata, and in all areas of human endeavor. (U.S. Department of Education, 1993, p. 3)

Compare the definitions for these two groups of children. Would you expect them to learn in the same manner? Will their grade school teachers treat them similarly? To underscore the "no" answer to each of these questions, consider the following descriptions of educational programs for children who are autistic and gifted.

The development of an *individual educational plan (IEP),* having communication and social skills as core components, is a must for children with autism. Efforts should be made to integrate children with autism into the regular classroom to help "prepare individuals with autism to live in their home

---

*Space prohibits us from covering all special needs categories; however, children with mental retardation, emotional or behavior disorders, learning disabilities, communication disorders, hearing loss, vision loss, or physical and health disabilities also are included in this group of persons with special needs.

community and in the least restrictive setting" (Hardiman, Drew, & Egan, 1996, p. 380). To facilitate the adaptation of children with autism to school, teachers must be extrasensitive and attentive to these students' unique characteristics and needs. For example, because children with autism do not deal well with change and confusion, it is advisable to spend some *extra* time with these pupils, showing them how to get around the school, where they can go, and whom they can see if they become confused and upset.

Because "gifted and talented elementary school children have mastered from 35 to 50 percent of the curriculum to be offered in five basic subjects before they begin the school year" (U.S. Department of Education, 1993, p. 2), the educational picture is much different when we consider this group. When dealing with gifted children, two frequently encountered concepts are *acceleration* and *enrichment.* The basic philosophy behind acceleration is to allow gifted students to achieve at their own levels and capabilities. Originally acceleration was equated with grade skipping; however, the frequent display of social maladjustment resulted in the decline of this practice. Currently, acceleration may be accomplished by a variety of other techniques: curriculum compacting (elimination of curriculum components that have been mastered already [Reis & Renzulli, 1992]), enrolling in extra courses, taking university courses while still in high school, and so forth. Enrichment activities are designed to challenge and broaden the knowledge and skills of gifted students. Such activities might include special classes and unique activities and assignments. For example, a gifted student in an art class might undertake a special project to learn more about a painter she is interested in. Unlike children with autism, gifted students are very independent and thrive on ambiguity, change, and challenges.

The education of students with special needs highlights the fact that diversity is broad and encompasing. It is present in how we deal with all aspects of our lives, from learning needs and styles to the development of social behaviors.

Evaluating techniques for improving memory naturally led psychologists to look for the physiological basis of memory. We consider their findings next.

Review Summary

1. Craik and Lockhart proposed only one type of memory. The **level of processing** may determine the permanence of the storage of this memory.

2. Other researchers have proposed that there is more than one type of long-term memory. Four types have been identified: **procedural, semantic, episodic,** and **priming** or **implicit memory.** Each serves to store a different kind of information.

3. The **tip-of-the-tongue (TOT) phenomenon** has been used to study the network of semantic memories, whereas the study of **flashbulb memories** has provided information about episodic memory.

4. Research on the **retrieval** of memories has shown

that we scan both STM and LTM to locate an item we wish to recall.

5. Encoding specificity has a great deal to do with the ease with which a memory is retrieved. If the cues that were present when a memory was encoded or stored are not present during retrieval, it is difficult to retrieve that memory.

6. Encoding specificity appears to be at work in such situations as **state-dependent learning.** State-dependent learning theory states that we recall information better when we learn and are tested in the same physiological/psychological state.

7. It has been suggested that memories of childhood sexual abuse may be repressed and recalled during adulthood. Many of these repressed memories appear to have been induced during therapy sessions by suggestions made by the therapist.

8. The number of sessions, distribution of practice, meaningfulness of items, similarity of items, and **serial position** of items influence human learning.

9. Our memory can be improved by using a **mnemonic device** such as **imagery.** The **method of** loci and the **pegword technique** are two popular mnemonic devices.

10. Grouping and coding are two other techniques that can be used as memory aids. **Acronyms,** words formed by the first letter(s) of the items to be remembered, and **acrostics,** a verse or saying in which the first letter(s) of each word stands for a bit of information, are two popular forms of coding.

11. Considerable attention is being given to educating children with special needs.

Study Break

1. If your strategy in studying for a test is to memorize all the material, you may not do as well as someone else who relates the course material to real-life events. Why?
2. What is the main problem with the levels-of-processing approach to the study of memory?
3. What type of memory occurs when you remember how to change the oil in an antique pickup truck?
   a. semantic
   b. procedural
   c. episodic
   d. implicit
4. What type of memory occurs when you remember where you were on Halloween night in 1992?
   a. semantic
   b. procedural
   c. episodic
   d. implicit
5. What type of memory occurs when you remember that the reciprocal of a number is equal to 1 divided by the number?
   a. semantic
   b. procedural
   c. episodic
   d. implicit
6. Explain the relationship between priming or implicit memory and improving recall by elderly people.
7. How have psychologists demonstrated the retrieval of memories from STM?
8. What is the relationship between encoding specificity and the failure of retrieval? In this regard, how should you study to optimize your chances of earning a good grade?
9. What is state-dependent learning? Give an original example of this process.
10. What is the "repressed-memory controversy"? What problem might this controversy be creating?
11. There is an important history exam tomorrow. Amy has been studying a little each day for the past two weeks, whereas you have reserved the two nights before the exam for studying. Who will do better on the exam? Explain your reasoning.
12. Psychologists who speak of working memory are referring to
   a. short-term memory.
   b. long-term memory.
   c. episodic memory.
   d. primary memory.

The Physiological Basis of Learning and Memory

When H.M. was 7 years old, he was struck by a bicycle, fell, and injured his head. Although there appeared to be only minimal damage, several years later H.M. began experiencing minor but intense brain seizures. A major seizure occurred when he was 16. By the time he was 27, the frequency and intensity of the seizures warranted surgery to remove large portions of his hippocampus and amygdala (see Chapter 2). The operation took place in 1953. ***What can an operation to control seizures tell us about memory?***

In addition to identifying and studying the processes that occur during learning and memory, psychologists have attempted to isolate the physical changes that accompany those processes. In other words, they have attempted to pinpoint and describe the physiological basis of learning and memory. Their research has focused on patients who suffer memory loss as a result of head injuries or operations like the one just described.

Amnesias

After experiencing a physical or psychological trauma, a person can lose his or her memory of people, places, and things. Such memory losses are called **amnesias.** We discuss amnesias caused by psychological traumas in Chapter 14. The study of amnesias resulting from physical trauma provides insight into the nature of memory. Two types of amnesias have been identified: *anterograde* and *retrograde*.

Anterograde Amnesia and The Hippocampus.   The inability to store new information after a traumatic physical event is known as **anterograde amnesia.** The case of H.M. is a well-known example of anterograde amnesia (Scoville & Milner, 1957). What can this case tell us about memory?

As it turned out, H.M.'s operation, in which large portions of the hippocampus and amygdala were removed, provided a great deal of information about the nature of memory. Since the operation, H.M., who is now in his seventies, has been unable to form new memories; his entire world consists of memories that were formed before 1953. He does not remember such things as the names of people he has just met, what he ate for lunch, what was on television last night, or what year it is. In short, his daily experience consists exclusively of STM, of living from moment to moment, except for his pre-1953 memories.

Psychological Detective

On the basis of this case, you should be able to reach two tentative conclusions. One has to do with the stages of memory processing discussed earlier; the second concerns the physiological basis of memory. Spend a few moments reviewing this information; then write down the two conclusions.

If you believe that H.M.'s problem has to do with the memory storage process, you are correct. For H.M., new information is not reaching long-term storage. Thus we are led to the second conclusion: The hippocampus or amygdala is involved in the process of storing new memories. Notice we said that these structures are *involved in the process* of storing new memories, not that new memories are stored in these structures. If memories were stored in the hippocampus or amygdala, H.M.'s operation would have erased memories stored before 1953.

The conclusion that the hippocampus is involved in the storing of memories is supported by research using animals. When the hippocampus is removed from both hemispheres of the brain in laboratory animals, the animals have difficulty holding information about a learning task they have just mastered in STM (Baddeley, 1988).

Retrograde Amnesia and the Consolidation Hypothesis.   Physical trauma may also result in the loss of memory of events that occurred before the

amnesia
Loss of memory that occurs as a result of physical or psychological trauma

anterograde amnesia
Inability to store new memories after a traumatic event

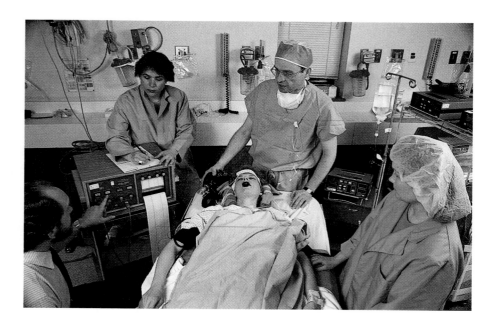

A human patient undergoing electroshock therapy may suffer from retrograde anmesia. According to the consolidation hypothesis, this loss of memory occurs because consolidation and transfer to long-term memory do not take place.

trauma. In such cases we are dealing with **retrograde amnesia.** The fact that the greatest memory loss is for events that occurred just before the trauma suggests an interesting and testable hypothesis. Based on the notion that memories must "set" or "consolidate" to be stored in LTM, the **consolidation hypothesis** predicts that memories that are interfered with before they have consolidated will not be stored. This process is analogous to baking a cake: If the oven door is opened, the cake will fall. The blow on the head that produces retrograde amnesia has interrupted the consolidation process for recent memories.

Both human and animal studies have provided evidence to support the consolidation hypothesis. For example, in some cases of severe depression, *electroconvulsive therapy (ECT),* also known as *electroshock therapy,* may be used (see Chapter 14). This procedure involves passing an electric current through the patient's brain. In addition to reducing the depression, ECT produces strong retrograde amnesia. Early studies found that the application of electroconvulsive shock (ECS) to animals shortly after a learning task also produced retrograde amnesia, suggesting that it interferes with the formation of a memory. What's more, the longer the delay between completion of the task and the application of ECS, the less the effect of ECS. In the longer delay conditions, we assumed that the memory had more time to consolidate and therefore ECS did not interfere with it as much.

retrograde amnesia
Loss of memories that were stored before a traumatic event

consolidation hypothesis
Hypothesis that memories must be consolidated or "set" before they can be stored

FIGURE 7-11 The longer the delay between original learning and an electroconvulsive shock, the greater the percentage of animals who avoided foot shock by staying on the platform.

Source: Chorover & Schiller, 1965.

In one study of the effects of ECS (Chorover & Schiller, 1965), rats were placed on small platforms. The normal response of a rat in this situation is to step down from the platform. When the rats stepped down, however, they received an electric shock to their feet. The rats' task was to learn to stay on the platform to avoid a foot shock. Five groups of rats were tested. These groups received ECS (by passing a mild electric current through the brain) either 3, 5, 7, 10, or 30 seconds after

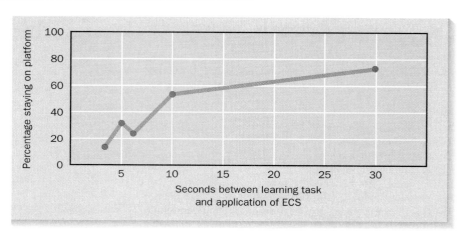

stepping off the platform and receiving a foot shock. Figure 7-11 shows that the longer the interval between the learning task and the delivery of ECS, the greater the percentage of animals staying on the platform on the next trial. Thus it appears that the memory of receiving the foot shock after stepping off the platform was consolidated more strongly when ECS was applied either 10 or 30 seconds after a foot shock. Although not all animal studies have supported the consolidation hypothesis as well (Maki, 1986), there is no doubt that ECS impairs memory storage.

Review Summary

1. Physical trauma may result in a loss of memory known as **amnesia. Anterograde amnesia** occurs when new information cannot be stored, although old memories remain intact. It can result from damage to the hippocampus. **Retrograde amnesia** occurs when memories for events that happened *before* the traumatic event are lost. It may occur when memories are not allowed to **consolidate** or set.

Study Break

1. Loss of memory owing to a physical trauma is known as
   a. consolidation.
   b. habituation.
   c. amnesia.
   d. long-term potentiation.
2. Inability to store new information after a traumatic physical event is known as
   a. retrograde amnesia.
   b. anterograde amnesia.
   c. retroactive amnesia.
   d. proactive amnesia.
3. H.M. lost the ability to form new memories because of an operation that removed portions of his
   a. cerebellum and cerebrum.
   b. hypothalamus and thalamus.
   c. hippocampus and amygdala.
   d. corpus callosum and cortex.
4. Which kind of amnesia results from damage to the hippocampus? Why?
5. Laboratory rats prefer to be in dark places; hence they move readily from a brightly lit chamber to a dark one. Assume that a foot shock is administered when the rats enter the dark compartment. What should the rats learn from this experience? What will happen if they receive an ECS three seconds after receiving a foot shock in the dark compartment? What would happen if an ECS was administered one hour after the rats received a foot shock in the dark compartment?

ANSWERS TO STUDY BREAKS

Page 289

1. Nonsense syllables. Nonsense syllables are used to avoid the presence of previous associations influencing learning.
2. Serial learning
3. There is an input stage, encoding process, and retrieval process in both the information system and human memory.
4. a. Sensory memory
   b. Short-term memory
   c. Long-term memory
   d. Sensory memory
   e. Short-term memory
   f. Short-term memory
5. Working memory follows the initial 10–20 seconds of short-term memory. During working memory, attention and conscious effort are brought to bear on the material.

6. *Maintenance rehearsal* is rehearsal that ensures that a memory remains until it has been used. *Elaborative rehearsal* is rehearsal that results in added meaning being given to the material to be remembered; it results in more permanent storage.
7. Proactive interference
8. Retroactive interference
9. a
10. b
11. b

Page 311

1. You are processing at a very shallow level. The person who relates the material to real-life events is processing at a much deeper level.

2. The term *level of processing* has never been clearly defined.

3. b

4. c

5. a

6. Priming memory sensitized persons to the information that is to be retrieved. Thus an elderly person may find it easier to retrieve memories.

7. By measuring the time it takes to respond with a yes or a no to the presence of a letter in STM. As more letters are added to the stimulus, the time required to identify a given letter as one that was present increased.

8. *Encoding specificity* means that memory retrieval is tied to cues that are present when the memory was encoded and when the memory is to be retrieved. To optimize the chances of earning a good grade, you should study in the same room where the test will be given or, if that procedure is not possible, in a variety of locations so that a number of cues will elicit the memories.

9. State-dependent learning is the storage of a memory under a certain physiological state. Learning the material for your next psychology test when you are extremely tired would be an example of state-dependent learning.

10. The *repressed-memory controversy* refers to the truthfulness of the sudden recall of repressed memories of childhood abuse by teenagers and adults undergoing therapy.

Because there is no way to distinguish between true and false repressed memories, this controversy may be leading to false allegations and the likelihood that true instances of repressed memories will not be believed.

11. Amy will do better on the exam because she has studied more often (increased number of study sessions is superior to one session) and because she has spread her studying out over the two-week period before the exam (spaced practice is more effective than massed practice).

12. a

Page 314

1. c

2. b

3. c

4. Anterograde amnesia. Damage to the hippocampus results in the inability to form new memories.

5. The rats should learn not to enter the dark compartment. If an ECS is administered three seconds after the shock in the dark compartment, there may be considerable disruption of consolidation. If an ECS is administered one hour after the shock in the dark compartment, the memory will have set, and an ECS will have no effect.

ANSWERS TO PSYCHOLOGICAL DETECTIVE

Page 294

1. Pacific Ocean
2. Oak
3. Internal combustion engine
4. Hibernate
5. Missouri River

ANSWERS TO HANDS ON EXERCISE

Page 294

How many capitals were on the tip of your tongue the first time you went through the list of states? Did the first letter help you recall any additional names?

State	Capital
Alabama	Montgomery
Connecticut	Hartford
Florida	Tallahassee
Georgia	Atlanta
Idaho	Boise
Iowa	Des Moines
Kentucky	Frankfort
Louisiana	Baton Rouge
Maryland	Annapolis
Massachusetts	Boston
Mississippi	Jackson
Nebraska	Lincoln
New Jersey	Trenton
Oregon	Salem
Texas	Austin
Wyoming	Cheyenne

Thinking and Intelligence

Chapter in Perspective

The brain plays a key role in basic processes such as sensation and perception of our environment, our emotional reactions, and our states of consciousness. Most of the basic processes we have discussed thus far are also found in lower animals, so we may wonder what separates lower animals from human beings.

The human brain endows us with remarkable abilities to solve problems and to make decisions. In this chapter we explore some of the remarkable abilities seen in human beings. As we explore these abilities, we also find that humans can be misled by some of the methods we use to solve problems and make decisions. One way to view the intellectual achievements of human beings is to consider this fact: Only human beings are capable of creating methods to measure their intellectual achievements. One of the more contentious issues we discuss is the measurement of intelligence. Our analysis of this topic shows us how the study of a topic changes over time and how new ways of conceptualizing intelligence are offered. ■

cognitive psychology
The subfield of psychology concerned with the study of higher mental processes such as thinking, knowing, and deciding

thinking
Manipulation of information in the form of mental images or concepts

Thinking

After agreeing to take part in an experiment, Sara was asked to sit in front of a computer screen and view a series of geometric figures that were presented in pairs (see Figure 8-1). Her task was simple: Determine whether the paired figures are the same or different. In some cases she quickly made the determination; in others the process took longer. Although she guessed that the experiment was designed to study thinking, she wondered how psychologists could study such an unseen process. ***How do psychologists study thinking?*** ■

In Chapter 1 we described how John B. Watson, the founder of behaviorism, redirected psychology to focus on the observation of external events. Because conscious experience could not be observed directly, he concluded that it was not worthy of scientific investigation. Moreover, terms such as *thinking* or *thoughts* were not precise, so Watson turned to the study of the muscle movements of subvocal speech as the basis of what we call *thinking*. Does Watson's proposal to study the muscle movements related to speech seem far-fetched? Ask someone a question (preferably one requiring some deliberation), and watch the person's lips as he or she considers how to respond. Do the person's lips move? As part of his effort to make psychology more objective, Watson claimed that psychologists could study thinking if it consisted of observable muscle movements like those that occur when we speak silently to ourselves.

If thinking consists of barely detectable motor movements, it would be impossible to think if all your motor muscles were paralyzed. To test this notion, Scott Smith injected himself with curare, a poison that blocks conduction in motor neurons and therefore causes paralysis (Smith et al., 1947). Had he not been connected to a respirator that could breathe for him, he would have died. While he was paralyzed, his colleagues asked him questions and even gave him some problems to solve. After the effects of the curare wore off, Smith told his colleagues what he had been thinking while he was paralyzed. His courageous efforts demonstrated that thinking consists of more than just muscle movements.

Cognitive Psychology

Although the results reported by Smith and his colleagues were striking, behaviorism remained a dominant force in psychology for more than half of the twentieth century (Guenther, 1998). Eventually a new perspective, *cognitive psychology*, gained prominence. **Cognitive psychology** is a branch of psychology that examines thinking: how we know and understand the world, solve problems, make decisions, combine information from memory and current experience, use language, and communicate our thoughts to others. **Thinking** is a mental process involving the

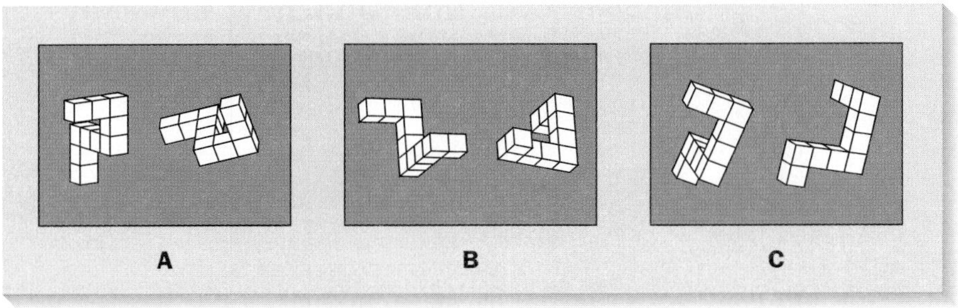

FIGURE 8-1 Pictures of three-dimensional objects shown to participants by Shepard and Metzler (1971). For each, look at the object on the left and determine whether the object on the right is a rotated view of the same object.

Source: Shepard & Metzler, 1971.

manipulation of information in the form of images or concepts that is inferred from our behavior. Thinking is evident, for example, when we solve a problem or make a decision.

Richard Mayer says that if cognitive psychology is to be scientific, "the data we use must be public—any reasonable person should be able to find the same data by following the same procedure" (Mayer, 1990, p. 1). Cognitive psychologists infer mental processes from the observable behaviors of the people they study. For example, to uncover problem-solving strategies, they may ask people to think aloud as they solve problems. In the following discussion we consider one way in which cognitive psychologists draw inferences about thinking—through the study of images.

Images. What route do you follow when you walk from your front door to your bedroom? What is the shape and color of a highway "yield" sign? Many people report that they visualize events and objects to answer such questions. *Visual imagery,* the experience of seeing even though the event or object is not actually viewed, can activate brain areas responsible for visual perception, such as the occipital lobe (Kosslyn & Koenig, 1992). Images do not have to be visual, however; they can be auditory or even olfactory (involving the sense of smell).

Before the development of sophisticated equipment to study brain activation, two researchers, Roger Shepard and Jacqueline Metzler (1971), investigated how people answer questions about visually presented material. Look again at Figure 8-1, and examine the paired drawings to determine whether the objects on the right are the same as those on the left. If you rotated the objects on the left, would they be the same as those on the right? The pairs of geometric figures used by Shepard and Metzler differed in orientation to each other between 0 and 180 degrees. Half of the pairs were matches that had been rotated; the other half were mirror images that could not be rotated to match. How would you go about answering questions about these pairs of figures? Would you create a visual image of the objects in your mind?

Visual imagery can activate various areas of the brain (indicated in red on this PET scan), especially the occipital lobe, which is responsible for processing visual information.

Psychological Detective

The study of visual imagery poses a difficulty for researchers: The process of thinking cannot be directly observed. How could researchers draw inferences about the mental processes involved in answering questions about the paired objects in Figure 8-1? Give this question some thought, and write down your answer before reading further.

Shepard and Metzler found that people were accurate in judging whether the pairs of figures were the same or different. When the object had been rotated a great deal, however, participants took longer to decide whether it was the same or different. Why? The researchers inferred that the increased time was spent mentally rotating the figures. Support for this conclusion is found in data showing that the greater the degree of rotation, the longer people take to rotate the configuration back to the original orientation. To behaviorists, such inferences about unseen mental processes are not a legitimate part of science. In science, however, inference is common: Geologists use the Earth's sediment layers to infer past events, and physicists cannot observe gravity directly, even though they study its effects.

Visual images allow us to scan information stored in memory and answer questions like the ones we asked earlier; they help us plan a course of action. For example, Albert Einstein's insight into the theory of relativity occurred when he created a visual image of chasing after and matching the speed of a beam of light (Kosslyn & Koenig, 1992). Later he turned this visual image into words. The following examples illustrate the value of imagery in our thinking, as well as its potential application in sports.

Suppose we need to describe the size of an acre. How might we convey this information? We could tell you that there are 43,560 square feet in an acre. Would that help you understand how large an acre is? Perhaps not. If, however, we used a visual image by telling you that an acre is about the size of a football field without the end zones, we would probably make it much more understandable.

Allan Paivio found that words like *book, house,* and *pencil* readily give rise to visual images and are easier to remember than low-imagery words like *ambition, integrity,* and *responsibility* (Paivio, 1971, 1986). High-imagery words offer two pegs on which to hang our memories: visual images and meaning (see Chapter 7). By contrast, low-imagery words must be remembered from their meaning alone.

Sports psychologists have found that visual imagery can be used as a practice technique to enhance performance in a number of sports (Romero & Silvestri, 1990). How does visual imagery enhance performance? Measures of blood flow in the brain show that mental practice can activate certain brain structures without actual physical movement; this activation appears to improve control and execution of movement (Decety & Ingvar, 1990).

Although images play an important role in cognition, not all of our thinking involves imagery. Much of it involves the formation and use of concepts. Next let's look at the role of concepts in thinking.

Visualizing a football field (without the end zones) makes it easier to comprehend the size of an acre.

Concepts. What would life be like if we had to deal separately with each individual animal, object, and person in our environment? How could we learn the names of all of them? We avoid such problems by using **concepts**—mental representations of a class (chairs, dogs, teachers) of things. Cabbage, peppers, and string beans are examples of the concept "vegetables." Concepts reduce the load on memory and enhance our ability to communicate; they also allow us to make predictions about our world.

Imagine sitting behind the wheel of an unfamiliar car. You can predict how the car operates, know the type of fuel needed, understand what happens when you put the key in the ignition, and locate several controls. You can do these things because you understand the concept "car." Much of what we learn in school, especially grade school, involves concepts such as colors, letters, species of living organisms, whole numbers and fractions, time, and distance. The use of such concepts makes communicating a great deal of information possible with relative ease.

One way we classify something as an example of a concept is to use rules that tell us what is and what is not an instance of the concept. Objects that follow the rules and have certain properties are called *positive instances* of the concept; the absence of such properties is the mark of a *negative instance* of the concept. Such rules work well for defining a concept such as "triangles" (closed, two-dimensional figures with three sides and angles that sum to 180 degrees) (Ross & Spalding, 1994).

Psychological Detective

An example of the rules approach to concepts can be found in Figure 8-2, where we have provided positive and negative instances of a concept. Your job is to figure out the set of rules we used. The first and fourth examples illustrate the concept (positive instances); the second and third examples do not illustrate the concept (negative instances). Write down the rule (or rules) that you believe define the concept before you go on. (The correct answer appears at the end of the chapter.)

One way you might learn this new concept is to use trial-and-error learning: You suggest a preliminary idea of what the concept might be; then you systematically test this idea or hypothesis on new examples. Researchers have used this approach in laboratory studies on concept formation. Were you able to identify the concept illustrated in Figure 8-2? As you thought about this concept, you probably noticed that it is not like those you encounter in everyday life, which usually are more complicated and not defined by neat sets of rules.

concepts

Mental categories that share common characteristics

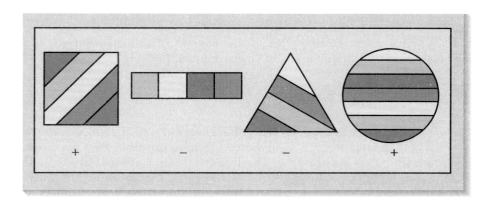

FIGURE 8-2 Sample material used in concept formation experiments.

FIGURE 8-3 All the animals in the photo on the left can be classified under the concept of "dog." Does the fox pictured on the right also belong to this concept? Why or why not?

Now try to list the properties that could be used to classify an animal as a dog. You might suggest four legs, some fur, a tail—but so far the list of properties still includes cats, foxes, and wolves. You can see that listing a set of properties as the rules for defining a concept may not work well. Why? As the dog example shows us, many concepts have fuzzy or unclear boundaries (see Figure 8-3). It seems that we do not form concepts the way participants in laboratory research do, by creating a list of properties. Instead we often rely on a **prototype,** or best example, of each concept. When we encounter a new object, we compare it to the prototype.

Think of the concept "fruit." What prototype (image or word) do you have in mind right now? Did you think of an orange, a plum, a date? Think of the concept "sports." Which of the following best fits your prototype of a sport: car racing, chess, or baseball? Now think of a bird. What do you have in mind? When psychologist Eleanor Rosch (1975) asked people to rate the degree to which various fruits represented the concept "fruit," they rated orange and apple as the best examples; tomato and avocado were least likely to serve as the prototype of a fruit. When we asked you to think of a bird, did you think of a cardinal, a robin, or a sparrow? You probably did not think of a chicken or a penguin.

We classify new objects according to their similarity to our prototypes. Thus membership in a concept category is not an all-or-nothing matter; rather, there are often varying degrees of similarity to the prototypes. The concepts we encounter and use every day tend not to have sharp boundaries and are not based on a specific, concrete set of properties.

Our concepts do not exist independently, isolated one from another; rather, they are organized into a hierarchy. Let's take the concept of furniture, for example, where related concepts organized under it become increasingly more specific. At the next-lower level, we might have different types of furniture, including one labeled "chair." Below this heading is yet another level that would include "recliner," "rocking chair," "desk chair," and so forth (Ross & Spalding, 1994).

We have discussed two types of raw material of thinking—images and concepts. Next we turn to the use of language in our thinking.

Thinking and Language

As we have seen, thinking can involve visual images as well as concepts, which are elements of our language. In addition, language can have even more dramatic influences on our thinking. The *linguistic relativity hypothesis* put forward by Benjamin Lee Whorf (1897–1941) suggests that syntax (word order) and vocabulary can mold our thinking. There is little doubt that elements of

prototype
A specific example of a particular concept that is readily brought to mind; viewed as the most typical or best example of a particular concept

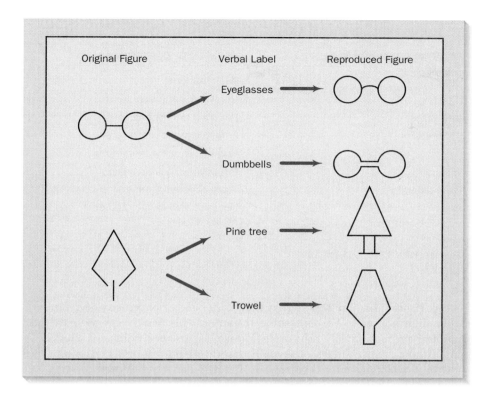

FIGURE 8-4 Effects of verbal labels on reproduction of drawings. The figures on the left were shown to participants along with one of the two verbal labels. The figures that these individuals drew later were influenced by the verbal labels they had been given.

Source: Carmichael, Hogan, & Walter, 1932.

language can influence how we perceive and remember our world. For example, in one study, people were shown drawings that could represent either of two objects; the experimenters gave the objects either of two names. As you see in Figure 8-4, the original language labels used by the experimenters influenced the participants' memory for and subsequent drawings of the objects (Carmichael, Hogan, & Walter, 1932).

Using Language to Limit Thought. Author George Orwell considered language to be a potential weapon that could be used to exploit, oppress, or manipulate people. Published in 1949, Orwell's novel *Nineteen Eighty-four* describes how a totalitarian state created an official state language called Newspeak to reduce the range of thought among its citizens. Although Orwell's account of language as a tool for political control was fictional, there are many current examples of the use of language to influence and control thinking (see Chapter 16).

William Lutz has collected examples of the use of language by business, educational, and governmental organizations to mislead or control perception and thinking. He uses the term *doublespeak* to describe language that is purposely designed to make the bad seem good, to turn a negative into a positive, or to avoid or shift responsibility (see Table 8-1). "Doublespeak is not a slip of the tongue, or language used out of ignorance, but is instead a very conscious use of language as a weapon or tool by those in power to achieve their ends at our expense," he claims (Lutz, 1990, p. xii).

One form of doublespeak is the *euphemism,* an acceptable or inoffensive word or phrase used in place of an unacceptable or offensive one. We frequently use "passed away" when talking to a bereaved person to demonstrate sensitivity for that person's feelings; no one is misled by this use of language. But when a Pentagon spokesperson announces that a military unit was "servicing the target," few of us realize that the unit was killing the

TABLE 8-1   **Examples of Doublespeak**

TERM IN ORDINARY ENGLISH	TERM IN DOUBLESPEAK
Desks	Pupil stations
Dead	Nonviable condition
New taxes	Revenue enhancement
Bar bouncer	Entertainment coordinator
Gym	Human resource laboratory
Invasion	Predawn vertical insertion
Farm animals	Grain-consuming animal units
Fired	Nonpositively terminated or reclassified

Sources: Lutz, 1990; Lederer, 1991.

enemy. Politicians may report that their cities have "pavement deficiencies" rather than potholes. Perhaps some readers of this book work as "part-time scanning professionals," otherwise known as grocery checkout clerks. In sum, although words may not actually determine our thoughts, examples like these indicate that careful selection of words can be designed to steer our thoughts in certain directions.

As we have seen, concepts can reduce the load on our memory because we don't have to remember every instance of objects separately. At times, we rely on memory to help us solve problems that are related to similar ones we have seen before. Even when a problem is not similar to past problems, we can turn to some problem-solving methods that have generally stood the test of time.

Problem Solving

Every day we encounter a variety of minor problems; occasionally we face major ones. You may find that the wheels of your car spin on the ice, a zipper on your luggage breaks as you wait to board a flight, or your lawnmower won't start. Some problems are easy to solve, others require great effort, and some may be unsolvable.

The problems we must solve can differ along several dimensions. One way in which problems differ is that some are well defined and others are ill defined. Well-defined problems have three specified characteristics: a clearly specified beginning state *(the starting point)*, a set of clearly specified tools or techniques for finding the solution *(the needed operations)*, and a clearly specified solution state *(the final product)* (Guenther, 1998). A well-defined problem might take the form of "How should I program my word processor to fit a 500-word essay on two pages?"

Here's another example of a well-defined problem. A certain psychologist (with little training in mechanics) took his lawnmower to a repair shop for a spring adjustment. The mechanic got the mower running but said it appeared that the battery might be going bad. The battery was then replaced. When the psychologist tried to start the mower, however, nothing happened. He reasoned that because it was unlikely that the new battery was bad, the problem must be elsewhere. Because the motor would not turn over at all, the psychologist deduced that the new battery was not properly connected. Once the battery's connecting cables were tightened, this well-defined problem was solved.

Ill-defined problems, on the other hand, have a degree of uncertainty about the starting point, needed operations, and final product. An ill-defined question might take the form of "How can I write the type of paper that will earn a grade of A?"

Problem-Solving Methods.   When you recognize that a problem exists, you can remember whether you faced a similar problem in the past; if so, you can retrieve the solution from memory and apply it to the current problem (see Chapter 7). If the problem is new and there is no solution in long-term memory, you can use several strategies to attack the problem. High-speed computers have provided scientists with a model that can be used to understand human thinking. To use the computer as a model of human thought, however, researchers need to know what human beings do when they solve problems. Two general approaches to solving problems can be programmed into a computer: algorithms and heuristics.

Algorithms.   One strategy you could use to solve some problems guarantees a correct solution in time (provided that a solution exists). An **algorithm** is a systematic procedure for solving a problem by evaluating all possible solutions. This approach guarantees a solution, if there is one. A simple example of an algorithm is the mathematical formula used to determine the area enclosed by a rectangle: Length multiplied by width gives the answer. Here is an opportunity for you to solve a problem that could involve use of an algorithm.

Psychological Detective

 An anagram *is a collection of letters that can be rearranged to form one or more words. Here's an anagram for you to solve:*

O E V S L

How would you go about finding the word? As you try to solve this problem, pay attention to exactly what you do.

Finding the solution to our anagram problem is a bit more complicated than using the formula for the area of a rectangle. Before you start writing all the possible arrangements of the five letters, be aware that they can be arranged in 120 different ways.

Algorithms tell you exactly what to do to reach a solution, but they can be time-consuming. If you spent one second on each combination of five letters, you could spend two minutes solving this simple anagram. Because most people solve the anagram in considerably less than two minutes, they probably use a method other than an algorithm. (The possible answers to the anagram are *solve, loves,* and *voles.*)

Algorithms do not provide answers when the problems are not clearly specified. There are no procedures that can be set up in advance to guarantee a solution for such problems. Moreover, some problems are so vast that algorithms are simply impractical. For example, chess players could not rely on algorithms because it would take centuries to examine all possible arrangements of the chess pieces, even if the players could evaluate them at a rate of several million per second.

Heuristics.   While you were trying to solve the anagram, you may have decided that the vowels O and E should be separated. It might also be a good idea to separate the V and the S because this combination of letters does not occur

algorithm
Systematic procedure for solving a problem by evaluating all possible solutions until the correct one is found

frequently in English words; on the other hand, SO is a common combination. These "rules of thumb" are examples of a problem-solving approach known as **heuristics.** Heuristics do not guarantee solutions, but they make more efficient use of time. Using heuristics may lead to quick solutions or to no solution at all.

Obstacles and Aids to Problem Solving.   Researchers have compared the problem solving of experts and nonexperts and found that experts know more information to use in solving problems. More important, experts know how to collect and organize information and are better at recognizing patterns in the information they gather. We can use the knowledge researchers have gained to improve our own problem-solving capabilities and avoid obstacles.

Setting Subgoals.   As we have noted, one way to study problem solving is to ask people to think aloud. This procedure enables a researcher to follow a person's problem-solving efforts. Using this technique, psychologists have found that expert problem solvers are adept at breaking problems down into subgoals, which can be attacked and solved one at a time. These intermediate subgoals can make problems more manageable and increase the chance of reaching a solution.

Psychological Detective

 Try this problem (adapted from Wickelgren, 1974). Nine adults and two children want to cross a river, using a raft that will carry either one adult or two children. The raft must be paddled by a person; it cannot be pulled across the river by a rope. How many times must the raft cross the river to accomplish this goal? (A round trip equals two crossings.) Write down your answer before reading further.

This is not an easy problem. Remember that effective problem solvers break down large problems into smaller subgoals; it is difficult to solve such a massive problem in one swipe. First you need to know how many crossings are required to transport one adult across the river. You find that it takes four crossings to move one adult across the river and return the boat to the original dock. If the two children cross the river, one of the children can return the boat. When the child returns, an adult can cross alone and the other child returns the boat. To move the nine adults across the river you must repeat that sequence of four trips eight more times—it will take 36 trips to move nine adults. One final trip is needed to move the two children across, for a total of 37 trips.

The keys to solving this problem are (1) to identify the sequence needed to transport one adult across the river and (2) to determine that the sequence can be repeated. Finding the solution requires that you break the problem into manageable intermediate subgoals (one person at a time).

Approach to Representing Problems.   Information that is not organized effectively can hinder problem solving. At times we may rely on memory; at other times external representations of a problem are helpful.

Consider the following problem (adapted from Bransford & Stein, 1984). There are three boxes of equal size. Inside each box are two smaller boxes. Inside each of the smaller boxes are four even smaller boxes. How many boxes are there all together?

The chances of solving this problem improve if the problem is represented somewhere other than in our heads. Students who were prompted to draw the problem solved it more frequently. (The correct answer is 33 boxes.)

heuristics
Educated guesses or rules of thumb for solving problems

What is ⅔ of ½? When you first read this problem, you may become confused and conclude that it is too difficult to solve. Now let's represent the problem as ⅔ × ½. This shows us that we could just as soon represent it as "What is ½ of ⅔?" This small change in representation converts a moderately difficult problem into a simple one whose answer almost jumps off the page (Bransford & Stein, 1984). Now try to solve a slightly different kind of problem.

Psychological Detective

Connect the nine dots in Figure 8-5 with four straight lines without lifting your pencil from the page. Try to solve this problem before reading further.

What did you see when you looked at the dots? Your perception of the dots probably followed the Gestalt principles of perceptual organization we discussed in Chapter 3. One difficulty that many people face in solving this problem is the tendency to see the dots as a boundary that encloses a rectangle. Thus our perception can lead us astray; however, nothing in the problem prevents us from taking our pencil outside the imaginary boundary that our mind creates. Try the problem; then turn to the end of the chapter for some solutions.

Here's another problem to solve. How would you put 27 pigs into 4 pens with an odd number of pigs in each pen? Most problem solvers try to figure a way to divide 27 into four odd numbers. This approach seems reasonable until you realize it is not possible. You tried this approach because you perceived the solution to involve four separate and distinct pens. *Hint:* Try looking at the relationship among the pens again. Consult the end of the chapter for the answer to this problem.

Now try to solve the problems presented in Figure 8-6.

Rigidity. Using our past experience is often helpful in solving problems, but sometimes it can block the path of our problem-solving efforts. **Rigidity** is the tendency to rely too heavily on past experience in solving problems.

A specific example of rigidity is the difficulty we experience in using familiar objects in new ways; this is termed **functional fixedness.** One example of functional fixedness, shown in Figure 8-7, is Maier's two-string problem (Maier, 1931). The two strings hanging from the ceiling are to be tied together. Among the objects in the room are a chair and a set of pliers.

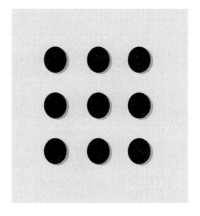

FIGURE 8-5 The nine-dot problem.

rigidity
Tendency to rely too heavily on past experiences in solving problems

functional fixedness
Inability to see new uses for familiar objects

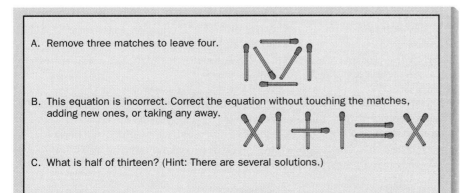

A. Remove three matches to leave four.

B. This equation is incorrect. Correct the equation without touching the matches, adding new ones, or taking any away.

C. What is half of thirteen? (Hint: There are several solutions.)

FIGURE 8-6 Try your hand at solving three more problems. The key to solving them is to break away from obvious ways of looking at things. Consider other perspectives; otherwise you will box yourself in, as you did if you treated the nine dots in Figure 8-5 as a rectangle. The answers appear at the end of the chapter.

Source: Michalko, 1991.

FIGURE 8-7 The Maier two-string problem. The two strings hanging from the ceiling are to be tied together, using only the chair and the pliers.

Source: Maier, 1931.

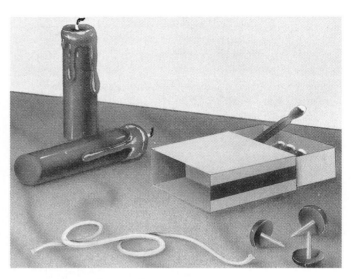

FIGURE 8-8 The candle problem. Using only the materials pictured, find a way to mount the candle on the wall.

Source: Duncker, 1945.

The strings are too far apart to allow the person to grasp both of them and tie them together. Not surprisingly, most of the solutions tried by participants in Maier's study involved the chair, although unsuccessfully. What is the solution? Think about it for a while.

The solution to this problem is to tie the pliers to the end of one string, set the string in motion like a pendulum, then catch it and tie it to the other string. The solution may seem obvious to you now, but only 39 percent of Maier's research participants solved the problem in the 10 minutes he allotted them. Why did they experience so much trouble with this problem? They displayed functional fixedness: They did not see that the pliers could be used in an unusual way. Now look at Figure 8-8.

Psychological Detective

Your task is to solve the problem presented in Figure 8-8. Imagine that you are in a small, nearly empty room. On the floor are the following objects: a box of wooden kitchen matches, a piece of string, a candle, and several thumbtacks. There is no electricity in the room. The task is to use the materials in the figure to mount the candle on the wall (Duncker, 1945). Write down your solution to the problem before reading further.

The solution is presented at the end of the chapter. Many people fail to solve this problem as a result of functional fixedness. Because the matches are shown in the box, people attempting to solve this problem often fail to see the box as a possible support for the candle.

The Set Effect. As we have shown, problem solvers can experience difficulty in representing a problem and may also rely only on common uses of objects. Depending on prior experience is another way we restrict ourselves to certain problem-solving approaches even if they are not the most effective. Such a bias is called the **set effect.**

set effect

Bias toward the use of certain problem-solving approaches because of past experience

TABLE 8-2 **The Luchins Water Jug Problem**

The goal is to obtain the desired quantity of water by using the jugs specified.

| | JUGS OF WATER | | | REQUIRED WATER |
Problem	A	B	C	D
1	29	3	0	20
2	21	127	3	100
3	14	163	25	99
4	18	43	10	5
5	9	42	6	21
6	20	59	4	31
7	23	49	3	20
8	28	59	3	25

Source: Luchins, 1946.

Luchins (1942) presented individuals with the problem outlined in Table 8-2. In this problem, the goal is to obtain the specified amount of water in Column D by using the jugs shown. After the first warm-up problem, the solution takes the form of B minus A minus 2C: Fill Jug B, then pour enough water to fill Jug A, and fill Jug C twice. This solution works for Problems 2 through 6.

Success in solving the first few water jug problems creates a "set" or tendency to use the same approach for the rest of the problems; after all, that approach worked. Nevertheless, there is an easier way to solve Problems 7 and 8. Those problems can be solved with fewer steps by first filling Jug A and then using it to fill Jug C. You may have failed to see this easier solution as you routinely applied the method that had worked so well for the earlier problems.

The problems we have described here have solutions. In problem solving we search for solutions; however, our thinking does not involve just solving problems. Sometimes we are asked to weigh advantages and disadvantages of different courses of action. Here there is no problem to be solved, but there is a decision to be made.

Making Decisions

Each day we make dozens—perhaps hundreds—of decisions. What is the easiest mode of transportation to take to the family reunion next week? Should I go to the bank today, or can it wait until tomorrow? Some of these decisions are easy; others are more difficult. How do we make such decisions?

The human brain enables us to process vast amounts of information quickly and accurately. Heuristics are often helpful and economical and can lead to good decisions; at times, however, they may also lead to bad decisions. The same principles that allow us to make judgments easily and often successfully are also responsible for some of our errors (Gilovich, 1991). In this section we look closely at some of the most important heuristics and their usefulness in making decisions.

Seeking Information to Confirm a Solution. The series 2, 4, 6 follows a rule concerned with how the numbers relate to one another. Your task is to discover the rule by suggesting other sets of numbers that follow it. Because the numbers increase by 2, many people suggest a series such as 12, 14, 16, followed by one like 22, 24, 26. Both series follow the rule. Buoyed by these two confirmations of the proposed rule, you might feel confident in announcing that the rule requires that the numbers increase by 2; however, you would be wrong. In fact, 79 percent of participants in a study by P. C. Wason (1960) confidently stated an incorrect rule when given this problem.

A common mistake in testing hypotheses is to commit to one hypothesis without adequately testing other possibilities—this is known as **confirmation bias.** In our example, the correct rule is that the series must consist of three positive numbers that increase. If you tried a series like 1, 2, 3, we would tell you that the series follows the rule and you could modify your initial hypothesis. People who found the correct rule earliest had generated more *negative instances,* which provided them with information that they could use to modify their hypotheses. This example illustrates an important aspect of our problem-solving and decision-making behavior: the tendency to seek instances that seem to confirm our beliefs, solutions, or hypotheses and to avoid instances that might disconfirm them.

John Hold (quoted in Gilovich, 1991) described children's reactions to a game of 20 questions in which the goal was to find a number between 1 and 10,000. The children cheered when the teacher said, "Yes, it is between 5,000 and 10,000," and groaned when the answer was "No, it is not between 5,000 and 10,000." Although both answers conveyed the same amount of information, confirmation was met with jubilation, and lack of confirmation was greeted with disappointment. As adults we do not outgrow the tendency to seek confirmation.

Representativeness. When we use the **representativeness heuristic,** we determine whether an event, an object, or a person resembles (or represents) a prototype. Suppose that Ted, a college graduate, is very careful and concerned about details. He rarely tells jokes and seems to lack creativity. Give him a task, and he will carry it out according to the rules. Is Ted an accountant or a writer? Your conclusion would most likely be based on the similarity you perceive between Ted's characteristics and those you believe are common among accountants and writers; you would be using the representativeness heuristic. In essence you are looking for a match between Ted and the prototype of either an accountant or a writer. Kahneman and Tversky (1973) found that including information about the number of accountants (30 percent) and writers (70 percent) in a group did not alter predictions of Ted's occupation. Participants were swayed by the similarity of Ted's personality characteristics to the commonly held stereotype of an accountant, which is quite different from the stereotype of a writer, who may be perceived as creative, tolerant, and open to experience. Because Ted's profile sounds like one we associate with accountants, it therefore represents our prototype of accountants. In this case the representativeness heuristic—a rule of thumb—leads us to assume that the similarity in the personality profile is a more powerful predictor than the odds of selecting an accountant from a group with a small number of accountants.

Now take out a few pennies from your pocket and drop them on the table. Here is a simple exercise that will illustrate the representativeness heuristic.

Psychological Detective

Suppose that you and a friend are tossing coins. Your friend tosses five heads in a row. It is your turn to bet on the next coin toss. Will it be heads or tails? Write down your choice and your reason for making the choice before reading further.

---

confirmation bias
Committing to one hypothesis without adequately testing other possibilities

representativeness heuristic
Heuristic in which one determines whether a particular instance represents a certain class or category

We expect the numbers of heads and tails to be approximately equal in the long run. Research findings and our own experience tell us that fair coins behave this way across many tosses. However, we also expect to find this approximate equality in the short run, although chance does not operate that way. Betting that the next toss will be tails after your friend has tossed five heads in a row is like saying the coin "knows" what happened on the previous five tosses. Although a run of five heads does not seem to be representative of a random distribution of heads and tails, the odds on the next coin toss are still 50:50. Those prior tosses do not affect the odds. This faulty assumption, which is quite common, is often called the gambler's fallacy—another example of the representativeness heuristic. With this fallacy, a series of heads and tails that does not look like chance is taken as evidence that some nonchance process is operating. Surprisingly, consecutive runs of heads and tails in random sequences can appear to be quite ordered. Some of the following computer-generated sequences look more random than the others:

Bets placed by gamblers are sometimes influenced by their observations of runs of numbers or colors. They assume that a run that does not appear to be random (i.e., a repeated sequence) will reverse itself in the short run.

HHHTT THHTT HTTTT HHTHH THTHH

Some gamblers may misread the series of heads and tails and assume they have a better chance of predicting the next toss than is actually the case.

Availability.   The **availability heuristic** involves making judgments or evaluations based on what comes to mind first (Kahneman & Tversky, 1973). Consider the following: Are there more words with *r* as the first letter than as the third letter? A quick word inventory leads you to conclude that there are more words that begin with *r*, but you are wrong. Why? Words that begin with *r*—*rich, reward, right*—come to mind more easily than words such as *fare, street,* and *word.*

We assume that easily recalled items occur more frequently than ones that do not come to mind readily. Moreover, we assume that what comes to mind easily is also more likely to occur in the future (MacLeod & Campbell, 1992). Ease of recall often is correlated with actual data—but not always. Who is most likely to be killed in a drunk-driving accident? Most people believe the answer is an *innocent victim.* According to the National Highway Traffic Safety Administration (1997), however, the person most likely to die in a drunk-driving accident is a *drunk driver.* Why do we give the wrong answer? It is easier to recall incidents in which an innocent person was the victim of a drunk-driving accident because such events are considered newsworthy. Drunk drivers die on the nation's highways every day, yet few of those accidents receive media attention.

Although the events covered by the media may not affect us directly, they play a role in how we assess our risk of accidents, catastrophes, or diseases. Imagine two of your friends discussing the relative safety of traveling to a vacation destination by either plane or automobile. News coverage of a recent plane crash leads them to decide in favor of travel by car, which they believe is safer. We may be misled because examples of airline accidents are dramatic and thus easy to recall. Yet more people are killed in cars and trucks during a single week than in plane crashes over the course of an entire year. For example, in 1994 there were 42,524 deaths in motor vehicle accidents (an average of more than 800 a week), whereas aviation-related accidents caused 723 deaths (U.S. Bureau of the Census, 1997).

Comparison.   We often make decisions by comparing the information we have obtained to some standard. Your standards are constantly changing, and these changes can affect your judgments. For example, a temperature of 68°F seems pleasant in the winter but cool in the summer.

availability heuristic
Heuristic in which the probability of an event is determined by how readily it comes to mind

Would you drive 20 minutes to save $5? Your answer may depend on the basis of comparison. If a toaster costs $45 at one store and the same toaster is available for $40 at another, are you likely to drive to the store with the lower price? Would you make the drive to buy a suit priced at $295 instead of $300 (Tversky & Kahneman, 1981)? Most people say they would make the drive for the toaster but not for the suit, yet the amount of money saved would be the same in both cases. These choices are examples of the just noticeable difference (see Chapter 3). In short, we tend to see the benefits or gains of a comparison in relative rather than absolute terms.

Framing. When we make decisions we are also influenced by whether our attention is drawn to positive or negative outcomes; psychologists refer to this presentation of an issue as **framing** (Guenther, 1998). When we make decisions we try to be risk averse; that means we want to stay away from negative outcomes. Unfortunately, this tendency has the potential to mislead us at times, causing us to fail to see that the way identical information is framed can make a dramatic difference in decision making. Let's consider an example. Imagine that you have lung cancer, and the treatment options are surgery or radiation. To help you make an informed decision, your physician tells you the results for lung cancer patients who selected surgery: 68 percent are alive after one year, and 34 percent are alive after five years. For lung cancer patients who selected radiation, 77 percent are alive after one year, and 22 percent are alive after five years. Given this information, which treatment do you select? The vast majority of people would select surgery.

Now let's change the framing a bit and see what happens. Suppose you are given the following information: Among patients who selected surgery, 32 percent are dead after one year and 66 percent are dead after five years.

On July 17, 1996 TWA flight 800, bound for Paris, exploded off the coast of Long Island (east of New York City) 10 minutes after it took off from JFK International Airport. All 230 passengers and crew members were killed. Media helicopters hovered over the scene and broadcast live footage that showed jet fuel burning on water that was littered with wreckage. In subsequent days and weeks there were numerous additional media reports on the search for survivors and wreckage. The extensive coverage given to such accidents leads us to overestimate the frequency of airplane accidents because examples are easy to recall.

framing

The tendency for decision making to be influenced by presentation of negative or positive outcomes; our decision making tends to be risk averse

> The outcomes for lung cancer patients who selected surgery were:
> 68% were alive after one year
> 34% were alive after five years

> The outcomes for lung cancer patients who selected radiation were:
> 77% were alive after one year
> 22% were alive after five years

> The outcomes for lung cancer patients who selected surgery were:
> 32% were dead after one year
> 66% were dead after five years

> The outcomes for lung cancer patients who selected radiation were:
> 23% were dead after one year
> 78% were dead after five years

FIGURE 8-9 The way an issue is framed can influence our decision-making process.

Among patients who selected radiation, 23 percent are dead after one year and 78 percent are dead after five years. Which treatment do you select now? Only a slight majority would select surgery. Note that the choices framed in terms of living or dying are identical (see Figure 8-9), yet the framing affects the option selected.

Keep in mind that the scenarios we have just described did not result from stupidity or a malfunctioning brain: "They illustrate how the mind actually works. Put in evolutionary terms, the mind has evolved to be effective in situations that are most likely to arise" (Restak, 1988, p. 238). We have developed some tried-and-true methods of making decisions that work most—but not all—of the time.

Creativity

Although we often face difficulties when trying to solve problems or in making decisions, we are capable of impressive and creative solutions and judgments. Yet **creativity,** or the ability to produce work that is both novel and appropriate, is a difficult concept to actually explain.

Defining Creativity.   Which of the mosaic designs in Figure 8-10 would you judge to be creative? Show these drawings to several friends, and ask for their opinions. Do they agree that some of them are creative and others are not? Which ones? Although you may find consensus, you and your friends might be unable to report the precise criteria that you used in deciding what constitutes creativity.

If there is no absolute standard for creativity, how can we judge whether a work is creative? Teresa Amabile (1982) has proposed a consensual assessment of creativity. She asked a group of judges to make global ratings based on their own definitions of creativity. The judges' ratings of both verbal and artistic products were consistent and reliable. People seem to agree on what is and is not creative.

creativity
The ability to produce work that is both novel and appropriate

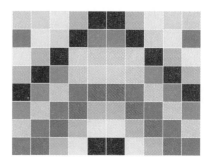
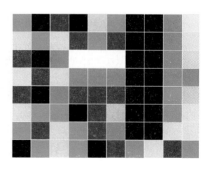
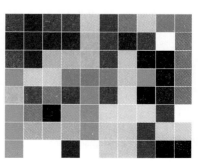

FIGURE 8-10 Judging creativity. These mosaics were constructed by individuals with different levels of creativity. Which would you judge to be creative?

Source: Barron, 1958.

Measuring Creativity. Intelligence tests were not designed to measure creativity, so it should not be surprising that the correlation between measures of creativity and intelligence is not strong (it is generally positive but low) (Sternberg, 1998). High intelligence does not guarantee high creativity, and low intelligence does not halt creativity. As psychologist Frank Barron (1988) points out, "The creative solution is not known beforehand, and there is an immense range of possibility for new developments once we get into a problem. Not only are there no 'right or wrong' answers, there really are no 'answers' at all, until they have been tested in someone else's perception, or by external reality." (p. 85). Barron's analysis suggests that many examples of creativity begin as ill-defined problems.

Imagine that thinking is like a line. When all lines of thought converge on one correct answer, we have an example of *convergent thinking*. By contrast, *divergent thinking* takes our thinking in different directions in search of multiple answers to a question. Of the two, divergent thinking is related more closely to creativity.

Sarnoff Mednick (1962) suggested that creativity involves seeing nontypical yet plausible ways of associating items or seeing aspects of an item that are real and useful but not usually the primary focus of our attention. You can gain insight into this process by completing items from the Remote Associates Test in Table 8-3. This test was designed to measure the process of making new associations. Success on the test calls for flexibility in making associations, fluency in the use of language, and originality.

Psychologists have devised other ways to measure creativity. In the Unusual Uses Test, for example, you would be asked to think of unusual uses for a common object such as a brick or a ball. In another measure of creativity, the Consequences Test, you would offer responses to the questions "What would happen if people could become invisible at will?" "What would happen if all electrical generating plants closed at noon each day?" "What would happen if everyone could read everyone else's mind?" The responses are judged on the basis of novelty and appropriateness. For example, in response to the first item, you could say, "It would rain for 40 days and 40 nights." Although this

---

TABLE 8-3   Sample Items from the Remote Associates Test

In this test you are presented with three words and asked to find a fourth word that is related to the other three. For example, what word do you think is related to these three?

cookies	sixteen	heart

The answer in this case is sweet. Cookies are sweet; sweet is part of the phrase *sweet sixteen* and part of the word *sweetheart.* Here is another example:

poke	go	molasses

The answer is *slow:* slow poke, go slow, slow as molasses. As you can see, the fourth word may be related to the other three for various reasons. Now try these.

1.	flap	tire	beanstalk
2.	mountain	up	school
3.	package	cardboard	fist
4.	surprise	line	birthday
5.	madman	acorn	bolt

Source: Mednick and Mednick, 1967.

response is novel (statistically rare), it is not appropriate in the context of the question. Conversely, if someone replied, "We couldn't see other people," the response would be appropriate but not creative. Thus there are two key elements in the definition of creativity as the ability to produce work that is both novel and appropriate.

Personal Factors in Creativity.   Are there other keys to understanding creativity? Several personal characteristics distinguish creative people from less creative people. Creative people are not afraid of hard work; they give it their undivided attention and often persevere in the face of obstacles: "Almost every major creative thinker has surmounted obstacles at one time or another, and the willingness not to be derailed is a crucial element of success" (Sternberg & Lubart, 1991, p. 13). For example, Thomas Edison conducted more than 2,000 experiments with different possible filaments for a light bulb before finding one that would not burn out quickly.

Another mark of a creative person is a willingness to take risks and make mistakes. Such people can put their self-esteem on the line for the prospects of rewards greater than others might ever dream about. For example, the experts declared Fred Smith's concept for Federal Express to be unworkable. Today Federal Express is the world leader in delivering packages (from letters to jet engines) anywhere in the world overnight. Creative people seem able to tolerate ambiguity, complexity, or lack of symmetry. According to one expert, "It is clear that creative persons are especially disposed to admit complexity and even disorder into their perceptions without being made anxious by the resulting chaos. It is not so much that they like disorder per se, but that they prefer the richness of the disordered to the stark barrenness of the simple" (MacKinnon, 1978, p. 62).

Situational Factors in Creativity.   Creativity often emerges when people rearrange what is known in new and unusual ways. These rearrangements can yield creative ideas, goods, and services (Michalko, 1991). Humor and playfulness provide fertile ground for forming new associations and arrangements. Mozart recognized this possibility when he wrote, "When I feel well and in a good humor, or when I am taking a drive or walking after a good meal, . . . thoughts crowd into my mind as easily as you could wish" (Ghiselin, 1952, p. 44).

Alice Isen and colleagues asked college students to solve the candle problem presented in Figure 8-8 (Isen, Daubman, & Nowicki, 1987). Before trying to solve the problem, some students watched a comedy film; 75 percent of them found the solution. By contrast, only 13 percent of students who did not watch a comedy film solved the problem. In another experiment, Isen and her colleagues placed students into three groups. The students in the first group watched a comedy film; those in the second group exercised for two minutes; and the third group, the control group, had no special preparation. All the students then tried to solve items similar to those in the Remote Associates Test in Table 8-3. The first group solved more items than the other two; Isen and her colleagues concluded that induced positive feelings can facilitate creativity.

Teresa Amabile and her colleagues (Amabile, Hennessey, & Grossman, 1986) asked participants to tell a story or make a collage. Some of them completed the work in exchange for a reward; others were not rewarded. Judgments of the creativity exhibited in the stories or collages were lower when the participants had received a reward. This result was consistent with other studies that have found that extrinsic rewards (as opposed to intrinsic rewards) can change the perceptions of activities and also lower interest in them.

A new perspective on the motivation underlying creativity focuses on how the motivator actually affects the person: Does it direct attention toward the task rather than the goal? A *task-focusing* motivator energizes a person to work and keeps the person's attention on the task. By contrast, a *goal-focusing* motivator leads a person to focus attention on rewards such as money to the detriment of the task. Intrinsic motivators tend to be task-focusing because a goal such as personal fulfillment is integrated with the task. Extrinsic motivators tend to be goal-focusing because the rewards are noticeable and distinct from the task. People vary, however, as to how they focus. Some people focus on the goals, which may distract them from the task; others focus on the task. Thus extrinsic motivators may have either benefits or negative effects, depending on how they influence the person's focus (Lubart, 1994).

Creativity often flourishes under the right mix of intrinsic and extrinsic motivation. Thomas Edison's first invention was an automatic vote recorder for Congress. When he presented it to a member of Congress, he was told that efficiency in lawmaking was the last thing Congress wanted. From that point on, Edison stated that the only reason he invented was to make a lot of money; he didn't have the time or interest to modify the world to fit his inventions.

Enhancing Creativity at Work. Businesses grow and prosper by adapting and creating new products and markets. Consequently, the business community has shown growing interest in developing their employees' creativity (Fontenot, 1993). Such companies as Frito-Lay and Texas Instruments have introduced creativity-enhancing methods into their training programs with outstanding results. Frito-Lay, for example, attributes significant cost savings to its creativity programs (Van Gundy, 1995). There is no magic in enhancing creativity; it takes the right attitude and technology in a work climate that is receptive to creative thinking and new ideas (Van Gundy, 1995). Individual and organizational creativity are closely interlocked (Amabile, 1988). For example, environmental conditions at work—including freedom over one's work, sufficient time to think, and collaboration across divisions—facilitate creativity (Amabile, 1988).

One key to developing creativity is to be alert to potential problems that might be solved with creative solutions. For example, a track coach paid attention when his runners complained their running shoes were causing blisters. The coach, Bill Browerman, was confident he could improve the design of existing shoes. He cut patterns for the shoes out of grocery bags and found lightweight materials that improved cushion and traction. Browerman's shoes are known today as the brand name Nike (Parachin, 1992).

We could also learn from the story of Swiss inventor George de Mestral. The name may be unfamiliar, but his invention is well known. One day he went hunting with his dog; they accidentally brushed against a bush that left both of them covered with burrs. When he tried to remove them, they clung stubbornly to his clothes. To most of us this would be a minor annoyance, but not to de Mestral. After he got home, he looked at the burrs under a microscope and discovered that hundreds of tiny hooks on each burr had snagged the threads of his pants. The result of this accident was Velcro fasteners.

We may not all brush up against new ideas like de Mestral did, but we can set the table for creativity. Unfortunately, most people believe the world is divided into two types of people—the creative ones and the rest of us. Yet if you spend some time watching children play, you'll see a great deal of cre-

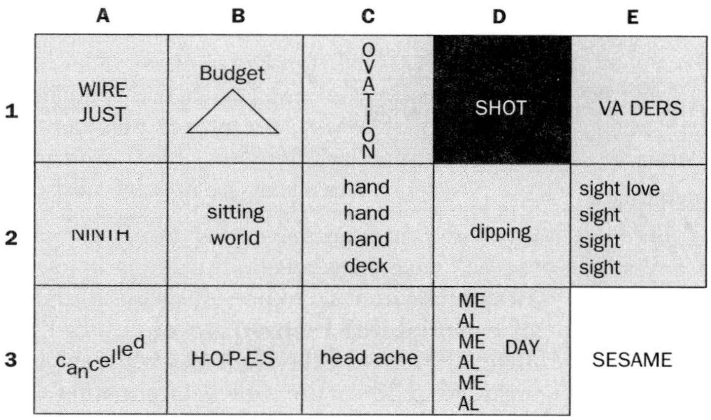

	A	B	C	D	E
1	WIRE JUST	Budget △	O V A T I O N	SHOT	VA DERS
2	NINTH	sitting world	hand hand hand deck	dipping	sight love sight sight sight
3	c a n c e l l e d	H-O-P-E-S	head ache	ME AL ME AL DAY ME AL	SESAME

FIGURE 8-11 Creativity consultants often suggest that their clients do some puzzle-solving exercises to prepare them to be more creative. In this puzzle, each box is a kind of puzzle for familiar words or phrases. For example, Box 1a can be read "Just under the wire." Try to decipher the other boxes. The solutions can be found at the end of the chapter.

Source: Wujec, 1995.

ativity (Wujec, 1995). What happens to diminish creativity as we become adults? Children's imaginations roam freely and are not limited by reality because they are not constrained by adult rules of thinking: "They don't know that they have to color inside the lines" (Wujec, 1995, p. 20). Adults are expected to be serious, yet playfulness and humor can help develop flexible thinking. We need to be open to "fooling around" with ideas to explore new mental connections.

There are a number of ways to stimulate a creative mind-set, including injecting a bit of humor and playfulness into the work situation. A related way is to get into a puzzle-solving frame of mind (see Figure 8-11).

Michael Michalko (1991), a full-time creativity consultant, believes that negative thoughts about one's potential for creativity are harmful. Quite often, people fail to develop creative ideas because they do not believe they can be creative (Parachin, 1992). The first step in developing the potential for creativity is to acknowledge and confront these negative thoughts and replace them with positive thoughts. For example, many workers say to themselves, "I'll never be able to do it." This thought can be altered to the following: "I'll do a little bit at a time to get started. There's no reason that I have to do it all on a crash schedule."

Creativity consultants aim to inject change into the lives of employees. They encourage employees to break habits by taking a different route to work, listening to a different radio station, or reading a different newspaper. These minor changes are designed to help employees break out of a rut, expose them to new things, and get them thinking rather than operating on automatic pilot. Employees are encouraged to look around, to make notes, to collect a lot of ideas.

We also need to recognize that creativity can take many forms in the business community. Henry Ford said he invented nothing new; he combined the inventions of others into a car. Ivory soap was run through an ice cream machine to add air that increased the sudsing and allowed the bar to float. Sometimes the creativity is remarkably simple: The key to the success of Domino's pizza was promising home delivery in 30 minutes or less.

Creative people can look at the same thing as everyone else but see something different (Wujec, 1995). For example, Arthur Fry, a chemist, was working with a glue that was to be used on fixed surfaces like bulletin boards. Unfortunately, it did not work well. One day while singing he had a creative insight: The adhesive could be used on a bookmark that would replace the little pieces of paper he used to mark his hymn book. Fry used the glue to develop Post-It notes.

Review Summary

1. Behavioral psychologists believed thinking could be equated with muscle movements of the vocal apparatus; however, research has shown that this is not correct.

2. Cognitive psychology is the study of thinking. **Thinking** involves manipulation of information that can take the form of images or concepts. **Visual imagery** is the experience of seeing without the object or event actually being viewed.

3. Concepts are mental representations that facilitate thinking and reduce the number of elements we must consider. Concepts may be defined by their properties; however, we usually identify specific examples as members of a concept by judging their degree of similarity to a **prototype,** or best example, of the concept.

4. An **algorithm** is a method of solving problems that involves systematically exploring all possible solutions until the correct one is reached. Algorithms can be time-consuming and do not work for problems that are not clearly defined.

5. Heuristics are educated guesses or rules of thumb that are used to solve problems. Although the use of heuristics does not guarantee a solution, it is more time-efficient than using algorithms.

6. Rigidity is the tendency to rely on past experiences to solve problems. One form of rigidity, **functional fixedness,** is the inability to use familiar objects in new ways. Likewise, **set effect** predicts that we will attempt to use solutions that have been successful in the past, even when they are not the most effective.

7. The **representativeness heuristic** predicts that we will base decisions on the similarity of characteristics of the situation to previously established concepts. The **availability heuristic** involves judging the probability of events by the readiness with which they come to mind. The way in which information is presented can dramatically alter our decision making; this effect is called **framing.** We also make decisions by comparing the information we have received to some standard. Heuristics facilitate good decisions but may sometimes result in bad ones.

8. Creativity seems to depend on divergent thinking, rather than the convergent thinking that is assessed in tests of intelligence. Creative people have a high capacity for hard work, a willingness to take risks, and a high tolerance for ambiguity and disorder.

9. The business community is interested in enhancing creativity to develop and market products and services. Various methods are used to enhance creativity, including encouraging employees to believe that they can be creative, breaking routines, and engaging in humorous and playful activities.

Study Break

1. Identify each of the following:
   a. Making an educated guess based on some rule of thumb to solve a problem
   b. Using a mechanical method to generate all possible solutions to a problem
   c. Relying heavily on past experience in solving current problems
   d. Deciding on the basis of a style of dress that she is an automobile mechanic
2. What is the advantage of creating an external representation when you are solving a problem?
3. You are engaged in a thought game in which your task is to discover the rule by which a series of numbers has been constructed. You are presented with the series 2, 5, 8. What is the next number? You answer 11. Which approach to problem solving does your guess illustrate? Why might this approach not be effective?
4. For an undergraduate research project, Sara decides to investigate the relationship between intelligence and creativity. Through consultation with her faculty supervisor, she selects measures of intelligence and creativity. When the data are collected, she correlates the scores for all the participants in her sample. What is the most likely outcome of her research?
   a. It is impossible to correlate creativity, so her research will not reveal any results.
   b. The tests of creativity and intelligence will reveal a low, positive correlation.
   c. The tests of creativity and intelligence will reveal a high, negative correlation.
   d. The tests of creativity and intelligence will reveal a moderate, negative correlation.
5. Which of the following has been found to facilitate creativity?
   a. Remarkable rote memory
   b. A history of childhood rebellion
   c. Positive feelings induced by humor
   d. The presence of the mental disorder schizophrenia

6. Teresa Amabile has developed a method of identifying creative works. Which of the following statements could summarize her work?
  a. Creativity is accomplished under conditions that focus on extrinsic motivation.
  b. Only experts in a given field are capable of offering legitimate opinions on creativity.
  c. People reliably identify what they think is creative even if they fail to describe a precise definition.
  d. There is no way to identify creative works; we must rely on the artist to make such judgments lest we inhibit free expression.

Intelligence

Alex's second-grade teacher gave him a letter to take to his parents. Because Alex is experiencing difficulty in class, the teacher consulted with the school psychologist. They agreed that it would be potentially beneficial to administer an intelligence test and other measures to Alex. They expect that the information obtained from the testing session will help them plan a better educational program to meet Alex's needs. ***Why were psychological tests first developed?*** ▣

You are familiar with psychological tests because you have taken such tests in school. A psychological test is an objective measure of a sample of behavior that is collected according to well-established procedures. Thus psychological tests are like the tests in other sciences: They are composed of observations made on a small but carefully chosen *sample* of a person's behavior (Anastasi & Urbina, 1997). Such tests are used for a range of purposes, including measuring differences among people in characteristics such as intelligence and personality. The primary purpose of one of the first psychological tests was to identify children with below-average intellectual ability so that they could be given schooling designed to improve that ability.

Psychological Detective

Think about what makes a person intelligent. What behaviors or characteristics do you expect to observe in someone who is judged to be intelligent? Write down your answer before reading further.

To answer this question, Robert Sternberg and his colleagues (1981) asked people in supermarkets, train stations, and a college library to record behaviors and characteristics related to the concept of intelligence. The researchers then gave the resulting list of behaviors and characteristics to other people, who rated the importance of each as an element of intelligence. The laypersons' descriptions of intelligence emphasized practical problem solving ("identifies connections among ideas"), verbal ability ("speaks clearly and articulately"), and social competence ("displays understanding of the world at large"). Experts who were asked similar questions viewed intelligence in a comparable fashion, with some minor differences of emphasis (Snyderman & Rothman, 1987).

Cultural Views of Intelligence

THE DESCRIPTIONS OF INTELLIGENCE OFFERED BY PEOPLE IN SUPERMARKETS OR college libraries were obtained in the United States. How a person defines intelligence depends on whom we ask, and the answers differ across time and place (Sternberg & Kaufman, 1998). Thus what behaviors are perceived as examples of intelligent behavior is influenced in part by culture. Moreover, culture can influence the processes that underlie intelligent behavior as well as the direction that intellectual development takes (Miller, 1997).

One study found that the Japanese place greater emphasis on the process of thinking than people in the United States (Tajima et al., 1991). Japanese people listed several characteristics of intelligence that deal with the process of thinking, such as "good judgment" and "good memory." Americans placed greater importance on external appearances and outcomes when listing characteristics that describe intelligence. The conceptions of intelligence among Taiwanese Chinese included interpersonal intelligence, intrapersonal intelligence, and self-assertion (Sternberg & Kautman, 1998). Differences such as these suggest that there may be some significant differences between Eastern and Western conceptions of intelligence—differences that may be due, in part, to the kinds of skills that cultures value (Srivastava & Misra, 1996).

Conceptions of intelligence in Africa focus on skills that facilitate and maintain harmonious group relations (Ruzgis & Grigorenko, 1994). For example, parents in Kenya emphasize responsible participation in family and social life as important aspects of intelligence (Super & Harkness, 1982). What's more, Kenyan children from a rural village perform better on tests of indigenous intelligence that require them to perform a task that is adaptive for them (recognizing how to use natural herbal medicines to fight illness) than they do on Western style vocabulary tests (Sternberg, 1998). In Zimbabwe the word for "intelligence," *ngware,* means to be prudent and cautious, particularly in social relationships (Sternberg & Kaufman, 1998).

As we discuss the concept of intelligence in the following section, it is important to be aware that the definition used in Western cultures, especially the United States, will not necessarily match definitions used in other parts of the world. Moreover, efforts to develop tests to quantify intelligence are primarily a Western phenomenon. Those tests may not be appropriate when translated and used in other cultures because the underlying definition of intelligence does not fit the culture's view.

In the United States, many experts do agree on the kinds of mental activities and knowledge that fall into the domain of intelligence. We can define **intelligence** as the overall ability to excel at a variety of tasks, especially those related to success in schoolwork.

Judging from the level of agreement in the United States on the characteristics of an intelligent person, the measurement and understanding of intelligence would not seem controversial. Nevertheless, this topic is one of the most contentious in psychology. The next section explores how psychologists measure intelligence, why these measures were developed, and why the concept of intelligence is controversial.

intelligence
The ability to excel at a variety of tasks, especially those related to academic success

The History of Intelligence Testing

We can trace the study of differences in intelligence to an Englishman, Francis Galton (1822–1911), an inventor and explorer. This wealthy man had a great passion for measurement and shared an interest in heredity with his cousin, Charles Darwin. Galton suggested that differences in levels of intellectual ability are due to hereditary factors. To check this notion, he traced the family trees of approximately 1,000 distinguished artists, judges, military commanders, poets, scientists, and statesmen and found that a large proportion of these eminent people had eminent family members. On the basis of such findings, Galton contended in his book *Hereditary Genius: An Inquiry into Its Laws and Consequences* (1869) that eminence and creativity run in families because they are inherited characteristics.

Galton set out to measure differences in degree of eminence and, presumably, in the level of intelligence in his anthropometric ("human measurement") laboratory in London. Beginning in 1884, visitors stopped in to have their keenness of eyesight and reaction time to stimuli measured. Galton believed that highly successful people perceive the world more accurately than less successful people. Thus their eyesight should be keener and their reactions quicker than those of less eminent people. Contrary to Galton's beliefs, the results showed that eminent people did not perceive the world any better than others.

Alfred Binet (1857–1911), a French psychologist, spent years considering ways to measure intelligence. Eventually he decided to assess more complex intellectual functions than sensory discrimination, including judgment, memory, and reasoning.

In 1881, the French Ministry of Education decreed that all children must attend school. Before that time the schools were not obligated to teach children with widely varying ability levels because slow learners usually did not attend school. Consequently, the curriculum was geared to average and above-average students. After the decision, teachers had to adapt their methods to teach children with a wide range of abilities. In 1904, a French commission studying the education of children with below-average ability decided that placing slower learners in special classes would be more effective than keeping them with learners performing at grade level or higher. Although teachers could offer judgments concerning their students' abilities, the commission recognized that such judgments might be tainted by factors (such as discipline problems) that were not related to ability. Their search for an objective measure as the basis for class placement decisions concerning the children led them to Binet.

Binet and his colleague Theophile Simon (1873–1961) collected simple problems that required higher mental processes such as reasoning, memory, and spatial thinking. In 1905, they developed the Binet-Simon scale. Typical items required children to define common words ("What is a pencil?"), name objects seen in pictures, tell how two objects are alike, ("How are a cow and a dog alike?"), draw designs from memory, and repeat a string of spoken digits. Completion of some items seemed to represent an ability level that was typical of children of a certain age, whereas completion of other items was associated with those of a different age. On the basis of this observation, Binet and Simon proposed the concept of **mental age.** To determine a child's mental age, they compared the child's performance to that of the average child at each age. For example, a mental age of 6 indicated that a child's performance was similar to the performance of other average 6-year-olds. A 6-year-old child with a mental age of 8 performed much better than the average 6-year-old. Binet thought the use of his scale would increase the likelihood that all children would receive an appropriate education. He fervently believed that one's attention, memory, and judgment could be improved with practice and appropriate methods.

Alfred Binet's pioneering work led to the development of the first widely used intelligence test.

mental age

Measure of intelligence derived by comparing an individual's score on an intelligence test with the average performance of individuals of the same age

intelligence quotient (IQ)
Score that indicates how an individual compares with others on an intelligence test

The Stanford-Binet Intelligence Scale. In the United States, Lewis Terman (1877–1957), a Stanford University psychologist, revised the Binet-Simon scale and extended it for use with adults. His Stanford-Binet Intelligence Scale was first published in 1916 and has been modified several times since then; the current version is the Stanford-Binet IV.

In 1912, the German psychologist William Stern (1871–1938) devised an index of intelligence by dividing a child's mental age (MA) by his or her chronological age (CA). Terman adopted this idea in the Stanford-Binet test and added one more feature; he multiplied the index by 100 to eliminate decimals. The resulting statistic is the **intelligence quotient (IQ),** calculated, as just explained, as MA/CA × 100. Thus one's IQ is a ratio of mental age divided by chronological age, multiplied by 100. For example, a 9-year-old child with a mental age of 9 would have an IQ of 100 (9/9 × 100 = 100). If the same child had a mental age of 6, the calculation of the IQ would be 6/9 × 100 = 67. Finally, if the child's mental age was 12, the IQ would be 12/9 × 100 = 133. The intelligence quotient made it possible to express a child's intellectual ability relative to that of children of the same age.

The Wechsler Scales. When David Wechsler (1896–1981) was chief psychologist at Bellevue Hospital in New York City, he found it difficult to test adults with the Stanford-Binet Intelligence Scale. Although the Stanford-Binet had been adapted for testing adults by adding more difficult items, time limits on some of the items handicapped a number of adults. So even though the concept of mental age could be applied to children, whose intellectual ability changes from year to year, it could not be applied to adults. The pace of change in intelligence slows considerably in the adult years, so the mental ages of the average 28- and 29-year-old are not likely to differ. For these reasons, Wechsler developed a new intelligence test for adults. Scores on this test are calculated by comparing a person's score with scores obtained by people of a range of ages rather than a single age. The current version of this test, known as the Wechsler Adult Intelligence Scale–III (WAIS–III), is used to assess people between the ages of 16 and 74 (Wechsler, 1997).

Wechsler's scales have also been adapted to cover earlier ages. The Wechsler Intelligence Scale for Children–III (WISC–III) tests children aged 6 to 16 (see Figure 8-12), and the Wechsler Preschool and Primary Scales of

The information from an intelligence test can reveal learning disabilities as well as identify a child's areas of strength.

SUBTEST (VERBAL)	DESCRIPTION	SAMPLE ITEMS
Information	Orally presented questions that tap knowledge of common events, objects, places, and people.	How many wings does a bird have? How many nickels make a dime?
Similarities	Child is asked to explain the similarity in pairs of words that are presented orally.	In what way are a lion and tiger alike? In what way are a saw and a hammer alike?
Arithmetic	A series of arithmetic questions are to be solved without use of pencil and paper or calculator.	Three women divided eighteen golf balls equally among themselves. How may golf balls did each person receive?
Vocabulary	Child must provide definitions for a series of orally presented words.	What does **near** mean? What does **slander** mean?
Comprehension	A series of orally presented questions that require the child to give solutions to everyday problems or to demonstrate understanding of social rules and concepts.	What should you do if you see someone forgot his book when he leaves a restaurant? Why is copper often used in electrical wires?
Digit Span	Number sequences are presented orally, and the child is asked to repeat them verbatim or in reverse order.	I am going to say some numbers. Listen carefully, and when I am through you say them right after me: 2, 4, 7. Repeat these numbers backward: 4, 6, 1, 7, 5.
SUBTEST (PERFORMANCE) Picture Completion	The child is asked to identify the important part that is missing in each of a set of colorful pictures of common objects and themes.	Look at this picture. What important part is missing?
Coding	Each of a series of shapes or numbers is paired with a simple symbol; based on a key, the child draws the symbol in its corresponding shape or under the corresponding number.	Look carefully at the key that matches numbers with symbols. Then write the symbol that goes with each number in the space below it.
Picture Arrangement	A set of colorful pictures is presented out of order, and the child rearranges them into a logical story sequence.	Arrange the pictures on these cards so they tell a story that makes sense.
Block Design	The child uses two-color blocks to replicate a design from a model or a picture.	Arrange the blocks so they look like the design in the picture.
Object Assembly	The child assembles a set of puzzles of common objects.	Put this puzzle together as quickly as you can.
Mazes	The child uses a pencil to solve a set of increasingly difficult mazes.	This is a maze. You are to start here (X) and finish here (y) without crossing any lines. Try your best not to go into any blind alleys.

FIGURE 8-12 The Wechsler Intelligence Scale for Children–III (WISC–III) consists of 12 subtests, divided into verbal and performance (perceptual-motor) subtests.

Source: Adapted from Wechsler, 1991.

Intelligence–Revised (WPPSI–R) is used to assess children aged 4 to 6½ (Wechsler, 1992, 1994). The multiple scores of the Wechsler subtests provide valuable information about individual strengths and weaknesses and can be helpful in identifying learning disabilities in children.

The Stanford-Binet Intelligence Scale and the Wechsler intelligence tests are individual tests (meaning that one person is tested at a time) that must be administered by a qualified examiner. Administering one of these tests takes between one and two hours. Individual intelligence tests offer several advantages as compared with group tests. The examiner can directly observe the examinee's reactions and put him or her at ease before beginning the test. The examiner can also determine whether the examinee understands the instructions. When large numbers of people must be tested, however, these measures of intelligence are time-consuming.

Principles of Psychological Tests

A psychological test is like a three-legged stool: If one leg is missing or broken, the stool collapses. Like that stool, psychological tests have three legs representing the essential elements for their effective and appropriate use: reliability, validity, and standardization. These principles apply to all psychological tests, whether they are designed to measure intelligence or personality (see Chapter 12).

Reliability.   To stand up to scrutiny, a psychological test must demonstrate **reliability;** that is, it must yield relatively consistent or repeatable results. Like other measuring devices, a psychological test is of little value if it provides inconsistent results. For example, you might be delighted to find that your bathroom scale reads 140 pounds, indicating that you lost the 12 pounds you wanted to shed. But when you step on the scale again to double-check the weight, the digits flash 154! Your scale is of little value because it is not reliable; it is time to buy a new one. If the scale were a psychological test, it would be time to look for a new measure.

Psychologists use several approaches to determine whether a test is reliable. They can administer a test twice to a group of people, separating the administrations by a short time period (a few days or a week). Using a correlation coefficient, they can measure the similarity in the scores obtained on the two occasions (see Chapter 1). If the scores are similar, they have established *test-retest reliability.* In another approach, known as the *alternate-forms method,* two different but equivalent forms of a test are administered to the same group of people. If the individuals' scores on the two forms are comparable, the test is reliable.

A psychological test has good reliability if the correlation coefficient that describes the similarity in pairs of scores is .80 or higher. The reliability of the Stanford-Binet and Wechsler intelligence tests is generally .90 or higher. Even if a measure provides reliable scores, however, we need to know whether the test is valid before we are ready to use it.

Validity.   A psychological test can be reliable, but it is of little value unless it is valid as well. **Validity** tells us whether the test actually measures what we intend it to measure. Suppose that we decide to measure anxiety by asking people to write down the names of the Seven Dwarfs. The written reports might be very reliable, yet those reports would have nothing to do with anxiety. Reliability does not guarantee validity.

How do psychologists establish test validity? The information they use varies with the type of test and the purpose for which it was designed. For example, for most of the tests you take in college, validity can be established by demonstrating that the test reflects the course content. Students who complain to professors that tests cover only a small part of the material or do not reflect the course material are questioning the *content validity* of the test. When a test

"You can't build a hut. You don't know how to find edible roots and you know nothing about predicting the weather. In other words, you do terribly on our I.Q. test."

reliability
Degree to which repeated administrations of a psychological test yield consistent scores

validity
Degree to which a psychological test measures what it intends to measure

is used to predict whether examinees will succeed in a particular task or job, the test should have high *predictive validity*.

Another way psychologists establish test validity is by demonstrating relationships between test scores and other measures or behaviors that should in theory be related to the test. For example, we would expect a valid test of anxiety while delivering a speech in front of a class to be related to physiological responses (e.g., how much you perspire), amount of uncertainty in a speech (say, the number of "ums" and "ahs"), ability to maintain eye contact with listeners, and several other behaviors. The relationship between the test and these various responses is known as *construct validity*.

Standardization.   The third crucial element of a well-developed psychological test is **standardization,** meaning that the test is administered the same way every time it is used. The instructions, time limits (if any), and scoring procedures must remain identical from one use to the next.

The development of norms is another important aspect of test standardization. At the beginning of Chapter 1 we met Patty who completed an IQ test on the internet. She wondered what her obtained score meant; perhaps she asked a friend, "What did you get?" If so, she was searching for information to help her interpret her score by comparing it to those obtained by others. **Norms** are scores obtained by a relatively large sample of similar people on the same test. They provide the frame of reference we need to interpret our own scores on that test.

The scores that describe many physical and psychological characteristics, including height, weight, anxiety, and intelligence, are distributed in the population in a certain way. Most people obtain scores near the middle of the distribution of test scores or physical measurements. The number of people obtaining a given score decreases as we move from the middle to the tails of the distribution (see Figure 8-13). For example, the height of an average adult American is about 68 inches. The heights of most adults tend to be close to this average; few adults are 38 inches or 88 inches tall. This commonly encountered distribution of scores is called the **normal distribution** (or *bell-shaped curve*; see Appendix A); measures of intelligence fit this distribution with the average (mean and median) score set at 100. About

standardization
The development of procedures for administering psychological tests and the collection of norms that provide a frame of reference for interpreting test scores

norms
Distribution of scores obtained by a large sample of people who have taken a particular psychological test

normal distribution
Symmetrical, bell-shaped distribution having half the above and below the mean

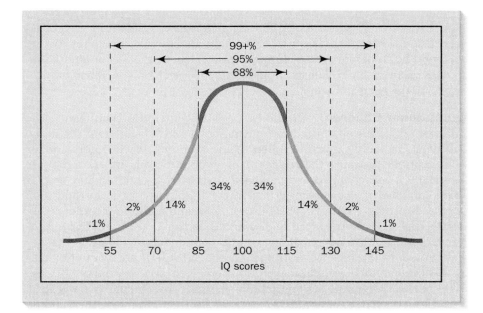

FIGURE 8-13 Normal curve of intelligence test scores. This curve has proved very useful to psychologists as well as to researchers in other disciplines. Although the curve is derived from theoretical mathematics, researchers found that many psychological and biological variables are distributed in the general population in a manner that fits the curve. As you can see, the majority of the population obtains IQ scores that are close to the mean of 100; scores further away from the mean occur less often.

STUDY CHART

Principles of Psychological Tests

Reliability: Does the test yield consistent results?

- If a test is administered on Monday to a group of fourth through eighth graders, will they obtain similar scores when the same test is readministered the following week?
- There are two forms of a test designed to measure test anxiety in college students; they are designated Form A and B. Will students' scores on Form A be similar to their scores on Form B?

Validity: Does the test measure what it was intended to measure?

- If a test is designed to measure spatial ability needed in the job of an airplane pilot, will the scores on the test predict which persons will make the best pilots?
- Are scores on tests of intelligence related to the grades students receive in various elementary and high school classes?
- Are persons who receive high scores on a test that seeks to identify characteristics related to depression likely to be diagnosed as depressed when they are interviewed by clinical psychologists and psychiatrists?

Standardization and Norms: Does the test have guidelines that specify the instructions, time limits, and scoring procedures? Are there norms to use in interpreting the scores?

- Does the test administrator know when to stop administering items on a particular subscale of an intelligence tests depending on the number of items failed in a row?
- Are the scores obtained on a test of general knowledge of public events different depending on the age of the people who take the test?

two-thirds of Americans have IQs between 85 and 115, in the large middle section of the bell-shaped curve.

Extremes of Intelligence

Intelligence test scores below 70 or above 130 occur in less than 5 percent of the population (see Figure 8-13); people with such statistically rare scores are designated as *exceptional*. Those with scores below 70 may be diagnosed as mentally retarded if they also exhibit significant deficits in adaptive behavior, such as self-care, social skills, or communication (American Psychiatric Association, 1994). The diagnosis of mental retardation also requires that the condition begin before age 18. In many cases, deficits that occur after age 18 are the result of brain damage from automobile accidents or other forms of trauma to the head and brain.

Exceptional Children. Public Law 94–142, includes significant provisions for educating all children with handicaps. This law brought the nature and needs of handicapped children to the attention of educators and the general public. Because the education of all children was affected, the term *handicapped* was changed to *exceptional*. Exceptional children may be classified into five major categories: learning disabilities, behavior and emotional disorders, sensory disabilities, communication disorders, and intellectual deviations (gifted and talented and mental retardation). Table 8-4 lists some of the major categories of exceptional individuals.

Standard intelligence tests such as the WISC–III are frequently used in the evaluation of children who are perceived as exceptional. Because there are many forms of exceptionality, however, psychologists have developed numerous assessment instruments in addition to direct observation of

TABLE 8-4   Some Categories and Characteristics of Exceptional Individuals

These categories represent deviations from the average in some aspect of intellectual functioning; both impaired intellectual functioning and superior abilities are represented. Many children who are identified as falling into one of these categories of exceptionality receive some form of special education. Traditional intelligence tests or tests specially developed for use with certain populations, such as the deaf, are often used to collect information that is helpful in identifying cases of exceptionality.

MENTAL RETARDATION

Level of Mental Retardation	IQ	Percentage of Total Group	Characteristics
Mild	50–55 to approximately 70	85%	• Often not distinguishable from other children until they begin school • Able to develop social and language skills and can acquire academic skills up to about the sixth-grade level • Usually live in the community or in a supervised group home
Moderate	30–40 to 50–55	10%	• Can learn to communicate during preschool years but are not likely to proceed past second-grade-level academic skills • Usually go through vocational training and may work in sheltered workshops
Severe	20–25 to 35–40	3–4%	• Poor motor development and poor communication skills • May learn to read "survival" words like *men, women,* and *stop* • Need protective living situation such as group homes
Profound	IQ below 20	1–2%	• Language and comprehension limited to simple requests and commands • Majority have some brain abnormality • Need constant supervision

LEARNING DISABILITY

Group of disorders manifested by significant difficulties in the acquisition and use of listening, speaking, reading, writing, reasoning, or mathematical abilities. About 4 percent of individuals between the ages of 6 and 21 are classified as having learning disabilities.

GIFTED AND TALENTED

The term *gifted* was first used to describe children whose scores on intelligence tests were well above average. The definition has been expanded to include talented individuals who display superlative skills in a specific area as evidenced by outstanding performance or products. These talents are typically not assessed by intelligence tests. The prevalence of the gifted and talented is difficult to determine because definitions vary greatly.

SAVANT SYNDROME

Designation for mentally retarded individuals who manifest at least one remarkable ability such as handling mathematical calculations quickly and without paper and pencil or calculators. This rare syndrome tends to occur more often among males and those diagnosed as autistic.

Sources: American Psychiatric Association, 1994; Haring, McCormick, & Haring, 1994.

behavior. For example, observation of classroom behaviors by teachers and aides is an important component of the assessment of children with behavior disorders.

As a child, artist Alonzo Clemons suffered a brain injury that left him with a lowered IQ and limited language development. Nevertheless, he has become an accomplished sculptor.

Exceptional children often require special attention and services, but there is no standard approach to dealing with their needs. For example, the verbal and physical aggression that may characterize children with emotional disturbances requires programs of intervention that differ from those appropriate for children with mental retardation. The school psychologist typically works with other professionals, such as classroom teachers and special education teachers, to determine appropriate plans and develop an individualized educational plan (IEP) for each child.

People with IQ scores of about 140 and above may be identified as gifted. Lewis Terman studied almost 1,500 children with IQs above 140. This longitudinal study enabled him to put to rest some myths about gifted people. They equaled or surpassed an unselected sample in terms of health, physique, athletic ability, and achievement. The survivors of Terman's study are still being followed as a gerontology project (Cravens, 1992).

Savant Syndrome.   In an 1887 lecture, J. Langdon Down (1828–1896) described a group of mentally retarded children who exhibited special abilities (Treffert, 1989). Down eventually became known for his description of *Down syndrome,* but in the 1887 lecture he offered a description of the savant syndrome.

Savant syndrome occurs in people who are severely handicapped in overall intelligence yet demonstrate exceptional ability in a specific area such as art, calculation, memory, or music. For example, despite very low scores on tests of intelligence, some savants can report calendar dates from hundreds of years ago. The essence of the savant syndrome is captured in the following case (Treffert, 1989):

Tom, a blind boy, had a vocabulary of less than 100 words. Yet he could play over 5,000 musical pieces from memory, including Bach, Beethoven, Chopin, and Rossini. At age 11, he played for the president of the United States. Some musicians felt that Tom had tricked the president and the pub-

savant syndrome

Case of a mentally retarded person who displays exceptional ability in a specific area

lic. They tested him: Tom was asked to listen to two unfamiliar musical pieces, of 13 and 20 pages each; he then played them perfectly from memory.

Most savants are male, and there is a higher frequency of this syndrome in the *autistic* population (O'Connor, 1989). *Autism* is characterized by failure to respond to people in socially appropriate ways and by serious deficits in the ability to use language. Although the cause of this rare phenomenon is largely a mystery, its existence should prompt us to reconsider the concept of general intelligence.

Kinds of Intelligence

We can divide theorists who study intelligence into two groups: "lumpers" and "splitters." Lumpers view intelligence as an overall ability to acquire knowledge, to reason, and to solve problems. As noted earlier, Galton is credited with originating the concept of intelligence. He could be considered a lumper. Most of the intelligence tests that were developed after his pioneering work yield a single number. A single number, however, may lead us to oversimplify the nature of intelligence. Splitters view intelligence as a collection of abilities that give rise to a diversity of individual strengths and weaknesses. They have developed several theories suggesting that there is more than one kind of intelligence.

Spearman's Model. Charles Spearman (1863–1945), a British psychologist, believed that there are two types of intelligence, one called *g* for general intelligence and the other, representing a number of specific abilities, called *s*. Spearman observed that people who perform well on one type of intelligence task tend to do well on most other tasks, although their scores on these tasks are seldom the same. He proposed that any given task reflects both types of intelligence. General intelligence cuts across specific kinds of items and accounts for similar levels of performance on a variety of items. By contrast, specific intelligence is related to the particular task and thus is responsible for the fact that each person does better on some tasks than on others.

In part because there is no universal agreement on the precise definition of intelligence and the way in which it should be measured, theorists differ in how they conceptualize intelligence. Let's say that you view intelligence not as a single overall ability (the kind that is represented by Spearman's *g*) but as a collection of abilities. It follows, then, that any single number on an intelligence test will provide, at best, an inadequate account of a person's ability (Sternberg, 2000).

Sternberg's Model. The kinds of intelligence that are rewarded in school may have little to do with success in life outside of school. Robert Sternberg (1988) believes that there are several ways to be adaptive or effective. He therefore proposed a new model of intelligence called the *triarchic theory of intelligence*. This model comprises (1) analytical intelligence, or the ability to break down a problem or situation into its components (the type of intelligence assessed by most current intelligence tests); (2) creative intelligence, or the ability to cope with novelty and to solve problems in new and unusual ways; and (3) practical intelligence, which is also known as common sense or "street smarts." The third type of intelligence is one that the public understands and values, yet it is missing in standard tests of intelligence (Sternberg et al., 1995)

Sternberg believes that most intelligence tests place a premium on speed, which is not relevant in most decisions we must make. This hurried approach to testing can discriminate against children who are not used to it, especially poor, minority, or immigrant children.

The triarchic theory of intelligence is the basis of efforts to match instruction to the strengths students exhibit in analytical, creative, or practical intelligence. Although these efforts are still in the early stage of development, they hold promise

TABLE 8-5 Questions Based on Sternberg's Triarchic Theory of Intelligence

The triarchic theory can be applied to teaching and the evaluation of students. These sample questions are based on the three components of the model.

DISCIPLINE	ANALYTIC	CREATIVE	PRACTICAL
Psychology	Compare Freud's theory of dreaming to Hall's.	Design an experiment to test a theory of dreaming.	How does Freud's theory of dreaming apply to your life?
Biology	Evaluate the validity of the bacterial theory of ulcers.	Design an experiment to test the bacterial theory of ulcers.	How would the bacterial theory of ulcers change conventional treatment regimens?
History	How did events in post–World War I Germany lead to the rise of Nazism?	How might President Truman have encouraged the surrender of Japan without dropping nuclear bombs on Hiroshima and Nagasaki?	What lessons does Nazism hold for events in Bosnia today?

Source: Adapted from Sternberg, 1997.

for increasing students' success. Students' strengths in one of the three components of the model are assessed; then students receive instruction that emphasizes their strength. At the end of the course, the students are evaluated; however, the focus of the evaluation is consistent with the component of the model that had been emphasized (Sternberg et al., 1996). See Table 8-5 for examples of the type of questions that different disciplines might use as a function of the triarchic component. According to Sternberg (1997), the early results demonstrate some "interesting trends; for example, students who were identified as creative, and were subsequently taught in a section emphasizing creative performance, outperformed the other two groups when assessed for creativity related to the course work."

Sternberg's perspective on intelligence emphasizes what could be called the *processes* of intelligence (in press). Next we turn to a theory of intelligence that focuses on what could be called the *domains* of intelligence.

Gardner's Multiple Intelligences. Tests of intelligence predict academic achievement because that is what they were designed to do. Had they been developed by artists, salespeople, or politicians, they might be quite different. To account for the broad range of achievements in a modern society, Howard Gardner (1983, 1993) originally proposed the existence of seven multiple intelligences. According to Gardner, there is more to intelligence than the verbal and mathematical abilities measured by current intelligence tests. Each person may have different strengths and weaknesses and thus manifest intelligence in various ways. Gardner (1998) has added one additional form of intelligence to the previous seven distinct kinds of intelligence:

1. *Linguistic:* Mastery and love of language and words; found in poets, speakers, writers, and rap singers
2. *Musical:* High level of competence in composing and performing; sensitivity to pitch and tone; evident in composers, singers, and musicians
3. *Logical-mathematical:* Used in solving mathematics problems and in logical thinking—for instance, in science
4. *Spatial reasoning:* Ability to grasp how objects orient in space, which can be very useful in art and navigation

Howard Gardner suggests that there is more to intelligence than scores on current intelligence tests. People can manifest intelligence in many ways that are not tapped by such tests. Oprah Winfrey's high level of interpersonal intelligence is evident to anyone who has seen her show. The Dallas Brass exhibit their musical intelligence in the many concerts they perform across the country.

5. *Movement or bodily kinesthetic:* Ability to control body motions and to handle objects skillfully; found in dancers and athletes

6. *Interpersonal intelligence:* Sensitivity to people and an ability to understand what motivates them, how to work effectively with them, and how to lead and to follow

7. *Intrapersonal intelligence:* Understanding one's emotions and being able to draw on them to guide one's behavior

8. *Naturalist:* Ability to recognize patterns in the way things are organized or function, or both; this ability is seen especially, although not exclusively, in the capacity to recognize flora and fauna

Although Sternberg's and Gardner's perspectives seem to be alternatives to traditional views of intelligence, they are in many ways actually complementary in their emphasis on different aspects of intelligence. As Robert Sternberg (in press) has noted, "One can think analytically, creatively, or practically, for example in the linguistic (or any other) domain, as when one analyzes a work of literature (analytic), writes a poem (creative), or discusses the relevance of the travails of a literary character for one's own life (practical)."

Sternberg and Gardner both suggest that people should be evaluated on the basis of factors other than their scores on tests of verbal and mathematical ability. Relying exclusively on these scores may cause us to overlook a person's other strengths, such as musical or athletic ability.

MULTIPLE INTELLIGENCES FOR THE 21ST CENTURY

| Programming a VCR so it does not flash 12-12-12 | Recalling the location of the remote control | Driving and speaking on a cellular phone |

Source: From *Eye on Psi Chi* (Winter 1997). Reprinted with the permission of Psi Chi. The National Honor Society in Psychology.

heritability
Percentage of differences among a group of people in a characteristic, such as intelligence, that is believed to be due to inherited factors.

Misuse of Intelligence Tests

Although current intelligence tests provide reliable scores, those tests and scores have been at the center of a controversy. What do intelligence scores mean? The high reliability coefficients that characterize most intelligence tests should not lead to the incorrect conclusion that assessments based on such tests are always accurate (valid). Psychological testing has the potential for abuse when the scores are applied without a full understanding of their meaning. The following examples show the misuse of psychological testing.

Earlier in this chapter we learned that Galton believed that intelligence was determined by heredity. Based on this belief, he proposed that the general intelligence of an entire nation could be increased if only the more intelligent citizens were allowed to have children. This movement, known as *eugenics*, was popularized by Galton and brought to the United States, where sterilization laws in more than 30 states soon barred people of low intelligence from having children (Colman, 1988). In Virginia alone more than 7,500 people were sterilized between 1924 and 1972, including one woman who was told that she was going to have her appendix removed (Gould, 1981). She did not discover the truth until after she had tried for years to bear a child.

In what has been called "one of the saddest chapters in the history of the testing of intelligence" (Sternberg, 1988, p. 7), intelligence test scores were used to prevent many European immigrants from entering the United States. The tests were usually administered in crowded conditions, and the items required a knowledge of U.S. culture that the foreign arrivals lacked. For example, one item asked examinees to look at a geometric figure and then use a pencil to copy it onto a piece of paper. This item seems easy to us, but many of the immigrants had never seen, let alone used, a pencil. Nevertheless, the results were used to classify large percents of immigrants as feebleminded (Gould, 1981).

Hereditary and Environmental Determinants of Intelligence

The people responsible for testing the immigrants' intelligence earlier in this century believed that the test scores reflected the operation of heredity rather than any environmental influences. The question of how heredity (nature) and environment (nurture) determine intelligence has sometimes mistakenly been posed as if one factor or the other alone accounted for intelligence. A more appropriate way to ask the question is, "To what degree is intelligence influenced by heredity, environment, and a combination of the two?"

Earlier in the twentieth century, intelligence tests were used to restrict U.S. immigration. This was done without a proper understanding of the influence of environmental conditions on test scores.

Hereditary Determinants.   One way researchers estimate the influence of heredity on intelligence is to use a mathematical measure called **heritability,** which can range from 0 to 100 percent. A characteristic that has a heritability of 0 is not influenced by inherited factors at all. When the heritability is 100 percent, inherited factors are completely responsible for that characteristic. Height has a heritability of 90 percent, which means that 90 percent of the differences in height among people are accounted for by variation in genetics; 10 percent are due to environmental factors such as diet (Horgan, 1993). Psychologist Arthur Jensen (1969) placed the heritability of intelligence at about 80 percent; however, more recent estimates put it in the range of 50 to 60 percent (Plomin et al., 1997; Snyderman & Rothman, 1987). Robert Plomin and his colleagues (Plomin et al., 1997) state, "The evidence for a strong genetic contribution to general cognitive ability (g) is clearer than for any other area of psychology" (p. 153). What's more, research identifying the specific genes responsible for a growing number of forms of mental retardation, reading disability, and late-onset Alzheimer's disease raise the possibility that in the near future breakthroughs will occur in the identification of genes responsible for general cognitive ability (Plomin et al., 1997; Plomin & DeFries, 1998; Plomin & Petrill, 1997).

Although we know the most about the heritability of intelligence at younger ages, it seems from new evidence that genetic factors can affect intelligence in older age populations. Moreover, researchers are now finding that heritability estimates are not constant across the life span; rather, they change with different age ranges (McClearn et al., 1997; Petrill et al., 1998). Researchers were able to locate a sample of twins from the Swedish Twin Registry; they were especially interested in twins who were 80 years of age or older and able to take part in a 1.5-hour testing period. The estimate of the heritability of general cognitive ability—based on an overall intelligence test—was quite high. As you can see from Figure 8-14, the estimates of heritability of intelligence tend to increase with age.

Even highly heritable characteristics can be influenced by environmental factors. For example, about 1 of every 10,000 American children is born with the genetic abnormality phenylketonuria (PKU) (Plomin et al., 1997). Their bodies are unable to produce the enzyme that breaks down phenylalanine, an amino acid found in many foods. Undigested phenylalanine accumulates in the body, causes damage to the nervous system (including the brain), and leads to retardation. The IQ scores of people with PKU who are left untreated is often below 50 (Plomin et al., 1997).

A diagnostic test performed shortly after birth can determine whether a baby has PKU. Babies found to have PKU are put on a low-phenylalanine diet (some phenylalanine is essential for the body). The general recommendation is

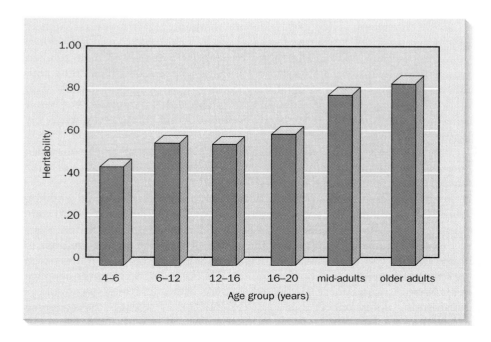

FIGURE 8-14 Influence of genetic factors across the life span.

Source: Plomin & Petrill, 1997.

to continue the special diet at least through the adolescent years (Plomin et al., 1997). In fact, the majority of treatment centers in the United States and Canada recommend that people with PKU continue their restricted diet throughout life (Fisch et al., 1997). This example shows that a disorder with a heritability of 100 percent can be modified by changing the environment (diets in this case). In short, heredity is not necessarily destiny.

Psychological Detective

PKU occurs relatively rarely, so it does not tell us a great deal about how heredity influences intelligence in most people. What other evidence could shed light on the way heredity influences intelligence? Give this question some thought, and write down your answer before reading further.

Another way in which researchers estimate the degree to which intelligence is affected by inherited factors is by examining correlations between the intelligence test scores of family members (Bouchard & McGue, 1981). If intelligence runs in families, the intelligence scores of family members should be correlated. The study of twins also plays a key role in investigating the influence of heredity and environment on characteristics such as intelligence. **Identical twins** (also known as *monozygotic twins*) have exactly the same genes and therefore are always of the same sex. **Fraternal twins** (also known as *dizygotic twins*) are no more similar than two siblings in the same family. They were born together but have only 50 percent of their genes in common. As you can see in Figure 8-15, the correlation between the intelligence scores of twins is quite high; the scores of less closely related people exhibit lower correlations. These statistics seem to provide evidence for inherited influences on intelligence.

Family members also share very similar environments, however, making it possible that the correlations among their test scores are due to environmental factors. Yet when twins are raised in separate environments, the correlation between their intelligence scores is still high. So it is unclear whether heredity or environment has a stronger influence on intelligence.

To disentangle the effects of similar environments and heredity, researchers have studied the intelligence test scores of adopted children. Figure 8-15 shows that the correlation between the scores of adoptive parents and their adopted children is approximately .30. Moreover, the intelligence scores of adopted children tend to correlate more highly with those of their biological parents than with those of their adoptive parents. In fact, the biological parent's IQ is a better predictor of a child's IQ than is the IQ of the adopting parent, even when the adoption occurs virtually at birth (Hunt, 1995).

What do these results tell us? Do they make a strong case for the influence of heredity on intelligence? Are there any problems with the conduct of such studies that could influence the results?

Typically, research that investigates the intelligence of adopted children does not tell us whether the environments in which the children were raised were similar to those that their biological parents would or could provide. Sandra Scarr and Richard Weinberg (1986) reported a study of several hundred children in Minnesota who had been placed in adoptive homes. In this case the children were either African American or of mixed racial background. Some of the adoptive parents were African American, but many were white, and most were college graduates with professional occupations. The intelligence scores of these adopted children were similar to those of other children brought up in the same homes. A

identical twins
Twins who develop from one ovum fertilized by one sperm; genetically identical to each other

fraternal twins
Twins who develop from two ova fertilized by two different sperm; genetically related as siblings

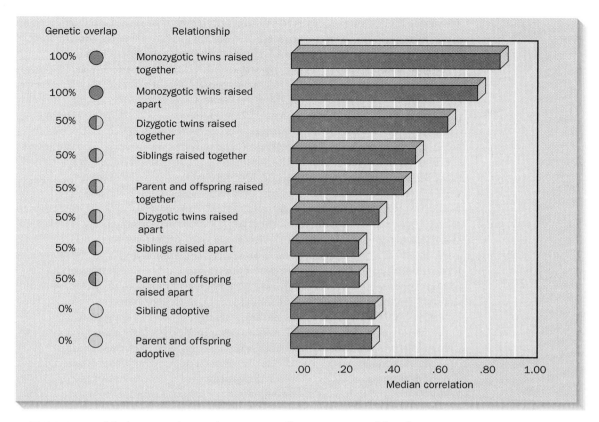

FIGURE 8-15 Median correlations between intelligence scores of family members. Degree of genetic overlap ranges from 100 percent for identical twins to 0 percent for unrelated children raised together.

Source: Plomin & Petrill, 1997.

follow-up of these children in their adolescent years indicated that being reared in a middle- or upper-middle-class environment that represents the culture of the test and schools has a significant effect on adoptees' IQ scores (Weinberg, Scarr, & Waldman, 1992). These findings suggest that the social environment plays a dominant role in determining the IQ of African American and interracial children and that both social and genetic variables contribute to individual variations among them (Weinberg, Scarr, & Waldman, 1992). Thus studies of adopted children suggest that the environment plays a role in intelligence. We next discuss a number of these environmental influences.

Environmental Determinants of Intelligence. A wide variety of environmental factors can affect intelligence. For example, exposure to lead is strongly linked to intellectual deficits (Needleman & Gatsonis, 1990). In Taiwan children who had been exposed prenatally to PCBs (chemicals used to insulate electrical equipment) had small but detectable intellectual deficits that did not decrease with age (Chen et al., 1992).

In the 1930s, Howard Skeels decided that tender loving care and stimulation could be beneficial for two children in an Iowa orphanage (Skeels & Dye, 1939). Skeels placed these quiet, slow, unresponsive sisters in a home for mentally retarded adolescents. On his return several months later, he was surprised to find that the sisters' intelligence test scores had increased and that they appeared alert and active. The attention and stimulation provided by the mentally retarded adolescents and the staff of the institution had made a difference.

This finding encouraged Skeels to provide a similar level of stimulation with a larger group of children; again the procedure was successful (Skeels, 1966). Skeels's success provided evidence that early stimulation could influence intelligence.

Psychologist James Flynn has reported a slow but steady rise in performance on IQ tests since the 1930s. The average number of correct responses in samples from 20 countries has risen by about 3 points per decade, or 15 points in 50 years. The *Flynn effect* (Flynn, 1998; Holloway, 1998) may be due to environmental factors, such as improved education, or perhaps it is the result of some glitch in the tests. Although performance has improved, the average test score has remained essentially the same. Why is this true? The answer is that IQ scores are a relative rather than an absolute measure; your score is compared with everyone else's. In other words, as the raw scores improve, the standard on which the IQ scores are based also rises. Thus if everyone else is improving, your relative score will not change much (Hunt, 1995). Put another way, a raw score that yielded an IQ of 100 in the 1930s would be equal to an 85 today.

What do you think happens if some children start school with weaker skills than other children? Can anything be done to increase their chances of success? One purpose of preschool programs such as Head Start is to provide these children with educational skills, social skills, and health care before they begin their formal schooling. Head Start is aimed at children around 4 years of age, especially those in low-income and minority populations. Head Start programs are delivered through 1,800 centers across the country (De Angelis, 1993).

Early evaluations of Head Start were not encouraging. Improvements were reported in verbal abilities, emotional maturity, and motivation, but they generally lasted only three to four years into elementary school—a fairly common phenomenon known as *fadeout*. However, some research on various forms of early childhood education, including Head Start, indicated that after participation in these programs, fewer of the children were placed in special education classes and fewer were held back in school (Consortium for Longitudinal Studies, 1983).

In retrospect, it seems that initial expectations for Head Start were too optimistic. Efforts to influence intellectual ability cannot overcome all other environmental influences (Lee et al., 1990), and early intervention does not guarantee success in life: "Early intervention simply cannot overpower the effects of poor living conditions, inadequate nutrition and health care, negative role models, and substandard schools" (Zigler & Styfco, 1994, p. 129). What's more, many Head Start teachers did not have adequate training, and parents were not as involved as they should have been. In addition, the quality of programs varied quite a bit. In the better programs, whose purpose was in part to enhance school readiness, the children often become better achievers by the time they left the program.

Despite its shortcomings, Head Start does have widespread public and bipartisan political support (Takanishi & De Leon, 1994; Zigler & Styfco, 1994). Programs such as the Carolina Abecedarian Project, however, have had greater success. In this project infants from low-income families were placed into intellectually enriched environments until they began school. Compared with controls, the enriched children scored higher on tests of intelligence, even seven years after the end of the intervention (Campbell & Ramey, 1994).

Psychological Detective

Look at the correlations in Figure 8-15. What evidence in those correlations points to the effects of the environment on intelligence? Why? Give this question some thought, and write down your answer before reading further.

A close look at the correlations in Figure 8-15 led some researchers to conclude that both heredity and environment strongly influence the development of intelligence (Plomin, 1989). Where is the support for the influence of the environment among those correlations? If two unrelated children are raised together, will their intelligence scores be similar? If heredity controls intelligence, the correlation between the intelligence scores of unrelated children should reflect their lack of family relationships—that is, it should be 0. Yet the correlation between the intelligence test scores of unrelated children raised together is greater than .30. Now look at the correlations for identical twins raised apart and raised together. The difference between those correlations also indicates that environmental factors have an effect on intelligence.

In most studies of intelligence (and other characteristics) of twins, researchers often assume that the twins (especially identical twins) are treated quite similarly. Researchers are increasingly finding, however, that twins and siblings in general are not treated as similarly as was once assumed. In fact, researchers have begun to use the terms *shared environment* and *nonshared environment* to describe the common and unique elements of the environment. They have found—sometimes to their surprise—that siblings tend to grow up in environments that are more different than similar. These differences in the environment—called nonshared environment—play a major role in accounting for differences among siblings in intelligence and, as we will see in Chapter 12, also in personality. Earlier we described a study of the similarity of intelligence scores in twins age 80 years and older. The major finding of that study was a high estimated heritability. From an environmental perspective, however, what is important is that the nonshared environment accounted for 27 percent of the differences in intelligence among older people. Thus even in old age differences in environment can play a role in shaping intelligence.

The growing list of potential environmental influences on intelligence includes how families conceptualize intelligence. For example, different ethnic groups have different conceptions of intelligence. As a result, they tend to socialize their children according to these conceptions. Researchers in one study (Okagaki & Sternberg, 1993) found that Latinos tended to emphasize the social-competence aspects of intelligence more, whereas Anglos tended to emphasize the cognitive-competence aspect of intelligence more.

Explaining Differences in Intelligence Scores.   The controversy surrounding intelligence testing continues today. Much of it concerns differences in the average intelligence scores attained by members of various racial and ethnic groups. For example, the average intelligence scores obtained by African Americans are lower than those for white Americans (MacKenzie, 1984). These group differences should not obscure the fact that there is a high degree of overlap in the distribution of intelligence scores for all groups.

Although individual differences in intelligence are due in part to heredity, the existence of group differences in IQ scores does not necessarily suggest that there are innate differences in intelligence among groups. Even characteristics that are affected by heredity can vary in response to environmental factors. Consider the analogy proposed by Richard Lewontin (1976): If we take a bag of seeds and sow half in fertile soil and the other half in barren soil, the plants that grow in barren soil will be shorter on average than the plants that grow in fertile soil. Even seeds with the genetic code for tallness are not likely to grow to their full potential if they are planted in barren soil. The differences among the plants within each group may be due to heredity, but the average difference between the two groups reflects environmental factors—in this case the quality of the soil. In the same way, differences in IQ scores among groups can reflect such environmental factors as academic background, quality of education, and the availability of resources such as books and educational toys.

For this reason, critics of intelligence tests argue that we must take a closer look at the tests themselves. These tests are designed to measure a quality known as "intelligence," but as we have seen, this quality can be difficult to define, let alone measure. Intelligence tests have good predictive validity; that is, they effectively predict the performance of children in school. Success in school, however, can reflect many influences besides innate intelligence. Therefore critics warn against drawing conclusions concerning students' mental abilities based on their test performance.

In fact, some experts have charged that group differences in test scores might reflect certain characteristics of the tests themselves. For example, Janet Helms (1992) suggests that intelligence tests reflect white, middle-class values and therefore are innately biased against members of other cultural groups. Tests assume that standard (white) English is best, so they are written in standard English. Similarly, some of the test questions are based on the assumption that the basic social unit is the nuclear family, which consists of a mother, a father, and their children. Thus children from groups that have a high rate of nonnuclear families are placed at a disadvantage in answering those questions.

Social scientist Claude Steele of Stanford University has recently proposed that students' attitudes and approach toward standardized tests can also affect their performance (Steele & Aronson, 1995). According to Steele, African-American students face additional pressures in that a poor performance can be interpreted so as to confirm negative stereotypes about African Americans as a group. Thus African-American students carry an extra burden that Steele calls stereotype vulnerability. To test this hypothesis, Steele and Joshua Aronson gave African-American and white students at Stanford a test composed of difficult verbal items from the Graduate Record Examination (GRE). Half of the students were told that the purpose of the exercise was to study "psychological factors involved in solving verbal problems." The remaining students were told that the exam was "a genuine test of your verbal abilities and limitations."

The results revealed that African-American students who thought they were simply solving problems performed as well as white students (who performed equally well in both situations). By contrast, the African-American students who had been told that the test measures their intellectual potential performed worse than all the other students. Significantly, all students had been asked to write down their race before taking the test. Thus African-American students who felt they were being evaluated as a group tried to deal with stereotype vulnerability by increasing their efforts, which led them to work inefficiently and inaccurately. Steele and Aronson (1995) concluded that they have uncovered "an underappreciated source of classic deficits in standardized test performance" (p. 810). Although Steele and Aronson's hypothesis has not been applied directly to IQ tests, it suggests an intriguing explanation for group differences in test scores.

The debate over how to interpret differences in test scores is not merely an intellectual exercise. Rather, it has significant scientific, political, and social implications. Consider, for example, the controversy surrounding the publication of *The Bell Curve* (1994) by Richard Herrnstein and Charles Murray. Herrnstein and Murray assert that there are genetically based differences in intelligence among socioeconomic, racial, and ethnic groups. They further argue that intelligence as measured by IQ scores determines such attributes and behaviors as employment, income, welfare dependence, and quality of parental behavior. Thus low IQ is the best explanation of why some people never get off welfare, why crime is rampant in the inner cities, and why so many teenage girls get pregnant. This argument has profound implications for political and social policy: It suggests that educational and social welfare programs will have limited effectiveness because heredity, rather than environment, is primarily responsible for the problems of low-income groups.

A number of researchers (e.g., Gottfredson, 1997) have in fact pointed out that intelligence does matter; for example, intelligence scores are related to job training and performance. Critics note, however, that Herrnstein and Murray fail to distinguish between correlation and causation (see Chapter 1) and thus draw inappropriate conclusions (Hunt, 1995; Kamin, 1995). It is true that people living below the poverty line are likely to have lower IQs and poorer health and to come from families of lower socioeconomic status. Although all of these behaviors are correlated, we do not know whether any cause-and-effect relationships exist among them (Hunt, 1995). For example, these behaviors could result from such environmental factors as inadequate schooling and lack of financial resources.

The controversy over how to interpret IQ scores will likely be with us for a long time. Although the issue is complex, the evidence suggests that performance on standardized tests reflects the interaction of genetic and environmental factors. Drawing conclusions about group differences based solely on test scores can be misleading and counterproductive. What's more, as we have already seen, there is a great deal of overlap among all groups in test scores.

Review Summary

1. Francis Galton initiated the intelligence testing movement. He developed tests based on the assumption that level of intelligence is related to sensory abilities.

2. Alfred Binet and Theophile Simon developed an intelligence test to evaluate French schoolchildren. They proposed the concept of **mental age,** which compared a child's performance with the average performance of children at a particular age. The **intelligence quotient (IQ)** is the ratio of mental age divided by chronological age and multiplied by 100.

3. Binet's tests became the widely used Stanford-Binet test. Another set of tests, the Wechsler Scales, yield verbal and performance appraisals of intelligence.

4. The three characteristics of a good psychological test are **reliability, validity,** and **standardization.** Reliability refers to the consistency of scores obtained on repeated administrations of the test. Validity refers to a test's ability to measure what it was designed to measure. **Standardization** refers to uniformity in testing procedures and test scoring. **Norms** provide the distribution of scores of a large sample of people who have previously taken a test.

5. Intelligence test scores are distributed in the shape of a **normal curve.** The majority of the scores are clustered around the middle, with fewer scores found at either extreme.

6. There may be several types of intelligence. Charles Spearman believed that we all possess general intelligence *(g)* along with specific abilities *(s)*. Both Robert Sternberg and Howard Gardner propose that we have several types of intelligence, most of which are not measured by current intelligence tests.

7. Intelligence tests can be misused. For example, they have been used by the United States to deny entry to immigrants and as a pretext for involuntary sterilization. The *eugenics movement* proposed that the intelligence of an entire nation could be increased if only the more intelligent citizens had children.

8. The **heritability** of intelligence is an estimate of the influence of heredity in accounting for differences among people. However, even clearly inherited characteristics or medical conditions, such as PKU, can be modified by altering a person's environment.

9. Correlations between the IQ scores of identical twins suggest that intelligence is strongly influenced by heredity. The closer the family relationship, the higher the correlation between the intelligence scores of family members. Studies of adopted children suggest that environmental factors also have an effect on intelligence.

10. Claude Steele has offered evidence that when taking standardized tests, African Americans may experience what he has termed *stereotype vulnerability.* This notion suggests that something as simple as a question about one's race may have much more significant meaning to African Americans than to other people.

Study Break

1. Match the following historical figures with their contributions to testing:

   a. Francis Galton
   b. Alfred Binet
   c. Lewis Terman
   d. David Wechsler

   1. Saw that intelligence is related to higher mental processes
   2. Devised a new test because the Binet test was difficult to use with adults
   3. Viewed intelligence as related to sensory ability
   4. Revised the Binet test for use in the United States

2. Distinguish between mental age and chronological age.

3. You have just completed your sophomore year in college, and you have no idea what you want to do when you graduate. Last week you took a test that was supposed to identify the things you enjoy doing. The results of the test strongly suggested that you should pursue a career in journalism. But you absolutely despise writing! What does the test apparently lack?

4. What do we mean when we say that intelligence scores are distributed like a normal curve? What does this interpretation tell us about extreme scores?

5. An expert on genetic influences on physical and psychological characteristics has been invited to campus to give a presentation. This expert has just finished a review of the evidence on genetics, heritability, and the public's knowledge of such concepts. Which of the following would be the best title for the presentation?
   a. "Heritability Does Not Equal Destiny"
   b. "Genetic Factors: How We Have Overstated Their Influence"
   c. "All in the Genes: Location of the Genes Responsible for Various Facets of Intelligence"
   d. "Genes Don't Influence Environmental Factors, and Environmental Factors Don't Influence Genes"

6. Your professor has given you an assignment to determine the estimates of the heritability of PKU, height, and intelligence. You are to turn in a list of these characteristics ranked from the one with the highest heritability to the one with the lowest. Of the following lists, which will you hand in?
   a. PKU, height, intelligence
   d. height, PKU, intelligence
   c. intelligence, PKU, height
   d. intelligence, height, PKU

7. What evidence supports the idea that intelligence is determined by heredity? What evidence supports the idea that intelligence results from environmental influences?

8. What is Claude Steele's stereotype vulnerability hypothesis?

ANSWERS TO STUDY BREAKS

Pages 338–339

1. **a.** heuristic **b.** algorithm **c.** rigidity **d.** representativeness heuristic
2. Reduces the burden on memory
3. You have generated a solution to the problem without considering that the sequence does not increase by three. Although you have found a solution that confirms your hypothesis, you have failed to generate other possibilities.
4. b
5. c
6. c

Page 360

1. **a.** 3, **b.** 1, **c.** 4, **d.** 2
2. Chronological age is simply how old a person is; mental age is how a child's intellectual development compares to other children's intellectual development.
3. validity
4. A normal curve tells us that most people obtain scores in the middle of a distribution, with fewer scores as we move away from the middle of the distribution.
5. a
6. a
7. The high correlation between intelligence scores of close relatives and especially the high correlation between identical twins separated at birth support the idea that intelligence is determined by heredity. Research on environmental factors such as lead, and programs such as Head Start, suggests that intelligence is influenced by environmental factors.
8. Claude Steele has proposed that when African-American students take standardized tests, they are subject to the effects of *stereotype vulnerability*. In addition to the pressures that occur for many students who take such tests, African-American students may feel pressure related to the possibility that poor performance on the test might be interpreted as confirming negative stereotypes about their race.

ANSWERS TO QUESTIONS AND PROBLEMS

Psychological Detective, page 321

The attribute that defines the concept is an odd number of segments within the geometric figure.

Problem in Figure 8-5, page 327

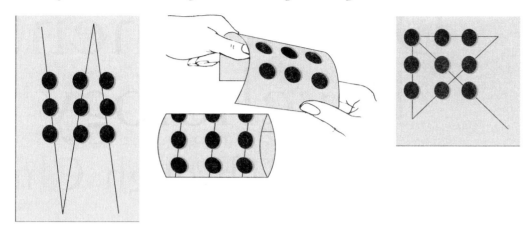

Problems in Figure 8-6, page 327

A. Remove the matches at the top, bottom, and right.

B. Turn the book upside down.

C. The obvious answer is six and a half. Less obvious answers are:
- halving 13 gives 1 and 3 (1/3)
- halving the word thirteen gives 4 letters on each side
- converting 13 to roman numerals and halving it gives 11 and 2 (XI/II)
- halving it a different way gives 8 (X̶I̶I̶I̶)

Problem in Figure 8-8, page 328

Pigs in A Pen Problem, page 327

Place nine pigs into each of three pens. Then place all three pens inside one large pen.

Exercise in Figure 8-11, page 337

Row 1
a. Just under the wire
b. Balanced budget
c. Standing ovation
d. Shot in the dark
e. Space invaders

Row 2
a. Bottom of the ninth
b. Sitting on top of the world
c. All hands on deck
d. Skinny-dipping
e. Love at first sight

Row 3
a. Canceled check
b. Dashed hopes
c. Splitting headache
d. Three square meals a day
e. Open sesame

Developmental Psychology I
Conception Through Childhood

Chapter in Perspective

So far we have established a biological basis for psychology, examined our sensory and perceptual processes, looked at emotions and states of consciousness, seen how learning takes place and memories are stored, and considered cognitive processes. As we continue our exploration of psychology, keep in mind that all of these processes take place in the context of a developing organism. Many newborns, including human infants, are helpless for a period of time after birth. Does this helplessness mean that they are incapable of engaging in the processes and activities we have covered? How well do their sensory receptors function? What, if anything, do they perceive? Can they think and learn? What types of emotions do they exhibit? How do these processes change as the child grows older? In this chapter we begin our discussion of development, in the interest of answering these, and other, questions for you. ■

To her 90-year-old great-grand-mother, this child probably seems to be growing "like a weed."

From the moment of conception until the moment of death, we change physically, cognitively, and psychosocially. **Developmental psychology** is concerned with the systematic physical and cognitive processes that lead to these changes that occur throughout life. The various periods of growth across the life span are shown in Table 9-1.

Because the subject matter of developmental psychology is diverse, you are likely to find developmental psychologists working in many settings. Some teach at colleges or universities, where they may also conduct research. Others consult with schools and day-care centers, write books on child rearing, or work with other professionals (such as social workers and physical therapists) to plan treatment programs. Developmental psychologists also conduct research for companies that sell baby food, diapers, and toys.

When we think of human development, we probably think first about physical changes that can be *quantified,* or measured. Many of us have watched our younger brothers and sisters or our own children "grow like weeds." One day a baby struggles to crawl across the floor; a few months later she is walking. We grow taller and heavier, run faster, and are able to lift heavier objects as we become adults; as old age approaches, some of these processes reverse themselves.

We also develop in *qualitative* ways that are *not* as easily measured as height, weight, and strength. Some of these qualitative changes involve cognitive processes and social interactions. As we grow older and add more information to long-term memory, our views on diverse topics such as pollution, love, and religion may change. We think in different and more complex ways about ourselves, our friends, and our environment.

In this chapter and the next we examine what is known about these quantitative and qualitative changes across the life span. This chapter discusses development from conception through childhood; adolescence, adulthood, and old age are discussed in Chapter 10.

Basic Issues in Developmental Psychology

John B. Watson (1924) proclaimed that "there is no such thing as an inheritance of capacity, talent, temperament, mental constitution, and characteristics. These things depend on training that goes on mainly in the cradle" (pp. 74–75). Watson was so convinced of the impact of the environment on development that he boldly declared that he could train any child to be a doctor, lawyer, artist, merchant or even beggar or thief if he could control the child's environment (Watson, 1928). *Was Watson correct? Do all of our abilities develop as a result of environmental influences?* ■

Nature and Nurture

developmental psychology
Study of physical, cognitive, and psychosocial changes throughout the life span, from conception until death

Watson had strong views about the power of the environment to influence development, but many parents, as well as most present-day psychologists, would disagree. According to Robert Plomin (1990a), "Parents are environmentalists [i.e., they stress nurture] until they have more than one child. With one

TABLE 9-1 Approximate Periods of Growth and Development across the Life Span

Zygote	Conception to 2 weeks
Embryo	2 to 9 weeks
Fetus	9 weeks to birth
Infancy	Birth to age 1 year
Toddler	1 to 3 years
Preschool period	3 to 6 years
Middle childhood	6 to 12 years
Adolescence	12 to 20 years
Young adulthood	20 to 40 years
Middle adulthood	40 to 65 years
Late adulthood	65 years to death

child, it seems possible to explain anything that happens. However, when their second child turns out to be different in many ways from the first child, parents realize that they did not treat the two children differently enough to account for the behavioral differences that are so apparent between them" (p. 8). The contrast between these two views illustrates a significant issue in developmental psychology: To what degree does development result from **nature** (heredity) and to what extent is it a product of **nurture** (environmental factors)?

In **behavior genetics,** a relatively new field that combines psychology and biology, researchers seek to provide answers to the nature-or-nurture question. Behavior geneticists, who advocate the evolutionary perspective (see Chapter 1), attempt to determine the extent to which individual differences in a particular behavior can be attributed to genetic causes.

Psychological Detective

To grasp how behavior geneticists examine how people behave, take a moment to consider some of the differences you see in such characteristics as musical ability, athletic ability, shyness, or activity level in your friends and relatives. To what extent are these characteristics genetically determined, and to what extent are they environmentally determined? Write down some of your observations before reading further.

Some of the people you describe may have exceptional musical talent, whereas others may describe themselves as tone-deaf. A few of your friends and relatives are outgoing; others are painfully shy. Why do these people differ in these ways? Environmental factors probably play a critical role in enabling people to develop their individual capabilities. But do some of the differences we observe owe to factors other than environmental influences?

Behavioral geneticists have found that heredity plays a significant role in intelligence, personality, and several patterns of abnormal behavior (Plomin et al., 1997). Yet "the same data that point to significant genetic influences provide the best available evidence for the importance of nongenetic factors" (Plomin, 1990a, p. 179). One of the most significant discoveries of behavior genetics is that environmental factors are experienced differently by children in the same family. Consider, for example, identical twins, who share the exact same genetic makeup. The fact that they do not have identical personalities points to the influence of environmental factors. Both nature and nurture play

nature

Theory that holds that physical and cognitive development is genetically determined

nurture

Theory that holds that physical and cognitive development is determined by environmental factors

behavior genetics

A new field, combining psychology and biology, that studies the influences of heredity and environment on behavior

longitudinal study
Research technique in which the same partcipants are tested or observed repeatedly over a period of time

cross-sectional study
Research technique in which participants, often of different ages, are tested or observed during a limited time span or only once

significant roles in development. If we are to understand the development of human thoughts, behaviors, motives, and emotions, we must learn to distinguish the influences of nature from those of nurture. Hence developmental psychologists are careful to use certain special research methods.

Research Methods

Psychologists conducting research on developmental processes face some unique challenges. First, psychologists cannot isolate their participants in cages like laboratory animals, allowing them to emerge only when it is time for their daily experimental sessions. What's more, ethical considerations prevent researchers from investigating some developmental processes. For example, in Chapter 6 we described the procedures John Watson and Rosalie Rayner used in 1921 to condition a long-lasting fear of white, furry objects in Little Albert. Such procedures are not permitted today. What is permissible? For example, is it acceptable to expose children to violent television programs to determine whether they will become violent or aggressive as a result? How does a researcher teach these children that their newly acquired aggressive behavior is wrong? These are the types of ethical questions that contemporary developmental researchers must address.

Longitudinal Versus Cross-Sectional Studies.   Research in human development may take longer than research in other areas of psychology. Developmental research may take months, years, or even decades. Long-term research projects in which the same participants are observed or tested repeatedly are called **longitudinal studies.** Studies that involve observing or testing participants of different ages at one moment in time are called **cross-sectional studies.** In other words, longitudinal projects study the same people over a period of time; cross-sectional studies cut across a section of the ages and types of people available at one moment in time (see Figure 9-1).

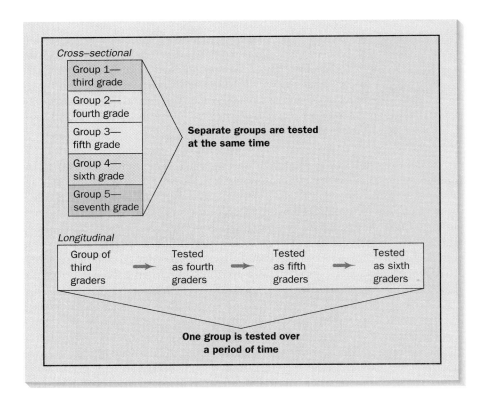

FIGURE 9-1   Comparison of cross-sectional and longitudinal research designs.

Psychological Detective

Consider the following research question: Are children who are shy at age 3 less shy at ages 6, 9, and 12? What type of research design will you need to answer this question—cross-sectional or longitudinal? Write down your answer and your reasons for choosing this particular research design before reading further.

cohort

Group of individuals born in the same period

Because cross-sectional research evaluates behavior at a given moment, it cannot determine whether the same children will be shy at different ages. Therefore a longitudinal design would be appropriate in this case. This design is diagrammed in Figure 9-2A. Although the need for a longitudinal design is obvious in this situation, such research presents some difficulties. Longitudinal studies involve a great deal of time; perhaps you are unable to devote the necessary time to the project. Also, will the participants always be available when you need to study them? Finally, how many participants can you afford to lose before the study is deemed not worth continuing?

Psychological Detective

Now look at the problem of shyness from a different vantage point. Is the average 3-year-old more shy than the average 6-year-old? Which research design is more suitable to answer this question? Write down your answer and your reasons for choosing this particular research design before reading further.

This research question requires information about the shyness of children of different ages at a particular point in time, so the cross-sectional design is appropriate. Measures of shyness (as evidenced in parents' reports) could be obtained from random samples of children in the various age groups. Then the measures from the separate groups could be compared (see Figure 9-2B).

The logic and conduct of cross-sectional research are clear and straightforward, but this type of research cannot provide information about changes over time. We would have information about shyness only at the time that we conducted our research.

Consider the research on shyness from a third perspective. In the 1950s, most middle-class children were reared in suburban homes by their mothers, relatively isolated from other children until they went to school. By the 1980s, children were more likely to spend 20 to 40 hours a week in communal day-care arrangements. Would this change make the whole population more or less shy?

To answer this question, we would need a measure of shyness in groups of 6-year-old children born in 1950, 1960, 1970, 1980, and 1990 before they attended first grade (see Figure 9-2C). Groups composed of participants born in the same year are called **cohorts** or cohort groups. In a *cohort design,* we compare the responses of different cohorts. By looking at differences among cohorts, we determine the effects on shyness of being born in different decades from 1950 to 1990. The cohort design is also used effectively in cross-cultural research in which same-age groups from different countries can be compared. The validity of a research finding is increased if it is verified across cultural groups as well as across age groups.

FIGURE 9-2 (A) Diagram of a longitudinal study designed to investigate shyness in a group of children at ages 3, 6, 9, and 12. The same group of participants is tested four different times. (B) Cross-sectional study designed to investigate shyness in 3- and 6-year-olds. The two groups of children are tested at the same point in time, and the results are compared. (C) Cohort study designed to investigate whether shyness has changed when children born in different decades enter first grade. Shyness is measured within each cohort, and then patterns of change are compared between cohorts.

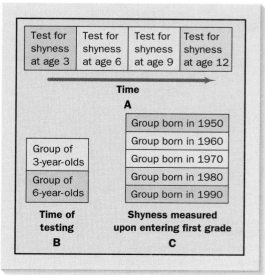

Because they are the same age, the children in this grade school class constitute a cohort.

Development from Conception to Birth

Bob and Liz are thinking about having a baby, but they are concerned about the possibility that their child will have chromosomal abnormalities. Bob's brother, who is 22, has Down syndrome and lives in a group home with six men and women who also have Down syndrome. Some birth defects may be inherited, so Bob and Liz want to know what their chances are of having a baby with Down syndrome. *What can be done to provide Bob and Liz with information about their chances of having a child with Down syndrome?* ■

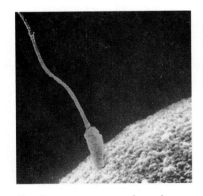

Fertilization occurs when the sperm penetrates the much larger ovum.

Great oaks grow from tiny acorns; a human grows from a cell that is smaller than the tip of a pin. Our lives can be traced to the union of our father's sperm (from the Greek word for "seed") and our mother's ovum ("egg").

In a single ejaculation, a man releases approximately 360 million sperm (Berk, 1998). The sperm immediately begin a journey from the woman's vagina to her fallopian tubes, where they may meet and penetrate an ovum, which is many times larger than the sperm. (One of the smallest cells in the body the sperm is approximately ⅙₀₀th of an inch from head to tail.) On the way to the fallopian tubes, most sperm fall victim to acidic vaginal secretions; some are caught in recesses, and others are attacked as foreign substances by the woman's white blood cells. In fact, it is remarkable that any sperm survive the journey to penetrate an ovum. A healthy couple having intercourse regularly without contraception has only a 25 to 30 percent chance of beginning a pregnancy in any given menstrual cycle. Most conceptions occur on the day of ovulation or during the two days that precede it (Wilcox, Weinberg, & Baird, 1995).

The task of penetrating the ovum is easier than the journey to the fallopian tubes. The ovum releases a substance that attracts the sperm and helps it adhere to the egg (Freedman, 1992). The head of the sperm, which contains the genetic material, penetrates the ovum and moves toward the genetic material within it. The union of the sperm and ovum forms a one-cell structure called a **zygote.**

zygote
One-celled organism formed by the union of a sperm and an ovum

The zygote moves from the fallopian tubes to the uterus (womb), a fist-sized, pear-shaped organ, and attaches itself to its inner wall. Through a process of cell division called **mitosis,** the zygote reproduces itself: One cell divides to become 2, then 4, and so on; after just 5 days the zygote contains about 100 cells (Moore, 1989). During the next 9 months, cell division continues at a furious pace, eventually producing an individual with billions of cells, all of which contain identical genetic information.

From the second to ninth weeks after fertilization, when the major organ systems are formed, the developing human is called an **embryo.** Not all zygotes become embryos, however, nearly one-third of implanted zygotes are rejected from the uterus through miscarriage (interruption of the pregnancy). Two of every three miscarriages occur before a woman is even aware that she is pregnant (Wilcox et al., 1988). The zygotes of most of these early miscarriages are defective in some way.

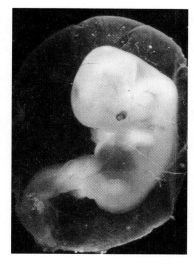

Between 2 weeks and 9 weeks following conception, the developing child is known as an embryo.

Heredity

As noted earlier, fertilization occurs when the sperm and ovum fuse, providing the zygote with the inherited (genetic) material that will influence its development. This material is arranged in structures called **chromosomes** located in the cell nuclei. All human cells except the sperm and ovum themselves contain 46 chromosomes, arranged in 23 pairs, with one member of each pair contributed by each parent. The chromosomes carry **genes,** which are the basic units of inheritance and the genetic blueprints for development.

There are about 100,000 genes on the 46 chromosomes. More than 5,000 of those genes have been identified so far. Among the recently identified genes are those responsible for cystic fibrosis, kidney disease, Huntington's chorea, some forms of Alzheimer's disease, and muscular dystrophy.

The general chemical name for genetic material is **deoxyribonucleic acid,** or **DNA.** Chromosomes are actually large segments of DNA. The unique genetic blueprint for your development is contained in the chromosomes located in the nucleus of each cell.

Our understanding of the mechanisms of genetics and heredity can be traced to the work of a monk, Gregor Mendel (1822–1884), who conducted a series of experiments using garden peas. Through these studies he unraveled the key principles of hereditary transmission; those principles are still relevant to the study of genetics.

During Mendel's time, people believed that a child's traits were simply a blend of the parents' traits; thus the child would have some intermediate or average value of a trait such as eye color. When Mendel bred peas having white flowers with peas having purple flowers, however, the offspring had purple flowers, rather than pink ones. This surprising finding led him to conclude that the offspring plant's traits were not merely blends of the parent plants' traits.

Mendel also concluded that each adult plant carries hereditary factors that govern the inheritance of a trait. As you just saw, we call these factors *genes,* and they are carried on *chromosomes.* The hereditary factors of the mother and father separate before the formation of their offspring. Thus each parent contributes only *half* of the genetic material to the trait in question.

Finally, Mendel suggested that hereditary factors could be either dominant or recessive. When a *dominant* gene and a *recessive* gene are present in a pea plant, the dominant gene expresses itself. A *recessive* gene can express itself only in the absence of a dominant gene.

A good example of this phenomenon in humans is the inheritance of sickle-cell anemia. Sickle-cell anemia occurs when a person's blood contains

mitosis
Process of cell division in which each cell contains the same genetic information as other cells

embryo
A developing organism during the stage when the major organ systems are formed

chromosomes
Segments of genetic material located in the nucleus of each cell; human cells have 23 pairs of chromosomes (numbered according to size), one of each pair being inherited from each parent

genes
Units of hereditary material that line the chromosomes and provide information concerning the form and function of each cell

deoxyribonucleic acid (DNA)
Chemical name for the genetic material located in the nucleus of each cell

Gregor Mendel's research with garden peas provided our basic understanding of genetics and heredity.

polygenic inheritance
Principle of heredity whereby complex traits, such as intelligence and personality, are determined by many genes

meiosis
Type of cell division that results in a reduction of the amount of genetic material in each of the resulting cells

too many abnormal hemoglobin molecules. Normal hemoglobin gives blood its red color and carries oxygen to body tissues. Too much abnormal hemoglobin (*hemoglobin 5*) causes the amount of oxygen in the blood to drop. The resulting low oxygen level causes the cells to become crescent- or sickle-shaped. An attack of sickle-cell anemia is accompanied by high fever, severe pain, and potential injury to body parts and tissue (Sullivan, 1987).

Sickle-cell anemia occurs in people who have two recessive genes for that trait. People who have one dominant gene and one recessive gene for sickle-cell anemia are called *carriers* (see Figure 9-3) because they can pass the recessive gene on to their children, even though they do not have symptoms of the disease themselves. Thus the children of two carriers would have a 1-in-4 chance of having normal hemoglobin, a 1-in-2 chance of being a carrier, and a 1-in-4 chance of having sickle-cell anemia. African Americans have a higher incidence of sickle-cell anemia than people of other races because they are more likely to carry the recessive gene.

Polygenic Heredity. Most human traits are controlled by a number of different genes, a phenomenon termed **polygenic inheritance.** To understand polygenic inheritance, we must consider the process of meiosis.

In **meiosis,** a process of cell division involving reduction of genetic material, the sex cells—the ovum and sperm—are formed. After meiosis, these cells have only half of the 46 chromosomes that were present before cell reduction occurred. Thus the ovum and sperm each contribute 23 chromosomes—one member of each pair—to the newly formed zygote (see Figure 9-4). When meiosis occurs, each member of a pair of chromosomes has an equal chance of being selected to form the sperm or ovum. Given that there are 23 pairs of chromosomes, it is unlikely that the exact same sequence of chromosomes will occur when each sperm or ovum is formed.

For example, if we numbered the pairs of chromosomes 1A and 1B, 2A and 2B, 3A and 3B, and so on up to 23A and 23B before meiosis, a sperm or ovum might contain chromosomes 1A, 2B, 3B, . . . 23A after meiosis. Another sperm or ovum from the same individual might contain chromosomes 1B, 2A, 3A, . . . 23B after meiosis. Obviously, millions of possible sequences exist, and this in part accounts for individual differences among siblings.

Fraternal (dizygotic) twins develop from two ova fertilized by two different sperm. These children have no more resemblance to each other than other children of the same parents. Identical (monozygotic) twins develop from one ovum fertilized by one sperm. The resulting cell immediately divides into two zygotes, each containing identical genetic material.

FIGURE 9-3 Parents who have a recessive gene for sickle-cell anemia are carriers for this disease. One-fourth of their children will be normal, one-half will be carriers, and one-fourth will have the disease.

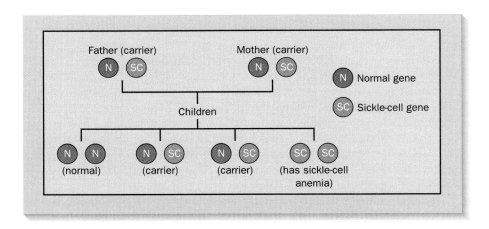

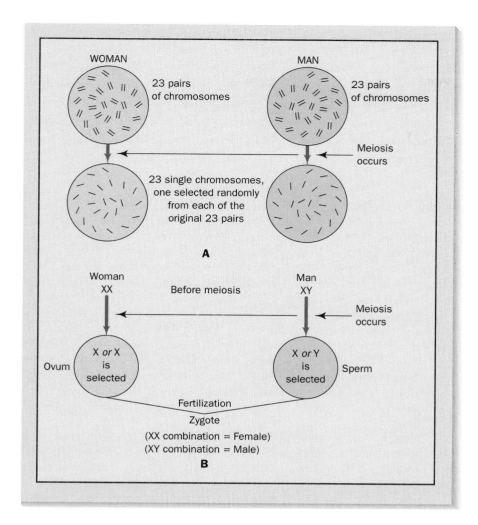

A

B

FIGURE 9-4 Diagram of genetic inheritance. The sex cell (sperm or ovum) of each parent contains 23 chromosomes. At conception, when the ovum is fertilized by the sperm, the 23 chromosomes from each parent combine to form the 23 pairs of chromosomes that characterize humans. (A) When sex cells are formed by meiosis, they contain 23 single chromosomes. (B) The sex of the child is determined by the 23rd pair of chromosomes.

Determination of Sex.

Although many societies have deemed a wife's failure to produce male offspring to be a basis for divorce, the sex of a child is actually determined by the father, not the mother. To understand this process, we need to examine the 23rd pair of chromosomes, the sex chromosomes.

In females, both sex chromosomes are the same; they are labeled XX. After meiosis, therefore, the ovum always contributes an X chromosome toward determining the child's sex. In males, the pair of sex chromosomes consists of a large chromosome and a smaller chromosome, which are labeled X and Y, respectively (the labels reflect the shapes of these chromosomes). After meiosis, the sperm may carry either an X or a Y sex chromosome.

When the sperm contributes an X chromosome, the pair of sex chromosomes will be XX, and the baby will be female. If the sperm contributes a Y chromosome, the pair of sex chromosomes will be XY, and the baby will be male.

Because they developed from a single ovum that was fertilized by one sperm, these sisters are indentical (monozygotic) twins.

Creating a Family Tree

HERE'S AN OPPORTUNITY FOR YOU TO EXPERIENCE HEREDITY FIRSTHAND BY MAKING a family tree. You will need to go back several generations. Be sure to include both sides of your family. In constructing this family tree, prepare a brief summary of both the physical characteristics and the personality traits of each person. Consider such attributes as hair color, eye color, height, intelligence, and personality traits. Once your family tree is complete, try to figure out what you have inherited.

Sex-Linked Traits. A gene located on a sex chromosome (X or Y) is called a *sex-linked gene*. The X chromosome is much larger than the Y chromosome and carries more genes. As a result, males are more vulnerable than females to some inherited disorders. In females, a recessive gene carrying a defect can be dominated by a gene on the other X chromosome; in males, however, the Y chromosome may not have the dominant gene, and the trait may appear. Such traits are called *sex-linked traits*.

Red-green colorblindness (see Chapter 3) is a sex-linked trait that occurs in about 8 of every 100 males in the United States. This most common form of colorblindness is controlled by genes on the X chromosome. A female may carry a gene for colorblindness on one X chromosome and a gene for normal vision, which is dominant, on the other X chromosome; she will have normal color vision. A male with a recessive gene for colorblindness, however, has no dominant gene for normal color vision on the Y chromosome, so he will be colorblind.

Hemophilia (also called *bleeder's disease*) is a sex-linked disorder that affects about 100,000 people (mostly males) in the United States. People with hemophilia lack a clotting factor in their blood; a small wound may cause them to bleed for hours. Internal bleeding can go undetected and result in death. Like colorblindness, hemophilia is carried on the X chromosome as a recessive gene (McKusick, 1986, 1995).

placenta
Organ that develops in the uterus during pregnancy; it produces hormones that maintain pregnancy, transmits nourishment to the fetus, and filters out certain harmful substances

FIGURE 9-5 During gestation, the developing baby (fetus) is suspended in the fluid-filled amniotic sac. The fetus is connected to the placenta by the umbilical cord.

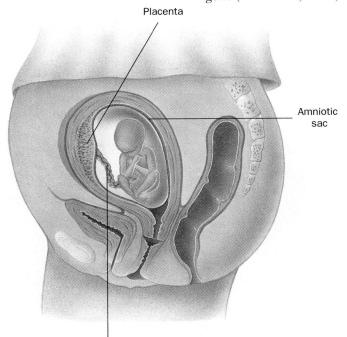

Placenta

Amniotic sac

Umbilical cord

Prenatal Development

The **placenta** (a Latin word meaning "flat cake") is an organ that develops even more rapidly than the fetus during the early months of pregnancy. The placenta allows an exchange of nutrients from the mother to the developing child and an exchange of waste products from the developing child to the mother. The mother's blood vessels intertwine with those that lead to the child through the umbilical cord. Because the blood vessels of the mother are separated by a membrane from those that lead to the child, however, not all substances can pass from one to the other. The three blood vessels of the *umbilical cord* connect the placenta and the fetus; one blood vessel provides nutrients and oxygen to the child; the two others remove waste (see Figure 9-5). Nutrients in the mother's blood are released into the placenta, where the fetus's blood takes them up and carries them, via the umbilical cord, to the fetus's body. Waste from the fetus goes in the opposite direction.

Testes develop in the embryo six to eight weeks after conception. If they start secreting testosterone (see Chapter 2), the developing baby will have male external genitals. The absence of testosterone leads to the development of a female (Halpern & Coren, 1993).

From the ninth week until birth, the developing child is called a **fetus.** By the end of the third month in the womb, the fetus is about three inches long and weighs about an ounce. Arms, legs, hands, and feet are visible and move in response to stimulation; the respiratory and digestive systems are functional. At the end of 6 months, the fetus is about 14 inches long and weighs 2 pounds. The eyes and eyelids are fully formed, and fat is beginning to form under the skin.

The fetus is suspended in a fluid-filled *amniotic sac* that cushions it against sudden movements or blows to the mother. Although it is immersed in amniotic fluid (which is 98 to 99 percent water), the fetus begins to move as early as the end of the third month of pregnancy (Moore & Persaud, 1993). However, the amniotic fluid retards the fetus's movement, which looks like those of "astronauts on the moon" (Hollander, 1979). Early in the pregnancy, the mother usually does not feel the motion of the fetus because the fetus is tiny and the uterus has no sense of touch; she begins to feel movement toward the middle of her pregnancy, when the fetus is large enough to be felt through the abdominal wall (Maurer & Maurer, 1988).

Barriers to Prenatal Development. If a pregnant woman's diet is inadequate, the baby is more likely to be born prematurely (at or before 37 weeks) or to have a low birth weight (less than 5.5 pounds). Low-birth-weight infants are 40 times more likely than normal-weight babies to die before their first birthday. Countries that have high numbers of low-birth-weight infants include Canada, Germany, Iran, Japan, China, and Norway. Compared with other industrialized countries, the United States has a relatively high infant mortality rate; in fact, 23 countries rank higher than the United States in the rate of infants who survive to their first birthday (Central Intelligence Agency, 1996).

Research conducted during the 1990s demonstrated that sufficient amounts of folic acid in the diets of pregnant women are important for the baby's development. For example, a large-scale study of 2,000 women who had previously given birth to a child with neural tube defects was conducted in seven countries. The researchers found that, when compared with women who received no supplement, 1,000 of the women who were randomly assigned to receive a folic acid supplement had a 72 percent reduction in neural tube defects in subsequent births.

Teratogens. Studies have demonstrated that a wide variety of factors, including drugs, alcohol, and viruses, can affect the developing fetus. A **teratogen** (from the Greek word for "monster") is any biological, chemical, or physical agent that can lead to birth defects. For example, the virus that causes *rubella* (German measles) can cross the placenta to the fetus. If a pregnant woman contracts rubella before the eleventh week of pregnancy, the baby is almost certain to have birth defects such as deafness or heart problems (Eberhart-Phillips, Frederick, & Baron, 1993). If the mother contracts rubella after 16 weeks, the chances of birth defects are near zero (Miller, Cradock-Watson, & Pollock, 1982).

We draw attention to the period during which rubella exerts its effects to introduce the concept of the critical period. A **critical period** is a specific time during development when certain processes should occur or when damage to normal development can take place. For example, most teratogens exert their most

fetus
The developing baby from about the ninth week after conception until birth

teratogen
Any biological, chemical, or physical agent capable of causing birth defects

critical period
A specific time during development when damage may occur or certain processes should take place

fetal alcohol syndrome (FAS)
Condition found in some children born to mothers who drank during pregnancy, characterized by lower birth weight, small head circumference, and mental retardation

damaging effects during the first eight weeks of development. Likewise, many neurons and neural circuits of the central nervous system develop between weeks 6 and 38 of prenatal development. If the developing child is exposed to teratogens, such as rubella, during the critical period, serious damage may result; if the critical period is successfully completed, damage from teratogens is much less likely.

A baby may also contract AIDS (acquired immunodeficiency syndrome) if the mother has the disease (Cohen, 1993; Grant, 1995). The virus that causes AIDS may pass through the placenta, or the baby may be exposed to the mother's infected blood during delivery (Weber, Redfield, & Lemon, 1986). Researchers do not fully understand why some infants contract AIDS in these situations and others do not. Most infants only live for a short time (five to eight months) after the AIDS symptoms appear (Chamberlain, Nichols, & Chase, 1991).

Drugs. Almost all drugs cross the placenta freely (Berk, 1998); among those that are harmful to the fetus are antibiotics (such as tetracycline), barbiturates, large doses of vitamins A and B6, and an acne preparation (Accutane). Even aspirin and caffeine are suspected of causing harm to the fetus. For example, heavy caffeine use is associated with miscarriage, low birth weight, and withdrawal symptoms in the newborn (Eskenazi, 1993).

In the 1950s and early 1960s, the tranquilizer thalidomide was used to treat nausea (morning sickness) occurring in the early stages of pregnancy. The drug was prescribed before it was known to be an extremely dangerous teratogen. Several thousand European women who had used thalidomide four to six weeks after conception (a critical period) gave birth to babies with severely deformed limbs (Moore & Persaud, 1993).

Babies born to mothers who are addicted to heroin are also addicted to those drugs and must undergo a painful withdrawal process. Marijuana use during pregnancy has been associated with decreased birth weight (Zuckerman et al., 1989).

Smoking. *Fetal tobacco syndrome,* a condition characterized by retarded fetal growth resulting in lower birth weight and hyperactivity (Cotton, 1994; Fried, 1993), can occur if a mother smokes as few as five cigarettes per day during pregnancy (Nieburg et al., 1985). Maternal smoking increases the level of carbon dioxide in the blood of the fetus and is also related to higher rates of infant death (U.S. Department of Health and Human Services, 1989). The number of fetal and infant deaths in the United States could be reduced by about 10 percent (4,000 fewer deaths) each year if all pregnant women stopped smoking (Kleinman et al., 1988).

Alcohol. Scientists have been aware for many years that children of alcoholic parents exhibit certain learning and developmental problems, such as low birth weight, small head size, and mental retardation. Until the early 1970s, many health professionals attributed these conditions to a disruptive home life and poor caretaking. Then physicians discovered that the mother's drinking behaviors could significantly affect her newborn's health. The identification of **fetal alcohol syndrome (FAS)** awakened the scientific community to the dangers of alcohol use during pregnancy (Jones & Smith, 1973). The signs of FAS include small head, flat midface, hearing loss, heart defects, and low intelligence (Aase, 1994; Day, 1992).

Ann Streissguth and her colleagues (Streissguth, Sampson, & Barr, 1989) completed two longitudinal studies of individuals whose mothers had been interviewed about their use of alcohol during pregnancy. The effects of prenatal exposure to moderate levels of alcohol were evident on the first day of life in indicators such as body tremors. The researchers also found that maternal alcohol use was associated with adolescent and adult handicaps such as intellectual deficiencies,

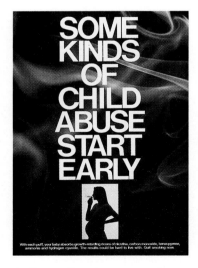

As few as five cigarettes a day can retard fetal growth

poor concentration, motor difficulties, and learning problems. Self-reported binge drinking (having five or more drinks on a single occasion) or drinking before becoming aware of a pregnancy were especially strong predictors of these problems (Streissguth, 1994; Streissguth, Sampson, & Barr, 1989).

Checking the Health of the Fetus.   Technological advances in the United States and other industrialized countries have greatly enhanced our ability to detect defects in the developing fetus (Moore & Persuad, 1993). Among the techniques available for this purpose are ultrasound and amniocentesis.

Ultrasound.   The **ultrasound procedure** involves directing high-pitched sound waves (more than 20,000 cycles per second) toward the fetus. We cannot hear these sounds, which pass through the body and bounce back like the sonar waves used by submarines. A computer converts these echoed sound waves into a **sonogram,** an outline image of the fetus, uterus, and placenta (see Figure 9-6).

Unlike X-rays, ultrasound appears to be harmless to the fetus. Physicians can use sonograms as early as five weeks after conception to determine the number of fetuses, the age of the fetus, the presence of gross deformities, and whether the fetus has died.

Amniocentesis.   The mother's age (especially if she is over 35), a family history of genetic defects, or detection of gross abnormalities by ultrasound may suggest the need for more precise testing by amniocentesis. **Amniocentesis** involves inserting a needle into the amniotic sac (see Figure 9-7) to withdraw about an ounce of amniotic fluid, which contains a small

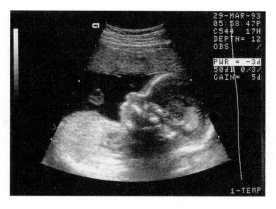

FIGURE 9-6 This sonogram shows the head and upper body of a 5-month-old fetus.

ultrasound procedure

Projection of sound waves onto the fetus, uterus, and placenta to construct a sonogram

sonogram

Outline picture constructed through use of the ultrasound procedure

amniocentesis

Withdrawal and analysis of amniotic fluid to detect genetic abnormalities in the fetus

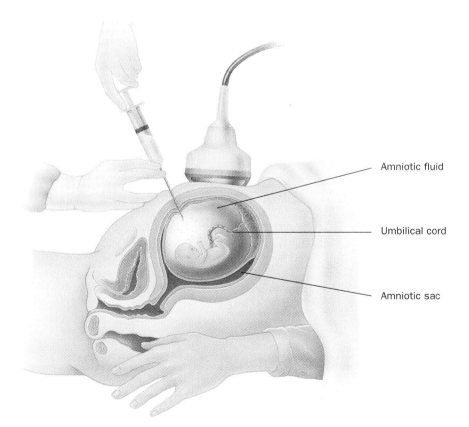

Amniotic fluid

Umbilical cord

Amniotic sac

FIGURE 9-7 In amniocentesis a needle is inserted into the amniotic sac and a small amount of amniotic fluid is withdrawn. The fetal cells in the amniotic fluid are analyzed to detect any genetic abnormalities that may be present.

number of fetal cells. The procedure can be done about 14 to 16 weeks after conception, when a sufficient amount of amniotic fluid is present. Fetal cells floating in the amniotic fluid are then analyzed. Amniocentesis is not risk-free. There is a 0.5 percent risk of a miscarriage; other risks include the possibility of introducing an infection into the uterus (Robinson & Henry, 1985).

Analysis of chromosomes can reveal the sex of the fetus as well as the presence of genetic defects such as Down syndrome, which occurs in about 1 in 800 births. In 95 percent of Down syndrome cases, the individual has three rather than two chromosomes in pair number 21 (Tingey, 1988). Children with Down syndrome are often in the mild-to-moderate range of mental retardation (see Chapter 8) (Plomin, De Fries, & McClearn, 1997) and find it difficult to distinguish between possible and impossible tasks (Pitcairn & Wishart, 1994). They have distinctive physical characteristics such as small skull, slanted eyes, protruding tongue, short neck, and enlarged abdomen. Heart defects and malformations of the digestive tract put them at risk for premature death (relative to normal children) unless these malformations are recognized and corrected. Despite difficulties such as these, early diagnosis and advances in medical technology have made it possible for individuals with Down syndrome to live longer and healthier lives (Carr, 1994).

Additional Genetic Tests.   Two additional methods of genetic testing are the *alphafetoprotein (AFP)* test and *chorionic villi sampling (CVS)*. The first test involves taking a blood sample to assess the level of AFP, a substance manufactured in the liver of the fetus, which eventually gets into the mother's bloodstream. High levels of AFP may indicate that the fetus has *spina bifida,* a disorder in which the spinal cord is exposed rather than covered by the backbone. Such high levels can also indicate that the brain is underdeveloped or that the fetus has Down syndrome. They may, however, mean nothing. Therefore additional testing is necessary. The second test, CVS, involves the removal of a small portion of the placental membrane, which can be analyzed in the same manner as the amniotic fluid obtained through amniocentesis. This technique has two advantages over amniocentesis: It can be done about eight weeks earlier, and it is less painful because it does not require puncturing the abdominal wall.

Returning to Bob and Liz, who are worried about having a Down syndrome baby because Bob's brother has the syndrome, amniocentesis will provide the answers they seek. However, the fact that Bob's brother has Down syndrome does not by itself mean that Bob and Liz are at risk. Liz's age is the most important risk factor. If she is well under the age of 40, her chances of having a Down syndrome child are greatly reduced.

Birth

A variety of drugs are used to reduce the pain of labor and delivery. Most of these drugs cross the placenta and are associated with a number of adverse short- and long-term effects on infants. As a result, "the use of medication in labor and delivery is a complicated and sensitive issue, because fetal risk, maternal pain, and physician need are at constant odds" (Bornstein & Lamb, 1992, p. 124). Concern about the effects of pain-reducing drugs has led some physicians to use these drugs more cautiously and in lower dosages than they did a few decades ago. Because it takes some time for drugs to cross the placenta, the longer the administration of drugs can be delayed, the better it is for the unborn child.

The growing popularity of a set of practices originally proposed by Grantly Dick-Read (1959) in England and Ferdinand Lamaze (1958) in France that are collectively known as *natural childbirth* has also reduced concern about the use of medication during labor and delivery. Actually, natural childbirth is a misnomer because any birth that occurs without surgical intervention is natural (Kime, 1992). *Prepared*

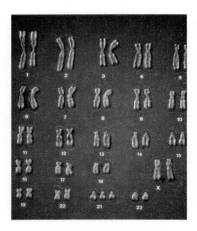

Because pair #21 has three chromosomes rather than two, this individual suffers from Down syndrome.

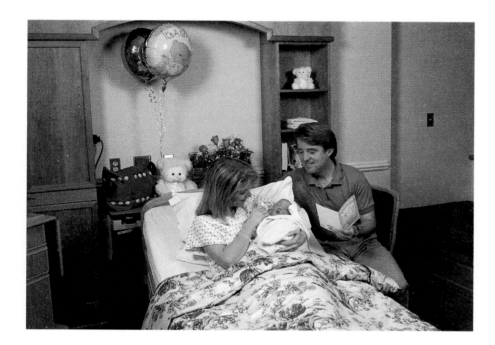

A delivery suite in modern hospitals allows family members to become more involved in the birth of a baby and in caring for the newborn immediately after birth.

childbirth involves special training in which the pregnant woman learns about the processes of labor and delivery and is taught relaxation techniques and breathing methods that help reduce the pain of labor and ease the process of delivery.

Unless the baby is premature, birth occurs approximately 266 days after fertilization or 280 days after the last menstrual period; depending on when the count begins, birth usually occurs after 38 or 40 weeks. Estimates of delivery dates are usually based on the date of the last menstrual period because it is easy to remember; it is usually impossible to know the precise time of fertilization. Hence birth may occur several days or even weeks before or after the "due date," keeping the expectant parents and their friends and relatives guessing until the last minute.

During the seventh month of pregnancy, the fetus usually moves into position for birth, usually with its head downward. At this stage, the mother may begin to experience some discomfort as the baby's head presses on her bladder. During the last month of pregnancy, the baby drops to a lower position in the uterus, a sign that birth is imminent.

The first stage of the birth process, labor, begins when the pituitary gland and uterus release a hormone called *oxytocin* that stimulates contractions of the muscles of the uterus (Mittendorf et al., 1990). Often the mother becomes aware of the onset of labor when her "water breaks"; this expression refers to a sudden release of amniotic fluid through the widening cervix (the narrow constricted portion of the uterus). Labor may last from a few hours to days; it is usually longer for a first birth than for later births. The second stage of the process is delivery, the actual birth of the baby. At birth, the average newborn in the United States weighs 7.5 pounds and is approximately 20 inches long. Delivery places tremendous force on the child's body, especially the head. Fortunately, the baby's skull is pliable, so that it can squeeze through the birth canal; however, the pressure created by the passage of the baby's head through the narrow birth canal can be very painful for the mother and is the main reason for the use of pain-relieving drugs during delivery.

During the birth process, some babies experience **anoxia,** or lack of oxygen. This occurs for several reasons: The contractions may compress the umbilical cord, the baby may squeeze the cord, or the cord may be wrapped around the baby. Medication given to the mother usually crosses the placenta and may interfere with the baby's breathing, thus depriving the baby of even

anoxia
Reduction or lack of oxygen

cesarean section
Procedure in which a baby is surgically removed from the uterus

more oxygen. Severe anoxia can cause cerebral palsy, a motor disability affecting the arms, head, and legs (Broman, 1979).

Expulsion of the placenta and related tissue mark the third stage of birth, called *afterbirth*.

Birth is a strenuous process for the infant as well as the mother. In fact, levels of the stress hormones epinephrine and norepinephrine are higher in infants than in women giving birth or in other adults during stressful events. This burst of stress hormones increases the infant's chances of survival by clearing the lungs for breathing, increasing the flow of blood to the brain and vital organs, and stimulating the liver to produce glucose (Lagercrantz & Slotkin, 1986).

When babies are in distress during delivery or are not in the head-down position, the physician may perform a **cesarean section,** or surgical removal of the baby from the uterus through an incision in the mother's abdomen. If the cesarean section is performed before the mother's contractions begin, the baby may not experience a surge of stress hormones. This may account for the breathing problems sometimes encountered in babies delivered by cesarean section. The rate of cesarean births in the United States is the highest in the world. For example, 23.5 percent of births in America in 1994 were by this method (U.S. Bureau of the Census, 1996).

Review Summary

1. Developmental psychologists are interested in the quantitative and qualitative changes that take place from conception until death. Both kinds of changes result from the interaction of genetic **(nature)** and environmental **(nurture)** influences.

2. Longitudinal studies are conducted to evaluate changes over a period of time. **Cross-sectional studies** are used to obtain information at a particular point in time.

3. A **cohort** study involves comparing individuals of the same age who were born in different generations. A comparison of cohorts yields information about the effects of growing up in different times.

4. Conception occurs when a sperm and an ovum unite. The child inherits half of its genetic makeup from each parent.

5. A **zygote** is produced by the union of a sperm and

an egg. The zygote embeds itself in the wall of the uterus and develops into a **fetus.** At birth, which occurs approximately 266 days after fertilization, the average baby weighs 7.5 pounds and is 20 inches long.

6. Despite the protection of the mother's body, the baby's development may be influenced by the mother's diet, her physical condition, and any drugs she may use, including tobacco and alcohol.

7. Both the **ultrasound procedure,** in which a sound-generated picture of the fetus (a **sonogram**) is produced, and **amniocentesis,** in which the genetic nature of fetal cells is analyzed, are used to determine the sex of the unborn child and whether any genetic defects are present. The *alphafetoprotein* and *chorionic villi sampling* procedures may also be used to determine genetic defects.

Study Break

1. Match the following terms with their definitions.

a. Developmental psychology

b. Nurture

c. Nature

d. Mitosis

1. Any substance that can lead to birth defects

2. The process by which a cell reproduces

3. Systematic changes that occur from conception to death

4. Lack of oxygen during childbirth

e. Meiosis

f. Gene

g. Hemophilia

h. Placenta

i. Teratogen

j. Anoxia

5. A sex-linked disorder

6. Environmental determinants of individual traits

7. Basic unit of inheritance

8. Hereditary determinants of individual development

9. Organ that provides nutrients to the fetus

10. Process of cell reduction

2. Name some situations in which developmental psychologists may be consulted or employed.
3. Distinguish between qualitative and quantitative aspects of development.
4. Distinguish between a longitudinal study and a cross-sectional study. What potential problems are associated with each of these research strategies?
5. Explain the concept of polygenic inheritance.
6. A sperm and an ovum unite to form
   a. a fetus.   **b.** a neonate.
   c. a zygote.   **d.** an embryo.
7. The sperm provides what percentage of the child's genetic inheritance?

8. Most human traits are controlled by a number of different genes, a phenomenon known as
   a. meiotic division.
   b. dizygotic genesis.
   c. multigenic inheritance.
   d. polygenic inheritance.
9. After the testes develop in the fetus, they secrete a substance that causes the fetus to be a male. What is the substance?
   a. Testosterone   **b.** Dopamine
   c. Estrogen   **d.** Estradiol

Development in Infancy

You are at the hospital visiting a friend who has just had a baby. You have visisted her several times and have seen her baby sleeping, crying, and just lying quietly in the crib. How utterly helpless and unable to interact with her environment she seems to be. *To what degree can newborns perceive and interact with their environment?* ■

Newborn infants (called *neonates*) may be quite different from those depicted in advertisements for baby products, which often use 3- or 4-month-old babies. The narrowness of the birth canal causes most newborns to emerge red and with facial bruises. The head is misshapen, and the baby is covered with a substance resembling cheese. This "bundle of joy" is apparently capable of little more than crying, sleeping, and excreting.

Just after birth, a baby's motor behavior appears to be uncoordinated and purposeless; however, newborns enter the world equipped with several reflexes (see Chapter 2; Knobloch & Pasamanick, 1974). The precise functions of some reflexes remain a mystery, but others, such as blinking or sucking, clearly offer protection or promote survival. Lightly stroke a baby's cheek and the baby turns toward the touch; this is the **rooting reflex**, which aids the newborn in finding the mother's nipple to obtain nourishment. Place a nipple in a baby's mouth and it begins sucking. Lightly press a finger in a baby's palm and it grasps with more force than you might imagine. In fact, the **palmar or grasp reflex** is so strong that you can lift an infant by its hands. Sudden noise or the sensation of being dropped elicits the **Moro reflex:** The startled infant flings out its arms and then brings them toward its body as if to hug something. When the bottom of a newborn's foot is stroked, the toes fan upward. This response, the **Babinski reflex,** is routinely used to test the functioning of the central nervous system.

Sensory Abilities

Unable to do more than move reflexively, a baby may look like the picture of psychological incompetence (Schaffer, 1977). A closer look at newborns, however, reveals that they are remarkably competent. Very young infants actively

rooting reflex
Reflex in which the infant turns its head in the direction of a touch on its face

palmar or grasp reflex
Reflex consisting of a very strong hold on any object placed in the palm

Moro reflex
Startle reflex in response to a loud noise or the sensation of being dropped

Babinski reflex
Reflex in which the infant's toes fan upward when the bottom of the foot is stroked

obtain information from their environment (Gibson, 1987). They can recognize their mother's voice just hours after birth. That recognition ability may actually develop before birth, while the baby is in the uterus.

Voice Recognition. Psychologists Anthony De Casper and Melanie Spence (1986) asked 12 women to read a Dr. Seuss story aloud twice a day during the last 5 to 6 weeks of pregnancy. Three days after birth, their babies varied the way they sucked on a pacifier according to whether they heard that story or another one through a loudspeaker. The babies sucked more actively in response to the story they had heard while in the womb, compared with a new story. Because a developing fetus constantly hears its mother's voice, it is not surprising that babies recognize their mother's voice long before they recognize their father's voice (De Casper & Prescott, 1984).

Vision. Estimates of the newborn's visual acuity range from 20/300 to 20/800 (Cole & Cole, 1993). Visual acuity improves to about 20/20 by 6 to 12 months (Cohen, De Loache, & Strauss, 1979).

Despite less than perfect vision, newborns can focus on objects that are about eight to ten inches away—the distance between the baby and the face of its caregiver during nursing or bottle feeding or when simply being held. They cannot reach out and touch objects, but their attention is riveted on faces and moving targets. Babies as young as two days prefer pictures of faces over pictures of other objects; complex patterns such as curved or wavy lines are favored over simple patterns like straight lines (Fantz, 1964).

Infants are attracted to and fascinated by faces, whether they are presented in two or three dimensions, in the flesh, or on film. Six-month-old babies prefer to look at attractive faces, even though they lack prior experience with cultural standards of beauty (Langlois et al., 1991).

Taste and Smell. Jacob Steiner (1979) carried out some simple yet fascinating studies of newborns' facial expressions in response to taste and smell. Some of the babies were only a few hours old and had not yet been nursed or fed. Steiner placed drops of chemical substances on each baby's tongue or under its nose and filmed the reactions. The babies' reactions to sour, bitter, and sweet substances were remarkably similar to those of adults.

In fact, it appears that both the taste and smell receptors are present and probably functioning by the fourth month of development. Studies have found that premature infants are capable of smell, suggesting that the fetus is capable of smell (Hughes & Noppe, 1991). Infant smell sensitivity seems to be present at birth for gross odor differences and rapidly increases in sensitivity during the first few weeks after birth (Porter et al., 1992).

How Newborns Learn

As we have seen, newborns are quite adept at perceiving the world around them (see Chapter 6). Research on newborns in the United States has shown that they are also quite capable of learning via classical conditioning, operant conditioning, and imitation.

Classical Conditioning. We saw in Chapter 6 that John Watson and Rosalie Rayner were able to classically condition fear in an older infant, Albert. Carolyn Rovee-Collier and Lewis Lipsitt (1982) have since demonstrated that newborn infants can also be classically conditioned (see also Blass, Ganchrow, & Steiner, 1984).

Psychological Detective

 How might you demonstrate classical conditioning in a newborn? First you must select a behavior that occurs frequently and automatically when appropriate stimulation is presented. What is such a behavior called? Then there are other components to be considered. Try to recall the name of each element. A review of Chapter 6 will assist you. Write down your answers before reading further.

Sucking is a frequent and automatic response that can serve as the unconditioned response (UR). A nipple placed in a baby's mouth elicits the sucking reflex, so the presence of the nipple in the mouth is an unconditioned stimulus (US). The sound of a particular phrase, such as "Are you hungry, baby?," spoken by the mother just before the baby begins to suck could be the conditioned stimulus (CS). Each time the baby loses the nipple and stops sucking, the mother could repeat the question. Then one day, when the baby has just been put down for a nap but is a little fussy, the mother says, "Are you hungry, baby?," and the baby starts sucking (conditioned response, CR), leading her mistakenly to think the baby really is still hungry. Try diagramming this arrangement of CS, US, UR, and CR as we did in Chapter 6.

Operant Conditioning. Operant conditioning has been demonstrated in three-day-old babies who learned to change the rate of their sucking (De Casper & Fifer, 1980). The reinforcer for changes in the rate of sucking was hearing the mother's voice rather than an unfamiliar one. Most of the babies learned the task quickly. By using other types of positive reinforcers, such as pictures or music, the researchers learned about the stimuli that served as reinforcers for newborns. The infants sucked more vigorously in response to some of those stimuli than they did in response to others. More recently, Carolyn Rovee-Collier (1993) demonstrated that as early as two months after birth, an infant can learn to make a kick response when it is reinforced by movement of a mobile suspended over the crib. Moreover, this research has shown that the memory of this learning session may be retained for several days after the conditioning session.

Imitating Others. Andrew Meltzoff and M. Keith Moore (1989) studied 40 babies less than 72 hours old to determine whether the newborns could imitate two behaviors modeled by an adult: protruding the tongue and moving the head. According to the authors, "The results show that infants systematically matched the adult display shown to them" (p. 966) (Figure 9-8). Sticking your tongue out and moving your head to imitate another person may not seem like much of an accomplishment, but think about the elements of the task that must be performed by a 3-day-old baby. First, the baby must be able to see the model's behavior well enough to discriminate between tongue protrusion and head movement. Then the baby must transform the perception of these behaviors into a behavioral imitation and store this sequence of perceptual discrimination and responding in memory in anticipation of the next occurrence of the situation. Thus the infant engages in complex processes, which provide the foundation for the even more complex activities it will learn later (Meltzoff & Moore, 1992).

FIGURE 9-8 A young infant is capable of imitating the behavior of an adult.

Maturation

Maturation is the biological unfolding of an organism according to the plan stored in its genes. In humans it refers primarily to the development of the motor and nervous systems. In the nervous system, myelin sheaths (see Chapter 2) begin to cover more axons after birth (Lipsitt, 1986), but myelination may not be complete until young adulthood. The sequence of myelination parallels the maturation of the entire nervous system (Yakovlev & Lecours, 1967). At birth or shortly afterward, the pathways connecting the senses and the brain are reasonably well myelinated, so the sensory equipment is in working order. As the nerve pathways between the brain and muscles myelinate, the developing person becomes capable of more complex motor activities. The lack of myelin explains why a child cannot jump or stand on one leg at a young age. As myelin sheaths cover more motor axons, children gain voluntary control over their behavior; at the same time, reflexes like rooting drop out of their repertoire.

Development of the Brain. Before birth, the brain develops at an amazing rate, adding as many as 250,000 new nerve cells each minute (Bornstein & Lamb, 1992). A spurt in cell development just before birth gives the newborn most, but not all, of its brain cells. The lower brain centers responsible for reflexes, breathing, digestion, and heartbeat are almost fully developed; cells in the cortex are numerous but not yet fully connected. The connections among these cells develop rapidly but are susceptible to environmental influences (Moore, 1989). Raising rats in an impoverished or enriched environment directly influences several aspects of brain growth and development; the development of the human brain is also influenced by such environmental factors.

Physical Development. As their daughter Yan approaches her third birthday, Chang and Mei Ling are amazed at how much she has changed since birth. She is more than twice as tall and weighs four times as much as she did when she was born. What's more, she has been walking on her own for almost two years and can climb stairs without assistance. Yan is not the seemingly helpless infant they brought home from the hospital.

Are such dramatic physical changes normal? Without question, the answer is yes. The rate of physical development immediately after birth is not equaled during the rest of a person's life. By the first birthday, height has increased from 20 to 30 inches and weight has tripled, from an average of 7.5 to over 22 pounds (Watson & Lowney, 1967).

As you might expect from our discussion of nature and nurture, inherited characteristics and the environment interact to determine the course of growth during this period (Mott, 1991; Scarr, 1992). Whether you will stand 42 inches tall and weigh 38 pounds by age 3 is determined by your genetic potential to attain this height and weight and the availability of a diet that allows you to realize that potential. The influence of environmental factors, especially nutrition, is evident in the relationship between family income and the height of children. A higher proportion of children with retarded growth is found in families with incomes below the poverty level (Brown, 1987).

Table 9-2 lists several physical skills that develop during the first two years of life and the approximate age at which they are mastered by children in the United States. Some babies and toddlers are able to perform motor behaviors at younger ages than those shown in Table 9-2. Such individuals are **precocious;** that is, they develop motor and cognitive abilities at an early age. Other children take longer than average to develop. Precocious development is frequently a source of pleasure and pride for parents, but slower motor develop-

maturation
Biological unfolding of the genetic plan for an individual's development

precocious
Developing motor and cognitive abilities at an early age

TABLE 9-2   **Physical Skills Acquired during the First Two Years of Life**

APPROXIMATE AGE AT WHICH SKILL IS MASTERED BY MOST CHILDREN

Rolling over	5.5 months
Sitting without support	7 months
Standing while holding on	8.5 months
Grasping with thumb and fingers	10.5 months
Standing alone	14 months
Walking well	15 months
Walking up steps	22 months
Kicking ball forward	23.5 months

Source: Adapted from Frankenburg et al., 1992.

Sinjin is an active 3-year-old whose physical development owes a lot to his backyard swing set.

ment is not necessarily a cause for concern or alarm. Children develop motor behaviors at widely varying ages.

When a baby's development is seriously delayed, remedial steps can be taken. To determine whether such steps are required, a psychologist or pediatrician may administer the Bayley Scales of Infant Development (Bayley, 1969; Kaplan-Estrin, Jacobson, & Jacobson, 1994). These scales provide indications of average, below-average, and above-average responses for a range of behaviors and stages of intellectual development for children between the ages of 2 months and 2.5 years. The Bayley Scales do not predict a child's future intelligence, but they do indicate whether development is lagging behind or is far ahead of what would normally be expected during early childhood.

Maturation is *not* an automatic process; cultural practices in infant rearing also can play an important role in physical development. For example, rapid motor development is actively discouraged by the Zinacanteco Indians of Mexico (Greenfield, 1992). On the other hand, babies in the West Indies are encouraged to sit up and walk much earlier than babies in North America (Hopkins & Westra, 1988; Super, 1981).

The physical development that occurs during infancy and childhood is impressive. As we see in the next sections, psychosocial development and cognitive development also occur at an impressive rate.

A Cross-Cultural Case for Breast Feeding and Good Infant Nutrition

Cultural & Diversity Perspective

During the 1970s, "more than 75 percent of American infants were bottle fed" (Berk, 1998, p. 124). Recently, along with an increase in the number of natural births, renewed interest in breast feeding has been demonstrated. In addition to being emotionally satisfying for both mother and infant, breast feeding offers some proven health advantages, especially in poverty-stricken countries.

First, the mother's milk transfers antibodies from the mother to the infant; hence breast-fed infants have fewer respiratory and intestinal illnesses (Ford & Labbok, 1993). Second, the mother's milk is more nutritious and appropriate for the infant's developing nervous system than milk from other animals (Raiha & Axelsson, 1995). This comparison is even more pronounced when breast feeding is compared with the *very* poor quality formulas that infants in economically depressed countries may be fed. The nutrition from breast feeding literally increases the chances these infants will survive. There are two potential problems with this conclusion, however. First, it assumes that the breast-feeding mother is in good health; if she isn't, then the quality of her milk may be inferior to a poor-quality formula, and the infant will suffer. Second, the 1990s have brought another problem to breast feeding. Because HIV can be transmitted through breast milk, confused new mothers in impoverished countries with very high HIV rates—women who were previously indoctrinated as to the benefits of breast milk—are now being told to return to infant formula, which is nutritionally inferior and very expensive.

Breast feeding also decreases the infant death rate in another way. Because women who are breast feeding are less likely to become pregnant, the number of children is reduced (Grant, 1995). The lower number of children competing for scarce resources results in a lower death rate.

This scenario paints a convincing picture for breast feeding. Infants do not continue breast feeding forever, however. What happens when they are weaned and begin eating solid foods? Unfortunately, the chances for malnutrition are high for many children in economically depressed countries. The most severe cases of malnutrition, associated with diets that are high in starch and low in protein, may lead to *kwashiorkor,* a condition that develops after weaning that is characterized by swelling, loss of hair, listlessness, and skin rashes. If this severe form of malnutrition is not corrected, brain development, especially myelination, is likely to be affected. Children who have kwashiorkor score low on intelligence tests and may have problems in school (Galler et al., 1990). Without question, the diet of the infant is crucial for development. Hence proper nutrition ultimately may be the cause of some cultural differences.

Review Summary

1. Newborn infants are able to recognize voices (audition) and faces (vision), to make appropriate facial reactions to taste and smell, and even to learn.

2. When a particular spoken phrase (CS) is paired with the presence of a nipple in the mouth (US), the infant can be classically conditioned to elicit a sucking response (CR) when just the phrase is spoken. Infants have also been operantly conditioned to change their rate of sucking in response to a stimulus they like (positive reinforcer), such as their mother's voice.

3. Imitation of such behaviors as tongue protrusion and head movement is shown in 3-day-old babies.

4. The biological development of a person according to his or her genetic makeup is termed **maturation.**

The rate of physical development right after birth is the highest it will be at any point during the individual's lifetime.

5. The interaction of genetic makeup and environmental factors determines the specific growth pattern for each individual. Some **precocious** babies develop physical and cognitive abilities at an early age; others are slower to develop.

6. Psychologists may use the Bayley Scales of Infant Development to determine whether an infant is average, above average, or below average in behavioral and intellectual development.

Study Break

1. Describe the evidence that supports the idea that infants have good visual ability.

2. In the classical conditioning study of infants, identify the role played by the nipple, the spoken phase, and sucking, respectively.

3. Research on operant conditioning in babies had the babies change the rate of their sucking in order to hear their mother's voice. What was the mother's voice in this research?
   a. stimulus
   b. response
   c. reinforcer
   d. goal
4. The biological unfolding of an individual according to a genetic plan is known as
   a. maturation.
   b. development.
   c. genetic inheritance.
   d. biological determinism.
5. Why are young children unable to perform complex motor behaviors?
6. What term describes babies who develop motor or cognitive activities at an early age?
   a. gifted
   b. precocious

   c. developmentally advanced
   d. motor capable
7. What is the name of the test that can be used to evaluate infant development?
8. If you classically condition a baby to fall asleep whenever it hears a lullaby on its crib music box, the song is serving as a(n)
   a. CR.
   b. CS.
   c. UR.
   d. US.
9. Which of the following skills is typically developed *last?*
   a. kicking ball forward
   b. walking up steps
   c. walking alone
   d. standing alone

Psychosocial Development in Childhood

Christiana is a single parent who works to support her 2-year-old daughter, Jerrie. The growing numbers of dual-career and single-parent families are increasingly relying on nonparental care for their children. Waiting lists at day-care centers are growing. Parents who cannot afford private day care may have to wait as long as two years for an opening at a subsidized day-care center. Despite the great demand for day care, little is known about the impact it may have on the development of young children. *Is day care harmful or beneficial to children?* ▨

The effects of day care are just one of the many topics studied by psychologists interested in the psychosocial development of young children. If you break the word psychosocial down into its two components, *psycho* and *social,* you have a good idea of what this section covers. We consider the development of the individual's unique personality (psycho) as well as factors that influence the ability to interact with the other people (social). Such abilities begin at an early age. For example, social behaviors begin to emerge by the time a child is a year old (Moore & Corkum, 1994).

Temperament

Physicians Alexander Thomas and Stella Chess (1980) were struck by the differences they observed in their own children; those differences were apparent even during the first few weeks of life. They were also impressed by the low correlations between environmental influences, such as parental attitudes and practices, and the child's psychological development. They decided to study the causes and consequences of differences in *temperament*. Temperament is the "how" of behavior: its quickness, ease of approach to new situations, intensity, and mood. A child's temperament is revealed in measures of activity level, regularity of biological functions, approach to or withdrawal from new situations, adaptability to new or altered situations, intensity of reaction, quality of mood, distractibility, and attention span and persistence. Thomas and Chess identified three types of temperament:

1. *Easy children* (40 percent) behaved in consistent ways, had a positive approach to new situations, and were highly adaptable to change. Their mood was mild to moderate and predominantly positive.
2. *Slow-to-warm-up children* (15 percent) displayed a combination of intense, negative responses to new stimuli with slow adaptability even after repeated contact.
3. *Difficult children* (10 percent) did not behave in consistent ways, were nonadaptable, and usually characterized by an intense negative mood.

As you can see from the percentages, not all children fit easily into one of these three groups.

Heredity seems to play an appreciable role in determining temperament (DiLalla, Kagan, & Reznick, 1994; Emde et al., 1992). Level of activity is especially enduring; in one study the children who were most active four days after birth were also most active eight years later (Korner et al., 1985). Difficult children are most vulnerable to behavior problems in early and middle childhood. Most of them improve with parental counseling and other therapeutic measures. A study of the enduring temperament of babies born in Finland also emphasized the importance of parental views (Lehtonen, Korhonen, & Korvenranta, 1994).

Although the work of Thomas and Chess has made important contributions to our understanding of temperament, it is not the only approach. For example, David Buss and Robert Plomin (1984) view temperament in behavior-genetic terms; temperament is inherited and forms the core of an individual's personality. What's more, Buss and Plomin believe there are only three dimensions of temperament: activity level, sociability, and emotionality.

Despite these different views of temperament, research has shown that an infant's temperament remains remarkably stable as the child gets older (Goldsmith et al., 1987). The most stable aspects of temperament appear to be sociability, emotionality, and level of activity (Goldsmith & Campos, 1982; Kagan, Reznick, & Snidman, 1987). Such stability suggests that temperament may influence the development of personality and the attachments that infants form with their caregivers.

Personality Development

Both Sigmund Freud and Erik Erikson proposed theories of personality development based on the idea that childhood experiences leave lasting marks on the individual's personality. Whereas both theorists believed that personality develops in a series of orderly stages and that childhood experiences are important, they differed in their emphasis. Freud stressed the individual's biological makeup, whereas Erikson stressed social interactions.

Sigmund Freud. During the late 1800s and early 1900s, Sigmund Freud radically influenced the way psychologists viewed the development of personality. Freud was the first person to propose that the early years of life are crucial to personality development. Freud's theory was concerned with the manner in which children resolve conflicts between their biological urges (primarily sexual) and the demands of society, particularly those of the parents. Freud viewed these conflicts as a series of developmental stages determined largely by the child's age. For example, he believed that during the first year of life, the mouth is the source of pleasure and sensual gratification. During this oral stage, the attitudes of the mother who breast-feeds her child and the timing of weaning are thought to have a significant effect on the infant's psychological development. (These developmental stages, along with their unique characteristics and demands, are described more fully in Chapter 12.) Freud, the first person to propose a stage theory of personality development, believed that each stage had the potential to affect the personality of the developing child.

Erik Erikson. Erik Erikson (1902–1994) also proposed a stage theory of personality development. Unlike Freud, however, Erikson did not stress the need to resolve conflicts created by biological needs. According to Erikson, our personality is molded by the way we deal with a series of psychosocial crises that occur as we grow older. A **psychosocial crisis** occurs when a psychological need conflicts with societal pressures and demands. Different cultures present different obstacles to the resolution of these psychosocial crises. Hence certain developmental paths will be more appropriate in one culture than in others.

Babies experience two psychosocial crises. The first occurs from birth until about 1.5 years of age, when the infant is establishing a pattern of **basic trust versus basic mistrust.** Put another way, can infants trust their environment? Will food be there when they are hungry? Will their diapers be changed? Will other sources of pain and discomfort be alleviated? The person who usually attends to the child's needs, the primary caregiver, plays a major role in the development of basic trust or mistrust. Consistent, loving caregivers facilitate the development of a sense of trust. Having trust in one's caregivers and one's environment is very important for developing trust in oneself. That is, infants who trust their caregivers and their environment begin to develop a sense that they are all right and that they fit into their environment in an appropriate manner.

Between the ages of about 1.5 and 3, children deal with a second psychosocial crisis, *autonomy versus shame and doubt. Autonomy* is the feeling that we can act independently and that we are in control of our own actions. Children start on the road to either autonomy or shame and doubt by developing a sense of how their behavior is controlled or determined. If children feel their behavior is not under their control but is determined by other people or external forces, they develop an external sense of control. Doubt and shame concerning one's ability to function frequently accompany an external sense of control. For example, if the parents always insist on feeding a child, the child may begin to doubt his or her ability to perform this important activity.

If children develop a sense of being in charge of what happens to them, they have developed an *internal* sense of control, or **autonomy.** The relationship between sense of control and autonomy is straightforward: The greater a child's internal sense of control, the greater the independence he or she will feel and exhibit.

The developing sense of independence allows children to begin doing things on their own. They decide what, when, and with whom they will play. This developing independence is the hallmark of the "terrible twos" and often brings children into conflict with their parents over such issues as what to eat and when to go to bed (Kopp, 1982). One cannot deny that the development of independence is necessary, yet it is also clear that the sense of independence must be achieved within certain rules and constraints. For example, children who are allowed to feed themselves in any manner they desire without being taught that throwing food is wrong may find it difficult to adapt to other social rules.

Erik Erikson proposed a stage theory of development that stresses the importance of psychosocial crises.

psychosocial crisis
Developmental problem or obstacle that is created when a psychological need conflicts with the demands of society

basic trust versus basic mistrust
Erikson's first psychosocial crisis (birth to 1.5 years), in which children learn through contact with their primary caregiver whether their environment can be trusted

autonomy versus shame and doubt
Erikson's second psychosocial crisis (1.5 to 3 years), in which children develop a sense of whether their behavior is under their own control or under the control of external forces

autonomy
The feeling of being able to act independently and having personal control over one's actions

initiative versus guilt
Erikson's third psychosocial crisis (3–7 years), in which children begin to evaluate the consequences of their behavior

industry versus inferiority
Erikson's fourth psychosocial crisis (7-10 years), in which children begin to acquire the knowledge and skills that will enable them to become productive members of society

The child's growing sense of morality forms the basis for Erikson's third psychosocial crisis, **initiative versus guilt** (approximately ages 3–7). A developing sense of right and wrong leads children to evaluate the consequences of the behaviors in which they might engage. Some behaviors, such as playing by the rules and obeying one's parents, can produce desirable consequences; others, such as cheating or not obeying one's parents, produce undesired consequences. To resolve this conflict successfully, children must take the initiative to adopt behaviors and goals that they enjoy *and* that society values. To do otherwise leaves the child (and later the adult) feeling guilty and fearful because his or her behaviors may not be appropriate or valued.

To make such decisions about the consequences of our behavior, we must successfully resolve the first two psychosocial crises: basic trust versus basic mistrust and autonomy versus shame and doubt. Unless children have some degree of trust in their own ability to take action, they will always be afraid of undertaking a new project or behavior.

The importance of developing a sense of competence also underlies Erikson's fourth psychosocial crisis, **industry versus inferiority** (approximately ages 7–10). Once children have developed basic trust, autonomy, and initiative, it is time to learn the skills and acquire the knowledge that will allow them to become productive members of society. The acquisition of such skills and knowledge reflects the development of industry. If a child is to become a productive member of society, the lessons taught in school must be learned, and learned well.

Erikson suggests that there are four additional psychosocial crises that continue beyond childhood; they are discussed in the next chapter. Although critics point out that Erikson's theory lacks precision, supporters note that it captures the reality of the changes that occur as we grow and develop throughout the life span. In addition, it is generally conceded that Erikson's theory is far more optimistic than Freud's.

STUDY CHART

Crises of Psychosocial Development During Childhood, as Proposed by Erik Erikson

Crisis	Approximate age	Characteristics
Basic trust versus basic mistrust	Birth to 1.5 years	Child learns whether to trust the environment. Ability to trust the environment is important for the development of trust in oneself.
Autonomy versus shame and doubt	1.5 to 3 years	Child develops a sense of control. The sense that control is internal (autonomy) helps the child develop independence. The sense that control is external fosters shame and doubt and hinders the growth of independence.
Initiative versus guilt	3 to 7 years	Child experiences conflict between the behaviors he or she wants to engage in and a growing sense of morality and begins to question whether certain behavior is right or good.
Industry versus inferiority	7 to 10 years	To become a productive member of society, the child must master certain skills and acquire a basic amount of knowledge. Successful learning and skill acquisition lead to the development of a sense of competence.

Source: Erikson, 1963.

FIGURE 9-9 The wire and terrycloth surrogate mothers used by Harry and Marguerite Harlow in their research on the development of attachment in infant monkeys.

If you read the sections about Freud and Erikson carefully, you noticed that personality develops in the context of significant other people, usually the parents. The attachments children form to their parents play a major role in shaping their developing personality.

Attachment

Attachment refers to an intense, reciprocal relationship occurring between two people, usually a child and an adult. The first experimental studies on the effects of attachment were reported by psychologists Harry and Marguerite Harlow (Harlow & Harlow, 1962). Approximately eight hours after birth, baby monkeys were separated from their mothers. The baby monkeys were raised in experimental chambers, where they were exposed to an inanimate object that served as a surrogate (substitute) mother. Some of the surrogate mothers were plain wire cylinders; others were covered with soft terrycloth (see Figure 9-9). Some of the infant monkeys were allowed to come into contact with both types of objects. When a bottle was attached, the baby monkey could be "fed" by the wire or cloth-covered "mother."

The Harlows found that the infant monkeys showed a definite preference for the soft, cloth-covered mother. For example, when confronted by a strange and frightening situation, they ran to the cloth-covered mother for safety and security. The monkeys showed this preference even when they were fed by the plain wire mother; apparently, the **contact comfort,** or warmth provided by the soft terrycloth, was a more important determinant of attachment than the provision of nourishment.

Although the Harlows' research demonstrated the role of contact comfort, it is clear that attachments are formed most often between children and their parents or primary caregivers. Parents and primary caregivers can return or reciprocate the love and affection that the child brings to the relationship. Inanimate objects do not return affection; the cloth mother provided only contact comfort and warmth.

In addition to demonstrating the importance of contact comfort, the Harlows also found that raising baby monkeys in isolation in the laboratory had a detrimental effect on the animals' social behavior (Suomi & Harlow, 1972; Suomi & Ripp, 1983). When the laboratory testing was complete, the juvenile monkeys were returned to a colony with other monkeys. The experimental monkeys,

attachment

Intense, reciprocal relationship formed by two people, usually a child and an adult

contact comfort

Preference for holding or clinging to objects, such as blankets or teddy bears, that yield physical comfort and warmth

however, did not adapt well in the colony. They avoided contact, fled from touch, curled up and rocked, or tried to attack the biggest, most dominant monkey in the group (often getting seriously injured in the process). Thus a major conclusion of the Harlows' research was that even though attachment was important, it did not ensure normal social development. Environmental contact (nurture) with members of one's own species is needed for this kind of development.

Ethological Theory. John Bowlby's **ethological theory** (1969) stresses the adaptiveness of attachment. Bowlby believes attachment evolved because of its adaptive value; infants are protected when parents or caregivers are near.

For Bowlby, attachment progresses through four stages:

Stage 1. Preattachment (birth to 6 weeks). Babies emit behaviors, such as smiling and crying, that bring them into close contact with humans. Attachment has *not* occurred because infants do not mind being left with unfamiliar adults.

Stage 2. Beginnings of Attachment (6 weeks to approximately 7 months). Infants begin to respond differentially to familiar adults but do not protest when separated.

Stage 3. Attachment (approximately 7 months to approximately 21 months). Attachment to the familiar caregiver is evident. Babies show distress when the primary caregiver leaves. Such *separation anxiety* appears to begin at approximately 6–7 months and increases until 15 months in cultures around the world (Kagan, Kearsley, & Zelazo, 1978).

Stage 4. Reciprocal Relationships (approximately 21 months). As language develops, separation anxiety decreases, and the child understands that the caregiver will return. Language allows the child to make requests of and bargain with the caregiver.

Bowlby (1980) believes that the experiences of these four stages result in the child's unique understanding of the parent-child bond. This understanding sets the stage for future close relationships.

The Strange Situation Test. Mary Salter Ainsworth observed the reactions of human infants confronted by strange situations (Ainsworth et al., 1978). At birth, infants are equipped with behaviors such as crying that promote closeness to a caregiver and operate to activate caregiving behaviors. "At first," Ainsworth (1989) notes, "these attachment behaviors are simply emitted, rather than directed toward any specific person, but gradually the baby begins to discriminate one person from another and to direct attachment behavior differentially" (p. 710).

Once attachment occurs, it can take several forms. One way to determine the kind of attachment a baby has developed is to observe the baby's reaction to being put in a *strange situation,* such as an unfamiliar playroom and the departure of the familiar caregiver. When Ainsworth and her colleagues did just that, they found that most babies (66 percent) were *securely attached.* When their mother was present to provide attention and support, securely attached babies explored and investigated their environment. A smaller group (20 percent) of babies did not want to be held; they also did not want to be put down. They ignored their mother or greeted her casually on her return. In fact, they seemed to interact with a stranger the same way they did with their mother. Such babies are termed *avoidant.* A third group, the *resistant* babies, sought closeness with the mother before she left. When she returned, these babies displayed angry, resistive behaviors. They often hit and pushed the mother. A fourth group consisted of *anxious-ambivalent* babies (see also Cassidy & Berline,

ethological theory of attachment

Theory stating that attachment evolved because of its adaptive value to the infant

1994) who became almost panic-stricken when their mother left. This panic reaction began before the mother left. When the mother returned, the baby actively sought, but at the same time actively resisted, contact and comfort.

It is important to remember that attachment is not a one-way process: The infant is only one-half of the interaction. The personality and temperament of the caregiver must also be considered. For example, the emotion and affect of the caregiver are related to the infant's pattern of attachment (Goldberg, MacKay-Soroka, & Rochester, 1994). Mothers of secure infants respond more frequently and are attentive to the full range of their baby's affective display, whereas mothers of avoidant infants are less responsive, especially to their baby's negative affect. Mothers of anxious-ambivalent babies are especially responsive to their baby's negative displays but unresponsive to positive displays.

The percentages of different types of attachment may vary from culture to culture (Van IJzendoorn & Kroonenberg, 1988). For example, more German infants than infants in the United States, Israel, or Japan are anxiously attached. Cultural practices such as German parents' stressing autonomy at an earlier age may produce such differences; they are not interpreted as deficiencies. However, sleeping out of the home in communal arrangements, such as those found in Israeli kibbutzim, may lead to an increase in anxious-ambivalent attachments (Sagi et al., 1994).

Infants' attachment styles are well documented, but not much is known about how these styles may influence individuals' behaviors as adults. Psychologists Judith Feeney and Patricia Noller (1990) found a relationship between the attachment style reported by the parents of college students and the students' preferred type of interpersonal relationship as adults (see also Vormbrock, 1993). For both men and women, there was a link between reported infant attachment style and preferred type of adult relationship. Securely attached babies grew into adults who had trusting attitudes toward others. Anxious-ambivalent babies were more dependent and in need of commitment in their relationships as adults. Babies with the avoidant style of attachment were more likely to mistrust others and feel uncomfortable in close relationships as adults. Likewise, early attachment patterns have been found to affect the behaviors of adults as old as 85 (Crose, 1994). What's more, Diane Benoit and Kevin Parker (1994) have shown that an attachment style can persist through at least three generations: We treat our children much as we were treated as children.

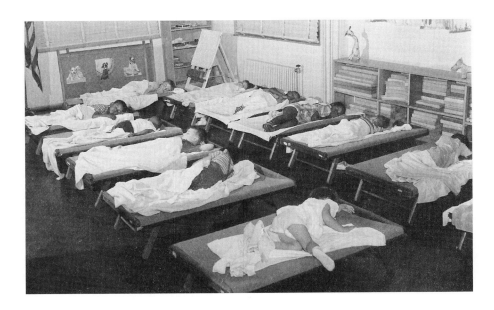

Children in an Israeli kibbutz sleep in a communal arrangement.

Finally, a longitudinal study of German children (Wartner et al., 1994) indicates that the lasting effects of attachment style occur in other cultures.

The Father's Role

We have repeatedly described the attachment established between an infant and its mother. What about the father? Do fathers form attachments with their children? There is some basis for the emphasis placed on the mother-infant attachment. As David Lynn (1974) pointed out, "One of the factors eroding the father's position in the family is the nature of work today in urban-industrial societies. Fathers now work away from the home, so that a degree of father absence is taken for granted. . . . In our society the absence of the father through death or divorce can be considered simply an extreme on the prevailing continuum of father absence" (p. 6). Despite this father-absent pattern, infants do establish attachments with their fathers at about the same age they form attachments with their mothers (Fox, Kimmerly, & Schafer, 1991). The types of interactions displayed by fathers with their infants may differ from those shown by the mother. Fathers are more likely to invest their time playing with their children than in cleaning or feeding them (Hossain & Roopnarine, 1994). It appears, however, that delaying having children until the father is older (i.e., age 35 and over) results in the father's spending more time with the child, having higher expectations for the child, and being more nurturant (Heath, 1994).

Culture and Fatherhood. The father-absent pattern does not occur in all cultures. For example, in the Chinese patriarchal (father-dominated) family, the most important relationship is between a father and his sons. Other cross-cultural research has found that infants in all cultures become attached to their parents despite widely varying child-rearing practices (Sagi, 1990).

In general, fathers tend to spend more time with their sons than with their daughters. Some psychologists (such as Pedersen, Rubenstein, & Yarrow, 1979) have found that a boy's cognitive development may be positively influenced by interaction with his father. As the number of dual-career and single-parent families increases, fathers are taking a more active role in caring for their babies.

Studies of Swedish (Lamb et al., 1982) and American (Belsky, Gilstrap, & Rovine, 1984) families have shown that the parent's sex is a more important

Both mothers and fathers form attachments with their children.

determinant of parent-child interaction than employment status and parental role. Mothers are more likely to have direct physical contact with infants (such as kissing, hugging, and holding them) than fathers are. Moreover, fathers spend only 20 to 35 percent as much time as mothers in one-on-one interaction with their children (Lamb et al., 1987). Because of increased employment among mothers and shrinking family size, this trend seems to be reversing itself; fathers are assuming more responsibility and spending more time caring for their children (Poussaint, 1990), even in cultures where such nurturance as known in the United States runs counter to the prevailing style (Nugent, 1991).

Day Care

In contemporary American society, "maternal employment is a reality. The issue today, therefore, is not whether infants should be in day care but how to make their experiences there and at home supportive of their development and of their parents' peace of mind" (Clarke-Stewart, 1989, p. 271). For example, some parents might be concerned that day care could weaken or change their child's attachment (Belsky, 1986). Karen McCartney and Deborah Phillips (1988) reviewed studies that compared the attachment of infants who attended day-care centers with that of infants who were cared for at home by their mothers. The results indicated that in the United States, infants who attended day-care centers did not differ from infants who were raised at home. Thus the concern that full-time day care results in more anxious and more insecure children seems unfounded (Roggman et al., 1994).

Children may actually derive some benefits from good day care. Such benefits may be more important for children from disadvantaged homes. Sandra Scarr and Marlene Eisenberg (1993) suggest that "good quality child care can enhance development of children from disadvantaged, stressed, and dysfunctional homes" (p. 618). In addition to contributing to children's cognitive and language development, placement in quality day care ensures that children receive appropriate inoculations and good nutrition. Good day care may also assist children's emotional development and help create better relationships between them and their parents. Day care provides some relief from the demands of parenting and can reduce stress because parents are assured that their children are receiving high-quality care. Also, it does not appear to matter if day care is done in a family setting or at a professional day-care center (Kontos, Hsu, & Dunn, 1994). What does matter is the quality of the day care.

What constitutes a good day-care center? A good day-care center functions as much like a good parent as possible. There is a high ratio of caregivers to children so that the caregivers can respond to each child's needs (Belsky, 1984). The emphasis is on teaching, as opposed to controlling the children (Miller & Bizzell, 1983), and day-care workers and children converse directly (McCartney, 1984). The social and cognitive foundations established in a high-quality day-care center carry over to the kindergarten and preschool experiences that mark the end of early childhood (Feagans & Farran, 1994). These experiences set the stage for the beginning of formal education in middle childhood.

Latchkey Children. Day-care centers are typically for younger children. Many older children who have a key to their house are expected to come home alone after school and do their homework and entertain themselves until their parents arrive. They are known as **latchkey children.** The media continually portray latchkey children as lonely and delinquent. Certainly, there is the potential for unauthorized, even delinquent behavior when children are left alone for long periods. The extent of such behavior is difficult to determine, however. To avoid such problems, parents should exercise great care in arranging for their

latchkey child
Child who is unsupervised after school

children's after-school activities. At the very least, children must be physically and emotionally capable of caring for themselves before they are allowed to come home to an empty house after school (Cole & Rodman, 1987). Concern over the growing number of latchkey children and the problems that their isolation and loneliness may create has led to the development of educational and organized after-school programs in many communities (Page, Scanlan, & Deringer, 1994).

Parenting Styles

Whether to place their children in a day-care center is only one of the many decisions parents face. How much television will the children be allowed to watch? Should children be spanked when they misbehave? How important to a child's diet are vitamins, vegetables, and milk? Such decisions reflect prevailing child-rearing practices and parenting styles (Darling & Steinberg, 1993) as well as the personalities and preferences of individual parents.

Diana Baumrind's (1971) research on parenting styles in the United States made use of interviews and observation. Trained observers recorded children's behaviors in nursery school. Another investigator interviewed the parents separately and then together about their child-rearing practices and beliefs. Then the investigator visited the home twice, staying from before dinner until after the child went to bed. On the basis of these observations and interviews, Baumrind concluded that 77 percent of the families studied would fit into one of three parenting styles (see also Steinberg et al., 1994):

1. *Authoritarian.* Parents shape and control their children's behavior according to a set standard; they emphasize the importance of obedience and use punitive measures to reduce misbehavior.
2. *Authoritative.* Parents know that they have more knowledge, skill, control, resources, and physical power than their children, yet they believe the rights of parents and children are reciprocal. They explain rules and decisions and are willing to listen to the child's point of view, although they do not always accept it. They are less likely to use physical punishment and less likely to stress obedience.
3. *Permissive.* Parents demonstrate less control than either authoritarian or authoritative parents because they believe children must learn how to behave through their own experience or because they do not take the time to discipline their children. They give children considerable leeway to set schedules and choose activities. They demand less achievement and are more willing to tolerate immature behavior.

Each of these parenting styles is associated with a different set of habits and behaviors. Children of authoritarian parents tend to be less sociable and friendly and more withdrawn than other children. Children of permissive parents are immature, moody, and dependent and have low self-control. Children of authoritative parents have good social skills and are well liked, independent, and cooperative.

Different cultures may emphasize different parenting styles (Bornstein, Tal, & Tamis-Lemonda, 1991). For example, the parenting styles of the Chinese are demanding and emphasize strict discipline and respect for elders (Chao, 1994). In turn, having been raised with a particular parenting style may assist one's adaptation to a particular culture. For example, children raised by authoritarian parents function well in that type of culture.

As you might expect, the parenting style to which a child is exposed at home has a significant impact on the development of self-esteem. Parents who have established clear, consistent rules but who are democratic in dealing with their children seem to have the most positive effect on the children's self-esteem. Suppose that a child's parents have told her that until she is 6 years old she may not cross the street by herself, but she may play with her friends on her side of the street. The child takes great pride in obeying these rules, and her parents reinforce her good behavior. When the rules are clear and the behavior is consistent, self-esteem and a sense of competence develop.

Keep in mind that parenting styles do not always include a husband and wife. As more gay and lesbian couples are choosing to have children by artificial insemination or adoption, research has focused on the effects that these non-traditional couples and their parenting styles have on children. A comparison of children born to 15 lesbian couples with children born to 15 similar heterosexual couples revealed no significant differences among the children. In fact, the lesbian couples had more parenting-awareness skills than the heterosexual couples (Flaks et al., 1995).

Other Influences.   In the middle to late years of childhood, growing independence and a decreasing need for parental supervision combine to increase the amount of leisure time available to most children in the United States. The majority of this time is taken up by peer-group activities and watching television. This pattern may not be seen in other cultures. For example, children in Japan and Taiwan, where the culture values academic achievement highly, spend more time reading (Stevenson & Lee, 1990).

The Peer Group.   Typically composed of classmates, selected friends, or other children in the neighborhood, the **peer group** offers children many opportunities for feedback concerning their abilities, intelligence, and values as they grow into young adults. Lessons about how to get along in a group may also be learned. Social skills are initially learned from parents; then, as interactions with other children become more frequent, newly acquired behaviors may be tested on the parents. Thus the peer group can foster the development of self-esteem and a sense of autonomy. Peer group influences can be negative, however. A youth may start to shoplift, smoke, and drink alcoholic beverages because of pressure from peer group members. For children with low prestige in the peer group, it will be nearly impossible to say no; to do so would surely mean the loss of what little status and popularity they might have.

Myth or Science

Although the media may portray gangs in present-day big cities as hardened young adults in their late teens or early twenties, this view may be far from accurate:

The average age of youth gang members continues to decline. Most experts place the figure at 13 to 15 years of age, whereas law enforcement officials in Los Angeles, Chicago, and other cities note that children as young as 9 or 10 are frequently found in today's gangs. (Rogers, 1991)

Today, the two most widely used approaches to combating gangs are suppression of drug use and sales and direct suppression of the gangs themselves. Neither of these approaches has been very effective. A more effective

peer group
Group of neighborhood children, classmates, or selected friends of the same age

Watching television has become an accepted part of the daily life of most children.

approach is to keep children from becoming involved with gangs in the first place.

Television. Does television really exert as great an influence on children as researchers and the media have led us to believe? The first step toward answering this question is to determine how much television children actually watch. According to Action for Children's Television (Nielsen Media Research, 1990), the rate of television viewing in the United States is extremely high. By the time the average child graduates from high school, he or she will have watched more than 25,000 hours of television, including more than 356,000 commercials. In the typical U.S. household the television is turned on 7.1 hours a day (Berk, 1998).

Although there is continuing debate over whether television viewing has intellectual benefits or leads to violence (see Chapter 16), one influence of television is firmly established. The stark reality of adult life portrayed on television has, to a great extent, removed the innocence from childhood (Winn, 1977). Any soap opera on any afternoon of the week displays the frailties and shortcomings of adults, leaving little to the imagination. The widespread acceptance of cable and satellite TV, as well as VCRs, has increased these options (Huston et al., 1992). Because children can learn all the "secrets" of adulthood (cursing, lying, romantic love, marriage, sexuality, stealing, violence) from television, they believe they are entitled to engage in these behaviors at a much earlier age. The result is a blurring of the distinction between childhood and adulthood.

So strong is the impact of television that some observers believe that television role models have undermined parents' ability to act effectively in this capacity (Friedrich-Cofer & Huston, 1986). With television modeling undesired behaviors, the task of raising children becomes much more difficult.

Psychological Detective

Are the critics right? Has television assumed a major portion of the parenting role? Do you want the television set to be a surrogate parent for your children in the same way that the wire and cloth forms were surrogate parents for the Harlows' monkeys? What could (or should) be done to correct the situation? Give these questions some thought, and write down your views before reading further.

You could restrict the amount of television that your children watch. This option is effective, and many parents impose such restrictions. What about the quality of the television programs viewed by children? It needs to be improved. Calls for television reform have led legislators to introduce several bills in Congress that are designed to regulate the amount of time allocated for commercials during children's programming *and* require that stations provide educational programming for children. Although such legislation would be helpful, parents are still ultimately responsible for the type and amount of television their children watch (American Academy of Pediatrics, 1986). Too much television can take away from other desired activities, such as reading and interacting with others (Singer & Singer, 1990).

Review Summary

1. Three types of temperament in young children—easy, slow-to-warm-up, and difficult—have been identified.

2. Sigmund Freud believed that the personality develops as a child deals with conflicts between biological urges and the demands of society.

3. Psychosocial crises, or conflicts between psychological needs and societal demands, were proposed as the main determinants of personality by Erik Erikson.

4. Erikson's psychosocial crises include **basic trust versus basic mistrust** (birth to age 1.5 years), **autonomy versus shame and doubt** (1.5 to 3 years), **initiative versus guilt** (3 to 7 years), and **industry versus inferiority** (7 to 10 years).

5. Studies of young monkeys conducted by Harry and Marguerite Harlow indicated that **attachment** was determined by contact comfort, not by the presence of food. Attachment to an inanimate object, however, is not sufficient for normal social development.

6. Infants form attachments with their caregivers. Mary Salter Ainsworth reports three main types of attachment: securely attached, avoidant, and anxious-ambivalent. The baby's style of attachment can influence relationships established during adulthood and may even persist through several generations. Infants form attachments with both the mother and the father.

7. The characteristics of the caregiver may also influence the type of attachment that develops.

8. Day-care centers have become more accepted as the demand for their services has grown. Good day care that is sensitive and responsive to each child's needs may be beneficial to the child's emotional development.

9. Diana Baumrind has found that over 77 percent of parents use one of three basic parenting styles: authoritarian, authoritative, or permissive. The particular parenting style has a major impact on the child's development of self-esteem.

10. Peer groups, television, and growing up in troubled areas all influence psychosocial development during middle childhood (ages 6 to 9).

11. Latchkey children are children who come home to an empty house after school. Concern about the growing number of unsupervised children has led to the development of organized after-school programs.

Study Break

1. Describe the three basic types of temperament that have been identified.
2. Name the four stages in Erikson's theory of development. Which basic psychosocial conflict is confronted during each stage?
3. Which of Erikson's psychosocial crises revolves around whether the child can depend on the primary caregiver?
 a. Initiative versus guilt
 b. Industry versus inferiority
 c. Autonomy versus shame and doubt
 d. Trust versus mistrust
4. What were the major findings of the Harlows' studies of attachment behavior in infant monkeys?
5. When Harlow and his colleagues completed their research with baby monkeys raised in isolation, they returned them to the monkey colony. What did they find?
 a. The monkeys immediately fit in socially.
 b. After some initial isolation, the monkeys adapted socially.
 c. The monkeys did not fit in socially at all.
 d. The monkeys eventually became social leaders.

6. Identify three main types of human attachment.
7. Which of the following factors should parents *not* look for in a good day-care center?
 a. an emphasis on teaching
 b. an emphasis on controlling children's behavior
 c. a high ratio of caregivers to children
 d. direct conversation between children and workers
8. You observe a parent who emphasizes obedience through guidelines and punishment. According to Baumrind, such a parent would be termed
 a. permissive.
 b. rigid.
 c. authoritative.
 d. authoritarian.
9. What evidence is there that television viewing may not be beneficial to young children?
10. An intense, reciprocal relationship between a child and an adult is called
 a. attachment.
 b. bonding.
 c. imprinting.
 d. connecting.

cognitive development
Changes that occur in our thought processes throughout life

assimilation
Piaget's term for the process of incorporating information into existing schemas

Cognitive Development in Childhood

In 1992, the American Psychological Association celebrated its hundredth anniversary. As part of this celebration, a traveling psychology exhibit that made stops in major cities was assembled. Many aspects of psychology were put on public display. Joe took his two daughters to see the exhibit. The children were fascinated by one of the exhibits, which consisted of two partially filled flasks. The flasks were very wide at the bottom and narrow at the top. They were mounted on a wall in such a way that they could be turned with the top up or down. When the flasks were turned bottom up, the children thought they were fuller than when they were turned bottom down. *What can this unusual display tell us about cognitive development in children?* ▪

Cognitive development refers to the changes that occur in our thought processes as we pass through life. Cognitive development and intelligence go hand in hand. As we saw in Chapter 8, intelligence has been measured by psychologists since 1905, when Alfred Binet developed a test to measure the intelligence of French schoolchildren. However, measuring the intelligence of babies and young children has been particularly difficult. Babies will not sit still for very long, and their ability to answer questions is very limited. Despite such obstacles, the Swiss scientist Jean Piaget (1896–1980) spent his professional career studying the cognitive development of young children.

Piaget's Theory

Do children perceive, think, and understand the world the way adults do? Early in the twentieth century psychologists attempted to measure an individual's intelligence and assign it a number (a quantitative approach). Binet began this approach, although he was wary of assigning intelligence scores to children because those scores might influence how the children were viewed by others, particularly teachers (see Chapter 8).

Early in his career, Piaget worked in Binet's laboratory, translating tests. As Piaget tried out test items on French children, he grew curious about the children's incorrect answers. Children of the same age tended to give the same wrong answers, suggesting that they shared a common way of thinking. Piaget interviewed and observed numerous children (including his own) over many years, concluding that a child's mind is not a miniature version of an adult's. Rather, children proceed through a series of *qualitative stages* of cognitive development.

Through his research Piaget identified the processes by which children gain new knowledge. Suppose a child has never seen a cow. The child tries to understand this new element or stimulus by using existing thought patterns or *schemas* (see Chapter 7). Being familiar with dogs, the child tries to understand the cow by using the schema for a dog. To use Piaget's terminology, the child assimilates the cow into the dog schema. **Assimilation** is the process by which we incorporate new information into our accustomed way of thinking (B. J. Wadsworth, 1979).

Jean Piaget spent much of his professional career studying cognitive development in young children.

Accommodation is the process of altering our ways of thinking (schemas) so we can include new information that does not fit into existing ways of thinking. For example, you probably found it difficult to include penguins in your schema for birds. Your schema had to be changed to include the fact that some birds do not fly. The processes of assimilation and accommodation operate throughout life.

Piaget proposed that all human beings proceed through a series of orderly and predictable stages of cognitive development at about the same ages. What's more, he claimed that a prior stage must be completed before progression to the next stage. Children proceed from concrete to more abstract thoughts as they grow older. In this section we examine each of Piaget's stages of cognitive development.

The Sensorimotor Stage. During the **sensorimotor stage** (birth to age 2) infants learn about their world through their senses and their motor behavior. They experience the world in a direct manner and learn basic lessons before proceeding to more complex thoughts. They do not yet use symbols or images to represent objects in the external world, so their world revolves around what they experience directly—the noise of a rattle, the sound of their mother's voice, the movement of a mobile hung over the crib.

Before symbolic communication is possible, infants must learn the principle of object permanence. **Object permanence** refers to the fact that a person or object does not cease to exist when it is not directly perceived. If a 4-month-old reaches for a small toy and you cover it with a cloth, the baby stops reaching and starts looking at something else. Lift the cloth, and the baby will be surprised to see the toy. If, however, you secretly remove the toy and then lift the cloth, the baby will look at the empty spot on the table without giving any sign of surprise or disappointment.

Contrast this response with the reaction of a 1-year-old. At this age, the child continues to reach for the cloth-covered toy and is not surprised to find it still there but would be surprised or upset if you had secretly removed it. At this age cognitive development centers on the ability to use **mental representation.** In other words, once the child begins to think about objects that are not physically present, the principle of object permanence has been established. The development of object permanence is related to the nature of the object

accommodation
Alteration of existing schemas to understand new information

sensorimotor stage
Piaget's first stage of cognitive development, in which children learn about their environment through direct sensory contact and motor activities

object permanence
Recognition that objects continue to exist even though they cannot be directly sensed

mental representation
An internal representation of an object or event that is not present

 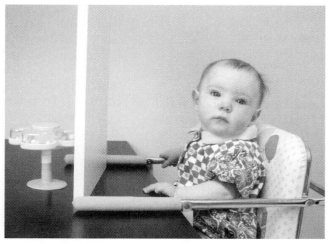

Because this young child does not look for the toy when it is hidden, object permanence has not been attained.

"Hi, Grandma! Betcha can't guess who this is!"

preoperational stage
Piaget's second stage of cognitive development, in which the child begins to think about objects that are not physically present

symbolic representation
Using a mental thought or activity as a substitute for an actual object

egocentrism
Inability to see a situation or event from another person's point of view

concrete operational stage
Piaget's third stage of cognitive development, in which the child is able to use mental representations to think about current objects and events but is not yet capable of abstract thought

conservation
Recognition that a physical change in a substance does not change the amount of that substance

that is hidden. One study showed that infants displayed better object permanence when searching for their mothers than for strangers or inanimate objects (Legerstee, 1994).

The Preoperational Stage. According to Piaget, the child is in the **preoperational stage** of cognitive development from ages 2 to 7. During this stage children become better able to represent events mentally; therefore they are less dependent on physical stimuli and physical reactions to guide their behavior. They begin to engage in pretend play, letting a doll represent a real baby or a toy car represent a real car. They use language (a symbol system) to ask for a drink rather than walking to the sink and pointing. In other words, the preoperational child is able to use **symbolic representation,** which occurs when a symbol is used to represent an actual object. If a toddler in the sensorimotor stage accidentally pushed a baby buggy against the wall, she might take a step back and thrust the buggy forward again and again, failing to reason out why her forward progress had been halted and what she could do to fix it. By contrast, a child in the preoperational stage would step back, look around, and think. Then she would reaim the buggy toward an open doorway. The use of symbolic representation also is shown in children's explanations of impossible events. Four-year-olds explain such events as "magic," whereas 5-year-olds explain such feats as "tricks" (Rosengren & Hickling, 1994). Thus children at this stage function increasingly in a conceptual and representational mode.

Children of this age should not, however, be given more credit than they are due. Their abilities have definite limitations. For example, the preoperational child's thought is characterized by **egocentrism,** or inability to see a situation or event from another person's point of view. Suppose a 3-year-old is talking on the phone to his grandfather. Grandpa asks, "Did you go to the circus yesterday?" The child nods his head silently. The child has failed to consider that Grandpa cannot see his head move. That is, he has failed to take Grandpa's point of view into account. Because preoperational children are not capable of reversible thinking, they frequently explain things by linking events together. This linking of often disconnected facts is called *transductive reasoning.* For example, when asked "why does it rain?" a preoperational child might reply "because we have an umbrella."

The Concrete Operational Stage. Children in the **concrete operational stage** are able to represent objects mentally and engage in logical reasoning about the world around them through the use of these mental representations, but they are not yet able to think abstractly. During this stage, thought becomes more logical. For example, at this stage, a child would be able to arrive at the conclusion that if she traded five baseball cards for one card, she would have fewer cards after the trade than before it. Baseball cards are things she is familiar with. Mental representations of such objects can be manipulated; objects can be added or subtracted. Likewise, the same child would deal with a question such as "What can be done to end world hunger?" by saying, "Drop food from parachutes" or "Grow more food."

Recall our description of the traveling psychology exhibit at the beginning of this section. What can the partially filled flasks tell us about the cognitive development of children? Piaget demonstrated that preoperational children do not grasp the principle of **conservation,** the understanding that a change in the size or shape of a substance does not change the amount of that substance. Consider Esther, a 4-year-old who does not like carrots. Esther's mother cuts the two carrots on Esther's plate into several smaller

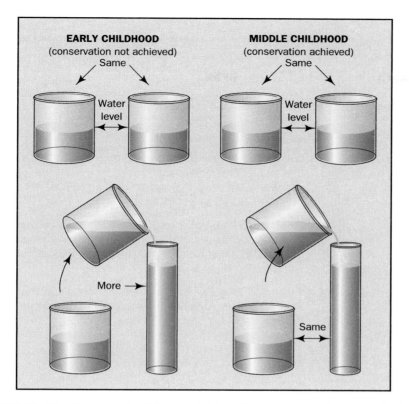

FIGURE 9-10 An example of the acquisition of conservation. During early childhood, children are typically unable to tell that the tall glass and the short glass contain the same amount of water. By middle childhood, the child has acquired the principle of conservation and will be able to tell that the two glasses contain the same amount of water.

pieces. Esther bursts into tears and complains bitterly, "Before I only had two carrots; now I've got lots!"

Look at Figure 9-10. The two glasses contain exactly the same amount of water. To a 4-year-old boy who has not acquired the principle of conservation, however, the tall glass has more water than the short one. He will say this even after seeing the water being poured from the short glass into the tall glass. Now think of the flasks at the psychology exhibit. When the flasks are turned base down, the fluid does not rise as high in the container. When the flasks are turned base up, the same fluid rises higher in the container, and the young child will say that there is more fluid. Until a child reaches the concrete operational stage and understands conservation, he or she will believe that changes in the shapes and sizes of objects indicate changes in quantity. Piaget's stages of cognitive development are summarized in the Study Chart on page 402.*

Challenges to Piaget's Theory.   Piaget has provided a comprehensive theory of cognitive development. As mentioned earlier, according to Piaget, a child will not move from one stage to the next unless there is a combination of biological maturation and appropriate environmental stimulation. Many

---

*We discuss Piaget's final stage, the *formal operational stage,* in Chapter 10. During this stage, which develops during adolescence, the individual begins to think abstractly.

STUDY CHART		
Stages of Cognitive Development, according to Jean Piaget		
Stage	**Age**	**Characteristics**
Sensorimotor	Birth to 2 years	Child explores the environment through sensory and motor behavior. Develops the concept of object permanence.
Preoperational	2 to 7 years	Child becomes able to think about people and objects that are not physically present. Even though mental representations are used, they cannot be manipulated logically. Child's thought reflects egocentrism.
Concrete operational	7 to 11 years	Even though thoughts are still limited to the immediate situation, the child is able to engage in logical reasoning through the use of mental representations. Principle of conservation is understood.
Formal operational	Adolescence and adulthood	The individual is able to use symbolic representations in abstract thought. Can create and logically think through hypothetical situations.

psychologists question, however, whether it is accurate to describe people as passing through a series of qualitatively different stages. On the other hand, they acknowledge the profound impact Piaget's theory has had on investigations of cognitive development, and they use his tasks and concepts to explore children's thinking.

Despite its impact and importance, Piaget's theory has not gone unchallenged. For example, the Russian psychologist Lev Vygotsky (1930, 1933, 1935/1978) stressed the social context in which a child learns (Berk, 2000). Whereas Piaget's theory deals with internal development, Vygotsky's theory emphasizes external factors such as society and culture. According to this researcher, the social interaction experienced by children facilitates learning and performing skills that are beyond their current capabilities. Because different cultures stress different types of social interactions, children may differ in their ability to solve various types of problems (Rogoff, 1990; Wahi & Johri, 1994). The role of the teacher or adult is to provide help or assistance (known as *scaffolding*) during a teaching session. As the child learns, the teacher changes or adapts the scaffolding to reflect the newly acquired skills (Berk & Spuhl, 1995; Wood, 1989); the child gradually assumes more responsibility for the task.

The ages at which the cognitive changes proposed by Piaget occur have also been challenged. For example, psychologist Renee Baillargeon reports that infants display object permanence much earlier than Piaget proposed; she has found this ability in infants as young as 10 weeks old (Baillargeon, 1993, 1994). Piaget's belief that object permanence does not stabilize until the end of the first year may be due to the fact that the motor task he required of the infants did not appear until later in development (Flavell, Miller, & Miller, 1993).

Without question, the child's cognitive growth is facilitated, if not made possible, by the rapid development of language. The development of language has enabled children to extend their cognitive powers to the point at which they can think symbolically and reason logically.

Language

You have agreed to take care of your 30-month-old niece while her parents go out for dinner. You are intrigued by some of the words she uses. For example, she says the word *mouses,* although you are fairly sure that no one taught her that word. While she is eating dinner she asks for more "chicken on the cob." When you realize that she delights in eating corn on the cob, you conclude that to her a chicken leg looks like a cob! ***How do children's speech errors help us understand the way they acquire language?*** ▪

The use of language to communicate is basic to the human ability to develop, refine, and exchange ideas. Language acquisition is therefore a critical component of the child's developing cognitive abilities. Both children and adults use language and images to create concepts and solve problems. This section examines the way language develops and how it both reflects and determines our thinking.

Language Development

Between birth and the beginning of formal schooling, children accomplish a monumental feat: They learn to speak and understand language (Collins & Kuczaj, 1991). *Speech* is what people actually say; *language* is the understanding of the rules of what they say. To understand the magnitude of this task, consider this: Apart from stock phrases and remarks such as "Thank you" or "How are you?," almost every sentence we speak or write has never before been spoken or written. Every day we read sentences that we have never encountered before, yet we understand almost every one of them (Lederer, 1991).

Acquiring any of the approximately 4,000 languages is a remarkable accomplishment because there is so much to learn. First, a child uses **phonemes** (from the Greek word for "sound"), which are the smallest units of basic sounds in a language. Most languages use 20 to 60 phonemes. English has 26 letters but 44 phonemes because the same letter, alone or in combination, can represent more than one sound. Perhaps you remember feeling confused when you first learned that the same symbol on the printed page—say, *c* or *gh*—could be pronounced in more than one way. A similar experience occurs when we learn a foreign language.

Although it is often convenient to think of words as the basic units of meaning in language, many words have more than one part that has meaning. A **morpheme** is the smallest unit of sound that has meaning. For example, the word *constructed* has three morphemes: *con, struct,* and *ed,* the last of which indicates past tense (Cole & Cole, 1993). When we learn to organize words into phrases and sentences, we are acquiring what is called **syntax.**

The Acquisition of Language. The baby's early cries and other sounds are probably responses both to the environment and to internal needs such as hunger. No matter what language their parents speak (and even if the parents are deaf), babies make the same sounds at about the same time. At about 2 months of age, an infant begins *cooing*—making squeals, gurgles, or vowel sounds of relatively short duration, such as "ahhh." At about 6 months of age, infants begin *babbling,* making one-syllable utterances that usually contain both vowels and consonants (Rice, 1995). As children move from

phonemes
The smallest units of sound understood as part of a language

morpheme
In a language, the smallest unit of sound that conveys meaning

syntax
The organization of words into phrases and sentences

babbling to pronouncing words, they vocalize more of the sounds used in their language community (Kuhl et al., 1992). Toddlers utter their first word that conveys meaning at about 1 year. Because parents are usually the child's primary caregivers, it is not surprising that the child's first words are usually *mama* or *dada*.

By the age of 18 months, the average toddler uses as many as 50 words. Most of these words are used for naming objects, such as *doggie*, but some are action words such as *bye-bye*. At about this age, toddlers combine two or more words to express a single idea, which results in the child's first sentence. Vocabulary development continues at a rapid pace during the preschool years.

Psychologists are especially interested in three characteristics of the infant's language. First, young children often use *telegraphic speech*—they leave words out of their sentences as in a telegraph message. Despite the missing words, the intent of the sentence is usually clear, especially if the nonverbal context helps listeners decipher the child's meaning. For example, Dad knows what his daughter wants when he hears "Daddy juice." Second, children seem to know how to string words together to convey the intended meaning in the correct sequence for their language. If a child sees a car run over a ball, the child might say, "Car hit ball." (The child would not say, "Ball hit car.") Third, children often overgeneralize grammatical rules, such as the use of *s* or *es* to create the plural. The plural of *house* is *houses,* so the plural of *mouse* should be *mouses*! Children also add *ed* at the end of verbs to indicate past tense. For example, young children will say, "Doggie runned away."

According to behaviorists, including B. F. Skinner (1957), language is learned like other behaviors: through imitation, conditioning, association, and reinforcement. Children hear others talk, and they imitate the sounds they hear. For example, parents will point to an object and name it, and children repeat the words. What's more, sounds that resemble words are reinforced; sounds that do not resemble words may be extinguished. For instance, the baby's babbling of *mama* produces such reinforcers as food, a smile, or a hug. The more often this sequence of behaviors and reinforcers is repeated, the more strongly *mama* is associated with the presence of the child's mother. Likewise, the correct sequencing of words to form sentences is reinforced, whereas incorrect sequences may be extinguished.

Although this behavioral theory of language acquisition explains how children can learn words from adults, it fails to explain how they create new and unique words and sentences. Cognitive scientist Steven Pinker (1994) considers it folklore that parents teach children language; parents do not provide explicit grammar lessons. The credit for the acquisition of language should go to the children.

The remarkable ability of children to master the complex rules of language and to use an extensive vocabulary within about 5 years suggests the existence of a built-in brain mechanism that makes this development possible. Except in situations in which access to language samples is denied, the acquisition of language is virtually guaranteed for children up to about age 5 or 6 and becomes more difficult thereafter. Thus there is a *critical period* during which language develops quite easily, as most adults in foreign language classes know quite well. According to this *nativist* theory of language, children are innately predisposed to acquire language (Greiser & Kuhl, 1989). The major advocate of this position, Noam Chomsky (1972), has called this innate ability our *language acquisition device* (LAD). When children hear speech, the LAD programs their brain to analyze what they are hearing and to extract the rules of grammar. The LAD is responsible for the

Although children appear to learn many elements of language from adults (as well as from other children), they also abstract rules of language that enable them to generate words that they have never heard spoken by adults.

TABLE 9-3 **The Sequence of Language Development in a Child**

AGE (MONTHS)	LANGUAGE DEVELOPMENT
2	Begins making vowel-like cooing sounds
4	Makes vowel-like sounds interspersed with consonant sounds
6	Engages in babbling (one-syllable utterances)
8	Uses two-syllable utterances such as *mama* and *dada;* imitates sounds
10	Understands some words and gestures (may say "no," shakes head)
12	Understands some simple commands; uses single words such as *baby;* has some control over intonation
18	Has a vocabulary of as many as 50 words; may use two-word utterances, still babbles; uses words of several syllables with intricate intonation patterns
24	Has a vocabulary over 50 words; uses two-word phrases
30	Aquires vocabulary rapidly; uses three- to five-word phrases
36	Has a vocabulary of 1,000 words, of which 80 percent are intelligible; makes fewer syntactic errors

Sources: Caplan, 1973; Lenneberg, 1973; Rice, 1995.

emergence of babbling and the imitation of speech sounds. Because of these experiences, children are able to apply those rules to their own sentences. Children are not taught grammar explicity; rather, they construct the rules from the examples they hear. The role of parents and other caregivers is to help this process along by providing models of appropriate language use (Sacks, 1989).

The LAD explains why children in different cultures follow the same (presumably innate) stages of language acquisition (McNeil, 1970; see Table 9-3); it also explains why deaf children pass through stages of language development that are analogous to those exhibited by hearing children (Meier, 1991).

Although the LAD explains how children learn the complex rules of their language, it does not explain why children who are raised by their parents at home show better language development than children raised in institutions. Learning theorists point to the greater availability of reinforcements at home than in institutions. As predicted by learning theory, much of the variety in children's language abilities can be attributed to differences in their environments.

Most psychologists currently favor a combination of learning and nativist theories. That is, some of our linguistic abilities seem to be innately determined, and others are acquired through learning. Researchers disagree, however, as to which behaviors belong in which category.

Moral Development

In addition to developing in the physical, cognitive, and linguistic realms, the child develops a sense of right and wrong. Consider the following example. Billy was told not to go into the dining room, but he wanted to help his mother set the table, so he entered the room, accidentally bumping into a tray of cups and breaking eight of them. Tommy had been told he could not go to the movies, so he was mad at his mother. He went into the dining room and deliberately broke a cup. Who is naughtier?

Lawrence Kohlberg (1973) proposed that there are three primary levels of moral development: the preconventional level, the level of conventional role conformity, and the level of autonomous moral principles. (As Kohlberg's assessment required verbal reasoning skills, his analysis and research did not include younger children who could not be tested.) Each of these levels has two stages associated with it; thus the individual progresses through a total of six stages of morality as the three major levels are mastered.

At the **preconventional level** (ages 4 to 10), the child observes external conventions or standards set by others in order to avoid punishment (Stage 1) or receive reinforcement (Stage 2). If a road sign says STOP, the child expects you to stop immediately. Parents frequently hear their 5- or 6-year-old children reprimanding them for not stopping completely at a stop sign or for driving faster than the speed limit. Consider our example of Billy and Tommy in the dining room. To a preconventional child, Billy is naughtier because he broke eight cups, whereas Tommy broke only one. At this level of moral development, intentionality is not as relevant as level of damage.

Level 2, **conventional role conformity** (ages 10 to 13), involves greater internalization of standards and values. *Internalization* occurs when we make external standards and values part of our own set of values and standards. Children at this level are still controlled by external rules, but they now want to behave well to please important people in their lives. Charlie wants to "be good" to please his grandfather because that is what his grandfather expects (Stage 3). Similarly, the song about Santa Claus says, "He's making a list, checking it twice. Gonna find out who's naughty or nice." Children behave nicely because Santa Claus expects them to. At Stage 4 we find children adhering to the rules of their peer group because they have promised to do so. The commitment is still to an external rule, but the promise to obey such rules has become even more internalized.

Kohlberg's third major level of moral development, **autonomous moral principles,** involves true morality. At the earliest, this level may be reached by age 13. Some people reach it in young adulthood; others never achieve it. The attainment of true morality involves complete internalization of control over moral conduct. At Stage 5 we find the adolescent or young adult following, say, the rules of her sorority because it benefits the group. Although these rules may not apply in all situations, in the long run it is better to follow them. At Stage 6 the person decides whether a particular behavior is good or bad, regardless of what others think or of any legal restrictions that exist. For example, one may adopt the belief that life is sacred and may feel that killing is to be avoided at any cost.

Despite its popularity, Kohlberg's theory of moral development has had its share of problems and critics. Prominent among the critics is Carol Gilligan (1982; Gilligan, Lyons, & Hanmer, 1990), who argues that Kohlberg's theory was developed only with male participants but has been applied to women as well. The assumption is that men and women view moral situations in the same manner; Gilligan argues that they do not. According to Gilligan, men tend to have a more absolute view of morality and are more concerned about not interfering with the rights of others. By

preconventional level
Kohlberg's first stage of moral development (ages 4 to 10), in which standards set by others are observed in order to receive reinforcement or avoid punishment

conventional role conformity
Kohlberg's second stage of moral development (ages 10 to 13), in which rules and standards are internalized and behaviors are performed in order to please others

autonomous moral principles
Kohlberg's third stage of moral development (age 13 or later, if at all), in which control over moral conduct is completely internalized

contrast, women are more concerned with the context in which a behavior occurs and the relationships involved.

Gilligan is not arguing that there are absolute differences between men and women in moral behavior; there is some degree of overlap. She believes, however, that a complete theory of moral development should stress both viewpoints. What's more, as men and women enter adulthood, their patterns of moral reasoning may become much more similar (Gilligan, Murphy, & Tappan, 1990). The complexity of life's experiences causes adults to view morality in a more relative and changeable manner than children do.

Cross-cultural research presents another challenge to Kohlberg's stage theory of moral development. For example, Fuchs and colleagues (1986) reported that more Israeli children raised in kibbutzim, in which they received training in the governmental structure and laws of the kibbutz, reached Stages 4 and 5 than did American children. Hence training in cultural laws influences the level of moral development that a person reaches. In a study of moral development in India, Vasudev and Hummel (1987) found that even though children may pass through the stages proposed by Kohlberg, their culture may dictate how they choose to deal with moral issues. For example, the resolution of moral dilemmas may be seen as a problem for the entire society (a collectivist view), not as an individual problem.

Review Summary

1. Jean Piaget proposed that cognitive development progresses through a series of qualitative stages. During the **sensorimotor stage,** infants and young children learn about their world through their senses and acquire the principle of **object permanence,** the recognition that objects do not cease to exist when we no longer have direct contact with them. The acquisition of object permanence is related to the nature of the object that is tested and the method of testing.

2. During the **preoperational stage,** the child gains the ability to use **symbolic representations** for objects and events that are not physically present. This stage is also characterized by **egocentrism,** the inability to see situations from another person's point of view.

3. Children continue to use mental representations but are not yet able to think abstractly during the **concrete operational stage.** The principle of **conservation**—the recognition that changes in size or shape do not change the amount of a substance—is acquired during this stage.

4. Piaget's theory has been challenged on the basis of lack of supportive cross-cultural data and major deviations from the proposed time lines.

5. Between birth and the beginning of formal schooling, children learn to speak and understand language. **Phonemes** are the individual sounds of a language; **morphemes** are its smallest meaning-bearing elements.

6. An understanding of the proper order of words in phrases and sentences demonstrates an understanding of **syntax.**

7. There are two major theories of language acquisition: the notion that language is a learned response acquired like any other behavior and the view that children are innately predisposed to acquire language through a built-in *language acquisition device (LAD)*.

8. A stage theory of moral development was proposed by Lawrence Kohlberg. The three major levels of morality are **preconventional** (adherence to standards to avoid punishment or receive reinforcement), **conventional role conformity** (internalization of standards and values), and **autonomous moral principles** (complete internalization of control over moral conduct).

Study Break

1. Match each of the following terms with its definition.

   a. Schema
   b. Assimilation
   c. Preoperational stage
   d. Egocentrism
   e. Conservation

   1. Principle that a change in size or shape does not change the amount
   2. Inability to see things from another person's point of view
   3. An existing thought pattern
   4. The process of understanding new stimulus elements in terms of existing stimuli
   5. Phase marked by an increase in representational thinking

2. Cognitive development refers to the lifelong changes that occur in our
   a. moral reasoning.
   b. learning abilities.
   c. personalities.
   d. thought processes.

3. A child has a pet kitten that runs away. The child's parents get the child a new kitten, but it is a different size and color. The child still recognizes it as a kitten and knows how to interact with it, thanks to Piaget's concept of
   a. accommodation.
   b. assimilation.

   c. schemas.
   d. object permanence.

4. You are trying to play hide-and-seek with your 6-month-old son. You hide behind the couch, expecting him to make some cooing noises while he looks for you. Nothing of the sort happens. In fact, your son acts as if you no longer exist. According to Piaget, what cognitive ability has your son not yet acquired?

5. What is meant by symbolic representation?

6. Describe the three levels of moral development proposed by Kohlberg.

7. At about what age do most children speak their first understandable word?
   a. 6 months
   b. 8 months
   c. 12 months
   d. 15 months

8. What are the two major competing theories of language acquisition?

9. All of the following are explained by the LAD *except*
   a. why home-reared children have better language development than children reared in institutions.
   b. why deaf children pass through language development stages analogous to hearing children.
   c. why children of different cultures follow the same stages of language acquisition.
   d. the emergence of babbling and the imitation of speech sounds.

ANSWERS TO STUDY BREAKS

Pages 378–379

1. a-3, b-6, c-8, d-2, e-10, f-7, g-5, h-9, I-1, j-4
2. Colleges or universities, public schools, day-care centers, consultants for companies
3. Quantitative changes (e.g., height and weight) can be measured easily. Qualitative developmental changes, such as cognitive processes, are not as easily measured.
4. The same participants are repeatedly tested or observed over a period of time in a longitudinal study. Cross-sectional studies test children of different ages at the same time. The cross-sectional study cannot tell us about the developmental trends of the same children. Longitudinal studies require a great deal of time to conduct.
5. Human traits are controlled by a number of different genes.
6. c
7. 50 percent

8. d
9. a

Pages 384–385

1. Infants can focus on objects eight to ten inches away. They can reach out and touch objects. They prefer to look at faces, as opposed to other objects.
2. US, CS, and UR, respectively
3. c
4. a
5. Their brain and muscles are not sufficiently developed to allow them to perform complex behaviors.
6. b
7. Bayley Scales of Infant Development
8. b
9. a

Page 397

1. *Easy:* Positive approach to new situations; highly adaptive to change. *Slow-to-warm-up:* Intense, negative responders to new situations; slow adaptability. *Difficult:* nonadaptable, intense, negative moods.

2. *Stage 1:* Basic trust versus mistrust. Can the environment be trusted? *Stage 2:* Autonomy versus shame and doubt. Development of an internal, as opposed to an external, sense of control. *Stage 3:* Initiative versus guilt. Questions whether certain behaviors are right or wrong. *Stage 4:* Industry versus inferiority. Acquisition of basic knowledge to become a productive member of society.

3. d

4. Warmth and contact comfort were important determinants of attachment. Social ability was harmed by raising the monkeys in isolation in the laboratory.

5. c

6. Securely attached, avoidant, anxious-ambivalent

7. b

8. d

9. The realistic portrayal of adult life has removed the innocence from childhood. Children can engage in adult behaviors at a much earlier age.

10. a

Page 408

1. a-3, b-4, c-5, d-2, e-1

2. d

3. b

4. Object permanence

5. When a symbol is used to represent an object

6. *Preconventional:* The child observes external standards set by others. *Conventional role conformity:* Individuals behave well to please important people in their lives. *Autonomous moral principles:* The individual acts according to abstract principles of fair play and justice.

7. c

8. The two major competing theories of language acquisition are the nativist theory, which postulates that children are innately predisposed to acquire language, and learning theory.

9. a

CHAPTER 10

Developmental Psychology II

Adolescence Through Old Age

Weddings, such as this Confucian wedding in Seoul, South Korea, reflect the development of intimacy during early adulthood.

Chapter in Perspective

In this chapter we continue our discussion of the physical, intellectual, social, and psychological changes that occur throughout the life span. In Chapter 9 we discussed development from conception through the end of childhood; this chapter covers the period from adolescence through old age. As we bring the developmental cycle to its inevitable conclusion, we examine the area of death and dying and our reactions to such losses. We also look at development from a cross-cultural perspective. As telecommunications and improved travel capabilities increase our knowledge of other cultures, it is important that we understand and appreciate that differences in birthing, child-rearing, and parenting practices—and in attitudes toward the elderly and death—can differ dramatically from one culture to another. Such differences can occur within large segments of the culture in the United States. Having dealt with developmental issues throughout the life span, we are prepared to consider the tasks the individual faces as a member of society. For example, we look at the area of sex and gender in Chapter 11 and then consider personality, psychological disorders, therapy, social psychology, and industrial/organizational psychology in subsequent chapters. ∎

Physical Changes

FIGURE 10-1 Bungee jumping. What does this practice have to do with developmental psychology? Why has it become so popular in modern societies?

You climb a ladder to the top of a crane that is nearly three stories tall. Once you reach the top, large rubber straps are attached to your ankles. Then you jump off. Luckily, the crane is suspended over water! Depending on how the straps have been adjusted, you may go completely below the surface of the water or just come close to it. In any event, you bounce back and forth several times before this daredevil feat is complete. Some people engage in this unusual behavior by jumping from hot-air balloons or bridges with the rubber straps attached to a waist harness. Known as bungee jumping, the practice is popular among teenagers around the world (see Figure 10-1). ***What can a phenomenon like bungee jumping tell us about developmental psychology?*** ■

To answer this question, imagine that people are not jumping from a crane or a hot-air balloon. Instead, they are jumping from a tall platform. Vines, not rubber straps, are attached to their ankles (see Figure 10-2). This event is dangerous and scary; some of the boys will not survive the jump—the vines may break or be too long. The survivors will be honored by their village. You can think of these events as graduation ceremonies that mark the start of adulthood. This custom has been practiced for centuries in some tribal societies, such as those in New Guinea. Although bungee jumping also offers teenagers and young adults in urban societies a chance to display their independence and demonstrate their "adult" status, it does not carry the same meaning.

In most modern societies, no single event or ceremony marks the passage from childhood to adulthood. Rather, we experience an extended transition period that links childhood and adulthood. That period is known as adolescence.

FIGURE 10-2 These boys are not jumping for the thrill of it. This is a rite of passage into adulthood. If the boys survive this jump, they will have become men.

Adolescence

Many adults remember **adolescence**—the years between approximately ages 12 and 20—as a period filled with trouble and turmoil. Although such memories may be accurate, "recent studies also indicate that the conflicts that do occur are best characterized as occasional bickering and squabbling over day-to-day topics, such as chores, personal appearance, curfew, and the like, rather than over major values" (Silverberg, Tennenbaum, & Jacob, 1992, p. 350; see also Workman & Johnson, 1994). In any event, adolescence is characterized by major physical, intellectual, psychological, and social changes. Coping with such changes is not easy (Blos, 1962; Galinsky, 1981).

The period (approximately two years long) that ends in the achievement of full sexual maturity, or **puberty,** is known as **pubescence.** During pubescence the sex organs mature and secondary sex characteristics appear. The dramatic physical maturation observed during pubescence, called the *growth spurt,* is second only to the one that occurs during infancy (see Chapter 9). Look at the picture of fifth-graders in Figure 10-3. One feature of the growth spurt is apparent: Not all children enter pubescence at the same time.

Among the most important factors determining the onset of pubescence is sex. Girls begin pubescence, and therefore achieve sexual maturity, earlier than boys. The age range for girls entering pubesence is from 8 to 14; the typical girl begins at age 10 or 11. The age range for boys entering pubescence is from 10 to 16, with the typical boy beginning at 12 or 13. Thus a person who has reached puberty is still considered an adolescent. Interestingly, the higher a family's standard of living, the earlier children in succeeding generations reach puberty. This effect, referred to as a **secular trend,** is due to better nutrition and health care. This trend appears to have leveled off in Europe and North America (Hopwood et al., 1990).

Although both boys and girls experience a growth spurt during pubescence, there are differences in the nature of that growth. In boys the shoulders broaden; in girls the hips broaden. Boys experience more large-muscle growth, giving them a strength advantage over girls for the first time in their lives. In other respects, growth is similar: Adolescents of both sexes may look gangly when their hands and feet grow more rapidly than their arms and legs (Katchadourian, 1977). In addition, the lips, nose, and ears grow more quickly than the head. Complex hormonal changes underlie the development seen during pubescence. For example, increased secretion of *growth hormone* and *thyroxine* produce the growth spurt. Sexual development is controlled by the secretion of the male and female sex hormones, *androgens* and *estrogen,* respectively.

Primary and secondary sex characteristics and capabilities develop to full maturity during pubescence. **Primary sex characteristics** are directly related to reproduction. The maturation of these characteristics in girls includes development of the ovaries, uterus, and vagina. The occurrence of **menarche** (the first menstrual period) signals that puberty has been reached. The maturation of primary sex characteristics in boys includes development of the testes, penis, seminal vesicles, and prostate gland. The ability to ejaculate semen, often in *nocturnal emissions,* or "wet dreams," signals that a boy has reached puberty.

You can think of **secondary sex characteristics** as signals or signs not directly related to reproduction that sexual maturity has been achieved. The secondary sex characteristics found in both girls and boys include the growth of axillary (underarm) hair and pubic hair and changes in the skin, which becomes coarser and oilier, sometimes resulting in complexion problems.

The maturational differences we have mentioned can lead to adjustment problems (Brooks-Gunn et al., 1994). Early-maturing girls and late-maturing boys face the most difficult adjustments. Early-maturing girls are taller and

FIGURE 10-3 The differences between these fifth graders indicate that children enter pubescence at different times.

adolescence
The years between approximately age 12 and age 20

puberty
The time at which an individual achieves full sexual maturity

pubescence
Period of rapid growth, maturation of sexual organs, and appearance of secondary sex characteristics that precedes puberty

secular trend
Tendency of members of one generation to begin puberty at an earlier age than their parents

primary sex characteristics
Characteristics directly related to reproduction

menarche
Beginning of menstruation

secondary sex characteristics
Sex-related characteristics that develop during adolescence and are not directly related to reproduction

The physical abilities of young adults are seen in their sports and leisure activities.

show the developmental aspects of pubescence more obviously than their classmates. For example, their large feet and developing breasts often provoke teasing. In the United States, early-maturing girls may also feel social pressure to begin dating and associating with older adolescents. In countries such as India, where many marriages are arranged, early maturation does not create such problems.

The late-maturing boy presents a different picture. First he sees himself physically outdistanced by the girls in his class, and then he is passed by most of the other boys. His lack of physical development becomes a source of scorn and shame. As a result, late-developing boys are sometimes less poised and less relaxed than their peers. One study (M. E. T. Wadsworth, 1979) found that a higher percentage of late-developing than normally developing boys became juvenile delinquents.

Adolescence ends when the individual becomes an adult. The exact point at which a person enters adulthood may vary considerably from society to society. As we saw in the opening vignette, a ritual, such as jumping off a platform, may mark the passage to adulthood. In some countries, such as the United States, the definition is arbitrary and based on age. Despite such variability, almost all countries have a developmental period that intervenes between childhood and adulthood (Schlegel & Barry, 1991). The longest of the major developmental stages, adulthood, lasts until death. It is usually divided into three periods: early adulthood, middle adulthood, and old age.

Early Adulthood

Early adulthood lasts roughly 20 years, from approximately age 20 until age 40. During this period most people embark on careers; marry and have children and become established members of society. Early adulthood is usually characterized by good health. It is also the time at which we reach the peak of physical and sensory fitness (Sinclair, 1978). In our early twenties we possess our maximum strength and our greatest sensitivity in both vision and hearing.

Nowhere are the physical and sensory abilities of young adults more evident than in professional athletes. By the time athletes are in their mid-thirties or early forties, most are considered old-timers on the threshold of retiring. At about age 30, a *gradual* decline in muscular strength, vision, and hearing begins. The decline in visual and auditory sensitivity may not be noticeable until middle adulthood; it may be of some comfort to know that your sensitivity to tastes, odors, and temperatures does not begin to decline until your late forties or early fifties.

As we will see in Chapter 15, good health, a good diet, and exercise help us cope with stress. Engaging in these healthy practices during early adulthood has a major impact on health later in life (Sloane, 1985). The way you treat your body during early adulthood directly affects your health during middle adulthood and old age. If you don't smoke, your lungs will be less susceptible to cancer; if you exercise, your risk of heart disease is decreased.

Middle Adulthood

Middle adulthood encompasses the period from approximately age 40 to age 65. Many of the changes of middle adulthood are in the form of a decline; hence adjustments are made, and coping strategies are adopted.

early adulthood
Period from approximately age 20 to age 40

middle adulthood
Period from approximately age 40 to age 65

The physical changes that began during early adulthood become more noticeable during middle adulthood. Many people now need reading glasses to adjust to **presbyopia,** the farsightedness that often accompanies aging (Whitbourne, 1985). Presbyopia occurs because of a stiffening of the lens of the eye, resulting in difficulty in focusing on near objects (Lemme, 1995). The most pronounced hearing deficit, **presbycusis,** is reduced ability to hear sounds at higher frequencies (see Chapter 3). Because sounds at these frequencies are not crucial to everyday behavior, such losses often go unnoticed until they begin to interfere with speech perception. A detectable loss of sensitivity in other senses, such as taste and smell, does not occur until at least age 50.

What about your fine physique and athletic prowess? The gradual decline that began in early adulthood eventually results in a reduction of slightly more than 10 percent in physical strength. For individuals who rarely exert themselves to their fullest extent, this decline in strength may not be detected. As we grow older, our reaction time slows (Birren, Woods, & Williams, 1980) and may be more noticeable than the decline in strength; for example, it may take longer to step on the brakes when necessary when driving.

Middle adulthood also brings with it a change in reproductive ability. During the late forties or early fifties, a woman's body undergoes a series of changes, known as **menopause,** that lead to the cessation of ovulation and menstrual periods. Menopause may result in important psychological reactions. Some women mourn the loss of their reproductive capacity (even if they have not given birth in many years); others rejoice in their freedom from worry about pregnancy and the discomfort of monthly periods. The physical changes that occur during menopause include a decrease in levels of estrogen, a hormone that plays a central role in the development of primary and secondary sex characteristics and the sexual drive. Unless preventive measures are begun before menopause, the decrease in estrogen can lead to **osteoporosis,** a condition in which the bones become thinner and are prone to fractures (Culliton, 1987; Prince et al., 1991).

Osteoporosis occurs in approximately 25 percent of American women after menopause. It can be prevented if calcium intake is high enough so that the bones do not lose strength. Dairy foods, soy products like tofu, and certain vegetables such as broccoli are excellent sources of calcium. Low-fat dairy products, such as yogurt, are also good sources. Because weight-bearing exercise in particular promotes new bone growth (and also reduces blood cholesterol and improves muscle mass, strength, and balance), it should be included in any regimen designed to combat the onset and progression of osteoporosis. However, Eastell (1998) believes that "estrogen-replacement therapy is the treatment of first choice" (p. 744).

The reproductive changes of middle adulthood are not as dramatic or obvious in men as they are in women. Men in their late fifties may experience fluctuations in hormone production (Kimmel, 1980; Whitbourne, 1985), as well as impotence and depression. The symptoms associated with this period, often called the *male climacteric,* vary considerably from one person to another. For example, there is a decrease in the amount of semen and sperm (Murray & Meacham, 1993), and an increasing number of men 60 and older suffer episodes of impotence (Whitbourne, 1996).

Late Adulthood

Whether you agree with the theory that we grow old because of wear and tear on the body or the theory that we are genetically programmed to grow old, aging is an inevitable part of the developmental cycle. At approximately age 65 we enter the final period of adulthood—**late adulthood** or old age.

This woman's posture suggests that she may be suffering from osteoporosis. This condition, in which the bones become thinner and are prone to fractures, occurs in 25 percent of American women after menopause.

presbyopia
Farsightedness that normally develops during middle adulthood; stiffening of the lens results in difficulty in focusing on near objects

presbycusis
Middle adulthood hearing disorder involving reduced ability to distinguish sounds at higher frequencies

menopause
Cessation of ovulation and menstruation; these changes mark the end of the childbearing years

osteoporosis
Condition in which the bones become thinner and more prone to fractures and breaks; typically appears in postmenopausal women

late adulthood
Period from approximately age 65 until death

Psychological Detective

The following statements will help you think about old age and put it in perspective. Mark each one as true or false before reading further.

- *All five senses decline in old age.*
- *Physical strength tends to decline with age.*
- *Older workers cannot perform as effectively as younger workers.*
- *At least 25 percent of elderly citizens are living in institutions such as nursing homes, psychiatric hospitals, and extended-care facilities.*
- *Medical practitioners tend to give low priority to senior citizens.*
- *It is almost impossible for most elderly people to learn new things.*

We will answer these questions throughout the rest of this chapter, but let's focus first on those that are related to physical changes. Despite the physical changes that occur in late adulthood, keep in mind that chronological age may not be a good predictor of ability or performance in elderly people. Hence researchers (such as Neugarten & Neugarten, 1987) now distinguish between the *young-old* and the *old-old*. The young-old appear physically young for their advanced years, whereas the old-old show definite signs of decline. Thus a person who is 85 or older could be classified as young-old, whereas a person in his late 60s might be classified as old-old.

Despite the young-old and old-old distinction, predictable physical changes come with advancing age. For example, many older people must contend with impaired vision and hearing. For many, the middle-adulthood problem of farsightedness is replaced by the development of more serious problems, such as **cataracts** (clouding of the lens of the eye), that may require corrective surgery (Segerberg, 1982). The need for hearing aids increases as hearing ability decreases. Because hearing aids are a visible sign of advancing age, however, many people refuse to use them (Olsho, Harkins, & Lenhardt, 1985).

The gradual decline in sensitivity to taste and smell that began in middle adulthood continues until the late seventies; after that, the majority of people experience a very sharp drop in olfactory ability (Doty, 1984). This decline explains why many older people do not enjoy eating as much as they once did; their food simply does not taste as good as it used to. Why? In Chapter 3 we saw that taste and olfaction influence each other. If we cannot smell our food, it does not taste as good or as we expect it to taste, and so we may not eat as much as we should. It is not surprising, therefore, that malnourishment may become a problem for some elderly people.

The ability to regulate body temperature also declines noticeably during old age. When you visit your older relatives or friends in the winter, you may find their homes very hot. Remember that it is hot for you but comfortable for them.

It is true that older people do not possess the physical strength that characterizes young adulthood, but this decline does not mean they are unable to perform such activities as taking care of their houses, doing yard work, and playing tennis. On the contrary, most of the same tasks and activities can still be carried out just as effectively and enjoyably, although they may take longer. Certainly, such activities, even aerobic dancing (Hopkins et al., 1990), are important in helping elderly people stay physically fit (Diamant, 1991).

The slowness of old age is also reflected in longer reaction times and an increase in the time required to process information. Thus older people are

cataracts
Clouding of the lens of the eye

increasingly likely to be involved in traffic accidents (Sterns, Barrett, & Alexander, 1985). This increase occurs because older individuals are unable to process information from traffic signals, such as stop signs and turn signals, as quickly or as well as they did when they were younger.

Physical appearance also changes with advancing age. People actually shrink as they grow older (Whitbourne, 1985). The shrinking results from compression of the disks between the vertebrae of the spinal column (see Chapter 2). In addition, older people tend to stoop when they stand, increasing the perception of shortness.

Elderly people also experience changes in their sleep patterns. As noted in Chapter 5, their sleep becomes less efficient; that is, they spend less of their time in bed actually sleeping. Their sleep is punctuated by more frequent awakenings, which result from a reduction of Stage 4 sleep and an increase in the light sleep of Stage 1. Older individuals may counteract the loss of deep sleep during the night by napping during the day.

Finally, most of the systems of the body become more susceptible to disease during old age. For example, heart disease is the most frequent cause of death for people over 65. Other prominent causes include cancer, stroke, diabetes, and kidney disease. These disorders are so prevalent that average life expectancy could be extended by more than 11 years if only heart and kidney disease were eliminated (Fries & Crapo, 1981).

Increasing susceptibility to disease is frequently accompanied by an increase in the amount or number of medications taken. In some cases these drugs may combine or interact with one another in unintended, and potentially deadly, ways. Drugs may be prescribed in larger doses than necessary or may be prescribed by different physicians who are not aware that any other drugs have been prescribed (Krupka & Vener, 1979).

Most medical practitioners give low priority to the aged population. Forgetfulness and declining abilities make many elderly people difficult to work with. Limited resources make them potential financial risks. Hence many elderly people receive less than adequate attention and care.

Snowshoeing is only one of many ways that older people can be active. Continued activity is important to maintaining physical fitness.

Experiencing Old Age

Hands On

HAVE YOU EVER WONDERED WHAT IT'S LIKE TO BE OLD? HERE'S AN EASY AND QUICK exercise that simulates some of the problems old age may bring that you and one or more friends can do just about anywhere. You will need the following supplies: plastic wrap, cotton, and masking tape. To simulate blurred vision owing to cataracts, cover your eyes (but not your nose or mouth!) with several layers of plastic wrap. Tape the wrap in place so that it will not fall off. Place cotton in your ears to simulate hearing loss, and put masking tape around your knuckles to simulate arthritis. Now try navigating around your dorm room, house, or apartment (try outdoors if you are really daring). Be sure someone is around to monitor your behavior. Once you have experienced this simulated old age, trade places with your friends. Once your entire group has had the "old-age experience," here are some questions you should try to answer (group collaboration is encouraged). What did it feel like to be old? Of all your senses, which would be worst to lose? Which the second worst? Can you now relate better to old people? If so, how?

Alzheimer's Disease. The overprescribing and misprescribing of drugs can lead to a number of problems, ranging from depression to dementia. These problems can occur at any age but are especially prevalent in elderly

dementia

General intellectual decline associated with old age; may be reversible when caused by medication or blood clots

Alzheimer's disease

Degenerative brain disorder that results in progressive loss of intelligence and awareness

people. **Dementia** is a condition of general intellectual decline involving loss of memory and disorientation (Erkinjuntti et al., 1997; Reisberg et al., 1985). Sometimes dementia is caused by a blood clot that prevents an adequate supply of blood from reaching the brain. Luckily, this problem can be corrected, and many people who have experienced dementia are able to resume normal functioning. Others are not as fortunate.

One form of dementia, Alzheimer's disease, is irreversible and is not treatable at present. **Alzheimer's disease** is a degenerative brain condition, which means that people suffering from this disorder show progressive loss of intelligence, memory, and general awareness. The exact cause of the ailment is unknown. Because Alzheimer's disease may affect nearly one-third of all people who live to be 85 or older (Heston & White, 1991; Holden, 1987b), it is receiving considerable attention from caregivers and researchers.

Autopsies show that the brains of Alzheimer's victims have changed or deteriorated. For example, many of the axons of neurons in the brain (see Chapter 2) are abnormally twisted and tangled; there may even be loss of complete cells (Roth et al., 1985). Under such conditions, the brain could hardly be expected to function well.

What causes Alzheimer's disease? To answer this question, we need to consider two variants of the disease. One type, which occurs at a somewhat earlier age (during middle adulthood), is thought to be caused by a genetic defect. If the gene responsible for the disorder could be identified and isolated, we would be well on the way toward finding a cure for this form of the disease. A second type of Alzheimer's disease usually occurs after age 65. It may be caused by factors such as an immune system deficiency, concentrations of aluminum in the brain (Cohen, 1987), or infection. Only continued research will provide a clear picture of this disease and how to combat it.

Culture and Life Expectancy. Even with all the physical problems associated with old age, the average life expectancy in the United States has increased at a steady rate. Better health and nutrition have extended the number of active years before illness or disability really begins. This increase is projected to continue at least through the year 2050 (Rosenfeld, 1985).

What's more, women have longer life expectancies than men. The disparity, which was small at the start of the 1900s, continues to grow. Currently women can expect to live approximately seven years longer than men. For a girl born in 1992, the average life expectancy is 79.0 years; a boy born in 1992 can expect to live 72.3 years (U.S. Bureau of the Census, 1994).

Although longer life expectancies are a relatively new phenomenon in the United States, some areas of the world—such as parts of Peru, Pakistan, the former Soviet Union, Japan, and Iceland—are famous for the longevity of their inhabitants. Among the very old people found living in the Abkhasia region of Russia was a woman who claimed to be 148 years old and whose daily routine included drinking vodka and smoking cigarettes (Beet, 1974). What is it about the cultural groups in which these people live that has produced longer average life expectancies? These people seem to share four characteristics: (1) Their diets are high in fruits and vegetables and low in meat and fat, (2) both relaxation and exercise are part of their daily routine, (3) they work throughout their lives, and (4) family and community activities are important to them (Pitskhelauri, 1982).

"Look you're 103 years old, you've got to start taking better care of youself."

Myth or Science

If we believe the popular media, individuals in their seventies and eighties are quite old. What does science say? Bennett S. Gurian (1993) disagrees. He says that "average life expectancy in the United States has doubled over the last century and is now approaching what has historically been the maximum human life span of 110 years." Just a few years ago, teenagers seemed to be the most rapidly growing group in our society, but not any longer. Currently people over 85 are the fastest-growing group; 50,000 Americans are over 100 years old. By 2030 there will be more than 8 million Americans over 85. Our conception of old age will change in the coming years.

This villager in Kirgiz in the former Soviet Union typifies the longevity of the region's inhabitants.

Intellectual Changes

During the past six months the dinner table has become a battle-ground. Susan and her teenage daughter, Alisha, have had very few peaceful meals. Their arguments frequently center on Susan's apparent hypocrisy. How can she profess to care about conserving the environment, Alisha asks, when she buys the products of companies that contribute to pollution? Susan's patience is being stretched thin. ***What can Susan do to alleviate her distress?*** ◼

This section examines the intellectual changes that occur from adolescence to adulthood (Hoyer & Rybash, 1994). For some young people, these changes may be characterized as a roller coaster; first intellectual ability increases to its highest point, then it declines substantially. For others, the decline is not inevitable.

Adolescence

By the time they reach adolescence, many individuals have entered Piaget's final stage of intellectual development, the **formal operational stage.** This stage is characterized by abstract thinking—the ability to think in terms of possibilities as opposed to concrete reality. At this stage of cognitive development, the individual is able to think about an issue in general terms and then deduce specific outcomes from these general considerations (Inhelder & Piaget, 1958). For example, a high school student may read about the problem of noise pollution and then design and conduct an experiment to determine the effects of exposure to loud noises.

   Although age may have something to do with entering this stage of development, merely having reached a certain age does not guarantee that a person will be capable of formal operations. Many adults remain at the level of concrete operations unless they are provided with appropriate educational opportunities and stimulation (Piaget, 1972; Neimark, 1982). What's more, our reasoning performance is higher when we are dealing with problems or issues that are relevant to our own lives (Sebby & Papini, 1994).

Adolescent Thought Patterns.
Although many adolescents can think and solve problems in an adult manner, much of their thought and behavior continues to be somewhat childish and contradictory. In his book *All Grown Up and No Place to Go,* David Elkind (1984) describes some of the thought patterns that characterize the adolescent years.

formal operational stage
Piaget's final stage of intellectual development, characterized by abstract thinking; achieved during adolescence or adulthood

This Custer Middle School Odyssey of the Mind team, shows off their pneumatic shoe invention on May 1, 1996, in Custer, S.D. They took the invention to the Abilities Festival of the Paralympic Games in Atlanta. They were inspired in their project by fellow student Natalie Molitor, center, who uses a wheelchair. Clockwise around Molitor are, from front right, Chris Kehr and Jenny Phillipe who hold the shoe, Matt Noble, Bradley Kehr, Dustin Kirk and Brandon Haug. These students are likely at the stage of cognitive development that Piaget termed formal operations.

According to Elkind, adolescents can envision ideal people, situations, and societies. Once such ideals are envisioned, the real world, with all its flaws and problems, becomes a target for criticism. Thus *criticizing and finding fault* are characteristic of adolescent thought. For example, Elkind (1984) indicates that "a boy who never washed, changed his shirt, or used a fork without a battle becomes a connoisseur of manners, dress, and behavior. Out of the blue, as it were, parents are told that they do not know how to walk, how to talk, how to dress, how to eat" (p. 30). If a better world can be envisioned, why has it not been created? When adolescents discuss such issues with adults, an argument is almost sure to develop; recall the dinner table arguments between Susan and her daughter, Alisha. What can Susan do to alleviate her distress? She and other parents can turn this *argumentativeness* into a growth experience for the adolescent. Rather than seeing them as a time for combat, parents should view these arguments as opportunities to help adolescents develop and extend their reasoning powers.

In contrast to such lofty ideals, adults often find a great deal of *apparent hypocrisy* among adolescents. For example, adolescents may join a peace movement during a war. Their vocal demonstrations may lead to violent confrontations with people who support the war. How can the adolescent espouse peace and engage in violent behavior at the same time? Just as an answer to that question is formulated, another aspect of adolescent thought becomes apparent.

Adolescent thought also becomes *self-centered* and *self-conscious*. Adolescents tend to create an **imaginary audience** that is constantly observing each and every one of their behaviors. Elkind (1984) describes the imaginary audience in the following manner:

> Because teenagers are caught up with the transformations they are undergoing—in their bodies, in their facial structure, in their feelings and emotions, and in their thinking powers—they become self-centered. They assume that everyone around them is concerned about the same thing they are concerned with, namely, themselves. I call this assumption the imaginary audience. It is the imaginary audience that accounts for the teenager's extreme self-consciousness. Teenagers feel that they are always on stage and that everyone around them is as aware and concerned about their appearance and behavior as they themselves are. (p. 33)

Through continuing interactions in which they become aware that other people have different, equally valid views and that their self-consciousness is greatly exaggerated, adolescents begin to establish the kind of understanding and empathy that form the basis for mature, adult relationships. An increase in self-disclosure to others (Windle, 1994; see Chapter 16) and the keeping of a diary in which adolescents express their thoughts, feelings, and emotions (Burt, 1994) may be important components of this maturing process.

Early Adulthood

If our physical abilities begin to decline during early adulthood, it seems likely that our intellectual abilities may also decline as we grow older. But whether intellectual abilities decline during adulthood is a subject of debate.

Psychological Detective

How would you investigate the prediction that intellectual abilities decline with age? What type of research would you conduct? Give this question some thought, review Chapter 9, and write down some answers before reading further.

imaginary audience
The adolescent's assumption that everyone else is concerned with his or her appearance and behavior

One possibility is to administer an intelligence test to a number of people in several age groups and compare the scores obtained by those groups (a cross-sectional approach; see Chapter 9). Will this procedure give us a valid answer to our question? No. The cohort effect that we discussed in Chapter 9 has not been taken into account. For example, people who are currently 80 to 90 years old are fairly unlikely to have finished high school, but today's 40-year-olds are likely to have received at least that much education. Therefore, when we compare present-day 40- and 80-year-olds, they differ in terms of both aging and educational experience. Consequently we cannot be sure whether any differences we observe are due to the different ages of our participants or to differences in their past experiences. We should be looking at changes in intelligence in the *same* individuals (a cohort) over a specified period.

K. Warner Schaie (1983, 1990) recognized the problems involved in conducting cross-sectional studies and conducted his own cohort studies to determine whether intelligence actually declines with age. His results indicated that most people actually improve in basic mental ability during adulthood. To avoid the possibilities that the improvement he observed was due to familiarity with the test and testing procedure and that only the most physically and mentally fit individuals returned for repeated testing, Schaie also tested a new group of individuals in each age category whenever he tested his original cohorts. After taking these possible problems into account, Schaie (1990) concluded that intelligence increases until the late thirties or early forties, remains stable until the mid-fifties or early sixties, and may not show any significant decline until the early seventies.

Types of Intelligence. Even though Schaie does not believe that a decline begins until late adulthood, others disagree with his view and suggest that intellectual abilities continually decline as a person grows older. John Horn and his colleagues (Horn & Donaldson, 1976; Horn & Hofer, 1992) believe that the answer to the question of whether intelligence declines with age is yes *and* no; it depends on the type of intelligence that is measured. There may well be a decline in **fluid intelligence,** which involves the ability to see new relationships, solve new problems, form new concepts, and use new information. Putting together a jigsaw puzzle falls into this category of intelligence. The best puzzle solvers can visualize what a particular piece must look like if it is going to fit into a certain spot in the puzzle. Likewise, creative solutions are required to solve environmental problems, such as the need to recycle (see Chapter 8). The ability to see new relationships reflects fluid intelligence in action. The decline in fluid intelligence appears to begin during young adulthood (approximately age 30) and continues gradually throughout the remainder of the individual's life.

A second type of intelligence, crystallized intelligence, appears to increase throughout life. **Crystallized intelligence** involves the ability to retrieve and use information that has been learned and stored. Solving a crossword puzzle is an example of the use of crystallized intelligence. Here are some examples from a crossword puzzle (the answers are given at the end of the chapter):

1. Acid found in apples (5 letters)
2. Chinese temple (6 letters)
3. Egg-shaped (5 letters)
4. Hambletonian gait (4 letters)

The best crossword puzzle solvers are those with the greatest usable store of knowledge. This type of intelligence favors older individuals who have been using their store of knowledge for years. The ability to remember words and

fluid intelligence
Intelligence involving the ability to see new relationships, solve new problems, form new concepts, and use new information

crystallized intelligence
Intelligence that involves the ability to retrieve and use information that has been learned and stored

FIGURE 10-4 As we grow older, fluid intelligence gradually declines, but crystallized intelligence continues to increase gradually.

Source: Horn & Donaldson, 1980.

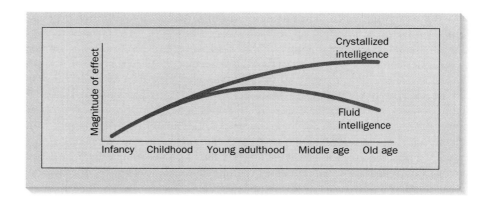

meanings that most people have never heard of reflects crystallized intelligence in action. Figure 10-4 depicts the relationship between changes in fluid and crystallized intelligence over the life span (Horn & Donaldson, 1980). The large number of politicians and judges who are over 65 demonstrates the importance of crystallized intelligence.

Nontraditional College Students. If there is a decline in intelligence with age, it does not seem to interfere with the desire or ability to obtain additional education. In recent years, more adults have been enrolling in college courses in the United States (as compared with many European universities, especially in Italy and Germany, where older students have always been prevalent). Because they do not fall into the traditional 17-to-24-year-old age bracket, these older students are classified as "nontraditional" (Long, 1980). Frequently, nontraditional students have spouses and children and hold full-time jobs. Such responsibilities, when added to the pressure of competing against younger students, could produce considerable stress.

Loretta McGregor and her colleagues (1991) investigated differences in anxiety, self-esteem, and self-perception of personality aspects in traditional and nontraditional American college students. The results indicated that both groups of students had similar levels of anxiety and self-esteem. In addition, these groups did not differ with regard to how they viewed their own scholastic ability, intellectual ability, social acceptance, appearance, creativity, and overall self-worth. McGregor and her colleagues concluded that traditional and nontraditional students do not differ appreciably. If differences exist, they are reflected in the need of nontraditional students for classes scheduled at appropriate times and for degree programs that lead to clear, obtainable career goals.

Middle Adulthood

If changes in intelligence are inevitable with aging, then we might expect the gradual decline in fluid intelligence and the gradual increase in crystallized intelligence that began in early adulthood to continue during middle adulthood. During this period, a person may not be able to answer as many questions concerning new facts and knowledge as a younger person, yet people in their forties and fifties are better at solving problems that require the use of a store of practical knowledge. When middle adulthood is reached, considerable information concerning everyday problems and ways to solve them has been accumulated. For example, a seasoned politician can draw on years of experience to help resolve a political issue. Likewise, when oil-well fires occur, established professionals, such as the legendary Red Adair, are hired to put them out; their expertise is highly valued.

Nontraditional students are a common sight in college classrooms.

Late Adulthood

The percentage of older people in the U.S. population is increasing rapidly; by 2030, an estimated 65 million or more Americans—upwards of 25 percent of the population—will be age 65 or older (see Figure 10-5). By 2050, 5.1 percent of the U.S. population will be age 85 or older (U.S. Bureau of the Census, 1996). The increase in the proportion of older people has been accompanied by an increase in research on the intelligence and personality of elderly people and the social aspects of old age.

As we have seen, fluid intelligence begins a gradual decline toward the end of young adulthood, whereas crystallized intelligence continues to increase gradually. Why does the decline in fluid intelligence occur? Does the brain simply wear out? If there is some general deterioration, it seems reasonable to predict a decrease in both types of intelligence. As this decrease does not occur for both, we must look for another explanation.

Recall our discussion of the encoding, storage, and retrieval of memory in Chapter 7. It is possible that the decline in fluid intelligence is related to a problem with one of these memory processes. Consider the alternatives. The

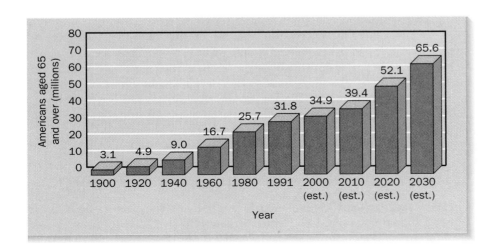

FIGURE 10-5 Population of the United States aged 65 and older, 1900–2030.

Source: American Association of Retired Persons, 1992, based on data from U.S. Bureau of the Census.

Continuing to be intellectually active may help prevent a decline in mental activities in old age.

excellent crystallized memory shown during late adulthood indicates that storage problems can be ruled out. Obviously, already stored memories are not being lost. What about encoding? It may be that, as we grow older, we begin to experience difficulties in successfully encoding new material. If encoding problems are the cause of the decline in fluid intelligence, it might be possible to increase memory abilities in the elderly by teaching them techniques that aid encoding. Research by Poon (1985) supported this prediction: Providing elderly individuals with encoding strategies such as arranging names alphabetically resulted in a level of retention similar to that shown by much younger persons.

What about retrieval? Do the elderly have difficulty with this process also? The results of a study in which elderly individuals were provided with memory prompts (Craik, Byrd, & Swanson, 1987) indicate that the answer is yes. When cues or prompts were presented, recall for words from a list improved significantly, as did performance on other verbal tasks. These results suggest that the memories had been encoded and stored but the participants had trouble retrieving them. This study also led to another interesting discovery: Not all of the elderly participants showed a loss in fluid intelligence. In fact, the memory abilities of elderly individuals who had been intellectually active and resourceful throughout their lives were comparable to those of undergraduate students. Results like these point to the advantage of continuing to be intellectually active throughout life. It is possible for older people to learn new things!

Unfortunately, many people do not hold this view. What images flash through your mind when you see or hear such terms as *senior citizens, older Americans,* or *elderly persons*? Do these phrases bring to mind positive or negative scenes? Perhaps you responded with images of feeble individuals hobbling with canes and not understanding what is said to them. The tendency to view the elderly in a negative manner is termed **ageism.** It seems to be triggered by common words, such as *old* (Perdue & Gurtman, 1990). Although the use of such adjectives may be unintentional, it can lead to discrimination.

In many instances, ageism leads to isolation of elderly citizens and keeps them from making valuable contributions to society. A person who sits in a retirement apartment watching television contributes less than someone who has a part-time job or is active in other ways. As the number of elderly people in our society increases and research findings help psychologists and others view them more realistically and positively, perhaps we will see a decrease in ageism (Perdue & Gurtman, 1990). Such isolation may be the product of our more affluent society; in less developed countries, where there are no pension plans or Social Security, older adults do not officially retire. Therefore they do not become as isolated and are afforded greater social status as "wise elders."

Schaie's Stages of Thought and Cognition

ageism

Viewing elderly people in a negative manner

Whereas Piaget's theory of intellectual development does not go beyond the period of formal operations, K. Warner Schaie (1977–78, 1990) has proposed that *adult* thought patterns progress through a series of stages.

STUDY CHART

Schaie's Stages of Thought and Cognition

Developmental Period	Stage	Perception
Adolescence	Acquisition	Knowledge, skills, and information are gained with minimal concern for importance or direct application.
Young adulthood	Achievement	Knowledge, skills, and information are used to achieve specific goals. Thoughts and cognition tend to be focused and intense.
Middle adulthood	Responsibility	Thoughts and cognition broaden to encompass long-range goals for both the individual and the family unit.
	Executive	Some individuals' thoughts and cognition broaden even further to include societal concerns.
Late adulthood	Reintegration	Thoughts and cognition are used to search for meaning in one's life.

Acquisition: Childhood and Adolescence. The importance of making a personal commitment influenced the development of Schaie's (1977–78) theory of adult thought, learning, and cognition. This theory stresses the different types of commitments that are made during adolescence, early adulthood, middle adulthood, and late adulthood. Each type of commitment brings with it a different cognitive orientation.

   The task of the adolescent is to acquire information, knowledge, and skills; minimal concern is attached to their importance or application. According to Schaie, the adolescent is in a period of *acquisition*. For example, the daily classes of a high school student might include algebra, American history, literature or poetry, and even the study of Latin. A commitment to the acquisition of knowledge is the key here; the acquired knowledge will be used later.

Achievement: Young Adulthood. We have seen that during young adulthood, the individual's commitment turns toward the achievement of specific goals. During Schaie's *achievement* stage, knowledge is used to attain specific goals. For example, one young adult may have set as her goal to be a senior vice president of a bank by age 40. Another individual's goal might involve owning his own business by age 35. Schaie feels that thought and cognition during the achievement stage of young adulthood tend to be quite focused and intense in the quest of specific goals.

Responsibility: Middle Adulthood. During middle adulthood, Schaie believes, an individual's thought becomes less achievement-oriented and more influenced by long-range plans. Such long-range plans include greater consideration of one's family unit than was true during the achievement stage. Professional goals become modified to include one's family. Is it more important to work until 10 P.M. every night to achieve a specific professional objective, or should one be at home with the family? This integration of personal and family goals represents the development of *responsibility* in thought, cognition, and commitment.

   For some people in middle adulthood, this sense of responsibility extends to society in general. Schaie believes that such social concerns take us beyond the stage of responsibility to the executive stage of thought. An individual in this stage may be employed as a school superintendent or the chief executive officer of a

reintegration
Schaie's fourth stage of cognition and thought, in which individuals in late adulthood come to grips with the meaning of their lives

company. Because diverse groups and interests must be taken into account, executive thoughts and cognition tend to be more complex and all-encompassing. For example, the mayor of New York City must deal with tourism, violence, the concerns and needs of merchants, pollution control, and unions of city employees.

Reintegration: Late Adulthood. During late adulthood, individuals come to grips with and try to make sense of the lives they have lived. Schaie feels that as we go through this process and seek meaning, our thoughts tend to turn either inward to seek meaning from our own lives or outward to seek the meaning of life in general. This final stage, called **reintegration,** focuses on the issue of why it is important to have gained knowledge and then used that knowledge.

Review Summary

1. No single event in contemporary society marks the passage from childhood to adulthood. Rather, children experience an extended period of adolescence, which lasts roughly from age 12 to age 20.

2. During **pubescence,** which takes approximately two years, the adolescent experiences a major growth spurt and the development of **primary** and **secondary sex characteristics. Puberty,** the achievement of full sexual maturity, marks the end of pubescence.

3. Physical changes during **middle adulthood** are characterized by a gradual decline. Visual and auditory sensitivity decline, muscle strength decreases about 10 percent, and reaction time becomes noticeably slower.

4. Women undergo a series of changes, known as **menopause,** that mark the end of childbearing. The decrease in estrogen production that accompanies menopause may result in **osteoporosis,** a condition in which the bones become thinner and prone to fractures.

5. The physical decline experienced during early and middle adulthood continues during **late adulthood.** Vision and hearing are most adversely affected.

6. Late adulthood is accompanied by an increase in susceptibility to disease. Nearly one-third of individuals age 85 or older may suffer from **Alzheimer's disease,** a degenerative brain disease.

7. According to Piaget, if adolescents are given appropriate educational opportunities and stimulation, they will enter the **formal operational stage** of cognitive development and be capable of abstract thought.

8. Fluid intelligence (the ability to solve new problems and form new concepts) may begin a gradual decline at about age 30. **Crystallized intelligence,** the ability to retrieve and use stored information, shows a gradual increase throughout adulthood.

9. If the elderly are taught strategies to enhance encoding and are provided with retrieval cues, their memory capability may not differ from that of a young adult. If a person remains intellectually active, fluid intelligence may not decline.

10. Ageism occurs when people in a particular age group, such as the elderly, are viewed in a negative light. According to Schaie, thought and cognition during adolescence are characterized by the *acquisition* of knowledge. In early adulthood, thought and cognition are used for *achievement.* During middle adulthood, the individual enters a period of *responsibility* with regard to thought and cognition. Long-range plans and the family unit are taken into account. The final stage of cognition and thought, **reintegration,** occurs when individuals attempt to put their lives in perspective.

Study Break

1. What is the name for the period that ends in sexual maturity? for the attainment of sexual maturity?

2. What is the effect of the secular trend on puberty?
   a. The higher the family's standard of living, the earlier children reach puberty.
   b. The lower the family's standard of living, the earlier children reach puberty.
   c. Girls reach puberty before boys.
   d. Boys reach puberty before girls.

3. Identify each of the following as a primary or secondary sex characteristic:
   a. Growth of axillary hair
   b. Development of the uterus
   c. Development of seminal vesicles
   d. Coarser and oilier skin
   e. Growth of pubic hair

4. During middle adulthood, strength decreases from its peak by about how much? What sort of decline may be even more noticeable?
5. Anita is in her late fifties. Recently she suffered several fractures in her arms and legs. The cause of these fractures is unknown. What condition may Anita be suffering from? How could she have avoided developing this condition?
6. All of the following are true of menopause *except*
   a. Estrogen levels increase.
   b. It occurs during one's late forties and early fifties.
   c. Women may react favorably or unfavorably to it.
   d. Osteoporosis may result from changing estrogen levels.
7. Maria, a researcher, is well known for her ability to develop new products at just the right time. She excels at what sort of intelligence?
8. Everyone at the factory respects Luis. He has been on the job longer than anyone else and can always help solve a problem because he remembers how he handled a similar problem several years ago. Luis has excellent _____ intelligence.
   a. learned
   b. environmental
   c. fluid
   d. crystallized
9. The fastest growing age group in our society is those who are
   a. over 65.
   b. teenagers.
   c. over 85.
   d. 21–34.

Personality and Social Changes

For 20 years, Janet, a clinical psychologist, has helped people solve emotional and psychological problems. She is quite good at her job and has become one of the most popular therapists at the mental health center. Lately, however, her work has been less satisfying. She is tired and discouraged all the time and does not feel that she is doing a good job. She is seriously thinking about leaving this line of work. ***What caused this change in Janet's feelings about her job? What can be done to improve her attitude?*** ▪

From adolescence through old age, social change appears to be the rule rather than the exception. Education, significant others, marriage, divorce, children, community involvement, career, and retirement are among the social factors to be dealt with. How we react to such changes and challenges may affect our personality (see Chapter 12). In this section we examine social and personality changes that occur from adolescence through old age.

Adolescence

In Chapter 9 we described Erik Erikson's theory of psychosocial development and saw that four psychosocial crises are experienced before the end of childhood. Erikson's fifth psychosocial crisis deals with **identity versus identity confusion.** For the adolescent, who is experiencing a major growth spurt and developing signs of adulthood, the search for an identity and a place in society is most important (Erikson, 1975). This search can also be extremely frustrating. For some individuals, the search for an identity may not end for years; for others, it never ends.

The new roles open to the adolescent are influenced by ethnic and racial background, geographic locale, family values, and societal values. It is quite unlikely that a 15-year-old girl from rural Nebraska will see her place in society in the same way as a 15-year-old girl from Los Angeles. Being raised on a farm in a small town in the Midwest gives one a different view of possible societal roles than does being raised in a major metropolitan area (Holland & Andre, 1994). Although both adolescents search for a place in society, their perceived options are quite different. The same could be said for the comparison of adolescents in the United States with adolescents in other countries. For example, in the United States,

identity versus identity confusion
Erikson's fifth psychosocial crisis, in which the adolescent faces the task of determining his or her identity and role in society

identity achievement
Adoption of a set of well-chosen values and goals

foreclosure
Uncritical acceptance of parental values and desires; hampers the development of a unique identity

negative identity
Adoption of behaviors that are the opposite of what is expected

identity diffusion
Failure to develop an identity because of lack of goals and general apathy

moratorium
Period during which an adolescent may try several identities without intending to settle on a specific one

young people tend to choose an occupation, whereas many adolescents in other cultures do not have a say in what their occupation will be. In some countries, such as Italy, the parents' occupation will likely become that of their children.

Possible Outcomes of Identity Formation.   In individualistic cultures such as the United States, adolescents who have explored the alternatives and adopted a well-chosen set of values and goals have reached **identity achievement** (Marcia, 1980). These adolescents have a good sense of psychological well-being. They know where they are headed and what it takes to get there.

In other instances, the frustrations of this stage of development may cause adolescents to accept uncritically the values and desires of their parents. In this situation, called **foreclosure,** the adolescent's unique identity is not allowed to develop. Consider Willard, a successful but frustrated surgeon. Willard grew up in a small town in southwestern Oklahoma. As a boy, he enjoyed electronics and building radios. He could easily have become an electronics engineer. However, he became a doctor because that was the occupation his family chose for him; nobody asked him what he wanted to do with his life. Remember, however, that in many societies, lack of choice may be the norm with regard to occupation, family, and role according to birth order; it does not have the same stigma that it does in the United States.

Some adolescents find the identity expected of them unacceptable but are unable to replace it with an acceptable alternative. In such situations, the adolescent may develop a **negative identity** by adopting behaviors opposite to those that are expected. For example, Ken's family always expected that he would become a lawyer. After a rebellious college career and a frustrating semester of law school, Ken dropped out of school; he now drives a cab to support his real passion, building computers.

Identity diffusion occurs when the adolescent has few goals and is generally apathetic about schoolwork, friends, and the future (Archer & Waterman, 1990). The individual lacks an identity and is not motivated to find one.

Finally, some adolescents may go through a period in which they try out several identities without intending to settle on a specific one. It is as if a **moratorium** had been called on actually selecting an identity. The years spent in college may be viewed as a moratorium. A student may sample several different subject areas before settling on a major and choosing a career.

The adolescent peer group promotes a sense of identity.

Adolescent Peer Groups.   During adolescence the peer group promotes a sense of identity and defends against identity confusion. The peer group can have a pronounced influence on an adolescent's attitudes, values, and behaviors. Belonging to groups such as the French club, the hiking club, or an athletic team may have a positive influence. Not all adolescent groups, however, help develop a strong and productive sense of identity and an appropriate adjustment to society. For example, the prevalence of teenage gangs has added to the crime and violence found in the nation's cities (Williams, Singh, & Singh, 1994).

John Coleman (1980) highlighted three functions that make peer groups so important to the adolescent:

1. Through the process of experimentation, adolescents find out which behaviors and personality characteristics will be accepted and praised and which ones will be rejected. Peer groups provide the all-important feedback.

2. The peer group serves as a support group of contemporaries who are also experiencing the same social and physical changes.

3. Because adolescence is a period of questioning the behavior, standards, and authority of adults, it is hard for adolescents to seek help and advice from their parents. The peer group serves this important function.

Any peer group can serve these three functions. Hence it is important for adolescents to be associated with a positive peer group if they are to become contributing members of society.

The importance of appropriate models for the adolescent was clarified in a study conducted by Brook and colleagues (1989). Their participants were 278 college students and their older brothers. All of the participants completed a questionnaire that dealt with the use of drugs by themselves, their parents, and their peers. The results indicated that drug use may be influenced by peers, parents, and older siblings but that these three sources do not exert the same degree of influence: "Drug modeling by peers and siblings was found to have a greater association with younger brother drug use than did drug modeling by parents" (p. 70). Likewise, John W. Graham, Gary Marks, and William B. Hansen (1991) reported that modeling by peers was related to cigarette smoking and alcohol use by seventh-grade boys and girls (see Chapter 15). Frequency of drug use among adolescents is related to frequency of parental drug use (Anderson & Henry, 1994; Denton & Kampfe, 1994).

Colorado psychologists Cynthia Tennant-Clark, Janet Fritz, and Fred Beauvais (1989) investigated the effects of adolescent participation in groups focusing on the occult. They defined occult participation as "belief in supernatural powers such as magic, . . . witchcraft or Satanism, and the practice of rituals associated with their beliefs" (p. 758). Adolescents who scored high in knowledge of occult rituals, literature, games, and paraphernalia were more likely to be involved with substance abuse, have a poor self-concept, and harbor negative feelings about the future. Adolescents who participate in occult activities may have difficulty adjusting to the demands of a society that does not condone such behaviors (Clark, 1994). Although we cannot say whether such participation causes problems like drug abuse and low self-esteem or whether those problems drive adolescents to participate in occult practices, it is clear that such groups are likely to have a negative influence.

Family Influences.   The importance of the adolescent's peer groups should not lead you to believe that the family has ceased to have an influence. For example, Kenneth Felkers and Cathie Stivers (1994) found that family attitudes play a major role in determining whether adolescents, especially girls, develop eating problems such as anorexia nervosa and bulimia. Family relations are also an important variable in predicting juvenile delinquency (Hoge, Andrews, & Leschied, 1994). A study of Norweigan adolescents indicated that good family relations were important in producing good mental health and reducing depression in adolescents (Pedersen, 1994); a study of Canadian adolescents has also shown the importance of family perceptions of adolescents in protecting them against depression (McFarlane et al., 1994).

Making a Commitment.   Adolescence is the stage of life in which most individuals begin to make sustained personal commitments. Such commitments may be to another person, a religious cause, career preparation, or a social program. Commitments help the adolescent develop a sense of identity and accomplishment.

The decision to become sexually active represents a major personal commitment that has important consequences. Nowhere is the importance of this decision more clearly seen than in the case of teenage pregnancy in the United States (Bingham, Miller, & Adams, 1990; Raeff, 1994; Rauch-Elnekave, 1994). The teenage pregnancy rate in the United States is more than 90 pregnancies per 1,000 girls, and that rate is over double the rate for Great Britain, Canada, France, Australia, and Sweden (United Nations, 1991). Additionally, a high teenage abortion rate (approximately 40 percent) and a high percentage of births to unwed teenage mothers (approximately 70 percent; Children's Defense Fund, 1997) are associated issues that must be dealt with. When careers and educational opportunities seem out of reach, many teenagers appear to turn to parenthood as a way of entering adulthood (Caldas, 1993; Murray, 1992).

To understand the factors involved in teenage pregnancy, researchers conducted in-depth interviews with five 14-year-old African-American adolescents who were pregnant or had recently given birth (Pete & De Santis, 1990). The interviews revealed three key factors in the decision to become sexually active: (1) The partner was someone the young woman trusted; (2) the risk of pregnancy was not taken seriously (contraceptive devices were rarely, if ever, used); and (3) family relationships were less than ideal (there was no parent or other adult with whom to talk). These three characteristics are consistent with the self-centered and self-conscious adolescent thought patterns described by David Elkind (1984).

Pete and De Santis (1990) highlight a major implication of their research when they indicate that "young teenagers need assistance . . . in communicating with their parents and partners about sexual matters. Parents also need assistance in developing these communication skills" (p. 153). The importance of teenage mothers maintaining good communication with their parents is seen clearly in the area of child abuse. Teenage mothers who have poor support and poor communication are more likely to abuse their children than mothers who have good support and good communication (Haskett, Johnson, & Miller, 1994).

Marion Howard and Judith McCabe (1990; see also Kirby et al., 1994; Zabin & Hayward, 1993) provide some helpful suggestions for encouraging teenagers not to be sexually active. Their procedure includes teaching teenagers to understand the problems of sexual activity; for example, the adolescent role-plays in various situations involving pressure to be sexually active and learns to say no. Role-playing the difficulties they are likely to face may help adolescents find it easier to say no when the actual situation presents itself.

Early Adulthood

Along with the physical and intellectual changes that characterize adulthood come important personality and social changes. In the United States and other individualistic cultures, the world is the adults' oyster; they can make of it what they want. For many persons, career and lifestyle choices are almost unlimited; *diversity* is a key word for the adult. Remember, however, that in collectivist cultures family responsibilities, group membership, and obligations to others may be the norm.

Intimacy Versus Isolation.   It may be difficult to believe that one can experience a psychosocial crisis when one is in the best of health and at the height of one's physical and intellectual powers. Yet this is exactly what Erikson suggests. He believes that young adults experience the crisis of **intimacy versus isolation.** *Intimacy* refers to the ability to make a strong commitment to other people. An individual who cannot establish intimate relationships becomes isolated. Adolescents who have developed a strong sense of personal identity and worth are better prepared to make the compromises and sacrifices required in a successful relationship. When they become young adults, such adolescents are more likely to establish close and satisfying relationships in the workplace when a career takes precedence over marriage and family (Weiland, 1993). Those who lack a strong personal identity are likely to feel insecure and to avoid close relationships.

The development of a strong sense of personal identity and intimacy may, however, take different courses for boys and girls. Susan Basow (1992) observes that, according to Erikson's life span perspective, "the sexes diverge during adolescence: boys generally establish a strong autonomous identity before establishing an intimate relationship, whereas girls frequently establish an intimate relationship first and may never establish a strong autonomous identity" (p. 120).

Marriage and Children.   A young adult who is able to establish intimate relationships faces a number of important decisions. Among those decisions are whether to marry or cohabit and whether to have children. Research on such topics as cohabitation has yielded some interesting results. Data from a sample of 180 college students indicated that the willingness to cohabit was shown by older students who had lower levels of religiosity, more liberal attitudes toward sexual behavior, and less traditional views of marriage and sex roles (Huffman et al., 1994).

Both marriage and cohabitation have benefits and costs. For example, married people are healthier and tend to be happier than unmarried people (Verbrugge, 1979). With nearly a million divorces granted each year in the United States, however, it is clear that marriage is difficult (Wallerstein, 1994) and may not always be beneficial or desirable. (The divorce rate in the United States is the highest in the world. It is almost double that of Sweden, the country that ranks second [Berk, 1998].) Although people who have divorced are likely to remarry, the rate of redivorce has increased to the point that there are now nearly as many redivorces as there are divorces (Norton & Moorman, 1987).

The Feminization of Poverty

IF SOMEONE ASKS YOU TO THINK ABOUT POVERTY, WHAT IMAGE COMES TO MIND? We asked a number of people, and the typical response was "minority *people.*" That view is far from accurate.

Because women, regardless of age, make up the majority of poverty-status adults, the term *feminization of poverty* is appropriate (Goldberg & Kremen, 1990). What's more, this situation is not limited to any specific ethnic group(s). The poverty differential between men and women becomes even greater in cases of divorce or separation in families with children. Because children typically remain with the mother, she is faced with significant added responsibilities and demands. Given the high rate of divorce in the United States, it should not surprise you that the feminization of poverty in the U.S. is ahead of that in other industrialized societies.

This sex difference in poverty is not, however, limited to the United States and other industrialized nations; it is a global problem (63 percent of the world's

intimacy versus isolation
Erikson's sixth psychosocial crisis, in which the young adult faces the task of establishing a strong commitment to others (intimacy) or having to deal with isolation

Cultural & Diversity Perspective

illiterate are women). According to a United Nations (1995) report, *fewer than 50 percent* of women in South Asia, Sub-Saharan Africa, and the Middle East and North Africa are literate. The same situation does not exist for men. Illiteracy sets a vicious cycle into motion: Illiterate women marry at an early age, take poor-paying jobs, have large families, are likely to experience divorce, and are faced with severe poverty. The cycle repeats itself for the daughters of these women.

One step toward solving these problems is simple: Decrease illiteracy among women. In addition to benefiting individuals, such education has a positive impact on the entire country.

Whether and when to have children is another major issue of young adulthood that has both costs and benefits. Statistics show that the average age at which women have their first child has been rising since the 1960s.

Psychological Detective

What are some of the advantages of having children when you are in your mid- to late twenties? Are there any advantages to becoming a parent at an earlier age? Write down some answers to these questions before reading further.

If you wait until you are in your mid- to late twenties or older to have children, you will have greater earning power, and you will be able to provide a better lifestyle and education for your children. Your career goals will be more fully developed. Your role and responsibilities as a parent will be clearer, and you are likely to have more time to enjoy your children.

Most of the advantages of having children when one is younger are related to the effects of aging. Younger parents are likely to be more active and energetic than older parents; hence they may be able to deal with the demands of caring for a baby more effectively than older parents. Health is another age-related factor. As the age of childbearing during young adulthood increases, the health risks to both mother and child increase (Fryns, 1987). For example, the risk of having a child with Down syndrome (see Chapter 9) increases from 1 in 2,000 for mothers age 25 to 1 in 40 for mothers age 45 and older. Age is not the only factor that affects the decision to have children, however; career aspirations may also play a major role.

Consider the case of Nancy and Charles. Nancy aspires to become an electrical engineer, and Charles is planning a career in advertising. As a dual-career marriage, they have been forced to make compromises; sometimes their schedules conflict and create tension between them.

But there are also several potential benefits. The sharing of child-care responsibilities can result in a closer relationship between a father and his children. Compared with wives who do not work outside the home, the wife in a dual-career couple has additional opportunities to develop her skills and build identity and self-esteem outside of her parenting role. Because neither partner dominates the family in terms of responsibility and earning power, dual careers can lead to a more egalitarian relationship. Dual careers can also result in a variety of problems, however, such as rivalry between husband and wife, conflicts between family and work roles, insufficient time to meet children's needs, and changes in family decision-making processes (Flanagan, 1990).

During young adulthood the main focus is on developing a well-paying, satisfying career.

Career Development.   As this discussion suggests, career development is one of the major tasks young adults face. Until fairly recently, a discussion of career development would have dealt exclusively with men. The dramatic increase of women entering previously male-dominated professions has changed this situation, however. For example, in 1972, only 3.8 percent of the lawyers in the United States were women; whereas in 1995, 21.4 percent of the lawyers were women. Likewise, in 1972, 9.3 percent of the physicians in the United States were women; whereas in 1995, 20.4 percent of the physicians were women (U.S. Bureau of the Census, 1996). Despite the dramatic increase in the number of women in the workforce, however, women continue to encounter barriers. Many more women than men are employed in clerical and sales positions (U.S. Department of Labor, 1985), and equity in salaries has not been achieved. Like Nancy, the aspiring electrical engineer, however, more women are entering traditionally male-dominated fields.

Middle Adulthood

During middle adulthood one's occupation takes on added significance. Because prestige, productivity, and earning power may never be greater, these are the "golden years" for many people. The importance of one's job during this stage has been revealed in two different types of research. One set of studies investigates what people feel they would do if they suddenly became millionaires. In one study, 80 percent of participants said they would keep working (Harpaz, 1985). The other type of research deals with the effects of unemployment. Workers who have been laid off report feelings of depression, emptiness, and being lost (Kelvin & Jarrett, 1985).

Burnout.   Even during these golden years, however, a person can experience job problems and dissatisfaction. Remember Janet, the clinical psychologist who had become dissatisfied with her job? What caused this change in her feelings about her job, and what can be done to improve her attitude?

For some people, employment during middle adulthood may be characterized by high levels of stress and frustration, eventually creating a condition known as *burnout*. **Burnout** is a feeling of emotional and physical exhaustion that interferes with job performance and can lead to reduced self-esteem and, eventually, depression. This condition is one of the hazards of high-stress occupations with long hours, such as medicine, police work, air traffic control, psychological counseling, teaching, and legal practice. For example, clinical psychologists who feel they are no longer able to help their clients often experience burnout (Maslach, 1978, 1982).

Many students enter the field of psychology with the goal of becoming clinical psychologists. Although this occupation can be very rewarding, the typical day of a clinical psychologist at a mental health center may be very stressful. The psychologist will see at least four or five clients for psychotherapy. Conducting psychotherapy sessions is a draining experience. In addition, there will be at least one meeting pertaining to the operation of the mental health center. Each of the numerous phone calls from patients will require 10 to 15 minutes of the psychologist's time. If student interns are studying at the center, the psychologist may be asked to supervise them. At some point during the day the psychologist will have to find time to write up therapy notes and prepare complete written reports on each patient for use by the mental health center, the consulting psychiatrist, or the local judge. In short, there is too much to accomplish and not enough time in which to accomplish it. Is it any wonder that there is a high rate of burnout among clinical psychologists?

What can be done to prevent or alleviate burnout? Many experts suggest that taking vacations and breaks from the job can help. Sophia Kahill (1986) suggests that adopting realistic expectations about one's job, developing outside

burnout
Emotional and physical exhaustion that interferes with job performance

Teaching reflects a concern for the next generation and helps to resolve the crisis of generativity versus stagnation.

interests, and establishing a social support system can also help counteract burnout. Hobbies can help, too. Consider Mark, a clinical psychologist who is also an avid collector of baseball cards. This hobby helps counteract burnout in several ways. Reading magazines about cards and going to card shows takes his mind away from the pressures of work. It also puts him in touch with new friends and acquaintances who do not talk about work-related problems. (See Chapter 13 for a discussion of coping with stress.)

Midlife Crisis.   For some men in Western countries such as the United States, middle adulthood brings with it the well-known midlife crisis (Levinson, 1986, 1996). The **midlife crisis** is a potentially stressful period that typically occurs during the mid-forties and is brought on when a person comes to grips with mortality issues and begins to review his or her life and accomplishments. Dissatisfaction with one's life may be accompanied by the feeling that rapid action is needed to correct the situation or regain one's youth. It is therefore not uncommon for persons who experience such a crisis to make radical changes in their jobs or lifestyles.

Consider the case of Paul. For a number of years, Paul was a successful business executive. His daily routine never varied, and most people saw him as rather dull. Then, at age 46, he made a dramatic change in his lifestyle. His gray and blue business suits and white dress shirts were replaced with bright-colored, trendy clothes. The family sedan was traded in for a small sports car. Many people are saying that Paul is not acting his age. What happened to cause these changes in Paul?

Paul's new car and flashy clothes suggest he is undergoing a midlife crisis. Is it possible that he is trying to deny his advancing age by adopting symbols of youth? How satisfying and productive has his life really been?

Although some experts feel that few men can avoid the midlife crisis (e.g., Levinson, 1986), other research does not paint as bleak a picture. The percentage who experience the classic midlife crisis may be quite low (less than 15 percent), and a sizable proportion (over 30 percent) report a satisfying adjustment to midlife (Farrell & Rosenberg, 1981). Thus only a small percentage of people change their lifestyle drastically (Wrightsman, 1994).

Research on midlife changes in women has revealed a different pattern (Reinke et al., 1985). For women, age-related stress tends to occur later, in the late forties and early fifties, when parenting responsibilities have decreased and there is time to cope with other issues (Helson & Roberts, 1994). As more women return to college and enter the labor force, however, the likelihood of a midlife crisis appears to be decreasing. College training and job satisfaction, in conjunction with women's family roles, provide important buffers against midlife difficulties (Baruch, 1984).

Erikson was not directly addressing the midlife crisis when he described the psychosocial crisis of middle adulthood, yet many of the same issues are involved. Erikson believes that during our early forties we face the crisis of **generativity versus stagnation.** To be generative is to have concern for the next generation and for the perpetuation of life. Because teaching, coaching, and parenting reflect an obvious desire to share one's talents and knowledge, this concern is frequently expressed through such activities.

Other Stresses During Middle Adulthood.   As their children grow older and leave home to begin their own careers, middle-aged American parents must confront another challenge. During the hustle and bustle of the

midlife crisis
Potentially stressful period that occurs during the mid-forties and is triggered by reevaluation of one's accomplishments

generativity versus stagnation
Erikson's seventh psychosocial crisis, which occurs during middle adulthood and reflects concern, or lack thereof, for the next generation

child-rearing years, communication between the parents may have diminished and in some cases faded entirely. Now that there are no children at home, the parents must become reacquainted. This adjustment is called the **empty nest syndrome.**

Psychological Detective

Many individuals report an improvement in marital satisfaction after their children have left home. What are some possible reasons for this increased satisfaction? Write down your answers before reading further.

Several factors appear to be responsible for the increase in marital satisfaction after the departure of children. First, the family's financial situation usually improves, and there are fewer worries about financial matters (Berry & Williams, 1987). Second, the goal of raising a family has been achieved. Once the children have left home, many of the anxieties associated with this goal are reduced. Finally, there is more time for the husband and wife to do things together.

Despite the benefits of having raised independent children, the aging parents of middle-aged Americans may begin to require additional care and attention, thus adding one more source of stress. The stress of attending to the needs of elderly parents is heightened when the parents live with their children. Such strains can, and do, lead to violence. As many as 1.5 million cases of elder abuse may occur in the United States each year (Baron & Welty, 1996). The magnitude of this problem and the intense stress it creates have led to the development of counseling and support groups for people who care for the elderly (Cantor, 1983).

Another source of stress that may be reintroduced after the empty nest adjustment period is the return of the birds to the nest. In times of economic hardship, many young couples are forced to return home to live with their parents. Similarly, a daughter and her young children may return to live with her parents after a divorce. For middle-aged parents who have adjusted to the empty nest, the interactions and demands of this newly refilled nest may be very stressful. Routines must be changed, and the needs and desires of additional family members must be addressed.

Late Adulthood

Erikson's final personality crisis, **integrity versus despair,** occurs during late adulthood. To accept one's impending death, one must be able to put one's life in perspective and attach meaning to it. Achieving this goal results in a sense of wholeness or integrity. People who are unable to find meaning in their lives may develop a sense of despair and anguish and wish they could have lived their lives differently.

Retirement. The crisis of integrity versus despair is reflected in the way an individual adapts to retirement. According to the American Association of Retired People (1992), more older Americans are choosing to retire than ever before. In addition, the age at which individuals retire is decreasing. Retirement may call forth visions of elderly people enjoying a vacationlike life in places with ideal climates such as Florida or Arizona. Although these images sell condominiums and retirement houses, they are not accurate. Retirement represents a major adjustment (Glick, 1980). Some people look forward to retirement and enjoy it greatly. For others, retirement is a time of frustration, anger, and possibly depression.

Why do people react so differently to retirement? A number of factors are involved. The keys to successful retirement include good planning and preparation,

empty nest syndrome
Period of adjustment for parents after all children have left home

integrity versus despair
Erikson's eighth psychosocial crisis, which occurs during late adulthood; integrity reflects a feeling that one's life has been worthwhile; despair reflects a desire to relive one's life

Erikson's Psychosocial Crises: Adolescence through Old Age

Crisis	Developmental Period	Characteristics
Identity versus identity confusion	Adolescence	The individual asks, "Who am I?" Adolescents seek to establish their sexual, career, and ethnic identities during this period. If these identities are not established, the individual will be confused about the roles he or she plays in the future.
Intimacy versus isolation	Early adulthood	Patterns of intimacy, companionship, and love are established during this period. Failure to develop such patterns results in an individual who lives in isolation from others.
Generativity versus stagnation	Middle adulthood	The individual's career and productivity reach a peak during this period. Families are formed, and children are raised. Failure to accomplish these objectives results in inactivity and stagnation.
Integrity versus despair	Late adulthood	One's life and its meaning are put in perspective. Individuals who feel that their lives lack meaning experience despair over unattained goals and unresolved problems.

This retired gardener in Goose Bay, Newfoundland, appears to have resolved the crisis of integrity versus despair in a productive manner.

satisfaction with one's accomplishments, good health, and freedom from financial worries. Individuals who begin to attend to these issues during middle adulthood make the transition to retirement much more easily than those who do not.

The Kansas City Study. Erikson's final crisis might lead you to believe there are only two personality types among elderly people—those who have achieved integrity in their lives and are reasonably satisfied, and those who have not achieved integrity and are angry or despondent. However, the results of an extensive study of aging conducted in Kansas City by Bernice Neugarten and her colleagues (1968) indicate that such a description may not be accurate. Through extensive interviews with 159 men and women ranging in age from 50 to 90, these investigators identified four main personality types: integrated, armor-defended, passive-dependent, and unintegrated. *Integrated* individuals (44 percent) have good cognitive abilities and generally lead active, complex, and satisfying lives. Individuals in the *armor-defended* category (25 percent) are achievement-oriented. They defend themselves against growing old and cling to the lifestyle of middle adulthood as long as possible. As long as they can maintain that lifestyle, they are satisfied with their lives.

The *passive-dependent* group (19 percent) comprises two types of individuals. People who are dependent on one or two others for their needs are categorized as *succorance-seeking*. As long as the support of those others is available, these people report a reasonably high level of satisfaction with life. Individuals who are inactive and have been passive throughout their lives are categorized as *apathetic*. These individuals typically report lower levels of satisfaction with their lives.

Unintegrated individuals (12 percent) fail to display a consistent or organized pattern of aging. Despite poor emotional and psychological control, such individuals are able to continue living in society, although with low levels of life satisfaction.

Over 90 percent of elderly U.S. citizens live in a community, rather than in an institution such as a nursing home. Most elderly people prefer to live in their own homes or apartments and maintain their independence as long as possible. With some careful planning, it is often possible to achieve this objective. Consider the case of Peggy, now 91, whose husband died 10 years ago. She continues to live in her own house, as she has for over 40 years. During the day a nurse assists her with meals and provides companionship, but Peggy is as independent as possible.

Owing to physical or financial limitations, however, not all elderly people are able to live in their own homes in this style. In many cultures such responsibilities are handled by the extended family. In other cultures, such as the United States, extended care facilities, retirement villages, and cooperative housing arrangements, in which elderly people share a house, enable them to live in a residential neighborhood. As the average life span increases, we can expect to see additional arrangements of this nature.

Review Summary

1. Adolescents experience major psychological and social changes. Erik Erikson proposes that as adolescents struggle to determine what their roles in society will be, they experience the psychosocial crisis of **identity versus identity confusion.**

2. The adolescent peer group provides feedback and helps adolescents achieve a sense of identity and belonging. Some peer groups, however, may interfere with satisfactory adaptation to society.

3. The establishment of a sustained personal commitment may provide adolescents with feedback concerning their identities and potential roles. Such commitments may involve major decisions, such as whether to be sexually active or use drugs.

4. According to Erikson, early adulthood is characterized by the psychosocial crisis of **intimacy versus isolation.** If individuals are not able to make the sacrifices and compromises needed to establish strong commitments, they will be isolated from others.

5. For many people, middle adulthood is a time of high job satisfaction. Some, however—especially those in high-stress occupations—experience **burnout.**

6. As people review their lives and achievements, they may experience a **midlife crisis,** which leads them to engage in radical behavior changes aimed at regaining youth.

7. The psychosocial crisis of middle adulthood, **generativity versus stagnation,** centers on concern for the well-being of future generations.

8. When their last child leaves home, parents may need to learn how to communicate and live as a couple once again. This adjustment is known as the **empty nest syndrome.** Other adjustments of middle adulthood include having to provide care for elderly parents.

9. The psychosocial crisis of **integrity versus despair** occurs during late adulthood. People who are unable to put their life in perspective may experience anger, bitterness, and despair.

10. The Kansas City study of aging revealed four personality types among the elderly: integrated, armor-defended, passive-dependent, and unintegrated.

Study Break

1. John is a college sophomore. During the past two years he has changed his major four times. According to Erik Erikson, John is trying to resolve which psychosocial crisis? What outcome seems likely at this point?

2. How can membership in a peer group be negatively related to substance abuse, low self-esteem, and negative feelings about the future?

3. Which of the following is not an advantage of postponing having children?
   a. Parents will have greater earning power.
   b. Parents' career goals will be more fully developed.
   c. Parents can provide better education for their children.
   d. Parents' health risks are reduced.
4. Peter was a loner in college. After graduation, he took a job that required minimal contact with other people. He has very few acquaintances and no real friends. It would seem that Peter has not been able to resolve which psychosocial crisis?
5. High-stress occupations may lead to what condition? What can be done to alleviate it?
6. Garland, a man in his forties, changed his appearance and image overnight! He now has a new hairstyle (and color), a new wardrobe, a new sports car with a sensational sound system, and new friends who are much younger than he is. What may Garland be experiencing?
7. Gib is in his mid-fifties. His job as a fifth-grade teacher is very satisfying. He enjoys coaching the baseball team at his school. It would appear that Gib has successfully resolved which psychosocial crisis?
8. How a person adjusts to retirement provides a good indication of how he or she has resolved which psychosocial crisis?
9. Erikson's psychosocial crisis that occurs during adolescence is called
   a. intimacy versus isolation.
   b. generativity versus stagnation.
   c. identity versus identity confusion.
   d. integrity versus despair.
10. Most individuals begin to make sustained personal commitments at the stage of
   a. early adulthood.
   b. late adulthood.
   c. adolescence.
   d. middle adulthood.

Death, Dying, and Bereavement

Galen and Shandra lost their daughter in a car accident over a year ago. You saw them at the funeral. Your studies have kept you busy however, and you haven't seen them since then. When you had dinner with them last week, all they could talk about was their daughter. After dinner, the conversation continued as you spent the rest of the evening watching home videos featuring their daughter. Their inability to take their minds off their loss struck you as morbid. *Is it typical for bereaved parents to dwell on the memory of their child for such a long time?* ■

For some people, death is seen as the final event in a person's life span. Although it marks the conclusion of a particular individual's developmental history, other people continue to be influenced by their memories of that person. In this section we examine attitudes toward death and the process of bereavement. We see that different attitudes toward death are associated with different stages of development.

Attitudes toward Death

Childhood. Before they attain the ability to perform concrete operations, children do not have an accurate conception of death. They believe that death is reversible—that a dead friend or pet can return to life. Before about age 6, children do not realize that all living things ultimately die and that all functions cease at the time of death. They believe death can be avoided.

Adolescence. Although adolescents understand the nature of death, they do not have a healthy respect for its implications (Corr, 1995). During adolescence, emphasis is on how one lives, not on how long. Death may even be glamorized and associated with daring deeds and heroic individuals (Pattison, 1977). For example,

Adolescents who idolize a seemingly indestructable hero, such as James Bond, may not see death as a feared event.

James Bond, the international spy created by Ian Fleming, is depicted as an individual whose daring deeds repeatedly bring him to the brink of death; Bond, however, never seems concerned. Adolescents frequently idolize individuals who express such feelings; hence death may not be regarded as an event to be feared.

For other adolescents, death may seem the only way out of an intolerable situation (Lennings, 1994). Their self-centered and self-conscious thoughts place a premium on how they lead their lives and who their friends are. Inability to lead one's life in a desired manner may be a major cause of teenage suicide. Having the right car, dating the right people, and being popular in school are very important to adolescents. Perhaps as a result of the increased pressures of our complex society, the number of teenage suicide has risen during recent years. Approximately 1 in every 10,000 adolescents commits suicide each year. Warning signs such as a sudden decrease in school attendance, withdrawal from social relationships, a breakup in a romantic relationship, having already attempted suicide, and publicized suicides by other adolescents should be taken seriously (King et al., 1990).

The egocentric thought of the adolescent also leads to the belief that "I am invulnerable; it will never happen to me." This view of not being subject to the same rules as others is called the **personal fable** (Elkind, 1984; Quadrel, Fischoff, & Davis, 1993). Although adolescents may think about death in the abstract, they frequently engage in high-risk behaviors, such as bungee jumping, skydiving, taking drugs, driving fast, or being members of gangs. Death simply is not considered a possibility.

Young Adulthood.   Young adults are at the peak of their physical and sensory abilities and believe that the future has much to offer them. They rarely think of their own death. Consequently, the occurrence of a life-threatening illness usually provokes extreme anger and rage. Young adults with a terminal illness are typically very poor hospital patients; they feel death is unfair and they are being robbed of their future.

Middle Adulthood.   During middle adulthood noticeable physical changes, coupled with the death of one's own parents, bring the realization that death is inevitable. This realization often results in changes in lifestyle. These changes may take one of two forms: The individual may adopt behaviors that are characteristic of an earlier developmental period, as in the reaction to a midlife crisis; or the individual may improve dietary and exercise habits to become more physically fit and live as long as possible.

Late Adulthood.   Even though death may be imminent, the elderly are more understanding and accepting of this eventuality than younger adults (Reker, Peacock, & Wong, 1987). Elderly people have put their lives in perspective and understand that death is a normal component of the developmental cycle. They have reached the integrity stage of development (Veroff & Veroff, 1980). Such integrity is shown in very different ways in different cultures. For example, the attainment of integrity for some Japanese might involve suicide to atone for one's sins and to save honor and face for one's family.

Confronting Death

Ultimately, we must all face our impending death. How will we react? Research on terminally ill patients conducted by Elisabeth Kübler-Ross has provided some answers. Terminally ill patients typically go through five stages in dealing with and understanding death (Kübler-Ross, 1969, 1975): denial, anger, bargaining for extra time, depression, and acceptance (see Table 10-1). Although a person is likely to

personal fable
Feeling shared by many adolescents that one is not subject to the same rules as other people

Research on terminally ill patients conducted by Elisabeth Kübler-Ross indicates that people may go through five stages in dealing with the approach of death.

TABLE 10-1 **Stages of Confronting Death**

STAGE	DESCRIPTION
Denial	The typical reaction is "This can't happen to me." Because friends and family members may also deny the reality of death, the patient feels isolated and has no one with whom to talk.
Anger	Once the reality has been confronted, the "Not me" attitude changes to an angry "Why me?" complaint. Young and healthy individuals are envied. To move beyond this stage, patients must express their anger and rage.
Bargaining	Once rage and anger have been expressed, the terminally ill person bargains for additional time. Such bargains often take the form of prayers, such as "I will lead a better life if I can only live until . . ."
Depression	Depression often follows the bargaining stage. As with anger, depression should not be hidden. Only by directly confronting and experiencing the normal feelings of sadness and grief will the person be able to progress to the stage of acceptance.
Acceptance	This stage is characterized by a feeling of being at peace with oneself. Unfinished business, such as setting one's finances in order and seeing old friends for a final time, has been taken care of, and the person accepts the fact that "the time is near."

experience each of these stages at one time or another, he or she will not necessarily proceed in an orderly manner from Stage 1 to Stage 5 (Corr, 1993; Kastenbaum, 1986, 1995). Individuals may experience these stages in different orders, and it is not uncommon to alternate between stages or to experience the emotions of two stages simultaneously. The nature of the disease leading to death also influences those emotions and the times when they are experienced. For example, a person suffering from a disease characterized by periods of remission may experience denial several times rather than once.

Cultural attitudes toward death differ significantly and influence the reactions toward it. For example, in several Native American cultures death is met with stoic self-control and a belief in the circular relation between life and death (Lewis, 1990). Buddhism also fosters self-acceptance of death (Truitner & Truitner, 1993).

Bereavement, Grief, and Support

Death brings numerous changes and adjustments for those who are left behind. Roles change—a wife becomes a widow, a husband a widower, a child an orphan. In addition to adjusting to living alone, widows and widowers must assume the responsibilities of the deceased spouse. Orphans must adjust to a totally new living environment. The emotional and role changes that follow a death are called **bereavement,** and the people whose emotions and roles change are known as the *bereaved*.

It may be quite difficult to adjust to these emotions and assume the new roles. **Grief,** encompassing the emotional changes associated with bereavement, is a normal part of this process and seems to progress through four stages (Kalish, 1985): shock and denial, intense concern, despair and depression, and recovery. First the bereaved person expresses *shock and denial*. These reactions serve to protect the individual from the pain of what has happened. This stage may last as long as two or three months.

bereavement
Emotional and role changes that follow death

grief
The emotional changes associated with bereavement

The emotional and role changes that follow a death are called bereavement. People whose emotions and roles change are the bereaved.

But what about Galen and Shandra, who were still grieving over the death of their daughter a year later? Is it typical to continue to dwell on the memory of a dead child for such a long time? The second phase of grief, which may last for six months to a year, is characterized by *intense concern* for perpetuating the memory of the dead person. The majority of the bereaved person's thoughts concern the person who has died. Thus the behaviors Galen and Shandra are displaying are entirely normal.

The third stage, *despair and depression,* is often characterized by confused thinking and anger. Irrational behaviors, such as suddenly selling one's house and moving to an area where one has no friends, may also be displayed during this phase. **Mourning** involves the behavioral changes associated with bereavement. Untimely deaths, such as the death of Galen and Shandra's daughter, may prolong or intensify the second and third phases, as compared with the natural death of an elderly parent who had been ill for a long time. When the bereaved person shows renewed interest in normal daily activities, he or she has reached the final stage—*recovery*—and the grief is resolved.

Social support is a key ingredient in successful coping with death and bereavement. In Western nations the hospice movement has taken the lead in the delivery of such support services. The **hospice** is more a philosophy of treatment than a set of buildings and equipment. In addition to providing normal medical services for the terminally ill, hospice physicians and staff are trained to give more personalized care and more time to terminally ill patients and their families (Armstrong-Daily, 1991). This philosophy of warm, personal concern and care is not confined to hospitals; it can be implemented just as effectively in the home (National Hospice Organization, 1992). The attitudes and adjustments of hospice patients and their families are superior to those of comparable patients receiving traditional hospital care.

The hospice movement is an excellent example of the application of psychology to the problems of society. According to Robert W. Buckingham (1983):

> Today, more than three-quarters of the terminally ill are consigned to institutions which are unprepared to deal with their final needs. The real terror of institutionalized dying is not death but mechanical maintenance without medical purpose and the ultimate indignity of having one's final days controlled by strangers. (p. 160).

The hospice movement began in the United States with the incorporation of Hospice, Connecticut, in 1971. It represents a revolution against the

mourning
The behavioral changes associated with bereavement

hospice
Institution where terminally ill patients and their families are given warm, friendly, personalized care

idea that a person must die in an institution surrounded by impersonal machines and technicians. The hospice is an application of humanistic psychology, which stresses the dignity of the individual. In the case of home care, a member of the family receives training in nursing methods. According to Buckingham (1983):

> There is a lot to be said for involving the family in the care of the dying patient; so many times families express the feeling of helplessness when a loved one is dying. Feelings of personal inadequacy and inferiority accompanied by negative expectancies concerning interpersonal contacts with others were much more characteristic of nonhospice than of hospice primary care persons. Being able to take care of, provide assistance for, and give comfort to the dying patient relinquished some of the guilt and helplessness felt by the family. (p. 162).

Highlighting Cultural Views and Practices

"David Shinn, 21, a Harvard senior, made a conscious decision to shun the science track in college even though he was brilliant at its disciplines and scored 1580 out of a possible 1600 on his college boards" (Allis, 1991). *What caused this outstanding Asian-American student to shy away from a promising career in science?* ▪

Although the majority of the material presented in Chapter 9 and this chapter thus far has dealt with the development of the so-called mainstream in the United States, parenting practices and patterns of development may differ from one cultural group to another. Only recently have developmental psychologists devoted much attention to the influence of culture. Their research has revealed a number of interesting cultural effects—for example, that Guyanese parents use authoritarian and punitive child-rearing techniques more frequently than Caucasian parents do (Deyoung & Zigler, 1994) and that noise pollution has caused auditory damage to occur more rapidly in the United States and Europe than in some African nations (Timiras, 1972). Reflecting the fact that cultural differences can occur within our own society, Ellen Rosen and her colleagues (1991) found that white college women are more dissatisfied with their body shape than African-American college women are. The white women also scored significantly higher on the bulimia scale.

We have also seen that better nutrition in developed nations hastens the onset of puberty. This section reveals that culture can influence birthing and parenting practices, intelligence, educational achievements and career choices, and the way the elderly population is perceived and treated.

Birthing and Parenting Practices

In the years after the Vietnam War, a large number of Southeast Asian refugees immigrated to the United States. Understanding the needs and values of these different cultural groups was a major challenge for child-care providers. Robert Morrow studied the child-rearing practices and customs of Cambodian, Vietnamese, Laotian, and Hmong families. He found that during their children's early years, Southeast Asian parents are more tolerant and permissive than

American parents: "The tendency is for parents to provide immediate gratification for their infants' early dependency needs" (Morrow, 1989, p. 276). For example, unlike many American children, most Southeast Asian children sleep in the same room and even in the same bed with their parents for an extended period. This practice may continue in Cambodian families until the child is 10 years old. Infants may be as old as 3 or 4 before they are weaned from breast feeding. Morrow views these child-rearing practices as giving the child "a safe, nurturant, and predictable environment" (p. 276) within the context of the family. These practices contrast with the emphasis on independence that characterizes Western societies. Table 10-2 summarizes several differences in birthing and pregnancy practices between American and Southeast Asian families.

Such parenting practices can influence social development. Unlike typical white middle-class Americans, who have a large number of friends outside their family, persons from other cultures may mistrust people outside the family. Parents serve as role models for their children, and their children, in turn, are more dependent on their parents, and for a longer period, than American children are. This pattern of heightened dependence has also been found in children in Tanzania (McGillicuddy-De Lisi & Subramanian, 1994). It is important for professionals in the United States, especially health care workers, to understand cultural differences so that they can be aware of changes that are taking place and provide the best possible services and advice (Sharma, Lynch, & Irvine, 1994).

Intelligence

In addition to influencing social development, culture may influence intellectual development.

TABLE 10-2 Birthing and Pregnancy Practices in American and Southeast Asian Cultures

AMERICAN	VIETNAMESE, CAMBODIAN, LAOTIAN	HMONG
Children are born in a hospital.	In the countryside, the Vietnamese prefer a midwife to deliver the child at home. She is often aided by female relatives (men, unmarried women, girls, and the husband are not present). In urban areas, the child is delivered in a hospital.	The husband delivers the baby with the help of a midwife. Then he stays home at least two or three days to care for his wife and child.
After delivery, women can go anywhere when able.	After delivery, a woman cannot visit relatives or friends and must stay at home. Vietnamese women usually stay home for one week. Cambodian women stay home for one week, then they can go anywhere when able.	After delivery, a woman cannot visit relatives or friends. She must stay inside the house for a month.
	In the countryside, a woman may deliver at home. In urban areas, the child is born in a hospital.	When a girl becomes pregnant, the parents build a temporary shelter for her outside her parents' house where she can deliver the baby. During the first month after delivery, she cannot enter any house but must stay in the shelter.

Source: Morrow, 1989.

Psychological Detective

Perhaps the most frequently used method for evaluating intelligence is administering an intelligence test (see Chapter 8). What problems might you encounter if you used this method to compare intelligence across cultures? Give this question some thought and write down your answers before reading further.

The biggest problem in cross-cultural comparisons of intelligence is the test itself. A test developed in one culture may not be a fair test of intelligence in another culture. Developing such a test would be most difficult; word meanings and connotations differ greatly from one culture to another. One solution might be to have the participant draw a picture and then evaluate the detail involved.

Despite the difficulty of creating a **culture-fair intelligence test,** cross-cultural comparisons of reading and math scores have been made (Stevenson et al., 1985). Such comparisons of science and math scores consistently place students from Hong Kong, Japan, Korea, and Taiwan among the top performers (Lapointe, Askew, & Meade, 1992). Elementary school children from the United States typically score at the average in science and math. Chinese children had the highest scores in reading ability.

Educational Achievement

Stanley Sue and Sumie Okazaki (1990) examined the educational achievements of Asian-American students (see also Stevenson & Lee, 1990). The high academic achievements of these students are remarkable; they are superior in nearly every category, and with every generation there is a greater likelihood that the parents will become more directly involved in their children's education (Shoho, 1994). The families of Asian-American students expect academic excellence (Chao, 1994); therefore such accomplishments are not surprising. Sue and Okazaki (1990), however, point to another factor that enhances the academic performance of Asian Americans. This factor is *upward mobility,* the ability to gain desirable employment and improve the family's economic condition:

> Although culture is certainly an important factor in achievements, education has been functional for upward mobility, especially when participation in other areas, such as sports, entertainment, and politics, has been difficult. One could argue that educational success, increased numbers of educated Asian role models, and limitations in mobility in other areas contribute to performance, above and beyond that which can be predicted from Asian cultural values. (p. 919)

Because all of the child's behavior and accomplishments occur within the context of the family, these children develop a strong sense of loyalty and obligation to their families. Their behaviors are always considered in terms of the shame or pride they will bring to the family. In contrast to the egocentrism of American children, the family comes first for Asian-American children.

Unfortunately, these high academic achievements and the stereotype that all outstanding Asian-American students are headed for careers in science are not without their drawbacks. Not all of these outstanding students are willing to be routed into such careers. According to Sam Allis (1991)

> Tohru Masamune, 31, grew up in a Japanese-American household distinguished by world-class scientists on both sides of his family. He graduated from M.I.T. in 1982 with a degree in chemical engineering. His success in the family tradition appeared assured. . . . Last year Masamune stunned his parents by dropping a well-paying job with a computer company to become an actor.

culture-fair intelligence test
An intelligence test that does not contain culturally loaded items

Recall David Shinn from the vignette at the beginning of this section. What caused him to shy away from a promising career in science?

> All my teachers were disappointed that I didn't go to M.I.T.," he says, "but I really wanted to avoid the stereotype of the science geek."

America's diverse Asian-American community is awash these days with stories like these. Asian-American students and graduates are increasingly chafing at the "model-minority myth." That image depicts them as a group of blinkered science-oriented achievers (Allis, 1991). Clearly both educational achievement and career choice may be influenced by an individual's cultural background. The diversity, abilities, and energy displayed by Asian-American students should be seen as assets to our educational system (Kim & Chun, 1994).

Aging

The form of prejudice known as *ageism* suggests that all elderly individuals are feeble and crotchety. As noted earlier in the chapter, this view is inaccurate; the majority of elderly people are active and productive. Likewise, the notion that aging occurs in a similar manner across all segments of society is inaccurate. Unfortunately, aging may pose additional problems for members of minority groups.

Whereas the likelihood of illness among elderly minorities is high, the chance of receiving treatment is low. Many elderly members of minority groups have incomes below the poverty level (American Association of Retired Persons, 1992). Moreover, many elderly minorities, especially first-generation immigrants, are unaware of or reluctant to take advantage of the social services available to them, such as legal counseling and low-cost health services at the local public health department (Gelfand, 1982).

In some cases these additional problems may be somewhat offset by the extended-family pattern that characterizes many minority groups. For example, Hispanic and African-American families tend to have active extended-kinship networks. These extended families can be counted on to provide emotional and financial support to their elder members (Gibson, 1986).

To be effective, psychologists, social workers, and other health care professionals who provide services to children, families, and elderly people from other cultures must be aware of differences like the ones we have described. As members of a multicultural society, we need to recognize and appreciate these differences. Only when such differences are appreciated will our society be able to function harmoniously.

Review Summary

1. Death brings the individual's developmental history to its conclusion. Attitudes toward death change with age. Young children believe that death is reversible; adolescents emphasize how one lives, not how long. The threat of death angers young adults and may cause substantial changes in the lifestyle of middle-aged individuals. The elderly are generally more understanding and accepting of the inevitability of death.

2. Elisabeth Kübler-Ross has identified five stages that an individual may go through in confronting death: denial, anger, bargaining for extra time, depression, and acceptance.

3. Role and status changes following a death constitute the process of **bereavement.**

4. Grief, which is a normal part of bereavement, progresses through four stages: shock and denial, efforts to perpetuate the memory of the deceased, despair, and recovery.

5. Child-rearing and other family-related practices may differ greatly from one culture to another. Knowledge of such differences is important for social workers and health-care providers who deal with families and children from other cultures.

Study Break

1. Describe how death is viewed during each of the stages of development. Be sure you can name each stage.
2. A high school senior has earned the reputation of being a very dangerous and reckless driver. Her reply to comments such as "You'll kill yourself" is always the same: "It will never happen to me." What is Elkind's name for this kind of attitude?
3. Which of the following is not a warning sign of possible adolescent suicide?
   a. A sudden decrease in school attendance
   b. Having already attempted suicide
   c. Highly publicized suicides by other adolescents
   d. A sudden clinging in social or love relationships
4. Describe the stages of confronting death outlined by Kübler-Ross.
5. Which of the following is not true of Kübler-Ross's stages of dealing with death?
   a. People may experience the stages in different orders.
   b. People may alternate between stages.
   c. People can experience the emotions of two stages simultaneously.
   d. People are likely to skip one or more of the stages.
6. What is the name for the emotional and role changes following a death?
7. Describe the stages through which people pass as they express grief over the death of a loved one.
8. Allowing a person to die with dignity, away from a cold and impersonal institution, is the goal of what type of institutions?
9. What practical reason is there for studying child-rearing practices in cultures other than our own?
10. A Southeast Asian child began first grade in an American school a year ago. Is it likely that this child made a large number of friends during the course of the year? Why or why not?

ANSWERS TO STUDY BREAKS

Pages 426–427

1. Pubesence, puberty
2. a
3. a. Growth of axillary hair—secondary sex characteristic
   b. Development of uterus—primary sex characteristic
   c. Development of seminal vesicles—primary sex characteristic
   d. Coarser and oiler skin—secondary sex characteristic
   e. Growth of pubic hair—secondary sex characteristic
4. 10 percent, reaction time
5. Osteoporosis: Maintain a sufficiently high level of calcium intake.
6. a
7. Fluid
8. d
9. c

Pages 437–438

1. Identity versus identity confusion. John probably will call a moritorium on actually selecting a major for the time being.
2. Appropriate, positive peer groups can reinforce acceptable behaviors, foster positive self-esteem, and provide optimism for the future.
3. d
4. Intimacy versus isolation
5. Burnout. Burnout can be dealt with by developing realistic expectations about your job, developing outside interests, and establishing a social support network.
6. Midlife crisis
7. Generativity versus stagnation
8. Integrity versus despair
9. c
10. c

Page 446

1. *Childhood:* Death is reversible.
   Adolescence: Implications of death are understood, but adolescents do not have a healthy respect for death.
   Young adulthood: Rarely think of death; life-threatening illnesses provoke anger.
   Middle adulthood: Realize that death is inevitable.
   Late adulthood: More understanding and accepting of death than younger adults.
2. Personal fable
3. d
4. *Denial:* "This can't happen to me!"
   Anger: "Why me!"
   Bargaining for extra time: Attempts to make bargains and gain extra time
   Depression: Feelings of sadness and grief
   Acceptance: Feelings of being at peace with oneself
5. d
6. Bereavement

7. *Shock and denial:* Protect one from the pain of what has happened
   Intense concern for perpetuating the memory of the deceased: May last six months to a year
   Despair and depression: Characterized by confused thinking, irrational behavior, and anger
   Recovery: Renewed interest in normal activities
8. Hospices

9. The United States and numerous other countries are becoming more culturally diverse. By understanding diverse cultures we are better able to understand our own.
10. The child probably did not develop a large number of friends during the first year of school because of strong attachments to the family unit and mistrust of people outside the family.

ANSWERS TO THE CROSSWORD PUZZLE CLUES

Page 421

1. Malic
2. Pagoda
3. Ovoid
4. Trot

Sex and Gender

Chapter in Perspective

To this point we have discussed a number of basic processes, such as learning, as well as the typical development of human beings across the life span. We now turn our attention to the study of how an individual's biological sex and a culture's gender expectations affect development. Although the biology of sex is the same throughout the world, culture can affect how individuals react to their biological sex by declaring certain behaviors and roles to be more consistent with one sex than with the other. As we will see, topics related to sex and gender have implications, ranging from what people view as appropriate occupations to the type of education they receive to how they are treated on the job.

In this chapter we discuss the biology of sex and then the development of gender roles. Many people have opinions concerning similarities and differences between men and women; we focus our discussion on research investigating cognitive and social behavior of males and females. Then we turn our attention to the influence of gender on education, work, and family responsibilities. ■

Sex and Gender: An Introduction

Several friends in a cafeteria are speculating about people sitting nearby. Sal decides that the workout clothes and muscular forearms of the young man at the next table indicate he is an athlete. To Andrea, the unusual clothing worn by a young woman seated a few tables away indicates she must be an art major. Everyone nods in agreement. Then a person at the far end of the cafeteria catches their attention. Clothing, haircut, and mannerisms offer no hints to suggest whether this person is male or female. After a while, the person of unknown sex is joined by a friend, and they leave the cafeteria, walking past the group of observers. Each member of the group listens to their conversation for clues to the mystery person's sex, but there are none. ***Why is it so important to know whether a person is male or female?*** ▪

When we meet or observe people in passing, we often rely on physical features such as their sex and race to categorize them. Of all the possible personal characteristics, we are most likely to notice whether people are male or female (Beal, 1994; Stangor et al., 1992). Why? If the only information you have about people is their sex, can you make more accurate predictions about them than if you did not have that information? Is a particular person likely to be an airline pilot? Do friends perceive the person to be warm and caring? Answers to these questions may be based on expectations about how males and females "should" act. In this chapter we discuss the biological factors that determine whether we are male or female. We also look at how beliefs about what behaviors are deemed appropriate for males and females influence our perception of others as well as our own behaviors.

The word **sex** refers to a biological classification based on genetic composition, anatomy, and hormones. The term **gender** recognizes that culture influences the raw material of biological sex through beliefs and expectations about what it means to be "masculine" and "feminine" (Paludi, 1998; Unger & Crawford, 1992). Thus the word *sex* refers to biological phenomena associated with being female or male. (Of course, the word sex also has a second meaning; we use it to refer to intimate acts that involve pleasure and express affection and love; see Chapter 4.) By contrast, *gender* refers to the psychological and social phenomena associated with being feminine or masculine as these concepts are defined in a given culture.

Here is one way to illustrate this distinction: The primary sex characteristics—a vagina or a penis—represent sex; a baby's pink or blue clothing or blankets represent gender. Why? The colors of the hats or blankets encourage us to treat an infant as a boy or a girl rather than as a "generic human" (Unger & Crawford, 1992). The difference between these words may appear subtle, but they are nonetheless important.

Imagine that you and your spouse are the parents of a newborn child. Your relatives live 1,000 miles away, so you telephone them to announce the news: "The baby was born three hours ago." The first question family members and friends ask when new parents announce the birth of child is, "Is it a boy or a girl?" (Intons-Peterson & Reddel, 1984). When Sigmund Freud claimed that "anatomy is destiny," he was suggesting that our biological makeup is the major determinant of our behavior. In other words, men and women behave differently because they differ in their genetic and hormonal makeup.

But consider the following: Most people who study art and music are women, yet can you name one famous female artist or composer? In fact, most

sex
Category based on biological differences in anatomy, hormones, and genetic composition

gender
Social and psychological phenomena associated with being "feminine" or "masculine" as these concepts are defined in a given culture

orchestras are made up largely of men. Women are said to be good at fine and delicate tasks performed with the hands, such as embroidery and weaving. Yet very few neurosurgeons in the United States are female, although this profession requires the skills we just described. Do biological factors account for these phenomena?

Individual and cultural expectations about feminine and masculine roles are significant influences. For example, suppose a friend tells you one of her parents is a dentist. Would you assume it was your friend's mother or her father? Chances are you would assume your friend's father was the dentist. Your answer, however, could depend on where you live. Most dentists in Sweden and in Russia are women; most dentists in the United States are men. The skills needed to be a dentist are not inherently male- or female-related, but different societies label them as such (Basow, 1992).

A classic study shows how beliefs about masculinity and femininity affect our perceptions. Jeffrey Rubin and colleagues (1974) interviewed the parents of newborns on the days the children were born. These parents rated their sons as stronger, better coordinated, and more alert than their daughters. Newborn girls were rated as more delicate, smaller, and softer than newborn boys. Actual physical differences between infant girls and boys might have accounted for these different perceptions and reactions. The newborn boys and girls, however, did not differ in height, weight, or other physical characteristics at birth. Increased concern about gender and sex stereotyping has not changed parents' attitudes a great deal (Reid, 1994). Merely changing the label of "boy" or "girl" can lead to differences in perceptions (Yoder, 1998). As noted in Chapter 3, our expectations have a powerful impact on our perception.

In this chapter we use the word *sex* when we are discussing biological factors primarily. When we refer to expectations about feminine and masculine ways of behaving, we use the term *gender*. Use of the term *gender* acknowledges that a particular difference between males and females is not an inevitable consequence of biological sex.

Blue or pink caps, booties, or blankets signal observers to react to children in different ways.

The Biology of Sex

What determines biological sex? Although most people are unmistakably male or female, the human embryo has the potential to develop as either male or female. Thus there is a potential for errors in sexual development beginning

cathy®   **by Cathy Guisewite**

at the embryonic stage, and some people—called *intersexes*—are born with various mixtures of male and female biological characteristics. For example, **hermaphrodites** have a combination of female and male internal and external genitalia, including one testis and one ovary. (The term *hermaphrodite* is derived from the name of the offspring of the mythological Greek gods, Hermes, messenger of gods and Aphrodite, the god of love and beauty). **Pseudohermaphrodites** possess two gonads (testes or ovaries) of the same kind, along with the usual male or female chromosomal makeup, but their external genitalia and secondary sex characteristics (see Chapter 10) do not match their chromosomal makeup (Fausto-Sterling, 1993).

The Genetics of Sex. Genetic factors are the first and most basic determinants of whether a person is male or female. The genetic blueprint that directs a person's development is established at fertilization by genes contained in the chromosomes of the ovum and sperm. As we saw in Chapter 9, the ovum and sperm each contribute 23 chromosomes to the zygote. One of the chromosomes is a sex chromosome. The ovum always contributes an X chromosome toward determining the child's sex, but the sperm may contribute either an X or a Y chromosome.

If the father contributes an X chromosome to the embryo at conception, the baby will be a girl (XX). If the father contributes a Y chromosome, the baby will be a boy (XY). The composition of our chromosomes is called our *genetic sex*.

Early in development, human embryos have an undifferentiated, or all-purpose, gonad (sex gland) that can become either a testis or an ovary. Approximately seven weeks after fertilization, genes located on a sex-determining region of the Y chromosome guide the development of the testes (Marx, 1995). These genes are also responsible for breaking down in males the embryonic structure that would lead to internal female organs. When no Y chromosome is present, the gonad begins developing as an ovary during the thirteenth week after fertilization.

Genetic Abnormalities. Genetic abnormalities that occur at conception can have major implications for later development (see Chapter 9). Some genetic abnormalities involve the sex chromosomes. For example, if the father's Y chromosome combines with an ovum carrying two X chromosomes, the result is an XXY chromosomal pattern known as *Klinefelter's syndrome*. The key features of this syndrome are smaller-than-normal male genitals, enlarged breasts, poor muscular development, and possible mental retardation. In *Turner syndrome*, the child has one X chromosome instead of two (a pattern referred to as XO); the second chromosome is either defective or missing. These individuals are usually characterized by short stature and a webbed neck; they do not undergo puberty or menstruate because their ovaries never function properly (Moore, 1989).

Sometimes a single X chromosome from the mother unites with two Y chromosomes from the father (XYY). The resulting individual is male, usually tall, and likely to have below-average intelligence. Past reports of an association between the XYY pattern and a tendency to commit violent crimes were not supported by subsequent research (Witkin et al., 1976). Compared with other criminals, those with the XYY pattern may be more likely to be caught, perhaps owing to their below-average intelligence. Less than 1 percent of the general population has the XYY chromosomal pattern, but the percentage of XYY individuals in prison is higher. However, this chromosomal pattern is not related to a significant amount of crime.

As mentioned in Chapter 9, some genetic disorders, such as colorblindness, are sex-linked, which means they are more likely to occur in one sex (usually males) than in the other. Because the Y chromosome is small compared with the X chromosome, it does not carry as many genes as the X chromosome. As a result, disorders or diseases carried on the X chromosome may not be countered by normal genes on the Y chromosome.

hermaphrodite
Individual who has both ovarian and testicular tissue

pseudohermaphrodite
Individual who possesses two gonads of the same kind along with the usual male or female chromosomal makeup, but has external genitalia and secondary sex characteristics that do not match his or her chromosomal makeup

Male Vulnerability.   More boys than girls are conceived (approximately 125 boys for every 100 girls), but at birth the ratio narrows to 106 boys for every 100 girls because more male embryos are miscarried (Pritchard, MacDonald, & Gant, 1985; Strickland, 1988). Longer maternal labor for boys than for girls is associated with several problems such as mental retardation, which occurs at a higher rate among males than among females (Vandenberg, 1987). What's more, the incidence of enuresis (bedwetting), stuttering, learning disabilities (see Chapter 8), and delayed speech development is higher in males than in females. Although the death rate for infant boys is higher than for infant girls, males constitute slightly more than 50 percent of the population prior to age 30. In fact, the death rate among males is higher than the rate among females throughout the life span. As a consequence, males constitute less than 50 percent of population beginning with the age interval 30 to 39 (see Figure 11-1). Females outnumber males by 3 to 1 among individuals aged 90 to 99.

Males have a greater chance of experiencing developmental difficulties such as reading problems, environmental health problems (such as cancer resulting from exposure to a toxic substance), and physical diseases (Jacklin, 1989). Compared with men, women have more disability days, physician visits, and surgical procedures. They are also more likely to be admitted to hospitals and to use more days of hospital care; only part of the difference is due to labor and delivery. Women are more likely to be treated for metabolic disorders; they are also prone to osteoporosis, which is an important factor in fractures (Travis, 1993). Although women are ill more frequently than men, they are more likely to suffer from serious but not life-threatening problems (Rodin & Ickovics, 1990). Men tend to develop more critical illnesses; they have higher rates of chronic diseases, such as heart disease, which are among the leading causes of death in the United States (see Chapter 15). Part of this increased vulnerability is due to risks associated with smoking, alcohol consumption, and job-related hazards (Verbrugge, 1989) that can lead to deaths from accidents, homicides, suicide, and AIDS (Rinzler, 1996). As we noted, however, males' heightened vulnerability begins early in life and may be in part genetically based.

Psychologist Bonnie Strickland (1988) notes that "females appear to have some biological or environmental advantage over males that makes them less vulnerable to major contemporary life-threatening physical disorders as well as accidents and suicides" (p. 382). For example, in most industrialized countries, the rate of heart disease is lower for females than for males. However, the leading cause of death among both men and women is heart disease. Women tend to suffer heart disease deaths at a later age than men.

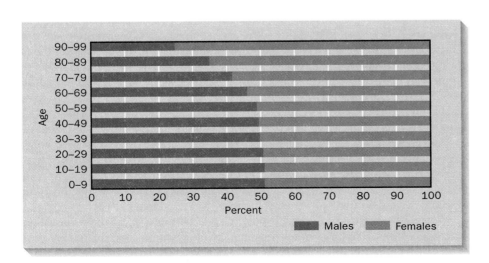

FIGURE 11-1 Percents of females and males across age groups. Although males and females constitute approximately half of the population at younger ages, the percentages begin to diverge with people in their 30's. Females make up an increasing percent of the population as age increases.

A common explanation for this finding is that women are protected by the hormone estrogen; the risk of heart disease increases in females as estrogen levels decrease (Rodin & Ickovics, 1990). Estrogen tends to raise the levels of "good" cholesterol and lower the levels of "bad" cholesterol in the blood (see Chapter 15). However, data do not consistently support this simple explanation. For example, one study suggests that women who take oral contraceptives (which contain estrogen) are at higher risk for developing heart disease, especially if they smoke (Rodin & Ickovics, 1990). It appears that lower female vulnerability to heart disease is not due to biological factors alone. Karen Matthews (1989) has proposed a model to explain the difference in heart disease rates that considers both hormonal and behavioral influences. Although hormones can influence the stress response, a person's behaviors are also important. Men are more likely to put themselves in situations in which the stress response is elicited. For example, men are more easily drawn into situations that elicit violent arguments and are more likely to view apparently meaningless events such as being passed on the highway by another driver as a form of competition requiring a response. Over time, and without the positive influence of estrogen, men are at greater risk for developing clogged arteries, a major cause of heart disease. The difference in heart disease rates between men and women shows us that hormones combine with behavior to affect health. Hormones also play a significant role in sex differentiation and sexual arousal.

The Hormonal Basis of Sex

As noted earlier, sexual differentiation does not begin until approximately the seventh week of embryonic development, when internal reproductive organs (testes or ovaries) develop in response to either the presence or the absence of genes carried on the Y chromosome. At that time, the testes produce hormones called *androgens* (of which the most important is testosterone), which direct development of the male genitals. If the male hormone is absent, the baby develops female genitals (ovaries, uterus, and vagina), regardless of chromosomal makeup. The action of hormones during the embryonic and fetal stages as well as during adolescence gives rise to what is termed *anatomical sex*. In males an increase in the level of testosterone at puberty is responsible for the development and growth of the penis and testes as well as the *secondary sex characteristics*. In females an increase in estrogen levels at puberty is responsible for the growth of the uterus and the vagina and the development of the secondary sex characteristics.

The foregoing analysis of sex differentiation seems straightforward. As noted earlier, however, just as problems can occur in the chromosomes, others can occur during the embryonic stage, as a result of the effects of hormones during early development, or during puberty. The hormonal environment of the womb, rather than the chromosomes, directly determines the sex of the fetus (Pool, 1994). For example, the mother may have ingested a drug that changes her hormone levels at a sensitive time for sex differentiation. In the 1950s, some pregnant women were prescribed a synthetic steroid that exposed their female fetuses to androgens; these genetic females (XX) were born with genitals resembling those of males. This condition, known as **adrenogenital syndrome,** often requires surgical correction. Individuals with this syndrome tend to exhibit more rough-and-tumble play, are more aggressive, and opt for more typically masculine toys than their unaffected sisters (Baxter, 1994).

A male embryo may fail to respond to male hormones, a condition called **androgen insensitivity syndrome.** The XY fetus will develop testes that produce testosterone; however, the rest of the body acts as if the hormones were

adrenogenital syndrome
Condition caused by exposure to excessive amounts of androgens during the fetal period; can result in a female with genitals resembling those of males

androgen insensitivity syndrome
Failure by a male embryo to respond to male hormones

not there, and the genetically male (XY) fetus heads down a mostly female track of development. Genital tissue is shaped into a clitoris and labia, so the child looks like a girl at birth. The only sign of a difference is the presence of testes, which can be missed without a close physical examination (Pool, 1994).

Sexual Behavior.   Researchers frequently use animals as models for studying the behavior of human beings. Sexual behavior in animals is controlled by genetically programmed factors, especially the levels of hormones that circulate in the bloodstream (see Chapters 2 and 4). Therefore female animals are receptive to sexual overtures only at certain biologically determined times, when they are said to be "in heat" (in *estrus*).

Psychological Detective

In what ways is sexual arousal in human beings different from sexual arousal in animals? What are the consequences of these differences in arousal? Give these questions some thought, and write down your answers before reading further.

Human sexual behavior—in contrast to that of many other living organisms—is a function of the complex interplay of genetic, prenatal, and environmental factors; thus human beings are not slaves to their hormone levels. We can become sexually aroused by a range of stimuli, from smells to sights to fantasies. This observation accounts for some unusual sexual behaviors and arousal patterns that can be seen in humans but not in lower animals; some of these are described further in Chapter 13.

Many people believe that men and women have entirely different sex hormones. In fact, both men and women have measurable quantities of the hormones estrogen, progesterone, and testosterone. The amounts of these hormones, however, differ in men and women.

An individual's potential to respond sexually to persons of the same sex, the opposite sex, or both is called **sexual orientation.** The most common cultural norm is *heterosexuality* (from the Greek word *hetero,* meaning "the other of two"), which means that an individual is sexually attracted to someone of the opposite sex. *Homosexuality* (from the Greek word homo, for "the same") means that an individual is sexually attracted to someone of the same biological sex. Homosexuals have adopted the term *gay* to put their sexual orientation in a more positive light than other terms. In common usage, this term refers to males and sometimes to females; the term *lesbian* is reserved exclusively for women who are sexually attracted to other women (Friedman & Downey, 1994). The sexual orientation known as *bisexuality* refers to attraction to people of both sexes. Many surveys overlook the category of bisexuality by classifying people with any same-sex behavior as homosexual.

The term *homophobia* (from the Greek word *phobia,* meaning "fear") was coined in 1967 to describe an irrational fear of homosexuality that is often manifested in prejudice and hate crimes against gay men and lesbians (Friedman & Downey, 1994; Strickland, 1995). Evidence of homophobia is found in a study of helping behavior. Imagine sitting at home when the telephone rings. The caller identifies himself as Mike and asks to speak to his girlfriend (Lisa) or boyfriend (Rick). After you tell him he has reached a wrong number, Mike explains that his car has a flat tire. For this reason he was trying to reach his friend to explain that he is running late. A statement about their anniversary clearly suggests they are romantically involved. Because he is out of change, he asks you to call his friend.

sexual orientation
Tendency for a person to be attracted to individuals of the same sex, opposite sex, or both

When Mike portrayed himself as gay (asked to call his boyfriend), only 33 percent of the respondents made the requested call. In contrast, when he portrayed himself as heterosexual, 80 percent of the respondents helped.

In some cases, people born with the genitals of one sex feel that they are of the other sex and are trapped in the wrong body; this condition is called *transsexualism*. Some of these people deliberately choose to change their sexual identity by having surgery. (We say more about transsexualism in Chapter 13.) Note that transsexuals do not have mixed or ambiguous sexual characteristics; they are clearly of a certain sex, but their gender doesn't match their biological sex.

Growing evidence suggests that biological factors play an important role in the development of sexual orientation. Researchers have discovered that a tiny portion of the hypothalamus is twice as large in men as in women and two to three times larger in heterosexual than in homosexual men (Le Vay & Hamer, 1994). The growth of the neurons in this region may be related to levels of androgens such as testosterone: The higher the level of androgens, the greater the number of neurons that survive, and hence the larger the region. Thus androgen levels may be unusually low in the fetuses of males who become gay and unusually high in the fetuses of females who become lesbian.

Research with twins also suggests a genetic component for homosexuality. Among males, researchers have found that when one identical twin is homosexual, the other twin is also homosexual in 57 percent of the cases. Among fraternal twins, in 24 percent of the cases both twins are homosexual. Among women, approximately 50 percent of identical twins, 16 percent of fraternal twins, and 13 percent of sisters of lesbians are also lesbian (Le Vay & Hamer, 1994). Although the data reported here are consistent with a genetic influence, they do not exclude environmental influences. Because all genetically identical women and men do not share the same sexual orientation, environmental influences are likely to have some effect (Yoder, 1998).

The Development of Gender Roles

Most children between the ages of 2 and 3 can label themselves as boys or girls; they can also classify other people as members of the same or the other sex. By age 3, most American children know the traditional expectations for males and females. Over and over they have heard that "boys don't play with dolls," "girls grow up to be nurses," and "it's OK if a boy gets dirty, but a girl should be dainty." They learn how these **gender roles,** or behaviors considered appropriate for males and females in a given culture, relate to clothing, games, tools, and toys (Biernat, 1991).

Children's letters to Santa Claus reveal they have clear notions of which toys are considered appropriate for boys and girls (Richardson & Simpson, 1982). Their requests mirror gender-related participation in career and domestic activities. For example, at an early age boys ask for guns and race cars and girls ask for dolls. A study of children's letters to Santa (Freeman et al., 1995) found that some, but not all, toy preferences have changed in recent years. For example, girls are now as likely as boys to enjoy riding bicycles and engaging in sports (see Table 11-1). Boys are as likely as girls to enjoy arts-and-crafts activities.

Between the ages of 4 and 5, children are aware that some occupations are "reserved" for men and others for women (Biernat, 1991). Children also learn that desires for autonomy and power are considered inappropriate for females and that feelings of vulnerability and dependency are considered inappropriate for males. For example, adults rarely notice or point out how strong a little girl may be or how nurturant a little boy is becoming, yet they readily note these attributes in the "appropriate" sex (Bem, 1993).

We label these differences "gender roles" because expectations seem to play a significant role in their development. How can we explain the development of

gender roles

Behaviors considered appropriate for males and females in a given culture

TABLE 11-1 **Types of Christmas Gifts Requested by 824 Boys and Girls**

GIFTS REQUESTED	BOYS (%)	GIRLS (%)
Items not associated with gender		
Real vehicles	29.7	28.7
Sports equipment	16.1	15.5
Communication items	12.2	14.3
Musical instruments	7.4	7.0
Items requested more by boys		
Games	41.6	25.7
Toy vehicles	19.3	6.2
Dolls (humanoid)	17.8	7.4
Military toys	6.2	0.4
Items requested more by girls		
Dolls (baby)	1.4	24.4
Dolls (female)	0.8	21.9
Clothing accessories	5.1	15.5
Stuffed animals	2.0	10.2

Source: Freeman et al., 1995.

gender roles in children? Four theories, each with a slightly different focus, have been proposed to explain the development of gender roles: psychodynamic theory, social learning theory, cognitive developmental theory, and gender-schema theory.

Psychodynamic Theory. According to Freud's psychodynamic theory, young boys develop a sexual attraction to their mother and young girls develop a similar attraction to their father. (This theory is discussed more fully in Chapter 12.) Freud's proposal follows from his view that even children are motivated by sexual instincts. Children soon learn, however, that they cannot prevail in any competition against the parent of the same sex. Thus the child settles for the attention that results from identifying with the parent of the same sex. If the child becomes like that parent, he or she will take on that parent's characteristics and acquire what society deems to be appropriate gender roles.

Psychological Detective

How do learning theorists explain the development of gender roles? Recall the principles of learning discussed in Chapter 6. Give this question some thought, and write down your answer before reading further.

Social Learning Theory. As we saw in Chapter 6, social learning theory is used to explain the development of a number of behaviors. When applied to gender roles, this theory proposes that children learn these roles from their parents (or other caregivers) through rewards and punishments (Mischel, 1966), along with imitation and role modeling (Bandura, 1969). Children learn to exhibit appropriate gender-related behaviors in the same way that they learn other behaviors. Mothers and fathers may encourage boys to be aggressive; they

Gender stereotypes influence children's choices of toys at an early age.

are not upset if their sons shout, fight, or get dirty because many parents believe that "boys will be boys." Consider the following:

> I remember when I was very little, maybe 5 or so. My brother and I were playing outside in the garden and mom saw us. Both of us were coated with dirt—our clothes, our skin, everything. Mom came up to the edge of the garden and shouted "Bishetta, you get out of that garden right now. Just look at you. Now what do you think folks would think of a dirty little girl? You don't want people to think you're not a lady, do you?" She didn't say a word to my brother who was just as dirty. (Wood, 1994, p. 22)

Fathers tend to discourage their sons from using "feminine" toys and games (Fagot & Hagan, 1991). Although 1-year-old boys and girls do not differ much in their use of forms of physical assertion such as hitting and are equally likely to communicate by whining or gesturing, adult reactions to these behaviors are quite different. Adults respond positively to 90 percent of girls' attempts to communicate and ignore 90 percent of girls' efforts to use physical assertion. In contrast, adults respond to boys' efforts to communicate only 15 percent of the time, but they respond to 41 percent of boys' attempts to use physical assertion (Fagot et al., 1985). Thus boys are encouraged to be physically assertive, whereas girls are taught to communicate verbally. Parents are not the only source of feedback concerning gender roles, however; relatives, peers, teachers, and the mass media are also important.

Cognitive Developmental Theory. Lawrence Kohlberg (1966) introduced the notion of gender identity as a critical component in his **cognitive developmental theory.** This approach adds to social learning theory by suggesting that in addition to the effects of role models and reinforcement, children might think, "If I'm a boy, I'd better figure out what kinds of things boys do" (Beal, 1994). Between the ages of 2 and 3, children acquire gender identity, which means that they develop a sense of themselves as male or female. Kohlberg places special emphasis on the notion of *gender permanence* between ages 5 and 7, which occurs when children realize that they are always going to be a male or a female. Understanding that gender is relatively unchanging motivates a child to learn how to be competent at his or her assigned gender (Wood, 1994). Critics point out, however, that a considerable amount of gender-role learning occurs before gender permanence develops.

Gender-Schema Theory. A fourth approach to explaining the development of gender distinctions, **gender-schema theory** (Bem, 1981, 1993), is a combination of social learning theory and cognitive developmental theory. A *schema* is a learned expectation that guides perceptions, memory, and inferences. Schemas are not limited to gender; they exist for a range of events. For example, we share schemas of a visit to the doctor, a dinner at a restaurant, or the purchase of a car (see Chapter 7).

Consider the case of a biologist and her 2-year-old son, who happened to have long blond hair. They were in a restaurant where a server remarked, "Oh, she's so cute. What a sweetie." The child's mother corrected the server, "Well, he's actually a boy." Without missing a beat, the server responded, "Tough little guy, huh!" (Baxter, 1994).

Gender-schema theory suggests that children form schemas of masculine and feminine attributes and activities on the basis of their accumulated experiences. According to this theory, we learn gender schemas early in life and they provide a lens through which we view the world. Thus we view attributes, behaviors, people, and things through our cultures's definitions of masculinity and femininity (Bem, 1993). In essence, we learn that some characteristics, behaviors, and roles are associated with being male and others with being female, and this knowledge influences our memory, perception, and behavior. The influence of gender schemas is evident in the following study. Children aged 5 and 6

cognitive developmental theory

Explanation for the learning of gender roles that holds that cognitive factors give rise to gender identity, gender stability, and gender constancy

gender-schema theory

Explanation for the learning of gender roles that suggests that children form schemas of masculine and feminine attributes, which influence memory, perception, and behaviors

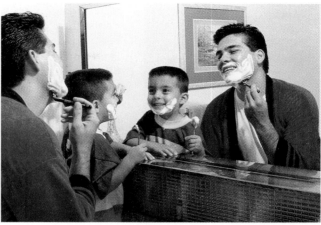

Imitating the gender-related behaviors of parents is one way that children learn to act in gender-appropriate ways.

watched films depicting male nurses and female doctors. Later the children rememered the males as the doctors and the females as the nurses (Drabman et al., 1981). Why? The schemas that the children had developed associated being a nurse with being female and being a doctor with being male. When they watched the film, they watched through the lens of their gender schemas.

A study conducted by Beverly Fagot and her colleagues (1992) provides additional insight into gender schemas. These researchers found that 2- to 3-year-old children who can discriminate between boys and girls on the basis of the labels of "boy" and "girl" are more adept than agemates who lack this ability at sorting nonhuman items in gender-stereotyped ways. As children acquire some labeling ability, they also acquire the dimensions that underlie gender distinctions: "How else would they think to give a fierce-looking bear to male subjects and a rather fluffy cat to female subjects?" (p. 229). The cultural association of objects and qualities with males or females does not depend solely on observing or being taught the specific associations: "Few men keep bears, and cats do not belong only to women. It appears that children, like the rest of us, make inferences on the basis of what they see or know about the nature of things. Children, even at these early ages, may have begun to connect certain qualities with males and other qualities with females" (p. 229). Each of the theoretical approaches to the development of the understanding of gender has strengths and weaknesses. All of them, however, suggest that children develop their understanding of gender concepts early in life and that this can have a significant impact on their lives.

Gender Stereotyping

Many broad-based personality measures feature a masculinity-femininity scale based on the assumption that men and women are psychologically different. What's more, these differences were perceived as being measurable by studying behaviors and characteristics that empirically distinguished men from women (Spence, 1993). This assumption had two important extensions: (1) that "normal" behavior was sex-appropriate, and any deviation from the norm was considered abnormal, and (2) that because masculinity and femininity were viewed as mutually exclusive categories, the more masculine a person was, the less feminine he or she must be. This way of conceptualizing masculinity and femininity forms the basis for terms like *other sex* and *opposite sex*.

A **stereotype** is a set of socially shared beliefs that we hold about members of a particular group (stereotypes and their role in social judgments are discussed more fully in Chapter 16). Distinctions based on biological sex are similar to stereotypes based on age, height, race, religion, and social class. When we use

stereotype

A set of beliefs about members of a particular group

Is this person a judge? Gender stereotyping is evident when we fail to recognize that judges can be male or female. Sandra Day O'Connor is a justice of the U.S. Supreme Court.

stereotypes, our responses to people are based on a category that describes them rather than on qualities of the individuals themselves. Stereotypes are both descriptive and prescriptive because they lead to expectations about what is and is not appropriate—in this case, for males or females. As such, stereotypes can be limiting and can constitute a form of social control (Fiske, 1993). The use of stereotypes based on sex is reflected in behaviors ranging from the courses students select to the occupations people enter. A male, for example, is unlikely to enroll in a course in home economics, and few construction workers are female.

Richard Restak, a neurologist, described an incident that illustrates how stereotypes influence our perceptions. While at a party, Restak was told to try to spend time with a judge who was attending the party. He looked around the room but did not see any one who looked like any judge he had ever encountered. After speaking to several guests, he met a woman who introduced herself as Sandra. Although Restak realized he had seen her in the media, he could not place her. During the conversation with Sandra, Restak considered asking her if she knew the identity of the judge. He saved himself from embarrassment by not asking the question; he eventually realized he was speaking with Supreme Court Judge Sandra Day O'Connor. Restak writes, "As I entered the room, my past experiences of dealing only with male judges precluded me from even considering that the judge mentioned . . . might be a woman. This unconscious sexism resulted in the creation of a semantic category which I used when scanning the room: judges are male, and no man here is very likely to be a judge" (Restak, 1994).

John Williams and Deborah Best (1990) enlisted the help of psychologists throughout the world for a cross-cultural investigation of gender stereotypes. They studied people in 30 countries including Australia, Brazil, Germany, Japan, Nigeria, and the United States. The participants were 5-, 8-, and 11-year-old children and college students.

Psychological Detective

At ages 5 and 8, children may not have the vocabulary needed to express their understanding of gender stereotypes. How would you design a study to investigate gender stereotypes among young children? Give this question some thought, and write down your answer before reading further.

To investigate gender stereotypes among 5- and 8-year-old children, the researchers told them stories. Each child was then presented with silhouettes of a male and female and was asked to select the person described in the story

---

TABLE 11-2   **Sample Stories Used to Study Children's Gender Stereotypes**

1. When you give one of these people a present, they appreciate it very much. They always say "Thank you." Which person says "Thank you"?
2. One of these people is a very affectionate person. When they like someone, they hug and kiss them a lot. Which person likes to hug and kiss a lot?
3. One of these people is a bully. They are always pushing people around and getting into fights. Which person gets into fights?

Note: The ungrammatical "they" was used to avoid giving cues about an expected answer.

Source: Williams & Best, 1990.

TABLE 11-3   Adjectives Used in a Study of Gender Stereotypes

Read each word and decide whether it is more frequently associated with males or females.

affectionate	fearful	rational
aggressive	gentle	softhearted
confident	nervous	tough
dependent	patient	witty

Source: Williams & Best, 1990.

(see Table 11-2). The 11-year-old children were given written versions of the stories told to the younger children. The college students were given a list of 300 adjectives and asked which were more frequently associated with being male and which were associated with being female (see Table 11-3).

Differing Views of Masculinity and Femininity

THE RESEARCHERS STUDYING GENDER STEREOTYPES AMONG 5- AND 8-YEAR-OLD children found remarkable consistencies in the characteristics associated with males and females in different countries. By the age of 5, most children around the world associate being aggressive and strong with males and being appreciative and soft-hearted with females. Developmental psychologists have found that gender stereotyping continues into middle adulthood. By age 8, children have learned a great deal about the concepts of masculinity and femininity. As these children grow older their stereotypes become more extreme and elaborate (Martin, Wood, & Little, 1990). By the age of 11, children associated being talkative with females and being confident with males. What's more, 77 to 100 percent of college students (mean of 93 percent) associated being adventurous with males. Between 62 and 98 percent of college students (mean of 88 percent) associated being emotional with females (Williams & Best, 1990).

Although this study of gender stereotypes revealed remarkable similarities, there were some differences among respondents in different countries. For example, Italians associated endurance with women; adults in other countries considered this a masculine characteristic. In contrast to college students in most countries, those in Thailand associated being submissive with males.

In earlier research, Margaret Mead (1935/1963) reported some dramatic differences in the characteristics exhibited by men and women in three New Guinea societies. Men and women among the mountain-dwelling Arapesh were remarkably similar in attitudes and behavior. Both were seen as cooperative and sensitive to others, or what many cultures view as feminine characteristics. Men and women among the Mundugumor were also remarkably similar; however, they shared what are often considered masculine characteristics such as aggressiveness and selfishness. Finally, the Tchambuli defined masculinity and femininity differently, and in contrast to views held in the United States, some of the characteristics were reversed. Among the Tchambuli, women were

Cultural & Diversity Perspective

dominant and rational; men were viewed as submissive, emotional, and nurturing toward children.

In most studies of gender stereotypes, the characteristics viewed as masculine (e.g., being adventurous) fall into a category often described as *instrumental* or *agentic* (task-oriented) because they emphasize achievement, assertiveness, and independence. The characteristics associated with being feminine (e.g., meekness) have been labeled *expressive* or *communal;* they are associated with emotional responses as well as interactions and relationships with other people. As Sandra Bem (1993) points out, however, these characteristics can be combined in either males or females. Individuals who have high levels of characteristics associated with both males and females are termed *androgynous.* Thus women and men can have high levels of both instrumental and expressive characteristics; they can be both assertive and sensitive, ambitious and compassionate. The term *androgyny* acknowledges a degree of flexibility in the characteristics people exhibit. For example, both men and women in the Tamang villages of Nepal do what we consider gender-specific tasks. Men do much of the cooking and child care; they seem especially nurturing and gentle with young children. Women also perform these tasks, but in addition they engage in heavy manual labor (Wood, 1994).

Language and Gender.   We use language to organize and communicate our thoughts; thus language reflects how we think and influences our thinking. Consider the following: "A skilled doctor makes an accurate diagnosis, and then he communicates the information to the patient." What images came to mind when you read this sentence?

Now read the following sentences, and pay attention to the images that come to mind:

- After a patient takes the prescribed medicine, he needs to rest.
- A teacher must be careful when he grades exams.
- A business executive must consider all aspects of an issue before he decides on a course of action.

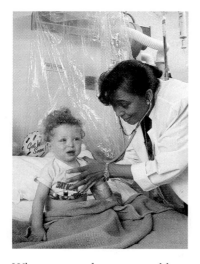

When you read a sentence like "A skilled doctor makes an accurate diagnosis, and then he communicates the information to the patient," you may not consider the possibility that the doctor is female.

The word *he* may not be intended to convey whether the person is a man or a woman, but most people assume the speaker meant the person was a man. If the images that came to your mind were primarily men, you are not alone: Most people call up such images when they read sentences like these (Gastil, 1990; Hamilton, 1991). Girls and women make up almost 52 percent of the human race, yet they are systematically left out in daily speech (Paludi, 1998). The words *he, his,* and *man* refer to men, but they are often also used to encompass both men and women.

Janet Hyde (1984a) asked grade school children to create a story about an individual whose job was that of "wudgemaker." Groups of children listened to descriptions of a wudgemaker that differed only in the pronouns used: *he, she, they,* and *he or she.* After hearing the story, the children created their own stories. Children who had heard stories with the pronoun *he* put women in their stories only 17 percent of the time. Apparently, the children understood *he* to refer exclusively to men. Moreover, children who heard *he* stories rated women as less competent than men in the job of wudgemaker. Thus the use of a single word can have a significant influence on children's ideas.

Psychological Detective

Read the following sentences:

- *The department chairman decided to schedule the course in the late afternoon.*
- *The chemical company spokesman will not answer questions concerning the spill in the river.*
- *Language separates mankind from other creatures.*

Rewrite these sentences to avoid the suggestion that the person or people in them must be male. Write down your answers before reading further.

Using the word *he* or words like *chairman* when gender is not relevant to the intended meaning conveys the inaccurate notion that gender is a relevant dimension. Minor wording changes may reduce the stereotyping that occurs when the words are associated with being male. For example, when the title of *chairman* is changed to *chairperson,* college students report fewer male images in describing this occupation; there was little difference in the images associated with *chairman* and *chair* (McConnell & Gavanski, 1994). Thus we could substitute *chairperson, spokesperson,* and *human beings* (*or humankind*) for the italicized words in the Psychological Detective exercise. Professional organizations such as the American Psychological Association, commercial publishers, and many newspapers and magazines have developed guidelines for unbiased (gender-inclusive) language. For example, using plural forms and the pronoun *they* and using gender-neutral job titles (*police officer, firefighter*) lets us include all people, and thus avoid stereotypes that can perpetuate prejudice.

Components of Gender Stereotypes.   Thus far we have addressed only one component of gender stereotypes: the tendency to believe that men and women exhibit different characteristics that can be summarized by the adjectives mentioned earlier. Gender stereotypes are not limited to a set of adjectives, however; they include prescriptions for behaviors, occupations, and physical appearance (Archer, 1989; Deaux & Lewis, 1984; Martin, Wood, & Little, 1990). As we pointed out earlier, an important implication of gender stereotyping is that movement away from what the stereotype prescribes is often viewed as movement toward the other sex. A woman who produces competent intellectual work at her job may be told that she "thinks like a man." Men who are hesitant to enter dangerous situations are very likely to be mocked with statements like "you old woman."

What happens if a woman becomes a weight lifter? Because physical appearance is such an important component of gender stereotypes, this deviation from the feminine stereotype is likely to prompt expressions of dismay from onlookers. Statements like "she doesn't look like a woman" seem designed to enforce the stereotype. In sum, gender stereotypes can have wide-ranging influences both on our perceptions and on other people's perceptions of us.

Mass Media and Gender Stereotypes.   Consider the following case: Three-year-old Rebecca's parents both have full-time jobs. Every night her father makes dinner for the family; her mother rarely cooks. Yet when it is dinnertime in Rebecca's doll house, she picks up the mommy doll and puts her to work in the kitchen (Shapiro, 1990). How did Rebecca acquire this element of gender stereotyping?

Rebecca's story reminds us that parents are not a child's only source of information about gender stereotypes; relatives, peers, teachers, and the mass media also influence stereotypes. For example, the major characters in television programs are more likely to be male than female. Moreover, these male

People whose behavior and body build run counter to gender stereotypes may be subject to criticism.

characters are generally more active than the female characters, who are less likely to be portrayed as working outside the home (Signorelli, 1989).

In the past, the narrator (voice-over) was male in 90 percent of television commercials (Bretl & Cantor, 1988; Lovdal, 1989). Compared with women, the men in television commercials were portrayed more often as authorities; the women were more often portrayed as users of the products being advertised (Bretl & Cantor, 1988; Lovdal, 1989). Women in commercials typically talked to people of inferior status and to other women about a more limited range of topics, such as body care products, clothing, and appliances. Some changes have occurred, however, in the portrayal of men and women in commercials. Men and women are now represented in approximately equal numbers as the primary character (as distinct from the voice-over) in television commercials. Women are now represented more often as primary characters in prime-time television programs, although the representation is still not equal.

The mass media also influence the stereotypes we hold about occupations. Roberta Wroblewski and Aletha Huston (1987) found that television was a major source of information about occupations for fifth- and sixth-grade students. These students were quite knowledgeable about occupations often shown on television, even when they did not have personal contact with those occupations in their everyday lives. The researchers found that nontraditional portrayals of television occupations may have altered the girls' aspirations. The girls preferred "masculine" television occupations (such as a police officer) over "feminine" real-life occupations. These nontraditional portrayals are not numerous, however; therefore their effectiveness in negating gender stereotyping may be limited.

The print media, from elementary school textbooks to newspapers to comic strips, present and strengthen messages about what is appropriate for women and men. For example, many preschool children learn from those media that "boys don't play with dolls" and "mommies can't be pilots," although such stereotypes are changing. Gender stereotypes can limit the choices individuals believe are open to them when making decisions such as which occupations to consider. Consequently, the mass media have increased efforts to ensure that their programming does not reflect stereotyped beliefs.

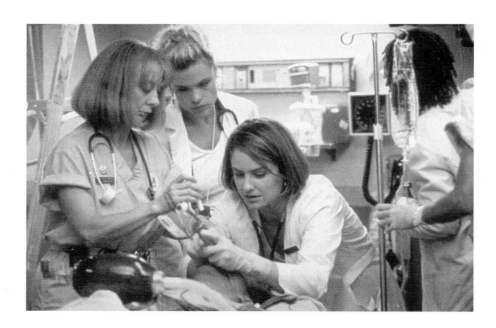

Television programs have changed in recent years to include more women in key roles. The television program *ER,* one of the most highly praised and watched shows, has several women in main character roles.

Review Summary

1. Sex refers to genetic, anatomical, and hormonal differences between males and females. **Gender** refers to the prescriptions for behaviors, characteristics, roles, and physical appearance that a culture encourages for members of each biological sex.

2. Hermaphrodites have both ovarian and testicular tissues; **pseudohermaphrodites** possess two gonads of the same kind, but their external genitalia and secondary sex characteristics do not match their chromosomal makeup.

3. Genetic inheritance is the most basic determinant of whether an individual is male or female. The 23rd pair of chromosomes determines a person's sex. A male has an X and a Y chromosome, whereas a female has two X chromosomes.

4. Early in development, the embryo's gonad (sex gland) can develop into either a testis or an ovary. The presence of a Y chromosome directs this undifferentiated gonad to develop into a testis. Exposure to excessively high levels of androgens during the fetal period can result in **adrenogenital syndrome. Androgen insensitivity syndrome** occurs when a male embryo does not respond to male hormones.

5. Genetic abnormalities include *Klinefelter's syndrome* (XXY), in which a male has smaller-than-normal genitals, and may be mentally retarded. Females with Turner syndrome (XO) do not achieve sexual maturation. Males with the XYY chromosomal pattern are usually tall, have below-average intelligence, and may be more likely to commit crimes.

6. The size of the Y chromosome is a significant factor in the inheritance of sex-linked disorders such as colorblindness. The smaller Y chromosome does not carry as many genes as the larger X chromosome.

7. Males are more vulnerable than females to developmental disorders and certain fatal diseases.

8. Hormonal factors are important determinants of sexual behavior in animals; they also play an important role in human behavior and in the development of the sex organs.

9. Sexual orientation is the tendency for a person to be attracted to individuals of the same or opposite sex or both. Homosexuality may have a genetic basis.

10. Among the explanations for the development of gender distinctions are psychodynamic theory, social learning theory, cognitive developmental theory, and gender-schema theory.

11. Stereotyping is the tendency to view people in terms of a set of beliefs about the groups or categories of which they are members. Gender stereotypes based on the assumption that masculinity and femininity are opposite and cannot occur in the same person have been replaced by broader conceptions of gender such as the notion of *androgyny.*

12. Although using the male pronoun *he* to refer to both men and women may be convenient, it can lead people to think that only men are being considered. Several organizations have developed guidelines for using language in a gender-neutral manner.

13. Children in all parts of the world learn gender stereotypes rapidly and at an early age. The mass media influence the learning of gender stereotypes.

Study Break

1. Which of the following represents sex, and which represents gender?
   a. A child has the XX chromosomal pattern.
   b. A part in a class play calls for a manager who is forceful in dealing with employees. The teacher selects John for the role.
   c. Rosa is having second thoughts about a career in computer programming despite having done well in her computer classes. She wonders whether she will fit in with the other programmers.
2. The XXY chromosomal pattern is associated with poor muscular development, small genitals, and possible mental retardation. What is this syndrome called?
3. What is the name of the chromosomal pattern found in tall males who are below average in intelligence and may be prone to criminal activities?
4. What is the name of the condition in which a male embryo does not respond to male hormones?
5. Identify the theory of gender-role development described in the following examples.
   a. A child develops gender identity and gender stability.
   b. A child understands that certain activities are associated with males and others are associated with females.
   c. A child learns which behaviors are appropriate for his or her sex via the parents' use of rewards and punishments.

6. Assertiveness, achievement, and independence, which are typically considered male traits, are categorized as
   a. primary.
   b. dominant.
   c. expressive.
   d. instrumental.

7. Pat possesses high levels of the characteristics associated with both males and females. Pat would be termed
   a. nonsexual.
   b. androgynous.
   c. gender-flexible.
   d. undifferentiated.

Similarities and Differences Between Males and Females

This morning's paper contained an article with the headline "Researchers Report That Boys Outperform Girls in Math." Because the researchers are affiliated with well-known universities, you are inclined to believe their findings. The significance of this finding hits home when your 12-year-old daughter says, "I always wanted to teach math. Does this mean that I can't?" That question makes you wonder what factors are responsible for the researchers' findings. *Do males and females differ in mathematical ability? If so, how can we explain this difference?* ∎

The study of male-female differences has been described as a "national preoccupation" (Jacklin, 1989). Everyone seems to want to know if differences exist and whether the differences are the result of biological factors. When considering these investigations, we must examine the possible causes of male-female differences as well as the actual *size* of the difference. Remember that sex differences are statistical in nature and say nothing about a given individual. Many reported differences are so small that they are not detected unless hundreds or thousands of people are tested.

Biological Differences

There are some obvious physical differences between males and females in hormones, physical size, and musculature. To begin with, men are taller than women. The average American man in his twenties is about 5 feet 10 inches; the average woman is about 5 feet 5 inches (Rinzler, 1996). The average man worldwide weighs approximately 150 pounds; the average women is approximately 120 pounds. Beginning at puberty, men achieve greater muscle mass than women, owing to the effects of testosterone. In women, estrogen prompts the development of breasts and the widening of hips during puberty (Pool, 1994). When it comes to athletic ability, males outperform females in the speed, distance, and accuracy of throwing a ball. In the ultimate game of life, however, females are the winners. Females have a longer life expectancy than males (U.S. Bureau of the Census, 1997).

Most physical differences have less impact today in industrialized and technologically advanced societies than was true in earlier eras. Owing to the wide use of mechanical equipment and computers, differences in physical size and strength are of limited importance for occupational success (Hare-Mustin & Marecek, 1990a, b; Lenski, Nolan, & Lenski, 1995). For example, in an earlier time, physical strength was an asset in piloting an airplane. Now the physical effort of piloting an aircraft has been replaced by the use of computerized equipment that can even land the plane if necessary.

Brain Differences.   The existence of biological differences like the ones just mentioned led some researchers to look for other differences. For example, a century ago scientists proposed that intelligence was a function of brain size. They reported that men had uniformly larger brains than women, which they claimed led to differences in intelligence and explained the greater accomplishments of men in fields such as politics and science. Some researchers who made these statements, however, knew whether the brains they examined were those of men or women. This made it possible that expectations influenced their observations. What's more, they failed to recognize the great degree of overlap in the brain sizes of men and women. For example, the average man is taller than the average woman, yet this difference in average height does not mean that all men are taller than all women. The overlap in the distribution of brain sizes is similar. In addition, subsequent research has found no relationship between brain size and intelligence in human beings.

Magnetic resonance imaging and PET scans (see Chapter 2) suggest the existence of some slight structural differences in the brains of men and women. One reported difference involves the corpus callosum, the bundle of nerves through which the two hemispheres of the brain communicate. The corpus callosum seems to be larger in women than in men (Burke & Yeo, 1994; Clarke & Zaidel, 1994). This difference may lead to differences in the communication between the hemispheres. One suggestion is that the left and right hemispheres of men do not communicate as much as they do in women. This proposal might explain why language abilities in women are more likely to survive a stroke in the left hemisphere. Women stroke victims may tap the language capacity of the right hemisphere (Begley, 1995), although other explanations have also been offered (Kimura, 1992).

Doreen Kimura (1992) suggests that "the effects of sex hormones on brain organization occur so early in life that from the start the environment is acting on differently wired brains in girls and boys" (p. 119). Men and women perform differently on a variety of tasks as a result of these early differences.

Are there significant differences in the brains of males and females? Many contemporary researchers have concluded that the differences, if any, are small and unlikely to account for differences in everyday behaviors. What's more, such differences are open to varying interpretations.

Early Analyses of Sex Differences

In 1974, Eleanor Maccoby and Carol Jacklin completed the first major research on male-female differences, which they published in the book *The Psychology of Sex Differences*. Their review of more than 1,000 studies led them to conclude that well-established differences exist between males and females in four areas: verbal ability, spatial ability, mathematical ability, and aggression.

How do researchers arrive at conclusions like these? In the past they counted the number of studies in each area that yielded a difference between males and females and noted the direction of the reported difference. This vote-counting method provided a general conclusion based on the overall trend of the findings (Eagly, 1995). Suppose, however, that we found two studies comparing males' and females' preferences for romantic films. One study of 10 women and 10 men yielded no difference in preference for type of film. The other study involved 500 participants, equally divided between men and women; this study found a difference. Using the vote-counting or box score method, these two studies cancel each other out, even though the size of the latter sample makes

"Because my genetic programming prevents me from stopping to ask directions—that's why!"

its findings far more compelling and more likely to be representative of the entire population than findings from a study of only 20 men and women.

A new and sophisticated statistical technique called *meta-analysis* has several advantages over older methods of analyzing research literature. Meta-analysis allows researchers to combine the results of a large number of studies on a single topic. More important, it enables researchers to assess the size and consistency of the findings—in this case the degree to which one's sex influences a range of abilities (Hyde, 1994; Hyde & Linn, 1986). This approach allows researchers to answer questions that take the form: If you know only a person's score on a test of *x*, how accurately could you guess whether the person is a male or a female (Fausto-Sterling, 1992)?

Meta-analyses have revealed a range of gender differences from small to large, depending on the particular behavior or characteristic examined (Hyde & Plant, 1995). For example, as we noted in Chapter 4, the frequent finding that women smile more than men do (Hall, 1984) has been confirmed by meta-analysis. Men perform better at mentally rotating objects and navigating through a route (although men seem to be quite reluctant to ask for directions when they are lost!); they are more accurate in guiding or intercepting projectiles. Women are better at rapidly identifying matching items (a skill called *perceptual speed*), precision manual tasks such as placing pegs in designated holes on a board, and verbal or associational fluency (Halpern, 1992; Linn & Peterson, 1985). Most differences, however, are close to zero or are classified as small; only 10 percent of them are considered large differences (Hyde & Plant, 1995).

Although meta-analysis can tell us whether a difference exists and its approximate size, it cannot tell us how the difference originated. In the following section we look at current research on differences between males and females.

The Cognitive Realm

People often wonder whether one sex is more intelligent than the other. On standard measures of intelligence, however (see Chapter 8), the scores obtained by females and males do not differ. Why? When Alfred Binet developed the first intelligence scale, he found boys were more likely than girls to obtain low scores. For a number of items, girls answered correctly at an earlier age than boys; the opposite pattern (boys outperforming girls) was found for a few items, although there weren't enough of those items to balance the test. Binet balanced the two types of items so that males and females performed equally well; this tradition has continued in modern tests of intelligence. Thus neither males nor females have an advantage stemming from the selection of items on intelligence tests. If, however, we look beyond overall intelligence scores and investigate *specific* abilities, some differences emerge.

Verbal Ability. The concept of *verbal ability* covers a number of different abilities, including vocabulary and verbal analogies. When the various components are analyzed separately, some differences do emerge. For example, women outperformed men on abilities such as anagrams, and verbal or associational fluency favored females (Halpern, 1992; Kimura, 1992). A meta-analysis of 165 studies that involved tests given to 1.4 million people found that women scored higher than men; the difference, however, is quite small (Hyde & Linn, 1988). Based on results such as these, psychologist Janet Hyde (1994) has suggested that "there are no longer any gender differences in verbal ability" (p. 454). She further pointed out that gender differences demonstrated by the more recent studies are smaller than those demonstrated by earlier studies. She concluded, "If this gender difference is biologically determined, it is difficult to see how it could get smaller over time!" (p. 455).

Mathematical Abilities.   In the early 1980s, two researchers, Camilla Benbow and Julian Stanley of Johns Hopkins University (1980, 1982), published several articles that created a stir in the popular press and in academic circles. For several years, Stanley had collected data on a group of very bright seventh- and eighth-grade students. Students who had scored in the top 2 to 5 percent of any standardized math test were invited to take the Scholastic Aptitude Test (SAT), which is widely used as one basis for college admission decisions (it is now known as the Scholastic Assessment Test). Benbow analyzed the results and found that the boys scored significantly higher than the girls on "mathematical reasoning ability." Most of this difference was already evident by the seventh grade. When reported in the press, however, the findings were exaggerated, as suggested by the vignette at the beginning of this section.

A meta-analysis of 254 samples sheds new light on the mathematical ability of boys and girls (Hyde, Fennema, & Lamon, 1990). This analysis involved the mathematics performance of more than 3 million students. Girls did better than boys at computation (addition, subtraction, multiplication, division); the difference, however, is small. There were no differences in the understanding of mathematical concepts at any age. A small to moderate difference in problem solving that favors boys was found to emerge in high school (Hyde, 1994). In some samples, such as those including highly precocious students, the differences favored males; these differences emerged in high school and college. In general, however, the differences between males and females were small and favored females in samples drawn from the general population.

Psychologist Meredith Kimball (1989) points out that most meta-analyses have used formal nonclassroom tests. When course *grades* are used as the basis for comparison, females' mathematical ability tends to be higher than that of males. Claude Steele's (1997) *stereotype vulnerability hypothesis* (see its application to racial differences in overall intellectual performance in Chapter 8) has been applied to females' performance on mathematical tasks. When female test takers are reminded of the stereotype of inferior performance before completing a test, they score lower on mathematical tests as compared with those in testing situations in which gender is not made a focus.

Visual-Spatial Abilities.   *Spatial ability* is a collection of related abilities. How do these abilities manifest themselves? You use visual-spatial abilities when you imagine how irregularly shaped objects would look if they were rotated in space or when you try to perceive the relationship among shapes and objects; the mental rotation task described at the beginning of Chapter 8 is a good example of a task requiring spatial ability. Skills such as these are helpful in certain types of mathematics and in engineering or architecture; they are also evident when we solve jigsaw puzzles or envision how furniture fits into a room before moving it in. The most consistent finding concerning spatial ability is that males outperform females on mental rotation tasks.

Expectations about computer skills and their relationship to mathematical ability could lead some young women to consider other fields of endeavor.

Psychological Detective

Some studies have demonstrated that males and females differ in mathematical and spatial abilities. Other than possible biological explanations, how might we account for the reported differences? Give this question some thought, and write down your answer before reading further.

A number of factors could be responsible for male-female differences in mathematical and visual-spatial abilities. Among those factors is math anxiety. Students with math anxiety often believe they lack the ability to solve math problems and are therefore doomed to fail. Other factors that may account for male-female differences in mathematical ability are parents' gender-stereotyped beliefs and students' perceptions of the value of mathematical and visual-spatial abilities for future studies. For example, after reading that girls don't perform well in math, many mothers subsequently lowered their expectations of their daughters' math competence (Eccles & Jacobs, 1986).

There is a relationship between spatial learning opportunities and performance on tests of spatial ability. Spatial training appears to improve scores on such tests for both males and females; the training does not differentially improve the scores of males compared with those of females (Baenninger & Newcombe, 1989). Moreover, most American parents believe that their sons are more talented than their daughters in mechanics and mathematics (Vetter, 1992). As a result, they are more likely to encourage interest in mathematics and visual-spatial activities in their sons than in their daughters. It is not surprising, therefore, that men are more likely than women to believe that they are good at mathematics and science even when their grades in these subjects are the same or lower (Adelman, 1991). Differences in the number of mathematics and science courses taken by boys and girls play a role in the poorer performance of females on the math portion of the SAT. Those differences may prevent many women from pursuing careers in science and technology (Basow, 1992).

With regard to general cognitive ability, Carol Tavris (1991) suggests that differences between males and females are small and usually not significant. The differences in verbal, spatial, and mathematical abilities are disappearing rapidly. The specific reasons for these changes are not clear, but they may be caused by societal changes that influence stereotyping and its effects on education.

The Social Realm

In addition to studying cognitive abilities, researchers have studied male-female differences in social behaviors such as communication, helping, and aggression. Here we examine some key findings of those studies.

Communication. A number of researchers have noted that men and women view communication differently. For most women, communication is a primary way to establish and maintain relationships. By contrast, men tend to view communication as a way of exerting control, preserving independence, and enhancing status (Wood, 1994). Consequently men are more likely to use speech to exhibit their knowledge, skill, or ability. Contrary to popular belief, research shows that males talk more than females (James & Drakich, 1993).

In the book *You Just Don't Understand: Women and Men in Conversation,* Deborah Tannen (1990) describes a difference between the conversations of men and women. According to Tannen, men often talk more easily in front of a group than with a spouse or a girlfriend. In public settings men feel challenged to demonstrate intelligence and expertise. At home or in a one-to-one setting, a man may feel he has nothing to prove; there is no one to defend against and hence no reason to talk. For women, dinner conversations may form a crucial bond of intimacy that can make or break a relationship.

Tannen's research suggests that there is one major difference between men and women in a social setting. She has found that men are less likely than women to ask questions. Women are more likely to add a question to the end of their statements (such as "I think Ted's teacher is giving the class too much work, don't you?"). Researchers have offered two explanations for this linguistic structure, known as a *tag question.* Tag questions may reveal tentativeness on the part of the speaker. They can also be viewed as a means of encouraging further conversation and inviting the participation of others (Paludi, 1998).

Helping Behavior. Women are generally regarded as caretakers and are thus expected to provide most of the care for infants, elderly relatives, and sick or disabled people. For example, if a school-age child is ill and needs to stay at home, it is generally the mother who takes time off from work (Wood, 1994).

Alice Eagly (Eagly & Crowley, 1986) conducted a meta-analysis of research on helping behavior. She found that most of the data had been collected in situations in which a person was called to give or not give aid to a stranger on a short-term basis. This kind of "heroic helping" is more consistent with the traditional masculine role than with the traditional feminine role that emphasizes helping within established relationships, as when a mother helps a daughter or her husband. Men helped more when the situation was dangerous and when the helping occurred in public than in private. By contrast, women were more likely to help when there were no observers and when a nurturing type of help was needed (see Belansky & Boggiano, 1994). This meta-analysis reveals that even an analysis of a very large number of studies can be misleading if the studies themselves have limitations: "In the twinkling of an eye, a gender difference can shift from large to zero, depending on the social context" (Hyde, 1994, p. 457).

Aggression. When Maccoby and Jacklin (1974) completed their review of sex differences in cognitive abilities, they noted that men exhibited higher levels of aggression than women. There is no doubt that the vast majority of crime committed in the United States is committed by men, who are also responsible for more violent crimes than are women.

Such a difference in violence and aggression may be due to biological factors. Other research, however, has challenged this conclusion. Anne Fausto-Sterling (1992) found that Maccoby and Jacklin's arguments are weaker than originally supposed. The first area in which male-female differences in aggression appears—physical aggression and rough-and-tumble play—could just as easily be caused by differential treatment of boys and girls as by biological factors. In fact, Maccoby and Jacklin's literature review revealed that parents were handling their sons more roughly than their daughters before the infants were 3 weeks old. What's more, data from studies of primates show that male-female differences in physical aggression occur only in some primate species, rather than in all of them. Even in species for which there is evidence of a sex difference, the difference is present only in some environments. Nevertheless, gonadal hormones do appear to influence the development of human behaviors such as aggression, in which sex differences can be seen (Collaer & Hines, 1995).

When comparing the helping behavior of women and men, researchers need to consider different types of help. Women tend to offer a nurturing type of help and often within established relationships. By contrast, men are more likely to offer what has been termed "heroic helping." Failure to consider these types of helping behavior have led to erroneous conclusions in past research.

In a meta-analysis of laboratory studies of aggression, Janet Hyde (1984b) found that a person's sex accounted for a small proportion of aggression in those studies. Alice Eagly and Valerie Steffen (1986) found that human males are more aggressive than human females, but the difference was noted mostly in aggression that produces physical harm rather than psychological or social harm. These differences appear early in childhood and continue into adulthood. Therefore broad generalizations about sex differences in aggression can be misleading. A second meta-analysis of gender differences in aggression (Bettencourt & Miller, 1996) found two trends in research on the topic: (1) In unprovoked situations, men are more aggressive than women, and (2) in provoked situations, the gender difference was much smaller. The influence of provocation seems to result from differences in appraisals of the intensity of the provocation and fear of danger from retaliation. What's more, the type of provocation also seems to influence the amount of aggression demonstrated by males and females.

The question "Are males more aggressive than females?" cannot be answered by a simple yes or no. An accurate answer would be that the level of aggression demonstrated by males and females depends on the type of aggression under consideration.

STUDY CHART

Male-Female Comparisons

Attribute	Comparison
Overall intelligence	There are no differences in the intelligence of males and females as assessed by standard intelligence tests. Items that favored one sex over the other are balanced out so as to eliminate bias toward either sex.
Verbal ability	Early research found that females outperformed males on tasks of verbal ability such as associational fluency. More recent research suggests that many of the differences have diminished or even ceased to exist.
Mathematical ability	Males show greater mathematical ability on standardized tests, especially at the highest ability level. Yet females tend to get higher grades in math in school. Current research indicates that these differences are small in the general population.
Visual-spatial ability	Differences in visual-spatial ability may be related to different opportunities to practice the skills involved or possibly to prenatal hormonal influences. The difference in mental rotation tasks is quite large, with males consistently outscoring females.
Communication	Contrary to popular belief, research shows that males talk more than females. Other differences, such as the use of tag questions, are open to varying interpretations. Such questions have been attributed to tentativeness among females; an alternative explanation is that these questions facilitate conversation.
Aggression	The overwhelming majority of crimes are committed by males. Laboratory research reveals, however, that knowing a person's biological sex tells us little about the level of aggression exhibited by that individual. There is little difference in aggression in unprovoked conditions; some differences in provoked situations seem related to appraisal of the provocation or fear of retaliation.

Review Summary

1. Apart from obvious differences in reproductive anatomy and genetics, there are few biological differences between men and women.

2. A wide range of behaviors has been investigated from the standpoint of male-female differences. Males and females do not to differ in overall intelligence, in part because intelligence tests were designed to equalize any differences.

3. In the past, females were reported to outperform males in verbal ability. The difference has narrowed to the point where it is essentially zero.

4. Males seem to perform better than females on tasks involving mathematical and spatial ability, although the difference is narrowing rapidly. The difference in mathematical ability seems limited to nonclassroom tests; in class, girls obtain higher grades in mathematics than boys. Gender stereotypes and differential opportunities may have an impact on differences in mathematical and spatial ability.

5. There seem to be some differences in the ways in which males and females communicate. Differences in helping behavior seem to be related to gender stereotypes. Differences in aggression may be quite narrow if one recognizes that there are different types of aggression.

Study Break

1. What part of the brain has been found in some studies to be larger in females than in males?
   a. pons
   b. thalamus
   c. amygdala
   d. corpus callosum
2. If you decided to summarize the results of a large number of studies, taking into account the magnitude of the results of each of the studies, what method would you use?
   a. box score
   b. vote counting
   c. bivariate analysis
   d. meta-analysis
3. What does current research say about differences between males and females in each of the following areas?
   a. Overall intelligence
   b. Verbal ability
   c. Mathematical and spatial abilities
4. How is meta-analysis different from more traditional research methods?
5. Describe how research on helping behavior depends on a careful analysis of different types of helping.

Social Issues

One day Elizabeth Hasanovitch's boss tried to rape her. She fled and did not return for her paycheck, even though she was left destitute. Later she wrote, "I felt what that glance in his eyes meant. It was quiet in the shop. Everybody had left, even the foreman. There in the office I sat on a chair. The boss stood near me with my pay in his hand, speaking to me in a velvety soft voice. Alas! Nobody around. I sat trembling with fear" (Fitzgerald, 1993b, p. 1). *Is the situation just described a common one?* ■

The perpetuation of gender stereotypes can produce what has been termed **sexism**—differential treatment of an individual on the basis of his or her sex. This term is often used to describe discrimination against women, such as differential treatment in educational settings and limited access to job opportunities, but it can also be applied to discrimination against men.

sexism
Differential treatment of an individual on the basis of his or her sex

Although women constitute more than half of the population, only 3 to 5 percent of senior positions of the largest U.S. corporations are held by women (Federal Glass Ceiling Commission, 1995). Despite changes in the norms and values of U.S. society, bias and discrimination based on sex still exist.

This section covers several aspects of sexism, beginning with the different educational experiences of males and females and a form of job-related discrimination called sexual harassment. The discussion then turns to the distribution of household responsibilities.

Education

Are boys and girls treated differently in educational settings? Psychologist Diane Halpern (1986) addressed this question with a story from her own experience in high school:

> I remember receiving a prize for serving as president of my high school's honor society. I was delighted with the bracelet I was given. I knew that all of the previous honor society presidents were male, and all of them had received a six-volume set of books by Winston Churchill. Yet, it had never occurred to me that the choice of this particular gift was an excellent example of sex differences in socialization practices. It wasn't until many years later that I was struck with the irony of the gift. (pp. 109–110)

In the late 1800s, scientists argued that the energy required for menstruation and childbearing made women unable to handle the rigors of an educational program; they therefore declared that educating women would be dangerous and damaging. What's more, they argued that women were less intelligent than men; as proof they pointed to differences in the size of the brain in men and women (Fausto-Sterling, 1992). Today such beliefs are considered absurd, and women are earning college degrees in increasing numbers (see Figure 11-2). In fact, since 1984–85, more women than men have earned undergraduate degrees.

Nevertheless, there is clear evidence that males and females receive differential treatment in educational settings starting early in life. As noted earlier, Beverly Fagot and her colleagues (1985) recorded the behaviors of teachers and children in a toddler play group. Although the 1-year-old children communicated to the teacher and to one another in similar ways, the teachers unwittingly reinforced the tendency for girls to communicate more gently and for boys to communicate more assertively.

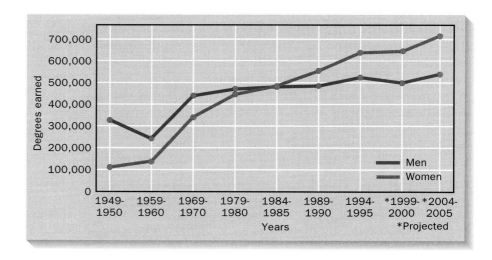

FIGURE 11-2 Numbers of men and women earning bachelor's degrees. Women now earn more undergraduate college/ university degrees than men; this trend is projected to continue and to accelerate in coming decades.

Elementary School. Other differences between the educational experiences of girls and boys emerge later. For example, teachers asked to nominate their best students are more likely to nominate boys than girls. They are especially likely to name boys as most skilled in mathematics, even though, as mentioned earlier, girls generally obtain higher grades than boys (Kimball, 1989). When asked to think of students who excel in language or social skills, teachers are more likely to name girls (Ben Tsvi-Mayer, Hertz-Lazarowitz, & Safir, 1989).

The materials used in teaching classes also reflect a gender bias. For example, a content analysis of children's readers in use in 1989 revealed that girls appeared as often as boys and that women appeared more often than they did in the 1970s. Still, however, women did not appear as often as men or in as wide a range of occupations (Purcell & Stewart, 1990).

Psychological Detective

 The study of possible gender bias in educational experiences has important implications for learning. How would you investigate the existence and extent of gender bias in classrooms? Would you ask teachers if such bias occurs? Are there better ways to investigate possible gender bias in classrooms? Give these questions some thought, and write down your answers before reading further.

Two professors of education, Myra and David Sadker (1985, 1993), have studied gender bias in classrooms. They observed 100 fourth-, fifth-, and eighth-grade classes in urban and rural school systems and found that even teachers "who care deeply about gender equity tend to interact differently with the boys and girls in their classrooms" (Sadker, Sadker, & Stulberg, 1993, p. 45). The teachers themselves were surprised by the findings.

What happens in these classrooms? Generally boys who call out in class are likely to get the teacher's attention. Girls who call out in class are more likely to be told to "remember the rule" to raise their hand before speaking. Although the teachers believed the girls talked more and participated more than the boys did, the observations showed that boys outtalked girls by a ratio of 3 to 1. Moreover, boys are eight times more likely than girls to call out answers in class. The stereotype of talkative females is so powerful, however, that the teachers failed to see this gender gap in communication in their classrooms.

Consistent with the gender stereotypes discussed earlier, boys are taught to be assertive and independent, whereas girls are taught to be dependent and passive: "Sexist treatment in the classroom encourages formation of patterns such as these, which give men more dominance and power than women in the working world" (Sadker & Sadker, 1986, p. 57). Boys and girls also receive different kinds of feedback, as revealed in the following classroom exchange taken from the Sadkers' research (p. 56):

TEACHER:	What is the capital of Maryland, Joel?
JOEL:	Baltimore.
TEACHER:	What's the largest city in Maryland, Joel?
JOEL:	Baltimore.
TEACHER:	That's good. But Baltimore isn't the capital. The capital is also the location of the U.S. Naval Academy. Joel, do you want to try again?
JOEL:	Annapolis.
TEACHER:	Excellent. Anne, what's the capital of Maine?
ANNE:	Portland.
TEACHER:	Judy, do you want to try?

JUDY: Augusta.
TEACHER: OK.

After Anne offered an incorrect answer, the teacher did not stay with her but moved on to Judy, who received a simple acceptance of her correct answer. In contrast, the teacher's reaction to Joel's answer was longer and more precise.

On the basis of these observations, the researchers offered the following conclusions:

1. Boys receive more attention from teachers and are given more time to talk in class.
2. Most educators are not aware of the existence or impact of this bias.
3. Brief but focused training can reduce or eliminate this bias.
4. Increasing equity in classroom interactions increases the effectiveness of teaching for all students. Equity and effectiveness are not competing concerns; they are complementary.

High School and Higher Education.   The patterns of sexism established in elementary school classrooms often continue into high school and higher education (American Association of University Women, 1992; Crawford & MacLeod, 1990). For example, girls and boys tend to take different courses in high school. Classes in home economics, health, and office occupations are filled with girls; those in technical, trade, and industrial programs are filled with boys. The consequence of these differences is that girls are being prepared for only a few jobs, especially those that are lower in status and salary (Basow, 1992).

A survey of social science graduate students at several large universities revealed that virtually all of the respondents had observed gender-biased behavior on the part of a professor, and that less than 5 percent had reported the problem to someone in an official capacity (Myers & Dugan, 1996). Examples of gender-biased behaviors include making more eye contact with men than with women, calling on men more often than women, calling on men by name more often, and addressing the class as if only men were present. Sexism is also seen in the selection and omission of course materials; women's achievements may be left to courses that deal specifically with gender (Myers & Dugan, 1996).

Between 1960 and the 1980s, the number of American women who earned science and engineering degrees increased; it then reached a plateau, and today it is still lower than the number of men earning degrees in these fields (Brush, 1991). Why? There is no simple answer. Discrimination against women in education has become more covert, but other factors may be at work as well.

Science textbooks tend to perpetuate gender stereotypes: They include numerous pictures of male scientists but very few of female scientists. What's more, when the latter are described, the portrayals are often inaccurate: "At the high school level, Marie Curie may be the only woman mentioned, perpetuating the belief that science has been created almost entirely by men" (Brush, 1991). A deep-seated cultural bias against science as an activity appropriate for women (La Follette, 1988) directs most girls away from science even before they begin their formal education. Those who desire to pursue a scientific career will find few role models in college (Sonnert & Holton, 1996).

Another possible cause of sex differences in higher education is the use of test scores as selection criteria. Colleges

Boys are taught from an early age to be assertive in requesting the teacher's attention in a classroom.

and universities use the SAT in selecting students for admission and for scholarship and financial aid awards. The SAT, however, has been shown to *underpredict* women's grades as compared with those of men. If a man and a woman have the same SAT scores, the woman will tend to earn higher grades in college. Giving significant weight to SAT scores in the admissions process or in awarding scholarships can lead to the rejection of women who would have done better in college courses than the men who were accepted.

Men and women often follow different majors in college. Men are more likely to be found in the natural sciences and business; women are more likely to be found in the humanities and fine arts. Rapidly developing areas such as computer science tend to enroll predominantly men.

Work and Careers

When students are ready to enter the job market, they continue to face the influence of gender stereotypes. In 1988, researchers asked undergraduates to rate several occupations as either masculine or feminine. Compared with ratings from 1975, there was a decline in the degree to which students stereotyped occupations according to gender. Traditionally masculine occupations, such as engineer, are still viewed as masculine, however, although the extent of such stereotyping has changed (White et al., 1989). It is perhaps ironic that during World War II, women entered the workforce in large numbers to replace men who had been drafted. Although they successfully produced the machinery needed during the war, when the war ended, most of these women were expected to return to their domestic roles of raising a family and taking care of the home (Adler, 1994).

During recent decades, large numbers of women have entered the workforce, for both personal and financial reasons (see Figure 11-3). The pervasive sexism they face has significant costs to them as individuals and to society as a whole. Sexism reduces the number of opportunities to enter the job market, which increases the risk of living a life of poverty. Looked at from a broader societal perspective, sexism also reduces the pool of talent and abilities available for employment by effectively cutting off more than half of the population.

A person's career choices are influenced by a number of factors, some of which can reduce the influence of sexism on the individual. Overcoming gender-role stereotypes is not easy; having a working mother, however,

This firefighter has broken the stereotype that suggests that firefighting is a male job; however, she is one of a tiny minority of women who work as firefighters. For centuries, stereotypes related to occupations have reduced women's access to many jobs, especially higher-paying ones.

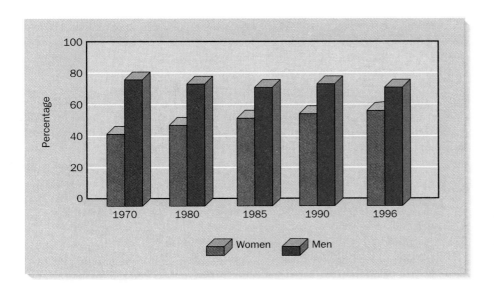

FIGURE 11-3 Percentages of men and women in the workforce. The percent of men who work has been relatively constant over the past decades, whereas women's rate of participation in the labor force has increased steadily.

TABLE 11-4   Major Barriers to and Facilitators of Women's Career Choices

BARRIERS	FACILITATORS
Environmental	
Gender-role stereotypes	Working mother
Occupational stereotypes	Supportive father
Gender bias in education	Highly educated parents
Barriers in higher education	Girls schools/women's colleges
Lack of role models	Female models
Individual	
Family-career conflict	Late marriage or single
Math avoidance	No or few children
Weak expectations or self-efficacy	Strong academic self-concept
Low expectations for success	Androgyny

Source: Adapted from Betz, 1994.

increases the chances that a young woman's career choices will be wider. The availability of female models in the family, school, or among friends and relatives often allows young women to pursue careers they might not have otherwise considered (see Table 11-4).

The stark reality of the working world is that women earn less than men. For example, compared with men who have similar credentials and experience, women scientists have lower salaries, are more likely to be in temporary positions, and find fewer opportunities to advance (Vetter, 1992). Although the difference in incomes earned by men and women has narrowed in recent years, a large gap still exists.

One reason for this gap is that women tend to work in a narrow range of occupations—for instance, as secretaries, child-care providers and in the food service and health-care fields (see Figure 11-4). Second, women tend to take on the primary responsibility of caring for the home and members of the family (which we discuss in greater detail later in this chapter). Finally, there's discrimination. Because discrimination is illegal, however, it tends to be practiced in subtle ways (Benokraitis & Feagin, 1995). For example, women working in large companies often encounter what has been called a *glass ceiling*. This term refers to barriers women face as they pursue jobs with greater responsibility and higher rates of pay in higher management. In the business world, gender stereotypes can have dramatic effects that are evident in humorous attempts to deal with a very serious subject (see Table 11-5).

Sexual Harassment. In 1980, the Equal Employment Opportunity Commission (EEOC), an agency of the U.S. government, issued guidelines on sex discrimination that provided the first legal definition of **sexual harassment** (see Table 11-6). The EEOC defined sexual harassment as

> unwelcome sexual advances, requests for sexual favors, and other verbal or physical conduct of a sexual nature . . . when (1) submission to the conduct becomes a condition of a person's employment; (2) employment decisions are based on the employee's submission to or rejection of such conduct; (3) the conduct substantially interferes with a person's work performance or creates an environment that is intimidating, hostile or offensive.

According to this definition, incidents of sexual harassment can take two forms: (1) *quid pro quo* (Latin for "this for that"), in which a sexual

sexual harassment
Under the law, either sexual coercion based on promised rewards or threatened punishments or creation of a hostile workplace environment

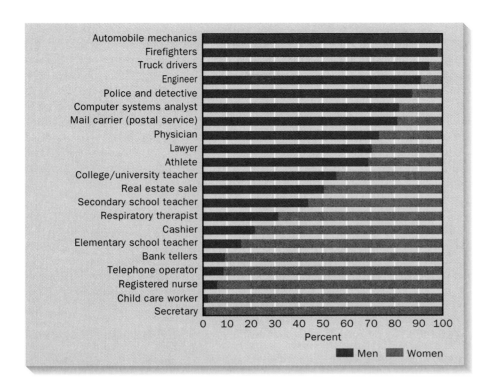

FIGURE 11-4 Percentages of men and women employed in various occupations. Many of the occupations with high percentages of women are lower-paying jobs. Despite societal changes, some occupations are still remarkably gender-typed as evident by the high percentage of either men or women, depending on how the occupation is gender typed.

TABLE 11-5   A Humorous Look at the Serious Subject of Gender Stereotyping

One reason we laugh at material intended to be humorous is that it can reveal elements of truth (the existence of gender stereotyping) about topics that are sometimes difficult to face.

How to tell a businessman from a businesswoman:

A businessman	A businesswoman
is aggressive	is pushy
is good on details	is picky
follows through	doesn't know when to quit
stands firm	is hard
is a man of the world	has been around
is not afraid to say what he thinks	is mouthy
exercises authority diligently	is power-mad
is close-mouthed	is secretive
is a stern taskmaster	is hard to work for
drinks because of the excessive job pressure	is a lush
loses his temper because he is so involved in his job	is bitchy
When he's depressed (hung over), everyone tiptoes past his office.	When she is moody, it must be "her time of the month."

Source: Dundes & Pagter, 1991.

---

proposition is tied to either a direct threat such as loss of a job or a direct offer such as a promotion, and (2) a hostile work (or educational) environment. A hostile environment is one pervaded by degrading, intimidating, or offensive behavior; explicit benefits, however, are not directly linked to sexual cooperation. In quid pro quo harassment, harassers use their power over their victims' employment to try to extort submission. Quid pro quo harassment can therefore only occur between a superior and a subordinate, and it can be based on a single incident (Conte, 1997). The hostile-environment form of sexual harassment can be based on the conduct of coworkers as well as supervisors. Thus sexual harassment involves a range of behaviors: verbal comments about a person's anatomy; the posting in the workplace of sexually suggestive or demeaning cartoons, drawings, photographs, and e-mail messages or the installation of pornographic software on company computers; touching someone in a sexually suggestive way; and rape, whether attempted or actual (Levy & Paludi, 1997).

An often-heard concern is that laws prohibiting sexual harassment take normal interpersonal encounters between men and women and make them illegal. Most experts agree, however, that consenting relationships that do not interfere with business are not illegal. Thus dating between co-workers is fine; dating between an employee and his or her direct supervisor is probably not acceptable (LaVelle, 1998). Moreover, under existing law an isolated incident

---

TABLE 11-6 Legal Decisions Concerning Sexual Harassment

1964 Civil Rights Act enacted; Title VII bans job discrimination based on sex. The act established the Equal Employment Opportunity Commission (EEOC), which is the agency of the federal government charged with enforcing Title VII.

1980 The EEOC issues a series of guidelines on sex discrimination and defined sexual harassment. The guidelines prohibit unwelcome sexual advances or requests made as a condition of employment. The guidelines also define a hostile work environment as illegal under the law.

1986 The U.S. Supreme Court *(Meritor Savings Bank v. Vinson)* upholds the validity of the EEOC guidelines and rules that sexual harassment that creates a hostile or abusive work environment is a violation of the Civil Rights Act.

1991 A California federal appeals court rules *(Ellison v. Brady)* that a hostile environment should be evaluated not from the standpoint of a "reasonable person" but of a "reasonable woman." The Civil Rights Act of 1991 authorizes compensatory damages (for pain, suffering, and emotional upset) in cases of intentional discrimination and punitive damages (punishment intended to discourage future behavior) against employers/companies that tolerate harassment.

1992 The U.S. Supreme Court *(Franklin v. Gwinnett County [Georgia] Public Schools)* determines that educational institutions can be held liable for compensatory damages under Title IX, which guarantees an educational environment free from sex discrimination.

1993 The U.S. Supreme Court rules *(Harris v. Forklift Systems, Inc.)* that Title VII does not require a showing of psychological injury to support a claim of hostile-environment sexual harassment. It is sufficient for the plaintiff to reasonably perceive the treatment as abusive.

1998 The U.S. Supreme Court rules *(Gebser v. Lago Vista Independent School District)* that a school district cannot be held liable for damages resulting from sexual harassment of students by teachers unless a school official has been notified of the misconduct and was deliberately indifferent to that misconduct.

Note: Every state and many cities and towns have civil rights laws that deal with sexual harassment in the workplace.

Sources: Davidhizar, Erdel, & Dowd, 1998; Eskenazi & Gallen, 1992; LaVelle, 1998; Levy & Paludi, 1997.

A sexual harassment lawsuit against Mitsubishi Company was settled when a judge approved a record $34 million payment by the company. Twenty-nine women filed a civil suit against the company in 1994. The EEOC filed a class action suit in 1996 on behalf of the workers after its investigation led to charges that the company created "a hostile and abusive work environment" and failed to take appropriate action when complaints were made. The women workers reported that they were called derogatory names and were subjected to groping, forced sex play, male flashing, and explicit sexual graffiti. Each of the workers involved can receive payments of up to $300,000, the maximum specified by the Civil Rights Act of 1991.

of general sexual harassment by co-workers or supervisors is not a violation unless the incident is extreme, as in assault or rape (Eskenazi & Gallen, 1992). The latter examples of sexual harassment are, of course, also violations of criminal law. A key in applying the law defining sexual harassment is that the behavior must be viewed as unwelcome.

Until recently, the widespread problem of sexual harassment received little public recognition. As one expert has written, "In a society where the sexual victimization of women has been so widespread as to be effectively invisible, sexual harassment remains the last great open secret" (Fitzgerald, 1993a, p. 1). This "open secret" has a long history; the incident described in the vignette at the beginning of this section took place in 1908.

In October 1991, Anita Hill, an attorney and professor of law, accused Clarence Thomas, who had been nominated to the U.S. Supreme Court, of having subjected her to sexual harassment on several occasions while she was in his employ. She testified before a Senate committee that was considering Thomas's nomination; Thomas denied the allegations in his testimony. The controversy generated a national debate on the issue of sexual harassment. Opinion polls taken during the hearings and shortly thereafter showed that the public believed Thomas by a wide margin. Within two years, however, more people said they believed Anita Hill than believed Justice Thomas (Levy & Paludi, 1997). Many people failed to understand that the hearings did not seek to determine whether sexual harassment had occurred. Members of the Senate Judiciary Committee could have felt that harassment did occur but nonetheless have chosen to approve Thomas's nomination as a Supreme Court Justice. The hearings did have an effect: "They raised the consciousness of every employer, manager, and employee, and heralded an unprecedented national preoccupation with an area of the law" (Levy & Paludi, 1997).

Shortly after the Thomas hearings sexual harassment was reported to have occurred at the September 1991 convention of the U.S. Navy's Tailhook Association, an organization of aircraft carrier pilots. Lieutenant Paula Coughlin, a helicopter pilot and aide to an admiral, described the sexual harassment of civilians and fellow officers. For example, dozens of women were forced to walk down a hotel hallway while male officers groped at them. Following these highly publicized reports, the number of claims of sexual harassment in the workplace, the military, and on college campuses increased significantly. For example, a survey of Fortune 500 companies found that 90 percent had received complaints of sexual harassment and that one-third had been sued. A typical Fortune 500 company loses millions of dollars each year in absenteeism, turnover, and lost productivity related to sexual harassment (Fisher, 1993).

In 1990, the EEOC declared that a person who claims to be the victim of a hostile environment must show there was a pattern of offensive behavior. The agency advocates using the "reasonable person" standard to determine whether a work environment is hostile. A federal circuit court, however, determined that a "reasonable woman" standard should be used in place of the sex-blind "reasonable person" approach. The court concluded that conduct that men might find acceptable may be objectionable to women (Watts, 1996). According to this standard, if a reasonable woman would have felt harassed in a given situation, the environment was hostile. In 1993, the Supreme Court ruled (*Harris v. Forklift Systems, Inc.*) that a person alleging sexual harassment does not have to prove that the conduct affected his or her psychological well-being.

Frequency of Sexual Harassment. To determine the frequency of sexual harassment among federal government employees, the Merit Systems Protection Board (MSPB) in 1981 surveyed more than 20,000 employees. Among its findings were the following:

1. Fully 42 percent of the federal government's female employees reported experiencing some form of sexual harassment during the two years preceding the survey.
2. Thirty-three percent of the women had experienced unwanted sexual remarks; 28 percent reported suggestive looks; and 26 percent reported being deliberately touched in a sexual manner. These incidents of sexual harassment were usually repeated over extended periods.

Several years later another survey was conducted, with virtually the same results (Merit Systems Protection Board, 1987).

Other surveys of the frequency of sexual harassment converge on the conclusion that approximately one out of every two U.S. women has been harassed during her working life (Gutek, 1985; Hesson-McInnis & Fitzgerald, 1997; Koss et al., 1994). Surveys reveal that the frequency and types of harassment in Canada and European countries are similar to those in the United States. In Scandinavian countries, however, rates of harassment appear lower than those of the United States. One possible explanation for this difference is that women in Scandinavian countries have high rates of participation in the labor force and greater income parity; there is a greater degree of gender equity there than in other parts of the world (Gruber, 1997). Sexual harassment of men is rare; however, reports of harassment of men tend to receive significant media attention when they result in legal proceedings.

Unwanted sexual advances are one example of sexual harassment. Recognition of the frequency of sexual harassment has led to the establishment of policies to reduce harassment and to provide victims with a means of having their complaints heard.

Women of all ages, races, and marital statuses have been harassed in the workplace and in educational settings from elementary school to medical school (Levy & Paludi, 1997; Wolf et al., 1991). For example, three-quarters of female medical residents and 82 percent of nurses report having been sexually harassed (Charney & Russell, 1994; Collins, 1996). The incidence of sexual harassment may be higher in workplaces where women have traditionally been underrepresented (Fitzgerald, 1993b), such as the trades, transit operations, and firefighting (Mansfield et al., 1991; Rosell, Miller, & Barber, 1995). The frequency of sexual harassment in the military has been described as "extraordinary" (Harris & Firestone, 1997).

The gender roles of the predominant group in a workplace influence expectations not only for the job but also for the treatment of women (Gutek, 1985). Lois Robinson's experiences as a shipyard worker in Jacksonville, Florida, illustrate this influence. The atmosphere at the shipyard was distinctly male; men controlled both social acceptance and tangible rewards. Outnumbered and perceived to be out of place, women were virtually powerless. The men used several methods to maintain their control: practical jokes, off-color jokes, visual displays of women in states of undress, vulgar graffiti, and the use of demeaning nicknames (such as "Honey" and "Babe"). These incidents occurred all day and every day throughout the shipyard (Fiske, 1993; Fiske & Stevens, 1993).

Here is how a 14-year-old girl described her experiences of sexual harassment at and on her way to school:

> I started being sexually harassed constantly by a group of guys on my bus. It was horrible. They would grab my breasts, thighs, and other places, and make rude comments and sexual gestures toward me. When I finally yelled at them to stop, hit them, or moved away, the bus driver would yell at me. I felt helpless because my parents worked and couldn't drive me to school. Finally I got the courage to do something about it: I told my principal what was happening. He was skeptical about the whole thing, and he didn't do much about it. (Stein, 1995, pp. 19–20)

Examples of such peer-to-peer harassment, which is common in elementary and secondary schools, include flipping up a girl's skirt; nasty, personalized graffiti on bathroom walls; sexualized jokes mocking women's bodies; physical assault; and attempted rape. Quite often such behavior has been tolerated "as a true-blooded, healthy American phenomenon, a normal stage of adolescent development" (Stein, 1995, p. 21) that is often perceived as "flirting." Yet one-third of college students asked to report on incidents of inappropriate behavior during their high school careers acknowledged the existence of dating relationships between students and teachers, and many reported other examples of sexual harassment (Corbett, Gentry, & Pearson, 1993).

Most victims of sexual harassment try to ignore the offensive behavior; consequently, they do not file formal complaints, often fearing retaliation or believing the organization will not respond to their complaint (Dansky & Kilpatrick, 1997). Victims of sexual harassment experience a number of work-related consequences: declines in job performance, decreased motivation, decreased morale, and increased absenteeism. Some victims have been fired after filing a complaint; others feel they must quit their jobs. Harassment in schools may lead victims to disrupt their academic experiences owing to changes in class schedules, major programs, or institution (Dansky & Kilpatrick 1997).

Over 90 percent of victims suffer psychological or physical symptoms (Charney & Russell, 1994; McKinney, 1994). The emotional reactions include anger, embarrassment, shock, and guilt; social withdrawal, fear of new people, and a lack of trust are common. The physical complaints include fatigue, headaches, inability to concentrate, nausea, and sleep and appetite disturbances (Paludi & Brickman, 1991). Compared with women who have not experienced sexual harassment, victims of sexual harassment have an elevated risk for posttraumatic stress disorder (see Chapter 15) and depression (Dansky & Kilpatrick, 1997).

Perceiving Sexual Harassment.   In a number of workplace and school surveys, significant numbers of women have described incidents that would qualify as instances of sexual harassment, yet only about 5 percent of them have reported these incidents to someone in authority, such as a work supervisor (Fitzgerald et al., 1988a; Fitzgerald et al., 1988b). Among the reasons for the low rate of complaints is that many women who tell researchers about such incidents do not perceive the incidents as sexual harassment (Fitzgerald et al., 1988a).

Psychologist Michele Paludi (Levy & Paludi, 1997) notes that general stereotypes are not left behind when men and women go to work each day. Women are typically seen as helpful, dependent, nurturing, and sexual, whereas men are perceived as independent, dominant, and aggressive: "Gender stereotypes imply that men should be sexually aggressive and women should be ready and willing to be sex objects. Sexual harassment may occur when these gender stereotypes spill over into the workplace" (p. 52).

Men and women do not differ in their perceptions of sexual harassment in explicitly coercive situations (e.g., stroking a woman's leg or fondling a student) (Baker, Terpstra, & Larntz, 1990; Fitzgerald & Ormerod, 1991). Men, however, tend to view less explicit instances (such as suggestive jokes or comments about a women's body) as trivial or innocuous (Fitzgerald & Ormerod, 1991). Many men view this kind of "so-called harassment" as part of the normal interaction between men and women (Reilly et al., 1992).

An emerging area of research is the extent to which cultures differ in their perceptions of sexual harassment (Pryor et al. 1997). Research has found that harassment occurs in all cultures that have been studied; there are some intriguing differences, however, in the perception of sexual harassment. College students from Australia, Brazil, Germany, and the United States were asked to judge the degree to which an interaction between a student and a professor might be sexual harassment. College women in the United States judged the situations to be more harassing than did college men. In the Brazilian sample, however, the opposite was true. College students' definitions of sexual harassment in Brazil were different from those in other countries. Brazilian men and women tended to define sexual harassment as less of an abuse of power, less related to gender discrimination, and more likely to be a relatively harmless sexual behavior. Some researchers (DeSouza & Hutz, 1995, 1996) suggest that sexual harassment is not necessarily unwelcome behavior in a society such as Brazil—a society that is more eroticized than the United States.

The way men and women perceive interpersonal behaviors, especially women's friendliness, may hold a key to understanding some incidents of sexual harassment (Stockdale, 1993). For example, college students were asked to observe a discussion group and then evaluate the participants. Compared with females' perception of males, males perceived more sexuality in the behavior of female participants (Saal, Johnson, & Weber, 1989).

Margaret Stockdale and her colleagues (1992) showed college-age men and women a videotape of a female training manager discussing a training program with a male sales manager. The interaction was staged to be friendly and professional. Viewers rated how flirtatious, seductive, and sexy they considered the female actor's behavior. Men were more likely than women to rate the woman actor as trying to behave sexually. In another study (Stockdale & Saal, 1990) viewers watched a videotape of actors portraying a male professor and a female student. Half of the viewers watched a portrayal of a friendly, nonharassing professor; the other half watched a portrayal of a harassing professor. The viewers who tended to misperceive the encounters were less repulsed by the harassing behavior than the accurate perceivers were.

The circumstances surrounding an event are also important in determining whether that event constitutes sexual harassment. A key factor is abuse of power. For example, a student who repeatedly asks another student for a date may be annoying. By contrast, a professor who pressures a student for a date is likely to be viewed as a threat, and the professor's persistence is therefore perceived as harassment. Surgeon Frances Conley (1993) resigned from a position at the Stanford University School of Medicine because of sexual harassment; she notes that "the unequal distribution of power on the basis of sex creates a climate for men who would use their position to exploit women" (p. 351).

A number of programs have been developed to train people to recognize and deal with incidents of sexual harassment. There have been, however, limited attempts to evaluate the effectiveness of such programs (Fitzgerald & Shullman, 1993). One study involving college student participants found that brief sexual harassment training could eliminate the common gender difference in the perception of incidents of sexual harassment (Moyer & Nath, 1998). It remains to be seen whether these results can be replicated and impact the rate and reporting of sexual harassment.

Gender Stereotyping on the Job. Psychological research on gender stereotyping can have a practical impact. Ann Hopkins, a manager at the accounting firm of Price Waterhouse, had brought the firm $25 million worth of business. Her clients praised her work, and her supporters at the firm described her as aggressive and hardworking. When she applied for partnership, the firm put her "on hold" for a year, despite the fact that she had generated more billable hours than any other candidate. The next year the firm did not recommend her for partnership. She claimed the reason was sex discrimination, and noted that only 7 of the firm's 662 partners were women. The firm countered that Hopkins had deficiencies in interpersonal skills—she was assertive and forceful. She had been described as "macho" and in need of a "course at charm school." A colleague offered her advice to improve her chances of becoming a partner: walk, talk, and dress more femininely, wear makeup, and wear jewelry (Fiske, 1993; Fiske & Stevens, 1993; Fiske et al., 1991).

Hopkins declined the advice and sued Price Waterhouse for violating her civil rights, protected under Title VII of the 1964 Civil Rights Act, which

The amount of business Ann Hopkins generated for the accounting firm that employed her indicated that she was highly successful. Nevertheless, the firm declined to recommend her for partnership. She filed a lawsuit in which she charged the firm with sex discrimination. The firm appealed all the way to the U.S. Supreme Court, which determined that the lower courts were correct in ruling in Hopkins's favor.

prohibits sex discrimination. Susan Fiske, a psychologist who investigates gender stereotypes, assisted in the lawsuit as an expert witness (Fiske et al., 1991). Research showed that stereotyping of behavior is more likely to occur when the targeted person is isolated or somehow stands out in a homogenous environment. Stereotyping is also more likely when there is a perceived lack of fit between a person's category and the occupation in question. For example, managers are expected to be aggressive and tough; however, these are not attributes typically expected of women. Hopkins's detractors perceived her as aggressive (a desirable attribute); her failure to conform to the gender stereotype, however, led them to conclude that she was therefore abrasive. Yet her supporters and clients saw her as a determined go-getter. Finally, stereotyping is more likely when ambiguous criteria are used to evaluate persons. The accounting firm used subjective judgments of Hopkins's interpersonal skills rather than objective criteria such as the amount of business she had generated (Fiske, 1993; Fiske et al., 1991).

The judge ruled in Hopkins's favor, asserting that "Price Waterhouse refused to make Ann Hopkins a partner. Gender-based stereotyping played a role in this decision" (*Hopkins v. Price Waterhouse*, 1990, p. 1). The company appealed this decision to the U.S. Supreme Court, which upheld it. The final ruling was issued in May 1990: Hopkins was awarded both the partnership that she had been denied and monetary damages.

Women as Leaders.   The main issue in the case of Ann Hopkins was straightforward: Are women in leadership positions evaluated differently from men in such positions? To answer this question, Alice Eagly and her colleagues (1992) conducted a meta-analysis of 147 studies that evaluated men and women in leadership roles. Those studies revealed a slight tendency for women leaders to be evaluated less highly than men in the same positions; women did not, however, receive lower evaluations in all situations. Instead the devaluation of women leaders was selective; it occurred when they occupied previously male-dominated roles and when the evaluators were men. What's more, women were evaluated less highly when they adopted more masculine styles of leadership, such as autocratic and nonparticipative management styles. A recent review of the effectiveness of men and women in the role of leaders or managers found that men and women were equally effective (Eagly, Karau, & Makhijani, 1995).

Gender has the potential to influence evaluations of managers, even though there may be no general tendency to devalue the managerial contributions of all women (Eagly, Makhijani, & Klonsky, 1992). How should a woman behave so as to avoid this devaluation? If women act like stereotypical males, their male colleagues may accuse them of not being feminine enough, yet if they behave in a stereotypically feminine manner, male colleagues are likely to accuse them of not being masculine enough (Tavris, 1991). Marilyn Loden and Judy Rosener (1990) suggest that women would prosper if they were encouraged to use their people-oriented skills instead of adapting male "command and control" styles of leadership.

Why is it so hard to overcome gender stereotypes in the workplace and elsewhere? One reason is that people often "fence off" individuals who do not fit their stereotypes. A person who disconfirms a stereotype is placed in a subtype, which serves to perpetuate the original stereotype. Women are not seen simply as doctors or professors but as female professors or lady doctors who are exceptions to the rule, thereby reinforcing gender stereotypes (Basow, 1992; Fiske & Stevens, 1993).

Eagly (Eagly, Mladinic, & Otto, 1991) investigated the social categories of "woman" and "man" as well as several others such as "Republican" and "Democrat." The general category of "woman" was evaluated quite favorably; in fact, it was evaluated more favorably than "man." How can we reconcile these findings with those of studies like the ones investigating the evaluation of women in the workplace? Recent societal changes in the status of women may cause people to evaluate women more favorably than they did when the first studies of gender stereotypes were conducted. But a more important question is this: If people have such positive evaluations of women as a social category, why do data on wages and promotions indicate that women are at a disadvantage? The answer is that although qualities such as being understanding and gentle are positive attributes, these qualities are valued more in close relationships than in the more highly paid sectors of the workforce. Compared with men, women managers tend to be more open, more democratic, and more likely to allow employees a voice in decision making.

Many women face workplace obstacles such as gender stereotyping that can have detrimental effects on their chances for advancement. In recent years more women are being hired and promoted into management-level positions. Changes in the sharing of family responsibilities, however, are slow in occurring.

When both wife and husband work outside the home, the majority of housework and child-care tasks remain the responsibility of the wife.

Family Responsibilities

"What do you do?" Perhaps you or your parents have been asked this question many times, and the answer most likely involved a statement about occupation. Many women are asked questions like "Do you work?" or "What does your husband do?" Such questions ignore the fact that more than half of all women in the United States now work outside the home. Many women, however, seem to have two jobs—one outside the home and one at home, where they are usually responsible for cooking, cleaning, and caring for children. Even in dual-career families, mothers continue to have the primary responsibility for child care. The tasks that men engage in at home tend to be sporadic, variable, and adjustable in terms of timing, such as repairing appliances and mowing the lawn. Women tend to engage in tasks that are repetitive, routine, and constrained by deadlines.

Monica Biernat and Camille Wortman (1991) conducted a longitudinal study of 139 married women professionals who had preschool children between the ages of 1 and 5. Most of the women and their husbands were in their thirties. All of these women worked at least 30 hours a week in high-status occupations (accounting, banking, higher education, law) that were equal in status to their husbands' occupations.

The wives and their husbands evaluated their participation in 8 different child-care tasks (e.g., caring for children's physical needs and getting up with them during the night) and 12 household activities (such as cooking and making repairs). They also rated their satisfaction with their role and their spouse's role in home labor.

The results indicated that the wives were more actively involved than their husbands with every one of the child-care tasks (see Figure 11-5). With the more enjoyable tasks (such as playing with children), however, there was greater equality. Unpleasant tasks, such as getting up in the middle of the night to care for a child, remained primarily the mother's responsibility.

These data revealed that couples were more likely to share household chores than child care. Wives were more likely to be responsible for finances, cleaning, and cooking; husbands handled some household chores related to laundry and repairs. Nevertheless, researchers concluded that although there was equality outside the home, substantial inequity existed in the home, particularly in the distribution of child-care tasks (Biernat & Wortman, 1991). This situation has the effect of producing a "second shift" of work at home for women around the world (Hochschild, 1989; Mednick, 1993).

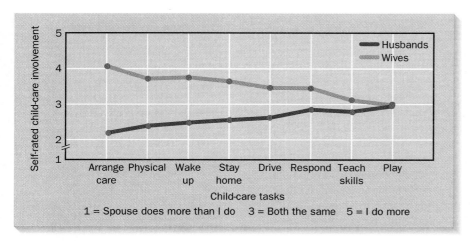

FIGURE 11-5 Differences in amount of time devoted to child care by wives and husbands.

Source: Biernat & Wortman, 1991.

Juggling. Many psychologists who have studied stress have focused on stressors affecting men, particularly stressors in the workplace. They have tended to view the home as a benign environment in which one recuperates from the rigors of working—a picture drawn from a traditional male perspective (Hare-Mustin & Marecek, 1990a). This type of research does not recognize that women are more concentrated in lower-paying jobs than are men, have less upward mobility, have less control over their more tedious jobs, and also experience sexual discrimination. For them, the home is a further source of stress as they struggle to perform household tasks after a difficult day at work.

Many married women may have hoped that when they entered the workplace, their husbands would take on more of the responsibility for caring for the children and the home. For many, however, this hope has not been realized. Instead of the envisioned role redefinition for men and women, the resulting situation has created a role expansion for women (Crosby & Jaskar, 1993). Faye Crosby (1991) uses the term *jugglers* to describe women who perform both job and family roles.

What are the consequences of these multiple roles for women? Contrary to expectations, Crosby (1991) found no evidence that role jugglers experience more stress than homemakers or other women with fewer roles. In fact, their multiple roles appear to insulate these women (and men also) against depression (Crosby & Jaskar, 1993). One likely reason for this effect is that multiple roles provide variety, change, and exposure to many viewpoints. These factors can buffer individuals against the impact of reversals and dissatisfactions in their daily lives (Crosby & Jaskar, 1993). Women in multiple roles do not wallow in self-pity; instead they "take pride in how well they cope" (Crosby & Jaskar, 1993, p. 162).

We have seen how gender stereotypes exert a powerful influence on a wide range of behaviors. Although biological aspects of sex are difficult to change, gender stereotypes and their influence on behavior can change. As they change, more opportunities become open to people of both sexes.

Review Summary

1. Continued reliance on gender stereotypes can result in **sexism**—differential treatment of individuals based on their sex.

2. Sexism has been noted in adults' interactions with toddlers in preschool settings. Observations of elementary school classrooms have found evidence that sexism pervades those settings as well. In schools boys tend to be reinforced for assertiveness; girls are reinforced for politeness. These differences can also be seen in high school and college classrooms.

3. Sexual harassment is not a new phenomenon. Two forms of sexual harassment have been defined: coercion of sexual favors by means of promised rewards

or threatened punishments (quid pro quo) and creation of a hostile environment.

4. Most studies reveal that more than half of working women have experienced some form of sexual harassment. Men and women differ in their interpretation of events as instances of sexual harassment.

5. Psychologists have applied what they have learned about gender stereotyping to claims of sex discrimination.

6. Women in leadership positions receive lower evaluations than men, although the difference is not large. There is evidence, however, that when evaluation criteria are ambiguous and the evaluators are men, there is a greater likelihood that women's leadership abilities will be devalued.

7. Despite the increase in the number of women who have entered the labor force in recent decades, little evidence exists that men and women share household and child-care responsibilities more equally than they did in the past.

8. Some psychologists have focused on the positive benefits that women derive from juggling work outside the home with household and other responsibilities. These benefits include increased ability to cope with stress.

Study Break

1. What are the major findings of observations of gender stereotyping in elementary school classrooms?
2. Which type of sexual harassment involves coerced sexual behavior in exchange for rewards or avoiding punishments?
  a. pro bono
  b. quid pro quo
  c. sexual exchange
  d. negotiated rape
3. Sexual harassment can have a wide range of physi-

cal and psychological consequences that include symptoms similar to those found in
  a. heart disease.
  b. schizophrenia.
  c. anorexia nervosa.
  d. posttraumatic stress disorder.
4. In what ways do men and women differ in their perceptions of sexual harassment?
5. In what ways do the typical household tasks done by husbands and wives differ?

ANSWERS TO STUDY BREAKS

Pages 465–466

1. a. Sex
  b. Gender
  c. Gender
2. Klinefelter's syndrome
3. XYY
4. Androgen insensitivity syndrome
5. a. Cognitive-developmental
  b. Gender-schema
  c. Social learning
6. d
7. b

Page 473

1. d
2. d
3. a. Intelligence tests were designed to eliminate items that were answered correctly more often by either boys or girls; thus there are no major differences in overall intelligence as assessed by standard measures of intelligence.
  b. Research reveals a slight superiority for girls/women in such verbal skills as spelling; however, the size of the current difference is very small.
  c. Girls actually earn higher grades in elementary school, but they do not do as well as boys on standardized tests. Differences in mathematical performance have

recently been found to be declining. Differences in spatial ability may be the result of differing opportunities to practice these skills.
4. A meta-analysis allows a researcher to draw conclusions from a large number of studies. When drawing these conclusions, however, meta-analysis allows the researcher to consider the size of the differences in each study rather than simply noting that there was or was not a difference.
5. Researchers have found that gender stereotypes affect the type of help that is offered. For example, women are more likely to offer help that might be called nurturing, whereas men are more likely to offer help that might be called heroic.

Page 489

1. Compared with girls, boys in elementary classrooms receive more attention and detailed feedback from teachers.
2. b
3. d
4. Men and women do not differ in their perception of the more serious forms of sexual harassment; men, however, tend to view less serious forms as examples of the normal relationships among men and women at work.
5. Women are more active on all child-care tasks. On the more enjoyable tasks such as playing with the children, there was greater equality. Generally, wives are more responsible for tasks such as finances, cleaning, and cooking; husbands are more responsible for tasks such as repairs.

Personality

Chapter in Perspective

To this point we have covered several basic processes, starting with how our nerves transmit information, how we sense and then understand information from our environment, and how we learn and remember information. We have also looked at how we develop physically and socially, and we briefly considered how personality develops. In this chapter we present an overview of the major theories of personality. The concept of personality is familiar because our language contains many words that describe how our friends, relatives, and strangers differ from one another in the ways they act and react to events. Psychologists have devised a number of methods to quantify such personality differences. How these differences occur is one of the key questions posed by psychologists. In previous chapters we have seen how biological factors such as heredity influence many basic processes. In this chapter we will see that heredity has important influences on personality. Next, we will look more closely at Freud's model for personality development. We will also consider the perspective of psychologists who have proposed that the basic processes of learning can account for some personality differences. Finally, we will see how social and cognitive factors influence what and how we learn and how these differences create what we call *personality*. ■

personality
A relatively stable pattern of behaving, feeling, and thinking that distinguishes one person from another

Analyzing Personality

Karin and her friends were in a shopping mall when they noticed a booth advertising "Personality Analysis by Computer." She completed a test called the GPA, which was a series of true-or-false questions (see Table 12-1). Although she thought some of the items were unusual, she was pleased with the analysis she received. After reviewing the analysis with her friends, however, Karin began wondering whether it was really accurate. *How could a computer generate a personality description based on a series of true-or-false questions?* ■

How would you describe a friend or relative without referring to his or her physical attributes? You might begin by saying that your friend has "a good personality." This statement usually means a person has made a positive impression on you and exhibits characteristics that you find desirable. In contrast, when we say that someone has "no personality," we usually mean we consider his or her characteristics disagreeable. People also use the term *personality* in another way—to refer to celebrities, especially those in the entertainment industry.

The question we posed earlier could be rephrased as "What is your friend like?" Think of another friend who is quite different from the first one you considered, and write a description of him or her. Now examine the words you used to describe these two individuals. You may have used words like *ambitious, happy,* and *sociable*. If your friends are indeed different, the words on the two lists should not overlap.

Defining Personality

The word *personality* is derived from the Latin word *persona,* which means "mask." In ancient Greece and Rome, actors wore masks to convey the personality characteristics of the roles they were playing. The masks made it easier for the small number of actors who played all the parts to portray their diverse roles.

To psychologists, **personality** refers to a relatively stable pattern of thinking, feeling, and behaving that distinguishes one person from another. This definition has two important components. First, each person's pattern of thinking, feeling, and behaving makes him or her distinctive. Thus each of us wears a mask that is different from those worn by others. The second component of the definition of personality is the notion that an individual's personality is relatively consistent. We are not completely consistent from one situation to the next; behavior varies across situations. The definition, however, proposes a certain degree of consistency in personality; people display levels of personality characteristics that are relatively stable across time. Psychologists have long debated and studied the issues of consistency across situations and stability across time, as we will see later in the chapter.

"I don't know why everyone says I don't have a personality."

TABLE 12-1 The Generalized Personality Analysis (GPA) Questionnaire

This personality questionnaire contains a series of statements. Read each one, decide how you feel about it, and mark your answer to the item. If you agree with the statement or feel it is true about you, answer *true*. If you disagree with the statement or feel it is not true about you, answer *false*.

1. Cats are antisocial.
2. Some roads never end.
3. Fast walkers are slow thinkers.
4. I get into the tub with my right foot first.
5. A circle is a square that has rounded edges.
6. Oak trees seem more friendly than pine trees.
7. The majority of right-thinking people are wrong.
8. There is more air in a loaf of bread than in a balloon.
9. Snow can turn to rain faster than rain can turn to snow.
10. Being able to flick a light switch gives me a feeling of power and strength.

Source: Palladino & Schell, 1980.

self-report inventory
Psychological tests in which individuals answer questions about themselves, usually by responding *yes* or *no* or *true* or *false*

Personality Tests

The methods psychologists use to examine personality include case studies, interviews, naturalistic observations, laboratory investigations, and psychological tests. To be useful, a psychological test must have three characteristics: reliability, validity, and standardization (see Chapter 8). Many of the tests published in magazines and newspapers lack all three characteristics; therefore you should be skeptical of the supposed meaning attached to such tests.

Self-Report Inventories.   Some of the best-known and most widely used personality measures are **self-report inventories** that require individuals to respond to questions about themselves in the form of yes-or-no, or true-or-false answers (e.g., "I am nervous when I speak to a large group of people").

We commonly use the word *personality* in two ways: (a) to refer to people who are outgoing, fun-loving, and very sociable, and (b) to refer to celebrities like Whoopi Goldberg.

"Might I point out, sir, that that one goes particularly well with your tie?"

This limited range of possible answers means that little, if any, judgment is required to score these tests. Two of the most frequently used self-report personality inventories are the Minnesota Multiphasic Personality Inventory (MMPI) and the California Psychological Inventory (CPI).

The Minnesota Multiphasic Personality Inventory. The most widely used self-report personality inventory, the MMPI (Butcher, Lim, & Nezami, 1998), was developed and first published in 1943 by Starke Hathaway and J. C. McKinley, both of the University of Minnesota. The test's long history of application is supported by evidence from thousands of studies, and its users have accumulated a great deal of experience (Helmes & Reddon, 1993). The purpose of the MMPI is to help diagnose psychological disorders such as depression and schizophrenia (see Chapter 13). Hathaway and McKinley began by collecting a large pool of items that could be answered "true" or "false" (e.g., "I wish I could be as happy as other people"). They retained items that were answered differently by normal people and those suffering from any of several psychological disorders. Most of the items deal with a range of psychological and physical symptoms (Groth-Marnat, 1990).

A revision of the MMPI, the MMPI-2, has 567 items and 10 clinical scales (see Figure 12-1) that were designed to assess characteristic symptoms associated with several of the major psychological disorders. Four validity scales were designed to detect tendencies for test takers to present themselves in a favorable light (such as answering "false" to "I do not read every editorial in the newspaper every day") or to assess other unusual ways of responding (Graham, 1990).

Many items from the earlier MMPI were rewritten to change outdated wording, improve clarity, and eliminate objectionable items dealing with topics such as religion and sex (Graham, 1990). The MMPI-2 has new norms, which were intended to reflect the entire population better than the norms of the original version (Duckworth, 1991; Helmes & Reddon, 1993).

The MMPI has been adapted for use in at least 22 languages and in many nations and cultures. Test developers follow a series of procedures when adapt-

FIGURE 12-1   MMPI profile of a 40-year old male. This profile reveals a mild to moderate level of depression and anxiety that suggests ambivalence, indecisiveness, and low self-confidence. Energy and activity levels are likely to be below average. Getting started on new tasks presents difficulty; after tasks are started, there is often self-blame over minor deficiencies in performance.

Sources: Friedman, Webb, & Lewak, 1989; Graham, 1990; Greene, 1991.

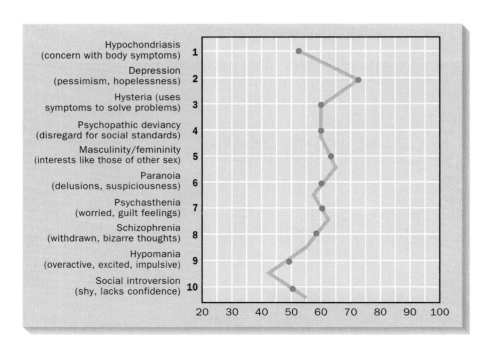

ing the test for use outside of the United States. The elimination of objectionable items during the MMPI-2 revision enhanced acceptability of the test by people in other cultures. The issue of item content, however, still must be addressed each time the test is adapted. For example, items referring to sex might be considered inappropriate by people taking the test in Arabic (Soliman, 1996). In addition to issues related to content, the items themselves must be translated; this process consists of several steps. First, items are translated from English. During this step, translators must take special care with words such as *frequently, sometimes,* and *usually* as well as slang or colloquial expressions like "muscle twitching and jumping." To ensure that the translation retains the original meaning, the translated version is translated back into English (a *back translation*). Any failures to convey the original meaning of the items are identified in this back-and-forth process. Once the translation is completed, the test adapters recheck to ensure that the test maintains its reliability and validity; the researchers check to determine if local norms must be used in place of norms based on a U.S. population (Butcher, Lim, & Nezami, 1998).

The California Psychological Inventory. The MMPI has served as the basis for the development of other personality inventories, including the California Psychological Inventory (CPI), which was designed for use with normal adolescents and adults. The 20 CPI scales, such as dominance, responsibility, and sociability (Gough & Bradley, 1996), have been used to predict academic achievement, to understand leadership (Day, Bedeian, & Conte, 1998), and to study individuals in various occupations. The CPI is widely used, and has been translated into 29 languages (Paunonen & Ashton, 1998).

Projective Tests. Have you ever stared at the sky and noticed a collection of clouds that reminded you of a crown? When you told a friend what you saw, she said it looked like a dog. Those clouds are similar to the stimuli used in projective tests to evaluate personality. **Projective tests** are assessment techniques that require individuals to respond to *unstructured* or *ambiguous* stimuli. In some projective tests, individuals respond to inkblots, make up stories about pictures, express themselves by drawing, or complete sentences such as "I think other people . . ."

   Because there are no correct or best answers, proponents of projective tests believe test takers will find it difficult to fake their responses. The assumption underlying projective tests is that people project their personality characteristics onto the ambiguous stimuli. These responses are thought to reflect unconscious aspects of personality that are not likely to be revealed in answers to more obvious self-report inventory items. One projective test, the *Thematic Apperception Test* (TAT), has been used to measure achievement motivation (see Chapter 4) and to make predictions of future achievement-related behaviors (McClelland, Koestner, & Weinberger, 1989). The 20 TAT cards contain vague black and white pictures (one card is blank). When administering the test, the psychologist asks the participant to make up a story to fit what is happening in the card and what the character is thinking and feeling and to give the outcome.

   One of the most widely used projective tests is the Rorschach inkblot test (Lubin et al., 1985), which was published in 1921 by a Swiss psychiatrist, Hermann Rorschach. Rorschach dropped ink onto a piece of paper and then folded the paper in half, thus creating a symmetrical pattern (see Figure 12-2). Five of the cards in the test are black, white, and gray; the remaining five cards include various colors.

   There are several steps in the administration of the Rorschach. First, the examiner displays the cards one at a time and asks the client to report what he or she sees in each card. The psychologist writes down the client's description of each

projective test
Psychological test that involves the use of unstructured or ambiguous stimuli in an effort to assess personality

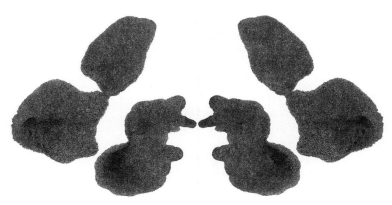

FIGURE 12-2 A card similar to those presented in the Rorschach inkblot test. Projective tests use unstructured or ambiguous stimuli (without obvious meaning or interpretation) like this inkblot, which require test takers to make sense of stimuli that do not have any specific meaning.

card and then asks for the aspects of each card that influenced the responses. Finally, the psychologist may code the responses on the basis of characteristics such as the part of the card used (e.g., whole blot or small details), the use of color, and the content of responses (e.g., humans or sex). Users of the Rorschach believe that these aspects of the responses yield information about an individual's personality. For example, heavy reliance on color might indicate impulsive behavior, and depressed people may use few, if any, colors in their responses.

Administering and interpreting projective tests requires extensive training. The degree of subjective judgment required to interpret them has led some psychologists to conclude that projective tests do not meet the same standards as many self-report inventories (Groth-Marnat, 1990). To address these concerns, more recent approaches to the interpretation of the Rorschach place greater emphasis on the quantification of Rorschach responses and comparisons to norms describing the responses (Exner, 1986, 1991).

The Barnum Effect.   The assortment of methods used to analyze personality is fascinating. Consider Karin's computer-generated personality analysis (Table 12-2). She believed that a computer had analyzed her answers to the GPA to produce an analysis just for her. The items on the GPA are not typical of self-report inventories; they were selected by researchers who wanted to determine if people would accept general personality feedback they thought was based on unusual items. Thus your responses to those items reveal little about your personality.

The computer-generated personality description that Karin received has much in common with those produced by several nonscientific methods of analyzing personality, such as handwriting analyses and horoscopes (Glick, Gottesman, & Jolton, 1989; McKelvie, 1990). Horoscopes contain statements that are similar to those found in Karin's personality analysis; the statements in Table 12-2 were collected from an astrology book (Forer, 1949). Although repeated evaluations have demonstrated that astrology has no scientific basis (Crowe, 1990), many people consult their horoscopes every day.

Psychological Detective

Can you provide reasons for people's acceptance of feedback from sources such as horoscopes or the GPA? Why would the statements in Table 12-2 lead an individual to report that his or her personality had been assessed accurately? Think about this question, and write down your answers before reading further.

Fortune-tellers rely on the Barnum effect; they often use favorable descriptions that apply to most people. They frequently phrase their statements as questions in order to elicit additional information from their clients.

In study after study, most people rate the personality statements in Table 12-2 as "good" or "excellent" descriptions of themselves (Forer, 1949; Snyder & Larson, 1972). Why? Let's examine the first statement in the personality analysis: "You have a great need for other people to like and admire you." Does this statement describe any of your friends? How many? Read the other statements and ask yourself the same questions. How many friends does each statement describe? In almost every case, the answer is "quite a few." These statements describe a considerable percentage of the population, and they are quite favorable (Furnham & Schofield, 1987; Glick, Gottesman, & Jolton, 1989). According to Paul Meehl (1956), these personality descriptions have something for every-

TABLE 12-2   Karin's Computer-Generated Personality Analysis

You have a great need for other people to like and admire you. You have a tendency to be critical of yourself. You have a great deal of unused capacity that you have not turned to your advantage. Although you have some personality weaknesses, you are generally able to compensate for them. Your sexual adjustment has presented problems for you. Disciplined and self-controlled outside, you tend to be worrisome and insecure inside. At times you have serious doubts as to whether you have made the right decision or done the right thing. You prefer a certain amount of change and variety and become dissatisfied when hemmed in by restrictions and limitations. You pride yourself as an independent thinker and do not accept others' statements without satisfactory proof. You have found it unwise to be too frank in revealing yourself to others. At times you are extroverted, affable, sociable, while at other times you are introverted, wary, reserved. Some of your aspirations tend to be pretty unrealistic. Security is one of your major goals in life.

Source: Forer, 1949, p. 120.

one. He coined the term **Barnum effect** to describe them (after P. T. Barnum, the showman who said a good circus has a "little something for everybody").

Researchers who study the Barnum effect typically ask individuals this question: "How accurate is the personality analysis in describing you?" An accurate answer to this question would be "The personality analysis describes me, but it also describes almost everyone I know." Karin recognized that her personality description did not distinguish her from her friends. Individuals who have been specifically asked about the general nature of such statements do recognize them as trivial (Furnham & Schofield, 1987; Greene, 1977).

The statements in Karin's personality analysis are similar to those found in analyses offered by fortune-tellers. How do fortune-tellers succeed in providing personality analyses their clients accept? In addition to relying on the Barnum effect, they use a method called *cold reading* to collect information from strangers. Fortune-tellers do not ask for information directly (Hyman, 1989; Randi, 1995) but use clues such as clothing, physical features, speech, gestures, and eye contact.

Myth or Science

 Can fortune-tellers see the future and analyze your personality? Fortune-tellers often memorize a "stock spiel" like the statements Karin received; they also recognize that most significant problems result from transitions like birth, marriage, and death. They use the techniques of cold reading to collect information that they formulate into their analyses and predictions. Although they present their analyses in general terms, clients assume that the information is specific and personal (Baker, 1993).

Here are some other keys that fortune-tellers use in providing feedback to their clients:

1. Tell the client that success depends on cooperation. Thus if the feedback is not accepted, fortune-tellers have a ready excuse—the client did not cooperate.

2. Present the analysis with confidence, but also profess modesty about the "talents" (of the fortune-teller) involved, and do not make excessive claims. Note that differentiating past, present, and future events and relationships is difficult. Clients will try to connect what they are told to the present and past; they often believe that statements or descriptions that are not currently accurate may become accurate in the future. Carefully observe the client's eye movement and bodily mannerisms for hints that you are on the right track.

Barnum effect
The tendency to accept generalized personality descriptions as accurate descriptions of oneself

3. *A gimmick such as a crystal ball or palm reading adds novelty and allows the fortune-teller to stall while formulating the next statement.*

4. *Fish for information by putting statements in the form of questions. Then use any acquired information in making additional statements to the client; most clients will later forget that they were the source of the information. Use vague language and modifiers such as possibly, maybe, and perhaps.*

Trait Approaches

When we asked you to describe a friend or relative, you probably used a number of words expressive of traits, such as *shy* or *friendly,* in your description. **Traits** are summary terms that describe tendencies to respond in particular ways that account for differences among people. Some people exhibit high levels of a given trait, and others exhibit low levels of the same trait. Most people, however, exhibit a moderate degree of a given trait, which are distributed according to the normal curve (see Chapter 8). Keep in mind that Barnum-type statements do not provide information about how much of a trait is exhibited (review the statements in Table 12-2). In contrast, most self-report inventories designed to measure a trait provide norms that allow us to determine the level of the trait that was assessed.

We begin our discussion of theoretical perspectives on personality with a look at traits. There are two reasons we decided on this structure to this chapter. First, you are very familiar with the concept of traits because you use them, probably every day to describe yourself as well as your friends and relatives. Second, from a historical perspective the concept of traits "may be as old as human language itself" (Matthews & Deary, 1998, p. 3). What's more, most approaches to personality make use of the concept of traits; where they differ is primarily in how they explain the development of individual differences.

Psychologist Gordon Allport (1897-1967) set out to compose a list of traits, which he described as the building blocks of personality (1961). To do this he examined everyday language because it seems likely we would encode the most important individual differences in human transactions as single terms in our language (John, 1990; McCrae & John, 1992). Trait words are pervasive in our language; we use them to describe people and read them in advertisements that extol the virtues of various products (*dependable, exciting*).

After eliminating words that referred to temporary moods (*frantic*), social evaluations (*worthy*), or physical attributes (*lean*), Allport found that 4,500 words remained (Allport & Odbert, 1936). The key question raised by these results is, Which trait terms are the most important? The large number of terms seemed to be more than were needed to describe a person's personality.

Factors of Personality: Raymond B. Cattell.   For some time, personality psychologists have been searching for a table of the key personality traits. Raymond B. Cattell (1990) decided that he would identify and measure the most important traits. Cattell's approach is to administer a wide variety of personality measures to many people and to use the results to identify the key personality traits. Cattell used data from a number of sources, including objective tests, records of his participants' lives (e.g., school and work records), and observations of their behaviors when placed in contrived situations. He then used a computer program to correlate the data. These correlations indicated that certain bits of information tended to cluster together. Cattell called these clusters *surface traits* because they were easy to identify from the correlations. Moreover, Cattell assumed that these surface traits were in turn directed by a smaller number of traits called *source traits.*

Cattell's *Sixteen Personality Factors Questionnaire (16PF)* (Cattell, Eber, & Tatsuoka, 1970) provides an assessment of the levels of a person's source

trait
A summary term that describes the tendency to behave, feel, and think in ways that are consistent across different situations

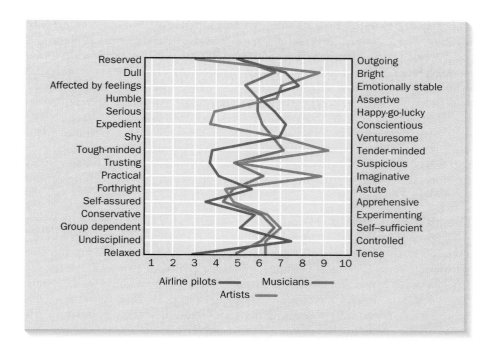

FIGURE 12-3 16PF profiles of airline pilots, artists, and musicians.

Source: Cattell, Eber, & Tatsuoka, 1970.

traits (see Figure 12-3); the latest version of this questionnaire is the 16PF5 (Conn & Rieke, 1994). According to Cattell, the same 16 traits can be used to describe each of us; the levels of those traits, however, vary from person to person, which accounts for our distinctiveness as individuals.

Hans Eysenck. Psychologist Hans Eysenck was always interested in how traits are organized. He concluded that one way to deal with the large number of traits is to organize them first into narrowly defined categories, which are in turn placed into broader categories (Eysenck & Eysenck, 1985; see Figure 12-4).

At the broadest level of abstraction, Eysenck said, we can describe personality as consisting of three basic traits: extraversion, neuroticism, and psychoticism. Neuroticism, or emotional instability, consists of traits such as anxiety, guilt feelings, low self-esteem, and shyness. Psychoticism consists of traits such as aggressiveness, impulsivity, and a lack of empathy. We will focus our attention on the trait of extraversion, which can be represented as a continuum from extreme extravert to extreme introvert. People we label as *extraverts* are more outgoing than *introverts,* who are oriented toward internal stimuli such as their own thoughts and moods. Because this trait is a continuum, however, many people have scores that would put them in the middle of the distribution.

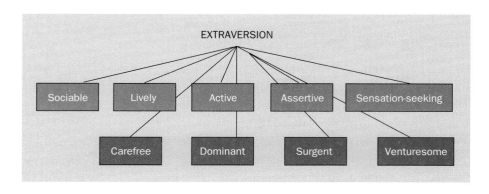

FIGURE 12-4 Eysenck's research focused on three major traits. A trait like extraversion encompasses several other traits, as illustrated here.

Source: Eysenck & Eysenck, 1985.

Extraverts and introverts differ in a number of ways and in a variety of settings. For example, researchers have investigated students' preferences for places to study (Campbell & Hawley, 1982). College students identified as introverts or extraverts were asked questions to determine their preferred levels of noise, crowding, and socializing opportunities while in the library. Take a moment to think about what conditions extraverts and introverts would prefer.

Introverts reported that they studied in quiet areas and used individual study carrels, which minimize noise and opportunities for socializing. Extraverts chose areas that provided opportunities for socializing as well as auditory and visual stimulation, such as large reading areas with sofas and lounge chairs.

The "Big Five" Traits. Despite the work of Cattell and Eysenck, there is a growing consensus that personality traits can be reduced to five basic ones, although there is some disagreement about the precise labels for the five (Goldberg, 1995). The most common names for the "big five" are (1) *openness to experience,* (2) *conscientiousness,* (3) *extraversion,* (4) *agreeableness,* and (5) *neuroticism* (Costa & McCrae, 1992a; Goldberg, 1995; McCrae & John, 1992). Table 12-3 lists and describes these five traits. Note that the names of the big five form the acronym OCEAN.

There are several reasons for concluding that these five traits represent basic dimensions of personality (Costa & McCrae, 1992c). These traits appear when peers provided ratings of Air Force officers, fraternity brothers, Peace Corps trainees, and spouses (McRae & Costa, 1987). They also appear in studies of individuals of different ages, in both men and women, in different races, in different language groups, and across cultures (Benet-Martínez & John, 1998; Paunonen et al., 1992; Trull & Geary, 1997). On the other hand, not all researchers agree on the specific names for the big five traits, and there is some disagreement on the meaning of the traits, especially the one called *openness to experience* (Matthews & Deary, 1998).

Some of the five major traits have a biological basis, especially extraversion (Viken et al., 1994). Conscientiousness has consistently been related to job performance in several occupations; extraversion correlates with job performance in occupations that involve social interaction such as management and sales (Barrick & Mount, 1991; Mount, Barrick, & Strauss, 1994). Personality measures, however, are not related to job performance across all occupations; extraversion is most useful in predicting job performance when employees have a significant amount of freedom in performing their jobs (Barrick & Mount, 1993). A high level of freedom may make personality traits more evident because one's behavior is less constrained by social demands.

Hands On

The "Big Five" Test

HERE IS AN OPPORTUNITY TO DETERMINE WHERE YOU FIT ON THE FIVE BIG TRAITS. Indicate how true each of the following terms is in describing you:

1 = Not at all true of me: I am never this way.

2 = Mostly not true of me: I am rarely this way.

3 = Neither true nor untrue of me, or I can't decide.

4 = Somewhat true of me: I am sometimes this way.

5 = Very true of me: I am very often this way.

TABLE 12-3   Names and Descriptions of the "Big Five" Traits

MAJOR TRAIT	DESCRIPTION OF PERSONALITY
Extraversion	People who score high are described as talkative and expressive as indicated by facial expressions and gestures. They are also assertive, gregarious, highly active, and have good skills in using humor. They like excitement and stimulation and tend to be energetic, optimistic, and upbeat. People with low scores tend to be described as solitary, quiet, having low energy, and reserved.
Agreeableness	People who score high are described as fundamentally altruistic. They are likely to yield in interactions with others. Others view them as sympathetic, straightforward, warm, and considerate. People who score low are described as antagonistic, unkind, suspicious, and unsympathetic.
Conscientiousness	People who score high are described as well organized, dependable, competent, and responsible. They are likely to get things done, able to delay gratification, exhibit highly ethical behavior, and have a high level of aspiration. People who score low are described as disorganized, careless, inefficient, and undependable.
Neuroticism	People who score high are described as self-defeating, basically anxious, and concerned about personal adequacy. They are subject to mood fluctuations and negative emotions, such as anger, guilt, and disgust. They are also prone to irrational ideas, are not always able to control impulses, and are less effective than others at coping with stress. People who score low are described as unemotional, calm, even-tempered, self-satisfied, and comfortable with themselves.
Openness to Experience	People who score high exhibit a preference for new and unfamiliar experiences reflected in appreciation of knowledge, various art forms, and nontraditional values as opposed to tradition and the status quo. They are considered highly introspective, attentive to inner feelings and fantasies, intellectual, and creative. People who score low are described as down-to-earth, conventional, preferring routine, and not intellectually oriented.

Sources: Adapted from Formy-Duval et al., 1995; McCrae & John, 1992; Costa & McCrae, 1992b; Matthews & Deary, 1998.

1. _____ imaginative
2. _____ organized
3. _____ talkative
4. _____ sympathetic
5. _____ tense
6. _____ intelligent
7. _____ thorough
8. _____ assertive
9. _____ kind
10. _____ anxious
11. _____ original
12. _____ efficient
13. _____ active
14. _____ soft-hearted
15. _____ nervous
16. _____ insightful
17. _____ responsible
18. _____ energetic
19. _____ warm
20. _____ worrying
21. _____ clever
22. _____ practical
23. _____ outgoing
24. _____ generous
25. _____ self-pitying

Instructions for scoring your answers to the "Big Five" Test can be found at the end of the chapter.
Source: Brody & Ehrlichman, 1998.

One aspect of research on the five major traits is especially relevant to the definition of personality: an investigation of their stability. Do the levels of these traits in an individual change over time, or do they remain similar through the adult years? Scores on a self-report inventory and personality ratings completed by spouses tended to remain stable into adulthood (Costa & McCrae, 1988). In fact, a growing body of research suggests that personality traits have considerable long-term stability (McCrae & Costa, 1990).

The strength of the trait approach is that it provides basic dimensions that describe the language of personality. Its weakness, however, is that it fails to explain behavior; that is, it does not help us understand *how* Jimmy became aggressive or *why* Anita is charitable. An even more serious criticism of the trait approach has been put forth by psychologists who argue that a basic assumption of the trait approach—consistency of behavior—is wrong. The following section looks at this debate.

Is Behavior Consistent?

As we have seen, one of the elements of the definition of personality is consistency in behavior. Are you consistent from day to day? Is the behavior of your family members and friends consistent from day to day? Consider these observations of some well-known people and imagine how psychologists interested in personality would evaluate such information.

> Albert Einstein was brilliantly intelligent and humorous. John F. Kennedy was ambitious and charming. Frank Sinatra was aggressive and emotional. Or so their biographers tell us. But perhaps they are wrong. Perhaps Einstein, Sinatra, Kennedy, you, and me and your cousin Frederick are equally intelligent, humorous, aggressive, emotional, ambitious, and moralistic. Perhaps personality traits . . . are mere fictions. (Kenrick & Funder, 1991, p. 150)

Challenges to the Idea of Consistency. On the basis of a study of the moral behavior of 11,000 elementary and high school students, Hugh Hartshorne and Mark May (1928) questioned whether behavior really is consistent. They developed a series of behavioral tests to measure the traits of altruism (defined as charitable concern for other people), honesty, and self-control, which they thought reflected children's moral behavior. When they analyzed the test scores, they found that the correlations among various behaviors in different settings and situations were quite low. Hartshorne and May concluded there was little consistency in the moral behavior of the children.

After analyzing reports of the relationship between traits and behavior, Walter Mischel (1968) suggested that personality traits do not lead to consistent behavior from one situation to the next. He concluded that "highly generalized behavioral consistencies have not been demonstrated, and the concept of personality traits as broad predispositions is thus untenable" (p. 140). He therefore advised psychologists to turn their attention from the search for traits to the study of *how situations influence behaviors.* For example, when you are out with your friends, your behavior with them may be quite different from your behavior during a dinner with relatives. An observer might find it hard to believe you are the same person in the two situations. That is Mischel's point: Behavior is a function of situations, not traits.

In Defense of Consistency. Although the idea of consistency of behavior was dealt some devas-

One reason we believe that personality is stable is that we observe stability in a variety of characteristics, including physical appearance, over time.

tating blows by Hartshorne and May (1928) and Mischel (1968), belief in this idea persisted. Darryl Bem and Andrea Allen (1974) offered several reasons for believing there is consistency in behavior. One reason is that we rely on preconceived notions of how behaviors are related and may jump to conclusions that are consistent with those preconceived notions. For example, if you expect "friendly" people to be "honest," you may conclude that a friendly person is honest even when you have no evidence to support such a conclusion.

Some characteristics, such as intelligence, emotional reactions, and physical appearance, are consistent over time. For example, Carroll Izard and colleagues (1993) found that tendencies to exhibit certain emotional reactions (e.g., anger or enjoyment) are stable across several years. What's more, after early childhood, scores on intelligence tests are quite stable into adulthood.

Another reason for the belief in consistency is that your presence may elicit particular behaviors in your friends or relatives. We often see other people in limited circumstances that can restrict the variety of behaviors that are likely to occur. For example, some parents may be shocked to learn that their child is disruptive in school. If a specific behavior is especially mischievous, their response may be, "Our child never does anything like that at home"—and they would be correct.

Although a number of studies have failed to demonstrate consistency of behavior related to traits across situations, there may be limitations in the methods used to study consistency (Bem & Allen, 1974; Small, Zeldin, & Savin-Williams, 1983). One problem can be illustrated by the following situation. Suppose your teacher decides that final grades for a course will be based on a single multiple-choice item. What do you think of this idea? We can hear the moans and groans. Let's examine the reasons for your objections. Your logic probably goes like this: "One multiple-choice item is not a good indicator of how much I have learned. What if I was sick the day the material in that item was covered in class? What if the item covers a topic that I found difficult?" Thus you have concluded that a single multiple-choice item is not a good indicator of your knowledge of the course material.

Following the same logic, Lewis Goldberg (1992) notes that arguments against the consistency of behaviors related to particular traits are often based on the false premise that "scientists in the field of personality seek to predict a single response of a particular individual in a completely novel situation" (p. 93).

Psychological Detective

 Suppose we have developed a self-report inventory to measure altruism. We could find out how many people volunteered to work for charity last year and then see whether volunteer work was related to scores on our altruism measure. There may be problems with this indicator of altruism, however. How could we provide more convincing evidence that this inventory measured altruism? Does volunteering to work for charity provide evidence of the consistency of altruism over time? Give these questions some thought, and write down your answer before reading further.

We begin by separating a large group of individuals into two smaller groups on the basis of their altruism scores (a group of high scorers and a group of low scorers). When we ask the individuals in each group if they volunteered to help a charity last year, we find few differences between the two groups. We can also ask, however, how many of them donated money to the poor, how many gave clothing to charitable organizations, and how many signed petitions requesting funds to build homeless shelters.

There may be few differences between the two groups of individuals on any one of the behaviors just mentioned. When we look at several behaviors

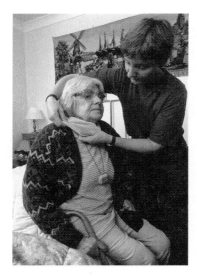

Psychologists are interested in the kind of helping behavior illustrated in this photograph. They avoid, however, relying on only one incident as an indicator of an individual's level of altruism.

together, however, a pattern emerges. A single behavior is a weak indicator of altruism, just as a single test item is a weak indicator of your knowledge of course material. When the behaviors are added together (like the items on that test), patterns become discernible.

Because a single example of any behavior is a weak indicator of any trait, Seymour Epstein (1979, 1980) suggests that researchers use the method of *aggregation,* in which they collect evidence of several behaviors, as we did in the example of altruism. The concept of aggregation is not new (Zuckerman, 1991). For example, psychologists who study operant conditioning do not study a single bar press in a Skinner box; instead they examine cumulative curves that are aggregations of a series of behaviors over time (see Chapter 6). Similarly, when we aggregate behaviors across situations, we can determine whether those behaviors are consistent over time.

Evidence of Consistency Based on Multiple Measures.
Epstein (1983) notes that both sides in the trait-situation debate believe they are correct and that consequently the other side must be wrong. Each side offers evidence to support its position, but a paradox exists here. Consider the following statements:

1. Behavior is specific to a situation.
2. People exhibit broad, stable tendencies to respond in certain ways across situations.

Behavior depends on the situation, but traits describe consistency in behavior across situations. Can we resolve this paradox? The situation also influences the likelihood that a person will exhibit a specific behavior. For example, because there are clear norms for acceptable behavior at a funeral, few people laugh at those events. If we were interested in the trait of a sense of humor and limited our observations to funerals, we might conclude that people with a high sense of humor were inconsistent. We need, however, to acknowledge the role of the situation. If we expanded our observations to other situations, it is likely that a pattern of consistency would emerge.

Stephen Small and his colleagues (1983) studied the traits of altruism and dominance in adolescents on a wilderness travel program. Counselors made observations of the campers' behaviors related to altruism (such as sharing possessions) and dominance (such as giving orders). A high degree of consistency was found for both altruistic and dominance behaviors when the behaviors were aggregated. The researchers concluded that revising the methods used by personality researchers can provide evidence in support of trait theories of personality.

The debate over traits versus situations has ended by revealing the existence of important regularities in individual behavior (Kenrick & Funder, 1990). David Funder (1991) notes that there are correlations between behaviors and traits, that agreement by different observers on the presence of particular traits supports their existence (Funder & Colvin, 1991), and that there is evidence that the levels of traits in an individual are stable across the life span. At the same time, researchers have come to realize that situations exert important influences on behavior.

Review Summary

1. Psychologists define **personality** as a stable pattern of thinking, feeling, and behaving that distinguishes one person from another. Two important components of this definition are distinctiveness and relative consistency.

2. Among the widely used **self-report inventories** of personality are the Minnesota Multiphasic Personality Inventory (MMPI) and the California Psychological Inventory (CPI). The MMPI was designed to help diagnose psychological disorders; the CPI is used to assess personality in the normal population.

3. **Projective tests** use ambiguous stimuli and require a great deal of interpretation by the test administrator. The most frequently used projective test is the Rorschach inkblot test.

4. The **Barnum effect** is the acceptance of generalized personality descriptions; it results from the use of favorable personality descriptions that apply to many people.

5. **Traits** are summary terms that describe tendencies to act and interact in particular ways that are consistent across situations. Gordon Allport developed a list of trait terms.

6. Raymond Cattell proposed 16 source traits to describe personality and make predictions of future behaviors.

7. Hans Eysenck proposed the existence of three major traits. Extraversion has been associated with a number of differences in everyday behavior.

8. Current research offers a model of five major traits that seem to be relatively stable across the life span and across cultures.

9. Critics of the concept of consistency in behavior based on traits argue that behavior is controlled by situations. In defense of the idea of consistency, some researchers note that there are some problems with the methods used and the assumptions made in this research.

10. Seymour Epstein proposes that both sides of the consistency issue are correct: Situations control behavior in a given instance, and broad consistencies do exist. Consistencies become visible when we add behaviors together, an approach termed *aggregation*.

Study Break

1. Which psychological test might be used in each of the following circumstances?
   a. A hospital needs to determine the most likely diagnosis of mental patients.
   b. A company wants to use a self-report inventory to select new salespeople.
   c. A psychologist is interested in assessing a person's unconscious thought processes but has no direct access to those processes.
2. Complete the following sentences.
   a. Hans Eysenck described personality as consisting of neuroticism, psychoticism, and . . .
   b. Raymond Cattell reduced the number of traits to . . .
3. Fortune-tellers use cues about people such as their clothing, speech, and gestures to persuade clients that they know a great deal about them. This process is known as
   a. cold reading.
   b. aggregation.
   c. standardization.
   d. projective testing.
4. Which of the following "big five" traits has been shown to be related to measures of job performance for several occupations?
   a. Neuroticism
   b. Agreeableness
   c. Consientiousness
   d. Openness to experience
5. What changes in research methods used by personality researchers have provided evidence to support trait theories of personality?

Biological Factors in Personality

The identical twins who live down the street—Kelly and Sharin—often dress alike. Family members, neighbors, and friends are amazed at how similar they are in their everyday behaviors. They both are on the high school basketball team, love to swim, and play in the school orchestra. Both sisters are outgoing and make friends easily. You wonder whether their similarities are due to the way they were raised ("nurture") or to hereditary influences ("nature"). *To what extent are our personalities influenced by nurture (factors in our environment) or nature (hereditary factors)?* ■

There is little doubt that people differ in the personality traits they exhibit. But why? Are differences a result of early child-rearing experiences? Does heredity influence differences in personality? If heredity plays a role in personality traits, can those traits change over time?

Early Biological Approaches

The idea that biological factors hold a key to personality has a long history. From the perspective of modern science, however, some of the earliest attempts to relate personality to biological factors appear primitive. The research tools were too crude and the hypotheses too broad; nevertheless, those efforts started a search that continues to this day.

Humors and Bumps. Hippocrates (460–377 B.C.E.), a Greek philosopher and physician, believed the human body contained four bodily "humors" or fluids: black bile, blood, phlegm, and yellow bile. The humor that predominated in a person was believed to determine that person's characteristics. For example, a predominance of black bile was thought to make a person depressed. Although we now know the body is not filled with humors, interest in the role of biological factors in personality has continued.

In the 1800s, phrenologists (*phrenology* was an attempt to study a person by analyzing bumps and indentations on the skull) attempted to link personality with features of the brain. Franz Joseph Gall (1758–1828) compared the brain to a muscle and tried to locate various characteristics by looking for well-developed parts of the brain. Bumps on the skull might signify the development of underlying brain tissue, which in turn should reflect higher levels of characteristics such as benevolence. Eventually it became clear that any bumps on the skull had no connection to personal characteristics, and interest in phrenology faded. Still, phrenology played an important role in encouraging the study of brain functions.

Body Types. William Sheldon (1899–1977), a psychologist with medical training, suggested that the shape of one's body determines one's personality (Sheldon & Stevens, 1942; Sheldon, Stevens, & Tucker, 1940). He developed a scheme consisting of three body types: *Endomorphs* are round, *mesomorphs* are rectangular, and *ectomorphs* are thin. Sheldon also collected information about the personalities of people representing each of the body types and reported high correlations between body type and personality characteristics. According to Sheldon, endomorphs love comfort and are outgoing, mesomorphs are assertive and energetic, and ectomorphs are restrained and lonely. When other researchers could not replicate these correlations, they suspected that preconceptions about the relationship of body type to personality (e.g., the stereotype of fat people as outgoing) had influenced Sheldon's results.

More recent research on physical characteristics has provided intriguing findings. For example, using the five-trait model, observers rated the personality traits of people whom they had never met (Borkenau & Liebler, 1992, 1995). The observers were exposed briefly to the target individuals in either a short videotape, a still photo, or an audiotape. Correlations between observers' ratings and participants' self-ratings revealed substantial agreement in the observers' judgment of the strangers' level of traits, such as extraversion. As expected, the more information provided, the more similar the ratings. What's more, the researchers found that the observers relied on several physical characteristics in making their trait ratings, although body size was not one of them. Physical features (such as voice quality, facial expressions, and presence or absence of smiling) bear a stronger relationship to self-reported extraversion than to other traits, and stronger ratings appropriately reflect this relationship. In fact, we can judge a stranger's degree of extraversion from nonverbal cues as well as we can judge someone's sex even when our exposure to strangers is limited to a brief videotape (Lippa, 1998).

Although there is little convincing evidence that body type is related to personality, researchers are investigating the role of other biological factors in personality. Among those factors is the person's general level of neural arousal.

Sensation Seeking. Organisms appear to seek an optimal level of arousal or stimulation that varies by individual. Stimulation that is too far above or below that level is perceived as unpleasant. Is it possible to measure a person's need for stimulation? Psychologist Marvin Zuckerman has developed a self-report inventory to measure what he calls *sensation seeking,* defined as a general tendency to seek stimulation from a variety of sources. Sensation seeking is related to the broad trait of extraversion (review Figure 12-4) as well as to conscientiousness (Zuckerman, 1994).

Sensation seeking can be divided into several related components. *Disinhibition* is the tendency to seek sensation through social activities such as parties; *thrill seeking* is the desire to engage in physically risky activities; *experience seeking* is the tendency to seek novel experiences through the mind and the senses; and *boredom susceptibility* is an intolerance for repetitive experience.

Sensation Seeking Scale

Hands On

YOU WILL BE ABLE TO ESTIMATE WHERE YOUR SCORE FALLS ON THE SENSATION Seeking Scale by completing the following items. The full scale consists of 40 items; we have reproduced 13 of them here so that you can get a feel for the types of items used to measure sensation seeking.

The Sensation Seeking Scale was designed to measure differences among individuals seeking stimulation from a variety of sources. For each of the following items, select the alternative that best indicates your preference. Then check your choices against the scoring key at the end of the chapter.

1. **a.** I would like a job that requires a lot of travel.
   b. I would prefer a job in one location.
2. **a.** I am invigorated by a brisk, cold day.
   b. I can't wait to get indoors on a cold day.
3. **a.** I get bored seeing the same old faces.
   b. I like the comfortable familiarity of everyday friends.
4. **a.** I would prefer living in an ideal society in which everyone is safe, secure, and happy.
   b. I would have preferred living in the unsettled days of our history.
5. **a.** I sometimes like to do things that are a little frightening.
   b. A sensible person avoids activities that are dangerous.
6. **a.** I would not like to be hypnotized.
   b. I would like to have the experience of being hypnotized.
7. **a.** The most important goal in life is to live it to the fullest and experience as much as possible.
   b. The most important goal in life is to find peace and happiness.
8. **a.** I would like to try parachute-jumping.
   b. I would never want to try jumping out of a plane, with or without a parachute.

Drag race champion Eddie Hill was the first person to go a quarter-mile from a standing start in less than five seconds. Drag racing is a high-risk occupation that probably attracts people with high scores on the Sensation-Seeking Scale.

9. **a.** I enter cold water gradually, giving myself time to get used to it.
   b. I like to dive or jump right into the ocean or a cold pool.
10. **a.** When I go on vacation, I prefer the comfort of a good room and bed.
   b. When I go on a vacation, I prefer the change of camping out.
11. **a.** I prefer people who are emotionally expressive even if they are a bit unstable.
   b. I prefer people who are calm and even-tempered.
12. **a.** A good painting should shock or jolt the senses.
   b. A good painting should give one a feeling of peace and security.
13. **a.** People who ride motorcycles must have some kind of unconscious need to hurt themselves.
   b. I would like to drive or ride a motorcycle.

Source: Zuckerman, 1994.

Research on sensation seeking reveals that high sensation seekers enjoy spicy, sour, and crunchy foods more than low sensation seekers. This preference is probably due to the varied experiences such foods can provide. High sensation seekers tend to use more drugs and alcohol than low sensation seekers (Simon et al., 1994; Stacy, Newcomb, & Bentler, 1991). Predictably, people in certain high-risk occupations—such as firefighters, race car drivers, riot squad police officers, and emergency room nurses—tend to score rather high on this scale. Sports and recreation reveal similar expected differences: Scores of skydivers soar above those of golfers and aerobics participants (Jack & Ronan, 1998; Wagner & Houlihan, 1994).

Biological differences may be at the root of differences in behavior related to sensation seeking, and these difference may have a genetic basis (Fulker, Eysenck, & Zuckerman, 1980; Tellegen et al., 1988). The enzyme MAO breaks down the neurotransmitter norepinephrine (see Chapter 2). Drugs that inhibit MAO increase levels of norepinephrine and cause individuals to be euphoric, impulsive, and aggressive. A negative correlation between MAO levels and sensation-seeking behavior (Zuckerman, Buchsbaum, & Murphy, 1980; Zuckerman, 1987) indicates that low levels of MAO (and hence high levels of norepinephrine) are associated with high sensation-seeking scores. For example, gamblers who are well known for their impulsiveness and risk taking exhibit low levels of MAO (Carrasco et al., 1994). Lest we forget, a correlation between a biological variable and a personality variable does not prove causation; nevertheless, the findings are intriguing.

A growing body of research points to the importance of biological factors in several personality characteristics. Is it possible that some of these personality characteristics are inherited? The study of twins can shed light on questions concerning the heritability of personality characteristics.

Twin Studies

One day in the 1980s, Oskar Stohr and Jack Yufe arrived in Minneapolis to participate in a study of identical twins reared apart. The twins had been separated shortly after birth, about 40 years earlier. Oskar was raised in Germany as a Nazi and a Catholic; Jack was reared by his Jewish father in Trinidad. The two men proved to have a great deal in common. Consider the following:

They both had mustaches.
Both wore wire-rimmed glasses.

They stored rubber bands on their wrists.

They read magazines from back to front.

They dipped buttered toast into their coffee.

Jim Springer and Jim Lewis had been adopted into separate working-class Ohio families in infancy. While in school, they both liked math but not spelling. Both had law enforcement training and worked part time as deputy sheriffs. They both vacationed in Florida, drove Chevrolets, and had dogs named Toy. Both had married and divorced women named Linda; their second marriages were to women named Betty. Both of them chew their fingernails and suffer late-afternoon headaches (Holden, 1980, 1987a).

The twins shown here are among those studied at the University of Minnesota. Many of those twins reported remarkable similarities across a range of experiences and behaviors.

These two stories depict remarkable similarities in twins who were separated at birth. Since 1979, the University of Minnesota Study of Twins Reared Apart has been recruiting twin pairs like those just described. Friends, relatives, or the twins themselves bring separated twin pairs to the attention of the researchers. Almost 1,000 twin pairs have agreed to participate in the research (Mann, 1994); most of them complete many hours of medical and psychological assessments.

Psychological Detective

How can we explain the similarities in the behavior of twins who were separated early in life? Do these similarities convince you that they are due to inherited factors? What other evidence could be gathered from these twins that would help us understand genetic influences on personality? Give these questions some thought, and write down your answers before reading further.

The stories of Oskar and Jack and the Jim twins are dramatic, but we should ask whether the remarkable similarities might be coincidences. The participants had many opportunities during the lengthy testing they underwent to discover similarities in their behaviors. Is there other evidence of similar personalities in identical twins who were separated early in life that cannot be explained as a series of coincidences?

Recall from Chapter 9 that fraternal twins are no more similar to each other than you are to your brother or sister; in contrast, identical twins have the same genes. Because identical twins share the same genes, we would expect their personalities to be similar. A problem often arises, however, in conducting research on twins: Identical twins may be treated more similarly than fraternal twins. Thus we cannot be sure whether similarities between identical twins are due to their identical heredity or to the similarity of their environments. The study of twins who were separated early in life allows researchers to isolate the effects of nature (heredity) from those of nurture (environment).

The University of Minnesota research team reported the results of a study of 44 pairs of identical twins who were separated early in life (Tellegen et al., 1988). The twins completed the Multidimensional Personality Questionnaire,

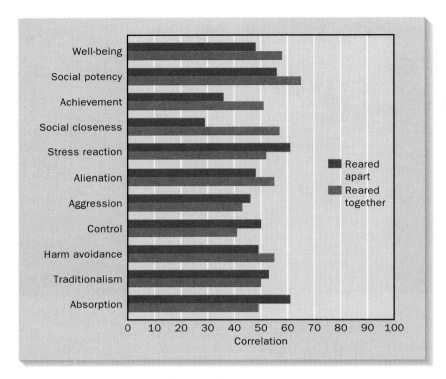

FIGURE 12-5 Correlations of personality characteristics for identical twins reared apart and identical twins reared together. The small differences suggest that environmental factors play a small role in determining these personality characteristics.

Source: Tellegen et al., 1988.

a self-report inventory that yields 11 scales. As you can see from Figure 12-5, the difference between the correlations for identical twins reared apart and for those reared together are very small. The correlations are similar whether the identical twins were reared apart or together.

In a second study of twins, Thomas Bouchard and Matthew McGue (1990) observed 45 sets of identical twins and 26 sets of fraternal twins who had been separated from each other early in life and had been reared in different homes. Their average age when studied was in the early forties; they ranged in age from 19 to 68. The correlations between scales of the California Psychological Inventory were higher for identical twin pairs than for fraternal twin pairs. This evidence, along with other research, led the investigators to conclude that parent-child relations and common environments have little effect on adult personality (Bouchard & McGue, 1990).

Let's turn to research focused on possible genetic influences on the big five traits we discussed earlier. Almost 1,000 twins took part in a study conducted in Germany and Poland. Each twin's personality was assessed by two different raters using the big five traits. A correlation of .63 between the raters demonstrated strong agreement in the assessments of the personalities by peers. The averaged peer ratings correlated .55 with the twins' self-report ratings. The correlations across identical twins were consistently higher than the correlations for fraternal twins, suggesting a genetic influence on personality (see Table 12-4). The researchers concluded that personality measured by either self-ratings or peer ratings shows a genetic influence with no evidence for a shared environmental influence (Angleitner, Riemann, & Strelau, 1995). Similar results were obtained in a study of twins in Canada and Germany, which the researchers interpreted as support for genetic influences in personality traits across cultures (Jang et al., 1998).

University of Minnesota researchers (McGue, Bacon, & Lykken, 1993) have also studied stability and change in the personalities of young adults. Their sample of 79 identical twins and 48 same-sex fraternal twins averaged 23 years old at the first testing. They were tested a second time at an average age of 30 years. Comparison of the two testings revealed both stability and change in personality during the transition from late adolescence to early adulthood. For example, mean scores for measures of positive emotionality (cheerfulness, forcefulness, warmth) were similar, and there was evidence of substantial genetic influence. Scores on measures of negative emotionality (such as nervousness, aggressiveness, and feeling mistreated) decreased, although there was again evidence of substantial genetic influence.

Before we are swept away by the research on the hereditary influences on personality, we should note that although heredity plays a substantial role in behavior, nongenetic factors are also important (Plomin, Owen, & McGuffin, 1994). The size of the genetic effect—estimated by what is called *heritability* (see Chapter 8)—rarely exceeds 50 percent; most cases are between 20 and 50 percent. Therefore differences among people in most personality characteristics are due at least as much to environmental factors as to heredity (Plomin, 1990b; Plomin & Rende, 1991). Even in the case of identical twins, about half

TABLE 12-4   **Similarity in Identical and Fraternal Twins in Personality Assessed Using the Big Five Traits**

BIG FIVE TRAIT	SELF-REPORT CORRELATION		PEER-RATING CORRELATION	
	Identical	Fraternal	Identical	Fraternal
Extraversion	.56	.28	.40	.17
Neuroticism	.53	.13	.43	−.03
Agreeableness	.42	.19	.32	.18
Conscientiousness	.54	.18	.43	.18
Openness to experience*	.54	.35	.48	.31

*Referred to as "Culture" by these researchers.
Source: Angleitner, Riemann, & Strelau, 1997.

of the differences in personality traits are not shared and hence are not due to hereditary factors. What's more, researchers have also found that siblings who grow up in the same family can be very different (Dunn & Plomin, 1990).

In trying to explain differences among siblings, researchers focused on differences across families. It now seems that what is important is not the environment shared by siblings but the *nonshared* environment. That is, each child experiences the environment differently, and these nonshared environmental factors appear to be more important than shared experiences (Plomin, Owen, & McGuffin, 1994; Plomin & Rende, 1991). For example, surveys of parents and children as well as naturalistic observations in the home suggest that parents may not treat each child alike, despite social pressure to do so. Even when parents are consistent in their responses to their children at the same age, however, siblings notice differences. For example, a parent's understandable attention directed to a newborn may be similar to what an older sibling received at the same age. The older sibling may protest for the same attention. Thus children may experience different environments as a function of differences in parental responses that are a function of age differences. What's more, each child's environment may be different as a result of social comparisons with siblings.

In a similar vein, John Loehlin and his colleagues (1990) found that the major influence on personality change in adopted and nonadopted children was neither genes nor shared environment, but individual experiences. Thus environmental influences may be specific to the child and not shared by all the siblings in a family (Dunn & Plomin, 1990; Plomin & Rende, 1991).

As we have seen, genetic factors present at birth can have important influences on the development of our personality. Next we turn to a very different approach to understanding personality. Sigmund Freud thought that our early experiences set the stage for personality throughout life; his focus, however, was on how unconscious factors could determine our personality.

Review Summary

1. Efforts to connect personality to biological factors can be traced to Hippocrates' theory of "humors" and later to phrenology.

2. William Sheldon suggested a relationship between body type and personality. Subsequent research demonstrated

that his findings were influenced by his preconceptions.

3. Additional support for the belief that biological factors influence personality is found in the negative correlation between sensation-seeking scores and levels of the enzyme MAO.

4. The study of identical twins reared apart allows researchers to identify the effects of heredity independently of the influence of environmental factors. Evidence from such studies indicates that heredity plays a role in a wide range of personality characteristics as evidenced by heritability estimates between 20 and 50 percent.

5. Recent evidence suggests that nonshared experiences exert a major influence on the personality of siblings.

Study Break

1. Who was the Greek philosopher who proposed that body fluids influenced personality? What name did he give those fluids?

2. While visiting a museum exhibit you notice a picture from the 1800s showing a man entering a shop that had a sign advertising *phrenology.* You ask a museum guide what the person is likely to have been doing. What will she tell you?
a. He was having excess humors drained.
b. A witch was to remove demons from the man's body.
c. The man's personality was to be analyzed by checking for bumps and indentations on his skull.

3. Why are identical twins reared apart so important in research designed to determine the influence of nature and nurture on personality?

4. Research on the question of why siblings in the same family are different has pointed to certain aspects of the environment as having a significant influence on these differences. Which aspects are these?

5. Researchers find that Ted's body has low levels of the enzyme MAO. Based on this finding, you conclude that Ted is likely to obtain a high score on a test designed to measure
a. achievement.
b. openness.
c. sensation seeking.
d. emotional stability.

6. A new self-report inventory assesses levels of the trait of complexity. The heritability of this trait is similar to most other personality traits. Which of the following heritability estimates would be most likely in this case?
a. 0 percent
b. 25 percent
c. 70 percent
d. 90 percent

The Psychodynamic Perspective

One morning, in Sally's philosophy class, the professor referred to the ideas of Sigmund Freud. Later in the day the professor in a literature class used Freud's ideas to explain hidden meanings in a poem about dreams. Then a sociology professor used Freud's ideas to explain aggressive behavior in some members of society. *Why have Freud's ideas been influential in so many disciplines?* ■

Sigmund Freud (1856–1939), a neurologist, developed both a theory of personality (psychodynamic theory) that emphasized unconscious factors and a therapy (psychoanalytic therapy) for patients exhibiting abnormal behaviors (see Chapter 14). Today almost everyone knows the name Sigmund Freud. Have you ever heard or used the terms *Freudian slip, unconscious,* or *repression?* If you have, you should recognize Freud's impact. As we saw in the case of Sally's classes, Freud's views and theories have found their way into several academic disciplines as well as into everyday speech. One reason for the pervasiveness of Freud's thinking is that he suggested that our behaviors may be determined by irrational forces outside of conscious awareness.

To understand Freud, it is important to understand the times in which he lived. Freud was born to Jewish parents in Austria in 1856 and grew up in Vienna. He lived during the Victorian era, a time notorious for its repressive views of sexuality. The prevailing social norms prohibited the discussion of sex. The time was also marked by extreme anti-Semitism (prejudice against Jews), which blocked Freud from pursuing a career as a scientist. His future looked bleak, and he needed money to get married, so he reluctantly went into private practice as a neurologist.

Most of Freud's patients were women who suffered from hysterical disorders. (As described in Chapter 13, these disorders involve physical symptoms such as blindness or paralysis that have no known physical cause.) Freud proposed that these disorders resulted from psychological conflicts, especially sexual ones. During therapy sessions, his patients related stories of sexual contact with an older male. At first Freud believed that these events had actually occurred, but later he changed his mind and concluded that they were fantasies. He believed his patients could not differentiate their sexual desires from what had actually happened earlier in their lives. Some critics believe Freud had uncovered evidence of sexual abuse of children, which he was either unwilling to report or unable to accept as true (Masson, 1985).

Freud believed that his patients were not consciously aware of these sexual conflicts. If these conflicts were not brought to conscious awareness, they would continue to exert an influence in the form of physical and psychological symptoms. To deal with these symptoms and to bring the conflicts to the conscious level, Freud developed a therapeutic approach called *psychoanalysis* or *psychoanalytic therapy* (see Chapter 14).

Sigmund Freud, a neurologist, developed both a theory of personality that emphasized unconscious factors and a therapy for patients exhibiting abnormal behaviors.

Basic Concepts

Three concepts form the backbone of Freud's theory: psychic determinism, instincts, and levels of consciousness. Let's look at each of these concepts.

Psychic Determinism.   **Psychic determinism** refers to the influence of the past on the present. Freud believed that much of our behavior, feeling, and thinking is determined by events that occurred earlier in our lives. For example, sexual conflicts occurring in childhood can bring on physical symptoms in adulthood.

Psychological Detective

What does the term Freudian slip *mean to you? What, if anything, do you think a Freudian slip reveals about a person? Give these questions some thought, and write down your answer before reading further.*

A Freudian slip is one example of the concept of psychic determinism. According to Freud, these errors in reading, speaking, or writing reveal something about our "inner" thoughts or "real" intent. Imagine attending an extremely boring party, which drags on for more hours than you can count. After several hours, you decide to leave and typically intend to say something like, "I'm sorry I have to leave now." Your true feelings, however, may be revealed in words such as "I'm glad I have to leave now."

Instincts.   What inner forces might lead to these Freudian slips? Freud believed we are driven by the energy of certain instincts in much the same way that a car is propelled by the energy contained in gasoline. He described two key instincts: *eros* for life-giving and pleasure-producing activities, including sex, and *thanatos* for aggression or destruction.

The Unconscious.   The third major concept in psychodynamic theory is Freud's proposal that there are various levels of consciousness. In Chapter 5 we defined *consciousness* as personal awareness of internal and external events.

psychic determinism
The psychodynamic assumption that all behaviors result from early childhood experiences, especially conflicts related to sexual instincts

unconscious

Part of the personality that lies outside of awareness yet is believed to be a crucial determinant of behavior

id

In psychodynamic theory, the most basic element of the personality; it is the source of the instincts and operates on the pleasure principle

Freud described three levels of consciousness (see Figure 12-6). The conscious level refers to the thoughts, wishes, and emotions you are aware of at this moment. The level just below consciousness is called the preconscious; its contents are waiting to be pulled into consciousness like fish from a pond.

The third, and in Freud's theory the most important, level of consciousness (or awareness) is below the preconscious and is called the **unconscious.** The unconscious consists of thoughts, wishes, and feelings that exist beyond our awareness; we can gain access to them only with great effort. The techniques of psychodynamic therapy are designed to gain access to the contents of the unconscious (see Chapter 14). Freud believed that much of our behavior is caused by unconscious forces, that the contents of conscious thought are only a small portion of our inner life.

The Structure of the Mind

According to Freud's comprehensive theory, the mind consists of three separate but interacting elements: the id, the ego, and the superego. (Note he was not describing actual parts of the brain but hypothetical concepts.) This model compares the mind to an iceberg (see Figure 12-6). Just as most of an iceberg lies beneath the surface of the water, much of what is truly significant in psychodynamic theory lies below conscious awareness. Figure 12-6 also depicts the relationship of the three components of the mind to the levels of consciousness discussed earlier. The next sections examine that relationship.

The Id.   The **id** represents the primitive, biological side of our personality. This reservoir of pleasure-seeking and aggressive instinctual energy aims to reduce tension that builds up when our wishes are thwarted. Moreover, the id is extremely selfish and has no concern for the needs or desires of others or for what society may want. As you can see in Figure 12-6, the id is entirely uncon-

FIGURE 12-6 Relationship of conscious, preconscious, and unconscious thought in Freudian theory.

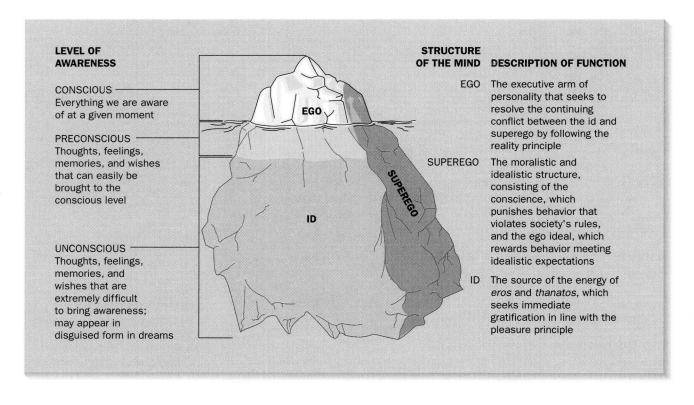

LEVEL OF AWARENESS

CONSCIOUS
Everything we are aware of at a given moment

PRECONSCIOUS
Thoughts, feelings, memories, and wishes that can easily be brought to the conscious level

UNCONSCIOUS
Thoughts, feelings, memories, and wishes that are extremely difficult to bring awareness; may appear in disguised form in dreams

EGO

SUPEREGO

ID

STRUCTURE OF THE MIND **DESCRIPTION OF FUNCTION**

EGO   The executive arm of personality that seeks to resolve the continuing conflict between the id and superego by following the reality principle

SUPEREGO   The moralistic and idealistic structure, consisting of the conscience, which punishes behavior that violates society's rules, and the ego ideal, which rewards behavior meeting idealistic expectations

ID   The source of the energy of *eros* and *thanatos*, which seeks immediate gratification in line with the pleasure principle

scious. Operating on the pleasure principle, it impulsively seeks immediate gratification of wishes through the ego.

The Ego.   As time passes, the id's relentless demands for instant gratification are reined in by a new structure, the ego. The **ego** is sometimes called the executive of the personality because it has a realistic plan for obtaining what the id wants; therefore it is said to operate on the reality principle. Seldom, however, do our surroundings provide immediate gratification of our needs, so the ego must tolerate some delay and occasional frustration.

The Superego.   The third element of the mind, the **superego,** has two components: the conscience and the ego ideal. Imagine yourself exceeding the speed limit while driving down a highway. Suddenly the red lights of a state police cruiser are reflected in your rear-view mirror. An anxious feeling spreads throughout your body, your heart beats rapidly, and you start to sweat as you wonder if the trooper is after you. When the cruiser zips by on its way to apprehend a "real" speeder, your heartbeat returns to normal. You reacted the way you did because you felt you had done something wrong and were about to be punished. This feeling stemmed from your conscience. This moral part of the superego is like a little voice that tells us when we have violated our parents' and society's rules. For many (but not all) of us, the conscience exacts punishment for even the possibility of violating those rules.

The second component of the superego, the ego ideal, represents the superego's positive side—the things that make us proud. Achieve excellent grades in school and the ego ideal "pats you on the back" in recognition of your accomplishment. The ego ideal aims for what is right, correct, and ideal; it motivates us to strive for perfection.

Interaction of Id, Ego, and Superego.   The relationship among the id, ego, and superego is like a car with some special features. Suppose that this car—call it IES (for id, ego, superego)—is designed to pull both to the left and to the right sides of the road, often at the same time. The left and right wheels represent the id and the superego, and they often try to turn in opposite directions. The id tries to satisfy basic biological drives; the superego strives to impose highly perfectionistic and moralistic goals in their place. Thus the id and the superego are unrealistic and irrational in separate but competing ways. The driver represents the ego and is responsible for making adjustments as the id and superego struggle against each other. The ego tries to find an acceptable middle road between these two divergent forces.

Defense Mechanisms

The ego is engaged in an ongoing battle to deal with the competing demands of the id and the superego. If you recall the iceberg model of the mind, you will realize that much of this conflict lies beneath the surface, in the unconscious.

Psychological Detective

Imagine that the id, ego, and superego are in conflict. How does a person know that this battle is happening? What does a person do when this conflict develops? Give these questions some thought, and write down your answers before reading further.

ego
In psychodynamic theory, the element of the mind that operates according to the reality principle and serves to satisfy the id and the superego

superego
In psychodynamic theory, the element of the mind that incorporates parental and societal standards in what is commonly referred to as the conscience as well as the idealistic ego ideal

defense mechanism

Psychodynamic term used to describe primarily unconscious methods of reducing anxiety or guilt that results from conflicts among the id, ego, and superego

repression

Defense mechanism in which anxiety-arousing ideas are pushed out of consciousness to the unconscious level of the mind

oral stage

The first stage of psychosexual development in which the mouth is the focus of pleasure-seeking activity

fixation

Cessation of further development, resulting in behaviors that are characteristic of the stage of development in which the fixation occurred

anal stage

Second stage of psychosexual development, during which the focus of pleasure is the anus and conflict often occurs as efforts are made to toilet-train the child

phallic stage

The third stage of psychosexual development, in which the genital organs become the focus of pleasure-seeking behavior

Oedipal complex

Process that occurs during the phallic stage in which a boy wishes to possess his mother sexually and fears retaliation by his father

Electra complex

Process that occurs during the phallic stage in which a girl wishes to possess her father sexually

Freud proposes that there is a never-ending battle between two irrational forces (the id and the superego) with a mediator (the ego) in the middle. Much of this conflict is unconscious, but when it becomes serious, an alarm goes off. In psychodynamic theory, anxiety or guilt is a warning to the ego that conflict is occurring.

When the anxiety or guilt alarm rings, the ego defends itself through unconscious efforts referred to as **defense mechanisms** (Freud, 1958) that tend to deny or distort reality (see Table 12-5). The effect of defense mechanisms is to reduce anxiety or guilt. The use of defense mechanisms, however, can be helpful or harmful, depending on how much a person relies on them.

One of the most basic defense mechanisms in psychodynamic theory is repression. **Repression** occurs when troublesome thoughts, such as the id's desire for immediate gratification of sexual desires, are pushed into the unconscious and kept there in order to reduce anxiety. Repressed thoughts, wishes, and memories are not lost forever, however. They may appear at another time disguised as dreams or slips of the tongue.

Stages of Psychosexual Development

Freud proposed that an individual's personality develops through a series of five stages stretching from infancy to adulthood. These stages are called *psychosexual stages* because each is characterized by efforts to obtain pleasure centered on one of several parts of the body called *erogenous zones*. According to Freud, the five stages of psychosexual development are the oral, anal, phallic, latency, and genital stages.

The Oral Stage.   Pleasure-seeking behavior in the **oral stage** focuses on the baby's mouth. Infants and toddlers can often be seen biting, sucking, or placing objects in their mouths. Freud hypothesized that if oral needs such as the need for food are delayed, the child's personality may become arrested or fixated. A person whose development is arrested will display behaviors as an adult that are associated with the time of life during which the **fixation** occurred. For example, fixation at the oral stage may be manifest in behaviors such as chewing on pencils or overeating and in personality characteristics such as excessive dependency, optimism, and gullibility.

The Anal Stage.   From about 18 months until about 3 years of age, the child is in the **anal stage.** As the child gains muscular control, the erogenous zone shifts to the anus, and the child derives pleasure from the retention and expulsion of feces. The key to this stage is toilet training. The way parents approach toilet training can have lasting effects on their children. If the parents are strict and demanding, the child may rebel, and the result will be fixation at this stage. Individuals who are fixated at this stage may be overly rigid and orderly as adults and are referred to as *anal-retentive.*

The Phallic Stage.   The phallic stage, which begins at about age 4 to 5, is ushered in by another shift in the erogenous zone and the child's pleasure-seeking behavior. During this stage, children derive pleasure from fondling their genitals. The **phallic stage** is also the time when the **Oedipal complex** (in boys) or the **Electra complex** (in girls) occurs.

Freud believed that young boys develop a sexual interest in their mothers, see their fathers as competitors for the mothers' affection, and therefore wish to get rid of their fathers. The name of this complex is derived from Oedipus, a character in an ancient Greek tragedy who had unwittingly killed his father and married his mother; when he discovered the truth, he gouged out his eyes and spent the rest of his life as a homeless wanderer.

The young boy fears his father's retaliation for these forbidden sexual and aggressive impulses. He fantasizes that the father's retaliation would involve injury

TABLE 12-5 Defense Mechanisms

Defense mechanisms protect the ego by distorting or otherwise altering reality. Although everyone uses defense mechanisms, excessive use of them is considered a sign of abnormality.

DEFENSE MECHANISM	DESCRIPTIONS	EXAMPLES
Denial	Refusing to acknowledge an undesirable experience, memory, or internal need that is anxiety-arousing and behaving as if it did not exist.	A physician tells a parent that her son has terminal cancer. Despite overwhelming evidence that the cancer is not treatable, the parent remains convinced that the child will recover.
Displacement	Shifting feelings from one object to a substitute that is not as gratifying but is less anxiety-arousing.	You want to retaliate against your boss for something she said to you during a performance evaluation. The ego, being relatively wise and in contact with reality, recognizes that such a course of action would be ill-advised. Later in the day, you find yourself yelling at the grocery clerk, cutting off other drivers on the way home, and hanging up on callers soliciting funds for a local charity. Each of these innocent bystanders is a safer outlet for aggression than your boss and hence is less threatening to the ego.
Projection	Attributing to others our own unwanted feelings, thoughts, or behaviors.	A person who is having difficulty making it to work on time because of procrastination and failure to meet deadlines says, "It's not my fault. My bosses are just too demanding, and my co-workers are uncooperative."
Rationalization	Proposing socially acceptable feelings or reasons in place of actual, unacceptable feelings or reasons for a behavior.	You did not do well on an exam in your economics course. You could admit that you found the material impossible to comprehend, but perhaps this admission would lead to additional anxiety. So you may tell yourself, and anyone else who is listening, that you "don't want to be an economist anyway."
Reaction formation	Defending against unacceptable feelings and behavior by exhibiting the opposite of one's true wishes or impulses.	A person may be attracted to pornographic material (id) yet be repulsed by the thought of such material (superego). Such a person may become involved in a censorship campaign that places him or her in the position of having having to review pornographic material.
Regression	Returning to forms of behavior that are indicative of an earlier level of development such as childhood (usually in response to an overwhelming stressor).	An adult has a temper tantrum (a common behavior of 3- or 4-year-olds).
Sublimation	A form of displacement in which a sexual or aggressive impulse is moved from an unacceptable object to one that is acceptable and ultimately has value to society.	A typical example of sublimation involves the direction of sexual energy toward the creation of works of art. Another example involves turning aggressive energy toward socially desirable goals such as surgery to save lives, rather than harming others.

The first stage of Freud's psychosexual stages—the oral stage—consists of attaining pleasure via the mouth.

to his genitals; as a result, he experiences what is called *castration anxiety*. To reduce the fear, the boy represses his sexual desire for his mother and begins to identify with his father, which means that he tries to be like dad in his behavior, values, attitudes, and sexual orientation. Successful resolution of the Oedipal complex, according to Freud, leads to acquisition of the male sex role (see Chapter 11).

The Electra complex is named for a character in another Greek tragedy who conspired to kill her mother to avenge her father's death. Young girls become aware that they do not have penises, which Freud believed they both value and desire. Thus girls experience *penis envy*, which leads to anger directed at their mothers and sexual attraction toward their fathers. A girl's attraction to her father is rooted in a fantasy that seducing him will provide her with a penis. She also fantasizes about having a baby as another means of gaining the valued organ. Resolution of this complex occurs when the girl represses her sexual desires and begins to identify with her mother.

Freud believed that the male superego receives an intense unconscious push from Oedipal castration fears and that the female superego ends up weaker than that of the male. This belief, however, like a number of Freudian ideas, has not been supported by research (Bower, 1991).

The Latency and Genital Stages. At about age 6, children enter a period when their sexual interests are suppressed. This period, which lasts until the beginning of adolescence, is called the **latency stage.** Sexual interests are reawakened at puberty and become stronger during the **genital stage.** In this stage sexual pleasure is derived from heterosexual relationships. At the beginning of the genital stage, most adolescents have difficulty developing true affection and caring for others; they still experience the selfish qualities of earlier stages of development. As they mature, they develop greater ability to establish such relationships, thus setting the foundation for adult relationships.

Freud in Perspective

Freud attracted both supporters and critics. Some of his most outspoken critics were formerly his greatest admirers who once espoused his views, but for a variety of reasons they developed new perspectives that nonetheless fit the psychodynamic mold. For example, they did not accept Freud's emphasis on the id and the role of sexual motives; instead they emphasized the ego and its role in the development of personality, as well as the social aspects of personality. These individuals are frequently referred to as neo-Freudians.

The Neo-Freudians. One of the best-known neo-Freudians, Carl Jung (1875–1961), split from Freud on more than one issue and developed his own psychodynamic viewpoint. Jung suggested that a *collective unconscious* contains images shared by all people. Jung's name for these images is *archetypes*. These archetypes are passed along genetically and cause us to respond to events in our environment in particular ways.

Karen Horney (1885–1952), an early disciple of Freudian thinking, rejected several Freudian notions and added several of her own. She viewed personality disturbances not as resulting from instinctual strivings to satisfy sexual and aggressive urges but as stemming from the basic anxiety that all people share. We all feel anxiety because we find ourselves isolated and sometimes helpless in an unfriendly world.

Alfred Adler (1870–1937) believed that Freud overemphasized the sexual drive in explaining personality. He argued that the primary drive is social rather than sexual. Specifically, it is a drive for superiority, which begins early in life because we are born with a sense of inferiority. Look at a very young child for a

latency stage
Stage of psychosexual development that extends from about age 6 until the onset of puberty and is characterized by low levels of sexual interest

genital stage
Stage of psychosexual development that begins at puberty and usually leads to normal adult sexual development

STUDY CHART

Freud's Stages of Psychosexual Development

Stage	Approximate Ages	Erogenous Zones	Major Characteristics
Oral	Birth to about 18 months	Mouth	Focus on oral gratification from sucking, chewing, eating, and biting
Anal	End of oral stage to 3 years	Anus	Gratification from holding and expelling feces at the time when these desires for gratification must meet societal demands to control the bladder and bowels (toilet training)
Phallic	End of anal stage to about 6 years	Genitals	Gratification focused on manipulation of genitals; development of sexual interest in the parent of opposite biological sex
Latency	End of phallic stage	None	Sexual desires not of paramount importance
Genital	Adolescence to adulthood	Genitals	Resurgence of sexual interests; focus on mature sexual adulthood relationships

moment; what you see is cute and cuddly and totally helpless as compared with adults. Adler suggested that children notice their helplessness and inferiority in relation to adults. This sense of inferiority motivates them to develop new skills and abilities that lead to a sense of superiority. Thus Adler shifted the emphasis in personality theory from the id to the ego, which strives to gain control over others. He noted that we spend much of our lives striving to compensate for our perceived shortcomings. For example, the Greek philosopher Demosthenes was embarrassed by his stuttering as a child, so he spent years practicing speaking clearly and eventually became a great orator.

Evaluation of Freudian Theory.   When Freud first published his ideas in the early 1900s, they met with strong negative reactions, especially his notions of sexuality in children. Most people were repulsed by the idea of viewing children as sexual beings. When Freud published his classic book on dreams, about 300 copies were sold.

Eventually Freud's ideas caught on, and they have had a lasting impact. Some researchers report that many of Freud's proposals such as unconscious influences on emotional responses, social behavior, and habitual behavior are supported by research (Westen, 1998); nevertheless, there are a great number of critics (Bower, 1998) who note that it is difficult to test psychodynamic concepts. For example, it is almost impossible to examine the effect of parenting practices on fixations because Freud did not specify the conditions that might lead to fixations. Even when such concepts can be tested, the tests have had mixed results. Significantly, Freud's theory is based on the study of a small number of disturbed people, who may not provide the basis for generalizations applicable to most people.

On the other side of the coin, Freud drew attention to the potential importance of early childhood experiences; he was the first to outline a stage theory of development and to identify key influences operating at each stage. Freud is also credited with drawing attention to the impact of sexuality on human behavior. It undoubtedly took courage for him to offer his ideas at a time when the public wanted to keep sexuality hidden and repressed. He noted the importance of unconscious factors in determining behavior. We are often unaware of the motivations and rationales that underlie our behavior. Some observers therefore view the concept of the unconscious as one of the enduring contributions of psychodynamic theory (Westen, 1998).

Freud's work also popularized counseling and psychotherapy in the United States and around the world. His ideas have been applied to the development of the form of psychotherapy called *psychoanalysis*, which strives to bring unconscious conflicts to the surface so that an individual can deal with them more effectively.

Still, critics note that Freud developed a theory that focused on concern for one's own desires, irresponsibility, and the denigration of women. For example, Freud saw women as more vain than men and having little sense of justice, along with a perpetual sense of inferiority owing to the lack of a penis. What's more, Freud's belief in unconscious instinctual drives may well have overstated the case for such influences.

Historically, a number of psychological perspectives developed, in part, in opposition to psychodynamic theory. Compared with Freud and his followers, these perspectives had very different views on the development of personality. We turn our attention to personality as viewed from the humanistic, cognitive, and learning perspectives.

Review Summary

1. Freud suggested that behaviors, feelings, and thoughts result from past events. Because this **psychic determinism** occurs at an unconscious level, we are often unaware of the true reasons for our behavior.

2. Freud compared the mind to an iceberg, with three levels of consciousness (*conscious, preconscious, and unconscious*) and three structures (**id, ego,** and **superego**). Conflicts among the structures of the mind occur beneath the level of conscious awareness.

3. Severe unconscious conflict produces anxiety or guilt that warn the ego. The ego uses **defense mechanisms** to protect itself from being overwhelmed by anxiety or guilt. **Repression** is the most basic defense mechanism.

4. According to Freud, at different stages of development the id centers its pleasure-seeking behavior on different parts of the body, called *erogenous zones*. The resulting psychosexual stages begin with the **oral stage** and continue through the **anal** and **phallic stages**. The **Oedipal** and **Electra complexes** occur during the phallic stage. This stage is followed by the **latency stage** and then by the **genital stage** and the emergence of adult sexual desires.

5. The neo-Freudians—including Jung, Horney, and Adler—disagreed with a number of Freud's views (e.g., those emphasizing the sexual and unconscious roots of behavior).

6. Freud is credited with pointing out the influence of early childhood experiences and with developing a stage theory of development. In addition, he noted the potential importance of unconscious experiences and the influence of sexuality on human behavior.

7. Critics of psychodynamic theory note that Freud based his ideas on small, unrepresentative samples of disturbed individuals.

Study Break

1. Consider each of the following situations, and determine whether the conflict involves the id, ego, and/or superego.
   a. You have not studied for an exam and are afraid that you will fail it. Your neighbor's paper is within sight, and you begin to think about "borrowing" some of her answers.
   b. You are late for an appointment on the other side of town. You are afraid that you will miss an important opportunity if you don't get there soon. While driving to your appointment, you spot a police cruiser just ahead of you.

2. Identify the stage of psychosexual development (oral, anal, phallic, latency, genital) described in each of the following statements:
   a. The Oedipus and Electra complexes occur during this stage.
   b. A child enjoys biting and chewing on almost any object.
   c. This period is relatively calm as far as sexual interests are concerned.

3. Identify the defense mechanism described in each of the following examples.
  a. Miguel did not get the job he wanted; he is having a temper tantrum.
  b. Amber turned her sexual and aggressive energies into an effort to create a sculpture.
  c. Bill forgot his appointment for root canal work for the fifth time this month.
  d. You just got a big fat F on your term paper, which means you are probably going to fail the class. On the way home from school, you cut off several drivers and you yell at your brother as soon as you walk in the house.

4. In which psychosexual stage do sexual interests reawaken and become stronger?
  a. latency
  b. genital
  c. phallic
  d. anal

5. What did Alfred Adler suggest as the primary motivating element in the development of personality?
  a. feelings of inferiority
  b. aggressive energy
  c. the "will to be"
  d. repressed sexuality

The Social-Cognitive and Humanistic Perspectives

A major exam is scheduled for next week. Alice and Gil overhear several students predicting they will fail; others say they expect to "ace" the test. These differing expectations seem puzzling because everyone will take the same exam. Later that day, Alice and Gil talk about trying to stop smoking. Alice is certain she will succeed, but Gil doubts he will be able to quit. After realizing they sound like the students who talked about the exam, they begin wondering why some people are sure they will "ace" an exam or quit smoking, whereas others are unsure. *What role do beliefs have in our understanding of personality?* ▪

Learning and Cognitive Perspectives

As we noted in Chapter 1, John B. Watson tried to rid psychology of terms like *thinking* and urged psychologists to avoid speculating about inner, unobservable processes. This behavioral or learning perspective was taken up by B. F. Skinner, who emphasized environmental contingencies in explaining human behavior. Skinner suggested the same principles that applied to rats and pigeons in his laboratory could be applied to humans (see Chapter 6).

According to Skinner, we can explain the distinctiveness of individual personalities without using terms like *traits*. Each person's behavior is distinctive because each one experiences different histories of reinforcement and punishment. Skinner focused attention on the environmental factors that initiate and maintain behaviors that ultimately distinguish one person from another. For example, John acts aggressively because he was probably reinforced for past aggressive behaviors. If Natasha's friends describe her as having a great sense of humor, her past joke telling probably resulted in reinforcement. According to behavioral or learning psychologists, there is no need to use a concept such as *traits* in explaining John's aggressiveness or Natasha's sense of humor.

Few psychologists would dismiss the importance of environmental influences like reinforcement. Even studies of the heritability of personality tell us that the environment plays a role; learning can influence personality. Some psychologists, however, say there is more to understanding personality than a person's learning experiences might suggest.

Rotter's Social Learning Theory.   Learning is a powerful tool for under-standing animal and human behavior; however, classical and operant conditioning do not explain all the learning that takes place. For example, research on modeling tells us that people can learn without direct experience (see Chapter 6).

Julian Rotter notes that reinforcement does not automatically stamp in a behavior. Most of the reinforcers we strive to obtain are social (e.g., hugs, attention, praise), and most learning occurs in social situations (Rotter, 1990). Rotter combined these observations in his social learning theory of personality, which incorporated cognitive factors. He acknowledges the role of cognitive factors in understanding human behavior, noting that behavior is often a function of *expectancies.*

The concept of *expectancy* is one of the most important elements of Rotter's theory. When you take an exam, apply for a job, or ask someone out on a date, you have some notion of the likelihood of success or failure. Generalized expectancies operate across a wide variety of situations; specific expectancies are limited to par-ticular situations. What's more, people differ in their tendencies to view them-selves as capable of influencing reinforcers or being subject to fate (Strickland, 1989). Some people, called *internals,* believe that they can influence their rein-forcers via their skill and ability. Others, called *externals,* believe that whether they attain a desired outcome is due primarily to chance or fate (Rotter, 1990).

Rotter (1966) devised the Internal-External (I-E) Scale to measure individuals' *locus of control* (internal or external); since then, locus of control has become one of the most studied concepts in psychology. Each of the 23 items on the I-E Scale offers a choice between an external alternative and an internal one (see Table 12-6).

Why does one person score in the external direction whereas another obtains a score indicating an internal locus of control? One factor that accounts for differences in locus of control is the individual's learning history. Thus Rotter continued Skinner's emphasis on the importance of learning; he carried it further, however, by recognizing that past learning affects not just behaviors but also *expectancies* about whether certain behaviors lead to desired outcomes. Cultural factors seem to influence locus-of-control scores. For example, people in Western countries tend to have more internal scores than people in Far Eastern countries, especially Japan (Berry et al., 1992). Low socioeconomic status tends to be linked with external locus of control.

TABLE 12-6   Sample Items from Rotter's Internal-External Control Scale

The total score is tabulated by adding 1 point for each item in which an individual selects the externally worded alternative. Thus high scores indicate an external locus of control, and low scores indicate an internal locus of control.

1. **a.** Becoming a success is a matter of hard work; luck has little or nothing to do with it.
   b. Getting a good job depends mainly on being in the right place at the right time.*
2. **a.** When I make plans, I am almost certain that I can make them work.
   b. It is not always wise to plan too far ahead because many things turn out to be a matter of good or bad fortune anyway.*
3. **a.** Most people don't realize the extent to which their lives are controlled by accidental happenings.*
   b. There really is no such thing as "luck."
4. **a.** What happens to me is my own doing.
   b. Sometimes I feel that I don't have enough control over the direction my life is taking.*
5. **a.** Many times I feel that I have little influence over the things that happen to me.*
   b. It is impossible for me to believe that chance or luck plays an important role in my life.

*External alternative.
Source: Rotter, 1966.

The concept of locus of control has a wide range of uses and applications (Strickland, 1989). For example, during the 1960s, researchers discovered that internals were more likely than externals to attend civil rights rallies, sign petitions, or participate in a "freedom ride" to challenge racial segregation in the South. Locus of control is related to measures of school achievement: Internals tend to outperform externals on standardized measures of achievement (Findley & Cooper, 1983).

Locus of control is also related to health behaviors. Internals are more likely to interpret threatening events as challenges. They are more likely to reduce their stress by solving problems that are threatening; by contrast, externals focus on their own emotional responses rather than on the threats. Consequently, internals' reactions to stress are less negative, and externals experience greater anxiety (Lefcourt & Davidson-Katz, 1991).

Bandura's Social Cognitive Theory.

Albert Bandura is well known for his research on observational learning or modeling of aggressive behavior and for using modeling to overcome phobias (see Chapter 6). A fundamental question that personality psychologists ask is, Why do people act as they do? According to Bandura (1986), the answer is that a combination of factors, including an individual's cognitions and the environment, interact to produce a particular behavior. These factors are not independent; they work together and influence one another (Bandura, 1986). This notion, known as **reciprocal determinism,** tells us that the person, environment, and behavior influence one another (see Figure 12-7). The behavioral/learning approaches focus on how environments (situations) influence behaviors (libraries are conducive to studying). An individual's personality also influences behavior, however, as the trait perspective has emphasized. Reciprocal determinism goes beyond these simple explanations of behavior as the result of either situations or personality by suggesting that our behavior can change the environment (studying instead of spending time with friends reduces social pressures or invitations to go out). Thus the environment is not only a cause of behavior, but it is also an effect of behavior. For example, one way personality influences situations is that we select situations differently, depending on our personalities. Achievement-oriented students are likely to spend their time in the library; extraverted people are likely to attend parties and other social gatherings. A complete understanding of personality requires recognition of the mutual influences among the person, the situation (environment), and behavior (Cloninger, 1996).

Another key concept in Bandura's theory is **self-efficacy,** a person's beliefs about his or her skills and ability to perform certain behaviors. The greater a person's sense of self-efficacy, the more confidence that person has in his or her ability to deal with life's challenges. A person's sense of self-efficacy has a powerful effect on his or her behavior, yet self-efficacy is not considered a trait. Why? Self-efficacy can be understood only in relation to specific behaviors and in specific situations. Unlike locus of control, it is not generalized across situations.

Four sources of information can influence self-efficacy. The first is past performance (successes or failures). The second is watching others in similar situations and noting the consequences they experience. The effect of observing others depends on factors such as one's similarity to the observed person. Third, verbal persuasion can also affect levels of self-efficacy; its effect depends on the persuader's trustworthiness and level of expertise. Finally, self-efficacy can be related to physiological arousal. For example, we may associate aversive emotional states with poor performance, perceived incompetence, or perceived failure (Maddux, 1991).

Albert Bandura added a concern for cognitive factors to the learning theorists' emphasis on external causes.

reciprocal determinism
Contention that person variables, situation variables, and behavior constantly interact

self-efficacy
A person's expectancy concerning his or her ability to engage in effective behaviors; such expectancies differ from one behavior to another

FIGURE 12-7 Bandura's model of reciprocal determinism.
Source: Bandura, 1986.

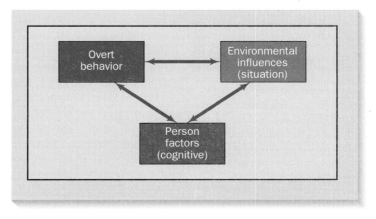

humanistic psychology
General approach to psychology, associated with Abraham Maslow and Carl Rogers, that emphasizes individuals' control of their behavior

self-actualization
Need to develop one's full potential

The concept of self-efficacy has been applied to a range of outcomes. For example, measures of self-efficacy predict final course grades among high school and college students (Hackett et al., 1992; Zimmerman, Bandura, & Martinez-Pons, 1992). Self-efficacy also predicts the ability to resist relapse after treatment for alcohol problems (Rchtarik et al., 1992), it is also related to a career outcomes such as career exploration (Solberg, 1998) and to how people attempt computer-related tasks (Brosnan, 1998).

The Humanistic Perspective

Not all psychologists believe that our behavior is determined by early childhood experiences, biological drives, or even learning histories. Some believe that to understand human behavior, we must look at unique human aspects and qualities. What sets us apart from lower animals is not objective reality but rather our ability to make choices and our individual perspectives on the world.

A group of theorists called **humanistic psychologists** oppose the basic beliefs of both psychodynamic theory and behaviorism. Rather than concentrate on unconscious motivation and past experience, they focus on the present and the healthy personality. What's more, they view the individual's perceptions of events as more significant than the learning theorist's or therapist's perceptions. For these reasons, they are often called *phenomenological psychologists*. (Phenomenology is the study of experience just as it occurs.) The two most notable representatives of this humanistic or phenomenological perspective are Abraham Maslow and Carl Rogers.

Abraham Maslow.   Abraham Maslow (1908–1970) described humanistic psychology as the "third force" in American psychology because it offered an alternative to psychodynamic theory and behaviorism. He viewed those perspectives as incomplete because they emphasized early childhood experience or viewed people as captives of their environments. In addition, he did not believe the study of laboratory animals or individuals suffering from psychological disorders provided a proper foundation for understanding human behavior.

Basic Needs.   According to Maslow, human beings have a set of needs that are organized in a hierarchy (see Chapter 4). Deficiency needs begin with physiological needs and move on to needs for safety, love and belongingness, and self-esteem. These basic needs exert a powerful pull on our behavior. Once you satisfy physiological needs, you can turn to needs for safety or to be loved by others. The basic biological needs exert a great deal of influence on our behavior, so much so that most people never reach the top level of the hierarchy.

Self-Actualization.   **Self-actualization** involves making "the full use and exploitation of talents, capacities, potentialities" (Maslow, 1970, p. 150). In other words, it is the need to develop one's full potential. Maslow believed that this need exists in everyone but is often thwarted by the environment. When our basic needs are met, energy is available for use in striving for greater understanding of ourselves and our surroundings. To illustrate these concepts, Maslow looked for healthy, self-actualized individuals who were doing the best that they are capable of doing.

Maslow's list of self-actualized people included Abraham Lincoln, Thomas Jefferson, Eleanor Roosevelt, and Albert Einstein. Because a number of them were deceased, he relied on historical documents to study them. The details of his analysis of these self-actualized individuals are sketchy, but he arrived at several general conclusions about their characteristics (see Table 12-7). For example, he found that these individuals tended to have accurate percep-

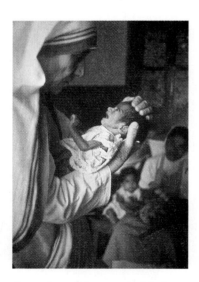

A number of the people Maslow identified as self-actualized were historical figures who he analyzed by studying historical documents. Although she is now dead, there is a great deal of evidence to suggest that Mother Teresa would fit Maslow's description of self actualization.

TABLE 12-7 **Characteristics of Maslow's Sample of Self-Actualized Individuals**

Accept their own natures

Are spontaneous and natural

Are deeply democratic in nature

Like privacy and tend to be detached

Focus on problems outside themselves

Exhibit a strong ethical and moral sense

Have close but limited number of friendships

Are independent of their cultural and social environment

Prefer a philosophical rather than a hostile type of humor

Have efficient perceptions of reality and are comfortable with those perceptions

Source: Maslow, 1970.

tions of their environments and were comfortable with those perceptions. Keep in mind that Maslow's selection process is subject to the same criticism that was directed at Freud's psychodynamic theory: The list of self-actualized individuals is not representative of the general population.

Maslow tried to move the study of personality away from the concern with pathology that was evident in Freud's work. He held a distinctly positive view of human nature. Many of his concepts, however, such as self-actualization, are difficult to test empirically.

Carl Rogers. Carl Rogers (1902–1987) shared Maslow's belief that people are innately good and are directed toward growth, development, and personal fulfillment. What's more, he believed there is an "inherent tendency of the organism to develop all its capabilities in ways which serve to maintain or enhance the person" (Rogers, 1959, p. 196). Unfortunately, his clinical experience told him that people are frequently derailed from their quests for fulfillment.

As we develop, our concept of self emerges. The *self* is our sense of "I" or "me"; it is generally conscious and accessible and is a central concept in Rogers's theory. The self-concept is our perception of our abilities, behaviors, and characteristics. Rogers believed that we act in accordance with our self-concept. If we have a positive self-concept, we tend to act in positive ways; if we have a negative self-concept, we often act in negative ways.

Maslow and Rogers agreed that people have a strong need to be loved, to experience affection. Sometimes, however, people experience affection that is conditional—given only if they engage in behaviors that are approved by others. Rogers contrasted this conditional regard with what he called *unconditional positive regard,* in which a person is accepted for what he or she is, not for what others would like the person to be. According to Rogers, if you grow up believing affection is conditional, you will distort your own experiences in order to feel worthy of acceptance from a wider range of people. For example, children may be told they are incapable of doing something or they are stupid, nasty, or disobedient. This may

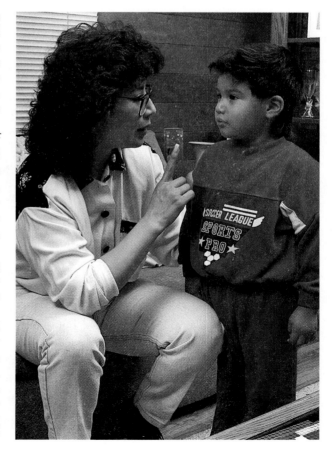

Conditional positive regard can have a negative impact on a child's developing self-concept.

lead them to understand that conditions are placed on their self-worth; as a result, they may begin to question themselves. This conditional positive regard, in which love and praise are not given unless the child conforms to the expectations of others, can have negative effects on the child's self-concept.

Think of the self as two sides of a coin. One side is the self as it really is, a product of our experiences; this is called the *real self*. The other side is the *ideal self,* the self we would like to be. Maladjustment results when there is a discrepancy between the real self and the ideal self—when the two sides of the coin do not match up.

Rogers used a technique called the Q-sort to measure the degree to which the real self-concept matched the ideal self-concept. To complete a Q-sort, the client is given a stack of cards with statements about the self such as "I am generally a happy person," "I am confident," or "I am upset much of the time." The client reads each card and then responds along a continuum that ranges from "Very characteristic of me" to "Not at all characteristic of me." In this way the client provides a picture of his or her real self-concept. The cards are then reshuffled and the client is given a new task—to place the cards on the same continuum in such a way as to indicate his or her ideal self-concept.

Psychological Detective

The Q-sort provides a great deal of information about a person. How could we analyze this information to determine the degree of congruence between a person's real and ideal selves? Remember that there are two sets of cards—one representing the real self and the other representing the ideal self. We are interested in determining the relationship between these two sets of cards. Give this question some thought, and write down your answer before reading further.

Correlations (see Chapter 1) between the two sets of card arrangements provide insight into the discrepancy or similarity between a person's real and ideal self-concepts. Higher correlations are found in well-adjusted individuals, lower correlations in disturbed individuals. This technique has also been used to demonstrate progress resulting from psychotherapy. As clients improve, their real and ideal self-concepts become more congruent; that is, the correlations become higher.

Cultural & Diversity Perspective

The Self in a Social Context

SUPPOSE WE ASKED YOU TO "DESCRIBE YOURSELF BRIEFLY." WHAT WOULD YOU write? Would descriptions written by you and your friends be similar or different from those written by people of similar ages in other countries and cultures? In essence, this question is designed to determine your self concept. "What people actually mean and understand as the self is dramatically different" depending on culture (Matsumoto, 1996).

American responses to this simple question tend to be more confident and elaborated. Japanese responses tend to be more tentative, and more concerned with the responses of others (Markus & Kitayama, 1998). What's more, most American respondents focus on ways that make them unique in comparisons to others. This way of responding is characteristic of what has been called an *individualist* (independent) conception of the self (Markus & Kitayama, 1991). In contrast, people in Asian cultures emphasize what has been called a *collectivist* (or interdependent) conception of the self (see Chapter 4).

These two ways of perceiving the self have significant consequences. For example, Japanese children in the second, third, and fifth grades were asked to evaluate a child who described his superb athletic talent in a modest, self-restrained way versus a self-enhancing way. The older children described the person who described his abilities modestly as a good person; fifth graders tended to view the self-enhancing description negatively. The older children tended to view the person who described his ability in a self-enhancing way as actually inferior to the modest description.

How do such differences in the evaluation of self develop? They reflect differences in socialization. Asian cultures tend to emphasize modesty and self-restraint, whereas American children are taught that "the squeaky wheel gets the oil." Conversely, Japanese children are taught, "The nail that stands out gets pounded down." These differences in socialization and their effects on behavior should serve as a reminder that when we speak of personality, we need to keep in mind the cultural context in which we ask questions concerning personality.

STUDY CHART

Overview of the Major Perspectives on Personality

Perspective	Key Figures	Strengths	Weaknesses
Trait	Gordon Allport, Raymond Cattell, Hans Eysenck	Describes the major dimensions on which individuals differ from one another	Sometimes emphasizes different traits as key ones; may not provide an explanation of the development of traits
Biological	William Sheldon, University of Minnesota Twins Reared Apart Project	Focuses on biological aspects of individuals' differences with a special emphasis on genetic influences	May misinterpret research to conclude that environmental factors are not important or that personality cannot change
Psychodynamic	Sigmund Freud, neo-Freudians	Uses case studies to provide in-depth assessment of individuals; focuses on the importance of unconscious processes and conflict as key factors in the development of personality	Uses concepts that are difficult to define and to study; overemphasizes the importance of early development
Social-cognitive	Julian Rotter, Albert Bandura	Adds a cognitive focus to learning-theory explanations of personality	Does not appear to account for broad consistencies in behavior; does not account for genetic influences on personality
Humanistic	Carl Rogers, Abraham Maslow	Focuses on conscious influences on behavior and on the more positive aspects of human nature	Uses concepts, such as self-actualization, that are difficult to define and to measure; takes an overly optimistic view of human nature

Review Summary

1. Behavioral and learning psychologists avoid commonly used terms such as *traits*. They explain the distinctiveness of a person's behavior as resulting from unique learning histories.

2. While acknowledging the importance of learning, Julian Rotter and Albert Bandura incorporated cognitive factors into their theories of personality.

3. Rotter's social learning theory recognizes that most reinforcers are social and that most learning takes place in social situations. Expectancy about obtaining a reinforcer in a given situation is an important cognitive variable. Individuals differ in the degree to which they see themselves or chance ("fate") as responsible for their successes and failures.

4. Measures of generalized expectancy, known as *locus of control,* are related to a variety of outcomes, including academic and health behaviors.

5. According to Albert Bandura, individuals not only are affected by the environment but also can influence it. Moreover, cognitive factors can influence the person's behavior and his or her environment. This combination of cognitive, behavioral, and environmental

effects is called **reciprocal determinism.**

6. Self-efficacy is a person's judgment about his or her ability to succeed in a given situation. Unlike a trait, self-efficacy is specific to the situation and can change over time.

7. Humanistic approaches evolved in opposition to the behavioral and psychodynamic perspectives. They propose that human beings are basically good and are directed toward development and growth.

8. Abraham Maslow's hierarchy begins with deficiency needs and leads to **self-actualization** at the top. The power of deficiency needs keeps most people from reaching the level of self-actualization, which Maslow defines as doing the best that an individual is capable of doing.

9. On the basis of his work with disturbed people, Carl Rogers concluded that efforts to achieve personal fulfillment were being stifled. He proposed that people's self-concepts had become distorted by conditions of worth imposed from the outside. In his theory, healthy individuals have a real self-concept that is consistent with their ideal self-concept.

Study Break

1. In what way do the views of Watson and Skinner concerning personality differ from the views of Bandura and Rotter?

2. Identify each of the following terms:
   a. Rotter's term for generalized expectancies
   b. In Rotter's social learning theory, a person who believes he or she can influence events
   c. Bandura's term for the relationship among person, behavior, and environment
   d. In Bandura's theory, a person's belief that he or she has the skills to succeed in a given situation

3. What are some of the characteristics that Maslow identified in self-actualized individuals?

4. How did Rogers use correlation coefficients to assess the similarity between real and ideal self-concepts? What type of correlation coefficient would suggest a high degree of similarity?

5. Which of the following terms is most likely to describe the self concepts of people in Asian cultures?
   a. dominant
   b. interdependent
   c. authoritarian
   d. reactive

ANSWERS TO STUDY BREAKS

Page 505

1. a. MMPI
   b. CPI
   c. Rorschach inkblot test or TAT

2. a. Extraversion
   b. 16 source traits
3. a
4. c

5. Rather than look at single behaviors and their relationship to trait levels, researchers have added behaviors together (aggregation) and found evidence for consistency in behavior related to individuals' levels of a given trait.

Page 512

1. Hippocrates, humors
2. c
3. High correlations between identical twins reared together could be the result of similarities in the environment. When the twins are separated, the high correlations reflect hereditary influences on personality.
4. Current research has focused on the nonshared aspects of the environment in which siblings are reared as important influences on personality.
5. c
6. b

Pages 520–521

1. a. Id and superego
   b. Id, ego, and superego
2. a. Phallic
   b. Oral
   c. Latency

3. a. Regression
   b. Sublimation
   c. Repression
   d. Displacement
4. b
5. a

Page 528

1. Watson and Skinner do not consider cognitive factors to be important. Bandura and Rotter consider learning and cognitive factors necessary in understanding personality.
2. a. Locus of control
   b. Internal
   c. Reciprocal determinism
   d. Self efficacy
3. Efficient perception of reality, preference for philosophical rather than hostile humor, and strong ethical and moral sense
4. Rogers used the Q-sort to assess a person's actual and ideal self-concepts. High positive correlations between the two indicated good convergence and hence an accepting and healthy personality.
5. b

THE "BIG FIVE" TEST

Pages 500–501

To compute your score for each of the five scales, simply add your scores for the items that contribute to each of the scales.
Openness to Experience: 1, 6, 11, 16, 21
Conscientiousness: 2, 7, 12, 17, 22
Extraversion: 3, 8, 13, 18, 23
Agreeableness: 4, 9, 14, 19, 24
Neuroticism: 5, 10, 15, 20, 25

Mean scores for men and women on each of the scales are listed below:

	Men	Women
Openness to Experience	20.3	19.4
Conscientiousness	18.8	20.2
Extraversion	18.8	19.0
Agreeableness	18.8	22.2
Neuroticism	16.3	18.5

Source: Brody & Erlichman, 1998.

SCORING KEYS

Pages 507–508

Add one point to your score for each of the following answers.
1. a
2. a
3. a
4. b
5. a
6. b
7. a
8. a
9. b
10. b
11. a
12. a
13. b
Use the following guidelines to compare your scores with others who have taken this questionnaire.
Score
0–3   Very low
4–5   Low
6–9   Average
10–11   High
12–13   Very high

Source: Zuckerman, 1978.

CHAPTER 13

Psychological Disorders

Chapter in Perspective

We have come a long way in developing an understanding of behavior. For many students, some of the most intriguing behaviors are those we label as *abnormal*. Perhaps they see some symptoms in themselves and wonder what causes such abnormal behaviors. We begin our discussion by describing how we decide which behaviors are to be labeled abnormal. The word *insanity* is one we have all heard; however, many people have a number of misconceptions related to this legal term. The disorders we will describe span a wide range, including those that seem close to our everyday experience—who has not experienced anxiety at some time? The symptoms of mood disorders include extreme examples of feelings and behaviors we have experienced and observed in others. Disorders like schizophrenia, involving symptoms such as delusions and hallucinations, are more difficult for many of us to understand because they are so different from anything we encounter.

Our discussion of basic processes such as how neurotransmitters operate will help us understand some unusual forms of behavior. We will also see that learning plays a role in the development of some forms of abnormal behavior. The types of abnormal behavior we describe, however, often have no simple explanations; they are the result of an interaction of factors within and outside the person. ▪

Abnormal Behavior

Above the din of traffic on a Chicago street, a voice filled with rage screams. A disheveled woman paces furiously back and forth, her shopping bag swinging as if to punctuate every angry word. A passerby approaches, offering to help; the woman tells the would-be helper she wants to be left alone. Later she is taken to a mental hospital because city officials claim she was exhibiting abnormal behavior. *What criteria can we use to distinguish between "normal" and "abnormal" behaviors?* ▪

What do we mean when we label a behavior "abnormal"? This is an important question. As we will see, the criteria we use to define abnormal behaviors influence the way we perceive and respond to other people. Thus the way we define abnormality is an important issue with serious consequences.

Criteria of Abnormality

Several criteria are used to distinguish between normal and abnormal behaviors. Sometimes one criterion will do; at other times we may rely on more than one. The most commonly used criteria for distinguishing between normal and abnormal behaviors are statistical rarity, interference with normal functioning, personal distress, and deviance from social norms.

Statistical Rarity.   A common way to define abnormal behavior is to determine how often the behavior occurs in the population. Abnormal literally means "away from the norm." Thus a behavior that is abnormal does not occur very often. A neighbor who checks the stove 26 times to be sure it has been turned off would be viewed as abnormal because such behavior is rare. Typing 150 words per minute is also rare and hence, by definition, is also abnormal. Some rare (and therefore statistically abnormal) behaviors, however, such as earning straight As or writing a novel, are acceptable and desirable. By itself, statistical rarity is clearly not a consistently useful indicator of what we should label abnormal.

Interference with Normal Functioning.   Behavior is said to be **dysfunctional** when it interferes with a person's ability to function on a daily basis. Everyone probably experiences some degree of anxiety every day, but imagine a level of anxiety that renders you unable to speak in the presence of others. That degree of anxiety is dysfunctional because it interferes with daily activities and affects others who depend on you. Behavior that is dysfunctional is generally considered abnormal.

dysfunctional
Term used to describe behaviors that adversely affect an individual's functioning

Personal Distress.   People may be diagnosed as suffering from a psychological disorder if their behavior is upsetting, distracting, or confusing to themselves. The criterion of personal distress is useful in cases in which the psychological disorder is accompanied by discomfort. Imagine the distress felt by someone who believes other people are "out to get" him or her or by a depressed person who sees suicide as "the only solution." Personal distress does not always accompany abnormal behavior, however. The woman screaming at unseen adversaries on a Chicago street was not distressed by her behavior; she wanted to be left alone. Her behavior would not be considered abnormal according to the criterion of personal distress, although it would be based on the criterion of statistical rarity.

Deviance from Social Norms.   All social groups, ranging from your neighborhood to an entire society, decide which behaviors are acceptable for group members. The resulting guidelines, called **social norms,** distinguish acceptable behaviors from unacceptable or deviant ones. Norms may be recorded as laws, like those that prohibit writing bad checks. Many social norms do not exist in written form, however; they still guide our behavior and influence opinions about the behavior of others. For example, there are no written laws dictating that people should use polite language such as "Excuse me," but many people consider these phrases an essential part of interacting with others.

How do social norms relate to the definition of abnormal behavior? Depending on the context—when and where they occur—certain behaviors are considered unacceptable. In other words, they are "against the norm," or abnormal. Norms differ from group to group and also change over time. For example, some groups of people view body piercing as self-mutilation; other groups see it as a valued expression of group solidarity or rebellion against conformity imposed from outside the group.

A Working Definition

Each of the criteria of abnormality we have discussed has advantages and disadvantages. We often use several criteria simultaneously in making judgments about particular behaviors; therefore we can define behaviors as **abnormal** when they are statistically unusual, are not socially approved, and cause distress to the person or interfere with his or her ability to function. Because different cultural groups have

social norms
Guidelines, usually unwritten, that define behavior that is acceptable or unacceptable within a particular group

abnormal
Term used to describe behavior that is rare or dysfunctional, causes personal distress, or deviates from social norms

We use several criteria to judge whether people are exhibiting abnormal behavior. By some standards the dress and behavior of these football fans would be judged abnormal. Many of the people in the stands, however, would judge these enthusiastic fans to be normal and perhaps even models to be emulated.

The jury's determination that John Hinckley Jr. was not guilty by reason of insanity led to changes in the application of the insanity plea across the country.

different social norms, definitions of abnormality using this criterion are culturally variable.

Keep the following points in mind when making such judgments. First, normality and abnormality are degrees of difference on a continuum; the point at which normal behavior becomes abnormal depends on how you define normality. When we perceive a behavior as abnormal, we are making a value judgment about the appropriateness of that behavior. Second, the person whose behavior is judged may not accept your perspective. (Recall the woman on the streets of Chicago described at the beginning of this section.) Finally, these judgments vary with social or cultural standards, which may change over time.

The Concept of Insanity

On March 30, 1981, radio and television stations flashed a news bulletin: John Hinckley Jr. had shot and wounded President Ronald Reagan and three other people. At the time when Hinckley came to trial, federal law required prosecutors to prove that a defendant was sane. Hinckley's lawyers argued their client had tried to kill the president to attract the attention of an actress. Experts testified that Hinckley suffered from a psychological disorder, but they disagreed about its severity. After deliberating the conflicting testimony, the jury returned a verdict of not guilty by reason of **insanity,** the legal ruling that a person accused of a crime is not responsible for it.

The key to understanding the Hinckley decision and others like it is the distinction between describing actions (Hinckley fired the shots) and holding someone responsible for those actions (Hinckley was responsible for firing the shots and should be punished). Suppose a 4-year-old child found the keys to the family car, managed to start and drive it, and hit and seriously injured a neighbor. Everyone agrees on the description, but would we hold the child responsible for the consequences? Because we believe a 4-year-old child is not capable of understanding a wrongful and deliberate act, our legal system would not punish the child.

Psychological Detective

Even before the Hinckley trial focused attention on the insanity plea, many people held strong opinions about the plea. What do you think most people believe about the frequency of use and success of the insanity plea? What are the primary sources of the information that lead to these opinions?

insanity

Legal ruling that a person accused of a crime is not held responsible for that act; defined in most states as the inability to tell the difference between right and wrong at the time the crime is committed

The Hinckley case showed the media to be a powerful source of information about the insanity defense. Millions of Americans saw newspaper and television pictures of the attempted assassination, which seemed to suggest that people with psychological disorders are dangerous. As many as 86 percent of newspaper stories that deal with former mental patients focus on a violent crime, usually murder (Shain & Phillips, 1991). Relying on such portrayals, many of us believe that defendants use the insanity plea as a loophole to escape punishment for their illegal acts: The public thinks that 37 percent of felony indictments involve an insanity plea and 44 percent of those pleas result in acquittal (Silver,

Cirincione, & Steadman, 1994). By contrast, an analysis of more than 1 million felony indictments found insanity pleas were used in less than 1 percent of the cases, and only one-quarter of those pleas were successful (Callahan et al., 1991).

How did the concept of an insanity plea develop? In 1843, an Englishman, Daniel M'Naughton, attempted to assassinate the British prime minister but killed the minister's secretary instead. Convincing testimony supported the defense's contention that M'Naughton believed the prime minister and others were conspiring against him. When the prosecution could not refute that testimony, the judge directed the jury to find M'Naughton "not guilty by reason of insanity."

In most states, the current basis for determining insanity is the M'Naughton or "right-wrong" rule (Steadman et al., 1993): An accused person is not held legally responsible if he or she was unable to tell the difference between right and wrong at the time of the crime. M'Naughton fired the gun in the belief that he was defending himself against people who were plotting to kill him. The determination of insanity is a legal decision (decided by a judge or a jury), rather than a psychological or psychiatric one, although psychologists and psychiatrists often offer testimony to the court in insanity cases.

Assault is the most frequent crime for which defendants plead not guilty by reason of insanity; only 15 percent of insanity verdicts occur in murder cases (Callahan et al., 1991). Most defendants who are ruled insane have a history of serious psychological disorders with prior hospitalizations. Release procedures are quite strict, so defendants who are judged insane spend as much or more time in confinement as people convicted of similar crimes. Thus these data contradict the widespread belief that the insanity plea is a legal loophole used by defendants to escape punishment.

In 1994 William Tager's delusion led him to the New York studio of the *Today* show armed with an assault rifle. He killed a stagehand who tried to alert police after spotting Tager with the gun as he tried to enter the studio. After his arrest, Tager told police that the television networks had been spying on him, tapping his phone, and sending rays and vibrations (through the television) toward him. He said he did not intend to harm celebrity performers or members of the audience; he was looking for high-ranking members of the networks he blamed for decades of spying and persecution. He was convicted of the shooting.

Models of Abnormal Behavior

Hundreds of years ago, many people believed that abnormal behaviors occurred when a person was "possessed" by demons. People who behaved in a bizarre fashion were often subjected to brutal treatments designed to drive the demons out. The belief in supernatural phenomena provided one way to understand disorders and also suggested possible treatments.

In their efforts to identify and explain abnormal behaviors, psychologists often adopt models, or general views of what causes those behaviors. Models help by pointing out which symptoms are most important, directing attention to their likely causes and suggesting possible treatments. We can organize the models under two general headings: the medical model and psychological models.

The Medical Model. Near the end of the eighteenth century, physicians began to document their patients' symptoms and to note which ones occurred together. The occurrence of groups of symptoms, called *syndromes,* helped physicians identify underlying diseases and develop treatments. Approaching abnormal behaviors just as one would approach medical illnesses is known as the **medical model.**

Psychiatrist Thomas Szasz (1993) argues for limiting the medical model to conditions resulting from actual brain dysfunctions. In his opinion, this model has been expanded to cover behaviors that are perhaps annoying or inappropriate but do not constitute diseases of the brain. For example, the list of proposed or recognized diseases includes shoplifting, pathological gambling, and nicotine dependence. According to Szasz, applying the medical model to such behaviors

medical model
The view that mental disorders are like physical illnesses and have underlying organic causes

psychodynamic model
The view that psychological disorders result from unconscious conflicts related to sex or aggression

behavioral model
The view that psychological disorders are learned behaviors that follow the principles of classical and operant conditioning or modeling

cognitive model
A view that emphasizes thinking as the key element in causing psychological disorders

sociocultural model
A view that emphasizes the importance of society and culture in causing psychological disorders

does not advance our understanding of the causes of the problems and allows people to avoid taking responsibility for their problems by attributing them to a disease process.

Accumulating evidence shows that a number of psychological disorders are related to elevated or reduced levels of certain neurotransmitters or structural abnormalities in the brain. What's more, evidence is increasing that heredity plays a significant role in the development of some psychological disorders.

The Psychological Models. In contrast to the medical model, various *psychological models* emphasize the importance of mental functioning, social experiences, and learning histories in trying to explain the causes of abnormal behaviors. Sigmund Freud's **psychodynamic model** focuses on unconscious conflicts involving the id, ego, and superego or fixations at an early stage of psychosexual development. For example, anxiety is seen as a warning that the ego is about to be overwhelmed by conflict. The **behavioral model,** by contrast, focuses on environmental factors that mold human and animal behaviors. Behavioral theorists such as John B. Watson and B. F. Skinner propose that we learn both normal and abnormal behaviors through the principles of classical conditioning, operant conditioning, and modeling (see Chapter 6). In contrast to the behavioral model, the **cognitive model** focuses on understanding the content and processes of human thought. Cognitive psychologists claim that to understand human behavior, we must look beyond actual events to understand how people interpret those events.

Cultural & Diversity Perspective

Culture Disorders

THE **SOCIOCULTURAL MODEL** EMPHASIZES THE ROLE OF SOCIAL AND CULTURAL influences on the frequency, diagnosis, and conception of psychological disorders. Among those influences are poverty and discrimination; these factors may promote a climate that increases the likelihood that psychological disorders will develop. Poverty is related to the prevalence of psychological disorders, and rates of psychological disorders are influenced by socioeconomic status (Bruce, Takeuchi, & Leaf, 1991; Dohrenwend et al., 1992).

The influence of culture is also seen in the fact that *anorexia nervosa* (a fear of being overweight associated with a failure to maintain appropriate weight; see Chapter 15) occurs primarily in the United States and other Western countries where thinness is considered a sign of female beauty. The lower rates of several psychological disorders in Taiwan compared with the United States may be due to cultural factors (Compton et al., 1991).

Some sets of symptoms, called *culture-bound syndromes,* tend to be limited to specific cultures. In Japan the syndrome called *taijin kyofusho* involves the intense fear that one's body or its functions are offensive to other people (American Psychiatric Association, 1994). This syndrome shares similarities with social phobias, which are concerns related to public scrutiny or possible embarrassment (Kleinknecht et al., 1997). The focus of *taijin kyofusho,* however, is on offending others rather than on the self; the difference in the focus of these related disorders is consistent with conceptions of the self as independent or interdependent in the two cultures (see Chapter 12).

In some Native American cultures, individuals may believe they can hear the voice of a dead person calling them as the spirit travels to the afterworld

(Lu, Lim, & Mezzich, 1995). *Ataque de nervios* (attacks of nerves) is particularly prominent among Spanish-speaking people from the Caribbean but also occurs among other Hispanic groups, most frequently women (Guarnaccia et al., 1993; Oquendo, Horwath, & Martinez, 1992; Oquendo, 1995). The symptoms of this brief-duration syndrome include shouting, crying, trembling, heat in the chest rising into the head, verbal or physical aggression, and seizurelike or fainting episodes. The symptoms follow family-related stressful events, such as news of the death of a close relative or witnessing an accident involving a family member (American Psychiatric Association, 1994); they typically begin in the presence of family members (Oquendo, Horwath, & Martinez, 1992). Although this "culturally condoned expression of distress" shares symptoms with several disorders (Guarnaccia et al., 1993; Oquendo, 1995), it would nonetheless not be properly understood by someone unfamiliar with the cultures in which it developed.

Do these various models of abnormal behavior appear to conflict with one another? There is a growing recognition that many disorders have multiple causes; thus the simultaneous use of several models is likely to advance our understanding. This emphasis on multiple causation is evident in the *biopsychosocial* model, which incorporates *bio*logical (medical-model) factors along with *psycho*logical and *socio*cultural (social) factors. Some people may have inherited a tendency to exhibit strong autonomic reactions, which may predispose them to develop a number of disorders. But will they actually develop any of them? Whether a disorder develops may depend on an interaction of psychological and social factors with an inherited predisposition. For example, exposure to repeated stressful experiences that bring out strong autonomic reactions may lead certain people to begin questioning their ability to cope. Growing up in a family that typically reacts to stressful situations by presenting physical symptoms can lead an individual to report similar symptoms. Thus any one model of abnormal behavior may be an oversimplification.

Classifying and Counting Psychological Disorders

You walk into a mental hospital and report that you heard a voice say "empty," "hollow," and "thud." You have no history of any psychological disorder, and except for giving the false report about hearing voices, you answer all questions truthfully. Will you be recognized as a fraud, or will you be diagnosed with a psychological disorder and treated for hearing voices in your head? *Can we tell the difference between normal and disturbed people?* ▪

Suppose someone tells you that your cousin has suffered a "nervous breakdown." You know something is wrong, but you also have a number of unanswered questions. What are the symptoms? How serious are they? Are treatments available? When you ask these questions, you are asking whether there is a diagnosis.

Diagnosis is the process of recognizing the presence of a disorder and naming it by using an existing classification system.

A major purpose of diagnosis is to make predictions. Given a particular diagnosis, what is the likely course of the disorder? Will the disorder respond to treatment? Which treatment? Success in making such predictions depends on the availability of a diagnostic system that can be used to classify disorders in a reliable fashion.

DSM-IV

The most frequently used system for classifying psychological disorders is the American Psychiatric Association's *Diagnostic and Statistical Manual of Mental Disorders,* known as the DSM. More than 200 psychological disorders are listed in the fourth edition of the DSM, called DSM-IV (1994). The major DSM-IV categories and examples of each category are listed in Table 13-1.

One reason for revising the DSM is that diagnoses based on the categories listed in earlier editions were not sufficiently reliable. At times, different mental health professionals who interviewed the same patient failed to agree on the diagnosis. To remedy this problem, the developers of the DSM added rules for making diagnoses. The DSM spells out the number, severity, and duration of symptoms that define each diagnosis. These detailed rules have had the desired effect: The reliability of diagnoses has improved. This improved reliability of the DSM, however, has not silenced critics who question the very act of making a diagnosis.

The Labeling Issue

Recall the vignette at the beginning of this section, in which we put you in the position of someone who walked into a mental hospital and reported hearing a voice say "empty," "hollow," and "thud." Do you believe the hospital staff could tell the difference between a normal person and a disturbed one?

Psychologist David Rosenhan (1973) and seven colleagues actually carried out this research. They entered mental hospitals and reported hearing voices. Except for giving false names, they answered all questions truthfully. Most of these "pseudopatients" were admitted to the hospital with the diagnosis of *schizophrenia,* a serious psychological disorder. Although they stopped reporting the symptom immediately after admission, they were hospitalized for an average of 19 days and were given a combined total of more than 2,000 pills (which they did not swallow).

Not surprisingly, Rosenhan's research generated controversy. Critics pointed out that patients do not walk into hospitals and fake symptoms, and hence the study was invalid on its face. Nevertheless, the pseudopatients' experiences reveal how labels such as "schizophrenia" can influence our perceptions of behavior. Once the label "schizophrenic" had been applied to the pseudopatients, it influenced the staff's perceptions of them. Some normal behaviors were perceived as abnormal when filtered through that diagnostic label. For example, while in the hospital, the pseudopatients wrote notes describing their experiences. The hospital staff viewed the writing as a symptom of schizophrenia. Several "real" patients, however, recognized the pseudopatients as normal people who were collecting information about life in a mental hospital. The reactions of staff members were quite different. For example, a pseudopatient might say, "Pardon me, Dr. X. Could you tell me when I am eligible for grounds privileges?" The response would be, "Good morning, Dave. How are you today?" Then the staff member would simply walk off (Rosenhan, 1973).

The pseudopatients could not escape the label, even when they were released from the hospital; they were given the diagnosis of "schizophrenia in remission." These results suggest the use of diagnostic labels can be a double-edged sword. Diagnosis can help advance our knowledge about the causes of disorders and

diagnosis
The process of deciding whether a person has symptoms that meet established criteria of an existing classification system

TABLE 13-1   Descriptions and Examples of Major Categories of Disorders Listed in the DSM-IV

DISORDER TYPE	DESCRIPTIONS AND EXAMPLES
Disorders usually first diagnosed in infancy, childhood, or adolescence	Disorders that begin before adulthood, including mental retardation, learning disorders, attention-deficit hyperactivity disorder, autistic disorder, enuresis (bedwetting), and separation anxiety
Delirium, dementia, and amnestic disorders	Disorders characterized by a significant deficit in cognition resulting from a medical condition or substance use. Delirium is a confused state of consciousness; dementia is characterized by multiple deficits in intellectual functioning, including memory deficits. Amnestic disorders affect memory but not other functioning
Substance-related disorders	Disorders resulting from excessive and persistent use of mind-altering substances such as alcohol, amphetamines, barbiturates, or cocaine
Schizophrenia and other psychotic disorders	Schizophrenia involves symptoms such as delusions, hallucinations, and deterioration from a previous level of functioning that last for at least six months (examples include catatonic schizophrenia and paranoid schizophrenia)
Mood disorders (affective disorders)	Disorders that involve extremes in mood that cause people to feel inappropriately sad or highly elated or to swing between these extremes; category includes major depressive episode and bipolar disorder (formerly called manic depression)
Anxiety disorders	A key symptom, anxiety, is manifested in phobias, generalized anxiety disorder, panic disorder, obsessive-compulsive disorder, or posttraumatic stress disorder
Somatoform disorders	Physical symptoms such as paralysis cause significant distress or impairment but do not have a medical explanation; examples include somatization disorder
Dissociative disorders	Disorders characterized by a sudden change in the usually integrated functions of consciousness, memory, identity, or perception; they include dissociative amnesia, dissociative fugue, and dissociative identity disorder (multiple personality)
Sexual and gender identity disorders	Disorders include the paraphilias, characterized by arousal involving unusual objects, activities, or situations, and sexual dysfunctions such as inhibition of orgasms; category also includes gender identity disorder
Personality disorders	Pervasive, inflexible patterns of inner experience and behavior beginning in adolescence or early adulthood that are stable over time, resistant to treatment, and lead to distress or impairment; category includes antisocial personality disorder

Source: Reprinted with permission from the *Diagnostic and Statistical Manual of Mental Disorders, Fourth Edition.* © 1994 American Psychiatric Association.

aid in making treatment decisions, but diagnostic labels may also create a stigma that can be difficult to overcome when looking for housing or a job or simply interacting with other people. Labels inevitably affect how we perceive and respond to others; our responses to those persons labeled as having a psychological disorder are often different from our responses to other people.

The Prevalence of Psychological Disorders

Just as it is difficult to define abnormal behavior, it is also difficult to collect accurate information about the number of people who experience psychological disorders. Many people who suffer from these disorders do not seek treatment; others seek help from family physicians rather than mental health professionals and thus are not readily identified and counted among those who have psychological disorders. Nevertheless, there have been several major efforts to determine the frequency of these disorders in the general population.

Epidemiologists study the distribution and factors associated with accidents, diseases, and psychological disorders. The data they collect are our best estimates of the numbers of people who suffer from various ailments and disorders.

epidemiologist
Scientist who studies the distribution and causes of accidents, diseases, and psychological disorders in a given population

FIGURE 13-1 Lifetime prevalence rates of selected psychological disorders based on results of the Epidemiologic Catchment Area Study, which is the most comprehensive survey of the prevalence of psychological disorders ever conducted.

Sources: Eaton, Dryman, & Weissman, 1991; Karno & Golding, 1991; Keith, Regier, & Rae, 1991; Robins, Tipp, & Przybeck, 1991; Weissman et al., 1991.

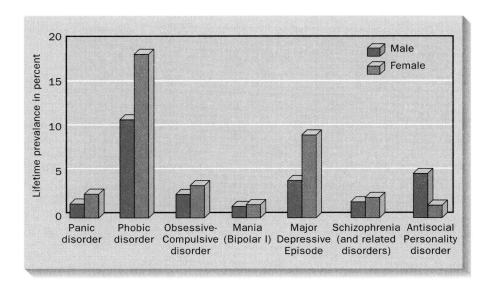

prevalence
Number or percentage of people in a population that ever had a particular disorder during a specified period

incidence
Number or percentage of newly diagnosed cases of a particular disorder in a given population

The information is also used to identify subgroups (such as adolescents) that are susceptible to particular disorders, to plan and evaluate treatments, and to determine the need for additional health care services.

Epidemiologists are interested in the **prevalence** of disorders—the percentage of a population experiencing a given disorder during some specified period. For example, if 500 people in a population of 10,000 had the flu during the past 6 months, the 6-month prevalence for flu would be 5 percent (500/10,000). Questions like "Did you have the flu at any time during your life?" yield lifetime prevalence figures.

The **incidence** of a disorder is the rate (or number) of new cases reported during a given period. If there were 100 newly diagnosed cases this year, the incidence of flu in our population of 10,000 would be 1 percent.

One very useful method for estimating the number of people who have psychological disorders is the face-to-face survey (see Chapter 1). This method was used in two surveys of more than 27,000 respondents: the Epidemiologic Catchment Area Study (Robins & Regier, 1991) and the National Comorbidity Survey (Kessler et al., 1994). In both surveys trained interviewers asked a series of questions designed to elicit information that would establish the presence of various psychological disorders. It is common in the United States for people to have a history of psychological disorders: Between 32 and 48 percent of the adult population has had at least one psychological disorder at some time (lifetime prevalence). Between 20 and 30 percent of the respondents reported having had active psychological disorders within the 12 months before the interview (Kessler et al., 1994; Robins, Locke, & Regier, 1991). In both surveys the most frequent diagnoses were phobias, alcohol and drug abuse or dependence (see Chapter 5), and major depressive episodes. Lifetime prevalence estimates for some of the disorders are presented in Figure 13-1.

These and other psychological disorders, however, often occur with other disorders. Figure 13-2 illustrates the frequency of these concurrent or *comorbid* diagnoses in the same people (Kessler et al., 1994). Approximately one-half of all people with psychological disorders have more than one disorder; comorbidity is even higher in sam-

FIGURE 13-2 Comorbid psychological disorders. Many people who have one psychological disorder experience other disorders at the same time. The simultaneous occurrence of disorders, or comorbidity, increases the difficulty associated with making appropriate diagnoses and developing effective treatment plans.

Source: Kessler et al., 1994.

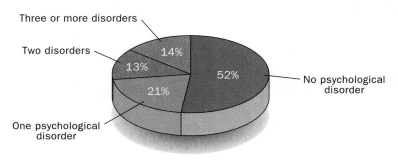

ples of people drawn from those who seek treatment (Clark, Watson, & Reynolds, 1995). The existence of several disorders in a person has important implications in treatment planning. Compared to those with a single diagnosis, individuals with comorbid diagnoses have a more chronic history of psychological disorders, report more physical health problems, and experience greater overall impairment (Newman et al., Moffitt, 1998).

Most people with psychological disorders do not seek treatment. Yet psychological disorders are associated with significant disability as measured by the number of days individuals are unable to carry out their usual activities or experience restrictions in their social or occupational roles (Ormel et al., 1994).

Review Summary

1. By the standard of statistical rarity, behavior is abnormal when it is infrequent. Behavior is **dysfunctional** when it interferes with the person's ability to function in day-to-day life. The criterion of personal distress is frequently used in identifying the presence of a psychological disorder. Departures from **social norms** are used to define deviant, and therefore **abnormal,** behaviors; social norms, however, can change over time and vary across cultures.

2. Insanity is a legal ruling that an accused individual will not be held responsible for a crime. The public's understanding of the insanity plea is not consistent with data showing that such pleas are infrequently used and rarely successful.

3. The **medical model** views abnormal behaviors as no different from illnesses and seeks to identify symptoms and prescribe medical treatments. The **psychodynamic model** considers abnormal behavior as the result of unconscious conflicts, often dating from childhood. The **behavioral model** views abnormal behaviors as learned through classical conditioning, operant conditioning, and

modeling. The **cognitive model** suggests that our interpretation of events and our beliefs influence our behavior. The **sociocultural model** emphasizes the importance of social and cultural factors in the frequency, diagnosis, and conception of disorders.

4. The American Psychiatric Association's *Diagnostic and Statistical Manual of Mental Disorders* (DSM) provides rules for diagnosing psychological disorders that have increased reliability.

5. Rosenhan's pseudopatient study raises questions about our ability to identify normal and abnormal behaviors and shows how labels affect the perception of behavior.

6. Epidemiologists study the prevalence and incidence of accidents, diseases, and psychological disorders. Phobias, alcohol and drug abuse or dependence, and major depressive episodes are among the most common psychological disorders. Many people suffer from more than one psychological disorder (comorbidity).

Study Break

1. Decide which criterion of abnormality—statistical rarity, dysfunctional, personal distress, deviance from social norms—could be used to judge each of the following cases. (More than one criterion may be applicable.)

   a. Sally spends much of her time daydreaming about "nothing in particular." Her work has suffered, and she has been put on probation because of her declining productivity.

   b. Tim spends most of his money on beer and has been neglecting his appearance. When a friend suggested that he seek help, Tim responded, "Mind your business. I'm not bothering anyone."

2. Decide which model of abnormal behavior—medical, psychodynamic, behavioral, cognitive, sociocultural—is most useful in understanding each of the following cases.

   a. Several students observed some patients at a mental hospital, including one who announced he was the "Creator." The students paid attention to this patient for hours; when they left, the patient walked away without saying anything.

   b. After Cara got a D on an exam, she concluded that the low grade "proves that I'm stupid." She ignored the fact that a bout of flu had prevented her from studying.

3. In most states, what is the most commonly used definition of insanity?

4. Which disorder seems to occur primarily in the United States and other Western countries?
   a. Depression
   b. Schizophrenia
   c. Bipolar disorder
   d. Anorexia nervosa

5. A newspaper editor asked a reporter to write an article to coincide with the trial of a man accused of a gruesome murder. The editor wants the reporter to determine how many insanity cases are tried in the area. What is the reporter likely to find?
   a. The plea of "not guilty by reason of insanity" is reserved for multiple murders.
   b. A majority of those accused of crimes plead "not guilty by reason of insanity" and are found "not guilty."
   c. Very few accused persons plead "not guilty by reason of insanity"; those who do, however, are very likely to be found "not guilty."
   d. Very few people accused of crimes plead "not guilty by reason of insanity" and few of them are successful in using this plea.

6. Your roommate, a psychology major, is completing an internship at the mental health center. Today he told you of a client who was described during a case conference as *comorbid*. You do not want to reveal your ignorance, so you look up the word later. What will the dictionary entry say?
   a. More than one disorder has been diagnosed in this client.
   b. The client shares some of the same symptoms that his or her family members have reported.
   c. The client was suffering from a serious condition that is life threatening.
   d. The word appears to be made-up and probably is used by someone suffering a psychotic disorder.

7. Rosenhan and his colleagues presented themselves as patients with just one symptom—hearing a voice say "empty," "hollow," and "thud." What diagnosis were these pseudopatients given? What is the most significant implication of Rosenhan's pseudopatient study?

8. In a survey conducted in a city of 20,000 people, researchers found that 200 of them had been diagnosed with ulcers during the past year. A total of 1,000 people reported having had an ulcer at some time during their life.
   a. What is the incidence of ulcers in this city?
   b. What is the lifetime prevalence of ulcers?

Anxiety, Somatoform, and Dissociative Disorders

One day while driving home, Deborah realized that her heart had suddenly begun racing; she was also short of breath and sweating profusely. Afraid that she might pass out, she rolled down the car window to let cold air rush across her face. Over the next several months, the attacks occurred more often. She opted to drive the side streets to and from work out of fear that she might be caught in traffic during an attack. Deborah began to think she was "going crazy" or was about to die. As she read the obituaries in the newspaper, she thought the deceased were lucky because "they didn't have to go on anymore." Eventually she was unable to leave home; she was even afraid to walk across the backyard to her neighbor's house. ***Could symptoms like a racing heart indicate a psychological disorder?*** ■

In this and the following sections, we focus on specific types or categories of psychological disorders. In doing so, we might list some symptoms you may see in yourself. Like medical students who sometimes believe they have the diseases covered in their textbooks and courses, you may conclude you have one or more of the disorders discussed in this chapter. Be aware of this tendency to diagnose yourself, and don't conjure up a lot of unnecessary worries. If you have some troubling symptoms, however, do not hesitate to discuss them with a teacher, a counselor, or a therapist. These professionals can help you evaluate the severity of your symptoms and determine whether you need treatment.

The disorders described in the first part of this section are related to anxiety. People with anxiety disorders maintain good contact with reality, are not grossly disturbed, and usually are not hospitalized. Their symptoms, however, can be disturbing and may interfere with day-to-day living. After discussing the anxiety disorders, we will turn to the somatoform and dissociative disorders.

Anxiety Disorders

Giving a speech in class, interviewing for a job—what do these experiences have in common? You may feel a bit apprehensive and uncomfortable in both situations. Does the word *anxious* come to mind? At moderate levels, anxiety is normal and expected; it often provides the motivation needed to give an outstanding speech or get a good job. High levels of **anxiety** or a general feeling of apprehension, however, are distressing and interfere with effective functioning. Severe anxiety that disrupts a person's life indicates the presence of an *anxiety disorder.* According to one survey, 19 percent of men and 31 percent of women have had at least one anxiety disorder at some time (Kessler et al., 1994).

But how do we recognize anxiety? There are three categories of indicators: behavioral, cognitive, and physiological. The behavioral indicators include shakiness and stuttering. Physiological signs like a rapid heart rate and dry mouth reflect activation of the sympathetic nervous system. Cognitive signs include difficulty concentrating and thoughts or beliefs that can fuel the anxiety (such as "I'll make a fool of myself when I give my speech").

Phobias. As we saw in Chapter 6, a **phobia** is an intense, excessive fear of an activity, object, or situation. The fear in a phobia is out of proportion to the real danger, and it is difficult to overcome. If your concern about facing fear-arousing stimuli leads to efforts to avoid those stimuli, you may have a phobia. The DSM-IV organizes phobias into three categories: *agoraphobia, social phobia,* and *specific phobia.* Phobias are very common disorders; the lifetime prevalence is 10 percent for men and 17 percent for women (Eaton, Dryman, & Weissman, 1991).

Agoraphobia (literally "fear of the marketplace") is the most common phobia treated in mental health clinics. Most people with agoraphobia are women who avoid public places or situations from which it would be difficult to escape if they developed embarrassing or incapacitating symptoms such as dizziness or vomiting. They prefer the safety of a private place, quite often their home.

Different phobias tend to develop at different ages. Agoraphobia usually begins in one's twenties; **social phobias,** such as fear of speaking in front of a group, usually emerge between late adolescence and early adulthood (15 to 25 years of age) (Schneier & Johnson, 1992). **Specific phobias**—fears of particular objects or situations—often begin between ages 5 and 9 (Ost, 1987). Examples of specific phobias are the fear of blood (*hemophobia*), fire (*pyrophobia*), and heights (*acrophobia*) (see Table 13-2).

anxiety
General feeling of apprehension characterized by behavioral, cognitive, or physiological symptoms

phobia
Irrational fear of an activity, object, or situation that is out of proportion to the actual danger

agoraphobia
Avoidance of public places or situations in which escape may be difficult should the individual develop incapacitating or embarrassing symptoms of panic

social phobia
A fear related to being seen or observed by others

specific phobia
Any phobia other than agoraphobia or the social phobias, including the fear of specific animals, of elements of the natural environment, and of such things as blood, injections, or injury

TABLE 13-2
Common Specific Phobias, by Type

PHOBIAS	FOCUS OF THE FEAR
Animal type	
Ailurophobia	Cats
Arachnophobia	Spiders
Cynophobia	Dogs
Entomophobia	Insects
Natural environment type	
Amathophobia	Dust
Frigophobia	Cold weather
Phonophobia	Loud noises
Photophobia	Light
Blood-injection-injury type	
Hemophobia	Blood
Odynephobia	Pain
Poinephobia	Punishment
Situation type	
Apeirophobia	Infinity
Claustrophobia	Closed spaces
Topophobia	Stage fright
Gephyrophobia	Crossing bridges
Other	
Catoptrophobia	Mirrors
Kakorrhaphiophobia	Failure
Logophobia	Words
Triskaidekaphobia	Number 13

Source: Andreasen & Black, 1995, p. 310.

"Looks like your fears of people, speaking, computers, and all forms of transportation might limit your career opportunities."

More than 50 percent of people with a blood-injection-injury phobia report a history of fainting. In contrast to the typical phobic reaction, their blood pressure drops dramatically when they are unable to avoid situations such as having blood drawn. Many victims of a blood phobia share the fear with a close family member, which may result from similar or common stressful experiences or genetic factors predisposing them to faint (Ost, 1992).

How do phobias develop? On the basis of their study of Little Albert (see Chapter 6), John B. Watson and Rosalie Rayner (1920) proposed that phobias are learned through classical conditioning. A phobia may result when a formerly neutral stimulus (such as a white rat) becomes associated with a fear-producing stimulus (such as a loud noise). Through this association, the neutral stimulus becomes a feared stimulus; that is, it is now the conditioned stimulus (CS) or phobic stimulus.

During World War II, London was subjected to very heavy aerial bombardment. Despite the frequent occurrence of unconditioned stimuli (loud explosions), few Londoners developed phobias. The situation in London is one example of our tendency to develop phobias to some stimuli more readily than to others. According to the concept of *preparedness* (see Chapter 6), we are more likely to learn to fear stimuli that our ancestors had reason to fear, such as snakes, than nonharmful objects like flowers or stimuli that did not exist in our ancestors' time—for instance, aerial bombardments.

Phobias may also develop by observing (modeling) the behaviors and emotional reactions of others; this indirect form of learning is often called *vicarious conditioning.* Few people who fear mice or snakes have actually had adverse encounters with such creatures. They may have seen other people react fearfully in the presence of these stimuli, however, or perhaps they have heard discussions of the awful things such animals might do to humans. This type of modeling can be beneficial when it enables us to learn reasonable fears without directly encountering dangerous objects; still, it can lead us to fear stimuli simply because we have been exposed to the fears of others.

Panic Disorder. At the beginning of the section we met Deborah, who experienced symptoms such as a racing heart and difficulty breathing while driving home. Do these symptoms suggest she is suffering from a psychological disorder?

Deborah had several panic attacks, which are intense physiological reactions that occur even in the absence of an emergency. Within seconds the heart rate of a person with this disorder can accelerate by 50 or more beats per minute (see Figure 13-3). In addition to rapid heartbeat, victims also report sweating, dizziness, shortness of breath, and shaking. An episode of panic lasts between 5 and 20 minutes, although victims perceive the duration of the attack to be endless (Rachman, 1998). Many victims believe they are going crazy, losing control, or having a heart attack, yet there is no medical evidence of a heart condition. Frequent panic attacks are diagnosed as **panic disorder,** the most severe anxiety disorder. The rate among women is more than twice of that for men (Eaton et al., 1994); panic disorder is often comorbid with other anxiety disorders or

panic disorder

The most severe anxiety disorder, characterized by intense physiological arousal not related to a specific stimulus

Source: Courtesy of Joseph Palladino

"Ignore him. He's a hypochondriac."

zation disorder) tend to agree with statements such as "Bodily complaints are always a sign of disease" and "Red blotches on the skin are a threatening sign of skin cancer." (Rief, Hiller, & Margraf, 1998). Their beliefs are genuine; they do not voluntarily produce their symptoms. Despite repeated assurances of good health, they are never convinced and continually consult one physician after another.

The following is a typical case. A radiologist is sure that twinges in his abdomen were evidence of cancer. When a specialist referred him to a diagnostic center, extensive tests revealed no disease. Yet the patient was disappointed rather than relieved. Every few days he spends 15 to 20 minutes checking his stomach as he lies in bed at home (Spitzer et al., 1994).

Somatization Disorder. People with **somatization disorder** present vague but complicated and dramatic medical histories, usually beginning in their teenage years. In contrast to hypochondriasis, which centers on some specific disease, somatization disorder involves a large number of symptoms (e.g., gastrointestinal, pain, sexual, and neurological). The symptoms cause significant distress that leads victims to consult physicians who inevitably fail to find a medical basis for the physical complaints. The disorder occurs more frequently in women than in men, although physicians may be less likely to recognize it in men.

Conversion Disorder. A loss or impairment of motor or sensory function that does not coincide with the organization of the nervous system is a **conversion disorder.** For example, a patient who reports paralysis of the wrist may still be able to move the fingers, even though the fingers and wrist are on the same nerve pathway. Sensory symptoms include blindness, deafness, and inability to feel sensations in some parts of the body, even though the sensory system is not damaged. Such symptoms are real to these individuals, who do not feel they produce them voluntarily. Nevertheless, there is no obvious medical explanation for the symptoms and the disability they produce.

This rare disorder is often a response to stressful situations such as war or the death of a loved one. For example, a group of Cambodian women all had

somatization disorder
Somatoform disorder involving multiple physical complaints that do not have a medical explanation and do not suggest a specific known disease

conversion disorder
Somatoform disorder in which a person presents sensory or motor symptoms that do not have a medical explanation

unexplained blindness. When they were interviewed, they related horrifying tales of having been forced to watch relatives being tortured and killed during political conflicts in their native country (Cooke, 1991).

Modeling may occur in some cases of conversion disorder (Mucha & Reinhardt, 1970). Naval aviators who developed conversion disorders during their stressful training were likely to have parents who had physical problems in the same body parts in which the aviators developed symptoms.

How can we explain the development of somatoform disorders? First, the symptoms may be a defense against the distress of difficult situations. Second, when we have physical problems, relatives and friends often offer attention and sympathy, and these reactions can act as reinforcers for continued presentation of the symptoms. For example, conversion reactions often disappear without treatment in hours or days, sometimes in response to changes in the availability of attention and sympathy.

Dissociative Disorders

Dissociative disorders involve a disruption in a particular function of the mind, such as memory or self-awareness, usually in response to extreme stress. These rare disorders are dramatic and have been the basis of plots for movies, books, and television shows. Dissociative disorders include dissociative amnesia, dissociative fugue, and dissociative identity disorder (multiple personality).

Dissociative Amnesia and Dissociative Fugue. An individual with **dissociative amnesia** is unable to recall important personal information. The memory impairment is too extensive to be due to normal forgetting; it may involve a specific traumatic event, most of the person's life, or a stretch of time ending in the present. Dissociative amnesia occurs suddenly, does not affect storage of new information, and frequently ends as abruptly as it began.

Psychological Detective

When Ed took his friends for a ride, he drove too fast on a hairpin turn, and the car flipped over. Rescue crews found three dead passengers; Ed survived, sustaining several broken bones and chest injuries. After he recovered from his injuries, he had no memory of the accident. The memory loss was too profound to be attributed to ordinary forgetfulness. How can we explain Ed's failure to recall the events? Use the medical and psychodynamic models to explain Ed's failure to recall events surrounding the car accident.

According to the medical model, amnesia results from physical causes such as a head injury or ingestion of large quantities of alcohol. Memory loss in these forms of amnesia is often permanent. Ed did not suffer a head injury and had no alcohol in his body, so we must consider another explanation. The psychodynamic explanation tells us that amnesia may occur as a defense against or escape from the anxiety caused by a traumatic event. In Ed's case, it appears that his recall failure was caused by the trauma of seeing his friends killed and feeling responsible for their deaths.

When amnesia is accompanied by travel, the person is suffering from **dissociative fugue.** People with this disorder may leave a stressful environment and take up residence in a distant city, with a new identity and no memory of their past life. Recovery is often sudden, and the victim's recall of the episode is no better than a dream. Cases of dissociative fugue are fascinating but rare; more typical cases, although still infrequent, involve wandering away from a natural disaster.

---

dissociative disorders
Disorders affecting a function of the mind, such as memory for events, knowledge of one's identity, or consciousness

dissociative amnesia
Dissociative disorder that involves a sudden inability to recall important personal information; often occurs in response to trauma or extreme stress

dissociative fugue
Dissociative disorder involving amnesia and flight from the workplace or home; may involve establishing a new identity in a new location

Dissociative Identity Disorder. The presence of more than one personality in a single individual, **dissociative identity disorder** (*multiple personality*), is the most dramatic dissociative disorder. Although it was once considered to be extremely rare, mental health professionals report significant numbers of cases of dissociative identity disorder, which they argue indicates that the disorder is not rare but underdiagnosed (Fahy, 1988; Kluft, 1987). Some psychologists, however, are cautious and note that this increase in diagnoses coincides with the recovered-memory movement, which has been implicated in a number of false reports of abuse (see Chapter 7) (Ofshe & Watters, 1994).

Most cases of dissociative identity disorder are associated with an early childhood history of sexual or physical abuse (Coons, Bowman, & Milstein, 1988; Lowenstein, 1994). Children are ill-equipped to cope with the trauma of abuse and may split off new personalities in an attempt to deal with it, in much the same way some children invent imaginary playmates. There are usually three or four personalities, although more than 100 have been reported in a single individual.

The personalities in dissociative identity disorder often contrast sharply with one another. For example, in the classic case described in *The Three Faces of Eve* (Thigpen & Cleckley, 1957), Eve White was shy and inhibited. At one point during psychotherapy, she put her hands on her temples and pressed hard, as if she was experiencing a severe headache. She dropped her hands, smiled, and said in an unfamiliar voice, "Hi, there, Doc!" A few minutes later she introduced herself as Eve Black. A subsequent publication by Chris Sizemore (Eve's real name) revealed that she actually had 21 separate personalities (Sizemore & Pittillo, 1977).

In most instances, it is not easy to identify cases of dissociative identity disorder. Typically, 6 to 12 years elapse between the first occasion on which a person seeks treatment and the eventual diagnosis of dissociative identity disorder (Lowenstein, 1994). During that time several diagnoses may be suggested; the most common are depression, schizophrenia, and alcohol or drug abuse (Coons, Bowman, & Milstein, 1988).

Cheryl Ann Tomiczek (*right*) is reunited with her mother, Irene. Ms. Tomiczek, who disappeared seven years earlier, was found naked and near starvation in a state park.

dissociative identity disorder (multiple personality)
Dissociative disorder in which a person has two or more separate personalities, which usually alternate

Eve of *The Three Faces of Eve* is one of the best-known cases of dissociative identity disorder (multiple personality disorder). New cases are often publicized on television talk shows.

Psychodynamic theorists describe multiple personality as resulting from early traumas such as sexual assault or physical punishment. They regard patients with this disorder as passive victims of unconscious processes that suddenly take over when the individual faces a stressor. Conversely, psychologist Nicholas Spanos and his colleagues (Spanos, Weekes, & Bertrand, 1985) suggest that the presentation of multiple personalities is a learned role. If multiple personality involves role playing, how does a person acquire the knowledge needed to portray the various roles? Suppose you were asked to act the part of a multiple personality. What would you say and do?

College students who are asked to act the part of a multiple personality are successful when they have the necessary information. Movies, television shows, and books like *The Three Faces of Eve* provide vivid descriptions of people who have suffered from this disorder. The student can create several roles based on those descriptions, giving each a different name, age, and personality. The roles are learned in the same way one learns a role in a school play.

Spanos and his colleagues (1985) do not deny that people who suffer from dissociative identity disorder have experienced traumas early in life, but they offer an alternative explanation of the development and maintenance of key elements of the disorder. In their view, people with dissociative identity disorder have been reinforced for revealing those personalities. For example, some therapists are so intrigued with the symptoms of this disorder they may inadvertently reinforce their clients for revelations concerning other personalities. Moreover, psychologist Richard Ofshe (Ofshe & Watters, 1994) has found that many of the symptoms of the disorder occur for the first time during the course of treatment. Using hypnosis in treatment may create a situation in which suggestible individuals turn the therapist's questions about other possible personalities into a belief of their existence. Group therapy sessions with dissociative identity disorder patients provide opportunities to observe the symptoms and perhaps offer some encouragement to report them.

The disorders we have discussed so far rarely lead to hospitalization, although the symptoms can interfere with daily living. Other psychological disorders, which we discuss in the next sections, have more serious consequences.

Review Summary

1. Anxiety involves behavioral, cognitive, and physiological elements. **Phobias** are excessive, irrational fears of activities, objects, or situations. The most frequently diagnosed phobia is **agoraphobia**. The DSM-IV also lists **social phobia** and **specific phobia**. Classical conditioning and modeling have been offered as explanations for the development of phobias.

2. Frequent panic attacks (which resemble heart attacks) are the main symptom of **panic disorder**. Biological and cognitive explanations for this disorder have been proposed. A person with a chronically high level of anxiety may suffer from **generalized anxiety disorder**.

3. Most people who have the diagnosis of **obsessive-compulsive disorder** have both obsessions and com-

pulsions. Obsessions are senseless thoughts, images, or impulses that occur repeatedly; they are often accompanied by compulsions, which are irresistible, repetitive acts.

4. Somatoform disorders involve the presentation of physical symptoms that have no known medical causes, but psychological factors are involved. Among these disorders are **hypochondriasis, somatization disorder, and conversion disorder.**

5. Dissociative disorders involve disruptions in some function of the mind. In **dissociative amnesia**, memories cannot be recalled; in **dissociative fugue**, memory loss is accompanied by travel. **Dissociative identity disorder** (*multiple personality*) is characterized by the presence of two or more personalities in the same individual.

Study Break

1. Identify the most likely diagnosis for each of the following conditions.
   a. Every day Brad thinks about hurting a family member. These thoughts are so repulsive that he begins counting backward from 1,000.
   b. Maria's 12 physical symptoms don't reflect any disease her physician has ever seen, and she is angry when the physician suggests that she make an appointment to see a psychologist.
   c. A week after reporting for military duty, Dan cannot use his arm to fire a gun. Medical causes have been ruled out.
   d. Andrea reports symptoms such as a racing heart and difficulty breathing that last for 10–15 minutes several times a week. She thinks she is having a heart attack.
2. What is the difference between an obsession and a compulsion?
3. Psychophysiological disorders are likely to affect parts of the body controlled by which part of the nervous system? Somatoform disorders are likely to be found in parts of the body controlled by which part of the nervous system?
4. Match the following:

a. Blindness without medical explanation	1. Ulcers
b. Serotonin	2. Somatization disorder
c. Multiple physical symptoms	3. Dissociative identity disorder
d. *The Three Faces of Eve*	4. Obsessive-compulsive disorder
e. Psychophysiological disorder	5. Conversion disorder

5. While watching a talk show, you hear the announcer describe today's guests as suffering from multiple personality. What is the current name for this disorder? It takes several years before a proper diagnosis is made; give examples of typical diagnoses made during the meantime.

Mood Disorders

Two years ago, Jim, a 58-year-old mechanic, tried to commit suicide by hanging himself; a neighbor found him in time. Last week he told a co-worker, "There's no reason to live. I've got a gun and I'm going to use it." Jim has lived alone since his wife died three years ago; his two daughters live in another state. Fellow workers often detected signs that Jim had been drinking. One co-worker sought the advice of others, who asserted, "Don't worry. People who talk about suicide don't do it." ***Do people who commit suicide give advance warning of their plans?*** ■

Mood is like a brush that paints a wide swath across our lives. Minor changes in our mood are normal and add variety to life. One day we feel fine, the next we feel blue. These feelings are minor, however, compared with the depths of despair experienced by seriously depressed people or the wild elation of those who suffer mania. Mood disorders occur at both ends of a continuum ranging from severe depression to excessive euphoria. In this section we discuss (unipolar) depression and bipolar (manic-depressive) disorder, both disorders that involve extremes of mood.

Depression

A lack of understanding of depression and the failure to recognize and treat this disorder costs $43 billion every year, primarily for treatment, absenteeism, lost productivity, and premature death (Hirschfeld et al., 1997). Clinical forms of depression are more severe than what we might term "the blues." How do we recognize depression, and how common is it?

TABLE 13-4 Depression Questionnaire

We all feel blue at times, but serious depression is qualitatively different and much more severe. This questionnaire will help you gauge the presence of the symptoms of depression. If five or more symptoms persist for more than two weeks or cause impairment in your daily functioning at work or in the family setting, it might be a good idea to discuss them with a counselor or a therapist. Read each symptom and decide whether it has occurred during the past two weeks or longer.

- Excessive crying
- Persistent sad or "empty" mood
- Feelings of guilt, worthlessness, helplessness
- Thoughts of death or suicide, suicide attempts
- Decreased energy, fatigue, feeling "slowed down"
- Difficulty concentrating, remembering, making decisions
- Chronic aches and pains that don't respond to treatment
- Loss of interest or pleasure in ordinary activities, including sex
- Eating disturbances (loss of appetite and weight, weight gain)
- Sleep disturbances (insomnia, early-morning waking, oversleeping)

Source: U.S. Department of Health and Human Services, 1994A.

Symptoms. The most obvious symptoms of **depression** are sadness, a lack of interest in previously pleasurable activities, and reduced energy. Depressed people often describe themselves in unflattering terms such as inferior and unattractive. They do not see themselves as capable of completing intellectually demanding tasks; reports of difficulty in concentrating and complaints of memory problems are common. This negative self-evaluation extends to their views of the world and the future. They torture themselves with guilt over what they see as past failures and inadequacies, and the future holds no promise of improvement. What's more, they may blame themselves for negative events, including ones that have no connection to them, yet they rarely credit themselves for any achievements. This sense of worthlessness and hopelessness makes them vulnerable to thoughts of suicide. The essence of depression is captured in the following quotation: "I am now the most miserable man living. If what I feel were equally distributed to the whole human family, there would not be one cheerful face on earth. Whether I shall ever be better, I cannot tell; I awfully forebode I shall not. To remain as I am is impossible. I must die or be better" (Oats, 1977, p. 62).

Other symptoms of depression can occur in different and even opposite ways. Two forms of insomnia are frequently associated with depression: difficulty falling asleep (sleep-onset insomnia) and awakenings early in the morning with an inability to return to sleep (see Chapter 5). Conversely, about 10 to 20 percent of depressed people greatly extend their sleep, perhaps to provide temporary refuge (Kupfer & Reynolds, 1992). Most people who are depressed find their appetites affected and consequently lose weight; a few people eat excessively. Depression is typically evident in *psychomotor retardation:* a slowed rate of speaking (in extreme cases, the person may stop speaking altogether), slow walking, frequent crying, and stooped posture. Symptoms such as wringing of the hands, pacing, and bemoaning one's fate, called *agitated depression,* can also be present, however.

Depression seems to occur in all cultures; the similarities in depression across culture are more apparent than the differences. Nevertheless, some differences are noteworthy. For example, depressed people in Western countries report guilt and self-reproach more often than people in non-Western countries such as Nigeria (Marsella et al., 1985). Another common difference is the manifestation

depression

Mood disorder characterized by sadness; feelings of guilt; changes in sleep, appetite, and motor behavior; and sometimes thoughts of suicide

of the symptoms. Although "feelings" may be important in our culture, depressed people in cultures such as China do not necessarily "feel" depressed, but tend to report more somatic problems. The reasons for such differences are some cultures have few words to convey emotions such as sadness. In addition, different cultures locate feeling states in different parts of the body, which may explain why some cultural groups emphasize somatic complaints in the expression of depression (Matsumoto, 1996).

If you have not experienced these symptoms yourself, you have undoubtedly observed them in others. The questionnaire in Table 13-4 is helpful in assessing the presence of depressive symptoms.

Abraham Lincoln exhibited numerous symptoms of depression.

Prevalence and Course.   Depression strikes rich and poor, young and old, men and women, the famous (the quote on p. 554 is by Abraham Lincoln) and the unknown. Approximately 6 percent of adults have experienced at least one episode of major depression (Weissman et al., 1991). The onset of the first episode of a major depressive disorder occurs in the late twenties (Judd, 1997). A milder, yet highly chronic, form of depression *(dysthymic disorder)* is so common it is known as the "common cold of psychological disorders." In some cases, major depressive disorder and dysthymic disorder occur together in what has been called *double depression* (Hammen, 1997; Keller, Hirschfeld, & Hanks, 1997). Affected people are chronically dysthymic, and then occasionally experience a major depressive episode. As the episode passes (as it typically does), they return to their chronic level of dysthymia, rather than to a normal mood.

In many cultures, the rate of depression is generally twice as high among women as men (Weissman & Olfson, 1995); however, accumulating evidence suggests that the sex difference occurs in developed countries, rather than in developing countries, where the male to female ratio is closer to 1:1 (Culbertson, 1997). The disparity in developed countries begins around puberty and continues throughout life (Leon, Klerman, & Wickramaratne, 1993; Weissman & Olfson, 1995). The American Psychological Association's Task Force on Women and Depression cites several points to explain the higher rate of depression among women. Depression occurs more frequently when a person engages in passive and dependent behaviors and focuses on the depressed feelings instead of acting to overcome the depression. Given the traditional gender roles in most societies (see Chapter 11), women are more likely to assume a passive role. Sexual and physical abuse is another factor that puts women at risk for depression. Although marriage may create a protective buffer against depression, the advantage is greater for men than it is for women. Mothers of young children are especially vulnerable to depression. Finally, poverty is a "pathway to depression," and the rate of poverty is especially high among women and children (McGrath et al., 1990).

The rate of depression has risen dramatically over the past century. Surveys of people in the United States, Western Europe, the Middle East, Asia, and the Pacific Rim yielded two major findings: (1) rates of depression have risen steadily for each successive generation since 1915, and (2) depression is beginning at an earlier age with each successive generation (Cross-National Collaborative Group, 1992).

What accounts for this "epidemic of depression"? Close family and community ties are important in preventing depression. For example, the Amish people have maintained their customs in rural farming communities for generations. Their supportive families and community provide comfort and aid in times of need. When an Amish family loses a barn to a fire, neighbors join together to rebuild it. Depression occurs among the Amish at about one-fifth to one-tenth the rate as it does among people in, say, the city of Baltimore (Seligman, 1989).

Phototherapy involves the use of broad-spectrum fluorescent lamps (incandescent lights may damage the retina); the light is 10 to 20 times brighter than ordinary indoor light. Patients suffering from Seasonal Affective Disorder (SAD) have daily therapy sessions from fall into the spring. They begin with a single 10- to 15-minute session per day and gradually increase session length to 30 to 45 minutes. This treatment typically leads to a reduction in the depression within two to four days. Note that tanning beds, where the eyes are generally covered and the skin is exposed to light, have no effect on the symptoms of SAD.

Although depression usually diminishes with time (typically within six months), episodes tend to recur. Most people who experience one episode of major depression will experience another one (Judd, 1997). Compared to patients with chronic medical illnesses such as heart disease, people with depression report more physical pain, feel less well, and experience more social limitations. What's more, their impaired functioning and diminished sense of well-being often linger after an episode lifts (Hays et al., 1995). Depression tends to be comorbid with anxiety disorders, substance abuse, and eating disorders (Cicchetti & Toth, 1998). Comorbidity is associated with poorer functioning and longer course of the disorder than what is termed "pure" depression (Hammen, 1997).

The symptoms of depression are somewhat more likely to occur at certain times during the year. Although a majority of people notice mood changes related to the seasons, some are so susceptible to these changes that they develop a form of depression called *seasonal affective disorder (SAD)*. SAD typically occurs during the fall and winter months (October through February) and remits in the spring (Bhatia & Bhatia, 1997; Saeed & Bruce, 1998). This "winter depression" is associated with increased sleep length, increased appetite, weight gain, fatigue, and social withdrawal. The symptoms may be related to levels of the hormone *melatonin,* which is secreted by the pineal gland. In animals, melatonin seems to regulate hibernation. As the hours of light decrease with the approach of winter, the animal's body secretes more melatonin, which slows bodily processes in preparation for hibernation. Like hibernating animals, some humans also slow down as their melatonin levels increase. People who suffer from this disorder can be helped by being exposed to greater amounts of bright light during winter, a treatment known as *phototherapy.*

Suicide.   The most serious complication of severe depression is the possibility of suicide. Consider the following statistics:

- In the United States, someone commits suicide every 17 minutes (approximately 31,000 deaths); 1.4 percent of all deaths are suicides.

- Hungary has the highest rate of suicide; other countries with high suicide rates are Denmark, Finland, and Sweden. Italy, Spain, and Greece have low rates of suicide. Compared with other countries, the suicide rate in the United States is moderate.

- In the United States, more people die by suicide than from murder. Suicide is the ninth most frequent cause of death overall but the third most frequent cause of death for people aged 15 to 24.

- In most Western countries, women have a higher rate of suicidal thoughts and behavior, yet men have a higher rate of completed suicide. Married people have the lowest suicide rates; divorced people have the highest rates.

- About 50 percent of college students have thought about suicide, and 5 to 6 percent have made suicide attempts.

- The majority of suicide victims were suffering from a psychological disorder, most often depression, alcohol abuse/dependence, or schizophrenia.

(U.S. Bureau of the Census, 1997; Hawton, 1992; Kochanek & Hudson, 1995; Krug et al., 1998; Lester, 1989, 1992; *The Harvard Mental Health Letter,* 1996)

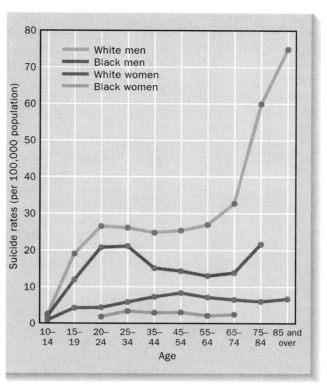

FIGURE 13-5 Variations in suicide rates by race, sex, and age. The suicide rate is significantly higher among men than among women. Suicide rates tend to increase with age; most of this increase, however, is due to suicides among white men.

Source: U.S. Bureau of the Census, 1997.

Women attempt suicide more frequently than men, but men succeed more often because they tend to use more lethal methods. A psychiatrist's chillingly blunt words make this point: "You can pump pills out of someone's stomach, you can't pump buckshot out of someone's brain." Suicide rates vary significantly with race and sex (see Figure 13-5); white men have the highest suicide rate. Suicide rates also tend to rise with age.

Myth or Science

 Recall that Jim, the mechanic whom we met at the beginning of this section, described his suicide plan to a co-worker. The co-worker sought guidance and was told not to worry because "people who talk about suicide don't do it." Was this guidance correct, or should talk of suicide be taken seriously? Contrary to common belief, suicide is often preceded by a warning. About 80 to 90 percent of suicide victims give direct warnings like "I'm going to end it all" or indirect clues such as giving prized possessions to friends and relatives. Statements about hopelessness and helplessness are especially common signs of suicidal thinking (Rudestam, 1971; Wrobleski, 1989). Unfortunately, people who hear or see evidence of suicidal potential often overlook or deny its significance.

Suicide researchers and prevention centers have accumulated information to assess an individual's suicidal potential. Jim closely matches the profile of the likely suicide victim (Hawton, 1992): An older white man suffering from depression who has made a prior suicide attempt and now has a plan, has recently experienced stressful life events, abuses alcohol, and has few sources of social support. You can see that Jim is at high risk for committing suicide.

Suicide rates are higher among men than among women. Part of this difference can be attributed to the more lethal methods used by men. The man seen here climbed over a protective steel barrier and fell to his death.

mania
Excessive activity, accelerated speech, poor judgment, elevated self-esteem, and euphoria that occur in bipolar disorder

bipolar disorder
Mood disorder in which a person experiences episodes of mania and depression, which usually alternate

What should you do if you suspect that someone you know might attempt suicide? You should not be afraid to ask, "Are you thinking about suicide?" If someone asked you that question, your likely response might be, "Are you nuts!" What should you do if your depressed friend's response is yes or a halfhearted no? According to one expert, "People who talk about or attempt suicide need immediate medical and psychological help" (Wrobleski, 1989, p. 45). Most suicidal people are ambivalent about committing suicide; they are experiencing pain, helplessness, and hopelessness. Help them understand that their current stressors make it difficult for them to think clearly.

Time is an important ally in the effort to prevent a suicide because people do not usually remain seriously suicidal for long. Surprisingly, suicide may be less likely when individuals are in the depths of depression. Helplessness and passivity sap motivation and energy so much that depressed people are unlikely to carry out their suicide plans. When the depression lifts and the person seems to feel better, suicide may actually be more likely. In the event that any of your friends talks about suicide, be sure that he or she knows that someone cares and that the person seek professional help from a suicide prevention or crisis intervention center.

Bipolar Disorder

Two weeks ago, 20-year-old Will's mood switched from friendly to irritable. When he thought some money was missing, he accused a friend of taking it. After determining he had misplaced the money himself, Will refused to apologize. Although he had no knowledge of music, he impulsively purchased an expensive guitar. As his need for sleep decreased, he spent hours making long-distance calls to friends and planning to write the definitive work on "existentialism, divine providence, and the collective unconscious." After deciding to reconcile with his girlfriend, he knocked on her door at 2 A.M. She refused to let him in, so he began shouting and pounding on the door. The noise woke neighbors who telephoned the police; they took Will to a hospital emergency room. While there, his speech was rapid, he shifted topics abruptly, and he was restless. A few weeks after his release from the hospital, he was extremely depressed (Andreasen, 1984).

Patty Duke, the actress, seeks to educate the public about bipolar disorder and its treatment. Before she was correctly diagnosed and treated with lithium, she attempted suicide several times, usually with pills. She also used alcohol and drugs to suppress her manic highs.

Will experienced an episode of poor judgment, excessive activity, accelerated speech, and extreme euphoria known as **mania.** Manic symptoms can result from cocaine or amphetamine use or hyperthyroidism; therefore these possibilities must be considered when making a diagnosis and planning treatment (Werder, 1995). The knowledge that mood disorders run in families is helpful: Will's mother had been treated for depression, and an uncle was hospitalized several times for mania and depression. Will's episode of mania was a mood disorder; it was followed by depression, and the diagnosis was **bipolar disorder** (occurrence of episodes at both ends of the mood spectrum). *Cyclothymic disorder* is a less severe, yet chronic, form of bipolar disorder (American Psychiatric Association, 1994).

The depression and mania in bipolar disorder may occur simultaneously, but they usually alternate—often separated by periods of relative normalcy. During a manic episode, boundless energy replaces the fatigue of depression; sadness and despair give way to euphoria and elevated self-esteem. Depression often reduces the desire for sex; mania often brings uncharacteristic promiscuity (reflecting increased sexual drive or libido). During an episode of mania people become highly sociable, although irritability lurks beneath the surface should anyone question their plans. They ignore painful or harmful consequences of their behavior and may incur huge debts, break the law, or make unwise business and personal decisions. Fortunately, bipolar disorder responds quite effectively to treatment with lithium (see Chapter 14), which was the treatment prescribed for Will.

Bipolar disorder is less prevalent than depression; it affects about 1 percent of the population with equal rates in men and women. Most often, the symptoms begin in a person's early twenties (Werder, 1995), as they did for Will. Like many other disorders, bipolar disorder often occurs with other disorders, especially substance abuse or dependence (Tohen, 1994).

Causes of Mood Disorders

Biological Explanations. For several reasons, experts believe that biological factors play a role in the development of mood disorders. First, as noted earlier, the symptoms of depression tend to be rather similar across cultures, suggesting a common underlying biological cause. Second, certain drugs such as Elavil and Prozac reduce depression, and mania responds to lithium treatment. The effects of neurotransmitters seem to be reflected in the dramatic differences in the activity levels of the brains of people during depressive and manic episodes (see Figure 13-6). Third, mood disorders tend to run in families, which suggests genetic transmission. Nevertheless, researchers agree that rising rates of depression during this century are unlikely to result from genetic factors; psychological and social factors also must be considered.

One way researchers study possible genetic influences on mood disorders is to compare the prevalence of these disorders in families with and without a family member with a mood disorder. Mood disorders occur more often in the first-degree relatives (parents, children, siblings) of family members with a mood disorder than among relatives of individuals who do not have such disorders (Gershon & Nurnberger, 1995). Compared with relatives of patients with unipolar disorder, relatives of bipolar patients exhibit higher rates of bipolar disorder but about the same rate of unipolar depression (see Figure 13-7). In general, the evidence for genetic transmission seems stronger for bipolar disorders than it does for unipolar depression.

In their efforts to understand the role of genetic factors in mood disorders, researchers have also studied identical and fraternal twins. They begin by identifying a twin who has a mood disorder, called an *index case*. Then they determine whether the second twin in each pair (the co-twin) also has a mood

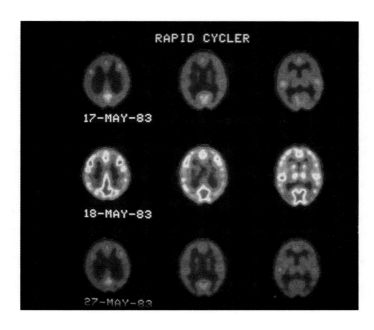

FIGURE 13-6 PET scans of the brain of a person who cycled from depression to mania reveal remarkably different patterns of activity associated with the two mood states. Activity levels are indicated by a spectrum ranging from blue (low) through green to yellow and red (high). It is not clear if the brain activity levels associated with depression and mania cause the mood disorders or whether they reflect underlying changes in mood (in which case they may be correlated with the mood).

Source: Nemeroff, 1998.

FIGURE 13-7 Prevalence of unipolar depression and bipolar disorder in families at different levels of risk. Being born into a family with a member who has a mood disorder raises the risk of having a mood disorder.

Source: Gershon & Nurnberger, 1995, p. 407.

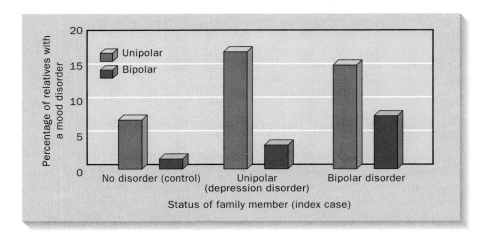

disorder. A twin pair is said to be *concordant* when both twins have mood disorders. The **concordance rate** is the percentage of twin pairs in which both twins have the disorder. The concordance rate for mood disorders among identical twins is approximately 65 percent; the rate among fraternal twins is about 14 percent (Andreasen & Black, 1995).

These findings strengthen the belief that genetic factors are involved in depression. But what exactly is inherited? To answer that question, we need to know that two neurotransmitters, norepinephrine and serotonin, seem to play significant roles in depression (Nemeroff, 1998). Antidepressant drugs increase the availability of norepinephrine or serotonin at synapses in the brain. The increased availability of these neurotransmitters alters neural transmission and can lead to increased activity and a lifting of the depression. These neurotransmitters may also be involved in altering levels of certain hormones, which could lead to depression.

Explaining mood disorders as the result of abnormal levels of certain neurotransmitters seems to be simple and straightforward. This theory cannot account for an interesting finding, however: Antidepressant drugs alter neurotransmitter levels almost immediately, yet depression may take as long as two weeks to lift after the start of drug treatment. What's more, the levels of certain neurotransmitters could change in response to environmental factors such as the disappointment after a major personal failure or after the death of a loved one. Thus, although people with mood disorders may inherit a tendency to develop these disorders, other factors need to be understood to complete the picture.

The Psychodynamic Explanation. The psychodynamic model emphasizes early childhood experiences as the foundation of adult behavior and emotional reactions. An infant depends on its caregiver, usually its mother. As its needs are met, the infant feels supported and loved, and attachment develops (see Chapter 9). The mother, however, must leave at times, temporarily or perhaps permanently. When this happens, the child may experience rage at being abandoned yet be ambivalent (feeling both love and rage) because the mother was also a source of comfort and love. The rage is turned against a more convenient and acceptable target—the child itself. According to Freud, this inwardly directed anger can cause depression. Later in life, depression may reappear when losses such as the death of a loved one or the loss of a job reactivate the earlier experiences of loss.

Cognitive and Behavioral Explanations. Suppose you have been looking for a job for over a year, to no avail. Some job seekers might decide they simply cannot get a job. They give up because they believe that no amount of searching will succeed. In short, if nothing they do makes a difference, why do anything at

concordance rate
Percentage of twin pairs in which both twins have a disorder that is of interest to an investigator

all? Under such circumstances, according to Martin Seligman (1975/1992), a psychological state known as **learned helplessness** may develop. Learned helplessness occurs when you believe you have no control over the reinforcements in your life, such as finding a job or getting a good grade on an exam. The result is often reduced efforts to attain those reinforcers. This model of depression explains the lethargy and lack of motivation seen in depressed individuals; one problem with this model, however, is that even in research situations designed to render people helpless, some individuals do not succumb. Hence there must be another variable that influences the development of depression.

A reformulation of Seligman's learned helplessness model, called the *hopelessness model,* focuses on people's beliefs about the situations in which they find themselves. Some people become depressed not because they lack control over a situation but because of the way they explain the situation. We differ in explanatory style—that is, the habitual way we explain good and bad events (see Chapter 14). Explanatory style is much more powerful than just the words a person uses. From the time we learn our explanatory style in childhood or adolescence, it serves as the mediator of whether we will suffer greatly from helplessness and possibly depression.

Explanatory style consists of three dimensions: permanent versus temporary, universal versus specific, and internal versus external. When bad events happen, we may view them as permanent or temporary. If you think about bad things in terms of "always" and "never," you have a permanent pessimistic style. Explanations may also be specific to the situation or universal, applying to all situations. People who rely on universal explanations for their failures often give up on everything when a failure strikes in one area. Finally, our explanations may be either internal (we blame ourselves) or external (we believe outside forces are at work); people who use internal explanations find their self-esteem is lowered significantly.

One combination of the dimensions of explanatory style is especially self-defeating: permanent, universal, and internal. People with this very pessimistic style who encounter bad events are more likely to become depressed, whereas those who have the opposite "optimistic" style and experience bad events will tend to resist depression.

Psychological Detective

Suppose you got back an exam with a big red F on it. How would you explain that F? Use the three dimensions of explanatory style, and write down your explanation. How do you think a person who is prone to depression might explain a bad grade?

A person who is likely to become depressed might give reasons like the following for a bad grade:

"I've always lacked ability." (permanent)

"I do poorly in everything I try." (universal)

"I'm just plain stupid." (internal)

Research suggests that depression may be related to the tendency to use permanent, universal, and internal explanations for negative events (Sweeney, Anderson, & Bailey, 1986).

The hopelessness model has much in common with the cognitively oriented theories of researchers who view depression as stemming from problems in the way people think. University of Pennsylvania psychiatrist Aaron Beck, for example, concluded that depression results from the way people think about themselves and

learned helplessness
Belief that one cannot control outcomes through one's actions; usually leads to passivity and reduced motivation and may cause depression

arbitrary inference
Conclusion drawn in the absence of supporting information

about what happens to them. They often blame themselves for events, so they focus on the negative. Depressed people hold negative views of themselves, their current experiences, and the future. They find themselves in this predicament because they are prone to commit errors in logic, which perpetuate their negative views. For example, depressed people may decide that no one likes them because no one spoke to them on the bus on the way to work. In this case, they have drawn an **arbitrary inference**—a conclusion based on insufficient evidence. They may also overgeneralize, like the student who decides she will never get a good grade because she earned a C on her first exam.

Beck has devised a therapy that deals directly with these cognitive elements of depression. We discuss Beck's cognitive therapy in Chapter 14.

Multiple Causes. To sum up, it appears that genetic factors play a role in mood disorders; clearly, however, they are not the only factors. As we have seen, factors such as explanatory style are also important components of depression. The levels of neurotransmitters may be influenced by a style of explaining negative events. One lesson is clear: The study of mood disorders leads us to recognize that there are no simple answers to questions about the causes of disorders; more often than not, biological, psychological, and social factors interact to affect the development and course of disorders. For example, researchers have suspected that stressful life events have been linked to the incidence of depression. Recent clarifications of this link, however, suggest that only some forms of depression are strongly related to stressful events (Brown, Harris, & Hepworth, 1994; Frank et al., 1994). What's more, stressful life events may also play a role in the frequency and timing of future episodes of bipolar disorder (Johnson & Roberts, 1995).

Review Summary

1. The symptoms of **depression** include sadness, reduced pleasure and energy levels, feelings of guilt, sleep disturbances, and suicidal thinking. The lifetime prevalence of depression is twice as high among women as among men; prevalence rates around the world are increasing.

2. Suicide, which is often associated with depression, is one of the leading causes of death in the United States. Suicide rates are higher among men than among women. The risk factors for suicide include being male, being unmarried, and being depressed.

3. Bipolar disorder involves swings between depression and **mania.** The symptoms of mania include euphoria, increased energy, poor judgment, decreased sleep, and elevated self-esteem.

4. Mood disorders tend to run in families, which suggests genetic transmission. Depression may involve low levels of norepinephrine or serotonin. According to the **learned helplessness** model, depression can also be brought on when people believe that they cannot control outcomes. A refinement of this model, the *hopelessness model*, suggests that typical ways of explaining negative events may be at the root of depression.

Study Break

1. What have epidemiological surveys revealed about the rate of depression around the world?

2. Identify the symptoms of depression in each of the following areas.
   a. Appetite
   b. Sleep
   c. Self-descriptions

3. Certain demographic characteristics are related to the probability of suicide. State the major predic-

tor of suicide in each of the following demographic categories.
   a. Sex
   b. Age
   c. Marital status
   d. Psychological disorders

4. A psychologist reported on research to determine the extent of genetic influences on mood disorders. During the presentation, the psychologist said that "50 percent of twin pairs shared mood disorders." What term is used to describe this figure?

   a. bipolarity rate
   b. shared incidence
   c. prevalence rate
   d. concordance rate

5. Which pair of neurotransmitters has been implicated in the development of depression?

   a. dopamine and GABA
   b. GABA and epinephrine
   c. norepinephrine and serotonin
   d. acetylcholine and norepinephrine

6. For the past three weeks, Rod has not slept more than an hour a day, yet he is energetic. He is developing plans for what he describes as "Las Vegas on the Ohio River." When a friend asked about his plans, Rod berated the man and physically attacked him. The police were called and took Rod to an emergency room, where a physician suspected bipolar disorder. The physician decided to run some tests, however, to rule out physical causes such as

   a. angina.
   b. hyperthyroidism.
   c. Alzheimer's disease.
   d. marijuana intoxication.

7. Buddy graduated from college three months ago. His grades were generally good, in the B range, and he is well liked. His efforts to find a job have been unsuccessful. Using the explanatory model, write a universal-internal-permanent explanation of his situation. Then write a specific-external-temporary explanation.

Schizophrenia

Although he was sometimes mischievous and moody, George usually appeared to be normal until the end of high school. At that time muffled sounds seemed to insult him, sudden movements were viewed as physical threats, and he saw a stove become "the Devil alive." After graduating from high school, George enlisted in the navy, where the symptoms continued. He thought the cook was Satan and his food was poisoned. His babbling was difficult to understand: "Got one to seven—see, the life in the drain—it's all butaco." After George wandered from a marching formation, an officer took him to the hospital, where he was diagnosed as suffering from schizophrenia (Heston, 1992). *What are the symptoms of schizophrenia?* ▪

The Swiss psychiatrist Eugen Bleuler coined the word *schizophrenia,* which literally means "splitting of the mind." **Schizophrenia** is a psychotic disorder that is characterized by positive symptoms (excesses) or negative symptoms (deficits). **Psychosis** is a general term for disorders in which severely disturbed people lose contact with reality and may require hospitalization.

The symptoms of schizophrenia usually appear around age 20, although deficiencies in attention and emotional responses are noted frequently during childhood. Approximately 1-1.5 percent (2 million) of the U.S. adult population has had the disorder (Carpenter & Buchanan, 1994). Although the rate of schizophrenia is approximately equal in men and women, it strikes men earlier and with greater severity (Beratis, Gabriel, & Hoidas, 1994). The symptoms frequently lead to significant social and occupational impairment (Breier et al., 1991), at an estimated cost for treatment and lost productivity of over $70 billion (Wyatt et al., 1991). The overall death rate among victims of schizophrenia is twice the expected rate, in part because the suicide rate is ten times higher than it is among the general population (Allebeck, 1989).

Schizophrenia is often confused with dissociative identity disorder. The "split" in schizophrenia, however, is not among different personalities; it is a split

schizophrenia
Psychotic disorder characterized by positive symptoms (excesses) such as delusions, hallucinations, and fluent but disorganized speech or negative symptoms (deficits) such as flat or blunted affect

psychosis
Any disorder in which a severely disturbed individual loses contact with reality

from reality as well as a split between thoughts and emotions. As we discuss this disorder in detail, keep these two points in mind: Schizophrenia is not dissociative identity disorder, and it is far more prevalent.

Symptoms of Schizophrenia

Schizophrenia involves a range of symptoms, none of which is present in all cases. There may be disturbances in perception, language, thinking, and emotional expression. How do we make sense of this array of symptoms? One approach to classifying symptoms holds promise; it is based on two types of symptoms: positive and negative.

Positive Symptoms. The *positive symptoms* of schizophrenia are distortions or excesses of normal functions, such as fluent but disorganized speech, delusions, and hallucinations. While listening to the speech of a patient with schizophrenia, you may struggle to follow his or her pattern of thought. The ideas expressed can be like a train that has slipped off its track onto another track; this pattern of speech is called *loose associations.* Some patients use *neologisms,* common words used in uncommon ways ("I wrote the letter with my writing toy") or newly created words ("I wrote the letter with my zemps"). Words may be strung together in ways that seem to follow grammatical rules, yet the words form an incoherent collection called a *word salad.* A simple question like "What brought you here?" can give rise to an odd response like "The, my, not, rode, for, new, cold, it, what, may, so" (Othmer & Othmer, 1989). Speech may also be characterized by *clang associations,* word connections dictated by sound similarity, not by logic or meaning. For example, one patient, when asked what he was doing, responded, "Eating wires and lighting fires" (Spitzer et al., 1994).

Among the most frequently observed positive symptoms are **delusions,** or false beliefs that cannot be corrected despite evidence. Delusions can appear in numerous forms. Individuals with *persecutory delusions* (the most common kind) believe that others are tormenting, following, or ridiculing them. Some delusions are bizarre, as is evident in the case of a patient who said she was "persecuted by a secret insect from the District Office" (Spitzer et al., 1994). A *delusion of grandeur* is a person's belief that he or she has special powers or abilities; for example, a computer programmer imagined the end of the world was coming and *he* determined which of his colleagues would survive in the afterlife by the keys he pressed on his keyboard.

Delusions are real to the people who experience them, so it is difficult to convince patients that they are false. What's more, if you believe others are persecuting or controlling you, you may feel a need to protect yourself. Delusions have led some persons to take action against people or institutions perceived to be intent on causing them harm or interfering with their lives (see photo on p. 535).

Cultural factors influence the content of delusions. For example, delusions of being controlled often involve reports of ghosts and witches in underdeveloped countries and nonindustrial areas; the mechanism of control in developed countries is more likely to be X-rays and lasers (Maher & Spitzer, 1993).

Schizophrenia often alters perceptions of the world. Objects take on unusual dimensions, and sensations seem to materialize from thin air. A frequent perceptual symptom is the **hallucination** (from a Latin word meaning "to wander mentally"). Hallucinations are perceptions that are not caused by stimulation of the relevant sensory organ. They can occur in any of the senses, although *auditory hallucinations* are the most common. The person may hear

delusion
An obviously false belief that is difficult to change

hallucinations
Sensory experiences that are not caused by stimulation of the relevant sensory organ

Schizophrenia is marked by a number of symptoms that can have profound effects on a person's ability to function effectively. Symptoms such as hallucinations and delusions seem inexplicable and extremely distressing to victims of this disorder.

voices that give orders, criticize, or offer ongoing commentary. *Visual hallucinations,* such as George's seeing a stove turn into a devil, are less common. Hallucinations seem real to the person experiencing them and can be quite frightening, as they were to George.

Negative Symptoms.   *Negative symptoms* are reductions or losses of function. These behavior deficits or defects include *poverty of speech* as well as disturbances in affect and volition or will (McGlashan & Fenton, 1992). These symptoms are associated with more cognitive impairment and poorer prognoses than positive symptoms (Andreasen et al., 1990; Fenton & McGlashan, 1991).

The speech of people with schizophrenia may be adequate in amount yet convey little information: Language that is vague, too abstract, too concrete, or repetitive is termed *poverty of content.* A restriction in the amount of spontaneous speech that is evident in brief and unelaborated replies to questions is called *poverty of speech.* Interviewers frequently find it necessary to prompt the person for additional information (Andreasen & Black, 1995).

Failure to experience any emotion is called *flat affect*—no ups or downs at all; an inability to experience the typical range of emotions is called *blunted affect.* Disturbances in affect are evident in rigid facial expressions, few expressive gestures, poor eye contact, and a lack of vocal inflection. *Avolition* (difficulty making decisions) and *apathy* are characterized by a lack of energy and drive such that a person is unable to initiate or persist in tasks. Unlike the lack of energy in depression, however, the apathy associated with schizophrenia is not accompanied by sadness. A number of disturbances in motor movements and a lack of self-care also characterize some forms of schizophrenia.

Subtypes of Schizophrenia

The DSM-IV describes five subtypes of schizophrenia: catatonic, disorganized, paranoid, residual, and undifferentiated (see Table 13-5). Although the prevalence of schizophrenia is similar around the world, rates of diagnosis of the subtypes differ. For example, disorganized schizophrenia accounts for about 50 percent of diagnoses of schizophrenia in Japan but only about 10 percent in other countries (Nakane, Ohta, & Radford, 1992). Such differences may be due to diagnostic, social, or cultural factors.

Each subtype of schizophrenia is characterized by a different set of symptoms, although distinctions among the types are not always clear-cut. Indeed, one subtype—undifferentiated—is a catchall category for cases that do not fit into

TABLE 13-5   Subtypes of Schizophrenia

SUBTYPE	KEY SYMPTOMS
Catatonic	Unusual motor symptoms ranging from rigidity to wild hyperactivity and occasional alterations between inactivity and excitement. Seldom seen today because drug treatments reduce or eliminate the symptoms.
Disorganized	Incoherent speech with highly unusual verbal associations along with flat or inappropriate affect (emotional expressions that are often the opposite of expected reactions). Patients often seem silly and childlike and may grimace, giggle inappropriately, and appear absorbed in thought. The onset of symptoms usually occurs during adolescence—the earliest onset of the subtypes. The symptoms do not seem to be reactions to stressful life events. The continuous nature of the disorder leads to a downhill progression that often results in long-term institutionalization.
Paranoid	Delusions of grandeur or persecution with possible auditory hallucinations. Has the latest age of onset of the subtypes. Develops in individuals who often have demonstrated good functioning before the relatively acute onset of symptoms. Has a generally good outcome and good recovery rates.
Residual	Delusions, hallucinations, and incoherent language are absent, but continuation of the disorder is evident in social withdrawal or odd beliefs.
Undifferentiated	Symptoms may include prominent delusions, hallucinations, and disorganized speech that do not fit other subtypes. Long-term outcomes of this subtype are highly variable.

Sources: American Psychiatric Association, 1994; Beratis, Gabriel, & Hoidas, 1994; Fenton & McGlashan, 1991.

other subtypes. A patient may exhibit the symptoms of different subtypes of schizophrenia at different times during the course of the disorder.

Causes of Schizophrenia

The search for what causes schizophrenia is difficult because there are no physical tests for the disorder, and no animal models exist. What's more, researchers are not sure if schizophrenia results from a single process or several processes. There have been many false leads and potential breakthroughs. Currently considered to be among the possible causes are genetic factors, brain abnormalities, altered neurotransmitter levels, and environmental factors.

Genetic Factors.   When Beth was 3 years old, her father died in a mental hospital, where he was being treated for schizophrenia. Beth, who is expecting a baby, wants to know whether her family history means that her child is at risk for developing schizophrenia. To help answer Beth's question, let's suppose that we randomly selected a person from the general population. What are the chances that this person will develop schizophrenia? Suppose we randomly select another person from a family with a member who has been diagnosed as suffering from schizophrenia. Does the risk change?

We noted earlier that approximately 1-1.5 percent of the population develops schizophrenia, so the answer to the first question is about 1-1.5 percent. Because schizophrenia runs in families, the odds that it will occur in a person selected from a family with a member who has the diagnosis are greater than 1 percent. How much greater depends on the person's relationship to the family member with schizophrenia. Figure 13-8 lists the risk (odds) of developing schizophrenia for various family members. The risk increases with the degree of genetic relatedness (Gottesman, 1991). Thus having a brother or sister with schizophrenia raises the risk to 9 percent; the risk spirals to 46 percent for children of two parents with the disorder. Beth's baby has about a 5

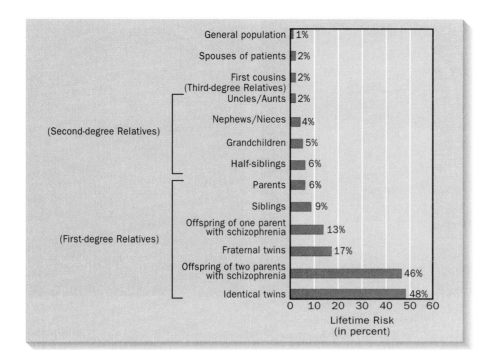

FIGURE 13-8 Degree of genetic relationship and average risk for developing schizophrenia. The risk varies as a function of genetic relatedness to a person afflicted with the disorder as compared with the risk in the general population. The highest risk occurs among co-twins of identical (monozygotic) twins who suffer from schizophrenia, which suggests that genetic factors play a role in schizophrenia. The fact that the risk is not 100 percent for identical twins, however, suggests that non-gentic (environmental) factors also play a role.

Source: Gottesman, 1991.

percent chance of developing schizophrenia because the grandfather (Beth's father) had the disorder; the risk for the grandchild of a person with schizophrenia is 5 percent. The concordance rates (both twins diagnosed with schizophrenia) across several reports are 48 percent for identical twins and 17 percent for fraternal twins (Gottesman, 1991). This 3:1 ratio in the concordance rates for identical to fraternal twins strongly implicates genetic factors. In sum, this research has produced evidence suggesting that schizophrenia may be transmitted genetically.

When children are reared by parents diagnosed with schizophrenia, we cannot separate genetic factors from the effects of being raised by parents with the disorder (environmental factors). For this reason, psychologists rely on studies of adopted children to distinguish the effects of genetics (nature) from those of the environment (nurture). In one study of children with at least one biological parent diagnosed with schizophrenia, rates of the disorder among the children were similar, regardless of whether they were raised by the biological parents or adopted parents (Wender et al., 1974). These results suggest that nature plays a more significant role than nurture in the development of schizophrenia.

Psychological Detective

 Is schizophrenia a genetically transmitted disorder? Can you identify reasons that genetic factors may not be the entire story? Twins are often reared in similar environments, raising the issue of nature versus nurture. What's more, if one twin has schizophrenia the other (co-twin) twin does not always develop the disorder. If schizophrenia were transmitted entirely by genes, what concordance rate would you expect to find in identical twins? Why?

If genetic factors provided the complete answer to the cause of schizophrenia, we would expect a concordance rate of 100 percent among identical twins because such twins share all their genetic material. The less than 100 percent

FIGURE 13-9 MRI scans of the brains of identical twins, one with schizophrenia (left) and the other normal. Note the difference in the size of the ventricles (fluid-filled spaces in the brain).

Source: Suddath et al., 1990.

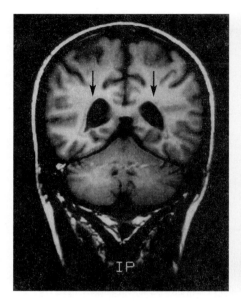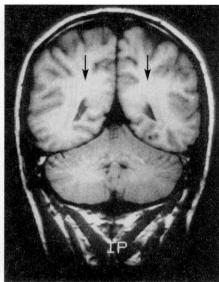

concordance rate for identical twins suggests a role for non-genetic factors (Moldin & Gottesman, 1997).

Brain Abnormalities.   A promising area of research on the causes of schizophrenia is the study of brain abnormalities. A number of studies using different methods have demonstrated that some patients with schizophrenia have significantly larger cerebral ventricles—fluid-filled chambers in the brain—than nonschizophrenic people and therefore have smaller brain areas (Lickey & Gordon, 1991; Suddath et al., 1990). For example, limbic-area brain structures such as the hippocampus are smaller in some people with schizophrenia (Cannon & Marco, 1994). The limbic system plays a role in emotional response, memory, and other functions (see Chapter 2).

Psychiatrist Nancy Andreasen and her colleagues (1994) compared the brains of patients diagnosed with schizophrenia with those of normal individuals. A procedure called MRI averaging calculates the average of images of the brains of patients and compares it with the average image of the brains of nonschizophrenic individuals. The results showed that the thalamus and surrounding areas in the patients with schizophrenia were smaller. Why is this finding important? The thalamus is a major relay station for information to and from brain structures that are important to emotion and memory. An abnormality in this structure could cause a flood of information to a person and make it difficult to respond appropriately. If this finding can be replicated, it may help us understand the wide array of symptoms seen in schizophrenia.

Are brain abnormalities associated with schizophrenia genetically transmitted? MRI pictures of the brains of discordant twin pairs—twin pairs in which one twin had schizophrenia and the other did not—have revealed clear differences in their brains. The ventricles in the twin with schizophrenia were larger than in the normal twin (see Figure 13-9). A difference in the ventricle size in identical twins could not be the result of genetic factors and provides further evidence that genetic factors are not the sole cause of schizophrenia. Men and women diagnosed with schizophrenia both show this pattern of ventricle enlargement; ventricle enlargement in men, however, is greater and may account for the common finding that the symptoms of schizophrenia are more severe in men than in women (Nopoulos, Flaum, & Andreasen, 1997).

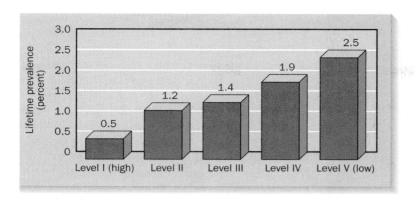

FIGURE 13-10 Socioeconomic status and prevalence of schizophrenia. (Socioeconomic status decreases from left to right.)

Source: Robins & Regier, 1991.

The exact cause of the differing size of the ventricles has not been identified; one proposed cause is viral infection very early in life (Torrey, 1991). An association of viral infections with schizophrenia was demonstrated in a follow-up of children born in 1966 in northern Finland. There was a strong association between the risk of developing schizophrenia and infections. According to the data, however, less than 6 percent of those in the sample with a diagnosis of schizophrenia had experienced infection. This finding suggests that viral infections may be one of many factors that could lead to the development of schizophrenia (Rantakallio et al., 1997).

Neurotransmitters. Another focus of research is the role of neurotransmitters. Not long ago, patients could be seen roaming the halls of mental hospitals, behaving in erratic, sometimes violent ways, because available therapies were ineffective in controlling their behavior. Many patients were confined in straitjackets to prevent them from harming themselves and others. In the 1950s, a powerful group of antipsychotic drugs was developed (see Chapter 14); these drugs made most patients more cooperative and easier for the hospital staff to manage. The effectiveness of these drugs suggested another possible cause: biochemical abnormalities.

Available evidence suggests that the neurotransmitter dopamine plays a role in schizophrenia. Certain drugs, such as amphetamines and cocaine, can induce some of the symptoms of schizophrenia, and these drugs are known to increase dopamine levels in the brain. The brains of people with schizophrenia may have more dopamine receptors, or their dopamine receptors may be more sensitive than those of a person not suffering from the disorder. What's more, levels of dopamine activity may differ in different parts of the brain, and this could account for some of the variations in the symptoms of schizophrenia.

Of course, genetic factors may influence either dopamine levels or sensitivity to dopamine. The evidence, however, does not prove that schizophrenia is caused by biochemical factors alone.

Environmental Causes. Genetic and various biological factors are not the only possible causes of schizophrenia. Consider the following: Schizophrenia runs in families, and identical twins are concordant for schizophrenia more often than fraternal twins. Yet 89 percent of all people with schizophrenia do *not* have a parent who suffers from schizophrenia (Gottesman, 1991).

The failure of genetic factors to provide a full explanation of why some people develop schizophrenia has fueled interest in environmental, including psychological, explanations. Stressful events and conditions have been shown to play a role in schizophrenia (Dohrenwend & Ergi, 1981). We

Psychologists have studied the Genain quadruplets for more than three decades in an attempt to unravel the mystery of schizophrenia. All of the sisters were diagnosed as suffering from schizophrenia, although their level of adjustment and length of hospitalization varied.

know that schizophrenia is diagnosed more frequently among people in lower socioeconomic classes than among those in higher classes (see Figure 13-10). Low-income people experience many stressors, including inadequate housing, substandard medical care, and poor diet. What's more, schizophrenia is more prevalent in urban areas than in rural ones—a tendency not attributed to differences in hospitalization policies (Torrey & Bowler, 1990). A study of the rate of schizophrenia in the Netherlands near the end of World War II suggests that prenatal nutritional deficiencies may play a role in the origin of some cases. Residents of the Netherlands endured severe famine as a result of the Nazi blockade of ports and other supply routes. Compared with people conceived at other times during the study period, individuals conceived at the height of the famine exhibited twice the rate of schizophrenia (Susser et al., 1996).

A series of studies has demonstrated a relationship between home environment and the risk of relapse for patients with schizophrenia. These studies have focused on *expressed emotion (EE)*, the degree to which family members' spontaneous talk about the patient is described as critical, hostile, or overinvolved. EE levels are assessed by interviewing family members and examining the content and vocal qualities of speech. A meta-analysis (see Chapter 11) of 27 studies found that EE was a significant predictor of relapse among patients with schizophrenia, and an even stronger predictor of relapse among patients with mood disorders and eating disorders (Butzlaff & Hooley, 1998). Expressed emotion, however, is a controversial topic because it can be viewed as blaming family members for the disorder and its relapses. Moreover, the direction of the effect is not clear: The family's emotional climate may be a reaction to the patient's symptoms rather than a result of those symptoms. For example, patients from families with high levels of EE are more likely to display odd and disruptive behavior within the family than patients from low-EE families (Rosenfarb et al., 1995).

But can stressors like poverty, urban life, or family conflict actually cause schizophrenia? Thousands of people have gone off to wars, suffered in major natural disasters, or been victims of violent crimes; few of them have developed schizophrenia. Researchers now believe that schizophrenia may result from several causes rather than a single cause.

Multiple Causes.　In 1930, four baby girls were born in a midwestern town. Known as the Genain quadruplets (not their real name), they had a turbulent family life. By the time they reached the age of 25, all four had been hospitalized with the diagnosis of schizophrenia. The Genain sisters were studied extensively by mental health experts, who attributed their common disorder to the interaction of several factors, including genetics and dysfunctional family life (Mirsky & Quinn, 1988; Mirsky et al., 1987).

In sum, it appears that no one inherits the specific symptoms of schizophrenia, although genetic factors play a role in a person's chances of developing the disorder. Despite past reports isolating a specific gene related to schizophrenia, the consensus of researchers suggests that multiple genes are involved in the disorder's development (Moldin & Gottesman, 1997). What is inherited?

Irving Gottesman (1991) suggests that "what is inherited is a predisposition toward developing the disorder—a loading of nature's dice that increases the risk of developing schizophrenia" (p. 91). The child of a parent with schizophrenia is at higher risk for developing the disorder than the cousin of an individual with schizophrenia. Whether a child actually develops schizophrenia is determined by a number of environmental factors, none of which has been clearly identified to date.

Review Summary

1. Schizophrenia affects approximately 1-1.5 percent of the population. It is often confused with dissociative identity disorder; however, the two are different disorders. Schizophrenia is characterized by a split between thoughts and emotions and a separation from reality.

2. The symptoms of schizophrenia can be classified as positive (excesses) or negative (deficits). Positive symptoms include fluent but disorganized speech, **delusions,** and **hallucinations.** Negative symptoms include disturbances in emotional expression such as flat affect along with disturbances in volition.

3. The DSM-IV lists five subtypes of schizophrenia: catatonic, disorganized, paranoid, residual, and undifferentiated.

4. Schizophrenia tends to run in families; the risk of developing the disorder increases with the degree of genetic relatedness between an individual and a family member who has schizophrenia.

5. Evidence of various brain abnormalities, including larger ventricles and a smaller thalamus, in people with schizophrenia suggests a possible cause. The neurotransmitter, dopamine, seems to be involved in the development of schizophrenia.

6. Environmental influences on schizophrenia include stress and hostile family communication. A predisposition to schizophrenia may be inherited, with the actual development of the disorder requiring the presence of other factors such as poverty or family conflict.

Study Break

1. Identify the following symptoms of schizophrenia as either positive or negative.
   a. The patient hears voices in an empty house.
   b. The patient believes others are controlling his thoughts.
   c. The patient rarely smiles, does not change her tone of voice, and does not maintain eye contact.
2. On the basis of the following symptoms, identify the most likely subtype of schizophrenia.
   a. The patient grimaces and assumes unusual postures.
   b. The patient is suspicious and has delusions of persecution.
   c. There are no prominent symptoms, but the patient is withdrawn.
3. What is the risk of developing schizophrenia for someone in the general population?
4. What concordance rate among identical twins would you expect if schizophrenia were entirely a genetic disorder?
5. What parts of the brain have been found to be smaller in individuals with schizophrenia as compared with those without the disorder?
6. Which neurotransmitter has been implicated in the development of schizophrenia?
7. What evidence suggests that schizophrenia is not entirely genetically based?

Personality and Sexual Disorders

When he was younger, Chuck spent plenty of time in the principal's office for fighting. One night during Christmas vacation, Chuck left his house and stole decorations from neighbors' homes. Footprints in the freshly fallen snow led the police to Chuck, who nonetheless denied knowledge of the incident. When he was 14, Chuck vandalized cars; when he was 18, he was arrested for dangling an acquaintance from a bridge. When asked why he committed such acts, he said that he was bored and wanted to "stir up some excitement." *Does Chuck's long-standing pattern of deviant behavior indicate that he exhibits a psychological disorder?* ▨

Personality Disorders

Personality disorders are long-standing patterns of maladaptive behavior that are usually evident during the adolescent years and are resistant to treatment, which is seldom sought. Approximately 10 percent of the adult population may have one or more personality disorders. The high rate of comorbidity of personality disorders with other psychological disorders as well as with medical conditions complicates diagnosis and treatment (Oldham, 1994). What's more, people with personality disorders are convinced that if a problem exists, it lies not in them but in other people's reactions to their behaviors. For example, the key feature of *narcissistic personality disorder* is an inflated sense of self-importance and superiority. Narcissistic individuals are preoccupied with fantasies of success, power, beauty, or ideal love. They are sure that other people recognize their special qualities and are therefore envious. Expectations of attention, admiration, and compliance with their wishes are frequently expressed. Yet a lack of empathy leaves them unable to understand other's reactions to their behavior.

The DSM-IV describes several personality disorders, but a great deal of attention has focused on one of them: the antisocial personality disorder. About 5 to 6 percent of adult men and 1 percent of adult women would meet the criteria for this diagnosis (Kessler et al., 1994; Robins, Tipp, & Przybeck, 1991). Consider Chuck, whom we described at the beginning of the section. Is his long-standing pattern of deviant behavior characteristic of a psychological disorder?

Chuck was eventually diagnosed as exhibiting **antisocial personality disorder;** in the past, he would have been called a *psychopath* or a *sociopath*. People exhibiting this disorder are often selfish, impulsive, manipulative, and remorseless. Robert Hare (1993), who has spent his career investigating these individuals, concluded that "lying, deceiving, and manipulation are natural talents" for them (p. 46). For example, one antisocial individual spotted a couple admiring a sailboat that had a For Sale sign on it. He introduced himself as the owner and invited them aboard for a closer look. They liked what they saw and handed him a deposit of $1,500. That was the last time they saw their money and the man (Hare, 1993).

The signs of disturbance seen in other disorders—anxiety, depression, or hallucinations—are absent in antisocial personality disorder. Individuals with this disorder rarely seek professional help unless their goal is to obtain an excuse to be absent from work, to acquire drugs, or to avoid prison by submitting to court-ordered treatment. They can appear so normal that psychiatrist Hervey Cleckley (1976) titled his classic book about them *The Mask of Sanity.*

Because antisocial individuals do not experience the warning signals of anxiety, they are prone to act impulsively, without regard for the feelings or well-being of others. They want immediate gratification, fail to develop emotional attachments, and have no remorse for their actions: "They leave in their

personality disorders
Disorders characterized by long-standing, difficult-to-treat, dysfunctional behaviors that are typically first observed in adolescence

antisocial personality disorder
Personality disorder characterized by deceitful, impulsive, reckless actions for which the individual feels no remorse

wakes a huge amount of human suffering. The pain [these individuals] wreak on other human beings can be physical, or it can be the mental anguish often felt by those who try to form relationships" with them (Magid & McKelvey, 1987, p. 4). Yet these individuals can be charming and ingratiating when it is to their advantage. Serial killer Ted Bundy used his charm to lure dozens of young women to accompany him to isolated places; only one of them was ever seen alive again.

Many antisocial people do not come into contact with law enforcement agencies. These con men, unethical business leaders, and crooked politicians are less dramatic but more numerous than the Ted Bundy type of killer. Nevertheless, our understanding of this disorder is based largely on studies of the unlucky or unsuccessful antisocial individuals found in prisons.

Cathy Spatz Widom (1977) devised a clever plan to identify antisocial people who are not in prison. She placed the following advertisement in newspapers: "Are you adventurous? Psychologist studying adventurous carefree people who've led exciting impulsive lives" (p. 675). A number of respondents to the advertisement met the criteria for antisocial personality disorder. Almost 50 percent of them had a history of heavy drinking and considerable experience with other drugs. Many had been arrested but had spent little time in jail, preferring court-ordered psychotherapy. Widom concluded that many people outside of prisons could be diagnosed as exhibiting antisocial personality disorder.

Antisocial behavior may occur in two forms (Moffitt, 1993). *Adolescence-limited antisocial behavior* is a common form that may be adaptive in some circumstances; it often disappears by the time the person reaches adulthood. This type of behavior presumably accounts for most antisocial behavior; it is not, however, related to antisocial personality disorder. The second type, *life-course persistent antisocial behavior,* occurs when the person engages in antisocial behavior into adulthood. The childhood and adolescent years of people diagnosed as exhibiting antisocial personality disorder as adults are marked by hyperactivity, impulsivity, attention problems, and neuropsychological impairment (Lynam, 1998). Nevertheless, many of them tend to engage in fewer criminal activities after age 40 (Hare, McPherson, & Forth, 1988). The specific reasons for this decrease are not clear. Perhaps these people continue their antisocial activities but have developed better strategies for staying out of prison.

Because people with antisocial personalities do not conform to social norms, researchers have turned their attention to the socializing agent that is primarily responsible for instilling social norms in the young: the family. They have found that during childhood, many antisocial people were subjected to inconsistent discipline or no discipline at all. As in Chuck's case, their future course was evident in early episodes of fighting, lying, stealing, and vandalism. Many children who are raised with little or no discipline, however, do not develop antisocial tendencies. Thus it appears that lack of discipline during childhood is not a complete explanation of the emergence of antisocial tendencies.

Psychological Detective

Over the years researchers have found that antisocial individuals have a low level of physiological arousal, a condition that is so uncomfortable that they will do almost anything to change it. As Chuck said, he was just trying to "stir up some excitement." How could researchers determine that an individual has a low level of arousal? How could they determine whether level of arousal is related to anti-social activity? Before reading further, design a study to gather evidence that might show that physiological arousal is or is not related to antisocial behavior.

gender identity disorder (transsexualism)
Sexual disorder characterized by a person's belief that he or she was born with the wrong biological sex organs

paraphilia
Sexual arousal by objects or situations not considered sexual by most people

fetishism
Paraphilia involving sexual arousal by unusual objects or body parts

Doris Richards (*top*) was a high school physical education teacher who changed her gender identity to become Steve Dain (*bottom*).

Just such a study was conducted by Adrian Raine, Peter Venables, and Mark Williams (1990). They recruited 101 young men between the ages of 14 and 16 to take part in a program to measure heart rate and brain waves, which served as indicators of arousal. Assessing the relationship of physiological arousal to antisocial behavior required a longitudinal research design. The criminal records of the young men were checked when they reached age 24. The men with a criminal record at that age were more likely to have had low arousal levels when they were teenagers than the men with no criminal record. Using only the indicators of physiological arousal, the researchers correctly classified 75 percent of the men as criminal or noncriminal.

Sexual Disorders

The DSM-IV divides sexual disorders into several categories: gender identity disorder (transsexualism), the paraphilias, and sexual dysfunctions. In this section we discuss the first two categories.

Gender Identity Disorder. Are you a male or a female? Although this seems like a silly question, for some people it is a serious matter. Beginning in childhood, some people believe their anatomical sex does not match their gender identity. Many cases of **gender identity disorder (transsexualism)** in childhood cease by the time the individual reaches adolescence, but some cases progress into what is known as transsexualism.

Transsexualism is a disorder in which a person is uncomfortable with his or her anatomical sex, views it as inappropriate, and wants to be a member of the other sex. This rare disorder occurs in 1 in 30,000 biological males and 1 in 100,000 biological females (American Psychiatric Association, 1994). One treatment, sex-reassignment surgery, involves surgically creating external sex organs that are characteristic of the other biological sex. Mental health professionals screen the candidates for sex reassignment surgery to ensure that disorders like schizophrenia are not present. If no psychotic disorder is found, the individual begins hormone treatment to alter secondary sex characteristics such as the presence (or absence) of facial hair. Before having the surgery, he or she spends one to two years dressing and behaving as a member of the other sex. Although evidence suggests that transsexuals who have undergone the operation are generally quite satisfied (Pauly, 1990), controversy surrounds the treatment because it is radical and irreversible.

Paraphilias. **Paraphilia** literally means "love beyond the usual" (Money, 1984). People with paraphilias are sexually aroused by objects or situations that are considered unusual or bizarre by most people, ranging from animals to dressing in the clothes of the other sex. Most of these individuals are men; their unusual activity is typically harmless or involves consenting others. Some of these people, however, can be dangerous and may come into contact with legal authorities.

Table 13-6 lists some of the more common paraphilias.

Fetishism. Derived from a French word for a magical charm, a fetish is an object that arouses sexual passion in some people. **Fetishism** is a sexual disorder in which an object or body part becomes associated with sexual arousal. A wide variety of objects may serve as fetishes; among them are boots, fur, and underwear. Some of these objects are associated with sexual activity; others are rarely associated with sexual excitement by most people. Fetishists may kiss, taste, or smell the fetish and masturbate while fondling it.

Consider the case of a 32-year-old man who was sexually excited at a young age by pictures of women wearing panties. At the age of 13, he ejaculated for the first time while fantasizing about panties. Thereafter he began to steal panties from his sister and her friends. His preferred pattern of sexual excitement involved panties, which he used while masturbating. Dating made him uncomfortable because he feared that if he and his date became intimate, she would not understand his sexual practices (Spitzer et al., 1994).

Psychodynamic theorists see paraphilias as associated with early childhood experiences or, in some cases, as alternatives that arouse less anxiety than sexual encounters with adult partners. Behavioral psychologists, in contrast, believe that most fetishes, and probably many of the paraphilias, develop through classical conditioning. Perhaps the object that becomes a fetish was accidentally paired with sexual arousal and thus acquired the power to elicit arousal later in life. In laboratory experiments, psychologists have paired pictures of boots with slides of nudes (Rachman, 1966). The participant's level of sexual arousal was measured by a device placed on the penis. The results showed that the arousal caused by the nudes was transferred to the boots.

TABLE 13-6 Paraphilias

Exhibitionism (indecent exposure, flashing): Repeated exposure of genitals to unsuspecting strangers, usually women and children. The exhibitionist may masturbate while exposing his genitals but usually does not pursue further sexual activity. Exhibitionists seem to desire surprise or shock in victims but are usually not physically dangerous to them.

Fetishism: Sexual arousal associated with nonliving objects, called fetishes, such as stockings, shoes, or boots. The fetishist often masturbates while fondling the desired object.

Frotteurism: Sexual arousal as a result of rubbing against or touching a nonconsenting person. The behavior usually occurs in crowded places like busy sidewalks or on public transportation. Victims may not protest at first because they cannot believe that such provocative acts are occurring in a public place.

Klismaphilia: Sexual arousal resulting from receiving or giving an enema.

Mysophilia: Sexual arousal that involves the presence of or use of filth.

Necrophilia: Sexual pleasure from viewing or having sexual contact with a corpse.

Partialism: Intense sexual attraction to specific body parts (most often legs or feet, and excluding genitals, breasts, and buttocks).

Pedophilia: Sexual activity with a child who has not reached puberty. Attraction to girls is twice as common as attraction to boys.

Sexual masochism: Sexual arousal that involves being humiliated, beaten, bound, or made to suffer in other ways.

Sexual sadism: Sexual arousal associated with the physical or psychological suffering of victims.

Transvestic fetishism: Sexual arousal associated with cross-dressing; that is, dressing in the clothes of the opposite sex.

Voyeurism (peeping): Sexual arousal as a result of observing unsuspecting individuals, most often strangers, who are either naked, in the process of undressing, or engaging in sexual activity. The voyeur usually does not seek any sexual liaison with the observed person.

Zoophilia: Sexual activity with animals.

Sources: American Psychiatric Association, 1994; Money, 1984.

Review Summary

1. **Personality disorders** are long-standing dysfunctional patterns of behavior. A person with antisocial personality disorder displays few of the signs usually associated with psychological disorders, such as anxiety. They are often described as deceitful, impulsive, and remorseless. Low levels of arousal may play a role in the development of this disorder.

2. **Gender identity disorder (transsexualism)** is a sexual disorder in which a person believes that he or she should have been a member of the opposite sex.

3. **Paraphilias** are disorders involving sexual arousal in unusual situations or in response to unusual objects. **Fetishism** is a paraphilia in which a person is sexually aroused by an object such as boots. One of the explanations for fetishism and perhaps other paraphilias is classical conditioning.

Study Break

1. What are the key symptoms of antisocial personality disorder? In what ways do antisocial individuals appear to be quite normal?
2. What are the key symptoms of transsexualism?
3. Give the name of each of the following sexual disorders.
   a. Sexual activity with a child
   b. Sexual contact with animals
   c. Sexual contact with dead bodies
   d. Sexual arousal from rubbing against a person
   e. Sexual arousal from receiving or giving an enema
   f. Sexual arousal related to boots or fur

ANSWERS TO STUDY BREAKS

Pages 541–542

1. a. Dysfunctional or personal distress
   b. Deviance from social norms
2. a. Behavioral
   b. Cognitive
3. Right-wrong or M'Naughton definition
4. d
5. d
6. a
7. Schizophrenia. Labels can influence our perceptions of behavior.
8. a. 200 cases in a year
   b. 1,000 is the lifetime prevalence

Page 553

1. a. Obsessive-compulsive disorder
   b. Somatization disorder
   c. Conversion disorder
   d. Panic disorder
2. An obsession is a recurrent, intrusive thought, impulse or image that is unwanted and inappropriate; a compulsion is a repeated, irresistible behavior or mental act that often follows obsessions.
3. Autonomic, central
4. a-5 b-4 c-2 d-3 e-1
5. Dissociative identity disorder; schizophrenia, depression, and alcohol or drug abuse

Pages 562–563

1. The rate of depression around the world is increasing and people are experiencing the first episode at a younger age.
2. a. Either increased appetite or loss of appetite
   b. Increased sleep (hypersomnia) or insomnia
   c. Depressed people often see themselves as unattractive and incapable of completing intellectually demanding tasks
3. a. The rate of suicide is higher among men.
   b. The rate of suicide tends to increase with age.
   c. Divorced people have a higher rate of suicide than married people.
   d. The rate of suicide is highest among people suffering from depression, alcohol abuse/dependence or schizophrenia
4. d
5. c
6. b
7. *Universal:* "I am able to deal successfully with difficult situations." *Internal:* "My success in dealing with difficult situations is due to my ability to stay calm and assess the situation accurately." *Permanent:* "My ability to handle my course work does not vary from one course or challenge to another." *Specific:* "I tend to do well in classes that I like when I have friends to call upon." *External:* "It is a good thing that I selected one of the easier teachers and got a class that met early in the morning." *Temporary:* "My ablity to handle challenges can change rapidly, almost at a moment's notice."

Page 571

1. **a.** Positive
   b. Positive
   c. Negative
2. **a.** Catatonic
   b. Paranoid
   c. Residual
3. Approximately 1-1.5 percent
4. 100 percent
5. Limbic system, thalamus
6. Dopamine
7. The concordance rate for identical twins is not 100 percent, and some identical twins (one with schizophrenia and one without) have been shown to have different-sized brain ventricles.

Page 576

1. The individual with antisocial personality disorder is described as irresponsible, deceitful, manipulative, and remorseless. People with this disorder do not, however, exhibit anxiety or depression and do not experience hallucinations.
2. A transsexual is a person who has no genetic abnormality yet believes he or she has the sex organs of the wrong sex.
3. **a.** Pedophilia
   b. Zoophilia
   c. Necrophilia
   d. Frotteurism
   e. Klismaphilia
   f. Fetishism

Therapy

Chapter in Perspective

By now you have seen that our earlier discussions of basic processes such as learning provide the background necessary to understand more complex topics such as the causes and treatment of psychological disorders. We can now appreciate the role biological mechanisms play in shaping both normal and abnormal behaviors. In addition, our growing awareness of human diversity helps us recognize how ethnicity and culture affect both our choice of treatment and the effectiveness of the therapies we choose. As we shall see, even biomedical treatments can be influenced by these factors.

The psychological disorders discussed in Chapter 13 sometimes become so distressing that the people who experience them seek treatment or therapy. Where do these people seek help? What kinds of therapies are available? Do current therapies reduce or eliminate the patients' symptoms? In this chapter we attempt to answer these questions. As we do so, keep in mind that our beliefs about the nature and origins of psychological disorders often determine which therapies we deem appropriate and useful. ■

Therapy through the Ages

The morning sun radiates across the sky; the birds greet the new day with a chorus of song. A young man, Oag, rises from sleeping quarters he shares with others. Although all the adults in the community are attending to their chores, the young man wanders off. On a typical day he sits and stares for long periods; then suddenly he seems propelled into a frenzied state. His behavior is unpredictable, and everyone is afraid of him. The elders decide the time has come to deal with his strange behavior. ***How did our earliest ancestors treat abnormal behaviors?*** ▪

The History of Therapy

Thousands of years ago, our ancestors attributed earthquakes, lightning, and thunder to evil spirits or demons. A successful hunt might have been viewed as the work of good spirits. Similarly, a person's bizarre behavior was often viewed as the work of a demon (bad spirit) that had "possessed" or taken command of the person's body. Techniques such as exorcism were used to rid the body of demons, which is how the elders treated Oag. Such beliefs are evident today in our use of language, as when we ask someone who has engaged in unusual behavior, "What got into you?" This question suggests earlier notions of demon possession.

The Greek philosopher and physician Hippocrates (460–377 B.C.) proposed that physical and psychological disorders have natural causes. He suggested that some disorders result from imbalances among four "humors" (liquids) in the body: black bile, blood, phlegm, and yellow bile (see Chapter 12). For example, elevated levels of black bile were thought to lead to *melancholia,* a term we use today to denote an especially severe form of depression. The Greek emphasis on naturalistic explanations continued in ancient Rome, where people received treatments such as baths, exercise, and massage.

Asylums and Hospitals.   During the sixteenth and seventeenth centuries, some people whose only "crimes" may have been that they suffered from psychological disorders were accused of being witches. The body of an accused witch might be examined for marks, which were considered evidence of a pact with Satan. The "witch" was often brutally tortured and was frequently killed.

Not all mentally ill people were tortured or put to death. Some were housed in institutions like St. Mary of Bethlehem Hospital in London, where patients were often kept in chains and slept on straw beds. On weekends visitors could pay a penny to amuse themselves by watching these patients. The hospital was known for its disorganization, unsanitary conditions, and inhumane treatment of patients. The word *bedlam,* a contraction of *Bethlehem,* came into the language to describe such conditions.

Moral Therapy.   In the eighteenth century, mentally ill people in Paris were often chained to walls. The attendants, or "keepers" as they were called, rarely showed compassion and even administered punishment when they deemed it necessary. A physician, Philippe Pinel (1745–1826), argued that what these patients needed was humane care and treatment. His ideas, however, ran counter to the prevailing notion that mental hospitals should function to protect society from the insane. Many of Pinel's ideas were derived from the work of Jean-Baptiste Pussin, a former patient at a hospital in which Pinel worked. After he was discharged, Pussin was given a job at

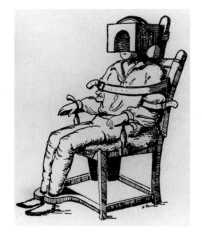

Tranquilizer chair. Benjamin Rush, recognized as the "Father of American Psychiatry," recommended use of the tranquilizer chair for patients suffering from mania. He also used bloodletting to treat the symptoms of mania; some of his patients died when he removed too much of their blood.

St. Mary of Bethlehem Hospital in London. Visitors amused themselves by watching patients.

a hospital in Paris. When he became superintendent of a ward for incurable mental patients, he insisted that the staff should be kind and gentle, he dismissed those who mistreated patients, and he removed the patients' chains.

After being named chief physician at another hospital, Pinel followed in the footsteps of Pussin and removed the patients' chains, directed the staff to treat the patients kindly, and stopped the use of bloodletting and punishment. Pinel's efforts led to a treatment philosophy called *moral management* or *moral therapy.* The term did not suggest any moralistic content of the treatment; rather, it reflected the belief that providing a humane and relaxed environment could produce positive changes in a person's behavior (Grob, 1994).

Benjamin Rush (1745–1813) introduced moral therapy at Philadelphia's Pennsylvania Hospital, the first general hospital in the United States with a separate unit for the mentally ill (Talbott, 1994). Rush expected staff members to be friends to the patients. Yet he restrained manic patients in his tranquilizer chair, which he thought was more humane than other restraints used at the time.

State Mental Hospitals.   In the mid-nineteenth century, Dorothea Lynde Dix (1802–1887), a former teacher, became concerned about the plight of the homeless and disturbed people. Her survey of Massachusetts institutions that housed the mentally ill yielded numerous examples of misery and horror. Armed with knowledge and determination, Dix insisted that the states had an obligation to provide care for the mentally ill. She convinced legislatures in 20 states to establish or enlarge mental hospitals (Grob, 1994).

As the states assumed more responsibility for custodial care of the mentally ill, economics dictated they build larger institutions to handle more patients. As the institutions expanded, conditions deteriorated, and the use of restraining devices increased. The institutions became more like warehouses for patients who were less likely to recover.

New Forms of Treatment.   Franz Anton Mesmer and his notion of animal magnetism offered a very different view of psychological disorders and their treatment (see Chapter 5). Mesmer believed he could harness this magnetism

As institutions for the mentally ill became larger and more crowded, staff members resorted to restraint devices like this criblike enclosure from the 1800s and various straps used through the 1950s.

The determined efforts of Dorothea Dix convinced many states to build institutions to treat people suffering from mental disorders. When she agreed to teach a religious class in a Massachusetts jail, she observed mentally ill persons confined in facilities with hardened criminals. She spent more than a year traveling throughout Massachusetts inspecting places where mentally ill patients were housed. Her observations became part of a petition to the legislature to expand the Worcester Hospital and to build other facilities. She followed a similar strategy in other states, where she would gather data and then present her findings to the legislature.

Source: Grob, 1994.

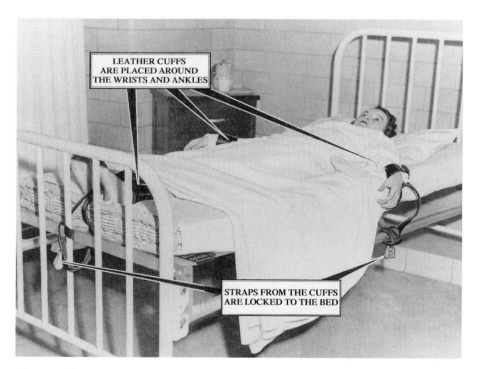

LEATHER CUFFS ARE PLACED AROUND THE WRISTS AND ANKLES

STRAPS FROM THE CUFFS ARE LOCKED TO THE BED

The use of restraints declined dramatically with the development of antipsychotic drugs.

as a form of therapy to treat patients. With modifications, his techniques evolved into hypnotism. Sigmund Freud, an early advocate of hypnotism as a therapeutic technique, developed the notion that psychological disorders result from unconscious feelings and conflicts, which required a different approach to therapy. At first he believed that hypnosis was an appropriate way to deal with these feelings and conflicts, but he later turned to other techniques when hypnosis proved less effective than he had hoped.

While Freud was exploring the unconscious for clues to the causes and treatment of psychological disorders, others were exploring the biological roots of such disorders. Early in the twentieth century, the disorder known as *general paresis,* which included symptoms such as paralysis and memory difficulties, was found to result from syphilis. This finding stimulated the search for biological causes of other psychological disorders, as well as the development of biomedical treatments such as psychosurgery and electroconvulsive (shock) therapy, which are described later in this chapter.

Deinstitutionalization.   Despite the availability of new treatments, many seriously disturbed patients continued to be housed in overcrowded and understaffed mental hospitals. Beginning in the 1950s, the populations of mental hospitals began to decline. One reason for this decline was the use of antipsychotic drugs, which made it possible to control many serious symptoms (Talbott, 1994). At the same time, there was a growing belief that community care was more effective than hospitalization (McGubbin, 1994). What's more, during the 1960s, state and federal courts restricted the grounds for committing people to hospitals. Generally speaking, states could commit patients involuntarily only if the patients were judged to be dangerous to themselves or others or in need of treatment. The courts also insisted that institutionalized patients had rights to minimum levels of treatment and care. These factors led to **deinstitutionalization,** a policy of discharging large numbers of patients from mental hospitals and then closing part or all of those hospitals. As a result of deinstitutionalization, the population of mental hospitals declined (see Figure 14-1) from more than 500,000 in the 1950s to less than 100,000 in 1995, despite a substantial increase in the overall population and the number of people suffering from psychological disorders (Torrey, 1997). If we consider the rate of increase in the overall population and the associated increase in the number of people with disorders, an estimated 90 percent of the people who would have been institutionalized in the 1950s are now living outside of institutions.

The Community Mental Health Movement.   In 1963, Congress passed the Community Mental Health Centers Act. This law provided funds for the establishment of community mental health centers in which patients would be treated on an outpatient basis.

In addition, the 1963 law helped finance community-based programs to prevent mental illness. Thus mental health professionals placed more emphasis on preventing as well as treating psychological disorders. Psychologists recognize three forms of prevention: primary, secondary, and tertiary. *Primary prevention* is designed to prevent disorders from occurring. Such efforts might include workshops on stress reduction or community recreation programs. *Secondary prevention* is designed to detect existing disorders and provide treatment at early stages. A crisis telephone line for individuals experiencing extreme stress is an example.

deinstitutionalization

The policy of discharging mentally ill patients from institutions on the assumption that they can be cared for in their communities; the policy also led to the closing of part or all of these institutions

FIGURE 14-1   The number of patients with mental illness began to decline with the development of antipsychotic drugs.

Source: Torrey, 1997.

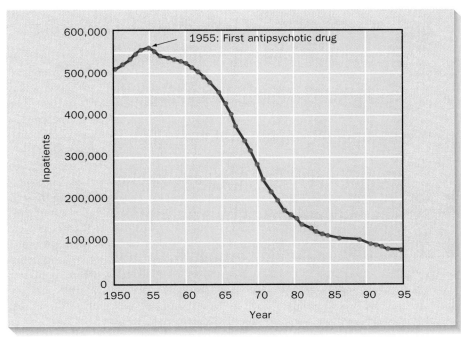

The policy of deinstitutionalization has added to the number of people who are homeless. The rates of schizophrenia and alcohol/drug abuse among the homeless tend to be higher than in the general population.

The goal of *tertiary prevention* is to reduce the damage caused by disorders for both the patients and society. An after-care program for former patients of mental hospitals is an example of tertiary prevention.

Several decades after the passage of the Community Mental Health Centers Act, many of the reformers' goals have not been achieved. The act proposed the construction of 2,000 community-based health centers; fewer than half this number were built. Consequently, many mentally ill people have been moved from mental hospitals to nursing homes and board-and-care facilities. What's more, thousands of former patients have wound up on the streets and in jails that are not equipped to deal with their needs (Torrey, 1997). After-care services for these patients have generally been inadequate, in part because of insufficient funding.

This poster is intended to prevent a substance abuse problem from developing. It is an example of primary prevention.

Therapy and Therapists

Not everyone who seeks therapy suffers from a psychological disorder. Some people need help to cope with such lifestyle events as the loss of a job, school-related difficulties, or family disagreements. During a one-year period, 28.1 percent of U.S. adults (about 50 million) would qualify for a diagnosis of some psychological disorder, and 14.7 percent received some mental health service (Bourdon et al., 1994). Of those people who had a disorder, however, only about 30 percent sought treatment (Figure 14-2). Of the people who sought treatment, 55 percent were suffering from a disorder. The remainder did not meet the diagnostic criteria for any psychological disorder during the year, although many had a previous disorder during their lifetimes. In any case, the actual mental health services provided fall short of the potential need (Regier et al., 1993).

What factors influence the decision to seek (or not to seek) mental health treatment? One key factor is the nature of the disorder. For example, the use of mental health services is high among people diagnosed with schizophrenia (64 percent), bipolar disorder (61 percent), and panic disorder (59 percent). By contrast, only 24 percent of individuals with a substance-use disorder seek help. In addition, people with multiple disorders are more likely to seek treatment (Regier et al., 1993).

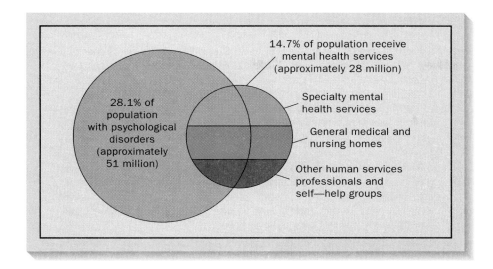

14.7% of population receive
mental health services
(approximately 28 million)

28.1% of
population
with psychological
disorders
(approximately
51 million)

Specialty mental
health services

General medical and
nursing homes

Other human services
professionals and
self—help groups

FIGURE 14-2 The annual prevalence of psychological disorders and treatment seeking. Only a small percentage of adults who had a psychological disorder sought some form of treatment; many people who sought mental health treatment did not have a psychological disorder.

Source: Bourdon et al., 1994.

Where do people go to receive treatment? Most receive outpatient rather than inpatient treatment. Five percent of patients receive inpatient care only, 10 percent receive a combination of inpatient (usually hospital) and outpatient treatment, and 85 percent are exclusively outpatients (Bourdon et al., 1994).

There are more than 400 different treatments for psychological disorders in the United States. These treatments can be divided into two broad categories: **biomedical therapies** and **psychological therapies.** The biomedical therapies use psychotropic drugs, electroconvulsive therapy, and psychosurgery to alter brain functioning and thus reduce symptoms. Psychological therapies range from "talk therapies" to treatments based on the principles of learning.

Psychotherapy is a general term that describes psychological treatments designed to help people resolve behavioral, emotional, and interpersonal problems and improve the quality of their lives (Engler & Goleman, 1992). The primary means of achieving these goals is for a therapist to engage a client in discussions and interactions. Some of these forms of therapy, often called *behavior therapy,* are based on the principles of classical conditioning, operant conditioning, and modeling (see Chapter 6).

Types of Therapists. Members of several professions as well as paraprofessionals provide psychotherapeutic services. The term *therapist* encompasses a diverse group of people with different backgrounds. Included here are people with a master's or doctoral degree in psychology and people with a medical degree and special training in psychiatry, as well as self-designated psychotherapists (Altshuler, 1994). Among the most common types of licensed psychotherapists are clinical and counseling psychologists, psychiatric nurses, psychiatrists, and social workers. Table 14-1 describes the qualifications and roles of these and other mental health professionals.

Although states regulate many mental health professions, they do not regulate terms like *psychotherapist* or *counselor.* Consequently, some practitioners who offer psychotherapeutic services may have little or no training. In addition, a state license does not guarantee that a therapist will have qualities such as patience and empathy. Licensed therapists, however, are accountable to a professional licensing board for maintaining professional standards and keeping up with advances in knowledge through continuing education. Most health insurance policies that pay for psychotherapy require the services to be provided by licensed professionals (Engler & Goleman, 1992).

biomedical therapies
A set of treatments for mental illness that include drugs, psychosurgery, and electroconvulsive therapy

psychological therapies
Treatments for psychological disorders such as psychotherapy or therapies based on classical or operant conditioning principles

psychotherapy
A special relationship between a distressed person and a trained therapist in which the therapist aids the client in developing awareness and changing his or her thinking, feeling, and behavior

TABLE 14-1   Types of Therapists and Their Training

Clinical psychologists	Have earned a doctoral degree (Ph.D., Psy.D., or Ed.D.), which usually takes four or more years after an undergraduate degree. Their training includes completion of a dissertation based on research and a one-year internship in a mental hospital or community mental health center. During their schooling, they take courses on the diagnosis and treatment of psychological disorders. They must meet state certification or licensing requirements that typically require doctoral training, an internship, a number of hours of supervised clinical work in addition to the internship, and a national licensing examination.
Counselors	Have a range of educational backgrounds, from a bachelor's degree to a doctorate. They may be members of the clergy (pastoral counselors) or professional educators; some counselors are trained to work with specific populations such as drug and alcohol abusers. Some people who identify themselves as counselors, however, have little formal training in providing psychotherapeutic services.
Marriage and family therapists	Usually, but not always, complete a two-year master's program. Their training focuses on therapy with couples and families and is typically followed by two or more years of supervised work. These therapists are specially trained to deal with marital problems and child-parent conflicts. Some states license marriage and family therapists.
Psychiatric nurses	Are registered nurses who usually have earned a master's degree from a psychiatric nursing program, which usually takes about two years. Psychiatric nurses are especially proficient in evaluating the effects of a person's environment and physical functioning on his or her mental health status.
Psychiatrists	Are medical doctors (holders of an M.D.) who have completed a three-year residency in psychiatry, usually in a psychiatric hospital or community mental health center. As physicians, they can prescribe drugs and hospitalize patients. They treat problems ranging from mild emotional problems to severe psychotic disorders. In addition to drug and other medical treatments, they can use a full range of individual and group psychotherapies; some psychiatrists also use behavior therapy.
Psychoanalysts	Often (but not always) hold an M.D. and have additional training in the psychoanalytic tradition of therapy developed by Sigmund Freud. A person without an M.D. can qualify as a psychoanalyst by completing the required training and undergoing psychoanalysis, a costly and time-consuming process.
Social workers	Constitute the largest group of professionals in the mental health field. Most have earned a master's degree in social work (M.S.W.), which usually takes two years of full-time study; a few social workers have earned a doctorate. Their course work includes practical experience (called "field placement") in social work agencies or mental health facilities. As part of their training, they learn to use the services of agencies and groups to meet their clients' needs. They may direct clinics or have private practices. Licensing requirements vary from state to state. Psychiatric social workers specialize in treating mentally ill patients.

Review Summary

1. Throughout history, prevailing views of the causes of psychological disorders have influenced treatments. Some people believed in "possession" by evil spirits, so they used treatments such as exorcism. The ancient Greeks proposed natural causes and treatments.

2. Belief in demon possession was common during the sixteenth and seventeenth centuries. Some accused witches may have suffered from psychological disorders. Asylums and hospitals did not always provide a humane refuge for afflicted people.

3. Jean-Baptiste Pussin removed the chains from mental patients in France. Philippe Pinel and Benjamin Rush advocated kind treatment of individuals with psychological disorders.

4. Dorothea Dix spearheaded a movement that led to state-operated custodial institutions. As state mental hospitals grew larger, however, their effectiveness declined.

5. The community mental health movement recommended community-based treatment and emphasized prevention. Use of psychotropic drugs coupled with growing awareness of the ineffectiveness of large institutions led to a policy of **deinstitutionalization,** the release of patients from mental hospitals.

6. Many people who seek mental health treatment do not have a psychological disorder. About 30 percent of individuals with a psychological disorder seek treatment. Those with schizophrenia, bipolar disorder, or panic disorder are more likely to seek treatment than individuals with substance-use disorders.

7. There are two treatment categories for psychological disorders: **biomedical** and **psychological therapies.** Among the licensed practitioners who provide therapy for psychological disorders are clinical psychologists and psychiatrists.

Study Break

1. How did the ancient Greeks view psychological disorders?
   a. The ancient Greeks focused on the influence of the weather.
   b. Disorders in ancient Greece were viewed as punishment from the gods.
   c. The ancient Greeks offered naturalistic explanations for the disorders.
   d. Disorders in ancient Greece were viewed as failures to live a life consistent with sound philosophical principles.
2. A student was asked to describe the treatment approach called moral management. Which of the following would be the best brief description?
   a. Provide a humane and relaxed environment and patients will recover.
   b. Focus on a person's failure to live a moral and ethical life.
   c. Strict discipline from morning to night is the path to a sound mind.
   d. Patients need to accept a set of philosophical principles for any treatment to be successful.
3. A group of students is asked to develop a vignette about the life and accomplishments of Dorothea Dix. Which of the following is likely to be included in that vignette?
   a. She is ministering to those she believes are possessed by demons.

   b. She meets with state legislators to convince them to approve funds for mental hospitals.
   c. She is shown removing chains from patients housed in hospitals throughout the United States.
   d. She is being interviewed for a newspaper article focused on her beliefs in the genetic causes of mental illness.
4. What factors led to significant reductions in the number of hospitalized mental patients beginning in the 1950s?
5. Which psychological disorder is associated with a high rate of seeking treatment?
   a. Schizophrenia
   b. Conversion disorder
   c. Substance-use disorders
   d. Generalized anxiety disorder
6. Identify the type of therapist (clinical psychologist, psychiatrist, social worker, counselor, marriage and family therapist, psychoanalyst) described in each of the following:
   a. Prescribes drugs for the symptoms of anxiety
   b. Has undergone personal therapy and strives to uncover unconscious conflicts that are believed to cause distress
   c. Completed an internship at a community mental health center, earned a Ph.D., and currently maintains a private practice

Psychologically Based Therapies

Curita is overwhelmed with doubt, does not sleep well, cannot relax, and feels isolated from friends and co-workers. For more than a year, she has realized that something has been "wrong." After deciding to see a psychotherapist, she begins to wonder what therapy will be like. She recalls the bewildering array of therapies discussed

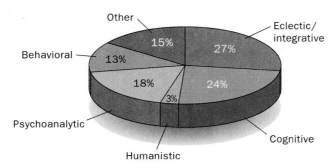

FIGURE 14-3 The primary theoretical orientations of clinical psychologists. More therapists now use elements from different therapeutic approaches in their work.

Source: Adapted from Norcross, Karg-Bray, & Prochaska, 1995.

in the psychology course she took three years ago. *What are the common forms of psychotherapy?* ■

Some forms of psychotherapy focus on individuals; others focus on groups. In some forms of therapy the therapist is quite active; in others the therapist is more passive. Some psychotherapies try to help clients develop insight into their troubling behavior; others aim squarely at changing the client's distressing behaviors. Although it is convenient to distinguish among various forms of psychotherapy, clinical psychologists are increasingly using elements of different therapeutic approaches in treating their clients (see Figure 14-3). The use of components from several therapies is called an *eclectic* or *integrative* approach (Norcross, Karg-Bray, & Prochaska, 1995; Norcross & Newman, 1992).

Most forms of psychotherapy have two key characteristics. First, psychotherapy is a special relationship between a distressed person and a trained therapist. The relationship is special because the therapist tries to create an atmosphere in which the distressed person feels comfortable expressing important and often confidential information. Second, therapists help their clients develop awareness and bring about changes in their behavior, feeling, and thinking (Strupp, 1986).

Psychoanalytic Therapy

Several of the forms of psychotherapy used in the United States can be traced to Sigmund Freud, who developed **psychoanalytic therapy** near the end of the nineteenth century. As we saw in Chapter 12, Freud contended that the symptoms of psychological disorders are due to unconscious feelings and conflicts, especially those involving sexual or aggressive urges that conflict with societal prohibitions. This view of psychological disorders called for a new treatment approach that could uncover unconscious feelings and conflicts that were protected by defense mechanisms (see Chapter 12). Freud searched for ways to probe beneath the surface of a patient's conscious feelings and thoughts. This probing not only proved to be time-consuming and painstaking but it also required the development of special therapeutic techniques and processes that are the hallmarks of psychoanalytic therapy. We discuss four of these processes: free association, dream interpretation, resistance, and transference.

Free Association. After Freud graduated from medical school, he became interested in using hypnosis as a technique for treating his patients. While treating a patient suffering from a conversion disorder (see Chapter 13) who could not be hypnotized, he found that free association could be used to recall the repressed memories he believed to be at the heart of the disorder. In **free association** patients are asked to relate thoughts, feelings, or images without modifying them in any way. Psychoanalysts believe that in freely discussing their feelings, patients will reveal unconscious thoughts, fears, and desires.

The operation of various defense mechanisms makes it difficult to see connections between a patient's current problems and what is revealed during free association. However, free association provides clues that psychoanalysts use to help their patients identify hidden conflicts. As the clues are revealed, the therapist asks questions or offers suggestions that are designed to help the patient gain insight into these unconscious conflicts.

Dream Interpretation. Freud called dreams "the royal road to the unconscious" and distinguished between two forms of dream content: manifest and

psychoanalytic therapy
Treatment of maladaptive behavior developed by Sigmund Freud; its goal is to uncover unconscious conflicts and feelings and bring them to the conscious level

free association
A psychoanalytic technique in which the patient is asked to say whatever comes to mind without censoring anything

The setting of psychoanalytic therapy was conceived to foster free association. Note how the therapist sits out of the patient's line of vision.

latent (see Chapter 5). *Manifest content* is the dream you recall when you awaken; *latent content* is the underlying meaning of that dream. The manifest content is a disguised version of the latent content of the dream. The psychoanalyst's task is to interpret dreams by discovering the latent content. Consider an adult male's dream of riding in the back seat of a car driven by another man; this is the manifest content. Like an archaeologist, the psychoanalyst tries to uncover the deeper (latent) meaning of the dream. One possible interpretation of this dream is that the man wants someone (most likely his father) to stop running his life.

Resistance.   Freud used free association to ask patients to report whatever came to mind without censoring anything. An uninterrupted flow of words, thoughts, and images spilled forth, but often the flow was halted. Why? Freud believed that the patient was coming closer to significant information that needed to be uncovered if the therapy was to succeed. **Resistance** occurs during free association when the patient's flow of words and thoughts stops. The cessation of associations might indicate that the defense mechanism of repression is operating to protect the ego from the anxiety generated by the thoughts and feelings revealed through the associations.

Transference.   People undergoing psychoanalytic therapy often reveal highly confidential and emotionally wrenching information to someone who just a short time earlier was a complete stranger. The bond that often develops between the patient and the therapist can foster strong feelings. Sometimes during psychoanalysis a patient transfers feelings about a significant person (such as a parent or sibling) to the psychoanalyst. The psychoanalyst thus becomes a screen onto which a patient projects feelings about other people. The psychoanalyst searches for the meaning of this **transference** because it is one more clue to the conflicts in a person's life. In *countertransference* the psychoanalyst transfers feelings to the client. This transfer is based on the psychoanalyst's responses to significant persons in his or her life.

Evaluation of Psychoanalysis.   One problem that researchers of psychoanalytic therapy face is the difficulty of defining the essential elements of the treatment and knowing when they are present. For example, how does a researcher investigate whether a patient has gained insight into unconscious conflicts? If the therapist interprets a statement by the patient, does the patient's acceptance of that interpretation constitute support for the effectiveness of psychoanalytic therapy? Suppose the patient rejects the psychoanalyst's interpretation. Does this mean that the therapy is not working or the patient is resisting the analysis?

resistance
A stage of psychoanalysis in which blocking of free association occurs because critical unconscious material is close to conscious awareness

transference
In psychoanalysis, the patient's positive or negative reaction to the therapist, which is believed to reflect the patient's relationship to a significant person outside of therapy

Carl Rogers developed client-centered therapy, which is designed to establish an environment in which individuals can solve their own problems. To create this environment the therapist demonstrates unconditional positive regard for clients, is genuine, and demonstrates empathy.

humanistic therapies

Therapies that emphasize the present and the ability of clients to solve their own problems once they are able to accept themselves

client-centered therapy

Therapy designed to create an environment in which the client is able to find solutions to his or her problems

The psychoanalytic approach assumes that if a symptom is addressed before the patient can deal with it effectively, new symptoms will appear in its place because the basic underlying conflict or feeling was not resolved. Despite this belief, the evidence suggests that *symptom substitution* does not typically occur.

Psychoanalytic therapy is costly and may require therapy sessions five days a week, sometimes for years. Thus psychoanalytic therapy seems to be more suited to clients with less serious problems, especially those who have been described as *yavis*—young, attractive, verbal, intelligent, and successful. Psychoanalytic therapy is not effective with patients who have lost contact with reality, as in schizophrenia.

Humanistic Therapies

In contrast to psychoanalytic therapies, humanistic therapies emphasize the here and now, the subjective interpretation of experience, and the human capacity for self-determination (Rice & Greenberg, 1992). **Humanistic therapies** seek to reduce blocks to growth that can create a poor self-concept. Humanistic therapists believe that clients who are more accepting will be better able to solve their own problems.

Client-Centered Therapy.   Early in his career, Carl Rogers (1902–1987) practiced psychoanalysis, but his growing dissatisfaction with that form of therapy led him to create a different approach. Rather than delving into unconscious conflicts, Rogers's **client-centered therapy** focuses on the conscious level.

According to Rogers, personal problems can develop when a person's ideal self differs from his or her real self (see Chapter 12). These discrepancies can occur if a person trusts other people's evaluations rather than his or her own. Rogers steadfastly believed in the innate goodness of human beings and saw people as capable of curing themselves provided they were in the right environment—one that was caring and accepting. The goal of client-centered therapy is to provide just such an environment (Rogers, 1957).

Client-centered therapists are guided by several assumptions (Patterson, 1985):

1. People are basically good and possess an innate drive toward self-actualization.
2. Clients can assume responsibility for themselves. Therapists do not initiate therapy, ask questions, give advice, or encourage clients to make certain choices. They respond to the client, and this responsiveness helps the client develop self-understanding. Consequently, this form of therapy is often called *nondirective therapy.*
3. Clients can resolve their own problems within a facilitating relationship.
4. The therapist's basic attitude is deep respect for the client as a person of worth. This is known as *unconditional positive regard.*

The key to successful client-centered therapy is the therapist's ability to create an environment in which the client feels accepted and able to find solutions to his or her problems. Client-centered therapists create such an environment by demonstrating unconditional positive regard, empathy, and genuineness in their sessions.

Therapists show unconditional positive regard by not evaluating, judging, or criticizing. They listen to the client without interrupting. Sitting back, listening, and not offering advice may be difficult for some therapists; however, the act of offer-

"So, while extortion, racketeering, and murder may be bad acts, they don't make you a bad person."

ing advice conveys the message that the client cannot solve problems without outside help. Client-centered therapists also show *empathy*—sensing how the client feels at every moment. Finally, the therapist must be *genuine* and not put on airs or try to be something he or she is not.

The following dialogue demonstrates how client-centered therapy proceeds. Note how the therapist reflects the message and emotion heard from the client and does not direct the flow of the conversation or ask questions.

CLIENT: I'm feeling lousy today.

THERAPIST: You're feeling pretty bad.

CLIENT: Yeah. I'm really ticked about something, and that made me feel bad. But I can't do much about it; I think I've got to live with it.

THERAPIST: You're angry and feel like there's nothing you can safely do with your feelings.

CLIENT: Uh-huh. If I yell at my boss, he yells back even louder. If I don't speak up, he continues to get on my case.

THERAPIST: You feel like you're between a rock and a hard place. No matter what, you end up feeling bad.

CLIENT: Every day he chews me out for something. I want to say something because he's getting on my nerves. I don't think I can take it any longer. I wonder if I make as many mistakes as he says; the boss is supposed to know what he's doing.

THERAPIST: So even when you finally say something, you feel bad.

CLIENT: Yeah. I can't say anything to him without getting mad and saying more than I probably should. And then I cause more trouble.

Gestalt Therapy.   The psychoanalyst Fritz Perls (1893–1970) made revisions in psychoanalytic therapy that developed into **Gestalt therapy,** which focuses on emotions and feelings. Perls believed that psychological difficulties can develop when people are unwilling to accept or express themselves because they are avoiding their real selves. This lack of self-awareness, coupled with a fear of other people's judgments, causes people to behave defensively. The primary goal of therapy is therefore to increase awareness and self-acceptance. Like client-centered therapy, Gestalt therapy focuses on the present. Unlike client-centered therapists, however, Gestalt therapists will confront, frustrate, or challenge their clients' beliefs and feelings. They offer opinions or hunches about what a client is experiencing while also providing support as the client discovers what he or she feels and needs (Rice & Greenberg, 1992). Gestalt therapists look for nonverbal clues that may reveal hidden feelings and then dramatize the clients' feelings by having them sit in different chairs to play various "parts" of themselves, such as a guilty conscience or a resentful but submissive child. By making these "parts" obvious, the therapist helps the client bring them into harmony.

Although their methodologies differ in some ways, client-centered therapy and Gestalt therapy share the common goal of helping clients develop greater personal insights. The number of therapists who practice either of these forms of humanistic therapy is small (Norcross, Karg-Bray, & Prochaska, 1995). As we shall see, however, client-centered therapy has made a major contribution in identifying some of the conditions conducive to effective therapy.

Cognitive Therapies

Gayle is so upset with her therapist that she storms into the office of the director of the community mental health center. "All she does is question me and make me feel stupid," she complains. "I didn't come here to be made to feel like a

Gestalt therapy
A humanistic form of therapy developed by Fritz Perls in which therapists may frustrate and challenge clients to lead them toward self-acceptance

cognitive therapies
Therapies designed to change cognitions in order to eliminate maladaptive behaviors

rational-emotive behavior therapy (REBT)
A cognitive therapy in which the therapist challenges and questions the client's irrational ideas

fool." The director explains that the therapist is using one of the **cognitive therapies,** called *rational-emotive behavior therapy,* which is quite different from many other therapies and is clearly different from Gayle's expectations. In these therapies, cognitions (thoughts and beliefs) hold the keys to understanding psychological disorders; these therapies have been quite effective in treating phobias and depression and in helping patients cope with medical procedures.

The goal of cognitive therapy is to change distorted cognitions in order to eliminate maladaptive behaviors. The cognitive therapist's targets are the client's thoughts and beliefs, which are more accessible than the unconscious feelings and conflicts that psychoanalysts seek to uncover. Compared with the methods used by client-centered therapists, a cognitive therapist's techniques are quite directive. Although the targets of cognitive therapy are closer to the surface, clients may not recognize these things until they are asked to confront their thought patterns.

Rational-Emotive Behavior Therapy. A basic assumption of **rational-emotive behavior therapy (REBT)** is that our emotional responses are an outgrowth of our cognitions (Ellis & Tafrate, 1998; Salovey & Singer, 1991). This principle is not new—it was proposed centuries ago by the Greek philosopher Epictetus, who said "What disturbs people's minds is not events but their judgments on events." Shakespeare made the point in *Hamlet:* "There's nothing either good or bad but thinking makes it so."

The pioneer of rational-emotive behavior therapy, Albert Ellis (1987), describes the basis for this therapy: "I have stubbornly held the near-pollyannaish position that humans largely disturb themselves" (p. 364). To illustrate, suppose you see a job advertised in the newspaper and become excited because you feel it is the perfect job for you. With great anticipation, you apply for the job. You expect the phone to ring, but three weeks later a form letter arrives announcing that your perfect job was offered to someone else. You are devastated.

Ellis argues that failing to get that job should not in itself make you unhappy or depressed. If, however, you interpret the situation as being due to lack of ability on your part, you are on your way to inappropriate negative consequences. You could recognize there were hundreds of applicants for the job and that not getting it is not a reflection on your ability. What's more, the employer will not have the benefit of your hard work. Now you may feel very different about the same event.

Rational-emotive behavior therapy is understood best in terms of what Ellis calls the *ABC* framework (see Figure 14-4). *A* represents an *activating* event related to an important desire, goal, or preference (getting the job, in our example); *B* is the *belief,* usually related to failure to attain the goal, that follows the activating event ("I'm no good because I didn't get the job"). That belief determines *C, consequences,* such as feelings of anger, anxiety, and depression.

According to Ellis, we hold a large number of irrational beliefs that interfere with our ability to perceive events clearly and often lead to negative feelings. Irrational beliefs often take the form of dogmatic *shoulds, oughts, musts, commands,* and *demands:* "If you understand how you upset yourself by slipping into irrational shoulds, oughts, demands, and commands, unconsciously sneaking them into your thinking, you can just about always stop disturbing yourself about anything" (Ellis, 1990, p. 17). Several irrational beliefs that Ellis identified on the basis of his clinical experience are listed in Table 14-2.

FIGURE 14-4 The *ABC* framework, the cornerstone of REBT practice.

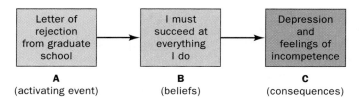

A (activating event)	B (beliefs)	C (consequences)
Letter of rejection from graduate school	I must succeed at everything I do	Depression and feelings of incompetence

Rational-emotive behavior therapy is a very active, directive form of psychotherapy. The REBT therapist does not sit back and accept everything the client says but instead plays the role of a persistent questioner who raises issues about the client's interpretations of events. This method teaches clients to detect their unrealistic, self-defeating, and irrational thoughts

TABLE 14-2   **Examples of Irritational Beliefs Described by Albert Ellis**

FOCUS	IRRATIONAL BELIEF
Competence and success	"Because I strongly desire to perform important tasks competently and successfully, I absolutely must perform them well (and am an inadequate, incompetent person if I don't)."
Love and approval	"Because I strongly desire to be approved by people I find significant, I absolutely must have their approval (and am an unlovable and worthless person if I do not)."
Fair treatment	"Because I strongly desire people to treat me considerately and fairly, they absolutely must do so (and they are evil, damnable people who deserve to be severely condemned and punished when they don't)."
Safety and comfort	"Because I strongly desire to have a safe, comfortable, and satisfying life, the conditions under which I live absolutely must be easy, convenient, and gratifying (and it is awful, I can't bear it, and can't be happy at all when they are unsafe and frustrating)."

Source: Ellis, 1987.

and to develop alternate rational beliefs (Kendall et al., 1995). A glimpse of REBT is captured in the following dialogue taken from one of Ellis's sessions:

CLIENT: I don't know! I'm not thinking clearly at the moment. I'm too nervous!

ELLIS: Well, but you can think clearly. Are you saying, "It's hopeless! I can't think clearly"? You see you're blaming yourself.

CLIENT: (*visibly upset, can't seem to say anything and then nods*)

ELLIS: No! You'll never get better unless you think. And you're saying, "Can't we do something magical to get me better?" And the answer is No! (Ellis, 1973, p. 186)

Beck's Cognitive Therapy.   Aaron Beck has devoted a lifetime to treating psychological disorders, especially depression. Beck notes that depressed people have negative views of their world, themselves, and their future—called the *cognitive triad*. They often interpret events in ways that lead to self-blame, and they also rely on cognitive distortions that can maintain their negative views. These

Two of the leading proponents of cognitive therapy are Aaron Beck *(left)* and Albert Ellis *(right)*. This very active form of therapy has been used to treat a variety of psychological disorders, including depression.

distorted interpretations and errors are fueled by automatic thoughts (negative sentences repeated to oneself) that occur despite their being contrary to objective reality (Beck, 1979).

Automatic thoughts arise quickly and are perceived as plausible. Although they are frequently followed by unpleasant emotions, we are generally not aware of their influence on our emotional reactions (Beck, 1991). After their attention was directed to such thoughts, Beck's clients reported a variety of automatic thoughts, such as "I'm not capable of having any friends," that can intervene between outside events and a person's emotional reactions. These thoughts are repeated so often that they become part of the way the person thinks.

Other cognitive distortions include *selective abstraction* and *overgeneralization* (see Table 14-3). Someone who focuses only on the negative aspects of an event and ignores the positive details is relying on selective abstraction. For example, a student who becomes depressed because he focuses on a single error in an otherwise excellent term paper is using selective abstraction. Overgeneralization occurs when a person makes a generalization based on limited information.

Psychological Detective

Take a moment to reflect on a situation that is probably close to home. Throughout your years in school, you have taken a number of tests. Think about an example of overgeneralization that might follow your receipt of a poor grade on an exam.

After receiving a poor grade, you may conclude, "I am just not college material" and "There is no use trying, I'm going to fail at everything I do." If your conclusions are similar to these then your thought processes reveal overgeneralization. You have taken a single incident and exaggerated its significance for your life.

Beck's goal is to have the depressed person consider these automatic thoughts and cognitive distortions from a more scientific perspective. The fol-

TABLE 14-3   Typical Cognitive Distortions Treated with Forms of Cognitive Therapies

DISTORTION	DEFINITION	EXAMPLE
Arbitrary inference	Drawing an erroneous conclusion without sufficient evidence.	When your hairdresser suggests you try a new hairstyle, you assume he or she believes you are becoming older-looking and unattractive.
Selective abstraction	Taking a detail out of context and using it to misrepresent the entire experience.	A politician gives a rousing speech at a rally but mispronounces one word in the 30-minute talk. She concludes, "There's proof that I'm not cut out to be a political leader."
Overgeneralization	Drawing a general conclusion on the basis of a single incident.	A student fails the first quiz of his college career and concludes that "I'm just not college material."
Magnification and minimization	Altering the significance of specific events in a way that yields negative interpretations.	The significance of a success may be minimized (a good grade is considered trivial because the exam was easy), and the significance of a failure is maximized (losing a tennis match is seen as evidence that you will never succeed at anything).

Sources: Andreasen & Black, 1995; Beck & Weishaar, 1989.

lowing dialogue (adapted from Young, Beck, & Weinberger, 1993, pp. 263–64) provides a glimpse of this form of therapy:

THERAPIST: Let's do an experiment and see if you can respond to the automatic thought and then let's see what happens to your feeling. See if responding rationally makes you feel worse or makes you feel better. OK, why didn't I answer that question right?

CLIENT: Why didn't I answer that question? Because I thought for a second that that was what I was supposed to say, and then when I heard the question over again, then I realized that was not what I heard. I didn't hear the question right, that's why I didn't answer it right.

THERAPIST: OK, so that is the fact situation. And so is the fact situation that you look dumb or you just didn't hear the question right?

CLIENT: I didn't hear the question right.

THERAPIST: Or is it possible that I didn't say the question in such a way that it was clear? I'm not perfect, so it's very possible that I didn't express the question properly.

CLIENT: But instead of saying you made a mistake, I would still say I made a mistake.

THERAPIST: We'll have to watch the video and see. Whichever. Does it mean if I didn't express the question, if I made a mistake, does it make me dumb?

CLIENT: No.

THERAPIST: And if you made the mistake, does it make you dumb?

CLIENT: No, not really.

THERAPIST: But you felt dumb?

CLIENT: But I did, yeah.

THERAPIST: Do you feel dumb still?

CLIENT: No.

Psychologists Steven Hollon, Richard Shelton, and Peter Loosen (1991) reviewed research comparing cognitive therapy to drug therapy for depression. They concluded that cognitive therapy is at least as effective as antidepressant drugs. What's more, cognitive therapy may prevent the return of depression after the completion of treatment if it helps clients learn new coping skills that can be useful in warding off the return of symptoms.

Stress Inoculation Training.   Another form of cognitive therapy, **stress inoculation training,** teaches cognitive skills that enable people to cope with stressful events that can lead to anger, anxiety, or pain (Meichenbaum, 1993). The word *inoculation* suggests that clients can be exposed to milder stressors in order to increase their ability to cope with higher levels of stress later. In the first phase of the three-phase training, the therapist and client examine situations that cause stress. This examination enables them to uncover beliefs and attitudes that lead the client to view those situations as stressful. The focus of this phase is on what clients say to themselves (*self-talk*) during encounters with stressful situations. The essential feature is tracking self-statements such as "This situation is too much for me."

The second phase of stress inoculation training focuses on coping skills and rehearsal. The clients practice new self-talk statements suggested by the therapist, such as "I know I can handle it." In the final stage clients apply these new self-statements in real-world situations (see Table 14-4). Stress inoculation training has been used with clients facing a variety of stressful situations, including medical procedures, chronic pain, and high-stress jobs like police work.

stress inoculation training
A cognitive therapy that helps clients learn ways to interpret stressful events and develop self-talk that reduces stress levels

TABLE 14-4   **Examples of Self-Talk Coping Statements in Stress Inoculation Training**

Phase 1: Facing or confronting the stressor

"I will take a few slow, deep breaths and relax."

"If I take one step at a time, I can handle this situation."

"The therapist told me I would feel anxious. This reminds me to do my coping exercises."

Phase 2: Coping with the stressor

"If I feel fear, I will pause."

"It is not necessary for me to eliminate my fear; I just have to control it."

"I will keep my mind focused on what is happening now, and concentrate on what I have to do."

Phase 3: When the coping attempt is finished

"I am making progress."

"This was easier than I thought it would be."

"This is working. It gets easier every time I use the exercises."

Source: Meichenbaum & Cameron, 1983.

Behavior Therapies

Behavior therapists do not delve into unconscious conflicts derived from early experiences; instead they focus on current factors such as reinforcers that are maintaining maladaptive behaviors. The terms *behavior modification* and *behavior therapy* are sometimes used interchangeably to describe techniques based on the principles of classical conditioning, operant conditioning, and modeling. Behavior modification is the broader of the two; it covers the application of behavioral techniques to a variety of behaviors in nonclinical settings. For example, behavior modification might include programs to reduce littering or increase the use of seat belts. Behavior therapy involves application of behavioral principles to change maladaptive behaviors, often in clinical settings (Martin & Pear, 1996).

Most behavioral techniques derive from the work of well-known psychologists such as John B. Watson and B. F. Skinner. Among the most frequently used behavioral techniques are systematic desensitization, aversion therapy, modeling, extinction, punishment, and the token economy.

Systematic Desensitization.   John B. Watson and Rosalie Rayner (1920) used the case of Little Albert, described in Chapter 6, to demonstrate how classical conditioning principles could be used to create an emotional response (phobia). Mary Cover Jones (1924) used a technique called *counterconditioning* to reduce a young child's fear of a rabbit. Jones presented the child Peter with his favorite food. Then she slowly inched a caged rabbit closer to the child. Eventually the pleasant feelings evoked by the food became associated with the rabbit, and the child's fear diminished. Today counterconditioning of phobias has been replaced by techniques such as **systematic desensitization,** which was developed by psychiatrist Joseph Wolpe in the 1950s.

The first step in systematic desensitization is to find a procedure that counters the anxiety people experience when they confront feared objects such as snakes. Hypnosis, biofeedback, and even drugs have been used to counter

systematic desensitization
A behavioral technique, based on classical conditioning, that is used to treat phobias; the technique usually combines training in relaxation with exposure to imagined scenes related to a phobia

the anxiety, but the most popular choice is progressive relaxation (see Chapter 15). Instruction in progressive relaxation during the first few therapy sessions, accompanied by practice outside of the sessions, enables most people to reach a state of calm that they may not have known they could achieve.

There are two versions of systematic desensitization: *in vivo* (real-life) graduated exposure to the feared stimuli and *imaginal* graduated exposure. In either case, the client and therapist work together to construct a list of scenes related to the phobic object or situation. An example of a scene related to ophidiophobia (fear of snakes) is looking up the word *snake* in a dictionary and then reading the definition. Here's another possible scene: walking into a room with a dozen snakes on the floor and hearing the door lock behind you. The scenes are arranged in a hierarchy, starting with one that arouses no fear and progressing to one that causes great fear (see Table 14-5).

Psychological Detective

How could psychologists combine progressive relaxation with scenes related to a particular phobia to reduce the fear? Give this question some thought, and write down a procedure that you think might work.

In imaginal graduated exposure the relaxed client is asked to imagine one scene at a time, starting with the scene that arouses no anxiety. Then the client moves through the hierarchy to scenes that create more and more anxiety (see

---

TABLE 14-5 Systematic Desensitization Hierarchy Used in Treating the Fear of Flying

The scenes are listed in order, starting with the one that causes the least fear and ending with the one that causes the greatest fear.

The plane has landed and stopped at the terminal.

A trip has been planned, and I have decided to travel by plane.

I call a travel agent for times and flight numbers.

I pack my suitcase the day before the trip.

On the day of the flight, I am leaving home. I lock the door, put the bags in the car, and check my tickets.

As I drive to the airport, I am aware of many planes.

With my bags in hand, I enter the terminal.

I walk to the counter, wait in line, and have the agent check my ticket and bags.

I am waiting in the lounge for my flight to be called over the intercom.

After hearing my flight number called, I proceed to the security checkpoint.

I walk down the ramp leading to the plane and enter the door of the plane.

I walk down the aisle and sit down in my assigned seat.

The plane is in flight and I decide to walk to the restroom.

I notice that the seat belt signs are illuminated and the pilot announces that we are preparing to land.

The plane is descending to the runway for a landing.

Source: Adapted from Martin & Pear, 1996, p. 341.

Figure 14-5). During systematic desensitization, it is quite likely that the client will experience some degree of anxiety as the scenes are imagined. When this happens, the therapist returns to the instructions for relaxation to ensure that the client is completely relaxed before proceeding. The client does not proceed to the next scene in the hierarchy until he or she is able to maintain a relaxed state while imagining the current one. Thus the client slowly learns to associate relaxation with scenes related to the phobias as he or she proceeds through the list to the scene that arouses the greatest fear. Eventually the fear is markedly reduced or completely eliminated and is replaced with more relaxed feelings.

In conducting systematic desensitization, therapists now rely more on real objects than on imagined scenes because greater fear reduction is achieved with real objects (Rachman, 1990). Although there is debate about the theoretical explanation of the success of systematic desensitization, there is little doubt that it is very effective in reducing a number of phobias (Nietzel, Bernstein, & Milich, 1994).

FIGURE 14-5   The components of systematic desensitization. Individuals with a phobia are often very anxious when they think about or are near the feared object. The purpose of systematic desensitization is to replace the symptoms of anxiety with a relaxed state while the individuals contemplate scenes that have caused significant anxiety (2, 3). After treatment, many individuals can approach the previously feared stimulus (4).

aversion therapy

Classical conditioning technique for reducing or eliminating behavior by pairing the behavior with an unpleasant (aversive) stimulus

Aversion Therapy.   **Aversion therapy** uses unpleasant or painful stimuli such as electrical shock, nausea-inducing drugs, or repugnant tastes or smells to decrease unwanted behavior. Aversion therapy is based on classical conditioning principles; it involves the repeated pairing of a problem behavior with an aversive stimulus. For example, in treating alcoholism, a person is given a drug, Antabuse (disulfiram), that will induce nausea. Just before the drug takes effect, the person is given a sip of an alcoholic beverage (see Figure 14-6). Thus the sight, smell, and taste of the drink are followed by nausea. This pairing of alcohol with the nausea-inducing drug is repeated over several sessions. Eventually the alcohol itself elicits nausea, which may cause the person to avoid alcohol in the future. One problem with this treatment occurs when unsupervised clients fail to take the Antabuse, thus reducing the chances for successful treatment. One form of aversion therapy, *covert sensitization,* involves having clients visualize or imagine adverse consequences that might accompany unwanted behavior.

Aversion therapy has been used to reduce and sometimes eliminate cigarette smoking, overeating, alcoholism, and sexual deviations such as exhibitionism. Because this procedure involves aversive stimulation, only qualified personnel should carry it out to guard against potential side effects (Martin & Pear, 1996).

FIGURE 14-6   Aversion therapy for alcoholics. The repeated pairing of an alcoholic drink with the nausea induced by the drug Antabuse may reduce the desire to continue drinking. Some courts have sentenced convicted drunk drivers who have a serious problem with alcohol to undergo this form of treatment.

Modeling.   One of the most effective techniques for treating phobias is *modeling,* or observational learning (see Chapter 6). Modeling is so common in our everyday behavior that we may miss its potential as a therapeutic technique. In this procedure a person—live or on videotape—demonstrates gradual contact with the feared object under controlled or protected circumstances. The client observes these behaviors and is given the opportunity to engage in similar behaviors. In one version, called *participant modeling,* a therapist model

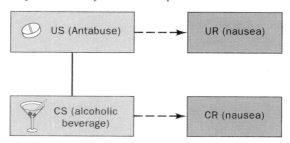

encourages and guides the client in taking a progressively more active role in interacting with the anxiety-provoking stimuli. Albert Bandura (1977) has explained the success of this therapy as the result of providing experiences that enhance perceptions of self-efficacy.

Extinction.   Recall from Chapter 6 that *extinction* occurs when reinforcers that maintained an undesired behavior no longer follow that behavior. Under these circumstances, the frequency of the behavior is likely to drop to zero. The speed with which a behavior is extinguished, however, depends on the schedule of reinforcement and the amount of reinforcement that maintained the behavior in the past. As noted in Chapter 6, intermittent or partial reinforcement schedules and larger reinforcements result in greater resistance to extinction.

Richard Foxx (1982) described the use of extinction in the case of Bruce, an institutionalized, severely retarded adolescent who constantly demanded his instructors' attention. Bruce did almost anything to gain their attention, including exposing himself.

Psychological Detective

Suppose you are one of Bruce's instructors. What would you and your fellow instructors do to extinguish this inappropriate behavior?

To extinguish a behavior, you must know what reinforcer is maintaining it. Bruce's instructors were convinced their attention maintained this behavior. Before making any efforts to extinguish the behavior, they recorded the frequency of the behavior for one week and found that Bruce engaged in the behavior about 14 times a day. Then they agreed they would not look at or speak to Bruce when he exposed himself. Instead they guided him in raising his pants without speaking or looking at him directly. On the first day of extinction training Bruce exposed himself 30 times; on the second day he began having temper tantrums; on the third day he exposed himself 40 times. Nevertheless, the instructors continued their extinction efforts; two and a half weeks later Bruce stopped exposing himself.

As the example of Bruce demonstrates, it is important to recognize "at the beginning of extinction, the frequency of a response may become greater than it was while the response was reinforced. The increase in responding at the beginning of extinction is referred to as a 'burst' of responses" (Kazdin, 1989, p. 179). This extinction burst can be startling to unsuspecting users of this technique, but it is consistent with theories that explain how people react to frustration.

Punishment.   Another procedure used by behavior therapists is punishment, which can be either the withdrawal of a positive stimulus or event (such as candy) or the presentation of a negative stimulus or event (such as an electric shock). As noted in Chapter 6, when used as a technique for altering maladaptive behaviors, punishment can have serious shortcomings and is not always effective. What's more, ethical and legal considerations mandate that less distressing forms of treatment be tried before punishment is considered. Nevertheless, some serious maladaptive behaviors are so resistant to change that punishment may be used as a last resort. Consider the following case:

> Susan, a profoundly retarded child, hit her face with her fist four or five times a minute, 3,000 times a day. Drug treatment reduced the hitting, but when Susan began to cry frequently, the neurologist reduced the medication. The hitting increased, and the crying remained. Increased doses and trials of other

drugs did not alter the behavior. When psychologists found that various behavioral techniques such as extinction had been tried and failed, they wired Susan's legs so she would receive electrical shocks when she hit herself. On the first day, Susan hit herself 45 times compared to the usual 3,000 times. The rate of hitting dropped to 6 hits a day, and the apparatus was removed. During the next 5 years, Susan hit herself 250 times compared to the 5 million hits she might have delivered. (Prochaska & Norcross, 1994, pp. 284–85)

In Chapter 6 we discussed several factors that influence the effectiveness of punishment in reducing behaviors. One of these factors was evident in this case: delivery of the punishment *each* time Susan hit herself. Susan did not find hitting herself to be aversive, but when control of a punisher was in the therapist's hands, it became aversive.

Token Economy.   A number of patients in mental hospitals, especially the larger and more impersonal ones, tend to lose their social skills. Everyday social skills such as knowing how to greet another person and respond when spoken to are necessary for getting along outside the hospital. Psychologists have found it is important to reward patients for displaying such skills immediately after the desired behaviors occur. To do so, they have used a method known as the **token economy,** a behavior therapy system in which desired behaviors are reinforced with tokens. Almost any object—poker chips, gold stars, or checkmarks on a graph—can be called a token (Baldwin & Baldwin, 1998).

Psychological Detective

Awarding poker chips may seem an unlikely way to alter maladaptive behaviors. Such tokens have little or no intrinsic value, yet they are a key ingredient in the success of this method. What are the advantages of using tokens to alter behaviors? How could tokens be used so they do have value? In answering these questions, recall our discussion of secondary reinforcers in Chapter 6. Give these questions some thought, and write down your answers before reading further.

There are three major steps in establishing a token economy (Corrigan, 1995). First the psychologist must identify the target behaviors; then the contingencies for each target must be established (e.g., how many tokens are presented for each of the target behaviors). Tokens (or points) are usually awarded as soon as they are earned to facilitate rapid learning (Morisse et al., 1996). Finally, the developer of the token economy must set the exchange rules for using the tokens.

Patients can use tokens as a medium of exchange to acquire desired reinforcers such as candy, television time, and grounds privileges. The tokens are used in the same way that money is used outside the hospital. They are *secondary* reinforcers that can be exchanged for other reinforcers, especially *primary* reinforcers such as candy. If psychologists used primary reinforcers to reward each occurrence of a desired behavior, patients might grow tired of them; they would then lose their reinforcing value. As learned or secondary reinforcers, however, tokens are less likely to lose their value because patients can accumulate them and exchange them later for the primary reinforcers they desire.

A token economy can also be used in educational settings to develop and maintain desired behaviors such as increasing attention to schoolwork (Sullivan & O'Leary, 1990). In a school-based token economy, students earn points or tokens for on-task behaviors and exchange them for extra recess time. Token economies

token economy
A technique that reinforces desirable behaviors with tokens (secondary reinforcers), which can be redeemed for other reinforcers, especially primary reinforcers

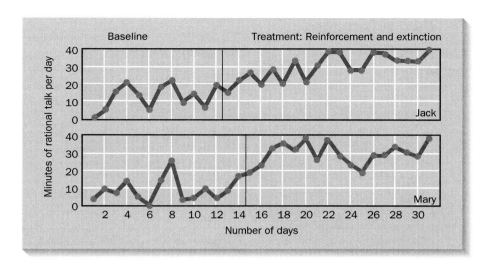

FIGURE 14-7 Effect of the combination of extinction and reinforcement on the duration of rational speech (non delusional) by patients diagnosed as suffering schizophrenia.

Source: Liberman et al., 1973.

are not solely used with large groups or in institutions. A home-based token economy might be used to encourage children to complete their household chores.

Combining Behavior Therapy Techniques.   In many cases it is necessary to use several behavior therapy techniques. For example, patients with schizophrenia may exhibit a variety of delusions—they may believe they are being persecuted or poisoned, that they are secret agents, and so on. What do you think might happen if staff members immediately left the room whenever a patient engaged in delusional speech?

Figure 14-7 shows that a combination of extinction and positive reinforcement increased the total time that patients spent engaging in rational speech (Liberman et al., 1973). The desired behavior was reinforced by the opportunity to have an evening chat with a therapist. The amount of time devoted to the chat depended on how much nondelusional conversation had occurred earlier in the day.

STUDY CHART

Behavior Therapy Techniques

Technique	Description
Systematic Desensitization	Treatment for phobias that combines relaxation training with graduated exposure to the feared stimuli.
Aversion therapy	A technique based on classical conditioning that associates an undesired behavior with aversive (unpleasant) stimuli such as shock or nausea-inducing drugs.
Modeling	A form of learning—also known as observational learning—that occurs by observing and imitating a model; it is an effective treatment for phobias.
Extinction	A technique used to eliminate an undesirable behavior, consisting of withholding reinforcers that had maintained a behavior.
Punishment	Either the removal of a positive stimulus or event (such as candy) or the presentation of a negative stimulus or event (such as a shock).
Token economy	Application of positive reinforcement using tokens (secondary reinforcers) that can be exchanged for other reinforcers.

group therapy
Therapy in which clients discuss problems in groups that may include individuals with similar problems

Group Therapies

Most forms of psychotherapy and behavior therapy involve interactions between a therapist and a client. Therapy sessions may not, however, reflect life outside the therapist's office. Clients are not likely to have a psychoanalyst available to offer interpretations of their actions; a behavior therapist will not be available to reinforce appropriate behaviors, nor will a client-centered therapist be present to offer unconditional positive regard. Problems that bring clients to therapists do not occur in a vacuum; often those problems reflect the clients' difficulties in interacting with family, friends, co-workers, and even strangers.

Group therapy can be a primary form of treatment or an adjunct to individual sessions; its different forms depend on the individuals who compose the groups, the problems or disorders they are confronting, the role the group leader takes, and the therapeutic goals that have been established (Andreasen & Black, 1995). Group therapy can be very valuable in treating a number of psychological disorders such as depression, phobias, and alcohol or drug abuse. It is useful in reducing problems related to stress and anger as well as resolving difficulties in social behavior that can also cause distress.

One advantage of group therapy is that clients have an opportunity to try out new behaviors in the group setting and receive feedback from other people who may be very different from the therapist. Thus it can facilitate the generalization of behaviors to everyday situations. In comparison to individual therapy sessions, group sessions are also cost-effective because several people are treated at the same time.

Group therapy has proved especially effective in developing the social and coping skills necessary to improve the quality of clients' relationships with others and to help them cope more effectively with stressors. The following is a description of a group therapy session designed to help single people cope more effectively with the unique stressors in their lives (Rose & Le Croy, 1991):

> The five women and three men in the group were all between 26 and 40 and unmarried or separated. The therapist asked each of them to review what he or she had done during the week and to complete the week's assignment. Members took turns describing their social achievements, their successes in coping with anxiety, and the frequency with which they used the relaxation

Some of the advantages of group therapy are social support and opportunities to practice coping skills and to receive feedback.

technique they had learned. Several members also described very stressful situations they had experienced during the week. One member gave details of her feelings of helplessness at work, where her supervisor gives her instructions on even minor items. The group member said, "It was as if she thought I was stupid, and frankly, I'm beginning to believe it." Other members of the group indicated that there was no reason to believe that she was dumb in any way. Then they offered several strategies that she could use to deal with the situation and what she might say to herself and to her supervisor.

Marital and Family Therapy. Two forms of group therapy—marital and family therapy—are based on the assumption that problems presented for treatment should be addressed within the context of a larger family unit. These therapies are among the most common forms of treatment; therapists from all mental health professions use them to treat a variety of problems (Lebow & Gurman, 1995). *Marital therapy* typically attempts to stabilize and improve the relationship of two individuals who regard themselves as partners in a marital relationship. In contemporary society, this form of therapy has expanded from clients who are husband and wife to unmarried or homosexual couples who are cohabiting (Andreasen & Black, 1995), in which case the therapy is often called *couples therapy*.

Family therapy focuses on the larger family unit: a parent and a child at a minimum, or both parents, stepparents, or grandparents, depending on the environment in which the child lives. Quite often a child is brought in for therapy for a specific problem, such as school difficulties, delinquency, or aggressive behavior, and the therapist finds that the problems exist in the context of the family setting, especially in the ways parents and children interact (Andreasen & Black, 1995). Returning the child to the family without changing those interaction patterns does not alleviate the problems. Therefore parents, spouses, and children should play a role in therapy for the client's problems.

STUDY CHART

Major Types of Psychological Therapies

Therapy Type	Description
Psychoanalytic therapy	A form of therapy developed by Sigmund Freud that is intended to bring unconscious influences on behavior to the conscious level. Key techniques and processes include free association, resistance, dream interpretation, and transference. This therapy is costly and often requires a significant time commitment. Most of the individuals who seek this form of therapy are articulate and suffer from relatively minor problems.
Humanistic therapies	Therapies that emphasize the present and are based on the assumption that people can solve their own problems after they develop self-awareness. Client-centered therapy aims to develop self-awareness in a nondirective manner; Gestalt therapy relies on more active elements, including confronting and frustrating clients.
Cognitive therapies	A related series of therapies that focus on clients' thinking about problems they encounter, especially logical errors that might be made. Cognitive therapies are quite effective in treating anxiety disorders, depression, and stress-related problems.
Group therapy	A form of therapy that may be used alone or in combination with individual therapy. It provides opportunities to obtain both social support and feedback while developing new skills for dealing with problem behaviors. Marital and family therapy is based on the assumption that problem behaviors are best treated in the context of the couple or the family.

"No one understands me. So as a last resort, my shrink referred me to you."

Self-Help

A person who feels overwhelmed by life's problems may turn to friends, relatives, or perhaps teachers for guidance and support. Professional therapists are not the only source of assistance for people in need of help. In fact, professional therapists alone could not meet the need for mental health services. Paraprofessionals are another source of assistance; they can be found in a variety of roles, such as talking to those who call telephone crisis lines. An additional source of help, the self-help group, provides assistance to an estimated 7 to 15 million people (Christensen & Jacobson, 1994).

Most self-help groups are developed and run by laypersons, although some invite professional therapists to help with unusual cases. A guiding principle is that compassion and understanding do not require advanced degrees. People in these groups pool their knowledge, share their experiences with common problems, and help one another. What's more, self-help groups have the potential to prevent more serious problems by providing social support during a time of need and by helping people develop coping skills (Jacobs & Goodman, 1989).

There are many kinds of self-help groups. Some of the best known are designed for people suffering from specific medical conditions, for people facing acute crises, and for individuals coping with mental illness. For example, the typical member of the National Alliance for the Mentally Ill is the parent of an adult child with schizophrenia. The oldest and largest self-help group is Alcoholics Anonymous, with about 60,000 chapters and several hundred thousand members.

Two rapidly expanding sources of self help are telephone and internet based groups. The internet communications of on-line groups focus on requests for information and provision of emotional support. A major advantage of internet self-help groups is that they are available at times when traditional sources of support have limited or no availability, such as at night (Winzelberg, 1997). Users of telephone self-help programs comment favorably on the program's flexibility, accessibility, and the autonomy afforded by telephone-based guidance for problems such as binge eating (Wells et al., 1997). Table 14-6 lists contact data for some self-help groups.

TABLE 14-6   Some Self-Help Groups

Most of these national organizations maintain files of local self-help groups. They also can provide literature on the problem that is their focus.

GROUP	PHONE NUMBER	WEB SITE
OC Foundation (for obsessive-compulsive disorder)	(203) 878-5669	www.ocdhelp.org
Alcoholics Anonymous	(212) 870-3400	www.alcoholics-anonymous.org
Anxiety Disorders Association of America	(301) 231-8368	www.adaa.org
Cocaine Anonymous	(800) 347-8998	www.ca.org
National Alliance for the Mentally Ill (families of mentally ill)	(800) 950-NAMI	www.nami.org
National Association of Anorexia Nervosa and Associated Disorders	(847) 831-3438	www.healththouch.com
National Depressive and Manic-Depressive Association	(312) 642-0049	www.ndmda.org
SIDS Alliance (sudden infant death syndrome)	(800) 221-7437	www.sidsalliance.org
Suicide Awareness Voices of Education (SAVE)	(612) 946-7998	www.save.org
Widowed Persons Services	(202) 434-2260	www.aarp.org

Review Summary

1. Psychotherapy involves a special relationship between a distressed person and a therapist in which the therapist helps the client make changes in his or her thinking, feeling, and behavior.

2. Psychoanalytic therapy aims to help the patient develop insight into unconscious feelings and conflicts by using **free association,** dream interpretation, and interpretation of **resistance** and **transference.**

3. Humanistic therapies emphasize the ability of each person to solve his or her problems. **Client-centered therapy** seeks to develop an accepting environment for the client. **Gestalt therapy** helps clients develop self-acceptance, but Gestalt therapists are more directive than client-centered therapists.

4. Cognitive therapies are designed to change the way the client thinks. Albert Ellis, the founder of **rational-emotive behavior therapy (REBT),** assumes that people are disturbed by the way they interpret events. Therefore, the role of the therapist is to challenge the client's irrational beliefs. Aaron Beck's cognitive therapy has been applied to depression with promising results.

5. Stress inoculation training helps clients deal with stressful situations by teaching them to examine their beliefs and develop self-talk to reduce the impact of stressful events.

6. Behavior therapists view maladaptive behaviors as learned and rely on classical and operant conditioning and modeling to teach the client new behaviors.

7. Systematic desensitization is an effective treatment for phobias in which clients are taught relaxation techniques and then asked to imagine or approach feared situations gradually. Modeling is also an effective treatment for phobias. **Aversion therapy** reduces undesirable behaviors by pairing them with an aversive (unpleasant) stimulus.

8. Extinction is an operant conditioning technique used to reduce the occurrence of maladaptive behaviors. Reinforcers are withheld after the maladaptive behavior has occurred.

9. Ethical and legal concerns restrict the use of punishment to cases in which a maladaptive behavior is highly resistant to other forms of therapy.

10. Token economies are used to provide secondary reinforcement of desired behaviors. The tokens can be exchanged for primary reinforcers.

11. Group therapy is based on the assumptions that behavior does not occur in a vacuum and that behaviors learned in group settings are more likely to generalize to everyday situations. Marital therapy and family therapy are two forms of group therapy.

12. A significant number of people find support and comfort in self-help groups.

Study Break

1. Identify the form of psychotherapy described in each of the following statements:
   a. The therapist seeks to uncover the patient's unconscious conflicts.
   b. The therapist reflects the emotional content of the client's statements.
   c. Therapists use a scientific approach to help clients assess the validity of statements made during sessions.
   d. Staff members at a mental hospital ignore patients when they use odd words.
   e. The therapist works with the client to develop self-talk to deal with stressful situations.
2. According to client-centered therapists, what are the major characteristics that a therapist should demonstrate to create the type of environment that leads to success in therapy?
3. Using Ellis's *ABC* framework, suggest two contrasting interpretations of the following situation: You tried out for the class play but were not selected. What consequences is each interpretation likely to have?
4. Suggest the behavior therapy that is most likely to be used in each of the following situations:
   a. A teenager is afraid of dogs of all sizes.
   b. A child hits himself repeatedly; the forms of treatment attempted so far have failed to change the behavior.
   c. A hospitalized patient does not greet people and lacks other social skills.

The Effectiveness of Psychotherapy

Tim has been having some difficulties adjusting to college and getting along with his roommates. He also has trouble making decisions and often feels lonely. At times Tim feels that "life is one big vacuum waiting to suck me up." His level of distress is rising daily, and he wants to do something about it, but he wonders whether psychotherapy is worth the time and effort. ***Is psychotherapy an effective treatment for psychological disorders?*** ▪

Does therapy work, and if so, why? Is one form of therapy superior to another? These questions are not easy to answer, for several reasons. First, it is difficult to define clearly what we mean by "success" in psychotherapy. Some therapies, such as psychoanalytic therapy, define success as the development of insight. It is difficult, however, to determine when a person has developed insight. Second, therapies are used in treating a wide variety of problems that may have little in common. When people seek therapy, they have made a decision to change some important aspect of their lives—an aspect that may differ greatly from one individual to another. Third, there is the ever-present placebo effect. Clients may improve during therapy because they expect to improve, regardless of any specific aspects of the therapy.

Eysenck's Challenge

A British psychologist, Hans Eysenck, published the first major study of the effectiveness of psychotherapy in 1952. Eysenck examined 24 studies involving more than 8,000 clients who had moderately severe disorders and received either psychoanalytic therapy, eclectic therapy, or no psychotherapy. Some of the clients seemed to improve without treatment, a phenomenon called *spontaneous remission.* Eysenck (1952) reported that the results "show that roughly two-thirds of a group of . . . patients will recover, whether they are treated by means of psychotherapy or not" (p. 322). The publication of Eysenck's report caused a furor among psychotherapists, and his review was subjected to numerous appraisals. Critics noted that the therapists who had published the studies Eysenck reviewed had different goals and orientations in evaluating therapy and probably used different criteria when judging success (Garfield, 1980).

After the uproar had diminished, the issue of success in psychotherapy was examined more closely. It appeared that Eysenck had overestimated the rate of spontaneous remission in the studies he reviewed. Subsequent estimates of the percentage of clients who improve without treatment were closer to 30 percent (Bergin, 1971).

Meta-Analysis.   One way to answer questions about the effectiveness of psychotherapy is to combine the results of a large number of different studies, using *meta-analysis* (see Chapter 11). Mary Smith and colleagues (1980) reported a meta-analysis of the results of 475 studies of the effectiveness of psychotherapy involving more than 25,000 patients. To rule out the influence of spontaneous remission, all the studies they analyzed involved comparisons of clients treated with psychotherapy to similar clients who received no therapy at all. In each study, the therapists made judgments of success using definitions and measures that were appropriate for the clients they treated. Consequently, there was no common measure across all the studies.

It sounds as if these researchers were comparing apples, oranges, and grapefruits. Each study, however, involved a comparison of a treated group with a nontreated group. Therefore the researchers used the difference in the degree of improvement between the groups (control and treated), regardless of the measure of success. The average of these differences provided an average improvement rate across all the studies.

By averaging the improvements across all the studies, the researchers found that treated individuals were better off than about 80 percent of those who did not receive therapy. The results of several meta-analyses have been reported and support the conclusion that "psychotherapy is generally effective" although "we are uncertain as to why" (Kopta, et al. 1999, p. 461).

Keep in mind that these conclusions about the effectiveness of psychotherapy are limited to therapies that have been formally evaluated (Lambert & Bergin, 1992). The new therapies that are touted on a regular basis are often inadequately tested—their effectiveness often supported by testimonials from satisfied clients, which should give us pause (see "Guidelines for the Psychological Detective" in Chapter 1). The history of therapies for psychological disorders, often with cruel and ineffective treatments, offers an important lesson: Maintain caution and care when evaluating claims for new therapies. Although we no doubt consider ourselves more enlightened than our predecessors, past generations thought the same about previous ones and the therapies that they offered (Dawes, 1994).

Carefully designed studies of the effectiveness of psychotherapy may not capture what happens in typical settings. For example, clients assigned to a control group may decide to seek therapy rather than wait for the end of a study on the effectiveness of therapy. The editors of *Consumer Reports* decided to ask clients if they were satisfied with their therapy (Seligman, 1996). A sample of 7,000 subscribers responded to a questionnaire designed to assess their satisfaction with psychotherapy and psychotropic drug treatment. This group of respondents consulted a range of mental health specialists. In general they reported being quite satisfied with the treatment they received. Two findings are of special note: (1) There were few differences among the specialists in providing satisfactory treatment, and (2) The use of drugs did not add significantly to satisfaction. Concerning the latter finding, it is important to note that by the nature of this type of research (mailed surveys), many clients who may have needed drugs or hospitalization may have been excluded.

Characteristics of Effective Psychotherapy

Which form of psychotherapy works best? This question has been asked repeatedly. Most studies of the effectiveness of various forms of psychotherapy show that differences among them are small and sometimes nonexistent (Smith, Glass, & Miller, 1980; Lambert, Shapiro, & Bergin, 1986), a finding supported by the *Consumer Reports* survey. This view has been termed the "Dodo bird verdict," after the Dodo bird in *Alice in Wonderland* who organized a race among various Wonderland creatures and concluded that "everyone has won and all must have prizes" (Luborsky, Singer, & Luborsky, 1975). What's more, a recent meta-analysis supported the idea that there is little difference among psychotherapy treatments (Wampold, et. al, 1997), although a number of research issues remain to be resolved (Howard, et al. 1997).

Certain characteristics of therapy may contribute to improvement, regardless of the form of therapy we are considering. For example, the therapist's ability to communicate empathy to clients is important (Luborsky et al., 1971). A therapeutic relationship characterized by warmth, acceptance, and trust facilitates psychotherapy. Even when therapists use the same techniques (based on a treatment manual) and are monitored and supervised throughout the course of treatment, some have significantly better outcomes than others (Lambert, 1989). We cannot escape the fact that some people are simply better than others at establishing a caring relationship and instilling hope.

The evidence also suggests that particular therapies are effective in alleviating certain problem behaviors. For example, behavioral therapies such as systematic desensitization are the treatment of choice for phobias, especially the specific phobias (Lambert & Bergin, 1992, 1994). Another interesting finding is that the effects of psychotherapy are equal to or surpass a variety of antidepressant drugs in the treatment of depression (Lambert & Bergin, 1994). Cognitive therapies may be especially effective if they provide coping skills that depressed individuals can use to ward off future episodes.

Changing Psychotherapy to Meet the Needs of Diversity

Culture, ethnicity, and sex have significant effects on our behavior, values, and attitudes; therefore it is not surprising that they influence psychotherapy in significant ways (Yamamoto et al., 1993). For example, *Nai-Kan* ("look within at oneself"), a therapy practiced in Japan, is designed to discover how a client has been ungrateful and troublesome to people who have extended themselves, such as parents and teachers. The therapy's primary goal is to find ways for the client to demonstrate gratitude and alliance to these people (Foulks, Bland, & Shervington, 1995). We cannot fully understand this therapy unless we have some knowledge of Japanese culture, in which the focus is on the group rather than the individual, as is the case in the United States.

There is a growing appreciation that the United States is a multicultural nation with a diversity of ethnic and cultural backgrounds. This reality affects patterns of therapy. In general, ethnic minority group members in the United States neither use nor provide psychotherapy in anything like their proportion in the population (Mays & Albee, 1992) (see Table 14-7). Do not, however, confuse this pattern of use with the need for help for emotional problems. Several minority groups experience a higher proportion of poverty and social stressors that can contribute to psychological disorders. Mental health services for U.S. minority groups are generally inadequate (Sue & Zane, 1987). For example, African Americans, Native Americans, Asian Americans, and Latinos terminate psychotherapy earlier and also average fewer sessions than

TABLE 14-7   Clinical Psychologists and the U.S. Population Compared

CHARACTERISTIC	CLINICAL PSYCHOLOGISTS (%)	U.S. POPULATION (%)
Sex		
Female	30	51
Male	70	49
Race or ethnicity		
Caucasian	93	83
Other	7	17

Sources: Norcross, Karg-Bray, & Prochaska, 1995; U.S. Bureau of the Census, 1997.

whites (Sue, 1992). Between 42 and 55 percent of minority clients failed to return after a single session, as compared with a 30 percent dropout rate for white clients.

Psychotherapy requires intimate conversations between socially distant individuals. Many ethnic groups and cultures reserve such intimate conversations for family members. Formal and polite but nonrevealing patterns of communication are used with outsiders. For example, Latino clients tend to use Spanish at home and English in psychotherapy, even when the therapist is bilingual. The formality of the therapy situation and the therapist's customary use of English may lead clients to see the relationship as similar to previous formal relationships that minimized self-disclosure (Foulks, Bland, & Shervington, 1995).

Language discrepancies between therapists and clients whose native language is not English can affect treatment in a number of ways. For example, identification with the therapist is an important factor in the way the client and therapist relate. Language is an important factor in establishing the existence of common cultural experiences that enable clients to feel comfortable and develop a therapeutic alliance (Yamamoto et al., 1993). Clients may seek therapists of the same ethnic group, race, and sex because they anticipate a feeling of shared values and understanding that will make them more comfortable in revealing intimate details of their lives (Nadelson & Zimmerman, 1993).

Among the reasons ethnic clients terminate psychotherapy so early are a lack of bilingual therapists and therapists' stereotypes about ethnic clients. The single most important reason may be that therapists do not provide culturally responsive forms of therapy. They may be unaware of values and customs within a culture that would help in understanding and treating certain behaviors. Consider the case of a young Latino who went through assertiveness training at the suggestion of his therapist. When the young man went home and asserted himself with his father, he faced a very negative reaction. Therapy should be undertaken with an understanding of cultural values, which in this case included properly respectful behavior toward one's father (Yamamoto et al., 1993).

To counter the high rate of early termination of treatment by minority clients, some psychologists have suggested that therapists develop greater cultural understanding and knowledge. In addition, therapists from diverse ethnic

Clients are often more comfortable with a therapist of the same sex or ethnic background.

backgrounds and ethnic-specific therapeutic services are needed. There is also a need for more bilingual and bicultural personnel who could work more effectively with clients from different cultures and those for whom English is a second language. Does responsiveness to cultural factors work? Sue and his colleagues (1991) analyzed the services, length of treatment, and outcomes of therapy for several ethnic groups in Los Angeles. Ethnic match (in which client and therapist were members of the same ethnic group) was related to the length and success of treatment among Mexican Americans. Among clients for whom English was not their first language, when the therapist had the same ethnic background and spoke the same language as the client, treatment tended to last longer and was more likely to be successful. Thus matching is important because it is related to length of treatment (Sue et al., 1991).

Steven Lopez and his colleagues (1989) suggest that most therapists are initially unaware of how cultural issues influence their work. As they are presented with pertinent information, they often pass through a period in which they see such considerations as a burden that distracts them from their work. Finally, they are able to integrate cultural considerations into their treatment decision making. This final stage is illustrated in the following vignette:

> I worked at a camp for emotionally disturbed children where most of the children were African American or Hispanic, low-income, and from the inner city. A problem arose with a five-year-old Hispanic girl who refused to take showers and had difficulty dressing and undressing with other people around. She would throw temper tantrums and required considerable attention from the counselors. The counselors were about to begin a behavior therapy program to get her to take showers and dress; they viewed her behavior as a consequence of her emotional disturbance. However, it was not clear to me that her tantrums were symptoms of emotional disturbance. She seemed terrified of being violated. I wondered if there were some issues related to cultural background and/or upbringing so I called her parents. They confirmed that the child was brought up to be very modest and not to expose herself to anyone except her mother. Imagine the terror that this child felt when the counselors tried to get her into a shower. They were asking her to violate her parents' code of honor and to adopt ways of behaving that had previously resulted in punishment. We took cultural factors into consideration and modified camp rules to allow her to shower with just one other adult and to dress quickly after other children had left the bunk. The temper tantrums stopped. (Lopez et al., 1989, p. 374)

Consideration of cultural factors made a big difference in the treatment of this young girl, for whom the supervisor had determined it was not appropriate to impose an unfamiliar set of values. Growing appreciation of the ethnic and racial diversity of the population has led therapists to consider these factors in providing various forms of treatment.

When to Begin Psychotherapy and What to Expect

How does someone like Tim, described at the beginning of this section, decide whether to enter psychotherapy? The answer to this question should be based on a range of considerations. People may decide to enter psychotherapy for shyness, anxiety, depression, an inner conflict, a traumatic or stressful event, or a marital or family problem. Others may find they continually develop self-destructive relationships or that their strong need to control others creates problems. Still others may have physical symptoms that are caused by emotional problems.

In *The Consumer's Guide to Psychotherapy,* Jack Engler and Daniel Goleman (1992) suggest three key issues to consider when deciding to enter psychotherapy:

1. Is your distress level intense enough that you want to do something about it now?
2. Are you no longer able to handle your problems on your own? Do you feel the need for more support?
3. Is your distress affecting your personal life, family, or work?

If the answer to any or all of these questions is yes, you may want to consider entering psychotherapy. One of the best ways to start is to seek recommendations from friends, relatives, or other professionals. Another good starting point is to call the community mental health center in your area.

Having decided on psychotherapy, what can you expect? Most clients do not anticipate lengthy treatment and become disenchanted with its slow progress. Long-term psychotherapy offers little to patients who are in the middle of crises that require immediate intervention (Strupp, 1992). One response to these concerns has been short-term psychotherapy, which is carried out in fewer sessions (Bloom, 1992). At the beginning of therapy the therapist states that there will be a fixed number of sessions—usually no more than 25 and often fewer. Short-term psychotherapy focuses on a few goals, such as removal or reduction of the client's most troubling symptoms. The new short-term forms of psychotherapy are quite active; clients should be prepared to listen to suggestions for changes in their behavior. Because time is limited, the therapist is likely to give the client homework assignments such as analyzing emotional reactions or practicing relaxation techniques. These assignments enable client and therapist to make maximum use of their limited time together. The image of the client stretched out on a couch has become outdated as therapies have become shorter and more active.

But just how active are the more modern forms of psychotherapy? Kenneth Howard and his colleagues (1986) analyzed the results of 15 studies involving more than 2,400 psychotherapy patients, most of them suffering from anxiety and depressive disorders. They found that about 50 percent of the patients improved after only 8 sessions; after 26 sessions, approximately 75 percent of the patients improved. The number of sessions stands in stark contrast to the years of expected therapy that was common with "traditional" psychoanalytic therapy, which has also adapted with a faster, problem-oriented modes of operation.

Stephen Kopta and colleagues (1994) studied the recovery rates among 854 psychotherapy clients. At the beginning of psychotherapy and at several points during treatment, the clients reported the severity of their symptoms on a checklist. The 62 symptoms on the checklist were divided into three categories: acute distress (feeling restless, crying easily), chronic distress (feeling guilty, being nervous when alone), and characterological (feeling watched, having frequent arguments). A client's symptoms were judged to be improved when the rating of severity was similar to the ratings provided by a group of normally functioning individuals. The researchers found that 58 sessions (a little more than one session a week for a year) produced recovery among 75 percent of the patients. Many of the individual symptoms, however, responded much more quickly than that (see Figure 14-8).

Finally, we live in a culture that urges us to make changes in our lives. Flick on the television and you see no end to the talk shows touting new forms of therapy for old and newly discovered problems. When considering how to make changes in some aspect of your life, it would be helpful to know the likelihood

FIGURE 14-8 The symptoms frequently treated with psychotherapy respond at different rates.

Source: Kopta et al., 1994.

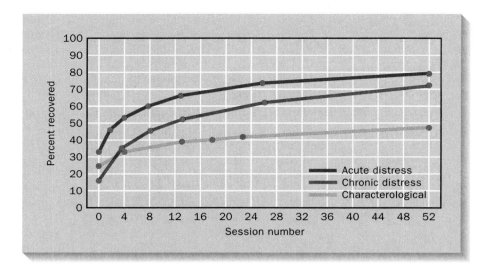

that change is possible. Some problem behaviors are easier to change than others. Some behaviors are very difficult to change because "our biology can make changing despite our efforts almost impossible" (Seligman, 1993). Having this kind of information helps you assess your situation; perhaps you will decide that you like yourself the way you are. Such a decision can save you from the self-reproach and remorse that often accompany failed efforts to alter problem behaviors. Here is a partial list of various problems and the likelihood of improvement:

Curable: panic

Almost curable: specific phobias

Moderate or mild relief: agoraphobia, depression, obsessive-compulsive disorder

Marginal relief: posttraumatic stress disorder

Temporary change: overweight

Unchangeable: sexual orientation (Seligman, 1993)

Review Summary

1. After Eysenck concluded that psychotherapy clients are just as likely to improve without it, psychotherapists sought to provide better information about the success of therapy.

2. Meta-analysis allows researchers to combine the results of a number of studies. Using this technique, researchers have found that therapy does lead to greater improvement than no treatment and that differences among the various forms of therapy are not great.

3. The search for the keys to successful therapy has led researchers to focus on factors such as the therapist's ability to communicate empathy, which can lead to improvement in distressed individuals.

4. Therapists are becoming increasingly aware of the influence of ethnic and cultural factors on psychother-

apy. Members of many ethnic groups drop out early from psychotherapy, in part because there is a dearth of therapists who share their native language as well as a failure to provide appropriate forms of therapy.

5. The decision to enter psychotherapy should involve asking questions about the degree of distress one is experiencing; one's ability to cope with that distress; and the effect of the symptoms on oneself, one's family, and one's work. Current forms of psychotherapy are offered in fewer sessions than in the past. Many symptoms, especially distress symptoms, respond rather quickly to treatment. There is also a growing recognition that there are limits to what aspects of our behavior can be changed.

Study Break

1. What conclusions did Eysenck draw from his study of the effectiveness of psychotherapy? What was the impact of his research?
2. What term describes the tendency for improvement in problems without therapy?
   a. double blind
   b. biased response
   c. spontaneous remission
   d. extinction
3. Which of the following titles might best convey the overall findings of the research by Kopta and his colleagues who studied how various symptoms improve after about a year of psychotherapy?
   a. What a difference a year makes!
   b. Why bother? It has little effect on symptoms.
   c. Prescribe medications; skip the psychotherapy.
   d. It takes years to develop symptoms; it will take years to stop them.
4. What do meta-analyses reveal about the effectiveness of psychotherapy?
5. Name some problem behaviors that can be changed with moderate difficulty. What problem behavior is considered curable?

Biomedical Therapies

While walking through a mall, Alice decides to stop in the bookstore, where she pauses at the magazine section. The cover story in major magazines is touting the latest "wonder drugs" for treating psychological disorders. Alice wonders if the drugs really work and whether they are safe. *What are the benefits and the costs associated with drug therapies for psychological disorders?* ▪

The brain plays a crucial role in every breath you take, every word you utter—every experience of each day of your life. Thus the proposal that altering the brain may be useful in treating psychological disorders is not radical. Although some past efforts to alter brain functioning appear drastic, more recent efforts, primarily psychotropic drugs, have been hailed as breakthroughs in treating psychological disorders. Even drug therapies, however, are not without problems—namely, harmful side effects. In this section we describe several biomedical therapies for psychological disorders.

Drug Therapy

As we saw in Chapters 2 and 5, neurotransmitters have powerful effects on behavior, emotions, and thinking. Most drugs affect neurotransmitter levels and thus can play a prominent role in treating psychological disorders. In this section we examine the psychotropic drugs most frequently prescribed to treat psychological disorders.

Antianxiety Drugs.   Anxiety is the primary symptom in several of the disorders discussed in Chapter 13. Although opinions vary on what causes anxiety disorders, **antianxiety drugs** can reduce the severity of many of the symptoms, especially physiological ones like increased heart rate. Antianxiety drugs are frequently prescribed to treat generalized anxiety disorder; they are also used to treat agitation, alcohol withdrawal, insomnia, and muscle spasms (Klerman et al., 1994).

The major class of antianxiety drugs (also known as minor tranquilizers) are the *benzodiazepines,* such as Valium, Librium, and Xanax (Smock, 1999). These drugs increase the ability of GABA, an inhibitory neurotransmitter, to bind to receptor sites at synapses in the brain. The resulting increase in the

antianxiety drugs
Minor tranquilizers, such as the benzodiazepines, used to reduce anxiety, usually by increasing the ability of the neurotransmitter GABA to bind at synapses

firing of inhibitory neurons lowers levels of the neurological activity that produces anxiety.

Antianxiety drugs are relatively safe because a lethal overdose requires a very large amount of the drug (Yudofsky, Hales, & Ferguson, 1991). Combining antianxiety drugs with alcohol or other drugs, however, can produce severe depression and can sometimes lead to suicide (Maxmen, 1991). The most common side effects of antianxiety drugs—drowsiness and impaired ability to acquire or store information—are usually temporary (Shader & Greenblatt, 1993). Some patients develop a tolerance for these drugs, which means they need larger doses to maintain the initial effect. Most patients who take antianxiety drugs every day for three months or longer run the risk of developing a dependence, which will be followed by withdrawal symptoms if they stop taking the drugs (Winger, Hofmann, & Woods, 1992).

Antidepressant Drugs. Significant strides have been made in the treatment of depression since the era when bloodletting was a common treatment. Antidepressant drugs are the most frequently prescribed psychotropic drugs in the United States, having recently surpassed antianxiety drugs (Pincus et al., 1998). This increase is, in part, a result of the increasing number of disorders for which antidepressant drugs are prescribed. There are three classes of antidepressant drugs: tricyclic antidepressants, monoamine oxidase (MAO) inhibitors, and selective serotonin reuptake inhibitors.

The chemical structure of *tricyclic antidepressants* resembles three connected circles, hence the name. Drugs in this class, such as Elavil, reduce the reuptake of the neurotransmitters serotonin and norepinephrine, thus making more of these chemical messengers available at synapses. Although these changes at the synapse occur immediately, 10 to 14 days usually pass before there is a reduction in the symptoms of depression. The side effects of antidepressants include constipation, dizziness, and dry mouth.

The enzyme MAO breaks down the neurotransmitters norepinephrine and serotonin before they can be repackaged for future use. When MAO is blocked, the levels of these neurotransmitters increase. A second class of drugs used to treat depression, *MAO inhibitors*, prevent MAO from breaking down norepinephrine and serotonin and thus increase their levels in the brain. Patients who do not respond to tricyclic antidepressants may be switched to one of the MAO inhibitors. Although the side effects of MAO inhibitors are similar to those of the tricyclic antidepressants, they tend to be more serious. For example, MAO inhibitors can produce a dangerous rise in blood pressure if taken at the same time as tyramine, a substance found in alcoholic beverages (beer and red wine), aged cheese, beans, liver, salami, pepperoni, and yogurt (Bhatia & Bhatia, 1997; Preston, O'Neal, & Talaga, 1998).

As we have seen, many drugs have side effects that range from annoying to life-threatening. Many of the side effects of tricyclic antidepressants result from their effects on the neurotransmitter norepinephrine. The third group of drugs used to treat depression, however, the *selective serotonin reuptake inhibitors* (SSRIs), have little, if any, effect on norepinephrine levels. The best known drug in this class, Prozac (fluoxetine), is the most widely prescribed drug for the treatment of depression. One reason for its popularity is a low rate of short-term side effects. Despite this popularity, it is not certain that Prozac is actually superior to other drugs used to treat depression (Gram, 1994). Nevertheless, Prozac (as well as other SSRIs) is prescribed for a growing number of problems, including anorexia nervosa, bulimia nervosa, obsessive-compulsive disorder, and panic disorder (Bailey, 1998; Osborn, 1998; Pies, 1998).

Mood Stabilizers. Drugs used to treat bipolar disorder (reduce mania and raise depressive mood) are called *mood stabilizers*. Three widely used mood sta-

Prozac, an antidepressant drug (selective serotonin reuptake inhibitor), has been hailed as a breakthrough. It is the most frequently used drug in the treatment of depression.

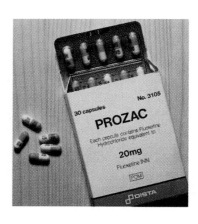

bilizers are lithium and the anticonvulsants carbamazepine and valproic acid (Preston, O'Neal, & Talaga, 1998; Rush & Suppes, 1998).

The natural mineral salt, *lithium,* is the drug of choice for treating the acute manic episodes of bipolar disorder, it tends to reduce the wild mood swings associated with this disorder (Price & Heninger, 1994). About 70 to 80 percent of patients respond to lithium treatment, usually within 5 to 14 days (Hopkins & Gelenberg, 1994; Price & Heninger, 1994). Bipolar patients often continue taking lithium even when they no longer display symptoms of mania or depression to prevent a recurrence.

Lithium has a narrow margin of safe use: The level of lithium in the blood required for effective treatment is close to the toxic level that can result in symptoms such as vomiting, nausea, and even death. Therefore patients must have periodic blood tests to check lithium levels and to adjust the dosage (Rybacki & Long, 1998). Therapeutic levels of lithium are associated with side effects such as hand tremor, excessive thirst and urination.

A number of mechanisms have been proposed to explain how lithium reduces mood swings. For example, lithium influences the passage of ions in and out of cell membranes (see Chapter 2); it may also regulate levels of norepinephrine (and perhaps other neurotransmitters).

Despite lithium's general effectiveness (Schou, 1997), some patients do not respond adequately to lithium therapy; therefore the search continues for other treatments. Among the alternative treatments are anticonvulsant drugs (Dubovsky & Buzan, 1997; Post et al., 1996), which are especially effective for the rapid cycling form of bipolar disorder (four or more episodes of disturbed mood in one year).

Antipsychotic Drugs. The first antipsychotic drug was discovered in France in 1952 when a surgeon, Henri Laborit, observed that a new anesthetic calmed his patients without a loss of consciousness. He persuaded several psychiatrists to try the drug on patients with schizophrenia. The drug, Thorazine (chlorpromazine), was soon widely adopted for treating schizophrenia, although it has now been replaced by more potent drugs. The discovery of **antipsychotic drugs** was a major factor in the deinstitutionalization of psychiatric patients. These drugs became the principal method for treating schizophrenia (Kane, 1996).

Antipsychotic drugs seem to work by occupying receptor sites in neurons that respond to dopamine, a neurotransmitter that has been implicated in the development of schizophrenia (see Chapter 13). When these receptor sites are occupied, nerve conduction is reduced. Antipsychotic drugs are very effective at decreasing positive symptoms such as delusions and hallucinations; they are less effective at reducing negative symptoms such as apathy (Torrey, 1988). Although antipsychotic drugs do not cure schizophrenia and other psychotic disorders, they are effective in controlling many of the symptoms.

The development of antipsychotic drugs was a major change in the treatment of mentally ill patients, but their use is not without problems. Movement disorders such as restlessness, tremors, and shuffling gait are major reasons that many patients stop taking their medications. The long-term use of antipsychotic drugs can lead to **tardive dyskinesia** ("late-appearing movement disorder"), which is characterized by symptoms such as persistent, involuntary chewing movements, lip smacking, and rolling movements of the tongue. This chronic and sometimes irreversible effect of antipsychotic drugs is considered a serious problem. Elderly patients and those with brain damage or diabetes have an elevated risk for developing tardive dyskinesia The symptoms typically develop gradually, so this condition can be recognized in its early stages, and treatment can be altered. The changes in treatment include tapering the dose of the antipsychotic drug to the lowest effective level or adding Vitamin E to the treatment (Egan,

antipsychotic drugs
Drugs that reduce the symptoms of schizophrenia by blocking dopamine receptors in the brain; the typical antipsychotic drugs work by blocking dopamine, whereas the atypical drugs (such as Clozapine) also block serotonin

tardive dyskinesia
A serious adverse effect of antipsychotic drugs characterized by involuntary motor symptoms such as lip smacking

Apud, & Wyatt, 1997). Another serious, although rare, adverse effect of antipsychotic drugs, *neuroleptic malignant syndrome,* can lead to a sudden high fever with sweating, high or unstable blood pressure, extreme muscle rigidity, and even death (Rosebush, 1994).

An estimated 30 to 40 percent of patients with schizophrenia do not respond adequately to typical antipsychotic drugs. Some of these patients, however, respond to the atypical antipsychotic Clozapine, which was introduced in 1990 (several more atypical antipsychotic drugs have been developed since that time). In addition to its effectiveness in some patients who do not respond to other antipsychotic drugs, Clozapine produces low rates of tardive dyskinesia (Meltzer, 1993; Pickar & Hsiao, 1995). One reason for this low rate of motor effects is that Clozapine affects serotonin as well as the dopamine receptors affected by most antipsychotic drugs (Pickar & Hsiao, 1995). Clozapine, however, can seriously impair the ability of the bone marrow to produce white blood cells, which leaves individuals highly vulnerable to infections (Rybacki & Long, 1998). This problem, which occurs in about 1 percent of patients, develops rapidly and can be lethal. Because the reduction in white blood cells is potentially life-threatening, patients who take Clozapine must have weekly blood tests to determine if their white-blood-count is within normal limits (Haber et al., 1997).

Although Clozapine does not lead to symptoms such as tardive dyskinesia, it is associated with side effects such as dizziness, drowsiness, and seizures that have led some psychiatrists to describe it as "not a user-friendly medication" (Pies, 1998). Clozapine is recommended for use only in patients who have failed to respond adequately to two or more typical antipsychotic drugs; consequently, it should never be the first antipsychotic drug prescribed (Pies, 1998; Rybacki, 1997). The history of antipsychotic drugs shows us that no drug is absolutely free of risk.

Evaluating Drug Therapy.   Table 14-8 summarizes the psychotropic drugs commonly used to treat psychological disorders. Proponents of drug therapy believe that the increased use and effectiveness of drugs heralded a new era in treating psychological disorders. In *Mind, Mood, and Medicine* (1981), Paul Wender and Donald Klein call the use of psychotropic drugs a "virtual revolution." Seymour Fisher and Roger Greenberg (1989), however, report that psychotherapy is often equally or more effective than drugs in treating many psychological disorders. They suggest that drugs are used more frequently and more quickly than psychotherapy because of their greater availability.

Drugs can make some patients more manageable for therapists and hospital staff, reduce patients' anxiety levels, lift a depressed mood, and eliminate some delusions. But they cannot replace lost social skills or teach patients how to interact with family members and other people. Therapy programs that combine drug therapy with efforts to enhance patients' social skills and to assist family members in dealing with former patients have shown promise (Hogarty et al., 1991).

As we have indicated, many psychotropic drugs reduce the symptoms of various psychological disorders; however, they are also often associated with side effects. For example, antipsychotic drugs can lead to adverse effects such as tardive dyskinesia. But withdrawing the drug can lead to a worsening of the symptoms or a relapse (return of symptoms). One study of the use of antipsychotic drugs found that about half of the patients with schizophrenia who were taking antipsychotic drugs suffered a relapse when the drugs were withdrawn. Because about half of the patients did not suffer a relapse, researchers suggest a program of slowly tapering the dosage to the lowest effective dosage that controls the symptoms, which may be zero (Gilbert et al., 1995).

TABLE 14-8   **Major Categories of Psychotropic Drugs Used in Treating Psychological Disorders**

TYPE OF DRUG	CHEMICAL GROUP	GENERIC NAME	BRAND NAME	SIDE EFFECTS	MODE OF ACTION
Antianxiety drugs	Benzodiazepines	alprazolam chlordiazepoxide diazepam	Xanax Librium Valium	Dizziness, drowsiness, unsteadiness, impaired memory and concentration	Enhances the action of inhibitory neurotransmitter GABA, which in turn reduces arousal of higher brain centers
Anti-depressants	Tricyclics	amitriptyline clomipramine imipramine	Elavil Anafranil Tofranil	Drowsiness, dry mouth, blurred vision, constipation, weight gain	Increase availability of the neurotransmitters norepinephrine and serotonin by blocking their reuptake
	Selective serotonin reuptake inhibitors (SSRI)	fluoxetine paroxetine sertraline	Prozac Paxil Zoloft	Gastrointestinal side effects (nausea, vomiting, and diarrhea), dizziness, dry mouth, sexual dysfunctions (e.g., decreased libido, erectile dysfunction)	Enhance the activity of serotonin by preventing its uptake
	Monoamine oxidase (MAO) inhibitors	isocarboxazid phenelzine	Marplan Nardil	Excessive thirst, increased frequency of urination, altered blood pressure	Block the action of the enzyme MAO, which breaks down norepinephrine
Mood stablizers		lithium	Eskalith	Increased thirst and urination, drowiness, dizziness, tremors, weight gain, nausea, vomiting	Lithium has diverse actions on several neurotransmitters and may alter neuronal function through effects on ion distribution
	Anticonvulsants	carbamazepine valproic acid	Tegretol Depakote	Increased thirst and urination, drowiness, dizziness, tremors, weight gain, nausea, vomiting	Valproic acid may increase levels of GABA. Carbamazepine may have widespread effects on neural function via its blocking of sodium channels
Antipsychotic drugs	Typical	chlorpromazine fluphenazine haloperidol	Thorazine Prolixin Haldol	Drowsiness, dizziness, dry mouth, tardive dyskinesia, restlessness	Generally block dopamine receptors in the brain
	Atypical	clozapine risperidone	Clozaril Riserdal	Dizziness, drowsiness, weight gain, loss of capacity of the bone marrow to make white blood cells, seizures	Atypical antipsychotic drugs affect serotonin and dopamine receptors

Sources: Bailey, 1998; Bhatia & Bhatia, 1997; Leavitt, 1995; Pies, 1998; Seeley, Stephens, & Tate, 1995.

**Cultural &
Diversity
Perspective**

Psychiatrist Keh-Ming Lin is a pioneer in the study of cultural and ethnic influences on the effectiveness of drugs used to treat psychological disorders.

Variations in Drug Response Related to Ethnicity and Sex

ETHNIC GROUPS DIFFER IN THEIR SUSCEPTIBILITY TO CERTAIN PHYSICAL DISORDERS such as Tay-Sachs disease and sickle-cell anemia; men and women also differ in their susceptibility to certain diseases. Given these general findings, we may also find differences in the response to psychotropic drugs.

Ethnicity and culture can interact in a complex manner to affect a person's response to drug treatment (Yamamoto & Lin, 1995). When Keh-Ming Lin arrived in the United States from Taiwan in 1974 for a residency in psychiatry, he noted that Caucasian patients with schizophrenia were given drug dosages ten times higher than those given in Taiwan.

Lin and his colleagues have been investigating ethnic differences in response to drug treatment for psychological disorders. Accumulating evidence reveals the existence of some *pharmacokinetic differences* among ethnic groups; these are group differences in the concentration of a drug in the blood after taking similar doses. Such ethnic differences may be a significant cause of the different response to drug therapies. For example, East Asian patients suffering from schizophrenia require lower doses of Haldol (haloperidol) to produce an optimal response. What's more, the side effects of antipsychotic drugs become evident in East Asian patients at lower doses than in Caucasian patients (Lin et al., 1989). The differential response to Haldol does not seem to result from lifestyle factors; similar responses were found in American- and foreign-born East Asians living in the United States (Lin et al., 1988b). East Asian men also seem to be more sensitive to the drug Xanax (alprazolam, a benzodiazepine), which is used to treat anxiety and panic symptoms. Levels of Xanax and Haldol reach significantly higher concentrations in East Asian patients and remain in the body longer than they do in Caucasian patients after both oral and intravenous administration (Chien, 1993).

These results suggest that East Asians may require lower doses than Caucasians to achieve comparable results. Moreover, there is evidence that Asians require lower doses of tricyclic antidepressants and lithium to yield the same effects (Yamamoto & Lin, 1995).

What accounts for such differences in the drug response among ethnic groups? There may be differences in the number or type of drug receptors in the brain, in the effects of enzymes in the body, or the way the body metabolizes (breaks down) drugs (Smith & Lin, 1996). Regardless of the actual causes of the differences, remember that the ultimate goal of this research is not to stereotype any individual or group; rather, it is to provide more appropriate treatment for all individuals suffering from psychological disorders.

Can a person's biological sex affect his or her response to psychotropic drug therapy? The answer is important in making treatment decisions; however, the question is not easy to answer. The Food and Drug Administration's (FDA) 1977 guidelines prohibited inclusion of "women of childbearing potential" in drug studies until the drugs had been tested on animals and been shown to be effective in men or older women. In 1993, the FDA replaced the earlier guidelines with new ones requesting the study of possible sex differences (Sherman, Temple, & Merkatz, 1995).

Drugs taken by the usual oral route are metabolized by the digestive tract; most of the drug travels to the liver, where it is metabolized and excreted, and some is eliminated through the kidneys. As little as 10 percent of a psychotropic drug remains to reach the brain. Differences between women and men may arise at any of these steps (Yonkers & Hamilton, 1995a).

Given the same dose, women generally have higher levels of a drug in their bloodstreams because they tend to weigh less than men. Complicating the picture, however, are the hormones estrogen and progesterone because they slow down the emptying time of the stomach, which can lower the amount of a drug that reaches the brain. Thus women can require higher doses of some drugs than men do. Conversely, women secrete less stomach acid than men do, and tricyclic antidepressants, benzodiazepines, and certain antipsychotic drugs are more likely to be absorbed by the body before they are neutralized by stomach acid. Thus women often require lower doses of these drugs (Yonkers & Hamilton, 1995a, 1995b).

In sum, sex differences are difficult to categorize; sometimes women require higher levels of drugs than men do, and sometimes they require lower levels. The new FDA guidelines will make more information available about sex differences in determining the appropriate levels of specific drugs.

Electroconvulsive Therapy

In 1938, the police in Rome found a man who suffered from schizophrenia wandering through a train station. They sent him to two psychiatrists, Ugo Cerletti and Lucio Bini, who had been experimenting with a new procedure to induce seizures. Seizures were thought to be beneficial in treating schizophrenia. The psychiatrists applied an electrical current to the man's head; the current triggered a seizure that jolted his body. After the third shock-induced seizure, the man appeared to recover from his schizophrenia (Valenstein, 1986). Cerletti and Bini's technique became known as **electroconvulsive therapy (ECT),** but it is also called *shock therapy.*

When ECT was first used, the seizures it induced were so violent that some patients suffered broken bones and a few even died. Consequently, it has been stigmatized by past misapplications and overuse (Banazak, 1996). Today, repeated evaluations of ECT indicate that it is a successful treatment for major depression, especially in cases that have not responded to antidepressant drugs (Kellner et al., 1997). Moreover, ECT is frequently used when there is a great risk of suicide because it works faster than drug therapies (Andreasen & Black, 1995; Fink, 1992).

Beginning in the 1950s, ECT was modified to reduce the more serious side effects. For example, before ECT is administered, patients are given an anesthetic and muscle relaxants to eliminate the chance of broken bones. Because the seizure can impede or prevent the flow of air to the lungs, patients also receive oxygen during the procedure to prevent the death of neurons in the brain. A rubber mouth guard inserted between the patient's teeth prevents patients from choking or biting their tongue.

After the patient is prepared for the treatment, electrodes are attached to the patient's head. In bilateral ECT the electrodes are attached to each of the patient's temples; in unilateral ECT they are attached to one side of the head. The electrodes deliver a current of electricity about equal to that required to light a 20-watt bulb for 2 seconds (Andreasen & Black, 1995). The equipment now in use delivers shorter bursts of electricity than those used before the

electroconvulsive therapy (ECT)

A biomedical treatment in which an electric current is passed through the brain to induce a seizure; most often used to treat severe depression

1950s. The current causes the patient to experience a convulsion, which should last at least 25 seconds to be effective (Fink, 1992). The recommended procedure is 3 treatments per week, for a total of 8 to 12 treatments.

Psychological Detective

What effects do you think ECT would have on a patient immediately after the treatment? What psychological processes would be affected? Give these questions some thought, and write down your answers before reading further.

After undergoing ECT, patients are confused, do not remember what happened during the treatment, and may experience memory impairment for about an hour (Fink, 1993). These effects occur because administration of the electrical shock disrupts the process of consolidation, which is crucial to the formation of long-term memories (see Chapter 7). The use of unilateral ECT may reduce the memory impairment because the treatment is usually not administered to the brain hemisphere that is responsible for language. There is concern, however, that unilateral ECT may not be as effective as bilateral treatment (Andreasen & Black, 1995; Fink, 1992).

Myth or Science

The application of electrodes to a person's skull to induce a seizure as a form of therapy has been controversial. Critics question the treatment because it looks like punishment; they also wonder if ECT damages the brain. Earlier research could not provide definitive answers to questions about the effects of ECT on the brain because researchers often did not have data on the condition of the patient's brain before ECT was administered. They have now obtained magnetic resonance images (MRIs) before and after administration of bilateral ECT. Comparison of these images reveals no evidence of changes in the brain a few days or six months after the treatment (Coffey et al., 1991). Although this finding is encouraging, it cannot tell us whether ECT causes subtle changes that are not detectable by the MRI.

The reason for the effectiveness of ECT is still not known (Kellner et al., 1997). It has been suggested (but not proven) that ECT increases the levels of several neurotransmitters, such as norepinephrine, in the brain. These biochemical changes are thought to reverse processes that occur during depression and are similar to the changes that occur with drug treatments. ECT, however, has many other effects on the central nervous system and hormone levels that might be responsible for the lifting of the depression (Andreasen & Black, 1995; Fink, 1992).

Psychosurgery

In *Great and Desperate Cures,* Elliot Valenstein (1986) describes a procedure from the 1930s: "After drilling two or more holes in a patient's skull, a surgeon inserted into the brain any of various instruments—some resembling an apple corer, a butter spreader, or an ice pick—and, often without being able to see what he was cutting, destroyed parts of the brain" (p. 3). This depiction is neither science fiction nor fiendish torture. Valenstein was describing an early version of **psychosurgery,** surgical alteration of brain tissue.

In 1935, Egas Moniz, a Portuguese neurologist, suggested that psychological problems might result from what he termed "reverberating circuits" in the brain. To break these circuits, Moniz proposed a simple surgical procedure that involved cutting nerve fibers of the brain's frontal lobes (see Chapter 2). Moniz coined the term *psychosurgery,* and his procedure became known as a *prefrontal lobotomy.* Psychosurgery found its way to the United States as a treatment for significantly impaired patients when Walter Freeman, a neurosurgeon, read an article by Moniz and decided to try the procedure in 1936. Yet "there was nothing compelling about any of his arguments that should have persuaded a prudent man to attempt psychosurgery" (Valenstein, 1986, p. 100).

Why was such a radical and irreversible treatment used on thousands of patients? (The full number of patients operated on will never be known.) For one reason, there were no alternative treatments available for the thousands of chronically ill patients in increasingly overcrowded hospitals. In addition, these procedures were evaluated by surgeons whose enthusiasm may have overridden their objectivity. Dramatic changes in a few patients were widely reported; some patients who were given local anesthesia reported almost immediate symptom relief (Swayze, 1995). According to Dawes (1994), "Without doing anything even remotely close to a scientific examination of the procedure, the doctors performing it advocated its widespread use" (p. 48). Eventually, more objective and long-term evaluations were conducted. These studies were less enthusiastic about psychosurgery and noted possible severe complications such as hemorrhage, seizures, and major personality changes (Swayze, 1995). The development of psychotropic drugs beginning in the 1950s provided a less drastic alternative to psychosurgery.

Present-day psychosurgical procedures are more refined than the earlier, crude operations; nevertheless, they are rarely performed, and then only as a last resort. Some cases of obsessive-compulsive disorder are so debilitating and unresponsive to drug or behavioral treatments that patients seek a surgical alternative. In an operation called a *cingulotomy,* the surgeon cuts a bundle of nerve fibers that play a role in the obsessions and compulsions (Baer et al., 1995; Sachdev & Hay, 1996). Although this surgical procedure has reduced symptom severity in some cases, most patients exhibit little, if any, change as a result of this surgery.

psychosurgery

The alteration of brain tissue in an attempt to alleviate psychological disorders

Review Summary

1. The major category of **antianxiety drugs,** the benzodiazepines, affect the ability of the inhibitory neurotransmitter GABA to bind to receptor sites in the brain.

2. Three categories of drugs are used to treat depression: tricyclic antidepressants, MAO inhibitors, and selective serotonin reuptake inhibitors. Tricyclic antidepressants prevent reuptake of norepinephrine and serotonin. MAO inhibitors prevent an enzyme from breaking down norepinephrine and serotonin. Drugs such as Prozac reduce the reuptake of serotonin. Lithium and anticonvulsant drugs are effective treatments for mania.

3. Antipsychotic drugs occupy dopamine receptor sites in the brain. These drugs are more effective at reducing the positive symptoms of schizophrenia than the negative ones. The use of antipsychotic drugs can lead to **tardive dyskinesia,** a serious adverse reaction involving involuntary motor movements.

4. There are some significant ethnic differences in responses to some drugs used to treat psychological disorders. The Food and Drug Administration has issued new guidelines for the study of possible sex differences in responses to drugs.

5. Electroconvulsive therapy (ECT) is effective for major depression. Modified procedures for administering ECT, such as use of muscle relaxants, have reduced the severity of side effects. The most prominent side effect is memory disturbance immediately following ECT administration.

6. In 1935, Egas Moniz devised the first **psychosurgery,** the prefrontal lobotomy. The few psychosurgical operations done today involve alteration of much smaller areas of brain tissue.

Study Break

1. Identify the categories of drugs that are most likely to be prescribed for each of the following disorders.
   a. Mania
   b. Schizophrenia
   c. Major depression
2. Identify the neurotransmitter that is affected by each of the following categories of drugs.
   a. Antipsychotic drugs
   b. Benzodiazepines
   c. Tricyclic antidepressants
3. What is the most serious side effect of treatment with Clozapine?
   a. insomnia
   b. memory impairment
   c. inability to manufacture white blood cells
   d. behavioral changes such as increased aggression
4. Which of the following drugs works by inhibiting the reuptake of serotonin?
   a. Valium
   b. Thorazine
   c. Lithium
   d. Prozac

5. A psychiatrist prescribed a drug for your uncle's psychological disorder. As part of the treatment regimen, the psychiatrist periodically checks the level of the drug in your uncle's blood. Based on your knowledge of drug therapy, you conclude the prescribed drug is
   a. Lithium.
   b. Valium.
   c. Elavil.
   d. Haldol.
6. What is the most prominent side effect of ECT?
   a. delusions
   b. infection
   c. hemorrhage
   d. memory impairment
7. The first psychosurgery involved severing nerve tracts in the
   a. occipital lobes.
   b. thalamus.
   c. frontal lobes.
   d. corpus callosum.
8. What has research shown concerning the possible influence of ethnicity and sex on response to psychotropic drug therapy?

ANSWERS TO STUDY BREAKS

Page 587

1. c
2. a
3. b
4. The availability of new drug therapies made it possible to reduce the symptoms experienced by some patients and allow them to leave hospitals.
5. a
6. **a.** Psychiatrist
   b. Psychoanalyst
   c. Clinical psychologist

Page 605

1. **a.** Psychoanalytic therapy
   b. Client-centered therapy

   c. Rational-emotive behavior therapy
   d. Behavioral (extinction)
   e. Stress inoculation therapy
2. unconditional positive regard, genuineness, empathy
3. You could interpret the failure to be selected as evidence that you have no ability at all, and consequently you may feel depressed. On the other hand, you might recognize that there were many qualified actors who have more experience than you and that you have skills that are apparent in other areas besides acting.
4. **a.** Systematic desensitization or modeling
   b. Punishment
   c. Token economy

Page 613

1. Eysenck reported that patients suffering from a variety of disorders improved whether they received psychotherapy or not. Researchers subsequently were challenged to present evidence for the effectiveness of therapy and identify its key elements.
2. c
3. a
4. The meta-analyses of psychotherapy generally show that psychotherapy is more effective than no treatment at all. They also tend to show that a wide range of therapies are effective.
5. Agoraphobia and depression can be changed with moderate difficulty; panic is considered curable.

Page 622

1. **a.** Mood stabilizers (especially lithium but also anticonvulsants)
   b. Antipsychotic
   c. Tricyclic antidepressant drugs, MAO inhibitors, or selective serotonin reuptake inhibitors
2. **a.** Dopamine; atypical antipsychotic drugs also affect serotonin
   b. GABA
   c. Norepinephrine and serotonin
3. c
4. d
5. a
6. d
7. c
8. Both ethnicity and a person's sex may impact the recommended dose of a drug; these factors also influence the effectiveness of certain drugs.

Health Psychology

Chapter in Perspective

To this point we have covered basic processes that include communication in the nervous system, how we sense and understand the physical world, and how we learn. We have also discussed how we develop across the lifespan, and looked at various psychological disorders and how they may be treated. Now we turn our attention from psychological disorders to those affecting our physical health. Progress over recent decades has altered the threats to our health. Many of the current causes of illness and death are related to decisions we make about our behaviors, such as those regarding diet and exercise. We are, in fact, endowed with a powerful built-in response to threats to our well-being that has served us well over the centuries. As we shall see, however, that biological response is now often elicited at times when it is not needed. Therefore we must learn to redirect it to our benefit. How we react to difficult situations is also a function of how we interpret events; thus our cognitive capabilities are as important in understanding our health as biological factors are.

Every day we ask and answer questions about physical and psychological well-being: "How are you today?" "You don't look good. Is something wrong?" These questions usually arise from routine courtesy; however, when serious health problems occur, our questions become more searching. We probe for the reasons one person becomes ill whereas another person exposed to similar circumstances does not. As awareness of our personal vulnerability to illnesses increases, we try to determine what we can do to reduce our risk and maintain good health. In this chapter we explore some of the issues surrounding disease and health. ▪

Health Psychology: An Overview

Outside a small town just before the turn of the century, a family struggles for survival. Pitted against the forces of nature, family members try to grow the food they need as they hope to be spared the illnesses that have affected other people in the town. For example, an epidemic of influenza swept through the community last year and took a heavy toll. *How have the diseases experienced by Americans changed over the years?* ▪

Dramatic changes in the causes of death in the United States over the past century have led to a focus on how emotional reactions, social influences, and overt behaviors affect our health. In 1900, the major causes of death were contagious diseases, such as influenza, pneumonia, and tuberculosis. By about 1950, changes in sanitation and the introduction of mass vaccinations had enabled Americans to avoid or at least to recover from many of these diseases. Today the leading causes of death, heart disease and cancer (U.S. Bureau of the Census, 1997), are noncontagious diseases that are linked to our behaviors or lifestyle. Our behavior has a powerful influence on our health; behavior changes might have prevented half the deaths in the United States in 1990 (see Table 15-1).

Although noncontagious diseases are now responsible for most deaths, deaths owing to infectious diseases have increased 58 percent from 1980 to 1992. Much of this increase was the result of *acquired immunodeficiency syndrome (AIDS)*, in which certain behaviors put individuals at risk for a disease caused by a virus.

Health psychology is the subfield of psychology devoted to understanding how psychological and social variables affect health and how we respond when we become ill. Health psychologists focus on how emotions, social factors, and behavior influence health and illness. They also develop programs to reduce the levels of risk factors related to diseases. For example, health psychologists have developed school-based programs to strengthen students' ability to resist social pressures to start smoking cigarettes (Botvin et al., 1992).

We are still subject to attacks from bacteria and viruses, such as the virus that causes *AIDS*. In today's world, however, the "new germs" are more often personal habits like smoking, a sedentary lifestyle, excessive intake of dietary fat, and strong emotional reactions to life events such as job loss or divorce that can produce the affliction we call stress (Ornstein & Sobel, 1987). Behavior and lifestyle affect our health, and culture affects our behavior and lifestyle; consequently, there are major cultural differences in health and disease around the world. Several times we have pointed to the importance of the cultural concepts of collectivism and individual-

health psychology
Subfield of psychology that is concerned with how psychological and social variables affect health and illness

TABLE 15-1 Deaths from Preventable Causes in the United States, 1990

A significant number of deaths could be prevented each year by changes in behaviors that are related to our risk of disease and death.

CAUSE	ESTIMATED DEATHS	PERCENTAGE OF TOTAL DEATHS
Smoking tobacco	400,000	19
Dietary factors and physical inactivity	300,000	14
Use of alcohol	100,000	5
Microbial agents	90,000	4
Toxic agents	60,000	3
Firearms	35,000	2
High-risk sexual behavior	30,000	1
Motor vehicle injuries	25,000	1
Illicit use of drugs	20,000	less than 1
Total	1,060,000	50

Source: McGinnis & Foege, 1993.

ism. Whether a culture is described as collectivistic or individualistic can influence the types and prevalence of diseases. For example, individualistic cultures such as the United States have lower rates of infectious and parasitic diseases compared to collectivistic cultures. On the other hand, individualistic cultures have higher rates of various types of cancer (Matsumoto, 1996).

A government report, *Healthy People 2000: National Health Promotion and Disease Prevention Objectives* (Public Health Service, 1990, 1995), applauds recent improvements in the health of Americans and offers goals to continue the movement toward a healthier nation. One goal is to reduce fat intake (measured in calories) to 30 percent of our diet—a 17 percent decrease from current levels. There is reason to be optimistic that such changes will lead to significant benefits. Past behavioral changes have been associated with notable improvements in health. For example, recent declines in deaths owing to heart disease and stroke are related to the increased detection and treatment of high blood pressure, reduction in the number of smokers, and decreases in the consumption of fat (Public Health Service, 1990).

Joseph Matarazzo (1984), a health psychologist, has offered a list of behaviors that are related to good health (see Table 15-2). These behaviors should not surprise you. Although initiating them seems difficult, they can easily become part of your daily routine. Begin each day by eating breakfast, and you will be less likely to eat snack foods to tide you over until lunch. Once you start buckling your seat belt, it becomes as automatic as putting the key in the ignition.

Stress and Illness

Almost every day, Beth relates another story about school and job pressures. Her courses this semester are especially difficult. A reduction in the size of the sales force at work means she is on the go from the time she arrives until closing. According to the newspaper, a virus is spreading

TABLE 15-2   **Behaviors That Have a Positive Influence on Health**

- Do not smoke.
- Engage in 30 minutes of physical activity almost every day.
- Eat breakfast every day.
- Get your weight to a normal level.
- Learn and follow a healthful diet.
- If you drink alcohol, do so in moderation.
- Get the amount of sleep that your body needs.
- Use seat belts every time you are in a vehicle.
- Do not drive at excessive speeds.
- Women, do a regular breast exam; men, get a regular prostate exam.
- Find a physician with whom you can communicate openly and effectively.

Source: Adapted from Matarazzo, 1984.

through the area. Yesterday Beth sensed that she was developing a cold and wondered if the stress she is experiencing has left her more vulnerable to that virus. ***Can stress make us more vulnerable to illness?*** ■

Just about every day we hear or use the word *stress* in conversations, yet the term did not come into widespread use until 1936, when a Canadian endocrinologist, Hans Selye (1907–1982), published a book titled *The Stress of Life* (1978). While he was in medical school, Selye noticed that many patients had similar symptoms—fatigue, loss of appetite, fever—regardless of the particular disease that was diagnosed.

Later in his career, Selye injected laboratory rats with an extract from ovarian cells and found some intriguing results. No matter what he did to the rats—whether it was injecting them with extracts or exposing them to extreme temperatures or shock—their biological response was similar. These experiments and observations led Selye to conclude that regardless of the external or internal event, the body (whether of a rat or a human being) responds in comparable ways, which he described as a "stress syndrome." He defined **stress** as the nonspecific response of the body to any demand. A **stressor** is anything that causes an organism to adjust and display this nonspecific stress response.

The General Adaptation Syndrome

stress
Nonspecific response of the body to any demand made on it

stressor
Anything that causes an organism to adjust and display the nonspecific stress response

general adaptation syndrome (GAS)
Typical series of responses to stressful situations that includes the alarm, resistance, and exhaustion stages

Selye outlined a series of biological responses, called the **general adaptation syndrome (GAS),** that occur as the body deals with stressors. The nervous and endocrine systems orchestrate this series of responses or stages: the alarm stage, the resistance stage, and the exhaustion stage.

Alarm Stage.   The *alarm stage* of the GAS is equivalent to the well-known fight-or-flight response (see Chapter 2). During this "call to arms," the hypothalamus signals the sympathetic nervous system and the pituitary (see Figure 15-1). The combination of the activation of the sympathetic nervous system and an outpouring of stress hormones prepares the body for a brief period of physical action in response to a threat. One consequence of the release of these hormones is easily recognized—your heart races. You may also experience "butterflies" in your stomach because digestion slows and blood is redirected to the muscles in prepa-

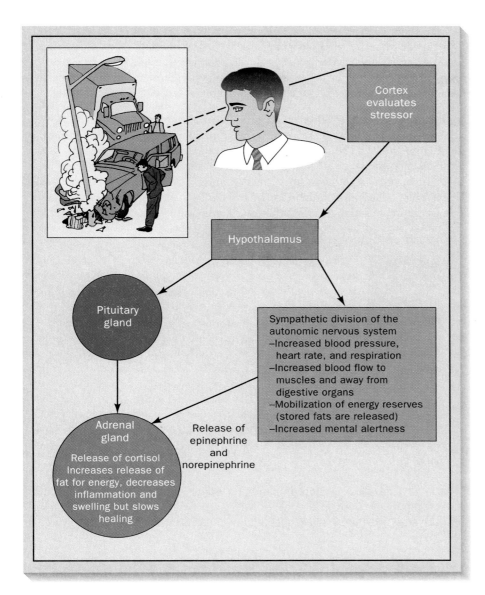

FIGURE 15-1 Once an event is interpreted as a potential stressor, the sympathetic division of the autonomic nervous system and the endocrine system prepare the body to respond.

ration for action. The body burns more energy, which may provide physical strength we did not believe we possessed. The last time you faced a stressor, you probably experienced many, perhaps all, of the following reactions:

- A pounding heart. The adrenal gland releases epinephrine (adrenaline) and norepinephrine (noradrenaline) to increase heart rate and blood pressure, which forces more blood and oxygen to where it is most needed.
- A tensing of your muscles. The liver releases stored fat into the bloodstream to provide energy to the muscles so that they are prepared for action.
- More perspiration than usual. Increased perspiration cools the body, which is burning more energy than usual.
- Faster blood clotting. Chemicals released into the bloodstream reduce possible blood loss by hastening the clotting process.
- Rapid breathing. Breathing becomes more rapid to supply more oxygen to the muscles.

FIGHT OR FLIGHT

The fight-or-flight response prepared our ancestors exceptionally well for physical actions such as fleeing from a dangerous woolly mammoth, but this response is not always useful today. Modern stressors like mammoth traffic jams do not call for physical responses; nevertheless, our biological equipment and responses to stressors are the same as those of our ancestors (Chrousos & Gold, 1992).

Resistance Stage. When a stressor continues past the alarm stage, the body moves to the second stage of the general adaptation syndrome, *resistance* (see Figure 15-2). The body maintains a moderate level of arousal, which enhances our ability to withstand the original stressor. If new stressors are introduced, however, the ability to resist the demands of all these stressors decreases. For example, a laboratory animal in the resistance stage may have greater ability to resist extreme cold, but it becomes more vulnerable to bacterial infections.

Myth or Science

Have you wondered if feeling overwhelmed by a set of circumstances—term papers, exams, job searching—could make you more vulnerable to a virus that can cause a cold? Such circumstances can affect your ability to resist new stressors, such as problems with a roommate; they may also reduce the ability of your immune system to fight a virus. Sheldon Cohen and his colleagues (1991) intentionally exposed students (with their informed consent) to one of several types of respiratory viruses. Did all the students develop colds after being infected? No. Students who were experiencing high levels of stressors were more likely to develop colds than students who were experiencing low levels of stressors. A similar finding in a second study reinforces these findings (Cohen, Tyrrell, & Smith, 1993). Thus the belief that stress makes us more vulnerable to colds is not *a myth: High levels of stressors can make us more vulnerable to a virus.*

Exhaustion Stage. When demands for adjustment exceed the body's ability to respond, the body enters the third stage of the GAS, *exhaustion*. At this point the stress response has lost its adaptive quality and actually contributes to

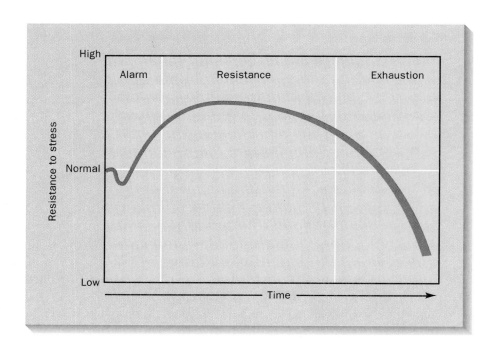

FIGURE 15-2 Selye's general adaptation syndrome (GAS). Hans Selye outlined three phases of the typical biological response to stressors.

pathological changes that result in disease. For example, continued high levels of heart rate and blood pressure raise the risk of heart disease. In fact, the stress response actually suppresses the body's immune system, which leaves us more vulnerable to diseases (Maier, Watkins, & Fleshner, 1994). When the body has reached the limits of its ability to adapt to stress, various physical disorders known as *psychophysiological disorders* (formerly called *psychosomatic disorders*) may develop. A wide range of diseases has been linked to stress, including asthma, herpes, and hypertension (high blood pressure). In short, certain diseases are influenced by our inability to adapt to excessive stress.

Stress is not, however, something that needs to be—or even can be—avoided. As Selye (1978) noted, "Since stress is the nonspecific response of the body to any demand, everybody is always under some degree of stress. . . . Stress can be avoided only by dying" (p. 63). Stress can impair your performance on exams and papers, but it can also provide the energy and zest to propel you to a first-rate performance.

Consider an example. Chantel prepares to ride what has been described as the "most thrilling, spine-tingling roller coaster on the planet." Her friends watch as the ride takes her up, down, and even upside down. They can hear her scream at the top of her lungs; nevertheless, when the ride stops Chantel sprints past you to line up for another go!

When Chantel experiences the fight-or-flight response during the roller coaster ride, the stress is positive, and the physiological arousal is pleasant and exciting. Under some conditions, this arousal can lead to emotional or intellectual growth and development. Selye called this pleasant, positive kind of stress *eustress* (from the Greek *eu,* meaning "good," as in *euphoria*); the damaging form of stress is called *distress.* Thus we should not seek to avoid stress altogether; instead we should find ways to channel the physiological arousal of the stress response more effectively. Some stressful events, however, are easier to avoid or channel than others.

Sources of Stress

Although in modern times we are not likely to have to flee from wild animals, we are at the mercy of sudden, unpredictable catastrophes, such as fires and hurricanes, and we may experience major changes in our lives: We move our homes, change jobs, get married, raise children. In addition, every day we encounter minor irritations: The toaster doesn't work, a careless driver backs into our car and dents it, and so on. Such minor annoyances can affect our sense of well-being and our health.

Catastrophes.   Catastrophes test our ability to adapt. Natural disasters like earthquakes, hurricanes, and tornados can cause devastation over vast areas. To this list of natural disasters we add a growing number of disasters caused by human error, such as toxic spills, nuclear accidents, and transportation accidents.

In 1979, a nuclear reactor accident at Three Mile Island in Pennsylvania caused a two-week state of emergency that required the people living in the area to make major adaptive responses. Psychologist Andrew Baum and his colleagues (1983) wondered whether the effects of the incident might extend beyond the emergency period. To answer this question, they compared people who lived near Three Mile Island to three other groups: people living near an undamaged nuclear reactor, people living near a coal-fired power plant, and people living more than 20 miles from any power plant. The people who lived near Three Mile Island reported more stress symptoms, responded poorly on tasks that required concentration, and had elevated levels of the stress hormones epinephrine and norepinephrine. The worry and uncertainty experienced in the aftermath of the accident persisted for about a year and a half.

A wide range of events can affect our psychological and physical health. These potential stressors range from unpredictable catastrophes such as fires to everyday hassles such as having to wait in lines.

Major Life Events. Dave, a 44-year-old laborer, has rarely experienced any illnesses. The past six months, however, have been "unbearable." He lost his job, the family home was damaged by a tornado, and his daughter was killed in an automobile accident. After he started experiencing insomnia, dizziness, and loss of appetite, Dave decided to see his physician. He wondered whether his symptoms were caused by the major life events he had recently experienced.

Major life events require significant adjustments in almost all aspects of our lives; therefore they can be powerful stressors. Thomas Holmes and Richard Rahe (1967) wished to determine how much adjustment such events require. To accomplish their goal, they developed the 43-item Social Readjustment Rating Scale, which is often printed in magazines, newspapers, and textbooks. A number expressed in life change units (LCUs) indicates the amount of adjustment each item requires. Holmes and Rahe determined the LCUs by asking groups of people to compare the amount of adjustment required by each item to the amount of adjustment that occurs when a person is married. (The amount of adjustment required by marriage was set at 50 LCUs.)

The death of a spouse was rated as the item requiring the greatest adjustment (100 LCUs). A study of almost 96,000 widowed people in Finland supports this assessment. The death rate for recently widowed people was higher than average; the greatest increase (twofold) occurred during the week after the loss of their spouse (Kaprio, Koskenvuo, & Rita, 1987).

Holmes and Rahe administered the Social Readjustment Rating Scale to many people who were also asked to report their illnesses across some span of time, usually one year. Those with high scores reported more illnesses than those with low scores. This dramatic finding seemed to support the notion that too much change really is bad for us.

The excitement generated by these findings turned to skepticism as subsequent investigators could not replicate the original strong relationships. The relationship between major life events and illness still existed, but it was not as strong as originally reported.

Psychological Detective

Not everyone who is exposed to numerous major life events develops physical or psychological symptoms. Think of reasons that might explain why people differ in their responses to similar sets of life events. Here is a hint: Imagine both you and your roommate have exams next week. If you both rated the degree of stress the exams cause, would you give similar ratings? Write down your answer before reading further.

Does everyone interpret major life events in the same way? Probably not (see Table 15-3). The circumstances of a divorce, for example, often determine whether it is viewed positively or negatively. Culture also seems to play a role in how people interpret and react to major life events. Compared with Americans and Japanese, Europeans gave lower ratings (indicating less change) to divorce (Ornstein & Sobel, 1987). What's more, some events on the Social Readjustment Rating Scale could be viewed as positive and therefore are not necessarily troublesome or disturbing. Starting a new job and moving to a new city can signify exciting opportunities that are likely sources of eustress, not distress. Also, events that do *not* occur can be just as stressful—perhaps more so—than events that do occur. To take just one example, imagine being jilted at the altar.

As we see later in the chapter, people differ in the way they interpret and respond to change. Some individuals are able to call friends and relatives for support in times of need; others may be more vulnerable to stres-

TABLE 15-3   **Differences in the Amount of Change Caused by the Same Life Events**

The life-change units used in the Social Readjustment Rating Scale may not reflect a given individual's assessment of a particular event. As you can see, assessments of the same life events vary widely.

	PERCENTAGE OF INDIVIDUALS REPORTING EACH AMOUNT OF CHANGE (ROUNDED)			
Event	Large	Moderate	Little	None
Relations with mate got worse	41	47	0	12
Relative died (not child or spouse)	8	8	29	54
Close friend died	5	16	30	49
Financial loss (not work-related)	16	44	19	21
Broke up with a friend	0	26	37	37
Was laid off from job	13	63	13	10
Had trouble with boss	18	35	33	15
Involved in a court case	10	10	29	52

Source: Adapted from Dohrenwend et al., 1990, p. 182.

sors because they must bear the full weight of major life changes with no support from others.

Posttraumatic Stress Disorder.   Some events are so far beyond our usual experience they would deeply disturb almost anyone who encountered them. Events like being raped or observing a violent death are not included in the Social Readjustment Rating Scale, yet their impact can be so great that they may result in **posttraumatic stress disorder (PTSD)**. The primary symptom of PTSD is experiencing intense fear while reliving a shocking event in dreams, flashbacks, or intrusive thoughts. Victims of PTSD are often anxious and irritable, find it difficult to concentrate, suffer from sleep disturbances, and experience guilt. (This disorder is classified as an anxiety disorder; the other anxiety disorders, were discussed in Chapter 13.) Consider the following case, and imagine how you might react if you were Ed:

> A man was standing on his tiptoes on the curb so Ed slowed the bus as he approached. Just before the bus reached the corner, the man flung himself against the windshield and was killed. For weeks after, Ed cried and could not function on the job; eventually he was admitted to a hospital with the diagnosis of posttraumatic stress disorder. He said, "I felt like somebody put a gun in my hand, pointed it at his head, and pulled the trigger." (Miller et al., 1988, p. 43)

Although most people exposed to trauma will do well, some experience severe symptoms as a result of their experience (Fullerton & Ursano, 1997). What today is termed PTSD has its roots in observations of the oldest non-natural disaster: war. The initial focus on war experiences dominated research until other traumatic situations such as railway accidents were added to the list of potential sources of PTSD. We now recognize that not only are the victims of such disasters at risk for PTSD, so are those who rush in to aid in a time of great need (McCarroll, Ursano, & Fullerton, 1997). Consider the following:

posttraumatic stress disorder (PTSD)
Set of symptoms that may follow deeply disturbing events; symptoms include reliving the event, difficulty in concentrating, sleep disturbances, anxiety, and guilt

There is growing awareness that the symptoms of PTSD can strike not only immediate victims of disasters such as the Oklahoma City bombing but also their rescuers. At a moment's notice, rescue workers can be summoned to the scene of a horrible disaster. The social support they provide to one another is often a major factor in helping them to deal with the human tragedies they observe firsthand.

Rescue workers are traumatized through the senses: viewing, smelling, and touching, experiencing the grotesque. Following a mass-casualty airplane crash, a disaster worker shut his eyes to go to sleep and saw one of the dead bodies from the crash. Many firefighters continued to smell the burning flesh long after they had gone home. Some washed repeatedly to get rid of the smell, but to no avail. (Ursano & McCarroll, 1994, pp. 65–66).

The effects of such traumas can last for long after the original event. Many victims of PTSD exhibit sympathetic nervous system and hormonal changes (Southwick, Yehuda, & Charney, 1997). Victims of PTSD often become highly sensitive; events that would not have evoked a response in the past now evoke cognitive and physical responses as if the original trauma was being experienced again. For example, Gulf War veterans with posttraumatic stress disorder were found to exhibit an exaggerated startle response to sound, which did not occur in veterans or civilians without PTSD (Morgan et al., 1991). Not surprisingly, most victims of PTSD avoid circumstances associated with the shocking event because such circumstances can cause these victims to relive the experience. For example, some Vietnam veterans suffered flashbacks of their war experiences after watching televised coverage of Operation Desert Storm in 1991.

Posttraumatic stress disorder occurs in about 5 men and 13 women per 1,000 American adults. Being in combat and seeing someone hurt or die are the most common traumatic events that bring on PTSD in men; common events that precipitate PTSD in women are physical attacks, especially rape (Helzer, Robins, & McEvoy, 1987). The level of violence in urban areas has created a climate that is likely to lead to PTSD. In a sample of more than 1,000 young adults in Detroit, researchers found that 39 percent had been exposed to traumatic events; 24 percent of this group developed PTSD. Thus the rate of PTSD in this sample was 9 percent (Breslau et al., 1991).

Everyday Hassles. Hassles are minor, everyday occurrences that are distressing, frustrating, and irritating; they include slow-moving traffic, long lines at the supermarket, and lost keys. Each hassle may elicit a minor alarm reaction; thus we can say that some people have their alarms going off continuously! Although such minor alarms may not seem capable of major consequences, psychologist Richard Lazarus and his colleagues have found that hassles can accumulate and become associated with physical and psychological problems. In one investigation, researchers found a correlation between the occurrence of daily hassles and the presence of current and subsequent health problems such as flu, headaches, and sore throats (De Longis, Folkman, & Lazarus, 1988).

A number of hassles may involve **conflict** (see Chapter 4) among competing desires or motives. Some conflicts require that we select between two attractive alternatives. These *approach-approach conflicts* are usually easy to resolve. In an *approach-avoidance conflict* the goal's positive values attract us while its negative features repulse us. Such conflicts often result in vacillation; one moment the answer is *yes,* the next moment it is *no.* Only when one motive (attraction or repulsion) becomes stronger than the other will this conflict be resolved. In an *avoidance-avoidance conflict* you must choose between two unpleasant alternatives. *Multiple approach-avoidance conflicts* are similar to many everyday experiences in which we are attracted and repulsed by a variety of goals. When such conflicts occur over interpersonal relationships that may have several positive and several negative factors, such as marriage or divorce, they can have serious, long-lasting effects.

How could minor annoyances like waiting in line or resolving conflicts have significant health consequences? An important clue is found in research conducted by Phillip Brantley and his colleagues (1988) in which volunteers

conflict
A state that occurs when an individual must choose between two or more competing goals

reported the frequency of their daily hassles over a nine-day period. During that time the researchers also collected measurements of these individuals' endocrine activity (see Chapter 2). They found that when the volunteers' daily hassles were frequent, their endocrine levels were elevated as compared with the levels on low-hassle days. Apparently the effect of several minor daily annoyances can accumulate and raise the levels of your body's stress hormones, which are released early in the GAS.

What Makes Events Stressful?

Consider the following real-life event: Your younger brother arrives home breathless and with a bit of apprehension to recount how "another car hit mine." You quickly determine it was *your* car, driven by your brother, that hit the other car. How do you react? You examine the damage and imagine $100 bills exiting your wallet. The alarm reaction has kicked into gear. Your interpretation of this event, however, can dramatically influence your physical reaction to it. If you focus on damage, costs, and inconvenience, anger builds within and is fueled by the actions of the sympathetic nervous system and the release of stress hormones. Now imagine you take a moment to reevaluate the situation. No one was hurt (which is important), cars can be repaired, and the inconvenience will not be excessive. If you adopt this approach, your physical response to the same event will be quite different.

Richard Lazarus and Susan Folkman (1984) believe that the way we deal with potential stressors begins with our appraisal of the event. When faced with a potential stressor like the one we just described, our first task is to determine whether the event or situation is stressful. In other words, should we be upset? This evaluation, called **primary appraisal,** can result in several conclusions. We may determine that an event or situation is irrelevant because it is of little or no consequence to us. In other cases we may determine that an event is actually beneficial (a form of eustress). Finally, we may determine that an event or situation is stressful, is potentially harmful, or creates a loss such as illness or injury. Potentially harmful events such as living in a violent neighborhood or facing a difficult exam involve an expectation of future physical or psychological harm. When we decide an event is a stressor, we must determine how we will deal with it—a process called **secondary appraisal** (see Figure 15-3).

Jobs that demand a great deal of responsibility but do not permit workers to control their time are more likely to lead to stress-induced illnesses (Bernard & Krupat, 1994). Air traffic controllers at large airports, medical interns, police officers, and secretaries experience high levels of stress for these reasons. Race car drivers may not be bothered by speeds that reach more than 200 miles per hour, but they tense up when they pull off the track and turn over control of their car to their pit crew. The same is true of employees whose companies are being acquired by other firms. Their sense of control is lost for a time, and as a result they may experience a variety of stress symptoms.

primary appraisal
The first step in coping with stress; consists of determining whether an event is a threat

secondary appraisal
The second step in coping with stress; consists of deciding how to deal with the stress-producing situation

FIGURE 15-3 The two-stage process of primary and secondary appraisal helps us determine whether an event is stressful, and if so, how we might cope.

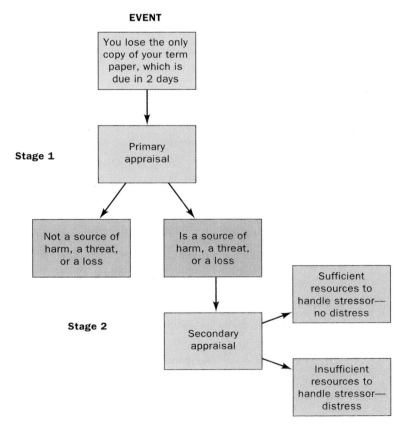

How Stress and Disease May Be Related

The immune system can be described as a sense organ because its job is to "sense" cells and substances that don't belong in our body. Thus the **immune system** is the body's major defense against foreign invaders like bacteria or viruses. The specialized cells and organs that make up this complex system are located throughout the bloodstream and the lymphatic system. To do its job properly, the immune system must first distinguish between cells that are part of the organism and those that are not. If the immune system fails to make this distinction, it can become too active and attack harmless cells, thereby aggravating conditions such as allergies and arthritis. In some cases the immune system may be so impaired that a person can become vulnerable to a range of diseases.

The immune system recognizes foreign invaders and then deactivates them and removes them from the body (Maier, Watkins, & Fleshner, 1994). The substances that trigger an immune response are called **antigens;** these include bacteria, fungi, parasites, and viruses. The task of ridding the body of these substances falls to a variety of specialized cells, including two forms of white blood cells: *lymphocytes,* small white cells produced in the bone marrow or the thymus, and *phagocytes* (literally "eater cells"), large white cells that engulf foreign matter, such as viruses.

Psychoneuroimmunology. A new science called *psychoneuroimmunology (PNI)* focuses on how the body defends itself against foreign substances and how psychological and physiological factors influence the immune system. The term focuses attention on the interactions of the brain, endocrine system, and immune system.

How can stress affect the immune system? We know that stress leads to activity in the sympathetic nervous system and the release of the hormones cortisol, epinephrine, and norepinephrine. These hormones help us resist stress, but in the long run they reduce the effectiveness of the immune system. A variety of stressful events—loss of a spouse, divorce, depression, exams—have been found to suppress the functioning of the immune system and make people more susceptible to disease (Evans et al., 1992; Glaser et al., 1993; Kiecolt-Glaser & Glaser, 1992). Long-term stressors are also associated with lowered immune system functioning. For example, Janice Kiecolt-Glaser and her colleagues (1991) studied the health status of caregivers who had been providing daily care for spouses suffering from Alzheimer's disease for an average of five years. Compared with a group of people with similar demographic characteristics who were not caring for such patients, the caregivers had lowered immune functioning and reported more days of infectious illnesses. In a literature review, researchers concluded that in the relationship between stress levels and immune system functioning, there were "relatively strong and consistent associations" (Herbert & Cohen, 1993).

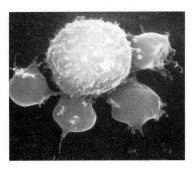

The specialized cells and organs that make up the immune system serve to recognize and destroy foreign substances called *antigens.* Among the specialized cells are *lymphocytes* that are shown here attacking bacteria.

immune system
System that protects the body against foreign substances such as viruses and bacteria

antigens
Foreign substances such as bacteria that trigger an immune response

---

Dear Mom and Dad,

I'm sorry for not writing but hope you will understand. First, sit down before you read further.

I'm doing much better now after recovering from the concussion and the broken leg I received when I jumped from the window of my dorm after it caught fire last month. I can almost see and walk normally thanks to the loving care of the wonderful man who risked his life to save me. He more than saved me; he has become my whole family. You see, I have been living with him since the fire, and we are planning to get married. We haven't set a date yet but plan to have one soon, before my pregnancy starts to show.

Love always,

Mary-

P.S.: There was no fire, I am perfectly healthy, and I'm not pregnant. In fact, I do not even have a boyfriend. However I did get a D in German, a D- in physics, and an F in algebra. I wanted you to keep this all in perspective.

Review Summary

1. Health psychology is a rapidly developing subfield that is concerned with the social and psychological factors that influence health and illness.

2. Hans Selye developed the concept of **stress** as the nonspecific response of the body to demands to adjust to a wide range of changes.

3. Stressors are demands that give rise to the **general adaptation syndrome (GAS),** which consists of three stages: *alarm, resistance,* and *exhaustion.*

4. Among the circumstances that could lead to stress are catastrophes, major life changes such as divorce, traumatic events such as criminal victimization, and hassles. They have been associated with physiological responses such as increased levels of stress hormones.

5. Researchers found that high levels of life change were associated with illness. Subsequent investigation showed that the relationship between major life events and illness is not as strong as originally reported. One explanation is that a person's interpretation of events is an important determinant of the event's impact.

6. Posttraumatic stress disorder (PTSD) occurs in the aftermath of deeply disturbing experiences such as rape and combat. Victims of PTSD often relive the traumatic event in dreams, flashbacks, or intrusive thoughts.

7. Hassles are everyday minor annoyances that can accumulate and become associated with subsequent health problems.

8. Interpretation or appraisal of an event often determines whether that event is stressful. **Primary appraisal** occurs when we determine whether an event is a threat; in **secondary appraisal** we decide how to deal with the threat.

9. The immune system is the body's major defense against bacteria and viruses. *Psychoneuroimmunology* is the study of how psychological and physiological factors interact to influence the immune system. A wide variety of stressful events can affect immune system functioning.

Study Break

1. Which of the following was one of the leading causes of death in the United States in 1900?
   a. stroke
   b. suicide
   c. influenza
   d. accidents
2. Which of the following is one of the leading causes of death in the United States during the last decade of the twentieth century?
   a. accidents
   b. childbirth
   c. heart disease
   d. suicide
3. A researcher for the National Institute of Health is asked to review the causes of death in the United States and report on the potential for efforts to reduce the deaths. She is asked to write a report to Congress. Which of the following would make for the best title for that report?
   a. Leading Cause of Death: Environmental Pollution
   b. Toxins Are Taking a Greater Toll than Was Suspected
   c. Growing Influence of Genetic Factors on Death Rates
   d. Focus on Behavior: Half of Deaths Could Be Prevented

4. Identify the GAS stage described in each of the following situations:
   a. A motorist cuts you off on the interstate, and you must slam on the brakes to avoid a collision. Your heart rate accelerates, your muscles tense, and your mouth is dry.
   b. Your uncle has had a series of significant financial and social setbacks in the past two years. His physician just told him that he has hypertension and ulcers.
   c. For several weeks Jane has been fighting a "flu bug." She seemed to be succeeding, but then her husband asked for a divorce and she lost her job. Shortly afterward she came down with the flu.
5. Describe the effects of the fight-or-flight response (alarm stage) on each of the following: heart rate, blood flow, breathing, hormones, muscles, and perspiration.
6. Which of the following parts of the brain plays a significant role in the fight-or-flight response?
   a. fornix
   b. pineal gland
   c. hypothalamus
   d. corpus callosum

7. After a stressful event has occurred, which part of the brain sends a chemical signal to the adrenal gland to tell it to release its hormones?
   a. thalamus
   b. pituitary
   c. amygdala
   d. hippocampus
8. Answer the following questions.
   a. A person who is deciding whether an event is stressful is engaged in what process?
   b. Jill decides she will be able to complete the papers that are due next week because her friends can give her some advice and she has learned how to use a word processor. Jill's thinking can be described as what process?
9. What are the key symptoms of posttraumatic stress disorder? What types of situations seem most likely to lead to it?

Lifestyle Influences on Disease Risk

Rich, 60, has been smoking for as long as he can remember. He knows the health risks associated with smoking because he has heard them "a million times." Yet he is hesitant to stop his 15-cigarette-a-day habit out of fear that he will gain weight. "Why stop smoking if all I'll do is gain weight and trade one risk factor for another?" ***Do people usually gain weight when they stop smoking?*** ▪

An illness or an accident can occur at any time. In some cases they result primarily from chance or genetic factors, which we really can't control. Our decisions to engage in certain behaviors, however, can have a profound effect on our health. *Lifestyle* refers to our daily voluntary decisions about how to act that can affect our risk of developing health problems (Bernard & Krupat, 1994). We look closely at several behaviors that can influence our risk of developing certain diseases. This section focuses on smoking, the development of heart disease, AIDS, and nutrition and weight.

The importance of lifestyle decisions is evident in a longitudinal study of more than 10,000 men who were between 45 and 84 years of age in 1977, when the study began. When these men were again studied in 1985, researchers found death rates were lower for those who had done one or more of the following: started moderate physical activity, quit smoking, or avoided obesity (Paffenbarger et al., 1993).

Smoking

Smoking-related illnesses are the single most preventable cause of death and illness in the United States (McGinnis & Foege, 1993). The current concern about the hazards of smoking was foreshadowed decades ago. Beginning in 1893, several states outlawed the sale, manufacture, advertising, or use of cigarettes (Tate, 1989).

A single puff of a cigarette sends the stimulant nicotine on a ten-second journey to your brain, where it causes a release of norepinephrine that increases your heart rate and blood pressure. Over time, the damage resulting from this nicotine-induced heart acceleration coupled with the effects of components of cigarette smoke such as tar can help bring on cancer, heart disease, and pulmonary diseases (McGinnis & Foege, 1993). Smoking is considered extremely addictive; few people who have smoked regularly for a year or more find it easy to quit (Schelling, 1992). Even nonsmokers suffer some consequences of smoking. Passive (secondhand or involuntary) smoking is a potential cause of lung cancer (U.S. Department of Health and Human Services, 1986) and also

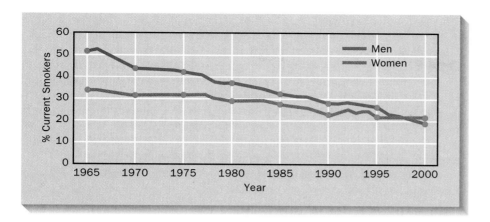

FIGURE 15-4 Rate of smoking among persons age 18 and older since 1965 and projection of smokers in 2000.

Sources: Centers for Disease Control and Prevention, 1997; Giovino et al., 1995; Pierce et al., 1989.

reduces the blood's ability to deliver oxygen to the heart. In this section we discuss the risks associated with smoking and describe efforts to reduce the number of Americans who smoke.

Who Smokes and Why? Despite repeated warnings about the risks associated with smoking, about one in four U.S. adults continues to smoke. The number of smokers has been declining, however. If this trend continues, 22 percent of the adult population (about 40 million people) will be smokers by the year 2000, which will still exceed the 15 percent goal in *Healthy People 2000*. The decline has not been equal among all groups; however, the rate of decline is greater for men than it is for women (see Figure 15-4). The rate of smoking among Americans with less education is declining at a slower rate than among those with more education. Although the number of smokers is declining in the United States, other countries report significant increases. For example, China's rate of cigarette production is increasing 11 percent a year to keep up with demand (Bartecchi, MacKenzie, & Schrier, 1995).

Smoking typically begins in the adolescent years: About 90 percent of smokers smoked their first cigarette before age 18. The majority of first-time smokers are between 11 and 13 years of age; almost no regular smoking begins

Because the smoking habit often begins in adolescence, more effort is being directed toward preventing smoking by people in this age group.

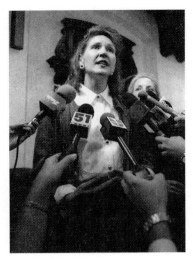

Norma Broin was the lead plaintiff in a class-action lawsuit filed by flight attendants against the tobacco companies. Part of one of her lungs was removed because of cancer. The lawsuit claimed that flight attendants breathed secondhand smoke that caused various illnesses. This lawsuit was one of many filed against the tobacco companies in the last decade. The most notable lawsuits (in terms of requested damages) were those filed by a number of states seeking reimbursement of the costs for medical care for illnesses caused by tobacco products.

after the age of 20 (Giovino et al., 1995). Peer-group identification has a strong effect on the probability that children and adolescents will begin smoking (Mosbach & Leventhal, 1988). An estimated 6 million teenagers and another 100,000 children under 13 years of age smoke (Bartecchi, MacKenzie, & Schrier, 1995). Peers and family members provide children with models of smoking behavior. What's more, in the past the tobacco industry targeted adolescents with promotional activities and advertising designed to entice them to begin smoking (King et al., 1998; Pierce et al., 1996). Such promotional activities and advertising aimed at adolescents is now banned as part of the tobacco settlement between the federal government and the tobacco industry.

Young people overestimate the percentage of adults and peers who smoke. One sample of urban adolescents estimated that 66 percent of adults smoke; they also underestimated their peers' negative attitudes toward smoking. Young people also believe that they are less likely than others to develop smoking-related illnesses if they become smokers (see the discussion of the personal fable in Chapter 10) (Leventhal, Glynn, & Fleming, 1987). The effect of peer influence on the initiation of smoking is strongest among adolescents who have not yet become established members of a friendship group. In these cases smoking may be seen as a vehicle for entering such a group (Aloise-Young, Graham, & Hansen, 1994).

Psychological Detective

Evidence clearly shows that the number of smokers has declined in the past decade. What factors do you believe account for this trend? Give this question some thought, and write down your answers before reading further.

Quitting the Smoking Habit.   A telephone survey of residents in eight states found increasing support for restricting tobacco use in public places such as restaurants. The respondents also favored efforts to restrict teenagers' access to cigarettes by banning cigarette advertising, stopping the sale of cigarettes via vending machines, and increasing the price of cigarettes (Centers for Disease Control and Prevention, 1994b). At least 46 states now restrict smoking in public places. Smoking has become unfashionable and is often perceived as rude or socially unacceptable.

Mark Twain said, "Quitting smoking is easy; I've done it a thousand times." Although Twain's comment is an exaggeration, most people stop and resume smoking several times before they quit for good (Farquhar & Spiller, 1990). People who finally quit often proceed through several steps during which they collect information and become attuned to quitting. The process continues until a trigger such as the death of a close friend or family member or strong social pressure makes the smoker especially sensitive to the drawbacks of smoking. Although a variety of aids and programs are available to help people stop smoking, about 90 percent of ex-smokers quit on their own (U.S. Department of Health and Human Services, 1989). A study sponsored by the National Cancer Institute (Orleans et al., 1991) found that the availability of telephone counseling increased the probability that people would quit smoking. Nevertheless, quitting rates were uniformly low across all treatments; there does not seem to be one best method for quitting. Group or individual counseling, multiple contacts with clinicians, and treatments focused on coping skills and stress management can, however, increase cessation rates (Wetter et al., 1998).

One reason often cited by smokers for their reluctance to quit is the fear of gaining weight. At the beginning of this section, we met Rich, who has been smoking for years and knows the risks. He would like to quit but is afraid he will gain weight if he does.

Weight gain after quitting smoking is fact, not folklore. On average, men gain about six pounds and women about eight pounds after quitting; 10 percent of men and 13 percent of women gain more than 28 pounds. The risk of gaining weight is greater for those who smoke 15 or more cigarettes a day (Williamson et al., 1991). Why do people gain weight? The primary reason is that smoking increases the number of calories burned, which in turn suppresses body weight (Perkins, 1993; Talcott et al., 1995). After people stop smoking, they burn fewer calories. If ex-smokers increase their physical activity, however, they will burn more calories (Rodin, 1987); limiting intake of foods that are high in fat and sugar is also helpful.

Another reason that many people are reluctant to quit smoking is nicotine dependence, which is listed as a mental disorder (American Psychiatric Association, 1994). The degree of nicotine dependence, which is related to the amount and duration of smoking, can be assessed by using questionnaires such as the one found in Table 15-4. The sudden cessation of smoking and the elimination of nicotine from the body can lead to a variety of symptoms: depressed mood, insomnia, irritability, anxiety, concentration difficulties, and increased appetite that can lead to the weight gain already mentioned (Danis & Seaton, 1997). People who are heavily dependent on nicotine can reduce the symptoms of withdrawal by using one of several methods of supplementing nicotine while they are quitting. The currently available methods are a nicotine gum, a nicotine patch, and a nicotine nasal spray (Danis & Seaton, 1997). There is now sufficient evidence on the effectiveness of nicotine gum and the nicotine patch to show they both increase cessation rates (Wetter et al., 1998).

Heart Disease

In the United States, someone dies of heart disease about every 34 seconds (American Heart Association, 1993). Many of these deaths could be prevented because several risk factors for heart disease can be modified (see Table 15-5).

TABLE 15-4   Fagerstrom Test for Nicotine Dependence

	0	1	2	3
1. How soon after you wake up do you smoke your first cigarette?	More than 1 hour	1/2 to 1 hour	6 to 30 minutes	5 minutes or less
2. Do you find it difficult to refrain from smoking in places where it is forbidden (in church, at the library, in a movie theater)?	No	Yes		
3. Which cigarette (i.e., morning, evening) would you hate to give up the most?	Any other	The first one in the morning		
4. How many cigarettes do you smoke per day?	10 or less	11 to 20	21 to 30	More than 31
5. Do you smoke more frequently during the first hours after waking than during the rest of the day?	No	Yes		
6. Do you smoke if you are so ill that you are in bed most of the day?	No	Yes		

Scoring: Add all of your scores. A score of 7 or greater indicates a high degree of dependence, possibly more severe withdrawal symptoms, greater difficulty quitting, and possibly the need for higher doses of nicotine supplements.

Source: Heatherton et al., 1991, as adapted by Danis & Seaton, 1997.

TABLE 15-5 **Major Risk Factors for Heart Disease**

RISK FACTORS THAT CANNOT BE MODIFIED

Heredity   The tendency to develop heart disease seems to be inherited.

Gender   Men are at greater risk for heart disease and are likely to have heart attacks earlier in life than women.

Increasing age   More than half of all heart attack victims are 65 or older. The increase in heart disease with age seems to be due, however, to the longer time available for other risk factors to have an impact rather than being an inevitable part of aging.

RISK FACTORS THAT CAN BE MODIFIED

Cigarette smoking   A smoker's risk of heart disease is twice that of a nonsmoker. What's more, after cardiac arrest, smokers are more likely to die within an hour than nonsmokers. How rapidly smoking cessation reduces the risk of heart disease is a matter of controversy.

High blood pressure (hypertension)   Elevated blood pressure increases the heart's workload and causes the heart to weaken over time. High blood pressure in combination with obesity, smoking, high cholesterol, or diabetes raises the risk of heart disease.

Blood cholesterol levels   The risk of heart disease rises as blood cholesterol levels increase. A growing focus of attention is levels of HDL (high-density lipoprotein) and LDL (low-density lipoprotein), also known as "good cholesterol" and "bad cholesterol," respectively. Higher HDL levels are associated with lower rates of heart disease. Cholesterol levels are affected by age, sex, heredity, and diet.

Obesity   Although some studies show increasing risk of heart disease with increased weight, the studies are inconsistent. Certain population subgroups, however, seem to be at greater risk than others. For example, those with male-type (apple-shape) obesity are at higher risk than those with female-type (pear-shape) obesity, in which excess fat is distributed more evenly. What's more, obesity is related to other risk factors such as high blood pressure, cholesterol levels, and physical inactivity.

Physical inactivity   When combined with overeating, physical inactivity can lead to excess weight and higher cholesterol levels.

Stress   Although life would be impossible without some stress, how we react to stressors can put us at increased risk for heart disease, either directly or by influencing other risk factors.

Sources: American Heart Association, 1993; Smith & Leon, 1992; National Institutes of Health Consensus Conference, 1993.

Cultural & Diversity Perspective

ALTHOUGH MOST OF THE RESEARCH ON HEART DISEASE HAS BEEN DONE ON MEN, it is important to realize that both men and women are susceptible to heart disease. The fact that men experience heart attacks earlier in life than do women leads to a strong association between men and heart attacks, which sometimes makes it difficult to recognize the signs of heart disease when they occur early in women. The risk of heart disease also varies with race (see Figure 15-5). One of the risk factors for heart disease, hypertension, occurs at a higher rate among African Americans than among other Americans and Africans. What's more, the difference in hypertension is most pronounced between urban African Americans and rural Nigerians, which suggests that the disease is primarily one of modern life (Cooper, Rotimi, & Ward, 1999). Taking a global perspective, the rate of heart disease is much lower in Japan compared to the United States (Bureau of the Census, 1997). What accounts for such differences? One clue comes from research conducted on Japanese Americans. Those who were described as "traditionally Japanese" (spoke Japanese at home, retained traditional values, and behaviors) had lower rates of heart disease that were comparable to Japanese people living in Japan. The group that was "least" Japanese had a three to five times great incidence of heart disease (Matsumoto, 1996).

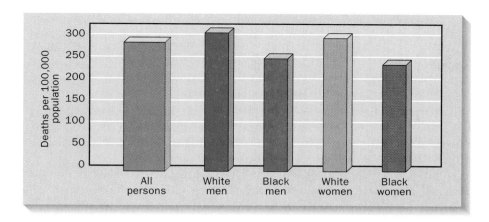

FIGURE 15-5 Death rates from heart disease. Both sex and race have significant effects on the rate of death owing to heart disease.

Source: National Center for Health Statistics, 1994.

One of the processes that leads to heart disease is *atherosclerosis,* in which a fatty substance called *cholesterol* lines the walls of arteries near the heart, eventually choking off the supply of blood to the heart. This process often begins in childhood (Hajjar & Nicholson, 1995).

To move through the blood, cholesterol molecules are attached to special transport systems called *lipoproteins* (Hajjar & Nicholson, 1995). About two-thirds of the cholesterol in our blood is carried on *low-density lipoproteins (LDL),* which are most responsible for atherosclerosis. The cholesterol carried on *high-density lipoproteins (HDL)* tends to be carried to the liver, where it is disposed of in the form of bile; hence HDL is often called "good cholesterol." In contrast, LDL is called "bad cholesterol" because it is more likely to clog our arteries and thus increase our risk for heart disease.

The influence of blood cholesterol levels on heart disease was studied in a group of more than 1,000 individuals (average age 22 years) who were followed for more than 30 years. These individuals' cholesterol levels were strongly associated with their incidence of heart disease, deaths owing to heart disease, and deaths from all causes (Klag et al., 1993).

One source of the cholesterol in our blood is dietary fat. The chances of developing atherosclerosis is a function, in part, of our intake of animal fats, but our behavior also plays a role. Some people frequently interpret events in ways that lead to anger and hostility, which invokes the fight-or-flight response and puts them at greater risk for developing heart disease. How? Fat deposited in the blood for the purposes of fueling the fight-or-flight response can harden and build up in the arteries.

Left: Blood can flow easily through the opening of a normal artery (red center area). *Right:* Over the course of many years, cholesterol deposited along the inner wall of an artery can harden and restrict the passage of blood ("hardening of the arteries"). Note the difference in the size of the opening in the two arteries. The blockage can severely impair the flow of blood to the heart and result in cardiac arrest (heart attack), during which some of the heart muscle dies.

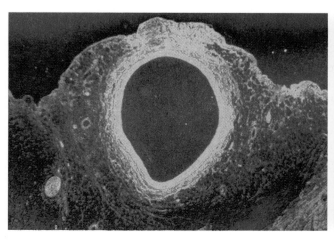

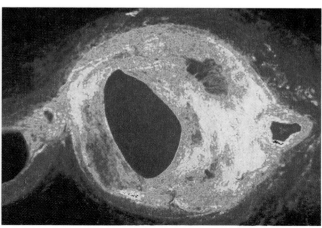

Two cardiologists, Meyer Friedman and Ray Rosenman (1974), found that many new cases of heart disease could not be predicted from known medical risk factors. They concluded that there must be another piece to the puzzle of heart disease; our thoughts, emotions, and behaviors could play a role in the development of heart disease. They labeled this piece of the heart-disease puzzle Type A behavior.

Type A behavior is a collection of personality characteristics and behaviors that includes aggressiveness, competitiveness, impatience, irritability, and the inability to relax. In contrast, a more easygoing and relaxed person is called a Type B person.

Is Type A behavior related to the incidence of heart disease? A study designed to answer that question, the Western Collaborative Group Study, involved more than 3,000 healthy men between the ages of 39 and 59 (Rosenman et al., 1975). After 8.5 years, the Type A men had twice the rate of heart disease as the Type B men. This increased risk was evident even after the effects of other risk factors, such as diet and smoking, were considered.

The emerging picture of the Type A person was someone under stress who had an increased risk of developing heart disease. At the beginning of the 1980s, Type A was recognized as an independent risk factor for heart disease, yet several studies did not replicate the findings of the Western Collaborative Group Study (Matthews & Haynes, 1986).

The Toxic Component of Type A Behavior.   The inconclusive results of the various Type A studies led some researchers to consider that perhaps some of the characteristics that make up Type A behavior are related to heart disease but others are not. The focus of research on Type A behavior thus switched to identifying the "toxic" component of Type A behavior. The prime candidate seems to be hostility, which has been related to early death, especially from heart disease (Barefoot, Dahlstrom, & Williams, 1983; Barefoot et al., 1989). Hostile individuals tend to perceive the behavior of others as intended to provoke or harm them; consequently they often interact with others in an antagonistic manner (see Table 15-6). They react quickly and strongly to potential threats; not surprisingly, they secrete greater amounts of the stress hormone cortisol during the day (Pope & Smith, 1991). The hostile person is like a power keg waiting to explode. Here is an example of such an explosion:

> A medical writer was riding with a very hostile Type A surgeon. When the surgeon was slow to step on the gas pedal after a traffic light turned green, the driver behind him honked. The surgeon's temper flared; he bolted from his car, walked to the car behind his, grabbed the keys from the ignition, and threw them into a snowbank. (Adapted from Friedman & Ulmer, 1984, p. 35)

Imagine the surgeon's internal reactions as he grabbed the keys and tossed them into the snow.

In sum, Timothy Smith (1992) has noted that although several studies have not supported the relationship between hostility and health, "considerable support has accumulated for the centuries-old hypothesis that hostility is a threat" (p. 147). Hostility is an independent risk factor for the development of heart disease and premature death from all causes (Miller et al., 1996). How often have you heard that the best advice when faced with a difficult situation is to count to ten and reassess? We suspect that hostile people count quickly to ten and then get angry. Perhaps the better advice is count very slowly!

Reducing the Risk of Heart Disease.   Can the behavior of a Type A person be changed to decrease the risk of a heart attack? Meyer Friedman and his colleagues (1984) attempted to do just that in the Recurrent Coronary

Type A behavior
Behavioral and personality characteristics that include competitiveness, aggressiveness, achievement drive, and inability to relax

TABLE 15-6 Are You a Hostile Person?

Each question describes a specific or general situation that you have probably encountered. If you haven't encountered it, imagine as vividly as you can how you would react in the situation. After each description you are presented with two responses, A or B, describing how that situation might affect you, or how you might behave under those circumstances. In some instances neither response may seem to fit, or both may appear equally desirable. This is normal; go ahead and answer anyway, choosing as best you can the single response that is *more likely* for you in that situation.

1. The person who cuts my hair trims off more than I wanted.
   A. I tell him or her what a lousy job he or she did.
   B. I figure it'll grow back, and I resolve to give my instructions more forcefully next time.

2. I am in the express checkout line at the supermarket, where a sign reads "No more than 10 items, please!"
   A. I pick up a magazine to pass the time.
   B. I glance ahead to see if anyone has more than 10 items.

3. I am struck in a traffic jam.
   A. I usually am not particularly upset.
   B. I quickly start to feel irritated and annoyed.

4. Another driver butts ahead of me in traffic.
   A. I usually flash my lights or honk my horn.
   B. I stay farther back behind such a driver.

5. Someone treats me unfairly.
   A. I usually forget it rather quickly.
   B. I am likely to keep thinking about it for hours.

6. I am caught in a slow-moving bank or supermarket line.
   A. I usually start to fume at people who dawdle ahead of me.
   B. I seldom notice the wait.

7. Someone is being rude or annoying.
   A. I am apt to avoid him or her in the future.
   B. I might have to get rough with him or her.

8. An elevator stops too long on a floor above where I am waiting.
   A. I soon start to feel irritated and annoyed.
   B. I start planning the rest of my day.

9. I am riding as a passenger in the front seat of a car.
   A. I take the opportunity to enjoy the scenery.
   B. I try to stay alert for obstacles ahead.

10. Someone is speaking very slowly during a conversation.
    A. I am likely to finish his or her sentence.
    B. I am likely to listen until he or she finishes.

11. I am requesting a seat assignment for an airline flight.
    A. I usually request a seat in a specific area of the plane.
    B. I generally leave the choice to the agent.

12. I recall something that angered me previously.
    A. I feel angry all over again.
    B. The memory doesn't bother me nearly as much as the actual event did.

13. I see people walking around in shopping malls.
    A. Many of them are either shopping or exercising.
    B. Many are wasting time.

14. Someone is hogging the conversation at a party.
    A. I look for an opportunity to put him or her down.
    B. I soon move to another group.

15. Slow-moving lines can often be found in banks and supermarkets.
    A. They are an unavoidable part of modern life.
    B. They are often due to someone's incompetence.

Scoring instructions: Give yourself one point each time your answer agrees with the letter in parentheses after each item number. 1(A), 2 (B), 3 (B), 4 (A), 5 (B), 6 (A), 7 (B), 8 (A), 9 (B), 10 (A), 11 (A), 12 (A), 13 (B), 14 (A), 15 (B).

Source: Adapted from Williams & Williams, 1993.

Prevention Project. This program involved a group of individuals who should be highly motivated to reduce their risk: people who had suffered heart attacks. Friedman and his colleagues assigned 270 patients to counseling sessions designed to increase their compliance with physician-prescribed drug, dietary, and exercise programs. Another group of 592 patients received standard counseling plus training to reduce Type A behaviors. The training included practice in relaxation along with instruction in recognizing and altering emotional reactions. At the end of 3 years, 44 percent of the patients who received the combined treatment had reduced their Type A behavior; they were also less likely to

FIGURE 15-6 Reductions in recurring heart attacks. Efforts to change Type A behaviors reduced the rate of recurrent heart attacks as compared with the rate among heart attack victims who received the typical counseling given to all heart attack patients.

Source: Friedman & Ulmer, 1984.

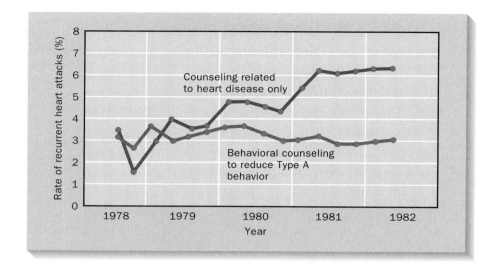

human immunodeficiency virus (HIV)

A virus that is usually contracted through the transfer of semen, blood, or vaginal secretions and is the cause of AIDS

acquired immunodeficiency syndrome (AIDS)

Viral disease transmitted via bodily fluids such as blood and semen usually during sexual relations or by sharing needles used by a person infected with the human immunodeficiency virus (HIV); the virus attacks the body's immune system, resulting in vulnerability to infections and diseases, which eventually cause death

These pamphlets encourage sexually active people to take precautions to prevent being infected by the AIDS virus.

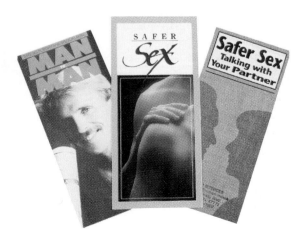

experience recurrent heart attacks as patients in the group that received only counseling (see Figure 15-6).

The researchers concluded that Type A behavior can be changed in many heart attack victims. For example, Type A people can reduce their risk by becoming aware of their cynical, hostile, and mistrustful thoughts, perhaps by keeping a daily log of such thoughts. Then they can apply the lessons we learned in our earlier discussion of the appraisal of potential stressors. They can reason with themselves about these thoughts. If that sounds silly, think about the following: Do you really believe the people two flights up are holding the elevator to spite you? That really sounds silly! Perhaps once we can laugh at the folly of our own stressful thoughts and emotions, we are on the way toward reducing hostility (Williams, 1989; Williams & Williams, 1993).

Acquired Immunodeficiency Syndrome (AIDS)

On June 5, 1981, the U.S. Centers for Disease Control reported that five gay men in Los Angeles had lost their ability to fight infections; they had acquired an immune deficiency of unknown origin. Two years later scientists isolated the **human immunodeficiency virus (HIV)** that causes **acquired immunodeficiency syndrome (AIDS).** A test developed in 1985 detects antibodies produced by the immune system to fight the virus (Newton, 1992). A person infected with HIV as indicated by the test is designated as HIV+ (positive).

HIV: A Global Perspective. AIDS is the tenth leading cause of death in the United States. Most of its victims are young adults and members of minority groups. In 1994 AIDS was the leading cause of death for men between the ages of 25 and 44 and the fifth leading cause for women in this age range (U.S. Bureau of the Census, 1997).

The year 1996 was a watershed in the history of AIDS in the United States: After more than a decade of increases, deaths from AIDS declined, and similar reductions in AIDS-related deaths were noted in France and Great Britain (Mann & Tarantola, 1998). A major reason for this drop in deaths and disease was the introduction of several powerful drugs that retard the activity of HIV (Mann & Tarantola, 1998; Bartlett & Moore, 1998), with special importance attached to the increasing use of therapies that combine several drugs (Palella et al., 1998).

The picture of the HIV epidemic is not as encouraging in other parts of the world. Consider the following:

- More than 40 million individuals have contracted HIV since the early 1980s.
- Almost 12 million have died (leaving at least eight million orphans) since the early 1980s.
- In 1997, nearly 6 million people (approximately 16,000 a day) were infected with HIV, and 2.3 million died as a result. (Mann & Tarantola, 1998)

HIV infection is spreading most rapidly in sub-Saharan Africa and parts of Asia, especially in India and Thailand (Gangakhedkar et al., 1997; Mann & Tarantola, 1998; Quinn, 1996) (see Figure 15-7). Two-thirds of all the world's HIV-infected children live in the regions below the Sahara. In Botswana, Swaziland, and several provinces of South Africa, one in four adults is afflicted with HIV. Unprotected heterosexual sex accounts for most of the cases of HIV in sub-Sahara Africa (Mann & Tarantola, 1998) and is a significant factor in India (Gangakhedkar et al., 1997). Most of the countries experiencing a rapid spread of HIV infection do not have funds for the expensive new drug therapies (estimated to be $10,000 to $12,000 per person per year) or the infrastructure to deliver the drugs if they had the money (Mann & Taratola, 1998).

How accurate is your information about AIDS? Health educators trying to reduce the incidence of HIV have found that the public has a great deal of misinformation. A wide variety of educational programs have been developed to provide accurate information that can be used to make prudent choices. The following statements set the record straight on a number of topics related to HIV and AIDs.

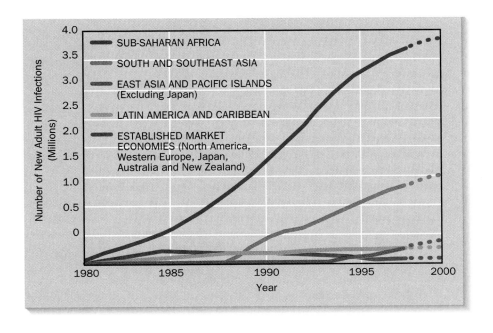

FIGURE 15-7 Number of new HIV infections. The number of people infected with HIV is growing rapidly in sub-Saharan Africa, South Asia, and Southeast Asia.

Source: Mann & Tarantola, 1998.

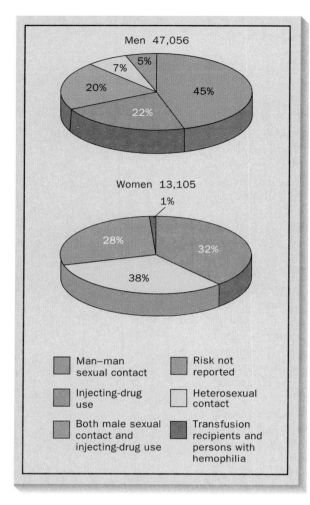

Men 47,056

5%
7%
20%
22%
45%

Women 13,105

1%
28%
32%
38%

- ■ Man–man sexual contact
- ■ Injecting-drug use
- ■ Both male sexual contact and injecting-drug use
- ■ Risk not reported
- □ Heterosexual contact
- ■ Transfusion recipients and persons with hemophilia

FIGURE 15-8 Number and percentages of American adolescents and adults with AIDS reported in 1997 and mode of exposure to HIV. The number of AIDS cases among men is substantially higher than the number of cases among women. Men and women differ in their likelihood of being exposed to infection with HIV.

Source: Centers for Disease Control and Prevention, 1997.

1. AIDS is a fatal disease for which there is currently no cure.

2. AIDS is caused by a virus.

3. You can get AIDS by sharing a needle with a drug user who has the disease.

4. You can contract AIDS by having sex with someone who has AIDS.

5. Using a condom during sex can lower the risk of getting AIDS.

6. HIV is not spread by using someone's personal belongings, such as a comb or a hairbrush.

HIV is actually a fragile virus that does not survive well outside of the body: It does not survive in the air, on plates or cups, on the skin, on door knobs, on toilet seats, or in drinking water. Thus HIV cannot be transmitted by casual social contact like shaking hands, hugging, or being in the same room with an infected person (Newton, 1992). HIV can be transmitted only by direct contact with bodily fluids that contain HIV-infected cells. The most common means of transmitting the virus are contact with semen or vaginal secretions and sharing hypodermic needles (Figure 15-8). The risk of HIV infection from blood transfusions is very small because all blood is now screened by a sensitive test for the presence of HIV (Lackritz et al., 1995).

Once HIV infects a person, it sets up a mammoth struggle between the immune system and the virus, which destroys white blood cells called *T lymphocytes*. Shortly after a person is infected, HIV replicates rapidly and can cause symptoms resembling the flu (Fackelmann, 1995). The immune system fights back and gains the upper hand, and the victim may then enjoy years of relatively good health. The immune system continues fighting valiantly, generally for 8 to 10 years (see Figure 15-9), until HIV replicates so rapidly that it destroys too many T cells (Fackelmann, 1995; Nowak & McMichael, 1995).

Why does HIV defeat the immune system? A major reason is that HIV mutates (alters its genetic material) continuously into a vast number of different forms that overwhelm the immune system. Thus a disease that would not be a threat to a healthy person can become a serious concern for someone with HIV. Once the immune system becomes compromised, infected individuals are subject to *opportunistic infections* such as pneumonia (Fackelmann, 1995). Whether HIV develops into AIDS slowly or quickly depends on a number of factors, including the level of stress in a person's life. As we have seen, stress can reduce the functioning of the immune system. Combining stress, which weakens the immune system, with HIV, which attacks it directly, can hasten the onset of AIDS.

Despite the availability of information about AIDS, many people fail to modify their sexual behavior to protect themselves from becoming infected. Bruce Roscoe and Tammy Kruger (1990) wondered whether college students' sexual attitudes and behaviors had changed as a result of the threat of AIDS. They asked a group of 750 juniors and seniors to complete a questionnaire. The results indicated that the students were very knowledgeable regarding AIDS and that about one-third of them had adopted such precautions as using condoms. These results are somewhat encouraging, but obviously more sexually active people need to be convinced to use condoms and other procedures associated with safe sex (Walter & Vaughn, 1993). The National Commission

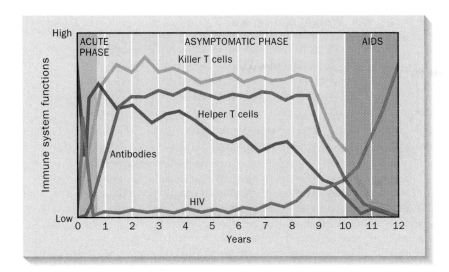

FIGURE 15-9 Immune system activity following HIV infection. Immediately after infection with HIV, an individual may have symptoms that are similar to those of the flu. After this acute phase, the immune system remains strong and symptoms are few for as long as ten years. Ultimately, however, the virus replicates rapidly and defeats the immune system.

Source: Nowak & McMichael, 1995.

on Acquired Immune Deficiency Syndrome (1991) wrote, "Until a cure or a vaccine is found, education and prevention are the only hope for altering the course of the HIV epidemic" (p. 19). There must be frank talk about sexual and drug-related behaviors that risk the spread of HIV. The language must move beyond expressions like "exchange of bodily fluids" that were not understood previously.

Nutrition and Eating

A few decades ago the major dietary problem of Americans was obtaining a sufficient amount of vitamins and nutrients. Today the major problems are excesses and imbalances in the types of food we consume. Dietary factors and physical inactivity play a role in five of the ten leading causes of death in the United States, including heart disease, some types of cancer, and strokes. In addition to being associated with the risk of **obesity** or weighing 20 percent or more than one's recommended weight, high intake of dietary fat is associated with increased risk for some types of cancer and, possibly, gallbladder disease (U.S. Department of Health and Human Services, 1988b).

Significant changes in what we eat and how much we weigh have taken place since the beginning of the twentieth century. Consider the following (Brownell & Wadden, 1991):

- Americans have grown heavier during the past century.
- Despite a stable or even reduced caloric intake since the early 1900s, obesity has increased.
- Our diet now contains a greater percentage of fat than the diet consumed early in this century.
- We eat more of our food away from home, much of it fast food—which is higher in fat than food eaten at home.

These changes have spawned concern about weight and seem to be responsible for a number of serious weight-related problems. It is not surprising that 41 percent of men and 55 percent of women in the United States are dissatisfied with their weight (Cash, Winstead, & Janda, 1986). Thus it is not surprising that Americans spend approximately $40 billion per year on weight-loss programs, primarily for diets and dietary foods (Wickelgren, 1998).

obesity
Body weight of 20 percent or more in excess of desirable body weight

How Does My Weight Compare?   Am I overweight? Am I obese? And just what is the difference? How much *should* I weigh?

Psychological Detective

Like most people, you probably wonder how your weight compares with that of other people. How can you collect information to make those comparisons, and how can you be sure such comparisons are meaningful? Write down your answer before reading further.

The most common way of finding a desirable weight is to look it up in tables first published by the Metropolitan Life Insurance Company in 1959. Historically, data collected by insurance companies have shown that weight levels are related to death rates. As an aid in setting premiums and assigning risk, insurance companies have published ranges of desirable weights for men and women that are related to height. People are classified as *overweight* if their weight exceeds the range in the table by 10 to 20 percent. If it exceeds the range by more than 20 percent, they are classified as *obese*. The insurance company tables of desirable weights (e.g., 126 pounds for a woman who stands 5'4" and 154 for a man of 5'10") are considered quite lean; about 80% of Americans would exceed the standards today (Wickelgren, 1998).

Consulting insurance company tables is the most common method of comparing our weight to that of others, but it is not the ideal one. Typically, these tables are based on a sample of people who can afford insurance—people who are likely to come from the middle or upper class and to be young or middle-aged. Thus the tables do not accurately represent the entire population. What's more, as people grow older, they tend to weigh more owing to metabolic and other factors; this increase in weight may be greater than the tables suggest because people over 55 are not well represented in the samples used to establish the tables.

The Body Mass Index (BMI).   For decades we have checked insurance charts to determine where we stand in the battle of the bulge, but now there is a new tape measure in use. In 1998, the National Heart, Lung, and Blood Institute announced a new set of numbers defining healthy and unhealthy body weights, which basically replaces the insurance company charts. These new federal government guidelines, intended for the identification and treatment of those who are overweight or obese, are based on **body mass index (BMI)** (Shapiro, 1998), which is a ratio between height and weight (Piper, 1996). Body mass index is a single number that represents your height and weight without regard to gender; it correlates with body fat. This index seems to be a better predictor of disease risk than body weight alone. Elevated BMI is associated with increased risk for hypertension, cardiovascular disease, adult-onset diabetes, and sleep apnea.

Psychological Detective

Would you like to calculate your BMI? It is actually quite easy. You will need a calculator. Follow this formula:

$$BMI = \frac{703 \times \text{weight in pounds}}{(\text{height in inches})^2}$$

body mass index (BMI)
A numerical index calculated from a person's height and weight that is used to indicate health status and disease risk

It is important to note that BMI should not be used by everyone. For example, competitive athletes and body builders often have a high BMI owing to their

TABLE 15-7   The Shape Up America! Guidelines for Interpreting Your BMI

BMI CATEGORY	HEALTH RISK BASED ON BMI
Less than 25	Minimal
25 to less than 27	Low
27 to less than 30	Moderate
30 to less than 35	High
35 to less than 40	Very high
Over 40	Extremely high

Source: Shape Up America! Web site at www.shapeup.org/

C. Everett Koop, former U.S. Surgeon General, founded the public health organization Shape Up America!, which is dedicated to improving health. The organization maintains a Web site where you can obtain information on a healthy diet, risk factors related to weight, and the body mass index (BMI).

relatively large amount of muscle tissue, which weighs more than fat tissue. Consequently, their disease risk would be overestimated by their BMI. In addition, the following individuals should not use the BMI: women who are pregnant or lactating, children, and frail and sedentary individuals. For everyone else, the meaning of your BMI can be determined by checking Table 15-7, which contains guidelines from Shape Up America!, a public health organization founded by former Surgeon General C. Everett Koop. Note that these guidelines avoid use of the terms *obese* and *overweight* when presenting the health risk associated with a given BMI.

The Biology of Obesity.   To understand our efforts to control weight, we need to know about calories. A *calorie* (popular shorthand for the term *kilocalorie*) is a measure of energy: One calorie is the amount of heat needed to raise the temperature of one kilogram of water one degree Celsius.

Have you ever heard people say that they were "born to be fat" or that they inherited their weight problem from their parents? There is considerable evidence to support such statements. Only about 5 percent of all cases of obesity result from physical causes such as endocrine dysfunctions or brain damage (Grilo & Pogue-Geile, 1991). What about the other cases? Albert Stunkard and his colleagues (1986) studied 540 adult adoptees and found no relationship between the adoptees' weights and those of their adoptive parents. They found a strong relationship, however, between the weights of adoptees and those of their biological parents. In another study Stunkard and his colleagues (1990) found that the correlations between the weights of adult twins who had been raised apart were 0.70 for men and 0.66 for women. These correlations were only slightly lower than those for twins who had been reared together. Such evidence indicates that inherited factors have a strong influence on what we weigh. As Judith Rodin (1992) notes, "Body size and weight are highly determined by our genes. Picking the right parents is far more important than picking the right diet" (p. 175). Carlos Grilo and Michael Pogue-Geile (1991) completed a review of the literature on environmental and hereditary influences on obesity. They reached the following conclusions:

Although genetic factors play a major role in determining how much we weigh, obese people have suffered discrimination. A federal appeals court ruled that Bon Cook had been discriminated against when she was denied a job because of her obesity.

1. There was no correlation between the weights of adoptive siblings who share the same environment but share no genes.
2. The correlation between the weights of identical twins varied little whether they were raised together or were separated and raised in different environments.

Fat cells expand quite easily, and they are easy for the body to maintain.

3. Spouses who lived together did not show increased resemblance in weight as compared with engaged couples who had not yet lived together.

Thus heredity seems to play a significant role in what we weigh. But what exactly is inherited? Everyone has a certain amount of body fat, but the amount varies from one individual to another. Fat accounts for 21 to 27 percent of body weight in women; in men it accounts for 14 to 20 percent (Gilbert, 1989). Obese people have more fat cells than normal-weight individuals, possibly owing to genetic factors. The number of fat cells in our body does not change except under unusual circumstances, such as *lipectomy,* in which fat is surgically scooped out of the body. Fat cells can, however, swell (become larger). When cells swell to hold additional fat, they require little energy to maintain themselves.

Obese and normal-weight people may inherit different setpoint weights (see Chapter 4; Bennett & Gurin, 1982). A *setpoint* is a weight level (actually a small range) that the body seems to defend by adjusting its *resting metabolic rate,* the rate at which the body uses energy to run basic functions when we are at rest. Obese people may not necessarily eat more than normal-weight individuals; they do, however, tend to have lower metabolic rates and hence burn calories more slowly. Slowing the metabolic rate has advantages during times of famine because it allows the body to conserve its resources while maintaining bodily functions and getting along on fewer calories. Unfortunately, the human body cannot tell if the reduced caloric intake is due to dieting or to famine.

Psychological Detective

Setpoint theory has important implications for dieters. Suppose you are trying to lose weight by dieting. Your body reacts to the reduction in calories. What are the implications? Write down your answer before reading further.

If you suggested that slowing the metabolic rate makes losing weight more difficult, you understand one of the problems that overweight people face when they try to diet. Their metabolism adjusts to keep their body weight close to its setpoint; in other words, the body works hard to protect itself when calories are restricted (Leibel, Rosenbaum, & Hirsch, 1995; Rodin, 1992). Men and women have different resting metabolic rates; women tend to have lower rates than men, which is due partly to differences in body size. Our metabolic rates also slow with age; this is one reason that we tend to gain weight as we grow older (see Figure 15-10).

Even if setpoint theory is valid, it does not mean that obese people are powerless to lose weight. The setpoint can be reset through techniques such as

Reprinted with special permission of King Features Syndicate.

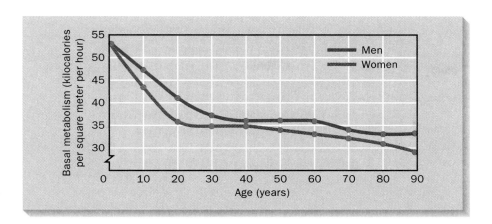

FIGURE 15-10 Basal (resting) metabolic rates. The rate at which the body burns energy is different for men and women and changes as we grow older.

Source: Hegarty, 1995.

exercise. Keep in mind, however, that burning a pound of fat is a slow process. To lose that pound, an average-sized person would have to do one of the following: play tennis for nine hours, jump rope for six hours, or swim for eight hours (Hegarty, 1995). Thus losing weight involves patience and the commitment to make significant changes in one's lifestyle.

Social Factors and Weight. Jeffery Sobal and Albert Stunkard (1989) believe that biological factors alone do not fully explain obesity; we must also consider social and cultural factors. According to *Healthy People 2000* (Public Health Service, 1990), 26 percent of the U.S. population is overweight; however, the problem does not strike evenly across the population. Among women, obesity is related to social class. For example, 37 percent of all women living in poverty are overweight. Rates of obesity are much higher among people in the lower socioeconomic classes than among those in the middle and upper socioeconomic classes. The relationship between obesity and social class is inconsistent for men and for children (Sobal & Stunkard, 1989).

Dieting. Our culture has an insatiable desire for new books, devices, medicines, and programs designed to make us fitter, healthier, and slimmer. When considering diets, it is important to note that the body does not treat all calories alike (Rodin, 1992). One gram of carbohydrates or protein contains four calories each, whereas one gram of fat contains nine calories (Bernard & Krupat, 1994). What's more, diets that are high in fat require fewer calories for digestion than high-carbohydrate diets. Once the fat is deposited in the body, few calories are needed to maintain it, and therefore it is difficult to remove.

Remember, overweight people "inherit only a tendency to develop obesity, the expression of which is affected by diet and exercise" (Brownell & Wadden, 1992, p. 506). For example, there is an association between the amount of time people spend watching television and the likelihood of obesity, which points to the importance of physical activity to burn calories. In two studies involving more than 10,000 adults, Larry Tucker and his colleagues (Tucker & Bagwell, 1991; Tucker & Friedman, 1989) found that men and women who watched three or more hours of television a day had twice the risk for obesity as those who spent less time in front of the TV.

Do not be discouraged if you are having trouble shedding pounds. Be realistic, however, about the amount of weight you can lose and your chances of keeping it off. Table 15-8 lists some helpful suggestions. Keep in mind that weight loss early in any diet is due almost entirely to loss of water; the fat cells have not yet begun to shrink. As you maintain the diet, real weight loss may occur, but the body will adjust its metabolism to accommodate the reduction in caloric intake. Subsequent weight loss may become more and more difficult.

TABLE 15-8 Behaviors That Contribute to Weight Reduction

- Most diets fail because they take the pleasure out of eating. The fat in most foods makes them more flavorful, creamy, and juicy. We can, however, enhance the taste of reduced-fat meals by adding spices and thus boost the effectiveness of diets without boosting the calories.

- Eat more slowly. Discover exactly how food tastes and thus allow the body's signals (e.g., a feeling of fullness) more time to work.

- Contrary to folklore, not all sugars are bad for us. The fructose found in fruits and honey tends to make us feel full. We tend to consume more calories after a glucose snack (glucose is a common form of sugar found in many foods) than after a fructose snack with equal calories. Thus a piece of fruit can decrease your appetite.

- Reduce the percentage of calories derived from fat. Even if you replace those calories with carbohydrates, your body uses more calories to break down carbohydrates than it does to break down fat.

- Reduce cues that tempt you to eat. Store food out of sight; do not shop on an empty stomach. Eat more low-calorie foods like carrots and popcorn that provide bulk and thus make you feel full.

- Engage in physical activity, which enhances long-term weight loss because it burns calories.

- Enlist the support of family members and friends. Tell them that you want to lose weight and that it is important to you. Ask them to refrain from offering you an extra piece of pie or a second serving of pork chops. Friends and relatives can also provide emotional support when needed.

- Set realistic goals. Few of us are going to look like the models in magazine advertisements. Positive physical and psychological benefits of weight loss often occur at levels above a proposed ideal weight.

- Recognize that weight control demands permanent lifestyle change and not a temporary diet.

Sources: Brownell & Wadden, 1992; Ornstein & Sobel, 1987; Spitzer & Rodin, 1987.

Eating Disorders. Two eating disorders are so serious that they are potentially life-threatening: **anorexia nervosa** (anorexia) and **bulimia nervosa** (bulimia). Many people who suffer from one or both of these disorders are dieting to control their weight, often in response to social and cultural pressure to be thin.

The literal meaning of anorexia nervosa—"nervous loss of appetite"—is misleading; people with this disorder are hungry, yet they deny their hunger owing to an intense fear of becoming fat. Their self-starvation is not due to any known physical disease. They maintain a body weight that is less than 85 percent of their expected weight, often by exercising compulsively. The average victim of anorexia nervosa loses 25 to 30 percent of normal body weight (Hsu, 1990). The weight loss is associated with a number of medical complications. Female victims of anorexia nervosa often experience *amenorrhea,* which is the absence of at least three consecutive menstrual cycles. Their self-imposed semistarvation may also lead to anemia, constipation, abdominal pain, and lethargy. The lack of nutrients causes the body to compensate; for example, calcium extracted from the bones often leads to stress fractures that may occur while simply walking (American Psychiatric Association, 1994; Pomeroy, 1996). Alterations in potassium and sodium levels can lead to cardiac arrest or kidney failure. Nevertheless, after losing so much weight that bones protrude, their body image is so distorted that they continue to believe they weigh too much.

anorexia nervosa

A potentially life-threatening eating disorder occurring primarily in adolescent and young adult females; an intense fear of becoming fat leads to self-starvation and weight loss; accompanied by a strong belief that one is fat despite objective evidence to the contrary

bulimia nervosa

Eating disorder in which a victim alternately consumes large amounts of food (gorging) and then empties the stomach (purging), usually by inducing vomiting

Tragically, some victims literally starve themselves to death.

Anorexia nervosa occurs most often in young women; the mean age of onset of the disorder is 17 (American Psychiatric Association, 1994). Men comprise less than 10 percent of all the cases of the disorder. Anorexia occurs more frequently in upper socioeconomic classes and is found almost exclusively in industrialized countries (Devlin & Walsh, 1992). A survey of more than 2,000 twins in Virginia found that about one-half of 1 percent of women met all the criteria for anorexia. More than 3 percent of the women, however, had some symptoms associated with the disorder. Anorexia is associated with depression, low self-esteem, and bulimia nervosa (Walters & Kendler, 1995; Rastam, Gillberg, & Gillberg, 1995). The twins of people with anorexia have an elevated risk for anorexia, bulimia, and depression, but it is not clear if this is due to environmental or genetic factors (Walters & Kendler, 1995).

Several possible causes of anorexia have been suggested. Among them are imbalances in levels of neurotransmitters, strong social pressure to be slim, and a very poor image of one's body. The treatment of anorexia focuses on psychological factors. The immediate goals of treatment are resumption of eating and weight gain, but weight gain by itself is not a cure. Individuals who suffer from anorexia must develop insight into their negative feelings about their bodies and the behaviors that accompany those feelings. Without this insight, any weight gain will probably be temporary, and the patient will revert to anorectic habits. Cognitive therapy, which helps patients understand the thoughts and feelings associated with the disorder, and behavior therapy, which helps change patients' undesirable behavior, are effective treatments.

Bulimia nervosa (literally, "continuous nervous hunger") is an urge to eat huge quantities of food (as much as 20,000 calories) in a short time span; it often develops during adolescence or early adulthood. A feeling of lack of control over eating is common during an episode. Depression and guilt often set in after the episode and lead to purging through self-induced vomiting or excessive use of laxatives or diuretics, or extreme exercise in what becomes a gorging-purging cycle. The vomiting can bring stomach acid in contact with the teeth, which corrodes the enamel and encourages tooth decay. Other medical complications include alteration of the gag reflex so that it is triggered too easily or unintentionally, enlargement of the salivary glands, and imbalances in potassium, sodium, and calcium.

Like anorexia, bulimia is most common among young women. Unlike anorectic women, however, bulimic women are not underweight. Rather, their weight is usually normal or sometimes just above the normal range. For this reason, bulimia is easier to hide than anorexia, and hence it is more difficult to calculate the number of people who suffer from this disorder.

In order to attain a better understanding of bulimia, researchers (Brown, Cash, & Lewis, 1989) compared reports of a large sample of bulimic adolescent

Left: Gymnast Christy Henrich, during the period when she was training for the Olympics. *Right:* Henrich later, when she was suffering from anorexia nervosa, which eventually killed her. Despite numerous hospitalizations for anorexia, Christy's weight dropped from 95 pounds to 47 pounds. Her desire to be thin stemmed from many social and personal factors.

women to those of a control sample of nonbulimic adolescents who were similar in age and weight. The women with bulimia were more concerned with their appearance and rated their appearance much more negatively than the controls. They also overestimated their current weight and were more fearful of gaining weight.

In sum, people with bulimia have a very distorted and negative image of their bodies. They face continuous self-imposed pressure to do something about their weight. If only the weight would come off, they believe, happiness and popularity will follow. That situation never materializes; therefore bulimic individuals can never be satisfied with their appearance.

Review Summary

1. Smoking-related illnesses are the most preventable cause of death in the United States. The number of smokers is declining, but people with less education are more likely to smoke than people with more education. Most smokers tried their first cigarette before age 18. Peer pressure is a major factor leading individuals to start smoking.

2. Although there are many programs to help people stop smoking, most people who quit do so on their own, usually after several unsuccessful attempts. Anticipated weight gain after quitting is often cited as a reason for continuing to smoke.

3. The concept of **Type A behavior** has been used to explain the development of heart disease. Type A individuals tend to be aggressive, competitive, impatient, and have difficulty relaxing.

4. The Western Collaborative Group Study indicated that a Type A individual was twice as likely to develop heart disease as the more relaxed and easygoing Type B person. Subsequent studies did not replicate this finding, and it became apparent that not all the components of Type A impart risk. Current research focuses on hostility as the toxic component of Type A behavior.

5. **Obesity** is associated with several physical illnesses. Factors such as gender and poverty play a role in the prevalence of obesity among certain groups in the population. The **body mass index (BMI)** is a single number derived from a person's height and weight; it is a better predictor of disease risk than insurance company tables of desirable weights.

6. Genetic factors play a key role in determining how much a person weighs. The *resting metabolic rate* is the rate at which a person burns calories to keep the body functioning. The body defends a setpoint weight, making it difficult, though not impossible, to lose weight.

7. A person with **anorexia nervosa** will lose a significant amount of weight. A person with **bulimia nervosa** will engage in a gorging-purging cycle, which involves taking in large amounts of food and then vomiting.

Study Break

1. Describe several factors that have been associated with the decline in the number of smokers in the United States in the past two decades.
2. Some people who want to stop smoking are afraid they will put on weight if they quit. What information and advice would you give them about the relationship between quitting smoking and gaining weight?
3. How does the body react in most cases shortly after being infected with HIV?
   a. Sleep difficulties occur.
   b. Flu-like symptoms are likely.
   c. Calcium is lost from the bones.
   d. Cholesterol levels increase significantly.
4. What is the leading cause of death among men between the ages of 25 and 44 in the United States?
   a. heart disease
   b. cancer
   c. accidents
   d. AIDS
5. The immune system seems capable of fighting off HIV infection for eight to ten years or more. Why does the virus eventually destroy the effectiveness of the immune system?
   a. Unprotected sex causes localized infections.
   b. The virus invades brain areas responsible for breathing.
   c. Reduced appetite caused by the virus saps energy reserves needed to fight the virus.
   d. Genetically altered forms of the virus are too much for the immune system to fight.

6. Imagine a Type A person of your age and another person of the same age with a Type B personality. Suppose that these individuals are extreme examples of the two personality types. Trace the differences in how they would react to the events of a typical day.

7. Imagine a person waiting to have a meal served at a local restaurant. The meal is slow to arrive, and when it does arrive, it is cold. Describe how an individual with a high level of the toxic component of a Type A personality might react. What is that component?

8. Genetic factors seem to play a major role in how much we weigh, but they are not the only factors. What evidence is there that social and cultural factors play a role in determining weight levels?

Coping with Stress

The news conference is about to begin. The grim faces around the small room suggest that the company will be cutting back over the next six months. Nevertheless, employees throughout the facility are listening to the live news feed, hoping against hope. The initial reaction, as expected, is shock. Several weeks later some of the employees are weathering the storm much better than others. Some continue to be just as devastated as they were on the day the cutbacks were announced. *What factors predict the different reactions of people facing stressors such as the loss of a job?* ■

Some people seem to crumble after catastrophes, major life events, traumatic occurrences, or hassles; others "roll with the punches." One reason people react so differently to the same situations is that some individuals produce higher levels of stress hormones during the alarm stage of the GAS. Many people try to deaden or drown the pain and anxiety produced by stress by drinking alcoholic beverages or taking antianxiety drugs.

As we have seen, the concept of control is important in determining what we perceive as stressful. Let's extend that concept by noting that one way to control stress is to control our emotional reactions, alter our interpretations of events, and engage in behaviors such as physical activity that reduce the effects of stress. These various cognitive and behavioral efforts to control stress are called **coping.** In this section we take a closer look at some of the ways people cope with stress.

Psychological Moderators of Stress

Many people benefit from certain psychological and social characteristics that reduce their vulnerability to the harmful effects of stress. Among them are hardiness, explanatory style, distraction, social support, and a sense of humor.

Hardiness.   To explain why some people cope with stress better than other people, psychologist Suzanne Kobasa (1982; Maddi & Kobasa, 1984) focuses on a characteristic she calls **hardiness.** For example, when the Illinois Bell Telephone Company was undergoing a major reorganization, the employees were very uncertain about their jobs. Kobasa and her colleagues studied Illinois Bell executives and found that some of them had frequent bouts of illness, whereas others, who were subjected to the same stressors, did not become ill. Demographic variables could not explain the different responses of the two groups. What was the key?

coping
Cognitive and behavioral efforts that are used to reduce the effects of stress

hardiness
A psychological characteristic that can reduce the impact of stressors; it consists of commitment, belief in a sense of control, and viewing change as a challenge

Kobasa found that the executives who had few or no illnesses during the period of uncertainty could be characterized as hardy individuals. Hardiness is a psychological characteristic composed of three elements: *commitment* to self, work, and family; belief in a sense of *control* over one's life, no matter what may happen; and a view of change as a normal process and as a *challenge* that offers opportunities rather than threats. These three Cs—*commitment, control,* and *challenge*—seemed to make the hardy executives more resistant to the negative effects of stressors. They experienced the same events as others, yet they saw them in a different light and consequently reacted in a healthier manner.

Explanatory Style. Hardy executives faced the future with some optimism even when confronting a serious stressor such as job loss. Accumulating research suggests that the influence of optimism is not wishful thinking. Martin Seligman writes, "Laboratories around the world have produced a steady flow of scientific evidence that psychological traits, particularly optimism, can produce good health" (1990, p. 1992). A person's perspective on current and future events can also influence health status in both the short and long terms. For example, the tendency to use pessimistic explanations for bad events has been associated with poorer health than an optimistic style. What makes this finding remarkable is that the health status of people in their sixties was related to how they explained events when they were 25 (Peterson, Seligman, & Valliant, 1988). Consider what happened to individuals who took part in the Terman Life-Cycle Study (see Chapter 8), a longitudinal study of a sample of persons who had obtained exceptionally high scores on tests of intelligence. Questionnaires they had answered in 1936 and 1940 were analyzed to determine how they tended to explain events. Those who gave broadly negative interpretations (called *catastrophizing*) were more likely to die early (Peterson et al., 1998).

Although the precise mechanism for findings such as these is not known, we know that optimists do not become depressed easily when they fail. They are more likely to stick to medical regimens and to seek medical advice, and they tend to have their major life events buffered by higher levels of social support than pessimists (Seligman, 1990).

Distraction. One way to deal with stressful situations is to ignore them: Go to a movie, take a ride, wander through a shopping mall. Getting away may not eliminate stressful events, but the distraction or diversion can make difficult situations more tolerable, at least for a while. A recently widowed individual who volunteers at a community service center may find that this activity reduces the frequency of memories of the deceased spouse (Rice, 1992).

Some cancer treatments, such as chemotherapy, have side effects that add to the pain and suffering of cancer victims. In an attempt to distract children who have cancer from these side effects, hospital staff gave pediatric cancer patients the opportunity to play video games after receiving nausea-producing chemotherapy (Redd et al., 1987). Children who played distracting video games experienced significant reductions in nausea after chemotherapy. This approach can be integrated into most chemotherapeutic procedures.

Is distraction an effective technique for coping with stress in other situations? To find out, psychologists Darragh Devine and Nicholas Spanos (1990) asked 96 students to use one of several strategies to reduce the pain of immersing an arm in a tank of ice-cold water. The strategies included reinter-

Social support in the form of comfort, information, recognition, companionship, approval, and even financial assistance can have an important impact on the development and reduction of stress symptoms.

preting the event, using imagination, or distracting themselves. For example, some students were asked to imagine they were in a desert on a very hot day and were feeling uncomfortably hot and tired (imagination and reinterpretation). Others were asked to imagine distracting scenes such as being at a carnival and riding a merry-go-round. All of the students reported less pain when they used any of these strategies than when they used no strategy. Distraction led to a reduction in pain comparable to the reduction found with imagination and reinterpretation.

Social Support. Where do you turn when you need help, want a shoulder to cry on, need a favor, or are looking for advice? The answer may be your spouse or significant other, a close relative, or a friend—someone who can provide support in time of need. **Social support** is the availability of comfort, information, recognition, companionship, approval, advice, money, and encouragement from others.

When we face difficult situations, our thinking may be unclear, so it helps to have someone to help us focus our thoughts or to speak from experience. For example, coronary bypass patients placed with hospital roommates who were already recovering from the same sort of surgery had better and quicker recoveries than patients not placed with such roommates (Kulik & Mahler, 1987).

Social support can play a role in reducing the possible negative side effects of major life events, and it can also play a role in reducing the influence of daily hassles. Anita De Longis and her colleagues (1988) found that individuals with social support experienced fewer detrimental effects from daily hassles. Longitudinal research designs involving thousands of people reveal that those with the fewest social ties had the highest death rates, whereas those with the most social ties had the lowest rate. Such research demonstrates the "enormous role sociocultural factors may play in the maintenance of physical health and illness" (Matsumoto, 1996, p. 224).

But social support is not a bed of roses. Although research emphasizes the positive value of supportive friends, relatives, and co-workers, there may be some drawbacks as well. Well-intentioned friends or relatives can sometimes be annoying, irritating, or overly involved and can actually become additional sources of stress (Pagel, Erdly, & Becker, 1987).

social support
Availability of comfort, recognition, approval, advice, money, or encouragement from others

FIGURE 15-11 Relationship between sense of humor and depression. If a sense of humor serves as a buffer against stress, persons with little sense of humor will have higher levels of depression in response to negative life events.

Source: Nezu, Nezu, & Blissett, 1988.

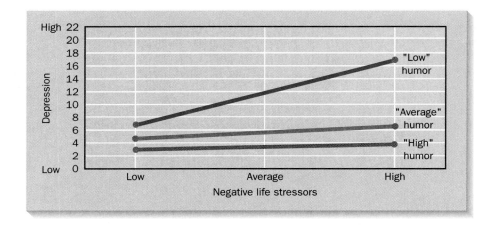

Sense of Humor. The belief that humor can enhance health is not new. The Bible tells us, "A merry heart doeth good like a medicine; but a broken spirit drieth the bones" (Proverbs 17:22). Norman Cousins (1979) drew attention to the potential of humor to reduce stress in *Anatomy of an Illness as Perceived by the Patient.* Cousins had contracted a connective tissue disease that leads to spinal deterioration and paralysis. After learning that his chances for recovery were 1 in 500, Cousins devised a regimen that included viewing comedy films and reading humorous materials. A few minutes of laughter gave him an hour or more of pain-free sleep, and he eventually recovered from the illness (Cousins, 1989). When writing about his experience, he was careful to point out that he did not regard the use of laughter as a substitute for traditional medical care.

Several lines of research seem to support the notion that humor and laughter can have positive psychological and physical benefits. Arthur Nezu, Christine Nezu, and Sonia Blissett (1988) found that undergraduate students with an average or high sense of humor reported few increases in depression over time (see Figure 15-11). In contrast, students with a low sense of humor were more likely to become depressed in response to negative life events. Thus it appears that a sense of humor may function to reduce the impact of some stressful events.

Humor has several applications as a stress modifier: It reduces built-up tension, it can offer a new perspective on stressful situations, it assists in appraising them, and it uses up the products of the GAS such as the hormones epinephrine and norepinephrine (Klein, 1989). Joel Goodman (1993) provides an illustration of how humor can alter the perception of a situation from abusing to amusing:

> Minneapolis was hit by tornados in 1981. Trees were uprooted and tossed about, smashing everything in their path including cars. At times like this, the fight-or-flight response is of little use. One person decided to roll with the punches in the aftermath of the tornados. He stood in front of his smashed car waving and pointing to a hand-lettered sign, "Compact Car." (pp. 6-7)

What could this person do? He could become angry (but at whom?), cry, or become depressed. Instead he decided to laugh at his situation and thus render it less stressful. Laughter exercises the lungs and circulatory system and increases the amount of oxygen in the blood. When the laughter dies down, the heart rate slows to a lower rate than before the laughter, and the muscles become more relaxed.

Humor has been shown to be effective in reducing pain (Cogan et al., 1987). This effect may be due to the tendency of humor to produce relaxation. The laughter accompanying the reading or viewing of humorous material may also distract people who are facing stressful situations. Another possibility is that laughter leads to a release of endorphins (Fry, 1986), the brain's natural painkillers, which in turn reduces the experience of pain (see Chapter 2). In any case, it is clear that humor and laughter have positive benefits.

Ways of Reducing Arousal: Relaxation and Physical Activity

Stressful situations can quickly elicit the alarm reaction of the GAS; however, many people have difficulty activating the parasympathetic nervous system to counter a heightened arousal and thereby cope more effectively. As one psychologist has noted, "The fight-or-flight response . . . is not an appropriate method for coping with traffic jams . . . and interpersonal conflict. If humans still inhabit the earth a million years from now, they very well may develop a natural relaxation response to daily frustrations and hassles" (Kleinke, 1991, p. 32). There is no need to wait to learn to relax and cope more effectively with stressful situations. Several approaches that reduce arousal are available now. They include relaxation techniques, biofeedback, and exercise.

Relaxation Techniques.   Imagine this scene: You are sitting in class when the instructor strolls in armed with a stack of exams. Your heart begins to race, your muscles become tense, and you start to perspire. You try relaxing, but to no avail! As your tension escalates, you silently admit you do not know how to relax.

Few ways of reducing stress reactions are as powerful and widely applicable as relaxation techniques. These techniques differ in complexity but have similar effects on the body. As with any skill, relaxation techniques require practice. How do you select the relaxation technique that is right for you? Try it and see how it feels.

Edmund Jacobson (1888–1983), a psychologist and physician, developed a method for learning to reduce muscle tension. Psychiatrist Joseph Wolpe modified Jacobson's techniques in order to reduce the training time (Bernstein & Carlson, 1993). The resulting series of exercises is called **progressive relaxation.** To become relaxed, you repeatedly tense and then relax each major muscle group one by one, such as the shoulders, thighs, and legs for a total of about 20 minutes. After several sessions, most people find they reach levels of relaxation they have never experienced before.

Some individuals have turned to various forms of meditation to reduce their arousal levels. In one popular form, called *transcendental meditation (TM)*, an individual silently repeats a sound (om), a word (one), a phrase (may I be peaceful), or a prayer, called a *mantra*, over and over. The use of this mantra in rhythm with inhaling or exhaling is intended to divert attention from one's surroundings and to keep one from thinking about anything that could be arousing. Many meditators report that they feel refreshed after meditating and that it reduces their arousal.

Another approach to relaxation is based on techniques that have been known for hundreds of years. Herbert Benson (1975, 1984) combined these techniques in a procedure designed to bring forth the **relaxation response,** or

progressive relaxation
Series of exercises consisting of alternately tightening and relaxing major muscle groups

relaxation response
Relaxation technique that involves the use of a mental device

biofeedback
Providing information about some ongoing biological process such as muscle tension in the hope that a person will learn to adjust the process

the calm resulting from activation of the parasympathetic branch of the autonomic nervous system. The key components of the procedure are as follows:

1. *Find a quiet environment.* Put yourself in a comfortable position in a calm and quiet environment that offers few distractions. The quiet environment enhances your ability to relax, but as you develop the skill, you may be able to relax even in noisy, distracting environments.
2. *Use a mental device.* The device could be as simple as repetition of the word *one,* although other sounds or phrases work nicely, including the rhythm of your breathing. Focus on the mental device to shift your attention away from external demands and thoughts. Close your eyes to enhance your ability to reduce external distractions. Later you can use these images in other situations to elicit relaxation.
3. *Adopt a passive attitude.* Relaxation is not a competitive sport. Trying harder to relax makes as much sense as trying harder to sleep. Adopt a "let it happen" attitude. When distracting thoughts occur, return to your mental device.

Several physiological changes result from the relaxation response. The brain's electrical activity changes to include more alpha waves (see Chapter 2), breathing slows, the heart rate slows, and blood pressure decreases. Using techniques like the relaxation response can lead to lower levels of sympathetic nervous system arousal during stressful situations.

A number of biological changes, such as increased muscle tension, occur in reaction to stressors. The technique of **biofeedback** involves attaching special electronic sensors to a person's body to detect these changes. The information detected is then fed to an electronic device that selects the appropriate signals and amplifies them for feedback to the person, usually in the form of sound or digital read-outs (see Figure 15-12). The feedback is helpful in guiding bodily changes that typically lead to a greater degree of relaxation.

Several types of biofeedback equipment that detect different biological responses are available. For example, the *electromyograph (EMG)* provides feedback on the electrical activity of the muscles as they contract. Placing electrodes on the skin surface of the head provides biofeedback that can be used to treat muscle tension headaches. Temperature biofeedback involves the use of temperature-sensitive sensors that reflect constriction and dilation of the blood vessels. This form of biofeedback has been used to treat migraine headaches.

Exactly how people use biofeedback is not clear. We know some forms of biofeedback, such as that provided about muscle tension in tension headaches, can be quite valuable. Other forms of biofeedback, such as information about alpha brain waves, add little to a person's ability to enhance relaxation.

Physical Activity. The tempo of everyday life and the rate of change have accelerated in recent decades. We move our households more times, change jobs more frequently, and travel at greater speeds than previous generations. Yet we live a more sedentary life than our grandparents and thus spend less time engaging in physical activity.

FIGURE 15-12 Electrodes (sensors) gather information about changes in the levels of biological processes such as muscle tension (in the forehead in this example) or temperature. This information is filtered and amplified before it is returned to the client in the form of auditory or visual feedback that can be used to alter these indicators of level of relaxation.

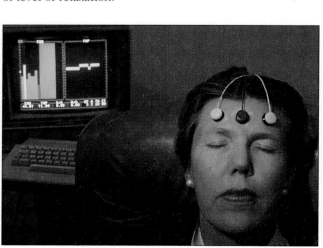

The benefits of exercise include stress reduction and weight control.

Why engage in physical activity? Consider this information as you reach for the remote control: A sedentary lifestyle can lower your life expectancy and contribute to the development of chronic diseases (Dubbert, 1992; Pate et al., 1995).

The benefits of physical activity are evident in a study of 17,000 Harvard University graduates. Those who walked 9 miles or more per week had a 21 percent lower risk of death than those who walked less than 3 miles per week. Those who burned less than 2,000 calories per week in physical activity had a 38 percent higher risk of death than those who burned more than 2,000 calories per week (Paffenbarger et al., 1986).

In another study, almost 2,000 healthy men between the ages of 40 and 59 were studied at two points separated by about 16 years. Their level of physical fitness was determined by the amount of work they could perform on a bicycle. Figure 15-13 compares the death rates for individuals whose level of physical fitness put them in either the top or the bottom 25 percent of the group. The individuals' level of physical fitness was related to death rate; those in the poorest physical condition had the highest death rate (Sandvik et al., 1993).

The government report *Healthy People 2000* (Public Health Service, 1990) sets a goal of increasing the percentage (to at least 30 percent) of people

FIGURE 15-13 Relationship of high and low levels of physical fitness to deaths from all causes. A sample of men had their levels of physical fitness evaluated. The men in the top 25 percent had a high level of physical fitness; the bottom 25 percent of the sample had a low level of physical fitness. The cumulative mortality percentages (an indication of the number who died over time) is strongly related to these individuals' levels of fitness.

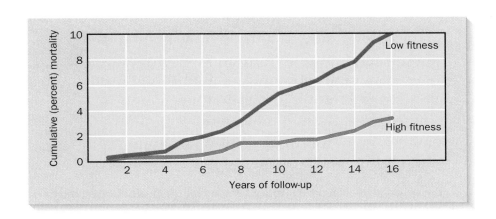

> TABLE 15-9 **Some Effects of Physical Activity on Physical and Psychological Well-Being**
>
> 1. Helps reduce weight by burning calories.
> 2. Produces endorphins, the body's opiatelike painkillers.
> 3. Strengthens the heart muscle so it works more efficiently.
> 4. Improves the sense of well-being; reduces anxiety, depression, and anger.
> 5. Improves the functioning of the heart and lungs and reduces blood pressure.
> 6. Burns stress-produced epinephrine, which provides quicker recovery from acute stress.
> 7. Increases levels of high-density lipoprotein (HDL) and reduces low-density lipoprotein (LDL) in the blood.
>
> *Sources:* Czajkowski et al., 1990; Hegarty, 1995; National Institutes of Health Consensus Conference, 1993; Plante & Rodin, 1990; Schafer, 1987.

age 6 or older who engage in moderate physical activity for the 30 minutes per day recommended for health benefits. Despite the apparent benefits of physical activity (see Table 15-9), only one out of five adults in the United States engages in physical activity at a level sufficient to attain these benefits (Dubbert, 1992).

Why don't more people engage in physical activity? One reason is that most of us believe that to attain benefits, we must engage in rigorous, continuous exercise. Exercise is planned, structured, and repetitive body movements done to improve or maintain physical fitness (Pate et al., 1995). You don't have to go to the gym to accumulate 30 minutes of physical activity. If you are not physically active now and want to boost your activity level, here are some suggestions:

1. The average adult watches 30 hours of television a week, yet many who do not engage in physical activity cite a lack of time. Therefore, build physical activity into your daily routine. Use the stairs instead of an elevator. Park your car at the far end of the lot at work or the shopping mall so you'll have some exercise both coming and going.

2. Do not set unrealistic goals that almost guarantee failure. You will not be ready to run a marathon after one week of physical activity! Go slowly, and select activities that are enjoyable and within your current ability. For example, walking is the most popular form of physical activity in America, and nature has provided just about everything you need to get started.

3. Add variety to your program. Among the pleasures of a physically active lifestyle are the experiences you would have missed otherwise. Vary your route if you are walking or running, and enjoy the sights.

4. Adopt an activity that fits your social needs. People who need time to think by themselves may find a solitary jog to their liking; others may benefit from the support and encouragement of a group of joggers, especially when motivation wanes, as it inevitably does.

5. Depend on physical activity as a replacement for unhealthy habits, such as smoking, overeating, excessive television watching, or other behaviors you wish to change. This strategy can compound the benefit and satisfaction derived from the time spent exercising.

Physical activity can have positive benefits for the heart because the heart responds to exercise like other muscles—it gets stronger. As a result of activity, the heart beats at a slower rate, yet it can pump more blood with each beat. In other words, physical activity makes the heart a more efficient pump.

Does Physical Activity Reduce Stress?   Some research suggests that exercise helps reduce the negative effects of stress. For example, Beth McGilley and David Holmes (1988) found that individuals who were physically fit had lower cardiovascular and subjective responses to psychological stress than individuals who were not physically fit.

Psychological Detective

What are some of the difficulties researchers face in trying to demonstrate the effects of physical activity on stress reactions? How might you overcome those difficulties? Write down some answers to these questions before reading further.

One of the major difficulties in demonstrating the effects of physical activity is that much of the evidence is correlational; that is, it shows that two variables are related. It is impossible, however, to draw cause-and-effect conclusions from correlational data. If the data reveal that people who engage in physical activity handle stress better than people who do not, we do not know whether they have better coping skills, can obtain more social support, or are different in other ways. The effects of physical activity on stress reduction may also be related to the specific activity involved.

To overcome some of these problems, James Blumenthal and his colleagues (1988) compared aerobic exercise to exercise designed to enhance strength and flexibility. They randomly assigned 36 men to either aerobic or strength and flexibility training. After 12 weeks, the individuals in the aerobic exercise group increased their levels of cardiovascular fitness as indicated by decreases in both heart rate and blood pressure. What's more, men in the aerobic exercise group had lower blood pressure and heart rates during mental stress. In this case correlational and experimental research converged on a similar finding: Exercise aids in dealing with stress.

As the day progresses, you may find that you wear down physically and mentally. When this happens, do you look for a "picker upper" to tide you over to the end of the workday? Robert Thayer (1987) has advice for people who use sugary snacks to raise their energy levels. In his study volunteer participants either consumed a candy bar or took a 10-minute walk on 12 selected days. Those who ate the candy bar reported increased energy afterward, but the effect was short-lived. One hour after eating the candy bar, they felt more tense and more tired than before eating it. In contrast, those who took a 10-minute walk felt increased energy and decreased tension for as long as 2 hours after this moderate activity. Thus physical activity, even in moderate amounts, has both short- and long-term benefits.

Review Summary

1. A number of psychological factors have been shown to modify stress reactions. **Hardiness** is a psychological characteristic composed of commitment, a sense of control, and a tendency to view change as a challenge. Hardy individuals react differently to stressful events and experience fewer illnesses than less hardy individuals.

2. Distraction has been used to reduce the side effects of chemotherapy in pediatric cancer patients. Experimental research reveals that distraction has benefits in dealing with other stressful situations.

3. Social support is the availability of approval, advice, money, or encouragement from others. Social support may reduce the negative effects of stressful events.

4. There is growing support for the notion that humor and laughter can reduce mood disturbances, buffer the effects of life events, and aid in dealing with pain.

5. Many people have never developed the skill of relaxing. Among the techniques used to produce relaxation are **progressive relaxation,** the **relaxation response,** and **biofeedback.** Relaxation activates the parasympathetic nervous system and is helpful in reducing stress reactions.

6. Physical activity is associated with increased longevity and positive benefits on physical and psychological health. Current recommendations call for at least 30 minutes of physical activity per day, which can be accumulated in short bouts throughout the day.

Study Break

1. What are the components of hardiness?
2. What are the key benefits of social support for people under stress?
3. What evidence supports the notion that a good sense of humor has positive benefits for health?
4. Identify the technique for inducing relaxation, described in each of the following.
   a. You tense and then relax each of the major muscle groups in your body.
   b. A technician connects a small device to your forehead. A wire from that device is connected to a box with a digital display.
   c. You find a quiet spot and repeat a sound silently again and again.
5. After years of suffering, Alice finally decided to seek the help of a therapist who has recommended a program of biofeedback involving temperature.

Which of the following is the most likely disorder Alice has at this time?
   a. ulcers
   b. depression
   c. hypertension
   d. migraine headache
6. What is the current recommendation for the amount of physical activity that will lead to health benefits?
   a. Anything short of a full exercise program is a waste of time.
   b. Exercise rigorously to raise the heartbeat to 150 beats per minute.
   c. Accumulate 30 minutes of physical activity in short bouts throughout the day.
   d. Only a physical trainer can determine the amount of exercise required for benefits.

ANSWERS TO STUDY BREAKS

Pages 637–638

1. c
2. c
3. d
4. a. Alarm
   b. Exhaustion
   c. Resistance
5. Heart rate and blood pressure increase, breathing becomes deeper, perspiration increases to cool the body, most muscles are engorged with blood, epinephrine and norepinephrine are released to power these changes.
6. c
7. b
8. a. Primary appraisal
   b. Secondary appraisal

9. The symptoms of posttraumatic stress disorder include anxiety, irritability, difficulty in concentrating, sleep disturbances, guilt, and reliving the shocking event in dreams or flashbacks. Among men, the most common circumstances leading to posttraumatic stress disorder are being in combat and seeing someone hurt or die; physical attacks, especially rape, are the most common circumstances leading to posttraumatic stress disorder among women.

Pages 656–657

1. Among the factors that have been associated with the decline in the number of smokers are growing awareness of the dangers of smoking and decreases in the number of places that smoking is permitted.

2. People who stop smoking do tend to gain weight, but the amount of weight gain is not great in most cases. Increases in exercise can control this weight gain.

3. b

4. d

5. d

6. The Type A person is likely to be impatient, hostile, and unable to relax. The Type B person would be exactly the opposite and would probably wonder why the Type A person seems so upset by minor inconveniences or delays.

7. The toxic element of Type A—hostility—would lead the Type A person to lash out at the server.

8. There is an association between social class and weight among women. Women in the lower socioeconomic classes are more likely than those in the upper classes to be overweight.

Page 666

1. The components of hardiness are commitment, control, and challenge.

2. Social support involves providing comfort, information, advice, money, and encouragement, which can help reduce the impact of stressful events.

3. Case studies initially pointed to the benefits of a sense of humor. Now both longitudinal and experimental studies have provided evidence of the benefits of humor and laughter in reducing depression and in dealing with pain.

4. **a.** Progressive relaxation
   b. Biofeedback
   c. Relaxation response

5. d

6. c

Social Psychology: The Individual in Society

Chapter in Perspective

In most of the preceding chapters we have considered the behavior of individuals independently of the groups to which they belong. In this chapter our focus expands to the individual as a member of various groups, including society as a whole; we describe the domain of social psychology. We examine the ways we view others and their behavior; interpersonal relations, such as attraction, friendship, love, helping others, and aggression; social influences on behavior; and how the individual functions as part of a social group. As you read this chapter, you will encounter familiar terms and concepts from previous chapters. In a very real sense, social psychology is psychology in action. It applies what you have already learned to real-life behaviors in social settings. ■

social psychology
Study of the causes, types, and consequences of human interaction

ethnocentrism
Belief that one's own country or culture is superior to all other countries and cultures

individualism
Placing one's own goals above those of the group

collectivism
Placing group goals above individual goals

Social Psychology and Culture

Several students in your psychology class are discussing a new research finding. The results are exciting and seem to add considerably to our understanding of patterns of human interaction. You find the research particularly interesting because it was conducted in a foreign country. After further discussion, one of your classmates suggests that the results are presented in an ethnocentric manner. *What does the term* ethnocentric *mean?* ■

The study of social psychology is nearly as old as scientific psychology itself. The results of the first social-psychological experiment were published in 1898, just 19 years after Wilhelm Wundt founded the science of psychology (see Chapter 1). In that experiment Norman Triplett (1898) found that the presence of other people could enhance or facilitate the performance of a behavior requiring skill, such as bicycle racing. This effect, known as *social facilitation,* is still being studied by social psychologists. Social psychologists also study aspects of human interaction such as the formation of impressions, the development of attitudes, the effects of group pressure, the bases of interpersonal attraction, and the causes of prejudice and discrimination. Thus **social psychology** may be defined as the study of the causes, types, and consequences of human interaction.

As you read this chapter, keep in mind that the human interactions we are discussing do not occur in isolation; they occur in a specific cultural context. As you are aware, cultures can be very different; hence it should not surprise you to find that the results of a research project conducted in one culture may not be the same when the project is conducted in a different culture. Unfortunately, researchers are sometimes guilty of **ethnocentrism;** they forget about cultural differences and see other cultures as an extension of their own, "superior" culture. As Smith and Davis (1997) point out, such researchers "interpret research results in accord with the values, attitudes, and behaviors that define their own culture and assume that these findings are applicable in other cultures as well" (p. 148). Because culture can influence the type of research problem we choose to investigate, the nature of our research hypothesis, and the selection of the variables we choose to manipulate (the independent variable; see Chapter 1) and record (the dependent variable), researchers must guard against ethnocentrism (Matsumoto, 1994).

Consider the issue of individualism and collectivism. **Individualism** is defined as placing one's own goals over those of the group, whereas **collectivism** is

Social facilitation occurs when the presence of other people enhances an individual's performance.

defined as placing group goals above individual goals. The degree of individualism or collectivism of a culture can influence many aspects of behavior, such as interpersonal relations, self-concept, parenting practices, self-esteem, and emotional expression (Kim & Choi, 1994; Triandis, 1995; Triandis, Brislin, & Hui, 1988).

Because cultures vary so widely, social psychologists need to conduct cross-cultural studies to determine whether the results of research conducted in one culture can be *generalized* to other cultures (Smith & Bond, 1993). Even with cross-cultural studies, however, you must learn to be a good psychological detective. In addition to ascertaining effects of culture, you need to ask about the conditions under which the research was conducted and even the nature of the research participants. For example, many psychologists rely on college students as participants because they constitute a convenient population for drawing a sample. What about a study from another culture that used college students as participants? Are college students in Iran or South Africa comparable to those in the United States? (Closer to home, we can ask if college students in different parts of the United States are comparable to one another. Remember, our own country is composed of different subcultures.) Questions such as these are difficult to answer. Yet they must be addressed if we are truly committed to developing a general body of knowledge. Although the problem is real and the need genuine, the amount of cross-cultural information is limited; we point to relevant findings throughout this chapter.

How We View Others and Their Behavior

Last week you attended a party and made several new acquaintances, including Antonio and Roberto. Something about Antonio attracted other people to him immediately; he was the life of the party. By contrast, Roberto blended into the background; you hardly knew he was there. You left the party with very definite but different impressions of each of your new acquaintances. *What factors influenced your impressions of Antonio and Roberto?* ▧

Impression formation is the process of developing an opinion about another person. In addition to forming impressions of others, we also make judgments, called *attributions,* about the reasons for or causes of this person's behavior. In this section we discuss these two processes and their effects, as well as the larger category, *attitudes,* that includes both impressions and judgments.

Impression Formation

The process of impression formation requires an actor and a perceiver. As the perceiver, you form an impression about the actor. The views and thoughts of the perceiver and the appearance and behaviors of the actor influence the impressions that are formed. Let us take a closer look at each of these dimensions of impression formation.

Aspects of the Perceiver.   Have you ever made a snap judgement about someone you just met? We do not enter into interpersonal relationships with a completely blank mind; we bring preconceived ideas or stereotypes to every

impression formation
The process of forming an opinion about another person

stereotype
Set of beliefs about members of a particular group

self-fulfilling prophecy
Phenomenon whereby our expectations elicit behaviors in others that confirm those expectations

situation. A **stereotype** is a set of beliefs about members of a particular group (Hamilton & Sherman, 1994). Stereotypes can be either negative or positive. Examples of negative stereotypes are "Jocks are dumb" and "Film stars are temperamental." "Beautiful people are good people" is an example of a positive stereotype (Feingold, 1991, 1992).

Why do we form stereotypes? In Chapter 3 we saw that the nervous system is not capable of processing all the sensory information to which we are exposed at any given time. To reduce this "information overload," we create perceptual categories, such as "red objects," "square objects," "sweet objects," and "loud objects." The same logic applies to the formation of stereotypes. If you put people into categories, you have fewer items of information to deal with—you can think about a small number of categories rather than a large number of individuals (Kaplan, Wanshula, & Zanna, 1992). Those categories are stereotypes.

Obviously a lot of information about an individual is lost when he or she is viewed as part of a category. Take the "beautiful is good" stereotype as an example. When we meet an attractive person, we may unconsciously put him or her in the beautiful-is-good category and assume that he or she possesses all the positive characteristics associated with that stereotype (Patzer, 1985). Does your personal experience support this stereotype?

Psychological Detective

Continued interactions with people should demonstrate that individuals in a given category do not necessarily share the same personality traits. Yet stereotypes persist, often in the face of contradictory evidence. Why do we continue to hold stereotypes? Write down at least one reason before reading further.

There are two reasons for the persistence of stereotypes. First, if we believe that a group of people (such as community leaders) possesses certain characteristics, we may selectively note behaviors that are consistent with that characteristic (such as volunteering to serve in the chamber of commerce) and fail to notice behaviors that are inconsistent (such as driving under the influence of alcohol). The second reason that stereotypes are durable involves the effects of our own reactions and behaviors on the individuals in question. Do you treat attractive people and unattractive people differently? Perhaps you treat individuals in ways that bring forth behaviors consistent with your stereotype. For example, grade school teachers who are told that the children in their classes are slow learners treat those children differently from the children they are told are gifted (Rosenthal & Jacobson, 1968). These different instructor reactions result in different behaviors on the part of the students, even if the students are not different in any appreciable manner. When your behaviors influence others to respond the way you expect, a **self-fulfilling prophecy** is at work (Jones, 1986).

If we view beautiful people as good, the "beautiful is good" stereotype may be influencing our attitudes.

Clearly the perceiver can and does play an active role in the process of impression formation. Certain characteristics of the actor, however, also play a prominent role in this process.

Aspects of the Actor.   Four features of the actor have been shown to influence impression formation. Those features are (1) physical appearance, (2) style and content of speech, (3) nonverbal mannerisms and nonverbal communication, and (4) the perceiver's prior information about the actor.

Appearance.   The "beautiful is good" stereotype assumes that attractive people have positive characteristics—they are witty and intelligent and have pleasing personalities (Feingold, 1991). Therefore attractive people can be expected to make better impressions. Research has shown that these expectations are borne out in reality (Dion & Stein, 1978); our first impressions of attractive people are more favorable than those of less attractive individuals.

Speech.   A verse in a popular rock-and-roll song of the 1950s went, "It ain't what you eat, it's the way how you chew it; it ain't what you do, it's the way how you do it." Although the songwriters could have used some help with their grammar, there is a message for the social psychologist in this lyric. *How* you do things makes a difference. With regard to impression formation, an actor's style of speech is important. Among the aspects of speech that are influential are speed, loudness, and inflections (variations). For example, a New Yorker's rapid, clipped speech may not appeal to a native of Atlanta, whose slower style may make the New Yorker impatient. When we meet someone with a foreign accent, we tend to talk more slowly and loudly. In addition, straightforward and clear speech is more appealing than speech that contains numerous qualifiers and hesitations, such as *like, maybe, kinda, I guess,* and *you know* (Erickson et al., 1978).

The content of speech is also important. Research on **self-disclosure,** the amount of personal information a person is willing to share with others, indicates that the more a person reveals, the more positive the impression others form (Jourard & Friedman, 1970). Although self-disclosure by one individual prompts self-disclosure by another (Miller, 1990), too much self-disclosure early in a relationship can create a negative impression (Cozby, 1972). How have you reacted when people whom you have just met told you highly personal information? Your reaction was probably unfavorable because you were unwilling to disclose the same kind of information about yourself. Most people are not willing to share intimate experiences and feelings with others whom they know only casually. As the relationship develops, they are more likely to reveal private information. Whereas self-disclosure is valued in Western, industrialized cultures like the United States that stress individualism (especially on radio and television talk shows), it is not as highly valued in Asian cultures like Japan that stress collectivism.

Favorable impressions are also created by people who respond appropriately to what has just been said to them. Suppose you have just told a new acquaintance what your major is. How would you react if the response to this self-disclosure was silence or a comment on an unrelated topic? Would your impression be different if the other person had said something positive about your choice of a major?

Nonverbal Communication.   Instructors often say that the first class session in a course is the most important one. As a student, your initial impression of the teacher may greatly influence your enjoyment of that first class. The instructor's nonverbal communication plays an important role in determining this initial impression. Which course would you rather take, one in which the instructor never looks the students in the eye and has unusual mannerisms (such as blinking rapidly, a behavior associated with anxiety) or one in which the instructor looks each student in the eye, smiles frequently, and has an easygoing, relaxed manner? People's mannerisms and other nonverbal communications influence our impressions of them (see Chapter 4).

self-disclosure
An individual's decision to share personal information

Nonverbal communication can tell us a lot about other people.

Mark Snyder and his colleagues (Snyder & Gangestad, 1986) have developed the Self-Monitoring Scale to measure the degree to which individuals manipulate the nonverbal signals they send to others in social situations and how well they are able to adjust their behaviors to fit the specific situation. The Self-Monitoring Scale is reproduced in Table 16-1; see how you score on this dimension.

Prior Information.   Information that is available to you before you meet someone can affect your impression of that person. For example, if a label is applied to an individual, it may stick, whether or not it is accurate. A classic study by psychologist Harold Kelley (1950) illustrates this point. The students in a class were told they would be hearing a visiting lecturer. Half of the students received a written description that portrayed the lecturer as "warm." The rest received a description that portrayed the lecturer as "cold." After the lecture the students who had read the "warm" description had a more favorable impression of the speaker than the students who had read the "cold" description.

Social Judgments: Attributing Causes to Behaviors

In addition to forming impressions of others, we seek to discern the causes of their behavior (Hamilton, Smith, & Kin, 1995). **Attribution** is the process by which we decide why certain events occurred or why a particular person acted in a certain manner (Weiner, 1993). Several factors influence our attributions. Among them are internal versus external causes, consistency, consensus, and our role as actor or perceiver in the situation.

Internal Versus External Causes.   In attempting to determine the cause of a particular event or behavior, we first decide whether it was due to internal factors, such as personality traits (see Chapter 12), or to external, situational factors, such as the stressors a person is experiencing. Because the determinants of many social events and behaviors are unclear, these attributions are not always automatic or trivial.

Psychological Detective

Consider each of the following events:
1. *Your best friend made an excellent grade on her midterm exam.*
2. *An automobile was stolen from the parking lot of a fancy restaurant.*
3. *An anonymous benefactor made a large donation to the local hospital.*
Write a likely explanation (attribution) for each event before reading further.

What causes did you assign to each of these situations? Here are some possibilities:

attribution
The process of assigning causes to events and behaviors

1. Your best friend earned an excellent grade on her midterm exam. Was her grade due to effort (internal cause) or an easy test (external cause)?

TABLE 16-1   **Self-Monitoring Scale**

The following statements concern your personal reactions to a number of situations. No two statements are exactly alike, so consider each statement carefully before answering. If a statement is true or mostly true as applied to you, mark T as your answer. If a statement is false or not usually true as applied to you, mark F as your answer. It is important that you answer frankly and honestly. Scoring instructions and interpretive comments are found at the end of the chapter.

 1. I find it hard to imitate the behavior of other people.
 2. My behavior is usually an expression of my true inner feelings, attitudes, and beliefs.
 3. At parties and social gatherings I do not attempt to do or say things that others will like.
 4. I can only argue for ideas I already believe.
 5. I can make impromptu speeches even on topics about which I have almost no information.
 6. I guess I put on a show to impress or entertain people.
 7. When I am uncertain how to act in a social situation, I look to the behavior of others for cues.
 8. I would probably make a good actor.
 9. I rarely need the advice of my friends to choose movies, books, or music.
10. I sometimes appear to others to be experiencing deeper emotions than I actually am.
11. I laugh more when I watch a comedy with others than when alone.
12. In a group of people, I am rarely the center of attention.
13. In different situations and with different people, I often act like very different persons.
14. I am not particularly good at making other people like me.
15. Even if I am not enjoying myself, I often pretend to be having a good time.
16. I'm not always the person I appear to be.
17. I would not change my opinions (or the way I do things) in order to please someone else or to win his or her favor.
18. I have considered being an entertainer.
19. In order to get along and be liked, I tend to be what people expect me to be rather than anything else.
20. I have never been good at games like charades or improvisational acting.
21. I have trouble changing my behavior to suit different people and different situations.
22. At a party I let others keep the jokes and stories going.
23. I feel a bit awkward in company and do not show up quite so well as I should.
24. I can look anyone in the eye and tell a lie with a straight face (if for a right end).
25. I may deceive people by being friendly when I really dislike them.

Source: Snyder & Gangestad, 1986.

2. An automobile was stolen from the parking lot of a fancy restaurant. Did the theft result from a premeditated plan (internal cause) or peer pressure (external cause)?

3. An anonymous benefactor made a large donation to the local hospital. Was the donation prompted by the desire to help sick people (internal cause) or by the need to have a large tax deduction (external cause)?

Deciding whether the cause of an event or behavior is internal or external has a major impact on the attributional process. If we decide that the behavior has an internal cause, we attribute it to the individual in question; if the behavior has an external cause, we attribute it to the environment. According to Harold Kelley (1967, 1971), factors such as *distinctiveness* (How do the person's responses vary from situation to situation?), *consistency* (Has this behavior occurred before?), and *consensus* (Have others also observed this behavior?) influence our decisions about internal or external causes.

Distinctiveness.   *Distinctiveness* refers to the extent to which a person's responses vary from situation to situation (e.g., Paul likes this modern painting, but not that one). The greater the variability, the higher the distinctiveness.

Consistency.   Our confidence in making attributions regarding internal or external causes is greatest when the behaviors we observe are consistent. For example, suppose that one of the roommates from two doors down the hall on your dormitory floor just came in from class and you hear him yelling at his roommate about the mess in their room. Was the student's angry outburst a reflection of a nasty disposition (internal cause), or does his roommate provoke similar reactions in everyone (external cause)? Unless we have seen the angry student's reactions or the roommate's behavior in similar situations, consistency will be low, and we will not be especially confident in our attribution of a cause.

Consensus.   *Consensus* refers to the reactions of other people to the external object or behavior in question. If everyone agrees that the roommate is a messy slob, there would be a high degree of consensus. If the angry student is the only one who accuses his roommate of being a slob, there would be a low level of consensus. When consensus is high and everyone views the behavior or object in the same manner, we tend to make external attributions; when it is low and no one agrees about the behavior or object in question, we tend to make internal attributions.

High distinctiveness and high consensus lead to an external attribution, whereas low distinctiveness and low consensus lead to an internal attribution. High consistency enables a person to make an attribution, whereas low consistency makes the process of attribution difficult.

The percentage of internal attributions in an individualistic society, such as the United States, increases dramatically starting at about age 11, whereas internal attributions increase only slightly in a collectivist society, such as India (Miller, 1984). The converse pattern is true for external attributions.

Attributional Biases.   We are not as objective as we might think when we make attributions about the causes of behaviors, events, and situations. Various biases can and do influence our attributions. Some of those biases are described in the following pages.

Myth or Science

One of the most prominent myths in our society concerns the belief that individuals can control chance. Dice players believe that throwing the dice in a certain manner results in a high number, whereas throwing the dice in a different manner results in a low number. In one study, college students believed that once a particular number had been rolled with the dice, the person who rolled could roll that number again (Fleming & Darley, 1990). This feeling of control is not limited to dice; it has also been shown for picking lottery numbers (Langer, 1977) and flipping a coin. Despite such widespread belief in one's ability to beat the odds, such behavior is only an illusion of control. In the long run, an unbiased coin always averages half heads and half tails. Fair dice yield high and low numbers regardless of how they are thrown. A particular selection of lottery numbers has no bearing on those actually selected. Why does this illusion persist? Every once in a while a person is reinforced with an appropriate number on a roll of the dice, a lottery ticket pays off, or a coin toss ends as predicted. Behavior does not change the odds. As we saw in Chapter 6, partial reinforcement can cause people to repeat a behavior for a long time.

The Fundamental Attribution Error.   Fritz Heider (1958) pointed out that people tend to pay more attention to the behavior and characteristics of an actor than to the situation in which the behavior occurs. This tendency biases them toward making internal attributions. Think back to the Psychological Detective on page 674. When you wrote explanations about your friend's midterm grade, the automobile that was stolen from the parking lot, and the anonymous benefactor, did you focus on the individuals more than on the situations? This internal attribution bias, which occurs even when strong situational determinants are not present, is termed the **fundamental attribution error.** It becomes especially pronounced when the actor's behavior is unclear and ambiguous (Gilbert et al., 1992).

   Imagine that you have volunteered to participate in a psychology experiment. You arrive at the designated testing room and find it decorated like a television studio. As you enter the room, you are randomly designated as either a contestant or a quizmaster. The quizmasters prepare several general questions, which the contestants try to answer. Without fail, the contestants find themselves unable to answer the questions. When the quiz is over, the intelligence of the quizmasters and contestants is rated. Quizmasters are always rated as smarter than contestants.

Psychological Detective

Is this internal attribution accurate, or are there situational factors that have not been taken into account? If there are such factors, what are they, and why were they overlooked? Jot down some possibilities before reading further.

   Recall that the participants were randomly assigned to either the quizmaster or the contestant role at the beginning of the experiment. The two groups should therefore have been comparable. What occurred next? The quizmasters created the questions that the contestants attempted to answer. This arrangement may have created a problem for the contestants. Who chose the categories of the questions? The quizmasters did. Why might this have created a problem? The contestants were forced to answer questions derived from the quizmasters' areas of greatest knowledge. Because the contestants' areas of greatest knowledge were different, they were placed at a disadvantage. (If you are an expert on sports trivia, it should not be surprising to find that your questions stump people who are not sports enthusiasts.) Yet in making their attributions, both the contestants and the quizmasters overlooked this aspect of the situation. The quizmasters repeatedly stumped the contestants, so they were seen as more intelligent; that is, an internal attribution was made. This experiment (Ross, Amabile, & Steinmetz, 1977) provides a clear example of the fundamental attribution error.

The Actor-Perceiver Bias.   Any behavior that is observed by others can have two attributions—the attribution of the person who performed the behavior (the actor) and the attribution of someone who witnessed the behavior (a perceiver). Are these two attributions likely to be the same?

   Consider the following situations, first from the standpoint of the perceiver and then from that of the actor:

1. A person stumbles and falls down a flight of stairs.
2. A middle-aged man is stopped for speeding.

If you adopt the role of the perceiver and then that of the actor in each of these situations, you should find a difference in your attributions. Perceivers are more

fundamental attribution error
The tendency to attribute behaviors to internal causes

The self-serving bias suggest that we are quick to accept credit for our successes but tend to blame our failures on factors beyond our control.

likely to make internal attributions: *The person* stumbled because he or she is clumsy; *the driver* was stopped for speeding because he did not believe traffic laws applied to him. In the role of the actor, you are more likely to make an external attribution: *I* fell down the stairs because the heel of my shoe came off; *I* was speeding because my speedometer is not accurate. Thus the fundamental attribution error may be committed more frequently by perceivers than by actors.

Self-Serving Bias.   Attributional differences between actors and perceivers lead to the prediction that perceivers make more internal attributions than actors. Another bias, however, may influence the attributions of the actors. So far we have not considered the impact of success and failure on a person's attributions.

Psychological Detective

Will an actor's attributions be different for successful experiences than for failures? Put yourself in each of the following situations:

1. *Your short story has just been accepted for publication in a regional literary magazine.*
2. *Your psychology exam was just returned with a D on it.*

Write down the attribution you would make in each situation before reading further.

Who was responsible for the success of the short story, and who is to blame for the D on the exam? Generally, we are quick to accept credit for our successes and equally quick to blame our failures on factors beyond our control. In short, we tend to make internal attributions when our behaviors are successful and external attributions when we fail (Miller & Ross, 1975). This attributional pattern is called the **self-serving bias.** We can see this bias at work in divorces in which each person claims to be the victim and blames the other person for the breakup (Gray & Silver, 1990). The self-serving bias occurs more often in individualistic societies, such as the United States, but less often in collectivist societies, such as Japan, that stress interdependence, not independence (Markus & Kitayama, 1991).

It is easy to focus on just internal and external issues and lose sight of contextual and cultural factors when considering the process of attribution. Such judgments always take place within a specific context or cultural background, and researchers have shown that these factors can influence the attribution process as much, if not more, than specific internal or external factors that are attended to (Branscombe et al., 1997). These researchers showed that the degree to which individuals identify themselves with the particular culture that is present affects the attribution process. Likewise, the operation of the fundamental attribution error has been shown in several individualistic Western societies (Gilbert & Malone, 1995), but not in the more collectivist culture of India (Miller, 1984).

self-serving bias
The tendency to make internal attributions when we are successful and external attributions when we fail

attitudes
Evaluative judgments about objects, people, and thoughts that include affective, knowledge, and behavioral components

Attitudes

Earlier in the chapter we saw that impression formation involves the judgment of an actor's character by a perceiver. Because impressions are evaluative judgments, they could also be included in the larger category that we call attitudes. **Attitudes** are evaluative judgments, but they are not limited to judgments about people. We form attitudes about objects, people, and thoughts (Petty & Cacioppo, 1996; Petty & Krosnick, 1995). What is your attitude about AIDS, religion, soccer, abortion, opera, politicians, crossword puzzles, plastic surgery, and the death penalty? As these examples indicate, attitudes can be positive, negative, or neutral; they can also vary greatly in intensity. For example, some people feel very strongly about abortion; others do not. Some people are passionate about soccer; others find the game boring. You may have attitudes of differing intensity about a wide variety of subjects, and those attitudes influence many of your thoughts, behaviors, and interactions. For example, intense political attitudes influence our thoughts about society, our behavior toward others with dissimilar views, and the people whom we call our friends.

Components of Attitudes: Affect, Cognition, and Behavior.   Let's say you love rollerblading. Just the thought of strapping on your "blades" brings a smile to your face. For you, there is no greater fun than rollerblading. You also know that rollerblading is excellent exercise and a great way to stay in shape. You have a positive attitude about it.

This description of rollerblading illustrates the three components of an attitude: affect, cognition, and behavior. You love the activity; it's great fun. These feelings highlight the *affective* or *emotional* component; they are an important ingredient in attitudes. The knowledge we have about the object or the focus of our attitude (in this case, rollerblading) constitutes the second, or cognitive, component of an attitude. You understand the health benefits that the activity can bring. Finally, attitudes have a *behavioral* component (McGuire, 1985). Our attitudes prompt us to do or say something. You strap on the "blades" and go outside to enjoy rollerblading.

Now, we don't want to leave you with the impression that these three components always work together perfectly. They don't; sometimes they clash. For example, let's say you love pizza (affective component); however, you have high cholesterol and understand (knowledge component) that eating pizza is bad for your health. Which behavior will your attitude result in, eating pizza or avoiding it? The answer depends on which component happens to be stronger. If you are walking past a pizza restaurant at lunchtime, your emotions and feelings probably will be stronger than your knowledge that pizza may not be the best food for your health. In that instance, you have pizza for lunch. If you are at home trying to decide where to go for dinner, however, the knowledge component may be stronger, and you decide to go where you can eat a healthier meal.

Functions of Attitudes.   Although it is easy to see that we all have attitudes, it is more difficult to understand why we have them and what their purpose is. Attitudes serve several distinct functions (Katz, 1960): ego defense, adjustment, and knowledge.

Ego Defense.   Attitudes protect us from threats to the self or ego. If a person makes statements that we perceive as threatening, we might say, "He makes comments like that because he's a dumb jock (writer, bookworm, musician)." Attributing threatening statements to the type of individual making them allows us to avoid confronting the possibility that the statements are accurate.

Adjustment.   Attitudes are used to maximize reinforcements and minimize punishments from the environment. People and behaviors that yield reinforcement are viewed positively; those that yield unpleasant effects are viewed negatively. For example, an individual who is being reinforced on a new job would be likely to say, "I am very impressed with the supervisors on my new job. They are friendly, fair, and understanding people."

Knowledge.   Attitudes can help bring order and meaning to one's world. For example, the following attitudes may help a person who is trying to understand

Likert scale

Questionnaire that requires individuals to indicate their degree of agreement or disagreement with a set of statements

an apparently unjust situation: "Most football players have skills that others lack. That's why they are paid such incredibly high salaries."

Measuring Attitudes. Theoretically, it should be simple to measure attitudes—just ask individuals to tell you their attitudes. Self-reports are often used to measure attitudes, but this method is far from simple. The types of questions asked, as well as the way they are asked, can influence the responses. For example, some people may try to hide their true feelings about sensitive topics such as AIDS, abortion, or the death penalty. Therefore psychologists have developed several other measurement techniques. Among them are Likert scales and behavioral measures.

Likert Scales. **Likert scales** are questionnaires that require participants to indicate the extent to which they agree or disagree with particular statements. As with other types of self-report, honesty of responses can't really be ascertained with these scales. See Figure 16-1 for examples of Likert scale items. The advantage of Likert scales is that they are easily quantified, which enables investigators to make comparisons among different groups of individuals. In addition, several items can be combined to form an attitude scale. For example, the question about recycling could be used in a scale that measured attitudes toward various aspects of environmental protection. Such scales can be developed to measure attitudes toward literally any topic.

Behavioral Measures. The saying "actions speak louder than words" indicates that we place considerable value on the behavioral component of attitudes. For example, if we tell others that energy conservation is a good cause, we are expected to be willing to invest time and effort in conservation activities, such as planting trees or stuffing envelopes to raise funds for conservation.

The attitudes we express to others may not, however, coincide with our actual behaviors. For example, in a study of academic dishonesty (cheating), Stephen Davis and his colleagues (1992) found that over 90 percent of their college-student respondents felt that cheating is wrong. However, between 40 and 60 percent of the same participants reported they had cheated on at least

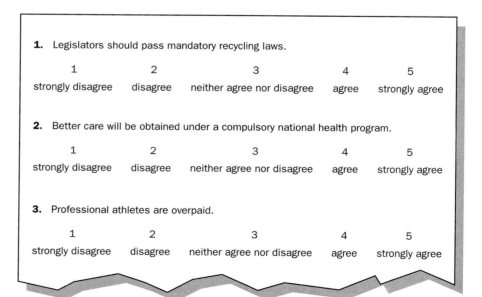

FIGURE 16-1 Examples of Likert scale items.

one exam (Davis & Ludvigson, 1995). Clearly these participants' expressed attitudes did not coincide with their behaviors. Because expressed attitudes do not always coincide with behaviors, it is important to observe the behavior of participants in addition to obtaining self-reports of their attitudes.

How Are Attitudes Formed?   The process of attitude formation has been of interest to social psychologists for many years. If we understood this process, we could apply it in numerous real-life situations. For example, we could create favorable attitudes about particular politicians, toothpastes, and automobiles. In turn, those attitudes might lead to behaviors that would be financially rewarding to us. Because of the attitudes we had created, people would now be purchasing the toothpaste and automobiles that we manufactured and electing politicians who shared our views.

Learning.   Attitudes can be acquired through the process of classical conditioning (see Chapter 6), in which a conditioned stimulus (CS) comes to elicit a conditioned response (CR). When classical conditioning takes place, we also develop an attitude toward the CS; we either like it or dislike it. For example, assume that the sight of food (CS) has been paired with a mild electric shock (unconditioned stimulus, US). After this procedure has been repeated several times with several different types of food, what is your attitude toward the sight of food? It should be rather negative. This procedure is used in weight-reduction programs in cases of extreme obesity.

Operant conditioning can also serve as a basis for the establishment of attitudes. Behaviors that result in reinforcement produce positive attitudes, whereas behaviors that result in punishment produce negative attitudes. For example, children whose schoolwork is praised develop positive attitudes toward school; children whose schoolwork is continually criticized develop negative attitudes toward school.

Cognitive Dissonance.   In 1957, Leon Festinger proposed that a condition known as **cognitive dissonance** occurs when a person experiences an inconsistency between thoughts and behaviors. Because cognitive dissonance is an unpleasant or aversive state, we seek to reduce it and instead create *cognitive consonance*—the state in which behaviors and thoughts are compatible. Recall the example of the person who was concerned about cholesterol and high-fat foods but who loved to eat pizza. Here we have dissonant thoughts and behaviors. The dissonance in this situation could be resolved by finding reasons to distrust the medical advice about cholesterol or by finding new reasons to avoid eating pizza. In either instance, the individual would strengthen an attitude about an object or event in his or her environment. Thus the formation of new attitudes is involved in the reduction of cognitive dissonance.

Attitudes are at the core of interpersonal relations. We consider this topic in the next section.

cognitive dissonance
Aversive state produced when an individual has two incompatible thoughts or cognitions simultaneously

Review Summary

1. Social psychology examines the causes, types, and consequences of human interaction.

2. Cultural differences, such as **individualism** (in which the individual's goals are most important) versus **collectivism** (in which group goals are most important), can influence the results of social psychological research.

Researchers need to avoid **ethnocentrism** (viewing all cultures as an inferior extension of their own).

3. Impression formation requires an actor and a perceiver. The views of the perceiver, as well as the appearance and behaviors of the actor, influence the impression of the actor that is formed by the perceiver.

4. Stereotypes are negative or positive sets of beliefs about members of particular groups. They reduce the amount of information that must be processed and are very resistant to change because we tend selectively to notice behaviors that confirm our stereotypes. What's more, our treatment of other people as prompted by our stereotypes often brings forth the very behaviors that we associate with our stereotypes of those people.

5. Some **self-disclosure** fosters a positive impression, but excessive self-disclosure early in a relationship may result in a negative first impression.

6. The process of **attribution** involves deciding why certain events occurred and why certain people behaved as they did. With internal attributions, behavior is seen as being caused by factors that reside within a person. With external attributions, the causes of behavior are viewed as residing outside an individual. We are more confident in

our attributions when behaviors are consistent and have also been witnessed by others. The **fundamental attribution error** occurs when internal factors are emphasized to the exclusion of external or situational factors.

7. Perceivers' attributions may be biased toward internal attributions, whereas actors are biased toward external attributions, especially when failure is involved.

8. Attitudes are evaluative judgments (negative, positive, or neutral) that are formed about people, places, and things. Affect, cognition, and behavior are the three components of an attitude.

9. Attitudes can serve ego-defensive, adjustment, and knowledge functions. They can be measured by **Likert scales** and evaluation of observed behaviors. Learning (classical and operant conditioning) and reduction of **cognitive dissonance** lead to the formation of attitudes.

Study Break

1. What factor makes social psychology different from other areas of psychology?
2. Viewing other cultures as an extension of one's own culture best describes
   a. ethnocentrism.
   b. cultural bias.
   c. nationalism.
   d. the just-world stereotype.
3. Match the following terms with their definitions.
   a. Forming an opinion about another person
   b. Set of beliefs about members of a particular group
   c. Amount of personal information an individual is willing to share
   d. Process by which we assign a cause to events and behaviors
   e. Bias toward internal attribution
   f. Evaluative judgment of a person or object

   1. Self-disclosure
   2. Attitudes
   3. Impression formation
   4. Fundamental attribution error
   5. Stereotype
   6. Attribution
4. Describe the "beautiful is good" stereotype.
5. When your behaviors influence others to respond the way you expect them to respond, what has occurred?
   a. a stereotype
   b. an expectation
   c. a self-fulfilling prophecy
   d. a behavioral-outcome prediction
6. You spend a few minutes talking with a new acquaintance after class. He tells you several interesting things about himself, and you form a favorable impression of him. What process has facilitated impression formation in this case?
7. Your best friend has been acting rather cool toward you lately. As you try to decide why your friend is acting in this manner, you are engaging in
   a. attribution.
   b. causality analysis.
   c. ascribing values.
   d. stereotyping.
8. Explain how consistency and consensus are related to the attribution process.
9. What types of attributions do perceivers tend to make? What types do actors tend to make?
10. Evaluative judgments about people, objects, or things are known as
    a. stereotypes.
    b. cognitions.
    c. attitudes.
    d. attributions.
11. Attitudes serve all the following functions except
    a. value knowledge.
    b. adjustment.
    c. ego defense.
    d. insulation.
12. When we watch *Jeopardy* and conclude that Alex Trebek must be a genius, we fall prey to
    a. the internal attribution bias.
    b. the fundamental attribution error.
    c. the attribution illusion.
    d. stereotyping.

Interpersonal Relations

attraction
The extent to which we like or dislike other people

Whenever Bonny has a problem that she cannot solve, she calls her best friend, Kathleen. Kathleen does the same. These two friends originally met nearly 20 years ago. Since then Bonny and her family have moved several times; they now live thousands of miles from Kathleen. Despite the distance and very infrequent visits, their friendship remains as strong as ever. *What factors or behaviors serve to maintain friendships?* ▪

During their lives, people form several kinds of interpersonal relationships. Some individuals become close friends; others remain casual acquaintances. The establishment of good interpersonal relationships is one key to a successful adjustment to society. In this section we examine the factors that cause us to be attracted to others (interpersonal attraction), as well as those that lead us to help or hurt others.

Attraction

Attraction refers to the extent to which we like or dislike other people. In this instance, our attitudes deal exclusively with others. How often do you find yourself saying, "I was naturally attracted to that person"? If someone asked you exactly what you meant by that statement, what would you say? What are the factors that attract us to others?

Proximity. Proximity to others is positively related to the establishment of friendships; people who live or work near us tend to become our friends. For example, apartment dwellers are often attracted to individuals who live in nearby apartments (Nahemow & Lawton, 1975; see Figure 16-2). Likewise, police trainees who were assigned alphabetically to seats in a class reported having friends whose last names started with the same letter as theirs or with the adjacent letters (Segal, 1974).

Proximity is an important determinant of attraction because it encourages interaction and repeated exposure (Moreland & Zajonc, 1982). The more frequent the contact, the greater the positive attraction; repeated contact turns a stranger into a familiar individual. (Just to make the picture complete, keep in mind that frequent contact can also intensify negative feelings. For example, repeated interaction with an annoying co-worker may increase dislike for that person.)

Affect and Emotions. "Laugh, and the world laughs with you," wrote the poet Ella Wheeler Wilcox. Research supports her observation—a person's affect or emotional state can influence attraction (Forgas, 1992; Zajonc & McIntosh, 1992). We are attracted to people who arouse positive feeling in us; we avoid individuals who arouse negative feelings. For example, what are you likely to do when you hear someone laugh? Most people join in the laughter, even if they don't know why they are laughing (see Chapter 4) (Provine, 1992). The converse can be said for the effect of sad moods (Sullins, 1991).

In addition to one's emotional state, the nature of our social interaction is an important ingredient in

FIGURE 16-2 People who live in apartment buildings tend to have friends who live in nearby apartments.

Source: Adapted from Nahemow & Lawton, 1975.

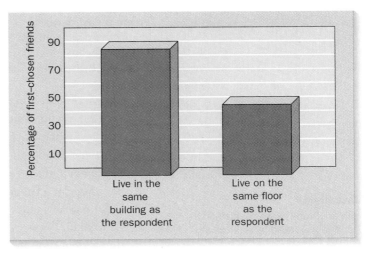

creating affect. For example, the type of opening line that is used in speaking to a stranger can determine attraction. Consider the following: You are sitting next to a stranger in the local laundromat waiting for your clothes to finish washing. Which of the following lines would elicit a positive response from you (Kleinke, Meeker, & Staneski, 1986): "Want to have a cup of coffee while we're waiting?" or "Those are some nice undies you have there"? Generally, direct opening lines are rated as more likable (positive) than cute or flippant opening lines (Kleinke & Dean, 1990).

Why are emotions and affect important to attraction? The principle of reinforcement (see Chapter 6) gives us a clue.

Reinforcement. Let's say that you're having a conversation with a new acquaintance. If that person pays you several compliments that make you feel good (positive reinforcers), you are more likely to be attracted to that person. Similarly, positive *affects,* such as laughing and smiling, also make us feel good. We like people who reward us and tend to dislike or avoid those who do not (Reisbult, 1980).

Similarity. We are also attracted to and make friends with people who are similar to ourselves (Moghaddam, 1994; Neimeyer & Mitchell, 1988). It has been shown that, in addition to such observable characteristics as race, age, and sex, similarity of attitudes, beliefs, and values is very important in the development of attraction. For example, Theodore Newcomb (1961) found that attitude similarity played a major role in the development of friendships among transfer students living in a boardinghouse at the University of Michigan. Research has shown, however, that similarity may not be such a powerful determinant of attraction in all cultures. For example, because the Japanese culture recognizes and values status more highly than our equality-oriented American culture does, the Japanese are more attracted to individuals of superior status (Nakao, 1987).

Our feelings toward another person can affect our perceptions of similarity. In general, the more we like an individual, the more we perceive that person as being similar to us. For example, men overestimate the similarity between themselves and a woman in whom they have a romantic interest (Gold, Ryckman, & Mosley, 1984).

Similarity can have positive benefits in a relationship. For example, the more similar a husband and wife, the lower the likelihood they will divorce, and the less their personalities change over time (Caspi & Herbener, 1990).

As we have suggested, being positively attracted to someone can lead to the development of a friendship. How does friendship differ from attraction?

Friendship

Unlike a casual relationship or chance attraction, a **friendship** is an interpersonal attraction that involves a set of rules, often informal, that must be followed if the friendship is to survive. Michael Argyle and Monica Henderson (1984) identified nine such rules:

1. Show emotional support.
2. Volunteer help in time of need.
3. Strive to make a friend happy when in each other's company.
4. Trust and confide in each other.
5. Share news of success with a friend.
6. Stand up for a friend in his or her absence.
7. Don't nag a friend.
8. Be tolerant of (other) friends.
9. Repay debts and favors.

friendship

Form of interpersonal attraction that is governed by an implicit set of rules

Friendships do not simply happen. Certain factors are important in the development of a friendship. In addition to the factors such as proximity, affect and emotions, reinforcement, and similarity that are important for establishing the attraction that underlies a friendship, self-disclosure is also an important factor.

Self-disclosure.   We saw earlier that self-disclosure influences the process of impression formation; it also influences the formation of friendships. We are more likely to form friendships with people who are willing to disclose information about themselves. Our level of self-disclosure evolves through several stages as a friendship develops. In the initial stage, we disclose relatively unimportant information. If these self-disclosures are reciprocated, subsequent disclosures will be more personal. Through this process the self-disclosures become progressively more personal, and the friendship becomes stronger. If the level of self-disclosure does not become more intimate or personal, the friendship stagnates. This is why we tend to have a group of casual friends who are in the category of "speaking acquaintances"; our level of self-disclosure with these individuals probably will not increase.

Love

Although most of us would agree that there is a difference between friendship and love, defining love is difficult. Is love the emotion that accompanies sexual attraction? Is it a stronger form of friendship that we reserve for our children, our parents, and other family members? Theorists have proposed that there are actually several types of love. For example, a distinction is often made between passionate and companionate love (E. Walster & G. W. Walster, 1978). **Passionate love** is a transitory form of love characterized by strong emotional reactions and arousal, sexual desires, and fantasies. Passionate love is another area in which researchers have found cultural differences. For example, German and American students place a higher value on romantic love than Japanese students do (Simmons, vom Kolke, & Shimizu, 1986). This difference may be due to the fact that Japanese women assume a more dependent role than American and German women or to the fact that love does not have as positive a connotation in Japan as in the other two countries. There is a tendency for more expressions of intimacy in individualistic countries, such as the United States, than in collectivist countries, such as Japan (Ting-Toomey, 1991).

Companionate love is characterized by a long-term relationship and commitment. Even though most relationships begin with passionate love, companionate love must develop if the relationship is to survive.

The passionate-companionate distinction is not the only psychological model of love. For example, Clyde and Susan Hendrick (1986) propose the existence of six different types of love, giving them names derived from their ancient Greek equivalents:

> *eros*—romantic, passionate love
> *ludus* (loo´dus)—game-playing love
> *storge* (stor´gay)—friendship love
> *mania*—possessive, dependent love
> *pragma*—logical, "shopping list" love
> *agape* (ah´gah-pay)—all-giving, selfless love

Use of the Hendricks' (1986) questionnaire designed to measure these six types of love has revealed cultural differences in the expression of *storge* (friendship love) (Murstein, Merighi, & Vyse, 1991). American students score higher on this type of love than French students do. This difference may be due to the

passionate love
Transitory form of love that involves strong emotional reactions, sexual desires, and fantasies

companionate love
Long-lasting form of love that involves commitment

fact that Americans are more expressive and have lower levels of self-control than the French.

Despite the complexity of love relationships and the difficulty of defining them, researchers have identified a number of factors that influence love relationships. These factors include sex roles, the presence of children, and the degree of dependence of each partner on the other.

Sex Roles.   As shown in Chapters 9 and 11, boys and girls learn to engage in different patterns of behavior. These childhood sex roles influence their behavior as adults. The sex roles of men and women often reflect the stereotypes of maleness and femaleness prevailing in the culture in which they were raised. For example, Abbey (1982) found that men perceived the dating behaviors of women more sexually than women perceived those of men; friendliness on a woman's part was seen as reflecting a desire for sex. What's more, men in our society traditionally have been expected to initiate sexual activity, and women are expected to react to their advances. Research has verified this predicted pattern: Men made sexual advances, and women resisted (Muehlenhard & Hollabaugh, 1988). Although such sex role stereotypes are still prevalent, however, recent research indicates that they are changing. For example, Robin Kowalski (1993) has shown that men who have accepted the changing roles of women in our society do not misperceive the dating behaviors of women.

Marital Satisfaction and Dissatisfaction.   A longitudinal view of the love relationship is provided through the study of marital satisfaction. Typically, marital satisfaction is described as a U-shaped function; satisfaction is high during the early years of marriage, decreases during the middle years, and increases during the later years (Spanier, Lewis, & Cole, 1975). The decrease in satisfaction during the middle years of marriage is associated with having and raising children (Glenn & McLanahan, 1982); the responsibilities of raising children can take a significant toll on a marriage. Predictably, the increase in marital satisfaction during the later years is linked to the fact that the children have grown up and left home, thus enabling the partners to rediscover that which brought them together initially.

Unfortunately, some marriages go beyond mere dissatisfaction. A conservative estimate places the number of women in the United States who are beaten by their intimate partners at 1.6 million annually (Gelles & Strauss, 1988): "That a tremendous amount of violence takes place within intimate relationships, the very relationships integral to human existence, is a given reality in our society" (Stuart & Campbell, 1989, p. 246).

Psychological Detective

Glenda is a battered spouse. For the past seven years her marriage has been a nightmare. More often than not, she goes to work with several black-and-blue marks. It is difficult to cover the signs of the abuse she receives. Several of her friends have pleaded with her to leave her husband, but for some reason she cannot bring herself to make the break. Why does Glenda continue to stay in an abusive marriage? Write down some possible reasons before you continue reading.

interdependence theory
Theory of interpersonal relationships that stresses the costs and rewards involved

Social psychologists have provided some insight into why such abusive relationships persist. **Interdependence theory** (Thibault & Kelley, 1959) takes into account the costs and rewards involved in a relationship, as well as the available alternatives. Here's how the theory works. Each person develops a

comparison level (CL); this CL is the general outcome you expect from a relationship. Your CL is based on your past experiences and the experiences of others (such as your parents and friends) in similar situations. You are satisfied with a relationship when the outcomes are equal to or above your CL. You become dissatisfied when the outcomes fall below your CL. The more the outcomes in a relationship fall below your CL, the more dissatisfied you become. It is important to remember that different individuals may have very different CLs. We cannot assume that everyone sees the world exactly as we do.

When do you leave a relationship? It is predictable that we would leave a relationship when the outcomes fall below our CL. Surprisingly, this action seldom occurs; we continue to find ourselves in relationships that are not satisfying. Why? According to interdependence theory, we also develop a CL for alternative relationships. Given this information, we can say that we will leave a relationship when the outcomes for that relationship fall below our CL for relationships in general and our CL for alternative relationships.

Why does Glenda continue to stay in an abusive marriage? Although we would expect that the outcomes of this relationship are below her CL, the alternatives are even worse: Glenda has no family, her self-esteem is low (Blackman, 1990), and her educational training prepared her only for jobs that pay the minimum wage. There also may be cultural imperatives that place a premium on the intact family unit and view divorce as unacceptable. Thus the outcomes for the current relationship do not fall below Glenda's CL for the alternative relationships she perceives as available to her. To test your understanding of interdependence theory, try turning the tables and ask the question, "Why does Glenda's husband continue to batter?" What factors keep this behavior above his CL for other relationships?

Prosocial Behavior: Helping Others

Behavior that benefits society or helps others is called **prosocial behavior.** One of the most widely studied forms of prosocial behavior is **altruism,** or helping behavior that is performed voluntarily for the benefit of another person, with no anticipation of reward (Walster & Piliavin, 1972). Examples of altruistic behaviors abound. Individuals have faced great danger to save others from situations such as drowning or being hurt in an automobile accident, burned in a fire, or injured in combat.

True instances of altruism are rare and difficult to document. It is virtually impossible to prove that an altruistic person is not rewarded in some way for his or her actions. Some theorists, such as Robert Cialdini and his colleagues (1987), feel that altruistic behavior always involves a reward of some kind. The reward may be extrinsic (money or praise) or intrinsic (a boost to the ego). Because it cannot be shown that intrinsic rewards are lacking, Cialdini and his colleagues question the existence of true altruism.

In contrast, Daniel Batson and his colleagues (1988; Batson, 1991) contend that altruism is a genuine phenomenon. The defining characteristics of altruism are empathy (an emotional reaction to the suffering of another person that produces the desire to help) and exceptionally small and uncertain rewards. When these characteristics are not present, Batson agrees with Cialdini that some selfish motive is involved and that true altruism is not being shown. Thus soldiers who cover an exploding grenade with their own bodies to protect their comrades are showing altruism, whereas a person who donates blood, wears a sticker announcing this fact, and receives the admiration of friends may not be altruistic.

Regardless of whether a reinforcer or a selfish motive is involved, individuals who display high levels of prosocial behavior have certain characteristics. For

comparison level
General outcome expected from a particular relationship

prosocial behavior
Behavior that benefits society or helps others

altruism
Helping behavior performed voluntarily with no anticipation of reward

bystander effect
The tendency for a group of bystanders to be less likely than an individual to provide assistance to a person in trouble

example, a study of female Japanese undergraduate students conducted by Takako Suzuki (1992) indicated that higher levels of prosocial behavior are positively correlated with empathy, social skills, and extraversion. The positive influence of empathy on prosocial behavior has also been shown in research on children (Bengtson & Johnson, 1992) and may even be related to parenting style (Dekovic & Janssens, 1992). These positive characteristics also are shown by individuals who have accepted the care of a spouse who is suffering from a long-term, chronic illness (Thompson & Pitts, 1992). Notice that we are using cross-cultural research to reach a generalized conclusion; prosocial people may be similar across cultures.

Situational and Personal Influences on Helping Behavior.   Most of us do not demonstrate prosocial behavior whenever an opportunity presents itself. We are reluctant to stop for hitchhikers on the highway; we give the cold shoulder to people asking for handouts on street corners; appeals from the Big Brothers and Big Sisters fall on deaf ears. Why? Research has shown that situational and personal influences may determine whether we are willing to help.

Much of the research on the factors influencing helping behavior has focused on the so-called bystander effect. We all hope that someone will come to our aid if we are in trouble—say, if we are being robbed. Unfortunately, this does not always happen. In a famous incident that occurred in 1964 in the Queens borough of New York City, a young woman named Kitty Genovese was stabbed to death. An especially horrifying aspect of her murder was the fact that the killer attacked the woman three separate times over the course of half an hour, during which time at least 38 people saw the attacks or heard the woman's screams. The killer was frightened off twice when people turned on their lights or called from their windows. On both occasions, however, he resumed his attack. None of the people who witnessed the attack came to the victim's aid, and no one called the police while she was being attacked. Why?

Two social psychologists, John Darley and Bibb Latané, provided some of the answers. Their laboratory studies demonstrated that individuals are more likely to give assistance when they are alone than when other people are present (Darley & Latané, 1968). As you can see in Figure 16-3, a person who appeared to be having a seizure was very likely to receive assistance when the person providing the assistance was alone. The finding that groups of bystanders are less likely than individuals to aid a person in trouble is known as the **bystander effect.**

Among the factors that determine the bystander effect are degree of danger, embarrassment, not knowing how to help, and diffusion of responsibility.

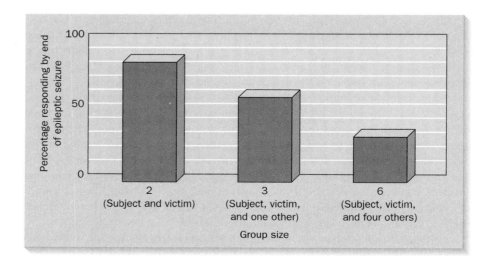

FIGURE 16-3 Effect of group size on the likelihood of helping the victim of an apparent epileptic seizure. As group size increased, the likelihood of helping decreased.

Source: Darley & Latané, 1968.

Certainly there was a potential for great danger in the Kitty Genovese situation; the involved risks prevented many of the bystanders from coming to her aid. Likewise, it would be difficult to know how to help in such a situation.

Potential embarrassment can also cause people to avoid lending assistance. Suppose a man has fallen in a subway car. Would you help him if he was carrying a cane? What if he was carrying a bottle in a brown paper sack and reeked of alcohol? An experiment was conducted to answer these questions. Even though the same person played both roles, help was given much more often when he carried the cane than when he carried the brown bag (Piliavin, Rodin, & Piliavin, 1969). Bystanders may have been unwilling to help in the latter case because the unpredictable behavior of the "drunk" could have created an embarrassing situation. One explanation of the way embarrassment operates in such situations is particularly intriguing. According to Darley and Latané, many emergency situations are ambiguous. To define the situation, people look to others. While doing this they want to avoid embarrassment, so they "act cool." Everyone else does the same thing. So what you see is everyone acting cool; no one appears concerned. This situation results in *pluralistic ignorance;* everyone is fooled into thinking that there is nothing to be concerned about.

Similarly, research has shown that people are less likely to help when the situation is perceived as serious (Staub & Baer, 1974). Most of us are not competent to help seriously injured people; we could do more harm than good. Likewise, most people are more reluctant to offer assistance in a foreign country. They fear that they will do something wrong. Such factors, however, should not prevent us from calling the police for assistance.

Finally, when other people are present, the responsibility for acting is shared. Therefore the responsibility of each member of the group is lower than it would be for an individual. As a result of this diffusion of responsibility, each person is less likely to help the person in distress.

Aggression

The converse of prosocial behavior is aggression. **Aggression** is any physical or psychological behavior that is performed with the intent of harming someone or something. This definition indicates that aggressive behavior is intentional; there is a deliberate intent to do harm. Deliberately hitting someone and yelling at an annoying driver are both aggressive behaviors.

At least two major types of aggression have been identified (Buss, 1961). **Hostile aggression** occurs when a person is angry or annoyed with someone else; the goal is to harm the other person (Berkowitz, 1994). Most murders tend to be impulsive, emotional acts of hostile aggression. **Instrumental aggression** is performed to achieve a goal. For example, a robber may attack a victim to steal something, not because the robber is angry with the victim, but because the aggressive behavior is instrumental in achieving the intended goal.

Biological Views of Aggression. Ethologists believe that at least some forms of aggression are inherited. Most territorial disputes among animals, however, do not result in physical damage or death. Konrad Lorenz (1966) believes that animals instinctively refrain from using their natural weapons, such as claws, horns, and fangs, to kill their opponents in aggressive conflicts. The conflict ends when the loser acknowledges defeat by displaying submissive behavior. Modern wars, in which thousands of people are killed, demonstrate that humans have not developed a comparable instinct.

Another biological view of aggression was suggested by the sociobiologist Edward O. Wilson (1975). According to *sociobiology,* the goal of all behavior is

aggression
Physical or psychological behavior that is performed with the intent of doing harm

hostile aggression
Aggressive behavior that is performed with the specific intent of harming another person

instrumental aggression
Aggression that causes harm in the process of achieving another goal

frustration-aggression hypothesis

The hypothesis that aggression is likely to occur when a person is frustrated

to increase the survival of one's own genes. The winner of an aggressive encounter has access to food, shelter, and mates. Winners survive to perpetuate their genes, whereas losers may perish. Hence sociobiologists see aggression as an adaptive response.

Environmental Conditions and Aggression. Although ethologists and sociobiologists argue that aggression is part of human nature, other psychologists stress the importance of environmental factors in producing aggressive behavior. Among the explanations they have proposed is the **frustration-aggression hypothesis** (Dollard et al., 1939). According to this hypothesis, an individual, when frustrated, is likely to act aggressively. *Frustration* is defined as being blocked from attaining a goal.

Consider an example. The decision to take a summer job as a construction worker seemed like a great idea at the time. The pay was reasonably good, and the physical labor would keep you in shape. After two days on the job, you are questioning your sanity. Your body aches, the heat is unbearable, and you feel as though you are about to die of thirst. Finally it's time for a break. You head for the water cooler stored in your car, only to find that you forgot to refill it this morning. No problem, a cool soft drink will do just as well. But after three tries, you find that the vending machine is still returning your money. How will you respond?

The chances are quite good that you will direct some aggressive responses toward the machine. Some of those responses may be verbal; others, such as shoves, kicks, and hits, may be physical. Your frustration has led to aggression.

Since its publication in 1939, the frustration-aggression hypothesis has generated considerable research. Much of this research indicates that aggression results from a variety of frustrating conditions.

Psychological Detective

 Put yourself in the following situation. You have been waiting in line for a long time to purchase concert tickets; you are now second in line. Your turn is next, but someone cuts in ahead of you. Is this frustrating? Will you act aggressively? Would you be less aggressive if you were twelfth in line when someone cut in? Write down your answers to these questions before reading further.

Mary Harris (1974) conducted this experiment in theater and grocery store lines. She found that cutting in front of the second person in line resulted in more aggression than cutting in front of the twelfth person. In other words, the closer you are to your goal, the more frustrated you become when you are blocked from attaining it. Harris concluded that aggressiveness is directly related to level of frustration: The greater the frustration, the greater the aggression.

After several decades of research on the frustration-aggression hypothesis, it became apparent that a third factor must be involved. Why does frustration lead to aggression in some instances but not in others? Anger seems to be the answer. If the frustrating event does not result in anger, the probability that aggressive behavior will be displayed is reduced (Krebs & Miller, 1985).

Leonard Berkowitz (1984) contends that in addition to frustration and anger, cues for aggressive responding must also be present. Those cues elicit an aggressive response when frustration has caused anger. What are those cues? Visual images that suggest aggression may be one such cue. Although some studies have shown that there is a relationship between viewing violence on television and engaging in violent behavior (e.g., Friedrich-Cofer & Huston,

1986; Roberts & Maccoby, 1985), this relationship may not be universal. Other studies have shown that television violence does not lead to increased displays of violence in all societies (Huesmann & Eron, 1986). Cultural differences (Levine, 1996) and personality differences (Bushman, 1996) are important factors in determining the effects of television violence.

Additional Environmental Cues.   Anger and cues for aggressive behavior do not occur only in conjunction with frustration. We can expect aggressive behavior to occur in other situations besides those that are frustrating. For example, verbal and physical attacks frequently provoke aggressive behaviors (Berkowitz, 1965; Taylor & Pasano, 1971). How do many drivers react to motorists who yell and make rude gestures on a congested highway? How would you react to someone who rear-ended your brand-new car?

Inequity, the perception of unfair treatment, is frequently overlooked as a cause of aggression (Walster, Walster, & Berscheid, 1978). The civil strife that broke out in South Africa in the late 1980s and early 1990s reflects aggressive behaviors designed to protest racial inequities. The same analysis can be applied to inner-city riots in the United States. The riots that erupted in Los Angeles in March 1992, when four police officers on trial for beating a black motorist were found not guilty, are a good example of the latter situation.

Adverse environmental conditions can also lead to aggression (Ulrich & Azrin, 1962). Let the air-conditioning fail on a hot summer day and you will see a dramatic rise in anger and aggressive behavior. Similarly, the number of batters hit by pitches during baseball games is directly related to the temperature: As the temperature increases, the number of batters who are hit also increases (Reifman, Larrick, & Fein, 1991).

An individual's level of general arousal also may contribute to aggression (Zillman, 1979). Even though the precipitating event may have occurred at an earlier time, sufficient arousal may remain to enhance or strengthen a subsequent aggressive response. Imagine that you completed a five-mile jog a few minutes ago and are quietly resting on the grass before heading home. Someone comes by and insults you. You are more likely to become aggressive under these conditions than you would if you had not jogged (Bryant & Zillman, 1979). Why? Some of the arousal that was generated during your jog is still present and serves to energize the aggressive response.

So far we have considered aggression from the standpoint of individuals. This approach reflects an American view of conflict and aggression, but it is not the only approach to understanding such behaviors. European psychologists, for example, place more emphasis on the extent to which groups and socioeconomic levels influence conflict (Hewstone, 1988). Social psychologist Fathali Moghaddam (1990) has effectively drawn our attention to the need for psychologists to study the concerns, values, and needs of other cultures. Only when other cultures are taken into account will our picture of these and other behaviors be complete.

Sexual Aggression.   As discussed earlier, many marriages are characterized by abuse and aggression, which is most often directed toward the wife. The dramatic increase in the incidence of rape indicates that such aggression and abuse are not limited to marital relationships (Goodman, Koss, & Russo, 1993a, 1993b). The extent of this problem is staggering. For example, crime reports from the Federal Bureau of Investigation indicate that in the early 1990s, rapes occurred at the rate of one every five minutes. These are the known cases of rape; many others go unreported (Bachman, 1994; Koss, 1992).

Motivated by both scientific and social concerns, psychologists have investigated sexual aggression. What have they learned? What factors contribute to the increasing number of rapes?

The increased availability and tolerance of pornography, especially pornography depicting violence and domination, are correlated with the increase in sexual assaults. For example, one study found that sales of sexually explicit magazines were positively correlated with the rape rate in all 50 states (Baron & Straus, 1984). A Canadian investigation (Marshall, 1989) found that rapists and child molesters viewed pornographic materials more often than non–sex offenders. Because pornography supports the myth that women enjoy sexual abuse and aggression, these findings should not be surprising.

What can be done to reduce sexual aggression toward women? One obvious answer would be to bring the creation and distribution of pornography under the control of state or federal laws. John Court (1984) reports that in countries in which pornography is controlled, the incidence of rape is lower. Other psychologists, such as Edward Donnerstein, feel that increasing the public's awareness of women's true feelings about sexual aggression and the psychological devastation created by rape would also be an effective deterrent (Donnerstein, Linz, & Penrod, 1987). Does this view represent wishful thinking? Can a media awareness campaign really have an effect? The answer may be yes. Alcohol and tobacco are not illegal, yet health concerns, highlighted by extensive media coverage, have resulted in a substantial decrease in consumption of both products.

Many unreported rapes fall into the category of date or acquaintance rape (Benson, Charlton, & Goodhart, 1992; Craig, 1990; Wiehe & Richards, 1995). In many instances date rape may be a result of misperceptions, especially on the part of the man. For example, research conducted by Tracy Bostwick and Janice De Lucia (1992) investigated perceived desire for sex. They presented their participants with several dating scenarios. Except for varying the party who asked for the date and the party who paid for it, the scenarios were the same. Even though there is no proven relationship between these behaviors and desire for sex, when the woman asked for the date and paid the bill, she was perceived as having a greater desire for sex than when the man asked and paid the bill. Likewise, men believed that sexual aggression was more justified when the man had paid all of the date's expenses (Cornett & Shuntick, 1991). In short, some women may be trapped in the dating relationship: If a woman asks and pays for the date, she is assumed to desire sex; if the man pays for the date, he may feel that he has the right to demand sex.

There are additional factors that contribute to the prevalence of date rape. The length of the steady dating relationship is positively related to men's perception of the acceptability of date rape: The longer the dating relationship, the more acceptable date rape is perceived to be (Bridges, 1991). Heavy alcohol consumption is another factor that often leads to date rape on college campuses (Abbey, 1991). Again, the explanations for this joint occurrence of alcohol consumption and date rape suggest that men often misinterpret the sexual desires of women and that men frequently use the supposed liberating effects of alcohol as a justification for sexual behavior (see Chapter 5).

To help college women deal with the threat of date or acquaintance rape, some authorities (Cummings, 1992) have advocated courses in defense training. Critics argue that such programs do not adequately prepare the women and thus give them a false sense of security. Other authorities (Lenihan, Rawlins, & Eberly, 1992) have explored the effectiveness of a date or acquaintance rape education program. Although such a program was effective in raising women's sensitivity to potentially dangerous situations, it had no influence on the men's attitudes. More effective solutions for this problem are needed.

Having looked at interpersonal relations, we next examine the effects of social influences on our behaviors. Have you ever bought something only to get home and wonder why you made that purchase? We will find out what makes a good salesperson in the next section.

Review Summary

1. Attraction is the extent to which we like or dislike other people. Attraction is determined by proximity, affect and emotions, reinforcement, and similarity.

2. Friendship is a form of interpersonal attraction that involves a set of unwritten rules.

3. Passionate love is characterized by strong emotional reactions, sexual desire, and fantasies. **Companionate love** is characterized by a long-term relationship and commitment. Several other types of love have been proposed. Sex roles can influence the love relationship.

4. Interdependence theory takes into account the costs and rewards in a relationship. Each person develops a **comparison level** (CL), or expected outcome, for the relationship. Dissatisfaction occurs when the outcomes of the relationship fall below the CL. People leave a relationship when the outcomes fall below their CLs for other relationships.

5. Prosocial behavior benefits society or helps others. **Altruism** occurs when a person helps others with no thought of reward. Because it is difficult to prove that no reward is present when a person behaves altruistically, the genuineness of this behavior has been questioned.

6. The **bystander effect** refers to the fact that people are less likely to provide assistance in an emergency when others are present than when they are alone. The bystander effect is attributable to potential embarrassment, fear of failure, and diffusion of responsibility.

7. Aggression is any behavior that is performed with the intent of doing harm. **Hostile aggression** occurs when the goal is specifically to harm another individual. **Instrumental aggression** occurs when someone hurts another person in the pursuit of another goal—for example, during a robbery.

8. Biological views stress the inherited nature of aggressive behaviors. *Sociobiologists* view aggression as an adaptive behavior that promotes the survival of one's species.

9. The **frustration-aggression hypothesis** predicts that frustration, or being blocked from attaining a goal, results in aggression. In addition to frustration, the presence of anger and certain cues may be necessary for aggression to occur.

10. Physical and verbal attacks, as well as adverse environmental conditions, may also elicit aggressive behavior. A high level of general arousal can facilitate aggressive responding.

11. Current statistics underestimate the prevalence of sexual aggression directed toward women. Viewing of pornography is positively related to sexual aggression.

12. Many incidents of rape can be classified as date or acquaintance rape. Date rape appears to result from misperceptions, especially on the part of men, about the acceptability of sexual relations in certain situations.

Study Break

1. What is attraction? Explain the factors that influence or determine whether we will be attracted to another person.
2. The interpersonal attraction that involves a set of rules, often informal, that must be followed if the relationship is to persist is called
   a. altruism.
   b. friendship.
   c. love.
   d. admiration.
3. You have just moved into a new apartment building. What two groups of people in the building are most likely to become your friends?
4. Distinguish between passionate and companionate love.
5. Hendrick and Hendrick proposed six different types of love. Which name and description are mismatched?
   a. *ludus*—game-playing love
   b. *storge*—logical, "shopping-list" love
   c. *mania*—possessive, dependent love
   d. *agape*—all-giving, selfless love
6. What is a CL, and how is it developed? How is the CL related to satisfaction and dissatisfaction with a relationship? Why would you stay in an unsatisfying relationship? What would cause you to leave such a relationship?
7. Your anger at your upstairs neighbor, who plays loud music at 3 A.M., has finally hit the boiling point; you are on your way upstairs to punch him

in the jaw. This is an example of what type of aggression? The statement "Only a few people will be hurt in the accomplishment of this objective" is an example of what type of aggression?

8. All week long you have thought about the dinner you are going to have on Saturday night. You and your date will be at your favorite restaurant, one with a great atmosphere and the best food in town. You arrive at the restaurant only to find a sign in the window saying "Closed for Remodeling." How are you likely to react? Why?

9. What is the biological approach that views aggression as an adaptive response that increases the survival of one's own species?
   a. behaviorism
   b. acculturation
   c. ethology
   d. sociobiology

10. All of the following factors contribute to date rape *except*
   a. men paying expenses.
   b. alcohol consumption.
   c. males' misinterpretation of females' desires.
   d. brief dating relationships.

Social Influences on Behavior

It's Saturday morning, time for your weekly trip to the local discount store. A large crowd has gathered around a display case. A handsome young man in a neatly pressed business suit and tie is encouraging the crowd to buy the brand-new Ronco Veg-O-Matic. "No more hassles with carrots, radishes, peppers, beets, or tomatoes—a perfect salad every time!" You listen to the sales pitch and even watch the salesman perform wonders with the Veg-O-Matic. You decide not to take advantage of his "wonderful introductory offer," however. There is something about him that just doesn't seem right. ***Why was the salesman unsuccessful in his attempt to persuade you to take a chance on his product?*** ■

Other people are constantly trying to influence us. Sales pitches are just one example of the numerous social influences and pressures on our behavior. In this section we examine three kinds of social influences: those designed to persuade us to change our attitudes and behaviors, to produce obedience, and to induce conformity.

Persuasion

Persuasion is the use of social influence to cause other people to change their attitudes and behaviors (Perloff, 1993). We are bombarded with hundreds of persuasive messages every day: Buy this car, join that group, support our cause, vote for this political candidate, give to that charitable organization. Some persuasive messages are effective; others are not. Social psychologists have identified four main factors that influence persuasion: source, message, channel, and audience. Let's take a closer look at each.

Source Factors.   Certainly the source of a persuasive message plays a role in determining whether the message changes our attitudes and behaviors. What is it about the source that is important in facilitating persuasion? Among the characteristics of sources that have been found to increase the impact of persuasive messages are expertise, attractiveness, and trustworthiness.

persuasion
The use of social influence to cause people to change attitudes or behavior

Would this salesperson be sucessful in convincing you to buy one of his used cars?

Expertise.   The greater the perceived expertise of the source of a message, the more persuasive the message (Hovland & Weiss, 1951). To demonstrate the importance of expertise, the following experiment has been conducted numerous times. First, participants are randomly assigned to one of two groups, and an initial appraisal of their attitudes on a particular subject, such as the dependability of American-made cars, is made. Then both groups read a message designed to change their attitude. The only difference is that the message for one group is attributed to a recognized expert (e.g., *Road and Track*), whereas the message for the second group is attributed to a questionable source (e.g., *Better Homes and Gardens*). After the message has been read, the participants' attitudes are measured again. The results indicate that the message from the recognized authority has produced significantly more attitude change. Assuming the attitudes of the two groups were comparable on the first measurement, any differences that appear in the second must reflect the influence of the perceived expertise of the source.

Attractiveness.   The source's attractiveness also influences the likelihood of persuasion; the more attractive the source, the more effective the message. The same physical factors that influence impression formation also influence persuasion (Dion & Stein, 1978). That is, the better your impression of the source, the more likely you are to be persuaded.

Psychological Detective

How would you conduct a research project to evaluate the influence of attractiveness on persuasion? Would it be possible to use the same research strategy that has been used to evaluate expertise? As you think about this research project, you might want to diagram your proposed study on a sheet of paper. Be sure to take all the important possibilities into account. When you are satisfied with your research design, continue reading.

To evaluate the influence of attractiveness, we would start with two randomly formed groups of participants and measure their attitudes. Then both groups would be given the same persuasive message, but the message would be

sleeper effect

Occurs when the message and its source become detached; messages from sources low in expertise, attractiveness, and trustworthiness may increase in effectiveness

delivered by individuals who differed in attractiveness. What other major influences must be controlled if our conclusions are to be valid? What about the level of expertise of the individuals who deliver the message? If we wish to measure only attractiveness, the degree of perceived expertise must be the same for both groups. What's more, the individuals delivering the message should be of the same sex. The ideal condition would be for the same individual to present the message to both groups. With a change of clothes, a pair of last year's running shoes, and mussed hair, the attractive expert would become less attractive. This research strategy is shown in Table 16-2.

Trustworthiness.   A persuasive message may fail to produce a change in attitude even if it is presented by an attractive expert. It takes more than an attractive expert to persuade us; the source of the persuasive message must also be trustworthy (Smith & Shaffer, 1991). Most individuals are very conscious of the prevalence and intent of persuasive communications and are skeptical of the vast array of claims they are exposed to. To be persuaded, they must trust the source of the message.

One of the major factors contributing to trustworthiness is the listener's perception of whether the speaker stands to gain from acceptance of the message. When speakers do not have anything to gain from presenting a particular message, they are more likely to be perceived as trustworthy. For example, suppose a series of TV commercials features a famous athlete urging you to buy a certain type of running shoe. Is this a trustworthy source? Probably not. The more shoes that are sold, the more high-paying commercials the athlete will be hired to make. But what if the same athlete appears in a series of public-service announcements about AIDS? In the latter instance the athlete's credibility may be enhanced; in this role the athlete does not stand to gain from urging listeners to practice safe sex.

Recall the Veg-O-Matic salesman described at the beginning of this section. Why was he unable to persuade you to take a chance on his product? He was attractive; that's a point in his favor. What about his level of expertise? World-class chefs do not usually demonstrate products in local discount stores; thus the salesman's level of expertise is questionable. How trustworthy is the salesman? Because his only reason for being in the store is to sell as many Veg-O-Matics as possible, you immediately question his claims. His apparent lack of expertise and trustworthiness have greatly reduced his persuasiveness.

If a *sleeper effect* occurs, however, his message may be more effective than we have led you to believe. The **sleeper effect** occurs when the message becomes detached from its source. For example, over time an audience member may forget which person presented which message. In such instances messages from sources low in expertise, attractiveness, or trustworthiness increase in effectiveness and result in potentially flawed decision making. Thankfully, the sleeper effect does not appear to play a major role in everyday life (Pratkanis et al., 1988).

TABLE 16-2   Design of an Experiment to Determine the Influence of Attractiveness on Persuasion

	STEP 1	STEP 2	STEP 3	RESULTS
Group 1 (attractive source)	Evaluate the attitude in question	Message presented by the attractive source	Reevaluate the attitude in question	Greater persuasion for attractive source
Group 2 (unattractive source)	Evaluate the attitude in question	Message presented by same source but unattractive	Reevaluate the attitude in question	Less persuasive for unattractive source

Message Factors. Features of the message itself also influence whether we are persuaded. Those factors include attention, drawing conclusions, and message acceptance.

Attention. To be persuaded by a message, you must pay attention to that message. This simple fact has led to the development of numerous procedures designed to attract attention, such as printing signs upside down or backwards, using vivid colors, using unusual music and sounds, and featuring sexually arousing stimuli. Unless the sights and sounds are the message, however, the story does not end here. The audience must attend to the message that accompanies these attention-getters. Therefore the message itself must be powerful enough to command attention. If we continue to attend to the unusual sights and sounds and never hear the message, persuasion will not occur. If the music is too catchy, for example, we may remember the music rather than the product that is being advertised.

Advertisers use bright colors, unusual scenes, and unusual shapes to attract attention.

Drawing Conclusions. Messages are designed to change our attitudes and thereby cause us to reach a particular conclusion. A basic research question concerns who draws the conclusion, the person delivering the message or the individuals receiving it. Should conclusions be part of the message, or should members of the audience be allowed to draw their own conclusions? The answer depends on the involvement of the audience. If the audience simply receives the message without being actively involved in processing it, explicitly drawn conclusions are more effective (Linder & Worchel, 1970). This situation fits the majority of television commercials. Conversely, when people are actively involved in processing persuasive messages, greater persuasion is achieved by allowing them to draw their own conclusions. For example, individuals who were in the market for compact disc players were influenced more by magazine ads that presented relevant facts and allowed readers to draw their own conclusions than by ads that presented the same facts and then stated conclusions (Kardes, 1988).

Reactance advertising tries to make consumers believe that their freedom to purchase goods and pay low prices is limited; hence, you buy their products so you will not feel that you have missed an opportunity.

Message Acceptance. The fact that someone attends to a message does not ensure that it will be persuasive. How many times have you heard a televised speech and said something like "That's absolute nonsense"? For a message to be persuasive, it should not differ drastically from the attitudes of the audience. Thus during a recession, when people are losing their jobs, television commercials urging us to buy imported goods are less likely to be persuasive. Messages that do not differ from our beliefs too much appear to result in the greatest amount of attitude change (Hovland, Harvey, & Sherif, 1957).

reactance
The tendency to react in the opposite direction to a persuasive message when compliance might place limits on personal freedom

subliminal
Below the level of conscious awareness

Reactance is another means by which message acceptance is manipulated. **Reactance** theory states that individuals tend to react rather strongly in the opposite direction to a persuasive appeal that has the potential to restrict their freedom (Brehm, 1972; Engs & Hanson, 1989). For example, most people are unlikely to react favorably to a proposal to raise taxes, regardless of the need for added revenue, because the resulting loss of income would limit their financial freedom. It should be evident that reactance is another name for what is popularly known as "reverse psychology."

Psychological Detective

Consider the ads we encounter every day on television, in newspapers and magazines, online, and in stores. Do those ads use the reactance principle to encourage us to make purchases? As you answer this question, try to think of as many specific examples as possible, and write them down before reading further.

We encounter reactance advertising every day in the form of proclamations such as "Sale! Everything Must Go," "Prices Will Never Be Lower," and "Limited Edition." Ads like these are designed to make us believe that our freedom to pay such low prices or purchase scarce merchandise is being restricted. It is expected that you will react to the threat of such restrictions by attending the sale or purchasing the scarce product.

Unconscious Motivation. If a persuasive message can arouse our unconscious motives, it may stand a better chance of succeeding because we will not consciously try to resist it. This is the premise behind the use of subliminal advertising. Because **subliminal** stimuli are below the level of conscious awareness, they should have a direct effect on unconscious motivation. To accomplish this goal, visual stimuli may be presented so rapidly that we do not consciously see them, or tape recordings may be played during sleep (Silverman & Lachmann, 1985).

The most famous *apparent* demonstration of the effectiveness of subliminal advertising occurred in 1956, when ads for popcorn and soft drinks were supposedly shown at 1/3,000-second intervals during a movie. Because this interval is too short for conscious awareness, moviegoers would have been unaware they had seen the ads. Yet popcorn and soft drink sales supposedly rose dramatically (McConnell, Cutler, & McNeil, 1958). Despite the claim of the success for subliminal advertising in that instance, convincing data were never presented. Moreover, more adequately controlled studies have failed to reproduce those results (Moore, 1982).

Although a limited number of presentations of a subliminal stimulus, as in the popcorn and soft drink example, may not alter our behaviors dramatically and immediately, there is some evidence that repeated subliminal presentations may change our attitudes and opinions (Bornstein, 1992). Recall that the more frequent our contact with a person, object, or idea is, the more likely we are to be positively attracted to that person, object, or idea. Thus frequent subliminal exposure to a stimulus may influence our attitudes. Perhaps this is why advertisers continue to use subliminal techniques, especially in magazine ads. For example, many liquor ads appear to contain cleverly disguised sexual stimuli. The advertisers hope that unconscious attraction to these stimuli will persuade the reader to purchase a particular brand of liquor.

Primacy and Recency Effects. We noted in Chapter 7 that items that are presented first (*primacy effect*) or last (*recency effect*) are remembered best.

If your audience is receiving two persuasive messages that oppose each other, would you prefer to have your message delivered first or last? The answer to this question depends on when the audience is required to act. If there is a delay between the presentation of the message and the required action, the first message is typically more effective (primacy). If action is required immediately after the message has been delivered, however, the last message has the advantage (recency). For example, suppose that you are the campaign manager for a political candidate. Your candidate and the opposing candidate are scheduled to debate the issues. Should your candidate speak first or last? If the election is a couple of weeks away, your candidate should speak first. If the election is tomorrow, your candidate should speak last.

Channel Factors. Persuasive messages are presented through a variety of channels—printed words, spoken words, pictures, movies, and videos. The term *channel* can refer to any means by which a message is presented to the audience. Often two or more channels are used simultaneously. For example, television is popular with advertisers because it combines visual and auditory channels (French & Richards, 1996; Macbeth, 1996). Some channels, such as radio, television, newspapers, and electronic media, make it possible to present messages to large audiences.

Psychological Detective

Are persuasive messages more effective when they are delivered to a group or when they are delivered on a personal (one-to-one) basis? If a message can be delivered as effectively to a group as to an individual, much time and effort can be saved by delivering it to a large number of people simultaneously. Recall several situations in which you were the recipient of a persuasive message. Was the message more effective when you were by yourself or when others were present? Write down your answers to these questions before reading further.

Time and again, it has been demonstrated that the person-to-person approach is more effective than appealing to a larger group (Maccoby & Alexander, 1980). Why? The same message is received in both cases. What factor of the one-on-one situation is lacking in a group presentation? When we are in a one-on-one situation, questions can be asked and answers given. In addition, the person who is presenting the message can extract a commitment from the receiver on the spot. This approach is known as the *foot in the door* technique. We say more about this phenomenon later in this chapter.

The persuasive supremacy of one-on-one communication accounts for the recent growth of telemarketing, or direct telephone solicitation. The next time your phone rings and you find yourself being asked to subscribe to a magazine, switch long-distance telephone service, or purchase credit card insurance, see how many features of effective persuasion are present in the message you are receiving.

Audience Factors. So far we have discussed the nature of the source, message, and channel factors that influence persuasion. The nature of the audience also influences persuasion.

The knowledge and past experiences of the receiver of a persuasive message are important. If the audience is naive and unaware that the message is intended to persuade—as in the case of young children watching Saturday morning television programs—the message is more likely to persuade. This effect is seen in the attempts of children to get their parents to buy the toys and foods they see advertised on TV. In general, the most persuasive messages differ only moderately from the attitudes of the audience.

Research has shown that audiences can defend themselves against persuasion. The most frequently used procedure is analogous to vaccination—giving people a mild case of a disease (such as measles) to inoculate them against that disease. With this method, the audience is exposed to a mild form of the persuasive message before the main or real message is presented. For example, exposing teenagers to a mild form of peer pressure to smoke, in anticipation of the pressure they will encounter later, has been shown to reduce the likelihood that they will smoke (Evans, 1980). Inoculation effects work best when the audience is encouraged to develop counterarguments to the message being presented.

The Cognitive Approach.   The factors involved in persuasion that we have so far considered all deal with more concrete issues, such as *what, when,* and *how* messages are transmitted and by whom. The *cognitive approach* takes a different view of persuasion (Petty & Cacioppo, 1986). The goal of this approach is to determine which cognitive processes take place when persuasion is effective. Thus research on the cognitive approach is concerned with what people think about during persuasion and how these thoughts result in a change in attitude. If a television commercial persuades you to buy a particular new car, a cognitive psychologist would be interested in what you thought during the commercial. The content of the commercial and how it was presented would be of secondary importance.

Obedience

In Chapter 1 we met Keith, who was learning in his history class about the atrocities of war. He left the class wondering whether his psychology class would provide any answers to why people commit such terrible acts. The psychology instructor asked the students, "How much electrical shock, from 0 to 450 volts, would you be willing to administer to another person as part of a scientific experiment on learning?" This question refers to one of the most famous series of studies in the history of social psychology, a study of obedience to authority conducted by Stanley Milgram in the 1960s.

More than 800 townspeople in New Haven, Connecticut, served as the participants in these experiments. Upon arrival at the laboratory, each participant was greeted by two people—a rather serious looking scientist (the experimenter) wearing a white laboratory coat and a middle-aged man who was actually a confederate of the experimenter. The scientist informed the participant and the confederate that they were about to participate in a study of teaching and learning and that one of them would play the role of the teacher. The confederate assumed the role of the learner; the real participant was the teacher.

The teacher read a list of pairs of words, then gave the learner the first word of a pair and asked the learner to identify the second word from among four words. Each time the learner gave an incorrect answer, the teacher was instructed to administer an electric shock to him. Before the session began, each teacher experienced a mild (45-volt) shock to appreciate what the learner would feel. Then the questioning began. As the session progressed and the learner began to make mistakes, the scientist (experimenter) demanded that the intensity of the shock be increased. The teachers followed these instructions until the learner had received a large number of what *appeared* to be very painful shocks. After the initial "shocks" were administered by the teacher, the learner protested and also indicated he had a heart condition. In many instances the teachers became tense and faced a real conflict. They wanted to stop, but felt they could not. The stress they faced raised ethical issues about the conduct of this experiment.

When behavior is initiated or changed in response to the direct command of a person with authority, **obedience** has occurred. In the experiment just described, no electric shocks were actually administered to the learners, but the teachers were unaware that this was the case. All the teachers obeyed the instructions of the experimenter until the 300-volt shock level was reached. (The electric current in your house is 110 to 120 volts.) In one experiment, 65 percent of the teachers obeyed the experimenter's commands all the way to the 450-volt level (see Figure 16-4).

Why did the teachers repeatedly administer shocks to the learners? "Because they were told to" seems to be the best answer to this question. Before you say, "I'd never do that," bear in mind that Milgram's research involved more than 800 participants. Equal percentages of men and women continued to administer shocks up to the 450-volt level.

Now consider two even more horrifying situations. In 1978, hundreds of people in Jonestown, Guyana, poisoned their own children with cyanide-laced Kool-Aid and then poisoned themselves. On April 19, 1993, several fires broke out in the Branch Davidian compound in Waco, Texas (Davidson & Harlan, 1993). More than 75 people, including several individuals who may have set the fires, perished. Why did these tragedies occur? The most plausible answer is that charismatic leaders—Jim Jones in Guyana and David Koresh in Waco (Lacayo, 1993)—gave commands that were obeyed.

Research like Milgram's and events like the Jonestown and Waco tragedies lead us to conclude that people can be too obedient. Several factors, including proximity to the victim, proximity to the authority figure, and assumption of responsibility, influence how obedient we are. The closer the victim is to the participant, the lower the percentage of participants who obey a command to harm the victim. This factor is known as *victim proximity.* In the Milgram studies fewer shocks were administered when the learner was in the same room with the teacher. Likewise, the closer the person commanding obedience (*authority proximity*), the more obedient participants are. In the Milgram studies obedience was

obedience

Initiating or changing a behavior in response to a direct command of an authority

FIGURE 16-4 The teachers (participants) in the Milgram experiment believed they were administering electric shocks to the learners when incorrect answers were given. (A) The machine that "controlled" the shock intensity. (B) Preparing the "learner" for the experiment. (C) The experimenter directs the "teacher" to administer the shock. (D) The "teacher" checks on the status of the "learner."

Source: Milgram, 1974.

Obedience to authority can be incredibly powerful. In 1978 Jim Jones persuaded his followers to give cyanide-laced Kool-Aid to their children and then poison themselves.

greater if the experimenter was in the same room as the teacher but decreased greatly if the experimenter telephoned the commands from another room.

Responsibility is also directly related to level of obedience. If the experimenter assumes responsibility for any harm that befalls the victim, as was the case in the Milgram studies, obedience is high. When responsibility is shifted to the participant, however, the likelihood of obedience drops dramatically. Similarly, if one of the experimenter's assistants defies the experimenter, the obedience of the teachers is reduced appreciably.

Conformity and Compliance

Imagine that you are a participant in an experiment. You and seven other students are seated around a table. You have been told that the experiment is on visual judgments. Your task is to determine which of three lines is the same length as a fourth line, the standard (see Figure 16-5). The person at the far end of the table answers first. Looking down the row, you see that you will be the next to last to answer. You think to yourself, "This is a piece of cake—the answer is obvious." Then something astonishing happens. All the students give the wrong answer; no one picks the line that matches the standard. Now it's your turn.

In the case of obedience, the *commands* to change behavior are clear, and the authority issuing the commands is obvious. In the case of **conformity,** there are *pressures,* often indirect, to change behavior and thoughts. The nature of the authority behind pressures for conformity is not as obvious as it is in commands for obedience. Think about the study just described. What would your response be under its conditions?

As with the obedience studies, many of us say that we would choose the correct line. However, Solomon Asch (1956), who conducted these studies, found that participants conformed to the rest of the group—that is, chose the wrong line—30 percent of the time. In case you have not already guessed, there was only one real participant in each group: the next-to-last person to answer. All the other students in the group were confederates of the experimenters. Asch (1955) also varied the number of confederates who were present; he found that as few as three people giving the wrong answer was sufficient to produce conformity. It was important that the confederates be *unanimous* in their wrong answers. If one of the confederates gave

conformity
Initiating or changing a behavior in response to indirect social pressures

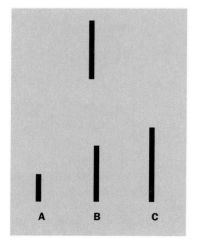

FIGURE 16-5 An example of the lines used in Asch's experiments. Although selecting the matching line might seem simple approximately one-third of the participants chose the wrong answer to conform with the group.

the correct answer, there was a significant decrease in the rate of conformity by the real participants. Having only one other person support you can wipe out most of the effects of group influence.

Psychological Detective

 Let's examine the Asch studies to see if we have all the information we need to demonstrate that conformity has occurred. We tentatively concluded that individuals make wrong choices because other members of the group have made the same choices. This does not necessarily mean that conformity has occurred, however. What other information is required? How would you acquire that information? Write down your answers before reading further.

Additional data showing how the real participants perform under conditions that do not demand conformity are needed. Perhaps the line-judging task is rather difficult, and an error rate of over 30 percent is normal. To evaluate this possibility, Asch asked participants to judge the lengths of the lines when they were alone. He found their judgments were wrong less than 1 percent of the time. There is a big difference between 1 percent and 30+ percent. Therefore it is reasonable to conclude that these experiments illustrated the effects of conformity. In an individualistic society, such as the United States, where conformity might be expected to be low, a conformity rate of 30+ percent is impressive. Conformity among people in other cultures, such as the Bantu of Rhodesia (now Zimbabwe) and the Fijians, is higher (Chandra, 1973; Matsuda, 1985).

Asch's classic studies soon gave rise to other research dealing with the effects of groups on judgments. Although group pressures do result in conformity, James Stoner (1961) showed that decisions reached by a group may be riskier than the independent decisions reached by individual members of the group. In many of the research projects conducted in this area, individuals were asked to read a situation in which the central character faced a potentially risky decision, such as conducting a lengthy and time-consuming research project to enhance a career. For a time, the results of such studies tended to support the notion of a **risky-shift phenomenon:** Groups make riskier decisions than individuals. This general conclusion was soon questioned, however.

Imagine changing the situation just mentioned. Instead of simply expending time and effort on an experiment that may enhance a career, the central character faces the decision of whether to sell a life insurance policy to invest in a risky but potentially very high-paying stock. What is your reaction to this situation? Most people would advise against selling the life insurance policy to play the stock market. What will the group decision be? Contrary to the risky-shift prediction, the group decision will be more strongly opposed to selling the life insurance policy than the individual opinions.

Findings like these prompted some researchers, such as Serge Moscovici and Marisa Zavalloni (1969), to propose that a group's influence is to strengthen or intensify preexisting attitudes, not simply to produce riskier decisions. In the case of the life insurance policy, the initial attitude was not to sell the policy; group discussion served to intensify this non–risk-taking attitude. In the case of expending time and effort on an experiment that may enhance one's career, the initial attitude might be favorable because there is nothing to lose. A group discussion would further enhance this preexisting attitude and lead to greater risk-taking. The effect of group discussion enhancing preexisting attitudes is known as **group polarization** (Pascarella & Terenzini, 1991).

risky-shift phenomenon
The finding that groups make riskier decisions than individuals

group polarization
Phenomenon in which group decision making enhances or amplifies the original opinions of the group's members

A woman hands out samples of a juice to shoppers at Passage, in St. Petersburg, Russia. The principle of reciprocity predicts that giving you a free sample of a product will increase your compliance with a subsequent request to buy that product

As a group's cohesiveness or shared values increase, so does conformity on the part of its members. For example, as sorority members grow closer, they are more likely to share such behaviors as binge eating (Crandall, 1988). Yet the presence of just one person who resists the pressure to conform can reduce conformity by others. For example, the presence of a nonjaywalking confederate reduced jaywalking to 17 percent; when the confederate jaywalked, the number of jaywalkers rose to 44 percent (Mullen, Copper, & Driskell, 1990).

Culture also influences the likelihood that a person will conform. For example, when Asch's line-judging experiment was replicated, similar rates were found in cultures, such as industrialized Europe, that have comparable views of conformity. However, in cultures that value conformity more highly, such as the Bantu culture of Zimbabwe, the rate of conformity rose appreciably (Whittaker & Meade, 1967). In all cultures, as the spirit of individualism increases, the rate of conformity decreases (Alwin, 1990; Remley, 1988).

When we conform, we yield to group pressures in the absence of direct requests to change behavior. Obedience involves a direct request to change behavior, but the request is in the form of an order. **Compliance** refers to behavior that is initiated or changed in response to a request, but the request is not a command or direct order. Compliance may sound rather simple: Requests are made, and behaviors result. It is actually more complicated than that, however, social psychologists have studied—and salespeople have exploited—numerous strategies designed to increase compliance. It is common lore among salespeople that if they are successful in getting a customer to comply with a small request, the chances of compliance with a larger request (a sale) are greatly increased. For example, if you can be talked into taking a test ride in a new car, the chances of your buying the car go up. This phenomenon is known as the **foot-in-the-door effect.**

Compliance may be influenced by what another person has done for you. Consider the following situation. Suppose that a computer salesperson has come to your apartment to discuss a new computer system. She arrives with details about several systems based on your current and projected needs. How will you respond when she asks which configuration you want to invest in? With all the work that went into preparing these proposals for you, don't you feel obligated to purchase one of the packages she has prepared? This tactic for increasing compliance is known as **reciprocity.** With reciprocity, the person seeking compliance does something for you to make you feel obligated when he or she makes a request.

One of the most common examples of reciprocity occurs in supermarkets. Suppose that while doing your grocery shopping you see a person handing out free samples of chips and cheese dip. It is late in the afternoon, and a bite to eat would taste good; you accept the sample. How will you respond to a request to buy some chips and dip? The salesperson anticipates that your acceptance of the free samples will put pressure on you to make a purchase.

In sum, we have seen how social influences affect persuasion, obedience, conformity, and compliance in individuals. In the next section we examine the effects of group membership.

compliance
Initiating or changing a behavior in response to a request

foot-in-the-door effect
Phenomenon in which a person who has agreed to a small request is more likely to comply with a subsequent larger request

reciprocity
Tactic for increasing compliance that involves doing something for others to create a feeling of obligation on their part

The Individual as Part of a Social Group

Many college students pride themselves on their ability to play pool. Pool balls can be heard being racked and shot at all hours in the student center. Perhaps you are a campus pool shark. It is Friday afternoon, and you and a friend are playing a casual game of pool. Halfway through the game some friends from your dorm drop by and decide to watch the rest of the game. It is your turn to shoot. *Will the presence of your friends help or hinder your game?* ▪

Most people have a strong need for affiliation; they enjoy being with others. Hence people frequently join and interact in groups like the group of friends just described. Being a member of a social group implies that there are membership criteria, responsibilities, privileges, and statuses. You are aware of your group memberships and responsibilities, as well as who does and does not belong to your group. The extent to which the members share the values of the group is known as *cohesion*. When there is high cohesion, group values are shared by all members. Low cohesion indicates that group values are not shared by all members and that conflict is likely.

In this section we examine group influences on individual behavior. We begin by looking at the effects of the simple presence of other people on the behavior of individuals.

Social Facilitation

Robert Zajonc (1965) proposed that the presence of other people increases arousal (general physiological or psychological excitement). Greater arousal increases the likelihood that the most dominant response for a particular behavior will be shown. If you have performed a task many times in the past, the correct response dominates, and the increased arousal causes you to perform even better when other people are present. As noted at the beginning of this section, the increase in performance that occurs when others are present is called **social facilitation** (Guerin, 1993). If, however, the task has not been practiced or learned very well and the correct response is not dominant, the presence of others tends to reduce the level of performance. This effect can be seen in the performance of children in a piano recital: Those who have practiced carefully perform as if inspired, while those who have devoted as little time as possible to practicing are plagued by wrong notes and memory lapses.

In the example at the beginning of the section, will the presence of your friends help or hinder your game of pool? As you now know, the answer to this question is "it depends." It depends on how good a pool player you are. If you are an above-average player, your performance should improve when others are present. If you are a below-average player, your performance should decline when others are present. As you can see from Figure 16-6, a study conducted by James Michaels and his colleagues (1982) verified this prediction. The accuracy of above-average players increased from making their shots 71 percent of the time when they were not watched closely to making their shots 80 percent of the time when friends were nearby. By contrast, the performance of the below-average players fell from 36 to 25 percent accuracy when their friends were watching.

social facilitation
An increase in performance that occurs when other people are present

FIGURE 16-6 The presence of others can improve your game of pool, if you are a good player. This effect is known as social facilitation. If you are a poor player, the presence of others may hurt your game.

Source: Michaels et al., 1982.

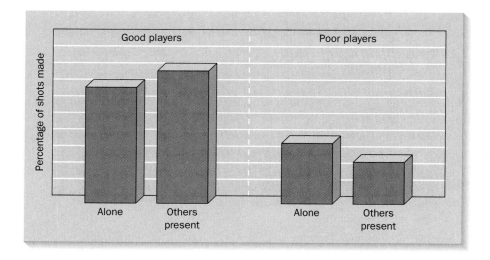

Social facilitation does not *always* occur, however. If the pressure is too great, even professional athletes falter in front of their fans. Davis and Harvey (1992) found that major league baseball players have lower batting averages in critical situations.

Social Loafing

The presence of others does not automatically guarantee that performance will improve. When one's individual efforts are being evaluated, social facilitation can be predicted to occur. When a group collectively works toward a common goal and individual efforts are not monitored or evaluated, however, social loafing is likely to occur.

Social loafing is the tendency to exert less effort when working on a group task if individual contributions are not evaluated. In an unusual laboratory test of this phenomenon, Alan Ingham and his colleagues (1974) asked individuals to take part in a tug-of-war. All of the participants were blindfolded. When they believed they were the only ones pulling on the rope, they pulled harder than when they thought other individuals were pulling also. Laboratory research has shown that people clap and cheer louder when they believe they are alone, even when they are high school cheerleaders (Hardy & Latané, 1986). Social loafing has also been shown in relay swimming performance (Everett, Smith, & Williams, 1992) and by novice rowers paired with experienced rowers (Hardy & Crace, 1991).

Social loafing can be reduced by making the task more involving, challenging, or appealing (Brickner, Harkins, & Ostrom, 1986). The coach of a good athletic team is well aware of social loafing and uses pep talks to counteract it. These motivational speeches are designed to challenge the team members to become more involved in the contest.

Audiences and Coactors

So far we have seen that the presence of other people may cause an individual to perform better at a task or to "goof off," depending on the situation. We need to add a clarification, however, about the other people who are present. In discussing social facilitation we assumed that the "others" constituted an audience. Sometimes the other people present are doing the same thing you are

social loafing

The tendency to exert less effort when working on a group task that does not involve evaluation of individual participants doing. In these instances they are called **coactors.** What happens when there are many coactors and few, if any, people in the audience? The answer is that the process known as *deindividuation* is likely to occur.

Deindividuation. When everyone is doing the same thing (i.e., there are many coactors) and no one is watching (there is no audience), **deindividuation,** or a loss of personal identity and decrease in responsibility in the presence of a group, frequently occurs (Diener, 1980). Deindividuation is the feeling of being lost in a crowd. Students at very large universities who complain about being a number instead of a name are experiencing deindividuation. Deindividuation often leads to uninhibited behavior. In some instances this behavior is positive, but the most frequent outcome is destructive or unauthorized behavior. The wild and destructive behavior of crowds after a major victory by the hometown sports team is an example of such behavior. Extra police and security guards must be hired to control the crowds.

Edward Diener and his colleagues (1976) reported an unusual experiment in which deindividuation resulted in unauthorized behavior. Their juvenile participants were 1,352 Halloween trick-or-treaters. A bowl of candy bars was at one end of a table located just inside the front door. A second bowl containing pennies and nickels was placed at the other end of the table. Concealed observers watched the children. All of the trick-or-treaters were greeted by a female experimenter who remarked on their costumes, instructed them to take only one candy bar, and then indicated that she needed to return to her work in another room.

There were two conditions in this experiment. In the anonymity (deindividuation) condition, no attempt was made to identify any of the children. In the nonanonymity (decreased-deindividuation) condition, however, the experimenter carefully asked each child's name and where he or she lived. The concealed observers recorded the number of children; whether a parent was present, and whether extra candy, money, or both were taken. The results indicated that "of the 416 transgressions . . . 65.4 percent were cases of extra candy being taken, 13.9 percent were cases where a child took only money, and the remaining 20.9 percent took both extra candy and money. Whenever a parent was present, the frequency of transgression was very low (8.3 percent)" (Diener et al., 1976, p. 180).

What effects did anonymity and group presence have on the frequency of this unauthorized behavior? As you can see from Table 16-3, the percentage of transgressions was higher in the anonymous condition—that is, more money and candy were taken when the identity of the children was not known.

Predictably, more transgressions took place among groups than with children alone. Also compare the percentages of transgressions in anonymous and nonanonymous groups. According to the concept of deindividuation, individuals in the anonymous groups would feel less inhibited; therefore these individuals should be more likely to take extra candy or money. This is exactly what happened: 20.8 percent of the children transgressed in the nonanonymous group, whereas nearly three times as many (57.2 percent) transgressed in the anonymous group.

Deindividuation has a powerful influence on the behavior of both adults and children. Some more extreme examples of deindividuation include the behavior of Ku Klux Klan members (they wear white sheets), military training (it is easier to kill an unseen, unnamed enemy), and mob behavior (most destruction and looting take place at night).

coactors

Other people who are present and are engaging in the same behaviors as an individual at the same time

deindividuation

Phenomenon in which the presence of a group results in a loss of personal identity and a decrease in responsibility

TABLE 16-3 Percentage of Trick-or-Treaters Who Transgressed

CONDITION	PERCENTAGE TRANSGRESSING
Anonymous	
Alone	21.4
Group	57.2
Nonanonymous	
Alone	7.5
Group	20.8

Source: Adapted from Diener et al., 1976.

The sheets and masks of the Ku Klux Klan hide personal identities and promote deindividuation.

Fathali Moghaddam (1998) has proposed an alternate interpretation of the effects of deindividuation. Rather than losing themselves or experiencing diffusion of responsibility in such situations, "deindividuated" individuals, Moghaddam suggests, have not abandoned all group norms and social controls; they simply have adopted new, antisocial norms and values. This view is supported by research on street gangs in which members, who might be seen as deindividuated, now obey a new code of behavior (Sanders, 1994; Sheldon, Tracy, & Brown, 1997).

Group Interactions and Group Decisions

There are many instances in which cooperation among group members is required. Families could not function, juries could not reach verdicts, and teams could not win games without interaction and cooperation among members. As we have seen, the presence of groups may result in riskier decisions or the strengthening of preexisting attitudes. The rest of this section explores several of the dynamics and processes of group interaction.

Group Formation and Effectiveness. When a group of unacquainted individuals is formed, certain predictable behaviors occur. First, the group will need a leader if it is to function effectively. Robert F. Bales (1950) found that two types of leaders emerge in a group. One leader is task-oriented; the business of the group is of primary importance to that individual. Another leader is socially oriented; he or she is more likely to show concern for the feelings and emotions of group members (Dabbs & Ruback, 1984). What else do we know about people who emerge as leaders of groups? The individuals who become leaders typically talk more, talk first, and sit at the head of the table. Studies of leadership in India, Iran, and Taiwan have also emphasized the importance of task and social leadership (Smith & Tayeb, 1989).

Brainstorming. In some situations group leaders may defer their leadership role in an attempt to involve all the members of the group. Because of the different viewpoints and experiences that a group's members bring to a situation, it is reasonable to predict that groups should be more effective than individuals in solving problems (Hill, 1982). Most research on this topic has dealt with the effects of a technique known as brainstorming. **Brainstorming** is a problem-solving technique involving the free expression of ideas by group members. Once ideas have been expressed, they lead to the generation of other, related ideas. Ultimately, the collection of ideas is pooled and a solution is achieved. For free expression of ideas to occur, it is important that brainstorming be conducted in an uncritical atmosphere. No ideas may be labeled as "dumb" or "stupid."

brainstorming
Free expression of ideas by members of a group to solve a problem

Psychological Detective

Brainstorming sounds impressive: Several individuals working together should be able to solve problems very effectively. This prediction has not proved to be true, however. It has been shown that the same number of individuals working independently actually generate more ideas than a brainstorming group (Madsen & Finger, 1978). Imagine yourself in a brainstorming session, and then imagine yourself trying to solve a problem by yourself. What is there about the brainstorming session that actually decreases the number of ideas generated? Write down some possibilities before reading further.

In this brainstorming session, three company executives pool their ideas concerning how to increase productivity.

In a brainstorming situation everyone is encouraged to express opinions in an uncritical atmosphere. Problems may arise, however, when several people are ready to express their ideas. In a group, only one person can talk at a time, whereas many ideas can be generated simultaneously by individuals working alone. The presentation of ideas in the group setting may have a second unwanted effect as well. When one's train of thought is interrupted, it may be impossible to return to an idea that came to mind earlier. This situation often happens in groups but not when people work alone. Clearly brainstorming is not always the best way to generate ideas.

Groupthink.   Are there any other factors that might cause a group to be less effective than individuals? Yes—when maintaining harmony among group members becomes more important than carefully analyzing the problem at hand, the group's effectiveness decreases. The process of making decisions that tend to promote the harmony of the group is known as **groupthink** (Janis, 1972). Groupthink occurs most often in very cohesive groups that are insulated from other opinions and groups, feel that they are invulnerable, have a respected or important leader, and are placed under time constraints to reach a decision concerning a threat to the group (Turner et al., 1992). In these circumstances groups tend to make premature and poorly considered decisions; the first suggestion proposed by the leader is usually adopted, especially if there is little hope of finding a better solution. For example, analyses of the decisions to cross the 38th parallel during the Korean War, to invade Cuba at the Bay of Pigs in 1961, and to escalate the Vietnam War in the mid-1960s have concluded that these were poor decisions prompted by groupthink (Janis, 1972). The activities of the Ku Klux Klan and lynch mobs also reflect groupthink in action.

Prejudice and Discrimination

Membership in a group such as a volleyball league team or a political action committee is usually voluntary. Some forms of group identification, however, are beyond our control. Most people are members of a variety of social categories of this type; they may be students, teachers, bricklayers, Italians, actors, rock musicians, alcoholics, Jews, or Catholics. When membership in such

groupthink
The tendency to make decisions intended primarily to promote the harmony of the group

groups or categories determines how other people feel about us and act toward us, we are dealing with prejudice and discrimination. These are important aspects of interpersonal relations and deserve a closer look.

Prejudice.   Think about the country you live in. Now think about several other countries. The chances are good that your feelings were more positive when you thought about your own country than when you thought about others. This occurs because the group to which we belong is the ideal against which other groups are compared and evaluated. Other groups naturally fall short of ours. When we make such comparisons between our nation or culture and others, we are being ethnocentric. Ethnocentrism is a form of prejudice.

Often our judgments of other individuals are based on only one characteristic—their social category or group membership. We do not need to know anything about the individual in question; all that matters is the category. Several examples of such group memberships were mentioned earlier; others are young, old, rich, poor, and intellectual. Judgments based solely on such characteristics are examples of **prejudice.** Ethnocentrism is an example of positive prejudice. Our thoughts about other countries and cultures probably reflect negative prejudice.

Psychological Detective

 As we have described it, the negative or positive evaluation that is at the heart of prejudice is quite general. Still, we all know that prejudices can be very specific. They enable us to describe exactly why a certain person is desirable or undesirable. If prejudice creates a general negative appraisal, where do the specifics come from? Give this question some thought, and write down your answer and your reasons for selecting it before reading further. Here's a hint: The answer involves a topic discussed earlier in this chapter.

If you agree that these specifics are a set of beliefs concerning the members of a particular group, you already know the answer: We are dealing with stereotypes. Recall the examples at the beginning of this chapter: All actors are temperamental; all jocks are dumb. These general views can be directed toward individuals: The softball player in your history class is seen as a dumb jock; your friend the theater major is regarded as temperamental by the algebra instructor. Stereotypes are a major component of prejudice.

Discrimination.   The experience of prejudice frequently results in behaviors that adversely affect members of the targeted group; such behaviors are known as **discrimination.** In turn, prejudice can result in the belief that discrimination is acceptable; hence a vicious cycle is created (Bowser & Hunt, 1996). Discrimination can occur along many dimensions, including age, sex, religion, race, and political views. For example, for all the faculty members at a certain college to be men, despite the fact that many qualified women had applied for faculty positions, would be an instance of sex discrimination.

Sources and Functions of Prejudice.   Prejudice serves several functions and springs from a variety of sources. Here we examine both social and emotional sources and functions of prejudice.

Social Function.   Prejudice frequently justifies social standing or maintains self-esteem. For example, by holding a negative, degrading prejudice toward certain groups, individuals can rationalize mistreatment of (discrimination against) members of those groups. Consider the treatment of slaves, women, racial minorities,

prejudice
Judging a person on the basis of stereotypes about the group to which the person belongs

discrimination
Behaviors that adversely affect members of a particular group

and people of different religions. Such discrimination implies the existence of two groups: "us" and "them," or ingroup and outgroup. Members of the *ingroup* share common values, goals, and beliefs, whereas members of the *outgroup* are seen as different from members of the ingroup. The perception of ingroups and outgroups is relative, however; your ingroup may be our outgroup, and vice versa. What's more, the size of the ingroup influences the strength of members' feelings toward that group; smaller ingroups result in stronger favorable attitudes toward other members of the group (Mullen, 1991). An example of the effect of ingroup size is frequently experienced when a small group of fans travels to a neighboring school for an athletic contest. Each member's ties to the group seem closer and stronger in the face of the large home crowd ("them").

Emotional Function. Earlier in this chapter we saw that frustration can lead to aggression. When we are frustrated, who becomes the target of our aggression? Who can serve this function better than the objects of prejudice and discrimination, especially if they are competing with us for scarce resources (Pettigrew, 1978)? Are there prejudices and discrimination in the business world? What happens when there is a union strike and nonunion employees are hired? What would happen if a professor announced that there would be only four A grades in a class of 20 students? Which groups would be the targets of prejudice and discrimination in these situations?

Because it makes us feel superior, prejudice can also satisfy our emotional need for status. In fact, an increase in the feeling of insecurity often results in our judging others more harshly. For example, students who wrote a short essay about dying (designed to increase feelings of insecurity) showed stronger prejudice against members of outgroups (Greenberg et al., 1990). Prejudice is prevalent and can have quite negative effects. Can it be reduced?

How to Reduce Prejudice. Prejudice and its outward manifestation, discrimination, are common occurrences that almost everyone has experienced in one form or another. Nearly five decades ago, Gordon Allport (1954/1979) proposed that "equal status contact between majority and minority groups in the pursuit of common goals" (p. 281) would reduce prejudice. His hypothesis predicts that close and extensive contact between group members will result in greater understanding because such contact shows that stereotypes are inaccurate. Before this hypothesis becomes workable, however, several additional qualifications are needed. First, for contact to be effective in reducing prejudice, the parties in both groups must be of equal status. The importance of this factor is shown in the problems encountered in attempting to integrate public schools and urban neighborhoods. When one group is perceived as having lower social or economic status than another, it is difficult to overcome prejudice.

Second, contact is more effective in breaking down stereotypes and reducing prejudices when both groups are united in the pursuit of a common goal. For example, Muzafer Sherif and his colleagues (1961) demonstrated that competition between groups at a summer boys' camp resulted in strong prejudice and discrimination. But when the groups were forced to cooperate to achieve a common goal (starting the water-tank truck on which the camp's water supply depended), prejudice and discrimination decreased. In sum, cooperation that is successful in achieving a goal generally leads to reduced prejudice and discrimination.

When the city commissioned several different gangs to paint these murals, cooperation in this activity led to a decrease in prejudice and violence among the gangs.

**Cultural &
Diversity
Perspective**

Taking Off the Ethnocentric Blinders

BECAUSE THE TYPICAL DEFINITION AND CONSIDERATION OF CULTURE INCLUDES many of the same issues and topics (e.g., attitudes, beliefs, behaviors, and values) that interest the social psychologist, you probably were not surprised to find that this chapter contained many such considerations. We seem , however, to have come full circle to the beginning of the chapter, where *ethnocentrism* was discussed. Because the majority of psychological research is conducted in the United States, many of the results have been seen through ethnocentric eyes—that is, it has been *assumed* that the results produced in our culture are characteristic of other cultures. The results of cross-cultural studies are helping us remove these blinders. We have selected several findings to illustrate how culture can influence social psychological research.

Social loafing provides a clear example of the influence of culture. We presented research results (see p. 706) that support the contention that people do not work as hard in groups as they do individually. These results, however, appear to be valid in *individualist* cultures where individual performance is valued. In *collectivist* cultures, such as China and Japan, where contributing to the group and group performance are valued, just the opposite is observed; research participants performed better in groups than individually (Gabrenya, Wang, & Latané, 1985).

The results of research, such as the Milgram obedience and the Asch conformity studies, are often presented as if they reflected the true state of affairs. Would we expect similar results if these studies were conducted in a collectivist culture? Because collectivist cultures endorse obedience and conformity, the results should be *even more pronounced* than they were in the original studies conducted in the United States.

Thus far we have suggested that culture may influence the display of social loafing and obedience and conformity. Can culture also influence impression formation and even love?

How do you react to a person you have just met who does not make eye contact with you? What is your reaction to a person who you have just met who insists on "getting in your face" to talk. In both instances you are likely to form a negative impression. Depending on the cultural background of the person you have just met, however, your impression may not be accurate. In some cultures children are taught not to look directly at other people (Watson, 1970). Likewise, the confortable distance for *casual* conversation is much shorter in other countries than it is in the United States (E. T. Hall, 1966; J. A. Hall, 1978).

What about love? Because *everyone* values love, maybe it is not influenced by culture. Wrong again; culture has an influence, even here. For example, romantic love is valued more highly in individualistic cultures, such as the United States and Germany, than in collectivist, family oriented cultures, such as Japan (Simmons, vomKolke, & Shimizu, 1986).

We have mentioned only a few of the many cultural differences in social psychology. Clearly increased cross-cultural research is needed to help establish the boundaries and generalities of research in this and other areas of psychological investigation.

Review Summary

1. The use of social influence to cause other people to change their attitudes and behaviors defines **persuasion.** The expertise, attractiveness, and trustworthiness of the source of a message are important determinants of persuasion.

2. The most persuasive messages are those that attract attention, draw conclusions (if the audience is passively involved), differ only moderately from the attitudes of the audience, are the last message heard (if action is required immediately), and are presented on a one-to-one basis.

3. Naive audiences that are unaware of the intent of persuasive messages are more likely to be influenced by these messages. If the audience has previously been exposed to a mild form of the persuasive message, persuasion will be more difficult.

4. The cognitive approach to persuasion seeks to determine the thought processes that occur during persuasion.

5. **Obedience** is the initiating or changing of behavior in response to a direct command. In cases in which obedience will result in harm to another person, obedience increases with proximity to the source of the commands but decreases with proximity to the victim. If the source of the commands takes responsibility for any harm resulting from obedience to those commands, the likelihood of obedience is high.

6. **Conformity** results from indirect pressure on an individual to change his or her behaviors and thoughts. The authority behind these pressures is less obvious than in cases of obedience.

7. The decisions of a group may be riskier than those of individuals. This **risky-shift phenomenon** is attributable to the **group polarization** effect, in which the original attitudes of the group's members are enhanced during group discussions.

8. **Compliance** refers to behavior that is initiated or changed as a result of a request. The compliance technique known as **reciprocity** involves doing something for someone else to make that person feel obligated to do something in return.

9. The presence of other people increases arousal, which may result in enhanced ability to perform a desired response. This effect is known as **social facilitation.**

10. **Social loafing** occurs when people working on a group task that lacks individual evaluation perform at a lower level than they would if they worked alone.

11. When there is no audience and only **coactors** are present, deindividuation may occur. **Deindividuation** is the feeling of being lost in a crowd; it may lead to uninhibited behavior that is often unauthorized and destructive.

12. Two types of leaders emerge in a group. One leader is concerned with the tasks confronting the group; the other is concerned with the interpersonal needs of the group's members.

13. **Brainstorming,** or free expression of ideas by the members of a group, is often not as effective in solving problems as the generation of ideas by individuals.

14. The process of making group decisions that promote group harmony is known as **groupthink.** Groupthink may hinder effective solution of problems.

15. **Prejudice** is judging others solely on the basis of their group membership. Stereotypes about the members of certain groups are an integral part of prejudice. Prejudice may be reduced through contact among members of different groups. Such contact is most effective where status is equal and common goals are being pursued.

16. **Discrimination** consists of behaviors directed at members of a particular group that affect them adversely.

Study Break

1. "The use of social influences to cause other people to change their attitudes and behaviors" is a definition of
   a. obedience.
   b. persuasion.
   c. brainstorming.
   d. discrimination.

2. Companies advertising motor oil often use race car drivers as spokespersons because they are
   a. perceived as experts.
   b. perceived as trustworthy.
   c. attractive sources.
   d. able to attract listeners' attention.

3. What is the relationship between attractiveness and persuasion?

4. Attention, acceptance, primacy, and recency all pertain to which factor of persuasion?
   a. source
   b. channel
   c. audience
   d. message

5. When should the person presenting a persuasive message draw specific conclusions for the audience?

6. The _____ occurs when the source of a message is forgotten and the effectiveness of the message increases.
   a. dissociation effect
   b. sleeper effect
   c. channel effect
   d. audience effect

7. Describe the goal of the cognitive approach to persuasion.

8. Subliminal advertising is proposed to work based on which message factor?
   a. unconscious motivation
   b. reaction formation
   c. persuasion
   d. reactance

9. What is the risky-shift phenomenon? How is it related to group polarization?

10. The tendency for group discussion to enhance preexisting attitudes is known as
    a. group polarization.
    b. risky shift.
    c. group compliance.
    d. group conformity.

11. Under what conditions does social loafing occur? What can be done to counteract it?

12. You are one of 327 students taking a Heritage of Western Culture course in a large auditorium. Each student has an assigned seat. When you interact with the professor, you are addressed by your seat number, not by name. Describe the process that you are experiencing.

13. Give the term that matches each of the following definitions:
    a. The process of making decisions that tend to promote the harmony of the group
    b. Judging others negatively because they are members of a particular group
    c. Adopting behaviors that adversely affect members of a targeted group

14. All of the following would help reduce prejudice *except*
    a. heightened group awareness.
    b. equal status groups.
    c. pursuit of common goals.
    d. close and extensive contact.

ANSWERS TO STUDY BREAKS

Page 682

1. Social psychology studies the individual as part of a group, whereas other areas tend to study individuals in isolation.
2. a
3. a-3,   b-5,   c-1,   d-6,   e-4,   f-2
4. Many people assume that all attractive people are also good and that they possess all the positive characteristics of good people.
5. c
6. Self-disclosure
7. a
8. The greater the consistency and consensus regarding a particular behavior, the more confident one feels in attributing the behavior to an external cause.
9. Internal, external
10. c
11. d
12. b

Pages 693–694

1. Attraction is the extent to which we like or dislike other people. The features that influence attraction are *proximity* (nearness is positively related to attraction), *affect and emotions* (we are attracted to people who arouse positive emotions in us), *reinforcement* (we are attracted to those who reinforce us), and *similarity* (we like those who are similar to us).
2. b
3. People who are similar to you (similarity) and people who live near you (proximity)
4. *Passionate love*—transitory, characterized by strong emotional reactions and sexual desires/fantasies. *Companionate love*—characterized by a long-term relationship and commitment.
5. b
6. A *comparison level* is the general outcome you expect from a relationship. It is based on your own experiences and the experiences you have seen others have in similar situations. If the outcomes of a situation are at or above your comparison level, you are satisfied with the relationship. When the outcomes of a relationship fall below your comparison level, you are dissatisfied. If the outcomes for the unsatisfying relationship do not fall below the comparison level for the alternatives, you will stay in that relationship. When the outcomes for the unsatisfying relationship fall below the comparison level for the alternatives, you will leave it.

7. Hostile, instrumental

8. According to the frustration-aggression hypothesis, an aggressive action would be predicted because the goal of going to your favorite restaurant has been blocked.

9. d

10. d

Pages 713–714

1. b

2. a

3. The more attractive the source, the more persuasive the message

4. d

5. Conclusions should be drawn when the audience is passive and simply receiving the message.

6. b

7. The goal of the cognitive approach is to determine the thought processes that occur during persuasion.

8. a

9. *Risky shift phenomenon* —the feeling that under some circumstances groups make more risky decisions than do individuals. *Group polarization*—indicates that if the preexisting attitude is toward risk, group discussions may intensify or polarize this attitude. The converse reaction (intensifying nonrisk attitudes) also may occur.

10. a

11. *Social loafing* occurs when people work in groups and are not subject to individual evauation. Social loafing can be reduced by making the task more involving, challenging, and appealing.

12. Deindividuation, the feeling of being lost in a crowd, is the process you are feeling.

13. Groupthink, prejudice, discrimination

14. a

SCORING FOR TABLE 16-1

Page 675

Give yourself 1 point for every answer that corresponds to the following key:

1. F

2. F

3. F

4. F

5. T

6. T

7. T

8. T

9. F

10. T

11. T

12. F

13. T

14. F

15. T

16. T

17. F

18. T

19. T

20. F

21. F

22. F

23. F

24. T

25. T

High self-monitoring scores range from 15 to 22, whereas intermediate scores range from 9 to 14. Scores of 0 to 8 are in the low range. Individuals with high scores are sensitive to situational cues, can detect deception on the part of others, and know how to influence other people's emotions.

CHAPTER 17

Industrial and Organizational Psychology

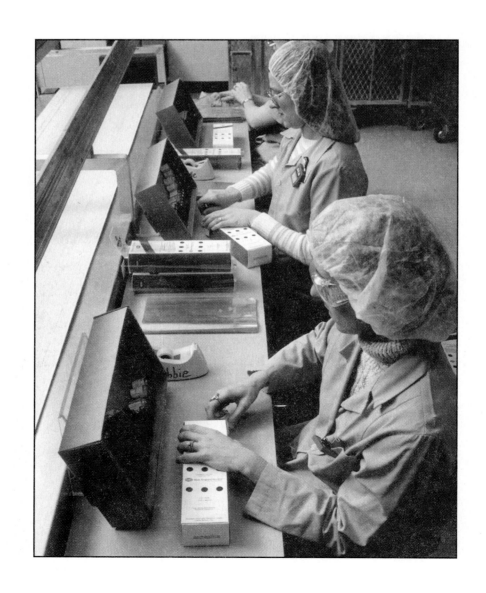

Chapter in Perspective

Psychology is not a stagnant discipline that resides only in textbooks. Many of the theories, techniques, and methods discussed throughout the text have been and continue to be applied every day in the real world. In Chapter 1 you were briefly introduced to industrial and organizational psychology; this subfield of psychology uses the knowledge of psychology to improve the workplace. In Chapter 8 we examined the role of intelligence tests, and in Chapter 12 we discussed personality tests. Both types of tests are used in the selection of personnel. In Chapter 11 we saw how gender stereotypes may influence career choices and career advancement, and we explored the legal implications of sexual harassment. In this chapter we look again at the interaction of psychology and the legal system. Chapter 5 discussed the implications of shift work as it related to safety and sleep. In this chapter we discuss human-factors psychology, which uses our knowledge of human behavior to design safer machines and more efficient workplaces. In short, in this chapter we consider some of the ways in which psychology is applied to our lives on a daily basis. ■

industrial/organizational (I/O) psychology
The scientific study and application of psychology to the workplace

personnel psychology
The study and analysis of individual differences in relation to jobs and the development and maintenance of an organization's human resources (its workers)

Industrial/Organizational Psychology

The year is 1917, and the United States has entered World War I. The secretary of war assigns you the task of identifying, classifying, and selecting army recruits based on the area in which they could best be used (e.g., infantry, officers, artillery). To complicate your job, many of the recruits are either illiterate or do not speak English. *How would you go about fulfilling your commissioned duties?* ■

This scenario represents one of the key steps in the development of industrial and organizational (I/O) psychology. Although I/O psychology had been developing since the turn of the century, it was not used on a large scale until World War I. The Committee on Classification of Personnel in the Army was headed by Robert M. Yerkes, who was assisted by two other psychologists, Walter Bingham and Edward Thorndike. By 1918, almost 2 million soldiers were tested using the first large-scale group intelligence test, *Army Alpha,* developed by the committee (see Chapter 8). Several months later the committee developed a second, nonlanguage version, called *Army Beta,* for illiterate and non–English-speaking soldiers. After the war psychologists began to develop other tests for the selection of civilian personnel.

Industrial and organizational psychology is the scientific study and application of psychology to the workplace. Industrial and organizational psychologists examine all aspects of the worker, the organization, and the work itself. One of the biggest challenges I/O psychologists face is the rapid change occurring in the workplace (Erez, 1994), including a more diverse labor force and the effects of globalization and new technologies (Schultz & Schultz, 1998). More and more minorities, women, and people with disabilities in America are entering the workforce. In the future employers will face a "skills gap"—not enough qualified applicants to fill positions that require high-level skills (Offermann & Gowing, 1990). What's more, workplace violence affecting more than 2 million U.S. residents a year has led to a concern for identifying violence-prone employees and for defusing incidents that could escalate (Warchol, 1998). I/O psychologists confront a daunting task: to increase compatibility between employees and jobs at a time when the composition of the labor force and the workplace is rapidly changing in a competitive and global marketplace.

Industrial and organizational psychology includes a variety of areas that can be explored in relation to the workplace, including job satisfaction, performance appraisal, training, personnel selection, and work-related law. For our purposes, we divide the field into three broad subcategories: personnel psychology, organizational psychology, and human-factors psychology (Schrader, 2000).

Newspaper advertisements such as these are often the beginning of the process of searching for a job. For many companies, the advertisements represent a significant amount of effort to identify the knowledge, skills, and abilities needed to perform the job.

Personnel Psychology

The word *personnel* means "people," thus the focus of **personnel psychology** is the study and analysis of individual differences in relation to jobs and the development and maintenance of an organization's human resources (its workers). A key responsibility of personnel psychologists is determining the knowledge, skills, and abilities (*KSAs*) needed to perform a given job. Once KSAs are established, personnel psychologists try to match the "right" employee to the "right" job, often by using personality, cognitive, and physical ability tests (see Chapters 8 and 12). Personnel psychologists must also be knowledgeable of employment law, which affects their work in a variety of ways (Cascio, 1998). Table 17-1 summarizes some of the most important laws and their impact on the field.

The basic goal of any selection system is to predict the success of job candidates before offering them a job (or turning them down). Some of the more recognized procedures include interviews, work samples, applications, letters of recommendation, tests, and situational exercises. Although many of these methods are beyond the scope of an introductory psychology text, we discuss the interview in some depth.

TABLE 17-1   U.S. Laws and Their Effects on Personnel Psychology

LAW	EFFECTS
U.S. Constitution	Fifth Amendment requires "due process" under the law; it gives individuals the right to a legal hearing and covers employment law. Thirteenth Amendment abolished slavery and involuntary servitude. It has been interpreted to include issues of racial discrimination in the workplace that can be legally viewed as a form of slavery. Fourteenth Amendment requires that all people be given equal and fair treatment under state laws in terms of both liabilities and privileges.
Equal Pay Act of 1963	Passed as an amendment to an earlier act, this law prohibits sex discrimination in wages. It states that equal jobs require equal pay regardless of gender.
Civil Rights Act of 1964	This landmark antidiscrimination law is composed of sections or *titles,* each of which deals with a different aspect of discrimination. Title VII, which focuses on employment-related issues, prohibits discrimination based on race, color, religion, sex, or national origin. To enforce these mandates, the act created the Equal Employment Opportunity Commission (EEOC), which was empowered to investigate charges of job discrimination. The Equal Employment Opportunity Act of 1972 amended Title VII by granting the EEOC the power to initiate lawsuits against employers accused of practicing discrimination. As amended by the 1972 law, Title VII now applies to virtually all employers with 15 or more employees, including state and local governments and educational institutions.
Age Discrimination in Employment Act of 1967	This act, later amended in 1986, extended discrimination protection on the basis of age for workers over the age of 40. Companies can present arguments that age is a factor if they can show that older people cannot successfully perform the job. Employers, however, must pass a rigorous legal test to prove their case. The key objective was to prevent companies from singling out older employees (with higher salaries) and terminating them or replacing them with younger workers to save money.
Americans with Disabilities Act of 1990	Passed to protect the estimated 43 million Americans with disabilities, this law prohibits discrimination against qualified job applicants with disabilities and requires employers to make "reasonable accommodations" for disabled workers. It also requires new businesses to be accessible to the disabled and existing businesses to make improvements where possible. The law applies to people with AIDS and, in some instances, those with substance abuse disorders.
Civil Rights Act of 1991	The most current piece of civil rights legislation altered a variety of employment practices. For example, results of employment tests used in personnel selection cannot be adjusted on the basis of race ("race-norming") or gender to increase the representation of minorities or women. In addition, employees may not object to certain employment practices if notice was given in advance and the employees failed to challenge them at that time. The law also changed the way "adverse impact" (employment policies that negatively affect minority groups) is interpreted in the courtroom.

Psychological Detective

Interviews are the most commonly used selection procedure, yet research shows that they have poor validity (little ability to predict which job candidates become good workers). Nevertheless, employers continue using interviews for selecting workers. What are some reasons that employers continue using such a poor selection device? Consider this question from a company recruiter's perspective. Write your reasons before proceeding further.

Selection procedures vary in terms of their validity, fairness, applicability, time requirements, and cost. For example, job application forms have good validity, fairness, and applicability and low time and cost factors. Consequently, application forms are a standard part of job selection. By contrast, interviews are less valid owing to their subjective nature unless the interview is *structured* (all candidates are asked the same questions in the same format) and contains situational questions (hypothetical situations requiring respondents to "think on their feet" to answer). Yet *unstructured* interviews continue to be a mainstay in business because many companies are reluctant to hire people without first meeting them face to face and observing their "personality" (Arvey & Campion, 1982). In addition, most interviewers (and the public) believe that they can "size people up" through an interview and accurately determine whether they will be good employees. Interviews are also relatively cost- and time-efficient.

Because the interview is so well established, it is hard to abandon. And research is beginning to cast more positive light on interviews, especially situational interviews (McDaniel et al., 1994). Structured interviews and situational interviews produce higher validity coefficients than unstructured interviews. What's more, employers who use structured interviews are in a better position to defend their selection procedures against allegations of discrimination in the hiring process (Williamson et al., 1997).

Testing is another common practice, and personnel psychologists have a wide variety of tests available. Sample questions from some of these tests can be found in Figure 17-1. Recall from Chapter 8 that successful tests must be reliable, valid, and standardized. These requirements extend to personnel tests

The interview is the most frequently used selection procedure despite its shortcomings; its ability to predict which applicants will be successful is rather low. In recent years, researchers have found that the validity of the interview can be improved by using a standard set of questions (structured interview) and situational questions.

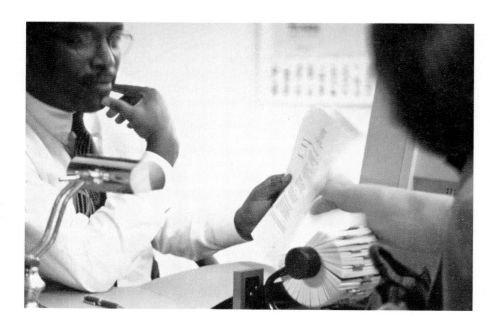

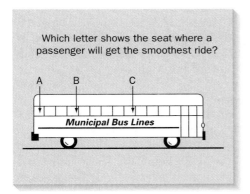

When the two numbers or names in a pair are exactly the same, make a check mark on the line between them.

66273894 _____ 66273984
527384578 _____ 527384578
New York World _____ New York World
Cargill Grain Co. _____ Cargil Grain Co.

Which letter shows the seat where a passenger will get the smoothest ride?

A   B   C

Municipal Bus Lines

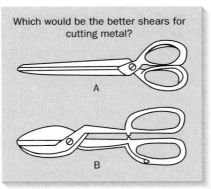

Which would be the better shears for cutting metal?

A

B

FIGURE 17-1 Sample items from several tests commonly used in job selection. Psychologists have a wide variety of tests that could be used as part of the selection process. Employers are required to demonstrate that the test is related to meaningful aspects of job performance.

Source: Sample items from the Bennett Mechanical Comprehension test. Copyright 1942, 1967, 1970, 1980 by the Psychological Corporation. Reproduced by permission. All rights reserved. Sample items from the Minnesota Clerical Test. Copyright 1933, renewed 1961 by The Psychological Corporation. Reproduced by permission. All rights reserved

as well. Cognitive (intelligence), personality, and physical (e.g., hand-eye coordination) tests that lack reliability and validity could be considered unfair or discriminatory. Ultimately a personnel psychologist must decide which methods will yield the best predictions. By combining the most applicable methods, personnel psychologists can determine which applicants should be hired.

Using Personality Tests in Selecting Police Officers

The selection of law enforcement officers is a major societal concern. Could psychological tests play a role in these selections? In the past psychological tests, such as the MMPI (see Chapter 12), were used to screen out applicants for consideration (Barrick & Mount, 1991; Hogan et al., 1985). These tests could not be used, however, to select applicants who had qualities that would make them good officers because there was no evidence that the test scores were related to job performance.

George Hargrave and Deirdre Hiatt (1989) studied police cadets who were selected for training without the use of any psychological test. While at the police academy, these cadets completed the California Psychological Inventory (CPI) (see Chapter 12). At the end of training their instructors rated each cadet's suitability for work in law enforcement. The 13 percent of cadets who were rated as "psychologically unsuited" differed from suitable cadets on nine scales of the CPI.

The researchers also studied officers (not cadets) who had experienced serious job problems such as physical confrontations with other officers. These officers also differed from other officers on several CPI scales, leading the researchers to conclude that the "CPI has potential value as a selection instrument" (Hargrave & Hiatt, 1989, p. 276). The CPI is used as a component in the selection of officers in the United States, Canada, and Australia (Hargrave & Hiatt, 1989; James, 1993).

Robert Tett and his colleagues (1991) reviewed the use of personality tests as predictors of job performance in several occupational groups. They caution that there must be a clear basis for using a particular personality characteristic in the selection process. Administering a psychological test in the hope that it will yield information useful in selecting future employees can be both inefficient and illegal. The Equal Employment Opportunity Commission (EEOC) requires test users to provide evidence that a test is related to meaningful aspects of job performance before it can be used to select employees.

Psychologists have also investigated drug testing and genetic screening as predictors of future work performance. One study found that employees who tested positive for illegal drugs had a job absenteeism rate almost 60 percent greater than those testing negative, and the turnover rate (as evidenced by employees quitting or being fired) was 47 percent greater for drug users as compared with non–drug users (Normand, Salyards, & Mahoney, 1990). The successful application of a drug-testing system can save a company millions of dollars. Drug testing remains controversial, however, critics argue that it violates a person's right to privacy and that such tests are not sufficiently accurate.

Genetic screening is a relatively new technique that allows employers to identify candidates who may be predisposed to develop diseases if exposed to certain environmental substances, such as toxic chemicals. These individuals could be screened out and placed in jobs that offer little chance of exposure (Olian, 1984). Like drug testing, genetic screening is controversial.

Once an applicant has been selected, the next step for the new recruit is to be placed into a job and trained.

Training

Training is the deliberate and planned process by which employees are exposed to learning experiences designed to teach new skills and improve job performance. Training typically follows personnel selection because new employees need to be trained in company procedures, policies, and equipment. *On-the-job training* may be sufficient for some jobs; more complex jobs may require weeks or months of intensive training. Technical fields, such as computer systems, involve continuous training because the knowledge becomes obsolete in a short time period (Coutts, 1991). Thus training is not just for new recruits; experienced personnel also benefit from new training programs and refresher courses.

A comprehensive training program involves several steps. The first step, a *needs assessment,* is equivalent to a job analysis in personnel selection. The needs assessment determines who needs to be trained, what training program to use, and what is to be taught. Unfortunately, most companies do not conduct a needs assessment to determine their training requirements (Rynes & Rosen, 1995; Saari, et al., 1988). Once the needs assessment is completed, the company has established the training objectives. At this point trainers select the training methods (see Table 17-2) and design the training program.

Training programs often combine several methods, and most involve a mix of learning principles (see Chapter 6). The last step, after the actual training program has been implemented, is to evaluate the training program. Four types of measures are used in evaluating a training program (Kirkpatrick 1976). *Reaction measures* indicate whether participants liked the training program. *Learning measures* test retention of new skills and knowledge from the training program. *Behavior measures* determine the extent to which the training transferred to the job environment (i.e., can the trainee now perform satisfactorily in the "real" work situation?). *Results measures* show whether certain predetermined organizational goals (e.g., increased productivity) were attained.

training
The deliberate and planned process by which employees are exposed to learning experiences designed to teach new skills and improve job performance

TABLE 17-2 Training Methods

On-the-job-training (OJT) Lectures	The trainee mimics the behavior of other employees, who instruct the trainee on the correct behaviors while working on the job.
	The trainer addresses a group of trainees by speaking to them.
Vestibule training	Common in production line work, vestibule training involves a smaller version of the production line that employees can practice on without affecting the real production line.
Audiovisual material	The trainee may be exposed to films, slides, videotapes, audiotapes, transparencies on an overhead projector, or computer presentations as a training technique. The trainee may also be filmed on a videotape, which is later analyzed to provide feedback.
Job rotation	Similar to OJT, job rotation involves having the trainee learn by performing several different jobs over an extended time period, thereby gaining a "bigger picture" of the overall process.
Conferences (discussion method)	Multiple trainers and trainees interact as if in a conference room or discussion group. A variation of this method is the training group (or T-group), often incorporating role-playing or sensitivity training to accomplish the training goals.
Apprentice training	A trainee is paired up with a more experienced worker and serves as the worker's apprentice. In white-collar jobs, this approach is referred to as *mentoring*. Typically, the one-to-one relationship is maintained over an extended period of time until the trade has been mastered.
Programmed instruction	The older version of this technique involved booklets (like study guides); newer versions usually use computers (i.e., computer-assisted instruction). The trainee proceeds through a series of stages of self-teaching, using the booklets or the computer. Answering a battery of questions at each stage determines advancement to the next stage.
Simulators	Simulations involve a modeled version of a "real life" scenario that the trainee can practice with or without actually being exposed to the consequences. Flight simulators for pilots are an excellent example. Games can be used to simulate situations in financial or business environments. Military simulators are quite common in training soldiers for the battlefield. Much of this technology is now employed in video and arcade games available to the public.

Unfortunately, few companies evaluate their training programs, and those that do often merely evaluate trainee's *attitudes* reaction measures about the training program rather than the program's effectiveness.

The ultimate purpose of recruiting, selecting, and training workers is to enable them to perform satisfactorily on the job; however, the hiring institution cannot take this for granted. Management must invest the time to determine that employees are performing as desired.

Performance Appraisal

If you have ever held a job, you have experienced a performance evaluation or appraisal. **Performance appraisal** is the evaluation of a person's functioning on job-related tasks; it usually includes some formal assessment and feedback. Typically, the evaluation involves ratings across a series of performance dimensions or criteria. Accurate performance appraisals are important because they can affect decisions about promotions, raises, and layoffs (Cleveland, Murphy, & Williams, 1989). One of the greatest challenges in appraisal is to make the evaluations fair and systematic (Arvey & Murphy, 1998). For example, supervisors may give ratings that are inconsistent with employees' actual performance (Longenecker, Sims, & Gioia, 1987). In the worst cases, they may give a favorable rating to get a troublesome employee transferred to another department or a poor evaluation to punish an employee. One way to increase interrater agreement

performance appraisal
The evaluation of a person's functioning on job-related tasks; this usually includes some formal assessment and feedback

in performance appraisals is to provide explicit instructions and standards against which employee performance is based (Schrader & Steiner, 1996).

There are two types of performance appraisal criteria: objective and subjective. *Objective or hard criteria* consist of variables that can be measured numerically, such as the number of sales made, televisions made, or data entry speed. Objective criteria are easily observed and totaled, so different raters should arrive at the same numeric rating. For example, if two production managers watch a worker assemble radios, both should determine accurately the number of radios assembled by counting the number of radios produced at the end of the day. By contrast, subjective or "soft" criteria are personal evaluations as when a rater makes a judgment of the quality of work performed. *Subjective criteria* are more variable than *objective criteria*. In our radio assembly example, managers may arrive at different estimates of the *quality* of a worker's performance in assembling the radios. The actual performance appraisal instrument used to record subjective ratings is also highly variable in the sense that it can be affected by a range of personal styles.

Performance ratings can be influenced by a number of errors and biases (Arvey & Murphy, 1998). *Leniency error* involves a rater's giving only favorable, above-average marks to all ratees. The opposite of this is *severity error,* whereby the rater systematically gives only unfavorable, below-average ratings to almost all employees. *Central tendency error* occurs when raters consistently rank all employees in the middle of the rating scale. Another error, the *halo error,* involves rating a person favorably on all performance dimensions because the rater has a favorable impression of the person in general. Some biases are unconscious on the part of the rater and thus can be difficult to detect. I/O psychologists have devised a number of ways of reducing these types of errors; these approaches include improving the rating instruments by clearly specifying the meaning associated with each numeric rating.

Next we turn our attention to how I/O psychologists work to improve the effectiveness of the entire organization.

Organizational Psychology

organizational psychology
The scientific study of organizations and their social processes

Organizational psychology is the scientific study of organizations and their social processes. Thus it blends work-related psychology, social psychology, human relations, and business. Organizational psychology developed during the 1960s from the study of social conditions in the workplace. This subfield of I/O psychology is concerned primarily with the organization itself and issues like organizational structure and culture, leadership, and motivation. Two key subfields of organizational psychology that merit further discussion are motivation and job satisfaction.

Motivation

Every year thousands of motivation seminars are held around the world to convey the secrets to motivating people. Why? Most people believe a motivated workforce performs better. The secret to motivating people, however, is more complex than many seminars convey. *Work motivation* is an internal state that activates and energizes job behavior such that it is directed and sustained toward a job or organizational goal. Many of the concepts discussed in Chapter 4 on motivation and in Chapter 6 on learning can be applied to work motivation. For example, several behavior modification programs in manufacturing plants use reinforcement to increase performance and enhance productivity. Some common workplace reinforcers are bonuses, promotions, more vacation time, and new equipment.

Setting goals, a widely accepted technique for increasing work motivation, is often coupled with reinforcement. *Goal-setting theory* proposes that managers should establish difficult but attainable, specific goals for employees rather than just telling them "to do the best you can" (Locke & Latham, 1990). To be effective, employees must be committed to achieving the work goals. This outcome can be accomplished in several ways: (1) providing employees with feedback on their work performance, (2) allowing employees to participate in the goal-setting process, and (3) rewarding employees for attaining goals.

Other motivational theories suggest that we have different needs and motives (see Chapter 4). Some people have a greater need for achievement and prefer challenging tasks, whereas others have a pronounced need for power, as defined by status and control over their jobs. Finally, certain workers have a need for affiliation; they desire to be part of a team. Organizations can capitalize on these needs by matching appropriate rewards to the employee's requisite motivation. For example, employees with a high need for affiliation could be incorporated into work teams that solve problems.

Equity theory, a cognitive theory of motivation, suggests that motivation involves comparing what we invest in work with what we get out of it (Adams, 1965). We mentally weigh our inputs, such as education, time, and experience, and skills, against our work outputs: job satisfaction, pay, and recognition. If our outputs are equal to or exceed our perceived inputs—if the situation seems to provide *equity*—our motivation is likely to remain constant. If, however, our inputs exceed our outputs (inequity), we are likely to be motivated in a different direction. Thus we might demand a raise, decrease our workload, alter our perception of the situation, or look for another job. Equity theory also states that in addition to analyzing our own situation cognitively, we compare our input-output ratio to other workers' ratios. If we perceive others as having more favorable ratios, we may be motivated to increase performance so as to gain the rewards they have.

Another cognitively based motivation theory, *expectancy theory* (or *VIE theory*), suggests that we are motivated to work hard only when we experience positive valence (*V*), high instrumentality (*I*), and high expectancy (*E*) (Vroom, 1964). Positive valence occurs when employees believe that their increased motivation will lead to a beneficial outcome (i.e., a reward). High instrumentality occurs when employees believe that they have the skills and abilities to perform the behaviors needed to achieve the outcome. High expectancy is the belief that using those skills and behaviors will in fact lead to the desired outcome. Thus workers will be motivated only if they believe that they have both the means and the opportunity to succeed in pursuit of a desired outcome.

Ultimately motivating workers is a tricky proposition because motivation is a highly individualized phenomenon: What motivates Employee A may have little effect on Employee B. What's more, motivation can be sustained only for short periods of time because it causes physiological arousal. As we saw in Chapter 15, extensive arousal can be stressful to the human body. This finding might explain why people who attend motivational seminars often come out of them all pumped up, but three months later they have noticed little change in their work behaviors.

Job Satisfaction

The most widely researched work attitude in organizational psychology is job satisfaction, which is linked to productivity, turnover, and absenteeism. *Job satisfaction* is defined as relatively stable positive feeling toward one's job. Ultimately job satisfaction is a measure of the discrepancy between expected levels of satisfaction and the actual satisfaction an employee feels. High levels of job satisfaction are likely when adequate resources are provided, when the work is interesting and challenging, when good working relationships exist with supervisors and co-workers, when opportunities exist for advancement and recognition, and when the job offers security and a perception of equitable pay.

Although common sense suggests that satisfied workers are productive workers, research does not consistently support this assumption. In one study researchers found a correlation of only +.17 between job satisfaction and productivity (Iaffaldano & Muchinsky, 1985). This relatively low correlation suggests that satisfaction is not a key ingredient in employee productivity. Similarly, the relationship between job satisfaction and absenteeism is not particularly strong either (Cotton & Tuttle, 1986). So what does job satisfaction lead to? Job satisfaction may have stronger ties to personal health; job dissatisfaction has been linked with elevated stress and poorer health (Ivancevich & Matteson, 1980). What's more, satisfied workers are more likely than dissatisfied workers to help co-workers, to improve their own skills, and to provide constructive criticism for the betterment of the company (George & Brief, 1992). The relationship between job satisfaction and productivity increases substantially when the organization has an effective reward system. Sustaining satisfied employees is desirable but often can be maintained only when compensation systems reflect actual productivity. Some researchers have been moving toward an integrated theory of job satisfaction that encompasses equity, need, discrepancy, and the expectancy theories to help explain how satisfaction should be measured and what correlates are related to high and low satisfaction (Nagy, 1996).

One new avenue of research suggests that certain people may be genetically predisposed to be more or less satisfied with their lives and jobs. Termed *positive* and *negative affectivity,* these personality dimensions have been found to be measurable and correlated with satisfaction (George, 1990; Levin & Stokes, 1989). Someone with negative affectivity is predisposed to have lower job satisfaction levels, whereas a person with positive affectivity is genetically inclined toward high job satisfaction levels. A study of identical twins found that as much as 30 percent of job satisfaction could be traced to a genetic predisposition to be satisfied (Arvey et al., 1989). Further research in this area is needed, but perhaps tests for positive and negative affectivity may find their way into the personnel selection process.

Human-Factors Psychology

Computers, robots, and other technological innovations are changing the way we work. One division within psychology focuses on interactions among people, machines, and the work environment; it is called human-factors psychology. Also known as *engineering psychology,* **human-factors psychology** is the science of engineering and designing equipment and machines for human use and modifying human behavior so that workers can operate machines more efficiently. British psychologists use the term *ergonomics*, which means "laws of work." The primary functions of human-factors psychology are reducing stress in workers confronted with new technology and making machines safer, more efficient, and more comfortable to use. Human-factors psychology is a combination of industrial engineering and applied psychology.

Human-factors psychology began developing during World War II. Previously people had to adapt to a machine no matter how unsafe, inefficient, or uncomfortable it was. Even when the machines functioned properly and the people were highly skilled, costly errors occurred. With the coming of the war, human-machine interactions had to be better coordinated. Over time, physicians, physiologists, and psychologists joined military engineers in redesigning tank and submarine stations, military uniforms, and aircraft cockpits.

At the beginning of the war different aircraft had different cockpit arrangements. This situation is analogous to trying to drive different cars in which the brakes, gas pedal, and clutch are rearranged; a safe response in one may lead to death in another. Today the military uses a uniform and more efficient system of cockpit controls for aircraft.

Human-factors psychology has helped in the redesign of cars, work cubicles, chairs, computer keyboards, nuclear power plant control rooms, and air traffic control rooms. Despite this progress, we have a long way to go. Video-cassette recorders (VCRs) still confuse us, we don't use all the features on our camera, some doors push and others pull, and many people have trouble figuring out how to turn on the water in a hotel shower (Norman, 1988).

At times, most of us deal with machines that were not designed according to the priniciples of good design. For example, this ATM will be much easier to use if each button has only one function and if the machine provides immediate feedback so users know if they are on the right track.

Human-Machine System

The combination of a machine and the person operating it is referred to as a *human-machine system* (or *person-machine system*). Examples of human-machine systems are a person typing on a computer keyboard and a construction worker driving a bulldozer. Ideally, the integration of the person and the machine results in the *principle of compatibility*: Machines follow certain guidelines that are compatible with our expectations. For example, red lights mean "stop" or "danger." Using a green light on a control panel to show danger would cause problems. Similarly we are accustomed to turning knobs and screwdrivers clockwise (to the right). Machines or tools that require the reverse, a counterclockwise turn (to the left), could be problematic.

By now you have probably determined that many human-factors designs involve display systems (speedometer, computer screen) or control systems (knobs, buttons) (see Figure 17-2). There are three criteria for the good design of these systems. First, each control should have *only one function*. For example, separate controls in showers and sinks for hot and cold water were converted to a single control that adjusts hot and cold water simultaneously to reduce the likelihood of being scalded or frozen. The second criterion is *immediate feedback*. The control or display should immediately signal us when an action is being or has been performed. In other words, when you push a button,

human-factors psychology
The science of engineering and designing equipment and machines for human use and modifying human behavior so that workers can operate machines more efficiently (also known as *engineering psychology* and *ergonomics*)

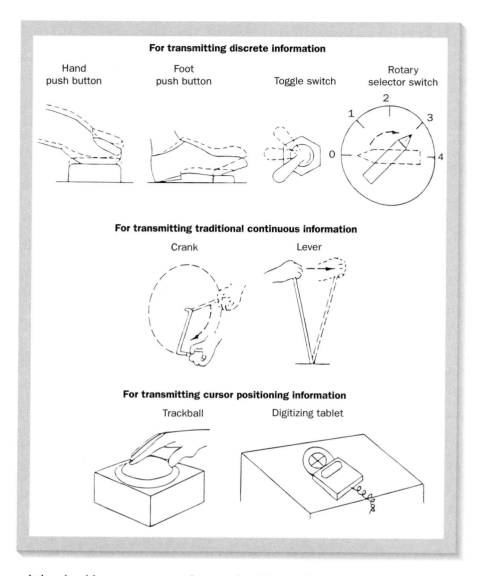

a light should come on or a buzzer should sound. Modern automated teller machines (ATMs) are good examples; in response to any button you press, a message appears on the screen giving you more choices from which to select. The ultimate feedback to show that you did everything right is getting your money. Perhaps this is why VCRs are so commonly singled out for humor—we often don't know our actions were wrong until it is too late (the VCR didn't record the show we thought we programmed it to record). The last criterion for good design is *visibility*: Systems should be easily understood through visual clues. A light switch provides just an on-off position and requires no extensive labels or instructions. As controls get more complicated, they may still possess good visibility if they are well designed.

Imagine that you had to redesign a stovetop to make it more useful. How might you redesign burner control knobs using visual cues? You can apply the principle of *proximity*. As shown in Figure 17-3, the knobs should be positioned in a staggered, square pattern corresponding to the pattern of the burners on the stovetop as opposed to being in a straight line. Donald Norman (1995), a leading human-factors psychologist, says that many accidents blamed on human error may be due to poor machine design.

The combination of person and machine may also be stressful for the individual. Imagine the stress experienced by an engineer working in a nuclear power

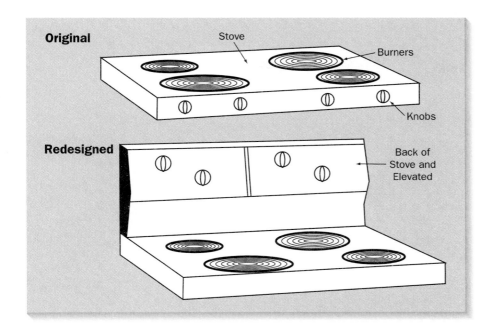

FIGURE 17-3 Engineering redesign of a stove.

Source: Adapted from Sanders & McCormick (1987).

plant or an air traffic controller at a busy airport like Chicago or Atlanta. Both jobs require that the worker be vigilant; a mistake could endanger many lives. You should not be surprised, then, to learn that human-factors psychologists have studied both occupations extensively. Human-engineering specialists will continue to revise, improve, and upgrade our physical world to make a safer and more efficient environment for all—from aspects as tiny and simple as a knob or a switch to the complexity of an engine room in a nuclear-powered submarine.

Workplace Design

In some cases human-machine interaction can be improved by redesigning a single knob or control. In other cases the entire workplace needs to be revised. Workplace design should adhere to several key principles:

1. All tools, materials, equipment, and supplies should be positioned in order of use so that employees' movements are continuous from beginning to end; items should be positioned so that they are accessible and placed within a comfortable reaching distance from any work position so that there is minimal need to change positions.

2. The most important operations or functions should be positioned in a central location. Any crucial displays or controls on the workstation should be located in the middle, directly in front of the worker.

3. Workstations that are used the most frequently should be centrally located to reduce the amount of travel necessary to reach them.

4. Work areas should be grouped according to the similarity of their function. Similar stations or controls and displays should be near one another.

Consider the poor design of the U.S. Army's M-1 Abrams tank, which was built in the mid-1980s without using human-engineering research. When the tank's turret blowers and engine were operating, approximately 50 percent of the tank crews reported that they could not hear one another over the noise. The work consoles for each crew member created visibility problems. The front fenders

Proper design of chairs, keyboards, and computer screens should be based on knowledge of human physical characteristics. Using information such as height, weight, eye level, and reaching distance in the design of equipment can make the equipment easier to use and also reduce errors and injuries.

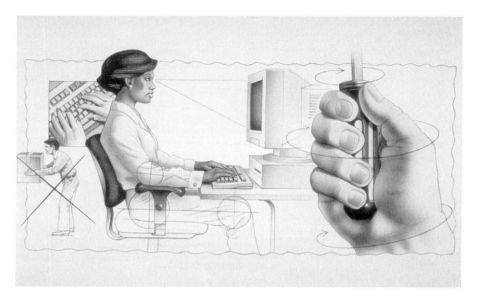

were so badly designed that they did not protect the tank commander or driver from mud, rocks, and other debris kicked up by the treads when riding in an open hatch. Finally, from their position in the tank, drivers were able to see the ground only about 25 feet in front of the tank. This huge blind spot made negotiating obstacles very difficult. The design of the tank's workspace area would have benefited from a subfield of engineering psychology known as *anthropometry.*

Engineering anthropometry, a major subset of human-factors psychology and engineering, involves measurement of human physical characteristics and development of machines and equipment to fit those characteristics. When designing equipment and workstations, engineers must consider people's height, weight, eye level, reaching distance, and so forth. A common use of engineering anthropometry is in the development of chairs. The clothing and shoe industries also make use of anthropometry because they need to know the most common shapes and sizes of the human body.

Safety

Safety is a major concern for human-factors psychologists. Equipment and machines must be designed so that our bodies are not subjected to undue stress or physical damage. Work-related musculoskeletal disorders, collectively referred to as *cumulative trauma disorders (CTDs),* involve damage to tendons, joints, and muscles. One of the most common and widely publicized CTDs is *carpal tunnel syndrome,* a very painful condition of the wrist and hand resulting from compression of the nerve that controls movements of the thumb and some of the fingers. The disorder is more common among women and is especially associated with repetitive work such as keyboard entry (McCann & Sulzer-Azaroff, 1996; Rinzler, 1996). Approximately 200,000 cases of carpal tunnel syndrome are reported per year in the United States. On a broader scale, approximately 7 workers per 100 experience an occupational injury or illness each year. There were more than 6,000 deaths due to occupational injuries in 1996, and in 1997 there were 125,000,000 days lost from work due to injuries. The total cost of work-related deaths and injuries in 1997 was $128 billion, which includes wage and productivity losses, medical costs, and administrative expenses (National Safety Council, 1998).

Human-factors psychologists (sometimes referred to as *safety psychologists*) use several approaches to make work environments safer. One approach is to distinguish accidents caused by unsafe conditions from those caused by

engineering anthropometry
The measurement of human physical characteristics and development of machines and equipment to fit those characteristics

unsafe acts. *Unsafe conditions* can be any degraded or deteriorating environmental state, such as a chemical spill or faulty equipment. Human-factors psychologists can prevent unsafe conditions by redesigning tools, machines, or the workplace environment. This approach is called the *ergonomic approach* to accident reduction.

By contrast, unsafe *acts* are caused by human error. As many as 50 to 80 percent of all accidents may fall into this category (Spettell & Liebert, 1986). Psychologists have proposed two strategies for reducing these types of accidents. According to the *personnel selection approach,* companies should hire only people who possess a safety-conscious personality. Several dimensions of personality (e.g., thrill seeking) account for up to 35 percent of the variance in accidents owing to risky driving (Beirness, 1993). That is, people who scored high on these personality traits had significantly higher incidents of automobile accidents than those who scored low. Insurance companies have long been aware that single males under the age of 25 are more likely to be involved in driving accidents than any other demographic group. The accident rate decreases, however, if the young, single male driver has a good grade-point average, is a nonsmoker, and has graduated from a driver education class. Although driving style does not necessarily conform to workplace practices, many of the same personality dimensions may account for workplace accidents. Hence companies may want to screen applicants for traits and habits that reflect an accident-prone or risk-taking personality.

The second strategy for accident reduction is to train workers to be more safety-conscious. This *personnel training approach* rewards employees for engaging in safe behaviors. Common characteristics of good safety programs are active management and better selection and retention of quality employees.

The Occupational Safety and Health Act, passed by Congress in 1970, created the Occupational Safety and Health Administration (OSHA) to establish and enforce health and safety regulations, to enhance safety education and training, and to promote safety research. This administration inspects worksites and assesses fines and penalties against employers who violate safety regulations. It has also established standards, ranging from the correct height for fire extinguishers to the amount and density of particles in the air. The most difficult challenge for OSHA is enforcing its guidelines and standards. Critics charge that its budget is inadequate and its inspection force is overworked. How has OSHA fared over the years? Congressional investigations of OSHA, have found few lasting reductions in injury rates or lost workdays (Cascio, 1995).

Safety is a major concern for all businesses. On-the-job injuries and deaths cost $128 billion in 1997. Safety psychologists use several approaches to make work environments safer for everyone.

Review Summary

1. **Industrial and organizational psychology** is the application of scientific principles to all aspects of work, including personnel selection and training.

2. **Personnel psychology** focuses on the ways to recruit, select, train, and evaluate workers. Several selection instruments, such as the interview and tests are available to assist psychologists. Personnel psychologists must also know employment law.

3. The planned process of systematically teaching employees new skills so as to enhance job perfor-

mance is called **training.** Training should begin with a needs assessment and end with an evaluation of the training program.

4. **Performance appraisal** is the evaluation of how well employees perform on the job. Job performance may be rated according to objective or subjective criteria. Raters are prone to a variety of rating errors, including *leniency error* and *halo error*.

5. **Organizational psychology** emphasizes an organization's social processes. *Work motivation* involves internal states that activate and direct behavior toward a goal. The prominent work motivation theories are *goal-setting, equity,* and *expectancy*. A pleasant attitude toward one's work indicates job satisfaction. Many work factors correlate with job satisfaction, but it is a very complex attitude.

6. The science of designing human-machine interactions to be safer and more efficient is called **human-factors psychology.**

7. The development of new technology and equipment should follow certain principles, such as compatibility. The design of workplaces is especially important to prevent disastrous outcomes such as the U.S. Army's M-1 tank.

8. **Engineering anthropometry** involves the measurement of human physical characteristics to determine the fit of equipment built for people to use.

9. Safety is a key concern of human-factors psychology. Statistics have shown that the workplace can be a dangerous environment. The Occupational Safety and Health Administration is a government agency that seeks to establish and regulate safety laws for businesses. Safety specialists can pick from the ergonomic approach, personnel selection approach, and personnel training approach to maximize worker safety.

Study Break

1. For eight years Alice has worked for a company that issues credit cards. Last year she was seriously injured in a boating accident. After several months she was able to return to work, although she is now disabled. Under the Americans with Disabilities Act of 1990 what is the company's responsibility to Alice?
   a. They must offer her a schedule of days only.
   b. They must make reasonable accommodations for her as a disabled employee.
   c. They must offer her new training to be able to compete for other jobs within the company.
   d. They must give her job back to her but can reduce her pay in accordance with her level of disability.
2. What changes could be made to interviews to improve their validity as selection procedures?
3. What term is used for the first step in the training process?
   a. ergonomics
   b. needs assessment
   c. beta testing
   d. behavioral measure
4. For years, a local manufacturing company with more than 500 employees has been using a "personality test" to select new employees. They report a high rate of success in using the test.

When they ask a psychologist to examine their personnel policies, what concern is she likely to raise in her report?
   a. The test may not be valid and if so its use is probably illegal.
   b. A protective test would be a better choice because personality tests tend to be transparent.
   c. A test that is used by only one company does not meet legal and professional guidelines for proper personnel selection.
   d. The Civil Rights Act of 1991 prohibited the use of personality tests in the selection process of companies with more than 15 employees.
5. Classify each of the following examples as either an objective or a subjective measure of performance:
   a. Number of days absent
   b. Number of televisions sold
   c. Supervisor's assessment of work quality
6. How can we motivate employees according to goal-setting theory?
7. List the major factors that an engineering psychologist would have to keep in mind when designing even something as simple as an office desk.
8. Compare and contrast the different approaches to safety.

ANSWERS TO STUDY BREAK

Page 732

1. b

2. Research suggests that the use of structured interviews and situational questions can improve validity of interviews for job selection.

3. b

4. a

5. **a.** Objective
   b. Objective
   c. Subjective

6. We must provide them with difficult but attainable goals. The goals must also be specific (not ambiguous). Additionally, feedback, employee participation, and rewards for good performance should be used.

7. Important factors:
   a. Everything should be positioned so that it is easily accessible, comfortable, in order, and requires little movement/effort to use.

b. Important things should be located centrally and at a level easily viewed by the operator.

c. The object itself should be centrally located in the room if used by all.

d. Similar items or work areas should be grouped together.

8. The ergonomic approach emphasizes redesign of the workplace or machines. The personnel selection and personnel training approaches emphasize changing the worker (not the machines). The personnel selection approach, however, argues that we should hire more safety-conscious people, whereas the personnel training approach suggests that we should continuously train and monitor employees with regard to safety.

Statistics
and Psychology

statistics
Branch of mathematics that involves the collection, analysis, and interpretation of data

descriptive statistics
Procedures used to summarize any set of data

inferential statistics
Procedures used to analyze data after an experiment is completed; used to determine if the independent variable has a significant effect

I n Chapter 1 you found that becoming a good psychological detective involved using and understanding statistics. We expand on that discussion here.

Let's begin with a definition of statistics. **Statistics** is a branch of mathematics that involves the collection, analysis, and interpretation of data. As we said in Chapter 1, you can and should use statistics to aid in the decision-making process about knowledge claims. The two main branches of statistics assist your decisions in different ways. **Descriptive statistics** are used to summarize any set of numbers so you can understand and talk about them more intelligibly. **Inferential statistics** are used to analyze data after an experiment is conducted to determine if an independent variable had a significant effect. ■

Decriptive Statistics

We use descriptive statistics when we want to summarize a set of numbers (often referred to as a *distribution*) so that their essential characteristics can be communicated. As we saw in Chapter 1, one of these essential characteristics is a measure of the typical score (called a measure of central tendency). The *mode, median,* and *mean* are the measures of central tendency used by psychologists. A second essential characteristic that we need to know about a distribution is how much variability or spread exists. ■

Measures of Central Tendency

Measures such as the mode, median, and mean tell us about the typical score in a distribution.

Mode.   The **mode** is the number or event that occurs most frequently in a distribution. If students reported the following work hours

12, 15, 20, 20, 20

the mode would be 20.

Mode = 20

Median.   The **median** (mdn) is the number or score that divides the distribution into equal halves. To be able to calculate the median, you must first rank order the scores. Thus if you started with the scores

56, 15, 12, 20, 17

you would need to rank order them as

12, 15, 17, 20, 56

Now, it's an easy task to determine that 17 is the median.

mdn = 17

What if you have an even number of scores, as in the following distribution?

1, 2, 3, 4, 5, 6

In this case the median lies halfway between the two middle scores (3 and 4). Thus the median would be 3.5, halfway between 3 and 4.

Mean.   The **mean** is defined as the arithmetic average. To find the mean we add all the scores in the distribution and then divide by the number of scores we added. For example, we start with

12, 15, 18, 19, 16

We use the Greek letter sigma, Σ, to indicate the sum. If X stands for the numbers in our distribution, then $\Sigma X = 80$. If N stands for the number of scores in the distribution, the mean would equal $\Sigma X/N$. For the preceding example, $\Sigma X(80)/N(5) = 16$. The sum of these numbers is 80, and the mean is 16 (80/5). The mean is symbolized by $\overline{X}$ (X bar). Thus

$$\overline{X} = 16$$

Which measure of central tendency should you choose? The answer depends on the type of information you seek. If you want to know which score occurred most often, then the mode is the choice. The mode may not, however,

mode
Score in a distribution that occurs most often

median
Number that divides a distribution in half

mean
Arithmetic average of a set of numbers; found by adding all the scores in a set and then dividing by the number of scores

be very *representative* of the other scores in your distribution. Consider the following distribution:

$$1, 2, 3, 4, 5, 11, 11$$

The mode is 11. The other scores, however, are considerably smaller; therefore the mode does not accurately describe the typical score.

In this case the median may be a better choice to serve as the representative score because it takes all of the data in the distribution into account. There are drawbacks to this choice, however. The median treats all scores alike; differences in magnitude are not taken into account. Thus the median for *both* of the following distributions is 14. Other than rank ordering the numbers, the values of the other scores do not enter into our calculations.

Distribution 1: 11, 12, 13, 14, 15, 16, 17   mdn = 14
Distribution 2: 7, 8, 9, 14, 23, 24, 25   mdn = 14

When we calculate the mean, however, the value of each number is taken into account. Although the medians for the two preceding distributions are the same, the means are not.

Distribution 1: 11, 12, 13, 14, 15, 16, 17
$$\Sigma X = 98 \quad \bar{X} = 98/7 \quad \bar{X} = 14.00$$

Distribution 2: 7, 8, 9, 14, 23, 24, 25
$$\Sigma X = 110 \quad \bar{X} = 110/7 \quad \bar{X} = 15.71$$

The fact that the mean of Distribution 2 is larger than that of Distribution 1 indicates that the value of each individual score has been taken into account.

Because the mean takes the value of each score into account, it usually is seen as providing a more accurate picture of the typical score and is favored by psychologists. The mean can be misleading, however. Consider the following distribution of charitable donations:

Charitable donations: $1, 1, 1, 5, 10, 10, 100
mode = $1.00
mdn = $5.00
mean = $128.00/7 $\bar{X}$ = $18.29

If you wanted to report the "typical" gift, would it be the mode? Probably not. Even though $1.00 is the most frequent donation, this amount is substantially smaller than any of the other donations, and more people made contributions larger than $1.00 than those who made the $1.00 contribution. What about the median? Five dollars appears to be more representative of the typical donation; there are equal numbers of higher and lower donations. Would the mean be better? In this example the mean is substantially inflated by one large ($100.00) donation; it is $18.29, although six of the seven donations are $10.00 and under. Reporting the mean in this case may look good on a report of giving, but it does not reflect the typical donation.

When you have only a limited number of scores in your distribution, the mean may be inflated (or deflated) by extremely large (or extremely small) scores. The median may be a better choice as your measure of central tendency in such instances. As the number of scores in your distribution increases, the effect of extremely large (or extremely small) scores decreases. Look what happens when we add two additional $5.00 donations:

Charitable donations: $1, 1, 1, 5, 5, 5, 10, 10, 100
mode = $1.00 and $5.00
mdn = $5.00
mean = $138.00/9 $\bar{X}$ = $15.33

Note that we now have two values for the mode ($1.00 and $5.00). The median stays the same ($5.00). The mean, however, has decreased to $15.33; the addition of only two scores moved it appreciably closer to the median.

Graphing Your Results

Once a measure of central tendency has been calculated, this information can be conveyed to others. If you have only one set of scores, the task is simple; you write down the values as part of your paper or report.

What if you are dealing with several groups or sets of numbers? The task becomes complicated, and the inclusion of several numbers in a paragraph of text might be confusing. In such cases a graph or figure can be used advantageously; a picture may be worth a thousand words. You may choose one of several types of graphs.

Pie Chart. If you are dealing with percentages that total 100 percent, then the familiar **pie chart** may be a good choice. The pie chart depicts the percentage represented by each alternative as a slice of a circular pie. The larger the slice, the greater the percentage. A pie chart depicting TV preferences for college men is shown in Figure A-1.

Bar Graph. We use the **bar graph** to present our data in terms of frequencies per category. For example, Figure A-2 shows the sports and fitness preferences of (1) men and boys and (2) women and girls who are frequent participants in such activities.

You can see at a glance that the type of activities and number per category differ drastically between the two groups. (If the sports and fitness categories in Figure A-2 could be quantified and arranged numerically, the columns depicting the frequencies would touch each other and the figure would be known as a *histogram*.) How many words would it take to write about these results rather than present them as a graph?

Frequency Polygon. If we mark the middle of the cross-piece of each bar in a bar graph, connect the dots, and remove the bars, we have constructed a **frequency polygon** (see Figure A-3). The frequency polygon, like the bar graph, displays the frequency of each number or score.

pie chart
Diagram in which the percentage allocated to each alternative is graphically represented as a slice (%) of a circular pie

bar graph
Presents the frequencies for each category as a vertical column or bar

frequency polygon
Line graph that is used to represent the frequencies for each category

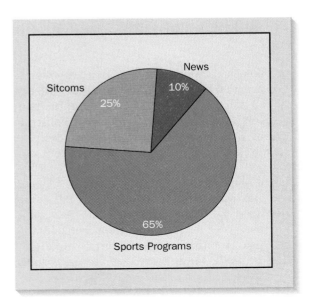

FIGURE A-1
A pie chart depicting TV preferences (percentages) for college men.

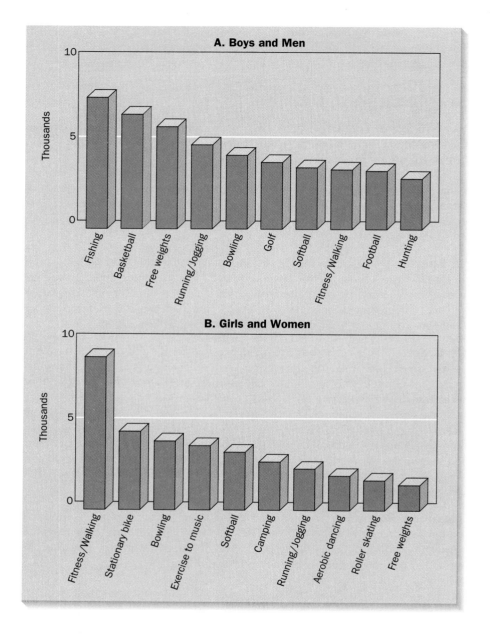

A. Boys and Men

Thousands

Fishing, Basketball, Free weights, Running/Jogging, Bowling, Golf, Softball, Fitness/Walking, Football, Hunting

B. Girls and Women

Thousands

Fitness/Walking, Stationary bike, Bowling, Exercise to music, Softball, Camping, Running/Jogging, Aerobic dancing, Roller skating, Free weights

Line Graph.   The results of psychological experiments are often presented as a line graph. Let's examine the construction of the line graph. We start with two axes or dimensions. The vertical or *Y* axis is known as the **ordinate;** the horizontal or *X* axis is known as the **abscissa** (see Figure A-4). When we construct a line graph, our scores or data (the dependent variables) are plotted on the ordinate. The values of the variable we are manipulating (the independent variable) are plotted on the abscissa.

How tall should the *Y* axis be; how long should the *X* axis be? A good rule of thumb is for the *Y* axis to be approximately two-thirds as tall as the *X* axis is long (see Figures A-4 and A-5). Other configurations give a distorted picture of the data. For example, if the ordinate is considerably shorter, differences between groups or treatments are obscured (see Figure A-6A), whereas lengthening the ordinate tends to exaggerate differences (see Figure A-6B).

ordinate
Vertical or *Y* axis of a graph

abscissa
Horizontal or *X* axis of a graph

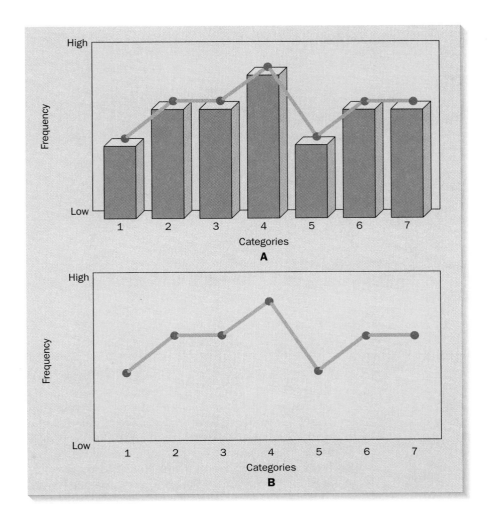

The frequency polygon is constructed by placing a dot in the center of each bar of a bar graph and connecting the dots (A) and removing the bars (B). The frequency polygon, like the bar graph, displays the frequency of each score or number.

In Figure A-5 we have plotted the results of a hypothetical experiment in which the effects of different levels of stress on correct responding in air traffic controllers were evaluated. As stress increased, the number of correct responses increased.

Although measures of central tendency and graphs convey considerable information, we can learn still more about the numbers we have gathered. We also need to know about the variability in our data.

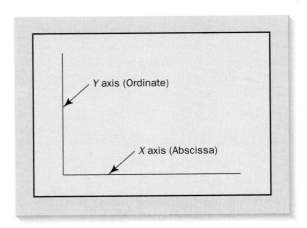

FIGURE A-4
The ordinate, or Y axis, and abscissa, or X axis. The ordinate should be about two-thirds the size of the abscissa to portray the data as clearly as possible.

FIGURE A-5
Results of a hypothetical experiment investigating the effects of stress on correct responding in air traffic controllers.

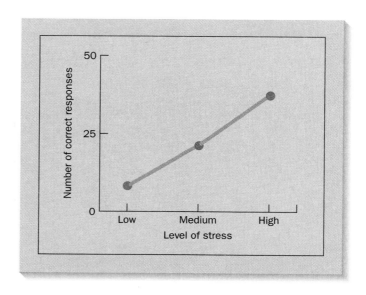

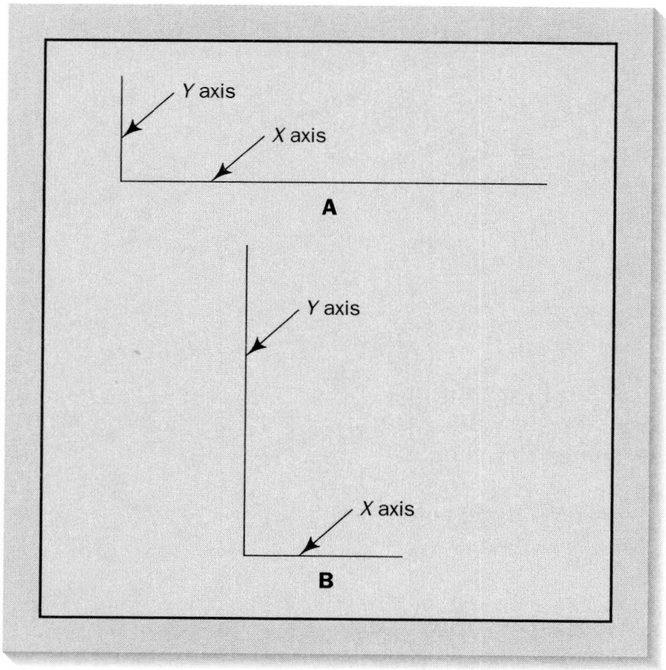

FIGURE A-6
Altering the X (abscissa) or Y (ordinate) axis can distort the results of an experiment. (A) If the ordinate is considerably shorter than the abscissa, significant effects can be obscured. (B) If the ordinate is considerably longer than the abscissa, very small effects can be exaggerated.

Measures of Variability

You just got your last psychology test back; your score was 64. What does that number tell you? By itself it may not mean very much. You ask your professor for additional information and find that the class mean was 56. You feel better because you were above the mean. After a few moments of reflection, however, you realize that you still need more information. How were the other scores grouped? Were they all clustered close to the mean, or did they spread out considerably? The amount of variability or spread in the other scores has a bearing on the meaning of your score. If most of the other scores are very close to the mean, then your score is among the highest in the class. If the other scores are spread out widely around the mean, then your score is not one of the strongest. These situations are diagrammed in Figure A-7.

Obviously we need a measure of variability. The range and standard deviation are two measures of variability frequently reported by psychologists.

Range. The **range** is the easiest measure of variability to calculate; you rank order the scores in your distribution and then subtract the smallest score from the largest. Consider the following distribution:

$$1, 1, 1, 1, 5, 6, 6, 8, 25$$

When we subtract 1 (smallest score) from 25 (largest score), we find that the range is 24.

$$\textbf{range: } 25 - 1 = 24$$

Other than telling us the difference between the largest and smallest scores, however, the range does not provide much information. Knowing that the range

range
Measure of variability that is computed by subtracting the smallest score from the largest score

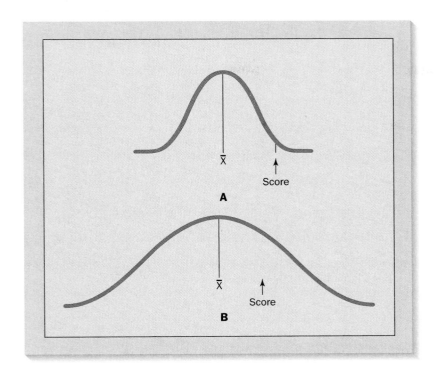

A

B

FIGURE A-7
The spread of scores in a distribution can influence the relative standing of a score. (A) When scores are clustered closely around the mean, a score may be one of the highest in the distribution. (B) When scores are spread out, the same score may not be one of the highest.

FIGURE A-8
The range does not provide much information about the distribution under consideration. Even though the range is the same, these two distributions differ drastically.

is 24 does not tell us about the distribution of the scores we just considered. Consider Figure A-8.

The range is the same for parts A and B; however, the spread of the scores differs drastically between these two distributions. Most of the scores are clustered in the center of the first distribution (Figure A-8A), whereas the scores are spread out more evenly in the second distribution (Figure A-8B). We must turn to another measure, the standard deviation, to provide this additional information.

Variance and Standard Deviation.   To obtain the standard deviation, we must first calculate the **variance.** You can think of the variance as a single number that represents the total amount of variability in our distribution. The larger this number, the greater the spread of the scores. The variance and standard deviation are based on how much each score in the distribution deviates from the mean. To calculate the variance for the distribution we just considered:

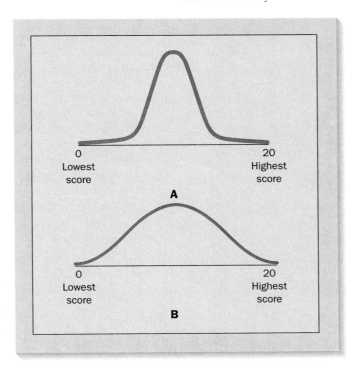

A

B

1. Find the mean. Mean = 54/9 = 6.

$\Sigma X = 54$ $N = 9$ $\overline{X} = \dfrac{\Sigma X}{N}$ $\overline{X} = 54/9$ $\overline{X} = 6$

2. Subtract the mean (column 2) from each score (column 1). This procedure yields a deviation score (x, column 3).

3. Square each deviation score (x^2, column 4).

variance
Single number that represents the total amount of variation in a distribution

standard deviation

Square root of the variance; has important relations to the normal curve

normal distribution

Symmetrical, bell-shaped distribution having half the scores above and half below the mean

SCORE	−	MEAN	=	DEVIATION SCORE (x)	x^2
1	−	6	=	−5	25
1	−	6	=	−5	25
1	−	6	=	−5	25
1	−	6	=	−5	25
5	−	6	=	−1	1
6	−	6	=	0	0
6	−	6	=	0	0
8	−	6	=	2	4
25	−	6	=	19	361
$\Sigma X = 54$				$\Sigma x = 0$	$\Sigma x^2 = 466$

To calculate the variance, all we have to do is take the sum of the squared deviations and divide by the number of scores.

$$\text{variance} = \frac{\Sigma x^2}{N} = 466/9$$
$$= 51.78$$

To find the **standard deviation,** take the square root of the variance.

$$\text{standard deviation (SD)} = \sqrt{\text{variance}}$$
$$= \sqrt{51.78}$$
$$= 7.20$$

As with variance, the larger the standard deviation, the greater the variability or spread of scores.

Now that we have calculated the standard deviation, what does it tell us? To answer that question, we must consider the normal distribution (also called the *bell curve*). The concept of the **normal distribution** is based on the finding that as we increase the number of scores in our sample, many distributions of interest to psychologists become symmetrical or bell shaped. The majority of the scores are clustered around the measure of central tendency, with fewer and fewer scores occurring as we move away from it. As you can see from Figure A-9, the mean, median, and mode of a normal distribution have the same value.

Normal distributions also have some interesting relationships to the standard deviation. For example, distances from the mean of a normal distribution can be measured in standard deviation units. Consider a distribution with an $\overline{X}$

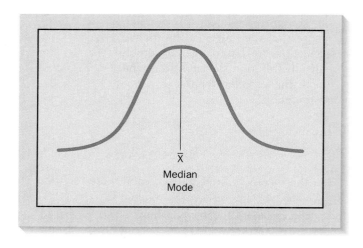

FIGURE A-9

A symmetrical or bell-shaped normal distribution. Note that the mean, median, and mode coincide in a normal distribution.

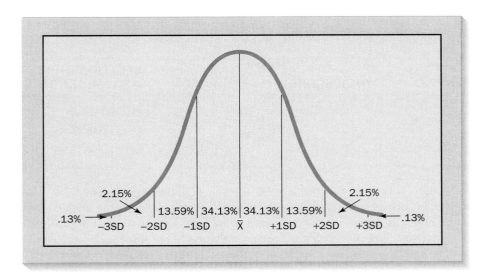

of 56 and SD of 4; a score of 60 can be described as falling one SD above the mean (+1 SD), whereas a score of 48 is two SDs (−2 SD) below the mean. As Figure A-10 shows, approximately 34 percent of all the scores in *all* normal distributions occur between the mean and one SD *above* the mean. Likewise, 34 percent of all the scores in all normal distributions occur between the mean and one SD *below* the mean. About another 13.5 percent of the scores occur between one and two SDs above the mean, whereas another 13.5 percent of the scores occur between one and two SDs below the mean. Thus, about 95 percent of all the scores in a normal distribution occur between two SDs below the mean and two SDs above the mean. Approximately 2.5 percent of the scores occur beyond two SDs above the mean, and another 2.5 percent of the scores occur beyond two SDs below the mean. It is important to remember that these percentages hold true for *all* normal distributions.

Let's return to your test score of 64 (see p. 740). You know that the mean of the class is 56. What if the instructor tells you that the SD is 4; what would your reaction be? Your score of 64 would be two SDs above the mean; you should feel happy. Your score of 64 puts you in the top 2.5 percent of the class (50 percent of the scores below the mean plus 34 percent from the mean to one SD above the mean plus 13.5 percent that occur between one and two SDs above the mean; see Figure A-11A).

What if your instructor had told you that the SD was 20? Your score of 64 does not stand up as well as it did when the SD was 4. You are above the mean but a long way from being even one SD above it (see Figure A-11B).

Because the percentage of the scores that occurs from the mean to the various SD units is the same for all normal distributions,

FIGURE A-11
(A) A score of 64 is exceptionally good when the mean is 56 and the SD is 4. (B) The same score is not as highly regarded when the SD is 20.

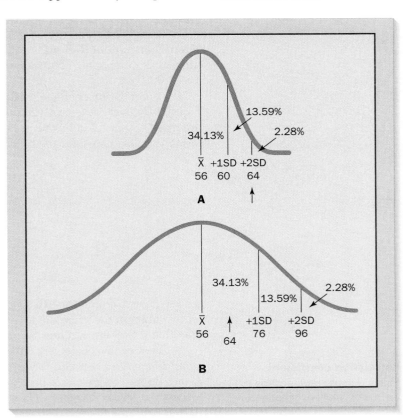

we can compare scores from different distributions by discussing them in terms of SDs above or below the mean. Consider the following scores:

TEST NO.	YOUR SCORE	$\overline{X}$	SD	RELATIONSHIP OF YOUR SCORE TO $\overline{X}$
1	46	41	5	One SD above
2	72	63	4	Over 2 SDs above
3	43	71	10	Over 2 SDs below

Even though your scores, the means, and the SDs differ considerably, we can determine how many SD *units* away from the mean each of your scores is. In turn, these differences can be compared. When these comparisons are made, we find that your first two scores are consistently one SD or more above the mean; you are in at least the top 16 percent of the class. Test 3 is a different matter! By comparing scores from various distributions in this manner, we are able to see patterns and possibly even make predictions about the nature of future scores.

Correlation

We can also use descriptive statistics for predictive purposes. Prediction forms an important part of psychology. For example, you probably took a college entrance examination while you were in high school. Based on the results of this exam, a prediction about your grades in college might be made. Similarly, should you plan to go on for graduate training after you complete your undergraduate degree, you probably will take another entrance examination. Depending on your area of interest, you might take the Graduate Record Examination (GRE), the Law School Aptitude Test (LSAT), the Medical College Aptitude Test (MCAT), or some similar test.

Such predictions are based on the calculation of a correlation coefficient. A **correlation coefficient** is a single number that represents the degree of relationship ("co-relation") between *two* variables; it can range in value from −1.00 to +1.00.

A correlation coefficient of −1.00 indicates there is a *perfect negative relationship* between the two variables of interest. That is, whenever we see an increase of one unit in one variable, there is a proportional decrease in the other variable. Consider the following scores on Texts *X* and *Y*:

	TEST *X*	TEST *Y*
Student 1	49	63
2	50	61
3	51	59
4	52	57
5	53	55

For each unit of increase in a score on Test *X*, there is a corresponding decrease of two units in the score on Test *Y*. Given this information, you are able to predict that if Student 6 scores 54 on Test *X*, the score on Test *Y* will be 53.

A correlation coefficient of 0.00 (or close to this number) indicates that there is *no relationship* between the two variables. As scores on one variable increase, scores on the other variable may increase, decrease, or be the same. Hence we are not able to predict how you will do on Test *Y* by knowing your score on Test *X*. Two sets of scores that have a 0.00 correlation might look like the following:

correlation coefficient

Single number representing the degree of relationship between two variables

	TEST X	**TEST Y**
Student 1	58	28
2	59	97
3	60	63
4	61	15
5	62	50

A correlation coefficient of +1.00 indicates that there is a *perfect positive relationship* between the two sets of scores. When we see an increase of one unit in one variable, we will see a proportional increase in the other variable. Consider the following scores on Texts X and Y:

	TEST X	**TEST Y**
Student 1	25	40
2	26	41
3	27	42
4	28	43
5	29	44
	$\Sigma X = 135$	$\Sigma Y = 210$
	$\overline{X} = 27$	$\overline{Y} = 42$

In this example there is an increase of one unit in the score on Test Y for every unit increase on Test X. The perfect positive correlation leads you to predict that if Student 6 scores 30 on Test X, then the score on Test Y will be 45.

The most common correlation coefficient is the Pearson product moment correlation coefficient. To calculate a Pearson product moment correlation coefficient, we use the following formula:

$$r = \frac{\Sigma(X - \overline{X})(Y - \overline{Y})}{\sqrt{\Sigma(X - \overline{X})^2 \Sigma(Y - \overline{Y})^2}}$$

The steps involved in calculating the correlation coefficient (r) may be summarized as follows:

Numerator

1. Subtract $\overline{X}$ from each X to get $(X - \overline{X})$.
2. Subtract $\overline{Y}$ from each Y to get $(Y - \overline{Y})$.
3. For each pair, multiply $(X - \overline{X})$ by $(Y - \overline{Y})$ to get $(X - \overline{X})(Y - \overline{Y})$.
4. Add to get $\Sigma(X - \overline{X})(Y - \overline{Y})$.

Denominator

1. Square each $(X - \overline{X})$ to get $(X - \overline{X})^2$.
2. Add all of the $(X - \overline{X})^2$s to get $\Sigma(X - \overline{X})^2$.
3. Square each $(Y - \overline{Y})$ to get $(Y - \overline{Y})^2$.
4. Add all of the $(Y - \overline{Y})^2$s to get $\Sigma(Y - \overline{Y})^2$.
5. Multiply $\Sigma(X - \overline{X})^2$ by $\Sigma(Y - \overline{Y})^2$.
6. Take the square root.

Then divide the numerator by the denominator to get r. Using the data from the preceding example, we can calculate the correlation where:

$$\Sigma X = 135 \quad \overline{X} = 27 \quad \Sigma Y = 210 \quad \overline{Y} = 42$$

Numerator

$$\frac{(X - \overline{X}) \quad (Y - \overline{Y})}{}$$

$(25 - 27)(40 - 42) = (-2)(-2) = 4$
$(26 - 27)(41 - 42) = (-1)(-1) = 1$
$(27 - 27)(42 - 42) = (0)(0) = 0$
$(28 - 27)(43 - 42) = (1)(1) = 1$
$(29 - 27)(44 - 42) = (2)(2) = 4$

$$\Sigma(X - \overline{X})(Y - \overline{Y}) = 10$$

Denominator

$(X - \overline{X})^2$				$(Y - \overline{Y})^2$			
$(25 - 27)^2 =$	$(-2)^2$	$=$	4	$(40 - 42)^2 =$	$(-2)^2$	$=$	4
$(26 - 27)^2 =$	$(-1)^2$	$=$	1	$(41 - 42)^2 =$	$(-1)^2$	$=$	1
$(27 - 27)^2 =$	$(0)^2$	$=$	0	$(42 - 42)^2 =$	$(0)^2$	$=$	0
$(28 - 27)^2 =$	$(1)^2$	$=$	1	$(43 - 42)^2 =$	$(1)^2$	$=$	1
$(29 - 27)^2 =$	$(2)^2$	$=$	4	$(44 - 42)^2 =$	$(2)^2$	$=$	4
	$\Sigma(X - \overline{X})^2 = 10$				$\Sigma(Y - \overline{Y})^2 = 10$		

$$r = \frac{\Sigma(X - \overline{X})(Y - \overline{Y})}{\sqrt{\Sigma(X - \overline{X})^2 \Sigma(Y - \overline{Y})^2}}$$

$$r = \frac{10}{\sqrt{(10)(10)}} = \frac{10}{\sqrt{100}} = \frac{10}{10} = 1$$

In this case our correlation coefficient is 1.00, indicating a perfect positive relationship between these two variables. For every increase of one unit in a score on Test X, there is a corresponding increase of one unit in the Test Y score. Our ability to predict a score on Test Y, knowing a corresponding score on Test X, is perfect. The following is an example in which the correlation is very high and positive, but not perfect.

	TEST X	**TEST Y**
Student 1	67	71
2	71	77
3	77	83
4	80	86
5	84	93
	$\Sigma X = 379$	$\Sigma Y = 410$
	$\overline{X} = 75.8$	$\overline{Y} = 82.0$

Numerator

$$\frac{(X = \overline{X})(Y = \overline{Y})}{}$$

$(67 - 75.8)(71 - 82) = (-8.8)(-11) = 96.8$
$(71 - 75.8)(77 - 82) = (-4.8)(-5) = 24.0$
$(77 - 75.8)(83 - 82) = (1.2)(1.0) = 1.2$
$(80 - 75.8)(86 - 82) = (4.2)(4.0) = 16.8$
$(84 - 75.8)(93 - 82) = (8.2)(11.0) = 90.2$

$$\Sigma(X - \overline{X})(Y - \overline{Y}) = 229.0$$

Denominator

$(X - \overline{X})^2$		
$(67 - 75.8)^2 = (-8.8)^2$	$=$	77.44
$(71 - 75.8)^2 = (-4.8)^2$	$=$	23.04
$(77 - 75.8)^2 = (1.2)^2$	$=$	1.44
$(80 - 75.8)^2 = (4.2)^2$	$=$	17.64
$(84 - 75.8)^2 = (8.2)^2$	$=$	67.24
	$\Sigma(X - \overline{X})^2 = 186.80$	

$(Y - \overline{Y})^2$		
$(71 - 82)^2 = (-11)^2$	$= 121$	
$(77 - 82)^2 = (-5)^2$	$= 25$	
$(83 - 82)^2 = (1)^2$	$= 1$	
$(86 - 82)^2 = (4)^2$	$= 16$	
$(93 - 82)^2 = (11)^2$	$= 121$	
	$\Sigma(Y - \overline{Y})^2 = 284.00$	

$$r = \frac{\Sigma(X - \overline{X})(Y - \overline{Y})}{\sqrt{\Sigma(X - \overline{X})^2 \Sigma(Y - \overline{Y})^2}}$$

$$r = \frac{229}{\sqrt{(186.80)(284.00)}} = \frac{229}{\sqrt{53051.20}} = \frac{229}{\sqrt{230.33}} = .99$$

The scatter diagrams in Figure A-12 will help you visualize the various correlations we have discussed. Perfect positive and perfect negative correlations always fall on a straight line, whereas nonperfect correlations do not. For positive correlations the trend of the points is from lower left to upper right; the trend is from upper left to lower right for negative correlations. As you can see, there is no consistent pattern for a 0.00 correlation.

Although descriptive statistics can tell us much about the data we have collected, they cannot tell us everything. For example, if we have conducted an experiment, descriptive statistics cannot tell us if the independent variable we manipulated had a significant effect on the behavior of the participants we were testing or if the results we obtained would have occurred by chance. To make such determinations we must conduct an inferential statistical test.

Inferential Statistics

The results of an inferential statistical test tell us whether our results would occur frequently or rarely by chance. If the results would occur often by chance, we say they are *not significant* and conclude that our independent variable did not affect the dependent variable. If, however, the results of our inferential statistical test would occur rarely by chance, then our result is *significant*, and we conclude that some factor besides chance is operative. If we have conducted our experiment properly and have exercised good control, then our significant statistical result gives us reason to believe that the independent variable we manipulated was effective.

For example, we might be interested in determining if a new method of studying will improve scores in introductory psychology. Twenty students are randomly selected from an introductory psychology

FIGURE A-12
Scatter diagram showing (A) perfect positive and perfect negative correlations, (B) positive and negative correlations, and (C) a 0.00 correlation.

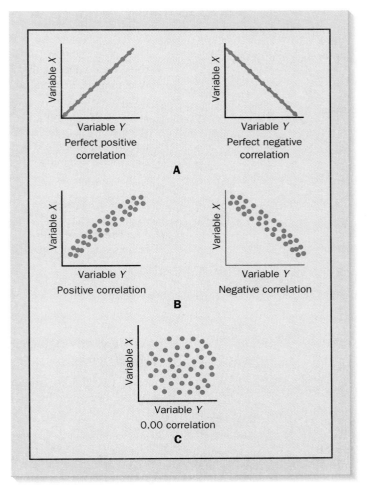

class. In turn, these students are randomly assigned to one of two groups of ten students each. Because the groups are *randomly* formed at the start of the experiment, we assume that they are comparable. ▨

The students in Group A use the new method of studying, whereas the students in Group B use the old method. All students take the same comprehensive final examination at the end of the course. We compare the scores of the two groups on this exam to see if the new method of studying was superior to the old. The scores for these two groups are

GROUP A (NEW STUDY METHOD)	GROUP B (OLD STUDY METHOD)
63	58
71	64
74	68
77	71
85	71
88	73
88	73
91	74
94	78
97	86
$\Sigma A = 828$	$\Sigma B = 716$
$\overline{X}_A = 82.8$	$\overline{X}_B = 71.6$

Was the new study method effective? Just looking at the differences between the groups suggests that it might be; the mean score of Group A is higher than that of Group B. On the other hand, there is considerable overlap between the two groups; several of the students using the old method scored as well as or better than some students using the new method. Is the difference we obtained large enough to be genuine, or is it just a chance happening? Simply looking at the results will not answer that question. An inferential statistical test is needed to determine if our difference is significant or if it can be attributed to chance.

The *t* Test

The ***t* test** is an inferential statistical test used to evaluate the difference between two means. The formula for the *t* test is

$$t = \frac{\overline{X}_A - \overline{X}_B}{\sqrt{\dfrac{(N_A - 1)V_A + (N_B - 1)V_B}{N_A + N_B - 2} \left(\dfrac{1}{N_A} + \dfrac{1}{N_B}\right)}}$$

Although this formula may look a bit intimidating, it really is easy. Just follow along, step by step.

1. Calculate the following:
   a. mean for each group

   $\overline{X}_A =$ mean Group A $\qquad\qquad \overline{X}_B =$ mean Group B
   $\quad = 82.80$ $\qquad\qquad\qquad\qquad\quad = 71.60$

   b. variance for each group

   $V_A =$ variance for Group A $\qquad V_B =$ variance for Group B
   $\quad = 121.73$ $\qquad\qquad\qquad\qquad = 57.16$

t test
Inferential statistical test used to evaluate the difference between two means

2. Determine N for each group

$$N_A = 10 \qquad\qquad\qquad N_B = 10$$

3. Plug the values you have calculated into the above formula.

$$t = \frac{82.80 - 71.60}{\sqrt{\dfrac{(10-1)121.73 + (10-1)57.16}{10 + 10 - 2}\left(\dfrac{1}{10} + \dfrac{1}{10}\right)}}$$

$$t = \frac{11.20}{\sqrt{\dfrac{1095.57 + 514.44}{18}\left(\dfrac{2}{10}\right)}} = \frac{11.20}{\sqrt{\dfrac{1610.01}{18}}\,(.20)}$$

$$t = \frac{11.20}{\sqrt{89.445(.20)}} = \frac{11.20}{\sqrt{17.889}} = \frac{11.20}{4.23} = 2.647$$

Once the t value is calculated, you are ready to determine if it occurs frequently or *rarely by chance*.

When do we consider that an event occurs rarely by chance? Traditionally psychologists have said that any event that occurs by chance alone 5 times or fewer in 100 occasions is a rare event. Thus you will see frequent mention of the ".05 level of significance" in journal articles. This statement means that a result is considered significant if it would occur five or fewer times by chance in 100 replications of the experiment. The experimenter decides on the level of significance before the experiment is conducted.

If we say that a result occurs rarely by chance, what caused it? If we have conducted the experiment properly and exercised good control to rule out unwanted effects, we hope that the manipulation of the independent variable is responsible for the differences we have observed. Was the independent variable (type of study method) responsible for the differences we observed in the experiment just described? Recall that our t value is 2.647. Once we have obtained our t value, several steps must be followed to interpret its meaning:

1. Determine the degree of freedom (df) involved. For our study method problem

$$\begin{aligned} df &= (N_A - 1) + (N_B - 1) \\ &= (10 - 1) + (10 - 1) \\ &= 18 \end{aligned}$$

2. The degrees of freedom are used to enter a t table. The t table contains values that occur by chance. We compare our t value to these chance values. To be significant, the calculated t must be equal to or larger than the one in the table. An example of a t table follows.

	LEVEL OF SIGNIFICANCE		
df	**.05**	**.02**	**.01**
4	2.776	3.747	4.604
10	2.228	2.764	3.169
15	2.131	2.602	2.947
18	2.101	2.552	2.878
21	2.080	2.518	2.831

We enter the *t* table on the row for 18 degrees of freedom. Reading across this row, we find that a value of 2.101 occurs by chance 5 percent of the time (.05 level of significance). Because our value of 2.647 is larger than the value in the table, we can conclude that our result is significant. The type of study method had a significant effect on examination scores. This result is one that occurs 5 or fewer times in 100 by chance. Had we chosen a different level of significance (such as twice in 100 occurrences, .02, or once in 100 occurrences, .01), we would have used one of those columns to determine significance instead of the .05 column.

Clearly inferential statistics play an important role in the scientific process. They provide much of the confidence with which we make our decisions as consumers of psychological information. The *t* test is only one example of an inferential statistic. If you continue your coursework in psychology, you will encounter others.

References

A

Aase, J. M. (1994). Clinical recognition of FAS: Difficulties of detection and diagnosis. *Alcohol Health and Research World, 18,* 5–9.

Abbey, A. (1982). Sex differences in attributions for friendly behavior: Do males misperceive females' friendliness? *Journal of Personality and Social Psychology, 42,* 830–838.

Abbey, A. (1991). Acquaintance rape and alcohol consumption on college campuses: How are they linked? *Journal of American College Health, 39,* 165–169.

Abplanalp, J. M., Rose, R. D. M., Donnelly, A. F., & Livingston-Vaughan, L. (1979). Psychoneuroendocrinology of the menstrual cycle: 2. The relationship between enjoyment of activities, moods, and reproductive hormones. *Psychosomatic Medicine, 41,* 605–615.

Ackerman, D. (1990). *A natural history of the senses.* New York: Random House.

Adelman, C. (1991). *Women at thirty-something: Paradoxes of attainment.* Washington, DC: U.S. Department of Education, Office of Educational Research and Development.

Ader, R., & Cohen, N. (1981). Conditioned immunopharmacologic responses. In R. Ader (Ed.), *Psychoneuroimmunology.* New York: Academic.

Ader, R., & Cohen, N. (1982). Behaviorally conditioned immunosuppression and murine systemic lupus erythematosus. *Science, 215,* 1534–1536.

Ader, R., & Cohen, N. (1985). CNS–immune system interactions: Conditioning phenomena. *Behavior and Brain Science, 8,* 379–394.

Adler, L. L. (1994). Women and gender roles. In L. L. Adler & U. P. Gielen, *Cross-cultural topics in psychology* (pp. 89–101). Westport, CT: Praeger.

Ahn, W., Brewer, W. F., & Mooney, R. J. (1992). Schema acquisition from a single example. *Journal of Experimental Psychology: Learning, Memory, and Cognition, 18,* 391–412.

Ainsworth, M. D. S. (1989). Attachments beyond infancy. *American Psychologist, 44,* 709–716.

Ainsworth, M. D. S., Blehar, M. C., Waters, E., & Wall, S. (1978). *Patterns of attachment: A psychological study of the strange situation.* Hillsdale, NJ: Erlbaum.

Akerstedt, T. (1991). Sleepiness at work: Effects of irregular work hours. In T. M. Monk (Ed.), *Sleep, sleepiness and performance* (pp. 129–152). New York: Wiley.

Akutsu, P. D., Sue, S., Zane, N. W. S., & Nakamura, C. Y. (1989). Ethnic differences in alcohol consumption among Asians and Caucasians in the United States: An investigation of cultural and physiological factors. *Journal of Studies on Alcohol, 50,* 261–267.

Alberti, R. E., & Emmons, M. L. (1990). *Your perfect right* (6th ed.). San Luis Obispo, CA: Impact.

Alcock, J. E. (1981). *Parapsychology: Science or magic?* Oxford: Pergamon.

Alcock, J. E. (1989). *Science and supernature: A critical appraisal of parapsychology.* Buffalo, NY: Prometheus.

Allebeck, P. (1989). Schizophrenia: A life-shortening disease. *Schizophrenia Bulletin, 15,* 81–89.

Allen, L. S., Richey, M. F., Chai, Y. M., & Gorski, R. A. (1991). Sex differences in the corpus callosum of the living human being. *Journal of Neuroscience, 11,* 933–942.

Allen, R. P. (1997). The significance and interpretation of the polysomnogram. In M. R. Pressman & W. C. Orr (Eds.), *Understanding sleep: The evaluation and treatment of sleep disorders* (pp. 193–208). Washington, DC: American Psychological Association.

Allis, S. (1991, March 25). Kicking the nerd syndrome. *Time,* p. 64.

Allport, G. W. (1979). *The nature of prejudice.* Reading, MA: Addison-Wesley. (Originally published in 1954)

Allport, G. W. (1961). *Pattern and growth in personality.* Austin, TX: Holt, Rinehart & Winston.

Allport, G. W., & Odbert, H. S. (1936). Trait names: A psycho-lexical study. *Psychological Monographs, 47*(1, Whole No. 211).

Aloise-Young, P. A., Graham, J. W., & Hansen, W. B. (1994). Peer influence on smoking initiation during early adolescence: A comparison of group members and group outsiders. *Journal of Applied Psychology, 79,* 281–287.

Altshuler, K. Z. (1991). Psychotherapy, 1945–1995. In J. M. Oldham & M. B. Riba (Eds.), *Review of psychiatry* (Vol. 13, pp. 55–72). Washington, DC: American Psychiatric Association.

Alwin, D. F. (1990). Historical changes in parental orientations to children. In N. Mandell (Ed.), *Sociological studies of child development* (Vol. 3). Greenwich, CT: JAI Press.

Amabile, T. M. (1982). Social psychology of creativity: A consensual assessment technique. *Journal of Personality and Social Psychology, 43,* 997–1013.

Amabile, T. M. (1988). A model of creativity and innovation in organizations. *Research in Organizational Behavior, 10,* 123–167.

Amabile, T. M., Hennessey, B. A., & Grossman, B. S. (1986). Social influences on creativity: The effects of contracted-for reward. *Journal of Personality and Social Psychology, 50,* 14–23.

American Academy of Pediatrics (1986). *How to be your child's TV guide: Guidelines for constructive viewing.* Elk Grove Village, IL: Author.

American Association of Retired People. (1992). *A profile of older Americans.* Washington, DC: Author.

American Association of University Women. (1992). *How schools short-change girls.* Washington, DC: AAUW Educational Foundation.

American Heart Association. (1993). *1992 heart and stroke facts.* Dallas: Author.

American Narcolepsy Association. (n.d.). *Facts about narcolepsy.* San Francisco: Author.

American Psychiatric Association. (1994). *Diagnostic and statistical manual of mental disorders* (4th ed.). Washington, DC: Author.

American Psychological Association. (1992). Ethical principles of psychologists and code of conduct. *American Psychologist, 47,* 1597–1611.

American Sleep Disorders Association. (1994). *Coping with shift work.* Rochester, MN: Author.

Amoore, J. E. (1970). *Molecular basis of odor.* Springfield, IL: Thomas.

Amsel, A. (1962). Frustrative nonreward in partial reinforcement and discrimination learning: Some recent history and a theoretical extension. *Psychological Review, 69,* 306–328.

Anastasi, A., & Urbina, S. (1997). *Psychological testing* (7th ed.). Upper Saddle River, NJ: Prentice Hall.

Anch, A. M., Browman, C. P., Mitler, M. M., & Walsh, J. K. (1988). *Sleep: A scientific perspective.* Upper Saddle River, NJ: Prentice Hall.

Anderson, A. R., & Henry, C. S. (1994). Family system characteristics and parental behaviors as predictors of adolescent substance use. *Adolescence, 29,* 405–420.

Anderson, J. R., & Bower, G. H. (1974). A propositional theory of recognition memory. *Memory and Cognition, 2,* 406–412.

Anderson, J. R., & Fincham, J. M. (1994). Acquisition of procedural skills from examples. *Journal of Experimental Psychology: Learning, Memory, and Cognition, 20,* 1322–1340.

Andreasen, N. C. (1988). Brain imaging: Applications in psychiatry. *Science, 239,* 1381–1388.

Andreasen, N. C. (1984). *The broken brain: The biological revolution in psychiatry.* New York: Harper & Collins.

Andreasen, N. C., Arndt, S., Swayze, V., III, Cizadlo, T., Flaum, M., O'Leary, D., Ehrhardt, J. C., & Yuh, W. T. C. (1994). Thalamic abnormalities in schizophrenia visualized through magnetic resonance image averaging. *Science, 266,* 294–298.

Andreasen, N. C., & Black, D. W. (1995). *Introductory textbook of psychiatry* (2nd ed.). Washington, DC: American Psychiatric Association.

Andreasen, N. C., Flaum, M., Swayze, V. W., II, Tyrrell, G., & Arndt, S. (1990). Positive and negative symptoms in schizophrenia. *Archives of General Psychiatry, 47,* 615–621.

Angleitner, A., Riemann, R., & Strelau, J. (1995). A study of twins using the self-report and peer-report NEO-FFI scales. Paper presented at the seventh meeting of the International Society for the Study of Individual Differences, July 15–19. Warsaw, Poland.

Archer, D., & Akert, R. M. (1984). Nonverbal factors in person perception. In M. Cook (Ed.), *Issues in person perception* (pp. 114–144). New York: Methuen.

Archer, J. (1989). The relationship between gender-role measures: A review. *British Journal of Social Psychology, 28,* 173–184.

Archer, S. L., & Waterman, A. S. (1990). Varieties of identity diffusions and foreclosures: An exploration of the subcategories of the identity statures. *Journal of Adolescent Research, 5,* 96–111.

Ardrey, R. (1966). *The territorial imperative.* New York: Atheneum.

Argyle, M., & Henderson, M. (1984). The rules of friendship. *Journal of Social and Personal Relationships, 1,* 211–237.

Armstrong-Daily, A. (1991). Hospice care for children: The families and health care providers. In D. Papadatos & C. Papadatos (Eds.), *Children and death* (pp. 225–229). New York: Hemisphere.

Aronson, E., & Mills, J. (1959). The effect of severity of initiation of liking for a group. *Journal of Abnormal and Social Psychology, 59,* 177–181.

Arrigo, J. M., & Pezdek, K. (1997). Lessons from the study of psychogenic amnesia. *Current Directions in Psychological Science, 6,* 148–152.

Arvey, B. D., Bouchard, T. J., Segal, N. L., & Abraham, L. M. (1989). Job satisfaction: Environmental and genetic components. *Journal of Applied Psychology, 74,* 187–192.

Arvey, B. O., & Campion, J. E. (1982). The employment interview: A summary and review of recent research. *Journal of Applied Psychology, 39,* 281–322.

Arvey, R. D., & Murphy, K. R. (1998). Performance evaluation in work settings. In J. T. Spence, J. M. Darley, & D. J. Foss (Eds.) (pp. 141–168). *Annual Review of Psychology, 49.* Palo Alto, CA: Annual Reviews.

Asch, S. E. (1955). Opinions and social pressure. *Scientific American, 193,* 31–35.

Asch, S. E. (1956). Studies of independence and conformity: A minority of one against a unanimous majority. *Psychological Monographs, 70*(9, Whole No. 416).

Aserinsky, E., & Kleitman, N. (1953). Regular occurring periods of eye motility and concomitant phenomena during sleep. *Science, 118,* 273–274.

Ash, M. G. (1995). *Gestalt psychology in German culture, 1890–1967: Holism and the quest for objectivity.* New York: Cambridge University Press.

Ashcraft, M. H. (1994). *Human memory and cognition* (2nd ed.). New York: HarperCollins.

Atkinson, R. C., & Shiffrin, R. M. (1971). The control of short-term memory. *Scientific American, 225,* 82–90.

Atkinson, J. W. (1974). The mainsprings of achievement-oriented activity. In J. W. Atkinson & J. O. Raynot (Eds.). *Motivation and achievement.* New York: Wiley.

Atkinson, J. W., & Walker, E. L. (1956). The affiliation motive and sensitivity to faces. *Journal of Abnormal and Social Psychology, 53,* 38–41.

Axelrod, S., & Apsche, J. (1983). *The effects of punishment on human behavior.* New York: Academic.

Ayers, M. S., & Reder, L. M. (1998). A theoretical review of the misinformation effect: Predictions from an activation-based memory model. *Psychonomic Bulletin & Review, 5,* 1–21.

Azrin, N. H., & Holz, W. C. (1966). Punishment. In W. K. Honig (Ed.), *Operant behavior: Areas of application* (pp. 380–447). New York: Appleton-Century-Crofts.

B

Bach, M., Bach, D., Bohmer, F., & Nutzinger, D. O. (1994). Alexithymia and somatization: Relationship to *DSM-III-R* diagnosis. *Journal of Psychosomatic Research, 38,* 529–538.

Bachman, J. G., Johnston, L. D, & O'Malley, P. M. (1998). Explaining recent increases in students' marijuana use: Impace of perceived risks and disapproval, 1976 through 1996. *American Journal of Public Health, 88,* 887-892.

Bachman, J. G., Johnston, L. D, & O'Malley, P. M. (1990). Explaining the recent decline in cocaine use among young adults: Further evidence that perceived risks and disapproval lead to reduced drug use. *Journal of Health and Social Behavior, 31,* 173–184.

Bachman, J. G., Johnston, L. D., O'Malley, P. M., & Humphrey, R. H. (1988). Explaining the recent decline in marijuana use: Differentiating the effects of perceived risks, disapproval, and general lifestyle factors. *Journal of Health and Social Behavior, 29,* 92–112.

Bachman, R. (1994). *Violence against women: A National Crime Victimization Survey report.* Washington, DC: U.S. Department of Justice.

Baddeley, A. (1998). *Human memory.* Boston: Allyn & Bacon.

Baddeley, A. D.(1988). Cognitive psychology and human memory. *Trends in Neurosciences, 11,* 176–181.

Baddeley, A. D. (1992a). Is working memory working? *Quarterly Journal of Experimental Psychology, 44A,* 1–31.

Baddeley, A. D. (1992b). Working memory. *Science, 255,* 556–559.

Baddeley, A. D., Papagno, C., & Andrade, J. (1993). The sandwich effect: The role of attentional factors in serial recall. *Journal of Experimental Psychology: Learning, Memory, and Cognition, 19,* 862–870.

Badia, P. (1993). Learning. In M. A. Carskadon (Ed.), *Encyclopedia of sleep and dreaming* (pp. 327–328). New York: Macmillan.

Baenninger, M., & Newcombe, N. (1989). The role of experience in spatial test performance: A meta-analysis. *Sex Roles, 20,* 327–344.

Baer, L., Rauch, S. L., Ballantine, T., Martuza, R., Cosgrove, R., Cassem, E., Giriunas, I., Manzo, P. A., Dimino, C., & Jenike, M. A. (1995). Cingulotomy for intractable obsessive-compulsive disorder. *Archives of General Psychiatry, 1995, 52,* 384–392.

Baillargeon, R. (1993). The object concept revisited: New directions in the investigation of infants' physical knowledge. In C. Granrud (Ed.), *Visual perception and cognition in infancy: Carnegie Mellon symposia on cognition* (pp. 265–315). Hillsdale, NJ: Erlbaum.

Baillargeon, R. (1994). How do infants learn about the physical world? *Current Directions in Psychological Science, 3,* 133–140.

Baker, D. D., Terpstra, D. E., & Larntz, K. (1990). The influence of individual characteristics and severity of harassing behavior on reactions to sexual harassment. *Sex Roles, 22,* 305–325.

Baker, R. A. (1990). *They call it hypnosis.* Buffalo, NY: Prometheus.

Baker, R. A. (1993). *The art of cold reading.* Lexington, KY: Author.

Baldwin, E. (1993). The case for animal research in psychology. *Journal of Social Issues, 49,* 121–131.

Baldwin, J. D., & Baldwin, J. I. (1998). *Behavior principles in everyday life* (3rd ed.). Upper Saddle River, NJ: Prentice Hall.

Bales, R. F. (1950). *Interaction process analysis: A method for the study of small groups.* Reading, MA: Addison-Wesley.

Banazak, D. A. (1996). Electroconvulsive therapy: A guide for family physicians. *American Family Physician, 53,* 273–278.

Bandura, A. (1977). Self-efficacy: Toward a unifying theory of behavior change. *Psychological Review, 84,* 191–215.

Bandura, A. (1986). *Social foundations of thought and action: A social-cognitive theory.* Upper Saddle River, NJ: Prentice Hall.

Bandura, A., Blanchard, E. B., & Ritter, B. (1969). Relative efficacy of desensitization and modeling approaches for inducing behavioral, affective, and attitudinal changes. *Journal of Personality and Social Psychology, 13,* 173–199.

Bandura, A., Ross, D., & Ross, S. (1963). Imitation of film-mediated aggressive models. *Journal of Abnormal and Social Psychology, 66,* 3–11.

Barefoot, J. C., Dahlstrom, W. G., & Williams, R. B., Jr. (1983). CHD incidence and total mortality: A 25-year follow-up study of 255 physicians. *Psychosomatic Medicine, 45,* 59–63.

Barefoot, J. C., Dodge, K. A., Peterson, B. L., Dahlstrom, W. G., & Williams, R. B., Jr. (1989). The Cook-Medley Hostility Scale: Item content and ability to predict survival. *Psychosomatic Medicine, 51,* 46–57.

Barinaga, M. (1994). To sleep, perchance to . . . learn? New studies say yes. *Science, 265,* 603–604.

Barlow, D. H., Vermilyea, J. Blanchard, E. B., Vermilyea, B. B., Di Nardo, P. A., & Cerny, J. A. (1985). The phenomenon of panic. *Journal of Abnormal Psychology, 94,* 320–328.

Barnett, R. C., Grahame, N. J., & Miller, R. R. (1993). Temporal encoding as a determinant of blocking. *Learning and Motivation, 22,* 253–268.

Barnlund, D. C. (1989). *Public and private self in Japan and the United States.* Tokyo: Intercultural Press.

Baron, S., & Welty, A. (1996). Elder abuse. *Journal of Gerontological Social Work, 25,* 33–57.

Baron, L., & Straus, M. A. (1984). Sexual stratification, pornography, and rape in the United States. In N. M. Malamuth & E. Donnerstein (Eds.), *Pornography and sexual aggression.* San Diego, CA: Academic Press.

Barrick, M. R., & Mount, M. K. (1991). The big five personality dimensions and job performance: A meta-analysis. *Personnel Psychology, 44,* 1–26.

Barrick, M. R., & Mount, M. K. (1993). Autonomy as a moderator of the relationships between the Big Five personality dimensions and job performance. *Journal of Applied Psychology, 78,* 111–118.

Barron, F. (1958). The psychology of imagination. *Scientific American, 199,* 150–166.

Barron, F. (1988). Putting creativity to work. In R. J. Sternberg (Ed.), *The nature of creativity* (pp. 76–98). New York: Cambridge University Press.

Bartecchi, C. E., MacKenzie, T. D., & Schrier, R. W. (1995). The global tobacco epidemic. *Scientific American, 272,* 44–51.

Barth, D. S., & MacDonald, K. D. (1996). Thalamic modulation of high-frequency oscillating potentials in auditory cortex. *Nature, 383,* 78–81.

Bartlett, F. C. (1932). *Remembering: A study in experimental and social psychology.* Cambridge: Cambridge University Press.

Bartlett, J. G., & Moore, R. D. (1998). Improving HIV therapy. *Scientific American, 279,* 84–87, 89.

Barton, A. (1992). Humanistic contributions to the field of psychotherapy: Appreciating the human and liberating the therapist. *Humanistic Psychologist, 20,* 332– 348.

Bartoshuk, L. M. (1991). Taste, smell, and pleasure. In R. C. Bolles (Ed.), *The hedonics of taste* (pp. 15–28). Hillsdale, NJ: Erlbaum.

Baruch, G. K. (1984). The psychological well-being of women in the middle years. In G. K. Baruch & J. Brooks-Gunn (Eds.), *Women in midlife.* New York: Plenum.

Basow, S. (1992). *Gender stereotypes and roles* (3rd ed.). Pacific Grove, CA: Brooks/Cole.

Batsell, W. R., Jr., & Best, M. R. (1992). Variations in the retention of taste aversion: Evidence for retrieval competition. *Animal Learning and Behavior, 20,* 146–159.

Batsell, W. R., Jr., & Best, M. R. (1993). One bottle too many? Method of testing determines the detection of overshadowing and retention of taste aversion. *Animal Learning and Behavior, 21,* 154–158.

Batson, C. D. (1991). *The altruism question: Toward a social-psychological answer.* Hillsdale, NJ: Erlbaum.

Batson, C. D., Dyck, J. L., Brandt, J. R., Batson, J. G., Powell, A. L., McMaster, M. R., & Griffitt, C. (1988). Five studies testing two new egoistic alternatives to the empathy-altruism hypothesis. *Journal of Personality and Social Psychology, 55,* 52–77.

Baum, A., Gatchel, R. J., & Schaeffer, M. A. (1983). Emotional, behavioral, and physiological effects of chronic stress at Three Mile Island. *Journal of Consulting and Clinical Psychology, 51,* 565–572.

Baumrind, D. (1983). Rejoinder to Lewis reinterpretation of parental firm control affects: Are authoritative families rarely harmonious? *Psychological Bulletin, 94,* 132– 142.

Baumrind, D. (1971). Harmonious parents and their preschool children. *Developmental Psychology, 41,* 92–102.

Baxter, S. (1994, March-April). Gender differences. *Psychology Today,* pp. 50–53, 85–86.

Bayley, N. (1969). *Bayley Scales of Infant Development.* New York: Psychological Corporation.

Beach, F. A. (1950). The snark was a boojum. *American Psychologist, 19,* 115– 124.

Beal, C. R. (1994). *Boys and girls: The development of gender roles.* New York: McGraw-Hill.

Beaumont, J. H. (1988). *Understanding neuropsychology.* New York: Blackwell.

Beck, A. T. (1979). *Cognitive therapy and the emotional disorders.* Cleveland, OH: Meridian.

Beck, A. T. (1991). Cognitive therapy: A 30-year retrospective. *American Psychologist, 46,* 369–375.

Beet, S. (1974). *Abkhasians: The long-lived people of the Caucasus*. Austin, TX: Holt, Rinehart & Winston.

Beirness, O. J. (1993). Do we really drive as we live? The role of personality factors in road crashes. *Alcohol, Drugs, and Driving, 9,* 129–143.

Begley, S. (1995, March 27). Gray matters. *Newsweek,* pp. 48–54.

Bekesy, G., von. (1956). Current status of theories of hearing. *Science, 123,* 779–783.

Belansky, E. S., & Boggiano, A. K. (1994). Predicting helping behaviors: The role of gender and instrumental/expressive self-schemata. *Sex Roles, 30,* 647–661.

Belsky, J. (1984). Two waves of day-care research: Developmental effects and conditions of quality. In R. Ainslie (Ed.), *The child and the day-care setting.* New York: Praeger.

Belsky, J. (1986). Infant day care: A cause for concern? *Zero to Three, 6,* 1–9.

Belsky, J., Gilstrap, B., & Rovine, M. (1984). The Pennsylvania Infant and Family Development Project: 1. Stability and change in mother-infant and father-infant interaction in a family setting—1-to 3- to 9-months. *Child Development, 55,* 692–705.

Bem, D. J., & Honorton, C. (1994). Does psi exist? Replicable evidence for an anomalous process of information transfer. *Psychological Bulletin, 115,* 4–18.

Bem, S. L. (1981). Gender schema theory: A cognitive account of sex typing. *Psychological Review, 88,* 354–364.

Bem, S. L. (1993). *The lenses of gender.* New Haven, CT: Yale University Press.

Benbow, C. P., & Stanley, J. C. (1980). Sex differences in mathematical ability: Fact or artifact? *Science, 210,* 1262–1264.

Benbow, C. P., & Stanley, J. C. (1982). Consequences in high school and college of sex differences in mathematical reasoning ability: A longitudinal perspective. *American Educational Research Association Journal, 19,* 598–622.

Bengtson, H., & Johnson, L. (1992). Perspective taking, empathy, and pro-social behavior in late childhood. *Child Study Journal, 22,* 11–22.

Bennett, W., & Gurin, J. (1982). *The dieter's dilemma: Eating less and weighing more.* New York: Basic Books.

Benoit, D., & Parker, K. C. H. (1994). Stability and transmission of attachment across three generations. *Child Development, 65,* 1444–1456.

Benokraitis, N., & Feagin, J. (1995). *Modern sexism: Blatant, subtle, and overt discrimination* (2nd ed.). Englewood Cliffs, NJ: Prentice Hall.

Benson, D., Charlton, C., & Goodhart, F. (1992). Acquaintance rape on campus: A literature review. *Journal of American College Health, 40,* 157–165.

Benson, H. (1975). *The relaxation response.* New York: Morrow.

Benson, H. (1984). *Beyond the relaxation response.* New York: Times Books.

Ben Tsvi–Mayer, S., Hertz-Lazarowitz, R., & Safir, M. P. (1989). Teachers' selection of boys and girls as prominent pupils. *Sex Roles, 21,* 231–245.

Beratis, S., Gabriel, J., & Hoidas, S. (1994). Age at onset in subtypes of schizophrenic disorders. *Schizophrenia Bulletin, 20,* 287–296.

Berenbaum, H., & James, T. (1994). Correlates and retrospectively reported antecedents of alexithymia. *Psychosomatic Medicine, 56,* 353–359.

Bergin, A. E. (1971). The evaluation of therapeutic outcomes. In A. E. Bergin & S. L. Garfield (Eds.), *Handbook of psychotherapy and behavior change: An empirical analysis.* New York: Wiley.

Berk, L. E. (1998). *Development through the life span.* Boston: Allyn & Bacon.

Berk, L. E. (2000). Development. In S. F. Davis & J. S. Halonen (Eds.), *The many faces of psychological research in the twenty-first century.* Washington, DC: American Psychological Association.

Berk, L. E., & Spuhl, S. T. (1995). Maternal interaction, private speech, and task performance in preschool children. *Early Childhood Research Quarterly, 10,* 145–169.

Berkowitz, L. (1965). The concept of aggressive drive: Some additional considerations. In L. Berkowitz (Ed.), *Advances in experimental social psychology* (Vol. 2). San Diego, CA: Academic Press.

Berkowitz, L. (1984). Some effects of thoughts on anti- and pro-social influences of media events: A cognitive neoassociation analysis. *Psychological Bulletin, 95,* 410–427.

Berkowitz, L. (1994). On the escalation of aggression. In M. Potegal & J. F. Knutson (Eds.), *The dynamics of aggression: Biological and social processes in dyads and groups* (pp. 33–41). Hillsdale, NJ: Erlbaum.

Berman, M. O. (1990). Severe brain dysfunction: Alcoholic Korsakoff's syndrome. *Alcohol Health and Research World, 14,* 120–129.

Bernard, L. C., & Krupat, E. (1994). *Health psychology.* Fort Worth, TX: Harcourt Brace.

Bernstein, D. A., & Carlson, C. R. (1993). Progressive relaxation: Abbreviated methods. In P. M. Lehrer & R. L. Woolfolk (Eds.), *Principles and practice of stress management* (2nd ed.) (pp. 53–88) New York: Guilford Press.

Bernstein, I. L. (1978). Learned taste aversions in children receiving chemotherapy. *Science, 200,* 1302–1303.

Bernstein, I. L., & Webster, M. M. (1980). Learned taste aversions in humans. *Physiology and Behavior, 25,* 363–366.

Bernstein, I. L., & Webster, M. M. (1982). Food aversions in children receiving chemotherapy for cancer. *Cancer, 50,* 2961–2963.

Berry, J. W., Poortinga, Y. H., Segall, M. H., & Dasen, P. R. (1992). *Cross-cultural psychology: Research and applications.* New York: Cambridge University Press.

Berry, R. E., & Williams, F. L. (1987). Assessing the relationship between quality of life and marital and income satisfaction: A path analytic approach. *Journal of Marriage and the Family, 49,* 107–116.

Bettencourt, B. A., & Miller, N. (1996). Gender differences in aggression as a function of provocation: A meta-analysis. *Psychological Bulletin, 119,* 422–447.

Betz, N. E. (1994). Basic issues and concepts in carer counseling for women. In W. B. Walsh & S. H. Osipow (Eds.), *Career counseling for women* (pp. 1–41). Hillsdale, NJ: Lawrence Erlbaum Associates.

Bhatia, S. C., & Bhatia, S. K. (1997). Major depression: Selecting safe and effective treatment. *American Family Physician, 55,* 1683–1694.

Biernat, M. (1991). Gender stereotypes and the relationship between masculinity and femininity: A developmental analysis. *Journal of Personality and Social Psychology, 61,* 351–365.

Biernat, M., & Wortman, C. (1991). Sharing of home responsibilities between professionally employed women and their husbands. *Journal of Personality and Social Psychology, 60,* 844–860.

Bingham, C. R., Miller, B. C., & Adams, G. R. (1990). Correlates of age at first sexual intercourse in a national sample of young women. *Journal of Adolescent Research, 5,* 18–33.

Birren, J. E., Woods, A. M., & Williams, M. V. (1980). Behavioral slowing with age: Causes, organization and consequences. In L. W. Poon (Ed.), *Aging in the 80's: Psychological issues.* Washington, DC: American Psychological Association.

Bishop, G. F., Tuchfarber, A. J., & Oldendick, R. W. (1986). Opinions on fictitious issues: The pressure to answer survey questions. *Public Opinion Quarterly, 50,* 240–250.

Björk, R. A. (1975). Short-term storage: The ordered output of a central processor. In F. Restle, R. M. Shiffrin, N. J. Castellad, H. R. Lindman, & D. B. Pisoni (Eds.), *Cognitive theory,* Vol. 1. Hillsdale, NJ: Erlbaum.

Björk, D. W. (1997). *B. F. Skinner: A life.* Washington, DC: American Psychological Association.

Björklund, A. (1992). Dopaminergic transplants in experimental parkinsonism: Cellular mechanisms of graft-induced functional recovery. *Current Opinion in Neurobiology, 2,* 683–689.

Blackman, J. (1990). Emerging images of severely battered women and the criminal justice system. *Behavioral Sciences and the Law, 8,* 121–130.

Blackmore, S. J. (1992). Psychic experiences: Psychic illusions. *Skeptical Inquirer, 16,* 367–376.

Blackmore, S. J. (1994). Psi in psychology. *Skeptical Inquirer, 18,* 351–355.

Blackmore, S. J., & Troscianko, T. (1985). Belief in the paranormal: Probability judgments, illusory control, and the "chance baseline shift." *British Journal of Psychology, 76,* 459–468.

Blaisdell, A. P., Denniston, J. C., & Miller, R. R. (1998). Temporal encoding as a determinant of overshadowing. *Journal of Experimental Psychology: Animal Behavior Processes, 24,* 72–83.

Blass, E. M., & Ganchrow, J. R., & Steiner, J. E. (1984). Classical conditioning in newborn infants 2-48 hours of age. *Infant Behavior and Development, 7,* 223–235.

Block, J. R., & Yuker, H. E. (1989). *Can you believe your eyes?* Lake Worth, FL: Gardner Press.

Block, R. I., Farinpour, R., & Braverman, K. (1992). Acute effects of marijuana on cognition: Relationships to chronic effects and smoking techniques. *Pharmacology Bulletin, 43,* 907–917.

Block, R. I., & Ghoneim, M. M. (1993). Effects of chronic marijuana use on human cognition. *Psychopharmacology, 110,* 219–228.

Bloom, B. L. (1992). Planned short-term psychotherapy: Current status and future challenges. *Applied and Preventive Psychology, 1,* 157–164.

Blos, P. (1962). *On adolescence: A psychoanalytic interpretation.* New York: Free Press.

Blount, R. L., Dahlquist, L. M., Baer, R. A., & Wuori, D. (1984). A brief, effective method for teaching children to swallow pills. *Behavior Therapy, 15,* 381–387.

Blum, D. (1998). Face it! *Psychology Today, 31*(5), 32–39, 66–67, 69–70.

Blumenthal, J. A., Emery, C. F., Walsh, M. A., Cox, D. R., Kuhn, C. M., Williams, R. B., & Williams, R. S. (1988). Exercise training in healthy Type A middle-aged men: Effects on behavioral and cardiovascular responses. *Psychosomatic Medicine, 50,* 418–433.

Bohan, J. S. (1992a). *Replacing women in psychology: Readings toward a more inclusive history.* Dubuque, IA: Kendall-Hunt.

Bohan, J. S. (1992b). *Seldom seen, rarely heard: Women's place in psychology.* Boulder, CO: Westview Press.

Bohn, M. J., Babor, T. F., & Kranzler, H. R. (1995). The Alcohol Use Disorders Identification Test (AUDIT): Validation of a screening instrument for use in medical settings. *Journal of Studies on Alcohol, 56,* 423–432.

Bolles, R. C. (1979). *Learning theory* (2nd ed.). Austin, TX:: Holt, Rinehart & Winston.

Booth-Kewley, S., & Friedman, H. S. (1987). Psychological predictors of heart disease: A quantitative review. *Psychological Bulletin, 101,* 343–362.

Bootzin, R. R., Epstein, D., & Wood, J. M. (1991). Stimulus control instructions. In P. J. Hauri (Ed.), *Case studies in insomnia* (pp. 19–28). New York: Plenum.

Borkenau, P., & Liebler, A. (1992). Trait inferences: Sources of validity at zero acquaintance. *Journal of Personality and Social Psychology, 62,* 645–657.

Borkenau, P., & Liebler, A. (1995). Observable attributes as manifestations and cues of personality and intelligence. *Journal of Personality, 63,* 125.

Bornstein, M. H., & Lamb, M. E. (1992). *Development in infancy* (3rd ed.). New York: McGraw-Hill.

Bornstein, M. H., Tal, J., & Tamis-Lemonda, C. S. (1991). Parenting in a cross-cultural perspective: The United States, France, and Japan. In M. H. Bornstein (Ed.), *Cultural approaches to parenting.* Hillsdale, NJ: Erlbaum.

Bornstein, R. F. (1992). Subliminal mere exposure effects. In R. F. Bornstein (Ed.), *Perception without awareness: Cognitive, clinical, and social perspectives* (pp. 191–210). New York: Guilford Press.

Bostwick, T. D., & De Lucia, J. L. (1992). Effects of gender and specific dating behaviors on perceptions of sex willingness and date rape. *Journal of Social and Clinical Psychology, 11*, 14–25.

Botvin, G. J., Dusenbury, L., Baker, E., James-Ortiz, S., Botvin, E. M., & Kerner, J. (1992). Smoking prevention among urban minority youth: Assessing effects on outcome and mediating variables. *Health Psychology, 11*, 290–299.

Bouchard, T. J., Jr., & McGue, M. (1981). Familial studies of intelligence. *Science, 212*, 1055–1059.

Bourdon, Rae, D. S., Narrow, W. E., Manderscheid, R. W., & Regier, D. A. (1994).

Bourne, L. E., Dominowski, R. L., Loftus, E. F., & Healy, A. F. (1986). *Cognitive processes.* Englewood Cliffs, NJ: Prentice Hall.

Bousfield, W. A. (1953). The occurrence of clustering in the recall of randomly arranged associates. *Journal of General Psychology, 49*, 229–240.

Bouton, M. E., & Brooks, D. C. (1993). Time and context effects on performance in a Pavlovian discrimination reversal. *Journal of Experimental Psychology, 19*, 165–179.

Bowd, A. D., & Shapiro, K. J. (1993). The case against laboratory animal research in psychology. *Journal of Social Issues, 49*, 133–142.

Bower, B. (1991). Oedipus wrecked. *Science News, 140*, 248–250.

Bower, B. (1993). Sudden recall: Adult memories of child abuse spark a heated debate. *Science News, 144*, 184–186.

Bower, G. H. (1981). Mood and memory. *American Psychologist, 36*, 129–148.

Bowlby, J. (1969). *Attachment and loss: Vol. 1. Attachment,* New York: Basic Books.

Bowlby, J. (1980). *Attachment and loss: Vol. 3. Loss: Sadness and depression.* New York: Basic Books.

Bowser, B. P., & Hunt, R. G. (Eds.) (1996). *Impacts of racism on white Americans* (2nd ed.). Beverly Hills, CA: Sage.

Bradshaw, J. L., & Nettleton, N. C. (1981). The nature of hemispheric specialization in man. *Behavioral and Brain Sciences, 4*, 51–91.

Branscombe, N. R., N'gbala, A., Kobrynowicz, D., & Wann, D. L. (1997). Self and group protection concerns influence attributions but they are not determinants of counterfactual mutation focus. *British Journal of Social Psychology, 36*, 387–404.

Bransford, J. D., Franks, J. J., Morris, C. D., & Stein, B. S. (1979). Some general constraints on learning and memory research. In L. S. Cermak & F. I. M. Craik (Eds.), *Levels of processing in human memory* (pp. 331–354). Hillsdale, NJ: Erlbaum.

Bransford, J. D., & Stein, B. S. (1984). *The ideal problem solver.* New York: Freeman.

Brantley, P. J., Dietz, L. S., McKnight, G. T., Jones, G. N., & Tulley, R. (1988). Convergence between the Daily Stress Inventory and endocrine measures of stress. *Journal of Consulting and Clinical Psychology, 56*, 549–551.

Braun, S. (1996). *Buzz: The science and lore of alcohol and caffeine.* New York: Oxford University Press.

Breer, H., & Boekhoff, I. (1992). Second messenger signaling in olfaction. *Current Opinion in Neurobiology, 2*, 439–443.

Brehm, J. W. (1956). Post-decision change in the desirability of alternatives. *Journal of Abnormal and Social Psychology, 52*, 384–389.

Brehm, J. W. (1972). *Responses to loss of freedom: A theory of psychological reactance.* Morristown, NJ: General Learning Press.

Breier, A., & Paul, S. M. (1990). The GABA$_A$/benzodiazepine receptor: Implications for the molecular basis of anxiety. *Journal of Psychiatric Research, 24*, 91–104.

Breier, A., Schreiber, J. L., Dyer, J., & Pickar, D. (1991). National Institute of Mental Health longitudinal study of chronic schizophrenia: Prog-

nosis and predictors of outcome. *Archives of General Psychiatry, 48*, 239–246.

Breslau, N., Davis, G. C., Andreski, P., & Peterson, E. (1991). Traumatic events and posttraumatic stress disorder in an urban population of young adults. *Archives of General Psychiatry, 48*, 216–222.

Bretl, D. J., & Cantor, J. (1988). The portrayal of men and women in U.S. television commercials: A recent content analysis and trends over 15 years. *Sex Roles, 18*, 595–609.

Breukelaar, J. W. C., & Dalrymple-Alford, J. C. (1998). Timing ability and numerical competence in rats. *Journal of Experimental Psychology: Animal Behavior Processes, 24*, 84–97.

Brickner, M. A., Harkins, S. G., & Ostrom, T. M. (1986). Effects of personal involvement: Thought-provoking implications for social loafing. *Journal of Personality and Social Psychology, 51*, 763–769.

Bridges, J. S. (1991). Perceptions of date and stranger rape: A difference in sex role expectations and rape-supportive beliefs. *Sex Roles, 24*, 291–307.

Bringmann, W. G., Bringmann, N. J., Ungerer, G. A. (1980). The establishment of Wundt's laboratory: An archival and documentary study. In W. G. Bringmann & R. D. Tweney (Eds.), *Wundt studies: A centennial collection* (pp. 123–157). Toronto: C. J. Hogrefe.

Brock, E. T., & Shucard, D. W. (1994). Sleep apnea. *American Family Physician, 49*, 385–394.

Brock, G. W., & Barnard, C. P. (1992). *Procedures in marriage and family therapy* (2nd ed.). Boston: Allyn & Bacon.

Brody, N., & Ehrlichman, H. (1998). *Personality psychology: The science of individuality.* Upper Saddle River, NJ: Prentice Hall.

Brody, L. R., & Hall, J. A. (1993). Gender and emotion. In M. Lewis & J. M. Haviland (Eds.), *Handbook of emotions* (pp. 447–460). New York: Guilford Press.

Broman, S. (1979). Prenatal anoxia and cognitive development in early childhood. In T. Field, A. Sostek, S. Goldberg, & H. Shuman (Eds.), *Infants born at risk* (p. 29). New York: Spectrum.

Brook, J. S., Whiteman, M., Gordon, A. S., & Brook, D. W. (1989). The role of older brothers in younger brothers' drug use viewed in the context of parent and peer influences. *Journal of Genetic Psychology, 151*, 59–75.

Broughton, R. S. (1991). *Parapsychology: The controversial science.* New York: Ballantine.

Brown, G. W., Harris, T. O., & Hepworth, C. (1994). Life events and endogenous depression. *Archives of General Psychiatry, 51*, 525–534.

Brown, J. A. (1958). Some tests of the decay theory of immediate memory. *Quarterly Journal of Experimental Psychology, 10*, 12–21.

Brown, J. L. (1987). Hunger in U.S. *Scientific American, 256*, 37–41.

Brown, J. S. (1942). Factors determining conflict reactions in different discriminations. *Journal of Experimental Psychology, 31*, 272–292.

Brown, P. K., & Wald, G. (1964). Visual pigments in single rods and cones in the human retina. *Science, 144*, 45–52.

Brown, T. A., Antony, M. M., & Barlow, D. H. (1995). Diagnostic comorbidity in panic disorder: Effect on treatment outcome and course of comorbid diagnoses following treatment. *Journal of Consulting and Clinical Psychology, 63*, 408–418.

Brown, T. A., Cash, T. F., & Lewis, R. L. (1989). Body-image disturbances in adolescent female binge-purgers: A brief report of the results of a national survey in the U.S.A. *Journal of Child Psychology and Psychiatry, 30*, 605–613.

Brownell, K. D., & Wadden, T. A. (1991). The heterogeneity of obesity: Fitting treatments to individuals. *Behavior Therapy, 22*, 153–177.

Bruce, M. L., Takeuchi, D. T., & Leaf, P. J. (1991). Poverty and psychiatric status. *Archives of General Psychiatry, 48*, 470–474.

Bruck, M., Cavanagh, P., & Ceci, S. J. (1991).

Fortysomething: Recognizing faces at one's 25th reunion. *Memory and Cognition, 19*, 221–228.

Bruck, M., & Ceci, S. J. (1997). The suggestibility of young children. *Current Directions in Psychological Science, 6*, 75–79.

Brush, S. G. (1991). Women in science and engineering. *American Scientist, 79*, 404–419.

Bryant, J., & Zillmann, D. (1979). The effect of the intensification of annoyance through residual excitation from unrelated prior stimulation on substantially delayed hostile behavior. *Journal of Experimental Social Psychology, 15*, 470–480.

Buck, L., & Axel, R. (1991). A novel multigene family may encode odorant receptors: A molecular basis for odor recognition. *Cell, 65*, 175–187.

Buckingham, R. W. (1983). Hospice care in the United States: The process begins. *Omega, 13*, 159–171.

Buckley, K. W. (1989). *Mechanical man: John Broadus Watson and the beginnings of behaviorism.* New York: Guilford.

Burke, H. L., & Yeo, R. A. (1994). Systematic variations in callosal morphology: The effects of age, gender, hand preference, and anatomic asymmetry. *Neuropsychology, 8*, 563–571.

Burns, R. A., & Gordon, W. U. (1988). Some further observations on serial enumeration and categorical flexibility. *Animal Learning and Behavior, 16*, 425–428.

Burt, C. D. B. (1994). An analysis of self-initiated coping behavior: Diary-keeping. *Child Study Journal, 24*, 171–189.

Bushman, B. J. (1996). Individual differences in the extent and development of aggressive cognitive-association networks. *Personality and Social Psychology Bulletin, 22*, 811–819.

Buss, A. H. (1961). *The psychology of aggression.* New York: Wiley.

Buss, A. H., & Plomin, R. (1984). *Temperament: Early developing personality traits.* Hillsdale, NJ: Erlbaum.

Butcher, J. N., Lim, J., & Nezami, E. (1998). Objective study of abnormal personality in cross-cultural settings: The Minnesota Multiphasic Personality Inventory (MMPI-2). *Journal of Cross-Cultural Psychology, 29*, 189–211.

Butler, R. A., & Harlow, H. F. (1954). Persistence of visual exploration in monkeys. *Journal of Comparative and Physiological Psychology, 47*, 258–263.

Butzlaff, R. L., & Hooley, J. M. (1998). Expressed emotion and psychiatric relapse: A meta-analysis. *Archives of General Psychiatry, 55*, 547–552.

Buxbaum, L. J., & Coslett, H. B. (1996). Deep dyslexic phenomena in a letter-by-letter reader. *Brain and Language, 54*, 136–167.

Buysse, D. J., Reynolds, C. F., III, Kupfer, D. J., Thorpy, M. J., Bixler, E., Manfredi, R., Kales, A., Vgontzas, A., Stepanski, E., Roth, T., Hauri, P., & Mesiano, D. (1994). Clinical diagnoses in 216 insomnia patients using the International Classification of Sleep Disorders (ICSD), DSM-IV, and ICD-10 categories: A report from the APA/NIMH DSM-IV field trial. *Sleep, 17*, 630–637.

C

Cacioppo, J. T., Bush, L. K., & Tassinary, L. G. (1992). Microexpressive facial actions as a function of affective stimuli: Replication and extension. *Personality and Social Psychology Bulletin, 18*, 515–526.

Cacioppo, J. T., KLein, D. J., Berntson, G. G., & Hatfield, E. (1993). The psychophysiology of emotion. In M. Lewis & J. M. Haviland (Eds.), *Handbook of emotions* (pp. 119–142). New York: Guilford Press.

Cain, W. S. (1982). Odor identification by males and females: Predictions versus performance. *Chemical Senses, 7*, 129–142.

Caldas, S. J. (1993). Current theoretical perspectives on adolescent pregnancy and childbearing in the United States. *Journal of Adolescent Research, 8,* 4–20.

Callahan, L. A., Steadman, H. J., McGreevy, M. A., & Robbins, P. C. (1991). The volume and characteristics of insanity defense pleas: An eight-state study. *Bulletin of the Academy of Psychiatry and the Law, 19,* 331–338.

Campbell, F. A., & Ramey, C. T. (1994). Effects of early intervention on intellectual and academic achievement: A follow-up on children from low-income families. *Child Development, 65,* 684–698.

Campbell, J. B., & Hawley, C. W. (1982). Study habits and Eysenck's theory of extraversion-introversion. *Journal of Research in Personality, 16,* 139–146.

Cannon, T. D., & Marco, E. (1994). Structural brain abnormalities as indicators of vulnerability to schizophrenia. *Schizophrenia Bulletin, 20,* 89–102.

Cannon, W. B. (1927). The James-Lange theory of emotions: A critical examination and an alternative. *American Journal of Physiology, 39,* 106–124.

Cantor, M. H. (1983). Strain among caregivers: A study of experience in the United States. *Gerontologist, 23,* 597–604.

Capaldi, E. D., & Sheffer, J. D. (1992). Contrast and reinforcement in consumption. *Learning and Motivation, 23,* 63–79.

Capelli, C. A., Nakagawa, N., & Madden, C. M. (1990). How children understand sarcasm: The role of context and intonation. *Child Development, 61,* 1824–1841.

Caplan, F. (1973). *The first twelve months of life.* New York: Grosset & Dunlap.

Carew, T. J., Walters, E. T., & Kandel, E. R. (1981). Classical conditioning in a simple withdrawal reflex in *Aplysia Californica. Journal of Neuroscience, 1,* 1426–1437.

Carmichael, L., Hogan, H. P., & Walter, A. A. (1932). An experimental study of the effect of language on the reproduction of visually perceived forms. *Journal of Experimental Psychology, 15,* 73–86.

Carpenter, W. T., & Buchanan, R. W. (1994). Schizophrenia. *New England Journal of Medicine, 330,* 681–690.

Carr, J. (1994). Long-term outcome for people with Down's syndrome. *Journal of Child Psychology and Psychiatry and Allied Disciplines, 35,* 425–439.

Carrasco, J. L., Saiz-Ruiz, J., Hollander, E., & Cesar, J. (1994). Low platelet monoamine oxidase activity in pathological gambling. *Acta Psychiatrica Scandinavica, 90,* 427–431.

Cartwright, R. D., & Lamberg, L. (1992). *Crisis dreaming: Using your dreams to solve your problems.* New York: HarperPerennial.

Cascio, W. F. (1995). *Managing human resources* (4th ed.). New York: McGraw-Hill.

Cash, T. F., Winstead, B. A., & Janda, J. H. (1986, April). Body image survey report: The great American shape-up. *Psychology Today,* pp. 30–37.

Caspi, A., & Herbener, E. S. (1990). Continuity and change: Assortative marriage and the consistency of personality in adulthood. *Journal of Personality and Social Psychology, 58,* 250–258.

Cassidy, J., & Berline, L. J. (1994). The insecure/ambivalent pattern of attachment: Theory and research. *Child Development, 65,* 971–981.

Catania, A. C., & Reynolds, G. S. (1968). A quantitative analysis of the responding maintained by interval schedules of reinforcement. *Journal of the Experimental Analysis of Behavior, 11,* 327–383.

Cattell, R. B., Eber, H. W., & Tatsuoka, M. M. (1970). *Handbook for the Sixteen Personality Factor Questionnaire (16PF).* Champaign, IL: Institute for Personality and Ability Testing.

Ceci, S. J., & Loftus, E. F. (1994). "Memory work". A royal road to false memories. *Applied Cognitive Psychology, 8,* 351–364.

Centers for Disease Control and Prevention. (1994a). AIDS among racial/ethnic minorities—United States, 1993. *Morbidity and Mortality Weekly Report, 43,* 644–647, 653–655.

Centers for Disease Control and Prevention. (1994b). Attitudes toward smoking policies in eight states—United States, 1993. *Morbidity and Mortality Weekly Report, 43,* 786–789.

Central Intelligence Agency (1996). *The world fact book.* Washington, DC: U.S. Government Printing Office.

Challis, B. H. (1993). Spacing effects on cued-memory tests depend on level of processing. *Journal of Experimental Psychology: Learning, Memory, and Cognition, 19,* 389–396.

Challis, B. H., & Brodbeck, D. R. (1992). Level of processing affects priming in word fragment completion. *Journal of Experimental Psychology: Learning, Memory, and Cognition, 18,* 595–607.

Chalsma, A. L., & Boyum, D. (1994). *Marijuana situation assessment.* Washington, DC: Office of National Drug Control Policy.

Chamberlain, M. C., Nichols, S. L., & Chase, C. H. (1991). Pediatric AIDS: Comparative cranial MRI and CT scans. *Pedriatric Neurology, 7,* 357–362.

Chandra, S. (1973). The effects of group pressure in perception: A cross-cultural conformity study in Fiji. *International Journal of Psychology, 8,* 37–39.

Chao, R. K. (1994). Beyond parental control and authoritarian parenting style: Understanding Chinese parenting through the cultural notion of training. *Child Development, 65,* 1111–1119.

Charney, D. A., & Russell, R. C. (1994). An overview of sexual harassment. *American Journal of Psychiatry, 151,* 10–17.

Chen, Y.-C. J., Guo, Y.-L., Hsu, C.-C., & Rogan, W. J. (1992). Cognitive development of yu-cheng ("oil disease") children prenatally exposed to heat-degraded PCBs. *Journal of the American Medical Association, 268,* 3213–3218.

Chermack, S. T., & Taylor, S. P. (1995). Alcohol and human physical aggression: Pharmacological versus expectancy effects. *Journal of Studies on Alcohol, 56,* 449–456.

Cherry, C. J., & Bowles, J. (1960). Contribution to the study of the cocktail-party phenomenon. *Journal of Acoustical Society of America, 32,* 884.

Chien, C.-P. (1993). Ethnopsychopharmacology. In A. C. Gaw (Ed.), *Culture, ethnicity, and mental illness* (pp. 413–430). Washington, DC: American Psychiatric Association.

Children's Defense Fund. (1997). *The state of America's children: Yearbook 1997.* Washington, DC: Author.

Chomsky, N. (1972). *Language and mind* (2nd ed.). San Diego, CA: Harcourt Brace.

Chorover, S., & Schiller, P. (1965). Short-term retrograde amnesia in rats. *Journal of Comparative and Physiological Psychology, 59,* 73–78.

Christensen, A., & Jacobson, N. S. (1994). Who (or what) can do psychotherapy: The status and challenge of nonprofessional therapies. *Psychological Science, 5,* 8–14.

Chrousos, G. P., & Gold, P. W. (1992). The concepts of stress and stress system disorders: Overview of physical and behavioral homeostasis. *Journal of the American Medical Association, 267,* 1244–1252.

Cialdini, R. B., Schaller, M., Houlihan, D., Arps, K., Fultz, J., & Beaman, A. L. (1987). Empathy-based helping: Is it selflessly or selfishly motivated? *Journal of Personality and Social Psychology, 52,* 749–758.

Cicchetti, D., & Toth, S. L. (1998). The development of depression in children and adolescents. *American Psychologist, 53,* 221–241.

Clark, L. A., Watson, D., & Reynolds, S. (1995). Diagnosis and classification of psychopathology: Challenges to the current system and future directions. *Annual Review of Psychology, 46,* 121–153.

Clark, C. M. (1994). Clinical assessment of adolescents involved in Satanism. *Adolescence, 29,* 461–468.

Clark, W. C., & Clark, S. B. (1980). Pain responses in Nepalese porters. *Science, 209,* 410–412.

Clarke, S., Assal, G., & deTribolet, N. (1993). Left hemisphere strategies in visual recognition, topographical orientation and time planning. *Neuropsychologia, 31,* 99–113.

Clarke, J. M., & Zaidel, E. (1994). Anatomical-behavioral relationships: Corpus callosum morphometry and hemispheric specialization. *Behavioral Brain Research, 64,* 185–202.

Clarke-Stewart, K. A. (1989). Infant day care: Maligned or malignant? *American Psychologist, 44,* 266–273.

Cleckley, H. (1976). *The mask of sanity* (5th ed.). St. Louis: Mosby.

Cleveland, J. N., Murphy, K. B., & Williams, B. E. (1989). Multiple uses of performance appraisal: Prevalence and correlates. *Journal of Applied Psychology, 74,* 130–135.

Cloninger, S. C. (1996). *Theories of personality: Understanding persons* (2nd ed.). Upper Saddle River, NJ: Prentice Hall.

Coffey, C. E., Weiner, R. D., Djang, W. T., Figiel, G. S., Soady, S. A. R., Patterson, L. J., Holt, P. D., Spritzer, C. E., & Wilinson, W. E. (1991). Brain anatomic effects of electroconvulsive therapy: A prospective magnetic resonance imaging study. *Archives of General Psychiatry, 48,* 1013–1021.

Cogan, D., & Cogan, R. (1984). Classical salivary conditioning: An easy demonstration. *Teaching of Psychology, 11,* 170–171.

Cogan, R., Cogan, D., Waltz, W., & McCue, M. (1987). Effects of laughter and relaxation on discomfort thresholds. *Journal of Behavioral Medicine, 10,* 139–144.

Cohen, A. S., Barlow, D. H., & Blanchard, E. B. (1985). The psychophysiology of relaxation-associated panic attacks. *Journal of Abnormal Psychology, 94,* 96–101.

Cohen, D. B., & Wolfe, G. (1973). Dream recall and repression: Evidence for an alternative hypothesis. *Journal of Consulting and Clinical Psychology, 41,* 349–355.

Cohen, F. L. (1993). Epidemiology of HIV infection and AIDS in children. In F. L. Cohen & J. D. Durham (Eds.), *Women, children, and HIV/AIDS* (pp. 137–155). New York: Springer.

Cohen, G. D. (1987). Alzheimer's disease. In G. L. Maddox (Ed.), *The encyclopedia of aging.* New York: Springer.

Cohen, J. D., Noll, D. C., & Schneider, W. (1993). Functional magnetic resonance imaging: Overview and methods for psychological research. *Behavioral Research Methods, Instruments, & Computers, 25,* 101–113.

Cohen, L. B., De Loache, J. S., & Strauss, M. S. (1979). Infant perceptual development. In J. D. Osofky (Ed.), *Handbook of infant development.* New York: Wiley.

Cohen, S., Tyrrell, D. A. J., & Smith, A. P. (1991). Psychological stress and susceptibility to the common cold. *New England Journal of Medicine, 325,* 606–612.

Cohen, S., Tyrrell, D. A. J., & Smith, A. P. (1993). Negative life events, perceived stress, negative affect, and susceptibility to the common cold. *Journal of Personality and Social Psychology, 64,* 131–140.

Cole, C., & Rodman, H. (1987). When school-age children care for themselves: Issues for family life education and parents. *Family Relations, 36,* 92–96.

Cole, M., & Cole, S. R. (1993). *The development of children* (2nd ed.). New York: Freeman.

Coleman, J. C. (1980). Friendship and the peer group in adolescence. In J. Adelson (Ed.), *Handbook of adolescent psychology.* New York: Wiley.

Coleman, R. M. (1986). *Wide awake at 3:00 A.M.: By choice or by chance?* New York: Freeman.

Coleman, R. M. (1995). *The 24-hour business: Maximizing productivity through round-the-clock operations.* New York: American Management Association.

Collaer, M. L., & Hines, M. (1995). Human behavioral sex differences: A role for gonadal hormones during early development. *Psychological Bulletin, 118,* 55–107.

Collier, G., Hirsch, E., & Hamlin, P. H. (1972). The ecological determinants of reinforcement in the rat. *Physiology and Behavior, 9,* 705–716.

Collins, A. M., & Loftus, E. F. (1975). A spreading activation theory of semantic processing. *Psychological Review, 82,* 407–428.

Collins, A. M., & Quillian, M. R. (1972). How to make a language user. In E. Tulving & W. Donaldson (Eds.), *Organization of memory* (pp. 383–415). San Diego, CA: Academic Press.

Collins, D. (1996). Legal update: Can't you take a joke? Sexual harassment in health care. *Caring, 15*(5), 78–80.

Collins, W. A., & Kuczaj, S. A., II. (1991). *Developmental psychology: Childhood and adolescence.* New York: Macmillan.

Colman, A. M. (1988). *Facts, fallacies and frauds in psychology.* London: Unwin Hyman.

Compton, W. M., III, Helzer, J. E., Hwu, H.-G., Yeh, E.-K., McEvoy, L., Tipp, J. E., & Spitznagel, E. L. (1991). New methods in cross-cultural psychiatry: Psychiatric illness in Taiwan and the United States. *American Journal of Psychiatry, 148,* 1697–1704.

Conley, F. K. (1993). Toward a more perfect world: Eliminating sexual discrimination in academic medicine. *New England Journal of Medicine, 328,* 351–352.

Conn, S. R., & Rieke, M. L. (1994). *The 16PF fifth edition technical manual.* Champaign, IL: Institute for Personality and Ability Testing.

Consortium for Longitudinal Studies (1983). *As the twig is bent: Lasting effects of preschool programs.* Hillsdale, NJ: Erlbaum.

Conte, A. (1997). Legal theories of sexual harassment. In W. O'Donohue (Ed.), *Sexual harassment: Theory, research and treatment* (pp. 50–83). Boston: Allyn & Bacon.

Cook, M., Mineka, S., Wolkenstein, B., & Laitsch, K. (1985). Observational conditioning of snake fear in unrelated rhesus monkeys. *Journal of Abnormal Psychology, 94,* 591–610.

Cook, R. G., Cavoto, B. R., Katz, J. S., & Cavoto, K. K. (1997). Pigeon perception and discrimination of rapidly changing texture stimuli. Journal of Experimental Psychology: *Animal Behavior Processes, 23,* 390–400.

Cooke, P. (1991, June 23). They cried until they could not see. *New York Times Magazine,* pp. 24–25, 45–48.

Coon, D. J. (1993). Standardizing the subject: Experimental psychologists, introspection, and the quest for a technoscientific ideal. *Technology and Culture, 34,* 757–783.

Coons, P. M., Bowman, E. S., & Milstein, V. (1988). Multiple personality disorder: A clinical investigation of 50 cases. *Journal of Nervous and Mental Disease, 176,* 519–527.

Corbett, K., Gentry, C. S., & Pearson, W., Jr. (1993). Sexual harassment in high school. *Youth & Society, 25,* 93–103.

Coren, S. (1992). *The left-hander syndrome: The causes and consequences of left-handedness.* New York: Free Press.

Coren, S., & Halpern, D. F. (1991). Left-handedness: A marker for decreased survival fitness. *Psychological Bulletin, 109,* 90–106.

Cornelissen, P., Hansen, P., Hutton, J., Evangelinou, V., & Stein, J. (1998). Magnocellular visual function and children's single word reading. *Vision Research, 38,* 471–482.

Cornett, M. B., & Shuntick, R. (1991). Sexual aggression: Perceptions of its likelihood of occurring and some correlates of self-admitted perpetration. *Perceptual and Motor Skills, 73,* 499–507.

Corr, C. A. (1993). Coping with dying: Lessons that we should and should not learn from the work of Elisabeth Kubler-Ross. *Death Studies, 7,* 69–83.

Corr, C. A. (1995). Entering into adolescent understandings of death. In E. A. Grollman (Ed.), *Bereaved children and teens* (pp. 21–35). Boston: Beacon Press.

Corrigan, P. W. (1995). Use of token economy with seriously mentally ill patients: Criticisms and misconceptions. *Psychiatric Services, 46,* 1258–1263.

Costa, P. T., Jr., & McCrae, R. R. (1988). Personality in adulthood: A six-year longitudinal study of self-reports and spouse ratings on the NEO Personality Inventory. *Journal of Personality and Social Psychology, 54,* 853–863.

Costa, P. T., Jr., & McCrae, R. R. (1992a). Four ways five factors are basic. *Personality and Individual Differences, 13,* 653–665.

Costa, P. T., Jr., & McCrae, R. R. (1992b). *NEO-PI-R and NEO-FFI professional manual.* Odessa, FL: Psychological Assessment Resources.

Costa, P. T., Jr., & McCrae, R. R. (1992c). Trait psychology comes of age. In T. B. Sonderegger (Ed.), *Nebraska symposium on motivation: Psychology and aging* (pp. 169–204). Lincoln: University of Nebraska Press.

Costanzo, M., & Archer, D. (1989). Interpreting the expressive behavior of others: The Interpersonal Perception Task. *Journal of Nonverbal Behavior, 13,* 225–245.

Cotton, J. L., & Tuttle, J. M. (1986). Employee turnover: A meta-analysis and review with implications for research. *Academy of Management Review, 11,* 55–70.

Cotton, P. (1994). Smoking cigarettes may do developing fetus more harm than ingesting cocaine, some experts say. *Journal of the American Medical Association, 263,* 2865–2869.

Court, J. H. (1984). Sex and violence: A ripple effect. In N. M. Malamuth & E. Donnerstein (Eds.), *Pornography and sexual aggression.* San Diego, CA: Academic Press.

Cousins, N. (1979). *Anatomy of an illness as perceived by the patient.* New York: Norton.

Cousins, N. (1989). *Head first: The biology of hope.* New York: Dutton.

Coutts, L. M. (1991). The organizational psychologist. In B. Gifford (Ed.), *Applied psychology: Variety and opportunity* (pp. 273–299). Needham Heights, MA: Allyn & Bacon.

Cowley, G. (1997, February 3). Can marijuana be medicine? *Newsweek,* 22–23, 26–27.

Cozby, P. C. (1972). Self-disclosure, reciprocity and liking. *Sociometry, 35,* 151–160.

Craig, M. E. (1990). Coercive sexuality in dating relationships: A situational model. *Clinical Psychology Review, 10,* 395–423.

Craik, F. I. M., Byrd, M., & Swanson, J. M. (1987). Patterns of memory loss in three elderly samples. *Psychology and Aging, 2,* 79–86.

Craik, F. I. M., & Lockhart, R. S. (1972). Levels of processing: A framework for memory research. *Journal of Verbal Learning and Verbal Behavior, 11,* 671–684.

Crandall, C. S. (1988). Social contagion of binge eating. *Journal of Personality and Social Psychology, 55,* 588–598.

Cravens, H. (1992). A scientific project locked in time. *American Psychologist, 47,* 183–189.

Crawford, M., & MacLeod, M. (1990). Gender in the college classroom: An assessment of the "chilly climate" for women. *Sex Roles, 23,* 101–122.

Cremers, C. W. R. J., & van Rijn, P. M. (1991). Acquired causes of deafness in childhood. *Annals of the New York Academy of Sciences, 630,* 197–202.

Crichton-Browne, J. (1880). On the weight of the brain: Its component parts in the insane. *Brain, 2,* 42–67.

Crews, F. (1996). The verdict on Freud. *Psychological Science, 7,* 63–68.

Crosby, F. J. (1991). *Juggling: The unexpected advantages of balancing a career and home for women and their families.* New York: Free Press.

Crosby, F. J., & Jaskar, K. L. (1993). Women and men at home and at work: Realities and illusions. In S. Oskamp & M. Costanzo (Eds.), *Gender issues in contemporary society* (pp. 143–171). Newbury Park, CA: Sage.

Crose, R. (1994). Family bonding and attachment patterns late in life. *Family Therapy, 21,* 217–221.

Cross-National Collaborative Group. (1992). The changing rate of major depression. *Journal of the American Medical Association, 268,* 3098–3105.

Crowe, L. C., & George, W. H. (1989). Alcohol and human sexuality: Review and integration. *Psychological Bulletin, 105,* 374–386.

Crowe, R. A. (1990). Astrology and the scientific method. *Psychological Reports, 67,* 163–191.

Cruser, L., & Klein, S. B. (1984). The role of schedule-induced polydipsia on temporal discrimination learning. *Psychological Reports, 58,* 443–452.

Crystal, J. D., Church, R. M., & Broadbent, H. A. (1997). Systematic nonlinearities in the memory representation of time. *Journal of Experimental Psychology: Animal Behavior Processes, 23,* 267–282.

Culbertson, F. M. (1997). Depression and gender: An international review. *American Psychologist, 52,* 25–31.

Culliton, B. (1987). Osteoporosis reexamined: Complexity of bone biology is a challenge. *Science, 235,* 833–834.

Cummings, N. (1992). Self-defense training for college women. *Journal of American College Health, 40,* 183–188.

Cupp, M. J. (1977). Melatonin. American *Family Physician, 56,* 1421–1425.

Curran, T., & Keele, S. W. (1993). Attentional and nonattentional forms of sequence learning. *Journal of Experimental Psychology: Learning, Memory, and Cognition, 19,* 189–202.

Cutler, B. L., Moran, G., & Narby, D. J. (1992). Jury selection in insanity defense cases. *Journal of Research in Personality, 26,* 165–182.

Czeisler, C. A., Allan, J. S., Strogatz, S. H., Ronda, J. M., Sanchez, R., Rios, C. D., Freitag, W. O., Richardson, G. S., & Kronauer, R. E. (1986). Bright light resets the human circadian pacemaker independent of the timing of the sleep-wake cycle. *Science, 233,* 667–671.

Czeisler, C. A., Moore-Ede, M. C., & Coleman, R. M. (1982). Rotating shift work schedules that disrupt sleep are improved by applying circadian principles. *Science, 217,* 460–463.

Czeisler, C. A., Weitzman, E. D., Moore-Ede, M. C., Zimmerman, J. C., & Knauer, R. S. (1980). Human sleep: Its duration and organization depend on its circadian phase. *Science, 210,* 1264–1267.

D

Dabbs, J. M., Jr., & Morris, R. (1990). Testosterone and antisocial behavior in a sample of 4462 men. *Psychological Science, 1,* 209–211.

Dabbs, J. M., Jr., & Ruback, R. B. (1984). Vocal patterns in male and female groups. *Personality and Social Psychology Bulletin, 10,* 518–525.

Damasio, A. R. (1994). *Descartes' error: Emotion, reason, and the human brain.* New York: Avon Books.

Damasio, H., Grabowski, T., Frank, R., Galaburda, A. M., & Damasio, A. R. (1994). The return of Phineas Gage: Clues about the brain from the skull of a famous patient. *Science, 264,* 1102–1105.

Danis, P. G., & Seaton, T. L. (March, 1997). Helping your patients to quit smoking. *American Family Physician,* 1207–1214.

Dansky, B. S., & Kilpatrick, D. G. (1997). Effects of sexual harassment. In W. O'Donohue (Ed.) *Sexual harassment: Theory, research, and treatment* (pp. 152–174). Boston: Allyn & Bacon.

Darley, J. M., & Latané, B. (1968). Bystander intervention in emergencies: Diffusion of responsibility. *Journal of Personality and Social Psychology, 8,* 377–383.

Darling, N., & Steinberg, L. (1993). Parenting style as context: An integrative model. *Psychological Bulletin, 113,* 487–496.

Dartnall, H. J. A., Bowmaker, J. K., & Mollen, J. D. (1983). Human visual pigments: Microspectrophotometric results from the eyes of seven persons. *Proceedings of the Royal Society of London, B, 220,* 115–130.

Darwin, C. J., Turvey, M. T., & Crowder, R. G. (1972). An auditory analogue of the Sperling partial report procedure: Evidence for brief auditory storage. *Cognitive Psychology, 3,* 255–267.

Darwin, C. R. (1965). *The expression of emotions in man and animals.* Chicago: University of Chicago Press. (Originally published in 1872)

Davidhizar, R., Erdel, S., & Dowd, S. (February, 1998). Sexual harassment: Where to draw the line. *Nursing Management,* 40–43.

Davidson, J., & Harlan, C. (1993, April 20). As Waco ends, Clinton's leadership comes under scrutiny. *Wall Street Journal,* pp. A1, A6.

Davidson, R. J. (1993). The neuropsychology of emotion and affective style. In M. Lewis & J. M. Haviland (Eds.), *Handbook of emotions* (pp. 143–154). New York: Guilford Press.

Davis, G. A. (1993). *A survey of adult aphasia and related language disorders.* Englewood Cliffs, NJ: Prentice Hall.

Davis, S. F. (1997). Internet addiction disorder. Peregrine Publishers: http://www.psychplace.com/ life/iad/intro.html.

Davis, S. F., Evans, S. E., & Farris, J. S. (1997). Road rage. Peregrine Publishers,: http://www.psychplace.com/life/roadrage/intro.html.

Davis, S. F., Grover, C. A., Becker, A. H., & McGregor, L. N. (1992). Academic dishonesty: Prevalence, determinants, techniques, and punishments. *Teaching of Psychology, 19,* 16–20.

Davis, S. F., & Ludvigson, H. W. (1995). Additional data on academic dishonesty and a proposal for remediation. *Teaching of Psychology, 22,* 119–122.

Dawes, R. M. (1994). *House of cards: Psychology and psychotherapy built on myth.* New York: Free Press.

Day, N. L. (1992). The effects of prenatal exposure to alcohol. *Alcohol Health and Research World, 16,* 238–244.

De Angelis, T. (1992, April). Health psychology grows both in stature, influence. *APA Monitor,* pp. 10–11.

De Angelis, T. (1993, April). Psychologists have tradition of helping kids get Head Start. *APA Monitor,* pp. 8–9.

Deaux, K., & Lewis, L. (1984). Structure of gender stereotypes: Interrelationships among components and gender label. *Journal of Personality and Social Psychology, 46,* 991–1004.

DeCarvalho, R. J. (1991). *The founders of humanistic psychology.* New York: Praeger.

DeCarvalho, R. J. (1992). The institutionalization of humanistic psychology. *Humanistic Psychologist, 20,* 124–135.

De Casper, A. J., & Fifer, W. (1980). Newborns prefer their mothers' voices. *Science, 208,* 1174–1176.

De Casper, A. J., & Prescott, P. A. (1984). Human newborns' perception of male voices: Preference, discrimination, and reinforcing value. *Developmental Psychobiology, 17,* 481–491.

De Casper, A. J., & Spence, M. J. (1986). Prenatal maternal speech influences newborns' perception of speech sounds. *Infant Behavior and Development, 9,* 133–150.

Decety, J., & Ingvar, D. H. (1990). Brain structures participating in mental simulation of motor behavior: A neuropsychological interpretation. *Acta Psychologica, 73,* 13–34.

Dekovic, M., & Janssens, J. M. (1992). Parents' child-rearing style and child's sociometric status. *Developmental Psychology, 28,* 925–932.

Delagrnage, P., & Guardiola-Nemaitre, B. (1997). Melatonin, its receptors, and relationships with biological rhythm disorders. *Clinical Neuropharmacology, 20,* 482–501.

Delemater, A. R. (1995). Outcome-selective effects of intertrial reinforcement in a Pavlovian appetitive conditioning paradigm with rats. *Animal Learning and Behavior, 23,* 31–39.

De Longis, A., Folkman, S., & Lazarus, R. S. (1988). The impact of daily stress on health and mood: Psychological and social resources as mediators. *Journal of Personality and Social Psychology, 54,* 486–495.

Dement, W. C. (1978). *Some must watch while some must sleep.* New York: Norton.

Dement, W. C. (1986). Normal sleep, disturbed sleep, transient and persistent insomnia. *Acta Psychiatrica Scandinavica Supplement, 74,* 41–46.

Dennett, D. C., & Kinsbourne, M. (1992). Time and the observer: The where and when of consciousness in the brain. *Behavioral and Brain Sciences, 15,* 183–200.

Denton, G. C. (1980). The influence of visual patterns on perceived speed. *Perception, 9,* 393–402.

Denton, R. E., & Kampfe, C. M. (1994). The relationship between family variables and adolescent substance abuse: A literature review. *Adolescence, 29,* 475–495.

De Reamer, B. (1980). *Modern safety and health technology.* New York: Wiley.

Deregowski, J. B. (1980). *Illusions, pattern, and pictures: A cross-cultural perspective.* New York: Academic Press.

De Silva, P., & Rachman, S. (1992). *Obsessive compulsive: The facts.* Oxford: Oxford University Press.

DeSouza, E. R., & Hutz, C. S. (1995). Responses toward sexual stimuli in Brazil as a function of one's gender role identity and sex. *InterAmerican Journal of Psychology, 29,* 13–21.

DeSouza, E. R., & Hutz, C. S. (1996). Reactions to sexual advances among U.S. and Brazilian men and women. *Sex Roles, 34,* 549–565.

De Valois, R. L., & Jacobs, G. H. (1968). Primate color vision. *Science, 162,* 533–540.

Devine, D. P., & Spanos, N. P. (1990). Effectiveness of maximally different strategies and expectancy in attenuation of reported pain. *Journal of Personality and Social Psychology, 58,* 672–678.

Devlin, M. J., & Walsh, B. T. (1992). Anorexia nervosa and bulimia nervosa. In P. Björntorp & B. N. Brodoff (Eds.), *Obesity* (pp. 436–444). Philadelphia: Lippincott.

Dewhurst, S. A., & Conway, M. A. (1994). Pictures, images, and recollective experiences. *Journal of Experimental Psychology: Learning, Memory, and Cognition, 20,* 1088–1098.

Deyoung, Y., & Zigler, E. F. (1994). Machismo in two cultures: Relation to punative child-rearing practices. *American Journal of Orthopsychiatry, 64,* 386–395.

Diamond, R., White, R. F., Myers, R. H., & Mastromauro, C. (1992). Evidence of pre-symptomatic cognitive decline in Huntington's disease. *Journal of Clinical and Experimental Neuropsychology, 14,* 961–975.

Diamant, L. (Ed.). (1991). *Mind-body maturity.* Washington, DC: Hemisphere.

Dick-Read, G. (1959). *Childbirth without fear.* New York: Harper & Row.

Di Clemente, R. J., Zorn, J., & Temoshok, L. (1986). Adolescents and AIDS: A survey of knowledge, attitudes and beliefs about AIDS in San Francisco. *American Journal of Public Health, 76,* 1443–1445.

Diener, E. (1980). Deindividuation: The absence of self-awareness and self-regulation in group members. In P. B. Paulus (Ed.), *Psychology of group influence.* Hillsdale: NJ: Erlbaum.

Diener, E., Fraser, S. C., Beaman, A. L., & Kelem, R. T. (1976). Effects of deindividuation variable on stealing among Halloween trick-or-treaters. *Journal of Personality and Social Psychology, 33,* 178–183.

DiLalla, L. F., Kagan, J., & Reznick, J. S. (1994). Genetic etiology of behavioral inhibition among 2-year-old children. *Infant Behavior and Development, 17,* 405–412.

Diller, L. (1992). Introduction to the special section of neuropsychology and rehabilitation: The view from New York University. *Neuropsychology, 6,* 357–359.

Dinges, D. F. (1989). Napping patterns and effects in human adults. In D. F. Dinges & R. J. Broughton (Eds.), *Sleep and alertness: Chronobiological, behavioral, and medical aspects of napping* (pp. 171–204). New York: Raven Press.

Dion, K. K., & Stein, S. (1978). Physical attractiveness and interpersonal influence. *Journal of Experimental Social Psychology, 14,* 97–108.

Dohrenwend, B. P., & Ergi, G. (1981). Recent stressful life events and episodes of schizophrenia. *Schizophrenia Bulletin, 7,* 12–23.

Dohrenwend, B. P., Levav, I., Shrout, P. E., Schwartz, S., Naveh, G., Link, B. G., Skodol, A. E., & Stueve, A. (1992). Socioeconomic status and psychiatric disorders: The causation-selection issue. *Science, 255,* 946–951.

Dollard, J., Doob, L., Miller, N., Mowrer, O., & Sears, R. (1939). *Frustration and aggression.* New Haven, CT: Yale University Press.

Domhoff, G. W. (1996). *Finding meaning in dreams: A quantitative approach.* New York: Plenum.

Domjan, M., & Purdy, J. E. (1995). Animal research in psychology: More than meets the eye of the general psychology student. *American Psychologist, 50,* 496–503

Donnerstein, E. (1995, January). *Mass media violence: Research, solutions, and policy implications.* Paper presented at the Seventeenth Annual National Institute on the Teaching of Psychology. St. Petersburg Beach, FL.

Donnerstein, E., Linz, D., & Penrod, S. (1987). *The question of pornography.* London: Free Press.

Dopkins, S., Pollatsek, A., & Nordlie, J. (1994). Role of an abstract order schema in conceptual judgment. *Journal of Experimental Psychology: Learning, Memory, and Cognition, 20,* 1283–1295.

Doty, R. L. (1984). Smell identification ability: Changes with age. *Science, 226,* 1441–1443.

Drabman, R., Robertson, S., Patterson, J., Jarvie, G., Hammer, D., & Cordua, G. (1981). Children's perceptions of media-portrayed sex roles. *Sex Roles, 7,* 379–389.

Dubbert, P. M. (1992). Exercise in behavioral medicine. *Journal of Consulting and Clinical Psychology, 60,* 613–618.

Dubovsky, S. L., & Buzan, R. D. (1997). Novel alternatives and supplements anticonvulsants for bipolar affective disorder. *Journal of Clinical Psychiatry, 58,* 224–242.

Duckworth, J. C. (1991). The Minnesota Multiphasic Personality Inventory—2: A review. *Journal of Counseling and Development, 69,* 564–567.

Dufour, M. C. (1995). Twenty-five years of alcohol epidemiology: Trends, techniques, and limitations. *Alcohol Health and Research World, 19,* 77–84.

Duncker, K. (1945). On problem-solving. *Psychological Monographs, 58* (5 Whole No. 270).

Dundes, A., & Pagter, C. R. (1991). *Never try to teach a pig to sing.* Detroit, MI: Wayne State University.

Dunn, J., & Plomin, R. (1990). *Separate lives: Why siblings are so different.* New York: Basic Books.

Dwyer, T., Ponsonby, A.-L., Blizzard, L., Newman, N. M., & Cochrane, J. A. (1995). The contribution of changes in the prevalence of prone sleeping position to the decline in sudden infant death syndrome in Tasmania. *Journal of the American Medical Association, 273,* 783–789.

D'Zmura, M. ((1991). Color in visual search. *Vision Research, 31,* 951–966.

D'Zmura, M., Lennie, P., & Tiana, C. (1997). Color search and visual field segregation. *Perception and Psychophysics, 59,* 381–388.

E

Eagly, A. H. (1995). The science and politics of comparing women and men. *American Psychologist, 50,* 145–158.

Eagly, A. H., & Crowley, M. (1986). Gender and helping behavior: A meta-analytic review of the social psychology literature. *Psychological Bulletin, 100,* 283–308.

Eagly, A. H., Karau, S. J., & Makhijani, M. G. (1995). Gender and the effectiveness of leaders: A meta-analysis. *Psychological Bulletin, 117,* 125–145.

Eagly, A. H., Makhijani, M. G., & Klonsky, B. G. (1992). Gender and the evaluation of leaders: A meta-analysis. *Psychological Bulletin, 111,* 3–22.

Eagly, A. H., Mladinic, A., & Otto, S. (1991). Are women evaluated more favorably than men? *Psychology of Women Quarterly, 15,* 203–216.

Eagly, A. H., & Steffen, V. J. (1986). Gender and aggressive behavior: A meta-analytic review of the social psychological literature. *Psychological Bulletin, 100,* 309–330.

Eastell, R. (1998). Treatment of postmenopausal osteoporosis. *New England Journal of Medicine, 338,* 736–746.

Eaton, W. W., Dryman, A., & Weissman, M. M. (1991). Panic and phobia. In L. N. Robins & D. A. Regier (Eds.), *Psychiatric disorders in America: The Epidemiologic Catchment Area Study* (pp. 155–179). New York: Free Press.

Eaton, W. W., Kessler, R. C., Wittchen, H. U., & Magee, W. J. (1994). Panic and panic disorder in the United States. *American Journal of Psychiatry, 151,* 413–420.

Ebbinghaus, H. (1885). *On memory.* Leipzig: Duncker & Humblot.

Eccles, J. S., & Jacobs, J. E. (1986). Social forces shape math attitudes and performance. *Signs, 11,* 367–380.

Eden, G., VanMeter, J., Rumsey, J., Maisog, J., Woods, R., & Zeffiro, T. (1996). Abnormal processing of visual motion in dyslexia revealed by functional brain imaging. *Nature, 382,* 66–69.

Edwards, K. (1998). The face of time: Temporal cues in facial expression of emotion. *Psychological Science, 9,* 270–276.

Egan, M. F., Apud, J., & Wyatt, R. J. (1997). Treatment of tardive dyskinesia. *Schizophrenia Bulletin, 23,* 583–609.

Eich, J. E., Weingartner, H., Stillman, R. C., & Gillin, J. C. (1975). State-dependent accessibility of retrieval cues in the retention of a categorized list. *Journal of Verbal Learning and Verbal Behavior, 14,* 408–417.

Eidelberg, D., & Galaburda, A. M. (1982). Symmetry and asymmetry in the human posterior thalamus. *Archives of Neurology, 39,* 325–332.

Ekman, P. (1992a). Facial expression of emotion: New findings, new questions. *Psychological Science, 3,* 34–38.

Ekman, P. (1993). Facial expressions and emotion. *American Psychologist, 48,* 384–392.

Ekman, P. (1994b). Strong evidence for universals in facial expressions: A reply to Russell's mistaken critique. *Psychological Bulletin, 115,* 268–287.

Ekman, P., Davidson, R. J., & Friesen, W. V. (1990). The Duchenne smile: Emotional expression and brain physiology II. *Journal of Personality and Social Psychology, 58,* 342–353.

Ekman, P., & Friesen, W. V. (1971). Constants across cultures in the face and emotion. *Journal of Personality and Social Psychology, 17,* 124–129.

Ekman, P., Friesen, W. V., & Bear, J. (1984, May). The international language of gestures. *Psychology Today,* pp. 64–69.

Ekman, P., Friesen, W. V., & O'Sullivan, M. (1988). Smiles when lying. *Journal of Personality and Social Psychology, 54,* 414–420.

Ekman, P., Friesen, W. V., O'Sullivan, M., Chan, A., Diacoyanni-Tarlatzis, I., Heider, K., Krause, R., LeCompte, W. A., Pitcairn, T., Ricci-Bitti, P.E. Scherer, K.R., Tomita, M., & Tzavaras, A. (1987) Universals and Cultural Differences in the Judgments of Facial Expressions of Emotion. *Journal of Personality and Social Psychology, 53,* 712-717.

Ekman, P., Levenson, R. W., & Friesen, W. V. (1983). Autonomic nervous system activity distinguishes among emotions. *Science, 221,* 1208–1210.

Elkind, D. (1984). *All grown up and no place to go.* Reading, MA: Addison-Wesley.

Elliot, A. J., & Devine, P. G. (1994). On the motivational nature of cognitive dissonance: Dissonance as psychological discomfort. *Journal of Personality and Social Psychology, 67,* 283–294.

Ellis, A. (1973). *Humanistic psychotherapy: The rational-emotive approach.* New York: McGraw-Hill.

Ellis, A. (1977). The basic clinical theory of rational-emotive therapy. In A. Ellis and R. Grieger (Eds.), *Handbook of rational-emotive therapy* (pp. 3–34). New York: Springer.

Ellis, A. (1987). The impossibility of achieving consistently good mental health. *American Psychologist, 42,* 364–375.

Ellis, A. (1990). *How to stubbornly refuse to make yourself miserable about anything yes anything!* New York: Lyle Stuart.

Ellis, A., & Tafrate, R. C. (1997). *How to control your anger before it controls you.* Secaucus, NJ: Carol Publishing Group.

Ellis, H. C., Thomas, R. L., & Rodriguez, I. A. (1984). Emotional mood states and memory: Elaborative encoding, semantic processing, and cognitive effort. *Journal of Experimental Psychology: Learning, Memory, and Cognition, 10,* 470–482.

Ellsworth, P. (1994). Sense, culture, and sensability. In S. Kitayama & H. R. Markus (Eds.), *Emotion and culture: Empirical studies of mutual influence* (pp. 23–50). Washington, DC: American Psychological Association.

Emde, R. N., Plomin, R., Robinson, J., Corley, R., DeFries, J., Fulker, D. W., Reznick, J. S., Campos, J., Kagan, J., & Zahn-Waxler, C. (1992). Temperament, emotion, and cognition at fourteen months: The MacArthur Longitudinal Twin Study. *Child Development, 63,* 1437–1455.

Engle, R. W., Cantor, J., & Carullo, J. J. (1993). Individual differences in working memory and comprehension: A test of four hypotheses. *Journal of Experimental Psychology: Learning, Memory, and Cognition, 19,* 972–992.

Engen, T. (1987). Remembering odors and their names. *American Scientist, 75,* 497–503.

Engler, J., & Goleman, D. (1992). *The consumer's guide to psychotherapy.* New York: Simon & Schuster.

Engs, R., & Hanson, D. J. (1989). Reactance theory: A test with collegiate drinking. *Psychological Reports, 64,* 1083–1086.

Epstein, J. F., & Gfroerer, J. C. (1997) *Heroin abuse in the United States.* Rockville, MD: substance Abuse and Mental Health Services Administration, Office of Applied Studies.

Epstein, S. (1979). The stability of behavior: 1. On predicting most of the people much of the time. *Journal of Personality and Social Psychology, 37,* 1097–1126.

Epstein, S. (1980). The stability of behavior: 2. Implications for psychological research. *American Psychologist, 35,* 790–806.

Epstein, S. (1983). The stability of confusion: A reply to Mischel and Peake. *Psychological Review, 90,* 179–184.

Equal Employment Opportunity Commission. (1980). Discrimination because of sex under Title VII of the 1964 Civil Rights Act as amended: Adoption of interim guidelines—sexual harassment. *Federal Register, 45,* 25024–25025.

Erdelyi, M. (1994). Hypnotic hypermnesia: The empty set of hypermneasi. *International Journal of Clinical and Experimental Hypnosis, 42,* 379–390.

Erez, M. (1994). Toward a model of cross-cultural industrial-organizational psychology. In H. C. Triandis, M. D. Dunnette, & L. M. Hough (Eds.), *Handbook of industrial and organizational psychology* (Vol.4, pp. 559–608). Palo Alto, CA: Consulting Psychologists Press.

Erickson, R. P., DiLorenzo, P. M., & Woodbury, M. A. (1994). Classification of taste responses in brain stem: Membership in fuzzy sets. *Journal of Neurophysiology, 71,* 2139–2150.

Erickson, B., Lind, E. A., Johnson, B. C., & O'Barr, W. M. (1978). Speech style and impression formation in a court setting: The effects of powerful and powerless speech. *Journal of Experimental Social Psychology, 14,* 266–279.

Erikson, E. H. (1963). *Childhood and society* (2nd edition). New York: Norton.

Erikson, E. H. (1975). *Life history and the historical movement.* New York: Norton.

Erkinjuntti, T., Ostbye, T., Steenhuis, R., & Hachinski, V. (1997). The effect of different diagnostic criteria on the prevalence of dementia. *New England Journal of Medicine, 337,* 1667–1674.

Eskenazi, B. (1993). Caffeine during pregnancy: Grounds for concern? *Journal of the American Medical Association, 270,* 2973–2974.

Eskenazi, M., & Gallen, D. (1992). *Sexual harassment: Know your rights!* New York: Carroll & Graf.

Evans, D. L., Folds, J. D., Petitto, J. M., Golden, R. N., Pedersen, C. A., Corrigan, M., Gilmore, J. H., Silva, S. G., Quade, D., & Ozer, H. (1992). Circulating natural killer cell phenotypes in men and women with major depression. *Archives of General Psychiatry, 49,* 388–395.

Evans, R. I. (1980). Behavioral medicine: A new applied challenge to social psychologists. In L. Bickman (Ed.), *Applied social psychology annual* (Vol. 1). Newbury Park, CA: Sage.

Evans, W. A., Krippendorf, M., Yoon, J. H., Posluszny, P., & Thomas, S. (1990). Science on the prestige and national tabloid presses. *Social Science Quarterly, 71,* 105–117.

Everett, J. J., Smith, R. E., & Williams, K. D. (1992). Effects of team cohesion and identifiability on social loafing in relay swimming performance. *International Journal of Sport Psychology, 23,* 311–324.

Exner, J. E., Jr. (1986). *The Rorschach: A comprehensive system, Vol. 1, Basic foundations* (2nd ed.). New York: Wiley.

Exner, J. E., Jr. (1991). *The Rorschach: A comprehensive system, Vol. 2, Interpretation* (2nd ed.). New York: Wiley.

Eysenck, H. J. (1952). The effects of psychotherapy: An evaluation. *Journal of Consulting Psychology, 16,* 319–324.

Eysenck, H. J., & Eysenck, M. W. (1985). *Personality and individual differences.* New York: Plenum.

F

Fackelmann, K. A. (1993). Marijuana and the brain. *Science News, 143,* 88–94.

Fackelmann, K. A. (1995). Staying alive: Scientists study people who outwit the AIDS virus. *Science News, 147,* 172–174.

Fagot, B. I., & Hagan, R. (1991). Observations of parent reactions to sex-stereotyped behaviors: Age and sex effects. *Child Development, 62,* 617–628.

Fagot, B. I., Hagan, R., Leinbach, M. D., & Kronsberg, S. (1985). Differential reactions to assertive and communicative acts of toddler boys and girls. *Child Development, 56,* 1499–1505.

Fagot, B. I., Leinbach, M. D., & O'Boyle, C. (1992). Gender labeling, gender stereotyping, and parenting behaviors. *Developmental Psychology, 28,* 225–230.

Fahy, T. A. (1988). The diagnosis of multiple personality: A critical review. *British Journal of Psychiatry, 153,* 597–606.

Fancher, R. E. (1996). *Pioneers of psychology* (3rd ed.). New York: Norton.

Fantz, R. L. (1964). Visual experience in infants: Decreased attention to familiar patterns relative to novel ones. *Science, 146,* 668–670.

Faraday, A. (1972). *Dream power.* New York: Coward-McCann.

Farquhar, J. W., & Spiller, G. A. (1990). *The last puff.* New York: Norton.

Farrell, M. P., & Rosenberg, S. D. (1981). *Men at midlife.* Westport, CT: Auburn House.

Farwell, L. A., & Donchin, E. (1988). Talking off the top of your head: Toward a mental prosthesis utilizing event-related brain potentials. *Electroencephalography and Clinical Neurophysiology, 70,* 510–523.

Fausto-Sterling, A. (1992). *Myths of gender: Biological theories about women and men* (2nd ed.). New York: Basic Books.

Fausto-Sterling, A. (1993, March-April). The five sexes: Why male and female are not enough. *Sciences,* pp. 20–25.

Feagans, L. V., & Farran, D. C. (1994). The effects of daycare intervention in the preschool years on the narrative skills of poverty children in kindergarten. *International Journal of Behavioral Development, 17,* 503–523.

Feather, N. T. (1961). The relationship of persistence on a task to expectation of success and achievement-oriented motives. *Journal of Abnormal and Social Psychology, 63,* 552–561.

Feder, K. (1988). Trends in popular media: Credulity still reigns. *Skeptical Inquirer, 12,* 124–126.

Federal Glass Ceiling Commission (1995). *Good for business: Making full use of the nation's human capital.* Washington, DC: U.S. Department of Labor.

Feeney, J. A., & Noller, P. (1990). Attachment style as a prediction of adult romantic relationships. *Journal of Personality and Social Psychology, 58,* 281–291.

Feingold, A. (1992). Good-looking people are not what we think. *Psychological Bulletin, 111,* 304–341.

Feingold, A. (1991). Sex differences in the effects of similarity and physical attractiveness on opposite-sex attraction. *Basic and Applied Social Psychology, 12,* 357–367.

Felkers, K. R., & Stivers, C. (1994). The relationship of gender and family environment to eating disorder risk in adolescents. *Adolescence, 29,* 821–834.

Fenton, W. S., & McGlashan, T. H. (1991). Natural history of schizophrenia subtypes: 2. Positive and negative symptoms and long-term course. *Archives of General Psychiatry, 48,* 978–986.

Fernandez, E., & Turk, D. C. (1992). Sensory and affective components of pain: Separation and synthesis. *Psychological Bulletin, 112,* 205–217.

Ferster, C. B., & Skinner, B. F. (1957). *Schedules of reinforcement.* New York: Appleton-Century-Crofts.

Festinger, L. (1957). *A theory of cognitive dissonance.* New York: HarperCollins.

Fetterman, J. G. (1993). Numerosity discrimination: Both time and number matter. *Journal of Experimental Psychology: Animal Behavior Processes, 19,* 149–164.

Fetterman, J. G. (1996). Dimensions of stimulus complexity. *Journal of Experimental Psychology: Animal Behavior Processes, 22,* 3–18.

Fettiplace, R. (1990). Transduction and tuning in auditory hair cells. *Seminars in the Neurosciences, 2,* 33–40.

Findley, M. J., & Cooper, H. M. (1983). Locus of control and academic achievement: A literature review. *Journal of Personality and Social Psychology, 44,* 419–427.

Fink, M. (1992). Electroconvulsive therapy. In E. S. Paykel (Ed.), *Handbook of affective disorders* (2nd ed., pp. 359–367). New York: Guilford Press.

Fink, M. (1993). Post-ECT delirium. *Convulsive Therapy, 9,* 326–330.

Fisch, R. O., Matalon, R., Weisberg, S., & Michaels, K. (1997). Phenylketonuria: Current dietary treatment practices in the United States and Canada. *Journal of the American College of Nutrition, 16,* 147–151.

Fischbach, G. D. (1992). Mind and brain. *Science, 267,* 48–57.

Fischler, M. A., & Firschein, O. (1987). *Intelligence: The eye, the brain, and the computer.* Reading, MA: Addison-Wesley.

Fisher, A. (1993). Sexual harassment: What to do. *Fortune, 128,* 84–86.

Fisher, S., & Greenberg, R. P. (Eds.). (1989). *The limits of biological treatments for psychological distress.* Hillsdale, NJ: Erlbaum.

Fiske, S. T. (1993). Controlling other people: The impact of power on stereotyping. *American Psychologist, 48,* 621–628.

Fiske, S. T., Bersoff, D. N., Borgida, E., Deaux, K., & Heilman, M. E. (1991). Social science research on trial: The use of sex stereotyping research in *Price Waterhouse v. Hopkins. American Psychologist, 46,* 1049–1060.

Fiske, S. T., & Stevens, L. E. (1993). What's so special about sex? Gender stereotyping and discrimination. In. S. Oskamp & M. Costanzo (Eds.), *Gender issues in contemporary society* (pp. 173–196). Newbury Park, CA: Sage.

Fitzgerald, L. F. (1993a, February). *The last great open secret: The sexual harassment of women in the workplace and academia.* Science and Public Policy Seminar address presented to the Federation of Behavioral, Psychological and Cognitive Sciences, Washington, DC.

Fitzgerald, L. F. (1993b). Sexual harassment: Violence against women in the workplace. *American Psychologist, 48* 1070–1076.

Fitzgerald, L. F., & Ormerod, A. J. (1991). Perceptions of sexual harassment: The influence of gender and academic context. *Psychology of Women Quarterly, 15,* 281–294.

Fitzgerald, L. F., & Shullman, S. L. (1993). Sexual harassment: A research analysis and agenda for the 1990s. *Journal of Vocational Behavior, 42,* 5–27.

Fitzgerald, L. F., Shullman, S. L., Bailey, N., Richards, M., Swecker, J., Gold, Y., Ormerod, A. J., & Weitzman, L. (1988). The incidence and dimensions of sexual harassment in academia and the workplace. *Journal of Vocational Behavior, 32,* 152–175.

Fitzgerald, L. F., Weitzman, L. M., Gold, Y., & Ormerod, M. (1988). Academic harassment: Sex and denial in scholarly garb. *Psychology of Women Quarterly, 12,* 329–340.

Flaks, D. K., Ficher, I., Masterpasqua, F., & Joseph, G. (1995). Lesbians choosing motherhood: A comparative study of lesbian and heterosexual parents and their children. *Developmental Psychology, 31,* 105–114.

Flanagan, C. A. (1990). Change in family work status: Effects on parent-adolescent decision making. *Child Development, 61,* 163–177.

Flavell, J. H., Miller, P. H., & Miller, S. A. (1993). *Cognitive development* (3rd ed.). Upper Saddle River, NJ: Prentice Hall.

Fleming, J. H., & Darley, J. M. (1990). The purposeful-action sequence and the "illusion of control": The effects of foreknowledge and target involvement on observers' judgments of others' control over random events. *Personality and Social Psychology Bulletin, 16,* 346–357.

Flynn, J. R. (1998). IQ gains over time. Toward finding the causes. In U. Neisser (Ed.), *The Rising curve: Long-term gains in IQ and related measures,* pp. 25–66. Washingotn, DC: American Psychological Association.

Foa, E. B., & Kozak, M. J. (1995). *DSM-IV field trial: Obsessive-compulsive disorder. American Journal of Psychiatry, 152,* 90–96.

Fontenot, N. A. (1993). Effects of training in creativity and creative problem finding upon business people. *Journal of Social Psychology, 133,* 11–22.

Ford, C. V. (1996). *Lie! Lies! Lies!!! The psychology of deceit.* Washington, DC: American Psychiatric Association.

Ford, K., & Labbok, M. (1993). Breast-feeding and child health in the United States. *Journal of Biological Science, 25,* 187–194.

Forer, B. R. (1949). The fallacy of personal validation: A classroom demonstration of gullibility. *Journal of Abnormal and Social Psychology, 44,* 118–123.

Forgas, J. P. (1992). Mood and the perception of unusual people: Affective asymmetry in memory and social judgments. *European Journal of Social Psychology, 22,* 531–547.

Formy-Duval, D. L., Williams, J. E., Patterson, D. J., & Fogle, E. E. (1995). A "Big Five" scoring system for the item pool of the Adjective Check List. *Journal of Personality Assessment, 65,* 59–76.

Foulks, E. F., Bland, I., & Shervington, D. (1995). Psychotherapy across cultures. In J. M. Oldham & M. B. Riba (Eds.). *Review of psychiatry* (Vol. 14, pp. 511–528). Washington, DC: American Psychiatric Association.

Fowler, R. D. (1990). In memoriam: Burrhus Frederic Skinner, 1904–1990. *American Psychologist, 45,* 1203.

Fox, N. A., Kimmerly, N. L., & Schafer, W. D. (1991). Attachment to mother/attachment to father: A meta-analysis. *Child Development, 62,* 210–225.

Foxx, R. M. (1982). *Decreasing behaviors of severely retarded and autistic persons.* Champaign, IL: Research Press.

Frank, E. Anderson, B., Reynolds, C. F., III, Ritenour, A., & Kupfer, D. J. (1994). Life events and the research diagnostic criteria endogenous subtype. *Archives of General Psychiatry, 51,* 519–524.

Frank, M. G., & Gilovich, T. (1988). The dark side of self- and social perception: Black uniforms and aggression in professional sports. *Journal of Personality and Social Psychology, 54,* 74–85.

Franken, R. E. (1998). *Human motivation* (4th Ed.). Pacific Grove, CA: Brooks/Cole.

Frankenburg, W. K., Dodds, J., Archer, P., Bresnick, B., et al. (1992). *DENVER II Training manual.* Denver, CO: Denver Developmental Materials.

Fredrikson, M., & Gunnarsson, R. (1992). Psychobiology of stage fright: The effect of public performance on neuroendocrine, cardiovascular, and subjective reactions. *Biological Psychology, 22,* 51–61.

Freedman, D. H. (1992, June). The aggressive egg. *Discover,* pp. 61–65.

Freedman, D. H. (1993, June). In the realm of the chemical. *Discover,* pp. 69–76.

Freeman, G., Sims, T., Kutsch, K., & Marcon, R. A. (1995). *Linking gender-related toy preferences to social structure: Changes in children's letters to Santa since 1978.* Paper presented at the annual meeting of the Southeastern Psychological Association, Savannah, GA.

French, D., & Richards, M. (Eds.). (1996). *Contemporary television.* Thousand Oaks, CA: Sage.

Freud, A. (1958). *The ego and the mechanism of defense.* Madison, CT: International Universities Press.

Freud, S. (1965). *The psychopathology of everyday life* (A. Tyson, trans.). New York: Norton. (Originally published in 1901)

Fried, P. A. (1993). Prenatal exposure to tobacco and marijuana: Effects during pregnancy, infancy, and early childhoood. Clinical Obstetrics and Gynecology, 36, 319–337.

Friedman, A. F., Webb, J. T., & Lewak, R. (1989). *Psychological assessment with the MMPI.* Hillsdale, NJ: Erlbaum.

Friedman, M., & Rosenman, R. H. (1974). *Type A behavior and your heart.* New York: Knopf.

Friedman, M., Thoresen, C. E., Gill, J. J., Powell, L. H., Ulmer, D., Thompson, L., Price, V. A., Rabin, D. D., Breall, W. S., Dixon, T., Levy, R., & Bourg, E. (1984). Alteration of Type A behavior and reduction in cardiac recurrences in postmyocardial infarction patients. *American Heart Journal, 108,* 237–248.

Friedman, M., & Ulmer, D. (1984). *Treating Type A behavior and your heart.* New York: Knopf.

Friedman, M. I., & Stricker, E. M. (1976). The physiological psychology of hunger: A physiological perspective. *Psychological Review, 83,* 409–431.

Friedman, R. C., & Downey, J. I. (1994). Homosexuality. *New England Journal of Medicine, 331,* 923–930.

Friedrich-Cofer, L., & Huston, A. C. (1986). Television violence and aggression: The debate continues. *Psychological Bulletin, 100,* 364–371.

Friedman-Hill, S., & Wolfe, J. (1995). Second-order parallel processing: Visual search for the odd item in a subset. *Journal of Experimental Psychology: Human Perception and Performance, 21,* 531–551.

Fries, J. F., & Crapo, L. M. (1981). *Vitality and aging.* New York: Freeman.

Friman, P. C., & Warzak, W. J. (1990). Nocturnal enuresis: A prevalent, persistent, yet curable parasomnia. *Pediatrician, 1,* 38–45.

Fritz, R. (1993). *Sleep disorders: America's hidden nightmare.* Naperville, IL: National Sleep Alert.

Fry, W. F., Jr. (1986). Humor, physiology, and the aging process. In L. Nahemow, K. A. McCluskey-Fawcett, & P. E. McGhee (Eds.), *Humor and aging* (pp. 81–98). San Diego, CA: Academic Press.

Fryns, J. P. (1987). Chromosomal abnormalities and autosomal syndromes. In G. Evers-Kieboom, J. J. Cassiman, H. Van den Berghe, & G. d'Ydewalle (Eds.), *Genetic risk, risk perception, and decision making.* New York: Liss.

Fuchs, I., Eisenberg, N., Hertz-Lazarowitz, R., & Sharabany, R. (1986). Kibbutz, Israeli city, and American children's moral reasoning about prosocial moral conflicts.

Fulker, D. W., Eysenck, S. B. G., & Zuckerman, M. (1980). A genetic and environmental analysis of sensation seeking. *Journal of Research in Personality, 14,* 261–281. 37–50.

Fullerton, C. S., & Ursano, R. J. (1997). The other side of chaos: Understanding the patterns of post-traumatic responses. In C. S. Fullerton & R. J. Ursano (Eds.), *Posttraumatic stress disorder: Acute and long-term responses to trauma and disaster* (pp. 3–18). Washington, DC: American Psychiatric Association.

Funder, D. C. (1991). Global traits: A neo-Allportian approach to personality. *Psychological Science, 2,* 31–39.

Funder, D. C., & Colvin, C. R. (1991). Explorations in behavioral consistency: Properties of persons, situations, and behaviors. *Journal of Personality and Social Psychology, 60,* 773–794.

Furnham, A., & Schofield, S. (1987). Accepting personality test feedback: A review of the Barnum effect. *Current Psychological Research and Reviews, 6,* 162–178.

Furumoto, L. (1979). Mary Whiton Calkins (1863–1930): Fourteenth president of the American Psychological Association. *Journal of the History of the Behavioral Sciences, 15,* 346–356.

Furumoto, L. (1992). Joining separate spheres–Christine Ladd-Franklin, woman scientist (1847–1930). *American Psychologist, 47,* 175–182.

G

Gabrenya, W. K., Jr., Wang, Y.-E., & Latané, B. (1985). Social loafing on an optimizing task: Cross-cultural differences among Chinese and Americans. *Journal of Cross-Cultural Psychology, 16,* 223–242.

Galati, D., Scherer, K. R., & Ricci-Bitti, P. E. (1997). Voluntary facial expression of emotion: Comparing congenitally blind with normally sighted encoders. *Journal of Personality and Social Psychology, 73,* 1363–1379.

Galef, B. G., Jr. (1989). Enduring social enhancement of rats' preferences for the palatable and the piquant. *Appetite, 13,* 81–92.

Galef, B. G., Jr. (1996). Social enhancement of food preferences in Norway rats: A brief review. In C. M. Heyes & B. G. Galef, Jr. (Eds.), *Social learning in animals: The roots of culture* (pp. 49–64). San Diego, CA: Academic Press.

Galef, B. G., Jr., & Stein, M. (1985). Demonstrator influence on observer diet preference: Analyses of critical social interactions and olfactory signals. *Animal Learning & Behavior, 13,* 31–38.

Galef, B. G., Jr., Whiskin, E. E., & Bielavska, E. (1997). Interaction with demonstrator rats changes observer rats' affective responses to flavors. *Journal of Comparative Psychology, 111,* 393–398.

Galinsky, E. (1981). *Between generations: The six stages of parenthood.* New York: Berkley.

Galler, J. R., Ramsey, C. F., Morely, D. S., Archer, E., & Salt, P. (1990). The long-term effects of early kwashiorkor compared with marasmus. IV. Performance on the National High School Entrance Examination. *Pediatric Research, 28,* 235–239.

Gallup, G. H., Jr., & Newport, F. (1991). Belief in paranormal phenomena among adult Americans. *Skeptical Inquirer, 15,* 137–146.

Gallup Organization (1995). *Sleep in America: A national survey of U.S. adults* (poll conducted for the Natinal Sleep Foundation). Princeton, NJ National Sleep Foundation.

Galvin, S. L., & Herzog, H. A., Jr. (1992). Ethical ideology, animal rights activism, and attitudes toward the treatment of animals. *Ethics and Behavior, 2,* 141–149.

Gangakhedkar, R. R., Bentley, M. E., Divekar, A. D., Gadkari, D., Mehendale, S. M., Shepherd, M. E., Bolinger, R. C., & Quinn, T. C. (1997). Spread of HIV infection in married monogamous women in India. *Journal of the American Medical Association, 278,* 2090–2092.

Gantt, W. H. (1971). Experimental basis for neurotic behavior. In H. D. Kimmel (Ed.), *Experimental psychopathology: Recent research and theory.* San Diego, CA: Academic Press.

Garb, J. L., & Stunkard, A. J. (1974). Taste aversions in man. *American Journal of Psychiatry, 131,* 1204–1207.

Garcia, J., Ervin, F. R., & Koelling, R. A. (1966). Learning with prolonged delay of reinforcement. *Psychonomic Science, 5,* 121–122.

Garcia, J., & Koelling, R. A. (1966). Relation of cue to consequence in avoidance learning. *Psychonomic Science, 4,* 123–124.

Gardner, H. (1983). *Frames of mind.* New York: Basic Books.

Gardner, H. (1985). *The mind's new science: A history of the cognitive revolution.* New York: Basic Books.

Gardner, H. (1998). Are there additional intelligences? The case for naturalist, spiritual, and existential intelligences. In J. Kane (Ed.), *Education, information, and transformation.* Upper Saddle River, NJ: Prentice Hall.

Gardner, H. (1993). *Multiple intelligence: The theory in practice.* New York: Basic.

Gardner, H. (1956). *Mathematics, magic and mystery.* New York: Dover.

Garfield, S. L. (1980). *Psychotherapy: An eclectic approach.* New York: Wiley.

Garfinkel, D., Laudon, M., Nof, D., & Zisapel, N. (1995). Improvement of sleep quality in elderly people by controlled-release melatonin. *Lancet, 346,* 541–544.

Garma, L., & Marchand, F. (1994). Nonpharmacological approaches to the treatment of narcolepsy. *Sleep, 17,* S97–S102.

Gastil, J. (1990). Generic pronouns and sexist language: The oxymoronic character of masculine generics. *Sex Roles, 11/12,* 629–643.

Gazzaniga, M. S. (1967). The split brain in man. *Scientific American, 217,* 24–29.

Geertz, C. (1980, July 24). Sociosexology. *New York Review of Books,* pp. 3–4.

Geisler, W., & Chou, K. (1995). Separation of low-level and high-level factors in complex tasks: Visual Search. *Psychological Review, 102,* 356–378.

Geldard, F. A. (1972). *The human senses* (2nd ed.). New York: Wiley.

Gelfand, D. E. (1982). *Aging: The ethnic factor.* New York: Little, Brown.

Gelfand, T., & Kerr, J. (Eds.) (1992). *Freud and the history of psychoanalysis.* Hillsdale, NJ: Analytic Press.

Gelles, R., & Strauss, M. (1988). *Intimate violence.* New York: Simon & Schuster.

Gershberg, F. B., & Shimamura, A. P. (1994). Serial position effects in implicit and explicit tests of memory. *Journal of Experimental Psychology: Learning, Memory, and Cognition, 20,* 1370–1378.

Gershon, E. S., & Nurnberger, J. I. (1995). Bipolar illness. In J. M. Oldham & M. B. Riba (Eds.), *Review of psychiatry* (Vol. 14, pp. 405–424). Washington, DC: American Psychiatric Association.

Gesteland, R. C. (1986). Speculations on receptor cells as analyzers and filters. *Experientia, 42,* 287–291.

Ghiselin, B. (Ed.). *The creative process.* New York: Mentor.

Giambra, L. M. (1989). Task-unrelated-thought frequency as a function of age: A laboratory study. *Psychology and Aging, 4,* 136–143.

Giannelli, P. C. (1995). The admissibility of hypnotic evidence in U.S. courts. *International Journal of Clinical and Experimental Hypnosis, 43,* 212–233.

Gibson, E. J. (1987). Introductory essay: What does infant perception tell us about theories of perception? *Journal of Experimental Psychology: Human Perception and Performance, 13,* 515–523.

Gibson, E. J., & Walk, R. D. (1960). The "visual cliff." *Scientific American, 202,* 64–71.

Gibson, R. C. (1986). Older black Americans. *Generations, 10,* 35–39.

Gilbert, D. T., & Malone, P. S. (1995). The correspondence bias. *Psychological Bulletin, 117,* 21–38.

Gilbert, D. T., McNulty, S. E., Giuliano, T. A., & Benson, J. E. (1992). Blurry words and fuzzy deeds: The attribution of obscure behavior. *Journal of Personality and Social Psychology, 62,* 18–25.

Gilbert, B. (1990, December). Once a malcontent, Ruby has taken up brush and palette. *Smithsonian,* pp. 40–50.

Gilbert, P. L., Harris, M. J., McAdams, L. A., & Jeste, D. V. (1995). Neuroleptic withdrawal in schizophrenic patients: A review of the literature. *Archives of General Psychiatry, 52,* 173–188.

Gilbert, S. (1989). *The psychology of dieting.* London: Routledge.

Gilchrist, A., Humphreys, G., Riddock, M., & Neumann, H. (1997). Luminance and edge information in grouping: A study using visual search. *Journal of Experimental Psychology: Human Perception and Performance, 23,* 464–480.

Gilligan, C. (1982). *In a different voice: Psychological theory and women's development.* Cambridge, MA: Harvard University Press.

Gilligan, C., Lyons, N. P., & Hanmer, T. J. (Eds.). (1990). *Making connections: The relational worlds of adolescent girls at Emma Willard School.* Cambridge, MA: Harvard University Press.

Gilligan, C., Murphy, J. M., & Tappan, M. B. (1990). Moral development beyond adolescence. In C. N. Alexander & E. J. Langer (Eds.), *Higher stages of human development.* New York: Oxford University Press.

Gillin, J. C., & Byerley, W. F. (1990). The diagnosis and management of insomnia. *New England Journal of Medicine, 322,* 239–248.

Gilman, S. (1992). Advances in neurology. *New England Journal of Medicine, 326,* 1608–1616.

Gilovich, T. (1991). *How we know what isn't so.* New York: Free Press.

Ginsberg, M. D. (1995). Neuroprotection in brain ischemia: An update (part I). *The Neuroscientist, 1,* 95–103.

Giovino, G. A., Henningfield, J. E., Tomar, S. L., Escobedo, L. G., & Slade, J. (1995). Epidemiology of tobacco use and dependence. *Epidemiologic Reviews, 17,* 48–65.

Glaser, R., Pearson, G. R., Bonneau, R. H., Esterling, B. A., Atkinson, C., & Kicolt-Glaser, J. K. (1993). Stress and the memory T-cell response to the Epstein-Barr virus in healthy medical students. *Health Psychology, 12,* 435–442.

Glenn, N. D., & McLanahan, S. (1982). Children and marital happiness: A further specification of the relationship. *Journal of Marriage and the Family, 44,* 63–72.

Glick, P., Gottesman, D., & Jolton, J. (1989). The fault is not in the stars: Susceptibility of skeptics and believers in astrology to the Barnum effect. *Personality and Social Psychology Bulletin, 15,* 572–583.

Glick, R. (1980). Promoting competence and coping through retirement planning. In L. A. Bond

& J. C. Rosen (Eds.), *Competence and coping during adulthood*. Hanover, NH: University Press of New England.

Gold, J. A., Ryckman, R. M., & Mosley, N. R. (1984). Romantic mood induction and attraction to a dissimilar other: Is love blind? *Personality and Social Psychology Bulletin, 10,* 358–368.

Goldberg, A. M., & Frazier, J. M. (1989). Alternatives to animals in toxicity testing. *Scientific American, 261,* 24–30.

Goldberg, G. S., & Kremen, E. (1990). *The feminization of poverty: Only in America?* New York: Prager.

Goldberg, L. R. (1995). What the hell took so long? Donald W. Fiske and the big-five factor structure. In P. E. Shrout & S. T. Fiske (Eds.), *Personality research, methods, and theory: A festschrift honoring Donald W. Fiske* (pp. 29–43). Hillsdale, NJ: Erlbaum.

Goldberg, S., MacKay-Soroka, S., & Rochester, M. (1994). Affect, attachment, and maternal responsiveness. *Infant Behavior and Development, 17,* 335–339.

Goldinger, S. D. (1996). Words and voices: Episodic traces in spoken word identification and recognition memory. *Journal of Experimental Psychology: Learning, Memory, and Cognition, 22,* 1166–1183.

Goldsmith, H. H., Buss, A. H., Plomin, R., Rothbart, M. K., Thomas, A., Chess, S., Hinde, R. A., & McCall, R. B. (1987). Roundtable: What is temperament? Four approaches. *Child Development, 58,* 505–529.

Goldsmith, H. H., & Campos, J. J. (1982). Toward a theory of infant temperament. In R. N. Emde and R. J. Harmon (Eds.), *The development of attachment and affiliative systems: Psychobiological aspects.* New York: Plenum.

Goleman, D. (1995). *Emotional intelligence: Why it can matter more than IQ.* New York: Bantam Books.

Goodman, J. (1993). Ed-libs. *Laughing matters, 9(2),* 44–45.

Goodman, J., Loftus, E. F., & Greene, E. (1990). Matters of money: Voir dire in civil cases. *Forensic Reports, 3,* 303–329.

Goodman, L. A., Koss, M. P., & Russo, N. F. (1993a). Violence against women: Physical and mental health effects: 1. Research findings. *Applied and Preventive Psychology, 2,* 79–89.

Goodman, L. A., Koss, M. P., & Russo, N. F. (1993b). Violence against women: Physical and mental health effects: 2. Conceptualizations of posttraumatic stress. *Applied and Preventive Psychology, 2,* 123–130.

Goodwin, C. J. (1988). Selective attention with human earphones. *Teaching of Psychology, 15,* 104–105.

Gordon, H. (1987). *Extrasensory deception: ESP, psychics, Shirley MacLaine, ghosts, UFOs . . .* Buffalo, NY: Prometheus.

Goshen-Gottstein, Y., & Moscovitch, M. (1995a). Recognition priming for newly formed and preexisting associations: Perceptual and conceptual influences. *Journal of Experimental Psychology: Learning, Memory, and Cognition, 21,* 1229–1248.

Goshen-Gottstein, Y., & Moscovitch, M. (1995b). Repetition priming effects for newly formed associations are perceptually based: Evidence from shallow encoding and format specificity. *Journal of Experimental Psychology: Learning, Memory, and Cognition, 21,* 1249–1262.

Gottesman, I. I. (1991). *Schizophrenia genesis: The origins of madness.* New York: Freeman.

Gottfredson, L. S. (1997). Why g matters: The complexity of everyday life. *Intelligence, 24(1),* 79–132.

Gough, H. G., & Bradley, P. (1996). *Manual for the California Psychological Inventory* (2nd ed.). Palo Alto, CA: Consulting Psychologists Press.

Gould, S. J. (1981). *The mismeasure of man.* New York: Norton.

Gould, S. J. (1994, November 28). Curveball. *New Yorker,* pp. 139–149.

Graf, P. (1982). The memorial consequences of generation and transformation. *Journal of Verbal Learning and Verbal Behavior, 21,* 539–548.

Graham, J. R. (1990). *MMPI-2: Assessing personality and psychopathology.* New York: Oxford University Press.

Graham, J. W., Marks, G., & Hansen, W. B. (1991). Social influence processes affecting adolescent substance abuse. *Journal of Applied Psychology, 76,* 291–298.

Gram, L. F. (1994). Drug therapy: Fluoxetine. *New England Journal of Medicine, 331,* 1354–1361.

Grant, J. P. (1995). *The state of the world's children 1995.* New York: Oxford University Press.

Grant, B. F., Harford, T. C., Dawson, D. A., Chou, P., Dufour, M. C., & Pickering, R. (1994). Prevalence of *DSM-IV* alcohol abuse and dependence: United States, 1992. *Alcohol Health and Research World, 18,* 243–248.

Gray, J. D., & Silver, R. C. (1990). Opposite sides of the same coin: Former spouses' divergent perspectives in coping with their divorce. *Journal of Personality and Social Psychology, 59,* 1180–1191.

Gray, P. (1995, January). *Incorporating evolutionary theory into the teaching of psychology.* Paper presented at the Seventeenth Annual National Institute on the Teaching of Psychology, St. Petersburg Beach, FL.

Gray, W. D. (1991). *Thinking critically about New Age ideas.* Belmont, CA: Wadsworth.

Green, J. P., Lynn, S. J., & Lalinoski, P. (In press). Hypnotic pseudomemories: The effects of warnings and hidden observer instructions. *Applied cognitive psychology.*

Green, L. B. (1992). The use of imagery in the rehabilitation of injured athletes. *The Sport Psychologist, 6,* 416–428.

Greenberg, J., Pyszczynski, T., Solomon, S., Rosenblatt, A., Veeder, M., Kirkland, S., & Lyon, D. (1990). Evidence for terror management theory: 2. The effects of mortality salience on reactions to those who threaten or bolster the cultural worldview. *Journal of Personality and Social Psychology, 58,* 308–318.

Greene, R. L. (1977). Student acceptance of generalized personality interpretations: A reexamination. *Journal of Consulting and Clinical Psychology, 45,* 965–966.

Greene, R. L. (1991). *The MMPI-2/MMPI: An interpretive manual.* Needham Heights, MA: Allyn & Bacon.

Greenfield, P. (1992, June). *Notes and references for developmental psychology.* Conference on Making Basic Texts in Psychology More Culture-Inclusive and Culture-Sensitive. Western Washington University, Bellingham, WA.

Greenspoon, J., & Raynard, R. (1957). Stimulus conditions and retroactive inhibition. *Journal of Experimental Psychology, 53,* 55–59.

Greiser, D., & Kuhl, P. K. (1989). Categorization of speech by infants: Support for speech-sound prototypes. *Developmental Psychology, 25,* 577–589.

Gresty, M. A., Bronstein, A. M., Brandt, T., & Dieterich, M. (1992). Neurology of otolith function. *Brain, 115,* 647–673.

Griffin, K. (1992, November-December). A whiff of things to come. *Health,* pp. 34–35.

Grilo, C. M., & Pogue-Geile, M. F. (1991). The nature of environmental influences on weight and obesity: A behavior genetic analysis. *Psychological Bulletin, 110,* 520–537.

Grinspoon, L., & Bakalar, J. B. (1993). *Marihuana, the forbidden medicine.* New Haven, CT: Yale University Press.

Grob, G. N. (1994). *The mad among us: A history of the care of America's mentally ill.* New York: Free Press.

Gross, J. J., & John, O. P. (1998). Mapping the domain of expressivity: Multimethod evidence for a hierarchical model. *Journal of Personality and Social Psychology, 74,* 170–191.

Grossman, M., & Wood, W. (1993). Sex differences in intensity of emotional experience: A social role interpretation. *Journal of Personality and Social Psychology, 65,* 1010–1022.

Grossman, S. P. (1990). Brain mechanisms concerned with food intake and body-weight regulation. In M. M. Fichter (Ed.), *Bulimia nervosa: Basic research, diagnosis, and therapy.* Chichester, England: John Wiley & Sons.

Groth-Marnat, G. (1990). *Handbook of psychological assessment* (2nd ed.). New York: Wiley.

Gruber, J. E. (1997). An epidemiology of sexual harassment: Evidence from North America and Europe. In W. O'Donohue (Ed.), *Sexual harassment: Theory, research, and treatment* (pp. 84–98). Boston: Allyn & Bacon.

Guarnaccia, P. J., Canino, G., Rubio-Stipec, M., & Bravo, M. (1993). The prevalence of ataques de nervios in the Puerto Rico Disaster Study: The role of culture in psychiatric epidemiology. *Journal of Nervous and Mental Disease, 181,* 157–163.

Guenther, R. K. (1998). *Human cognition.* Upper Saddle River, NJ: Prentice Hall.

Guerin, B. (1993). *Social facilitation.* Cambridge: Cambridge University Press.

Gulevich, G., Dement, W. C., & Johnson, L. (1966). Psychiatric and EEG observations on a case of prolonged (264 hours) wakefulness. *Archives of General Psychiatry, 15,* 29–35.

Gur, R. C., Mozley, L. H., Mozley, P. D., Resnick, S. M., Karp, J. S., Alavi, A., Arnold, S. E., & Gur, R. E. (1995). Sex differences in regional glucose metabolism during a resting state. *Science, 267,* 528–531.

Gurian, B. G. (1993). What is old-old age? *Harvard Mental Health Letter, 11,* 8.

Gutek, B. A. (1985). *Sex and the workplace: The impact of sexual behavior and harassment on women, men, and organizations.* San Francisco: Jossey-Bass.

Guthrie, R. V. (1998). *Even the rat was white* (2nd ed.). Needham Heights, MA: Allyn & Bacon.

H

Haber, R. N. (1958). Discrepancy from adaption level as a source of affect. *Journal of Experimental Psychology, 56,* 370–375.

Haber, J., Krainovich-Miller, B., Leach McMahon, A. L., Price-Hoskins, P. (1997). *Comprehensive psychiatric nursing* (5th ed.). St. Louis: Mobsy.

Hackett, G., Betz, N. E., Casas, J. M., & Rocha-Singh, I. A. (1992). Gender, ethnicity, and social cognitive factors predicting the academic achievement of students in engineering. *Journal of Counseling Psychology, 39,* 527–538.

Haggard, E. A., As, A., & Borgen, C. M. (1970). Social isolates and urbanites in perceptual isolation. *Journal of Abnormal Psychology, 76,* 1–9.

Haines, V. J., Diekhoff, G. M., LaBeff, E. E., & Clark, R. E. (1986). College cheating: Immaturity, lack of commitment, and the neutralizing attitude. *Research in Higher Education, 25,* 342–354.

Haist, F., Shimamura, A. P., & Squire, L. R. (1992). On the relationship between recall and recognition. *Journal of Experimental Psychology: Learning, Memory, and Cognition, 18,* 691–702.

Hajjar, D. J., & Nicholson, A. C. (1995). Atherosclerosis. *American Scientist, 83,* 460–467.

Hall, C. S. (1966). *The meaning of dreams.* New York: McGraw-Hill.

Hall, E. G., & Lee, A. M. (1984). Sex differences in motor performance of young children: Fact or fiction? *Sex Roles, 10,* 217–230.

Hall, E. T. (1966). *The hidden dimension.* New York: Doubleday.

Hall, J. A. (1984). *Nonverbal sex differences: Communication accuracy and expressive style.* Baltimore: Johns Hopkins University Press.

Hall, J. A. (1978). Gender effects in decoding nonverbal cues. *Psychological Bulletin, 85,* 845–857.

Hall, E. G., & Davies, S. (1991). Gender differences in perceived intensity and affect of pain between athletes and nonathletes. *Perceptual and Motor Skills, 73,* 779–786.

Halpern, D. F. (1986). *Sex differences in cognitive abilities*. Hillsdale, NJ: Erlbaum.

Halpern, D. F. (1992). *Sex differences in cognitive abilities* (2nd ed.). Hillsdale, NJ: Erlbaum.

Halpern, D. F., & Coren, S. (1993). Left-handedness and life span: A reply to Harris. *Psychological Bulletin, 114*, 235–241.

Hamann, S. B., & Squire, L. R. (1996). Level-of-processing effects in word-completion priming: A neuropsychological study. *Journal of Experimental Psychology: Learning, Memory, and Cognition, 22*, 933–947.

Hamilton, D. L., & Sherman, J. W. (1994). Stereotypes. In R. S. Wyer & T. K. Krull (Eds.). *Handbook of social cognition* (2nd ed., Vol. 2, pp. 1–68). Hillsdale, NJ: Erlbaum.

Hamilton, M. C. (1991). Masculine bias in the attribution of personhood. *Psychology of Women Quarterly, 15*, 393–402.

Hammen, C. (1997). *Depression*. East Sussex, United Kingdom.

Hanson, S., & Hanson, P. (1989, April). Mean spirits: Why the strange friendship of Harry Houdini and Sir Arthur Conan Doyle didn't have a ghost of a chance. *Los Angeles Times Magazine*, pp. 94–104.

Hardy, C., & Crace, R. K. (1991). The effects of task structure and teammate competence on social loafing. *Journal of Sport and Exercise Psychology, 13*, 372–381.

Hardy, C., & Latané, B. (1986). Social loafing on a cheering task. *Social Science, 71*, 165–172.

Hare, R. D. (1993). *Without conscience: The disturbing world of the psychopaths among us*. New York: Basic Books.

Hare, R. D., McPherson, L. M., & Forth, A. E. (1988). Male psychopaths and their criminal careers. *Journal of Consulting and Clinical Psychology, 56*, 710–714.

Hare-Mustin, R. T., & Marecek, J. (1990a). Gender and the meaning of difference. In R. T. Hare-Mustin & J. Marecek (Eds.), *Making a difference: Psychology and the construction of gender* (pp. 22–64). New Haven, CT: Yale University Press.

Hare-Mustin, R. T., & Marecek, J. (1990b). On making a difference. In R. T. Hare-Mustin & J. Marecek (Eds.), *Making a difference: Psychology and the construction of gender* (pp. 1–21). New Haven, CT: Yale University Press.

Hargrave, G. E., & Hiatt, D. (1989). Use of the California Psychological Inventory in law enforcement officer selection. *Journal of Personality Assessment, 53*, 267–277.

Hari, R. (1994). Human cortical functions revealed by magnetoencephalography. *Progress in Brain Research, 100*, 163–168.

Haring, N. G., McCormick, L., & Haring, T. G. (1994). *Exceptional children and youth* (6th ed.). Upper Saddle River, NJ: Prentice Hall.

Harlow, H. F., & Harlow, M. K. (1962). The effect of rearing conditions on behavior. *Bulletin of Menninger Clinic, 26*, 213–224.

Harlow, H. F., Harlow, M. K., & Meyer, D. R. (1950). Learning motivated by a manipulation drive. *Journal of Experimental Psychology, 40*, 228–234.

Harlow, J. M. (1868). Recovery from the passage of an iron bar through the head. *Massachusetts Medical Society Publication, 2*, 329–347.

Harpaz, I. (1985). Meaning of working: Profiles of various occupational groups. *Journal of Vocational Behavior, 26*, 25–40.

Harris, L. J. (1993). Do left-handers die sooner than right-handers? Commentary on Coren and Halpern's (1991) "Left-handedness: A marker for decreased survival fitness." *Psychological Bulletin, 114*, 203–234.

Harris, M. B. (1974). Mediators between frustration and aggression in a field experiment. *Journal of Experimental Social Psychology, 10*, 561–571.

Harris, R. J., & Firestone, J. M. (1997). Subtle sexism in the U.S. military: Individual responses to sexual harassment. In N. V. Benokraitis (Ed.), *Subtle sexism: Current practice and prospects for change* (pp. 154–171). Thousand Oaks, CA: Sage Publications.

Hartmann, E. (1987). *The sleep book: Understanding and preventing sleep problems in people over 50*. Glenview, IL: Scott, Foresman.

Hartshorne, H., & May, M. A. (1928). *Studies in the nature of character* (Vol. 1). New York: Macmillan.

Hauri, P. J., & Linde, S. (1990). *No more sleepless nights*. New York: Wiley.

Hauri, P. J. (1991). Sleep hygiene, relaxation therapy, and cognitive interventions. In P. J. Hauri (Ed.), *Case studies in insomnia* (pp. 65–84). New York: Plenum.\

Harvard Mental Health Letter. (November, 1996). Suicide–Part I. *13*, 1–5.

Harvard Mental Health Letter. (August, 1998). Obsessive-compulsive disorder–Part I, *15(4)*, 1–4.

Hauri, P. J. (1992). *Sleep disorders*. Kalamazoo, MI: Upjohn.

Hawton, K. (1992). Suicide and attempted suicide. In E. S. Paykel (Ed.), *Handbook of affective disorders* (2nd ed., pp. 635–650). New York: Guilford Press.

Hayes, D. S., & Casey, D. M. (1992). Young children and television: The retention of emotional reactions. *Child Development, 63*, 1423–1436.

Heath, A. C., Kendler, K. S., Eaves, I. J., & Martin, N. G. (1990). Evidence for genetic influences on sleep disturbance and sleep patterns in twins. *Sleep, 13*, 318–335.

Heath, T. D. (1994). The impact of delayed fatherhood on the father-child relationship. *Journal of Genetic Psychology, 155*, 511–530.

Heatherton, T. F., Kozlowski, L. T., Frecker, R. C., & Fagerstrom, K. O. (1991). The Fagerstrom test for nicotine dependence: A revision of the Fagerstrom tolerance questionnaire. *British Journal of Addictions, 86*, 119–127.

Hegarty, V. (1995). *Nutrition, food, and the environment*. St. Paul, MN: Eagen Press.

Heider, F. (1958). *The psychology of interpersonal relationships*. New York: Wiley.

Helmes, E., & Reddon, J. R. (1993). A perspective on developments in assessing psychopathology: A critical review of the MMPI and MMPI-2. *Psychological Bulletin, 113*, 453–471.

Helms, J. E. (1992). Why is there no study of cultural equivalence in standardized cognitive ability testing? *American Psychologist, 47*, 1083–1101.

Helson, R., & Roberts, B. W. (1994). Ego development and personality change in adulthood. *Journal of Personality and Social Psychology, 66*, 911–920.

Helzer, J. E., Burnam, A., & McEvoy, L. T. (1991). Alcohol abuse and dependence. In L. N. Robins & D. A. Regier (Eds.), *Psychiatric disorders in America: The Epidemiologic Catchment Area Study* (pp. 81–115). New York: Free Press.

Helzer, J. E., Canino, G. J., Yeh, E.-K., Bland, R. C., Lee, C. K., Hwu, H.-G., & Newman, S. (1990). Alcoholism—North America and Asia. *Archives of General Psychiatry, 47*, 313–319.

Helzer, J. E., Robins, L. N., & McEvoy, M. A. (1987). Posttraumatic stress disorder in the general population. *New England Journal of Medicine, 317*, 1630–1634.

Henderson, P. H., Clarke, J. E., & Woods, C. (1998). Summary report 1996: Doctoral recipients from United States universities. Washington, DC: National Academy Press.

Hendrick, C., & Hendrick, S. (1986). A theory and method of love. *Journal of Personality and Social Psychology, 50*, 392–402.

Hennager, K. (1993). Senoi dream theory. In M. A. Carsakadon (Ed.), *Encyclopedia of sleep and dreaming* (pp. 532–533). New York: Macmillan.

Henning, H. (1916). *Der Geruch*. Leipzig: Barth.

Herbert, T. B., & Cohen, S. (1993). Stress and immunity in humans: A meta-analytic review. *Psychosomatic Medicine, 55*, 364–379.

Herzog, H. A. (1990). Discussing animal rights and animal research in the classroom. *Teaching of Psychology, 17*, 90–94.

Hesson-McInnis, M. S., & Fitzgerald, L. F. (1997). Sexual harassment: A preliminary test of an integrative model. *Journal of Applied Social Psychology, 27*, 877–901.

Heston, L. L. (1992). *Mending minds: A guide to the new psychiatry of depression, anxiety, and other serious mental disorders*. New York: Freeman.

Heston, L. L., & White, J. A. (1991). *Dementia* (2nd ed). New York: Freeman.

Hetherington, A. W., & Ranson, S. W. (1940). Hypothalamic lesions and adiposity in the rat. *Anatomical Record, 78*, 149–172.

Hettinger, T. P., & Frank, M. E. (1992). Information processing in mammalian gustatory systems. *Current Opinion in Neurobiology, 2*, 469–478.

Hewstone, M. (1988). Causal attribution: From cognitive processes to collective beliefs. *Psychologist, 8*, 323–327.

Heyes, C. M., Jaldow, E., & Dawson, G. R. (1993). Observational extinction: Observation of noninforced responding reduces resistance to extinction in rats. *Animal Learning and Behavior, 21*, 221–225.

Higbee, K. L. (1993). *Your memory: How it works and how to improve it*. New York: Paragon House.

Hilgard, E. R. (1991). Suggestibility and suggestions as related to hypnosis. In J. F. Schumaker (Ed.), *Human suggestibility: Advances in theory, research, and application* (pp. 38–58). New York: Routledge.

Hill, G. W. (1982). Group versus individual performance: Are N + 1 heads better than one? *Psychological Bulletin, 91*, 517–539.

Hilton, D. J., Smith, R. H., & Kin, S. H. (1995). Processes of causal explanation and dispositional attribution. *Journal of Personality and Social Psychology, 68*, 377–387.

Hines, T. (1988). *Pseudoscience and the paranormal: A critical examination of the evidence*. Buffalo, NY: Prometheus.

Hirschfeld, R., Keller, M., Panico, S., Arons, B., Barlow, D., Davidoff, F., Endicott, J., Froom, J., Goldstein, M., Gorman, J., Guthrie, D., Marek, R., Maureen, T., Meyer, R., Philips, K., Ross, J., Schwenk, T., Sharfstein, S., Thase, M., & Wyatt, R. (1997). The National Depressive and Manic-Depressive Association Consensus Statement on the Undertreatment of Depression. *Journal of the American Medial Association, 277*, 333–340.

Hobson, J. A. (1989). *Sleep*. New York: Scientific American Library.

Hobson, J. A., & McCarley, R. W. (1977). The brain as a dream state generator: An activation-synthesis hypothesis of the dream process. *American Journal of Psychiatry, 134*, 1335–1348.

Hochschild, A. (1989). *The second shift: Working parents and the revolution at home*. New York: Viking Penguin.

Hogan, R., Carpenter, B. N., Briggs, S. R., & Hansson, R. O. (1985). *Personality assessment and personnel selection*. In H. J. Bernardin & D. A. Bownas (Eds.), *Personality assessment in organizations* (pp. 21–52). New York: Praeger.

Hogarty, G. E., Anderson, C. M., Reiss, D. J., Kornblith, S. J., Greenwald, D. P., Ulrich, R. F., & Carter, M. (1991). Family psychoeducation, social skills training, and maintenance chemotherapy in the aftercare treatment of schizophrenia. *Archives of General Psychiatry, 48*, 340–347.

Hoge, R. D., Andrews, D. A., & Leschied, A. W. (1994). Tests of three hypotheses regarding the predictors of delinquency. *Journal of Abnormal Child Psychology, 22*, 547–559.

Holden, C. (1987a). The genetics of personality. *Science, 237*, 598–601.

Holden, C. (1987b). OTA cites financial disaster of Alzheimer's. *Science, 236*, 253.

Holden, C. (1990). Head Start enters adulthood. *Science, 247*, 1400–1402.

Holland, A., & Andre, T. (1994). The relationship of self-esteem to selected personal and environmental resources of adolescents. *Adolescence, 29*, 345–360.

Hollander, H. (1979). Historical review and clinical relevance of real-time observations of fetal movement. *Contributions to Gynecology and Obstetrics, 6*, 26–28.

Hollister, L. E. (1988). Marijuana and immunity. *Journal of Psychoactive Drugs, 20*, 3–8.

Hollon, S. D., Shelton, R. C., & Loosen, P. T. (1991). Cognitive therapy and pharmacotherapy for depression. *Journal of Consulting and Clinical Psychology, 59*, 88–99.

Holloway, K. S., & Domjan, M. (1993). Sexual approach conditioning: Unconditional stimulus factors. *Journal of Experimental Psychology: Animal Behavior Processes, 19*, 38–46.

Holloway, M. (1999). Flynn's effect. *Scientific American, 280*, 37–38.

Holmes, D. S. (1994). Is there evidence for repression? Doubtful. *Harvard Mental Health Letter, 10*(12), 5–6.

Holmes, T. H., & Rahe, R. H. (1967). The Social Readjustment Rating Scale. *Journal of Psychosomatic Research, 11*, 213–218.

Holway, A. F., & Boring, E. G. (1941). Determinants of apparent visual size with distance variant. *American Journal of Psychology, 54*, 21–37.

Honts, C. R., Roskin, D.C., & Kircher, J.C. (1994). Mental and physical countermeasures reduce the accuracy of polygraph tests, *Journal of Applied Psychology, 79*, 252–259.

Hooper, J., & Teresi, D. (1987). *The 3-pound universe*. New York: Dell.

Hopkins, B., & Westra, T. (1988). Maternal handling and motor development: An intracultural study. *Genetic, Social, and General Psychology Monographs, 14*, 377–420.

Hopkins, D. R., Murrah, B., Hoeger, W. W. K., & Rhodes, R. C. (1990). Effect of low-impact aerobic dance on the functional fitness of elderly women. *Gerontologist, 30*, 189–192.

Hopkins, H. S., & Gelenberg, A. J. (1994). Treatment for bipolar disorder: How far have we come? *Psychopharmacology Bulletin, 30*, 27–38.

Hopkins, K. D., Stanley, J. C., & Hopkins, B. R. (1990). *Educational and psychological measurement and evaluation* (7th ed.). Englewood Cliffs, NJ: Prentice Hall.

Hoptman, M. J., & Davidson, R. J. (1994). How and why do the two hemispheres interact? *Psychological Bulletin, 116*, 195–219.

Hopwood, N. J., Kelch, R. P., Hale, P. M., Mendes, T. M., Foster, C. M., & Beitins, I. Z. (1990). The onset of human puberty: Biological and environmental factors. In J. Bancroft and J. M. Reinisch (Eds.), *Adolescence and puberty*. New York: Oxford University Press.

Horgan, J. (1993). Eugenics revisited. *Scientific American, 268*, 122–131.

Horn, J. L., & Donaldson, G. (1976). On the myth of intellectual decline in adulthood. *American Psychologist, 31*, 701–719.

Horn, J. L., & Donaldson, G. (1980). Cognitive development II: Adulthood development of human abilities. In O. G. Brian & J. Kagan (Eds.), *Constancy and change in human development*. Cambridge, MA: Harvard University Press.

Horn, J. L., & Hofer, S. M. (1992). Major abilities and development in the adult period. In R. J. Sternberg & C. A. Berg (Eds.), *Intellectual development*. New York: Cambridge University Press.

Hossain, Z., & Roopnarine, J. L. (1994). African-American fathers' involvement with infants: Relationship to their functioning style, support, education, and income. *Infant Behavior and Development, 17*, 175–184.

Houts, A. C. (1991). Nocturnal enuresis as a biobehavioral problem. *Behavior Therapy, 22*, 133–151.

Hovland, C. I. (1937). The generalization of conditioned responses: 4. The effects of varying amounts of reinforcement upon the degree of generalization of conditioned responses. *Journal of Experimental Psychology, 21*, 261–276.

Hovland, C. I., Harvey, O. H., & Sherif, M. (1957). Assimilation and contrast effects in reactions to communication and attitude change. *Journal of Abnormal and Social Psychology, 55*, 244–252.

Hovland, C. I., Janis, I. K., & Kelley, H. H. (1953). *Communication and persuasion*. New Haven, CT: Yale University Press.

Hovland, C. I., & Weiss, W. (1951). The influence of source credibility on communication effectiveness. *Public Opinion Quarterly, 15*, 635–650.

Howard, A., Pion, G. M., Gottfredson, G. D., Flattau, P. E., Oskamp, S., Pfafflin, S. M., Bray, D. W., & Burstein, A. G. (1986). The changing face of American psychology: A report from the committee on employment and human resources. *American Psychologist, 41*, 1311–1327.

Howard, K. I., Kopta, S. M., Krause, M. S., & Orlinsky, D. E. (1986). The dose-effect relationship in psychotherapy. *American Psychologist, 41*, 159–164.

Howard, M., & McCabe, J. B. (1990). Helping teenagers postpone sexual involvement. *Family Planning Perspectives, 22*, 21–26.

Hoyenga, K. B., & Hoyenga, K. T. (1984) *Motivational explanations of behavior*. Belmont, CA: Brooks/Cole.

Hoyer, W. J., & Rybash, J M. (1994). Characterizing adult cognitive development. *Journal of Adult Development, 1*, 7–12.

Hsu, L. K. G. (1989). The gender gap in eating disorders: Why are the eating disorders more common among women? *Clinical Psychology Review, 9*, 393–407.

Hsu, L. K. G. (1990). *Eating disorders*. New York: Guilford.

Hubel, D. H., & Wiesel, T. N. (1979). Brain mechanisms in vision. *Scientific American, 241*, 150–162.

Huffman, T., Chang, K., Rausch, P., & Schaffer, N. (1994). Gender differences and factors related to the disposition toward cohabitation. *Family Therapy, 21*, 171–184.

Huesmann, L. R., & Eron, L. D. (Eds.)(1986). *Television and the aggressive child: A cross-national comparison*. Hillsdale, NJ: Erlbaum.

Hughes, F. P., & Noppe, L. D. (1991). *Human development across the life span*. New York: Macmillan.

Hughes, H. C., Nozawa, G., & Kitterle, F. (1996). Global precedence, spatial frequency channels, and the statistics of natural images. *Journal of Cognitive Neuroscience, 8*, 197–203.

Hughes, J., Smith, T. W., Kosterlitz, H. W., Fothergill, L. A., Morgan, B. A., & Morris, H. R. (1975). Identification of two related pentapeptides from the brain with the potent opiate agonist activity. *Nature, 258*, 577–579.

Hughes, J. R., Olivet, A. H., Helzer, T. E., Higgins, S. T., & Bickel, W. K. (1992). Should caffeine abuse, dependence, or withdrawal be added to DSM-IV and ICD-10? *American Journal of Psychiatry, 149*, 33–40.

Hull, C. L. (1943). *Principles of behavior*. New York: Appleton.

Hull, C. L. (1952.). *A behavior system*. New York: Appleton.

Humphreys, L. G. (1939). Acquisition and extinction of verbal expectancies in a situation analogous to conditioning. *Journal of Experimental Psychology, 25*, 294–301.

Hunt, E. (1995). The role of intelligence in modern society. *American Scientist, 83*, 356–368.

Hur, Y. M., Bouchard, T. J., Jr., & Lykken, D. T. (1998). Genetic and environmental influences on morningness-eveningness. *Personality and Individual Differences, 25*, 917–925.

Huston, A. C., Donnerstein, E., Fairchild, H., Feshbach, N. D., Katz, P. A., Murray, J. P., Rubenstein, E. A., Wilcox, B. L., & Zuckerman, D. (1992). *Big world, small screen: The role of television in American society*. Lincoln: University of Nebraska Press.

Hyde, J. S. (1984a). Children's understanding of sexist language. *Developmental Psychology, 20*, 697–706.

Hyde, J. S. (1984b). How large are gender differences in aggression? A developmental meta-analysis. *Developmental Psychology, 20*, 722–736.

Hyde, J. S. (1994). Can neta-analysis make feminist transformations in psychology? *Psychology of Women Quarterly, 18*, 451–462.

Hyde, J. S., Fennema, E., & Lamon, S. J. (1990). Gender differences in mathematics performance: A meta-analysis. *Psychological Bulletin, 107*, 139–155.

Hyde, J. S., & Linn, M. C. (Eds.). (1986). *The psychology of gender: Advances through meta-analysis*. Baltimore: Johns Hopkins University Press.

Hyde, J. S., & Linn, M. C. (1988). Gender differences in verbal ability: A meta-analysis. *Psychological Bulletin, 104*, 53–69.

Hyde, J. S., & Plant, E. A. (1995). Magnitude of psychological gender differences: Another side to the story. *American Psychologist, 50*, 159–161.

Hyde, T. S., & Jenkins, J. J. (1969). Differential effects of incidental tasks on the organization of recall of a list of highly associated words. *Journal of Experimental Psychology, 82*, 472–481.

Hyman, R. (1989). *The elusive quarry: A scientific appraisal of psychical research*. Buffalo, NY: Prometheus.

Hyman, R. (1994). Anomaly or artifact? Comments on Ben and Honorton. *Psychological Bulletin, 115*, 19–24.

I

Iacono, W. G., &Lykken, D. T. (1997). The validity of the lie detector: Two surveys of scientific opinion. *Journal of Applied Psychology, 82*. 426–433.

Iaffaldano, M. T., & Muchiosky, P M. (1985). Job satisfaction and job performance: A meta-analysis. *Psychological Bulletin, 97*, 251–273.

Iggo, A., & Andres, K. H. (1982). Morphology of cutaneous receptors. *Annual Review of Neuroscience, 5*, 1–31.

Ingham, A. G., Levinger, G., Graves, J., & Peckham, V. (1974). The Ringelmann effect: Studies of group size and group performance. *Journal of Experimental Social Psychology, 10*, 371–384.

Inhelder, B., & Piaget, J. (1958). *The growth of logical thinking from childhood to adolescence*. New York: Little, Brown.

Institute for Women's Policy Research (1997, January). *The wage gap: Women's and men's earnings* (briefing paper). Washington, DC: Institute for Women's Policy Research.

Intons-Peterson, M. J., & Reddel, M. (1984). What do people ask about a neonate? *Developmental Psychology, 20*, 358–359.

Isen, A. M., Daubman, K. A., & Nowicki, G. P. (1987). Positive affect facilitates creative problem solving. *Journal of Personality and Social Psychology, 52*, 1122–1131.

Ivancevich, J. M., & Matteson, M. T. (1980). *Stress and work: A managerial perspective*. Glenview, IL: Scott, Foresman.

Izard, C. E. (1990). Facial expression and the regulation of emotion. *Journal of Personality and Social Psychology, 58*, 487–498.

Izard, C. E. (1994). Innate and universal facial expressions: Evidence from developmental and cross-cultural research. *Psychological Bulletin, 115*, 288–299.

Izard, C. E., Libero, D. Z., Putnam, P., & Haynes, O. M. (1993). Stability of emotion experiences and their relations to traits of personality. *Journal of Personality and Social Psychology, 64*, 847–860.

J

Jacklin, C. N. (1989). Female or male: Issues of gender. *American Psychologist, 44*, 127–133.

Jacobs, M. K., & Goodman, G. (1989). Psychology and self-help groups. *American Psychologist, 44*, 536–545.

James, S. P. (1993). Neglected images of policing: Looking beyond the rhetoric of performance assessment. *Policing and Society, 3*, 73–89.

James, D., & Drakich, J. (1993). Understanding gender differences in amount of talk: A critical review of research. In D. Tannen (Ed.), *Gender and conversational interaction* (pp. 281–312). New York: Oxford University Press.

Jamieson, K. M., & Flanagan, T. J. (1988). *Sourcebook of criminal justice statistics, 1988.* Washington, DC: U.S. Department of Justice, Bureau of Justice Statistics.

Jang, K. L., McCrae, R. R., Angleitner, A., Riemann, R., Livesley, W. J. (1998). Heritability of facet-level traits in a cross-cultural twin sample: Support for a hierarchical model of personality. *Journal of Personality and Social Psychology, 74,* 1556–1565.

Janis, I. L. (1972). *Victims of groupthink.* Boston: Houghton Mifflin.

Jaroff, L. (1993, November 29). Lies of the mind. *Time,* pp. 52–59.

Jaskiw, G. E., & Weinberger, D. R. (1992). Dopamine and schizophrenia: A cortically corrective perspective. *Seminars in the Neurosciences, 4,* 179–188.

Jendreck, M. P. (1989). Faculty reactions to academic dishonesty. *Journal of College Student Development, 30,* 401–406.

Jenkins, J. G., & Dallenbach, K. M. (1924). Oblivicence during sleeping and waking. *American Journal of Psychology, 35,* 605–612.

Jensen, A. R. (1969). How much can we boost IQ and scholastic achievement? *Harvard Educational Review, 39,* 1–123.

Jewell, L. N. (1998). *Contemporary industrial/organizational psychology* (3rd ed.). Pacific Grove, CA: Brooks/Cole.

John, O. P. (1990). The search for basic dimensions of personality. In P. McReynolds, J. C. Rosen, & G. J. Chelune (Eds.), *Advances in psychological assessment* (Vol. 7, pp. 1–37). New York: Plenum.

Johnson, S. L., & Roberts, J. E. (1995). Life events and bipolar disorder: Implications from biological theories. *Psychological Bulletin, 117,* 434–449.

Johnston, J. C., & McClelland, J. L. (1973). Visual factors in word perception. *Perception and Psychophysics, 14,* 365–370.

Johnston, J. C., & McClelland, J. L. (1974). Perception of letters in words: Seek not and ye shall find. *Science, 184,* 1192–1194.

Johnston, L. D., O'Malley, P. M., Bachman, J. G. (1996). *Natinal survey results on drug use from the monitoring the future study, 1975–1995* (NIH Publication No. 96–4139). Rockville, MD: National Institute of Health and Human Services.

Jones, E. E. (1986). Interpreting interpersonal behavior: The effects of expectancies. *Science, 234,* 41–46.

Jones, J. C., & Barlow, D. H. (1990). Self-reported frequency of sexual urges, fantasies, and masturbatory fantasies in heterosexual males and females. *Archives of Sexual Behavior, 19,* 269–279.

Jones, J. M. (1994). The African American: A duality dilemma? In W. J. Lonner & R. Malpass (Eds.), *Psychology and culture* (pp. 17–21). Boston: Allyn & Bacon.

Jones, K. L., & Smith, D. W. (1973). Recognition of the fetal alcohol syndrome in early infancy. *Lancet, 2,* 999–1001.

Jones, M. C. (1924). A laboratory study of fear: The case of Peter. *Journal of Genetic Psychology, 31,* 308–315.

Jourard, S. M., & Friedman, R. (1970). Experimenter-subject "distance" and self-disclosure. *Journal of Personality and Social Psychology, 25,* 278–282.

Joyner, A. L., & Guillemot, F. (1994). Gene targeting and development of the nervous system. *Current Opinion in Neurobiology, 4,* 37–42.

Judd, L. L. (1997). The clinical course of unipolar major depressive disorders. *Archives of General Psychiatry, 54,* 989–991.

Julien, R. M. (1998). *A primer of drug action* (8th Ed.). New York: Freeman.

Julien, R. M. (1995). *A primer of drug action* (7th ed.). New York: Freeman.

Julien, R. M. (1998). *A primer of drug action* (8th Ed.). New York: Freeman.

K

Kafka, M. P. (1997). How are drugs used in the treatment of paraphilic disorders? *The Harvard Mental Health Letter,14(3),* 8.

Kagan, J., Kearsley, R. B., & Zelazo, P. R. (1978). *Infancy: Its place in human development.* Cambridge, MA: Harvard University Press.

Kagan, J., Reznick, J. S., & Snidman, N. (1987). The physiology and psychology of behavioral inhibition in children. *Child Development, 58,* 1459–1473.

Kahill, S. (1986). Relationship of burnout among professional psychologists to professional expectations and social support. *Psychological Reports, 59,* 1043–1051.

Kahneman, D. (1973). *Attention and effort.* Upper Saddle River, NJ: Prentice Hall.

Kahneman, D., & Tversky, A. (1973). On the psychology of prediction. *Psychological Review, 80,* 237–251.

Kalat, J. W. (1995). *Biological psychology* (5th ed.). Pacific Grove, CA: Brooks/Cole.

Kalat, J. W. (1998). *Biological psychology* (6th ed.). Pacific Grove, CA: Brooks/Cole.

Kalish, R. A. (1985). The social context of death and dying. In R. H. Binstock & E. Shanas (Eds.), *Handbook of aging in the social sciences.* New York: Van Nostrand Reinhold.

Kamin, L. J. (1969). Predictability, surprise, attention, and conditioning. In B. Campbill & R. Church (Eds.), *Punishment and aversive behavior.* New York: Appleton-Century-Crofts.

Kamin, L. J. (1994). Behind the curve (Book review of *The Bell Curve*). *Scientific American, 241,* 67–76.

Kane, J. M. (1996). Drug therapy: Schizophrenia. *New England Journal of Medicine, 334,* 34–41.

Kaplan, M. F., Wanshula, L. T., & Zanna, M. P. (1992). Time pressure and information integration in social judgment: The effect of the need for structure. In O. Svenson & J. Maule (Eds.), *Time pressure and stress in human judgment and decision making.* Cambridge: Cambridge University Press.

Kaplan-Estrin, M., Jacobson, S. W., & Jacobson, J. L. (1994). Alternative approaches to clustering and scoring the Bayley Infant Behavior Record. *Infant Behavior and Development, 17,* 149–157.

Kaprio, J., Koskenvuo, M., & Rita, H. (1987). Mortality after bereavement: A prospective study of 95,647 widowed persons. *American Journal of Public Health, 77,* 283–287.

Karch, S. B. (1998). *A brief history of cocaine.* Boca Raton, FL: CRC Press.

Kardes, F. R. (1988). Spontaneous inference processes in advertising: The effects of conclusion omission and involvement on persuasion. *Journal of Consumer Research, 15,* 225–233.

Karno, M., & Golding, J. M. (1991). Obsessive-compulsive disorder. In L. N. Robins & D. A. Regier (Eds.), *Psychiatric disorders in America: The Epidemiologic Catchment Area Study* (pp. 204–219). New York: Free Press.

Kastenbaum, R. J. (1986). *Death, society, and the human experience.* Columbus, OH: Merrill.

Kastenbaum, R. J. (1995). *Death, society, and human experience* (5th ed.). Boston: Allyn & Bacon.

Katchadourian, H. A. (1977). *The biology of adolescence.* New York: Freeman.

Katz, D. (1960). The functional approach to the study of attitudes. *Public Opinion Quarterly, 24,* 163–204.

Kazdin, A. E. (1989). *Behavior modification in applied settings* (4th ed.). Pacific Grove, CA: Brooks/Cole.

Kazdin, A. E. (1978). *History of behavior modification: Experimental foundations of contemporary research.* Baltimore: University Park Press.

Keefauver, S. P., & Guilleminault, C. (1994). Sleep terrors and sleepwalking. In M. Kryger, T. Roth, &

W. C. Dement (Eds.), *Principles and practices of sleep medicine* (2nd ed., pp. 567–573). Philadelphia: Saunders.

Keeling, R. P. (1987). Effects of AIDS on young Americans. *Medical Aspects of Human Sexuality, 21,* 22–33.

Keith-Lucas, T., & Guttman, N. (1975). Robust single-trial delayed backward conditioning. *Journal of Comparative and Physiological Psychology, 88,* 468–476.

Keller, M. B., Hirschfeld, R. M., & Hanks, D. (1997). Double depression: A distinctive subtype of unipolar depression. *Journal of Affective Disorders, 43,* 63–73.

Kelley, H. H. (1950). The warm-cold variable in first impressions of persons. *Journal of Personality, 18,* 431–439.

Kelley, H. H. (1967). Attribution theory in social psychology. In D. Levine (Ed.), *Nebraska symposium on motivation* (Vol. 15). Lincoln: University of Nebraska Press.

Kelley, H. H. (1971). *Attribution in social interaction.* Morristown, NJ: General Learning Press.

Kellner, C. H., Pritchett, J. T., Beale, M. D., & Coffey, C. E. (1997). *Handbook of ECT.* Washington, DC: American Psychiatric Association.

Kelvin, P., & Jarrett, J. A. (1985). *Unemployment: Its social and psychological effects.* Cambridge: Cambridge University Press.

Kendall, P. C., Haaga, D. A. F., Ellis, A., Bernard, M., DiGiuseppe, R., & Kassinove, H. (1995). Rational-emotive therapy in the 1990s and beyond: Current status, recent revisions, and research questions. *Clinical Psychology Review, 15,* 169–185.

Kenrick, D. T., & Funder, D. C. (1990). Profiting from controversy: Lessons from the person-situation debate. *American Psychologist, 43,* 23–34.

Kenrick, D. T., & Funder, D. C. (1991). The person-situation debate: Do personality traits really exist? In V. J. Derlega, B. A. Winstead, & W. H. Jones (Eds.), *Personality: Contemporary theory and research* (pp. 149–174). Chicago: Nelson-Hall.

Kessler, R. C., McGonagle, K. A., Zhao, S., Nelson, C. B., Hughes, M., Eshleman, S., Wittchen, H.-U., & Kenderl, K. S. (1994). Lifetime and 12-month prevalence of *DSM-III-R* psychiatric disorders in the United States. *Archives of General Psychiatry, 51,* 8–19.

Kiecolt-Glaser, J. K., Dura, J. R., Speicher, C. E., Trask, O. J., & Glaser, R. (1991). Spousal caregivers of dementia victims: Longitudinal changes in immunity and health. *Psychosomatic Medicine, 53,* 345–362.

Kiecolt-Glaser, J. K., & Glaser, R. (1992). Psychoneuroimmunology: Can psychological interventions modulate immunity? *Journal of Consulting and Clinical Psychology, 60,* 569–575.

Kihlstrom, J. F. (1985). Hypnosis. *Annual Review of Psychology, 36,* 385–418.

Kim, U., & Choi, S. H. (1994). Individualism, collectivism, and child development: A Korean perspective. In P. M. Greenfield & R. R. Cocking (Eds.), *Cross-cultural roots of minority child development* (pp. 227–257). Hillsdale, NJ: Erlbaum.

Kim, U., & Chun, M. B. J. (1994). Educational "success" of Asian Americans: An indigenous perspective. *Journal of Applied Developmental Psychology, 15,* 329–339.

Kimball, M. M. (1989). A new perspective on women's math achievement. *Psychological Bulletin, 105,* 198–214.

Kime, R. E. (1992). *Pregnancy, childbirth, and parenting.* Guilford, CT: Dushkin.

Kimmel, D. C. (1980). *Adulthood and aging* (2nd ed.). New York: Wiley.

Kimura, D. (1992). Sex differences in the brain. *Scientific American, Vol. 267,* 118–125.

King, C. A., Raskin, A., Gdowski, C. L., Butku, M., & Opipari, L. (1990). Psychosocial factors associated with urban adolescent female suicide attempts.

Journal of the American Academy of Child and Adolescent Psychiatry, 29, 289–294.

King, C., III, Siegel, M., Celebucki, C., & Connolly, G. N. (1998). Adolescent exposure to cigarette advertising in magazines. *Journal of the American Medical Association, 279,* 516–520.

King, D. B., & Viney, W. (1992). Modern history of pragmatic and sentimental attitudes toward animals and the selling of comparative psychology. *Journal of Comparative Psychology, 106,* 190–195.

King, D. B., Wertheimer, M., Keller, H., & Crochetiere, K. (1994). The legacy of Max Wertheimer and gestalt psychology. *Social Research, 61,* 907–935.

Kinney, H. C., Filiano, J. J., Sleeper, L. A., Mandell, F., Valdes-Dapena, M., & White, W. F. (1995). Decreased muscarinic receptor binding in the arcuate nucleus in sudden infant death syndrome. *Science, 269,* 1446–1450.

Kinsey, A. C. Pomeroy, W. B., & Martin, C. E. (1948). *Sexual behavior in the human male.* Philadelphia: W. B. Saunders.

Kinsey, A. C. Pomeroy, W. B., & Martin, C. E. (1953). *Sexual behavior in the human female.* Phildelphia: W. B. Saunders.

Kirby, D., Short, L., Collins, J., Rugg, D., Kolbe, L., Howard, M., Miller, B., Sonenstein, F., & Zabin, L. S. (1994). School-based programs to reduce sexual behaviors: A review of effectiveness. *Public Health Reports, 109,* 339–360.

Kirkpatrick, O. L. (1976). Evaluation of training. In B. L. Craig (Ed.), *Training and development handbook* (2nd ed.) (pp. 301–319). New York: McGraw-Hill.

Kirkpatrick-Steger, K., & Wasserman, E. A. (1996). Effects of spatial rearrangement of object components on picture recognition in pigeons. *Journal of the Experimental Analysis of Behavior, 65,* 60–67.

Kirkpatrick-Steger, K., Wasserman, E. A., & Biederman, I. (1998). Effects of geon detection, scrambling, and movement on picture recognition in pigeons. *Journal of Experimental Psychology: Animal Behavior Processes, 24,* 34–46.

Kixmiller, J. S., Wann, S. F., Weaver, K. A., Grover, C. A., & Davis, S. F. (1987). Effect of elaboration levels on content comprehension. *Bulletin of the Psychonomic Society, 26,* 32–33.

Klag, M. J., Ford, D. E., Mead, L. A., He, J., Whelton, P. K., Liang, K.-Y., & Levine, D. M. (1993). Serum cholesterol in young men and subsequent cardiovascular disease. *New England Journal of Medicine, 328,* 313–318.

Klare, R. (1990). Ghosts make news: How four newspapers report psychic phenomena. *Skeptical Inquirer, 14,* 363–370.

Klein, A. (1989). *The healing power of humor.* Los Angeles: Tarcher.

Klein, D. F. (1993). False suffocation alarms, spontaneous panics, and related conditions: An integrative hypothesis. *Archives of General Psychiatry, 50,* 306–317.

Klein, S. B., McGee-Davis, J., Cohen, L., & Weston, D. (1984). Relative influence of cue predictiveness and salience on flavor-aversion learning. *Learning and Motivation, 15,* 188–202.

Kleinke, C. L. (1986). *Meeting and understanding people.* New York: Freeman.

Kleinke, C. L. (1991). *Coping with life challenges.* Pacific Grove, CA: Brooks/Cole.

Kleinke, C. L., & Dean, G. D. (1990). Evaluation of men and women receiving positive and negative responses with various acquaintance strategies. *Journal of Social Behavior and Personality, 5,* 369–377.

Kleinke, C. L., Meeker, F. B., & Staneski, R. A. (1986). Preference for opening lines: Comparing ratings by men and women. *Sex Roles, 15,* 585–600.

Kleiknecht, R. A., Dinnel, D. L., Kleinknecht, E. A., Hiruma, N., Harada, N. (1997). Cultural factors in social anxiety: A comparison of social phobia symptoms and taijin kyofusho. *Journal of Anxiety Disorders, 11,* 157–177.

Kleinman, J. C., Pierre, M. B., Jr., Madans, J. H., Land, G. H., & Schramm, W. F. (1988). The effects of maternal smoking on fetal and infant mortality. *American Journal of Epidemiology, 127,* 274–282.

Kleinmuntz, B., & Szucko, J. J. (1984). Lie detection in ancient and modern times: A call for contemporary scientific study. *American Psychologist, 39,* 766–776.

Klerman, G. L., Weissman, M. M., Markowitz, J., Glick, I., Wilner, P. J., Mason, B., & Shear, M. K. (1994). Medication and psychotherapy. In A. E. Bergin & S. L. Garfield (Eds.), *Handbook of psychotherapy and behavior change* (4th ed., pp. 734–782). New York: Wiley.

Kliegl, R., & Lindenberger, U. (1993). Modeling intrusions and correct recall in episodic memory: Adult age differences in encoding of list context. *Journal of Experimental Psychology: Learning, Memory, and Cognition, 19,* 617–637.

Klinger, E. (1990). *Daydreaming: Using waking fantasy and imagery for self-knowledge and creativity.* Los Angeles: Tarcher.

Kluft, R. P. (1987). An update on multiple personality disorder. *Hospital and Community Psychiatry, 38,* 363–373.

Knierim, J. J., & Van Essen, D. C. (1992). Visual cortex: Cartography, connectivity, and concurrent processing. *Current Opinion in Neurobiology, 2,* 150–155.

Knobloch, H., & Pasamanick, B. (Eds.), (1974). *Gesell and Amatruda's developmental diagnosis.* Hagerstown, MD: Harper & Row.

Knowles, J. A., & Weissman, M. M. (1995). Panic disorder and agoraphobia. In J. M. Oldham and M. B. Riba (Eds.), *Review of psychiatry* (Vol. 14, pp. 383–404). Washington, DC: American Psychiatric Association.

Kobasa, S. C. (1982). Commitment and coping in stress resistance among lawyers. *Journal of Personality and Social Psychology, 42,* 707–717.

Kochanek, K. D., & Hudson, B. L. (1995). *Advance report of final mortality statistics, 1992* (Monthly Vital Statistics Report, 43, No. 6, Suppl.). Hyattsville, MD: National Center for Health Statistics.

Kohlberg, L. (1966). A cognitive-developmental analysis of children's sex role concepts and attitudes. In E. E. Maccoby (Ed.), *The development of sex differences* (pp. 82–173). Stanford, CA: Stanford University Press.

Kohlberg, L. (1973). Continuities in childhood and adult moral development revisited. In P. Baltes & K. W. Schaie (Eds.), *Life-span development psychology: Personality and socialization.* San Diego, CA: Academic Press.

Köhler, W. (1927). *The mentality of apes.* San Diego, CA: Harcourt Brace.

Kolb, B., & Whishaw, J. Q. (1990). *Fundamentals of human neuropsychology* (3rd ed). New York: Freeman.

Kontos, S., Hsu, H., & Dunn, L. (1994). Children's cognitive and social competence in child-care centers and family day-care homes. *Journal of Applied Developmental Psychology, 15,* 387–411.

Kopp, C. B. (1982). Antecedents of self-regulation. *Developmental Psychology, 18,* 199–214.

Kopta, S. M., Howard, K. I., Lowry, J. L., & Beutler, L. E. (1994). Patterns of symptomatic recovery in psychotherapy. *Journal of Consulting and Clinical Psychology, 62,* 1009–1016.

Korner, A., Zeanah, C., Lindin, J., Berkowitz, R., Krapmen, H., & Agras, W. (1985). The relation between neonatal and later activity and temperament. *Child Development, 56,* 38–42.

Koss, M. P. (1992). The underdetection of rape: Methodological choices influence incidence estimates. *Journal of Social Issues, 48,* 61–75.

Koss, M. P., Goodman, L. A., Browne, A., Fitzgerald, L. F., Keita, G. P., & Russo, N. F. (1994). *No safe haven: Male violence against women at home, at work, and in the community.* Washington, DC: American Psychological Association.

Kosslyn, S. M., & Koenig, O. (1992). *Wet mind: The new cognitive neuroscience.* New York: Free Press.

Kowalski, R. M. (1993). Inferring sexual interest from behavioral cues: Effects of gender and sexually relevant attitudes. *Sex Roles, 29,* 13–36.

Kracke, W. H . (1993). Cultural aspects of dreaming. In M. A. Carsakadon (Ed.), *Encyclopedia of sleep and dreaming* (pp. 151–155). New York: Macmillan.

Krebs, D. L., & Miller, D. T. (1985). Altruism and aggression. In G. Lindzey & E. Aronson (Eds.), *Handbook of social psychology* (3rd ed, Vol. 2). New York: Random House.

Kribbs, N. B. (1993). Siesta. In M. A. Carsakadon (Ed.), *Encyclopedia of sleep and dreaming* (pp. 544–545). New York: Macmillan.

Kring, A. M., & Gordon, A. H. (1998). Sex differences in emotion: Expression, experience, and physiology. *Journal of Personality and Social Psychology, 74,* 686–703.

Krug, E. G., Kresinow, M. J., Peddicord, J. P., Dahlberg, L. L., Powell, K. E., Crosby, A. E., & Annest, J. L. (1998). Suicide after natural disasters. *New England Journal of Medicine, 338,* 373–378.

Krupka, L., & Vener, A. M. (1979). Hazards of drug use among the elderly. *Gerontologist, 19,* 90–95.

Kübler-Ross, E. (1969). *On death and dying.* New York: Macmillan.

Kübler-Ross, E. (1975). *Death: The final stage of growth.* Upper Saddle River, NJ: Prentice Hall.

Kuhl, P. K., Williams, K. A., Lacerda, F., Stevens, K. N. & Lindblom, B. (1992). Linguistic experiences alter phonetic perception in infants by 6 months of age. *Science, 255,* 606–608.

Kulik, J. A., & Mahler, H. I. M. (1987). Effects of preoperative roommate assignment on preoperative anxiety and recovery from coronary-prone surgery. *Health Psychology, 6,* 525–543.

Kupfer, D. J., & Reynolds, C. F., III. (1992). Sleep and affective disorders. In E. S. Paykel (Ed.), *Handbook of affective disorders* (2nd ed., pp. 311–323). New York: Guilford Press.

L

Lacayo, R. (1993, May 3). In the grip of a psychopath. *Time,* pp. 34–35.

Lackritz, E. M., Satten, G. A., Aberle-Grasse, J., Dodd, R. Y., Raimondi, V. P., Janssen, R. S., Lewis, W. F., Notari, E. P., & Petersen, L. R. (1995). Estimated risk of transmission of the human immunodeficiency virus by screened blood in the United States. *New England Journal of Medicine, 333,* 1721–1725.

Ladouceur, R., Talbot, F., & Dugas, M. J. (1997). Behavioral expressions of intolerance of uncertainty in worry. *Behavior Modification, 21,* 355–371.

La Follette, M. C. (1988). Eye on the stars: Images of women scientists in popular magazines. *Science, Technology, and Human Values, 13,* 262–275.

Lagercrantz, H., & Slotkin, T. A. (1986). The "stress" of being born. *Scientific American, 254,* 100–107.

Lajunen, T., Hakkarainen, P., & Summala, H. (1996). The ergonomics of road signs: Explicit and embedded speed limits. *Ergonomics, 39,* 1069–1083.

Lamaze, F. (1958). *Painless childbirth.* London: Burke.

Lamb, M. E., Frodi, A. M., Frodi, A., & Hwang, C. P. (1982). Characteristics of maternal and paternal behavior in traditional and nontraditional Swedish families. *International Journal of Behavioral Development, 5,* 131–141.

Lamb, M. E., Pleck, J. H., Charnov, E. L., & Levine, J. A. (1987). A biosocial perspective on paternal behavior and involvement. In J. B. Lancaster, A. Rossi, J. Altmann, & L. R. Sherrod (Eds.), *Parenting across the lifespan: Biosocial perspectives.* Hawthorne, NY: Aldine de Gruyter.

Lamb, T. D., & Pugh, E. N., Jr. (1990). Physiology of transduction and adaptation in rod and cone photoreceptors. *Seminars in the Neurosciences, 2,* 3–13.

Lamberg, L. (1984). *The American Medical Association guide to better sleep.* New York: Random House.

Lambert, M. J. (1989). The individual therapist's contribution to psychotherapy process and outcome. *Clinical Psychology Review, 9,* 469–485.

Lambert, M. J., & Bergin, A. E. (1992). Achievements and limitations of psychotherapy research. In D. K. Freedheim (Ed.). *History of psychotherapy: A century of change* (pp. 360–390). Washington, DC: American Psychological Association.

Lambert, M. J., & Bergin, A. E. (1994). The effectiveness of psychotherapy. In A. E. Bergin & S. L. Garfield (Ed.), *Handbook of psychotherapy and behavior change* (4th ed., pp. 142–189). New York: Wiley.

Lambert, M. J., Shapiro, D. A., & Bergin, A. E. (1986). The effectiveness of psychotherapy. In S. L. Garfield & A. E. Bergin (Eds.), *Handbook of psychotherapy and behavior change* (3rd ed., pp. 157–211). New York: Wiley.

Laming, D. (1992). Analysis of short-term retention: Models for Brown-Peterson experiments. *Journal of Experimental Psychology: Learning, Memory, and Cognition, 18,* 1342–1365.

Landoldt, H. P., Werth, E., Borbely, A. A., & Dijk, D. J. (1995). Caffeine intake (200 mg) in the morning affects human sleep and EEG power spectra at night. *Brain Research, 675,* 67–74.

Landrum, R. E. (1992). College students' use of caffeine and its relationship to personality. *College Student Journal, 26,* 151–155.

Langer, E. J. (1977). The psychology of chance. *Journal of the Theory of Social Behavior, 7,* 346–357.

Langlois, J. H., Ritter, J. M., Roggman, L. A., & Vaughn, L. S. (1991). Facial diversity and infant preferences for attractive faces. *Developmental Psychology, 27,* 79–84.

Langton, P. A. (1991). *Drugs and the alcohol dilemma.* Boston: Allyn & Bacon.

Lapointe, A. E., Askew, J. M., & Meade, N. A. (1992). *Learning mathematics.* Princeton, NJ: Educational Testing Service.

Lashley, K. (1938). The thalamus and emotion. *Psychological Review, 45,* 42–61.

Latané, B., Bidwell, L. D. (1977). Sex and affiliation in college cafeterias. *Personality and Social Psychology Bulletin, 3,* 571–574.

Lauber, J. K., & Kayten, P. J. (1988). Sleepiness, circadian dysrhythmia, and fatigue in transportation system accidents. *Sleep, 11,* 503–512.

Laumann, E. O., Gagnon, J. H., Michael, R. T., & Michaels, S. (1994). *The social organization of sexuality.* Chicago: University of Chicago Press.

LaVelle, M. (1998). The new rules of sexual harassment. *US News & World Reports, 125(1),* 30–31.

Lazarus, R. S. (1994). Universal antecedents of the emotions. In P. Ekman & R. J. Davidson (Eds.), *The nature of emotion: Fundamental questions* (pp. 163–171). New York: Oxford University Press.

Lazarus, R. S., & Folkman, S. (1984). *Stress, appraisal and coping.* New York: Springer.

Leary, M. R., Britt, T. W., Cutlip, W. D., II, & Templeton, J. L. (1992). Social blushing. *Psychological Bulletin, 112,* 446–460.

Leary, M. R., & Meadows, S. (1991). Predictors, elicitors, and concomitants of social blushing. *Journal of Personality and Social Psychology, 60,* 254–262.

Leavitt, F. (1995). *Drugs and behavior* (3rd ed.). Newbury Park, CA: Sage.

Lebow, J. L., & Gurman, A. S. (1995). Research assessing couple and family therapy. In J. T. Spence, J. M. Darley, & Foss, D. J. (Eds.), *Annual Review of Psychology, Vol. 46* (pp. 27–57). Palo Alto, CA: Annual Reviews.

Lederer, R. (1991). *The miracle of language.* New York: Pocket Books.

Le Doux, J. E. (1994). Emotion, memory and the brain. *Scientific American, 270,* 50–57.

LeDoux, J. (1996). *The emotional brain.* New York: Simon & Schuster.

Lee, D. J., & Hall, C. C. I. (1994). Being Asian in North American. In W. J. Lonner & R. Malpass (Eds.), *Psychology and culture* (pp. 23–27). Boston: Allyn & Bacon.

Lee, V. E., Brooks-Gunn, J., Schnur, E., & Liaw, F. (1990). Are Head Start effects sustained? A longitudinal follow-up comparison of disadvantaged children attending Head Start, no preschool, and other preschool programs. *Child Development, 61,* 495–507.

Lefcourt, H. M., & Davidson-Katz, K. (1991). Locus of control and health. In C. R. Snyder & D. R. Forsyth (Eds.), *Handbook of social and clinical psychology* (pp. 246–266). New York: Pergamon.

Legerstee, M. (1994). The role of familiarity and sound in the development of person and object permanence. *British Journal of Developmental Psychology, 12,* 455–468.

Lehtonen, K., Korhonen, T., & Korvenranta, H. (1994). Temperament and sleeping patterns in colicky infants during the first year of life. *Journal of Developmental and Behavioral Pediatrics, 15,* 416–420.

Leibel, R. L., Rosenbaum, M., & Hirsch, J. (1995). Changes in energy expenditure resulting from altered body weight. *New England Journal of Medicine, 332,* 621–628.

Leitenberg, H., & Henning, K. (1995). Sexual fantasy. *Psychological Bulletin, 117,* 469–496.

Lemme, B. H. (1995). *Development in adulthood.* Needham Heights, MA: Allyn & Bacon.

Lenihan, G. O., Rawlins, M. E., & Eberly, C. G. (1992). Gender differences in rape supportive attitudes before and after a date rape education intervention. *Journal of College Student Development, 33,* 331–338.

Lenneberg, E. H. (1973). *Biological foundations of language.* New York: Wiley.

Lennings, C. J. (1994). A cognitive understanding of adolescent suicide. *Genetic, Social, and General Psychology Monographs, 120,* 287–307.

Lenski, G., Nolan, P., & Lenski, J. (1995). *Human societies: An introduction to macrosociology* (7th ed.). New York: McGraw Hill.

Leon, A. C., Klerman, G. L., & Wickramaratne, P. (1993). Continuing female predominance in depressive illness. *American Journal of Public Health, 83,* 754–757.

Lesch, M. F., & Pollatsek, A. (1993). Automatic access of semantic information by phonological codes in visual word recognition. *Journal of Experimental Psychology: Learning, Memory, and Cognition, 19,* 285–294.

Lester, D. (1989). *Questions and answers about suicide.* Philadelphia: Charles Press.

Lester, D. (1992). *Why people kill themselves: A 1990s summary of research findings on suicidal behavior* (3rd ed.). Springfield: IL: Thomas.

Le Vay, S., & Hamer, D. H. (1994). Evidence for a biological influence in male homosexuality. *Scientific American, 272,* 44–49.

Levenson, R. W. (1992). Autonomic nervous system differences among emotions. *Psychological Science, 3,* 23–27.

Levenson, R. W. (1994). The search for autonomic specificity. In P. Ekman & R. J. Davidson (Eds.), *The nature of emotion: Fundamental questions* (pp. 252–257). New York: Oxford University Press.

Levenson, R. W., Ekman, P., & Friesen, W. V. (1990). Voluntary facial action generates emotion-specific autonomic nervous system activity. *Psychophysiology, 27,* 363–384.

Levenson, R. W., Ekman, P. Heider, K., & Friesen, W. V. (1992). Emotion and autonomic nervous system activity in the Minangkabau of West Sumatra. *Journal of Personality and Social Psychology, 62,* 972–988.

Leventhal, H., Glynn, K., & Fleming, R. (1987). Is the smoking decision an "informed choice"? *Journal of the American Medical Association, 257,* 3373–3376.

Levine, J. D., Fields, H. L., & Basbaum, A. I. (1993). Peptides and the primary afferent nociceptor. *Journal of Neuroscience, 13,* 2273–2286.

Levine, M. (1996). *Viewing violence: How media violence affects your child's and adolescent's development.* New York: Doubleday.

Levinson, D. J. (1986). A conception of adult development. *American Psychologist, 41,* 3–13.

Levinson, D. J. (1996). *The seasons of a woman's life.* New York: Knopf.

Levitt, E. E., Baker, E. L., Jr., & Fish, R. C. (1990). Some conditions of compliance and resistance among hypnotic subjects. *American Journal of Clinical Hypnosis, 32,* 225–236.

Levy, A., & Paludi, M. (1997). *Workplace sexual harassment.* Upper Saddle River, NJ: Prentice Hall.

Levy, B. A., Campsall, J., Browne, J., Cooper, D., Waterhouse, C., & Wilson, C. (1995). Reading fluency: Episodic integration across texts. *Journal of Experimental Psychology: Learning, Memory, and Cognition, 21,* 1169–1185.

Levy, J. (1983). Language, cognition, and the right hemisphere: A response to Gazzaniga. *American Psychologist, 38,* 538–541.

Lewin, K. *The conceptual representation and the measurement of psychological forces.* Durham, NC: Duke University Press.

Lewis, M. (1992). *Shame: The exposed self.* New York: Free Press.

Lewis, M. (1993a). The emergence of human emotions. In M. Lewis & J. M. Haviland (Eds.), *Handbook of emotions* (pp. 223–235). New York: Guilford Press.

Lewis, M. (1993b). Self-conscious emotions: Embarrassment, pride, shame, and guilt. In M. Lewis & J. M. Haviland (Eds.), *Handbook of emotions* (pp. 563–573). New York: Guilford Press.

Lewis, M. (1995). Self-conscious emotions. *American Scientist, 83,* 68–78.

Lewis, R. (1990). Death and dying among the American Indians. In J. K. Parry (Ed.), *Social work practice with the terminally ill: A transcultural perspective* (pp. 23–32). Springfield, IL: Charles C. Thomas.

Lewontin, R. C. (1976). Race and intelligence. In N. J. Block & G. Dworkin (Eds.), *The IQ controversy* (pp. 78–92). New York: Pantheon.

Lezak, M. D. (1995). *Neuropsychological assessment* (3rd ed.). New York: Oxford University Press.

Liberman, R. P., Teigen, J., Patterson, R., & Baker, V. (1973). Reducing delusional speech in chronic, paranoid schizophrenics. *Journal of Applied Behavior Analysis, 6,* 57–64.

Lickey, M. E., & Gordon, B. (1991). *Medicine and mental illness: The use of drugs in psychiatry.* New York: Freeman.

Liebman, D. A. (1979). Behaviorism and the mind: A (limited) call for a return to introspection. *American Psychologist, 34,* 319–333.

Lin, K.-M., Poland, R. E., Lau, J. K., & Rubin, R. T. (1988). Haloperidol and prolactin concentrations in Asians and Caucasians. *Journal of Clinical Psychopharmacology, 8,* 195–201.

Lin, K.-M., Poland, R. E., Nuccio, I., Matsuda, K., Hathuc, N., Su, T.-P., & Fu, P. (1989). A longitudinal assessment of haloperidol doses and serum concentrations in Asian and Caucasian schizophrenic patients. *American Journal of Psychiatry, 146,* 1307–1311.

Lindberg, N. O., Coburn, C., & Stricker, E. M. (1984). Increased feeding by rats after subdiabetogenic streptozotocin treatment: A role for insulin in satiety. *Behavioral Neuroscience, 98,* 138–145.

Linden, W., Wen, F., & Paulhus, D. L. (1995). Measuring alexithymia: Reliability, validity, and prevalence. In J. N. Butcher & C. D. Spielberger (Eds.), *Advances in personality assessment* (Vol. 10, pp. 51–95). Hillsdale, NJ: Lawrence Erlbaum.

Linder, D. E., & Worchel, S. (1970). Opinion change as a result of effortfully drawing a counterattitudinal conclusion. *Journal of Experimental Social Psychology, 6,* 432–448.

Lindsay, D. S., & Read, J. D. (1993). Psychotherapy and memories of childhood sexual abuse: A cognitive perspective. *Applied Cognitive Psychology, 8,* 281–338.

Lindsay, P. H., & Norman, D. A. (1977). *Human information processing.* San Diego, CA: Academic Press.

Linn, M. C., & Petersen, A. C. (1985). Emergence and characterization of sex differences in spatial ability: A meta-analysis. *Child Development, 56,* 1479–1498.

Lippa, R. (1998). The nonverbal display and judgment of extraversion, masculinity, femininity, and gender diagnosticity: A lens model analysis. *Journal of Research in Personality, 32,* 80–107.

Lipsitt, L. (1986). Learning in infancy: Cognitive development in babies. *Journal of Pediatrics, 109,* 172–182.

Liu, Y. (1996). Interactions between memory scanning and visual scanning in display monitoring. *Ergonomics, 39,* 1038–1053.

Locke, E. A., & Latham, C. P. (1990). *A theory of goal-setting and task performance.* Englewood Cliffs, NJ: Prentice Hall.

Loden, M., & Rosener, J. B. (1990). *Workforce America! Managing employee diversity as a vital resource.* Burr Ridge, IL: Irwin.

Loftus, E. F. (1975). Leading questions and the eyewitness report. *Cognitive Psychology, 7,* 560–572.

Loftus, E. F. (1979). *Eyewitness testimony.* Cambridge, MA: Harvard University Press.

Loftus, E. F. (1984, February). Eyewitness: Essential but unreliable. *Psychology Today,* pp. 22–27.

Loftus, E. F. (1991). *Witness for the defense.* New York: St. Martin's Press.

Loftus, E. F. (1993). The reality of repressed memories. *American Psychologist, 48,* 518–537.

Loftus, E. F. (1997). Memory for a past that never was. *Current Directions in Psychological Science, 6,* 60–65.

Loftus, E. F., & Ketcham, K. (1994). *The myth of repressed memory: False memories and allegation of sexual abuse.* New York: St. Martin's Press.

Loftus, E. F., Miller, D. G., & Burns, H. J. (1978). Semantic integration of verbal information into a visual memory. *Journal of Experimental Psychology: Human Learning and Memory, 4,* 19–31.

Long, H. B. (1980). Characteristics of senior citizens' educational tuition waiver in twenty-one states: A follow-up study. *Educational Gerontology, 5,* 139–149.

Long, J. W., & Rybacki, J. J. (1994). *The essential guide to prescription drugs, 1994 edition.* New York: HarperPerennial.

Longenecker, C. O., Sims, H. P., & Cinia, O. A. (1987). Behind the mask: The politics of employee appraisal. *Academy of Management Executive, 1,* 183–193.

Lopez, S. R., Grover, K. P., Holland, D., Johnson, M. J., Kain, C. D., Kanel, K., Mellins, C. A., & Rhyne, M. C. (1989). Development of culturally sensitive psychotherapists. *Professional Psychology: Research and Practice, 20,* 369–376.

Lorenz, K. (1966). *On aggression.* San Diego, CA: Harcourt Brace.

Lovdal, L. T. (1989). Sex role messages in television commercials: An update. *Sex Roles, 21,* 715–724.

Lowenstein, R. J. (1994). Diagnosis, epidemiology, clinical course, treatment, and cost effectiveness of treatment for dissociative disorders and MPD: Report submitted to the Clinton Administration Task Force on Health Care Financing Reform. *Dissociation, 7,* 3–11.

Lu, F. G., Lim, R. F., & Mezzich, J. E. (1995). Issues in the assessment and diagnosis of culturally diverse individuals. In J. M. Oldham & M. B. Riba (Eds.) *Review of psychiatry* (Vol. 14, pp. 477–510). Washington, DC: American Psychiatric Association.

Lubart, T. I. (1994). Creativity. In R. L. Sternberg (Ed.), *Thinking and problem solving* (pp. 289–332). San Diego, CA: Academic Press.

Luborsky, L., Chandler, M., Auerbach, A. H., Cohen, J., & Bachrach, H. M. (1971). Factors influencing the outcome of psychotherapy: A review of quantitative research. *Psychological Bulletin, 75,* 145–185.

Luborsky, L., Singer, B., & Luborsky, L. (1975). Comparative studies of psychotherapy. *Archives of General Psychiatry, 32,* 995–1008.

Lubow, R., & Kaplan, O. (1997). Visual search as a function of prior experience with target and distractor. *Journal of Experimental Psychology: Human Perception and Performance, 23,* 14–24.

Luchins, A. S. (1942). Mechanization in problem solving: The effect of Einstellung. *Psychological Monographs, 54* (Whole No. 248).

Lutz, W. (1990). *Doublespeak.* New York: HarperCollins.

Lykken, D. T. (1981). *A tremor in the blood.* New York: McGraw-Hill.

Lynam. D. R. (1998). Early identification of the fledgling psychopath: Locating the psychopathic child in the current nomenclature. *Journal of Abnormal Psychology, 107,* 566–575.

Lynn, D. B. (1974). *The father: His role in child development.* Pacific Grove, CA: Brooks/Cole.

Lynn, S. J., Lock, T. G., Myers, B., & Payne, D. G. (1997). Recalling the unrecallable: Should hypnosis be used to recover memories in psychotherapy? *Current Directions in Psychological Science, 6,* 79–83.

Lynn, S. J., Myers, B., & Malinoski, P. (In press). Hypnosis, pseudomemories, and clinical guidelines: A sociocognitive perspective. In J. D. Read & D. S. Lindsay (Eds.), *Recollections of trauma: Scientific studies and clinical practice.* New York: Plenum Press.

Lynn, S. J., & Payne, D. G. (1997). Memory as the theater of the past: The psychology of false memories. *Current Directions in Psychological Science, 6,* 55.

Lynn, S. J., Rhue, J. W., & Weekes, J. R. (1989). Hypnosis and experienced nonvolition: A social-cognitive integrative model. In N. P. Spanos & J. F. Chaves (Eds.), *Hypnosis: The cognitive-behavioral perspective* (pp. 78–109). Buffalo, NY: Prometheus.

M

Maas, J. B. (1998). *Power sleep.* New York: Villard.

Maccoby, E. E., & Jacklin, C. N. (1974). *The psychology of sex differences.* Stanford, CA: Stanford University Press.

Macbeth, T. M. (Ed.) (1996). *Tuning in to young viewers: Social science perspectives on television.* Thousand Oaks, CA: Sage.

Maccoby, E. E., & Alexander, J. (1980). Use of media in lifestyle programs. In P. O. Davidson & S. M. Davidson (Eds.), *Behavioral medicine: Changing health lifestyles.* New York: Brunner/Mazel.

MacDonald, T. K., Zanna, M. P., & Fong, G. T. (1995). Decision making in altered states: Effects of alcohol on attitudes toward drinking and driving. *Journal of Personality and Social Psychology, 68,* 973–985.

MacKenzie, B. (1984). Explaining race differences in IQ: The logic, the methodology, and the evidence. *American Psychologist, 39,* 1214–1233.

MacKinnon, D. W. (1978). *In search of human effectiveness: Identifying and developing creativity.* Buffalo, NY: Creative Education Foundation.

Macuda, T., & Roberts, W. A. (1995). Further evidence for hierarchical chunking in rat spatial memory. *Journal of Experimental Psychology: Animal Behavior Processes, 21,* 20–32.

Maddi, S. R., & Kobasa, S. C. (1984). *The hardy executive: Health under stress.* Belmont, CA: Dorsey/Wadsworth.

Maddux, J. E. (1991). Self-efficacy. In C. R. Snyder & D. R. Forsyth (Eds.), *Handbook of social and clinical psychology* (pp. 57–78). New York: Pergamon.

Madigan, S., & O'Hara, R. (1992). Short-term memory at the turn of the century: Mary Whiton Calkins's memory research. *American Psychologist, 47,* 170–174.

Madsen, D. B., & Finger, J. R., Jr. (1978). Comparison of a written feedback procedure, group brainstorming, and individual brainstorming. *Journal of Applied Psychology, 63,* 120–123.

Magid, K., & McKelvey, C. A. (1987). *High risk: Children without a conscience.* New York: Bantam Books.

Maher, B. A., & Spitzer, M. (1993). Delusions. In C. G. Costello (Ed.), *Symptoms of schizophrenia* (pp. 92–120). New York: Wiley.

Maier, N. R. F. (1931). Reasoning in humans II: The solution of a problem and its appearance in consciousness. *Journal of Comparative Psychology, 12,* 181–194.

Maier, S. F., Watkins, L. R., & Fleshner, M. (1994). Psychoneuroimmunology: The interface between behavior, brain, and immunity. *American Psychologist, 49,* 1004–1017.

Maki, W. S. (1986). Distinction between new and used traces: Different effects of electroconvulsive shock on memories for places present and places past. *Quarterly Journal of Experimental Psychology: Comparative and Physiological Psychology, 38,* 397–423.

Mann, C. C. (1994). Behavioral genetics in transition. *Science, 264,* 1686–1689.

Mann, J. M., & Tarantola, D. J. M. (1998). HIV 1998: The global picture. *Scientific American, 279,* 82–83.

Mansfield, P. K., Koch, P. B., Henderson, J., & Vicary, J. R. (1991). The job climate for women in traditionally male blue-collar occupations. *Sex Roles, 25,* 63–79.

Marcia, J. E. (1980). Identity in adolescents. In J. Adelson (Ed.), *Handbook of adolescent psychology* (pp. 159–187). New York: Wiley.

Marin, G. (1994). The experience of being a Hispanic in the United States. In W. J. Lonner & R. Malpass (Eds.), *Psychology and culture* (pp. 29–33). Boston: Allyn & Bacon.

Mark, V. H., & Ervin, F. R. (1970). *Violence and the brain.* New York: HarperCollins.

Marks, D., & Kammann, R. (1980). *The psychology of the psychic.* Buffalo, NY: Prometheus.

Markus, H. R., & Kitayama, S. (1991). Culture and the self: Implications for cognition, emotion, and motivation. *Psychological Review, 98,* 224–253.

Markus, H. R., & Kitayama, S. (1998). The cultural psychology of personality. *Journal of Cross-Cultural Psychology, 29,* 63–87.

Marsella, A. J., Sartorius, N., Jablensky, A., & Fenton, F. R. (1985). Cross-cultural studies of depressive disorders: An overview. In A. Kleinman & B. Good (Eds.), *Culture and depression* (pp. 299–324). Berkeley, CA: University of California Press.

Marshall, W. L. (1989). Pornography and sex offenders. In D. Zillmann & J. Bryant (Eds.), *Pornography: Research advances and policy considerations.* Hillsdale, NJ: Erlbaum.

Martin, C. L., Wood, C. H., & Little, J. K. (1990). The development of gender stereotype components. *Child Development, 61,* 1891–1904.

Martin, G., & Pear, J. (1996). *Behavior modification: What it is and how to do it* (5th ed.). Upper Saddle River, NJ: Prentice Hall.

Martin, L. L., Harlow, T. F., & Strack, F. (1992). The role of bodily sensations in the evaluation of social events. *Personality and Social Psychology Bulletin, 18,* 412–419.

Martini, F.H. (1992) *Fundamentals of Anatomy and Physiology, 2/E* Upper Saddle River, NJ: Prentice Hall.

Marx, J. (1995). Snaring the genes that divide the sexes for mammals. *Science, 269,* 1824–1825.

Maslach, C. (1978). The client role in staff burnout. *Journal of Social Issues, 34,* 111–124.

Maslach, C. (1982). *Burnout: The cost of caring.* Upper Saddle River, NJ: Prentice Hall.

Maslow, A. H. (1970). *Motivation and personality* (2nd ed.). New York: HarperCollins.

Masson, J. M. (1985). *The assault on truth.* New York: Viking Penguin.

Masters, J. C., Burrish, T. G., Hollon, S. D., & Rimm, D. C. (1987). *Behavior therapy: Techniques and empirical findings* (3rd ed.). San Diego, CA: Harcourt Brace.

Masters, W. H., & Johnson, V. E. (1966). *Human sexual response*. Boston: Little, Brown.

Masters, W. J., et al. (1994). *Heterosexuality*. New York: HarperCollins.

Matarazzo, J. D. (1984). Behavioral immunogens. In B. L. Hammonds & C. J. Scheirer (Eds.), *Psychology and health* (pp. 9–43). Washington, DC: American Psychological Association.

Mather, M., Henkel, L. A., & Johnson, M. K. (In press). Evaluating characteristics of false memories: Remember/know judgements and memory characteristics questionnaire compared. *Memory & Cognition*.

Matthews, K. A. (1989). Interactive effects of behavior and reproductive hormones on sex differences in risk for coronary heart disease. *Health Psychology, 8*, 373–387.

Matthews, K. A., & Haynes, S. G. (1986). Type A behavior pattern and coronary disease risk: Update and critical evaluation. *American Journal of Epidemiology, 123*, 923–960.

Matsuda, L. A., Lolait, S. J., Brownstein, M. J., Young, A. C., & Bonner, T. I. (1990). Structure of cannabinoid receptor and functional expression of the cloned cDNA. *Nature, 346*, 561–564.

Matsuda, N. (1985). Strong, quasi-, and weak conformity among Japanese in the modified Asch procedure. *Journal of Cross-Cultural Psychology, 16*, 83–97.

Matsumoto, D. (1992). More evidence for the universality of a contempt expression. *Motivation and Emotion, 16*, 363–368.

Matsumoto, D. (1994). *People: Psychology from a cultural perspective*. Pacific Grove, CA: Brooks/Cole.

Matsumoto, D. (1996). Culture and psychology. Pacific Grove, CA: Brooks/Cole.

Matsumoto, D. (1997). *Culture and modern life*. Pacific Grove, CA: Brooks/Cole Publishers.

Matsumoto, D. (1998, March). *Culture, emotion, and the teaching of psychology*. Paper presented at the annual Great Plains Students' Psychology Convention, Lincoln, NE.

Matthews, G., & Deary, I. J. (1998). *Personality traits*. Cambridge: Cambridge University Press.

Maurer, D., & Maurer, C. (1988). *The world of the newborn*. New York: Basic Books.

Maxmen, J. S. (1991). *Psychotropic drugs: Fast facts*. New York: Norton.

Mayer, J. (1953). Glucostatic mechanism of regulation of food intake. *New England Journal of Medicine, 249*, 13–16.

Mayer, R. E. (1990). *The promise of cognitive psychology*. Lanham, MD: University Press of America.

Mays, V. M., & Albee, G. W. (1992). Psychotherapy and ethnic minorities. In D. K. Freedheim (Ed.), *History of psychotherapy: A century of change* (pp. 552–570). Washington, DC: American Psychological Association.

McBurney, D. H. (1986). Taste, smell, and flavor terminology: Taking the confusion out of fusion. In H. Meiselman & R. S. Rivlin (Eds.), *Clinical measurements of taste and smell* (pp. 117–125). New York: Macmillan.

McCarroll, J. E., Ursano, R. J., & Fullerton, C. S. (1997). Exposure to traumatic death in disaster and war. In C. S. Fullerton & R. J. Ursano (Eds.), *Posttraumatic stress disorder: Acute and long-term responses to trauma and disaster* (pp. 37–58). Washington, DC: American

McCartney, K. (1984). Effect of quality of day care environment on children's language development. *Developmental Psychology, 20*, 244–260.

McCartney, K., & Phillips, D. (1988). Motherhood and child care. In B. Birns & D. Hay (Eds.), *The different faces of motherhood*. New York: Plenum.

McClearn, G. E., Johansson, B., Berg, S., Pedersen, N. L., Ahern, F., Petrill, S. A., & Plomin, R. (1997). Substantial genetic influence on cognitive abilities in twins 80 or more years old. *Science, 276*, 1560–1563.

McClelland, D. C. (1958). Some social consequences of achievement motivation. In M. R.

Jones (Ed.). *Nebraska symposium on motivation*. Lincoln: University of Nebraska Press.

McClelland, D. C. (1985). *Human motivation*. Glenview, IL: Scott, Foresman.

McClelland, D. C., Koestner, R., & Weinberger, J. (1989). How do self-attributed and implicit motives differ? *Psychological Review, 67*, 690–702.

McClelland, J. L., Rumelhart, D. E., & Hinton, G. E. (1986). The appeal of parallel distributed processing. In D. E. Rumelhart, J. L. McClelland, & the PDP Research Group (Eds.), *Parallel distributed processing*: Explorations in the microstructure of cognition (Vol. 1). Cambridge, MA: Bradford.

McClelland, J. L., Rumelhart, D. E., & the PDP Research Group (Eds.). (1986). *Parallel distributed processing: Explorations in the microstructure of cognition* (Vol. 2). Cambridge, MA: Bradford.

McClintock, M. (1971). Menstrual synchrony and suppression. *Nature, 229*, 244–245.

McConnell, A. R., & Gavanski, I. (1994). *Women as "men" and "people": Occupation title suffixes as primes*. Paper presented at the annual meeting of the Midwestern Psychological Association, Chicago.

McConnell, J. B., Cutler, R. L., & McNeil, E. B. (1958). Subliminal stimulation: An overview. *American Psychologist, 13*, 229–239.

McCrae, R. R., & Costa, P. T., Jr. (1987). Validation of the five-factor model of personality across instruments and observers. *Journal of Personality and Social Psychology, 52*, 81–90.

McCrae, R. R., & Costa, P. T., Jr. (1990). *Personality in adulthood*. New York: Guilford Press.

McCrae, R. R., & John, O. P. (1992). An introduction to the five-factor model and its applications. *Journal of Personality, 60*, 175–215.

McDaniel, M. A., Whetzel, D. L., Schmidt, P. L., & Maurer, S. D. (1994). The validity of employment interviews: A comprehensive review and meta-analysis. *Journal of Applied Psychology 79*, 599–616.

McDonald, P. W., & Prkachin, K. M. (1990). The expression and perception of facial emotion in alexithymia: A pilot study. *Psychosomatic Medicine, 52*, 199–210.

McFarland, D. (Ed.). (1991). *The Guinness book of world records, 1991*. New York: Bantam Books.

McFarlane, A. H., Bellissimo, A., Norman, G. R., & Lange, P. (1994). Adolescent depression in a school-based community sample: Preliminary findings on contributing social factors. *Journal of Youth and Adolescence, 23*, 601–620.

McGilley, B. M., & Holmes, D. S. (1988). Aerobic fitness response to psychological stress. *Journal of Research in Personality, 22*, 129–139.

McGillicuddy–De Lisi, A. V., & Subramanian, S. (1994). Tanzanian and United States mothers' beliefs about parents' and teachers' roles in children's knowledge acquisition. *International Journal of Behavioral Development, 17*, 209–237.

McGinnis, J. M., & Foege, W. H. (1993). Actual causes of death in the United States. *Journal of the American Medical Association, 270*, 2207–2212.

McGlashan, T. H., & Fenton, W. S. (1992). The positive-negative distinction in schizophrenia: Review of natural history validators. *Archives of General Psychiatry, 49*, 63–72.

McGrath, E., Puryear-Keita, G., Strickland, B. R., & Russo, N. F. (Eds.). (1990). *Women and depression: Risk factors and treatment issues*. Washington, DC: American Psychological Association.

McGregor, L., Miller, H. R., Mayleben, M. A., Buzzanga, V. L., Davis, S. F., & Becker, A. H. (1991). Similarities and differences between "traditional" and "nontraditional" college students in selected personality characteristics. *Bulletin of the Psychonomic Society, 29*, 128–130.

McGubbin, M. (1994). Deinstitutionalization: The illusion of disillusion. *Journal of Mind and Behavior, 15*, 35–54.

McGue, M., Bacon, S., & Lykken, D. T. (1992). Personality stability and change in early adulthood:

A behavioral genetic analysis. *Developmental Psychology, 29*, 96–109.

McGuire, W. K. (1985). Attitudes and attitude change. In G. Lindzey & E. Aronson (Eds.), *The handbook of social psychology* (3rd ed., Vol. 2). New York: Random House.

McKelvie, S. J. (1990). Student acceptance of a generalized personality description: Forer's graphologist revisited. *Journal of Social Behavior and Personality, 5*, 91–95.

McKinney, K. (1994). Sexual harassment and college faculty members. *Deviant Behavior, 15*, 171–191.

McKim, W. A. (1997). *Drugs and behavior: An introduction to behavioral pharmacology* (3rd ed.). Upper Saddle River, NJ: Prentice Hall.

McKusick, V. A. (1986). *Mendelian inheritance in man* (7th ed.). Baltimore: Johns Hopkins University Press.

McKusick, V. A. (1995). *Mendelian inheritance in man: Catalogs of autosomal dominant, autosomal recessive, and X-linked phenotypes* (10th ed.). Baltimore: Johns Hopkins University Press.

McLaughlin, S., & Margolskee, R. F. (1994). The sense of taste. *American Scientist, 82*, 538–545.

McNally, R. J., Hornig, C. D., & Donnell, C. D. (1995). Clinical versus nonclinical panic: A test of suffocation false alarm theory. *Behaviour Research and Therapy, 33*, 127–131.

McNeil, D. (1970). Language development in children. In P. Mussen (Ed.), *Handbook of child psychology* (3rd ed.). New York: Wiley.

Mead, M. (1963). *Sex and temperament in three primitive societies*. New York: Morrow. (Original work published 1935).

Mednick, A. (1993, May). World's women familiar with a day's double shift. *APA Monitor*, pp. 32–33.

Mednick, S. A. (1962). The associative basis of the creative process. *Psychological Review, 69*, Boston; Houghton Mifflin, 220–232.

Mednick, M. T. S., & Mednick, S. A. (1967). *Examiner's manual for the Remote Associations Test*.

Meichenbaum, D. (1993). Stress inoculation training: A 20-year update. In P. M. Lehrer & R. L. Woolfolk (Eds.), *Principles and practice of stress management* (pp. 373–406). New York: Guilford Press.

Meier, R. P. (1991). Language acquisition by deaf children. *American Scientist, 79*, 60–70.

Meijer, J. H., & Rietveld, W. J. (1989). Neurophysiology of the suprachiasmatic circadian pacemaker in rodents. *Physiological Review, 69*, 671–707.

Mellinger, G. D., Balter, M. B., & Uhlenhuth, E. H. (1985). Insomnia and its treatment: Prevalence and its correlates. *Archives of General Psychiatry, 42*, 225–232.

Meltzer, H. Y. (1993). Clozapine: A major advance in the treatment of schizophrenia. *Harvard Mental Health Newsletter, 10* (2), 4–6.

Meltzoff, A. N., & Moore, M. K. (1992). Early imitation within a functional framework: The importance of person identity, movement, and development. *Infant Behavior and Development, 15*, 479–505.

Melzack, R., & Wall, P. D. (1965). Pain mechanisms: A new theory. *Science, 150*, 971–979.

Melzack, R., & Wall, P. D. (1982). *The challenge of pain*. Harmondsworth, England: Penguin.

Menco, B. (1992). Ultrastructural studies of membrane, cytoskeletal, mucous, and protective compartments in olfaction. *Microscopy Research and Technique, 22*, 215–224.

Mendelson, W. B. (1997). A critical evaluation of the hypnotic efficacy of melatonin. *Sleep, 20* (10), 916–919.

Merit Systems Protection Board. (1981). *Sexual harassment of federal workers: Is it a problem?* Washington, DC: U.S. Government Printing Office.

Merzenich, M., Jenkins, W., Johnston, P., Schreiner, C., Miller, S., & Tallal, P. (1996). Temporal processing deficits of language-learning children ameliorated by training. *Science, 271*, 77–81.

Merit Systems Protection Board. (1987). *Sexual harassment of federal workers: An update*. Washington, DC: U.S. Government Printing Office.

Mesquita, B., & Frijda, N. H. (1992). Cultural variations in emotions: A review. *Psychological Bulletin*, *112*, 179–204.

Messer, W. S., & Griggs, R. A. (1989). Student belief and involvement in the paranormal and performance in introductory psychology. *Teaching of Psychology*, *16*, 187–191.

Michaels, J. W., Blommel, J. M., Brocato, R. M., Linkous, R. A., & Rowe, J. S. (1982). Social facilitation and inhibition in a natural setting. *Replication in Social Psychology*, *2*, 21–24.

Michalko, M. (1991). *Thinkertoys*. Berkeley, CA: Ten Speed Press.

Milgram, S. (1974). *Obedience to authority*. New York: HarperCollins.

Miller, A., Springen, K., Gordon, J., Murr, A., Cohn, B., Drew, L., & Barrett, T. (1988, April 25). *Newsweek*, 40–45.

Miller, D. T., & Ross, M. (1975). Self-serving biases in attributions of causality: Fact or fiction? *Psychological Bulletin*, *82*, 213–225.

Miller, E., Cradock-Watson, J. E., & Pollock, T. M. (1982 October 9). Consequences of confirmed maternal rubella at successive stages of pregnancy. *The Lancet*, 781–784.

Miller, G. A. (1956). The magical number seven, plus or minus two: Some limits on our capacity for processing information. *Psychological Review*, *63*, 81–97.

Miller, J. G (1984). Culture and the development of everyday social explanation. *Journal of Persoanlity and Social Psychology*, *46*, 961–978.

Miller, J. G. (1997). A cultural-psychology perspective on intelligence. In R. J. Sternberg & E. L. Grigorenko (Eds.), *Intelligence, heredity, and environment* (pp. 269–302). New York: Cambridge University Press.

Miller, K. (1994, March 17). Safety quiz: Insurance claims data don't show advantage of some auto devices. *Wall Street Journal*, pp. Al, A7.

Miller, L. B., & Bizzell, R. P. (1983). Long-term effects of four preschool programs: Sixth, seventh, and eighth graders. *Child Development*, *54*, 727–741.

Miller, L. C. (1990). Intimacy and liking: Mutual influence and the role of unique relationships. *Journal of Personality and Social Psychology*, *59*, 50–60.

Miller, N. E. (1944). Experimental studies in conflict. In J. McV. Hund (Ed.), *Personality and the behavioral disorders* (Vol. 1, pp. 431–465). New York: Ronald Press.

Miller, N. E. (1985). The value of behavioral research on animals. *American Psychologist*, *40*, 423–440.

Miller, T. Q., Smith, T. W., Turner, C. W., Guijarro, M. L., & Hallet, A. J. (1996). A meta-analytic review of research on hostility and physical health. *Psychological Bulletin, 119*, 322–348.

Mirsky, A. F., & Quinn, O. W. (1988). The Genain quadruplets. *Schizophrenia Bulletin*, *14*, 595–612.

Mirsky, A. F., Quinn, O. W., De Lisi, L. E., Schwerdt, P., & Buchsbaum, M. S. (1987). The Genain quadruplets: A 25-year follow-up of four monozygous women discordant for the severity of schizophrenic illness. In N. E. Miller & G. D. Cohen, *Schizophrenia and aging* (pp. 83–94). New York: Guilford Press.

Mischel, W. (1966). A social-learning view of sex differences in behaving. In E. E. Maccoby (Ed.), *The development of sex differences* (pp. 56–81). Stanford, CA: Stanford University Press.

Mischel, W. (1968). *Personality and assessment*. New York: Wiley.

Mittendorf, R., Williams, M. A., Berkley, C. S., & Cotton, P. F. (1990). The length of uncomplicated human gestation. *Obstetrics and Gynecology*, *75*, 929–932.

Mlot, C. (1998). Probing the biology of emotion. *Science, 28*, 1005–1007.

Moffitt, T. E. (1993). Adolescence-limited and life-course-persistent antisocial behavior: A developmental taxonomy. *Psychological Review, 100*, 674–701.

Moghaddam, F. M. (1990). Modulative and generative orientations in psychology: Implications for psychology in the three worlds. *Journal of Social Issues*, *46*, 21–41.

Moghaddam, F. M. (1994). Ethnic segregation in a multicultural society: A review of recent trends in Montreal and Toronto and reconceptualization of "causal factors." In F. Frisken (Ed.), *The changing Canadian metropolis* (pp. 237–258). Berkeley, CA, and Toronto: University of California Press and Canadian Urban Studies Institute.

Moghaddam, F. M. (1998). *Social psychology: Exploring universals across cultures*. New York: W. H. Freeman.

Moldin, S. O., & Gottesman, I. I. (1997). At issue: Genes, experience, and chance in schizophrenia-Positioning for the 21st century. *Schizophrenia Bulletin*, *23*, 547–561.

Money, J. (1980). Endocrine influences and psychosexual status spanning the life cycle. In H. M. Van Praag, M. H. Lader, O. J. Rafaelsen, & E. H. Sachar (Eds.), *Handbook of biological psychiatry: Part 3. Brain mechanisms and abnormal behavior—genetics and neuroendocrinology*. New York: Dekker.

Money, J. (1984). Paraphilias: Phenomenology and classification. *American Journal of Psychotherapy*, *38*, 164–179.

Monk, T. M., & Folkard, S. (1992). *Making shift work tolerable*. London: Taylor & Francis.

Monti, P. M., & Smith, N. F. (1976). Residual fear of the conditioned stimulus as a function of response prevention after avoidance or classical defense conditioning in the rat. *Journal of Experimental Psychology: General*, *105*, 148–162.

Moorcraft, W. H. (1989) *Sleep, dreaming, and sleep disorders*. Lanham, MD: University Press of America.

Moore, C., & Corkum, V. (1994). Social understanding at the end of the first year of life. *Developmental Review*, *14*, 349–372.

Moore, B.N., Parker, R.(1995). *Critical thinking (4th ed)* Mountain View, Mayfield, CA:.

Moore, K. L. (1989). *Before we are born: Basic embryology and birth defects* (3rd ed.). Philadelphia: Saunders.

Moore, K. L., & Persaud, T. V. N. (1993). *Before we are born* (4th ed.). Philadelphia: Saunders.

Moore, T. E. (1982). Subliminal advertising: What you see is what you get. *Journal of Marketing*, *46*, 38–47.

Moore-Ede, M. C. (1993). *The twenty-four hour society*. Reading, MA: Addison-Wesley.

Moore-Ede, M. C., Sulzman, F. M., & Fuller, C. A. (1982). *The clocks that time us: Physiology of the circadian timing system*. Cambridge, MA: Harvard University Press.

Moravcsik, J. E., & Healey, A. F. (1995). Effect of meaning on letter detection. *Journal of Experimental Psychology: Learning, Memory, and Cognition*, *21*, 82–95.

Moreland, R. L., & Zajonc, R. B. (1982). Exposure effects in person perception: Familiarity, similarity, and attraction. *Journal of Experimental Social Psychology*, *18*, 395–415.

Morgan, C. A., III, Grillon, C., Southwick, S. M., Davis, M., Charney, D. S. (1996). Exaggerated acoustic startle reflex in Gulf War veterans with posttraumatic stress disorder. *American Journal of Psychiatry*, *153*, 64–68.

Morganstern, K. P. (1974). Cigarette smoke as a noxious stimulus in self-managed aversion therapy for compulsive eating: Technique and case illustration. *Behavior Therapy*, *5*, 255–260.

Morganthau, T. (1994, October 24). IQ: Is it destiny? *Newsweek*, pp. 53–55.

Mori, K., Mataga, N., & Imamura, K. (1992). Differential specificities of single mitral cells in rabbit olfactory bulb for a series of homologous series of fatty acid odor molecules. *Journal of Neurophysiology*, *67*, 786–789.

Morisse, D., Batra, L., Hess, L., Silverman, R., et al. (1996). A demonstration of a token economy for the real world. *Applied & Preventive Psychology*, *5*, 41–46.

Morris, D. (1994). *Bodytalk: The meaning of human gestures*. New York: Crown.

Morris, R. W. (1989). Chronobiology and health part I: Basic principles. *pharmindex* (January): 6–16. Copyright © 1989 by Skyline Publishers, Inc. Reprinted with the permission of Professor Ralph Morris, University of Illinois at Chicago.

Morrow, R. D. (1989). Southeast Asian child rearing practices: Implications for child and youth care workers. *Child and Youth Care Quarterly*, *18*, 273–287.

Mosbach, P., & Leventhal, H. (1988). Peer group identification and smoking: Implications for intervention. *Journal of Abnormal Psychology*, *97*, 238–245.

Moscovici, S., & Zavalloni, M. (1969). The group as a polarizer of attitudes. *Journal of Personality and Social Psychology*, *12*, 124–135.

Mott, F. L. (1991). Developmental effects of infant care: The mediating role of gender and health. *Journal of Social Issues*, *47*, 139–158.

Moulton, D. G. (1974). Dynamics of cell populations in the olfactory epithelium. *Annals of New York Academy of Sciences*, *237*, 52–61.

Mount, M. K., Barrick, M. R., & Strauss, J. P. (1994). Validity of observer ratings of the Big Five personality factors. *Journal of Applied Psychology*, *79*, 272–280.

Moyer, R. S., & Nath, A. (1998). Some effects of brief training interventions on perceptions of sexual harassment. *Journal of Applied Social Psychology*, *28*, 333–356.

Mozel, M. M., Smith, B., Smith, P., Sullivan, R., & Swender, P. (1969). Nasal chemoreception in flavor identification. *Archives of Otolaryngology*, *90*, 367–373.

Mucha, T. F., & Reinhardt, R. F. (1970). Conversion reactions in student aviators. *American Journal of Psychiatry*, *127*, 493–497.

Muehlenhard, C. L., & Hollabaugh, L. C. (1988). Do women sometimes say no when they mean yes? The prevalence and correlates of women's resistance to sex. *Journal of Personality and Social Psychology*, *54*, 872–879.

Mukerjee, M. (1997, February). Trends in animal research. *Scientific American*, 86–93.

Mullen, B. (1991). Group composition, salience, and cognitive representations: The phenomenology of being in a group. *Journal of Experimental Social Psychology*, *27*, 297–323.

Mullen, B., & Johnson, C. (1988). *The psychology of consumer behavior*. Hillsdale, NJ: Erlbaum.

Murphy, C., Cain, W. S., & Bartoshuk, L. M. (1977). Mutual action of taste and olfaction. *Sensory Processes*, *1*, 204–211.

Murphy, S. M. (1994). Imagery interventions in sport. *Medicine and Science in Sports and Exercise, 26*, 484–494.

Murray, M. J., & Meacham, R. B. (1993). The effect of age on male reproductive function. *World Journal of Urology*, *11*, 137–140.

Murray, V. M. (1992). Incident of first pregnancy among black adolescent females over three decades. *Youth & Society*, *23*, 478–506.

Murstein, B. I., & Fontaine, P. A. (1993). The public's knowledge about psychologists and other mental health professionals. *American Psychologist*, *48*, 839–845.

Murstein, B. L., Merighi, J. R., & Vyse, S. A. (1991). Love styles in the United States and France: A cross-cultural comparison. *Journal of Social and Clinical Psychology*, *10*, 37–46.

Murtagh, D. R. R., & Greenwood, K. M. (1995). Identifying effective psychological treatments for insomnia: A meta-analysis. *Journal of Consulting and Clinical Psychology*, *63*, 79–89.

Musen, G., & Squire, L. R. (1993). Implicit learning of color-word association using a Stroop paradigm. *Journal of Experimental Psychology: Learning, Memory, and Cognition*, *19*, 789–798.

Myers, D. J., & Dugan, K. B. (1996). Sexism in graduate school classrooms: Consequences for students and faculty. *Gender & Society, 19,* 330–350.

Myers, J. J., & Sperry, R. W. (1985). Interhemispheric communication after section of the forebrain commisures. *Cortex, 21,* 249–260.

N

Nadelson, C. C., Zimmerman , V. (1993) Culture and psychiatric care of women. In A. C. Gaw (Ed.), *Culture, ethnicity, and mental illness* (pp.501–515). Wahington, D.C: American Psychiatric Association.

Nagy, M. (1996, April). An integrated model of job satisfaction. Paper presented at the Annual Meeting of the Society for Industrial and Organizational Psychology, San Diego, CA.

Nahemow, L., & Lawton, M. P. (1975) Similarity and propinquity in friendship formation. *Journal of Personality and Social Psychology, 33,* 205– 213.

Nakajima, S. (1993). Asymmetrical effect of a temporal gap between feature and target stimuli on Pavlovian feature-positive and feature-negative discrimination. *Learning and Motivation, 24,* 255–265.

Nakane, Y., Ohta, Y., & Radford, M. H. B. (1992). Epidemiological studies of schizophrenia in Japan. *Schizophrenia Bulletin, 18,* 75–84.

Nakao, K. (1987). Analyzing sociometric preferences: An example of Japanese and U.S. business groups. *Journal of Social Behavior and Personality, 2,* 523–534.

National Center for Education Statistics. (1997). Digest of Education Statistics. Washington, DC: U.S. Department of Education.

National Commission on Acquired Immune Deficiency Syndrome. (1991). *America living with AIDS.* Washington, DC: U.S. Government Printing Office.

National Commission on Sleep Disorders Research. (1992). *Report of the National Commission on Sleep Disorders Research.* Washington, DC: U.S. Government Printing Office.

National Commission on Sleep Disorders Research (1993). *Report of the National Commission on Sleep Disorders Research.* Submitted to the secretary of the U.S. Department of Health and Human Services.

National Highway Traffic Safety Administration. (1997). *Traffic safety facts 1996: A compilation of motor vehicle crash data from the fatality analysis reporting system and the general estimates system.* Washington, DC: National Center for Statistics and Analysis, U.S. Department of Transportation.

National Hospice Organization (1992). Poll says hospice leads. *Hospice, 3(3),* 4.

National Institute on Alcohol Abuse and Alcoholism. (1991, October). Alcoholism and co-occurring disorders. *Alcohol Alert, 14* (PH302).

National Institute on Alcohol Abuse and Alcoholism. (1997, October). Alcohol, violence, and aggression. *Alcohol Alert,* No. 38.

National Institute on Drug Abuse (1997). Marijuana (Capsule 12). Rockville, MD: U.S. Department of Health and Human Services.

National Institutes of Health. (1995). Facts about sleep apnea (NIH Publication 95–3798). Bethesda, MD: U.S. Department of Health and Human Services.

National Sleep Foundation. (1998). *Women and sleep.* Washington, DC: National Sleep Foundation.

Needleman, H. L., & Gatsonis, C. A. (1990). Low-level lead exposure and the IQ of children. *Journal of the American Medical Association, 263,* 673–678.

Negus, B. (1956). The air-conditioning mechanism of the nose. *British Medical Journal, 1,* 367–371.

Neimark, E. D. (1982). Cognitive development in adulthood: Using what you've got. In T. M. Field, A. Huston, H. C. Quay, L. Troll, & G. E. Finley (Eds.), *Review of human development.* New York: Wiley.

Neimeyer, R. A., & Mitchell, K. A. (1988). Similarity and attraction: A longitudinal study. *Journal of Social and Personality Relationships, 5,* 131–148.

Neisser, U. (1967). *Cognitive psychology.* Upper Saddle River, NJ: Prentice Hall.

Neitz, M., Neitz, J., & Grishok, A. (1995). Polymorphism in the number of genes encoding long-wavelength sensitive cone pigments among males with normal color vision. *Vision Research, 35,* 2395–2407.

Neitz, J., Neitz, M., & Jacobs, G. (1993). More than three cone pigments among people with normal color vision. *Vision Research, 33,* 117–122.

Neitz, M., Neitz, J., & Jacobs, G. (1995). Genetic basis of photopigment variations in human dichromats. *Vision Research, 35,* 2095–2104.

Nelson, D. L., Bennett, D. J., Gee, N. R., Schreiber, T. A., & McKinney, V. M. (1993). Implicit memory: Effects of network size and interconnectivity on cued recall. *Journal of Experimental Psychology: Learning, Memory, and Cognition, 19,* 747–764.

Neugarten, B., Havighurst, R., & Tobin, S. (1968). Personality and patterns of aging. In B. Neugarten (Ed.), *Middle age and aging.* Chicago: University of Chicago Press.

Neugarten, B., & Neugarten, D. (1987, May). The changing meanings of age. *Psychology Today, 21(5),* 29–33.

Newcomb, T. M. (1961). *The acquaintance process.* Austin, TX: Holt, Rinehart & Winston.

Newman, D. L., Moffitt, T. E., Caspi, A., & Silva, P. A. (1998). Comorbid mental disorders: Implications for treatment and sample selection. *Journal of Abnormal Psychology, 107,* 305–311.

Newton, D. E. (1992). *AIDS issues: A handbook.* Hillsdale, NJ: Enslow.

Nezu, A. M., Nezu, C. M., & Blissett, S. E. (1988). Sense of humor as a moderator of the relation between stressful events and psychological distress: A prospective analysis. *Journal of Personality and Social Psychology, 54,* 520–525.

Nieburg, P., Marks, J. S., McLaren, N. M., & Remington, P. L. (1985). The fetal alcohol syndrome. *Journal of the American Medical Association, 253,* 2998–2999.

Nielsen Media Research. (1990). *Report on television.* Summarized in *American Enterprise,* July-August, 1990.

Nietzel, M. T., Bernstein, D. A., & Milich, R. (1994). *Clinical psychology* (4th ed.). Upper Saddle River, NJ: Prentice Hall.

Nisbett, R. E. (1972). Hunger, obesity, and the ventromedial hypothalamus. *Psychological Review, 79,* 433–453.

Nopoulos, P., Flaum, M., & Andreasen, N. C. (1997). Sex differences in brain morphology in schizophrenia. *American Journal of Psychiatry,154,* 1648–1654.

Norcross, J. C., Karg-Bray, R. S., & Prochaska, J. O. (1995). *Clinical psychologists in the 1990s.* Unpublished paper.

Norcross, J. C., & Newman, C. F. (1992). Psychotherapy integration: Setting the context. In J. C. Norcross & M. R. Goldfried (Eds.), *Handbook of psychotherapy integration* (pp. 3–45). New York: Basic Books.

Norman, D. A. (1988). *The psychology of everyday things.* New York: Basic Books.

Norman, D. A. (1995). Designing the future. *Scientific American, 273,* 194–198.

Norman, K. A., & Schachter, D. L. (In press). False recognition in younger and older adults: Exploring the characteristics of illusory memories. *Memory & Cognition.*

Normand, J., Salyards, S. D., & Mahoney, J. J. (1990). An evaluation of preemployment drug testing. *Journal of Applied Psychology, 75,* 629–639.

Norton, A. J., & Moorman, J. E. (1987). Current trends in marriage and divorce in American women. *Journal of Marriage and the Family, 49,* 3–14.

Nossiter, A. (1994, November 10). A daughter's death, a father's guilt. *New York Times,* p. A24.

Nothdurft, H. (1993). The role of features in preattentive vision: Comparison of orientation, motion, and color cues. *Vision Research, 33,* 1937–1958.

Nowak, M. A., & McMichael, A. J. (1995). How HIV defeats the immune system. *Scientific American, 273,* 58–65.

Nugent, J. K. (1991). Cultural and psychological influences on the father's role in infant development. *Journal of Marriage and the Family, 53,* 475–485.

Nymberg, J. H., & Van Noppen, B. (1994). Obsessive-compulsive disorder: A concealed diagnosis. *American Family Physician, 49,* 1129–1137.

O

Oats, S. B. (1977). *With malice toward none.* New York: NAL Penguin.

Obeso, J. A., Grandes, F., Vaamonde, J., Luquin, M. R., Artieda, J., Lera, G., Rodriguez, M. E., & Martinez-Lage, J. M. (1989). Motor complications associated with chronic levodopa therapy in Parkinson's disease. *Neurology, 39* (Suppl. 2), 11–19.

O'Connor, N. (1989). The performance of the "idiot savant": Implicit and explicit. *British Journal of Disorders of Communication, 24,* 1–20.

O'Conner, P. G., & Schottenfeld, R. S. (1998). Patients with alcohol problems. *New England Journal of Medicine, 1998, 338,* 592–602.

Offermano, L. B., & Cowing, M. K. (1990). Organizations of the future. *American Psychologist, 45,* 95–108.

Office of Technology Assessment. (1991). *Biological rhythms: Implications for the worker.* Washington, DC: U.S. Government Printing Office.

Ofshe & Watters, E. (1994). *Making monsters: False memories, psychotherapy, and sexual hysteria.* New York: Scribner.

Ohzawa, I., De Angelis, G. C., & Freeman, R. D. (1990). Stereoscopic depth discrimination in the visual cortex: Neurons ideally suited as disparity detectors. *Science, 249,* 1037–1041.

Okagaki, L., & Sternberg, R. J. (1993). Parental beliefs and children's school performance. *Child Development, 64,* 36–56.

Oldham, J. M. (1994). Personality disorders: Current perspectives. *Journal of the American Medical Association, 272,* 1770–1776.

Olian, J. D. (1984). Genetic screening for employment purposes. *Personnel Psychology, 37,* 423–438.

Olsho, L. W., Harkins, S. W., & Lenhardt, M. L. (1985). Aging and the auditory system. In J. E. Birren & K. W. Schaie (Eds.), *Handbook of the psychology of aging.* New York: Van Nostrand Reinhold.

O'Neill, W. M. (1995). American behaviorism: A historical and critical analysis. *Theory and Psychology, 5,* 285–305.

Oquendo, M. A. (1995). Differential diagnosis of ataque de nervios. *American Journal of Orthopsychiatry, 65,* 60–65.

Oquendo, M., Horwath, & Martinez, A. (1992). Ataques de nervios: Proposed diagnostic criteria for a cultur-specific syndrome. *Culture, Medicine & Psychiatry, 16,* 356–376.

Orleans, C. T., Schoenbach, V. J., Wagner, E. H., Quade, D., Salmon, M. A., Pearson, D. C., Fiedler, J., Porter, C. Q., & Kaplan, B. H. (1991). Self-help quit smoking interventions: Effects of self-help materials, social support instructions, and telephone counseling. *Journal of Consulting and Clinical Psychology, 59,* 439–448.

Ormel, J., Von Korff, M., Ustun, B., Pini, S., Korten, A., & Oldehinkel, T. (1994). Common mental disorders and disability across cultures: Results from the WHO Collaborative Study on Psychological Problems in General Health Care. *Journal of the American Medical Association, 272,* 1741–1748.

Ornstein, R., & Sobel, D. (1987). *The healing brain.* New York: Simon & Schuster.

Osborn, I. (1998). *Tormenting thoughts and secret rituals: The hidden epidemic of obsessive-compulsive disorder.* New York: Pantheon Books.

Oscar-Berman, M., Shagrin, B., Evert, D. L., & Epstein, C. (1997). Impairments of brain and behavior: The neurological effects of alcohol. *Alcohol Health & Research World, 21, (1),* 65–75.

Ost, L.-G. (1987). Age of onset in different phobias. *Journal of Abnormal Psychology, 96,* 223–239.

Ost, L.-G. (1992). Blood and injection phobia: Background and cognitive, physiological, and behavioral variables. *Journal of Abnormal Psychology, 101,* 68–74.

Othmer, E., & Othmer, S. C. (1989). *The clinical interview: Using DSM-III-R.* Washington, DC: American Psychiatric Association.

Overton, D. A. (1964). State-dependent or "dissociated" learning produced with pentobarbital. *Journal of Comparative and Physiological Psychology, 57,* 3–12.

Owens, J., Capaldi, E. D., & Sheffer, J. D. (1993). An exposure effect opposes flavor-nutrient learning. *Animal Learning and Behavior, 21,* 196–202.

P

Paffenbarger, R. S., Hyde, R. T., Wing, A. L., & Hsieh, C. (1986). Physical activity, all-cause mortality, and longevity of college alumni. *New England Journal of Medicine, 314,* 605–613.

Paffenbarger, R. S., Hyde, R. T., Wing, A. L., Lee, I.-M., Jung, D. L., & Kampert, J. B. (1993). The association of changes in physical-activity level and other lifestyle characteristics with mortality among men. *New England Journal of Medicine, 328,* 538–545.

Page, R. M., Scanlan, A., & Deringer, N. (1994). Childhood loneliness and isolation: Implications for childhood educators. *Child Study Journal, 24,* 107–118.

Pagel, J. F. (1994). Treatment of insomnia. *American Family Physician, 49,* 1417–1421.

Pagel, M. D., Erdly, W. W., & Becker, J. (1987). Social networks: We get by with (and in spite of) a little help from our friends. *Journal of Personality and Social Psychology, 53,* 793–804.

Paivio, A. (1971). *Imagery and verbal processes.* Austin, TX: Holt, Rinehart & Winston.

Paivio, A. (1986). *Mental representations: A dual coding approach.* New York: Oxford University Press.

Palella, F. J., Jr., Delaney, K. M., Moorman, A. C., Loveless, M. O., Fuhrer, J., Satten, G. A., Aschman, D. J., Holmberg, S. D., & HIV Outpatient study investigators. (1998). Declining morbidity and mortality among patients with advanced human immunodeficiency virus infections. *New England Journal of Medicine, 338,* 853–860.

Palladino, J. J., & Schell, K. A. (1980, March). *Student acceptance of personality descriptions based on the BRPI.* Paper presented at the meeting of the Southeastern Psychological Association, Washington, DC.

Paludi, M. A., & Brickman, R. B. (1991). *Academic and workplace sexual harassment: A resource manual.* Albany, NY: State University of New York Press.

Parachin, V. M. (1992, January). Seven ways to fire up your creativity. *Supervision,* pp. 3–4.

Parks, A. S., & Bruce, H. M. (1961). Olfactory stimuli in mammalian reproduction.

Pascarella, E. T., & Terenzini, P. T. (1991). *How college affects students: Findings and insights from twenty years of research.* San Francisco: Jossey-Bass.

Pascualy, R. A., & Soest, S. W. (1994). *Snoring and sleep apnea: Personal and family guide to diagnosis and treatment.* New York: Raven Press.

Pate, R. R., et al. (1995). Physical activity and public health: A recommendation from the Centers for Disease Control and Prevention and the American College of Sports Medicine. *Journal of the American Medical Association, 273,* 402–407.

Patterson, C. H. (1985). *The therapeutic relationship: Foundations for an eclectic psychotherapy.* Monterey, CA: Brooks/Cole.

Pattison, E. M. (1977). The experience of dying. In E. M. Pattison (Ed.), *The experience of dying.* Upper Saddle River, NJ: Prentice Hall.

Patzer, G. L. (1985). *The physical attractiveness phenomenon.* New York: Plenum.

Paulos, J. A. (1991). Coincidences. *Skeptical Inquirer, 15,* 382–385.

Pauly, I. B. (1990). Gender identity disorders: Evaluation and treatment. *Journal of Sex Education and Therapy, 16,* 2–24.

Paunonen, S. V., & Ashton, M. C. (1998). The structured assessment of personality across cultures. *Journal of Cross-Cultural Psychology, 29,* 150–170.

Paunonen, S. V., Jackson, D. N., Trzebinski, J., & Forsterling. F. (1992). Personality structure across cultures: A multimethod evaluation. *Journal of Personality and Social Psychology, 62,* 447–456.

Pavlov, I. (1928). *Lectures on conditioned reflexes: The higher nervous activity of animals* (Vol. 1), H. Gantt (Trans.). London: Lawrence and Wishart.

Pavlov, I. P. (1927). *Conditioned reflexes.* Oxford: Oxford University Press.

Payne, D. G., Elie, C. J., Blackwell, J. M., & Neuschatz, J. S. (1996). Memory illusions: Recalling, recognizing, and recollecting events that never occurred. *Journal of Memory and Language, 35,* 261–285.

Payne, D. G., Neuschatz, J. S., Lampinen, J. M., & Lynn, S. J. (1997). Compelling memory illusions: The qualitative characteristics of false memories. *Current Directions in Psychological Science, 6,* 56–60.

Pedersen, F. A., Rubenstein, J. L., & Yarrow, L. J. (1979). Infant development in father-absent families. *Journal of Genetic Psychology, 135,* 51–61.

Pedersen, W. (1994). Parental relations, mental health, and delinquency in adolescents. *Adolescence, 29,* 975–990.

Pepler, D. J., & Craig, W. M. (1995). A peek behind the fence: Naturalistic observatons of aggressive children with remote audiovisual recording. *Developmental Psychology, 31,* 548–553.

Perdue, C. W., & Gurtman, M. B. (1990). Evidence for the automaticy of ageism. *Journal of Experimental Social Psychology, 26,* 199–216.

Perkins, K. A. (1993). Weight gain following smoking cessation. *Journal of Consulting and Clinical Psychology, 61,* 768–777.

Perloff, R. M. (1993). *The dynamics of persuasion.* Hillsdale, NJ: Erlbaum.

Pert, C. B., & Snyder, S. H. (1973). The opiate receptor: Demonstration in nervous tissue. *Science, 179,* 1011–1014.

Peterson, C., Seligman, M. E. P., Yurko, K. H., Martin, L. R., & Friedman, H. S. (1998). Catastrophizing and untimely death. *Psychological Science, 9(2),* 127–130.

Pete, J. M., & De Santis, L. (1990). Sexual decision making in young black adolescent females. *Adolescence, 25,* 145–154.

Peterson, C., Seligman, M. E. P., & Vaillant, G. (1988). Pessimistic explanatory style is a risk factor for physical illness: A thirty-five-year longitudinal study. *Journal of Personality and Social Psychology, 55,* 23–27.

Peterson, L. R., & Peterson, M. J. (1959). Short-term retention of individual items. *Journal of Experimental Psychology, 58,* 193–198.

Petrill, S. A., Plomin, R., Berg, S., Johansson, B., Pedersen, N. L., Ahern, F., & McClearn, G. E. (1998). The genetic and environmental relationship between general and specific cognitive abilities in twins age 80 and older. *Psychological Science, 9,* 183–189.

Pettigrew, T. J. (1978). Three issues in ethnicity: Boundaries, deprivations, and perceptions. In J. M. Yinger & S. J. Cutler (Eds.), *Major social issues: A multidisciplinary view.* New York: Free Press.

Petty, R. E., & Cacioppo, J. T. (1986). The elaboration likelihood model of persuasion. In L. Berkowitz (Ed.), *Advances in experimental social psychology* (Vol. 19, pp. 123–205). San Diego, CA: Academic Press.

Petty, R. E., & Cacioppo, J. T. (1996). *Attitudes and persuasion: Classic and contemporary approaches.* Boulder, CO: Westview Press.

Petty, R. E., & Krosnick, J. A. (Eds.). (1995). *Attitude strength: Antecedents and consequences.* Hillsdale, NJ: Erlbaum.

Pfaffmann, C. (1955). Gustatory nerve impulses in rat, cat, and rabbit. *Neurophysiology, 18,* 429–440.

Phelps, M. E., & Mazziotta, J. C. (1985). Positron emission tomography: Human brain function and biochemistry. *Science, 228,* 799–809.

Piaget, J. (1972). Intellectual evolution from adolescence to adulthood. *Human Development, 15,* 1–12.

Piccione, C., Hilgard, E. R., & Zimbardo, P. G. (1989). On the degree of stability of measured hypnotizability over a 25-year period. *Journal of Personality and Social Psychology, 56,* 289–295.

Pick, D., & Reid, S. (1995, October). *The red in trichromatic theory.* Paper presented at the Mid-America Conference for Teachers of Psychology, Evansville, IN.

Pickar, D., & Hsiao, J. K. (1995). Clozapine treatment of schizophrenia. *Journal of the American Medical Association, 274,* 961–963.

Pierce, J. P., Choi, W. S., Gilpin, E. A., Farkas, A. J., & Berry, C. C. (1996). Tobacco industry promotion of cigarettes and adolescent smoking. *Journal of the American Medical Association, 279,* 511–515.

Piercey, M. F., Schroeder, L. A., Folkens, K., Xu, J. C., & Horig, J. (1981). Sensory and motor functions of spinal cord substance P. *Science, 187,* 1361–1363.

Pies, R. W. (1998). *Handbook of essential psychopharmacology.* Washington, DC: American Psychiatric Association.

Piliavin, I. M., Rodin, J., & Piliavin, J. A. (1969). Good Samaritanism: An underground phenomenon? *Journal of Personality and Social Psychology, 13,* 289–299.

Pillitteri, J. L., Kozlowski, L. T., Person, D. C., & Spear, M. E. (1994). Over-the-counter sleep aids: Widely used but rarely studied. *Journal of Substance Abuse, 6,* 315–323.

Pincus, H. A., Tanielian, T. L., Marcus, S. C., Olfson, M., Zarin, D. A., Thompson, J., & Zito, J. M. (1998). Prescribing trends in psychotropic medications: Primary care, psychiatry, and other medical specialties. *Journal of the American Medical Association, 279,* 526–531.

Pinker, S. (1994). *The language instinct: How the mind creates language.* New York: Morrow.

Pinner, R. W., Teutsch, S. M., Simonsen, L., Klug, L. A., Graber, J. M., Clarke, M. J., & Berkelman, R. L. (1996). Trends in infectious disease mortality in the United States. *Journal of the American Medical Association, 275,* 189–193.

Piper, B. (1996). *Diet and nutrition.* Chapman & Hall: London.

Pitcairn, T. K., & Wishart, J. G. (1994). Reactions of young children with Down's syndrome to an impossible task. *British Journal of Developmental Psychology, 12,* 485–489.

Pitskhelauri, R. Z. (1982). *The long-living of Soviet Georgia.* New York: Human Sciences Press.

Pittam, J., & Scherer, K. R. (1993). Vocal expression and communication of emotion. In M. Lewis & J. M. Haviland (Eds.), *Handbook of emotions* (pp. 185–197). New York: Guilford Press.

Plomin, R. (1989). Environment and genes. *American Psychologist, 44,* 105–111.

Plomin, R. (1990a). *Nature and nurture: An introduction to human behavioral genetics.* Pacific Grove, CA: Brooks/Cole.

Plomin, R. (1990b). The role of inheritance in behavior. *Science, 248,* 183–188.

Plomin, R., De Fries, J. C., & McClearn, G. E. (1990). *Behavioral genetics: A primer.* New York: Freeman.

Plomin, R., & DeFries, J. C. (1998). The genetics of cognitive abilities and disabilities. *Scientific American,* 62–69.

Plomin, R., DeFries, J. C., McClearn, G. E., & Rutter, M. (1997). *Behavioral genetics* (3rd ed.). New York: Freeman.

Plomin, R., Owen, M. J., & McGuffin, P. (1994). The genetic basis of complex human behaviors. *Science, 264,* 1733–1739.

Plomin, R., & Petrill, S. A. (1997). Genetics and intelligence: What's new. *Intelligence, 24,* 53–77.

Plomin, R., & Rende, R. (1991). Human behavioral genetics. In M. R. Rosenzweig & L. W. Porter (Eds.), *Annual review of psychology* (Vol. 42, pp. 161–190). Palo Alto, CA: Annual Reviews.

Plutchik, R. (1980). *Emotion: A psychoevolutionary synthesis.* New York: HarperCollins.

Plutchik, R. (1993). Emotions and their vicissitudes: Emotions and psychopathology. In M. Lewis & J. M. Haviland (Eds.), *Handbook of emotions* (pp. 53–66). New York: Guilford Press.

Poldrack, R. A., & Cohen, N. J. (1998). Priming of new associations in reading time: What is learned? *Psychonomic Bulletin & Review, 4,* 398–402.

Pomeroy, C. (1996). Anorexia nervosa, bulimia nervosa, and binge eating disorder. The assessment of physical status. In J. K. Thompson (Ed.), *Body image, eating disorders, and obesity* (pp. 177–204). Washington, DC: American Psychological Association.

Ponsonby, A., Dwyer, T., Gibbons, L. E., Cochrane, J. A., & Wang, Y. (1993). Factors potentiating the risk of sudden infant death syndrome associated with the prone position. *New England Journal of Medicine, 329,* 377–382.

Pool, R. (1994). *Eve's rib: Searching for the biological roots of sex differences.* New York: Crown.

Pope, H. G., & Katz, D. L. (1987). Bodybuilder's psychosis. *Lancet, 1,* 863.

Pope, M. K., & Smith, T. W. (1991). Cortisol excretion in high and low cynically hostile men. *Psychosomatic Medicine, 53,* 386–392.

Porter, R. H., Makin, J. W., Davis, L. B., & Christensen, K. M. (1992). An assessment of the salient olfactory environment of formula-fed infants. *Physiology & Behavior, 50,* 907–911.

Post, R. M., Ketter, T. A., Denicoff, K., & Pazzaglia, P. J. (1996). The place of anticonvulsant therapy in bipolar illness. *Psychopharmacology, 128,* 115–129.

Poussaint, A. F. (1990). Introduction. In B. Cosby, *Fatherhood.* New York: Berkley.

Pratkanis, A., & Aronson, E. (1991). *Age of propaganda: The everyday use and abuse of persuasion.* New York: Freeman.

Pratkanis, A. R., Greenwald, A. G., Leippe, M. R., & Baumgardner, M. H. (1988). In search of reliable persuasion effects: III. The sleeper effect is dead, long live the sleeper effect. *Journal of Personality and Social Psychology, 54,* 203–218.

Preston, J. D., O'Neal, J. H., & Talaga, M. C. (1998). *Consumer's guide to psychiatric drugs.* Oakland, CA: New Harbinger Publications.

Price, D. D., & Barber, J. (1987). An analysis of factors that contribute to the efficacy of hypnotic analgesia. *Journal of Abnormal Psychology, 96,* 46–51.

Price, L. H., & Heninger, G. R. (1994). Lithium in the treatment of mood disorders. *New England Journal of Medicine, 331,* 591–598.

Prince, R. L., Smith, M., Dick, I. M., Price, R. I., Webb, P. G., Henderson, K., & Harris, M. P. (1991). Prevention of postmenopausal osteoporosis. *New England Journal of Medicine, 325,* 1189–1195.

Pritchard, J. A., MacDonald, P. C., & Gant, N. F. (1985). *Williams obstetrics* (17th ed.). East Norwalk, CT: Appleton & Lange.

Prochaska, J. O. (1979). *Systems of psychotherapy: A transtheoretical analysis.* Belmont, CA: Dorsey/Wadsworth.

Prokasy, W. F., Jr., Grant, D. A., & Myers, N. A. (1958). Eyelid conditioning as a function of unconditioned stimulus intensity and intertrial interval. *Journal of Experimental Psychology, 55,* 242–246.

Provine, R. R. (1992). Contagious laughter: Laughter is a sufficient stimulus for laughs and smiles. *Bulletin of the Psychonomic Society, 30,* 1–4.

Provine, R. R. (1997). Yawns, laughs, smiles, tickles, and talking: Naturalistic and laboratory studies of facial action and social communication. In J. A. Russell & J. M. Fernandez (Eds.), *The psychology of facial expression* (pp. 158–175). Cambridge: Cambridge University Press.

Purcell, P., & Stewart, L. (1990). Dick and Jane in 1989. *Sex Roles, 22,* 177–185.

Q

Quadrel, M., J., Fischoff, B., & Davis, W. (1993). Adolescent (in)vulnerability. *American Psychologist, 48,* 102–116.

Quinn, T. C. (1996). Global burden of the HIV pandemic. *Lancet, 348,* 99–106.

R

Rachman, S. (1998). *Anxiety.* East Sussex: United Kingdom: Psychology Press.

Rachman, S. J. (1966). Sexual fetishism: An experimental analog. *Psychological Record, 18,* 25–27.

Rachman, S. J. (1990). *Fear and courage* (2nd ed.). New York: Freeman.

Raiha, N. C. R., & Axelsson, I. E. (1995). Protein nutrition in infancy. *Pediatric Clinics of North America, 42,* 745–763.

Rainnie, D. G., Grunze, H. C. R., McCarley, R. W., & Greene, R. W. (1994). Adenosine inhibition of mesopontine cholinergic neurons: Implications for EEG arousal. *Science, 263,* 689–692.

Raeff, C. (1994). Viewing adolescent mothers on their own terms: Linking self-conceptualization and adolescent motherhood. *Developmental Review, 14,* 215–244.

Raine, A., Venables, P. H., & Williams, M. (1990). Relationships between central and autonomic measures of arousal at age 15 years and criminality at age 24 years. *Archives of General Psychiatry, 47,* 1003–1007.

Rajaram, S., & Roediger, H. L., III. (1993). Direct comparison of four implicit memory tests. *Journal of Experimental Psychology: Learning, Memory, and Cognition, 19,* 765–776.

Raming, K., Krieger, J., Strotman, J., Boekhoff, I., Kubick, S., Baumstark, C., & Breer, H. (1993). Cloning and expression of odorant molecules. *Nature, 361,* 353–356.

Randi, J. (1987). *Flim-flam: Psychics, ESP, unicorns, and other delusions.* Buffalo, NY: Prometheus.

Randi, J. (1995). *An encyclopedia of claims, frauds, and hoaxes of the occult and supernatural.* New York: St. Martin's Press.

Rantakallio, P., Peter, J., Moring, J., & Von Wendt, L. (1997). Association between central nervous system infections during childhood and adult onset schizophrenia and other psychoses: A 28–year follow-up. *International Journal of Epidemiology, 26,* 837–843.

Rapoport, J. L. (1989). *The boy who couldn't stop washing: The experience and treatment of obsessive-compulsive disorder.* New York: Dutton.

Rastam, M., Gillberg, I., & Gillberg, C. (1995). Anorexia nervosa 6 years after onset: II. Comorbid psychiatric problems. *Comprehensive Psychiatry, 36,* 70–76.

Rauch-Elnekave, H. (1994). Teenage motherhood: Its relationship to undetected learning problems. *Adolescence, 29,* 91–103.

Razran, G. H. S. (1949). Stimulus generalization of conditioned responses. *Psychological Bulletin, 46,* 337–365.

Rchtarik, R. G., Prue, D. M., Rapp, S. R., & King, A. C. (1992). Self-efficacy, aftercare and relapse in a treatment program for alcoholics. *Journal of Studies on Alcoholism, 53,* 435–440.

Reason, J., & Mycielska, K. (1982). *Absent-minded? The psychology of mental lapses and everyday errors.* Upper Saddle River, NJ: Prentice Hall.

Records, R. E. (1979). Retina: Metabolism and photochemistry. In R. E. Records (Ed.), *Physiology of the human eye and visual system* (pp. 296–318). New York: HarperCollins.

Redd, W. H., Jacobsen, P. B., Die-Trill, M., Dermatis, H., McEvoy, M., & Holland, J. C. (1987). Cognitive/attentional distraction in the control of conditioned nausea in pediatric cancer patients receiving chemotherapy. *Journal of Consulting and Clinical Psychology, 55,* 391–395.

Regier, D. A., Narrow, W. E., Rae, D. S., Manderscheid, R. W., Locke, B. Z., & Goodwin, F. K. (1993). The de facto U.S. mental and addictive disorders service system. *Archives of General Psychiatry, 50,* 85–94.

Reichling, D. B., Kwait, G. C., & Basbaum, A. I. (1988). Anatomy, physiology, and pharmacology of the periaqueductal gray contribution to antinociceptive controls. In H. C. Fields & J. M. Benson (Eds.), *Progress in brain research* (pp. 31–46). Amsterdam: Elsevier.

Reid, G. M. (1994). Maternal sex-stereotyping of newborns. *Psychological Reports, 73,* 1443–1450.

Reifman, A. S., Larrick, R. P., & Fein, S. (1991). Temper and temperature on the diamond: The heat-aggression relationship in major league baseball. *Personality and Social Psychology Bulletin, 17,* 580–585.

Reilly, M. E., Lott, B., Caldwell, D., & De Luca, L. (1992). Tolerance for sexual harassment related to self-reported sexual victimization. *Journal of Social Issues, 38,* 99–110.

Reinke, B. J., Ellicott, A. M., Harris, R. L., & Hancock, E. (1985). Timing of psychosocial changes in women's lives. *Human Development, 28,* 259–280.

Reisberg, B., Ferris, S., de Leon, M. J., & Crook, T. (1985). Age-associated cognitive decline and Alzheimer's disease: Implications for assessment and treatment. In M. Bergener, M. Ermini, & H. B. Stahelin (Eds.), *Thresholds in aging.* London: Academic Press.

Reisbult, C. E. (1980). Commitment and satisfaction in romantic associations: A test of the investment model. *Journal of Experimental Social Psychology, 16,* 172–186.

Reite, M. L., Nagel, K. E., & Ruddy, J. R. (1990). *The evaluation and management of sleep disorders.* Washington, DC: American Psychiatric Association.

Reker, G. T., Peacock, E. J., & Wong, P. T. P. (1987). Meaning and purpose in life and well-being: A life-span perspective. *Journal of Gerontology, 42,* 44–49.

Remley, A. (1988, October). From obedience to independence. *Psychology Today,* pp. 56–59.

Report of the Presidential Commission on the Space Shuttle Challenger Accident. (1986). Washington, DC: U.S. Government Printing Office.

Rescorla, R. A. (1968). Probability of shock in presence and absence of CS in fear conditioning. *Journal of Comparative and Physiological Psychology, 66,* 1–5.

Restak, R. M. (1988). *The mind.* New York: Bantam Books.

Restak, R. M. (1994). *The modular brain.* New York: Charles A. Scribner's Sons.

Rice, F. P. (1995). *Human development: A life span approach* (2nd ed.). Upper Saddle River, NJ: Prentice Hall.

Rice, L. N., & Greenberg, L. S. (1992). Humanistic approaches to psychotherapy. In D. K. Freedheim (Ed.), *History of psychotherapy: A century of change.* Washington, DC: American Psychological Association.

Rice, P. L. (1992). *Stress and health* (2nd ed.). Pacific Grove, CA: Brooks/Cole.

Richardson, J. G., & Simpson, C. H. (1982). Children, gender, and social structure: An analysis of the contents of letters to Santa Claus. *Child Development, 53,* 429–436.

Richmond, V. P., & McCroskey, J. C. (1995). *Nonverbal behavior in interpersonal relations* (3rd ed.). Needham Heights, MA: Allyn & Bacon.

Richter, C. P. (Ed.). (1922). A behavioristic study of the activity of the rat. *Comparative Psychology Monographs, 1.*

Rief, W., Hiller., & Margrat, J. Cognitive aspects of hypochondriasis and the somatization syndrome. *Journal of Abnormal Psychology, 107,* 587–595.

Rime, B., & Schiaratura, L. (1991). Gesture and speech. In R. S. Feldman & B. Rime (Eds.), *Fundamentals of nonverbal behavior* (pp. 239–281). Cambridge: Cambridge University Press.

Rinzler, C. A. (1996). *Why Eve doesn't have an Adam's apple: A dictionary of sex differences.* New York: Facts on File.

Roberts, D. F., & Maccoby, N. (1985). Effects of mass communication. In G. Lindzey & E. Aronson (Eds.), *Handbook of social psychology* (3rd ed., Vol. 2). New York: Random House.

Robins, L. N., Locke, B. Z., & Regier, D. A. (1991). An overview of psychiatric disorders in America. In L. N. Robins & D. A. Regier (Eds.), *Psychiatric disorders in America: The Epidemiologic Catchment Area Study* (pp. 328–366). New York: Free Press.

Robins, L. N., & Regier, D. A. (Eds.). (1991). *Psychiatric disorders in America: The Epidemiologic Catchment Area Study.* New York: Free Press.

Robins, L. N., Tipp, J., & Przybeck, T. (1991). Antisocial personality. In L. N. Robins & D. A. Regier (Eds.), *Psychiatric disorders in America: The Epidemiologic Catchment Area Study* (pp. 258–290). New York: Free Press.

Robinson, A., & Henry, G. P. (1985). Prenatal diagnosis by amniocentesis. *Annual Review of Medicine, 36,* 13–26.

Roche, J. P. (1996). Path-leaving decisions in black-capped chickadees. *Animal Behaviour, 52,* 289–298.

Roche, J. P., & Timberlake, W. (1998). The influence of artificial paths and landmarks on the foraging behavior of Norway rats (Rattus norvegicus). *Animal Learning & Behavior, 26,* 76–84.

Rock, I., & Palmer, S. (1990). The legacy of Gestalt psychology. *Scientific American, 263,* 84–90.

Rodin, J. (1987). Weight gain following smoking cessation: The role of food intake and exercise. *Addictive Behaviors, 12,* 303–317.

Rodin, J. (1992). *Body traps.* New York: Morrow.

Rodin, J., & Ickovics, J. R. (1990). Women's health: Review and research agenda as we approach the 21st century. *American Psychologist, 45,* 1018–1034.

Roediger, H. L. (1990). Implicit memory: Retention without remembering. *American Psychologist, 45,* 1043–1056.

Roffwarg, H. P., Muzio, J. N., & Dement, W. C. (1966). Ontogenetic development of the human sleep-dream cycle. *Science, 37,* 604–619.

Rogers, C. (1959). My philosophy of interpersonal relationships and how it grew. *Journal of Humanistic Psychology, 28,* 3–15.

Rogers, C. R. (1957). The necessary and sufficient conditions of therapeutic personality change. *Journal of Consulting Psychology, 21,* 95–103.

Rogers, C. R. (1991, October). Children in gangs. *UNESCO Courier,* pp. 19–21.

Roggman, L. A., Langlois, J. H., Hubbs-Tait, L., & Reiser-Danner, L. A. (1994). Infant day-care, attachment, and the "file drawer problem." *Child Development, 65,* 1429–1443.

Rogoff, B. (1990). *Apprenticeship in thinking.* New York: Oxford University Press.

Rohrer, D., Wixted, J. T., Salmon, D. P., & Butters, N. (1995). Retrieval from semantic memory and its implications for Alzheimer's disease. *Journal of Experimental Psychology: Learning, Memory, and Cognition, 21,* 1127–1139.

Rollin, B. E. (1985). The moral status of research animals in psychology. *American Psychologist, 40,* 920–926.

Romero, K., & Silvestri, L. (1990). The role of mental practice in the acquisition and performance of motor skills. *Journal of Instructional Psychology, 17,* 218–221.

Rosch, E. H. (1975). Cognitive representations of semantic categories. *Journal of Experimental Psychology: General, 104,* 192–233.

Roscoe, B., & Kruger, T. L. (1990). AIDS: Late adolescents' knowledge and its influence on sexual behavior. *Adolescence, 25,* 39–48.

Rose, J. E., Brugge, J. F., Anderson, D. J., & Hind, J. E. (1967). Phase-locked response to low-frequency tones in single auditory nerve fibers of the squirrel monkey. *Journal of Neurophysiology, 30,* 769–793.

Rose, S. D., & Le Croy, C. W. (1991). Group methods. In F. H. Kanfer and A. P. Goldstein (Eds.), *Helping people change* (4th ed., pp. 422–453). New York: Pergamon.

Rosebush, P. (1994). What is neuroleptic malignant syndrome and how is it treated? *Harvard Mental Health Letter, 11(6),* 8.

Rosell, E., Miller, K., & Barber, K. (1995). Firefighting women and sexual harassment. *Public Personnel Management, 24,* 339–350.

Roseman, I. J., Dhawan, N., Rettek, S. I., Naidu, R. K., & Thapa, K. (1995). Cultural differences and cross-cultural similarities in appraisals and emotional responses. *Journal of Cross-Cultural Psychology, 26,* 23–48.

Rosen, E., Anthony, D. L., Booker, K. M., Brown, T. L., Christian, E., Crews, R. C., Hollins, V. J., Privette, J. T., & Reed, R. R. (1991). A comparison of eating disorder scores among African-American and white college students. *Bulletin of the Psychonomic Society, 29,* 65–66.

Rosenfarb, I. S., Goldstein, M. J., Mintz, J., & Neuchterlein, K. H. (1995). Expressed emotion and subclinical psychopathology observable within the transactions between schizophrenic patients and their family members. *Journal of Abnormal Psychology, 104,* 259–267.

Rosenfeld, A. (1985). *Prolongevity: 2. An updated report on the scientific prospectus for adding good years to life.* New York: Knopf.

Rosenfeld, P. (1995). Alternative views of Bashore and Rapp's (1993) alternatives to traditional polygraphy: A critique. *Psychological Bulletin, 117,* 159–166.

Rosengren, K. S., & Hickling, A. K. (1994). Seeing is believing: Children's explanations of commonplace, magical, and extraordinary transformations. *Child Development, 65,* 1605–1626.

Rosenhan, D. L. (1973). On being sane in insane places. *Science, 179,* 250–258.

Rosenthal, R., Hall, J. A., DiMatteo, M. R., & Rogers, P., & Archer, D. (1979). *Sensitivity to nonverbal communication: A profile approach to the measurement of differential abilities.* Baltimore: Johns Hopkins University Press.

Rosenthal, R., & Jacobson, L. (1968). *Pygmalion in the classroom: Teacher expectation and intellectual development.* Austin, TX: Holt, Rinehart & Winston.

Rosenzweig, M. R. (1992). Psychological science around the world. *American Psychologist, 47,* 718–722.

Rosenzweig, M. R., Bennett, E. L., & Diamond, M. C. (1976). Brain changes in response to experience. *Progress in psychobiology.* New York: Freeman.

Ross, B. H., & Spalding, T. L. (1994). Concepts and categories. In R. J. Sternberg (Ed.), *Thinking and problem solving* (pp. 119–148). San Diego, CA: Academic Press.

Ross, L., Amabile, T. M., & Steinmetz, J. L. (1977). Social roles, social control, and biases in social-perception processes. *Journal of Personality and Social Psychology, 35,* 485–494.

Roth, M., Wischik, C. M., Evans, N., & Mountjoy, C. (1985). Convergence and cohesion of recent neurobiological findings in relation to Alzheimer's disease and their bearing on its etiological basis. In M. Bergener, M. Ermini, & H. B. Stahelin (Eds.), *Thresholds in aging.* London: Academic Press.

Rotter, J. B. (1966). Generalized expectancies for internal versus external control of reinforcement. *Psychological Monographs, 80* (Whole No. 609).

Rotter, J. B. (1990). Internal versus external control of reinforcement. *American Psychologist, 45,* 489–493.

Rotton, J., & Kelly, I. W. (1985). Much ado about the full moon: A meta-analysis of lunar-lunacy research. *Psychological Bulletin, 97,* 286–306.

Rovee-Collier, C. (1993). The capacity for long-term memory in infancy. *Current Directions in Psychological Science, 2,* 130–135.

Rovee-Collier, C., & Lipsitt, L. (1982). Learning, adaptation, and memory in the newborn. In P. Stratton (Ed.), *Psychobiology of the human newborn.* New York: Wiley.

Roy-Byrne, P. P., & Katon, W. (1997). Generalized anxiety disorder in primary care: The precursor/modifier pathway to increased health care utilization. *Journal of Clinical Psychiatry, 38,* 34–40.

Rozin, P., Lowery, L., & Ebert, R. (1994). Varieties of disgust faces and the structure of disgust. *Journal of Personality and Social Psychology, 66,* 870–881.

Rubin, R. T., Provenzano, F. J., & Luria, Z. (1974). The eye of the beholder: Parents' views on sex of newborns. *American Journal of Orthopsychiatry, 43,* 720–731.

Ruchlis, H. (1990). *Clear thinking: A practical introduction.* Buffalo, NY: Prometheus.

Rudestam, K. E. (1971). Stockholm and Los Angeles: A cross-cultural study of the communication of suicidal intent. *Journal of Consulting and Clinical Psychology, 36,* 82–90.

Rush, J., & Suppes, T. (1998). What are the new treatments for bipolar disorder? *Harvard Mental Health Letter, 14(11),* 8.

Russell, J. A. (1991). Culture and the categorization of emotions. *Psychological Bulletin, 110,* 426–450.

Russell, J.A., & Sato, K. (1995). Comparing emotion words between languages. *Journal of Cross-Cultural Psychology, 26,* 384–391.

Ruzgis, P., & Grigorenko, E. L. (1994). Cultural meaning systems, intelligence, and personality. In R. J. Sternberg & P. Ruzgis (Eds.), *Personality and intelligence* (pp. 248–270). New York: Cambridge University Press.

Rybacki, J. J. (1997). *The concise essential guide to prescription drugs.* New York: Harper Paperbacks.

S

Saal, F. E., Johnson, C. B., & Weber, N. (1989). Friendly or sexy? It may depend on whom you ask. *Psychology of Women Quarterly, 13,* 263–276.

Saari, L. M., Johnson, T. R., McLaughlin, S. D., & Zimmerle, D. M. (1988). A survey of management training and education practices in U.S. companies. *Personnel Psychology, 41,* 731–744.

Sachdev, P., & Hay. P. (1996). Site and size of lesion and psychosurgical outcome in obsessive-compulsive disorder. A magnetic resonance imaging study. *Biological Psychiatry, 39,* 739–742.

Sacks, O. (1985). *The man who mistook his wife for a hat.* New York: Summit Books.

Sacks, O. (1989). *Seeing voices: A journey into the world of the deaf.* Berkeley, CA: University of California Press.

Sack, R. L., Hughes, R. J., Edgar, D. M., & Lewy, A. J. (1997). Sleep-promoting effects of melatonin: At what dose, in whom, under what conditions, and by what mechanisms? *Sleep, 20* 908–915.

Sadker, M., & Sadker, D. (1985, March). Sexism in the schoolroom of the '80s. *Psychology Today,* pp. 54–57.

Sadker, M., & Sadker, D. (1986, March). Sexism in the classroom: From grade school to graduate school. *Phi Delta Kappan,* pp. 512–515.

Sadker, M., & Sadker, D. (1993). *Failing at fairness.* New York: Scribner.

Sadker, M., Sadker, D., & Stulberg, L. M. (1993, March). Fair and square? Creating a nonsexist classroom. *Instructor*, pp. 45–46, 67–68.

Saeed, S. A., & Bruce, T. J. (1998). Seasonal affective disorder. *American Family Physician*, 57, 1340–1346.

Sagi, A. (1990). Attachment theory and research from a cross-cultural perspective. *Human Development*, 33, 10–22.

Sagi, A., Van Ijzendoorn, M. H., Aviezer, O., & Donnell, F. (1994). Sleeping out of home in a kibbutz communal arrangement: It makes a difference for infant-mother attachment. *Child Development*, 65, 992–1004.

Salive, M. E., Guralnik, J. M., & Glynn, R. J. (1993). Left-handedness and mortality. *American Journal of Public Health*, 83, 265–267.

Salminen, J.K., Saarijanvi, S., Aairela, E., & Tamminen, T. (1994) Alexithymia; State on trait? One–year follow–up study of general hospital psychiatric Consultation outpatients. *Journal of Psychosomatic Research*, 38, 681–685.

Salovey, P., & Singer, J. A. (1991). Cognitive behavior modification. In F. H. Kanfer & A. P. Goldstein (Eds.), *Helping people change* (4th ed., pp. 361–395). New York: Pergamon.

Samovar, L. A., & Porter, R. E. (1991). *Communication between cultures*. Belmont, CA: Wadsworth.

Sanders, W. B. (1994). *Gangbangs and drive-bys: Grounded culture and juvenile gang violence*. Hawthorne, NY: Aldine de Gruyter.

Sandvik, L., Erikssen, J., Thaulow, E., Erikssen, G., Mundal, R., & Rodahl, K. (1993). Physical fitness as a predictor of mortality among healthy middle-aged Norwegian men. *New England Journal of Medicine*, 328, 533–537.

Saunders, J. B., Aasland, O. G., Babor, T. F., de la Fuente, J. R., & Grant, M. (1993). Development of the Alcohol Use Disorders Identification Test (AUDIT): WHO Collaborative Project on Early Detection of Persons with Harmful Alcohol Consumption–II. *Addiction*, 88, 791–804.

Saxe, L. (1991). Lying: Thoughts of an applied social psychologist. *American Psychologist*, 46, 409–415.

Saxe, L. (1994). Detection of deception: Polygraph and integrity tests. *Current Directions in Psychological Science*, 3(3), 69–73.

Scarborough, E., & Furumoto, L. (1987). *Untold lives: The first generation of American women psychologists*. New York: Columbia University press.

Scarr, S. (1992). Developmental theories for the 1990s: Development and individual differences. *Child Development*, 63, 1–19.

Scarr, S., & Eisenberg, M. (1993). Child care research: Issues, perspectives, and results. *Annual Review of Psychology*, 44, 613–644.

Scarr, S., & Weinberg, R. A. (1986). The early childhood enterprise: Care and education of the young. *American Psychologist*, 41, 1140–1146.

Schaap, D., & Gerberg, M. (Eds.). (1992). *Joy in Mudville: The big book of baseball humor*. New York: Doubleday.

Schab, F. R. (1990). Odors and the remembrance of things past. *Journal of Experimental Psychology: Learning, Memory, and Cognition*, 16, 648–655.

Schachter, D. L. (1997). False recognition and the brain. *Current Directions in Psychological Science*, 6, 65–70.

Schachter, D. L., Curran, T., Galluccio, L., Milberg, W., & Bates, J. (1996). False recognition and the right frontal lobe: A case study. *Neuropsychologica*, 34, 793–808.

Schachter, S., & Singer, J. E. (1962). Cognitive, social, and physiological determinants of emotional state. *Psychological Review*, 69, 379–399.

Schafer, M., & Crichlow, S. (1996). Antecedents of groupthink. *Journal of Conflict Resolution*, 40, 415–435.

Schaffer, R. (1977). *Mothering*. Cambridge, MA: Harvard University Press.

Schaie, K. W. (1977–1978). Toward a stage theory of adult cognitive development. *Journal of Aging and Human Development*, 8, 129–138.

Schaie, K. W. (1983). The Seattle longitudinal study: A twenty-one year investigation of psychometric intelligence. In K. W. Schaie (Ed.), *Longitudinal studies of adult psychological development*. New York: Guilford Press.

Schaie, K. W. (1990). Intellectual development in adulthood. In J. E. Birren & K. W. Schaie (Eds.), *Handbook of the psychology of aging*. San Diego, CA: Academic Press.

Scheibel, A. B., Fried, I., Paul, L., Forsythe, A., Tomyasu, U., Silverman, K., Evans, S. M., Strain, E. C., & Griffiths, R. R. (1992). Withdrawal syndrome after the double-blind cessation of caffeine consumption. *New England Journal of Medicine*, 327, 1109–1114.

Schelling, T. C. (1992). Addictive drugs: The cigarette experience. *Science*, 255, 430–433.

Schenck, C. H., Hurwitz, T. D., & Mahowald, M. W. (1993). REM sleep behaviour disorder: An update on a series of 96 patients and a review of the world literature. *Journal of Sleep Research*, 2, 224–231.

Schenck, C. H., & Mahowald, M. W. (1990). Polysomnographic, neurologic, psychiatric, and clinical outcome report on 70 consecutive cases with REM sleep behavior disorder (RBD): Sustained clonazepam efficiency in 89.5% of 57 treated patients. *Cleveland Clinic Journal of Medicine*, 57, (Suppl.), S9–S23.

Scherer, K. R., & Wallbott, H. G. (1994). Evidence for universality and cultural variation of differential emotion response patterning. *Journal of Personality and Social Psychology*, 66, 310–328.

Schiffman, H. R. (1967). Size estimation of familiar objects under informative and reduced conditions of viewing. *American Journal of Psychology*, 80, 229–235.

Schiffman, S. S. (1983). Taste and smell in disease. *New England Journal of Medicine*, 308, 1275–1279.

Schildkraut, J. J., & Kety, S. S. (1967). Biogenic amines and emotion. *Science*, 156, 1129–1137.

Schindler, L. W. (1991). *Understanding the immune system*. Rockville, MD: National Institutes of Health.

Schlegel, A., & Barry, H., III (1991). *Adolescence: An anthropological inquiry*. New York: Free Press.

Schmidt-Nowara, W., & Jessop, C. (1995). *Increased mortality in sleep apnea syndrome*. Paper presented at the annual meeting of the Association for the Psychophysiological Study of Sleep, Nashville, TN.

Schneier, F. R., & Johnson, J. (1992). Social phobia: Comorbidity and morbidity in an epidemiological sample. *Archives of General Psychiatry*, 49, 282–288.

Schou, M. (1997). Forty years of lithium treatment. *Archives of General Psychiatry*, 54, 9–13.

Schrader, B. W., & Steiner, D. D. (1996). Common comparison standards: An approach to improving agreement between self and supervisory performance ratings. *Journal of Applied Psychology*, 81, 813–820.

Schreurs, B. G. (1993). Long-term memory and extinction of the classically conditioned rabbit nictitating membrane response. *Learning and Motivation*, 24, 294–302.

Schultz, D. P., & Schultz, S. E. (1998). *Psychology and work today: An introduction to industrial and organizational psychology* (7th ed.). Upper Saddle River, NJ: Prentice Hall.

Schuman, H., & Presser, S. (1981). *Questions and answers in attitude surveys: Experiments on question form, wording, and content*. San Diego, CA: Academic Press.

Schweinberger, S. R. (1996). How Gorbachev primed Yeltsin: Analyses of associative priming in person recognition by means of reaction times and event-related brain potentials. *Journal of Experimental Psychology: Learning, Memory, and Cognition*, 22, 1383–1407.

Scott, A. J. (1994). Chronobiological considerations in shiftworker sleep and performance and shiftwork scheduling. *Human Performance*, 7, 207–233.

Scott, T. R., & Plata-Salaman, C. R. (1991). Coding of taste quality. In T. V. Getchell, (Eds.), *Smell and taste in health and disease* (pp. 345–368). New York: Raven Press.

Scoville, W. B., & Milner, B. (1957). Loss of recent memory after bilateral hippocampal lesions. *Journal of Neurology, Neurosurgery, and Psychiatry*, 20, 11–19.

Sears, W. (1995). SIDS: *A parent's guide to understanding and preventing sudden infant death syndrome*. Boston: Little, Brown.

Sebby, R. A., & Papini, D. R. (1994). Postformal reasoning during adolescence and young adulthood: The influence of problem relevancy. *Adolescence*, 29, 389–400.

Secretary of Health and Human Services. (1997). *Ninth special report to the U.S. Congress on alcohol and health*. Washington, DC: U.S. Government Printing Office (NIH publication no. 97–4017).

Segal, M. W. (1974). Alphabet and attraction: An unobtrusive measure of the effect of propinquity in a field setting. *Journal of Personality and Social Psychology*, 30, 654–657.

Segerberg, O. (1982). *Living to be 100: 1,200 who did and how they did it*. New York: Scribner.

Seligman, M. E. P. (1970). On the generality of the laws of learning. *Psychological Review*, 77, 406–418.

Seligman, M. E. P. (1989). Research in clinical psychology: Why is there so much depression today? In I. S. Cohen (Ed.), *The G. Stanley Hall Lecture Series* (Vol. 9, pp. 75–96). Washington, DC: American Psychological Association.

Seligman, M. E. P. (1990). *Learned optimism: How to change your mind and your life*. New York: Pocket Books.

Seligman, M. E. P. (1992). *Helplessness: On depression, development and death*. New York: Freeman. (Originally published in 1975)

Seligman, M. E. P. (1993). *What you can change and what you can't*. New York: Knopf.

Seligman, M. E. P. (1995). The effectiveness of psychotherapy: The *Consumer Reports* study. (1995). *American Psychologist*, 50, 965–974.

Seligman, M. E. P. (1996). Long-term psychotherapy is highly effective: The Consumer Reports Study. *Harvard Mental Health Letter*, 5–7.

Selling it. (1991, April). *Consumer Reports*, p. 295.

Selye, H. (1978). *The stress of life*. New York: McGraw-Hill.

Shader, R. I., & Greenblatt, D. J. (1993). Use of benzodiazepines in anxiety disorders. *New England Journal of Medicine*, 328, 1398–1405.

Shain, R., & Phillips, J. (1991). The stigma of mental illness: Labeling and stereotyping in the news. In L. Wilkins & P. Patterson (Eds.), *Risky business: Communicating issues of science, risk, and public policy* (pp. 61–74). Westport, CT: Greenwood Press.

Shapiro, B. E., & Danly, M. (1985). The role of the right hemisphere in the control of speech prosody in propositional and affective contexts. *Brain and Language*, 25, 19–36.

Shapiro, E. S., & Ager, C. (1992). Assessment of special education students in regular education programs: Linking assessment to instruction. *School Psychology*, 92, 283–296.

Shapiro, L. (1990, May 28). Guns and dolls. *Newsweek*, pp. 56–65.

Shapiro, L. (1998, June 15). Fat, fatter, But who's counting? *Newsweek*, 55.

Sharma, A., Lynch, M. A., & Irvine, M. L. (1994). The availability of advice regarding infant feeding to immigrants of Vietnamese origin: A survey of families and health visitors. *Child: Care, Health, and Development*, 20, 349–354.

Shaw, J. I., Borough, H. W., & Fink, M. I. (1994). Perceived sexual orientation and helping behavior by males and females: The wrong number technique. *Journal of Psychology & Human Sexuality, 6,* 73–81.

Shean, G. (1978). *Schizophrenia: An introduction to research and theory.* Framingham, MA: Winthrop.

Shearn, D., Bergman, E., Hill, K., & Abel, A. (1990). Facial coloration and temperature responses in blushing. *Psychophysiology, 27,* 687–693.

Sheldon, R. G., Tracy, S. K., & Brown, W. B. (1997). *Youth gangs in American society.* New York: Wadsworth.

Sheldon, W. H., & Stevens, S. S. (1942). *The varieties of temperament: A psychology of constitutional differences.* New York: HarperCollins.

Sheldon, W. H., Stevens, S. S., & Tucker, W. B. (1940). *The varieties of human physique: An introduction to constitutional psychology.* New York: HarperCollins.

Shepard, R. N., & Metzler, J. (1971). Mental rotation of three-dimensional objects. *Science, 171,* 701–703.

Sherif, M., Harvey, O. J., White, B. J., Hood, W. E., & Sherif, C. W. (1961). *Intergroup conflict and cooperation: The Robber's Cave Experiment.* Norman, OK: Institute of Group Relations.

Sherman, J. E. (1978). US inflation with trace and simultaneous fear conditioning. *Animal Learning and Behavior, 6,* 463–468.

Sherman, L. A., Temple, R., & Merkatz, R. B. (1995). Women in clinical trials: An FDA perspective. *Science, 269,* 793–795.

Shipley, R. H. (1974). Extinction of conditioned fear in rats as a function of several parameters of CS exposure. *Journal of Comparative and Physiological Psychology, 87,* 699–707.

Shoho, A. R. (1994). A historical comparison of parental involvement of three generations of Japanese Americans (isseis, niseis, sanseis) in the education of their children. *Journal of Applied Developmental Psychology, 15,* 305–311.

Siegel, R. K. (1989). *Intoxication: Life in pursuit of artificial paradise.* New York: Dutton.

Signorelli, N. (1989). Television and conceptions about sex roles: Maintaining conventionality and the status quo. *Sex Roles, 21,* 341–360.

Silinsky, E. M. (1989). Adenosine derivatives and neuronal function. *Seminars in Neurosciences, 1,* 155–165.

Silver, E., Cirincione, C., & Steadman, H. J. (1994). Demythologizing inaccurate perceptions of the insanity defense. *Law and Human Behavior, 18,* 63–70.

Silverberg, S. B., Tennenbaum, D. L., & Jacob, T. (1992). Adolescence and family interaction. In V. B. Van Hasselt & M. Hersen (Eds.), *Handbook of social development: A life-span perspective.* New York: Plenum.

Silverman, L. H., & Lachmann, F. M. (1985). The therapeutic properties of unconsciousness oneness fantasies: Evidence and treatment implications. *Contemporary Psychoanalysis, 21,* 91–115.

Simmons, C. H., vom Kolke, A., & Shimizu, H. (1986). Attitudes toward romantic love among American, German, and Japanese students. *Journal of Social Psychology, 126,* 327–336.

Simon, L. (Ed.) (1996). *William James remembered.* Lincoln: University of Nebraska Press.

Simon, T. R., Stacy, A. W., Sussman, S., & Dent, C. W. (1994). Sensation seeking and drug use among high risk Latino and Anglo adolescents. *Personality and Individual Differences, 17,* 665–672.

Sinclair, D. (1978). *Human growth after birth* (3rd ed.). London: Oxford University Press.

Singer, D. G., & Singer, J. L. (1990). *The house of make-believe.* Cambridge, MA: Harvard University Press.

Sizemore, C. C., & Pittillo, E. S. (1977). *I'm Eve.* New York: Doubleday.

Skeels, H. M. (1966). Adult status of children with contrasting early life experiences: A follow-up study. *Monographs of the Society for Child Development, 31* (Serial No. 105).

Skeels, H. M., & Dye, H. B. (1939). A study of the effects of differential stimulation on mentally

retarded children. *Proceedings of the American Association for Mental Deficiency, 44,* 114–136.

Skinner, B. F. (1938). *The behavior of organisms: An experimental analysis.* Upper Saddle River, NJ: Prentice Hall.

Sleek, S. (1997, June). Can "emotional intelligence" be taught in today's schools? *APA Monitor,* 25.

Sloane, E. (1985). *Biology and women* (2nd ed.). New York: Wiley.

Small, S. A., Zeldin, S., & Savin-Williams, R. C. (1983). In search of personality traits: A multimethod analysis of naturally occurring prosocial and dominance behavior. *Journal of Personality, 51,* 1–16.

Smith, M., & Lin, K. M. (1996). Gender and ethnic differences in the pharmacogenetics of psychotropics. In M. F. Jensvold, U. Halbreich, & J. A. Hamilton (Eds.), *Psychopharmacology and women: Sex, gender, and hormones* (pp. 121–136). Washington, DC: American Psychiatric Association.

Smith, M. C., Coleman, S. R., & Gormezano, I. (1969). Classical conditioning of the rabbit's nictitating membrane response at back-ward, simultaneous, and forward CS-US intervals. *Journal of Comparative and Physiological Psychology, 69,* 226–231.

Smith, M. L., Glass, G. V., & Miller, R. L. (1980). *The benefits of psychotherapy.* Baltimore: Johns Hopkins University Press.

Smith, P. B., & Bond, N. H. (1993). *Social psychology across cultures.* Needham Heights, MA: Allyn & Bacon.

Smith, P. B., & Tayeb, M. (1989). Organizational structure and processes. In M. Bond (Ed.), *The cross-cultural challenge to social psychology.* Newbury Park, CA: Sage.

Smith, R. A., & Davis, S. F. (1996). *The psychologist as detective.* Upper Saddle River, NJ: Prentice Hall.

Smith, R. A., & Davis, S. F. (1997). *The psychologist as detective: An introduction to conducting research in psychology.* Upper Saddle River, NJ: Prentice Hall.

Smith, S. M., Brown, H. O., Toman, J. E. P., & Goodman, L. S. (1947). The lack of cerebral effects of d-tubocurarine. *Anesthesiology, 8,* 1–14.

Smith, S. M., Glenberg, A. M., & Björk, R. (1978). Environmental context and human memory. *Memory and Cognition, 6,* 342–353.

Smith, S. M., & Shaffer, D. R. (1991). Celerity and cajolery: Rapid speech may promote or inhibit persuasion through its impact on message elaboration. *Personality and Social Psychology Bulletin, 17,* 663–669.

Smith, T. W., & Leon, A. S. (1992). *Coronary heart disease: A behavioral perspective.* Champaign, IL: Research Press.

Snyder, C. R., & Larson, G. R. (1972). A further look at student acceptance of general personality interpretations. *Journal of Consulting and Clinical Psychology, 38,* 384–388.

Snyder, M., & Gangestad, S. (1986). On the nature of self-monitoring: Matters of assessment, matters of validity. *Journal of Personality and Social Psychology, 51,* 125–139.

Snyderman, M., & Rothman, S. (1987). Survey of expert opinion on intelligence and aptitude testing. *American Psychologist, 42,* 137–144.

Sobal, J., & Stunkard, A. J., Jr. (1989). Socioeconomic status and obesity: A review of the literature. *Psychological Bulletin, 105,* 260–275.

Soliman, A. M. (1996). Development of an Arabic translation of the MMPI-2: With clinical applications. In J. N. Butcher (Ed.), *International adaptation of the MMPI-2* (pp. 463–486). Minneapolis: University of Minnesota Press.

Solomon, R. L. (1980). The opponent-process theory of acquired motivation: The costs of pleasure and benefits of pain. *American Psychologists, 35,* 691–712.

Solomon, R. L. (1982). The opponent-process in acquired motivation. In D. W. Pfaff (Ed.), *The physiological mechanisms of motivation.* New York: Springer-Verlag.

Solso, R. L. (1998). *Cognitive psychology* (5th ed.). Boston: Allyn & Bacon.

Sonnert, G., & Holton, G. (1996). Career patterns of women and men in the sciences. *American Scientist, 84,* 63–71.

Sontheimer, H. (1995). Glial influences on neuronal signaling. *The Neuroscientist, 1,* 123–126.

Southwick, S. M., Yehuda, R., & Charney, D. S. (1997). Neurobiological alterations in PTSD: Review of the clinical literature. In C. S. Fullerton & R. J. Ursano (Eds.), *Posttraumatic stress disorder: Acute and long-term responses to trauma and disaster* (pp. 241–266).

Spanier, G. B., Lewis, R. A., & Cole, C. L. (1975). Marital adjustment over the family life cycle: The issue of curvilinearity. *Journal of Marriage and the Family, 37,* 263–275.

Spanos, N. P. (1987–1988). Past-life hypnotic regression: A critical review. *Skeptical Inquirer, 12,* 174–180.

Spanos, N. P. (1991). Hypnosis, hypnotizability, and hypnotherapy. In C. R. Snyder & D. R. Forsyth (Eds.), *Handbook of social and clinical psychology* (pp. 644–663). New York: Pergamon.

Spanos, N. P., Menary, E., Gabora, N. J., Du Breuil, S. C., & Dewhirst, B. (1991). Secondary identity enactments during hypnotic past-life regression: A sociocognitive perspective. *Journal of Personality and Social Psychology, 61,* 308–320.

Spanos, N. P., Weekes, J. R., & Bertrand, L. D. (1985). Multiple personality: A social psychological perspective. *Journal of Abnormal Psychology, 94,* 362–376.

Spence, J. T. (1993). Women, men, and society: *Plus ça change, plus c'est la même chose.* In S. Oskamp & M. Costanzo (Eds.), *Gender issues in contemporary society* (pp. 3–17). Newbury Park, CA: Sage.

Sperling, G. (1960). The information available in brief visual presentation. *Psychological Monographs, 74* (Whole No. 11).

Sperry, R. W. (1964). The great cerebral commissure. *Scientific American, 210,* 42–52.

Spetch, M. L., Kelly, D. M., & Lechelt, D. P. (1998). Encoding of spatial information in images of an outdoor scene by pigeons and humans. *Animal Learning & Behavior, 26,* 85–102.

Spettell, C. M., & Liehert, R. M. (1986). Training for safety in automated person-machine systems. *American Psychologist, 41,* 545–550.

Spiegel, D., & Scheflin, A. W. (1994). Dissociated or fabricated? Psychiatric aspects of repressed memory in criminal and civil cases. *International Journal of Clinical and Experimental Hypnosis, 42,* 411–432.

Spitzer, R. L., Gibbon, M., Skodol, A. E., Williams, J. B. W., & First, M. B. (Eds.). (1994). *DSM-IV case book: A learning companion to the Diagnostic and Statistical Manual of Mental Disorders, Fourth Edition.* Washington, DC: American Psychiatric Association.

Srivastava, A. K., & Misra, G. (1996). Changing perspectives on understanding intelligence: An appraisal. *Indian Psychological Abstract Review, 3,* 1–34.

Stacy, A. W., Newcomb, M. D., & Bentler, P. M. (1991). Social psychological influences on sensation seeking from adolescence to adulthood. *Personality and Social Psychology Bulletin, 17,* 701–708.

Stacy, A. W., Widaman, K. F., & Marlatt, G. A. (1990). Expectancy models of alcohol use. *Journal of Personality and Social Psychology, 58,* 918–928.

Stangor, C., Lynch, L., Duan, C., & Glass, B. (1992). Categorization of individuals on the basis of multiple social features. *Journal of Personality and Social Psychology, 62,* 207–218.

Stanovich, K. E. (1992). *How to think straight about psychology* (3rd ed.). New York: HarperCollins.

Stapel, D. A., & Koomen, W. (1997). Social categorization and perceptual judgement of size: When perception is social. *Journal of Personality and Social Psychology, 73,* 1177–1190.

Staub, E., & Baer, R. S., Jr. (1974). Stimulus characteristics of a sufferer and difficulty of escape as determinants of helping. *Journal of Personality and Social Psychology, 30,* 279–285.

Steadman, H. J., McGreevy, M. A., Morrissey, J. P., Callahan, L. A., Robbins, P. C., & Cirincione, C. (1993). *Before and after Hinckley: Evaluating insanity defense reform.* New York: Guilford Press.

Steblay, N., Mehrkens, N., & Bothwell, R. K. (1994). Evidence for hypnotically refreshed testimony: The view from the laboratory. *Law and Human Behavior, 18,* 635–651.

Steele, C. M. (1997). A threat in the air: How stereotypes shape intellectual identity and performance. *American Psychologist, 52,* 613–629.

Steele, C. M., & Aronson, J. (1995). Stereotype threat and the intellectual test performance of African Americans. *Journal of Personality and Social Psychology, 69,* 797–811.

Steele, C. M., & Josephs, R. A. (1990). Alcohol myopia: Its prized and dangerous effects. *American Psychologist, 45,* 921–933.

Stein, J., & Walsh, V. (1997). To see but not to read: The magnocellular theory of dyslexia. Trends in *Neuroscience, 20,* 147–152.

Stein, N. (1995). The definition of sexual harassment applies to schools. In K. L. Swisher (Ed.), *What is sexual harassment?* (pp. 19–24). San Diego: Greenhaven Press.

Steinberg, L., Lamborn, S. D., Darling, M., Mounts, N. S., & Dornbusch, S. M. (1994). Over-time changes in adjustment and competence among adolescents from authoritative, authoritarian, indulgent, and neglectful families. *Child Development, 65,* 754–770.

Steiner, J. (1979). Human facial expressions in response to taste and smell stimulation. In H. Reese & L. P. Lipsitt (Eds.), *Advances in child development and behavior* (Vol. 13, pp. 257–295). San Diego, CA: Academic Press.

Sternberg, R. J. (1988). *The triarchic mind: A new theory of human intelligence.* New York: Viking Penguin.

Sternberg, R. J. (1997). Educating intelligence: Infusing the Triarchic Theory into school instruction. In R. J. Sternberg & E. L. Grigorenko (Eds.), *Intelligence, heredity, and environment* (p. 343–362). New York: Cambridge University Press.

Sternberg, R. J., Conway, B. E., Ketron, J. L., & Bernstein, M. (1981). People's conceptions of intelligence. *Journal of Personality and Social Psychology, 41,* 37–55.

Sternberg, R. J., Ferrari, M., Clinkenbeard, P., & Brigorenki, E. L. (1996). Identification, instruction, and assessment of gifted children: A construct validation of a triachic model. *Gifted Child Quarterly, 40,* 129–137.

Sternberg, R. J., & Kaufman, J. C. (1998). Human abilities. In J. T. Spence, J. M. Darley, & D. J. Foss (Eds.), *Annual Review of Psychology, 49,* 479–502. Palo Alto, CA: Annual Reviewd.

Sternberg, R. J., & Lubbart, T. I. (1991). An investment theory of creativity and its development. *Human Development, 34,* 1–31.

Sternberg, R. J., Wagner, R. K., & Williams, W. M., & Horvath, J. A. (1995). Testing common sense. *American Psychologist, 50,* 912–927.

Sternberg, R. L. (1998). How intelligent is intelligence testing? *Scientific American Presents, 9(4),* 12–17.

Sternberg, S. (1966). High speed scanning in human memory. *Science, 153,* 652–654.

Sternberg, S. (1975). Memory scanning: New findings and current controversies. *Quarterly Journal Experimental Psychology, 27,* 1–32.

Sterns, H. L., Barrett, G. V., & Alexander, R. A. (1985). Accidents and the aging individual. In J. E. Birren & K. W. Schaie (Eds.), *Handbook of the psychology of aging.* New York: Van Nostrand Reinhold.

Stevenson, H. W., & Lee, S. Y. (1990). Contexts of achievement: A study of American, Chinese, and Japanese children. *Monographs of the Society for Research in Child Development, 55(1–2, Serial No. 221).*

Stevenson, H. W., Stigler, J. W., Lee, S. Y., Lucker, G. W., Kitamura, S., & Hsu, C. (1985). Cognitive performance and academic achievement of Japanese, Chinese, and American children. *Child Development, 56,* 718–734.

Stockdale, M. S. (1993). The role of sexual misperceptions of women's friendliness in an emerging theory of sexual harassment. *Journal of Vocational Behavior, 42,* 84–101.

Stockdale, M. S., Dewey, J. D., & Saal, F. E. (1992). *Evidence that misperception tendencies relate to a sexual harassment belief system.* Unpublished manuscript, Southern Illinois University, Carbondale.

Stockdale, M. S., & Saal, F. E. (1990, April). *The relationship between misperceiving friendly cues and condoning or tolerating sexual harassment.* Paper presented at the annual meeting of the Southeastern Psychological Association, Atlanta.

Stoner, G. R., & Albright, T. D. (1993). Image segmentation cues in motion processing: Implications for modularity in vision. *Journal of Cognitive Neuroscience, 5,* 129–149.

Stoner, J. A. F. (1961). *A comparison of individual and group decisions* involving risk. Unpublished master's thesis, Massachusetts Institute of Technology, Cambridge.

Strack, F., Martin, L. L., & Stepper, S. (1988). Inhibiting and facilitating conditions of the human smile: A nonobtrusive test of the facial feedback hypothesis. *Journal of Personality and Social Psychology, 54,* 768–777.

Streissguth, A. P. (1994). A long-term perspective of FAS. *Alcohol Health and Research World, 18,* 74–81.

Streissguth, A. P., Sampson, P. D., & Barr, H. M. (1989). Neurobehavioral dose-response effects of prenatal alcohol exposure in humans from infancy to adulthood. *Annals of the New York Academy of Sciences, 562,* 145–158.

Strickland, B. R. (1988). Sex-related differences in health and illness. *Psychology of Women Quarterly, 12,* 381–399.

Strickland, B. R. (1989). Internal-external control of expectancies: From contingency to creativity. *American Psychologist, 44,* 1–12.

Strickland, B. R. (1995). Research on sexual orientation and human development: A commentary. *Developmental Psychology, 31,* 137–140.

Strupp, H. H. (1986). Psychotherapy: Research, practice, and public policy (how to avoid dead ends). *American Psychologist, 41,* 120–130.

Strupp, H. H. (1992). The future of psychodynamic psychotherapy. *Psychotherapy, 29,* 21–27.

Stuart, E. P., & Campbell, J. C. (1989). Assessment of patterns of dangerousness with battered women. Issues in *Mental Health Nursing, 10,* 245–260.

Stunkard, A. J., Jr., Harris, J. R., Pedersen, N. L., & McClearn, G. E. (1990). The body-mass index of twins who have been reared apart. *New England Journal of Medicine, 322,* 1483–1487.

Stunkard, A. J., Jr., Sorensen, T. I. A., Hanis, C., Teasdale, T. W., Chakraborty, R., Schull, W. J., & Schulsinger, F. (1986). An adoption study of human obesity. *New England Journal of Medicine, 314,* 193–198.

Suddath, R. L., Christison, G. W., Torrey, E. F., Casanova, M. F., & Weinberger, D. R. (1990). Anatomical abnormalities in the brains of monozygotic twins discordant for schizophrenia. *New England Journal of Medicine, 322,* 789–794.

Sue, S. (1992). Ethnicity and mental health: Research and policy issues. *Journal of Social Issues, 48,* 187–205.

Sue, S., Fujino, D. C., Hu, L., Takeuchi, D. T., & Zane, N. W. S. (1991). Community mental health services for ethnic minority groups: A test of the cultural responsiveness hypothesis. *Journal of Consulting and Clinical Psychology, 59,* 535–540.

Sue, S., & Okazaki, S. (1990). Asian-American educational achievements: A phenomenon in search of an explanation. *American Psychologist, 45,* 913–920.

Sue, S., & Zane, N. W. S. (1987). The role of culture and cultural techniques in psychotherapy. *American Psychologist, 42,* 37–45.

Sullins, E. S. (1991). Emotional contagion revisited: Effects of social comparison and expressive style on mood convergence. *Personality and Social Psychology Bulletin, 17,* 166–174.

Sullivan, L. W. (1987). The risks of the sickle-cell trait: Caution and common sense. New England *Journal of Medicine, 317,* 830–831.

Sullivan, M. A., & O'Leary, S. G. (1990). Maintenance following reward and cost token programs. *Behavior Therapy, 21,* 139–149.

Suomi, S. J., & Harlow, H. (1972). Social rehabilitation of isolate-reared monkeys. *Developmental Psychology, 6,* 487–496.

Suomi, S. J., & Ripp, C. (1983). A history of motherless monkey mothering at the University of Wisconsin Primate Laboratory. In *Child abuse: The nonhuman primate data.* New York: Liss.

Super, C. M. (1981). Behavioral development in infancy. In R. H. Monroe, R. L. Monroe, & B. B. Whiting (Eds.), *Handbook of cross-cultural development* (pp. 181–270). New York: Garland.

Super, C. M., & Harkness, S. (1982). The infants' niche in rural Kenya and metropolitan America. In L. L. Adler (Ed.), *Cross-cultural research at issue,* (pp. 47–55). New York: Academic.

Susser, E., Neugebauer, R., Hoek, H. W., Brown, A. S., Lin, S., Labovitz, D., & Gorman, J. M. (1996). Schizophrenia after prenatal famine. *Archives of General Psychiatry, 53,* 25–31.

Suter, P. M., Schutz, Y., & Jequier, E. (1992). The effect of ethanol on fat storage in health subjects. *New England Journal of Medicine, 326,* 983–987.

Sutton, S., Teuting, P., Zubin, J., & John, E. R. (1967). Information delivery and the sensory evoked potentials. *Science, 155,* 1436–1439.

Suzuki, T. (1992). Some factors influencing prosocial behavior: Empathy, social skill and extraversion. *Japanese Journal of Experimental Social Psychology, 32,* 71–84.

Swayze, V. W., II. (1995). Frontal leukotomy and related psychosurgical procedures in the era before antipsychotics (1935–1954): A historical overview. *American Journal of Psychiatry, 152,* 505–515.

Sweeney, P. D., Anderson, K., & Bailey, S. (1986). Attributional style in depression: A meta-analytic review. *Journal of Personality and Social Psychology, 50,* 974–991.

Swets, J. A., Tanner, W. P., & Birdsall, T. G. (1961). Decision processes in perception. *Psychological Review, 68,* 301–340.

Swiller, H. I. (1988). Alexithymia: Treatment utilizing combined individual and group psychotherapy. *International Journal of Group Psychotherapy, 38(1),* 47–61.

Szasz, T. (1993). *A lexicon of lunacy: Metaphoric malady, moral responsibility, and psychiatry.* New Brunswick, NJ: Transaction.

T

Tajima, N., Hill, G. W., Willey, D. L., Asao, K., Uemura, K., & Firment, M. J. (1991, August). *A cross-cultural investigation of implicit concepts of intelligence.* Paper presented at the meeting of the American Psychological Association, San Francisco.

Takanishi, R., & De Leon, P. H. (1994). A head start for the 21st century. *American Psychologist, 499,* 120–122.

Talbott, J. A. (1994). Fifty years of psychiatric services: Changes in treatment of chronically mentally ill patients. In J. M. Oldham & M. B. Riba (Eds.), *Review of Psychiatry* (Vol. 13, pp. 93–120).

Talcott, G. W., Fiedler, E. R., Pascale, R. W., Klesges, R. C., Peterson, A. L., & Johnson, R. S. (1995). Is weight gain after smoking cessation inevitable? *Journal of Consulting and Clinical Psychology, 63*, 313–316.

Tallal, P. (1980). Auditory temporal perception, phonics, and reading disabilities in children. *Brain and Language, 9*, 182–198.

Tannen, D. (1990). *You just don't understand: Women and men in conversation*. New York: Ballantine.

Tate, C. (1989, July). In the 1800s, antismoking was a burning issue. *Smithsonian*, pp. 107–117.

Tavris, C. (1991). The mismeasure of women. In J. D. Goodchilds (Ed.), *Psychological perspectives on human diversity in America* (pp. 91–136). Washington, DC: American Psychological Association.

Taylor, G. J. (1994). The alexithymia construct: Conceptualization, validation, and relationship with basic dimensions of personality. *New Trends in Experimental and Clinical Psychiatry, 10*, 61–74.

Taylor, S. E. (1990). Health psychology: The science and the field. *American Psychologist, 45*, 40–50.

Taylor, S. P., & Pasano, R. (1971). Physical aggression as a function of frustration and physical attack. *Journal of Social Psychology, 84*, 261–267.

Teigen, K. H. (1986). Old truths or fresh insights? A study of students' evaluations of proverbs. *British Journal of Social Psychology, 25*, 43–49.

Teitelbaum, P. (1961). Disturbances in feeding and drinking behavior after hypothalamic lesions. In M. R. Jones (Ed.), *Nebraska symposium on motivation*. Lincoln: University of Nebraska Press.

Tellegen, A., Lykken, D. T., Bouchard, T. J., Jr., Wilcox, K. J., Segal, N. L., & Rich, S. (1988). Personality similarity in twins reared apart and together. *Journal of Personality and Social Psychology, 54*, 1031–1039.

Tennant-Clark, C. M., Fritz, J. J., & Beauvais, F. (1989). Occult participation: Its impact upon adolescent development. *Adolescence, 96*, 757–772.

Tetter, J., & Gold, G. H. (1988). A taste of things to come. *Nature, 331*, 298–299.

Thayer, R. E. (1987). Energy, tiredness, and tension effects of a sugar snack versus moderate exercise. *Journal of Personality and Social Psychology, 52*, 119–125.

Thibault, J. W., & Kelley, H. H. (1959). *The social psychology of groups*. New York: Wiley.

Thigpen, C. H., & Cleckley, H. M. (1957). *The three faces of Eve*. Augusta, GA: Authors.

Thomas, A., & Chess, S. (1980). *The dynamics of psychological development*. New York: Brunner/Mazel.

Thompson, S. C., & Pitts, J. S. (1992). In sickness and in health: Chronic illness, marriage, and spousal caregiving. In S. Spacaman & S. Oskamp (Eds.), H*elping and being helped: Naturalistic studies* (pp. 115–151). Newbury Park, CA: Sage.

Thorndike, E. L. (1911). *Animal intelligence*. New York: Macmillan.

Timiras, P. S. (1972). *Developmental physiology and aging*. New York: Macmillan.

Tinbergen, N. (1951). *The study of instinct*. Oxford: Claredon.

Tingey, C. (1988). *Down syndrome: A resource handbook*. Boston: College-Hill.

Ting-Toomey, S. (1991). Intimacy expressions in three cultures: France, Japan, and the United States. *International Journal of Intercultural Relations, 15*, 29–46.

Todd, G. E., & Cogan, D. C. (1978). Selected schedules of reinforcement in the black-tailed prairie dog (*Cynomys ludovicianus*). *Animal Learning and Behavior, 6*, 429–434.

Tohen, M. (1994). Bipolar disorder and comorbid substance use. *Decade of the Brain, 5*(3), 1–2.

Tolman, E. C., & Honzik, C. H. (1930). Introduction and removal of reward, and maze performance in rats. *University of California Publication in Psychology, 4*, 257–275.

Torrey, E. F. (1988). *Surviving schizophrenia: A family manual* (rev. ed.). New York: HarperCollins.

Torrey, E. F. (1991). A viral-anatomical explanation of schizophrenia. *Schizophrenia Bulletin, 17*, 15–18.

Torrey, E. F. (1997). Out of the shadows: *Confronting America's mental illness crisis*. New York: John Wiley & Sons.

Torrey, E. F., & Bowler, A. (1990). Geographical distribution of insanity in America: Evidence for an urban factor. *Schizophrenia Bulletin, 16*, 591–604.

Toufexis, A. (1990, December 17). Drowsy America. *Time*, pp. 78–85.

Toussaint, M., Luthringer, R., Schaltenbrand, N., Nicolas, A., Jacqmin, A., Carelli, G., Gresser, J., Muzet, A., & Macher, J. P. (1997). changes in EEG power density during sleep laboratory adaption. *Sleep, 20*, 1201–1207.

Travis, C. B. (1993). Women and health. In F. L. Denmark & M. A. Paludi (Eds.), *Psychology of Women: A handbook of issues and theories* (pp. 283–323). Westport, CT: Greenwood Press.

Treffert, D. A. (1989). *Extraordinary people: Understanding "idiot savants."* New York: HarperCollins.

Triandis, H. C. (1995). *Individualism and collectivism*. Boulder, CO: Westview Press.

Triandis, H. C., Brislin, R., & Hui, C. H. (1988). Cross-cultural training across the individualism-collectivism divide. *International Journal of Intercultural Relations, 12*, 269–289.

Triplett, N. (1898). The dynamogenic factors in pacemaking competition. *American Journal of Psychology, 9*, 507–533.

Trosman, H. (1993). Freud's dream theory. In M. A. Carskadon (Ed.), *Encyclopedia of sleep and dreaming* (pp. 251–254). New York: Macmillan.

True, R. M. (1949). Experimental control in hypnotic age regression states. *Science, 110*, 583–584.

Truitner, K., & Truitner, N. (1993). Death and dying in Buddhism. In D. P. Irish, K. F. Lundquist, & V. J. Nelson (Eds.), *Ethnic variations in dying, death, and grief* (pp. 125–136). Washington, DC: Taylor & Francis.

Trull, T. T., & Geary, D. C. (1997). Comparison of the big-five factor structure across samples of Chinese and American adults. *Journal of Personality Assessment, 69*, 324–341.

Tu, G. C., & Israel, Y. (1995). Alcohol sonsumption by Orientals in North America is predicted largely by a single gene. *Behavior Genetics, 25*, 59–65.

Tucker, L. A., & Bagwell, M. (1991). Television viewing and obesity in adult females. *American Journal of Public Health, 81*, 908–911.

Tucker, L. A., & Friedman, G. M. (1989). Television viewing and obesity in adult males. *American Journal of Public Health, 79*, 516–518.

Tulving, E. (1983). *Elements of episodic memory*. Oxford: Oxford University Press.

Tulving, E., & Schachter, D. L. (1990). Priming and human memory systems. *Science, 247*, 301–306.

Tulving, E., & Thomson, D. M. (1973). Encoding specificity and retrieval processes in episodic memory. *Psychological Review, 80*, 352–373.

Turnbull, C. M. (1961). Some observations concerning the experiences and behavior of the BaMbuti Pygmies. *American Journal of Psychology, 74*, 304–308.

Turner, M. E., Pratkanis, A. R., Probasco, P., & Leve, C. (1992). Threat, cohesion, and group effectiveness: Testing a collective dissonance reduction perspective on groupthink. *Journal of Personality and Social Psychology, 63*, 781–796.

Tversky, A., & Kahneman, D. (1981). The framing of decisions and the psychology of choice. *Science, 211*, 453–458.

U

Ullman, L. P., & Krasner, L. (1965). *Case studies in behavior modification*. Austin, TX: Holt, Rinehart & Winston.

Ulrich, R. E., & Azrin, N. H. (1962). Reflexive fighting in response to aversive stimulation. *Journal of the Experimental Analysis of Behavior, 5*, 511–520.

Unger, R., & Crawford, M. (1992). *Women and gender: A feminist psychology*. New York: McGraw-Hill.

United Nations. (1991). *World population trends and policies: 1991 monitoring report*. New York: Author.

United Nations. (1995). *Women in a changing global economy*. New York: Author.

U.S. Bureau of the Census. (1993). *Statistical abstract of the United States, 1993*. Washington, DC: U.S. Government Printing Office.

U.S. Bureau of the Census. (1996). *Statistical abstract of the United States* (118th ed.). Washington, DC: U.S. Government Printing Office.

U.S. Bureau of the Census. (1997). *Statistical abstract of the United States, 1997* (117th ed.). Washington, DC: U.S. Department of Commerce.

U.S. Department of Health and Human Services. (1988a). *The health consequences of smoking: Nicotine addiction*. Washington DC: U.S. Government Printing Office.

U.S. Department of Health and Human Services. (1988b). *The Surgeon General's report on nutrition and health*. (DHHS PHS Publication No. 88-50210). Washington, DC: U.S. Government Printing Office.

U.S. Department of Health and Human Services. (1989). *Reducing the health consequences of smoking: 25 years of progress*. Washington, DC: U.S. Government Printing Office.

U.S. Department of Health and Human Services. (1990). *Healthy people 2000: National health promotion and disease prevention objectives*. (DHHS PHS Publication No. 91-50212). Washington, DC: U.S. Government Printing Office.

U.S. Department of Health and Human Services. (1994a). *Depression, Effective treatments are available* (NIH Publication No. 94-3590). Rockville, MD: National Institutes of Health.

U.S. Department of Health and Human Services. (1997). *Preliminary results from the 1996 National Household Survey on Drug Abuse*. Rockville, MD: National Clearinghouse for Alcohol and Drug Information, Office of Appplied Studies.

U.S. Department of Health and Human Services. (1994b). *Preliminary estimates from the 1993 National Household Survey on Drug Abuse*. Washington, DC: U.S. Government Printing Office.

U.S. Department of Justice, Bureau of Justice Statistics (1995). *Criminal victimization in the United States, 1993*, NCJ-151657. Washington, DC: U.S. Department of Justice.

U.S. Department of Labor. (1985). *Employed persons by major occupational groups and sex*. Washington, DC: U.S. Government Printing Office.

Ursano, R. J., & McCarroll, J. E. (1994). Exposure to traumatic death: The nature of the stress. In R. J. Ursano, B. G. McCaughey, & C. S. Fullerton (Eds.), *Individual and community responses to trauma and disaster: The structure of human chaos* (pp. 46–71). London.

V

Valenstein, E. S. (1973). *Brain control*. New York: Wiley.

Valenstein, E. S. (1986). *Great and desperate cures*. New York: Basic Books.

Vandenberg, S. G. (1987). Sex differences in mental retardation and their implications for sex differences in ability. In J. M. Reinisch, L. A. Rosenblum, S. & A. Sanders (Eds.), *Masculinity/femininity: Basic perspectives* (pp. 157–171). New York: Oxford University Press.

Van Gundy, A. B. (1995). *Brain boosters for business advantage*. San Diego, CA: Pfeiffer.

Van IJzendoorn, M. H., & Kroonenberg, P. M. (1988). Cross-cultural patterns of attachment: A meta-analysis of the strange situation. *Child Development, 59*, 147–156.

Vasudev, J., & Hummel, R. C. (1987). Moral stage sequence and principled reasoning in an Indian sample. *Human Development, 30*, 103–118.

Verbrugge, L. M. (1979). Marital status and health. *Journal of Marriage and the Family, 41*, 467–485.

Verbrugge, L. M. (1989). The twain meet: Empirical explanations of sex differences in health and mortality. *Journal of Health and Social Behavior, 30*, 282–304.

Vernoy, M. W. (1987). Demonstrating classical conditioning in introductory psychology: Needles don't always make balloons pop! *Teaching of Psychology, 14*, 176–177.

Veroff, J., & Veroff, J. B. (1980). *Social incentives: A life-span developmental approach.* San Diego, CA: Academic Press.

Vetter, B. (1992). Ferment: yes; progress: maybe; change: slow. *Mosaic, 23*(3), 34–41.

Viken, R. J., Rose, R. J., Kaprio, J., & Koskenvuo, M. (1994). A developmental genetic analysis of adult personality: Extraversion and neuroticism from 18 to 59 years of age. *Journal of Personality and Social Psychology, 66*, 722–730.

Viney, W., King, D. B., & Berndt, J. (1990). Animal research in psychology: Declining or thriving? *Journal of Comparative Psychology, 104*, 322–325.

Volkmann, F. C., Riggs, C. A., & Moore, R. K. (1980). Eyeblinks and visual suppression. *Science, 207*, 1206–1208.

Vortac, O., Edwards, M., Fuller, D., & Manning, C. (1993). Automation and cognition in air traffic control: An empirical investigation. *Applied Cognitive Psychology, 7*, 631–651.

Vroom, V. H. (1964). *Work and motivation.* New York: John Wiley & Sons.

Vormbrock, J. K. (1993). Attachment theory as applied to wartime and job-related marital separation. *Psychological Bulletin, 114*, 122–144.

Vygotsky, L. S. (1978) Mind in society: *The development of higher psychological processes.* Cambridge, MA: Harvard University Press. (Original works published 1930, 1933, and 1935.)

W

Wadsworth, B. J. (1979). *Piaget's theory of cognitive development* (2nd ed.). White Plains, NY: Longman.

Wadsworth, M. E. T. (1979). *Roots of delinquency: Infancy, adolescence, and crime.* Oxford: Robertson.

Wagner, A. M., & Houlihan, D. D. (1994). Sensation seeking and trait anxiety in hang-glider pilots and golfers. *Personality and Individual Differences, 16*, 975–977.

Wahi, S., & Johri, R. (1994). Questioning a universal theory of mind: Mental-real distinctions made by Indian children. *Journal of Genetic Psychology, 155*, 503–510.

Wallen, K. (1990). Desire and ability: Hormones and the regulation of female sexual behavior. *Neuroscience and Biobehavioral Reviews, 14*, 233–241.

Wallerstein, J. S. (1994). The early psychological tasks of marriage I. *American Journal of Orthopsychiatry, 64*, 640–650.

Walsh, W. M. (1991). *Case studies in family therapy: An integrative approach.* Needham Heights, MA: Allyn & Bacon.

Walster, E., & Piliavin, J. A. (1972). Equity and the innocent bystander. *Journal of Social Issues, 28*, 165–189.

Walster, E., & Walster, G. W. (1978). *Love.* Reading, MA: Addison-Wesley.

Walster, E., Walster, G. W., & Berscheid, E. (1978). *Equity: Theory and research.* Needham Heights, MA: Allyn & Bacon.

Walter, H. J., & Vaughan, R. O. (1993). AIDS risk reduction among a multiethnic sample of urban high school students. *Journal of the American Medical Association, 270*, 725–730.

Walters, E. E., & Kendler, M. D. (1995). Anorexia nervosa and anorexic-like syndromes in a population-based female twin sample. *American Journal of Psychiatry, 152*, 64–71.

Wang, H.-W., Wysocki, C. J., & Gold, G. H. (1993). Induction of olfactory sensitivity in mice. *Science, 260*, 998–1000.

Wang, Q., Cavanagh, P., & Green, M. (1994). Familiarity and pop-out in visual search. *Perception and Psychophysics, 56*, 495–500.

Wang, Q., Schoenlein, R. W., Peteanu, L. A., Mathies, R. A., & Shank, C. V. (1994). Vibrationally coherent photochemistry in the femtosecond primary event of vision. *Science, 266*, 422–424.

Wann, D. L. (1997). *Sport psychology.* Upper Saddle River, NJ: Prentice Hall.

Warach, S. (1995). Mapping brain pathophysiology and higher cortical function with magnetic resonance imaging. *The Neuroscientist, 1*, 221–235.

Warchol, G. (1998). Workplace violence, 1992–96. *Bureau of Justice Statistics Special Report, NCJ 168634.* Washington, DC: U.S. Department of Justice.

Warm, J. S., Dember, W. N., & Parasuraman, R. (1991). Effects of olfactory stimulation on performance and stress in a visual sustained attention task. *Journal of Society of Cosmetic Chemists, 42*, 199–210.

Waterhouse, J., Reilly, T., & Atkinson, G. (1997). Jet-lag. *The Lancet, 350*, 1611–1616.

Warrington, E. K., & Weiskrantz, L. (1968). New method of testing long-term retention with special reference to amnesic patients. *Nature, 217*, 972–974.

Wartik, N. (1993, May). A question of abuse. *American Health*, pp. 62–67.

Wartner, U. G., Grossman, K., Fremmer-Bombik, E., & Suess, G. (1994). Attachment patterns at age six in south Germany: Predictability from infancy and implications for preschool behavior. *Child Development, 65*, 1014–1027.

Wason, P. C. (1960). On the failure to eliminate hypotheses in a conceptual task. *Quarterly Journal of Experimental Psychology, 12*, 129–140.

Watkins, M. J., & Le Compte, D. C. (1991). Inadequacy of recall as a basis for frequency knowledge. *Journal of Experimental Psychology: Learning, Memory, and Cognition, 17*, 1161–1176.

Watson, E. H., & Lowney, G. H. (1967). *Growth and development of children* (5th ed.). St. Louis, MO: Mosby–Year Book.

Watson, J. B. (1924). *Behaviorism.* New York: Norton.

Watson, J. B. (1928). *Psychological care of infant and child.* New York: Norton.

Watson, J. B., & Rayner, R. (1920). Conditioned emotional responses. *Journal of Experimental Psychology, 3*, 1–14.

Watson, O. M. (1970). *Proxemic behavior: A cross-cultural study.* The Hague: Mouton.

Watson, R. I. (1962). The experimental tradition and clinical psychology. In A. J. Bachrach (Ed.), *Experimental foundations of clinical psychology.* New York: Basic Books.

Watts, B. (1996). Legal issues. In M. A. Pauludi (Ed.), *Sexual harassment on college campuses: Abusing the ivory tower* (pp. 1–24). Albany, NY: State University of New York Press.

Weaver, K. A., & McNeill, A. N. (1992). Null effect of mood as a semantic prime. *Journal of General Psychology, 119*, 295–301.

Weaver, R. L., II. (1993). *Understanding interpersonal communication* (6th ed.). New York: HarperCollins.

Webb, W. B. (1992). *Sleep: The gentle tyrant* (2nd ed.). Bolton, MA: Anker.

Webb, W. B., & Campbell, S. S. (1983). Relationships in sleep characteristics of identical and fraternal twins. *Archives of General Psychiatry, 40*, 1093–1095.

Weber, D. J., Redfield, R. R., & Lemon, S. M. (1986). Acquired immuno-deficiency syndrome: Epidemiology and significance for the obstetrician and gynecologist. *American Journal of Obstetrics and Gynecology, 155*, 235–239.

Wechsler, D. (1992). *The Wechsler Preschool and Primary Scales of Intelligence-Revised.* San Antonio, TX: Psychological Corporation.

Wechsler, D. (1994). *The Wechsler Intelligence Scale for Children–Third Edition.* San Antonio, TX: Psychological Corporation.

Wechsler, D. (1997). *The Wechsler Adult Intelligence Scale–Third Edition.* San Antonio: TX: Psychological Corporation.

Wechsler, H., Davenport, A., Dowdall, G., Moeykens, B., & Castillo, S. (1994). Health and behavioral consequences of binge drinking in college: A national survey of students at 140 campuses. *Journal of the American Medical Association, 272*, 1672–1677.

Weinberg, R. A., Scarr, S., & Waldman, I. D. (1992). The Minnesota Transracial Adoption Study: A follow-up of IQ performance at adolescence. *Intelligence, 16*, 117–135.

Weiland, S. (1993). Erik Erikson: Ages, stages, and stories. *Generations, 17*(2), 17–22.

Weiner, B. (1993). On sin versus sickness: A theory of perceived social responsibility and social motivation. *American Psychologist, 48*, 957–965.

Weiner, I. B., & Hess, A. K. (Eds.). (in press). *Handbook of forensic psychology* (2nd ed.). New York: Wiley.

Weissman, M. M., Bruce, M. L., Leaf, P. J., Florio, L. P., & Holzer, C., III. (1991). Affective disorders. In L. N. Robins & D. A. Regier (Eds.), *Psychiatric disorders in America: The Epidemiologic Catchment Area Study* (pp. 53–80). New York: Free Press.

Weissman, M. M., & Olfson, M. (1995). Depression in women: Implications for health care research. *Science, 269*, 799–801

Weller, A., & Weller, L. (1992). Menstrual synchrony in female couples. *Psychoneuroendocrinology, 17*, 171–177.

Wells, A. M., Garvin, V., Dohm, F. A., & Striegel-Moore, R. H. (1997). Telephone-based guided self-help for binge eating disorders: A feasibility study. *International Journal of Eating Disorders, 21*, 341–346.

Wender, P. H., & Klein, D. F. (1981). *Mind, mood and medicine: A guide to the new psychiatry.* New York: Farrar, Straus & Giroux.

Wender, P. H., Rosenthal, D., Kety, S. S., Schulsinger, F., & Welner, J. (1974). Cross-fostering: A research strategy for clarifying the role of genetic and experiential factors in the etiology of schizophrenia. *Archives of General Psychiatry, 30*, 121–128.

Werder, S. F. (1995). An update on the diagnosis and treatment of mania in bipolar disorder. *American Family Physician, 51*, 1126–1136.

Westen, D. (1990). Psychoanalytic approaches to personality. In L. A. Pervin (Ed.), *Handbook of personality: Theory and research* (pp. 21–65). New York: Guilford Press.

Whitbourne, S. K. (1985). *The aging body.* New York: Springer-Verlag.

Whitbourne, S. K. (1996). *The aging individual: Physical and psychological perspectives.* New York: Springer.

White, M. J., Kruczek, T. A., Brown, M. T., & White, G. B. (1989). Occupational sex stereotypes among college students. *Journal of Vocational Behavior, 34*, 289–298.

Whittaker, J. O., & Meade, R. D. (1967). Social pressure in the modification and distortion of judgment: A cross-cultural study. *International Journal of Psychology, 2*, 109–113.

Wickelgren, W. A. (1974). *How to solve problems.* New York: Freeman.

Widom, C. S. (1977). A methodology for studying noninstitutionalized psychopaths. *Journal of Consulting and Clinical Psychology, 45*, 674–683.

Wiehe, V. R., & Richards, A. L. (1995). *Intimate betrayal: Understanding and responding to the trauma of acquaintance rape.* Thousand Oaks, CA: Sage.

Wilcox, A. J., Weinberg, C. R., & Baird, D. D. (1995). Timing of sexual intercourse in relation to ovulation: Effects on the probability of conception, survival of the pregnancy, and sex of the baby. *New England Journal of Medicine, 333*, 1517–1519.

Wilcox, A. J., Weinberg, C. R., O'Connor, J. F., Baird, D. D., Schlatterer, J. P., Canfield, R. E., Armstrong, E. G., & Nisula, B. C. (1988). Incidence of early loss of pregnancy. *New England Journal of Medicine, 319*, 189–194.

Wilcoxin, H. C., Dragoin, W. B., & Kral, P. A. (1971). Illness-induced aversion in rat and quail: Relative salience of visual and gustatory cues. *Science, 171*, 826–828.

Wilkie, D. M., & Willson R. J. (1995). More evidence of robust spatial associative memory in the pigeon, *Columba livia. Animal Learning and Behavior, 23*, 69–75.

Williams, B. A. (1994). Blocking despite changes in reinforcer identity. *Animal Learning and Behavior, 22*, 442–457.

Williams, J. E., & Best, D. L. (1990). *Measuring sex stereotypes: A multination study* (Vol. 6, rev. ed.). Newbury Park, CA: Sage.

Williams, J. S., Singh, B. K., & singh, B. B. (1994). Urban youth, fear of crime, and resulting defensive actions. *Adolescence, 29*, 323–330.

Williams, R..B. Jr. (1989). *The trusting heart: Great news about Type A behavior.* New York: Times Books.

Williams, R. B., Jr., & Williams, V. (1993). *Anger kills.* New York: Times Books.

Williamson, D. F., Madams, J., Ada, R. F., Kleinman, J. C., Giovino, G. A., & Byers, T. (1991). Smoking cessation and severity of weight gain in a national cohort. *New England Journal of Medicine, 324*, 739–745.

Williamson, L. G., Campion, J. E., Malos, S. B., Roehling, M. V., & Campion, M. A. (1997). Employment interview on trial: Linking interview structure with litigation outcomes. *Journal of Applied Psychology, 82*, 900–912.

Willinger, M. (1995). Sleep position and sudden infant death syndrome. *Journal of the American Medical Association, 273*, 818–819.

Wilson, E. O. (1975). *Sociobiology: The new synthesis.* Cambridge, MA: Harvard Univeristy Press.

Wilson, S. C., & Barber, T. X. (1983). The fantasy-prone personality: Implications for understanding imagery, hypnosis, and parapsychological phenomena. In A. A. Sheikh (Ed.), *Imagery: Current theory, research, and application.* New York: Wiley.

Windle, M. (1994). A study of friendship characteristics and problem behaviors among middle adolescents. *Child Development, 65*, 1764–1777.

Winger, G., Hofmann, F. G., & Woods, J. H. (1992). *A handbook on drug and alcohol abuse: The biomedical aspects* (3rd ed.). New York: Oxford University Press.

Winn, M. (1977). *The plug-in drug.* New York: Viking Penguin.

Winzelberg, A. (1997). The analysis of an electronic support group for individuals with eating disorders. *Computers in Human Behavior, 13*, 393407.

Witkin, H. A., Mednick, S. A., Schulsinger, F., Bakkestrom, E., Christiansen, K. O., Goodenough, D. R., Hirschhorn, K., Lundsteen, C., Owen, D. R., Philip, J., Rubin, D. B., & Stocking, M. (1976). Criminality in XYY and XXY men. *Science, 193*, 547–555.

Wolf, T. M., Randall, H. M., & von Almen, T. K., & Tynes, L. L. (1991). Perceived mistreatment and attitude change by graduating medical students: A retrospective study. *Medical Education, 25*, 182–190.

Wood, D. J. (1989). Social interaction as tutoring. In M. H. Bornstein & J. S. Bruner (Eds.), *Interaction in human development* (pp. 59–80). Hillsdale, NJ: Erlbaum.

Wood, J. M., & Bootzin, R. R. (1990). The prevalence of nightmares and their independence from anxiety. *Journal of Abnormal Psychology, 99*, 64–68.

Wood, J. T. (1994). *Gendered lives: Communication, gender, and culture.* Belmont, CA: Wadsworth.

Woods, C. B., & Krantz, J. H. (2000). Sensation and perception: A window into the brain and mind.

In S. F. Davis and J. Halonen (Eds.), *The many faces of psychological research in the 21st century.* Washington, DC: American Psychological Association.

Woods, S. C., Seeley, R. J., Porte, D., Jr., & Schwartz, M. W. (1998). Signals that regulate food intake and energy homeostasis. *Science, 280*, 1378–1382.

Workman, J. E., & Johnson, K. K. P. (1994). Effects of conformity and noncomformity to gender-role expectations for dress: Teachers versus students. *Adolescence, 29*, 207–223.

Wrightsman, L. S. (1994). *Adult personality development: (vol. 1), Theories and concepts.* Thousand Oaks, CA: Sage.

Wrightsman, L. S., Nietzel, M. T., & Fortune, W. H. (1994). *Psychology and the legal system* (3rd ed.). Pacific Grove, CA: Brooks/Cole.

Wrobleski, A. (1989). *Suicide: Why? 85 questions and answers about suicide.* Minneapolis: Afterwords.

Wroblewski, R., & Huston, A. C. (1987). Televised occupational stereotypes and their effects on early adolescents: Are they changing? *Journal of Early Adolescence, 7*, 283–297.

Wujec, T. (1995). *Five-star mind: Games and puzzles to stimulate your creativity and imagination.* New York: Doubleday.

Wyatt, R. J., Henter, I., Leary, M. C., & Taylor, E. (1991). An economic evaluation of schizophrenia-1991. *Social Psychiatry and Psychiatric Epidemiology, 30*, 196–205.

Y

Yakovlev, P. I., & Lecours, A. R. (1967). The myelogenetic cycles of regional maturation of the brain. In A. Minkowski (Ed.), *Regional development of the brain in early life.* Oxford: Blackwell.

Yamamoto, J., & Lin, K.-M. (1995). Psychopharmacology, ethnicity, and culture. In J. M. Oldham & M. B. Riba (Eds.), *Review of psychiatry* (Vol. 14, pp. 529–541). Washington, DC: American Psychiatric Association.

Yamamoto, J., Silva, J. A., Justice, L. R., Chang, C. Y., & Leong, G. B. (1993). Cross-cultural psychotherapy. In A. C. Gaw (Ed.), *Culture, ethnicity, and mental illness* (pp. 101–124). Washington, DC: American Psychiatric Association.

Yang, S. Y., & Sternberg, R. J. (1997). Taiwanese conceptions of intelligence. In Sternberg, R. J. & Kaufman, J. C. (1998). Human abilities, In J. T. Spence, J. M. Darley, & D. J. Foss (Eds.), *Annual Review of Psychology, 49*, 479–502. Palo Alto, CA: Annue Reviews.

Yapko, M. D. (1994). *Suggestions of abuse.* New York: Simon & Schuster.

Yoder, J. D. (1998). *Women and gender: Transforming psychology.* Upper Saddle River, NJ: Prentice Hall.

Yonelinas, A. P., Hockley, W. E., & Murdock, B. B. (1992). Test of the list-strength effect in recognition memory. *Journal of Experimental Psychology: Learning, Memory, and Cognition, 18*, 345–355.

Yonkers, K. A., & Hamilton, J. A. (1995a). Do men and women need different doses of psychotropic drugs? *Harvard Mental Health Letter, 11*(11), 8.

Yonkers, K. A., & Hamilton, J. A. (1995b). Psychotropic medications. In J. M. Oldham & M. B. Riba (Eds.), *Review of psychiatry* (Vol. 14, pp. 307–332). Washington, DC: American Psychiatric Association.

Youdim, M. B. H., & Riederer, P. (1997). Understanding Parkinson's disease. *Scientific American, 276*, 52–59.

Young, J. E., Beck, A. T., & Weinberger, A. (1993). Depression. In D. H. Barlow (Ed.), *Clinical handbook of psychological disorders: A step-by-step treatment manual* (2nd ed., pp. 240–277). New York: Guilford Press.

Young, T., Evans, L., Finn, L., & Palta, M. (1997). Estimation of the clinically diagnosed proportion of sleep apnea syndrome in middle-aged men and women. *Sleep, 20*, 705706.

Yudofsky, S. C., Hales, R. E., & Ferguson, T. (1991). *Psychiatric drugs.* New York: Ballantine.

Z

Zabin, L. S., & Hayward, S. C. (1993). *Adolescent sexual behavior and childbearing.* Newbury Park, CA: Sage.

Zajonc, R. B. (1965). Social facilitation. *Science, 149*, 269–274.

Zajonc, R. B. (1980). Feeling and thinking; Preferences need no inference. *American Psychologist, 35*, 151–175.

Zajonc, R. B., & McIntosh, D. N. (1992). Emotions research: Some promising questions and some questionable promises. *Psychological Science, 3*, 70–74.

Zakhari, A. (1997). Alcohol and the cardiovascular system: Molecular mechanisms for beneficial and harmful action. *Alcohol Health & Research World, 21*, 21–29.

Zeki, S. (1992). The visual image in mind and brain. *Scientific American, 267*, 69–76.

Zeki, S. (1993). *A vision of the brain.* London: Blackwell Scientific Publications.

Zhdanova, I. V., Lynch, H. J., & Wurtman, R. J. (1997). *Melatonin: sleep-promoting hormone. Sleep, 20*, 899–907.

Zigler, E., & Styfeo S. J. (1994) Head Start: Criticism in a constructive context. *American Psychologist, 49*, 127–132.

Zillman, D. (1979). *Hostility and aggression.* Hillsdale, NJ: Erlbaum.

Zimmerman, B., Bandura, A., & Martinez-Pons, M. (1992). Self-motivation for academic attainment: The role of self-efficacy beliefs and personal goal setting. *American Educational Research Journal, 29*, 663–676.

Zornetzer, S. F. (1985). Catecholamine system involvement in age-related memory dysfunction. *Annals of the New York Academy of Sciences, 44*, 242–254.

Zuckerman, B., Frank, D. A., Hingson, R., Amaro, H., Levenson, S. M., & Kayne, H. (1989). Effects of maternal marijuana and cocaine use on fetal growth. *New England Journal of Medicine, 320*, 762–768.

Zuckerman, M. (1978). The search for high sensation. *Psychology Today, 11*(8), 38–46.

Zuckerman, M. (1987). Biological connection between sensation seeking and drug abuse. In J. Engel and L. Oreland (Eds.), *Brain reward systems and abuse.* New York: Raven Press.

Zuckerman, M. (1991). *Psychobiology of personality.* Cambridge: Cambridge University Press.

Zuckerman, M. (1994). *Behavioral expression and biosocial bases of sensation seeking.* Cambridge: Cambridge University Press.

Zuckerman, M., Buchsbaum, M. S., & Murphy, D. L. (1980). Sensation seeking and its biological correlates. *Psychological Bulletin, 88*, 187–214.

Zusne, L., & Jones, W. H. (1982). *Anomalistic psychology: A study of extraordinary phenomena of behavior and experience.* Hillsdale, NJ: Erlbaum.

Credits

PHOTO CREDITS

Chapter 1 Page 21 Ken Fisher/Tony Stone Images; p. 2 Hulton Getty Picture Collection/Tony Stone Images; p. 6 UPI/Corbis; p. 15 Jeff Greenberg/Rainbow; p. 17 Mary Kate Denny/PhotoEdit; p. 28 Archives of the History of American Psychology; p. 30 (top) Culver Pictures, Inc., (bottom) , Archive Photos; p. 31 (top) Yvonne Hemsey/Liaison Agency, Inc., (bottom) Keystone/The Image Works; p. 33 (top) Partridge/Margaret Clapp Library, (bottom) Columbia University, Rare Book and Manuscript Library; p. 35 (top) The Bancroft Library, (bottom) AP/Wide World Photos; p. 36 Northside Center for Child Development, Inc; p. 39 Tom Pantages.

Chapter 2 Page 44 AP/Wide World Photos; p. 58 National Library of Medicine; p. 59 Peter Menzel/Stock Boston; p. 60 (margin) Ms. Michal Heron (bottom left & right) Dan McCoy/Rainbow; p. 61 (A) Pete Saloutos/The Stock Market, (B) Hank Morgan, Rainbow; p. 62 Scott Camazine/Photo Researchers, Inc.; p. 63 Corbis.

Chapter 3 Page 86 Cordon Art B.V.; p. 89 Richard Dunoff/The Stock Market; p. 90 The Granger Collection; p. 93 (left) Chris Rogers/Rainbow, (right) M. Antman/The Image Works; p. 99 Carolyn Smith; p. 101 Dick George/The Phoenix Zoo; p. 102 Martin Dohrn/Science Photo Library/Photo Researchers, Inc.;Hart-Davis/Science Photo Researchers, Inc.; p. 111 Science Source/Photo Researchers, Inc.; p. 116 Clive Brunskill/Allsport Photography (USA), Inc.; p. 121 Tom & Dee Ann McCarthy/The Stock Market; p. 122 Stephen F. Davis; p. 123 Catherine Karnow/Woodfin Camp & Associates; p. 125 (left) David Hundley/The Stock Market, (middle) Mark E. Gibson/The Stock Market, (right) Carolyn Smith, (bottom) Joseph Campos; p. 126 Clark/Monkmeyer Press; p. 128 P. Hasegawa/Impact Visuals Photo & Graphics, Inc; p. 130 Cyane Lowden; p. 136 AP/Wide-World Photos; p. 138 Stephen F. Davis-

Chapter 4 Page 140 Jim Erickson/The Stock Market; p. 144 The Image Bank; p 145 Harlow Primate Laboratory; p. 151 The Image Bank; p. 154 Michael Kaufman/Impact Visuals Photo & Graphics, Inc.; p. 158 Lawrence Migdale/Photo Researchers, Inc.; p. 159 Jeffrey Sylvester/FPG International LLC; p. 162 AP/Wide World Photos; p. 170 Mark C. Burnett/Photo Researchers, Inc; p. 174 (a) Liaison Agency, Inc., (b) Matsumoto/Paul Ekman, Ph.D., (c) Alan Weiner/Liaison Agency, Inc., (d) Matsumoto/ Paul Ekman, Ph.D. (e & f) Dr. David Matsumoto; p. 179 (top) Michael Klausman/Paul Ekman, Ph.D., (margin) Bob Daemmrich/Stock Boston; p. 180 UPI/Corbis; p. 184 Collins/Monkmeyer Press; p. 185 (top) Mark Stevenson/Picture Perfect USA, Inc., (middle) Steve Cavalier/Picture Perfect USA, Inc., (bottom) Kathleen Brown/Sharpshooters.

Chapter 5 Page 188 Larry Mulvehill/Rainbow; p. 198 Michael Nichols/Magnum Photos, Inc.; p. 200 Monte S. Buchsbaum, M.D.; p. 203 UPI Telephoto/Corbis; p. 207 Respironics, Inc.; p. 209 Huy Tran/National Heart, Lung, and Blood Institute; p. 217 AP/Wide World Photos; p. 222 Evan P. Scneider/Monkmeyer Press; p. 225 Dr. Adolf Pfefferbaum; p. 226 MarkReinstein/Uniphoto Picture Agency; p. 228 W. Geiersperger/Stock Boston; p. 230 Rick Gerharter/Impact Visuals Photo & Graphics,Inc.

Chapter 6 Page 232 Jon Reis/The Stock Market; p. 236 Sovfoto/Eastfoto; p. 239 Corbis; p. 242 Steve Powell/All-Sport Photographic Ltd.; p. 251 Lambert/Archive Photos; p. 252 Nina Leen/Life Picture Service; p. 265 William Johnson/Stock Boston; p. 268 John Eastcott/Yva Momatiuk/Stock Boston.

Chapter 7 Page 274 Tony Craddock/Science Photo Library/Photo Researchers, Inc.; p. 276 Corbis; p. 280 Rhoda Sidney/Stock Boston; p. 284 George A. Miller; p. 293 George Zimbel/Monkmeyer

Press; p. 295(left) John Iacono/Time Inc. Magazines, Sports Illustrated, (right) Jonathan Daniel/Allsport Photography (USA), Inc.; p. 301 Elizabeth Loftus; p. 302 Angela Maynard/PhotoDisc, Inc; p. 303 Paul Sakuma/AP/Wide World Photos; p. 313 James D. Wilson/Woodfin Camp & Associates.

Chapter 8 Page 316 Sotographs/Liaison Agency, Inc.; p. 319 Michael Fisher/Custom Medical Stock Photo, Inc.; p. 320 Herb Snitzer/Stock Boston; p. 322 (left) Ralph A. Reinhold/Animals/Earth Scenes, (right) EPA–Documerica; p. 331 Tom Campbell/Liaison Agency, Inc.; p. 332 Rommel Pecson/Impact Visuals Photo & Graphics, Inc.; p. 341 Culver Pictures, Inc., p. 342 Dr. Rose K. Gantner/Comstock; p. 348 Pam Driscol Gallery; p. 351 (left) Gregory Pace/Sygma, (right) Dallas Brass; p. 352 Culver Pictures, Inc.

Chapter 9 Page 362 M. Brodskaya/Impact Visuals Photo & Graphics, Inc; p. 364 John Coletti/Stock Boston; p. 368 (top) Mark Lunenberg., (margin) D. W. Fawcett/Photo Researchers, Inc.; p. 369 Petit Format/Nestle/Science Source/Photo Researchers, Inc.; p. 370 Archiv/Photo Researchers, Inc.; p. 371 Bob Daemmrich/Stock Boston; p. 374 American Heart Association; p. 375 Phototake NYC; p. 376 CNRI/Science Photo Library/Photo Researchers, Inc.; p. 377 ATC Productions/The Stock Market; p. 381 Suzanne Haldane/Stock Boston; p. 383 Stephen F. Davis; p. 387 UPI/Corbis-Bettmann; p. 389 Harlow Primate Laboratory; p.391Corbis-Bettmann; p. 392 Shackman/ Monkmeyer Press; p. 396 Joe DiMaggio/The Stock Market; p. 398 Corbis-Bettmann, p. 399 Goodman/Monkmeyer Press; p. 404 Erika Stone/Photo Researchers, Inc.

Chapter 10 Page 410 Alain Evrard/Liaison Agency, Inc.; p. 412 (top) Sylvain Grandadam/Tony Stone Images, (left & right) Henry Bagish/Anthro-Photo; p. 413 Bob Daemmrich/Stock Boston; p. 414

(left) Peter Cade/Tony Stone Images, (right) Charles Gupton/Stock Boston; p. 415 Owen Franken/Stock Boston; p. 417 Brian Bailey/Tony Stone Images; p. 418 Tom Pantages/Tom Pantages; p. 419 Steve Maines/Stock Boston; p. 420 AP/Wide World Photos; p. 423 Michael Hayman/Stock Boston; p. 424 The Image Bank; p. 428 Butch Martin/The Image Bank; p. 432 Gabe Palmer/The Stock Market; p. 434 Jose L Pelaez/The Stock Market; p. 436 Yva Momatiuk/John Eastcott/Woodfin Camp & Associates; p. 438 Liaison Agency, Inc.; p. 439 AP/Wide World Photos; p. 441 Andrew Lichtestein/Impact Visuals Photo & Graphics, Inc.

Chapter 11 Page 448 David R. Frazier/Photo Researchers, Inc.; p. 451 Mryleen Ferfuson/PhotoEdit; p. 457 David Young-Wolfe/PhotoEdit; p. 459 Tony Freeman/Photo Edit; p. 460 J. Trave/Liason Agency, Inc.; p. 462 Stock Boston; p 463 Bob Daemmrich/Stock Boston; p. 464 Archive Photos; p. 470 Loren Santow/Tony Stone Images; p. 471 Stock Boston; p. 476 Uniphoto Picture Agency; p. 477 Ellis Herwig/Stock Boston; p. 481 Seth Perlman/AP/Wide World Photos; p. 483 Mug Shots/The Stock Market; p. 485 Cynthia Johnson/Time Life Syndication; p. 487 G. Contorakes/Sharpshooters.

Chapter 12 Page 490 Herbert Migdoll/Rainbow; p. 493 (left) Joseph Palladino, (right) J. Bucklan/Sygma; p. 496 John Coletti/Stock Boston; p. 502 Joseph A. Chiodi; p. 504 Penny Tweedie/Tony Stone Images; p. 508 Focus on Sports Inc.; p. 509 T. K. Wanstal/The Image Works; p. 513 Corbis; p. 518 Nick Gunderson/Tony Stone Images; p. 523 Albert Bandura, Prof. of Psychology p. 524 J.P. Laffont-Sigma/Sygma; p. 525 Tony Freeman/PhotoEdit.

Chapter 13 Page 530 Sylvain Grandadam/Photo Researchers, Inc.; p. 533 Catherine Karnow/Woodfin Camp & Associates; p. 534 AP/Wide World Photos; p. 535 Mario Cabrera/AP/Wide World Photos; p. 551 (top) AP/Wide World Photos, (bottom) AP/Wide World Photos; p. 544 Joseph Palladino; p. 548 Lewis R. Baxter, Jr., M.D.; p. 555 Library of Congress; p. 556 Goldberg/Monkmeyer Press; p. 557 Michael Grecco/Stock Boston; p. 558 Frank Edwards/Fotos International/Archive Photos; p. 559 Lewis R. Baxter, Jr., M.D.; p. 565 Mary Ellen Mark Library; p. 568 Drs. E. Fuller Torrey and Daniel R. Weinberger; p. 570 Edna Morlok; p. 574 Bob McLeod/San Francisco Examiner.

Chapter 14 Page 578 Photo Researchers, Inc.; p. 580 Corbis; p. 581 Corbis; p. 582 (left) Culver Pictures, Inc., (right) Corbis, (middle) Temple University Libraries Urban Archives; p. 584 (top) Reuters/Steve Jaffe/Archive Photos/Archive Photos, (margin) Goodwin/Monkmeyer Press; p. 589 Goldberg Monkmeyer Press; p. 590 Carl Rogers Memorial Library; p. 593 (left) Aaron T. Beck, M.D., (right) Institute for Rational-Emotive Therapy; p. 602 Uniphoto Picture Agency; p. 609 Michael Newman/PhotoEdit; p. 614 Damien Lovegrove/Science Photo Library/Photo Researchers, Inc.; p. 618 Keh-Ming Lin.

Chapter 15 Page 624 John Coletti/Stock Boston; p. 631 Greg Smith, Stock Boston; p. 634 Charles H. Porter 4th/Sygma; p. 636 Benjamin Koziner/ Phototake NYC; p. 639 Rob Crandall; p. 640 Colin Braley/Archive Photos; p. 643 (left & right) Custom Medical Stock Photo, Inc.; p. 646 Frank LaBua/Simon & Schuster/PH College; p. 651Providence Journal Company (top) Jeffrey Markowitz/Sygma; p. 652 CNRI/Phototake NYC; p. 655 AP/Wide World Photos; p. 659 Stock Boston; p. 662 Dan McCoy/Rainbow; p. 663 L. Steinmark/Custom Medical Stock Photo, Inc.

Chapter 16 Page 668 George Disario/The Stock Market; p. 670 Dave Benett/Globe Photos, Inc.; p. 672 The Stock Market; p. 674 Bob Daemmrich/Stock Boston; p. 678 Mug Shots/Gabe Palmer/The Stock Market; p. 695 Donna Day/Tony Stone Images; p. 697 (top) Alan Schein/The Stock Market, (bottom) Ed Bohon/The Stock Market; p. 701 Alexandra Milgram; p. 702 Philippe Ledru/Sygma; p. 704 Steve Raymer/Corbis; p. 708 Bob Daemmrich/Stock Boston; p. 709 George Disario/The Stock Market; p. 711 Alan Reininger/Woodfin Camp & Associates.

Chapter 17 Page 716 John Coletti/Uniphoto Picture Agency; p. 718 Boden Ledingham/Masterfile Corporation; p. 720 White Packert/The Image Bank; p. 727 Weinberg Clark/The Image Bank; p. 730 Andy Zito; p. 731 David Austen/Stock Boston.

TEXT CREDITS

The publishers acknowledge the copyright owners for permission to reprint the following copyrighted materials:

Page 25, Figure 1-4: Halpern, D. (1991). Left-handedness: A marker for decreased survival fitness. *APA Psychological Bulletin* 109, 90-106. Reprinted with the permission of Professor Diane Halpern, California State University, San Bernardino.

Page 50, Figure 2-3: Shaver, K. G., & Tarpy, R. M. (1993). *Psychology.* New York: Macmillian. Copyright © 1993 by Macmillian Publishing Company. Reprinted with the permission of Prentice-Hall, Inc.

Page 51, Figure 2-4: Benjamin, Hopkins & Nation, 1989.

Page 53, Figure 2-6: Shaver, K. G., & Tarpy, R. M. (1993). *Psychology.* New York: Macmillian. Copyright © 1993 by Macmillian Publishing Company. Reprinted with the permission of Prentice-Hall, Inc.

Page 56, Figure 2-9: Shaver, K. G., & Tarpy, R. M. (1993). *Psychology.* New York: Macmillian. Copyright © 1993 by Macmillian Publishing Company. Reprinted with the permission of Prentice-Hall, Inc.

Page 57, Figure 2-10 (A & B): Benjamin, L. T., Hopkins, R. J., & Nation, J. R. (1989) *Psychology* (2nd ed.). New York: Macmillian. Copyright © 1990 by Macmillian Publishing Company. Reprinted with the permission of Prentice-Hall, Inc. © Shaver, K. G., & Tarpy, R. M. (1993). *Psychology.* New York: Macmillian. Copyright © 1993 by Macmillian Publishing Company. Reprinted with the permission of Prentice-Hall, Inc.

Page 64, Figure 2-17 (A): Shaver, K. G., & Tarpy, R. M. (1993). *Psychology.* New York: Macmillian. Copyright © 1993 by Macmillian Publishing Company. Reprinted with the permission of Prentice-Hall, Inc.

Page 66, Figure 2-18: Shaver, K. G., & Tarpy, R. M. (1993). *Psychology.* New York: Macmillian. Copyright © 1993 by Macmillian Publishing Company. Reprinted with the permission of Prentice-Hall, Inc.

Page 68, Table 2-3: From *Drugs And Behavior,* (3rd ed.) by Fred Leavitt. Copyright © 1995 by Sage Publications, Inc. Reprinted by permission of Sage Publications, Inc. Seeley, R.. R., Stephens, T.D., & Tate, P. (1995). *Anatomy and Physiology* (3rd ed.) St. Louis: Mosby-Year Book. Copyright © 1995. Reprinted with the permission of the publishers.

Page 70, Table 2-4: Landrum, R. E. (1992). College students' use of caffeine and its relationship to personality. *College Student Journal, 26,* 151-155. Reprinted with the permission of the College Student Journal, Project Innovation of Mobile, P.O. Box 8508, Mobile, AL 36608.

Page 72, Figure 2-20: Shaver, K. G., & Tarpy, R. M. (1993). *Psychology.* New York: Macmillian. Copyright © 1993 by Macmillian Publishing Company. Reprinted with the permission of Prentice-Hall, Inc.

Page 78, Figure 2-23: Shaver, K. G., & Tarpy, R. M. (1993). *Psychology.* New York: Macmillian. Copyright © 1993 by Macmillian Publishing Company. Reprinted with the permission of Prentice-Hall, Inc.

Page 95, Figure 3-3: Pinel, J. (1993). *Biopsychology* (2nd ed.) Allyn & Bacon. Reprinted by permission.

Page 95, Figure 3-4: Dowling, J.E. & Boycott, B.B. (1966). *Proceedings of the Royal Society of London,* B., pp. 80-111.

Page 106, Figure 3-14: Shaver, K. G., & Tarpy, R. M. (1993). *Psychology.* New York: Macmillian. Copyright © 1993 by Macmillian Publishing Company. Reprinted with the permission of Prentice-Hall, Inc.

Page 113, Figure 3-17: Shaver, K. G., & Tarpy, R. M. (1993). *Psychology.* New York: Macmillian. Copyright © 1993 by Macmillian Publishing Company. Reprinted with the permission of Prentice-Hall, Inc.

Page 130, Figure 3-26 (A): Seamon, J. G. & Kendrick, D. T. (1994). *Psychology* (2nd ed.) Reprinted by permission of Prentice-Hall, Inc., Upper Saddle River, NJ.

Page 132, Figure 3-27: Stapel, D. A. & Koomen, W. (1997). Social categorization and perceptual judgement of size: When perception is social. *Journal of Personality and Social Psychology, 73,* 1177–1190. Copyright © 1997 by the American Psychological Association. Reprinted with permission.

Page 163, Table 4-2: Scherer, K. R. & Wallbott, H. G. (1994). Evidence for universality and cultural variation of differential emotion response patterning. *Journal of Personality and Social Psychology, 66,* 310-328. Copyright © 1994 by The American Psychological Association. Reprinted with permission.

Page 164, Figure 4-8: From Levenson, R. W., Ekman, P., & Friesen, W.V. (1990). Voluntary facial action generates emotion-specific autonomic nervous system activity. *Psychophysiology, 27,* 363-384. Copyright © 1990 by The Society for Psychophysiology Research. Reprinted with the permission of Cambridge University Press.

Page 167, Figure 4-9: LeDoux, J. E. (1994, June). Emotion, Memory and the Brain. *Scientific American,* Reprinted by permission of Robert Osti.

Page 173, Table 4-3: Ekman, P., Friesen, W.V., O'Sullivan, M., Chan, A., Diacoyanni-Tarlatzis, I., Heider, K., Krause, R., LeCompte, W.A., Pitcairn, T., Ricci-Bitti, P.E., Sherer, K.R., Tomita, M. & Tzavaras, A. (1987). Universals and Cultural Differences in the Judgements of Facial Expressions of Emotion. *Journal of Personality and Social Psychology, 53,* 712717. Copyright © 1987 by the American Psychological Association. Reprinted with permission.

Page 176, Figure 4-12: Plutchik, R. (1980). *Emotion: A Psychoevolutionary Synthesis.* Copyright © 1980 by Robert Plutchik. Reprinted by permission of Addison-Wesley Educational Publishers Inc.

Page 178, Figure 4-13: Adapted from Martini, F. (1992). *Fundamentals of Anatomy and Physiology,* p. 335. Figure 11-4b. Upper Saddle River, NJ: Prentice Hall. Copyright © 1992 by Prentice-Hall, Inc. Reprinted with the permission of the publisher.

Page 192, Figure 5-1: Developed from Morris, R. W. (1989). Chronobiology and health part I: Basic principles. *pharmIndex* (January): 6-16. Copyright © 1989 by Skyline Publishers, Inc. Reprinted with the permission of Professor Ralph Morris, University of Illinois at Chicago.

Page 193, Figure 5-2: Moore-Ede, M. (1992). *The Twenty Four hour society,* p. 24. Reading, MA: Addison-Wesley. Copyright © 1992 by Martin Moore-Ede. Reprinted with the permission of Addison-Wesley Publishing Company, Inc.

Page 195, Figure 5-3: Waterhouse, Reilly & Atkinson, Jet Lag. *The Lancet* vol. 350, Nov 29, 1997, pp. 1611–1616. Copyright © 1997 by The Lancet Ltd. Reprinted by permission.

Page 199, Figure 5-4: Hauri, P.J. (1992). The sleep disorders: Current concepts. *A Scope Publications.* Kalamazoo, MI: Upjohn. Copyright © 1977 by the Upjohn Company. Reprinted with the permission of Pharmacia & Upjohn Inc., Kalamazoo, Michigan.

Page 200, Figure 5-7: American Medical Association, 1984. *From The American Medical Association Guide to Better Sleep* by American Medical Association. Copyright © 1984 by the American Medical Association. Reprinted by permission of Random House, Inc.

Page 201, Figure 5-8: Hartman, E. (1987). *The Sleep Book: Understanding and Preventing Sleep Problems in People Over 50.* Glenview, Ill.: Scott, Foresman and Company. Copyright © 1987 by Scott, Foresman and Company. Reprinted with the permission of Dr. Ernest Hartmann, Lemuel Shattuck Hospital, Boston, Mass.

Page 202, Figure 5-9: Moorcroft, W. H. (1993). *Sleep, Dreaming, and Sleep Disorders* (2nd ed.), p. 35. Lanham, Maryland: University Press of America. Copyright © 1989, 1993 by University Press of America. Reprinted with the permission of the publishers.

Page 226, Figure 5-12: Grant, Harford, Dawson et al., 1992.

Page 242, Figure 6-4: Hartman, T. T., & Grant, D. A., (1960) Effect of intermittent reinforcement on acquisition, extinction, and spontaneous recovery of the conditioned eyelid response. *Journal of Experimental Psychology, 60,* 89-96. Reprinted with the permission of the American Psychological Society.

Page 278, Figure 7-1: Jenkins, J. G. & Dallenbach, K. M. (1924). "Obliviscence during sleeping and waking," *American Journal of Psychology* 35. Copyright 1924 by the Board of Trustees of the University of Illinois. Reprinted with the permission of the University of Illinois Press.

Page 292, Figure 7-8: Hyde, T. S. & Jenkins, J. J. (1969). Differential effects of incidental tasks on the organization of recall on a list of highly associated words, *Journal of Experimental Psychology, 82,* 472-481. Copyright © 1969 by the American Psychological Association. Reprinted with permission.

Page 301, Figure 7-10: Loftus, E. (1979). The malleability of human memory. *American Scientist, 67,* p. 313. Reprinted with the permission of Dr. Elizabeth Loftus, University of Washington, Seattle.

Pages 507–508, Hands On: Zuckerman, M. (1994). "The Sensation Seeking Scale" from *Behavioral expressions and biosocial bases of sensation seeking.* New York: Cambridge University Press. Reprinted with the permission of Marvin Zuckerman, University of Delaware, Newark.

Page 510, Figure 12-5: Tellegen, A., et al. (1988). Personality similarity in twins reared apart and together. *Journal of Personality and Social Psychology, 54,* 1031–1039. Copyright © 1988 by the American Psychological Association. Reprinted with permission.

Page 511, Table 12-4: Angleitner, A., Riemann, R., & Strelau, J. (1997). "Genetic and environmental influences on personality: A study of twins reared together using the self-and peer report NEO-FFI scales," *Journal of Personality,* 65, pp. 449-475. Reprinted by permission of Blackwell Publishers.

Page 523, Figure 12-7: Bandura, A. (1986). *Social foundations of thought and action: A social-cognitive theory* by Albert Bandura. Copyright © 1986 by Prentice Hall, Inc. Reprinted with the permission of the publisher.

Page 533, Table 12-6: J. B. (1966). Generalized expectancies for internal versus external control of reinforcement. *Psychological Monographs, 80* (Whole No. 609.) Copyright © 1966 by Julian B. Rotter. Reprinted with the permission of the author.

Page 539, Table 13-1: Reprinted with permission from the *Diagnostic and Statistical Manual of Mental Disorders* (4th Ed.). Copyright 1994 American Psychiatric Association.

Page 543, Table 13-2: Andreasen, N. C. & Black, D. W. (1995). *Introductory Textbook of Psychiatry* (2nd ed.). Reprinted by permission of the American Psychiatric Press.

Page 545, Figure 13-3: Cohen, A., Barlow, D. & Blanchard, E. (1985). Psychophysiology of relaxation associated panic attacks. *Journal of Abnormal Psychology, 94,* 96101. Reprinted by permission of Plenum Publishing Corporation and the author.

Page 546, Table 13-3: DeSilva, P. & Rachman, S. (1992). *Obsessive compulsive: The facts,* 1994. Reprinted by permission of Oxford University Press.

Page 567, Figure 13-8: Gottesman, I. I. (1991). From Schizophrenic Genesis: *The Origins Of Madness* by Gottesman © 1991 by Irving l. Gottesman. Used with Permission by W. H. Freeman and Company.

Page 569, Figure 13-10: Robins, L. N. & Regier, D. A. (Eds.) (1981). *Psychiatric Disorders In America: The Epidemiologic Catchment Area Study,* p. 47. New York: The Free Press. Copyright © 1991 by Lee N. Robins and Darrell A. Regier. Reprinted with the permission of The Free Press, a Division of Simon & Schuster, Inc.

Page 583, Figure 14-1: Fuller Torrey, E, (1997). *Out of the Shadows: Confronting America's Mental Illness Crisis.* Reprinted by permission of John Wiley & Sons, Inc.

Page 593, Table 14-2: Ellis, A. (1987). The impossibility of achieving consistently good mental health. *American Psychologist, 42,* 364-375. Copyright © 1987 by the American Psychological Association. Reprinted with permission.

Page 594, Table 14-3: Beck, A. T. & Weishaar, M. (1989). Cognitive therapy. In A. Freeman, K. M. Simon, L. E. Beutler, & H. Arkowitz (Eds.) *Comprehensive handbook of cognitive therapy* (pp. 21-26). Reprinted by permission of Plenum Publishing Corporation, and from Andreasen, N. C. & Black, D. W. (1991). *Introductory Textbook of Psychiatry.* Reprinted by permission of the American Psychiatric Press.

Page 596, Table 14-4: Meichenbaum, D. H. & Cameron, R. (1983). Stress inoculation training: Toward a general paradigm for training coping skills. In D. H. Meichenbaum & M.E. Jaremko (eds.), *Stress reduction and prevention, 1983.* Reprinted by permission of Plenum Publishing Corporation and Professor Donald Meichenbaum.

Page 597, Table 14-5: Martin, G. & Pear, J. (1988). *Behavior modification: What it is and how to do it* (4th ed.), 344. Englewood Cliffs, NJ: Prentice Hall. Copyright © 1992 by Prentice-Hall, Inc. Reprinted with the permission of the publisher.

Page 601, Figure, 14-7: Liberman, R. P., Teigen, J., Patterson, R. & Baker, V. (1973). Reducing delusional speech in chronic, paranoid schizophrenics. *Journal of Applied Behavior Analysis, 6,* 57-64. Copyright © 1973. Reprinted with the permission of Journal of Applied Behavior Analysis.

Page 612, Figure 14-8: Kopta, S. M., Howard, K. I., Lowry, J. L., & Beutler, L. E. (1994). Patterns of symptomatic recovery in psychotherapy. *Journal of Consulting and Clinical Psychology, 62,* 1009-1016. Copyright © 1994 by the American Psychological Association. Reprinted with permission.

Page 628, Table 15-2: Matarazzo, J. D. (1984). Behavioral immunogens. In B. L. Hammonds & C. J. Scheirer (Eds.), *Psychology and Health* (pp. 9-43). Copyright © 1984 by the American Psychological Association. Reprinted with permission.

Page 633, Table 15-3: Dohrenwend, B. P., Link, B. G., Shrout, P. E. & Markowitz, J. (1990). Measuring Life Events: The problem of variability within event categories. *Stress Medicine, 6,* 179-187. Copyright © 1990. Reprinted with the permission of John Wiley & Sons, Ltd.

Page 645, Table 15-6: Williams, R. B. & Williams, V. (1993). *Anger Kills.* Copyright © 1993 by Redford B. WIlliams, M. D. and Virginia WIlliams, Ph.D. Reprinted by permission of Times Books, a division Random House, Inc.

Page 647, Figure 15-7: Figure from *Scientific American,* July 1998. Reprinted by permission of Laurie Grace.

Page 649, Figure 15-9: Nowak, M. A. & McMichael, A. J. (1995). How HIV Defeats the Immune System, *Scientific American, 273 (2).* Reprinted by permission of Dimitry Schildlovsky.

Page 653, Figure 15-10: Hegarty, V. (1995). *Nutrition: Food and the Environment.* St. Paul, MN: Eagan Press. Copyright © 1995. Reprinted with the permission of AAAC/Eagan Press.

Page 660, Figure 15-11: Nezu, A. M., Nezu, C. M., & Blissett, S. E. (1988). Sense of humor as a moderator of the relation between stressful events and psychological distress: A prospective analysis. *Journal of Personality and Social Psychology, 54,* 520-525. Copyright © 1988 by the American Psychological Association. Reprinted with permission.

Glossary & Index

applies psychology to law and legal proceedings. **40**

Forgetting
curve of, 277
directed, 286

Formal operational stage Piaget's final stage of intellectual development, characterized by abstract thinking; achieved during adolescence of adulthood. **419**

Fovea Indented spot in the center of the retina that contains only cones. **97**

Foxx, Richard, 599

Framing The tendency for decision making to be influenced by presentation of negative or positive outcomes. **332–333**

Fraternal twins Twins who develop from two ova fertilized by two sperm; genetically related as siblings. **354**
See also Twin studies

Free association Psychoanalytic technique in which the patient is asked to say whatever comes to mind without censoring anything. **588**

Free recall Learning procedure in which material that has been learned my be repeated in any order. **277**

Frequency theory Theory stating that the basilar membrane vibrates at different rates to create the perception of different pitches. **107–108**

Freud, Sigmund, 31, 211, 227, 386–387, 457, 512–520, 536, 560, 582–583
psychoanalytic therapy, 588–590

Friedman, Meyer, 644–645

Friendship Form of interpersonal attraction that is governed by an implicit set of rules. **684–685**

Fritz, Janet, 429

Front-in-the-door effect Phenomenon in which a person who has agreed to a small request is more likely to comply with a subsequent larger request. **704**

Frustration-aggression hypothesis Hypothesis that aggression is likely to occur when a person is frustrated. **690**

Functional fixedness Inability to see new uses for familiar objects. **327**

Functionalism Approach to psychology that focused on the functions of consciousness. **29**

Functional magnetic resonance imaging (fMRI) A modification of the standard MRI procedure that allows both structural and temporal images to be gathered. **61–62**

Fundamental attribution error Tendency to attribute behaviors to internal causes. **677**

G

GABA, 613

Gage, Phineas, 58

Galef, Bennett, Jr., 259–260

Gall, Franz Joseph, 506

Galton, Francis, 341, 349

Ganglion cells Cells in the retina whose axons form the optic nerve. **96**

Ganzfeld, 134

Garcia, John, 247

Gardner, Howard, 350–351

Gate control theory Theory of pain stating that the release of substance P in the spinal cord produces the sensation of pain. **116**

Gazzaniga, Michael, 76

Gender Social and psychological phenomena associated with being feminine or masculine as these concepts are defined in a given culture. **450**
language and, 462–463
permanence, 458

Gender differences
aggression and, 471–472
AIDS and, 646, 648
biological, 466–467
communication and, 470–471
depression and, 555
drug therapy and, 618–619
early analyses of, 467–468
emotions and, 181
family responsibilities and, 487–488
helping behavior and, 471
impact of, 33–36
intelligence and, 468–470
male-female comparisons, 472
obesity and, 653
schizophrenia and, 568
sense of smell and, 114
sex roles and, 686
social development and, 470–472
suicide and, 557

Gender identity disorder Sexual disorder characterized by a person's belief that he or she was born with the wrong biological sex organs. **574**

Gender roles Behaviors considered appropriate for males and females in a given culture. **456**
cultural differences, 461–462
development of, 456–459

Gender-schema theory Explanation for the learning of gender roles that suggests that children form schemas of masculine and feminine attributes which influence memory, perception, and behaviors. **458–459**

Gender stereotyping, 459–460
components of, 463
cultural differences, 461–462
language and, 462–463

mass media and, 463–464
in the workplace, 485–486

General adaptation syndrome (GAS) Responses to stressful situations that includes the alarm, resistance, and exhaustion stages. **628–631**

Generalization Occurrence of responses to stimuli that are similar to a CS. **243–244, 265–266**

Generalized anxiety disorder (GAD Chronically high level of anxiety that is not attached to a specific stimulus. **545–546**

Generativity versus stagnation Erikson's seventh psychosocial crisis which occurs during middle adulthood and reflects concern, or lack thereof, for the next generation. **434**

Genes Units of hereditary material that line the chromosomes and provide information concerning the form and function of each cell. **369**

Genetic abnormalities, 452

Genetics
depression and, 560
obesity and, 652
schizophrenia and, 566–568
of sex, 452
Genetic screening, 722

Genital stage Stage of psychosexual development that begins at puberty and usually leads to normal adult sexual development. **518**

Genovese, Kitty, 688

Gestalt psychology Approach to psychology most noted for emphasizing that our perception of a whole is different from our perception of the individual stimuli. **29–30**
principles of perceptual organization, 125–127

Gestalt therapy Humanistic form of therapy developed by Perls in which therapists may frustrate and challenge clients to lead them toward self-acceptance. **591**

Gibson, Eleanor, 124–125

Giftedness, 309–310, 346–349

Gilligan, Carol, 406–407

Glia cell Special type of cell found in the nervous system that forms the myelin sheath. **65**

Glucocorticoids, 82–83

Gluostatic theory, 153

Goal-setting theory, 725

Goldberg, Lewis, 503

Gonads, 82

Good continuation and direction Gestalt principle stating that smooth, flowing lines are more readily perceived than choppy, broken lines. **127**

Goodman, Joel, 660

Gordon, Walter, 259

Graham, John W., 429

careful observations of a phenomenon, proposes theories to explain the phenomenon, makes hypotheses about future behaviors, and then tests theses hypotheses through more research and observation. **13**–14

Scientific observations, role of, 9–10

Sclera, 94

Seasonal affective disorder (SAD), 556

Secondary appraisal Second step in coping with stress; consists of deciding how to deal with stress-producing situation. **635**

Secondary reinforcer Stimulus that acquires reinforcing properties by being associated with a primary reinforcer. **251**

Secondary sex characteristics Characteristics that develop during adolescence and are not directly related to reproduction. **413, 454**

Secular trend Tendency of members of one generation to begin puberty at an earlier age than their parents. **413**

Selective abstraction, 594

Selective serotonin reuptake inhibitors (SSRIs), 614

Self-actualization Need to develop one's full potential. **149, 524**–525

Self-disclosure Individual's decision to share personal information. **673**
  friendship and, 685

Self-efficacy A person's expectancy concerning his or her ability to engage in effective behaviors; such expectancies differ from one behavior to another. **523**

Self-fulfilling prophecy Our expectations elicit behaviors in others that confirm those expectations. **672**

Self-help groups, 604

Self-monitoring scale, nonverbal communication and, 674, 675

Self-report inventories Psychological tests in which individuals answer questions about themselves, usually by responding yes or no or true or false. **493**–495

Self-serving bias Tendency to make internal attributions when we are successful and external attributions when we fail. **678**

Self-talk, 595–596

Seligman, Martin, 248, 561, 658

Selye, Hans, 628

Semantic memory Memory for general knowledge. **293**

Semantic network Network of related concepts that are linked together. **298**

Semicircular canals Fluid-filled passages in the inner ear that detect movement of the head. **115**

Sensation Activation of receptors by

stimuli in the environment. **88**–89

Sensation seeking scale, 507–508

Sensorimotor stage Piaget's first stage of cognitive development in which children learn about their environment through direct sensory contact and motor activities. **399**

Sensorineural deafness Deafness resulting from disease and tumors in the auditory pathways of auditory cortex of the brain. **108, 109**

Sensory memory Very brief, extensive memory for sensory events. **282**–283

Sensory systems, 91
  hearing, 104–110
  in infants, 379–380
  other, 115–117
  smell, 112–115
  summary of, 118
  taste, 110–112
  vision, 92–103

Serial enumeration Ability to remember a series of events. **259**

Serial learning Learning procedure in which material that has been learned must be repeated in the order in which it was presented. **277**

Serial position effect Tendency for items at the beginning and end of a list to be learned better than items in the middle. **306**

Set effect Bias toward the use of certain problem-solving approaches because of past experience. **328**–329

Set point A range of weight that the body seems to maintain under most circumstances. **154**

Sex Category based on biological differences in anatomy, hormones, and genetic composition. **450**
  biology of, 451–454
  determination of, 371
  genetics of, 452
  hormonal basis of, 454–456
  -linked traits, 372
  motivation and, 154–157

Sex characteristics
  primary, 413
  secondary, 413, 454

Sex differences. *See* Gender differences

Sexism Differential treatment of an individual on the basis of his or her sex. **473**–474
  education and, 474–477
  family responsibilities and, 487–488
  work and careers and, 477–487

Sex roles, love and, 686

Sexual aggression, 691–692

Sexual disorders, 574–575

Sexual dysfunctions, 157

Sexual harassment Either sexual coercion based on promised rewards or threatened punishments or cre-

ation of a hostile workplace environment. **478**–482
  frequency of, 482–484
  legal decision concerning, 480
  perceiving, 484–485

Sexual orientation Tendency for a person to be attracted to individuals of the same, opposite, or both sexes. **455**–456

Sexual response surveys, 155–157

Shape constancy The tendency to perceive the shape of an object as constant even though its retinal image changes. **122**

Shaping A form of operant conditioning in which a desired response if taught by reinforcement of successive responses that more closely resemble the target response. **253**–254

Sheldon, William, 506

Shelton, Richard, 595

Shepard, Roger, 319

Sherif, Muzafer, 711

Sherrington, Charles Scott, 63, 66–67

Shiffrin, Richard, 281–288

Shift work, 195–196

Shinn, David, 445

Shinn, Milicent, 33

Shock therapy, 619

Short-term memory (STM) Memory stage in which information is held in consciousness for 10 to 20 seconds. **283**–285
  retrieval of, 297

Sickle-cell anemia, 369–370

Signal detection theory The contention that the threshold varies with the nature of the stimulus and background stimulation. **91**

Similarity Gestalt principle stating that perceptual elements that are similar are seen as a group. **127**
  attraction and, 684

Simon, Theophile, 341

Singer, Jerome, 183–184

Sixteen Personality Factors Questionnaire (Cattell), 498–499

Size constancy The tendency to perceive the size of an object as constant even though its retinal image changes. **122**–123

Sizemore, Chris, 551

Skeels, Howard, 355–356

Skin, 117

Skinner, B. F., 30–31, 252–253, 404, 536, 521, 596

Skinner box, 253

Sleep, 197
  deprivation, 202
  differences in individual needs/patterns, 200–202
  dreams, 210–212
  functions of, 202–203
  inertia, 201
  in late adulthood, 417